The Official *SCRABBLE*® Players Dictionary

Third Edition

MERRIAM-WEBSTER, INCORPORATED
Springfield, Massachusetts, U.S.A.

Copyright © 1995 by Milton Bradley Company, a division of
Hasbro, Inc.

Library of Congress Cataloging in Publication Data
Main entry under title:

The Official Scrabble® players dictionary. — 3rd ed.
   p. cm.
 ISBN 0-87779-220-8
 1. Scrabble® (Game) — Glossaries, vocabularies, etc.
GV1507.S3036 1995
793.73—dc20   95-20437
               CIP

The game board shown on the dust jacket is copyright © 1948
by Milton Bradley Company, a division of Hasbro, Inc.

SCRABBLE® is a registered trademark of Hasbro, Inc. in
the United States and Hasbro Canada, Inc. in Canada.
Used with permission in the United States and Canada.

Made in the United States of America

20 19 18 17   RRD 04 05

P ₃ **REFACE** ● This is the third edition of the enormously popular Official SCRABBLE® Players Dictionary, and it includes more than 1,000 words not included in the previous edition. This dictionary has been prepared especially for lovers of SCRABBLE® Brand crossword games and is endorsed by the National SCRABBLE® Association for recreational and school use.

It is important to remember that The Official SCRABBLE® Players Dictionary was edited solely with this limited purpose in mind. It is not intended to serve as a general dictionary of English; thus, such important features of general dictionaries as definitions of multiple senses, pronunciation respellings, etymologies, and usage labels are omitted.

It is the intention of the makers of SCRABBLE® Brand crossword games that they be enjoyed by children and adults alike. With this consideration in mind, words likely to offend players of the game have been omitted from this edition. The words omitted are those that would qualify for a warning usage note on the basis of standards applied in other Merriam-Webster dictionaries.

The detailed organization and special features of the dictionary are explained in the Introduction which follows. It should be read with care by all who use the dictionary. Now that this new updated work is available, we are confident that it will afford satisfaction and enjoyment to SCRABBLE® Brand crossword game players everywhere.

The Official SCRABBLE® Players Dictionary
has been endorsed by the
National SCRABBLE® Association.

For information on SCRABBLE® clubs, tournaments, publications, school programs, and other activities, contact:

National SCRABBLE® Association
Box 700
Greenport, NY 11944
Phone: (516) 477-0033
Fax: (516) 477-0294

INTRODUCTION ● MAIN ENTRIES ● Main entries are listed in boldface type and are set flush with the left-hand margin of each column. Except for an occasional cross-reference (such as **MISSPOKEN** past participle of misspeak), main entries contain from two to eight letters, since words within this range are considered to be most useful to SCRABBLE® crossword game players. Words that are not permissible in SCRABBLE® crossword games have not been included in this dictionary. Thus, proper names, words requiring hyphens or apostrophes, words considered foreign, and abbreviations have been omitted. Because dictionaries have different standards for selecting entries, several desk dictionaries were consulted in preparing the list of main entries for this book. Obsolete, archaic, slang, and nonstandard words are included because they are permitted by the rules of the game. All variant forms of a main entry are shown at their own alphabetical places and defined in terms of the principal form. Words that exceed eight letters in length and are not inflected forms of words entered in this dictionary should be looked up in a desk dictionary. The National SCRABBLE® Association recommends Merriam-Webster's Collegiate Dictionary, Tenth Edition, as a source of additional words.

RUN-ON ENTRIES ● A main entry may be followed by one or more derivatives in boldface type with a different part-of-speech label. These are run-on entries. Run-on entries are not defined since their meanings are readily derivable from the meaning of the root word.

FENDER *n* pl. -S a metal guard over the wheel of a motor vehicle
FENDERED *adj*

HAMULUS *n* pl. -LI a small hook
HAMULAR, HAMULATE, HAMULOSE, HAMULOUS *adj*

No entry has been run on at another if it would fall alphabetically more than three places from the entry. **When you do not find a word at its own place, it is always wise to check several entries above and below to see if it is run on.**

CROSS-REFERENCES ● A cross-reference is a main entry that is an inflected form (such as the plural form of a noun, the past tense form of a verb, or the comparative form of an adjective) of another word. An inflected form is entered as a main entry if it undergoes a spelling change in addition to or instead of suffixation *and* if it falls alphabetically more than three places away from the root word.

For example, in the entries reproduced below, **DICING** is a main entry because it involves a spelling change (the final *-e* of *dice* is dropped) besides the addition of the -ING ending and because it falls more than three places from the entry **DICE.** On the other hand, *dices* is not a main entry because it involves no spelling change beyond the addition of the ending -S. The word *diced,* although involving a spelling change (the final -*e* of *dice* is dropped), is not a main entry because it does not fall more than three places from **DICE. DICIER** and **DICIEST** are main entries because they involve a spelling change (the -*e*- is dropped and the final -*y* is changed to -*i*-) besides the addition of the -ER, -EST endings and they fall more than three places from the entry **DICEY.**

DICE	*v* DICED, DICING, DICES to cut into small cubes
DICENTRA	*n* pl. -S a perennial herb
DICER	*n* pl. -S a device that dices food
DICEY	*adj* DICIER, DICIEST dangerous
DICHASIA	*n/pl* flower clusters
DICHOTIC	*adj* affecting the two ears differently
DICHROIC	*adj* having two colors
DICIER	comparative of dicey
DICIEST	superlative of dicey
DICING	present participle of dice

This policy is intended to make the word desired as easy to find as possible without wasting space. Nevertheless, many inflected forms will appear only at the main entry.

You should always look at several entries above and below the expected place if you do not find the desired word as a main entry.

Cross-reference entries for present tense third person singular forms of verbs use the abbreviation "sing."

PARTS OF SPEECH ● An italic label indicating a part of speech follows each main entry except cross-references (such as **DICIER, DICIEST, DICING**), for which the label is given at the root word. The eight traditional parts of speech are indicated as follows:

n	noun	*pron*	pronoun
v	verb	*prep*	preposition
adj	adjective	*conj*	conjunction
adv	adverb	*interj*	interjection

The label *n/pl* is given to two kinds of nouns. One is the plural noun that has no singular form.

KINETICS *n/pl* a branch of science dealing with motion

The other is the plural noun of which the singular is not entered in this dictionary. Singular forms are omitted if they contain more than eight letters.

NUCLEOLI   *n/pl* nucleoles

Nucleolus, the singular form, has nine letters and is not entered.

When a word can be used as more than one part of speech, each part of speech is entered separately if the inflected forms are not spelled alike. For example, both the adjective *pale* and the verb *pale* are entered because the inflected forms vary.

PALE   *adj* PALER, PALEST lacking
               intensity of color
PALE   *v* PALED, PALING, PALES to
               make or become pale

On the other hand, the verb *leg* is entered while the noun *leg* is not because the inflected form *legs* at the verb is spelled the same as the plural form of the noun. In a dictionary for SCRABBLE® crossword game players, entry of the noun is therefore redundant. Homographs (words spelled alike) which may be used as the same part of speech are treated in the same way. For example, *gin* is entered as a verb twice because the inflected forms are spelled differently.

GIN   *v* GINNED, GINNING, GINS to
               remove seeds from cotton
GIN   *v* GAN, GUNNEN, GINNING,
               GINS to begin

If both set of inflected forms were spelled alike, only one *gin* would be entered in this dictionary. In this way the dictionary includes as many different spellings as possible yet avoids wasting space with repeated entry of words spelled in the same way. The SCRABBLE® crossword game player, after all, needs only one entry to justify a play.

INFLECTED FORMS   ●   Inflected forms include the past tense, past participle, present participle, and present tense third person singular of verbs, the plural of nouns, and the comparative and superlative of adjectives and adverbs. They are shown in capital letters immediately following the part-of-speech label. Irregular inflected forms are listed as main entries when they fall four or more alphabetical places away from the root word (see **Cross-References** above). All inflected forms are allowable for play in SCRABBLE® crossword games.

The principal parts of the majority of verbs are shown as -ED, -ING, -S (or -ES when applicable). This indicates that the past tense and past participle are formed simply by adding *-ed* to the entry word, that the present participle is formed simply by adding *-ing* to the entry word, and that the present third person singular is formed simply by adding *-s* (or *-es*) to the entry word.

NEATEN   *v* -ED, -ING, -S to make neat

When inflection of an entry word involves any spelling change in addition to the suffixal ending (such as the dropping of a final *-e,* the doubling of a final consonant, or the changing of a final *-y* to *-i-*) or when the inflection is irregular, the inflected forms given indicate such changes.

MOVE   *v* MOVED, MOVING, MOVES to change from one position to another

SUP   *v* SUPPED, SUPPING, SUPS to eat supper

PLY   *v* PLIED, PLYING, PLIES to supply with or offer repeatedly PLYINGLY *adv*

EAT   *v* ATE or ET, EATEN, EATING, EATS to consume food

For verbs of more than one syllable, either the last syllable or the last two syllables are shown.

MUMBLE   *v* -BLED, -BLING, -BLES to speak unclearly

BENEFIT   *v* -FITED, -FITING, -FITS or -FITTED, -FITTING, -FITS to be helpful or useful to

The plurals of nouns are preceded by the abbreviation "pl." Most plurals are shown as -S (or -ES when applicable) to indicate that the plural is formed simply by adding the given suffix to the entry word.

ACID   *n* pl. -S a type of chemical compound

When pluralizing a noun involves any spelling change in addition to the suffixal ending (such as the changing of a final *-y* to *-i-* or a final *-f* to *-v-*) or when the plural is irregular, the plural form shown indicates such change.

CITY   *n* pl. CITIES a large town

BEEF   *n* pl. BEEFS or BEEVES a steer or cow fattened for food

ORNIS   *n* pl. ORNITHES avifauna

In such cases involving polysyllabic nouns at least the last syllable is shown.

EULOGY   *n* pl. -GIES a formal expression of high praise

For the sake of clarity, two groups of nouns that are confusing to many, those ending in -*o* and those ending in -*y,* are always indicated in this dictionary by showing at least the last syllable, even though no spelling change is involved.

MUNGO   *n* pl. -GOS a low-quality wool

NAY   *n* pl. NAYS a negative vote

Variant plurals are shown wherever they add another word permissible in SCRABBLE® crossword games.

CELLO   *n* pl. -LOS or -LI a stringed
                  musical instrument

Plurals which have the same form as the singular are shown only when they are the only plural for that entry. This is done to show that for the entry in question it is not permissible to add -*s* (or -*es*) to the singular to create a plural.

TAKA   *n* pl. TAKA a monetary unit of
                  Bangladesh

VEG   *n* pl. VEG a vegetable

Otherwise, they are omitted and only the plural with the inflection is shown.

DEER   *n* pl. -S a ruminant mammal

The comparative and superlative forms of adjectives and adverbs are shown, when applicable, immediately following the part-of-speech label. Any spelling changes are indicated in the forms shown.

JUST   *adj* JUSTER, JUSTEST acting
                  in conformity with what is
                  morally good

FAR   *adv* FARTHER, FARTHEST or
                  FURTHER, FURTHEST at or to
                  a great distance

LACEY   *adj* LACIER, LACIEST lacy

Not all adjectives or adverbs can be inflected, and only those inflected forms shown are acceptable. None of the adjectives and adverbs listed as run-on entries in this dictionary have inflected forms.

DEFINITIONS   ●   In most cases, only one very brief definition is given for each main entry since definitions do not play a significant role in the SCRABBLE® crossword game. This definition serves only to orient the player in a general way to a single meaning of the word. It is not intended to have all the precision and detail of a definition in a good general dictionary.

When a word consisting of eight letters or less appears in a definition but is not an entry in this dictionary, it is glossed in parentheses. For example, at the entry for the verb *hand,* the noun "hand" is used in the definition and is glossed because the noun *hand* is not a separate entry.

HAND *v* -ED, -ING, -S to present with the hand (the end of the forearm)

A main entry that is a variant form of another entry is defined in terms of the most common form, which is entered and defined at its own alphabetical place.

MATZA *n* pl. -S matzo
MATZAH *n* pl. -S matzo
MATZO *n* pl. -ZOS, -ZOT, or -ZOTH an unleavened bread

SCRABBLE® crossword game players in Canada will be pleased to learn that variant forms such as *honour, centre,* and *cheque,* which are often omitted from general dictionaries, have also been included in this book.

LISTS OF UNDEFINED WORDS ● Lists of undefined words appear after the entries of the prefixes **RE-** and **UN-.** These words are not defined because they are self-explanatory: their meanings are simply the sum of a meaning of the prefix combined with a meaning of the root word. All of their inflected forms are given, however.

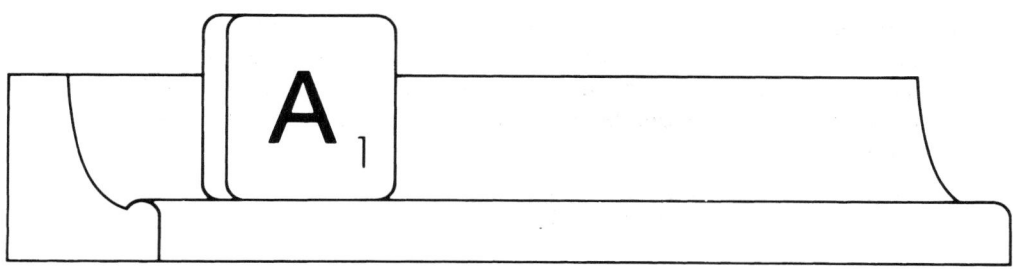

AA	*n* pl. -S rough, cindery lava
AAH	*v* -ED, -ING, -S to exclaim in amazement, joy, or surprise
AAL	*n* pl. -S an East Indian shrub
AALII	*n* pl. -S a tropical tree
AARDVARK	*n* pl. -S an African mammal
AARDWOLF	*n* pl. -WOLVES an African mammal
AARGH	*interj* — used to express disgust
AARRGH	*interj* aargh
AARRGHH	*interj* aargh
AASVOGEL	*n* pl. -S a vulture
AB	*n* pl. -S an abdominal muscle
ABA	*n* pl. -S a sleeveless garment worn by Arabs
ABACA	*n* pl. -S a Philippine plant
ABACK	*adv* toward the back
ABACUS	*n* pl. -CI or -CUSES a calculating device
ABAFT	*adv* toward the stern
ABAKA	*n* pl. -S abaca
ABALONE	*n* pl. -S an edible shellfish
ABAMP	*n* pl. -S abampere
ABAMPERE	*n* pl. -S a unit of electric current
ABANDON	*v* -ED, -ING, -S to leave or give up completely
ABAPICAL	*adj* directed away from the apex
ABASE	*v* ABASED, ABASING, ABASES to lower in rank, prestige, or esteem **ABASEDLY** *adv*
ABASER	*n* pl. -S one that abases
ABASH	*v* -ED, -ING, -ES to make ashamed or embarrassed
ABASIA	*n* pl. -S a defect in muscular coordination in walking
ABASING	present participle of abase
ABATE	*v* ABATED, ABATING, ABATES to reduce in degree or intensity **ABATABLE** *adj*
ABATER	*n* pl. -S one that abates
ABATIS	*n* pl. -TISES a barrier made of felled trees
ABATOR	*n* pl. -S one that unlawfully seizes an inheritance
ABATTIS	*n* pl. -TISES abatis
ABATTOIR	*n* pl. -S a slaughterhouse
ABAXIAL	*adj* situated away from the axis
ABAXILE	*adj* abaxial
ABBA	*n* pl. -S father — used as a title of honor
ABBACY	*n* pl. -CIES the office of an abbot
ABBATIAL	*adj* pertaining to an abbot
ABBE	*n* pl. -S an abbot
ABBESS	*n* pl. -ES the female superior of a convent of nuns
ABBEY	*n* pl. -BEYS a monastery or convent
ABBOT	*n* pl. -S the superior of a monastery
ABBOTCY	*n* pl. -CIES abbacy
ABDICATE	*v* -CATED, -CATING, -CATES to give up formally
ABDOMEN	*n* pl. -MENS or -MINA the body cavity containing the viscera
ABDUCE	*v* -DUCED, -DUCING, -DUCES to abduct
ABDUCENS	*n* pl. -CENTES a cranial nerve
ABDUCENT	*adj* serving to abduct
ABDUCING	present participle of abduce
ABDUCT	*v* -ED, -ING, -S to draw away from the original position
ABDUCTOR	*n* pl. -ES or -S an abducent muscle
ABEAM	*adv* at right angles to the keel of a ship

ABED	adv in bed
ABELE	n pl. -S a Eurasian tree
ABELIA	n pl. -S an Asian or Mexican shrub
ABELIAN	adj being a commutative group in mathematics
ABELMOSK	n pl. -S a tropical herb
ABERRANT	n pl. -S a deviant
ABET	v ABETTED, ABETTING, ABETS to encourage and support
ABETMENT	n pl. -S the act of abetting
ABETTAL	n pl. -S abetment
ABETTED	past tense of abet
ABETTER	n pl. -S abettor
ABETTING	present participle of abet
ABETTOR	n pl. -S one that abets
ABEYANCE	n pl. -S temporary inactivity
ABEYANCY	n pl. -CIES abeyance
ABEYANT	adj marked by abeyance
ABFARAD	n pl. -S a unit of capacitance
ABHENRY	n pl. -RIES or -RYS a unit of inductance
ABHOR	v -HORRED, -HORRING, -HORS to loathe
ABHORRER	n pl. -S one that abhors
ABIDANCE	n pl. -S the act of abiding
ABIDE	v ABODE or ABIDED, ABIDING, ABIDES to accept without objection
ABIDER	n pl. -S one that abides
ABIGAIL	n pl. -S a lady's maid
ABILITY	n pl. -TIES the quality of being able to do something
ABIOSIS	n pl. -OSES absence of life **ABIOTIC** adj
ABJECT	adj sunk to a low condition **ABJECTLY** adv
ABJURE	v -JURED, -JURING, -JURES to renounce under oath
ABJURER	n pl. -S one that abjures
ABLATE	v -LATED, -LATING, -LATES to remove by cutting
ABLATION	n pl. -S surgical removal of a bodily part
ABLATIVE	n pl. -S a grammatical case
ABLAUT	n pl. -S a patterned change in root vowels of verb forms
ABLAZE	adj being on fire

ABLE	adj ABLER, ABLEST having sufficient power, skill, or resources
ABLE	n pl. -S a communications code word for the letter A
ABLEGATE	n pl. -S a papal envoy
ABLER	comparative of able
ABLEST	superlative of able
ABLINGS	adv ablins
ABLINS	adv perhaps
ABLOOM	adj blooming
ABLUENT	n pl. -S a cleansing agent
ABLUSH	adj blushing
ABLUTED	adj washed clean
ABLUTION	n pl. -S a washing
ABLY	adv in an able manner
ABMHO	n pl. -MHOS a unit of electrical conductance
ABNEGATE	v -GATED, -GATING, -GATES to deny to oneself
ABNORMAL	n pl. -S a mentally deficient person
ABOARD	adv into, in, or on a ship, train, or airplane
ABODE	v ABODED, ABODING, ABODES to forebode
ABOHM	n pl. -S a unit of electrical resistance
ABOIDEAU	n pl. -DEAUS or -DEAUX a type of dike
ABOIL	adj boiling
ABOITEAU	n pl. -TEAUS or -TEAUX aboideau
ABOLISH	v -ED, -ING, -ES to do away with
ABOLLA	n pl. -LAE a cloak worn in ancient Rome
ABOMA	n pl. -S a South American snake
ABOMASAL	adj pertaining to the abomasum
ABOMASUM	n pl. -SA the fourth stomach of a ruminant
ABOMASUS	n pl. -MASI abomasum
ABOON	adv above
ABORAL	adj situated away from the mouth **ABORALLY** adv
ABORNING	adv while being born
ABORT	v -ED, -ING, -S to bring forth a fetus prematurely
ABORTER	n pl. -S one that aborts

ABORTION	*n* pl. -S induced expulsion of a nonviable fetus
ABORTIVE	*adj* failing to succeed
ABOUGHT	past tense of aby and abye
ABOULIA	*n* pl. -S abulia **ABOULIC** *adj*
ABOUND	*v* -ED, -ING, -S to have a large number or amount
ABOUT	*adv* approximately
ABOVE	*n* pl. -S something that is above (in a higher place)
ABRACHIA	*n* pl. -S a lack of arms
ABRADANT	*n* pl. -S an abrasive
ABRADE	*v* ABRADED, ABRADING, ABRADES to wear away by friction
ABRADER	*n* pl. -S a tool for abrading
ABRASION	*n* pl. -S the act of abrading
ABRASIVE	*n* pl. -S an abrading substance
ABREACT	*v* -ED, -ING, -S to release repressed emotions by reliving the original traumatic experience
ABREAST	*adv* side by side
ABRI	*n* pl. -S a bomb shelter
ABRIDGE	*v* ABRIDGED, ABRIDGING, ABRIDGES to reduce the length of
ABRIDGER	*n* pl. -S one that abridges
ABROACH	*adj* astir
ABROAD	*adv* out of one's own country
ABROGATE	*v* -GATED, -GATING, -GATES to abolish by authoritative action
ABROSIA	*n* pl. -S a fasting from food
ABRUPT	*adj* -RUPTER, -RUPTEST rudely brief **ABRUPTLY** *adv*
ABSCESS	*v* -ED, -ING, -ES to form an abscess (a localized collection of pus surrounded by inflamed tissue)
ABSCISE	*v* -SCISED, -SCISING, -SCISES to cut off
ABSCISIN	*n* pl. -S a regulatory substance found in plants
ABSCISSA	*n* pl. -SAS or -SAE a particular geometric coordinate
ABSCOND	*v* -ED, -ING, -S to depart suddenly and secretly
ABSEIL	*v* -ED, -ING, -S to rappel
ABSENCE	*n* pl. -S the state of being away
ABSENT	*v* -ED, -ING, -S to take or keep away
ABSENTEE	*n* pl. -S one that is not present
ABSENTER	*n* pl. -S one that absents himself
ABSENTLY	*adv* in an inattentive manner
ABSINTH	*n* pl. -S absinthe
ABSINTHE	*n* pl. -S a bitter liqueur
ABSOLUTE	*adj* -LUTER, -LUTEST free from restriction
ABSOLUTE	*n* pl. -S something that is absolute
ABSOLVE	*v* -SOLVED, -SOLVING, -SOLVES to free from the consequences of an action
ABSOLVER	*n* pl. -S one that absolves
ABSONANT	*adj* unreasonable
ABSORB	*v* -ED, -ING, -S to take up or in
ABSORBER	*n* pl. -S one that absorbs
ABSTAIN	*v* -ED, -ING, -S to refrain voluntarily
ABSTERGE	*v* -STERGED, -STERGING, -STERGES to cleanse by wiping
ABSTRACT	*adj* -STRACTER, -STRACTEST difficult to understand
ABSTRACT	*v* -ED, -ING, -S to take away
ABSTRICT	*v* -ED, -ING, -S to form by cutting off
ABSTRUSE	*adj* -STRUSER, -STRUSEST difficult to understand
ABSURD	*adj* -SURDER, -SURDEST ridiculously incongruous or unreasonable **ABSURDLY** *adv*
ABSURD	*n* pl. -S the condition in which man exists in an irrational and meaningless universe
ABUBBLE	*adj* bubbling
ABULIA	*n* pl. -S loss of will power **ABULIC** *adj*
ABUNDANT	*adj* present in great quantity
ABUSE	*v* ABUSED, ABUSING, ABUSES to use wrongly or improperly **ABUSABLE** *adj*
ABUSER	*n* pl. -S one that abuses
ABUSIVE	*adj* characterized by wrong or improper use
ABUT	*v* ABUTTED, ABUTTING, ABUTS to touch along a border
ABUTILON	*n* pl. -S a flowering plant
ABUTMENT	*n* pl. -S something that abuts
ABUTTAL	*n* pl. -S an abutment
ABUTTED	past tense of abut
ABUTTER	*n* pl. -S one that abuts

ABUTTING	present participle of abut
ABUZZ	*adj* buzzing
ABVOLT	*n* pl. -S a unit of electromotive force
ABWATT	*n* pl. -S a unit of power
ABY	*v* ABOUGHT, ABYING, ABYS to pay the penalty for
ABYE	*v* ABOUGHT, ABYING, ABYES to aby
ABYSM	*n* pl. -S an abyss
ABYSMAL	*adj* immeasurably deep
ABYSS	*n* pl. -ES a bottomless chasm **ABYSSAL** *adj*
ACACIA	*n* pl. -S a flowering tree or shrub
ACADEME	*n* pl. -S a place of instruction
ACADEMIA	*n* pl. -S scholastic life or environment
ACADEMIC	*n* pl. -S a college student or teacher
ACADEMY	*n* pl. -MIES a secondary school
ACAJOU	*n* pl. -S a tropical tree
ACALEPH	*n* pl. -LEPHAE or -LEPHS a jellyfish
ACALEPHE	*n* pl. -S acaleph
ACANTHUS	*n* pl. -THI or -THUSES a prickly herb
ACAPNIA	*n* pl. -S a lack of carbon dioxide in blood and tissues
ACARI	pl. of acarus
ACARID	*n* pl. -S a type of arachnid
ACARIDAN	*n* pl. -S acarid
ACARINE	*n* pl. -S acarid
ACAROID	*adj* resembling an acarid
ACARPOUS	*adj* not producing fruit
ACARUS	*n* pl. -RI a mite
ACAUDAL	*adj* having no tail
ACAUDATE	*adj* acaudal
ACAULINE	*adj* having no stem
ACAULOSE	*adj* acauline
ACAULOUS	*adj* acauline
ACCEDE	*v* -CEDED, -CEDING, -CEDES to consent
ACCEDER	*n* pl. -S one that accedes
ACCENT	*v* -ED, -ING, -S to pronounce with prominence
ACCENTOR	*n* pl. -S a songbird
ACCEPT	*v* -ED, -ING, -S to receive willingly
ACCEPTEE	*n* pl. -S one that is accepted
ACCEPTER	*n* pl. -S one that accepts
ACCEPTOR	*n* pl. -S accepter
ACCESS	*v* -ED, -ING, -ES to get at
ACCIDENT	*n* pl. -S an unexpected or unintentional occurrence
ACCIDIA	*n* pl. -S acedia
ACCIDIE	*n* pl. -S acedia
ACCLAIM	*v* -ED, -ING, -S to shout approval of
ACCOLADE	*n* pl. -S an expression of praise
ACCORD	*v* -ED, -ING, -S to bring into agreement
ACCORDER	*n* pl. -S one that accords
ACCOST	*v* -ED, -ING, -S to approach and speak to first
ACCOUNT	*v* -ED, -ING, -S to give an explanation
ACCOUTER	*v* -ED, -ING, -S to equip
ACCOUTRE	*v* -TRED, -TRING, -TRES to accouter
ACCREDIT	*v* -ED, -ING, -S to give official authorization to
ACCRETE	*v* -CRETED, -CRETING, -CRETES to grow together
ACCRUAL	*n* pl. -S the act of accruing
ACCRUE	*v* -CRUED, -CRUING, -CRUES to come as an increase or addition
ACCURACY	*n* pl. -CIES the quality of being accurate
ACCURATE	*adj* free from error
ACCURSED	*adj* damnable
ACCURST	*adj* accursed
ACCUSAL	*n* pl. -S the act of accusing
ACCUSANT	*n* pl. -S an accuser
ACCUSE	*v* -CUSED, -CUSING, -CUSES to make an assertion against
ACCUSER	*n* pl. -S one that accuses
ACCUSTOM	*v* -ED, -ING, -S to make familiar
ACE	*v* ACED, ACING, ACES to score a point against in a single stroke
ACEDIA	*n* pl. -S apathy
ACELDAMA	*n* pl. -S a place of bloodshed
ACENTRIC	*adj* having no center
ACEQUIA	*n* pl. -S an irrigation ditch or canal
ACERATE	*adj* acerose
ACERATED	*adj* acerose

ACERB	*adj* ACERBER, ACERBEST sour
ACERBATE	*v* -BATED, -BATING, -BATES to make sour
ACERBIC	*adj* acerb
ACERBITY	*n* pl. -TIES sourness
ACEROLA	*n* pl. -S a West Indian shrub
ACEROSE	*adj* needle-shaped
ACEROUS	*adj* acerose
ACERVATE	*adj* growing in compact clusters
ACERVULI	*n/pl* spore-producing organs of certain fungi
ACESCENT	*n* pl. -S something that is slightly sour
ACETA	pl. of acetum
ACETAL	*n* pl. -S a flammable liquid
ACETAMID	*n* pl. -S an amide of acetic acid
ACETATE	*n* pl. -S a salt of acetic acid **ACETATED** *adj*
ACETIC	*adj* pertaining to vinegar
ACETIFY	*v* -FIED, -FYING, -FIES to convert into vinegar
ACETIN	*n* pl. -S a chemical compound
ACETONE	*n* pl. -S a flammable liquid **ACETONIC** *adj*
ACETOSE	*adj* acetous
ACETOUS	*adj* tasting like vinegar
ACETOXYL	*n* pl. -S a univalent radical
ACETUM	*n* pl. -TA vinegar
ACETYL	*n* pl. -S a univalent radical **ACETYLIC** *adj*
ACHE	*v* ACHED, ACHING, ACHES to suffer a dull, continuous pain
ACHENE	*n* pl. -S a type of fruit **ACHENIAL** *adj*
ACHIER	comparative of achy
ACHIEST	superlative of achy
ACHIEVE	*v* ACHIEVED, ACHIEVING, ACHIEVES to carry out successfully
ACHIEVER	*n* pl. -S one that achieves
ACHILLEA	*n* pl. -S yarrow
ACHINESS	*n* pl. -ES the state of being achy
ACHING	present participle of ache
ACHINGLY	*adv* in an aching manner
ACHIOTE	*n* pl. -S a yellowish red dye
ACHOLIA	*n* pl. -S a lack of bile
ACHOO	*interj* ahchoo
ACHROMAT	*n* pl. -S a type of lens
ACHROMIC	*adj* having no color
ACHY	*adj* ACHIER, ACHIEST aching
ACICULA	*n* pl. -LAE or -LAS a needlelike part or process **ACICULAR** *adj*
ACICULUM	*n* pl. -LA or -LUMS a bristlelike part
ACID	*n* pl. -S a type of chemical compound
ACIDEMIA	*n* pl. -S a condition of increased acidity of the blood
ACIDHEAD	*n* pl. -S one who uses LSD
ACIDIC	*adj* sour
ACIDIFY	*v* -FIED, -FYING, -FIES to convert into an acid
ACIDITY	*n* pl. -TIES sourness
ACIDLY	*adv* sourly
ACIDNESS	*n* pl. -ES acidity
ACIDOSIS	*n* pl. -DOSES an abnormal condition of the blood **ACIDOTIC** *adj*
ACIDURIA	*n* pl. -S a condition of having excessive amounts of acid in the urine
ACIDY	*adj* sour
ACIERATE	*v* -ATED, -ATING, -ATES to turn into steel
ACIFORM	*adj* needle-shaped
ACING	present participle of ace
ACINUS	*n* pl. -NI a small, saclike division of a gland **ACINAR, ACINIC, ACINOSE, ACINOUS** *adj*
ACKEE	*n* pl. -S akee
ACLINIC	*adj* having no inclination
ACME	*n* pl. -S the highest point **ACMATIC, ACMIC** *adj*
ACNE	*n* pl. -S a skin disease **ACNED** *adj*
ACNODE	*n* pl. -S an element of a mathematical set that is isolated from the other elements
ACOCK	*adj* cocked
ACOLD	*adj* cold
ACOLYTE	*n* pl. -S an assistant
ACONITE	*n* pl. -S a poisonous herb **ACONITIC** *adj*
ACONITUM	*n* pl. -S aconite
ACORN	*n* pl. -S the fruit of the oak tree
ACOUSTIC	*n* pl. -S a hearing aid
ACQUAINT	*v* -ED, -ING, -S to cause to know
ACQUEST	*n* pl. -S something acquired

ACQUIRE   *v* -QUIRED, -QUIRING, -QUIRES to come into possession of

ACQUIRER   *n* pl. -S one that acquires

ACQUIT   *v* -QUITTED, -QUITTING, -QUITS to free or clear from a charge of fault or crime

ACRASIA   *n* pl. -S a lack of self-control

ACRASIN   *n* pl. -S a substance secreted by the cells of a slime mold

ACRE   *n* pl. -S a unit of area

ACREAGE   *n* pl. -S area in acres

ACRED   *adj* owning many acres

ACRID   *adj* -RIDER, -RIDEST sharp and harsh to the taste or smell

ACRIDINE   *n* pl. -S a chemical compound

ACRIDITY   *n* pl. -TIES the state of being acrid

ACRIDLY   *adv* in an acrid manner

ACRIMONY   *n* pl. -NIES sharpness or bitterness of speech or temper

ACROBAT   *n* pl. -S one skilled in feats of agility and balance

ACRODONT   *n* pl. -S an animal having rootless teeth

ACROGEN   *n* pl. -S a plant growing at the apex only

ACROLECT   *n* pl. -S a high form of a language

ACROLEIN   *n* pl. -S a flammable liquid

ACROLITH   *n* pl. -S a type of statue

ACROMION   *n* pl. -MIA the outward end of the shoulder blade **ACROMIAL** *adj*

ACRONIC   *adj* occurring at sunset

ACRONYM   *n* pl. -S a word formed from the initials of a compound term or series of words

ACROSOME   *n* pl. -S a thin sac at the head of a sperm

ACROSS   *prep* from one side of to the other

ACROSTIC   *n* pl. -S a poem in which certain letters taken in order form a word or phrase

ACROTISM   *n* pl. -S weakness of the pulse **ACROTIC** *adj*

ACRYLATE   *n* pl. -S an acrylic

ACRYLIC   *n* pl. -S a type of resin

ACT   *v* -ED, -ING, -S to do something

ACTA   *n/pl* recorded proceedings

ACTABLE   *adj* suitable for performance on the stage

ACTIN   *n* pl. -S a protein in muscle tissue

ACTINAL   *adj* having tentacles

ACTING   *n* pl. -S the occupation of an actor

ACTINIA   *n* pl. -IAE or -IAS a marine animal

ACTINIAN   *n* pl. -S actinia

ACTINIC   *adj* pertaining to actinism

ACTINIDE   *n* pl. -S any of a series of radioactive elements

ACTINISM   *n* pl. -S the property of radiant energy that effects chemical changes

ACTINIUM   *n* pl. -S a radioactive element

ACTINOID   *n* pl. -S an actinide

ACTINON   *n* pl. -S an isotope of radon

ACTION   *n* pl. -S the process of acting

ACTIVATE   *v* -VATED, -VATING, -VATES to set in motion

ACTIVE   *n* pl. -S a participating member of an organization

ACTIVELY   *adv* with activity

ACTIVISM   *n* pl. -S a doctrine that emphasizes direct and decisive action

ACTIVIST   *n* pl. -S an advocate of activism

ACTIVITY   *n* pl. -TIES brisk action or movement

ACTIVIZE   *v* -IZED, -IZING, -IZES to activate

ACTOR   *n* pl. -S a theatrical performer **ACTORISH** *adj*

ACTRESS   *n* pl. -ES a female actor **ACTRESSY** *adj*

ACTUAL   *adj* existing in fact **ACTUALLY** *adv*

ACTUARY   *n* pl. -ARIES a statistician who computes insurance risks and premiums

ACTUATE   *v* -ATED, -ATING, -ATES to set into action or motion

ACTUATOR   *n* pl. -S one that actuates

ACUATE   *adj* sharp

ACUITY   *n* pl. -ITIES sharpness

ACULEATE   *adj* having a sting

ACULEUS   *n* pl. -LEI a sharp-pointed part

ACUMEN   *n* pl. -S mental keenness

ACUTANCE   *n* pl. -S a measure of photographic clarity

ACUTE   *adj* ACUTER, ACUTEST marked by sharpness or severity **ACUTELY** *adv*

ACUTE   *n* pl. -S a type of accent mark

ACYCLIC   *adj* not cyclic

ACYL   *n* pl. -S a univalent radical

ACYLATE   *v* -ATED, -ATING, -ATES to introduce acyl into

ACYLOIN   *n* pl. -S a type of chemical compound

AD   *n* pl. -S an advertisement

ADAGE   *n* pl. -S a traditional saying expressing a common observation **ADAGIAL** *adj*

ADAGIO   *n* pl. -GIOS a musical composition or movement played in a slow tempo

ADAMANCE   *n* pl. -S adamancy

ADAMANCY   *n* pl. -CIES unyielding hardness

ADAMANT   *n* pl. -S an extremely hard substance

ADAMSITE   *n* pl. -S a lung-irritating gas

ADAPT   *v* -ED, -ING, -S to make suitable

ADAPTER   *n* pl. -S one that adapts

ADAPTION   *n* pl. -S the act of adapting **ADAPTIVE** *adj*

ADAPTOR   *n* pl. -S adapter

ADAXIAL   *adj* situated on the same side as

ADD   *v* -ED, -ING, -S to combine or join so as to bring about an increase **ADDABLE** *adj*

ADDAX   *n* pl. -ES a large antelope

ADDEDLY   *adv* additionally

ADDEND   *n* pl. -S a number to be added to another

ADDENDUM   *n* pl. -DA something added or to be added

ADDER   *n* pl. -S a venomous snake

ADDIBLE   *adj* capable of being added

ADDICT   *v* -ED, -ING, -S to devote or surrender to something habitually or compulsively

ADDITION   *n* pl. -S something added

ADDITIVE   *n* pl. -S a substance added to another to impart desirable qualities

ADDITORY   *adj* making an addition

ADDLE   *v* -DLED, -DLING, -DLES to confuse

ADDRESS   *v* -DRESSED or -DREST, -DRESSING, -DRESSES to speak to

ADDUCE   *v* -DUCED, -DUCING, -DUCES to bring forward as evidence

ADDUCENT   *adj* serving to adduct

ADDUCER   *n* pl. -S one that adduces

ADDUCING   present participle of adduce

ADDUCT   *v* -ED, -ING, -S to draw toward the main axis

ADDUCTOR   *n* pl. -S an adducent muscle

ADEEM   *v* -ED, -ING, -S to take away

ADENINE   *n* pl. -S an alkaloid

ADENITIS   *n* pl. -TISES inflammation of a lymph node

ADENOID   *n* pl. -S an enlarged lymphoid growth behind the pharynx

ADENOMA   *n* pl. -MAS or -MATA a tumor of glandular origin

ADENOSIS   *n* pl. -NOSES abnormal growth of glandular tissue

ADENYL   *n* pl. -S a univalent radical

ADEPT   *adj* ADEPTER, ADEPTEST highly skilled **ADEPTLY** *adv*

ADEPT   *n* pl. -S an adept person

ADEQUACY   *n* pl. -CIES the state of being adequate

ADEQUATE   *adj* sufficient for a specific requirement

ADHERE   *v* -HERED, -HERING, -HERES to become or remain attached or close to something

ADHEREND   *n* pl. -S the surface to which an adhesive adheres

ADHERENT   *n* pl. -S a supporter

ADHERER   *n* pl. -S one that adheres

ADHERING   present participle of adhere

ADHESION   *n* pl. -S the act of adhering

ADHESIVE   *n* pl. -S a substance that causes adhesion

ADHIBIT   *v* -ED, -ING, -S to take or let in

ADIEU   *n* pl. ADIEUS or ADIEUX a farewell

ADIOS   *interj* — used to express farewell

ADIPOSE   *n* pl. -S animal fat **ADIPIC** *adj*

ADIPOSIS   *n* pl. -POSES obesity

ADIPOUS   *adj* pertaining to adipose

ADIT   *n* pl. -S an entrance

ADJACENT   *adj* next to

ADJOIN *v* -ED, -ING, -S to lie next to

ADJOINT *n* pl. -S a type of mathematical matrix

ADJOURN *v* -ED, -ING, -S to suspend until a later time

ADJUDGE *v* -JUDGED, -JUDGING, -JUDGES to determine judicially

ADJUNCT *n* pl. -S something attached in a subordinate position

ADJURE *v* -JURED, -JURING, -JURES to command solemnly

ADJURER *n* pl. -S one that adjures

ADJUROR *n* pl. -S adjurer

ADJUST *v* -ED, -ING, -S to bring to a more satisfactory state

ADJUSTER *n* pl. -S one that adjusts

ADJUSTOR *n* pl. -S adjuster

ADJUTANT *n* pl. -S an assistant

ADJUVANT *n* pl. -S an assistant

ADMAN *n* pl. -MEN a man employed in the advertising business

ADMASS *adj* pertaining to a society strongly influenced by advertising

ADMIRAL *n* pl. -S a high-ranking naval officer

ADMIRE *v* -MIRED, -MIRING, -MIRES to regard with wonder, pleasure, and approval

ADMIRER *n* pl. -S one that admires

ADMIT *v* -MITTED, -MITTING, -MITS to allow to enter

ADMITTER *n* pl. -S one that admits

ADMIX *v* -MIXED or -MIXT, -MIXING, -MIXES to mix

ADMONISH *v* -ED, -ING, -ES to reprove mildly or kindly

ADNATE *adj* joined to another part or organ

ADNATION *n* pl. -S the state of being adnate

ADNEXA *n/pl* conjoined anatomical parts **ADNEXAL** *adj*

ADNOUN *n* pl. -S an adjective when used as a noun

ADO *n* pl. ADOS bustling excitement

ADOBE *n* pl. -S an unburnt, sun-dried brick

ADOBO *n* pl. -BOS a Philippine dish of fish or meat

ADONIS *n* pl. -ISES a handsome young man

ADOPT *v* -ED, -ING, -S to take into one's family by legal means

ADOPTEE *n* pl. -S one that is adopted

ADOPTER *n* pl. -S one that adopts

ADOPTION *n* pl. -S the act of adopting **ADOPTIVE** *adj*

ADORABLE *adj* worthy of being adored **ADORABLY** *adv*

ADORE *v* ADORED, ADORING, ADORES to love deeply

ADORER *n* pl. -S one that adores

ADORN *v* -ED, -ING, -S to add something to for the purpose of making more attractive

ADORNER *n* pl. -S one that adorns

ADOWN *adv* downward

ADOZE *adj* dozing

ADRENAL *n* pl. -S an endocrine gland

ADRIFT *adj* drifting

ADROIT *adj* ADROITER, ADROITEST skillful **ADROITLY** *adv*

ADSCRIPT *n* pl. -S a distinguishing symbol written after another character

ADSORB *v* -ED, -ING, -S to gather on a surface in a condensed layer

ADSORBER *n* pl. -S one that adsorbs

ADULARIA *n* pl. -S a mineral

ADULATE *v* -LATED, -LATING, -LATES to praise excessively

ADULATOR *n* pl. -S one that adulates

ADULT *n* pl. -S a fully developed individual

ADULTERY *n* pl. -TERIES voluntary sexual intercourse between a married person and someone other than his or her spouse

ADULTLY *adv* in a manner typical of an adult

ADUMBRAL *adj* shadowy

ADUNC *adj* bent inward

ADUNCATE *adj* adunc

ADUNCOUS *adj* adunc

ADUST *adj* scorched

ADVANCE *v* -VANCED, -VANCING, -VANCES to move or cause to move ahead

ADVANCER *n* pl. -S one that advances

ADVECT *v* -ED, -ING, -S to convey or transport by the flow of a fluid

ADVENT *n* pl. -S arrival

ADVERB	*n* pl. -S a word used to modify a verb, adjective, or other adverb	**AERATE**	*v* -ATED, -ATING, -ATES to supply with air
ADVERSE	*adj* acting in opposition	**AERATION**	*n* pl. -S the act of aerating
ADVERT	*v* -ED, -ING, -S to call attention	**AERATOR**	*n* pl. -S one that aerates
ADVICE	*n* pl. -S recommendation regarding a decision or action	**AERIAL**	*n* pl. -S an antenna
ADVISE	*v* -VISED, -VISING, -VISES to give advice to	**AERIALLY**	*adv* in a manner pertaining to the air
ADVISEE	*n* pl. -S one that is advised	**AERIE**	*n* pl. -S a bird's nest built high on a mountain or cliff **AERIED** *adj*
ADVISER	*n* pl. -S one that advises	**AERIER**	comparative of aery
ADVISING	present participle of advise	**AERIES**	pl. of aery
ADVISOR	*n* pl. -S adviser	**AERIEST**	superlative of aery
ADVISORY	*n* pl. -RIES a report giving information	**AERIFORM**	*adj* having the form of air
ADVOCACY	*n* pl. -CIES the act of advocating	**AERIFY**	*v* -FIED, -FYING, -FIES to aerate
ADVOCATE	*v* -CATED, -CATING, -CATES to speak in favor of	**AERILY**	*adv* in an aery manner
		AERO	*adj* pertaining to aircraft
ADVOWSON	*n* pl. -S the right of presenting a nominee to a vacant church office	**AEROBE**	*n* pl. -S an organism that requires oxygen to live **AEROBIC** *adj*
ADYNAMIA	*n* pl. -S lack of physical strength **ADYNAMIC** *adj*	**AEROBICS**	*n/pl* exercises for conditioning the heart and lungs by increasing oxygen consumption
ADYTUM	*n* pl. -TA an inner sanctuary in an ancient temple	**AEROBIUM**	*n* pl. -BIA aerobe
ADZ	*n* pl. -ES a cutting tool	**AERODUCT**	*n* pl. -S a type of jet engine
ADZE	*n* pl. -S adz	**AERODYNE**	*n* pl. -S an aircraft that is heavier than air
ADZUKI	*n* pl. -S the edible seed of an Asian plant	**AEROFOIL**	*n* pl. -S airfoil
AE	*adj* one	**AEROGEL**	*n* pl. -S a highly porous solid
AECIA	pl. of aecium	**AEROGRAM**	*n* pl. -S an airmail letter
AECIAL	*adj* pertaining to an aecium	**AEROLITE**	*n* pl. -S a meteorite containing more stone than iron
AECIDIAL	*adj* pertaining to an aecium	**AEROLITH**	*n* pl. -S aerolite
AECIDIUM	*n* pl. -IA an aecium	**AEROLOGY**	*n* pl. -GIES the study of the atmosphere
AECIUM	*n* pl. -IA a spore-producing organ of certain fungi	**AERONAUT**	*n* pl. -S one who operates an airship
AEDES	*n* pl. AEDES any of a genus of mosquitoes	**AERONOMY**	*n* pl. -MIES the study of the upper atmosphere
AEDILE	*n* pl. -S a magistrate of ancient Rome	**AEROSAT**	*n* pl. -S a satellite for use in air-traffic control
AEDINE	*adj* pertaining to an aedes	**AEROSOL**	*n* pl. -S a gaseous suspension of fine solid or liquid particles
AEGIS	*n* pl. -GISES protection	**AEROSTAT**	*n* pl. -S an aircraft that is lighter than air
AENEOUS	*adj* having a greenish gold color		
AENEUS	*adj* aeneous	**AERUGO**	*n* pl. -GOS a green film that forms on copper
AEOLIAN	*adj* eolian		
AEON	*n* pl. -S eon	**AERY**	*adj* AERIER, AERIEST airy
AEONIAN	*adj* eonian	**AERY**	*n* pl. AERIES aerie
AEONIC	*adj* eonian	**AESTHETE**	*n* pl. -S esthete
AEQUORIN	*n* pl. -S a protein secreted by jellyfish		

AESTIVAL	*adj* estival
AETHER	*n* pl. -S the upper region of the atmosphere **AETHERIC** *adj*
AFAR	*n* pl. -S a great distance
AFEARD	*adj* afraid
AFEARED	*adj* afeard
AFEBRILE	*adj* having no fever
AFF	*adv* off
AFFABLE	*adj* easy to talk to **AFFABLY** *adv*
AFFAIR	*n* pl. -S anything done or to be done
AFFAIRE	*n* pl. -S a brief amorous relationship
AFFECT	*v* -ED, -ING, -S to give a false appearance of
AFFECTER	*n* pl. -S one that affects
AFFERENT	*n* pl. -S a nerve that conveys impulses toward a nerve center
AFFIANCE	*v* -ANCED, -ANCING, -ANCES to betroth
AFFIANT	*n* pl. -S one who makes a written declaration under oath
AFFICHE	*n* pl. -S a poster
AFFINAL	*adj* related by marriage
AFFINE	*n* pl. -S a relative by marriage
AFFINED	*adj* closely related
AFFINELY	*adv* in the manner of a type of mathematical mapping
AFFINITY	*n* pl. -TIES a natural attraction or inclination
AFFIRM	*v* -ED, -ING, -S to state positively
AFFIRMER	*n* pl. -S one that affirms
AFFIX	*v* -ED, -ING, -ES to attach
AFFIXAL	*adj* pertaining to a prefix or suffix
AFFIXER	*n* pl. -S one that affixes
AFFIXIAL	*adj* affixal
AFFLATUS	*n* pl. -ES a creative inspiration
AFFLICT	*v* -ED, -ING, -S to distress with mental or physical pain
AFFLUENT	*n* pl. -S a stream that flows into another
AFFLUX	*n* pl. -ES a flowing toward a point
AFFORD	*v* -ED, -ING, -S to have sufficient means for
AFFOREST	*v* -ED, -ING, -S to convert into forest
AFFRAY	*v* -ED, -ING, -S to frighten
AFFRAYER	*n* pl. -S one that affrays
AFFRIGHT	*v* -ED, -ING, -S to frighten
AFFRONT	*v* -ED, -ING, -S to insult openly
AFFUSION	*n* pl. -S an act of pouring a liquid on
AFGHAN	*n* pl. -S a woolen blanket or shawl
AFGHANI	*n* pl. -S a monetary unit of Afghanistan
AFIELD	*adv* in the field
AFIRE	*adj* being on fire
AFLAME	*adj* flaming
AFLOAT	*adj* floating
AFLUTTER	*adj* nervously excited
AFOOT	*adv* on foot
AFORE	*adv* before
AFOUL	*adj* entangled
AFRAID	*adj* filled with apprehension
AFREET	*n* pl. -S an evil spirit in Arabic mythology
AFRESH	*adv* anew
AFRIT	*n* pl. -S afreet
AFT	*adv* toward the stern
AFTER	*prep* behind in place or order
AFTERS	*n/pl* dessert
AFTERTAX	*adj* remaining after payment of taxes
AFTMOST	*adj* nearest the stern
AFTOSA	*n* pl. -S a disease of hoofed mammals
AG	*adj* pertaining to agriculture
AGA	*n* pl. -S a high-ranking Turkish military officer
AGAIN	*adv* once more
AGAINST	*prep* in opposition to
AGALLOCH	*n* pl. -S the fragrant wood of a tropical tree
AGALWOOD	*n* pl. -S agalloch
AGAMA	*n* pl. -S a tropical lizard
AGAMETE	*n* pl. -S an asexual reproductive cell
AGAMIC	*adj* asexual
AGAMOUS	*adj* agamic
AGAPE	*n* pl. -PAE or -PAI the love of God for mankind **AGAPEIC** *adj*
AGAR	*n* pl. -S a viscous substance obtained from certain seaweeds
AGARIC	*n* pl. -S any of a family of fungi

AGAROSE   *n* pl. -S a sugar obtained from agar

AGATE   *n* pl. -S a variety of quartz **AGATOID** *adj*

AGATIZE   *v* -IZED, -IZING, -IZES to cause to resemble agate

AGAVE   *n* pl. -S a tropical plant

AGAZE   *adj* gazing

AGE   *v* AGED, AGING or AGEING, AGES to grow old

AGEDLY   *adv* oldly

AGEDNESS   *n* pl. -ES oldness

AGEE   *adv* to one side

AGEING   *n* pl. -S aging

AGEISM   *n* pl. -S discrimination based on age

AGEIST   *n* pl. -S an advocate of ageism

AGELESS   *adj* never growing old

AGELONG   *adj* lasting for a long time

AGENCY   *n* pl. -CIES an organization that does business for others

AGENDA   *n* pl. -S a list of things to be done

AGENDUM   *n* pl. -S an item on an agenda

AGENE   *n* pl. -S a chemical compound used in bleaching flour

AGENESIA   *n* pl. -S agenesis

AGENESIS   *n* pl. AGENESES absence or imperfect development of a bodily part **AGENETIC** *adj*

AGENIZE   *v* -NIZED, -NIZING, -NIZES to treat with agene

AGENT   *n* pl. -S one who is authorized to act for another **AGENTIAL** *adj*

AGENTING   *n* pl. -S the business or activities of an agent

AGENTIVE   *n* pl. -S a word part that denotes the doer of an action

AGENTRY   *n* pl. -RIES the office or duties of an agent

AGER   *n* pl. -S one that ages

AGERATUM   *n* pl. -S a flowering plant

AGGADIC   *adj* haggadic

AGGER   *n* pl. -S a mound of earth used as a fortification

AGGIE   *n* pl. -S a type of playing marble

AGGRADE   *v* -GRADED, -GRADING, -GRADES to fill with detrital material

AGGRESS   *v* -ED, -ING, -ES to commit the first act of hostility

AGGRIEVE   *v* -GRIEVED, -GRIEVING, -GRIEVES to distress

AGGRO   *n* pl. -GROS a rivalry or grievance

AGHA   *n* pl. -S aga

AGHAST   *adj* shocked by something horrible

AGILE   *adj* able to move quickly and easily **AGILELY** *adv*

AGILITY   *n* pl. -TIES the quality of being agile

AGIN   *prep* against

AGING   *n* pl. -S the process of growing old

AGINNER   *n* pl. -S one that is against change

AGIO   *n* pl. AGIOS a premium paid for the exchange of one currency for another

AGIOTAGE   *n* pl. -S the business of a broker

AGISM   *n* pl. -S ageism

AGIST   *v* -ED, -ING, -S to feed and take care of for a fee, as livestock

AGITATE   *v* -TATED, -TATING, -TATES to move with a violent, irregular action **AGITABLE** *adj*

AGITATO   *adj* fast and stirring — used as a musical direction

AGITATOR   *n* pl. -S one that agitates

AGITPROP   *n* pl. -S pro-Communist propaganda

AGLARE   *adj* glaring

AGLEAM   *adj* gleaming

AGLEE   *adv* agley

AGLET   *n* pl. -S a metal sheath at the end of a lace

AGLEY   *adv* awry

AGLIMMER   *adj* glimmering

AGLITTER   *adj* glittering

AGLOW   *adj* glowing

AGLY   *adv* agley

AGLYCON   *n* pl. -S a type of chemical compound

AGLYCONE   *n* pl. -S aglycon

AGMA   *n* pl. -S eng

AGMINATE   *adj* clustered together

AGNAIL   *n* pl. -S a piece of loose skin at the base of a fingernail

AGNATE   *n* pl. -S a relative on the father's side **AGNATIC** *adj*

AGNATION	*n* pl. -S the relationship of agnates
AGNIZE	*v* -NIZED, -NIZING, -NIZES to acknowledge
AGNOMEN	*n* pl. -MINA or -MENS an additional name given to an ancient Roman
AGNOSIA	*n* pl. -S loss of ability to recognize familiar objects
AGNOSTIC	*n* pl. -S one who disclaims any knowledge of God
AGO	*adv* in the past
AGOG	*adv* in a state of eager curiosity
AGON	*n* pl. -S or -ES the dramatic conflict between the main characters in a Greek play
AGONAL	*adj* pertaining to agony
AGONE	*adv* ago
AGONES	a pl. of agon
AGONIC	*adj* not forming an angle
AGONIES	pl. of agony
AGONISE	*v* -NISED, -NISING, -NISES to agonize
AGONIST	*n* pl. -S one that is engaged in a struggle
AGONIZE	*v* -NIZED, -NIZING, -NIZES to suffer extreme pain
AGONY	*n* pl. -NIES extreme pain
AGORA	*n* pl. -RAS or -RAE a marketplace in ancient Greece
AGORA	*n* pl. AGOROT or AGOROTH a monetary unit of Israel
AGOUTI	*n* pl. -S or -ES a burrowing rodent
AGOUTY	*n* pl. -TIES agouti
AGRAFE	*n* pl. -S agraffe
AGRAFFE	*n* pl. -S an ornamental clasp
AGRAPHA	*n/pl* the sayings of Jesus not found in the Bible
AGRAPHIA	*n* pl. -S a mental disorder marked by inability to write **AGRAPHIC** *adj*
AGRARIAN	*n* pl. -S one who favors equal distribution of land
AGRAVIC	*adj* pertaining to a condition of no gravitation
AGREE	*v* AGREED, AGREEING, AGREES to have the same opinion
AGRESTAL	*adj* growing wild
AGRESTIC	*adj* rural
AGRIA	*n* pl. -S severe pustular eruption
AGRIMONY	*n* pl. -NIES a perennial herb
AGROLOGY	*n* pl. -GIES the science of soils in relation to crops
AGRONOMY	*n* pl. -MIES the application of scientific principles to the cultivation of land
AGROUND	*adv* on the ground
AGRYPNIA	*n* pl. -S insomnia
AGUE	*n* pl. -S a malarial fever **AGUELIKE, AGUISH** *adj* **AGUISHLY** *adv*
AGUEWEED	*n* pl. -S a flowering plant
AH	*interj* — used to express delight, relief, or contempt
AHA	*interj* — used to express surprise, triumph, or derision
AHCHOO	*interj* — used to represent the sound of a sneeze
AHEAD	*adv* at or to the front
AHEM	*interj* — used to attract attention
AHIMSA	*n* pl. -S the Hindu principle of nonviolence
AHOLD	*n* pl. -S a hold or grasp of something
AHORSE	*adv* on a horse
AHOY	*interj* — used in hailing a ship or person
AHULL	*adj* abandoned and flooded, as a ship
AI	*n* pl. -S a three-toed sloth
AIBLINS	*adv* ablins
AID	*v* -ED, -ING, -S to help
AIDE	*n* pl. -S an assistant
AIDER	*n* pl. -S one that aids
AIDFUL	*adj* helpful
AIDLESS	*adj* helpless
AIDMAN	*n* pl. -MEN a corpsman
AIGLET	*n* pl. -S aglet
AIGRET	*n* pl. -S aigrette
AIGRETTE	*n* pl. -S a tuft of feathers worn as a head ornament
AIGUILLE	*n* pl. -S a sharp, pointed mountain peak
AIKIDO	*n* pl. -DOS a Japanese art of self-defense
AIL	*v* -ED, -ING, -S to cause pain or discomfort to
AILERON	*n* pl. -S a movable control surface on an airplane wing

AILMENT   *n* pl. -S a physical or mental disorder

AIM   *v* -ED, -ING, -S to direct toward a specified object or goal

AIMER   *n* pl. -S one that aims

AIMFUL   *adj* full of purpose **AIMFULLY** *adv*

AIMLESS   *adj* lacking direction or purpose

AIN   *n* pl. -S ayin

AINSELL   *n* pl. -S own self

AIOLI   *n* pl. -S garlic mayonnaise

AIR   *v* -ED, -ING, -S to expose to the air (the mixture of gases that surrounds the earth)

AIR   *adv* AIRER, AIREST early

AIRBOAT   *n* pl. -S a boat used in swampy areas

AIRBORNE   *adj* flying

AIRBOUND   *adj* stopped up by air

AIRBRUSH   *v* -ED, -ING, -ES to apply in a fine spray by compressed air, as paint

AIRBURST   *n* pl. -S an explosion in the air

AIRBUS   *n* pl. -BUSES or -BUSSES a passenger airplane

AIRCHECK   *n* pl. -S a recording made from a radio broadcast

AIRCOACH   *n* pl. -ES the cheaper class of accommodations in commercial aircraft

AIRCRAFT   *n* pl. AIRCRAFT any machine or device capable of flying

AIRCREW   *n* pl. -S the crew of an aircraft

AIRDATE   *n* pl. -S the scheduled date of a broadcast

AIRDROME   *n* pl. -S an airport

AIRDROP   *v* -DROPPED, -DROPPING, -DROPS to drop from an aircraft

AIRER   *n* pl. -S a frame on which to dry clothes

AIRFARE   *n* pl. -S payment for travel by airplane

AIRFIELD   *n* pl. -S an airport

AIRFLOW   *n* pl. -S a flow of air

AIRFOIL   *n* pl. -S a part of an aircraft designed to provide lift or control

AIRFRAME   *n* pl. -S the framework and external covering of an airplane

AIRGLOW   *n* pl. -S a glow in the upper atmosphere

AIRHEAD   *n* pl. -S a stupid person

AIRHOLE   *n* pl. -S a hole to let air in or out

AIRIER   comparative of airy

AIRIEST   superlative of airy

AIRILY   *adv* in an airy manner

AIRINESS   *n* pl. -ES the state of being airy

AIRING   *n* pl. -S an exposure to the air

AIRLESS   *adj* having no air

AIRLIFT   *v* -ED, -ING, -S to transport by airplane

AIRLIKE   *adj* resembling air

AIRLINE   *n* pl. -S an air transportation system

AIRLINER   *n* pl. -S a large passenger aircraft

AIRMAIL   *v* -ED, -ING, -S to send mail by airplane

AIRMAN   *n* pl. -MEN an aviator

AIRN   *n* pl. -S iron

AIRPARK   *n* pl. -S a small airport

AIRPLANE   *n* pl. -S a winged aircraft propelled by jet engines or propellers

AIRPLAY   *n* pl. -PLAYS the playing of a record on a radio program

AIRPORT   *n* pl. -S a tract of land maintained for the landing and takeoff of aircraft

AIRPOST   *n* pl. -S a system of conveying mail by airplane

AIRPOWER   *n* pl. -S the military strength of a nation's air force

AIRPROOF   *v* -ED, -ING, -S to make impermeable to air

AIRSCAPE   *n* pl. -S a view of the earth from an aircraft or a high position

AIRSCREW   *n* pl. -S an airplane propeller

AIRSHED   *n* pl. -S the air supply of a given region

AIRSHIP   *n* pl. -S a lighter-than-air aircraft having propulsion and steering systems

AIRSICK   *adj* nauseated from flying in an airplane

AIRSPACE   *n* pl. -S the portion of the atmosphere above a particular land area

AIRSPEED   *n* pl. -S the speed of an aircraft with relation to the air

AIRSTRIP   *n* pl. -S a runway

AIRT   *v* -ED, -ING, -S to guide

AIRTH   *v* -ED, -ING, -S to airt

AIRTIGHT	*adj* not allowing air to escape or enter	**ALANINE**	*n* pl. -S an amino acid
AIRTIME	*n* pl. -S the time when a broadcast begins	**ALANT**	*n* pl. -S alan
		ALANYL	*n* pl. -S a univalent radical
AIRWARD	*adv* toward the sky	**ALAR**	*adj* pertaining to wings
AIRWAVE	*n* pl. -S the medium of radio and television transmission	**ALARM**	*v* -ED, -ING, -S to frighten by a sudden revelation of danger
AIRWAY	*n* pl. -WAYS a passageway in which air circulates	**ALARMISM**	*n* pl. -S the practice of alarming others needlessly
AIRWISE	*adj* skillful in aviation	**ALARMIST**	*n* pl. -S one who alarms others needlessly
AIRWOMAN	*n* pl. -WOMEN a female aviator	**ALARUM**	*v* -ED, -ING, -S to alarm
AIRY	*adj* AIRIER, AIRIEST having the nature of air	**ALARY**	*adj* alar
AISLE	*n* pl. -S a passageway between sections of seats **AISLED** *adj*	**ALAS**	*interj* — used to express sorrow or regret
AISLEWAY	*n* pl. -WAYS an aisle	**ALASKA**	*n* pl. -S a heavy fabric
AIT	*n* pl. -S a small island	**ALASTOR**	*n* pl. -S an avenging deity in Greek tragedy
AITCH	*n* pl. -ES the letter H	**ALATE**	*n* pl. -S a winged insect
AIVER	*n* pl. -S a draft horse	**ALATED**	*adj* having wings
AJAR	*adj* partly open	**ALATION**	*n* pl. -S the state of having wings
AJEE	*adv* agee	**ALB**	*n* pl. -S a long-sleeved vestment
AJIVA	*n* pl. -S inanimate matter	**ALBA**	*n* pl. -S the white substance of the brain
AJOWAN	*n* pl. -S the fruit of an Egyptian plant	**ALBACORE**	*n* pl. -S a marine food fish
AJUGA	*n* pl. -S a flowering plant	**ALBATA**	*n* pl. -S an alloy of copper, nickel, and zinc
AKEE	*n* pl. -S a tropical tree		
AKELA	*n* pl. -S a leader of a cub scout pack	**ALBEDO**	*n* pl. -DOS or -DOES the ratio of the light reflected by a planet to that received by it
AKENE	*n* pl. -S achene		
AKIMBO	*adj* having hands on hips and elbows bent outward	**ALBEIT**	*conj* although
		ALBICORE	*n* pl. -S albacore
AKIN	*adj* related by blood	**ALBINAL**	*adj* albinic
AKVAVIT	*n* pl. -S aquavit	**ALBINIC**	*adj* pertaining to albinism
AL	*n* pl. -S an East Indian tree	**ALBINISM**	*n* pl. -S the condition of being an albino
ALA	*n* pl. ALAE a wing or winglike part	**ALBINO**	*n* pl. -NOS an organism lacking normal pigmentation
ALACK	*interj* — used to express sorrow or regret	**ALBITE**	*n* pl. -S a mineral **ALBITIC** *adj*
ALACRITY	*n* pl. -TIES cheerful promptness	**ALBIZIA**	*n* pl. -S a tropical tree
ALAE	pl. of ala	**ALBIZZIA**	*n* pl. -S albizia
ALAMEDA	*n* pl. -S a shaded walkway	**ALBUM**	*n* pl. -S a book for preserving photographs or stamps
ALAMO	*n* pl. -MOS a softwood tree		
ALAMODE	*n* pl. -S a silk fabric	**ALBUMEN**	*n* pl. -S the white of an egg
ALAN	*n* pl. -S a large hunting dog	**ALBUMIN**	*n* pl. -S a simple protein
ALAND	*n* pl. -S alan	**ALBUMOSE**	*n* pl. -S a proteose
ALANE	*adj* alone	**ALBURNUM**	*n* pl. -S sapwood
ALANG	*adv* along	**ALCADE**	*n* pl. -S alcalde
ALANIN	*n* pl. -S alanine	**ALCAHEST**	*n* pl. -S alkahest

ALCAIC	*n* pl. -S a type of verse form
ALCAIDE	*n* pl. -S the commander of a Spanish fortress
ALCALDE	*n* pl. -S the mayor of a Spanish town
ALCAYDE	*n* pl. -S alcaide
ALCAZAR	*n* pl. -S a Spanish fortress or palace
ALCHEMY	*n* pl. -MIES a medieval form of chemistry **ALCHEMIC** *adj*
ALCHYMY	*n* pl. -MIES alchemy
ALCID	*n* pl. -S a diving seabird
ALCIDINE	*adj* pertaining to a family of seabirds
ALCOHOL	*n* pl. -S a flammable liquid
ALCOVE	*n* pl. -S a recessed section of a room **ALCOVED** *adj*
ALDEHYDE	*n* pl. -S a type of chemical compound
ALDER	*n* pl. -S a shrub or small tree
ALDERFLY	*n* pl. -FLIES a winged insect
ALDERMAN	*n* pl. -MEN a member of a municipal legislative body
ALDOL	*n* pl. -S a chemical compound
ALDOLASE	*n* pl. -S an enzyme
ALDOSE	*n* pl. -S a type of sugar
ALDRIN	*n* pl. -S an insecticide
ALE	*n* pl. -S an alcoholic beverage
ALEATORY	*adj* pertaining to luck
ALEC	*n* pl. -S a herring
ALEE	*adv* toward the side of a vessel sheltered from the wind
ALEF	*n* pl. -S aleph
ALEGAR	*n* pl. -S sour ale
ALEHOUSE	*n* pl. -S a tavern where ale is sold
ALEMBIC	*n* pl. -S an apparatus formerly used in distilling
ALENCON	*n* pl. -S a needlepoint lace
ALEPH	*n* pl. -S a Hebrew letter
ALERT	*adj* ALERTER, ALERTEST ready for sudden action **ALERTLY** *adv*
ALERT	*v* -ED, -ING, -S to warn
ALEURON	*n* pl. -S aleurone
ALEURONE	*n* pl. -S protein matter found in the seeds of certain plants
ALEVIN	*n* pl. -S a young fish
ALEWIFE	*n* pl. -WIVES a marine fish
ALEXIA	*n* pl. -S a cerebral disorder marked by the loss of the ability to read
ALEXIN	*n* pl. -S a substance in the blood that aids in the destruction of bacteria
ALEXINE	*n* pl. -S alexin
ALFA	*n* pl. -S a communications code word for the letter A
ALFAKI	*n* pl. -S alfaqui
ALFALFA	*n* pl. -S a plant cultivated for use as hay and forage
ALFAQUI	*n* pl. -S a teacher of Muslim law
ALFAQUIN	*n* pl. -S alfaqui
ALFORJA	*n* pl. -S a leather bag
ALFRESCO	*adv* outdoors
ALGA	*n* pl. -GAE or -GAS any of a group of primitive aquatic plants **ALGAL** *adj*
ALGAROBA	*n* pl. -S the mesquite
ALGEBRA	*n* pl. -S a branch of mathematics
ALGERINE	*n* pl. -S a woolen fabric
ALGICIDE	*n* pl. -S a substance used to kill algae
ALGID	*adj* cold
ALGIDITY	*n* pl. -TIES coldness
ALGIN	*n* pl. -S a viscous substance obtained from certain algae
ALGINATE	*n* pl. -S a chemical salt
ALGOID	*adj* resembling algae
ALGOLOGY	*n* pl. -GIES the study of algae
ALGOR	*n* pl. -S coldness
ALGORISM	*n* pl. -S the Arabic system of arithmetic notation
ALGUM	*n* pl. -S almug
ALIAS	*n* pl. -ES an assumed name
ALIBI	*v* -BIED, -BIING, -BIES or -BIS to make excuses for oneself
ALIBLE	*adj* nourishing
ALIDAD	*n* pl. -S alidade
ALIDADE	*n* pl. -S a device used in angular measurement
ALIEN	*v* -ED, -ING, -S to transfer to another, as property
ALIENAGE	*n* pl. -S the state of being foreign
ALIENATE	*v* -ATED, -ATING, -ATES to make indifferent or unfriendly
ALIENEE	*n* pl. -S one to whom property is transferred

ALIENER *n* pl. -S alienor

ALIENISM *n* pl. -S alienage

ALIENIST *n* pl. -S a physician who treats mental disorders

ALIENLY *adv* in a foreign manner

ALIENOR *n* pl. -S one that transfers property

ALIF *n* pl. -S an Arabic letter

ALIFORM *adj* shaped like a wing

ALIGHT *v* ALIGHTED or ALIT, ALIGHTING, ALIGHTS to come down from something

ALIGN *v* -ED, -ING, -S to arrange in a straight line

ALIGNER *n* pl. -S one that aligns

ALIKE *adj* having close resemblance

ALIMENT *v* -ED, -ING, -S to nourish

ALIMONY *n* pl. -NIES an allowance paid to a woman by her divorced husband

ALINE *v* ALINED, ALINING, ALINES to align

ALINER *n* pl. -S aligner

ALIPED *n* pl. -S an animal having a membrane connecting the toes

ALIQUANT *adj* not dividing evenly into another number

ALIQUOT *n* pl. -S a number that divides evenly into another

ALIST *adj* leaning to one side

ALIT a past tense of alight

ALIUNDE *adv* from a source extrinsic to the matter at hand

ALIVE *adj* having life

ALIYA *n* pl. -S aliyah

ALIYAH *n* pl. -YAHS or -YOS or -YOT the immigration of Jews to Israel

ALIZARIN *n* pl. -S a red dye

ALKAHEST *n* pl. -S the hypothetical universal solvent sought by alchemists

ALKALI *n* pl. -LIES or -LIS a type of chemical compound **ALKALIC** *adj*

ALKALIFY *v* -FIED, -FYING, -FIES to alkalize

ALKALIN *adj* alkaline

ALKALINE *adj* containing an alkali

ALKALISE *v* -LISED, -LISING, -LISES to alkalize

ALKALIZE *v* -LIZED, -LIZING, -LIZES to convert into an alkali

ALKALOID *n* pl. -S a type of chemical compound

ALKANE *n* pl. -S a type of chemical compound

ALKANET *n* pl. -S a European plant

ALKENE *n* pl. -S a type of chemical compound

ALKIES pl. of alky

ALKINE *n* pl. -S alkyne

ALKOXIDE *n* pl. -S a type of chemical salt

ALKOXY *adj* containing a univalent radical composed of alkyl united with oxygen

ALKY *n* pl. -KIES one who is habitually drunk

ALKYD *n* pl. -S a synthetic resin

ALKYL *n* pl. -S a univalent radical **ALKYLIC** *adj*

ALKYLATE *v* -ATED, -ATING, -ATES to combine with alkyl

ALKYNE *n* pl. -S a type of chemical compound

ALL *n* pl. -S everything that one has

ALLANITE *n* pl. -S a mineral

ALLAY *v* -ED, -ING, -S to reduce in intensity or severity

ALLAYER *n* pl. -S one that allays

ALLEE *n* pl. -S a tree-lined walkway

ALLEGE *v* -LEGED, -LEGING, -LEGES to assert without proof or before proving

ALLEGER *n* pl. -S one that alleges

ALLEGORY *n* pl. -RIES a story presenting a moral principle

ALLEGRO *n* pl. -GROS a musical passage played in rapid tempo

ALLELE *n* pl. -S any of several forms of a gene **ALLELIC** *adj*

ALLELISM *n* pl. -S the state of possessing alleles

ALLELUIA *n* pl. -S a song of praise to God

ALLERGEN *n* pl. -S a substance capable of inducing an allergy

ALLERGIC *adj* pertaining to allergy

ALLERGIN *n* pl. -S allergen

ALLERGY *n* pl. -GIES a state of hypersensitive reaction to certain things

ALLEY *n* pl. -LEYS a narrow passageway

ALLEYWAY *n* pl. -WAYS an alley

ALLHEAL   *n* pl. -S a medicinal herb

ALLIABLE   *adj* capable of being allied

ALLIANCE   *n* pl. -S an association formed to further the common interests of its members

ALLICIN   *n* pl. -S a liquid compound

ALLIED   past tense of ally

ALLIES   present 3d person sing. of ally

ALLIUM   *n* pl. -S a bulbous herb

ALLOBAR   *n* pl. -S a change in barometric pressure

ALLOCATE   *v* -CATED, -CATING, -CATES to set apart for a particular purpose

ALLOD   *n* pl. -S allodium

ALLODIUM   *n* pl. -DIA land held in absolute ownership **ALLODIAL** *adj*

ALLOGAMY   *n* pl. -MIES fertilization of a flower by pollen from another

ALLONGE   *n* pl. -S an addition to a document

ALLONYM   *n* pl. -S the name of one person assumed by another

ALLOPATH   *n* pl. -S one who treats diseases by producing effects incompatible with those of the disease

ALLOT   *v* -LOTTED, -LOTTING, -LOTS to give as a share or portion

ALLOTTEE   *n* pl. -S one to whom something is allotted

ALLOTTER   *n* pl. -S one that allots

ALLOTTING   present participle of allot

ALLOTYPE   *n* pl. -S a type of antibody

ALLOTYPY   *n* pl. -TYPIES the condition of being an allotype

ALLOVER   *n* pl. -S a fabric having a pattern extending over the entire surface

ALLOW   *v* -ED, -ING, -S to put no obstacle in the way of

ALLOXAN   *n* pl. -S a chemical compound

ALLOY   *v* -ED, -ING, -S to combine to form an alloy (a homogenous mixture of metals)

ALLSEED   *n* pl. -S a plant having many seeds

ALLSPICE   *n* pl. -S a tropical tree

ALLUDE   *v* -LUDED, -LUDING, -LUDES to make an indirect reference

ALLURE   *v* -LURED, -LURING, -LURES to attract with something desirable

ALLURER   *n* pl. -S one that allures

ALLUSION   *n* pl. -S the act of alluding **ALLUSIVE** *adj*

ALLUVIA   a pl. of alluvium

ALLUVIAL   *n* pl. -S soil composed of alluvium

ALLUVION   *n* pl. -S alluvium

ALLUVIUM   *n* pl. -VIA or -VIUMS detrital material deposited by running water

ALLY   *v* -LIED, -LYING, -LIES to unite in a formal relationship

ALLYL   *n* pl. -S a univalent radical **ALLYLIC** *adj*

ALMA   *n* pl. -S almah

ALMAGEST   *n* pl. -S a medieval treatise on astrology or alchemy

ALMAH   *n* pl. -S an Egyptian girl who sings and dances professionally

ALMANAC   *n* pl. -S an annual publication containing general information

ALME   *n* pl. -S almah

ALMEH   *n* pl. -S almah

ALMEMAR   *n* pl. -S a bema

ALMIGHTY   *adj* having absolute power over all

ALMNER   *n* pl. -S almoner

ALMOND   *n* pl. -S the edible nut of a small tree

ALMONER   *n* pl. -S one that distributes alms

ALMONRY   *n* pl. -RIES a place where alms are distributed

ALMOST   *adv* very nearly

ALMS   *n* pl. ALMS money or goods given to the poor

ALMSMAN   *n* pl. -MEN one who receives alms

ALMUCE   *n* pl. -S a hooded cape

ALMUD   *n* pl. -S a Spanish unit of capacity

ALMUDE   *n* pl. -S almud

ALMUG   *n* pl. -S a precious wood mentioned in the Bible

ALNICO   *n* pl. -COES a magnetic alloy

ALODIUM   *n* pl. -DIA allodium **ALODIAL** *adj*

ALOE   *n* pl. -S an African plant **ALOETIC** *adj*

ALOFT   *adv* in or into the air

ALOGICAL   *adj* being outside the bounds of that to which logic can apply

ALOHA   *n* pl. -S love — used as a greeting or farewell

ALOIN   *n* pl. -S a laxative

ALONE   *adj* apart from others

ALONG   *adv* onward

ALOOF   *adj* distant in interest or feeling **ALOOFLY** *adv*

ALOPECIA   *n* pl. -S baldness **ALOPECIC** *adj*

ALOUD   *adv* audibly

ALOW   *adv* in or to a lower position

ALP   *n* pl. -S a high mountain

ALPACA   *n* pl. -S a ruminant mammal

ALPHA   *n* pl. -S a Greek letter

ALPHABET   *v* -ED, -ING, -S to arrange in the customary order of the letters of a language

ALPHORN   *n* pl. -S a wooden horn used by Swiss herdsmen

ALPHOSIS   *n* pl. -SISES lack of skin pigmentation

ALPHYL   *n* pl. -S a univalent radical

ALPINE   *n* pl. -S a plant native to high mountain regions

ALPINELY   *adv* in a lofty manner

ALPINISM   *n* pl. -S mountain climbing

ALPINIST   *n* pl. -S a mountain climber

ALREADY   *adv* by this time

ALRIGHT   *adj* satisfactory

ALSIKE   *n* pl. -S a European clover

ALSO   *adv* in addition

ALT   *n* pl. -S a high-pitched musical note

ALTAR   *n* pl. -S a raised structure used in worship

ALTER   *v* -ED, -ING, -S to make different

ALTERANT   *n* pl. -S something that alters

ALTERER   *n* pl. -S one that alters

ALTHAEA   *n* pl. -S althea

ALTHEA   *n* pl. -S a flowering plant

ALTHO   *conj* although

ALTHORN   *n* pl. -S a brass wind instrument

ALTHOUGH   *conj* despite the fact that

ALTITUDE   *n* pl. -S the vertical elevation of an object above a given level

ALTO   *n* pl. -TOS a low female singing voice

ALTOIST   *n* pl. -S one who plays the alto saxophone

ALTRUISM   *n* pl. -S selfless devotion to the welfare of others

ALTRUIST   *n* pl. -S one that practices altruism

ALUDEL   *n* pl. -S a pear-shaped vessel

ALULA   *n* pl. -LAE a tuft of feathers on the first digit of a bird's wing **ALULAR** *adj*

ALUM   *n* pl. -S a chemical compound

ALUMIN   *n* pl. -S alumina

ALUMINA   *n* pl. -S an oxide of aluminum

ALUMINE   *n* pl. -S alumina

ALUMINUM   *n* pl. -S a metallic element **ALUMINIC** *adj*

ALUMNA   *n* pl. -NAE a female graduate

ALUMNUS   *n* pl. -NI a male graduate

ALUMROOT   *n* pl. -S a flowering plant

ALUNITE   *n* pl. -S a mineral

ALVEOLAR   *n* pl. -S a sound produced with the tongue touching a place just behind the front teeth

ALVEOLUS   *n* pl. -LI a small anatomical cavity

ALVINE   *adj* pertaining to the abdomen and lower intestines

ALWAY   *adv* always

ALWAYS   *adv* at all times

ALYSSUM   *n* pl. -S a flowering plant

AM   present 1st person sing. of be

AMA   *n* pl. -S amah

AMADAVAT   *n* pl. -S an Asian songbird

AMADOU   *n* pl. -S a substance prepared from fungi for use as tinder

AMAH   *n* pl. -S an Oriental nurse

AMAIN   *adv* with full strength

AMALGAM   *n* pl. -S an alloy of mercury with another metal

AMANDINE   *adj* prepared with almonds

AMANITA   *n* pl. -S any of a genus of poisonous fungi

AMANITIN   *n* pl. -S a chemical compound

AMARANTH   *n* pl. -S a flowering plant

AMARELLE   *n* pl. -S a variety of sour cherry

AMARETTI   *n/pl* macaroons made with bitter almonds

AMARETTO   *n* pl. -TOS a kind of liqueur

AMARNA   *adj* pertaining to a certain historical period of ancient Egypt

AMASS   *v* -ED, -ING, -ES to gather

AMASSER	*n* pl. -S one that amasses
AMATEUR	*n* pl. -S one that engages in an activity for pleasure
AMATIVE	*adj* amorous
AMATOL	*n* pl. -S a powerful explosive
AMATORY	*adj* pertaining to sexual love
AMAZE	*v* AMAZED, AMAZING, AMAZES to overwhelm with surprise or wonder **AMAZEDLY** *adv*
AMAZON	*n* pl. -S a tall, powerful woman
AMBAGE	*n* pl. -S a winding path
AMBARI	*n* pl. -S ambary
AMBARY	*n* pl. -RIES an East Indian plant
AMBEER	*n* pl. -S tobacco juice
AMBER	*n* pl. -S a fossil resin
AMBERINA	*n* pl. -S a type of glassware
AMBEROID	*n* pl. -S ambroid
AMBERY	*n* pl. -BERIES ambry
AMBIANCE	*n* pl. -S ambience
AMBIENCE	*n* pl. -S the character, mood, or atmosphere of a place or situation
AMBIENT	*n* pl. -S ambience
AMBIT	*n* pl. -S the external boundary of something
AMBITION	*v* -ED, -ING, -S to seek with eagerness
AMBIVERT	*n* pl. -S a person whose personality type is intermediate between introvert and extravert
AMBLE	*v* -BLED, -BLING, -BLES to saunter
AMBLER	*n* pl. -S one that ambles
AMBO	*n* pl. AMBOS or AMBONES a pulpit in an early Christian church
AMBOINA	*n* pl. -S amboyna
AMBOYNA	*n* pl. -S the mottled wood of an Indonesian tree
AMBRIES	pl. of ambry
AMBROID	*n* pl. -S a synthetic amber
AMBROSIA	*n* pl. -S the food of the Greek and Roman gods
AMBRY	*n* pl. -BRIES a recess in a church wall for sacred vessels
AMBSACE	*n* pl. -S bad luck
AMBULANT	*adj* ambulating
AMBULATE	*v* -LATED, -LATING, -LATES to move or walk about
AMBUSH	*v* -ED, -ING, -ES to attack from a concealed place
AMBUSHER	*n* pl. -S one that ambushes
AMEBA	*n* pl. -BAS or -BAE amoeba **AMEBAN, AMEBIC, AMEBOID** *adj*
AMEBEAN	*adj* alternately responding
AMEER	*n* pl. -S amir
AMEERATE	*n* pl. -S amirate
AMELCORN	*n* pl. -S a variety of wheat
AMEN	*n* pl. -S a word used at the end of a prayer to express agreement
AMENABLE	*adj* capable of being persuaded **AMENABLY** *adv*
AMEND	*v* -ED, -ING, -S to improve
AMENDER	*n* pl. -S one that amends
AMENITY	*n* pl. -TIES the quality of being pleasant or agreeable
AMENT	*n* pl. -S a mentally deficient person
AMENTIA	*n* pl. -S mental deficiency
AMERCE	*v* AMERCED, AMERCING, AMERCES to punish by imposing an arbitrary fine
AMERCER	*n* pl. -S one that amerces
AMESACE	*n* pl. -S ambsace
AMETHYST	*n* pl. -S a variety of quartz
AMI	*n* pl. -S a friend
AMIA	*n* pl. -S a freshwater fish
AMIABLE	*adj* having a pleasant disposition **AMIABLY** *adv*
AMIANTUS	*n* pl. -ES a variety of asbestos
AMICABLE	*adj* friendly **AMICABLY** *adv*
AMICE	*n* pl. -S a vestment worn about the neck and shoulders
AMICUS	*n* pl. AMICI one not party to a lawsuit but permitted by the court to advise it
AMID	*n* pl. -S amide
AMIDASE	*n* pl. -S an enzyme
AMIDE	*n* pl. -S a type of chemical compound **AMIDIC** *adj*
AMIDIN	*n* pl. -S the soluble matter of starch
AMIDINE	*n* pl. -S a type of chemical compound
AMIDO	*adj* containing an amide united with an acid radical
AMIDOGEN	*n* pl. -S a univalent chemical radical

AMIDOL	*n* pl. -S a chemical compound
AMIDONE	*n* pl. -S a chemical compound
AMIDSHIP	*adv* toward the middle of a ship
AMIDST	*prep* in the midst of
AMIE	*n* pl. -S a female friend
AMIGA	*n* pl. -S a female friend
AMIGO	*n* pl. -GOS a friend
AMIN	*n* pl. -S amine
AMINE	*n* pl. -S a type of chemical compound **AMINIC** *adj*
AMINITY	*n* pl. -TIES the state of being an amine
AMINO	*adj* containing an amine united with a nonacid radical
AMIR	*n* pl. -S a Muslim prince or governor
AMIRATE	*n* pl. -S the rank of an amir
AMISS	*adj* being out of proper order
AMITIES	pl. of amity
AMITOSIS	*n* pl. -TOSES a type of cell division **AMITOTIC** *adj*
AMITROLE	*n* pl. -S an herbicide
AMITY	*n* pl. -TIES friendship
AMMETER	*n* pl. -S an instrument for measuring amperage
AMMINE	*n* pl. -S a type of chemical compound
AMMINO	*adj* pertaining to an ammine
AMMO	*n* pl. -MOS ammunition
AMMOCETE	*n* pl. -S the larva of a lamprey
AMMONAL	*n* pl. -S a powerful explosive
AMMONIA	*n* pl. -S a pungent gas
AMMONIAC	*n* pl. -S a gum resin
AMMONIC	*adj* pertaining to ammonia
AMMONIFY	*v* -FIED, -FYING, -FIES to treat with ammonia
AMMONITE	*n* pl. -S the coiled shell of an extinct mollusk
AMMONIUM	*n* pl. -S a univalent chemical radical
AMMONO	*adj* containing ammonia
AMMONOID	*n* pl. -S ammonite
AMNESIA	*n* pl. -S loss of memory
AMNESIAC	*n* pl. -S one suffering from amnesia
AMNESIC	*n* pl. -S amnesiac
AMNESTIC	*adj* pertaining to amnesia
AMNESTY	*v* -TIED, -TYING, -TIES to pardon
AMNION	*n* pl. -NIONS or -NIA a membranous sac enclosing an embryo **AMNIC, AMNIONIC, AMNIOTIC** *adj*
AMNIOTE	*n* pl. -S a vertebrate that develops an amnion during the embryonic stage
AMOEBA	*n* pl. -BAS or -BAE a unicellular microscopic organism **AMOEBAN, AMOEBIC, AMOEBOID** *adj*
AMOEBEAN	*adj* amebean
AMOK	*n* pl. -S a murderous frenzy
AMOLE	*n* pl. -S a plant root used as a substitute for soap
AMONG	*prep* in the midst of
AMONGST	*prep* among
AMORAL	*adj* lacking a sense of right and wrong **AMORALLY** *adv*
AMORETTO	*n* pl. -TI or -TOS a cupid
AMORINO	*n* pl. -NI an amoretto
AMORIST	*n* pl. -S a lover
AMOROSO	*adv* tenderly — used as a musical direction
AMOROUS	*adj* pertaining to love
AMORT	*adj* being without life
AMORTISE	*v* -TISED, -TISING, -TISES to amortize
AMORTIZE	*v* -TIZED, -TIZING, -TIZES to liquidate gradually, as a debt
AMOSITE	*n* pl. -S a type of asbestos
AMOTION	*n* pl. -S the removal of a corporate officer from his office
AMOUNT	*v* -ED, -ING, -S to combine to yield a sum
AMOUR	*n* pl. -S a love affair
AMP	*n* pl. -S ampere
AMPERAGE	*n* pl. -S the strength of an electric current expressed in amperes
AMPERE	*n* pl. -S a unit of electric current strength
AMPHIBIA	*n/pl* organisms adapted for life both on land and in water
AMPHIOXI	*n/pl* lancelets
AMPHIPOD	*n* pl. -S a small crustacean
AMPHORA	*n* pl. -RAE or -RAS a narrow-necked jar used in ancient Greece **AMPHORAL** *adj*

AMPLE	*adj* -PLER, -PLEST abundant **AMPLY** *adv*
AMPLEXUS	*n* pl. -ES the mating embrace of frogs
AMPLIFY	*v* -FIED, -FYING, -FIES to make larger or more powerful
AMPOULE	*n* pl. -S ampule
AMPUL	*n* pl. -S ampule
AMPULE	*n* pl. -S a small glass vial
AMPULLA	*n* pl. -LAE a globular bottle used in ancient Rome **AMPULLAR** *adj*
AMPUTATE	*v* -TATED, -TATING, -TATES to cut off by surgical means
AMPUTEE	*n* pl. -S one that has had a limb amputated
AMREETA	*n* pl. -S amrita
AMRITA	*n* pl. -S a beverage that bestows immortality in Hindu mythology
AMTRAC	*n* pl. -S a military vehicle equipped to move on land and water
AMTRACK	*n* pl. -S amtrac
AMU	*n* pl. -S a unit of mass
AMUCK	*n* pl. -S amok
AMULET	*n* pl. -S an object worn to protect against evil or injury
AMUSE	*v* AMUSED, AMUSING, AMUSES to occupy pleasingly **AMUSABLE** *adj* **AMUSEDLY** *adv*
AMUSER	*n* pl. -S one that amuses
AMUSIA	*n* pl. -S the inability to recognize musical sounds
AMUSIVE	*adj* amusing
AMYGDALA	*n* pl. -LAE an almond-shaped anatomical part
AMYGDALE	*n* pl. -S amygdule
AMYGDULE	*n* pl. -S a small gas bubble in lava
AMYL	*n* pl. -S a univalent radical
AMYLASE	*n* pl. -S an enzyme
AMYLENE	*n* pl. -S a flammable liquid
AMYLIC	*adj* pertaining to amyl
AMYLOGEN	*n* pl. -S amylose
AMYLOID	*n* pl. -S a hard protein deposit resulting from degeneration of tissue
AMYLOSE	*n* pl. -S the relatively soluble component of starch
AMYLUM	*n* pl. -S starch
AN	*indefinite article* — used before words beginning with a vowel sound
ANA	*n* pl. -S a collection of miscellaneous information about a particular subject
ANABAENA	*n* pl. -S a freshwater alga
ANABAS	*n* pl. -ES a freshwater fish
ANABASIS	*n* pl. -ASES a military advance
ANABATIC	*adj* pertaining to rising wind currents
ANABLEPS	*n* pl. -ES a freshwater fish
ANABOLIC	*adj* pertaining to a process by which food is built up into protoplasm
ANACONDA	*n* pl. -S a large snake
ANADEM	*n* pl. -S a wreath for the head
ANAEMIA	*n* pl. -S anemia **ANAEMIC** *adj*
ANAEROBE	*n* pl. -S an organism that does not require oxygen to live
ANAGLYPH	*n* pl. -S a type of carved ornament
ANAGOGE	*n* pl. -S a spiritual interpretation of words **ANAGOGIC** *adj*
ANAGOGY	*n* pl. -GIES anagoge
ANAGRAM	*v* -GRAMMED, -GRAMMING, -GRAMS to transpose the letters of a word or phrase to form a new one
ANAL	*adj* pertaining to the anus
ANALCIME	*n* pl. -S analcite
ANALCITE	*n* pl. -S a mineral
ANALECTA	*n/pl* analects
ANALECTS	*n/pl* selections from a literary work or group of works
ANALEMMA	*n* pl. -MAS or -MATA a type of graduated scale
ANALGIA	*n* pl. -S inability to feel pain
ANALITY	*n* pl. -TIES a type of psychological state
ANALLY	*adv* at or through the anus
ANALOG	*n* pl. -S analogue
ANALOGIC	*adj* pertaining to an analogy
ANALOGUE	*n* pl. -S something that bears an analogy to something else
ANALOGY	*n* pl. -GIES resemblance in some respects between things otherwise unlike
ANALYSE	*v* -LYSED, -LYSING, -LYSES to analyze
ANALYSER	*n* pl. -S analyzer

ANALYSIS   *n* pl. -YSES the separation of a whole into its parts

ANALYST   *n* pl. -S one that analyzes

ANALYTIC   *adj* pertaining to analysis

ANALYZE   *v* -LYZED, -LYZING, -LYZES to subject to analysis

ANALYZER   *n* pl. -S one that analyzes

ANANKE   *n* pl. -S a compelling necessity in ancient Greek religion

ANAPAEST   *n* pl. -S anapest

ANAPEST   *n* pl. -S a type of metrical foot

ANAPHASE   *n* pl. -S a stage of mitosis

ANAPHOR   *n* pl. -S a word or phrase that takes reference from a preceding word or phrase

ANAPHORA   *n* pl. -S the repetition of a word or phrase at the beginning of several successive verses or sentences

ANARCH   *n* pl. -S an advocate of anarchy

ANARCHY   *n* pl. -CHIES absence of government **ANARCHIC** *adj*

ANASARCA   *n* pl. -S a form of dropsy

ANATASE   *n* pl. -S a mineral

ANATHEMA   *n* pl. -MAS or -MATA a formal ecclesiastical ban or curse

ANATOMY   *n* pl. -MIES the structure of an organism **ANATOMIC** *adj*

ANATOXIN   *n* pl. -S a toxoid

ANATTO   *n* pl. -TOS annatto

ANCESTOR   *v* -ED, -ING, -S to be an ancestor (a person from whom one is descended) of

ANCESTRY   *n* pl. -TRIES a line or body of ancestors

ANCHOR   *v* -ED, -ING, -S to secure by means of an anchor (a device for holding a floating vessel in place)

ANCHORET   *n* pl. -S a recluse

ANCHOVY   *n* pl. -VIES a small food fish

ANCHUSA   *n* pl. -S a hairy-stemmed plant

ANCHUSIN   *n* pl. -S a red dye

ANCIENT   *adj* -CIENTER, -CIENTEST of or pertaining to time long past

ANCIENT   *n* pl. -S one who lived in ancient times

ANCILLA   *n* pl. -LAE or -LAS a helper

ANCON   *n* pl. -ES the elbow **ANCONAL, ANCONEAL, ANCONOID** *adj*

ANCONE   *n* pl. -S ancon

ANCRESS   *n* pl. -ES a female recluse

AND   *n* pl. -S an added condition or stipulation

ANDANTE   *n* pl. -S a moderately slow musical passage

ANDESITE   *n* pl. -S a volcanic rock

ANDESYTE   *n* pl. -S andesite

ANDIRON   *n* pl. -S a metal support for holding wood in a fireplace

ANDROGEN   *n* pl. -S a male sex hormone

ANDROID   *n* pl. -S a synthetic man

ANE   *n* pl. -S one

ANEAR   *v* -ED, -ING, -S to approach

ANECDOTE   *n* pl. -DOTES or -DOTA a brief story

ANECHOIC   *adj* neither having nor producing echoes

ANELE   *v* ANELED, ANELING, ANELES to anoint

ANEMIA   *n* pl. -S a disorder of the blood **ANEMIC** *adj*

ANEMONE   *n* pl. -S a flowering plant

ANEMOSIS   *n* pl. -MOSES separation of rings of growth in timber due to wind

ANENST   *prep* anent

ANENT   *prep* in regard to

ANERGIA   *n* pl. -S anergy

ANERGY   *n* pl. -GIES lack of energy **ANERGIC** *adj*

ANEROID   *n* pl. -S a type of barometer

ANESTRUS   *n* pl. -TRI a period of sexual dormancy

ANETHOL   *n* pl. -S anethole

ANETHOLE   *n* pl. -S a chemical compound

ANEURIN   *n* pl. -S thiamine

ANEURISM   *n* pl. -S aneurysm

ANEURYSM   *n* pl. -S an abnormal blood-filled dilation of a blood vessel

ANEW   *adv* once more

ANGA   *n* pl. -S any of the eight practices of yoga

ANGAKOK   *n* pl. -S an Eskimo medicine man

ANGARIA   *n* pl. -S angary

ANGARY   *n* pl. -RIES the right of a warring state to seize neutral property

ANGEL   *v* -ED, -ING, -S to support financially

ANGELIC   *adj* pertaining to an angel (a winged celestial being)

ANGELICA   *n* pl. -S an aromatic herb

ANGELUS   *n* pl. -ES a Roman Catholic prayer

ANGER   *v* -ED, -ING, -S to make angry

ANGERLY   *adv* in an angry manner

ANGINA   *n* pl. -S a disease marked by spasmodic attacks of intense pain **ANGINAL, ANGINOSE, ANGINOUS** *adj*

ANGIOMA   *n* pl. -MAS or -MATA a tumor composed of blood or lymph vessels

ANGLE   *v* -GLED, -GLING, -GLES to fish with a hook and line

ANGLEPOD   *n* pl. -S a flowering plant

ANGLER   *n* pl. -S one that angles

ANGLICE   *adv* in readily understood English

ANGLING   *n* pl. -S the sport of fishing

ANGORA   *n* pl. -S the long, silky hair of a domestic goat

ANGRY   *adj* -GRIER, -GRIEST feeling strong displeasure or hostility **ANGRILY** *adv*

ANGST   *n* pl. -S a feeling of anxiety or dread

ANGSTROM   *n* pl. -S a unit of length

ANGUINE   *adj* resembling a snake

ANGUISH   *v* -ED, -ING, -ES to suffer extreme pain

ANGULAR   *adj* having sharp corners

ANGULATE   *v* -LATED, -LATING, -LATES to make angular

ANGULOSE   *adj* angular

ANGULOUS   *adj* angular

ANHINGA   *n* pl. -S an aquatic bird

ANI   *n* pl. -S a tropical American bird

ANIL   *n* pl. -S a West Indian shrub

ANILE   *adj* resembling an old woman

ANILIN   *n* pl. -S aniline

ANILINE   *n* pl. -S a chemical compound

ANILITY   *n* pl. -TIES the state of being anile

ANIMA   *n* pl. -S the soul

ANIMAL   *n* pl. -S a living organism typically capable of voluntary motion and sensation **ANIMALIC** *adj*

ANIMALLY   *adv* physically

ANIMATE   *v* -MATED, -MATING, -MATES to give life to

ANIMATER   *n* pl. -S animator

ANIMATO   *adv* in a lively manner — used as a musical direction

ANIMATOR   *n* pl. -S one that animates

ANIME   *n* pl. -S a resin obtained from a tropical tree

ANIMI   *n* pl. -S anime

ANIMISM   *n* pl. -S the belief that souls may exist apart from bodies

ANIMIST   *n* pl. -S an adherent of animism

ANIMUS   *n* pl. -ES a feeling of hostility

ANION   *n* pl. -S a negatively charged ion **ANIONIC** *adj*

ANISE   *n* pl. -S a North African plant

ANISEED   *n* pl. -S the seed of the anise used as a flavoring

ANISETTE   *n* pl. -S a liqueur flavored with aniseed

ANISIC   *adj* pertaining to an anise

ANISOLE   *n* pl. -S a chemical compound

ANKERITE   *n* pl. -S a mineral

ANKH   *n* pl. -S an Egyptian symbol of enduring life

ANKLE   *v* -KLED, -KLING, -KLES to walk

ANKLET   *n* pl. -S an ornament for the ankle

ANKUS   *n* pl. -ES an elephant goad

ANKUSH   *n* pl. -ES ankus

ANKYLOSE   *v* -LOSED, -LOSING, -LOSES to unite or grow together, as the bones of a joint

ANLACE   *n* pl. -S a medieval dagger

ANLAGE   *n* pl. -GEN or -GES the initial cell structure from which an embryonic organ develops

ANLAS   *n* pl. -ES anlace

ANNA   *n* pl. -S a former coin of India and Pakistan

ANNAL   *n* pl. -S a record of a single year

ANNALIST   *n* pl. -S a historian

ANNATES   *n/pl* the first year's revenue of a bishop paid to the pope

ANNATTO   *n* pl. -TOS a yellowish-red dye

ANNEAL   *v* -ED, -ING, -S to toughen

ANNEALER   *n* pl. -S one that anneals

ANNELID   *n* pl. -S any of a phylum of segmented worms

ANNEX   *v* -ED, -ING, -ES to add or attach

ANNEXE	*n* pl. -S something added or attached
ANNOTATE	*v* -TATED, -TATING, -TATES to furnish with critical or explanatory notes
ANNOUNCE	*v* -NOUNCED, -NOUNCING, -NOUNCES to make known publicly
ANNOY	*v* -ED, -ING, -S to be troublesome to
ANNOYER	*n* pl. -S one that annoys
ANNUAL	*n* pl. -S a publication issued once a year
ANNUALLY	*adv* once a year
ANNUITY	*n* pl. -TIES an allowance or income paid at regular intervals
ANNUL	*v* -NULLED, -NULLING, -NULS to make or declare void or invalid
ANNULAR	*adj* shaped like a ring
ANNULATE	*adj* composed of or furnished with rings
ANNULET	*n* pl. -S a small ring
ANNULI	a pl. of annulus
ANNULLED	past tense of annul
ANNULLING	present participle of annul
ANNULUS	*n* pl. -LI or -LUSES a ring or ringlike part **ANNULOSE** *adj*
ANOA	*n* pl. -S a wild ox
ANODE	*n* pl. -S a positively charged electrode **ANODAL, ANODIC** *adj* **ANODALLY** *adv*
ANODIZE	*v* -IZED, -IZING, -IZES to coat with a protective film by chemical means
ANODYNE	*n* pl. -S a medicine that relieves pain **ANODYNIC** *adj*
ANOINT	*v* -ED, -ING, -S to apply oil to as a sacred rite
ANOINTER	*n* pl. -S one that anoints
ANOLE	*n* pl. -S a tropical lizard
ANOLYTE	*n* pl. -S the part of an electricity-conducting solution nearest the anode
ANOMALY	*n* pl. -LIES a deviation from the common rule, type, or form
ANOMIE	*n* pl. -S a collapse of the social structures governing a given society **ANOMIC** *adj*
ANOMY	*n* pl. -MIES anomie
ANON	*adv* at another time
ANONYM	*n* pl. -S a false or assumed name
ANOOPSIA	*n* pl. -S a visual defect
ANOPIA	*n* pl. -S anoopsia
ANOPSIA	*n* pl. -S anoopsia
ANORAK	*n* pl. -S a parka
ANORETIC	*n* pl. -S anorexic
ANOREXIA	*n* pl. -S loss of appetite
ANOREXIC	*n* pl. -S one affected with anorexia
ANOREXY	*n* pl. -OREXIES anorexia
ANORTHIC	*adj* denoting a certain type of crystal system
ANOSMIA	*n* pl. -S loss of the sense of smell **ANOSMIC** *adj*
ANOTHER	*adj* one more
ANOVULAR	*adj* not involving ovulation
ANOXEMIA	*n* pl. -S a disorder of the blood **ANOXEMIC** *adj*
ANOXIA	*n* pl. -S absence of oxygen **ANOXIC** *adj*
ANSA	*n* pl. -SAE the projecting part of Saturn's rings
ANSATE	*adj* having a handle
ANSATED	*adj* ansate
ANSERINE	*n* pl. -S a chemical compound
ANSEROUS	*adj* silly
ANSWER	*v* -ED, -ING, -S to say, write, or act in return
ANSWERER	*n* pl. -S one that answers
ANT	*n* pl. -S a small insect
ANTA	*n* pl. -TAE or -TAS a pilaster formed at the termination of a wall
ANTACID	*n* pl. -S a substance that neutralizes acid
ANTALGIC	*n* pl. -S an anodyne
ANTBEAR	*n* pl. -S an aardvark
ANTE	*v* ANTED or ANTEED, ANTEING, ANTES to put a fixed stake into the pot before the cards are dealt in poker
ANTEATER	*n* pl. -S any of several mammals that feed on ants
ANTECEDE	*v* -CEDED, -CEDING, -CEDES to precede
ANTED	a past tense of ante
ANTEDATE	*v* -DATED, -DATING, -DATES to be of an earlier date than
ANTEFIX	*n* pl. -FIXES or -FIXA an upright ornament at the eaves of a tiled roof

ANTELOPE   *n* pl. -S a ruminant mammal

ANTENNA   *n* pl. -NAE or -NAS a metallic device for sending or receiving radio waves **ANTENNAL** *adj*

ANTEPAST   *n* pl. -S an appetizer

ANTERIOR   *adj* situated in or toward the front

ANTEROOM   *n* pl. -S a waiting room

ANTETYPE   *n* pl. -S an earlier form

ANTEVERT   *v* -ED, -ING, -S to displace by tipping forward

ANTHELIA   *n/pl* halolike areas seen in the sky opposite the sun

ANTHELIX   *n* pl. -LICES or -LIXES the inner curved ridge on the cartilage of the external ear

ANTHEM   *v* -ED, -ING, -S to praise in a song

ANTHEMIA   *n/pl* decorative floral patterns used in Greek art

ANTHER   *n* pl. -S the pollen-bearing part of a stamen **ANTHERAL** *adj*

ANTHERID   *n* pl. -S a male reproductive organ of certain plants

ANTHESIS   *n* pl. -THESES the full bloom of a flower

ANTHILL   *n* pl. -S a mound formed by ants in building their nest

ANTHODIA   *n/pl* flower heads of certain plants

ANTHOID   *adj* resembling a flower

ANTHRAX   *n* pl. -THRACES an infectious disease

ANTI   *n* pl. -S one that is opposed

ANTIAIR   *adj* directed against attacking aircraft

ANTIAR   *n* pl. -S an arrow poison

ANTIARIN   *n* pl. -S antiar

ANTIATOM   *n* pl. -S an atom comprised of antiparticles

ANTIBIAS   *adj* opposed to bias

ANTIBODY   *n* pl. -BODIES a body protein that produces immunity against certain microorganisms or toxins

ANTIBOSS   *adj* opposed to bosses

ANTIBUG   *adj* effective against bugs

ANTIC   *v* -TICKED, -TICKING, -TICS to act in a clownish manner

ANTICAR   *adj* opposed to cars

ANTICITY   *adj* opposed to cities

ANTICK   *v* -ED, -ING, -S to antic

ANTICLY   *adv* in a clownish manner

ANTICOLD   *adj* effective against the common cold

ANTICULT   *adj* opposed to cults

ANTIDORA   *n/pl* holy breads

ANTIDOTE   *v* -DOTED, -DOTING, -DOTES to counteract the effects of a poison with a remedy

ANTIDRUG   *adj* opposed to illicit drugs

ANTIFAT   *adj* preventing the formation of fat

ANTIFLU   *adj* combating the flu

ANTIFOAM   *adj* reducing or preventing foam

ANTIFUR   *adj* opposed to the wearing of animal furs

ANTIGAY   *adj* opposed to homosexuals

ANTIGEN   *n* pl. -S a substance that stimulates the production of antibodies

ANTIGENE   *n* pl. -S antigen

ANTIGUN   *adj* opposed to guns

ANTIHERO   *n* pl. -ROES a protagonist who is notably lacking in heroic qualities

ANTIJAM   *adj* blocking interfering signals

ANTIKING   *n* pl. -S a usurping king

ANTILEAK   *adj* preventing leaks

ANTILEFT   *adj* opposed to leftism

ANTILIFE   *adj* opposed to life

ANTILOCK   *adj* designed to prevent the wheels of a vehicle from locking

ANTILOG   *n* pl. -S the number corresponding to a given logarithm

ANTILOGY   *n* pl. -GIES a contradiction in terms or ideas

ANTIMALE   *adj* opposed to men

ANTIMAN   *adj* antimale

ANTIMASK   *n* pl. -S a comic performance between the acts of a masque

ANTIMERE   *n* pl. -S a part of an organism symmetrical with a part on the opposite side of the main axis

ANTIMONY   *n* pl. -NIES a metallic element

ANTING   *n* pl. -S the deliberate placing, by certain birds, of living ants among the feathers

ANTINODE   *n* pl. -S a region between adjacent nodes

ANTINOMY   *n* pl. -MIES a contradiction between two seemingly valid principles

ANTINUKE *adj* opposing the use of nuclear power plants or nuclear weapons

ANTIPHON *n* pl. -S a psalm or hymn sung responsively

ANTIPILL *adj* opposing the use of contraceptive pills

ANTIPODE *n* pl. -S an exact opposite

ANTIPOLE *n* pl. -S the opposite pole

ANTIPOPE *n* pl. -S one claiming to be pope in opposition to the one chosen by church law

ANTIPORN *adj* opposed to pornography

ANTIPOT *adj* opposing the use of pot (marijuana)

ANTIPYIC *n* pl. -S a medicine that prevents the formation of pus

ANTIQUE *v* -TIQUED, -TIQUING, -TIQUES to give an appearance of age to

ANTIQUER *n* pl. -S one that antiques

ANTIRAPE *adj* concerned with preventing rape

ANTIRED *adj* opposed to communism

ANTIRIOT *adj* designed to prevent or end riots

ANTIROCK *adj* opposed to rock music

ANTIROLL *adj* designed to reduce roll

ANTIRUST *n* pl. -S something that prevents rust

ANTISAG *adj* designed to prevent sagging

ANTISERA *n/pl* serums that contain antibodies

ANTISEX *adj* opposed to sexual activity

ANTISHIP *adj* designed for use against ships

ANTISKID *adj* designed to prevent skidding

ANTISLIP *adj* designed to prevent slipping

ANTISMOG *adj* designed to reduce pollutants that cause smog

ANTISMUT *adj* opposed to pornography

ANTISNOB *adj* opposed to snobbery

ANTISTAT *adj* designed to prevent the buildup of static electricity

ANTITANK *adj* designed to combat tanks

ANTITAX *adj* opposing taxes

ANTITYPE *n* pl. -S an opposite type

ANTIWAR *adj* opposing war

ANTIWEAR *adj* designed to reduce the effects of long or hard use

ANTIWEED *adj* concerned with the destruction of weeds

ANTLER *n* pl. -S the horn of an animal of the deer family **ANTLERED** *adj*

ANTLIKE *adj* resembling an ant

ANTLION *n* pl. -S a predatory insect

ANTONYM *n* pl. -S a word opposite in meaning to another

ANTONYMY *n* pl. -MIES the state of being an antonym

ANTRA a pl. of antrum

ANTRAL *adj* pertaining to an antrum

ANTRE *n* pl. -S a cave

ANTRORSE *adj* directed forward or upward

ANTRUM *n* pl. -TRA or -TRUMS a cavity in a bone

ANTSY *adj* -SIER, -SIEST fidgety

ANURAL *adj* anurous

ANURAN *n* pl. -S a frog or toad

ANURESIS *n* pl. -RESES inability to urinate **ANURETIC** *adj*

ANURIA *n* pl. -S absence of urine **ANURIC** *adj*

ANUROUS *adj* having no tail

ANUS *n* pl. -ES the excretory opening at the end of the alimentary canal

ANVIL *v* -VILED, -VILING, -VILS or -VILLED, -VILLING, -VILS to shape on an anvil (a heavy iron block)

ANVILTOP *n* pl. -S an anvil-shaped cloud mass

ANXIETY *n* pl. -ETIES painful or apprehensive uneasiness of mind

ANXIOUS *adj* full of anxiety

ANY *adj* one, no matter which

ANYBODY *n* pl. -BODIES a person of some importance

ANYHOW *adv* in any way

ANYMORE *adv* at the present time

ANYONE *pron* any person

ANYPLACE *adv* in any place

ANYTHING *n* pl. -S a thing of any kind

ANYTIME *adv* at any time

ANYWAY *adv* in any way

ANYWAYS *adv* anyway

ANYWHERE *n* pl. -S any place

ANYWISE *adv* in any way

AORIST *n* pl. -S a verb tense **AORISTIC** *adj*

AORTA	*n* pl. -TAS or -TAE a main artery **AORTAL, AORTIC** *adj*
AOUDAD	*n* pl. -S a wild sheep
APACE	*adv* swiftly
APACHE	*n* pl. -S a Parisian gangster
APAGOGE	*n* pl. -S establishment of a thesis by showing its contrary to be absurd **APAGOGIC** *adj*
APANAGE	*n* pl. -S appanage
APAREJO	*n* pl. -JOS a type of saddle
APART	*adv* not together
APATETIC	*adj* having coloration serving as natural camouflage
APATHY	*n* pl. -THIES lack of emotion
APATITE	*n* pl. -S a mineral
APE	*v* APED, APING, APES to mimic
APEAK	*adv* in a vertical position
APEEK	*adv* apeak
APELIKE	*adj* resembling an ape (a large, tailless primate)
APER	*n* pl. -S one that apes
APERCU	*n* pl. -S a brief summary
APERIENT	*n* pl. -S a mild laxative
APERITIF	*n* pl. -S an alcoholic drink taken before a meal
APERTURE	*n* pl. -S an opening
APERY	*n* pl. -ERIES the act of aping
APETALY	*n* pl. -ALIES the state of having no petals
APEX	*n* pl. APEXES or APICES the highest point
APHAGIA	*n* pl. -S inability to swallow
APHANITE	*n* pl. -S an igneous rock
APHASIA	*n* pl. -S loss of the ability to use words
APHASIAC	*n* pl. -S one suffering from aphasia
APHASIC	*n* pl. -S aphasiac
APHELION	*n* pl. -ELIA or -ELIONS the point in a planetary orbit farthest from the sun **APHELIAN** *adj*
APHESIS	*n* pl. -ESES the loss of an unstressed vowel from the beginning of a word **APHETIC** *adj*
APHID	*n* pl. -S any of a family of small, soft-bodied insects
APHIDIAN	*n* pl. -S an aphid
APHIS	*n* pl. APHIDES an aphid
APHOLATE	*n* pl. -S a chemical used to control houseflies
APHONIA	*n* pl. -S loss of voice
APHONIC	*n* pl. -S one affected with aphonia
APHORISE	*v* -RISED, -RISING, -RISES to aphorize
APHORISM	*n* pl. -S a brief statement of a truth or principle
APHORIST	*n* pl. -S one that aphorizes
APHORIZE	*v* -RIZED, -RIZING, -RIZES to write or speak in aphorisms
APHOTIC	*adj* lacking light
APHTHA	*n* pl. -THAE a small blister in the mouth or stomach **APHTHOUS** *adj*
APHYLLY	*n* pl. -LIES the state of being leafless
APIAN	*adj* pertaining to bees
APIARIAN	*n* pl. -S an apiarist
APIARIST	*n* pl. -S a person who raises bees
APIARY	*n* pl. -ARIES a place where bees are kept
APICAL	*n* pl. -S a sound articulated with the apex (tip) of the tongue
APICALLY	*adv* at or toward the apex
APICES	a pl. of apex
APICULUS	*n* pl. -LI a sharp point at the end of a leaf
APIECE	*adv* for each one
APIMANIA	*n* pl. -S an excessive interest in bees
APING	present participle of ape
APIOLOGY	*n* pl. -GIES the study of bees
APISH	*adj* slavishly or foolishly imitative **APISHLY** *adv*
APLASIA	*n* pl. -S defective development of an organ or part
APLASTIC	*adj* not plastic
APLENTY	*adj* being in sufficient quantity
APLITE	*n* pl. -S a fine-grained rock **APLITIC** *adj*
APLOMB	*n* pl. -S self-confidence
APNEA	*n* pl. -S temporary cessation of respiration **APNEAL, APNEIC** *adj*
APNOEA	*n* pl. -S apnea **APNOEAL, APNOEIC** *adj*
APOAPSIS	*n* pl. -APSIDES the high point in an orbit

APOCARP *n* pl. -S a fruit having separated carpels

APOCARPY *n* pl. -PIES the state of being an apocarp

APOCOPE *n* pl. -S an omission of the last sound of a word **APOCOPIC** *adj*

APOCRINE *adj* pertaining to a type of gland

APOD *n* pl. -S an apodal animal

APODAL *adj* having no feet or footlike appendages

APODOSIS *n* pl. -OSES the main clause of a conditional sentence

APODOUS *adj* apodal

APOGAMY *n* pl. -MIES a form of plant reproduction **APOGAMIC** *adj*

APOGEE *n* pl. -S the point in the orbit of a body which is farthest from the earth **APOGEAL, APOGEAN, APOGEIC** *adj*

APOLLO *n* pl. -LOS a handsome young man

APOLOG *n* pl. -S apologue

APOLOGAL *adj* pertaining to an apologue

APOLOGIA *n* pl. -GIAS or -GIAE a formal justification or defense

APOLOGUE *n* pl. -S an allegory

APOLOGY *n* pl. -GIES an expression of regret for some error or offense

APOLUNE *n* pl. -S the point in the orbit of a body which is farthest from the moon

APOMICT *n* pl. -S an organism produced by apomixis

APOMIXIS *n* pl. -MIXES a type of reproductive process

APOPHONY *n* pl. -NIES ablaut

APOPHYGE *n* pl. -S a concave curve in a column

APOPLEXY *n* pl. -PLEXIES a sudden loss of sensation and muscular control

APORT *adv* on or toward the left side of a ship

APOSPORY *n* pl. -RIES a type of reproduction without spore formation

APOSTACY *n* pl. -CIES apostasy

APOSTASY *n* pl. -SIES an abandonment of one's faith or principles

APOSTATE *n* pl. -S one who commits apostasy

APOSTIL *n* pl. -S a marginal note

APOSTLE *n* pl. -S a disciple sent forth by Christ to preach the gospel

APOTHECE *n* pl. -S a spore-producing organ of certain fungi

APOTHEGM *n* pl. -S a maxim

APOTHEM *n* pl. -S the perpendicular from the center to any side of a regular polygon

APPAL *v* -PALLED, -PALLING, -PALS to appall

APPALL *v* -ED, -ING, -S to fill with horror or dismay

APPANAGE *n* pl. -S land or revenue granted to a member of a royal family

APPARAT *n* pl. -S a political organization

APPAREL *v* -ELED, -ELING, -ELS or -ELLED, -ELLING, -ELS to provide with outer garments

APPARENT *adj* easily seen

APPEAL *v* -ED, -ING, -S to make an earnest request

APPEALER *n* pl. -S one that appeals

APPEAR *v* -ED, -ING, -S to come into view

APPEASE *v* -PEASED, -PEASING, -PEASES to bring to a state of peace or contentment

APPEASER *n* pl. -S one that appeases

APPEL *n* pl. -S a feint in fencing

APPELLEE *n* pl. -S the defendant in a type of judicial proceeding

APPELLOR *n* pl. -S a confessed criminal who accuses an accomplice

APPEND *v* -ED, -ING, -S to add as a supplement

APPENDIX *n* pl. -DIXES or -DICES a collection of supplementary material at the end of a book

APPESTAT *n* pl. -S the mechanism in the central nervous system that regulates appetite

APPETENT *adj* marked by strong desire

APPETITE *n* pl. -S a desire for food or drink

APPLAUD *v* -ED, -ING, -S to express approval by clapping the hands

APPLAUSE *n* pl. -S the sound made by persons applauding

APPLE *n* pl. -S an edible fruit

APPLIED past tense of apply

APPLIER *n* pl. -S one that applies

APPLIQUE *v* -QUED, -QUEING, -QUES to apply as a decoration to a larger surface

APPLY   *v* -PLIED, -PLYING, -PLIES to bring into contact with something

APPOINT   *v* -ED, -ING, -S to name or assign to a position or office

APPOSE   *v* -POSED, -POSING, -POSES to place side by side

APPOSER   *n* pl. -S one that apposes

APPOSITE   *adj* relevant

APPRAISE   *v* -PRAISED, -PRAISING, -PRAISES to set a value on

APPRISE   *v* -PRISED, -PRISING, -PRISES to notify

APPRISER   *n* pl. -S one that apprises

APPRIZE   *v* -PRIZED, -PRIZING, -PRIZES to appraise

APPRIZER   *n* pl. -S one that apprizes

APPROACH   *v* -ED, -ING, -ES to come near or nearer to

APPROVAL   *n* pl. -S the act of approving

APPROVE   *v* -PROVED, -PROVING, -PROVES to regard favorably

APPROVER   *n* pl. -S one that approves

APPULSE   *n* pl. -S the approach of one moving body toward another

APRAXIA   *n* pl. -S loss of the ability to perform coordinated movements **APRACTIC, APRAXIC** *adj*

APRES   *prep* after

APRICOT   *n* pl. -S an edible fruit

APRON   *v* -ED, -ING, -S to provide with an apron (a garment worn to protect one's clothing)

APROPOS   *adj* relevant

APROTIC   *adj* being a type of solvent

APSE   *n* pl. -S a domed, semicircular projection of a building **APSIDAL** *adj*

APSIS   *n* pl. -SIDES an apse

APT   *adj* APTER, APTEST suitable

APTERAL   *adj* apterous

APTERIUM   *n* pl. -RIA a bare area of skin between feathers

APTEROUS   *adj* having no wings

APTERYX   *n* pl. -ES the kiwi

APTITUDE   *n* pl. -S an ability

APTLY   *adv* in an apt manner

APTNESS   *n* pl. -ES the quality of being apt

APYRASE   *n* pl. -S an enzyme

APYRETIC   *adj* having no fever

AQUA   *n* pl. AQUAE or AQUAS water

AQUACADE   *n* pl. -S a swimming and diving exhibition

AQUANAUT   *n* pl. -S a scuba diver trained to live in underwater installations

AQUARIA   a pl. of aquarium

AQUARIAL   *adj* pertaining to an aquarium

AQUARIAN   *n* pl. -S a member of the old sects that used water rather than wine in religious ceremonies

AQUARIST   *n* pl. -S one who keeps an aquarium

AQUARIUM   *n* pl. -IUMS or -IA a water-filled enclosure in which aquatic animals are kept

AQUATIC   *n* pl. -S an organism living or growing in or near water

AQUATINT   *v* -ED, -ING, -S to etch, using a certain process

AQUATONE   *n* pl. -S a type of printing process

AQUAVIT   *n* pl. -S a Scandinavian liquor

AQUEDUCT   *n* pl. -S a water conduit

AQUEOUS   *adj* pertaining to water

AQUIFER   *n* pl. -S a water-bearing rock formation

AQUILINE   *adj* curving like an eagle's beak

AQUIVER   *adj* quivering

AR   *n* pl. -S the letter R

ARABESK   *n* pl. -S a design of intertwined floral figures

ARABIC   *adj* derived from gum arabic

ARABICA   *n* pl. -S an evergreen shrub that produces coffee beans

ARABIZE   *v* -IZED, -IZING, -IZES to cause to acquire Arabic customs

ARABLE   *n* pl. -S land suitable for cultivation

ARACEOUS   *adj* belonging to the arum family of plants

ARACHNID   *n* pl. -S any of a class of segmented invertebrate animals

ARAK   *n* pl. -S arrack

ARAMID   *n* pl. -S a type of chemical compound

ARANEID   *n* pl. -S a spider

ARAPAIMA   *n* pl. -S a large food fish

ARAROBA   *n* pl. -S a Brazilian tree

ARB   *n* pl. -S a type of stock trader

ARBALEST   *n* pl. -S a type of crossbow

ARBALIST   *n* pl. -S arbalest

ARBELEST	*n* pl. -S arbalest
ARBITER	*n* pl. -S one chosen or appointed to judge a disputed issue **ARBITRAL** *adj*
ARBOR	*n* pl. -S a shady garden shelter
ARBOR	*n* pl. -ES a tree
ARBOREAL	*adj* living in trees
ARBORED	*adj* having trees
ARBORETA	*n/pl* places for the study and exhibition of trees
ARBORIST	*n* pl. -S a tree specialist
ARBORIZE	*v* -IZED, -IZING, -IZES to form many branches
ARBOROUS	*adj* pertaining to trees
ARBOUR	*n* pl. -S a shady garden shelter **ARBOURED** *adj*
ARBUSCLE	*n* pl. -S a dwarf tree
ARBUTE	*n* pl. -S an evergreen tree **ARBUTEAN** *adj*
ARBUTUS	*n* pl. -ES an evergreen tree
ARC	*v* ARCED, ARCING, ARCS or ARCKED, ARCKING, ARCS to move in a curved course
ARCADE	*v* -CADED, -CADING, -CADES to provide with an arcade (a series of arches)
ARCADIA	*n* pl. -S a region of simple pleasure and quiet
ARCADIAN	*n* pl. -S one who lives in an arcadia
ARCADING	*n* pl. -S an arcade
ARCANE	*adj* mysterious
ARCANUM	*n* pl. -NA or -NUMS a mystery
ARCATURE	*n* pl. -S a small arcade
ARCH	*v* -ED, -ING, -ES to bend like an arch (a curved structure spanning an opening)
ARCHAIC	*adj* pertaining to an earlier time
ARCHAISE	*v* -ISED, -ISING, -ISES to archaize
ARCHAISM	*n* pl. -S an archaic word, idiom, or expression
ARCHAIST	*n* pl. -S one that archaizes
ARCHAIZE	*v* -IZED, -IZING, -IZES to use archaisms
ARCHDUKE	*n* pl. -S an Austrian prince
ARCHER	*n* pl. -S one that shoots with a bow and arrow
ARCHERY	*n* pl. -CHERIES the sport of shooting with a bow and arrow
ARCHIL	*n* pl. -S orchil
ARCHINE	*n* pl. -S a Russian unit of linear measure
ARCHING	*n* pl. -S a series of arches
ARCHIVE	*v* -CHIVED, -CHIVING, -CHIVES to file in an archive (a place where records are kept) **ARCHIVAL** *adj*
ARCHLY	*adv* slyly
ARCHNESS	*n* pl. -ES slyness
ARCHON	*n* pl. -S a magistrate of ancient Athens
ARCHWAY	*n* pl. -WAYS a passageway under an arch
ARCIFORM	*adj* having the form of an arch
ARCKED	a past tense of arc
ARCKING	a present participle of arc
ARCO	*adv* with the bow — used as a direction to players of stringed instruments
ARCSINE	*n* pl. -S the inverse function to the sine
ARCTIC	*n* pl. -S a warm, waterproof overshoe
ARCUATE	*adj* curved like a bow
ARCUATED	*adj* arcuate
ARCUS	*n* pl. -ES an arch-shaped cloud
ARDEB	*n* pl. -S an Egyptian unit of capacity
ARDENCY	*n* pl. -CIES ardor
ARDENT	*adj* characterized by intense emotion **ARDENTLY** *adv*
ARDOR	*n* pl. -S intensity of emotion
ARDOUR	*n* pl. -S ardor
ARDUOUS	*adj* involving great labor or hardship
ARE	*n* pl. -S a unit of surface measure
AREA	*n* pl. AREAE a section of the cerebral cortex having a specific function
AREA	*n* pl. -S a particular **AREAL** extent of space or surface *adj* **AREALLY** *adv*
AREAWAY	*n* pl. -WAYS a sunken area leading to a basement entrance
ARECA	*n* pl. -S a tropical tree
AREIC	*adj* pertaining to a region of the earth contributing little surface drainage
ARENA	*n* pl. -S an enclosed area for contests

ARENITE	n pl. -S rock made up chiefly of sand grains	**ARIA**	n pl. -S an elaborate melody for a single voice
ARENOSE	adj sandy	**ARID**	adj -IDER, -IDEST extremely dry **ARIDLY** adv
ARENOUS	adj arenose		
AREOLA	n pl. -LAE or -LAS a small space in a network of leaf veins **AREOLAR, AREOLATE** adj	**ARIDITY**	n pl. -TIES the state of being arid
		ARIDNESS	n pl. -ES aridity
		ARIEL	n pl. -S an African gazelle
AREOLE	n pl. -S areola	**ARIETTA**	n pl. -S a short aria
AREOLOGY	n pl. -GIES the study of the planet Mars	**ARIETTE**	n pl. -S arietta
		ARIGHT	adv rightly; correctly
ARETE	n pl. -S a sharp mountain ridge	**ARIL**	n pl. -S an outer covering of certain seeds **ARILED, ARILLATE, ARILLOID** adj
ARETHUSA	n pl. -S a flowering plant		
ARF	n pl. -S a barking sound		
ARGAL	n pl. -S argol	**ARILLODE**	n pl. -S a type of aril
ARGALA	n pl. -S a type of stork	**ARIOSE**	adj characterized by melody
ARGALI	n pl. -S a wild sheep	**ARIOSO**	n pl. -SOS or -SI a musical passage resembling an aria
ARGENT	n pl. -S silver **ARGENTAL, ARGENTIC** adj		
		ARISE	v AROSE, ARISEN, ARISING, ARISES to get up
ARGENTUM	n pl. -S silver		
ARGIL	n pl. -S a white clay	**ARISTA**	n pl. -TAE or -TAS a bristlelike structure or appendage **ARISTATE** adj
ARGINASE	n pl. -S an enzyme		
ARGININE	n pl. -S an amino acid		
ARGLE	v -GLED, -GLING, -GLES to argue	**ARISTO**	n pl. -TOS an aristocrat
		ARK	n pl. -S a large boat
ARGOL	n pl. -S a crust deposited in wine casks during aging	**ARKOSE**	n pl. -S a type of sandstone **ARKOSIC** adj
ARGON	n pl. -S a gaseous element	**ARLES**	n/pl money paid to bind a bargain
ARGONAUT	n pl. -S a marine mollusk	**ARM**	v -ED, -ING, -S to supply with weapons
ARGOSY	n pl. -SIES a large merchant ship		
ARGOT	n pl. -S a specialized vocabulary **ARGOTIC** adj	**ARMADA**	n pl. -S a fleet of warships
		ARMAGNAC	n pl. -S a French brandy
ARGUABLE	adj capable of being argued about **ARGUABLY** adv	**ARMAMENT**	n pl. -S a military force equipped for war
ARGUE	v -GUED, -GUING, -GUES to present reasons for or against	**ARMATURE**	v -TURED, -TURING, -TURES to furnish with armor
		ARMBAND	n pl. -S a band worn around an arm (an upper appendage of the human body)
ARGUER	n pl. -S one that argues		
ARGUFIER	n pl. -S one that argufies		
ARGUFY	v -FIED, -FYING, -FIES to argue stubbornly	**ARMCHAIR**	n pl. -S a chair with armrests
		ARMER	n pl. -S one that arms
ARGUING	present participle of argue	**ARMET**	n pl. -S a medieval helmet
ARGUMENT	n pl. -S a discussion involving differing points of view	**ARMFUL**	n pl. ARMFULS or ARMSFUL as much as the arm can hold
ARGUS	n pl. -ES an East Indian pheasant	**ARMHOLE**	n pl. -S an opening for the arm in a garment
ARGYLE	n pl. -S a knitting pattern	**ARMIES**	pl. of army
ARGYLL	n pl. -S argyle	**ARMIGER**	n pl. -S one who carries the armor of a knight
ARHAT	n pl. -S a Buddhist who has attained nirvana		
		ARMIGERO	n pl. -GEROS armiger

ARMILLA	*n* pl. -LAE or -LAS a thin membrane around the stem of certain fungi
ARMING	*n* pl. -S the act of one that arms
ARMLESS	*adj* having no arms
ARMLET	*n* pl. -S an armband
ARMLIKE	*adj* resembling an arm
ARMLOAD	*n* pl. -S an armful
ARMLOCK	*n* pl. -S a hold in wrestling
ARMOIRE	*n* pl. -S a large, ornate cabinet
ARMONICA	*n* pl. -S a type of musical instrument
ARMOR	*v* -ED, -ING, -S to furnish with armor (a defensive covering)
ARMORER	*n* pl. -S one that makes or repairs armor
ARMORIAL	*n* pl. -S a treatise on heraldry
ARMORY	*n* pl. -MORIES a place where weapons are stored
ARMOUR	*v* -ED, -ING, -S to armor
ARMOURER	*n* pl. -S armorer
ARMOURY	*n* pl. -MOURIES armory
ARMPIT	*n* pl. -S the hollow under the arm at the shoulder
ARMREST	*n* pl. -S a support for the arm
ARMSFUL	*a* pl. of armful
ARMURE	*n* pl. -S a woven fabric
ARMY	*n* pl. -MIES a large body of men trained and armed for war
ARMYWORM	*n* pl. -S a destructive moth larva
ARNATTO	*n* pl. -TOS annatto
ARNICA	*n* pl. -S a perennial herb
ARNOTTO	*n* pl. -TOS a tropical tree
AROID	*n* pl. -S a flowering plant
AROINT	*v* -ED, -ING, -S to drive away
AROMA	*n* pl. -S a pleasant odor
AROMATIC	*n* pl. -S a fragrant plant or substance
AROSE	past tense of arise
AROUND	*prep* on all sides of
AROUSAL	*n* pl. -S the act of arousing
AROUSE	*v* AROUSED, AROUSING, AROUSES to stimulate
AROUSER	*n* pl. -S one that arouses
AROYNT	*v* -ED, -ING, -S to aroint
ARPEGGIO	*n* pl. -GIOS a technique of playing a musical chord
ARPEN	*n* pl. -S arpent
ARPENT	*n* pl. -S an old French unit of area
ARQUEBUS	*n* pl. -ES an early portable firearm
ARRACK	*n* pl. -S an Oriental liquor
ARRAIGN	*v* -ED, -ING, -S to call before a court of law to answer an indictment
ARRANGE	*v* -RANGED, -RANGING, -RANGES to put in definite or proper order
ARRANGER	*n* pl. -S one that arranges
ARRANT	*adj* outright **ARRANTLY** *adv*
ARRAS	*n* pl. ARRAS a tapestry **ARRASED** *adj*
ARRAY	*v* -ED, -ING, -S to place in proper or desired order
ARRAYAL	*n* pl. -S the act of arraying
ARRAYER	*n* pl. -S one that arrays
ARREAR	*n* pl. -S an unpaid and overdue debt
ARREST	*v* -ED, -ING, -S to seize and hold by legal authority
ARRESTEE	*n* pl. -S one that is arrested
ARRESTER	*n* pl. -S one that arrests
ARRESTOR	*n* pl. -S arrester
ARRHIZAL	*adj* rootless
ARRIS	*n* pl. -RISES a ridge formed by the meeting of two surfaces
ARRIVAL	*n* pl. -S the act of arriving
ARRIVE	*v* -RIVED, -RIVING, -RIVES to reach a destination
ARRIVER	*n* pl. -S one that arrives
ARROBA	*n* pl. -S a Spanish unit of weight
ARROGANT	*adj* overly convinced of one's own worth or importance
ARROGATE	*v* -GATED, -GATING, -GATES to claim or take without right
ARROW	*v* -ED, -ING, -S to indicate the proper position of with an arrow (a linear figure with a wedge-shaped end)
ARROWY	*adj* moving swiftly
ARROYO	*n* pl. -ROYOS a brook or creek
ARSENAL	*n* pl. -S a collection or supply of weapons
ARSENATE	*n* pl. -S a chemical salt
ARSENIC	*n* pl. -S a metallic element
ARSENIDE	*n* pl. -S an arsenic compound
ARSENITE	*n* pl. -S a chemical salt

ARSENO	*adj* containing a certain bivalent chemical radical
ARSENOUS	*adj* pertaining to arsenic
ARSES	pl. of arsis
ARSHIN	*n* pl. -S archine
ARSINE	*n* pl. -S a poisonous gas
ARSINO	*adj* containing a certain univalent chemical radical
ARSIS	*n* pl. ARSES the unaccented part of a musical measure
ARSON	*n* pl. -S the malicious or fraudulent burning of property **ARSONOUS** *adj*
ARSONIST	*n* pl. -S one that commits arson
ART	*n* pl. -S an esthetically pleasing and meaningful arrangement of elements
ARTAL	a pl. of rotl
ARTEFACT	*n* pl. -S artifact
ARTEL	*n* pl. -S a collective farm in Russia
ARTERIAL	*n* pl. -S a type of highway
ARTERY	*n* pl. -TERIES a vessel that carries blood away from the heart
ARTFUL	*adj* crafty **ARTFULLY** *adv*
ARTICLE	*v* -CLED, -CLING, -CLES to charge with specific offenses
ARTIER	comparative of arty
ARTIEST	superlative of arty
ARTIFACT	*n* pl. -S an object made by man
ARTIFICE	*n* pl. -S a clever stratagem
ARTILY	*adv* in an arty manner
ARTINESS	*n* pl. -ES the quality of being arty
ARTISAN	*n* pl. -S a trained or skilled workman
ARTIST	*n* pl. -S one who practices one of the fine arts
ARTISTE	*n* pl. -S a skilled public performer
ARTISTIC	*adj* characteristic of art
ARTISTRY	*n* pl. -RIES artistic quality or workmanship
ARTLESS	*adj* lacking cunning or guile
ARTSY	*adj* -SIER, -SIEST arty
ARTWORK	*n* pl. -S illustrative or decorative work in printed matter
ARTY	*adj* ARTIER, ARTIEST showily or pretentiously artistic
ARUGOLA	*n* pl. -S arugula
ARUGULA	*n* pl. -S a European annual herb

ARUM	*n* pl. -S a flowering plant
ARUSPEX	*n* pl. -PICES haruspex
ARVAL	*adj* pertaining to plowed land
ARVO	*n* pl. -VOS afternoon
ARYL	*n* pl. -S a univalent radical
ARYTHMIA	*n* pl. -S an irregularity in the rhythm of the heartbeat **ARYTHMIC** *adj*
AS	*adv* to the same degree
ASANA	*n* pl. -S a posture in yoga
ASARUM	*n* pl. -S a perennial herb
ASBESTOS	*n* pl. -ES a mineral **ASBESTIC** *adj*
ASBESTUS	*n* pl. -ES asbestos
ASCARID	*n* pl. -S a parasitic worm
ASCARIS	*n* pl. -RIDES ascarid
ASCEND	*v* -ED, -ING, -S to go or move upward
ASCENDER	*n* pl. -S one that ascends
ASCENT	*n* pl. -S the act of ascending
ASCESIS	*n* pl. -CESES the conduct of an ascetic
ASCETIC	*n* pl. -S one who practices extreme self-denial for religious reasons
ASCI	pl. of ascus
ASCIDIAN	*n* pl. -S a small marine animal
ASCIDIUM	*n* pl. -DIA a flask-shaped plant appendage
ASCITES	*n* pl. ASCITES accumulation of serous fluid in the abdomen **ASCITIC** *adj*
ASCOCARP	*n* pl. -S a spore-producing organ of certain fungi
ASCORBIC	*adj* relieving scurvy
ASCOT	*n* pl. -S a broad neck scarf
ASCRIBE	*v* -CRIBED, -CRIBING, -CRIBES to attribute to a specified cause, source, or origin
ASCUS	*n* pl. ASCI a spore sac in certain fungi
ASDIC	*n* pl. -S sonar
ASEA	*adv* at sea
ASEPSIS	*n* pl. -SEPSES the condition of being aseptic
ASEPTIC	*adj* free from germs
ASEXUAL	*adj* occurring or performed without sexual action

ASH	*v* -ED, -ING, -ES to convert into ash (the residue of a substance that has been burned)
ASHAMED	*adj* feeling shame, guilt, or disgrace
ASHCAN	*n* pl. -S a metal receptacle for garbage
ASHEN	*adj* consisting of ashes
ASHFALL	*n* pl. -S a deposit of volcanic ash
ASHIER	comparative of ashy
ASHIEST	superlative of ashy
ASHINESS	*n* pl. -ES the condition of being ashy
ASHLAR	*v* -ED, -ING, -S to build with squared stones
ASHLER	*v* -ED, -ING, -S to ashlar
ASHLESS	*adj* having no ashes
ASHMAN	*n* pl. -MEN one who collects and removes ashes
ASHORE	*adv* toward or on the shore
ASHPLANT	*n* pl. -S a walking stick
ASHRAM	*n* pl. -S a secluded dwelling of a Hindu sage
ASHTRAY	*n* pl. -TRAYS a receptacle for tobacco ashes
ASHY	*adj* ASHIER, ASHIEST covered with ashes
ASIDE	*n* pl. -S a comment by an actor intended to be heard by the audience but not the other actors
ASININE	*adj* obstinately stupid or silly
ASK	*v* -ED, -ING, -S to put a question to
ASKANCE	*adv* with a side glance
ASKANT	*adv* askance
ASKER	*n* pl. -S one that asks
ASKESIS	*n* pl. ASKESES ascesis
ASKEW	*adv* to one side
ASKING	*n* pl. -S the act of one who asks
ASKOS	*n* pl. ASKOI an oil jar used in ancient Greece
ASLANT	*adj* slanting
ASLEEP	*adj* sleeping
ASLOPE	*adj* sloping
ASOCIAL	*adj* avoiding the company of others
ASP	*n* pl. -S a venomous snake
ASPARKLE	*adj* sparkling
ASPECT	*n* pl. -S appearance of something to the eye or mind
ASPEN	*n* pl. -S any of several poplars
ASPER	*n* pl. -S a Turkish money of account
ASPERATE	*v* -ATED, -ATING, -ATES to make uneven
ASPERGES	*n* pl. ASPERGES a Roman Catholic rite
ASPERITY	*n* pl. -TIES acrimony
ASPERSE	*v* -PERSED, -PERSING, -PERSES to spread false charges against
ASPERSER	*n* pl. -S one that asperses
ASPERSOR	*n* pl. -S asperser
ASPHALT	*v* -ED, -ING, -S to coat with asphalt (a substance used for paving and roofing)
ASPHERIC	*adj* varying slightly from an exactly spherical shape
ASPHODEL	*n* pl. -S a flowering plant
ASPHYXIA	*n* pl. -S unconsciousness caused by lack of oxygen
ASPHYXY	*n* pl. -PHYXIES asphyxia
ASPIC	*n* pl. -S the asp
ASPIRANT	*n* pl. -S one that aspires
ASPIRATA	*n* pl. -TAE a type of plosive
ASPIRATE	*v* -RATED, -RATING, -RATES to pronounce with an initial release of breath
ASPIRE	*v* -PIRED, -PIRING, -PIRES to have an earnest desire or ambition
ASPIRER	*n* pl. -S an aspirant
ASPIRIN	*n* pl. -S a pain reliever
ASPIRING	present participle of aspire
ASPIS	*n* pl. -PISES aspic
ASPISH	*adj* resembling an asp
ASQUINT	*adv* with a sidelong glance
ASRAMA	*n* pl. -S ashram
ASS	*n* pl. -ES a hoofed mammal
ASSAGAI	*v* -GAIED, -GAIING, -GAIS to pierce with a light spear
ASSAI	*n* pl. -S a tropical tree
ASSAIL	*v* -ED, -ING, -S to attack
ASSAILER	*n* pl. -S one that assails
ASSASSIN	*n* pl. -S a murderer
ASSAULT	*v* -ED, -ING, -S to attack
ASSAY	*v* -ED, -ING, -S to attempt

ASSAYER	*n* pl. -S one that assays
ASSEGAI	*v* -GAIED, -GAIING, -GAIS to assagai
ASSEMBLE	*v* -BLED, -BLING, -BLES to come or bring together
ASSEMBLY	*n* pl. -BLIES the act of assembling
ASSENT	*v* -ED, -ING, -S to express agreement
ASSENTER	*n* pl. -S one that assents
ASSENTOR	*n* pl. -S assenter
ASSERT	*v* -ED, -ING, -S to state positively
ASSERTER	*n* pl. -S one that asserts
ASSERTOR	*n* pl. -S asserter
ASSESS	*v* -ED, -ING, -ES to estimate the value of for taxation
ASSESSOR	*n* pl. -S one that assesses
ASSET	*n* pl. -S a useful quality or thing
ASSIGN	*v* -ED, -ING, -S to set apart for a particular purpose
ASSIGNAT	*n* pl. -S one of the notes issued as currency by the French revolutionary government
ASSIGNEE	*n* pl. -S one to whom property or right is legally transferred
ASSIGNER	*n* pl. -S one that assigns
ASSIGNOR	*n* pl. -S one who legally transfers property or right
ASSIST	*v* -ED, -ING, -S to give aid or support to
ASSISTER	*n* pl. -S one that assists
ASSISTOR	*n* pl. -S assister
ASSIZE	*n* pl. -S a session of a legislative or judicial body
ASSLIKE	*adj* resembling an ass
ASSOIL	*v* -ED, -ING, -S to pardon
ASSONANT	*n* pl. -S a word or syllable that resembles another in sound
ASSORT	*v* -ED, -ING, -S to distribute into groups according to kind or class
ASSORTER	*n* pl. -S one that assorts
ASSUAGE	*v* -SUAGED, -SUAGING, -SUAGES to make less severe
ASSUME	*v* -SUMED, -SUMING, -SUMES to take on
ASSUMER	*n* pl. -S one that assumes
ASSURE	*v* -SURED, -SURING, -SURES to insure
ASSURED	*n* pl. -S an insured person
ASSURER	*n* pl. -S one that assures
ASSURING	present participle of assure
ASSUROR	*n* pl. -S assurer
ASSWAGE	*v* -SWAGED, -SWAGING, -SWAGES to assuage
ASTASIA	*n* pl. -S inability to stand resulting from muscular incoordination
ASTATIC	*adj* unstable
ASTATINE	*n* pl. -S a radioactive element
ASTER	*n* pl. -S a flowering plant
ASTERIA	*n* pl. -S a gemstone cut to exhibit asterism
ASTERISK	*v* -ED, -ING, -S to mark with an asterisk (a star-shaped printing mark)
ASTERISM	*n* pl. -S a property of certain minerals of showing a starlike luminous figure
ASTERN	*adv* at or toward the rear of a ship
ASTERNAL	*adj* not connected to the sternum
ASTEROID	*n* pl. -S a type of celestial body
ASTHENIA	*n* pl. -S lack of strength
ASTHENIC	*n* pl. -S a slender, lightly muscled person
ASTHENY	*n* pl. -NIES asthenia
ASTHMA	*n* pl. -S a respiratory disease
ASTIGMIA	*n* pl. -S a visual defect
ASTILBE	*n* pl. -S an Asian perennial
ASTIR	*adj* moving about
ASTOMOUS	*adj* having no stomata
ASTONISH	*v* -ED, -ING, -ES to fill with sudden wonder or surprise
ASTONY	*v* -TONIED, -TONYING, -TONIES to astonish
ASTOUND	*v* -ED, -ING, -S to amaze
ASTRAGAL	*n* pl. -S a convex molding
ASTRAL	*n* pl. -S a type of oil lamp
ASTRALLY	*adv* in a stellar manner
ASTRAY	*adv* off the right course
ASTRICT	*v* -ED, -ING, -S to restrict
ASTRIDE	*adv* with one leg on each side
ASTRINGE	*v* -TRINGED, -TRINGING, -TRINGES to bind or draw together
ASTUTE	*adj* shrewd **ASTUTELY** *adv*
ASTYLAR	*adj* having no columns
ASUNDER	*adv* into pieces
ASWARM	*adj* swarming

ASWIRL	*adj* swirling
ASWOON	*adj* swooning
ASYLUM	*n* pl. -LUMS or -LA an institution for the care of the mentally ill
ASYNDETA	*n/pl* omissions of certain conjunctions
AT	*prep* in the position of
ATABAL	*n* pl. -S a type of drum
ATACTIC	*adj* showing no regularity of structure
ATAGHAN	*n* pl. -S yataghan
ATALAYA	*n* pl. -S a watchtower
ATAMAN	*n* pl. -S a hetman
ATAMASCO	*n* pl. -COS a flowering plant
ATAP	*n* pl. -S the nipa palm tree
ATARAXIA	*n* pl. -S peace of mind
ATARAXIC	*n* pl. -S a tranquilizing drug
ATARAXY	*n* pl. -RAXIES ataraxia
ATAVIC	*adj* pertaining to a remote ancestor
ATAVISM	*n* pl. -S the reappearance of a genetic characteristic after several generations of absence
ATAVIST	*n* pl. -S an individual displaying atavism
ATAXIA	*n* pl. -S loss of muscular coordination
ATAXIC	*n* pl. -S one suffering from ataxia
ATAXY	*n* pl. ATAXIES ataxia
ATE	*n* pl. -S blind impulse or reckless ambition that drives one to ruin
ATECHNIC	*adj* lacking technical knowledge
ATELIC	*adj* pertaining to a type of verb form
ATELIER	*n* pl. -S a workshop or studio
ATEMOYA	*n* pl. -S a fruit of a hybrid tropical tree
ATHANASY	*n* pl. -SIES immortality
ATHEISM	*n* pl. -S the belief that there is no God
ATHEIST	*n* pl. -S a believer in atheism
ATHELING	*n* pl. -S an Anglo-Saxon prince or nobleman
ATHENEUM	*n* pl. -S a literary institution
ATHEROMA	*n* pl. -MAS or -MATA a disease of the arteries
ATHETOID	*adj* affected with a type of nervous disorder
ATHIRST	*adj* having a strong desire
ATHLETE	*n* pl. -S one skilled in feats of physical strength and agility **ATHLETIC** *adj*
ATHODYD	*n* pl. -S a type of jet engine
ATHWART	*adv* from side to side
ATILT	*adj* being in a tilted position
ATINGLE	*adj* tingling
ATLAS	*n* pl. ATLANTES or ATLASES a male figure used as a supporting column
ATLATL	*n* pl. -S a device for throwing a spear or dart
ATMA	*n* pl. -S atman
ATMAN	*n* pl. -S the individual soul in Hinduism
ATOLL	*n* pl. -S a coral island
ATOM	*n* pl. -S the smallest unit of an element **ATOMIC, ATOMICAL** *adj*
ATOMICS	*n/pl* the science dealing with atoms
ATOMIES	pl. of atomy
ATOMISE	*v* -ISED, -ISING, -ISES to atomize
ATOMISER	*n* pl. -S atomizer
ATOMISM	*n* pl. -S the theory that the universe is composed of simple, indivisible, minute particles
ATOMIST	*n* pl. -S an adherent of atomism
ATOMIZE	*v* -IZED, -IZING, -IZES to reduce to a fine spray
ATOMIZER	*n* pl. -S a device for atomizing liquids
ATOMY	*n* pl. -MIES a tiny particle
ATONAL	*adj* lacking tonality **ATONALLY** *adv*
ATONE	*v* ATONED, ATONING, ATONES to make amends or reparation **ATONABLE** *adj*
ATONER	*n* pl. -S one that atones
ATONIC	*n* pl. -S an unaccented syllable or word
ATONING	present participle of atone
ATONY	*n* pl. -NIES muscular weakness
ATOP	*adj* being on or at the top
ATOPY	*n* pl. -PIES a type of allergy **ATOPIC** *adj*
ATRAZINE	*n* pl. -S an herbicide
ATREMBLE	*adj* trembling
ATRESIA	*n* pl. -S absence or closure of a natural bodily passage

ATRIA	a pl. of atrium
ATRIAL	*adj* pertaining to an atrium
ATRIP	*adj* aweigh
ATRIUM	*n* pl. ATRIA or ATRIUMS the main room of an ancient Roman house
ATROCITY	*n* pl. -TIES a heinous act
ATROPHIA	*n* pl. -S a wasting away of the body or any of its parts **ATROPHIC** *adj*
ATROPHY	*v* -PHIED, -PHYING, -PHIES to waste away
ATROPIN	*n* pl. -S atropine
ATROPINE	*n* pl. -S a poisonous alkaloid
ATROPISM	*n* pl. -S atropine poisoning
ATT	*n* pl. ATT a monetary unit of Laos
ATTABOY	*interj* —used to express encouragement or approval
ATTACH	*v* -ED, -ING, -ES to connect as an associated part
ATTACHE	*n* pl. -S a diplomatic official
ATTACHER	*n* pl. -S one that attaches
ATTACK	*v* -ED, -ING, -S to set upon violently
ATTACKER	*n* pl. -S one that attacks
ATTAIN	*v* -ED, -ING, -S to gain or achieve by mental or physical effort
ATTAINER	*n* pl. -S one that attains
ATTAINT	*v* -ED, -ING, -S to disgrace
ATTAR	*n* pl. -S a fragrant oil
ATTEMPER	*v* -ED, -ING, -S to modify the temperature of
ATTEMPT	*v* -ED, -ING, -S to make an effort to do or accomplish
ATTEND	*v* -ED, -ING, -S to be present at
ATTENDEE	*n* pl. -S an attender
ATTENDER	*n* pl. -S one that attends
ATTENT	*adj* heedful
ATTEST	*v* -ED, -ING, -S to affirm to be true or genuine
ATTESTER	*n* pl. -S one that attests
ATTESTOR	*n* pl. -S attester
ATTIC	*n* pl. -S a story or room directly below the roof of a house
ATTICISM	*n* pl. -S a concise and elegant expression
ATTICIST	*n* pl. -S one who uses atticisms

ATTIRE	*v* -TIRED, -TIRING, -TIRES to clothe
ATTITUDE	*n* pl. -S a state of mind with regard to some matter
ATTORN	*v* -ED, -ING, -S to acknowledge a new owner as one's landlord
ATTORNEY	*n* pl. -NEYS a lawyer
ATTRACT	*v* -ED, -ING, -S to cause to approach or adhere
ATTRITE	*adj* attrited
ATTRITED	*adj* worn down by rubbing
ATTUNE	*v* -TUNED, -TUNING, -TUNES to bring into harmony
ATWAIN	*adv* in two
ATWEEN	*prep* between
ATWITTER	*adj* twittering
ATYPIC	*adj* atypical
ATYPICAL	*adj* not typical
AUBADE	*n* pl. -S a morning song
AUBERGE	*n* pl. -S an inn
AUBRETIA	*n* pl. -S aubrieta
AUBRIETA	*n* pl. -S a flowering plant
AUBURN	*n* pl. -S a reddish brown color
AUCTION	*v* -ED, -ING, -S to sell publicly to the highest bidder
AUCUBA	*n* pl. -S a shrub of the dogwood family
AUDACITY	*n* pl. -TIES boldness
AUDAD	*n* pl. -S aoudad
AUDIAL	*adj* aural
AUDIBLE	*n* pl. -S a type of play in football
AUDIBLY	*adv* in a way so as to be heard
AUDIENCE	*n* pl. -S a group of listeners or spectators
AUDIENT	*n* pl. -S one that hears
AUDILE	*n* pl. -S one whose mental imagery is chiefly auditory
AUDING	*n* pl. -S the process of hearing, recognizing, and interpreting a spoken language
AUDIO	*n* pl. -DIOS sound reception or transmission
AUDIT	*v* -ED, -ING, -S to examine with intent to verify
AUDITION	*v* -ED, -ING, -S to give a trial performance
AUDITIVE	*n* pl. -S an auditory
AUDITOR	*n* pl. -S one that audits
AUDITORY	*n* pl. -RIES a group of listeners

AUGEND	*n* pl. -S a number to which another is to be added
AUGER	*n* pl. -S a tool for boring
AUGHT	*n* pl. -S a zero
AUGITE	*n* pl. -S a mineral **AUGITIC** *adj*
AUGMENT	*v* -ED, -ING, -S to increase
AUGUR	*v* -ED, -ING, -S to foretell from omens
AUGURAL	*adj* pertaining to augury
AUGURER	*n* pl. -S one that augurs
AUGURY	*n* pl. -RIES the practice of auguring
AUGUST	*adj* -GUSTER, -GUSTEST inspiring reverence or admiration **AUGUSTLY** *adv*
AUK	*n* pl. -S a diving seabird
AUKLET	*n* pl. -S a small auk
AULD	*adj* AULDER, AULDEST old
AULIC	*adj* pertaining to a royal court
AUNT	*n* pl. -S the sister of one's father or mother
AUNTHOOD	*n* pl. -S the state of being an aunt
AUNTIE	*n* pl. -S aunt
AUNTIES	pl. of aunty
AUNTLIKE	*adj* resembling an aunt
AUNTLY	*adj* -LIER, -LIEST of or suggesting an aunt
AUNTY	*n* pl. AUNTIES aunt
AURA	*n* pl. -RAS or -RAE an invisible emanation
AURAL	*adj* pertaining to the sense of hearing **AURALLY** *adv*
AURAR	pl. of eyrir
AURATE	*adj* having ears
AURATED	*adj* aurate
AUREATE	*adj* golden
AUREI	pl. of aureus
AUREOLA	*n* pl. -LAS or -LAE a halo
AUREOLE	*v* -OLED, -OLING, -OLES to surround with a halo
AURES	pl. of auris
AUREUS	*n* pl. -REI a gold coin of ancient Rome
AURIC	*adj* pertaining to gold
AURICLE	*n* pl. -S an ear or ear-shaped part **AURICLED** *adj*
AURICULA	*n* pl. -LAS or -LAE an auricle
AURIFORM	*adj* ear-shaped
AURIS	*n* pl. AURES the ear
AURIST	*n* pl. -S a specialist in diseases of the ear
AUROCHS	*n* pl. -ES an extinct European ox
AURORA	*n* pl. -RAS or -RAE the rising light of the morning **AURORAL, AUROREAN** *adj*
AUROUS	*adj* pertaining to gold
AURUM	*n* pl. -S gold
AUSFORM	*v* -ED, -ING, -S to subject steel to a strengthening process
AUSPEX	*n* pl. -PICES a soothsayer of ancient Rome
AUSPICE	*n* pl. -S a favorable omen
AUSTERE	*adj* -TERER, -TEREST grave in disposition or appearance
AUSTRAL	*n* pl. -ES or -S a former monetary unit of Argentina
AUSUBO	*n* pl. -BOS a tropical tree
AUTACOID	*n* pl. -S a hormone
AUTARCHY	*n* pl. -CHIES absolute rule
AUTARKY	*n* pl. -KIES national economic self-sufficiency **AUTARKIC** *adj*
AUTECISM	*n* pl. -S the development of the entire life cycle of a parasitic fungus on a single host
AUTEUR	*n* pl. -S the creator of a film
AUTHOR	*v* -ED, -ING, -S to write
AUTISM	*n* pl. -S extreme withdrawal into fantasy
AUTISTIC	*n* pl. -S one who is affected with autism
AUTO	*v* -ED, -ING, -S to ride in an automobile
AUTOBAHN	*n* pl. -BAHNS or -BAHNEN a German superhighway
AUTOBUS	*n* pl. -BUSES or -BUSSES a bus
AUTOCADE	*n* pl. -S a parade of automobiles
AUTOCOID	*n* pl. -S autacoid
AUTOCRAT	*n* pl. -S an absolute ruler
AUTODYNE	*n* pl. -S a type of electrical circuit
AUTOGAMY	*n* pl. -MIES fertilization of a flower by its own pollen
AUTOGENY	*n* pl. -NIES the production of living organisms from inanimate matter
AUTOGIRO	*n* pl. -ROS a type of airplane
AUTOGYRO	*n* pl. -ROS autogiro
AUTOLYSE	*v* -LYSED, -LYSING, -LYSES to autolyze

AUTOLYZE	*v* -LYZED, -LYZING, -LYZES to break down tissue by the action of self-contained enzymes
AUTOMAN	*n* pl. -MEN an automobile maker
AUTOMATA	*n/pl* robots
AUTOMATE	*v* -MATED, -MATING, -MATES to convert to a system of automatic control
AUTOMEN	*n* pl. of automan
AUTONOMY	*n* pl. -MIES the state of being self-governing
AUTOPSIC	*adj* pertaining to an autopsy
AUTOPSY	*v* -SIED, -SYING, -SIES to examine a dead body to determine the cause of death
AUTOSOME	*n* pl. -S a type of chromosome
AUTOTOMY	*n* pl. -MIES the shedding of a damaged body part
AUTOTYPE	*n* pl. -S a type of photographic process
AUTOTYPY	*n* pl. -TYPIES autotype
AUTUMN	*n* pl. -S a season of the year **AUTUMNAL** *adj*
AUTUNITE	*n* pl. -S a mineral
AUXESIS	*n* pl. AUXESES an increase in cell size without cell division
AUXETIC	*n* pl. -S a substance that promotes auxesis
AUXIN	*n* pl. -S a substance used to regulate plant growth **AUXINIC** *adj*
AVA	*adv* at all
AVADAVAT	*n* pl. -S a small songbird
AVAIL	*v* -ED, -ING, -S to be of use or advantage to
AVANT	*adj* culturally or stylistically new
AVARICE	*n* pl. -S greed
AVAST	*interj* — used as a command to stop
AVATAR	*n* pl. -S the incarnation of a Hindu deity
AVAUNT	*interj* — used as an order of dismissal
AVE	*n* pl. -S an expression of greeting or farewell
AVELLAN	*adj* having the four arms shaped like filberts — used of a heraldic cross
AVELLANE	*adj* avellan
AVENGE	*v* AVENGED, AVENGING, AVENGES to exact retribution for
AVENGER	*n* pl. -S one that avenges
AVENS	*n* pl. -ES a perennial herb
AVENTAIL	*n* pl. -S ventail
AVENUE	*n* pl. -S a wide street
AVER	*v* AVERRED, AVERRING, AVERS to declare positively
AVERAGE	*v* -AGED, -AGING, -AGES to calculate the arithmetic mean of
AVERMENT	*n* pl. -S the act of averring
AVERRED	past tense of aver
AVERRING	present participle of aver
AVERSE	*adj* opposed; reluctant **AVERSELY** *adv*
AVERSION	*n* pl. -S a feeling of repugnance **AVERSIVE** *adj*
AVERT	*v* -ED, -ING, -S to turn away
AVGAS	*n* pl. -GASES or -GASSES gasoline for airplanes
AVIAN	*n* pl. -S a bird
AVIANIZE	*v* -IZED, -IZING, -IZES to make less severe by repeated culture in a chick embryo, as a virus
AVIARIST	*n* pl. -S the keeper of an aviary
AVIARY	*n* pl. -ARIES a large enclosure for live birds
AVIATE	*v* -ATED, -ATING, -ATES to fly an aircraft
AVIATION	*n* pl. -S the act of aviating
AVIATOR	*n* pl. -S one that aviates
AVIATRIX	*n* pl. -TRICES or -TRIXES a female aviator
AVICULAR	*adj* pertaining to birds
AVID	*adj* eager
AVIDIN	*n* pl. -S a protein found in egg white
AVIDITY	*n* pl. -TIES the state of being avid
AVIDLY	*adv* in an avid manner
AVIDNESS	*n* pl. -ES avidity
AVIFAUNA	*n* pl. -NAS or -NAE the bird life of a particular region
AVIGATOR	*n* pl. -S one that navigates aircraft
AVION	*n* pl. -S an airplane
AVIONICS	*n/pl* the science of electronics applied to aviation **AVIONIC** *adj*
AVISO	*n* pl. -SOS advice
AVO	*n* pl. AVOS a monetary unit of Macao

AVOCADO	*n* pl. -DOS or -DOES the edible fruit of a tropical tree
AVOCET	*n* pl. -S a shore bird
AVODIRE	*n* pl. -S an African tree
AVOID	*v* -ED, -ING, -S to keep away from
AVOIDER	*n* pl. -S one that avoids
AVOSET	*n* pl. -S avocet
AVOUCH	*v* -ED, -ING, -ES to affirm
AVOUCHER	*n* pl. -S one that avouches
AVOW	*v* -ED, -ING, -S to declare openly **AVOWABLE** *adj* **AVOWABLY, AVOWEDLY** *adv*
AVOWAL	*n* pl. -S an open declaration
AVOWER	*n* pl. -S one that avows
AVULSE	*v* AVULSED, AVULSING, AVULSES to tear off forcibly
AVULSION	*n* pl. -S the act of avulsing
AW	*interj* — used to express protest, disgust, or disbelief
AWA	*adv* away
AWAIT	*v* -ED, -ING, -S to wait for
AWAITER	*n* pl. -S one that awaits
AWAKE	*v* AWAKED or AWOKE, AWOKEN, AWAKING, AWAKES to wake up
AWAKEN	*v* -ED, -ING, -S to awake
AWAKENER	*n* pl. -S one that awakens
AWAKING	present participle of awake
AWARD	*v* -ED, -ING, -S to grant as due or merited
AWARDEE	*n* pl. -S one that is awarded something
AWARDER	*n* pl. -S one that awards
AWARE	*adj* having perception or knowledge
AWASH	*adj* covered with water
AWAY	*adv* from a certain place
AWAYNESS	*n* pl. -ES the state of being distant
AWE	*v* AWED, AWING or AWEING, AWES to inspire with awe (reverential fear)
AWEARY	*adj* weary
AWEATHER	*adv* toward the windward side of a vessel
AWED	past tense of awe
AWEE	*adv* awhile
AWEIGH	*adj* hanging just clear of the bottom — used of an anchor
AWELESS	*adj* lacking awe
AWESOME	*adj* inspiring awe
AWFUL	*adj* -FULLER, -FULLEST extremely bad or unpleasant **AWFULLY** *adv*
AWHILE	*adv* for a short time
AWHIRL	*adj* whirling
AWING	a present participle of awe
AWKWARD	*adj* -WARDER, -WARDEST lacking skill, dexterity, or grace
AWL	*n* pl. -S a pointed tool for making small holes
AWLESS	*adj* aweless
AWLWORT	*n* pl. -S an aquatic plant
AWMOUS	*n* pl. AWMOUS alms
AWN	*n* pl. -S a bristlelike appendage of certain grasses **AWNED, AWNLESS, AWNY** *adj*
AWNING	*n* pl. -S a rooflike canvas cover **AWNINGED** *adj*
AWOKE	a past tense of awake
AWOKEN	a past participle of awake
AWOL	*n* pl. -S one who is absent without leave
AWRY	*adv* with a turn or twist to one side
AX	*v* -ED, -ING, -ES to work on with an ax (a type of cutting tool)
AXAL	*adj* axial
AXE	*v* AXED, AXING, AXES to ax
AXEL	*n* pl. -S a jump in figure skating
AXEMAN	*n* pl. -MEN axman
AXENIC	*adj* free from germs
AXES	pl. of axis
AXIAL	*adj* pertaining to or forming an axis **AXIALLY** *adv*
AXIALITY	*n* pl. -TIES the state of being axial
AXIL	*n* pl. -S the angle between the upper side of a leaf and its supporting stem
AXILE	*adj* axial
AXILLA	*n* pl. -LAE or -LAS the armpit
AXILLAR	*n* pl. -S a feather on the undersurface of a bird's wing
AXILLARY	*n* pl. -LARIES an axillar
AXING	present participle of axe

AXIOLOGY	*n* pl. -GIES the study of values and value judgments
AXIOM	*n* pl. -S a self-evident truth
AXION	*n* pl. -S a hypothetical subatomic particle
AXIS	*n* pl. AXES a straight line about which a body rotates **AXISED** *adj*
AXIS	*n* pl. AXISES an Asian deer
AXITE	*n* pl. -S a fiber of an axon
AXLE	*n* pl. -S a shaft upon which a wheel revolves **AXLED** *adj*
AXLETREE	*n* pl. -S a type of axle
AXLIKE	*adj* resembling an ax
AXMAN	*n* pl. -MEN one who wields an ax
AXOLOTL	*n* pl. -S a salamander of Mexico and western United States
AXON	*n* pl. -S the central process of a neuron **AXONAL** *adj*
AXONE	*n* pl. -S axon
AXONEMAL	*adj* pertaining to an axoneme
AXONEME	*n* pl. -S a part of a cilium
AXONIC	*adj* pertaining to an axon
AXOPLASM	*n* pl. -S the protoplasm of an axon
AXSEED	*n* pl. -S a European herb
AY	*n* pl. AYS aye
AYAH	*n* pl. -S a native maid or nurse in India
AYE	*n* pl. -S an affirmative vote
AYIN	*n* pl. -S a Hebrew letter
AYURVEDA	*n* pl. -S a Hindu system of medicine
AZALEA	*n* pl. -S a flowering shrub
AZAN	*n* pl. -S a Muslim call to prayer
AZIDE	*n* pl. -S a type of chemical compound **AZIDO** *adj*
AZIMUTH	*n* pl. -S an angle of horizontal deviation
AZINE	*n* pl. -S a type of chemical compound
AZLON	*n* pl. -S a textile fiber
AZO	*adj* containing nitrogen
AZOIC	*adj* pertaining to geologic time before the appearance of life
AZOLE	*n* pl. -S a type of chemical compound
AZON	*n* pl. -S a radio-controlled aerial bomb
AZONAL	*adj* pertaining to a type of a soil group
AZONIC	*adj* not restricted to any particular zone
AZOTE	*n* pl. -S nitrogen **AZOTED** *adj*
AZOTEMIA	*n* pl. -S an excess of nitrogenous substances in the blood **AZOTEMIC** *adj*
AZOTH	*n* pl. -S mercury
AZOTIC	*adj* pertaining to azote
AZOTISE	*v* -TISED, -TISING, -TISES to azotize
AZOTIZE	*v* -TIZED, -TIZING, -TIZES to treat with nitrogen
AZOTURIA	*n* pl. -S an excess of nitrogenous substances in the urine
AZURE	*n* pl. -S a blue color
AZURITE	*n* pl. -S a mineral
AZYGOS	*n* pl. -ES an azygous anatomical part
AZYGOUS	*adj* not being one of a pair

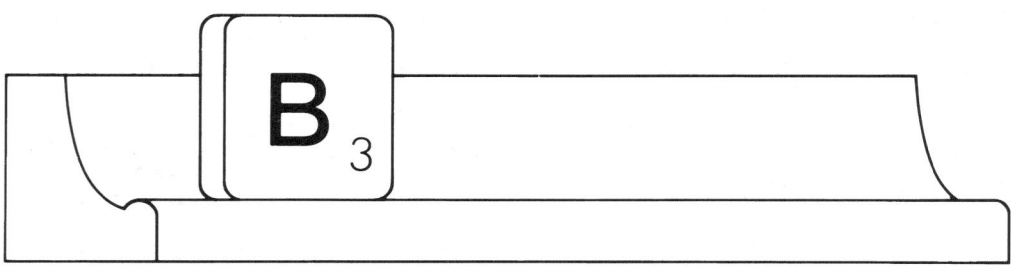

BA	*n* pl. -S the eternal soul, in Egyptian mythology
BAA	*v* -ED, -ING, -S to bleat
BAAL	*n* pl. -S or -IM a false god
BAALISM	*n* pl. -S the worship of a baal
BAAS	*n* pl. -ES master; boss
BAASKAAP	*n* pl. -S the policy of domination by white people in South Africa
BABA	*n* pl. -S a rum cake
BABASSU	*n* pl. -S a palm tree
BABBITT	*v* -ED, -ING, -S to line with babbitt (an alloy of tin, copper, and antimony)
BABBLE	*v* -BLED, -BLING, -BLES to talk idly or excessively
BABBLER	*n* pl. -S one that babbles
BABBLING	*n* pl. -S idle talk
BABE	*n* pl. -S a baby
BABEL	*n* pl. -S confusion
BABESIA	*n* pl. -S a parasitic protozoan
BABICHE	*n* pl. -S rawhide thongs
BABIED	past tense of baby
BABIES	present 3d person sing. of baby
BABIRUSA	*n* pl. -S a wild pig
BABKA	*n* pl. -S a coffee cake
BABOO	*n* pl. -BOOS a Hindu gentleman
BABOOL	*n* pl. -S babul
BABOON	*n* pl. -S a large ape
BABU	*n* pl. -S baboo
BABUL	*n* pl. -S a North African tree
BABUSHKA	*n* pl. -S a woman's scarf
BABY	*v* -BIED, -BYING, -BIES to coddle
BABYHOOD	*n* pl. -S the state of being a baby (an infant)
BABYISH	*adj* resembling a baby
BACALAO	*n* pl. -LAOS codfish
BACCA	*n* pl. -CAE a berry
BACCARA	*n* pl. -S baccarat
BACCARAT	*n* pl. -S a card game
BACCATE	*adj* pulpy like a berry
BACCATED	*adj* baccate
BACCHANT	*n* pl. -S or -ES a carouser
BACCHIC	*adj* riotous
BACCHIUS	*n* pl. -CHII a type of metrical foot
BACH	*v* -ED, -ING, -ES to live as a bachelor
BACHELOR	*n* pl. -S an unmarried man
BACILLAR	*adj* rod-shaped
BACILLUS	*n* pl. -LI any of a class of rod-shaped bacteria
BACK	*v* -ED, -ING, -S to support
BACKACHE	*n* pl. -S a pain in the back
BACKBEAT	*n* pl. -S a type of rhythm in music
BACKBEND	*n* pl. -S an acrobatic feat
BACKBITE	*v* -BIT, -BITTEN, -BITING, -BITES to slander
BACKBONE	*n* pl. -S the spine
BACKCAST	*n* pl. -S a backward movement in casting a fishing line
BACKCHAT	*n* pl. -S repartee
BACKDATE	*v* -DATED, -DATING, -DATES to predate
BACKDOOR	*adj* secretive
BACKDROP	*v* -DROPPED or -DROPT, -DROPPING, -DROPS to provide with a scenic background
BACKER	*n* pl. -S a supporter
BACKFILL	*v* -ED, -ING, -S to refill
BACKFIRE	*v* -FIRED, -FIRING, -FIRES to produce undesirable effects
BACKFIT	*v* -FITTED, -FITTING, -FITS to retrofit
BACKFLOW	*n* pl. -S a flowing back toward a source

BACKHAND	*v* -ED, -ING, -S to strike with the back of the hand
BACKHAUL	*v* -ED, -ING, -S to return after delivering a load
BACKHOE	*n* pl. -S an excavating machine
BACKING	*n* pl. -S support
BACKLAND	*n* pl. -S a region remote from cities
BACKLASH	*v* -ED, -ING, -ES to cause a reaction
BACKLESS	*adj* having no back
BACKLIST	*v* -ED, -ING, -S to include in a publisher's list of older book titles
BACKLIT	*adj* illuminated from behind
BACKLOG	*v* -LOGGED, -LOGGING, -LOGS to accumulate
BACKMOST	*adj* hindmost
BACKOUT	*n* pl. -S a reversal of launching procedures
BACKPACK	*v* -ED, -ING, -S to hike with a pack on one's back
BACKREST	*n* pl. -S a back support
BACKROOM	*adj* made or operating inconspicuously
BACKRUSH	*n* pl. -ES the seaward return of water from a wave
BACKSAW	*n* pl. -S a type of saw
BACKSEAT	*n* pl. -S a rear seat
BACKSET	*n* pl. -S a setback
BACKSIDE	*n* pl. -S the hind part
BACKSLAP	*v* -SLAPPED, -SLAPPING, -SLAPS to show much approval
BACKSLID	past tense of backslide (to revert to sin)
BACKSPIN	*n* pl. -S a backward rotation
BACKSTAB	*v* -STABBED, -STABBING, -STABS to attack or betray behind one's back
BACKSTAY	*n* pl. -STAYS a support for a mast
BACKSTOP	*v* -STOPPED, -STOPPING, -STOPS to bolster
BACKUP	*n* pl. -S a substitute
BACKWARD	*adv* toward the back
BACKWASH	*v* -ED, -ING, -ES to spray water backward
BACKWOOD	*adj* uncouth
BACKWRAP	*n* pl. -S a wraparound garment that fastens in the back
BACKYARD	*n* pl. -S an area at the rear of a house
BACON	*n* pl. -S a side of a pig cured and smoked
BACTERIA	*n* pl. -S a group of microscopic organisms
BACTERIN	*n* pl. -S a vaccine prepared from dead bacteria
BACULINE	*adj* pertaining to a rod
BACULUM	*n* pl. -LA or -LUMS a bone in the penis of many mammals
BAD	*adj* BADDER, BADDEST very good
BAD	*adj* WORSE, WORST not good
BAD	*n* pl. -S something that is bad
BADDIE	*n* pl. -S a bad person
BADDY	*n* pl. -DIES baddie
BADE	past tense of bid
BADGE	*v* BADGED, BADGING, BADGES to supply with an insignia
BADGER	*v* -ED, -ING, -S to harass
BADGERLY	*adj* bothersome
BADGING	present participle of badge
BADINAGE	*v* -NAGED, -NAGING, -NAGES to banter
BADLAND	*n* pl. -S a barren, hilly area
BADLY	*adv* in a bad manner
BADMAN	*n* pl. -MEN an outlaw
BADMOUTH	*v* -ED, -ING, -S to criticize
BADNESS	*n* pl. -ES the state of being bad
BAFF	*v* -ED, -ING, -S to strike under a golf ball
BAFFIES	pl. of baffy
BAFFLE	*v* -FLED, -FLING, -FLES to confuse
BAFFLER	*n* pl. -S one that baffles
BAFFY	*n* pl. -FIES a wooden golf club
BAG	*v* BAGGED, BAGGING, BAGS to put into a bag (a flexible container)
BAGASS	*n* pl. -ES bagasse
BAGASSE	*n* pl. -S crushed sugarcane
BAGEL	*n* pl. -S a ring-shaped roll
BAGFUL	*n* pl. BAGFULS or BAGSFUL as much as a bag can hold
BAGGAGE	*n* pl. -S luggage
BAGGED	past tense of bag
BAGGER	*n* pl. -S one that bags
BAGGIE	*n* pl. -S the stomach
BAGGING	*n* pl. -S material for making bags
BAGGY	*adj* -GIER, -GIEST loose-fitting **BAGGILY** *adv*

BAGHOUSE	*n* pl. -S a facility for removing particulates from exhaust gases
BAGMAN	*n* pl. -MEN a traveling salesman
BAGNIO	*n* pl. -NIOS a brothel
BAGPIPE	*n* pl. -S a wind instrument
BAGPIPER	*n* pl. -S one that plays bagpipes
BAGSFUL	a pl. of bagful
BAGUET	*n* pl. -S baguette
BAGUETTE	*n* pl. -S a rectangular gem
BAGWIG	*n* pl. -S a type of wig
BAGWORM	*n* pl. -S the larva of certain moths
BAH	*interj* — an exclamation of disgust
BAHADUR	*n* pl. -S a Hindu title of respect
BAHT	*n* pl. -S a monetary unit of Thailand
BAIDARKA	*n* pl. -S bidarka
BAIL	*v* -ED, -ING, -S to transfer property temporarily **BAILABLE** *adj*
BAILEE	*n* pl. -S a person to whom property is bailed
BAILER	*n* pl. -S bailor
BAILEY	*n* pl. -LEYS an outer castle wall
BAILIE	*n* pl. -S a Scottish magistrate
BAILIFF	*n* pl. -S a court officer
BAILMENT	*n* pl. -S the act of bailing
BAILOR	*n* pl. -S a person who bails property to another
BAILOUT	*n* pl. -S the act of parachuting from an aircraft
BAILSMAN	*n* pl. -MEN one who provides security for another
BAIRN	*n* pl. -S a child **BAIRNISH** *adj*
BAIRNLY	*adj* -LIER, -LIEST childish
BAIT	*v* -ED, -ING, -S to lure
BAITER	*n* pl. -S one that baits
BAITH	*adj* both
BAIZA	*n* pl. -S a monetary unit of Oman
BAIZE	*n* pl. -S a green, woolen fabric
BAKE	*v* BAKED, BAKING, BAKES to prepare food in an oven
BAKEMEAT	*n* pl. -S a pastry
BAKER	*n* pl. -S one that bakes
BAKERY	*n* pl. -ERIES a place where baked goods are sold
BAKESHOP	*n* pl. -S a bakery
BAKING	*n* pl. -S a quantity baked
BAKLAVA	*n* pl. -S a Turkish pastry
BAKLAWA	*n* pl. -S baklava
BAKSHISH	*v* -ED, -ING, -ES to give a tip
BAL	*n* pl. -S a balmoral
BALANCE	*v* -ANCED, -ANCING, -ANCES to weigh
BALANCER	*n* pl. -S one that balances
BALAS	*n* pl. -ES a red variety of spinel
BALATA	*n* pl. -S a tropical tree
BALBOA	*n* pl. -S a monetary unit of Panama
BALCONY	*n* pl. -NIES an elevated platform
BALD	*adj* BALDER, BALDEST lacking hair
BALD	*v* -ED, -ING, -S to become bald
BALDHEAD	*n* pl. -S a bald person
BALDIES	*pl.* of baldy
BALDISH	*adj* somewhat bald
BALDLY	*adv* in a plain and blunt manner
BALDNESS	*n* pl. -ES the state of being bald
BALDPATE	*n* pl. -S a baldhead
BALDRIC	*n* pl. -S a shoulder belt
BALDRICK	*n* pl. -S baldric
BALDY	*n* pl. BALDIES a bald person
BALE	*v* BALED, BALING, BALES to form into tightly compressed bundles
BALEEN	*n* pl. -S whalebone
BALEFIRE	*n* pl. -S a bonfire
BALEFUL	*adj* menacing
BALER	*n* pl. -S one that bales
BALING	present participle of bale
BALISAUR	*n* pl. -S a long-tailed badger
BALK	*v* -ED, -ING, -S to stop short and refuse to proceed
BALKER	*n* pl. -S one that balks
BALKLINE	*n* pl. -S the starting line in track events
BALKY	*adj* BALKIER, BALKIEST stubborn **BALKILY** *adv*
BALL	*v* -ED, -ING, -S to form into a ball (a spherical object)
BALLAD	*n* pl. -S a narrative poem or song **BALLADIC** *adj*
BALLADE	*n* pl. -S a type of poem
BALLADRY	*n* pl. -RIES ballad poetry
BALLAST	*v* -ED, -ING, -S to stabilize
BALLER	*n* pl. -S one that balls

BALLET	*n* pl. -S a classical dance form **BALLETIC** *adj*	**BANANA**	*n* pl. -S an edible fruit
BALLGAME	*n* pl. -S a game played with a ball	**BANAUSIC**	*adj* practical
BALLHAWK	*n* pl. -S a very good defensive ballplayer	**BANCO**	*n* pl. -COS a bet in certain gambling games
BALLIES	pl. of bally	**BAND**	*v* -ED, -ING, -S to decorate with flexible strips of material
BALLISTA	*n* pl. -TAE an ancient weapon	**BANDAGE**	*v* -DAGED, -DAGING, -DAGES to cover a wound with a strip of cloth
BALLON	*n* pl. -S lightness of movement		
BALLONET	*n* pl. -S a small balloon	**BANDAGER**	*n* pl. -S one that bandages
BALLONNE	*n* pl. -S a ballet jump	**BANDANA**	*n* pl. -S bandanna
BALLOON	*v* -ED, -ING, -S to swell out	**BANDANNA**	*n* pl. -S a large, colored handkerchief
BALLOT	*v* -ED, -ING, -S to vote		
BALLOTER	*n* pl. -S one that ballots	**BANDBOX**	*n* pl. -ES a lightweight box
BALLPARK	*n* pl. -S a facility in which ballgames are played	**BANDEAU**	*n* pl. -DEAUX or -DEAUS a headband
BALLROOM	*n* pl. -S a large room for dancing	**BANDER**	*n* pl. -S one that bands
BALLUTE	*n* pl. -S a small inflatable parachute	**BANDEROL**	*n* pl. -S a streamer
		BANDIED	past tense of bandy
BALLY	*n* pl. -LIES a noisy uproar	**BANDIES**	present 3d person sing. of bandy
BALLYHOO	*v* -ED, -ING, -S to promote by uproar	**BANDIT**	*n* pl. -DITS or -DITTI a robber
BALLYRAG	*v* -RAGGED, -RAGGING, -RAGS to bullyrag	**BANDITRY**	*n* pl. -TRIES robbery by bandits
		BANDOG	*n* pl. -S a watchdog
BALM	*n* pl. -S a fragrant resin **BALMLIKE** *adj*	**BANDORA**	*n* pl. -S bandore
BALMORAL	*n* pl. -S a type of shoe	**BANDORE**	*n* pl. -S an ancient lute
BALMY	*adj* BALMIER, BALMIEST mild **BALMILY** *adv*	**BANDSMAN**	*n* pl. -MEN a member of a musical band
BALNEAL	*adj* pertaining to baths	**BANDY**	*v* -DIED, -DYING, -DIES to throw to and fro
BALONEY	*n* pl. -NEYS bologna	**BANE**	*v* BANED, BANING, BANES to kill with poison
BALSA	*n* pl. -S a tropical tree		
BALSAM	*v* -ED, -ING, -S to anoint with balsam (an aromatic, resinous substance)	**BANEFUL**	*adj* poisonous
		BANG	*v* -ED, -ING, -S to hit sharply
BALSAMIC	*adj* containing balsam	**BANGER**	*n* pl. -S a sausage
BALUSTER	*n* pl. -S a railing support	**BANGKOK**	*n* pl. -S a straw hat
BAM	*v* BAMMED, BAMMING, BAMS to strike with a dull resounding noise	**BANGLE**	*n* pl. -S a bracelet
		BANGTAIL	*n* pl. -S a racehorse
		BANI	pl. of ban
BAMBINO	*n* pl. -NOS or -NI a baby	**BANIAN**	*n* pl. -S a Hindu merchant
BAMBOO	*n* pl. -BOOS a tropical grass	**BANING**	present participle of bane
BAN	*v* BANNED, BANNING, BANS to prohibit	**BANISH**	*v* -ED, -ING, -ES to expel
		BANISHER	*n* pl. -S one that banishes
BAN	*n* pl. BANI a monetary unit of Romania	**BANISTER**	*n* pl. -S a handrail
		BANJAX	*v* -ED, -ING, -ES to damage or ruin
BANAL	*adj* ordinary **BANALLY** *adv*		
BANALITY	*n* pl. -TIES something banal	**BANJO**	*n* pl. -JOS or -JOES a musical instrument
BANALIZE	*v* -IZED, -IZING, -IZES to make banal		
		BANJOIST	*n* pl. -S one who plays the banjo

BANK	*v* -ED, -ING, -S to keep money in a bank (an institution dealing in money matters) **BANKABLE** *adj*
BANKBOOK	*n* pl. -S a depositor's book
BANKCARD	*n* pl. -S a credit card issued by a bank
BANKER	*n* pl. -S one who works in a bank **BANKERLY** *adj*
BANKING	*n* pl. -S the business of a bank
BANKNOTE	*n* pl. -S a promissory note
BANKROLL	*v* -ED, -ING, -S to fund
BANKRUPT	*v* -ED, -ING, -S to impoverish
BANKSIA	*n* pl. -S an Australian plant
BANKSIDE	*n* pl. -S the slope of a river bank
BANNED	past tense of ban
BANNER	*v* -ED, -ING, -S to furnish with a flag
BANNERET	*n* pl. -S a small flag
BANNEROL	*n* pl. -S a banderol
BANNET	*n* pl. -S a bonnet
BANNING	present participle of ban
BANNOCK	*n* pl. -S a type of cake
BANNS	*n/pl* a marriage notice
BANQUET	*v* -ED, -ING, -S to feast
BANSHEE	*n* pl. -S a female spirit
BANSHIE	*n* pl. -S banshee
BANTAM	*n* pl. -S a small fowl
BANTENG	*n* pl. -S a wild ox
BANTER	*v* -ED, -ING, -S to exchange mildly teasing remarks
BANTERER	*n* pl. -S one that banters
BANTLING	*n* pl. -S a very young child
BANTY	*n* pl. -TIES a bantam
BANYAN	*n* pl. -S an East Indian tree
BANZAI	*n* pl. -S a Japanese battle cry
BAOBAB	*n* pl. -S a tropical tree
BAP	*n* pl. -S a small bun or roll
BAPTISE	*v* -TISED, -TISING, -TISES to baptize
BAPTISIA	*n* pl. -S a flowering plant
BAPTISM	*n* pl. -S a Christian ceremony
BAPTIST	*n* pl. -S one who baptizes
BAPTIZE	*v* -TIZED, -TIZING, -TIZES to administer baptism to
BAPTIZER	*n* pl. -S a baptist
BAR	*v* BARRED, BARRING, BARS to exclude
BARATHEA	*n* pl. -S a silk fabric
BARB	*v* -ED, -ING, -S to furnish with a barb (a sharp projection)
BARBAL	*adj* pertaining to the beard
BARBARIC	*adj* uncivilized
BARBASCO	*n* pl. -COS or -COES a tropical tree
BARBATE	*adj* bearded
BARBE	*n* pl. -S a medieval cloth headdress
BARBECUE	*v* -CUED, -CUING, -CUES to cook over live coals or an open fire
BARBEL	*n* pl. -S an organ of a fish
BARBELL	*n* pl. -S an exercise apparatus
BARBEQUE	*v* -QUED, -QUING, -QUES barbecue
BARBER	*v* -ED, -ING, -S to cut hair
BARBERRY	*n* pl. -RIES a shrub
BARBET	*n* pl. -S a tropical bird
BARBETTE	*n* pl. -S a platform
BARBICAN	*n* pl. -S an outer fortification
BARBICEL	*n* pl. -S a part of a feather
BARBITAL	*n* pl. -S a sedative
BARBLESS	*adj* having no barbs
BARBULE	*n* pl. -S a small barb
BARBUT	*n* pl. -S a type of helmet
BARBWIRE	*n* pl. -S barbed wire
BARCHAN	*n* pl. -S a type of sand dune
BARD	*v* -ED, -ING, -S to armor a horse
BARDE	*v* BARDED, BARDING, BARDES to bard
BARDIC	*adj* poetic
BARE	*adj* BARER, BAREST naked
BARE	*v* BARED, BARING, BARES to expose
BAREBACK	*adv* without a saddle
BAREBOAT	*n* pl. -S a pleasure boat rented without personnel
BAREFIT	*adj* barefoot
BAREFOOT	*adj* being without shoes
BAREGE	*n* pl. -S a sheer fabric
BAREHEAD	*adv* without a hat
BARELY	*adv* scarcely
BARENESS	*n* pl. -ES the state of being bare
BARER	comparative of bare
BARESARK	*n* pl. -S an ancient warrior

BAREST	superlative of bare
BARF	v -ED, -ING, -S to vomit
BARFLY	n pl. -FLIES a drinker who frequents bars
BARGAIN	v -ED, -ING, -S to discuss terms for selling or buying
BARGE	v BARGED, BARGING, BARGES to move by barge (a long, large boat)
BARGEE	n pl. -S a bargeman
BARGELLO	n pl. -LOS a needlepoint stitch that makes a zigzag pattern
BARGEMAN	n pl. -MEN the master or a crew member of a barge
BARGHEST	n pl. -S a goblin
BARGING	present participle of barge
BARGUEST	n pl. -S barghest
BARHOP	v -HOPPED, -HOPPING, -HOPS to visit a number of bars during an evening
BARIC	adj pertaining to barium
BARILLA	n pl. -S a chemical compound
BARING	present participle of bare
BARITE	n pl. -S a mineral
BARITONE	n pl. -S a male singing voice
BARIUM	n pl. -S a metallic element
BARK	v -ED, -ING, -S to cry like a dog
BARKEEP	n pl. -S a bartender
BARKER	n pl. -S one that barks
BARKLESS	adj having no bark; unable to bark
BARKY	adj BARKIER, BARKIEST covered with bark (tough outer covering of a root or stem)
BARLEDUC	n pl. -S a fruit jam
BARLESS	adj having no restraints
BARLEY	n pl. -LEYS a cereal grass
BARLOW	n pl. -S a jackknife
BARM	n pl. -S the foam on malt liquors
BARMAID	n pl. -S a female bartender
BARMAN	n pl. -MEN a male bartender
BARMIE	adj barmy
BARMY	adj BARMIER, BARMIEST full of barm; frothy
BARN	n pl. -S a large storage building
BARNACLE	n pl. -S a shellfish
BARNLIKE	adj resembling a barn

BARNY	adj BARNIER, BARNIEST resembling a barn in size, shape, or smell
BARNYARD	n pl. -S a yard near a barn
BAROGRAM	n pl. -S a barometric reading
BARON	n pl. -S a lower member of nobility
BARONAGE	n pl. -S the rank of a baron
BARONESS	n pl. -ES the wife of a baron
BARONET	n pl. -S the holder of a rank below that of a baron
BARONG	n pl. -S a broad knife
BARONIAL	adj pertaining to a baron
BARONNE	n pl. -S a baroness
BARONY	n pl. -ONIES the domain of a baron
BAROQUE	n pl. -S an ornate object
BAROUCHE	n pl. -S a type of carriage
BARQUE	n pl. -S a sailing vessel
BARRABLE	adj capable of being barred
BARRACK	v -ED, -ING, -S to shout boisterously
BARRAGE	v -RAGED, -RAGING, -RAGES to subject to a massive attack
BARRANCA	n pl. -S a steep ravine
BARRANCO	n pl. -COS barranca
BARRATER	n pl. -S barrator
BARRATOR	n pl. -S one who commits barratry
BARRATRY	n pl. -TRIES fraud committed by a master or crew of a ship
BARRE	v BARRED, BARRING, BARRES to play a type of guitar chord
BARRED	past tense of bar
BARREL	v -RELED, -RELING, -RELS or -RELLED, -RELLING, -RELS to move fast
BARREN	adj -RENER, -RENEST unproductive **BARRENLY** adv
BARREN	n pl. -S a tract of barren land
BARRET	n pl. -S a flat cap
BARRETOR	n pl. -S barrator
BARRETRY	n pl. -TRIES barratry
BARRETTE	n pl. -S a hair clip
BARRIER	n pl. -S an obstacle
BARRING	present participle of bar and barre
BARRIO	n pl. -RIOS a district
BARROOM	n pl. -S a room where liquor is sold

BARROW	*n* pl. -S a type of cart
BARSTOOL	*n* pl. -S a stool in a barroom
BARTEND	*v* -ED, -ING, -S to tend a barroom
BARTER	*v* -ED, -ING, -S to trade
BARTERER	*n* pl. -S one that barters
BARTISAN	*n* pl. -S bartizan
BARTIZAN	*n* pl. -S a small turret
BARWARE	*n* pl. -S barroom equipment
BARYE	*n* pl. -S a unit of pressure
BARYON	*n* pl. -S a type of subatomic particle **BARYONIC** *adj*
BARYTA	*n* pl. -S a compound of barium **BARYTIC** *adj*
BARYTE	*n* pl. -S barite
BARYTONE	*n* pl. -S baritone
BASAL	*adj* pertaining to the foundation **BASALLY** *adv*
BASALT	*n* pl. -S a volcanic rock **BASALTIC** *adj*
BASALTES	*n* pl. BASALTES unglazed stoneware
BASCULE	*n* pl. -S a type of seesaw
BASE	*adj* BASER, BASEST morally low
BASE	*v* BASED, BASING, BASES to found
BASEBALL	*n* pl. -S a type of ball
BASEBORN	*adj* of low birth
BASED	past tense of base
BASELESS	*adj* having no foundation
BASELINE	*n* pl. -S a line at either end of a court in certain sports
BASELY	*adv* in a base manner
BASEMAN	*n* pl. -MEN a certain player in baseball
BASEMENT	*n* pl. -S the part of a building below ground level
BASENESS	*n* pl. -ES the state of being base
BASENJI	*n* pl. -S a barkless dog
BASER	comparative of base
BASES	pl. of basis
BASEST	superlative of base
BASH	*v* -ED, -ING, -ES to smash
BASHAW	*n* pl. -S a pasha
BASHER	*n* pl. -S one that bashes
BASHFUL	*adj* shy; timid
BASHLYK	*n* pl. -S a cloth hood

BASIC	*n* pl. -S a fundamental
BASICITY	*n* pl. -TIES the state of being alkaline
BASIDIUM	*n* pl. -IA a structure on a fungus **BASIDIAL** *adj*
BASIFIER	*n* pl. -S one that basifies
BASIFY	*v* -FIED, -FYING, -FIES to alkalize
BASIL	*n* pl. -S an aromatic herb
BASILAR	*adj* basal
BASILARY	*adj* basilar
BASILIC	*adj* pertaining to a basilica
BASILICA	*n* pl. -CAS or -CAE an ancient Roman building
BASILISK	*n* pl. -S a fabled serpent
BASIN	*n* pl. -S a large bowl **BASINAL, BASINED** *adj*
BASINET	*n* pl. -S a medieval helmet
BASINFUL	*n* pl. -S as much as a basin can hold
BASING	present participle of base
BASION	*n* pl. -S a part of the skull
BASIS	*n* pl. BASES the foundation of something
BASK	*v* -ED, -ING, -S to lie in a pleasant warmth
BASKET	*n* pl. -S a wooden container
BASKETRY	*n* pl. -RIES basket weaving
BASMATI	*n* pl. -S a long-grain rice
BASOPHIL	*n* pl. -S a type of cell
BASQUE	*n* pl. -S a bodice
BASS	*n* pl. -ES an edible fish
BASSET	*v* -SETED, -SETING, -SETS or -SETTED, -SETTING, -SETS to outcrop
BASSI	a pl. of basso
BASSINET	*n* pl. -S a basket used as a baby's crib
BASSIST	*n* pl. -S a person who plays a double bass
BASSLY	*adv* in a low-pitched manner
BASSNESS	*n* pl. -ES lowness in pitch
BASSO	*n* pl. -SOS or -SI a low-pitched singer
BASSOON	*n* pl. -S a low-pitched instrument
BASSWOOD	*n* pl. -S a linden tree
BASSY	*adj* low in pitch
BAST	*n* pl. -S a woody fiber
BASTARD	*n* pl. -S an illegitimate child

BASTARDY	*n* pl. -TARDIES the state of being a bastard
BASTE	*v* BASTED, BASTING, BASTES to sew loosely together
BASTER	*n* pl. -S one that bastes
BASTILE	*n* pl. -S bastille
BASTILLE	*n* pl. -S a prison
BASTING	*n* pl. -S the thread used by a baster
BASTION	*n* pl. -S a fortified place
BAT	*v* BATTED, BATTING, BATS to hit a baseball
BATBOY	*n* pl. -BOYS a boy who minds baseball equipment
BATCH	*v* -ED, -ING, -ES to bring together
BATCHER	*n* pl. -S one that batches
BATE	*v* BATED, BATING, BATES to reduce the force of
BATEAU	*n* pl. -TEAUX a flat-bottomed boat
BATFISH	*n* pl. -ES a batlike fish
BATFOWL	*v* -ED, -ING, -S to catch birds at night
BATH	*n* pl. -S a washing
BATHE	*v* BATHED, BATHING, BATHES to wash
BATHER	*n* pl. -S one that bathes
BATHETIC	*adj* trite
BATHING	present participle of bathe
BATHLESS	*adj* not having had a bath
BATHMAT	*n* pl. -S a mat used in a bathroom
BATHOS	*n* pl. -ES triteness
BATHROBE	*n* pl. -S a housecoat
BATHROOM	*n* pl. -S a room in which to bathe
BATHTUB	*n* pl. -S a tub in which to bathe
BATHYAL	*adj* pertaining to deep water
BATIK	*n* pl. -S a dyeing process
BATING	present participle of bate
BATISTE	*n* pl. -S a sheer fabric
BATLIKE	*adj* resembling a bat (a flying mammal)
BATMAN	*n* pl. -MEN an orderly
BATON	*n* pl. -S a short rod
BATSMAN	*n* pl. -MEN one who bats
BATT	*n* pl. -S a sheet of cotton
BATTALIA	*n* pl. -S a military unit
BATTEAU	*n* pl. -TEAUX bateau
BATTED	past tense of bat
BATTEN	*v* -ED, -ING, -S to fasten with strips of wood
BATTENER	*n* pl. -S one that battens
BATTER	*v* -ED, -ING, -S to beat repeatedly
BATTERIE	*n* pl. -S a ballet movement
BATTERY	*n* pl. -TERIES a device for generating an electric current
BATTIER	comparative of batty
BATTIEST	superlative of batty
BATTIK	*n* pl. -S batik
BATTING	*n* pl. -S a batt
BATTLE	*v* -TLED, -TLING, -TLES to fight
BATTLER	*n* pl. -S one that battles
BATTU	*adj* pertaining to a ballet movement
BATTUE	*n* pl. -S a type of hunt
BATTY	*adj* -TIER, -TIEST crazy
BATWING	*adj* shaped like a bat's wing
BAUBEE	*n* pl. -S bawbee
BAUBLE	*n* pl. -S a cheap trinket
BAUD	*n* pl. -S a unit of data transmission speed
BAUDEKIN	*n* pl. -S a brocaded fabric
BAUDRONS	*n* pl. -ES a cat
BAUHINIA	*n* pl. -S a small tropical tree
BAULK	*v* -ED, -ING, -S to balk
BAULKY	*adj* BAULKIER, BAULKIEST balky
BAUSOND	*adj* having white marks
BAUXITE	*n* pl. -S an ore of aluminum **BAUXITIC** *adj*
BAWBEE	*n* pl. -S a Scottish coin
BAWCOCK	*n* pl. -S a fine fellow
BAWD	*n* pl. -S a madam
BAWDIER	comparative of bawdy
BAWDIES	pl. of bawdy
BAWDIEST	superlative of bawdy
BAWDILY	*adv* in a bawdy manner
BAWDRIC	*n* pl. -S baldric
BAWDRY	*n* pl. -RIES obscenity
BAWDY	*adj* BAWDIER, BAWDIEST obscene
BAWDY	*n* pl. BAWDIES obscene language
BAWL	*v* -ED, -ING, -S to cry loudly

BAWLER	*n* pl. -S one that bawls	**BEADY**	*adj* BEADIER, BEADIEST resembling beads
BAWSUNT	*adj* bausond	**BEAGLE**	*n* pl. -S a small hound
BAWTIE	*n* pl. -S a dog	**BEAK**	*n* pl. -S a bird's bill **BEAKED, BEAKLESS, BEAKLIKE** *adj*
BAWTY	*n* pl. -TIES bawtie		
BAY	*v* -ED, -ING, -S to howl	**BEAKER**	*n* pl. -S a large cup
BAYADEER	*n* pl. -S bayadere	**BEAKY**	*adj* BEAKIER, BEAKIEST resembling a beak
BAYADERE	*n* pl. -S a dancing girl		
BAYAMO	*n* pl. -MOS a strong wind	**BEAM**	*v* -ED, -ING, -S to emit in beams (rays of light)
BAYARD	*n* pl. -S a horse		
BAYBERRY	*n* pl. -RIES a berry tree	**BEAMIER**	comparative of beamy
BAYMAN	*n* pl. -MEN a person who fishes on a bay	**BEAMIEST**	superlative of beamy
		BEAMILY	*adv* in a beamy manner
BAYONET	*v* -NETED, -NETING, -NETS or -NETTED, -NETTING, -NETS to stab with a dagger-like weapon	**BEAMISH**	*adj* cheerful
		BEAMLESS	*adj* having no beam
		BEAMLIKE	*adj* resembling a beam
BAYOU	*n* pl. -S a marshy body of water	**BEAMY**	*adj* BEAMIER, BEAMIEST beaming
BAYWOOD	*n* pl. -S a coarse mahogany		
BAZAAR	*n* pl. -S a marketplace	**BEAN**	*v* -ED, -ING, -S to hit on the head
BAZAR	*n* pl. -S bazaar	**BEANBAG**	*n* pl. -S a small cloth bag
BAZOO	*n* pl. -ZOOS the mouth	**BEANBALL**	*n* pl. -S a baseball thrown at the head
BAZOOKA	*n* pl. -S a small rocket launcher		
BDELLIUM	*n* pl. -S a gum resin	**BEANERY**	*n* pl. -ERIES a cheap restaurant
BE	*v* present sing. 1st person AM, 2d ARE or ART, 3d IS, past sing. 1st and 3d persons WAS, 2d WERE or WAST or WERT, past participle BEEN, present participle BEING to have actuality	**BEANIE**	*n* pl. -S a small cap
		BEANLIKE	*adj* resembling a bean
		BEANO	*n* pl. BEANOS a form of bingo
		BEANPOLE	*n* pl. -S a thin pole
		BEAR	*v* BORE, BORNE or BORN, BEARING, BEARS to endure **BEARABLE** *adj* **BEARABLY** *adv*
BEACH	*v* -ED, -ING, -ES to drive ashore		
BEACHBOY	*n* pl. -BOYS a male beach attendant	**BEARCAT**	*n* pl. -S a small mammal
		BEARD	*v* -ED, -ING, -S to oppose boldly
BEACHY	*adj* BEACHIER, BEACHIEST sandy or pebbly	**BEARER**	*n* pl. -S one that bears
		BEARHUG	*n* pl. -S a rough tight embrace
BEACON	*v* -ED, -ING, -S to warn or guide	**BEARING**	*n* pl. -S demeanor
BEAD	*v* -ED, -ING, -S to adorn with beads (round pieces of glass)	**BEARISH**	*adj* resembling a bear (a large mammal)
		BEARLIKE	*adj* bearish
BEADIER	comparative of beady	**BEARSKIN**	*n* pl. -S the skin of a bear
BEADIEST	superlative of beady	**BEARWOOD**	*n* pl. -S a small tree of the buckthorn family
BEADILY	*adv* in a beady manner		
BEADING	*n* pl. -S beaded material	**BEAST**	*n* pl. -S an animal
BEADLE	*n* pl. -S a parish official	**BEASTIE**	*n* pl. -S a tiny animal
BEADLIKE	*adj* beady	**BEASTLY**	*adj* -LIER, -LIEST resembling a beast
BEADMAN	*n* pl. -MEN beadsman		
BEADROLL	*n* pl. -S a list of names	**BEAT**	*v* BEAT, BEATEN, BEATING, BEATS to strike repeatedly **BEATABLE** *adj*
BEADSMAN	*n* pl. -MEN one who prays for another		
BEADWORK	*n* pl. -S beading		

BEATER	*n* pl. -S one that beats
BEATIFIC	*adj* blissful
BEATIFY	*v* -FIED, -FYING, -FIES to make happy
BEATING	*n* pl. -S a defeat
BEATLESS	*adj* having no rhythm
BEATNIK	*n* pl. -S a nonconformist
BEAU	*n* pl. BEAUX or BEAUS a boyfriend **BEAUISH** *adj*
BEAUCOUP	*adj* many or much
BEAUT	*n* pl. -S something beautiful
BEAUTIFY	*v* -FIED, -FYING, -FIES to make beautiful
BEAUTY	*n* pl. -TIES one that is lovely
BEAUX	a pl. of beau
BEAVER	*v* -ED, -ING, -S to work hard
BEBEERU	*n* pl. -S a tropical tree
BEBLOOD	*v* -ED, -ING, -S to cover with blood
BEBOP	*n* pl. -S a type of jazz
BEBOPPER	*n* pl. -S one that likes bebop
BECALM	*v* -ED, -ING, -S to make calm
BECAME	past tense of become
BECAP	*v* -CAPPED, -CAPPING, -CAPS to put a cap on
BECARPET	*v* -ED, -ING, -S to cover with a carpet
BECAUSE	*conj* for the reason that
BECHALK	*v* -ED, -ING, -S to cover with chalk
BECHAMEL	*n* pl. -S a white sauce
BECHANCE	*v* -CHANCED, -CHANCING, -CHANCES to befall
BECHARM	*v* -ED, -ING, -S to hold under a spell
BECK	*v* -ED, -ING, -S to beckon
BECKET	*n* pl. -S a securing rope
BECKON	*v* -ED, -ING, -S to signal by sign or gesture
BECKONER	*n* pl. -S one that beckons
BECLAMOR	*v* -ED, -ING, -S to clamor loudly
BECLASP	*v* -ED, -ING, -S to embrace
BECLOAK	*v* -ED, -ING, -S to place a cloak on
BECLOG	*v* -CLOGGED, -CLOGGING, -CLOGS to clog thoroughly
BECLOTHE	*v* -CLOTHED, -CLOTHING, -CLOTHES to clothe
BECLOUD	*v* -ED, -ING, -S to make cloudy
BECLOWN	*v* -ED, -ING, -S to cause to appear ridiculous
BECOME	*v* -CAME, -COMING, -COMES to come to be
BECOMING	*n* pl. -S a process of change
BECOWARD	*v* -ED, -ING, -S to accuse of cowardice
BECRAWL	*v* -ED, -ING, -S to crawl over
BECRIME	*v* -CRIMED, -CRIMING, -CRIMES to make guilty of a crime
BECROWD	*v* -ED, -ING, -S to crowd closely
BECRUST	*v* -ED, -ING, -S to cover with a crust
BECUDGEL	*v* -GELLED, -GELLING, -GELS or -GELED, -GELING, -GELS to cudgel thoroughly
BECURSE	*v* -CURSED or -CURST, -CURSING, -CURSES to curse severely
BED	*v* BEDDED, BEDDING, BEDS to provide with a bed (a piece of furniture used for sleeping)
BEDABBLE	*v* -BLED, -BLING, -BLES to soil
BEDAMN	*v* -ED, -ING, -S to swear at
BEDARKEN	*v* -ED, -ING, -S to darken
BEDAUB	*v* -ED, -ING, -S to besmear
BEDAZZLE	*v* -ZLED, -ZLING, -ZLES to confuse
BEDBUG	*n* pl. -S a bloodsucking insect
BEDCHAIR	*n* pl. -S a chair near a bed
BEDCOVER	*n* pl. -S a cover for a bed
BEDDABLE	*adj* suitable for taking to bed
BEDDED	past tense of bed
BEDDER	*n* pl. -S one that makes up beds
BEDDING	*n* pl. -S material for making up a bed
BEDEAFEN	*v* -ED, -ING, -S to deafen
BEDECK	*v* -ED, -ING, -S to clothe with finery
BEDEL	*n* pl. -S an English university officer
BEDELL	*n* pl. -S bedel
BEDEMAN	*n* pl. -MEN beadsman
BEDESMAN	*n* pl. -MEN beadsman
BEDEVIL	*v* -ILED, -ILING, -ILS or -ILLED, -ILLING, -ILS to harass
BEDEW	*v* -ED, -ING, -S to wet with dew
BEDFAST	*adj* confined to bed

BEDFRAME	*n* pl. -S the frame of a bed	**BEDTIME**	*n* pl. -S a time for going to bed
BEDGOWN	*n* pl. -S a dressing gown	**BEDU**	*n* pl. BEDU a bedouin
BEDIAPER	*v* -ED, -ING, -S to ornament with a kind of design	**BEDUIN**	*n* pl. -S bedouin
BEDIGHT	*v* -ED, -ING, -S to bedeck	**BEDUMB**	*v* -ED, -ING, -S to render speechless
BEDIM	*v* -DIMMED, -DIMMING, -DIMS to make dim	**BEDUNCE**	*v* -DUNCED, -DUNCING, -DUNCES to make a dunce of
BEDIMPLE	*v* -PLED, -PLING, -PLES to dimple	**BEDWARD**	*adv* toward bed
		BEDWARDS	*adv* bedward
BEDIRTY	*v* -DIRTIED, -DIRTYING, -DIRTIES to make dirty	**BEDWARF**	*v* -ED, -ING, -S to cause to appear small by comparison
BEDIZEN	*v* -ED, -ING, -S to dress gaudily	**BEE**	*n* pl. -S a winged insect
BEDLAM	*n* pl. -S confusion	**BEEBEE**	*n* pl. -S a pellet
BEDLAMP	*n* pl. -S a lamp near a bed	**BEEBREAD**	*n* pl. -S a pollen mixture
BEDLESS	*adj* having no bed	**BEECH**	*n* pl. -ES a type of tree
BEDLIKE	*adj* resembling a bed		**BEECHEN** *adj*
BEDMAKER	*n* pl. -S one that makes beds	**BEECHNUT**	*n* pl. -S the nut of a beech
BEDMATE	*n* pl. -S a bed companion	**BEECHY**	*adj* BEECHIER, BEECHIEST abounding in beeches
BEDOTTED	*adj* covered with dots		
BEDOUIN	*n* pl. -S a nomadic Arab	**BEEF**	*n* pl. BEEFS or BEEVES a steer or cow fattened for food
BEDPAN	*n* pl. -S a toilet pan		
BEDPLATE	*n* pl. -S a frame support	**BEEF**	*v* -ED, -ING, -S to add bulk to
BEDPOST	*n* pl. -S a post of a bed	**BEEFALO**	*n* pl. -LOS or -LOES the offspring of an American buffalo and domestic cattle
BEDQUILT	*n* pl. -S a quilt for a bed		
BEDRAIL	*n* pl. -S a board at bedside		
BEDRAPE	*v* -DRAPED, -DRAPING, -DRAPES to drape	**BEEFCAKE**	*n* pl. -S pictures of male physiques
BEDRENCH	*v* -ED, -ING, -ES to drench thoroughly	**BEEFIER**	comparative of beefy
		BEEFIEST	superlative of beefy
BEDRID	*adj* bedfast	**BEEFILY**	*adv* in a beefy manner
BEDRIVEL	*v* -ELLED, -ELLING, -ELS or -ELED, -ELING, -ELS to cover with saliva	**BEEFLESS**	*adj* being without beef
		BEEFWOOD	*n* pl. -S a hardwood tree
BEDROCK	*n* pl. -S the rock under soil	**BEEFY**	*adj* BEEFIER, BEEFIEST brawny
BEDROLL	*n* pl. -S a portable roll of bedding	**BEEHIVE**	*n* pl. -S a hive for bees
BEDROOM	*n* pl. -S a room for sleeping	**BEELIKE**	*adj* resembling a bee
BEDRUG	*v* -DRUGGED, -DRUGGING, -DRUGS to make sleepy	**BEELINE**	*v* -LINED, -LINING, -LINES to go in a straight direct course
BEDSHEET	*n* pl. -S a sheet for a bed	**BEEN**	past participle of be
BEDSIDE	*n* pl. -S the side of a bed	**BEEP**	*v* -ED, -ING, -S to honk a horn
BEDSIT	*n* pl. -S a one-room apartment	**BEEPER**	*n* pl. -S a signaling device
BEDSONIA	*n* pl. -S a virus	**BEER**	*n* pl. -S an alcoholic beverage
BEDSORE	*n* pl. -S a type of sore	**BEERY**	*adj* BEERIER, BEERIEST affected by beer
BEDSTAND	*n* pl. -S a table next to a bed		
BEDSTEAD	*n* pl. -S a support for a bed	**BEESWAX**	*n* pl. -ES a type of wax
BEDSTRAW	*n* pl. -S a woody herb	**BEESWING**	*n* pl. -S a crust that forms on wines
BEDTICK	*n* pl. -S the cloth case of a mattress	**BEET**	*n* pl. -S a garden plant
		BEETLE	*v* -TLED, -TLING, -TLES to jut out

BEETLER   *n* pl. -S one that operates a cloth-finishing machine

BEETROOT   *n* pl. -S the root of the beet

BEEVES   a pl. of beef

BEEYARD   *n* pl. -S an apiary

BEEZER   *n* pl. -S the nose

BEFALL   *v* -FELL, -FALLEN, -FALLING, -FALLS to happen to

BEFINGER   *v* -ED, -ING, -S to touch all over

BEFIT   *v* -FITTED, -FITTING, -FITS to be suitable to

BEFLAG   *v* -FLAGGED, -FLAGGING, -FLAGS to deck with flags

BEFLEA   *v* -ED, -ING, -S to infest with fleas

BEFLECK   *v* -ED, -ING, -S to fleck

BEFLOWER   *v* -ED, -ING, -S to cover with flowers

BEFOG   *v* -FOGGED, -FOGGING, -FOGS to envelop in fog

BEFOOL   *v* -ED, -ING, -S to deceive

BEFORE   *adv* previously

BEFOUL   *v* -ED, -ING, -S to foul

BEFOULER   *n* pl. -S one that befouls

BEFRET   *v* -FRETTED, -FRETTING, -FRETS to gnaw

BEFRIEND   *v* -ED, -ING, -S to act as a friend to

BEFRINGE   *v* -FRINGED, -FRINGING, -FRINGES to border with a fringe

BEFUDDLE   *v* -DLED, -DLING, -DLES to confuse

BEG   *v* BEGGED, BEGGING, BEGS to plead

BEGALL   *v* -ED, -ING, -S to make sore by rubbing

BEGAN   past tense of begin

BEGAZE   *v* -GAZED, -GAZING, -GAZES to gaze at

BEGET   *v* -GOT or -GAT, -GOTTEN, -GETTING, -GETS to cause to exist

BEGETTER   *n* pl. -S one that begets

BEGGAR   *v* -ED, -ING, -S to impoverish

BEGGARLY   *adj* very poor

BEGGARY   *n* pl. -GARIES extreme poverty

BEGGED   past tense of beg

BEGGING   present participle of beg

BEGIN   *v* -GAN, -GUN, -GINNING, -GINS to start

BEGINNER   *n* pl. -S one that begins

BEGIRD   *v* -GIRT or -GIRDED, -GIRDING, -GIRDS to surround

BEGIRDLE   *v* -DLED, -DLING, -DLES to surround

BEGLAD   *v* -GLADDED, -GLADDING, -GLADS to gladden

BEGLAMOR   *v* -ED, -ING, -S to dazzle with glamor

BEGLOOM   *v* -ED, -ING, -S to make gloomy

BEGONE   *interj* — used as an order of dismissal

BEGONIA   *n* pl. -S a tropical herb

BEGORAH   *interj* begorra

BEGORRA   *interj* — used as a mild oath

BEGORRAH   *interj* begorra

BEGOT   a past tense of beget

BEGOTTEN   past participle of beget

BEGRIM   *v* -GRIMMED, -GRIMMING, -GRIMS to begrime

BEGRIME   *v* -GRIMED, -GRIMING, -GRIMES to dirty

BEGROAN   *v* -ED, -ING, -S to groan at

BEGRUDGE   *v* -GRUDGED, -GRUDGING, -GRUDGES to concede reluctantly

BEGUILE   *v* -GUILED, -GUILING, -GUILES to deceive

BEGUILER   *n* pl. -S one that beguiles

BEGUINE   *n* pl. -S a lively dance

BEGULF   *v* -ED, -ING, -S to engulf

BEGUM   *n* pl. -S a Muslim lady of high rank

BEGUN   past participle of begin

BEHALF   *n* pl. -HALVES interest, support, or benefit

BEHAVE   *v* -HAVED, -HAVING, -HAVES to act properly

BEHAVER   *n* pl. -S one that behaves

BEHAVIOR   *n* pl. -S demeanor

BEHEAD   *v* -ED, -ING, -S to cut off the head of

BEHELD   past tense of behold

BEHEMOTH   *n* pl. -S a large beast

BEHEST   *n* pl. -S a command

BEHIND   *n* pl. -S the buttocks

BEHOLD   *v* -HELD, -HOLDING, -HOLDS to view

BEHOLDEN   *adj* indebted

BEHOLDER *n* pl. -S one that beholds

BEHOOF *n* pl. -HOOVES use, advantage, or benefit

BEHOOVE *v* -HOOVED, -HOOVING, -HOOVES to be proper for

BEHOVE *v* -HOVED, -HOVING, -HOVES to behoove

BEHOWL *v* -ED, -ING, -S to howl at

BEIGE *n* pl. -S a tan color

BEIGNET *n* pl. -S a type of fritter or doughnut

BEIGY *adj* of the color beige

BEING *n* pl. -S something that exists

BEJABERS *interj* bejesus

BEJEEZUS *interj* bejesus

BEJESUS *interj* — used as a mild oath

BEJEWEL *v* -ELED, -ELING, -ELS or -ELLED, -ELLING, -ELS to adorn with jewels

BEJUMBLE *v* -BLED, -BLING, -BLES to jumble

BEKISS *v* -ED, -ING, -ES to cover with kisses

BEKNIGHT *v* -ED, -ING, -S to raise to knighthood

BEKNOT *v* -KNOTTED, -KNOTTING, -KNOTS to tie in knots

BEL *n* pl. -S a unit of power

BELABOR *v* -ED, -ING, -S to discuss for an absurd amount of time

BELABOUR *v* -ED, -ING, -S to belabor

BELACED *adj* adorned with lace

BELADY *v* -DIED, -DYING, -DIES to apply the title of lady to

BELATED *adj* late or too late

BELAUD *v* -ED, -ING, -S to praise

BELAY *v* -ED, -ING, -S to fasten a rope

BELCH *v* -ED, -ING, -ES to expel gas through the mouth

BELCHER *n* pl. -S one that belches

BELDAM *n* pl. -S an old woman

BELDAME *n* pl. -S beldam

BELEAP *v* -LEAPT or -LEAPED, -LEAPING, -LEAPS to leap upon

BELFRY *n* pl. -FRIES a bell tower
BELFRIED *adj*

BELGA *n* pl. -S a former Belgian monetary unit

BELIE *v* -LIED, -LYING, -LIES to misrepresent

BELIEF *n* pl. -S acceptance of the truth or actuality of something

BELIER *n* pl. -S one that belies

BELIEVE *v* -LIEVED, -LIEVING, -LIEVES to accept as true or real

BELIEVER *n* pl. -S one that believes

BELIKE *adv* perhaps

BELIQUOR *v* -ED, -ING, -S to soak with liquor

BELITTLE *v* -TLED, -TLING, -TLES to disparage

BELIVE *adv* in due time

BELL *v* -ED, -ING, -S to provide with a bell (a ringing device)

BELLBIRD *n* pl. -S a tropical bird

BELLBOY *n* pl. -BOYS a hotel's errand boy

BELLE *n* pl. -S an attractive woman

BELLEEK *n* pl. -S a very thin translucent porcelain

BELLHOP *n* pl. -S a bellboy

BELLIED past tense of belly

BELLIES present 3d person sing. of belly

BELLMAN *n* pl. -MEN a town crier

BELLOW *v* -ED, -ING, -S to shout in a deep voice

BELLOWER *n* pl. -S one that bellows

BELLPULL *n* pl. -S a cord pulled to ring a bell

BELLWORT *n* pl. -S a flowering plant

BELLY *v* -LIED, -LYING, -LIES to swell out

BELLYFUL *n* pl. -S an excessive amount

BELONG *v* -ED, -ING, -S to be a member of

BELOVED *n* pl. -S one who is loved

BELOW *n* pl. -S something that is beneath

BELT *v* -ED, -ING, -S to fasten with a belt (a strap or band worn around the waist)

BELTER *n* pl. -S one that belts

BELTING *n* pl. -S material for belts

BELTLESS *adj* having no belt

BELTLINE *n* pl. -S the waistline

BELTWAY *n* pl. -WAYS a highway around an urban area

BELUGA *n* pl. -S a white sturgeon

BELYING present participle of belie

BEMA   *n* pl. -MATA or -MAS a platform in a synagogue

BEMADAM   *v* -ED, -ING, -S to call by the title of madam

BEMADDEN   *v* -ED, -ING, -S to madden

BEMATA   a pl. of bema

BEMEAN   *v* -ED, -ING, -S to debase

BEMINGLE   *v* -GLED, -GLING, -GLES to mix together

BEMIRE   *v* -MIRED, -MIRING, -MIRES to soil with mud

BEMIST   *v* -ED, -ING, -S to envelop in a mist

BEMIX   *v* -MIXED or -MIXT, -MIXING, -MIXES to mix thoroughly

BEMOAN   *v* -ED, -ING, -S to lament

BEMOCK   *v* -ED, -ING, -S to mock

BEMUDDLE   *v* -DLED, -DLING, -DLES to confuse completely

BEMURMUR   *v* -ED, -ING, -S to murmur at

BEMUSE   *v* -MUSED, -MUSING, -MUSES to confuse

BEMUZZLE   *v* -ZLED, -ZLING, -ZLES to muzzle

BEN   *n* pl. -S an inner room

BENAME   *v* -NAMED, -NEMPT or -NEMPTED, -NAMING, -NAMES to name

BENCH   *v* -ED, -ING, -ES to take a player out of a game

BENCHER   *n* pl. -S a magistrate

BEND   *v* BENT or BENDED, BENDING, BENDS to curve **BENDABLE** *adj*

BENDAY   *v* -ED, -ING, -S to reproduce using a certain process

BENDEE   *n* pl. -S bendy

BENDER   *n* pl. -S one that bends

BENDWAYS   *adv* bendwise

BENDWISE   *adv* diagonally

BENDY   *n* pl. -DYS okra

BENE   *n* pl. -S benne

BENEATH   *prep* under

BENEDICK   *n* pl. -S benedict

BENEDICT   *n* pl. -S a newly married man

BENEFIC   *adj* kindly

BENEFICE   *v* -FICED, -FICING, -FICES to endow with land

BENEFIT   *v* -FITED, -FITING, -FITS or -FITTED, -FITTING, -FITS to be helpful or useful to

BENEMPT   a past participle of bename

BENEMPTED   a past participle of bename

BENIGN   *adj* kind **BENIGNLY** *adv*

BENISON   *n* pl. -S a blessing

BENJAMIN   *n* pl. -S benzoin

BENNE   *n* pl. -S the sesame plant

BENNET   *n* pl. -S a perennial herb

BENNI   *n* pl. -S benne

BENNY   *n* pl. -NIES an amphetamine tablet

BENOMYL   *n* pl. -S a chemical compound

BENT   *n* pl. -S an inclination

BENTHAL   *adj* benthic

BENTHIC   *adj* pertaining to oceanic depths

BENTHOS   *n* pl. -ES benthic sea life

BENTWOOD   *n* pl. -S wood bent for use in furniture

BENUMB   *v* -ED, -ING, -S to make numb

BENZAL   *adj* pertaining to a certain chemical group

BENZENE   *n* pl. -S a volatile liquid

BENZIDIN   *n* pl. -S a hydrocarbon

BENZIN   *n* pl. -S benzine

BENZINE   *n* pl. -S a volatile liquid

BENZOATE   *n* pl. -S a chemical salt

BENZOIN   *n* pl. -S a gum resin **BENZOIC** *adj*

BENZOL   *n* pl. -S a benzene

BENZOLE   *n* pl. -S benzol

BENZOYL   *n* pl. -S a univalent chemical radical

BENZYL   *n* pl. -S a univalent chemical radical **BENZYLIC** *adj*

BEPAINT   *v* -ED, -ING, -S to tinge

BEPIMPLE   *v* -PLED, -PLING, -PLES to cover with pimples

BEQUEATH   *v* -ED, -ING, -S to grant by testament

BEQUEST   *n* pl. -S a legacy

BERAKE   *v* -RAKED, -RAKING, -RAKES to rake all over

BERASCAL   *v* -ED, -ING, -S to accuse of being a rascal

BERATE   *v* -RATED, -RATING, -RATES to scold severely

BERBERIN   *n* pl. -S a medicinal alkaloid

BERBERIS   *n* pl. -ES a barberry

BERCEUSE   *n* pl. -S a lullaby

BERDACHE	*n* pl. -S an American Indian male transvestite
BEREAVE	*v* -REAVED or -REFT, -REAVING, -REAVES to deprive
BEREAVER	*n* pl. -S one that bereaves
BERET	*n* pl. -S a soft, flat cap
BERETTA	*n* pl. -S biretta
BERG	*n* pl. -S an iceberg
BERGAMOT	*n* pl. -S a citrus tree
BERGERE	*n* pl. -S an upholstered armchair
BERHYME	*v* -RHYMED, -RHYMING, -RHYMES to compose in rhyme
BERIBERI	*n* pl. -S a thiamine deficiency disease
BERIME	*v* -RIMED, -RIMING, -RIMES to berhyme
BERINGED	*adj* adorned with rings
BERLIN	*n* pl. -S a type of carriage
BERLINE	*n* pl. -S a limousine
BERM	*n* pl. -S a ledge
BERME	*n* pl. -S berm
BERMUDAS	*n/pl* knee-length walking shorts
BERNICLE	*n* pl. -S a wild goose
BEROBED	*adj* wearing a robe
BEROUGED	*adj* obviously or thickly rouged
BERRETTA	*n* pl. -S biretta
BERRY	*v* -RIED, -RYING, -RIES to produce berries (fleshy fruits)
BERSEEM	*n* pl. -S a clover
BERSERK	*n* pl. -S a fierce warrior
BERTH	*v* -ED, -ING, -S to provide with a mooring
BERTHA	*n* pl. -S a wide collar
BERYL	*n* pl. -S a green mineral **BERYLINE** *adj*
BESCORCH	*v* -ED, -ING, -ES to scorch
BESCOUR	*v* -ED, -ING, -S to scour thoroughly
BESCREEN	*v* -ED, -ING, -S to screen
BESEECH	*v* -SOUGHT or -SEECHED, -SEECHING, -SEECHES to implore
BESEEM	*v* -ED, -ING, -S to be suitable
BESET	*v* -SET, -SETTING, -SETS to assail
BESETTER	*n* pl. -S one that besets
BESHADOW	*v* -ED, -ING, -S to cast a shadow on

BESHAME	*v* -SHAMED, -SHAMING, -SHAMES to put to shame
BESHIVER	*v* -ED, -ING, -S to break into small pieces
BESHOUT	*v* -ED, -ING, -S to shout at
BESHREW	*v* -ED, -ING, -S to curse
BESHROUD	*v* -ED, -ING, -S to cover
BESIDE	*prep* next to
BESIDES	*adv* in addition
BESIEGE	*v* -SIEGED, -SIEGING, -SIEGES to surround
BESIEGER	*n* pl. -S one that besieges
BESLAVED	*adj* filled with slaves
BESLIME	*v* -SLIMED, -SLIMING, -SLIMES to cover with slime
BESMEAR	*v* -ED, -ING, -S to smear over
BESMILE	*v* -SMILED, -SMILING, -SMILES to smile on
BESMIRCH	*v* -ED, -ING, -ES to dirty
BESMOKE	*v* -SMOKED, -SMOKING, -SMOKES to soil with smoke
BESMOOTH	*v* -ED, -ING, -S to smooth
BESMUDGE	*v* -SMUDGED, -SMUDGING, -SMUDGES to smudge
BESMUT	*v* -SMUTTED, -SMUTTING, -SMUTS to blacken with smut
BESNOW	*v* -ED, -ING, -S to cover with snow
BESOM	*n* pl. -S a broom
BESOOTHE	*v* -SOOTHED, -SOOTHING -SOOTHES to soothe
BESOT	*v* -SOTTED, -SOTTING, -SOTS to stupefy
BESOUGHT	a past tense of beseech
BESPEAK	*v* -SPOKE or -SPAKE, -SPOKEN, -SPEAKING, -SPEAKS to claim in advance
BESPOUSE	*v* -SPOUSED, -SPOUSING, -SPOUSES to marry
BESPREAD	*v* -SPREAD, -SPREADING, -SPREADS to spread over
BESPRENT	*adj* sprinkled over
BEST	*v* -ED, -ING, -S to outdo
BESTEAD	*v* -ED, -ING, -S to help
BESTIAL	*adj* pertaining to beasts
BESTIARY	*n* pl. -ARIES a collection of animal fables
BESTIR	*v* -STIRRED, -STIRRING, -STIRS to rouse

BESTOW *v* -ED, -ING, -S to present as a gift

BESTOWAL *n* pl. -S a gift

BESTREW *v* -STREWED, -STREWN, -STREWING, -STREWS to scatter

BESTRIDE *v* -STRODE or -STRID, -STRIDDEN, -STRIDING, -STRIDES to straddle

BESTROW *v* -STROWED, -STROWN, -STROWING, -STROWS to bestrew

BESTUD *v* -STUDDED, -STUDDING, -STUDS to dot

BESWARM *v* -ED, -ING, -S to swarm all over

BET *v* BET or BETTED, BETTING, BETS to wager

BETA *n* pl. -S a Greek letter

BETAINE *n* pl. -S an alkaloid

BETAKE *v* -TOOK, -TAKEN, -TAKING, -TAKES to cause to go

BETATRON *n* pl. -S an electron accelerator

BETATTER *v* -ED, -ING, -S to tatter

BETAXED *adj* burdened with taxes

BETEL *n* pl. -S a climbing plant

BETELNUT *n* pl. -S a seed chewed as a stimulant

BETH *n* pl. -S a Hebrew letter

BETHANK *v* -ED, -ING, -S to thank

BETHEL *n* pl. -S a holy place

BETHESDA *n* pl. -S a chapel

BETHINK *v* -THOUGHT, -THINKING, -THINKS to consider

BETHORN *v* -ED, -ING, -S to fill with thorns

BETHUMP *v* -ED, -ING, -S to thump soundly

BETIDE *v* -TIDED, -TIDING, -TIDES to befall

BETIME *adv* betimes

BETIMES *adv* soon

BETISE *n* pl. -S stupidity

BETOKEN *v* -ED, -ING, -S to indicate

BETON *n* pl. -S a type of concrete

BETONY *n* pl. -NIES a European herb

BETOOK past tense of betake

BETRAY *v* -ED, -ING, -S to aid an enemy of

BETRAYAL *n* pl. -S the act of betraying

BETRAYER *n* pl. -S one that betrays

BETROTH *v* -ED, -ING, -S to engage to marry

BETTA *n* pl. -S a freshwater fish

BETTED a past tense of bet

BETTER *v* -ED, -ING, -S to improve

BETTING present participle of bet

BETTOR *n* pl. -S one that bets

BETWEEN *prep* in the space that separates

BETWIXT *prep* between

BEUNCLED *adj* having many uncles

BEVATRON *n* pl. -S a proton accelerator

BEVEL *v* -ELED, -ELING, -ELS or -ELLED, -ELLING, -ELS to cut at an angle

BEVELER *n* pl. -S one that bevels

BEVELLER *n* pl. -S beveler

BEVELLING a present participle of bevel

BEVERAGE *n* pl. -S a liquid for drinking

BEVIES pl. of bevy

BEVOMIT *v* -ED, -ING, -S to vomit all over

BEVOR *n* pl. -S a piece of armor for the lower face

BEVY *n* pl. BEVIES a group

BEWAIL *v* -ED, -ING, -S to lament

BEWAILER *n* pl. -S one that bewails

BEWARE *v* -WARED, -WARING, -WARES to be careful

BEWEARY *v* -WEARIED, -WEARYING, -WEARIES to make weary

BEWEEP *v* -WEPT, -WEEPING, -WEEPS to lament

BEWIG *v* -WIGGED, -WIGGING, -WIGS to adorn with a wig

BEWILDER *v* -ED, -ING, -S to confuse

BEWINGED *adj* having wings

BEWITCH *v* -ED, -ING, -ES to affect by witchcraft or magic

BEWORM *v* -ED, -ING, -S to infest with worms

BEWORRY *v* -RIED, -RYING, -RIES to worry

BEWRAP *v* -WRAPPED or -WRAPT, -WRAPPING, -WRAPS to wrap completely

BEWRAY *v* -ED, -ING, -S to divulge

BEWRAYER *n* pl. -S one that bewrays

BEY *n* pl. BEYS a Turkish ruler

BEYLIC *n* pl. -S the domain of a bey

BEYLIK *n* pl. -S beylic

BEYOND	*n* pl. -S something that lies farther ahead
BEZANT	*n* pl. -S a coin of ancient Rome
BEZAZZ	*n* pl. -ES pizazz
BEZEL	*n* pl. -S a slanted surface
BEZIL	*n* pl. -S bezel
BEZIQUE	*n* pl. -S a card game
BEZOAR	*n* pl. -S a gastric mass
BEZZANT	*n* pl. -S bezant
BHAKTA	*n* pl. -S one who practices bhakti
BHAKTI	*n* pl. -S a selfless devotion to a deity in Hinduism
BHANG	*n* pl. -S the hemp plant
BHARAL	*n* pl. -S a goatlike Asian mammal
BHEESTIE	*n* pl. -S bheesty
BHEESTY	*n* pl. -TIES a water carrier
BHISTIE	*n* pl. -S bheesty
BHOOT	*n* pl. -S bhut
BHUT	*n* pl. -S a small whirlwind
BI	*n* pl. -S a bisexual
BIACETYL	*n* pl. -S a chemical flavor enhancer
BIALI	*n* pl. -S bialy
BIALY	*n* pl. -ALYS an onion roll
BIANNUAL	*adj* occurring twice a year
BIAS	*v* -ASED, -ASING, -ASES or -ASSED, -ASSING, -ASSES to prejudice **BIASEDLY** *adv*
BIASNESS	*n* pl. -ES the state of being slanted
BIATHLON	*n* pl. -S an athletic contest
BIAXAL	*adj* biaxial
BIAXIAL	*adj* having two axes
BIB	*v* BIBBED, BIBBING, BIBS to tipple
BIBASIC	*adj* dibasic
BIBB	*n* pl. -S a mast support
BIBBED	past tense of bib
BIBBER	*n* pl. -S a tippler
BIBBERY	*n* pl. -BERIES the act of bibbing
BIBBING	present participle of bib
BIBCOCK	*n* pl. -S a type of faucet
BIBELOT	*n* pl. -S a trinket
BIBLE	*n* pl. -S an authoritative publication **BIBLICAL** *adj*
BIBLESS	*adj* having no bib (a cloth covering)
BIBLIKE	*adj* resembling a bib
BIBLIST	*n* pl. -S one who takes the words of the Bible literally
BIBULOUS	*adj* given to drinking
BICARB	*n* pl. -S sodium bicarbonate
BICAUDAL	*adj* having two tails
BICE	*n* pl. -S a blue or green pigment
BICEPS	*n* pl. -ES an arm muscle
BICHROME	*adj* two-colored
BICKER	*v* -ED, -ING, -S to argue
BICKERER	*n* pl. -S one that bickers
BICOLOR	*n* pl. -S something having two colors
BICOLOUR	*n* pl. -S bicolor
BICONVEX	*adj* convex on both sides
BICORN	*adj* having two horns
BICORNE	*n* pl. -S a type of hat
BICRON	*n* pl. -S one billionth of a meter
BICUSPID	*n* pl. -S a tooth
BICYCLE	*v* -CLED, -CLING, -CLES to ride a bicycle (a two-wheeled vehicle)
BICYCLER	*n* pl. -S one that bicycles
BICYCLIC	*adj* having two cycles
BICYCLING	present participle of bicycle
BID	*v* BADE, BIDDEN, BIDDING, BIDS to make a bid (an offer of a price)
BIDARKA	*n* pl. -S an Eskimo canoe
BIDARKEE	*n* pl. -S bidarka
BIDDABLE	*adj* obedient **BIDDABLY** *adv*
BIDDEN	past participle of bid
BIDDER	*n* pl. -S one that bids
BIDDING	*n* pl. -S a command
BIDDY	*n* pl. -DIES a hen
BIDE	*v* BIDED or BODE, BIDING, BIDES to wait
BIDENTAL	*adj* having two teeth
BIDER	*n* pl. -S one that bides
BIDET	*n* pl. -S a low basin used for washing
BIDING	present participle of bide
BIELD	*v* -ED, -ING, -S to shelter
BIENNALE	*n* pl. -S a biennial show
BIENNIAL	*n* pl. -S an event that occurs every two years
BIENNIUM	*n* pl. -NIA or -NIUMS a period of two years

BIER	*n* pl. -S a coffin stand
BIFACE	*n* pl. -S a stone tool having a cutting edge
BIFACIAL	*adj* having two faces
BIFF	*v* -ED, -ING, -S to hit
BIFFIN	*n* pl. -S a cooking apple
BIFFY	*n* pl. -FIES a toilet
BIFID	*adj* divided into two parts **BIFIDLY** *adv*
BIFIDITY	*n* pl. -TIES the state of being bifid
BIFILAR	*adj* having two threads
BIFLEX	*adj* bent in two places
BIFOCAL	*n* pl. -S a type of lens
BIFOLD	*adj* twofold
BIFORATE	*adj* having two perforations
BIFORKED	*adj* divided into two branches
BIFORM	*adj* having two forms
BIFORMED	*adj* biform
BIG	*adj* BIGGER, BIGGEST of considerable size
BIG	*n* pl. -S one of great importance
BIGAMIES	pl. of bigamy
BIGAMIST	*n* pl. -S one who commits bigamy
BIGAMOUS	*adj* guilty of bigamy
BIGAMY	*n* pl. -MIES the crime of being married to two people at once
BIGARADE	*n* pl. -S a citrus tree
BIGAROON	*n* pl. -S a type of cherry
BIGEMINY	*n* pl. -NIES the state of having a double pulse
BIGEYE	*n* pl. -S a marine fish
BIGFOOT	*n* pl. -FEET or -FOOTS a large hairy humanlike creature
BIGGER	comparative of big
BIGGEST	superlative of big
BIGGETY	*adj* biggity
BIGGIE	*n* pl. -S one that is big
BIGGIN	*n* pl. -S a house
BIGGING	*n* pl. -S biggin
BIGGISH	*adj* somewhat big
BIGGITY	*adj* conceited
BIGHEAD	*n* pl. -S a disease of animals
BIGHORN	*n* pl. -S a wild sheep
BIGHT	*v* -ED, -ING, -S to fasten with a loop of rope
BIGLY	*adv* in a big manner
BIGMOUTH	*n* pl. -S a talkative person
BIGNESS	*n* pl. -ES the state of being big
BIGNONIA	*n* pl. -S a climbing plant
BIGOT	*n* pl. -S a prejudiced person
BIGOTED	*adj* intolerant
BIGOTRY	*n* pl. -RIES prejudice
BIGWIG	*n* pl. -S an important person
BIHOURLY	*adj* occurring every two hours
BIJOU	*n* pl. -JOUX or -JOUS a jewel
BIJUGATE	*adj* two-paired
BIJUGOUS	*adj* bijugate
BIKE	*v* BIKED, BIKING, BIKES to bicycle
BIKER	*n* pl. -S one that bikes
BIKEWAY	*n* pl. -WAYS a route for bikes
BIKIE	*n* pl. -S biker
BIKING	present participle of bike
BIKINI	*n* pl. -S a type of bathing suit **BIKINIED** *adj*
BILABIAL	*n* pl. -S a sound articulated with both lips
BILANDER	*n* pl. -S a small ship
BILAYER	*n* pl. -S a film with two molecular layers
BILBERRY	*n* pl. -RIES an edible berry
BILBO	*n* pl. -BOS or -BOES a finely tempered sword
BILBOA	*n* pl. -S bilbo
BILE	*n* pl. -S a fluid secreted by the liver
BILGE	*v* BILGED, BILGING, BILGES to spring a leak
BILGY	*adj* BILGIER, BILGIEST smelling like seepage
BILIARY	*adj* pertaining to bile
BILINEAR	*adj* pertaining to two lines
BILIOUS	*adj* pertaining to bile
BILK	*v* -ED, -ING, -S to cheat
BILKER	*n* pl. -S one that bilks
BILL	*v* -ED, -ING, -S to present a statement of costs to **BILLABLE** *adj*
BILLBUG	*n* pl. -S a weevil
BILLER	*n* pl. -S one that bills
BILLET	*v* -ED, -ING, -S to lodge soldiers
BILLETER	*n* pl. -S one that billets
BILLFISH	*n* pl. -ES a fish with long, slender jaws

BILLFOLD	*n* pl. -S a wallet
BILLHEAD	*n* pl. -S a letterhead
BILLHOOK	*n* pl. -S a cutting tool
BILLIARD	*n* pl. -S a carom shot in billiards (a table game)
BILLIE	*n* pl. -S a comrade
BILLIES	pl. of billy
BILLING	*n* pl. -S the relative position in which a performer is listed
BILLION	*n* pl. -S a number
BILLON	*n* pl. -S an alloy of silver and copper
BILLOW	*v* -ED, -ING, -S to swell
BILLOWY	*adj* -LOWIER, -LOWIEST swelling; surging
BILLY	*n* pl. -LIES a short club
BILLYCAN	*n* pl. -S a pot for heating water
BILOBATE	*adj* having two lobes
BILOBED	*adj* bilobate
BILSTED	*n* pl. -S a hardwood tree
BILTONG	*n* pl. -S dried and cured meat
BIMA	*n* pl. -S bema
BIMAH	*n* pl. -S bema
BIMANOUS	*adj* two-handed
BIMANUAL	*adj* done with two hands
BIMBO	*n* pl. -BOS or -BOES a disreputable person
BIMENSAL	*adj* occurring every two months
BIMESTER	*n* pl. -S a two-month period
BIMETAL	*n* pl. -S something composed of two metals
BIMETHYL	*n* pl. -S ethane
BIMODAL	*adj* having two statistical modes
BIMORPH	*n* pl. -S a device consisting of two crystals cemented together
BIN	*v* BINNED, BINNING, BINS to store in a large receptacle
BINAL	*adj* twofold
BINARY	*n* pl. -RIES a combination of two things
BINATE	*adj* growing in pairs **BINATELY** *adv*
BINAURAL	*adj* hearing with both ears
BIND	*v* BOUND, BINDING, BINDS to tie or secure **BINDABLE** *adj*
BINDER	*n* pl. -S one that binds
BINDERY	*n* pl. -ERIES a place where books are bound
BINDI	*n* pl. -S a dot worn on the forehead by women in India
BINDING	*n* pl. -S the cover and fastenings of a book
BINDLE	*n* pl. -S a bundle
BINDWEED	*n* pl. -S a twining plant
BINE	*n* pl. -S a twining plant stem
BINGE	*v* BINGED, BINGEING or BINGING, BINGES to indulge in something without restraint
BINGER	*n* pl. -S one that binges
BINGO	*n* pl. -GOS a game of chance
BINIT	*n* pl. -S a unit of computer information
BINNACLE	*n* pl. -S a compass stand
BINNED	past tense of bin
BINNING	present participle of bin
BINOCLE	*n* pl. -S a binocular
BINOCS	*n/pl* binoculars
BINOMIAL	*n* pl. -S an algebraic expression
BINT	*n* pl. -S a woman
BIO	*n* pl. BIOS a biography
BIOASSAY	*v* -ED, -ING, -S to test a substance (as a drug)
BIOCHIP	*n* pl. -S a hypothetical computer component that uses proteins to store or process data
BIOCIDE	*n* pl. -S a substance destructive to living organisms **BIOCIDAL** *adj*
BIOCLEAN	*adj* free of harmful organisms
BIOCYCLE	*n* pl. -S a life-supporting region
BIOETHIC	*adj* pertaining to ethical questions arising from advances in biology
BIOGAS	*n* pl. -GASES or -GASSES fuel gas produced by organic waste
BIOGEN	*n* pl. -S a hypothetical protein molecule
BIOGENIC	*adj* produced by living organisms
BIOGENY	*n* pl. -NIES the development of life from preexisting life
BIOHERM	*n* pl. -S a mass of marine fossils
BIOLOGIC	*n* pl. -S a drug obtained from an organic source
BIOLOGY	*n* pl. -GIES the science of life
BIOLYSIS	*n* pl. -YSES death **BIOLYTIC** *adj*
BIOMASS	*n* pl. -ES an amount of living matter
BIOME	*n* pl. -S an ecological community

BIOMETRY   *n* pl. -TRIES the statistical study of biological data

BIONICS   *n/pl* a science joining biology and electronics **BIONIC** *adj*

BIONOMY   *n* pl. -MIES ecology **BIONOMIC** *adj*

BIONT   *n* pl. -S a living organism **BIONTIC** *adj*

BIOPIC   *n* pl. -S a biographical movie

BIOPLASM   *n* pl. -S living matter

BIOPSIC   *adj* pertaining to the examination of living tissue

BIOPSY   *v* -SIED, -SYING, -SIES to examine living tissue

BIOPTIC   *adj* biopsic

BIOSCOPE   *n* pl. -S an early movie projector

BIOSCOPY   *n* pl. -PIES a type of medical examination

BIOTA   *n* pl. -S flora and fauna

BIOTECH   *n* pl. -S applied biology

BIOTIC   *adj* pertaining to life

BIOTICAL   *adj* biotic

BIOTICS   *n/pl* a life science

BIOTIN   *n* pl. -S a B vitamin

BIOTITE   *n* pl. -S a form of mica **BIOTITIC** *adj*

BIOTOPE   *n* pl. -S a stable habitat

BIOTOXIN   *n* pl. -S poison made by a plant or animal

BIOTRON   *n* pl. -S a climate control chamber

BIOTYPE   *n* pl. -S a group of genetically similar organisms **BIOTYPIC** *adj*

BIOVULAR   *adj* derived from two ova

BIPACK   *n* pl. -S a pair of films

BIPAROUS   *adj* producing offspring in pairs

BIPARTED   *adj* having two parts

BIPARTY   *adj* of two parties

BIPED   *n* pl. -S a two-footed animal **BIPEDAL** *adj*

BIPHASIC   *adj* having two phases

BIPHENYL   *n* pl. -S a hydrocarbon

BIPLANE   *n* pl. -S a type of airplane

BIPOD   *n* pl. -S a two-legged support

BIPOLAR   *adj* having two poles

BIRACIAL   *adj* having members of two races

BIRADIAL   *adj* having dual symmetry

BIRAMOSE   *adj* biramous

BIRAMOUS   *adj* divided into two branches

BIRCH   *v* -ED, -ING, -ES to whip

BIRCHEN   *adj* made of birch wood

BIRD   *v* -ED, -ING, -S to hunt birds (winged, warm-blooded vertebrates)

BIRDBATH   *n* pl. -S a bath for birds

BIRDCAGE   *n* pl. -S a cage for birds

BIRDCALL   *n* pl. -S the call of a bird

BIRDER   *n* pl. -S a bird hunter

BIRDFARM   *n* pl. -S an aircraft carrier

BIRDIE   *v* BIRDIED, BIRDIEING, BIRDIES to shoot in one stroke under par in golf

BIRDING   *n* pl. -S bird-watching

BIRDLIKE   *adj* resembling a bird

BIRDLIME   *v* -LIMED, -LIMING, -LIMES to trap small birds

BIRDMAN   *n* pl. -MEN one who keeps birds

BIRDSEED   *n* pl. -S a mixture of seeds used for feeding birds

BIRDSEYE   *n* pl. -S a flowering plant

BIRDSHOT   *n* pl. -S small shot for shooting birds

BIRDSONG   *n* pl. -S the song of a bird

BIREME   *n* pl. -S an ancient galley

BIRETTA   *n* pl. -S a cap worn by clergymen

BIRK   *n* pl. -S a birch tree

BIRKIE   *n* pl. -S a lively person

BIRL   *v* -ED, -ING, -S to rotate a floating log

BIRLE   *v* BIRLED, BIRLING, BIRLES to carouse

BIRLER   *n* pl. -S one that birls

BIRLING   *n* pl. -S a lumberjack's game

BIRR   *v* -ED, -ING, -S to make a whirring noise

BIRR   *n* pl. BIRROTCH a monetary unit of Ethiopia

BIRRETTA   *n* pl. -S biretta

BIRSE   *n* pl. -S a bristle

BIRTH   *v* -ED, -ING, -S to originate

BIRTHDAY   *n* pl. -DAYS an anniversary of a birth

BIS   *adv* twice

BISCUIT   *n* pl. -S a small cake of shortened bread

BISE   *n* pl. -S a cold wind

BISECT   *v* -ED, -ING, -S to cut into two parts

BISECTOR	*n* pl. -S something that bisects
BISEXUAL	*n* pl. -S one who is attracted to both sexes
BISHOP	*v* -ED, -ING, -S to appoint as a bishop (the head of a diocese)
BISK	*n* pl. -S bisque
BISMUTH	*n* pl. -S a metallic element
BISNAGA	*n* pl. -S a type of cactus
BISON	*n* pl. -S an ox-like animal
BISQUE	*n* pl. -S a thick soup
BISTATE	*adj* pertaining to two states
BISTER	*n* pl. -S a brown pigment **BISTERED** *adj*
BISTORT	*n* pl. -S a perennial herb with roots used as astringents
BISTOURY	*n* pl. -RIES a surgical knife
BISTRE	*n* pl. -S bister **BISTRED** *adj*
BISTRO	*n* pl. -TROS a small tavern **BISTROIC** *adj*
BIT	*v* BITTED, BITTING, BITS to restrain
BITABLE	*adj* capable of being bitten
BITCH	*v* -ED, -ING, -ES to complain
BITCHERY	*n* pl. -ERIES bitchy behavior
BITCHY	*adj* BITCHIER, BITCHIEST malicious **BITCHILY** *adv*
BITE	*v* BIT, BITTEN, BITING, BITES to seize with the teeth **BITEABLE** *adj*
BITER	*n* pl. -S one that bites
BITEWING	*n* pl. -S a dental X-ray film
BITING	present participle of bite
BITINGLY	*adv* sarcastically
BITSTOCK	*n* pl. -S a brace on a drill
BITSY	*adj* tiny
BITT	*v* -ED, -ING, -S to secure a cable
BITTED	past tense of bit
BITTEN	a past participle of bite
BITTER	*adj* -TERER, -TEREST having a disagreeable taste **BITTERLY** *adv*
BITTER	*v* -ED, -ING, -S to make bitter
BITTERN	*n* pl. -S a wading bird
BITTIER	comparative of bitty
BITTIEST	superlative of bitty
BITTING	*n* pl. -S an indentation in a key
BITTOCK	*n* pl. -S a small amount
BITTY	*adj* -TIER, -TIEST fragmented

BITUMEN	*n* pl. -S an asphalt
BIUNIQUE	*adj* being a type of correspondence between two sets
BIVALENT	*n* pl. -S a pair of chromosomes
BIVALVE	*n* pl. -S a bivalved mollusk
BIVALVED	*adj* having a two-valved shell
BIVINYL	*n* pl. -S a flammable gas used in making synthetic rubber
BIVOUAC	*v* -OUACKED, -OUACKING, -OUACKS or -OUACS to make a camp
BIWEEKLY	*n* pl. -LIES a publication issued every two weeks
BIYEARLY	*adj* occurring every two years
BIZ	*n* pl. BIZZES business
BIZARRE	*n* pl. -S a strangely striped flower
BIZE	*n* pl. -S bise
BIZNAGA	*n* pl. -S bisnaga
BIZONE	*n* pl. -S two combined zones **BIZONAL** *adj*
BLAB	*v* BLABBED, BLABBING, BLABS to talk idly
BLABBER	*v* -ED, -ING, -S to blab
BLABBY	*adj* talkative
BLACK	*adj* BLACKER, BLACKEST being of the darkest color
BLACK	*v* -ED, -ING, -S to make black
BLACKBOY	*n* pl. -BOYS an Australian plant
BLACKCAP	*n* pl. -S a small European bird
BLACKEN	*v* -ED, -ING, -S to make black
BLACKFIN	*n* pl. -S a food fish
BLACKFLY	*n* pl. -FLIES a biting fly
BLACKGUM	*n* pl. -S a tupelo
BLACKING	*n* pl. -S black shoe polish
BLACKISH	*adj* somewhat black
BLACKLEG	*n* pl. -S a cattle disease
BLACKLY	*adv* in a black manner
BLACKOUT	*n* pl. -S a power failure
BLACKTOP	*v* -TOPPED, -TOPPING, -TOPS to pave with asphalt
BLADDER	*n* pl. -S a saclike receptacle **BLADDERY** *adj*
BLADE	*n* pl. -S a cutting edge **BLADED** *adj*
BLAE	*adj* bluish-black
BLAH	*n* pl. -S nonsense
BLAIN	*n* pl. -S a blister

BLAM	*n* pl. -S the sound of a gunshot
BLAMABLE	*adj* being at fault **BLAMABLY** *adv*
BLAME	*v* BLAMED, BLAMING, BLAMES to find fault with
BLAMEFUL	*adj* blamable
BLAMER	*n* pl. -S one that blames
BLAMING	present participle of blame
BLANCH	*v* -ED, -ING, -ES to whiten
BLANCHER	*n* pl. -S a whitener
BLAND	*adj* BLANDER, BLANDEST soothing **BLANDLY** *adv*
BLANDISH	*v* -ED, -ING, -ES to coax by flattery
BLANK	*adj* BLANKER, BLANKEST empty
BLANK	*v* -ED, -ING, -S to delete
BLANKET	*v* -ED, -ING, -S to cover uniformly
BLANKLY	*adv* in a blank manner
BLARE	*v* BLARED, BLARING, BLARES to sound loudly
BLARNEY	*v* -NEYED, -NEYING, -NEYS to beguile with flattery
BLASE	*adj* indifferent
BLAST	*v* -ED, -ING, -S to use an explosive
BLASTEMA	*n* pl. -MAS or -MATA a region of embryonic cells
BLASTER	*n* pl. -S one that blasts
BLASTIE	*n* pl. -S a dwarf
BLASTIER	comparative of blasty
BLASTIEST	superlative of blasty
BLASTING	*n* pl. -S the act of one that blasts
BLASTOFF	*n* pl. -S the launching of a rocket
BLASTOMA	*n* pl. -MAS or -MATA a type of tumor
BLASTULA	*n* pl. -LAS or -LAE an early embryo
BLASTY	*adj* BLASTIER, BLASTIEST gusty
BLAT	*v* BLATTED, BLATTING, BLATS to bleat
BLATANCY	*n* pl. -CIES something blatant
BLATANT	*adj* obvious
BLATE	*adj* timid
BLATHER	*v* -ED, -ING, -S to talk foolishly
BLATTED	past tense of blat
BLATTER	*v* -ED, -ING, -S to chatter
BLATTING	present participle of blat
BLAUBOK	*n* pl. -S an extinct antelope
BLAW	*v* BLAWED, BLAWN, BLAWING, BLAWS to blow
BLAZE	*v* BLAZED, BLAZING, BLAZES to burn brightly
BLAZER	*n* pl. -S a lightweight jacket
BLAZON	*v* -ED, -ING, -S to proclaim
BLAZONER	*n* pl. -S one that blazons
BLAZONRY	*n* pl. -RIES a great display
BLEACH	*v* -ED, -ING, -ES to whiten
BLEACHER	*n* pl. -S one that bleaches
BLEAK	*adj* BLEAKER, BLEAKEST dreary
BLEAK	*n* pl. -S a freshwater fish
BLEAKISH	*adj* somewhat bleak
BLEAKLY	*adv* in a bleak manner
BLEAR	*v* -ED, -ING, -S to dim
BLEARY	*adj* BLEARIER, BLEARIEST dimmed **BLEARILY** *adv*
BLEAT	*v* -ED, -ING, -S to utter the cry of a sheep
BLEATER	*n* pl. -S one that bleats
BLEB	*n* pl. -S a blister **BLEBBY** *adj*
BLEED	*v* BLED, BLEEDING, BLEEDS to lose blood
BLEEDER	*n* pl. -S one that bleeds
BLEEDING	*n* pl. -S the act of losing blood
BLEEP	*v* -ED, -ING, -S to blip
BLELLUM	*n* pl. -S a babbler
BLEMISH	*v* -ED, -ING, -ES to mar
BLENCH	*v* -ED, -ING, -ES to flinch
BLENCHER	*n* pl. -S one that blenches
BLEND	*v* BLENDED or BLENT, BLENDING, BLENDS to mix smoothly and inseparably together
BLENDE	*n* pl. -S a shiny mineral
BLENDER	*n* pl. -S one that blends
BLENNY	*n* pl. -NIES a marine fish
BLENT	a past tense of blend
BLESBOK	*n* pl. -S a large antelope
BLESBUCK	*n* pl. -S blesbok
BLESS	*v* BLESSED or BLEST, BLESSING, BLESSES to sanctify
BLESSED	*adj* -EDER, -EDEST holy
BLESSER	*n* pl. -S one that blesses

BLESSING	*n* pl. -S a prayer
BLEST	a past tense of bless
BLET	*n* pl. -S a decay of fruit
BLETHER	*v* -ED, -ING, -S to blather
BLEW	past tense of blow
BLIGHT	*v* -ED, -ING, -S to cause decay
BLIGHTER	*n* pl. -S one that blights
BLIGHTY	*n* pl. BLIGHTIES a wound causing one to be sent home to England
BLIMEY	*interj* — used as an expression of surprise
BLIMP	*n* pl. -S a nonrigid aircraft **BLIMPISH** *adj*
BLIMY	*interj* blimey
BLIN	*n* pl. BLINI or BLINIS a blintze
BLIND	*adj* BLINDER, BLINDEST sightless
BLIND	*v* -ED, -ING, -S to make sightless
BLINDAGE	*n* pl. -S a protective screen
BLINDER	*n* pl. -S an obstruction to sight
BLINDLY	*adv* in a blind manner
BLINI	a pl. of blin
BLINIS	a pl. of blin
BLINK	*v* -ED, -ING, -S to open and shut the eyes
BLINKARD	*n* pl. -S one who habitually blinks
BLINKER	*v* -ED, -ING, -S to put blinders on
BLINTZ	*n* pl. -ES blintze
BLINTZE	*n* pl. -S a thin pancake
BLIP	*v* BLIPPED, BLIPPING, BLIPS to remove sound from a recording
BLISS	*v* -ED, -ING, -ES to experience or produce ecstasy
BLISSFUL	*adj* very happy
BLISTER	*v* -ED, -ING, -S to cause blisters (skin swellings)
BLISTERY	*adj* having blisters
BLITE	*n* pl. -S an annual herb
BLITHE	*adj* BLITHER, BLITHEST merry **BLITHELY** *adv*
BLITHER	*v* -ED, -ING, -S to blather
BLITZ	*v* -ED, -ING, -ES to subject to a sudden attack
BLIZZARD	*n* pl. -S a heavy snowstorm
BLOAT	*v* -ED, -ING, -S to swell
BLOATER	*n* pl. -S a smoked herring
BLOB	*v* BLOBBED, BLOBBING, BLOBS to splotch
BLOC	*n* pl. -S a coalition
BLOCK	*v* -ED, -ING, -S to obstruct
BLOCKADE	*v* -ADED, -ADING, -ADES to block
BLOCKAGE	*n* pl. -S the act of blocking
BLOCKER	*n* pl. -S one who blocks
BLOCKISH	*adj* blocky
BLOCKY	*adj* BLOCKIER, BLOCKIEST short and stout
BLOKE	*n* pl. -S a fellow
BLOND	*adj* BLONDER, BLONDEST light-colored
BLOND	*n* pl. -S a blond person
BLONDE	*n* pl. -S blond
BLONDISH	*adj* somewhat blond
BLOOD	*v* -ED, -ING, -S to stain with blood (the fluid circulated by the heart)
BLOODFIN	*n* pl. -S a freshwater fish
BLOODIED	past tense of bloody
BLOODIER	comparative of bloody
BLOODIES	present 3d person sing. of bloody
BLOODIEST	superlative of bloody
BLOODILY	*adv* in a bloody manner
BLOODING	*n* pl. -S a fox hunting ceremony
BLOODRED	*adj* of the color of blood
BLOODY	*adj* BLOODIER, BLOODIEST stained with blood
BLOODY	*v* BLOODIED, BLOODYING, BLOODIES to make bloody
BLOOEY	*adj* being out of order
BLOOIE	*adj* blooey
BLOOM	*v* -ED, -ING, -S to bear flowers
BLOOMER	*n* pl. -S a blooming plant
BLOOMERY	*n* pl. -ERIES a furnace for smelting iron
BLOOMY	*adj* BLOOMIER, BLOOMIEST covered with flowers
BLOOP	*v* -ED, -ING, -S to hit a short fly ball
BLOOPER	*n* pl. -S a public blunder
BLOSSOM	*v* -ED, -ING, -S to bloom
BLOSSOMY	*adj* having blossoms
BLOT	*v* BLOTTED, BLOTTING, BLOTS to spot or stain

BLOTCH   *v* -ED, -ING, -ES to mark with large spots

BLOTCHY   *adj* BLOTCHIER, BLOTCHIEST blotched

BLOTLESS   *adj* spotless

BLOTTED   past tense of blot

BLOTTER   *n* pl. -S a piece of ink-absorbing paper

BLOTTIER   comparative of blotty

BLOTTIEST   superlative of blotty

BLOTTING   present participle of blot

BLOTTO   *adj* drunk

BLOTTY   *adj* -TIER, -TIEST spotty

BLOUSE   *v* BLOUSED, BLOUSING, BLOUSES to hang loosely

BLOUSON   *n* pl. -S a woman's garment

BLOUSY   *adj* BLOUSIER, BLOUSIEST blowsy **BLOUSILY** *adv*

BLOVIATE   *v* -ATED, -ATING, -ATES to speak pompously

BLOW   *v* BLEW, BLOWN, BLOWING, BLOWS to drive or impel by a current of air

BLOW   *v* BLEW, BLOWED, BLOWING, BLOWS to damn

BLOWBACK   *n* pl. -S an escape of gases

BLOWBALL   *n* pl. -S a fluffy seed ball

BLOWBY   *n* pl. -BYS leakage of exhaust fumes

BLOWDOWN   *n* pl. -S a tree blown down by the wind

BLOWER   *n* pl. -S one that blows

BLOWFISH   *n* pl. -ES a marine fish

BLOWFLY   *n* pl. -FLIES a type of fly

BLOWGUN   *n* pl. -S a tube through which darts may be blown

BLOWHARD   *n* pl. -S a braggart

BLOWHOLE   *n* pl. -S an air or gas vent

BLOWIER   comparative of blowy

BLOWIEST   superlative of blowy

BLOWN   past participle of blow

BLOWOFF   *n* pl. -S the expelling of gas

BLOWOUT   *n* pl. -S a sudden rupture

BLOWPIPE   *n* pl. -S a blowgun

BLOWSED   *adj* blowsy

BLOWSY   *adj* -SIER, -SIEST slovenly **BLOWSILY** *adv*

BLOWTUBE   *n* pl. -S a blowgun

BLOWUP   *n* pl. -S an explosion

BLOWY   *adj* BLOWIER, BLOWIEST windy

BLOWZED   *adj* blowzy

BLOWZY   *adj* -ZIER, -ZIEST blowsy **BLOWZILY** *adv*

BLUB   *v* BLUBBED, BLUBBING, BLUBS to blubber

BLUBBER   *v* -ED, -ING, -S to weep noisily

BLUBBERY   *adj* fat; swollen

BLUCHER   *n* pl. -S a half boot

BLUDGEON   *v* -ED, -ING, -S to hit with a club

BLUDGER   *n* pl. -S a loafer or shirker

BLUE   *adj* BLUER, BLUEST having the color of the clear sky

BLUE   *v* BLUED, BLUEING or BLUING, BLUES to make blue

BLUEBALL   *n* pl. -S a medicinal herb

BLUEBELL   *n* pl. -S a flowering plant

BLUEBILL   *n* pl. -S the scaup duck

BLUEBIRD   *n* pl. -S a songbird

BLUEBOOK   *n* pl. -S an examination booklet

BLUECAP   *n* pl. -S a flowering plant

BLUECOAT   *n* pl. -S a police officer

BLUED   past tense of blue

BLUEFIN   *n* pl. -S a large tuna

BLUEFISH   *n* pl. -ES a marine fish

BLUEGILL   *n* pl. -S an edible sunfish

BLUEGUM   *n* pl. -S a timber tree

BLUEHEAD   *n* pl. -S a marine fish

BLUEING   *n* pl. -S bluing

BLUEISH   *adj* bluish

BLUEJACK   *n* pl. -S an oak tree

BLUEJAY   *n* pl. -JAYS a corvine bird

BLUELINE   *n* pl. -S a line that divides a hockey rink

BLUELY   *adv* in a blue manner

BLUENESS   *n* pl. -ES the state of being blue

BLUENOSE   *n* pl. -S a puritanical person

BLUER   comparative of blue

BLUESIER   comparative of bluesy

BLUESIEST   superlative of bluesy

BLUESMAN   *n* pl. -MEN one who plays the blues

BLUEST   superlative of blue

BLUESTEM   *n* pl. -S a prairie grass

BLUESY	*adj* BLUESIER, BLUESIEST resembling the blues (a musical form)	**BOARFISH**	*n* pl. -ES a marine fish
		BOARISH	*adj* swinish; coarse
BLUET	*n* pl. -S a meadow flower	**BOART**	*n* pl. -S bort
BLUETICK	*n* pl. -S a hunting dog	**BOAST**	*v* -ED, -ING, -S to brag
BLUEWEED	*n* pl. -S a bristly weed	**BOASTER**	*n* pl. -S one that boasts
BLUEWOOD	*n* pl. -S a shrub	**BOASTFUL**	*adj* given to boasting
BLUEY	*n* pl. BLUEYS a bag of clothing carried in travel	**BOAT**	*v* -ED, -ING, -S to travel by boat (watercraft) **BOATABLE** *adj*
BLUFF	*v* -ED, -ING, -S to mislead	**BOATBILL**	*n* pl. -S a wading bird
BLUFF	*adj* BLUFFER, BLUFFEST having a broad front **BLUFFLY** *adv*	**BOATEL**	*n* pl. -S a waterside hotel
		BOATER	*n* pl. -S one that boats
BLUFFER	*n* pl. -S one that bluffs	**BOATFUL**	*n* pl. -S as much as a boat can hold
BLUING	*n* pl. -S a fabric coloring	**BOATHOOK**	*n* pl. -S a pole with a metal hook for use aboard a boat
BLUISH	*adj* somewhat blue		
BLUME	*v* BLUMED, BLUMING, BLUMES to blossom	**BOATING**	*n* pl. -S the sport of traveling by boat
BLUNDER	*v* -ED, -ING, -S to make a mistake	**BOATLIKE**	*adj* resembling a boat
		BOATLOAD	*n* pl. -S the amount that a boat holds
BLUNGE	*v* BLUNGED, BLUNGING, BLUNGES to mix clay with water	**BOATMAN**	*n* pl. -MEN one who works on boats
BLUNGER	*n* pl. -S one that blunges	**BOATSMAN**	*n* pl. -MEN boatman
BLUNT	*adj* BLUNTER, BLUNTEST not sharp or pointed **BLUNTLY** *adv*	**BOATYARD**	*n* pl. -S a marina
		BOB	*v* BOBBED, BOBBING, BOBS to move up and down
BLUNT	*v* -ED, -ING, -S to make blunt	**BOBBER**	*n* pl. -S one that bobs
BLUR	*v* BLURRED, BLURRING, BLURS to make unclear	**BOBBERY**	*n* pl. -BERIES a disturbance
BLURB	*v* -ED, -ING, -S to praise in a publicity notice	**BOBBIES**	pl. of bobby
		BOBBIN	*n* pl. -S a thread holder
BLURRY	*adj* -RIER, -RIEST unclear **BLURRILY** *adv*	**BOBBINET**	*n* pl. -S a machine-made net
		BOBBING	present participle of bob
BLURT	*v* -ED, -ING, -S to speak abruptly	**BOBBLE**	*v* -BLED, -BLING, -BLES to fumble
BLURTER	*n* pl. -S one that blurts		
BLUSH	*v* -ED, -ING, -ES to become red	**BOBBY**	*n* pl. -BIES a police officer
BLUSHER	*n* pl. -S one that blushes	**BOBCAT**	*n* pl. -S a lynx
BLUSHFUL	*adj* of a red color	**BOBECHE**	*n* pl. -S a glass collar on a candle holder
BLUSTER	*v* -ED, -ING, -S to blow violently	**BOBOLINK**	*n* pl. -S a songbird
BLUSTERY	*adj* windy	**BOBSLED**	*v* -SLEDDED, -SLEDDING, -SLEDS to ride on a bobsled (a racing sled)
BLYPE	*n* pl. -S a shred		
BO	*n* pl. BOS a pal		
BOA	*n* pl. -S a large snake	**BOBSTAY**	*n* pl. -STAYS a steadying rope
BOAR	*n* pl. -S a male pig	**BOBTAIL**	*v* -ED, -ING, -S to cut short
BOARD	*v* -ED, -ING, -S to take meals for a fixed price	**BOBWHITE**	*n* pl. -S a game bird
		BOCACCIO	*n* pl. -CIOS a rockfish
BOARDER	*n* pl. -S one that boards	**BOCCE**	*n* pl. -S boccie
BOARDING	*n* pl. -S a surface of wooden boards	**BOCCI**	*n* pl. -S boccie
BOARDMAN	*n* pl. -MEN a board member		

BOCCIA	*n* pl. -S boccie
BOCCIE	*n* pl. -S an Italian bowling game
BOCK	*n* pl. -S a dark beer
BOD	*n* pl. -S a body
BODE	*v* BODED, BODING, BODES to be an omen of
BODEGA	*n* pl. -S a grocery store
BODEMENT	*n* pl. -S an omen
BODHRAN	*n* pl. -S an Irish drum
BODICE	*n* pl. -S a corset
BODIED	past tense of body
BODIES	present 3d person sing. of body
BODILESS	*adj* lacking material form
BODILY	*adj* of the body
BODING	*n* pl. -S an omen
BODINGLY	*adv* ominously
BODKIN	*n* pl. -S a sharp instrument
BODY	*v* BODIED, BODYING, BODIES to give form to
BODYSUIT	*n* pl. -S a one-piece garment for the torso
BODYSURF	*v* -ED, -ING, -S to ride a wave without a surfboard
BODYWORK	*n* pl. -S a vehicle body
BOEHMITE	*n* pl. -S a mineral
BOFF	*n* pl. -S a hearty laugh
BOFFIN	*n* pl. -S a scientific expert
BOFFO	*n* pl. -FOS a boff
BOFFOLA	*n* pl. -S a boff
BOG	*v* BOGGED, BOGGING, BOGS to impede
BOGAN	*n* pl. -S a backwater or tributary
BOGBEAN	*n* pl. -S a marsh plant
BOGEY	*v* -GEYED, -GEYING, -GEYS to shoot in one stroke over par in golf
BOGEYMAN	*n* pl. -MEN a terrifying creature
BOGGED	past tense of bog
BOGGIER	comparative of boggy
BOGGIEST	superlative of boggy
BOGGING	present participle of bog
BOGGISH	*adj* boggy
BOGGLE	*v* -GLED, -GLING, -GLES to hesitate
BOGGLER	*n* pl. -S one that causes another to boggle
BOGGY	*adj* -GIER, -GIEST marshy
BOGIE	*n* pl. -S bogy
BOGIES	pl. of bogy
BOGLE	*n* pl. -S a bogy
BOGUS	*adj* not genuine; fake
BOGWOOD	*n* pl. -S preserved tree wood
BOGY	*n* pl. -GIES a goblin
BOGYISM	*n* pl. -S behavior characteristic of a bogy
BOGYMAN	*n* pl. -MEN bogeyman
BOHEA	*n* pl. -S a black tea
BOHEMIA	*n* pl. -S a community of bohemians
BOHEMIAN	*n* pl. -S an unconventional person
BOHUNK	*n* pl. -S an unskilled laborer
BOIL	*v* -ED, -ING, -S to vaporize liquid **BOILABLE** *adj*
BOILER	*n* pl. -S a vessel for boiling
BOILOFF	*n* pl. -S the vaporization of liquid
BOING	*interj* — used to express the sound of reverberation or vibration
BOISERIE	*n* pl. -S wood paneling on a wall
BOITE	*n* pl. -S a nightclub
BOLA	*n* pl. -S a throwing weapon
BOLAR	*adj* pertaining to bole
BOLAS	*n* pl. -ES bola
BOLD	*adj* BOLDER, BOLDEST daring **BOLDLY** *adv*
BOLD	*n* pl. -S a thick type
BOLDFACE	*v* -FACED, -FACING, -FACES to print in thick type
BOLDNESS	*n* pl. -ES the quality of being bold
BOLE	*n* pl. -S a fine clay
BOLERO	*n* pl. -ROS a lively Spanish dance
BOLETE	*n* pl. -S boletus
BOLETUS	*n* pl. -TUSES or -TI a fungus
BOLIDE	*n* pl. -S an exploding meteor
BOLIVAR	*n* pl. -S or -ES a monetary unit of Venezuela
BOLIVIA	*n* pl. -S a soft fabric
BOLL	*v* -ED, -ING, -S to form pods
BOLLARD	*n* pl. -S a thick post on a ship or wharf
BOLLIX	*v* -ED, -ING, -ES to bungle
BOLLOX	*v* -ED, -ING, -ES to bollix

BOLLWORM	*n* pl. -S the larva of a certain moth
BOLO	*n* pl. -LOS a machete
BOLOGNA	*n* pl. -S a seasoned sausage
BOLONEY	*n* pl. -NEYS bologna
BOLSHIE	*n* pl. -S a Bolshevik
BOLSHY	*n* pl. -SHIES bolshie
BOLSON	*n* pl. -S a flat arid valley
BOLSTER	*v* -ED, -ING, -S to support
BOLT	*v* -ED, -ING, -S to sift
BOLTER	*n* pl. -S a sifting machine
BOLTHEAD	*n* pl. -S a matrass
BOLTHOLE	*n* pl. -S a place or way of escape
BOLTONIA	*n* pl. -S a perennial herb
BOLTROPE	*n* pl. -S a rope sewn to a sail
BOLUS	*n* pl. -ES a large pill
BOMB	*v* -ED, -ING, -S to attack with bombs (explosive projectiles)
BOMBARD	*v* -ED, -ING, -S to bomb
BOMBAST	*n* pl. -S pompous language
BOMBAX	*adj* pertaining to a family of tropical trees
BOMBE	*n* pl. -S a frozen dessert
BOMBER	*n* pl. -S one that bombs
BOMBESIN	*n* pl. -S a combination of amino acids
BOMBING	*n* pl. -S an attack with bombs
BOMBLOAD	*n* pl. -S the quantity of bombs being carried
BOMBYCID	*n* pl. -S a moth
BOMBYX	*n* pl. -ES a silkworm
BONACI	*n* pl. -S an edible fish
BONANZA	*n* pl. -S a rich mine
BONBON	*n* pl. -S a sugared candy
BOND	*v* -ED, -ING, -S to join together **BONDABLE** *adj*
BONDAGE	*n* pl. -S slavery
BONDER	*n* pl. -S one that bonds
BONDING	*n* pl. -S the formation of a close personal relationship
BONDMAID	*n* pl. -S a female slave
BONDMAN	*n* pl. -MEN a male slave
BONDSMAN	*n* pl. -MEN bondman
BONDUC	*n* pl. -S a prickly seed
BONE	*v* BONED, BONING, BONES to debone
BONEFISH	*n* pl. -ES a slender marine fish
BONEHEAD	*n* pl. -S a stupid person
BONELESS	*adj* having no bones (hard connective tissue)
BONEMEAL	*n* pl. -S fertilizer or feed made from crushed bone
BONER	*n* pl. -S a blunder
BONESET	*n* pl. -S a perennial herb
BONEY	*adj* BONIER, BONIEST bony
BONEYARD	*n* pl. -S a junkyard
BONFIRE	*n* pl. -S an open fire
BONG	*v* -ED, -ING, -S to make a deep, ringing sound
BONGO	*n* pl. -GOS or -GOES a small drum
BONGOIST	*n* pl. -S a bongo player
BONHOMIE	*n* pl. -S friendliness
BONIER	comparative of bony or boney
BONIEST	superlative of bony or boney
BONIFACE	*n* pl. -S an innkeeper
BONINESS	*n* pl. -ES the state of being bony
BONING	present participle of bone
BONITA	*n* pl. -S bonito
BONITO	*n* pl. -TOS or -TOES a marine food fish
BONK	*v* -ED, -ING, -S to hit on the head with a hollow blow
BONKERS	*adj* crazy
BONNE	*n* pl. -S a housemaid
BONNET	*v* -ED, -ING, -S to provide with a bonnet (a type of hat)
BONNIE	*adj* bonny
BONNOCK	*n* pl. -S bannock
BONNY	*adj* -NIER, -NIEST pretty **BONNILY** *adv*
BONSAI	*n* pl. BONSAI a potted shrub that has been dwarfed
BONSPELL	*n* pl. -S bonspiel
BONSPIEL	*n* pl. -S a curling match or tournament
BONTEBOK	*n* pl. -S an antelope
BONUS	*n* pl. -ES an additional payment
BONY	*adj* BONIER, BONIEST full of bones
BONZE	*n* pl. -S a Buddhist monk
BONZER	*adj* very good
BOO	*v* -ED, -ING, -S to cry "boo"
BOOB	*v* -ED, -ING, -S to make a foolish mistake

BOOBISH *adj* doltish

BOOBOO *n* pl. -BOOS a mistake

BOOBY *n* pl. -BIES a dolt

BOODLE *v* -DLED, -DLING, -DLES to take bribes

BOODLER *n* pl. -S one that boodles

BOOGER *n* pl. -S a bogeyman

BOOGEY *v* -GEYED, -GEYING, -GEYS boogie

BOOGIE *v* -GIED, -GYING, -GIES to dance to rock music

BOOGY *v* -GIED, -GYING, -GIES boogie

BOOGYMAN *n* pl. -MEN bogeyman

BOOHOO *v* -ED, -ING, -S to weep noisily

BOOK *v* -ED, -ING, -S to engage services **BOOKABLE** *adj*

BOOKCASE *n* pl. -S a case which holds books (literary volumes)

BOOKEND *n* pl. -S a support for a row of books

BOOKER *n* pl. -S one that books

BOOKFUL *n* pl. -S as much as a book can hold

BOOKIE *n* pl. -S a bet taker

BOOKING *n* pl. -S an engagement

BOOKISH *adj* pertaining to books

BOOKLET *n* pl. -S a small book

BOOKLICE *n/pl* wingless insects that damage books

BOOKLORE *n* pl. -S book learning

BOOKMAN *n* pl. -MEN a scholar

BOOKMARK *n* pl. -S a marker for finding a place in a book

BOOKRACK *n* pl. -S a support for an open book

BOOKREST *n* pl. -S a bookrack

BOOKSHOP *n* pl. -S a store where books are sold

BOOKWORM *n* pl. -S an avid book reader

BOOM *v* -ED, -ING, -S to make a deep, resonant sound

BOOMBOX *n* pl. -ES a portable radio and tape or compact disc player

BOOMER *n* pl. -S one that booms

BOOMIER comparative of boomy

BOOMIEST superlative of boomy

BOOMKIN *n* pl. -S a bumkin

BOOMLET *n* pl. -S a small increase in prosperity

BOOMTOWN *n* pl. -S a prospering town

BOOMY *adj* BOOMIER, BOOMIEST prospering

BOON *n* pl. -S a timely benefit

BOONDOCK *adj* pertaining to a backwoods area

BOONIES *n/pl* a backwoods area

BOOR *n* pl. -S a rude person

BOORISH *adj* rude

BOOST *v* -ED, -ING, -S to support

BOOSTER *n* pl. -S one that boosts

BOOT *v* -ED, -ING, -S to load a program into a computer **BOOTABLE** *adj*

BOOTEE *n* pl. -S a baby's sock

BOOTERY *n* pl. -ERIES a shoe store

BOOTH *n* pl. -S a small enclosure

BOOTIE *n* pl. -S bootee

BOOTIES pl. of booty

BOOTJACK *n* pl. -S a device for pulling off boots

BOOTLACE *n* pl. -S a shoelace

BOOTLEG *v* -LEGGED, -LEGGING, -LEGS to smuggle

BOOTLESS *adj* useless

BOOTLICK *v* -ED, -ING, -S to flatter servilely

BOOTY *n* pl. -TIES a rich gain or prize

BOOZE *v* BOOZED, BOOZING, BOOZES to drink liquor excessively

BOOZER *n* pl. -S one that boozes

BOOZY *adj* BOOZIER, BOOZIEST drunken **BOOZILY** *adv*

BOP *v* BOPPED, BOPPING, BOPS to hit or strike

BOPEEP *n* pl. -S a game of peekaboo

BOPPER *n* pl. -S a bebopper

BORA *n* pl. -S a cold wind

BORACES a pl. of borax

BORACIC *adj* boric

BORACITE *n* pl. -S a mineral

BORAGE *n* pl. -S a medicinal herb

BORAL *n* pl. -S a mixture of boron carbide and aluminum

BORANE *n* pl. -S a chemical compound

BORATE *v* -RATED, -RATING, -RATES to mix with borax or boric acid

BORAX *n* pl. -RAXES or -RACES a white crystalline compound

BORDEAUX	*n* pl. BORDEAUX a red or white wine
BORDEL	*n* pl. -S a brothel
BORDELLO	*n* pl. -LOS a brothel
BORDER	*v* -ED, -ING, -S to put a border (an edge) on
BORDERER	*n* pl. -S one that borders
BORDURE	*n* pl. -S a border around a shield
BORE	*v* BORED, BORING, BORES to pierce with a rotary tool
BOREAL	*adj* pertaining to the north
BORECOLE	*n* pl. -S kale
BORED	past tense of bore
BOREDOM	*n* pl. -S tedium
BOREEN	*n* pl. -S a lane in Ireland
BOREHOLE	*n* pl. -S a hole bored in the earth
BORER	*n* pl. -S one that bores
BORESOME	*adj* tedious
BORIC	*adj* pertaining to boron
BORIDE	*n* pl. -S a boron compound
BORING	*n* pl. -S an inner cavity
BORINGLY	*adv* tediously
BORN	*adj* having particular qualities from birth
BORNE	a past participle of bear
BORNEOL	*n* pl. -S an alcohol
BORNITE	*n* pl. -S an ore of copper
BORON	*n* pl. -S a nonmetallic element **BORONIC** *adj*
BOROUGH	*n* pl. -S an incorporated town
BORROW	*v* -ED, -ING, -S to take on loan
BORROWER	*n* pl. -S one that borrows
BORSCH	*n* pl. -ES borscht
BORSCHT	*n* pl. -S a beet soup
BORSHT	*n* pl. -S borscht
BORSTAL	*n* pl. -S a reformatory
BORT	*n* pl. -S a low-quality diamond **BORTY** *adj*
BORTZ	*n* pl. -ES bort
BORZOI	*n* pl. -S a Russian hound
BOSCAGE	*n* pl. -S a thicket
BOSCHBOK	*n* pl. -S bushbuck
BOSH	*n* pl. -ES nonsense
BOSHBOK	*n* pl. -S bushbuck
BOSHVARK	*n* pl. -S a wild hog
BOSK	*n* pl. -S a small wooded area
BOSKAGE	*n* pl. -S boscage
BOSKER	*adj* fine; very good
BOSKET	*n* pl. -S a thicket
BOSKY	*adj* BOSKIER, BOSKIEST wooded; bushy
BOSOM	*v* -ED, -ING, -S to embrace
BOSOMY	*adj* swelling outward
BOSON	*n* pl. -S a subatomic particle
BOSQUE	*n* pl. -S bosk
BOSQUET	*n* pl. -S bosket
BOSS	*v* -ED, -ING, -ES to supervise
BOSSDOM	*n* pl. -S the domain of a political boss
BOSSIER	comparative of bossy
BOSSIES	pl. of bossy
BOSSISM	*n* pl. -S control by political bosses
BOSSY	*adj* BOSSIER, BOSSIEST domineering **BOSSILY** *adv*
BOSSY	*n* pl. BOSSIES a cow
BOSTON	*n* pl. -S a card game
BOSUN	*n* pl. -S a boatswain
BOT	*n* pl. -S the larva of a botfly
BOTA	*n* pl. -S a leather bottle
BOTANIC	*adj* pertaining to botany
BOTANICA	*n* pl. -S a shop that sells herbs and magic charms
BOTANIES	pl. of botany
BOTANISE	*v* -NISED, -NISING, -NISES to botanize
BOTANIST	*n* pl. -S one skilled in botany
BOTANIZE	*v* -NIZED, -NIZING, -NIZES to study plants
BOTANY	*n* pl. -NIES the science of plants
BOTCH	*v* -ED, -ING, -ES to bungle
BOTCHER	*n* pl. -S one that botches
BOTCHERY	*n* pl. -ERIES something botched
BOTCHY	*adj* BOTCHIER, BOTCHIEST badly done **BOTCHILY** *adv*
BOTEL	*n* pl. -S boatel
BOTFLY	*n* pl. -FLIES a type of fly
BOTH	*adj* being the two
BOTHER	*v* -ED, -ING, -S to annoy
BOTHRIUM	*n* pl. -RIA or -RIUMS a groove on a tapeworm
BOTHY	*n* pl. BOTHIES a hut in Scotland

BOTONEE	*adj* having arms ending in a trefoil — used of a heraldic cross
BOTONNEE	*adj* botonee
BOTRYOID	*adj* resembling a cluster of grapes
BOTRYOSE	*adj* botryoid
BOTRYTIS	*n* pl. -TISES a plant disease
BOTT	*n* pl. -S bot
BOTTLE	*v* -TLED, -TLING, -TLES to put into a bottle (a rigid container)
BOTTLER	*n* pl. -S one that bottles
BOTTLING	*n* pl. -S a bottled beverage
BOTTOM	*v* -ED, -ING, -S to comprehend
BOTTOMER	*n* pl. -S one that bottoms
BOTTOMRY	*n* pl. -RIES a maritime contract
BOTULIN	*n* pl. -S a nerve poison
BOTULISM	*n* pl. -S botulin poisoning
BOUBOU	*n* pl. -S a long flowing garment
BOUCHEE	*n* pl. -S a small patty shell
BOUCLE	*n* pl. -S a knitted fabric
BOUDOIR	*n* pl. -S a woman's bedroom
BOUFFANT	*n* pl. -S a woman's hairdo
BOUFFE	*n* pl. -S a comic opera
BOUGH	*n* pl. -S a tree branch **BOUGHED** *adj*
BOUGHPOT	*n* pl. -S a large vase
BOUGHT	past tense of buy
BOUGHTEN	*adj* purchased
BOUGIE	*n* pl. -S a wax candle
BOUILLON	*n* pl. -S a clear broth
BOULDER	*n* pl. -S a large rock **BOULDERY** *adj*
BOULE	*n* pl. -S buhl
BOULLE	*n* pl. -S buhl
BOUNCE	*v* BOUNCED, BOUNCING, BOUNCES to spring back
BOUNCER	*n* pl. -S one that bounces
BOUNCY	*adj* BOUNCIER, BOUNCIEST tending to bounce **BOUNCILY** *adv*
BOUND	*v* -ED, -ING, -S to leap
BOUNDARY	*n* pl. -ARIES a dividing line
BOUNDEN	*adj* obliged
BOUNDER	*n* pl. -S one that bounds
BOUNTY	*n* pl. -TIES a reward **BOUNTIED** *adj*
BOUQUET	*n* pl. -S a bunch of flowers
BOURBON	*n* pl. -S a whiskey
BOURDON	*n* pl. -S a part of a bagpipe
BOURG	*n* pl. -S a medieval town
BOURGEON	*v* -ED, -ING, -S to burgeon
BOURN	*n* pl. -S a stream
BOURNE	*n* pl. -S bourn
BOURREE	*n* pl. -S an old French dance
BOURRIDE	*n* pl. -S a fish stew
BOURSE	*n* pl. -S a stock exchange
BOURTREE	*n* pl. -S a European tree
BOUSE	*v* BOUSED, BOUSING, BOUSES to haul by means of a tackle
BOUSOUKI	*n* pl. -KIA or -KIS bouzouki
BOUSY	*adj* boozy
BOUT	*n* pl. -S a contest
BOUTIQUE	*n* pl. -S a small shop
BOUTON	*n* pl. -S an enlarged end of a nerve fiber
BOUVIER	*n* pl. -S a large dog
BOUZOUKI	*n* pl. -KIA or -KIS a stringed musical instrument
BOVID	*n* pl. -S a bovine
BOVINE	*n* pl. -S an ox-like animal
BOVINELY	*adv* stolidly
BOVINITY	*n* pl. -TIES the state of being a bovine
BOW	*v* -ED, -ING, -S to bend forward
BOWEL	*v* -ELED, -ELING, -ELS or -ELLED, -ELLING, -ELS to disbowel
BOWER	*v* -ED, -ING, -S to embower
BOWERY	*n* pl. -ERIES a colonial Dutch farm
BOWFIN	*n* pl. -S a freshwater fish
BOWFRONT	*adj* having a curved front
BOWHEAD	*n* pl. -S an arctic whale
BOWING	*n* pl. -S the technique of managing the bow of a stringed instrument
BOWINGLY	*adv* in a bowing manner
BOWKNOT	*n* pl. -S a type of knot
BOWL	*v* -ED, -ING, -S to play at bowling
BOWLDER	*n* pl. -S boulder
BOWLEG	*n* pl. -S an outwardly curved leg
BOWLER	*n* pl. -S one that bowls
BOWLESS	*adj* being without an archery bow
BOWLFUL	*n* pl. -S as much as a bowl can hold

BOWLIKE	*adj* curved	**BOZO**	*n* pl. -ZOS a fellow
BOWLINE	*n* pl. -S a type of knot	**BRA**	*n* pl. -S a brassiere
BOWLING	*n* pl. -S a game in which balls are rolled at objects	**BRABBLE**	*v* -BLED, -BLING, -BLES to quarrel noisily
BOWLLIKE	*adj* concave	**BRABBLER**	*n* pl. -S one that brabbles
BOWMAN	*n* pl. -MEN an archer	**BRACE**	*v* BRACED, BRACING, BRACES to support
BOWPOT	*n* pl. -S boughpot		
BOWSE	*v* BOWSED, BOWSING, BOWSES to bouse	**BRACELET**	*n* pl. -S a wrist ornament
		BRACER	*n* pl. -S one that braces
BOWSHOT	*n* pl. -S the distance an arrow is shot	**BRACERO**	*n* pl. -ROS a Mexican laborer
		BRACH	*n* pl. -ES or -S a hound bitch
BOWSPRIT	*n* pl. -S a ship's spar	**BRACHET**	*n* pl. -S a brach
BOWWOW	*v* -ED, -ING, -S to bark like a dog	**BRACHIAL**	*n* pl. -S a part of the arm
BOWYER	*n* pl. -S a maker of archery bows	**BRACHIUM**	*n* pl. -IA the upper part of arm
BOX	*v* -ED, -ING, -ES to put in a box (a rectangular container)	**BRACING**	*n* pl. -S a brace or reinforcement
		BRACIOLA	*n* pl. -S a thin slice of meat
BOXBERRY	*n* pl. -RIES an evergreen plant	**BRACIOLE**	*n* pl. -S braciola
BOXBOARD	*n* pl. -S stiff paperboard	**BRACKEN**	*n* pl. -S a large fern
BOXCAR	*n* pl. -S a roofed freight car	**BRACKET**	*v* -ED, -ING, -S to classify
BOXER	*n* pl. -S one that packs boxes	**BRACKISH**	*adj* salty
BOXFISH	*n* pl. -ES a marine fish	**BRACONID**	*n* pl. -S any of a family of flies
BOXFUL	*n* pl. -S as much as a box can hold	**BRACT**	*n* pl. -S a leaflike plant part **BRACTEAL, BRACTED** *adj*
BOXHAUL	*v* -ED, -ING, -S to veer a ship around	**BRACTLET**	*n* pl. -S a small bract
BOXIER	comparative of boxy	**BRAD**	*v* BRADDED, BRADDING, BRADS to fasten with thin nails
BOXIEST	superlative of boxy		
BOXINESS	*n* pl. -ES the state of being boxy	**BRADAWL**	*n* pl. -S a type of awl
BOXING	*n* pl. -S a casing	**BRADOON**	*n* pl. -S bridoon
BOXLIKE	*adj* resembling a box	**BRAE**	*n* pl. -S a hillside
BOXTHORN	*n* pl. -S a thorny shrub	**BRAG**	*adj* BRAGGER, BRAGGEST first-rate
BOXWOOD	*n* pl. -S an evergreen shrub		
BOXY	*adj* BOXIER, BOXIEST resembling a box	**BRAG**	*v* BRAGGED, BRAGGING, BRAGS to speak vainly of one's deeds
BOY	*n* pl. BOYS a male child	**BRAGGART**	*n* pl. -S one who brags
BOYAR	*n* pl. -S a former Russian aristocrat	**BRAGGER**	*n* pl. -S a braggart
		BRAGGEST	superlative of brag
BOYARD	*n* pl. -S boyar	**BRAGGING**	present participle of brag
BOYARISM	*n* pl. -S the rule of boyars	**BRAGGY**	*adj* -GIER, -GIEST tending to brag
BOYCHICK	*n* pl. -S boychik		
BOYCHIK	*n* pl. -S a young man	**BRAHMA**	*n* pl. -S a large domestic fowl
BOYCOTT	*v* -ED, -ING, -S to refuse to buy	**BRAID**	*v* -ED, -ING, -S to weave together
BOYHOOD	*n* pl. -S the state of being a boy	**BRAIDER**	*n* pl. -S one that braids
BOYISH	*adj* resembling a boy **BOYISHLY** *adv*	**BRAIDING**	*n* pl. -S something made of braided material
BOYLA	*n* pl. -S a witch doctor		
BOYO	*n* pl. BOYOS a boy	**BRAIL**	*v* -ED, -ING, -S to haul in a sail

BRAILLE	*v* BRAILLED, BRAILLING, BRAILLES to write in braille (raised writing for the blind)
BRAIN	*v* -ED, -ING, -S to hit on the head
BRAINIER	comparative of brainy
BRAINIEST	superlative of brainy
BRAINILY	*adv* in a brainy manner
BRAINISH	*adj* impetuous
BRAINPAN	*n* pl. -S the skull
BRAINY	*adj* BRAINIER, BRAINIEST smart
BRAISE	*v* BRAISED, BRAISING, BRAISES to cook in fat
BRAIZE	*n* pl. -S a marine fish
BRAKE	*v* BRAKED, BRAKING, BRAKES to slow down or stop
BRAKEAGE	*n* pl. -S the act of braking
BRAKEMAN	*n* pl. -MEN a trainman
BRAKING	present participle of brake
BRAKY	*adj* BRAKIER, BRAKIEST abounding in shrubs or ferns
BRALESS	*adj* wearing no bra
BRAMBLE	*v* -BLED, -BLING, -BLES to gather berries
BRAMBLY	*adj* -BLIER, -BLIEST prickly
BRAN	*v* BRANNED, BRANNING, BRANS to soak in water mixed with bran (the outer coat of cereals)
BRANCH	*v* -ED, -ING, -ES to form branches (offshoots)
BRANCHIA	*n* pl. -CHIAE a respiratory organ of aquatic animals
BRANCHY	*adj* BRANCHIER, BRANCHIEST having many branches
BRAND	*v* -ED, -ING, -S to mark with a hot iron
BRANDER	*n* pl. -S one that brands
BRANDISH	*v* -ED, -ING, -ES to wave menacingly
BRANDY	*v* -DIED, -DYING, -DIES to mix with brandy (a liquor)
BRANK	*n* pl. -S a device used to restrain the tongue
BRANNED	past tense of bran
BRANNER	*n* pl. -S one that brans
BRANNING	present participle of bran
BRANNY	*adj* -NIER, -NIEST containing bran
BRANT	*n* pl. -S a wild goose
BRANTAIL	*n* pl. -S a singing bird
BRASH	*adj* BRASHER, BRASHEST rash; hasty **BRASHLY** *adv*
BRASH	*n* pl. -ES a mass of fragments
BRASHY	*adj* BRASHIER, BRASHIEST brash
BRASIER	*n* pl. -S brazier
BRASIL	*n* pl. -S brazil
BRASILIN	*n* pl. -S brazilin
BRASS	*v* -ED, -ING, -ES to coat with brass (an alloy of copper and zinc)
BRASSAGE	*n* pl. -S a fee for coining money
BRASSARD	*n* pl. -S an insignia
BRASSART	*n* pl. -S brassard
BRASSICA	*n* pl. -S a tall herb
BRASSIE	*n* pl. -S a golf club
BRASSISH	*adj* resembling brass
BRASSY	*adj* BRASSIER, BRASSIEST resembling brass **BRASSILY** *adv*
BRAT	*n* pl. -S a spoiled child **BRATTISH** *adj*
BRATTICE	*v* -TICED, -TICING, -TICES to partition
BRATTLE	*v* -TLED, -TLING, -TLES to clatter
BRATTY	*adj* -TIER, -TIEST resembling a brat
BRAUNITE	*n* pl. -S a mineral
BRAVA	*n* pl. -S a shout of approval
BRAVADO	*n* pl. -DOS or -DOES false bravery
BRAVE	*adj* BRAVER, BRAVEST showing courage **BRAVELY** *adv*
BRAVE	*v* BRAVED, BRAVING, BRAVES to face with courage
BRAVER	*n* pl. -S one that braves
BRAVERY	*n* pl. -ERIES courage
BRAVEST	superlative of brave
BRAVI	a pl. of bravo
BRAVING	present participle of brave
BRAVO	*n* pl. -VOS or -VOES or -VI a hired killer
BRAVO	*v* -ED, -ING, -ES to applaud by shouting "bravo"
BRAVURA	*n* pl. -RAS or -RE fine musical technique
BRAW	*adj* BRAWER, BRAWEST splendid

BRAWL	*v* -ED, -ING, -S to fight
BRAWLER	*n* pl. -S a fighter
BRAWLIE	*adv* splendidly
BRAWLY	*adj* BRAWLIER, BRAWLIEST inclined to brawl
BRAWN	*n* pl. -S muscular strength
BRAWNY	*adj* BRAWNIER, BRAWNIEST muscular **BRAWNILY** *adv*
BRAWS	*n/pl* fine clothes
BRAXY	*n* pl. BRAXIES a fever of sheep
BRAY	*v* BRAYED, BRAYING, BRAYS to utter a harsh cry
BRAYER	*n* pl. -S a roller used to spread ink
BRAZA	*n* pl. -S a Spanish unit of length
BRAZE	*v* BRAZED, BRAZING, BRAZES to solder together
BRAZEN	*v* -ED, -ING, -S to face boldly
BRAZENLY	*adv* boldly
BRAZER	*n* pl. -S one that brazes
BRAZIER	*n* pl. -S one who works in brass
BRAZIL	*n* pl. -S a dyewood
BRAZILIN	*n* pl. -S a chemical compound
BRAZING	present participle of braze
BREACH	*v* -ED, -ING, -ES to break through
BREACHER	*n* pl. -S one that breaches
BREAD	*v* -ED, -ING, -S to cover with crumbs of bread (a baked foodstuff made from flour)
BREADBOX	*n* pl. -ES a container for bread
BREADNUT	*n* pl. -S a tropical fruit
BREADTH	*n* pl. -S width
BREADY	*adj* resembling or characteristic of bread
BREAK	*v* BROKE, BROKEN, BREAKING, BREAKS to reduce to fragments
BREAKAGE	*n* pl. -S the act of breaking
BREAKER	*n* pl. -S one that breaks
BREAKING	*n* pl. -S the change of a pure vowel to a diphthong
BREAKOUT	*n* pl. -S an escape
BREAKUP	*n* pl. -S the act of breaking up
BREAM	*v* -ED, -ING, -S to clean a ship's bottom
BREAST	*v* -ED, -ING, -S to confront boldly
BREATH	*n* pl. -S air inhaled and exhaled
BREATHE	*v* BREATHED, BREATHING, BREATHES to inhale and exhale air
BREATHER	*n* pl. -S one that breathes
BREATHY	*adj* BREATHIER, BREATHIEST marked by loud breathing
BRECCIA	*n* pl. -S a type of rock **BRECCIAL** *adj*
BRECHAM	*n* pl. -S a collar for a horse
BRECHAN	*n* pl. -S brecham
BRED	past tense of breed
BREDE	*n* pl. -S a braid
BREE	*n* pl. -S broth
BREECH	*v* -ED, -ING, -ES to clothe with breeches (trousers)
BREED	*v* BRED, BREEDING, BREEDS to cause to give birth
BREEDER	*n* pl. -S one that breeds
BREEDING	*n* pl. -S upbringing
BREEKS	*n/pl* breeches
BREEZE	*v* BREEZED, BREEZING, BREEZES to move swiftly
BREEZY	*adj* BREEZIER, BREEZIEST windy **BREEZILY** *adv*
BREGMA	*n* pl. -MATA a junction point of the skull **BREGMATE** *adj*
BREN	*n* pl. -S a submachine gun
BRENT	*n* pl. -S brant
BRETHREN	*a* pl. of brother
BREVE	*n* pl. -S a symbol used to indicate a short vowel
BREVET	*v* -VETED, -VETING, -VETS or -VETTED, -VETTING, -VETS to confer an honorary rank upon
BREVETCY	*n* pl. -CIES an honorary rank
BREVIARY	*n* pl. -RIES a prayer book
BREVIER	*n* pl. -S a size of type
BREVITY	*n* pl. -TIES shortness of duration
BREW	*v* -ED, -ING, -S to make beer or the like
BREWAGE	*n* pl. -S a brewed beverage
BREWER	*n* pl. -S one that brews
BREWERY	*n* pl. -ERIES a place for brewing
BREWING	*n* pl. -S a quantity brewed at one time
BREWIS	*n* pl. BREWISES broth
BRIAR	*n* pl. -S brier **BRIARY** *adj*
BRIARD	*n* pl. -S a large dog

BRIBE	*v* BRIBED, BRIBING, BRIBES to practice bribery **BRIBABLE** *adj*
BRIBEE	*n* pl. -S one that is bribed
BRIBER	*n* pl. -S one that bribes
BRIBERY	*n* pl. -ERIES an act of influencing corruptly
BRIBING	present participle of bribe
BRICK	*v* -ED, -ING, -S to build with bricks (blocks of clay)
BRICKBAT	*n* pl. -S a piece of brick
BRICKLE	*n* pl. -S a brittle candy
BRICKY	*adj* BRICKIER, BRICKIEST made of bricks
BRICOLE	*n* pl. -S a cushion shot in billiards
BRIDAL	*n* pl. -S a wedding
BRIDALLY	*adv* in a manner befitting a bride
BRIDE	*n* pl. -S a woman just married or about to be married
BRIDGE	*v* BRIDGED, BRIDGING, BRIDGES to connect
BRIDGING	*n* pl. -S a bracing
BRIDLE	*v* -DLED, -DLING, -DLES to control with a restraint
BRIDLER	*n* pl. -S one that bridles
BRIDOON	*n* pl. -S a device used to control a horse
BRIE	*n* pl. -S bree
BRIEF	*adj* BRIEFER, BRIEFEST short
BRIEF	*v* -ED, -ING, -S to summarize
BRIEFER	*n* pl. -S one that briefs
BRIEFING	*n* pl. -S a short lecture
BRIEFLY	*adv* in a brief manner
BRIER	*n* pl. -S a thorny shrub **BRIERY** *adj*
BRIG	*n* pl. -S a two-masted ship
BRIGADE	*v* -GADED, -GADING, -GADES to group together
BRIGAND	*n* pl. -S a bandit
BRIGHT	*adj* BRIGHTER, BRIGHTEST emitting much light **BRIGHTLY** *adv*
BRIGHT	*n* pl. -S a light-hued tobacco
BRIGHTEN	*v* -ED, -ING, -S to make bright
BRILL	*n* pl. -S an edible flatfish
BRIM	*v* BRIMMED, BRIMMING, BRIMS to fill to the top
BRIMFUL	*adj* ready to overflow
BRIMFULL	*adj* brimful
BRIMLESS	*adj* having no brim (an upper edge)
BRIMMED	past tense of brim
BRIMMER	*n* pl. -S a brimming cup or glass
BRIMMING	present participle of brim
BRIN	*n* pl. -S a rib of a fan
BRINDED	*adj* brindled
BRINDLE	*n* pl. -S a brindled color
BRINDLED	*adj* streaked
BRINE	*v* BRINED, BRINING, BRINES to treat with brine (salted water)
BRINER	*n* pl. -S one that brines
BRING	*v* BROUGHT, BRINGING, BRINGS to take with oneself to a place
BRINGER	*n* pl. -S one that brings
BRINIER	comparative of briny
BRINIES	pl. of briny
BRINIEST	superlative of briny
BRINING	present participle of brine
BRINISH	*adj* resembling brine
BRINK	*n* pl. -S an extreme edge
BRINY	*n* pl. BRINIES the sea
BRINY	*adj* BRINIER, BRINIEST salty
BRIO	*n* pl. BRIOS liveliness
BRIOCHE	*n* pl. -S a rich roll
BRIONY	*n* pl. -NIES bryony
BRIQUET	*v* -QUETTED, -QUETTING, -QUETS to mold into small bricks
BRIS	*n* pl. BRISSES a Jewish circumcision rite
BRISANCE	*n* pl. -S the shattering effect of an explosive **BRISANT** *adj*
BRISK	*adj* BRISKER, BRISKEST lively
BRISK	*v* -ED, -ING, -S to make brisk
BRISKET	*n* pl. -S the breast of an animal
BRISKLY	*adv* in a brisk manner
BRISLING	*n* pl. -S a small herring
BRISSES	pl. of bris
BRISTLE	*v* -TLED, -TLING, -TLES to rise stiffly
BRISTLY	*adj* -TLIER, -TLIEST stiffly erect
BRISTOL	*n* pl. -S a smooth cardboard
BRIT	*n* pl. -S a young herring
BRITCHES	*n/pl* breeches; trousers
BRITSKA	*n* pl. -S an open carriage
BRITT	*n* pl. -S brit

BRITTLE	*adj* -TLER, -TLEST likely to break
BRITTLE	*v* -TLED, -TLING, -TLES to become brittle
BRITTLY	*adv* in a brittle manner
BRITZKA	*n* pl. -S britska
BRITZSKA	*n* pl. -S britska
BRO	*n* pl. BROS a brother
BROACH	*v* -ED, -ING, -ES to pierce so as to withdraw a liquid
BROACHER	*n* pl. -S one that broaches
BROAD	*adj* BROADER, BROADEST wide
BROAD	*n* pl. -S an expansion of a river
BROADAX	*n* pl. -ES a broad-edged ax
BROADAXE	*n* pl. -S broadax
BROADEN	*v* -ED, -ING, -S to make broad
BROADISH	*adj* somewhat broad
BROADLY	*adv* in a broad manner
BROCADE	*v* -CADED, -CADING, -CADES to weave with a raised design
BROCATEL	*n* pl. -S a heavy fabric
BROCCOLI	*n* pl. -S a vegetable related to the cabbage
BROCHE	*adj* brocaded
BROCHURE	*n* pl. -S a pamphlet
BROCK	*n* pl. -S a badger
BROCKAGE	*n* pl. -S an imperfectly minted coin
BROCKET	*n* pl. -S a small, red deer
BROCOLI	*n* pl. -S broccoli
BROGAN	*n* pl. -S a heavy shoe
BROGUE	*n* pl. -S an Irish accent
BROGUERY	*n* pl. -ERIES the use of an Irish accent
BROGUISH	*adj* resembling a brogue
BROIDER	*v* -ED, -ING, -S to adorn with needlework
BROIDERY	*n* pl. -DERIES the act of broidering
BROIL	*v* -ED, -ING, -S to cook by direct heat
BROILER	*n* pl. -S a device for broiling
BROKAGE	*n* pl. -S the business of a broker
BROKE	past tense of break
BROKEN	*adj* shattered **BROKENLY** *adv*
BROKER	*v* -ED, -ING, -S to act as a broker (an agent who buys and sells stocks)
BROKING	*n* pl. -S the business of a broker
BROLLY	*n* pl. -LIES an umbrella
BROMAL	*n* pl. -S a medicinal liquid
BROMATE	*v* -MATED, -MATING, -MATES to combine with bromine
BROME	*n* pl. -S a tall grass
BROMELIN	*n* pl. -S an enzyme
BROMIC	*adj* containing bromine
BROMID	*n* pl. -S bromide
BROMIDE	*n* pl. -S a bromine compound
BROMIDIC	*adj* commonplace; trite
BROMIN	*n* pl. -S bromine
BROMINE	*n* pl. -S a volatile liquid element
BROMISM	*n* pl. -S a diseased condition of the skin
BROMIZE	*v* -MIZED, -MIZING, -MIZES to treat with bromine or a bromide
BROMO	*n* pl. -MOS a medicinal compound
BRONC	*n* pl. -S bronco
BRONCHI	pl. of bronchus
BRONCHIA	*n/pl* the main air passages of the lungs
BRONCHO	*n* pl. -CHOS bronco
BRONCHUS	*n* pl. -CHI a tracheal branch
BRONCO	*n* pl. -COS a wild horse
BRONZE	*v* BRONZED, BRONZING, BRONZES to make brown or tan
BRONZER	*n* pl. -S one that bronzes
BRONZING	*n* pl. -S a brownish coloring
BRONZY	*adj* BRONZIER, BRONZIEST of a brownish color
BROO	*n* pl. BROOS a bree
BROOCH	*n* pl. -ES a decorative pin
BROOD	*v* -ED, -ING, -S to ponder deeply
BROODER	*n* pl. -S one that broods
BROODY	*adj* BROODIER, BROODIEST tending to brood **BROODILY** *adv*
BROOK	*v* -ED, -ING, -S to tolerate
BROOKIE	*n* pl. -S a brook trout
BROOKITE	*n* pl. -S a mineral
BROOKLET	*n* pl. -S a small brook or creek
BROOM	*v* -ED, -ING, -S to sweep

BROOMY   adj BROOMIER, BROOMIEST abounding in broom (a type of shrub)

BROS   pl. of bro

BROSE   n pl. -S a porridge

BROSY   adj smeared with brose

BROTH   n pl. -S a thin clear soup

BROTHEL   n pl. -S a house of prostitution

BROTHER   n pl. -S or BRETHREN a male sibling

BROTHER   v -ED, -ING, -S to treat like a brother

BROTHY   adj resembling broth

BROUGHAM   n pl. -S a type of carriage

BROUGHT   past tense of bring

BROUHAHA   n pl. -S an uproar

BROW   n pl. -S the forehead **BROWED** adj

BROWBAND   n pl. -S a band designed to cross the forehead

BROWBEAT   v -BEAT, -BEATEN, -BEATING, -BEATS to intimidate

BROWLESS   adj lacking eyebrows

BROWN   adj BROWNER, BROWNEST of a dark color

BROWN   v -ED, -ING, -S to make brown

BROWNIE   n pl. -S a small sprite

BROWNIER   comparative of browny

BROWNIEST   superlative of browny

BROWNISH   adj somewhat brown

BROWNOUT   n pl. -S a power reduction

BROWNY   adj BROWNIER, BROWNIEST somewhat brown

BROWSE   v BROWSED, BROWSING, BROWSES to look at casually

BROWSER   n pl. -S one that browses

BRR   interj brrr

BRRR   interj — used to indicate that one feels cold

BRUCELLA   n pl. -LAE or -LAS any of a genus of harmful bacteria

BRUCIN   n pl. -S brucine

BRUCINE   n pl. -S a poisonous alkaloid

BRUGH   n pl. -S a borough

BRUIN   n pl. -S a bear

BRUISE   v BRUISED, BRUISING, BRUISES to injure without breaking the surface of the skin

BRUISER   n pl. -S a big, husky man

BRUIT   v -ED, -ING, -S to spread news of

BRUITER   n pl. -S one that bruits

BRULOT   n pl. -S a biting fly

BRULYIE   n pl. -S a noisy quarrel

BRULZIE   n pl. -S brulyie

BRUMAL   adj wintry

BRUMBY   n pl. -BIES a wild horse

BRUME   n pl. -S fog **BRUMOUS** adj

BRUNCH   v -ED, -ING, -ES to eat a late morning meal

BRUNET   n pl. -S a dark-haired male

BRUNETTE   n pl. -S a dark-haired female

BRUNIZEM   n pl. -S a prairie soil

BRUNT   n pl. -S the main impact

BRUSH   v -ED, -ING, -ES to touch lightly

BRUSHER   n pl. -S one that brushes

BRUSHIER   comparative of brushy

BRUSHIEST   superlative of brushy

BRUSHOFF   n pl. -S an abrupt dismissal

BRUSHUP   n pl. -S a quick review

BRUSHY   adj BRUSHIER, BRUSHIEST shaggy; rough

BRUSK   adj BRUSKER, BRUSKEST brusque

BRUSQUE   adj BRUSQUER, BRUSQUEST abrupt in manner

BRUT   adj very dry

BRUTAL   adj cruel; savage **BRUTALLY** adv

BRUTE   v BRUTED, BRUTING, BRUTES to shape a diamond by rubbing it with another diamond

BRUTELY   adv in a brutal manner

BRUTIFY   v -FIED, -FYING, -FIES to make brutal

BRUTING   present participle of brute

BRUTISH   adj brutal

BRUTISM   n pl. -S the state of being brutal

BRUXISM   n pl. -S a nervous grinding of the teeth

BRYOLOGY   n pl. -GIES the study of mosses

BRYONY   n pl. -NIES a climbing plant

BRYOZOAN   n pl. -S a type of small aquatic animal

BUB   n pl. -S young fellow

BUBAL   n pl. -S a large antelope

BUBALE   n pl. -S bubal

BUBALINE *adj* pertaining to the bubal

BUBALIS *n* pl. -LISES bubal

BUBBLE *v* -BLED, -BLING, -BLES to form bubbles (bodies of gas contained within a liquid)

BUBBLER *n* pl. -S a drinking fountain

BUBBLY *n* pl. -BLIES champagne

BUBBLY *adj* -BLIER, -BLIEST full of bubbles

BUBINGA *n* pl. -S an African tree

BUBO *n* pl. -BOES a swelling of a lymph gland **BUBOED** *adj*

BUBONIC *adj* pertaining to a bubo

BUCCAL *adj* pertaining to the cheek **BUCCALLY** *adv*

BUCK *v* -ED, -ING, -S to leap forward and upward suddenly

BUCKAROO *n* pl. -ROOS a cowboy

BUCKAYRO *n* pl. -ROS buckaroo

BUCKBEAN *n* pl. -S a marsh plant

BUCKEEN *n* pl. -S a poor man who acts as if wealthy

BUCKER *n* pl. -S a bucking horse

BUCKEROO *n* pl. -ROOS buckaroo

BUCKET *v* -ED, -ING, -S to hurry

BUCKEYE *n* pl. -S a nut-bearing tree

BUCKISH *adj* foppish

BUCKLE *v* -LED, -LING, -LES to bend under pressure

BUCKLER *v* -ED, -ING, -S to shield

BUCKO *n* pl. BUCKOES a bully

BUCKRAM *v* -ED, -ING, -S to stiffen

BUCKSAW *n* pl. -S a wood-cutting saw

BUCKSHEE *n* pl. -S something extra obtained free

BUCKSHOT *n* pl. -S a large lead shot

BUCKSKIN *n* pl. -S the skin of a male deer

BUCKTAIL *n* pl. -S a fishing lure

BUCOLIC *n* pl. -S a pastoral poem

BUD *v* BUDDED, BUDDING, BUDS to put forth buds (undeveloped plant parts)

BUDDER *n* pl. -S one that buds

BUDDIED past tense of buddy

BUDDIES present 3d person sing. of buddy

BUDDING *n* pl. -S a type of asexual reproduction

BUDDLE *n* pl. -S an apparatus on which crushed ore is washed

BUDDLEIA *n* pl. -S a tropical shrub

BUDDY *v* -DIED, -DYING, -DIES to become close friends

BUDGE *v* BUDGED, BUDGING, BUDGES to move slightly

BUDGER *n* pl. -S one that budges

BUDGET *v* -ED, -ING, -S to estimate expenditures

BUDGETER *n* pl. -S one that budgets

BUDGIE *n* pl. -S a small parrot

BUDGING present participle of budge

BUDLESS *adj* being without buds

BUDLIKE *adj* resembling a bud

BUDWORM *n* pl. -S a caterpillar that eats buds

BUFF *v* -ED, -ING, -S to polish **BUFFABLE** *adj*

BUFFALO *n* pl. -LOES or -LOS an ox-like animal

BUFFALO *v* -ED, -ING, -ES to intimidate

BUFFER *v* -ED, -ING, -S to cushion

BUFFET *v* -ED, -ING, -S to hit sharply

BUFFETER *n* pl. -S one that buffets

BUFFI a pl. of buffo

BUFFIER comparative of buffy

BUFFIEST superlative of buffy

BUFFO *n* pl. -FI or -FOS an operatic clown

BUFFOON *n* pl. -S a clown

BUFFY *adj* BUFFIER, BUFFIEST of a yellowish-brown color

BUG *v* BUGGED, BUGGING, BUGS to annoy

BUGABOO *n* pl. -BOOS a bugbear

BUGBANE *n* pl. -S a perennial herb

BUGBEAR *n* pl. -S an object or source of dread

BUGEYE *n* pl. -S a small boat

BUGGED past tense of bug

BUGGER *v* -ED, -ING, -S to damn

BUGGERY *n* pl. -GERIES sodomy

BUGGING present participle of bug

BUGGY *n* pl. -GIES a light carriage

BUGGY *adj* -GIER, -GIEST infested with bugs

BUGHOUSE *n* pl. -S an insane asylum

BUGLE	*v* -GLED, -GLING, -GLES to play a bugle (a brass wind instrument)
BUGLER	*n* pl. -S one that plays a bugle
BUGLOSS	*n* pl. -ES a coarse plant
BUGSEED	*n* pl. -S an annual herb
BUGSHA	*n* pl. -S buqsha
BUHL	*n* pl. -S a style of furniture decoration
BUHLWORK	*n* pl. -S buhl
BUHR	*n* pl. -S a heavy stone
BUILD	*v* BUILT or BUILDED, BUILDING, BUILDS to construct
BUILDER	*n* pl. -S one that builds
BUILDING	*n* pl. -S something that is built
BUILDUP	*n* pl. -S an accumulation
BUILT	a past tense of build
BUIRDLY	*adj* burly
BULB	*n* pl. -S an underground bud **BULBAR, BULBED** *adj*
BULBEL	*n* pl. -S bulbil
BULBIL	*n* pl. -S a small bulb
BULBLET	*n* pl. -S a small bulb
BULBOUS	*adj* bulb-shaped; bulging
BULBUL	*n* pl. -S a songbird
BULGE	*v* BULGED, BULGING, BULGES to swell out
BULGER	*n* pl. -S a golf club
BULGUR	*n* pl. -S crushed wheat
BULGY	*adj* BULGIER, BULGIEST bulging
BULIMIA	*n* pl. -S insatiable appetite **BULIMIAC** *adj*
BULIMIC	*n* pl. -S one who is affected with bulimia
BULK	*v* -ED, -ING, -S to gather into a mass
BULKAGE	*n* pl. -S a peristaltic stimulant
BULKHEAD	*n* pl. -S a partition in a ship
BULKY	*adj* BULKIER, BULKIEST massive **BULKILY** *adv*
BULL	*v* -ED, -ING, -S to push ahead
BULLA	*n* pl. -LAE a large blister
BULLACE	*n* pl. -S a purple plum
BULLATE	*adj* blistered in appearance
BULLBAT	*n* pl. -S a nocturnal bird
BULLDOG	*v* -DOGGED, -DOGGING, -DOGS to throw a steer
BULLDOZE	*v* -DOZED, -DOZING, -DOZES to bully
BULLET	*v* -ED, -ING, -S to move swiftly
BULLETIN	*v* -ED, -ING, -S to issue a news item
BULLFROG	*n* pl. -S a large frog
BULLHEAD	*n* pl. -S a freshwater catfish
BULLHORN	*n* pl. -S an electric megaphone
BULLIED	past tense of bully
BULLIER	comparative of bully
BULLIES	present 3d person sing. of bully
BULLIEST	superlative of bully
BULLION	*n* pl. -S uncoined gold or silver
BULLISH	*adj* stubborn
BULLNECK	*n* pl. -S a thick neck
BULLNOSE	*n* pl. -S a disease of swine
BULLOCK	*n* pl. -S a castrated bull **BULLOCKY** *adj*
BULLOUS	*adj* resembling bullae
BULLPEN	*n* pl. -S an enclosure for bulls
BULLPOUT	*n* pl. -S a bullhead
BULLRING	*n* pl. -S a bullfight arena
BULLRUSH	*n* pl. -ES bulrush
BULLSHOT	*n* pl. -S a drink made of vodka and bouillon
BULLWEED	*n* pl. -S knapweed
BULLWHIP	*v* -WHIPPED, -WHIPPING, -WHIPS to strike with a long whip
BULLY	*v* -LIED, -LYING, -LIES to treat abusively
BULLY	*adj* -LIER, -LIEST wonderful
BULLYBOY	*n* pl. -BOYS a ruffian
BULLYRAG	*v* -RAGGED, -RAGGING, -RAGS to bully
BULRUSH	*n* pl. -ES a tall marsh plant
BULWARK	*v* -ED, -ING, -S to fortify with a defensive wall
BUM	*v* BUMMED, BUMMING, BUMS to live idly
BUM	*adj* BUMMER, BUMMEST of little value; worthless
BUMBLE	*v* -BLED, -BLING, -BLES to bungle
BUMBLER	*n* pl. -S one that bumbles
BUMBLING	*n* pl. -S an instance of clumsiness
BUMBOAT	*n* pl. -S a boat used to peddle wares to larger ships

BUMF	*n* pl. -S paperwork
BUMKIN	*n* pl. -S a ship's spar
BUMMED	past tense of bum
BUMMER	*n* pl. -S one that bums
BUMMEST	superlative of bum
BUMMING	present participle of bum
BUMP	*v* -ED, -ING, -S to knock against
BUMPER	*v* -ED, -ING, -S to fill to the brim
BUMPH	*n* pl. -S bumf
BUMPKIN	*n* pl. -S an unsophisticated rustic
BUMPY	*adj* BUMPIER, BUMPIEST of uneven surface **BUMPILY** *adv*
BUN	*n* pl. -S a small bread roll
BUNCH	*v* -ED, -ING, -ES to group together
BUNCHY	*adj* BUNCHIER, BUNCHIEST clustered **BUNCHILY** *adv*
BUNCO	*v* -ED, -ING, -S to swindle
BUNCOMBE	*n* pl. -S nonsense
BUND	*n* pl. -S a political association
BUNDIST	*n* pl. -S a member of a bund
BUNDLE	*v* -DLED, -DLING, -DLES to fasten a group of objects together
BUNDLER	*n* pl. -S one that bundles
BUNDLING	*n* pl. -S a former courtship custom
BUNDT	*n* pl. -S a type of cake pan
BUNG	*v* -ED, -ING, -S to plug with a cork or stopper
BUNGALOW	*n* pl. -S a small cottage
BUNGEE	*n* pl. -S an elasticized cord
BUNGHOLE	*n* pl. -S a hole in a keg or barrel
BUNGLE	*v* -GLED, -GLING, -GLES to work, make, or do clumsily
BUNGLER	*n* pl. -S one that bungles
BUNGLING	*n* pl. -S something done clumsily
BUNION	*n* pl. -S a painful swelling of the foot
BUNK	*v* -ED, -ING, -S to go to bed
BUNKER	*v* -ED, -ING, -S to store in a large bin
BUNKMATE	*n* pl. -S a person with whom sleeping quarters are shared
BUNKO	*v* -ED, -ING, -S to bunco
BUNKUM	*n* pl. -S nonsense
BUNN	*n* pl. -S bun
BUNNY	*n* pl. -NIES a rabbit
BUNRAKU	*n* pl. -S a Japanese puppet show
BUNT	*v* -ED, -ING, -S to butt
BUNTER	*n* pl. -S one that bunts
BUNTING	*n* pl. -S a fabric used for flags
BUNTLINE	*n* pl. -S a rope used to haul up a sail
BUNYA	*n* pl. -S an evergreen tree
BUOY	*v* -ED, -ING, -S to mark with a buoy (a warning float)
BUOYAGE	*n* pl. -S a group of buoys
BUOYANCE	*n* pl. -S buoyancy
BUOYANCY	*n* pl. -CIES the tendency to float
BUOYANT	*adj* having buoyancy
BUPPIE	*n* pl. -S a black professional person working in a city
BUQSHA	*n* pl. -S a monetary unit of Yemen
BUR	*v* BURRED, BURRING, BURS to burr
BURA	*n* pl. -S buran
BURAN	*n* pl. -S a violent windstorm
BURBLE	*v* -BLED, -BLING, -BLES to speak quickly and excitedly
BURBLER	*n* pl. -S one that burbles
BURBLY	*adj* -BLIER, -BLIEST burbling
BURBOT	*n* pl. -S a freshwater fish
BURBS	*n/pl* the suburbs
BURD	*n* pl. -S a maiden
BURDEN	*v* -ED, -ING, -S to load heavily
BURDENER	*n* pl. -S one that burdens
BURDIE	*n* pl. -S burd
BURDOCK	*n* pl. -S a coarse weed
BUREAU	*n* pl. -REAUS or -REAUX a chest of drawers
BURET	*n* pl. -S burette
BURETTE	*n* pl. -S a measuring tube
BURG	*n* pl. -S a city or town
BURGAGE	*n* pl. -S a feudal tenure
BURGEE	*n* pl. -S a small flag
BURGEON	*v* -ED, -ING, -S to develop rapidly
BURGER	*n* pl. -S a hamburger
BURGESS	*n* pl. -ES a citizen of an English borough
BURGH	*n* pl. -S a Scottish borough **BURGHAL** *adj*
BURGHER	*n* pl. -S a citizen of a borough
BURGLAR	*n* pl. -S one who commits burglary
BURGLARY	*n* pl. -GLARIES a felonious theft

BURGLE	v -GLED, -GLING, -GLES to commit burglary
BURGONET	n pl. -S an open helmet
BURGOO	n pl. -GOOS a thick oatmeal
BURGOUT	n pl. -S burgoo
BURGRAVE	n pl. -S a German nobleman
BURGUNDY	n pl. -DIES a red wine
BURIAL	n pl. -S the act of burying
BURIED	past tense of bury
BURIER	n pl. -S one that buries
BURIES	present 3d person sing. of bury
BURIN	n pl. -S an engraving tool
BURKE	v BURKED, BURKING, BURKES to murder by suffocation
BURKER	n pl. -S one that burkes
BURKITE	n pl. -S a burker
BURL	v -ED, -ING, -S to finish cloth by removing lumps
BURLAP	n pl. -S a coarse fabric
BURLER	n pl. -S one that burls
BURLESK	n pl. -S a type of stage show
BURLEY	n pl. -LEYS a light tobacco
BURLY	adj -LIER, -LIEST heavy and muscular **BURLILY** adv
BURN	v BURNED or BURNT, BURNING, BURNS to destroy by fire
BURNABLE	n pl. -S something that can be burned
BURNER	n pl. -S one that burns
BURNET	n pl. -S a perennial herb
BURNIE	n pl. -S a brooklet
BURNING	n pl. -S the firing of ceramic materials
BURNISH	v -ED, -ING, -ES to polish
BURNOOSE	n pl. -S a hooded cloak
BURNOUS	n pl. -ES burnoose
BURNOUT	n pl. -S a destructive fire
BURNT	a past tense of burn
BURP	v -ED, -ING, -S to belch
BURR	v -ED, -ING, -S to remove a rough edge from
BURRED	past tense of bur
BURRER	n pl. -S one that burrs
BURRIER	comparative of burry
BURRIEST	superlative of burry
BURRING	present participle of bur

BURRITO	n pl. -TOS a tortilla rolled around a filling
BURRO	n pl. -ROS a small donkey
BURROW	v -ED, -ING, -S to dig a hole or tunnel in the ground
BURROWER	n pl. -S one that burrows
BURRY	adj -RIER, -RIEST prickly
BURSA	n pl. -SAS or -SAE a bodily pouch **BURSAL** adj
BURSAR	n pl. -S a college treasurer
BURSARY	n pl. -RIES a college treasury
BURSATE	adj pertaining to a bursa
BURSE	n pl. -S a small bag or pouch
BURSEED	n pl. -S a coarse weed
BURSERA	adj designating a family of shrubs and trees
BURSITIS	n pl. -TISES inflammation of a bursa
BURST	v BURST or BURSTED, BURSTING, BURSTS to break open suddenly or violently
BURSTER	n pl. -S one that bursts
BURSTONE	n pl. -S a heavy stone
BURTHEN	v -ED, -ING, -S to burden
BURTON	n pl. -S a hoisting tackle
BURWEED	n pl. -S a coarse weed
BURY	v BURIED, BURYING, BURIES to put in the ground and cover with earth
BUS	v BUSED, BUSING, BUSES or BUSSED, BUSSING, BUSSES to transport by bus (a large motor vehicle)
BUSBAR	n pl. -S a type of electrical conductor
BUSBOY	n pl. -BOYS a waiter's assistant
BUSBY	n pl. -BIES a tall fur hat
BUSH	v -ED, -ING, -ES to cover with bushes (shrubs)
BUSHBUCK	n pl. -S a small antelope
BUSHEL	v -ELED, -ELING, -ELS or -ELLED, -ELLING, -ELS to mend clothing
BUSHELER	n pl. -S one that bushels
BUSHER	n pl. -S a minor league baseball player
BUSHFIRE	n pl. -S a fire in a wooded area
BUSHGOAT	n pl. -S a bushbuck
BUSHIDO	n pl. -DOS the code of the samurai

BUSHIER	comparative of bushy
BUSHIEST	superlative of bushy
BUSHILY	*adv* in a bushy manner
BUSHING	*n* pl. -S a lining for a hole
BUSHLAND	*n* pl. -S unsettled forest land
BUSHLESS	*adj* having no bushes
BUSHLIKE	*adj* resembling a bush
BUSHMAN	*n* pl. -MEN a woodsman
BUSHPIG	*n* pl. -S a wild African pig
BUSHTIT	*n* pl. -S a titmouse
BUSHWA	*n* pl. -S nonsense
BUSHWAH	*n* pl. -S bushwa
BUSHY	*adj* BUSHIER, BUSHIEST covered with bushes
BUSIED	past tense of busy
BUSIER	comparative of busy
BUSIES	present 3d person sing. of busy
BUSIEST	superlative of busy
BUSILY	*adv* in a busy manner
BUSINESS	*n* pl. -ES an occupation, profession, or trade
BUSING	*n* pl. -S the act of transporting by bus
BUSK	*v* -ED, -ING, -S to prepare
BUSKER	*n* pl. -S a roaming entertainer
BUSKIN	*n* pl. -S a high shoe **BUSKINED** *adj*
BUSLOAD	*n* pl. -S a load that fills a bus
BUSMAN	*n* pl. -MEN a bus operator
BUSS	*v* -ED, -ING, -ES to kiss
BUSSED	a past tense of bus
BUSSES	a present 3d person sing. of bus
BUSSING	*n* pl. -S busing
BUST	*v* -ED, -ING, -S to burst
BUSTARD	*n* pl. -S a game bird
BUSTER	*n* pl. -S one that breaks up something
BUSTIC	*n* pl. -S a tropical tree
BUSTIER	*n* pl. -S a woman's undergarment
BUSTLE	*v* -TLED, -TLING, -TLES to move energetically
BUSTLINE	*n* pl. -S the distance around the bust (the upper torso of a woman)
BUSTY	*adj* BUSTIER, BUSTIEST full-bosomed
BUSULFAN	*n* pl. -S a medicine
BUSY	*adj* BUSIER, BUSIEST occupied
BUSY	*v* BUSIED, BUSYING, BUSIES to make busy
BUSYBODY	*n* pl. -BODIES a nosy person
BUSYNESS	*n* pl. -ES the state of being busy
BUSYWORK	*n* pl. -S active but valueless work
BUT	*n* pl. -S a flatfish
BUTANE	*n* pl. -S a flammable gas
BUTANOL	*n* pl. -S a flammable alcohol
BUTANONE	*n* pl. -S a flammable ketone
BUTCH	*n* pl. -ES a lesbian with mannish traits
BUTCHER	*v* -ED, -ING, -S to slaughter
BUTCHERY	*n* pl. -ERIES wanton or cruel killing
BUTE	*n* pl. BUTE a pain-relieving drug
BUTENE	*n* pl. -S butylene
BUTEO	*n* pl. -TEOS a hawk
BUTLE	*v* -LED, -LING, -LES to serve as a butler
BUTLER	*n* pl. -S a male servant
BUTLERY	*n* pl. -LERIES a storage room
BUTLES	present 3d person sing. of butle
BUTLING	present participle of butle
BUTT	*v* -ED, -ING, -S to hit with the head
BUTTALS	*n/pl* boundary lines
BUTTE	*n* pl. -S an isolated hill
BUTTER	*v* -ED, -ING, -S to spread with butter (a milk product)
BUTTERY	*adj* -TERIER, -TERIEST containing butter
BUTTERY	*n* pl. -TERIES a wine cellar
BUTTIES	pl. of butty
BUTTOCK	*n* pl. -S either of the two rounded parts of the rump
BUTTON	*v* -ED, -ING, -S to fasten with a button (a small disk)
BUTTONER	*n* pl. -S one that buttons
BUTTONY	*adj* resembling a button
BUTTRESS	*v* -ED, -ING, -ES to prop up
BUTTY	*n* pl. -TIES a fellow workman
BUTUT	*n* pl. -S a monetary unit of Gambia
BUTYL	*n* pl. -S a hydrocarbon radical
BUTYLATE	*v* -ATED, -ATING, -ATES to add a butyl to
BUTYLENE	*n* pl. -S a gaseous hydrocarbon
BUTYRAL	*n* pl. -S a chemical compound

BUTYRATE	*n* pl. -S a chemical salt
BUTYRIC	*adj* derived from butter
BUTYRIN	*n* pl. -S a chemical compound
BUTYROUS	*adj* resembling butter
BUTYRYL	*n* pl. -S a radical of butyric acid
BUXOM	*adj* -OMER, -OMEST healthily plump **BUXOMLY** *adv*
BUY	*v* BOUGHT, BUYING, BUYS to purchase **BUYABLE** *adj*
BUYBACK	*n* pl. -S the repurchase by a corporation of its own stock
BUYER	*n* pl. -S one that buys
BUYOUT	*n* pl. -S the purchase of a business
BUZUKI	*n* pl. -KIA or -KIS bouzouki
BUZZ	*v* -ED, -ING, -ES to make a vibrating sound
BUZZARD	*n* pl. -S a large bird of prey
BUZZER	*n* pl. -S a signaling device
BUZZWIG	*n* pl. -S a large, thick wig
BUZZWORD	*n* pl. -S a word used to impress someone
BWANA	*n* pl. -S master; boss
BY	*n* pl. BYS a pass in certain card games
BYE	*n* pl. -S a side issue
BYELAW	*n* pl. -S bylaw
BYGONE	*n* pl. -S a past occurrence
BYLAW	*n* pl. -S a secondary law
BYLINE	*v* -LINED, -LINING, -LINES to write under a byline (a line giving the author's name)
BYLINER	*n* pl. -S one that writes under a byline
BYNAME	*n* pl. -S a secondary name
BYPASS	*v* -ED, -ING, -ES to avoid by going around
BYPAST	*adj* past; gone by
BYPATH	*n* pl. -S an indirect road
BYPLAY	*n* pl. -PLAYS secondary action
BYRE	*n* pl. -S a cowshed
BYRL	*v* -ED, -ING, -S to birle
BYRNIE	*n* pl. -S an armored shirt
BYROAD	*n* pl. -S a side road
BYSSUS	*n* pl. BYSSUSES or BYSSI a fine linen
BYSTREET	*n* pl. -S a side street
BYTALK	*n* pl. -S small talk
BYTE	*n* pl. -S a group of adjacent binary digits
BYWAY	*n* pl. -WAYS a side road
BYWORD	*n* pl. -S a well-known saying
BYWORK	*n* pl. -S work done during leisure time
BYZANT	*n* pl. -S bezant

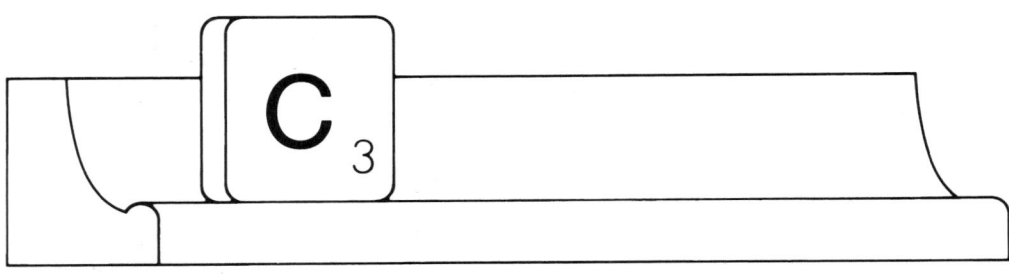

CAB	*v* CABBED, CABBING, CABS to take or drive a taxicab
CABAL	*v* -BALLED, -BALLING, -BALS to conspire
CABALA	*n* pl. -S an occult or secret doctrine
CABALISM	*n* pl. -S adherence to a cabala
CABALIST	*n* pl. -S one who practices cabalism
CABALLED	past tense of cabal
CABALLING	present participle of cabal
CABANA	*n* pl. -S a small cabin
CABARET	*n* pl. -S a music hall
CABBAGE	*v* -BAGED, -BAGING, -BAGES to steal
CABBALA	*n* pl. -S cabala
CABBALAH	*n* pl. -S cabala
CABBED	past tense of cab
CABBIE	*n* pl. -S cabby
CABBING	present participle of cab
CABBY	*n* pl. -BIES a driver of a cab
CABER	*n* pl. -S a heavy pole thrown as a trial of strength
CABERNET	*n* pl. -S a dry red wine
CABESTRO	*n* pl. -TROS a lasso
CABEZON	*n* pl. -S a large, edible fish
CABEZONE	*n* pl. -S cabezon
CABILDO	*n* pl. -DOS a town council
CABIN	*v* -ED, -ING, -S to live in a cabin (a roughly built house)
CABINET	*n* pl. -S a piece of furniture with shelves and drawers
CABLE	*v* -BLED, -BLING, -BLES to fasten with a cable (a heavy rope)
CABLET	*n* pl. -S a small cable
CABLEWAY	*n* pl. -WAYS a suspended cable
CABLING	present participle of cable
CABMAN	*n* pl. -MEN a driver of a cab
CABOB	*n* pl. -S kabob
CABOCHED	*adj* full-faced — used of an animal's head in heraldry
CABOCHON	*n* pl. -S a precious stone
CABOMBA	*n* pl. -S an aquatic plant
CABOODLE	*n* pl. -S a collection
CABOOSE	*n* pl. -S the last car of a freight train
CABOSHED	*adj* caboched
CABOTAGE	*n* pl. -S coastal trade
CABRESTA	*n* pl. -S cabestro
CABRESTO	*n* pl. -TOS cabestro
CABRETTA	*n* pl. -S a soft leather
CABRILLA	*n* pl. -S a sea bass
CABRIOLE	*n* pl. -S a curved furniture leg
CABSTAND	*n* pl. -S a place where cabs await hire
CACA	*n* pl. -S excrement
CACAO	*n* pl. -CAOS a tropical tree
CACHALOT	*n* pl. -S a large whale
CACHE	*v* CACHED, CACHING, CACHES to store in a hiding place
CACHEPOT	*n* pl. -S an ornamental container for a flowerpot
CACHET	*v* -ED, -ING, -S to print a design on an envelope
CACHEXIA	*n* pl. -S general ill health **CACHEXIC** *adj*
CACHEXY	*n* pl. -CHEXIES cachexia
CACHING	present participle of cache
CACHOU	*n* pl. -S catechu
CACHUCHA	*n* pl. -S a Spanish dance
CACIQUE	*n* pl. -S a tropical oriole
CACKLE	*v* -LED, -LING, -LES to make the sound of a hen
CACKLER	*n* pl. -S one that cackles

CACODYL	*n* pl. -S a poisonous liquid
CACOMIXL	*n* pl. -S a raccoon-like mammal
CACTUS	*n* pl. -TI or -TUSES a plant native to arid regions **CACTOID** *adj*
CAD	*n* pl. -S an ungentlemanly man
CADASTER	*n* pl. -S a public record of land ownership
CADASTRE	*n* pl. -S cadaster
CADAVER	*n* pl. -S a corpse
CADDICE	*n* pl. -S caddis
CADDIE	*v* -DIED, -DYING, -DIES to serve as a golfer's assistant
CADDIS	*n* pl. -DISES a coarse woolen fabric
CADDISH	*adj* resembling a cad
CADDY	*v* -DIED, -DYING, -DIES to caddie
CADE	*n* pl. -S a European shrub
CADELLE	*n* pl. -S a small, black beetle
CADENCE	*v* -DENCED, -DENCING, -DENCES to make rhythmic
CADENCY	*n* pl. -CIES a rhythm
CADENT	*adj* having rhythm
CADENZA	*n* pl. -S an elaborate musical passage
CADET	*n* pl. -S a student at a military school
CADGE	*v* CADGED, CADGING, CADGES to get by begging
CADGER	*n* pl. -S one that cadges
CADGY	*adj* cheerful
CADI	*n* pl. -S a Muslim judge
CADMIUM	*n* pl. -S a metallic element **CADMIC** *adj*
CADRE	*n* pl. -S a nucleus of trained personnel
CADUCEUS	*n* pl. -CEI a heraldic wand or staff **CADUCEAN** *adj*
CADUCITY	*n* pl. -TIES senility
CADUCOUS	*adj* transitory; perishable
CAECUM	*n* pl. -CA cecum **CAECAL** *adj* **CAECALLY** *adv*
CAEOMA	*n* pl. -S a spore-forming organ of a fungus
CAESAR	*n* pl. -S an emperor
CAESIUM	*n* pl. -S cesium
CAESTUS	*n* pl. -ES cestus
CAESURA	*n* pl. -RAS or -RAE a pause in a line of verse **CAESURAL, CAESURIC** *adj*
CAFE	*n* pl. -S a small restaurant
CAFF	*n* pl. -S a cafe
CAFFEIN	*n* pl. -S caffeine
CAFFEINE	*n* pl. -S a bitter alkaloid used as a stimulant
CAFTAN	*n* pl. -S a full-length tunic
CAGE	*v* CAGED, CAGING, CAGES to confine
CAGEFUL	*n* pl. -S the number held in a cage (an enclosure)
CAGELING	*n* pl. -S a caged bird
CAGER	*n* pl. -S a basketball player
CAGEY	*adj* CAGIER, CAGIEST shrewd
CAGIER	comparative of cagy
CAGIEST	superlative of cagy
CAGILY	*adv* in a cagey manner
CAGINESS	*n* pl. -ES the quality of being cagey
CAGING	present participle of cage
CAGY	*adj* CAGIER, CAGIEST cagey
CAHIER	*n* pl. -S a notebook
CAHOOT	*n* pl. -S partnership
CAHOW	*n* pl. -S a sea bird
CAID	*n* pl. -S a Muslim leader
CAIMAN	*n* pl. -S a tropical reptile
CAIN	*n* pl. -S kain
CAIQUE	*n* pl. -S a long, narrow rowboat
CAIRD	*n* pl. -S a gypsy
CAIRN	*n* pl. -S a mound of stones set up as a memorial **CAIRNED, CAIRNY** *adj*
CAISSON	*n* pl. -S a watertight chamber
CAITIFF	*n* pl. -S a despicable person
CAJAPUT	*n* pl. -S cajeput
CAJEPUT	*n* pl. -S an Australian tree
CAJOLE	*v* -JOLED, -JOLING, -JOLES to persuade by flattery
CAJOLER	*n* pl. -S one that cajoles
CAJOLERY	*n* pl. -ERIES persuasion by flattery
CAJOLING	present participle of cajole
CAJON	*n* pl. -ES a steep-sided canyon
CAJUPUT	*n* pl. -S cajeput
CAKE	*v* CAKED, CAKING, CAKES to form into a hardened mass

CAKEWALK *v* -ED, -ING, -S to step stylishly

CAKEY *adj* CAKIER, CAKIEST tending to form lumps

CAKY *adj* CAKIER, CAKIEST cakey

CALABASH *n* pl. -ES a gourd

CALADIUM *n* pl. -S a tropical plant

CALAMAR *n* pl. -S calamary

CALAMARI *n* pl. -S squid used as food

CALAMARY *n* pl. -MARIES a squid

CALAMI pl. of calamus

CALAMINE *v* -MINED, -MINING, -MINES to apply an ointment for skin ailments

CALAMINT *n* pl. -S a perennial herb

CALAMITE *n* pl. -S an extinct treelike plant

CALAMITY *n* pl. -TIES a grievous misfortune

CALAMUS *n* pl. -MI a marsh plant

CALANDO *adj* gradually diminishing

CALASH *n* pl. -ES a light carriage

CALATHOS *n* pl. -THI a fruit basket

CALATHUS *n* pl. -THI calathos

CALCANEA *n/pl* calcanei

CALCANEI *n/pl* bones of the heel

CALCAR *n* pl. -CARIA an anatomical projection

CALCAR *n* pl. -S a type of oven

CALCEATE *adj* wearing shoes

CALCES a pl. of calx

CALCIC *adj* pertaining to lime or calcium

CALCIFIC *adj* containing salts of calcium

CALCIFY *v* -FIED, -FYING, -FIES to harden

CALCINE *v* -CINED, -CINING, -CINES to reduce to a calx by heat

CALCITE *n* pl. -S a mineral **CALCITIC** *adj*

CALCIUM *n* pl. -S a metallic element

CALCSPAR *n* pl. -S a calcite

CALCTUFA *n* pl. -S a mineral deposit

CALCTUFF *n* pl. -S calctufa

CALCULUS *n* pl. -LI or -LUSES a branch of mathematics

CALDARIA *n/pl* rooms for taking hot baths

CALDERA *n* pl. -S a large crater

CALDRON *n* pl. -S a large kettle or boiler

CALECHE *n* pl. -S calash

CALENDAL *adj* pertaining to calends

CALENDAR *v* -ED, -ING, -S to schedule

CALENDER *v* -ED, -ING, -S to smooth by pressing between rollers

CALENDS *n* pl. CALENDS the first day of the Roman month

CALESA *n* pl. -S a calash

CALF *n* pl. CALVES or CALFS a young cow or bull **CALFLIKE** *adj*

CALFSKIN *n* pl. -S the skin of a calf

CALIBER *n* pl. -S the diameter of a gun barrel

CALIBRE *n* pl. -S caliber **CALIBRED** *adj*

CALICES pl. of calix

CALICHE *n* pl. -S a mineral deposit

CALICLE *n* pl. -S a cup-shaped, anatomical structure

CALICO *n* pl. -COES or -COS a cotton fabric

CALIF *n* pl. -S caliph

CALIFATE *n* pl. -S the domain of a calif

CALIPASH *n* pl. -ES an edible part of a turtle

CALIPEE *n* pl. -S an edible part of a turtle

CALIPER *v* -ED, -ING, -S to use a type of measuring device

CALIPH *n* pl. -S a Muslim leader **CALIPHAL** *adj*

CALISAYA *n* pl. -S the medicinal bark of the cinchona

CALIX *n* pl. -LICES a cup

CALK *v* -ED, -ING, -S to caulk

CALKER *n* pl. -S one that calks

CALKIN *n* pl. -S a gripping projection on a horseshoe

CALL *v* -ED, -ING, -S to summon **CALLABLE** *adj*

CALLA *n* pl. -S a tropical plant

CALLALOO *n* pl. -LOOS a crabmeat soup

CALLAN *n* pl. -S callant

CALLANT *n* pl. -S a lad

CALLBACK *n* pl. -S a recall of a defective product

CALLBOY *n* pl. -BOYS a bellboy

CALLER *n* pl. -S one that calls

CALLET *n* pl. -S a prostitute

CALLING *n* pl. -S a vocation or profession

CALLIOPE *n* pl. -S a keyboard musical instrument

CALLIPEE *n* pl. -S calipee

CALLIPER	*v* -ED, -ING, -S to caliper
CALLOSE	*n* pl. -S a part of a plant cell wall
CALLOUS	*v* -ED, -ING, -ES to make or become hard
CALLOW	*adj* -LOWER, -LOWEST immature
CALLUS	*v* -ED, -ING, -ES to form a hard growth
CALM	*adj* CALMER, CALMEST free from agitation **CALMLY** *adv*
CALM	*v* -ED, -ING, -S to make calm
CALMNESS	*n* pl. -ES the state of being calm
CALO	*n* pl. CALO a Spanish argot used by Chicano youths
CALOMEL	*n* pl. -S a chemical compound used as a purgative
CALORIC	*n* pl. -S heat
CALORIE	*n* pl. -S a unit of heat
CALORIZE	*v* -RIZED, -RIZING, -RIZES to coat steel with aluminum
CALORY	*n* pl. -RIES calorie
CALOTTE	*n* pl. -S a skullcap
CALOTYPE	*n* pl. -S a kind of photograph
CALOYER	*n* pl. -S a monk of the Eastern Church
CALPAC	*n* pl. -S a sheepskin hat
CALPACK	*n* pl. -S calpac
CALQUE	*v* CALQUED, CALQUING, CALQUES to model a word's meaning upon that of an analogous word in another language
CALTHROP	*n* pl. -S caltrop
CALTRAP	*n* pl. -S caltrop
CALTROP	*n* pl. -S a spiny plant
CALUMET	*n* pl. -S a ceremonial pipe
CALUMNY	*n* pl. -NIES a false and malicious accusation
CALUTRON	*n* pl. -S a device used for separating isotopes
CALVADOS	*n* pl. -ES a dry apple brandy
CALVARIA	*n* pl. -S the dome of the skull
CALVARY	*n* pl. -RIES a representation of the Crucifixion
CALVE	*v* CALVED, CALVING, CALVES to give birth to a calf
CALVES	a pl. of calf
CALX	*n* pl. -ES or CALCES a mineral residue
CALYCATE	*adj* calycine
CALYCEAL	*adj* calycine
CALYCES	a pl. of calyx
CALYCINE	*adj* pertaining to a calyx
CALYCLE	*n* pl. -S an outer calyx
CALYCULI	*n/pl* small, cup-shaped structures
CALYPSO	*n* pl. -SOS or -SOES an improvised song
CALYPTER	*n* pl. -S calyptra
CALYPTRA	*n* pl. -S a hood-shaped organ of flowers
CALYX	*n* pl. -LYXES or -LYCES the outer protective covering of a flower
CALZONE	*n* pl. -S a turnover with a savory filling
CAM	*n* pl. -S a rotating or sliding piece of machinery
CAMAIL	*n* pl. -S a piece of armor for the neck **CAMAILED** *adj*
CAMAS	*n* pl. -ES camass
CAMASS	*n* pl. -ES a perennial herb
CAMBER	*v* -ED, -ING, -S to arch slightly
CAMBIA	a pl. of cambium
CAMBIAL	*adj* pertaining to cambium
CAMBISM	*n* pl. -S the theory and practice of exchange in commerce
CAMBIST	*n* pl. -S a dealer in bills of exchange
CAMBIUM	*n* pl. -BIUMS or -BIA a layer of plant tissue
CAMBOGIA	*n* pl. -S a gum resin
CAMBRIC	*n* pl. -S a fine linen
CAME	*n* pl. -S a leaden window rod
CAMEL	*n* pl. -S a large, humped mammal
CAMELEER	*n* pl. -S a camel driver
CAMELIA	*n* pl. -S camellia
CAMELLIA	*n* pl. -S a tropical shrub
CAMEO	*v* -ED, -ING, -S to portray in sharp, delicate relief
CAMERA	*n* pl. -ERAS or -ERAE a judge's chamber **CAMERAL** *adj*
CAMION	*n* pl. -S a military truck
CAMISA	*n* pl. -S a shirt or chemise
CAMISADE	*n* pl. -S camisado
CAMISADO	*n* pl. -DOS or -DOES an attack made at night
CAMISE	*n* pl. -S a loose shirt or gown
CAMISIA	*n* pl. -S camise

CAMISOLE *n* pl. -S a brief negligee

CAMLET *n* pl. -S a durable fabric

CAMOMILE *n* pl. -S a medicinal herb

CAMORRA *n* pl. -S an unscrupulous secret society

CAMP *v* -ED, -ING, -S to live in the open

CAMPAGNA *n* pl. -PAGNE a flat, open plain

CAMPAIGN *v* -ED, -ING, -S to conduct a series of operations to reach a specific goal

CAMPER *n* pl. -S one that camps

CAMPFIRE *n* pl. -S an outdoor fire

CAMPHENE *n* pl. -S camphine

CAMPHINE *n* pl. -S an explosive liquid

CAMPHIRE *n* pl. -S a flowering plant

CAMPHOL *n* pl. -S borneol

CAMPHOR *n* pl. -S a volatile compound

CAMPI pl. of campo

CAMPIER comparative of campy

CAMPIEST superlative of campy

CAMPILY *adv* in a campy manner

CAMPING *n* pl. -S the act of living outdoors

CAMPION *n* pl. -S an herb

CAMPO *n* pl. -PI an open space in a town

CAMPO *n* pl. -POS a level, grassy plain

CAMPONG *n* pl. -S kampong

CAMPOREE *n* pl. -S a gathering of Boy Scouts

CAMPSITE *n* pl. -S an area suitable for camping

CAMPUS *v* -ED, -ING, -ES to restrict a student to the school grounds

CAMPY *adj* CAMPIER, CAMPIEST comically exaggerated

CAMSHAFT *n* pl. -S a shaft fitted with cams

CAN *v* CANNED, CANNING, CANS to put in a can (a cylindrical container)

CAN *v* present sing. 2d person CAN or CANST, past sing. 2d person COULD, COULDEST, or COULDST — used as an auxiliary to express ability

CANAILLE *n* pl. -S the common people

CANAKIN *n* pl. -S cannikin

CANAL *v* -NALLED, -NALLING, -NALS or -NALED, -NALING, -NALS to dig an artificial waterway through

CANALISE *v* -ISED, -ISING, -ISES to canalize

CANALIZE *v* -IZED, -IZING, -IZES to canal

CANALLED a past tense of canal

CANALLER *n* pl. -S a freight boat

CANALLING a present participle of canal

CANAPE *n* pl. -S a food served before a meal

CANARD *n* pl. -S a false story

CANARY *n* pl. -NARIES a songbird

CANASTA *n* pl. -S a card game

CANCAN *n* pl. -S a dance marked by high kicking

CANCEL *v* -CELED, -CELING, -CELS or -CELLED, -CELLING, -CELS to annul

CANCELER *n* pl. -S one that cancels

CANCER *n* pl. -S a malignant growth

CANCHA *n* pl. -S a jai alai court

CANCROID *n* pl. -S a skin cancer

CANDELA *n* pl. -S a unit of light intensity

CANDENT *adj* glowing

CANDID *adj* -DIDER, -DIDEST frank and sincere

CANDID *n* pl. -S an unposed photograph

CANDIDA *n* pl. -S a parasitic fungus

CANDIDLY *adv* in a candid manner

CANDIED past tense of candy

CANDIES present 3d person sing. of candy

CANDLE *v* -DLED, -DLING, -DLES to examine eggs in front of a light

CANDLER *n* pl. -S one that candles

CANDOR *n* pl. -S frankness; sincerity

CANDOUR *n* pl. -S candor

CANDY *v* -DIED, -DYING, -DIES to coat with sugar

CANE *v* CANED, CANING, CANES to weave or furnish with cane (hollow woody stems)

CANELLA *n* pl. -S a medicinal tree bark

CANEPHOR *n* pl. -S a Greek maiden bearing a basket on her head

CANER *n* pl. -S one that canes

CANEWARE *n* pl. -S a yellowish stoneware

CANFIELD *n* pl. -S a card game

CANFUL *n* pl. CANFULS or CANSFUL as much as a can holds

CANGUE   *n* pl. -S an ancient Chinese punishing device

CANID   *n* pl. -S a dog

CANIKIN   *n* pl. -S cannikin

CANINE   *n* pl. -S a dog

CANING   present participle of cane

CANINITY   *n* pl. -TIES the state of being a canine

CANISTER   *n* pl. -S a small, metal box

CANITIES   *n* pl. CANITIES the turning gray of the hair

CANKER   *v* -ED, -ING, -S to affect with ulcerous sores

CANNA   *n* pl. -S a tropical plant

CANNABIC   *adj* pertaining to cannabis

CANNABIN   *n* pl. -S a resin extracted from cannabis

CANNABIS   *n* pl. -BISES hemp

CANNED   past tense of can

CANNEL   *n* pl. -S an oily, compact coal

CANNELON   *n* pl. -S a stuffed roll

CANNER   *n* pl. -S one that cans food

CANNERY   *n* pl. -NERIES a place where food is canned

CANNIBAL   *n* pl. -S one who eats his own kind

CANNIE   *adj* -NIER, -NIEST canny

CANNIER   comparative of canny

CANNIEST   superlative of canny

CANNIKIN   *n* pl. -S a small can or cup

CANNILY   *adv* in a canny manner

CANNING   *n* pl. -S the business of preserving food in airtight containers

CANNOLI   *n/pl* a tube of pastry

CANNON   *v* -ED, -ING, -S to fire a cannon (a heavy firearm)

CANNONRY   *n* pl. -RIES artillery

CANNOT   the negative form of can

CANNULA   *n* pl. -LAS or -LAE a tube inserted into a bodily cavity **CANNULAR** *adj*

CANNY   *adj* -NIER, -NIEST prudent

CANOE   *v* -NOED, -NOEING, -NOES to paddle a canoe (a light, slender boat)

CANOEIST   *n* pl. -S one who canoes

CANOLA   *n* pl. CANOLA an oil from the seeds of a kind of herb

CANON   *n* pl. -S a law decreed by a church council **CANONIC** *adj*

CANONESS   *n* pl. -ES a woman who lives according to a canon

CANONISE   *v* -ISED, -ISING, -ISES to canonize

CANONIST   *n* pl. -S a specialist in canon law

CANONIZE   *v* -IZED, -IZING, -IZES to declare to be a saint

CANONRY   *n* pl. -RIES a clerical office

CANOODLE   *v* -DLED, -DLING, -DLES to caress

CANOPY   *v* -PIED, -PYING, -PIES to cover from above

CANOROUS   *adj* melodic

CANSFUL   a pl. of canful

CANSO   *n* pl. -SOS a love song

CANST   a present 2d person sing. of can

CANT   *v* -ED, -ING, -S to tilt or slant

CANTALA   *n* pl. -S a tropical plant

CANTATA   *n* pl. -S a vocal composition

CANTDOG   *n* pl. -S a device used to move logs

CANTEEN   *n* pl. -S a small container for carrying water

CANTER   *v* -ED, -ING, -S to ride a horse at a moderate pace

CANTHUS   *n* pl. -THI a corner of the eye **CANTHAL** *adj*

CANTIC   *adj* slanted

CANTICLE   *n* pl. -S a hymn

CANTINA   *n* pl. -S a saloon

CANTLE   *n* pl. -S the rear part of a saddle

CANTO   *n* pl. -TOS a division of a long poem

CANTON   *v* -ED, -ING, -S to divide into cantons (districts)

CANTONAL   *adj* pertaining to a canton

CANTOR   *n* pl. -S a religious singer

CANTRAIP   *n* pl. -S cantrip

CANTRAP   *n* pl. -S cantrip

CANTRIP   *n* pl. -S a magic spell

CANTUS   *n* pl. CANTUS a style of church music

CANTY   *adj* cheerful

CANULA   *n* pl. -LAS or -LAE cannula

CANULATE   *v* -LATED, -LATING, -LATES to insert a canula into

CANVAS   *v* -ED, -ING, -ES to canvass

CANVASER *n* pl. -S one that canvases

CANVASS *v* -ED, -ING, -ES to examine thoroughly

CANYON *n* pl. -S a deep valley with steep sides

CANZONA *n* pl. -S canzone

CANZONE *n* pl. -NI or -NES a form of lyric poetry

CANZONET *n* pl. -S a short song

CAP *v* CAPPED, CAPPING, CAPS to provide with a cap (a type of head covering)

CAPABLE *adj* -BLER, -BLEST having ability **CAPABLY** *adv*

CAPACITY *n* pl. -TIES the ability to receive or contain

CAPE *n* pl. -S a sleeveless garment **CAPED** *adj*

CAPELAN *n* pl. -S capelin

CAPELET *n* pl. -S a small cape

CAPELIN *n* pl. -S a small, edible fish

CAPER *v* -ED, -ING, -S to frolic

CAPERER *n* pl. -S one that capers

CAPESKIN *n* pl. -S a soft leather

CAPEWORK *n* pl. -S a bullfighting technique

CAPFUL *n* pl. -S as much as a cap can hold

CAPH *n* pl. -S kaph

CAPIAS *n* pl. -ES a judicial writ

CAPITA pl. of caput

CAPITAL *n* pl. -S the upper part of a column

CAPITATE *adj* head-shaped

CAPITOL *n* pl. -S a building occupied by a state legislature

CAPITULA *n/pl* flower clusters

CAPLESS *adj* being without a cap

CAPLET *n* pl. -S a coated tablet

CAPLIN *n* pl. -S capelin

CAPMAKER *n* pl. -S one that makes caps

CAPO *n* pl. -POS a pitch-raising device for fretted instruments

CAPON *n* pl. -S a gelded rooster

CAPONATA *n* pl. -S a relish made with eggplant

CAPONIER *n* pl. -S a type of defense

CAPONIZE *v* -IZED, -IZING, -IZES to geld a rooster

CAPORAL *n* pl. -S a coarse tobacco

CAPOTE *n* pl. -S a hooded cloak or overcoat

CAPOUCH *n* pl. -ES capuche

CAPPED past tense of cap

CAPPER *n* pl. -S a capmaker

CAPPING *n* pl. -S a wax covering in a honeycomb

CAPRIC *adj* pertaining to a goat

CAPRICCI *n/pl* caprices

CAPRICE *n* pl. -S a whim

CAPRIFIG *n* pl. -S a European tree

CAPRINE *adj* capric

CAPRIOLE *v* -OLED, -OLING, -OLES to leap

CAPRIS *n/pl* pants for women

CAPROCK *n* pl. -S an overlying rock layer

CAPSICIN *n* pl. -S a liquid used as a flavoring

CAPSICUM *n* pl. -S a tropical herb

CAPSID *n* pl. -S the outer shell of a virus particle **CAPSIDAL** *adj*

CAPSIZE *v* -SIZED, -SIZING, -SIZES to overturn

CAPSOMER *n* pl. -S a protein forming the capsid

CAPSTAN *n* pl. -S a machine used to hoist weights

CAPSTONE *n* pl. -S the top stone of a structure

CAPSULAR *adj* enclosed and compact

CAPSULE *v* -SULED, -SULING, -SULES to condense into a brief form

CAPTAIN *v* -ED, -ING, -S to lead or command

CAPTAN *n* pl. -S a fungicide

CAPTION *v* -ED, -ING, -S to provide with a title

CAPTIOUS *adj* tending to find fault

CAPTIVE *n* pl. -S a prisoner

CAPTOR *n* pl. -S one who takes or holds a captive

CAPTURE *v* -TURED, -TURING, -TURES to take by force or cunning

CAPTURER *n* pl. -S one that captures

CAPUCHE *n* pl. -S a hood or cowl **CAPUCHED** *adj*

CAPUCHIN *n* pl. -S a long-tailed monkey

CAPUT *n* pl. CAPITA a head or head-like part

CAPYBARA *n* pl. -S a large rodent

CAR	*n* pl. -S an automobile
CARABAO	*n* pl. -BAOS a water buffalo
CARABID	*n* pl. -S a predatory beetle
CARABIN	*n* pl. -S carbine
CARABINE	*n* pl. -S carbine
CARACAL	*n* pl. -S an African lynx
CARACARA	*n* pl. -S a large hawk
CARACK	*n* pl. -S carrack
CARACOL	*v* -COLLED, -COLLING, -COLS to caracole
CARACOLE	*v* -COLED, -COLING, -COLES to perform a half turn on a horse
CARACUL	*n* pl. -S karakul
CARAFE	*n* pl. -S a glass bottle
CARAGANA	*n* pl. -S an Asian shrub
CARAGEEN	*n* pl. -S an edible seaweed
CARAMBA	*interj* — used to express surprise or dismay
CARAMEL	*n* pl. -S a chewy candy
CARANGID	*n* pl. -S a marine fish
CARAPACE	*n* pl. -S a hard, protective outer covering
CARAPAX	*n* pl. -ES carapace
CARASSOW	*n* pl. -S curassow
CARAT	*n* pl. -S a unit of weight for gems
CARATE	*n* pl. -S a tropical skin disease
CARAVAN	*v* -VANED, -VANING, -VANS or -VANNED, -VANNING, -VANS to travel in a group
CARAVEL	*n* pl. -S a small sailing ship
CARAWAY	*n* pl. -WAYS an herb used in cooking
CARB	*n* pl. -S a carburetor
CARBAMIC	*adj* pertaining to a type of acid
CARBAMYL	*n* pl. -S a chemical radical
CARBARN	*n* pl. -S a garage for buses
CARBARYL	*n* pl. -S an insecticide
CARBIDE	*n* pl. -S a carbon compound
CARBINE	*n* pl. -S a light rifle
CARBINOL	*n* pl. -S an alcohol
CARBO	*n* pl. -S a carbohydrate
CARBOLIC	*n* pl. -S an acidic compound
CARBON	*n* pl. -S a nonmetallic element **CARBONIC** *adj*
CARBONYL	*n* pl. -S a chemical compound
CARBORA	*n* pl. -S a wood-boring worm
CARBOXYL	*n* pl. -S a univalent acid radical
CARBOY	*n* pl. -BOYS a large bottle **CARBOYED** *adj*
CARBURET	*v* -RETED, -RETING, -RETS or -RETTED, -RETTING, -RETS to combine chemically with carbon
CARCAJOU	*n* pl. -S a carnivorous mammal
CARCANET	*n* pl. -S a jeweled necklace
CARCASE	*n* pl. -S carcass
CARCASS	*n* pl. -ES the body of a dead animal
CARCEL	*n* pl. -S a unit of illumination
CARD	*v* -ED, -ING, -S to provide with a card (a stiff piece of paper)
CARDAMOM	*n* pl. -S a tropical herb
CARDAMON	*n* pl. -S cardamom
CARDAMUM	*n* pl. -S cardamom
CARDCASE	*n* pl. -S a case for holding cards
CARDER	*n* pl. -S one that does carding
CARDIA	*n* pl. -DIAS or -DIAE an opening of the esophagus
CARDIAC	*n* pl. -S a person with a heart disorder
CARDIGAN	*n* pl. -S a type of sweater
CARDINAL	*n* pl. -S a bright red bird
CARDING	*n* pl. -S the process of combing and cleaning cotton fibers; cleaned and combed fibers
CARDIOID	*n* pl. -S a heart-shaped curve
CARDITIS	*n* pl. -TISES inflammation of the heart **CARDITIC** *adj*
CARDOON	*n* pl. -S a perennial plant
CARE	*v* CARED, CARING, CARES to be concerned or interested
CAREEN	*v* -ED, -ING, -S to lurch while moving
CAREENER	*n* pl. -S one that careens
CAREER	*v* -ED, -ING, -S to go at full speed
CAREERER	*n* pl. -S one that careers
CAREFREE	*adj* being without worry or anxiety
CAREFUL	*adj* -FULLER, -FULLEST cautious
CARELESS	*adj* inattentive; negligent
CARER	*n* pl. -S one that cares
CARESS	*v* -ED, -ING, -ES to touch lovingly
CARESSER	*n* pl. -S one that caresses
CARET	*n* pl. -S a proofreaders' symbol

CARETAKE *v* -TOOK, -TAKEN, -TAKING, -TAKES to take care of someone else's house or land

CAREWORN *adj* haggard

CAREX *n* pl. CARICES a marsh plant

CARFARE *n* pl. -S payment for a bus or car ride

CARFUL *n* pl. -S as much as a car can hold

CARGO *n* pl. -GOS or -GOES conveyed merchandise

CARHOP *n* pl. -S a waitress at a drive-in restaurant

CARIBE *n* pl. -S the piranha

CARIBOU *n* pl. -S a large deer

CARICES pl. of carex

CARIES *n* pl. CARIES tooth decay **CARIED** *adj*

CARILLON *v* -LONNED, -LONNING, -LONS to play a set of bells

CARINA *n* pl. -NAS or -NAE a carinate anatomical part **CARINAL** *adj*

CARINATE *adj* shaped like the keel of a ship

CARING present participle of care

CARIOCA *n* pl. -S a South American dance

CARIOLE *n* pl. -S a small, open carriage

CARIOUS *adj* decayed

CARITAS *n* pl. -ES love for all people

CARK *v* -ED, -ING, -S to worry

CARL *n* pl. -S a peasant

CARLE *n* pl. -S carl

CARLESS *adj* being without a car

CARLIN *n* pl. -S an old woman

CARLINE *n* pl. -S carling

CARLING *n* pl. -S a beam supporting a ship's deck

CARLISH *adj* resembling a carl

CARLOAD *n* pl. -S as much as a car can hold

CARMAKER *n* pl. -S an automobile manufacturer

CARMAN *n* pl. -MEN a streetcar driver

CARMINE *n* pl. -S a vivid red color

CARN *n* pl. -S cairn

CARNAGE *n* pl. -S great and bloody slaughter

CARNAL *adj* pertaining to bodily appetites **CARNALLY** *adv*

CARNAUBA *n* pl. -S a palm tree

CARNET *n* pl. -S an official permit

CARNEY *n* pl. -NEYS carny

CARNIE *n* pl. -S carny

CARNIES pl. of carny

CARNIFY *v* -FIED, -FYING, -FIES to form into flesh

CARNIVAL *n* pl. -S a traveling amusement show

CARNY *n* pl. -NIES a carnival

CAROACH *n* pl. -ES caroche

CAROB *n* pl. -S an evergreen tree

CAROCH *n* pl. -ES caroche

CAROCHE *n* pl. -S a stately carriage

CAROL *v* -OLED, -OLING, -OLS or -OLLED, -OLLING, -OLS to sing joyously

CAROLER *n* pl. -S one that carols

CAROLI a pl. of carolus

CAROLLED a past tense of carol

CAROLLER *n* pl. -S caroler

CAROLLING a present participle of carol

CAROLUS *n* pl. -LUSES or -LI an old English coin

CAROM *v* -ED, -ING, -S to collide with and rebound

CAROTENE *n* pl. -S a plant pigment

CAROTID *n* pl. -S an artery in the neck

CAROTIN *n* pl. -S carotene

CAROUSAL *n* pl. -S a boisterous drinking party

CAROUSE *v* -ROUSED, -ROUSING, -ROUSES to engage in a carousal

CAROUSEL *n* pl. -S an amusement park ride

CAROUSER *n* pl. -S one that carouses

CAROUSING present participle of carouse

CARP *v* -ED, -ING, -S to find fault unreasonably

CARPAL *n* pl. -S carpale

CARPALE *n* pl. -LIA a bone of the wrist

CARPEL *n* pl. -S a simple pistil

CARPER *n* pl. -S one that carps

CARPET *v* -ED, -ING, -S to cover a floor with a heavy fabric

CARPI pl. of carpus

CARPING *n* pl. -S the act of one who carps

CARPOOL *v* -ED, -ING, -S to take turns driving a group of commuters

CARPORT *n* pl. -S a shelter for a car

CARPUS *n* pl. -PI the wrist

CARR *n* pl. -S a marsh

CARRACK *n* pl. -S a type of merchant ship

CARREL *n* pl. -S a desk in a library stack for solitary study

CARRELL *n* pl. -S carrel

CARRIAGE *n* pl. -S a wheeled, horse-drawn vehicle

CARRIED past tense of carry

CARRIER *n* pl. -S one that carries

CARRIES present 3d person sing. of carry

CARRIOLE *n* pl. -S cariole

CARRION *n* pl. -S dead and putrefying flesh

CARRITCH *n* pl. -ES a religious handbook

CARROCH *n* pl. -ES caroche

CARROM *v* -ED, -ING, -S to carom

CARROT *n* pl. -S an edible orange root

CARROTIN *n* pl. -S carotene

CARROTY *adj* -ROTIER, -ROTIEST resembling a carrot in color

CARRY *v* -RIED, -RYING, -RIES to convey from one place to another

CARRYALL *n* pl. -S a light covered carriage

CARRYON *n* pl. -S a small piece of luggage

CARRYOUT *n* pl. -S a take-out order of food

CARSE *n* pl. -S low, fertile land along a river

CARSICK *adj* nauseated from riding in a car

CART *v* -ED, -ING, -S to convey in a cart (a two-wheeled vehicle) **CARTABLE** *adj*

CARTAGE *n* pl. -S the act of carting

CARTE *n* pl. -S a menu

CARTEL *n* pl. -S a business organization

CARTER *n* pl. -S one that carts

CARTLOAD *n* pl. -S as much as a cart can hold

CARTON *v* -ED, -ING, -S to pack in a cardboard box

CARTOON *v* -ED, -ING, -S to sketch a cartoon (a humorous representation) of

CARTOONY *adj* resembling a cartoon

CARTOP *adj* able to fit on top of a car

CARTOUCH *n* pl. -ES a scroll-like tablet

CARUNCLE *n* pl. -S a fleshy outgrowth

CARVE *v* CARVED, CARVING, CARVES to form by cutting

CARVEL *n* pl. -S caravel

CARVEN *adj* carved

CARVER *n* pl. -S one that carves

CARVING *n* pl. -S a carved figure or design

CARWASH *n* pl. -ES an establishment equipped to wash automobiles

CARYATIC *adj* resembling a caryatid

CARYATID *n* pl. -S or -ES a sculptured female figure used as a column

CARYOTIN *n* pl. -S karyotin

CASA *n* pl. -S a dwelling

CASABA *n* pl. -S a variety of melon

CASAVA *n* pl. -S cassava

CASBAH *n* pl. -S the old section of a North African city

CASCABEL *n* pl. -S the rear part of a cannon

CASCABLE *n* pl. -S cascabel

CASCADE *v* -CADED, -CADING, -CADES to fall like a waterfall

CASCARA *n* pl. -S a medicinal tree bark

CASE *v* CASED, CASING, CASES to put in a case (a container or receptacle)

CASEASE *n* pl. -S an enzyme

CASEATE *v* -ATED, -ATING, -ATES to become cheesy

CASEBOOK *n* pl. -S a law textbook

CASED past tense of case

CASEFY *v* -FIED, -FYING, -FIES to caseate

CASEIN *n* pl. -S a milk protein **CASEIC** *adj*

CASELOAD *n* pl. -S the number of cases being handled

CASEMATE *n* pl. -S a bombproof shelter

CASEMENT *n* pl. -S a type of window

CASEOSE *n* pl. -S a proteose

CASEOUS *adj* cheesy

CASERN *n* pl. -S a barracks for soldiers

CASERNE *n* pl. -S casern

CASETTE *n* pl. -S cassette

CASEWORK *n* pl. -S a form of social work

CASEWORM *n* pl. -S an insect larva

CASH *v* -ED, -ING, -ES to convert into cash (ready money) **CASHABLE** *adj*

CASHAW	*n* pl. -S cushaw
CASHBOOK	*n* pl. -S a book of monetary records
CASHBOX	*n* pl. -ES a container for money
CASHEW	*n* pl. -S a nut-bearing tree
CASHIER	*v* -ED, -ING, -S to dismiss in disgrace
CASHLESS	*adj* having no cash
CASHMERE	*n* pl. -S a fine wool
CASHOO	*n* pl. -SHOOS catechu
CASIMERE	*n* pl. -S a woolen fabric
CASIMIRE	*n* pl. -S casimere
CASING	*n* pl. -S a protective outer covering
CASINO	*n* pl. -NOS or -NI a gambling room
CASITA	*n* pl. -S a small house
CASK	*v* -ED, -ING, -S to store in a cask (a strong barrel)
CASKET	*v* -ED, -ING, -S to place in a casket (a burial case)
CASKY	*adj* resembling a cask
CASQUE	*n* pl. -S a helmet **CASQUED** *adj*
CASSABA	*n* pl. -S casaba
CASSATA	*n* pl. -S an Italian ice cream
CASSAVA	*n* pl. -S a tropical plant
CASSETTE	*n* pl. -S a small case containing audiotape or videotape
CASSIA	*n* pl. -S a variety of cinnamon
CASSINO	*n* pl. -NOS a card game
CASSIS	*n* pl. -SISES a European bush
CASSOCK	*n* pl. -S a long garment worn by clergymen
CAST	*v* CAST, CASTING, CASTS to throw with force **CASTABLE** *adj*
CASTANET	*n* pl. -S a rhythm instrument
CASTAWAY	*n* pl. -WAYS an outcast
CASTE	*n* pl. -S a system of distinct social classes
CASTEISM	*n* pl. -S the use of a caste system
CASTER	*n* pl. -S a small, swiveling wheel
CASTING	*n* pl. -S something made in a mold
CASTLE	*v* -TLED, -TLING, -TLES to make a certain move in chess
CASTOFF	*n* pl. -S a discarded person or thing
CASTOR	*n* pl. -S caster
CASTRATE	*v* -TRATED, -TRATING, -TRATES to remove the testes of
CASTRATO	*n* pl. -TI a singer castrated in boyhood
CASUAL	*n* pl. -S one who works occasionally
CASUALLY	*adv* informally
CASUALTY	*n* pl. -TIES a victim of war or disaster
CASUIST	*n* pl. -S one who resolves ethical problems
CASUS	*n* pl. CASUS a legal occurrence or event
CAT	*v* CATTED, CATTING, CATS to hoist an anchor to the cathead
CATACOMB	*n* pl. -S an underground cemetery
CATALASE	*n* pl. -S an enzyme
CATALO	*n* pl. -LOS or -LOES a hybrid between a buffalo and a cow
CATALOG	*v* -ED, -ING, -S to classify information descriptively
CATALPA	*n* pl. -S a tree
CATALYST	*n* pl. -S a substance that accelerates a chemical reaction
CATALYZE	*v* -LYZED, -LYZING, -LYZES to act as a catalyst
CATAMITE	*n* pl. -S a boy used in sodomy
CATAPULT	*v* -ED, -ING, -S to hurl through the air
CATARACT	*n* pl. -S a tremendous waterfall
CATARRH	*n* pl. -S inflammation of a mucous membrane
CATAWBA	*n* pl. -S a variety of fox grape
CATBIRD	*n* pl. -S a songbird
CATBOAT	*n* pl. -S a small sailboat
CATBRIER	*n* pl. -S a thorny vine
CATCALL	*v* -ED, -ING, -S to deride by making shrill sounds
CATCH	*v* CAUGHT, CATCHING, CATCHES to capture after pursuit
CATCHALL	*n* pl. -S a container for odds and ends
CATCHER	*n* pl. -S one that catches
CATCHFLY	*n* pl. -FLIES an insect-catching plant
CATCHUP	*n* pl. -S ketchup
CATCHY	*adj* CATCHIER, CATCHIEST pleasing and easily remembered
CATCLAW	*n* pl. -S a flowering shrub

CATE	*n* pl. -S a choice food	**CATMINT**	*n* pl. -S catnip
CATECHIN	*n* pl. -S a chemical used in dyeing	**CATNAP**	*v* -NAPPED, -NAPPING, -NAPS to doze
CATECHOL	*n* pl. -S a chemical used in photography	**CATNAPER**	*n* pl. -S one that steals cats
CATECHU	*n* pl. -S a resin used in tanning	**CATNIP**	*n* pl. -S an aromatic herb
CATEGORY	*n* pl. -RIES a division in any system of classification	**CATSPAW**	*n* pl. -S a light wind
		CATSUP	*n* pl. -S ketchup
CATENA	*n* pl. -NAS or -NAE a closely linked series	**CATTAIL**	*n* pl. -S a marsh plant
CATENARY	*n* pl. -NARIES a mathematical curve	**CATTALO**	*n* pl. -LOS or -LOES catalo
		CATTED	past tense of cat
CATENATE	*v* -NATED, -NATING, -NATES to link together	**CATTERY**	*n* pl. -TERIES an establishment for breeding cats
CATENOID	*n* pl. -S a geometric surface	**CATTIE**	*n* pl. -S an Asian unit of weight
CATER	*v* -ED, -ING, -S to provide food and service for	**CATTIER**	comparative of catty
		CATTIEST	superlative of catty
CATERAN	*n* pl. -S a brigand	**CATTILY**	*adv* in a catty manner
CATERER	*n* pl. -S one that caters	**CATTING**	present participle of cat
CATERESS	*n* pl. -ES a woman who caters	**CATTISH**	*adj* catty
CATFACE	*n* pl. -S a deformity of fruit	**CATTLE**	*n/pl* domesticated bovines
CATFALL	*n* pl. -S an anchor line	**CATTLEYA**	*n* pl. -S a tropical orchid
CATFIGHT	*n* pl. -S a fight between two women	**CATTY**	*adj* -TIER, -TIEST catlike; spiteful
CATFISH	*n* pl. -ES a scaleless, large-headed fish	**CATWALK**	*n* pl. -S a narrow walkway
CATGUT	*n* pl. -S a strong cord	**CAUCUS**	*v* -CUSED, -CUSING, -CUSES or -CUSSED, -CUSSING, -CUSSES to hold a political meeting
CATHEAD	*n* pl. -S a beam projecting from a ship's bow		
CATHECT	*v* -ED, -ING, -S to invest with psychic energy	**CAUDAD**	*adv* toward the tail
		CAUDAL	*adj* taillike **CAUDALLY** *adv*
CATHEDRA	*n* pl. -DRAS or -DRAE a bishop's throne	**CAUDATE**	*n* pl. -S a basal ganglion of the brain
CATHETER	*n* pl. -S a medical instrument	**CAUDATED**	*adj* having a tail
CATHEXIS	*n* pl. -THEXES the concentration of psychic energy on a person or idea	**CAUDEX**	*n* pl. -DICES or -DEXES the woody base of some plants
		CAUDILLO	*n* pl. -DILLOS a military dictator
CATHODE	*n* pl. -S a negatively charged electrode **CATHODAL, CATHODIC** *adj*	**CAUDLE**	*n* pl. -S a warm beverage
		CAUGHT	past tense of catch
CATHOLIC	*n* pl. -S a member of the early Christian church	**CAUL**	*n* pl. -S a fetal membrane
		CAULD	*n* pl. -S cold
CATHOUSE	*n* pl. -S a brothel	**CAULDRON**	*n* pl. -S caldron
CATION	*n* pl. -S a positively charged ion **CATIONIC** *adj*	**CAULES**	pl. of caulis
		CAULICLE	*n* pl. -S a small stem
CATKIN	*n* pl. -S a flower cluster	**CAULINE**	*adj* pertaining to a stem
CATLIKE	*adj* resembling a cat; stealthy; silent	**CAULIS**	*n* pl. -LES a plant stem
		CAULK	*v* -ED, -ING, -S to make the seams of a ship watertight
CATLIN	*n* pl. -S catling		
CATLING	*n* pl. -S a surgical knife	**CAULKER**	*n* pl. -S one that caulks

CAULKING	n pl. -S the material used to caulk	**CAVIL**	v -ILED, -ILING, -ILS or -ILLED, -ILLING, -ILS to carp
CAUSABLE	adj capable of being caused	**CAVILER**	n pl. -S one that cavils
CAUSAL	n pl. -S a word expressing cause or reason	**CAVILLER**	n pl. -S caviler
		CAVILLING	a present participle of cavil
CAUSALLY	adv by way of causing	**CAVING**	n pl. -S the sport of exploring caves
CAUSE	v CAUSED, CAUSING, CAUSES to bring about	**CAVITARY**	adj pertaining to the formation of cavities in tissue
CAUSER	n pl. -S one that causes		
CAUSERIE	n pl. -S an informal conversation	**CAVITATE**	v -TATED, -TATING, -TATES to form cavities
CAUSEWAY	v -ED, -ING, -S to build a causeway (a raised roadway) over	**CAVITY**	n pl. -TIES an unfilled space within a mass **CAVITIED** adj
CAUSEY	n pl. -SEYS a paved road	**CAVORT**	v -ED, -ING, -S to frolic
CAUSING	present participle of cause	**CAVORTER**	n pl. -S one that cavorts
CAUSTIC	n pl. -S a corrosive substance	**CAVY**	n pl. -VIES a short-tailed rodent
CAUTERY	n pl. -TERIES something used to destroy tissue	**CAW**	v -ED, -ING, -S to utter the sound of a crow
CAUTION	v -ED, -ING, -S to warn	**CAY**	n pl. CAYS a small low island
CAUTIOUS	adj exercising prudence to avoid danger	**CAYENNE**	n pl. -S a hot seasoning **CAYENNED** adj
CAVALERO	n pl. -ROS a horseman	**CAYMAN**	n pl. -S caiman
CAVALIER	v -ED, -ING, -S to behave haughtily	**CAYUSE**	n pl. -S an Indian pony
		CAZIQUE	n pl. -S cacique
CAVALLA	n pl. -S a large food fish	**CEASE**	v CEASED, CEASING, CEASES to stop
CAVALLY	n pl. -LIES cavalla		
CAVALRY	n pl. -RIES a mobile army unit	**CEBID**	n pl. -S ceboid
CAVATINA	n pl. -NAS or -NE a simple song	**CEBOID**	n pl. -S one of a family of monkeys
CAVE	v CAVED, CAVING, CAVES to hollow out	**CECUM**	n pl. CECA a bodily cavity with one opening **CECAL** adj **CECALLY** adv
CAVEAT	v -ED, -ING, -S to enter a type of legal notice		
CAVEATOR	n pl. -S one that files a caveat	**CEDAR**	n pl. -S an evergreen tree **CEDARN** adj
CAVED	past tense of cave	**CEDE**	v CEDED, CEDING, CEDES to yield
CAVEFISH	n pl. -ES a sightless fish		
CAVELIKE	adj resembling a cave (an underground chamber)	**CEDER**	n pl. -S one that cedes
		CEDI	n pl. -S a monetary unit of Ghana
CAVEMAN	n pl. -MEN a cave dweller	**CEDILLA**	n pl. -S a pronunciation mark
CAVER	n pl. -S one that caves	**CEDING**	present participle of cede
CAVERN	v -ED, -ING, -S to hollow out	**CEDULA**	n pl. -S a Philippine tax
CAVETTO	n pl. -TOS or -TI a concave molding	**CEE**	n pl. -S the letter C
		CEIBA	n pl. -S a tropical tree
CAVIAR	n pl. -S the roe of sturgeon	**CEIL**	v -ED, -ING, -S to furnish with a ceiling
CAVIARE	n pl. -S caviar		
CAVICORN	adj having hollow horns	**CEILER**	n pl. -S one that ceils
CAVIE	n pl. -S a hencoop	**CEILING**	n pl. -S the overhead lining of a room
CAVIES	pl. of cavy	**CEINTURE**	n pl. -S a belt for the waist

CEL	n pl. -S a sheet of celluloid used in animation
CELADON	n pl. -S a pale green color
CELEB	n pl. -S a celebrity; a famous person
CELERIAC	n pl. -S a variety of celery
CELERITY	n pl. -TIES swiftness
CELERY	n pl. -ERIES a plant with edible stalks
CELESTA	n pl. -S a keyboard instrument
CELESTE	n pl. -S celesta
CELIAC	n pl. -S one that has a chronic nutritional disturbance
CELIBACY	n pl. -CIES abstention from sexual intercourse
CELIBATE	n pl. -S one who lives a life of celibacy
CELL	v -ED, -ING, -S to store in a honeycomb
CELLA	n pl. -LAE the interior of an ancient temple
CELLAR	v -ED, -ING, -S to store in an underground room
CELLARER	n pl. -S the steward of a monastery
CELLARET	n pl. -S a cabinet for wine bottles
CELLIST	n pl. -S one who plays the cello
CELLMATE	n pl. -S one of two or more prisoners sharing a cell
CELLO	n pl. -LOS or -LI a stringed musical instrument
CELLULAR	adj pertaining to a cell (a basic unit of life)
CELLULE	n pl. -S a small cell
CELOM	n pl. -LOMS or -LOMATA coelom
CELOSIA	n pl. -S a flowering plant
CELT	n pl. -S a primitive ax
CEMBALO	n pl. -LI or -LOS a harpsichord
CEMENT	v -ED, -ING, -S to bind firmly
CEMENTER	n pl. -S one that cements
CEMENTUM	n pl. -TA the hard tissue covering the roots of the teeth
CEMETERY	n pl. -TERIES a burial ground
CENACLE	n pl. -S a small dining room
CENOBITE	n pl. -S a member of a religious order
CENOTAPH	n pl. -S an empty tomb
CENOTE	n pl. -S a sinkhole in limestone
CENSE	v CENSED, CENSING, CENSES to perfume with incense
CENSER	n pl. -S a vessel for burning incense
CENSOR	v -ED, -ING, -S to delete an objectionable word or passage
CENSUAL	adj pertaining to the act of censusing
CENSURE	v -SURED, -SURING, -SURES to criticize severely
CENSURER	n pl. -S one that censures
CENSUS	v -ED, -ING, -ES to take an official count of
CENT	n pl. -S the 100th part of a dollar
CENTAL	n pl. -S a unit of weight
CENTARE	n pl. -S a measure of land area
CENTAUR	n pl. -S a mythological creature
CENTAURY	n pl. -RIES a medicinal herb
CENTAVO	n pl. -VOS a coin of various Spanish-American nations
CENTER	v -ED, -ING, -S to place at the center (the midpoint)
CENTESIS	n pl. -TESES a surgical puncture
CENTIARE	n pl. -S centare
CENTILE	n pl. -S a value of a statistical variable
CENTIME	n pl. -S the 100th part of a franc
CENTIMO	n pl. -MOS any of various small coins
CENTNER	n pl. -S a unit of weight
CENTO	n pl. -TONES or -TOS a literary work made up of parts from other works
CENTRA	a pl. of centrum
CENTRAL	n pl. -S a telephone exchange
CENTRAL	adj -TRALER, -TRALEST situated at, in, or near the center
CENTRE	v -TRED, -TRING, -TRES to center
CENTRIC	adj situated at the center
CENTRING	n pl. -S a temporary framework for an arch
CENTRISM	n pl. -S moderate political philosophy
CENTRIST	n pl. -S an advocate of centrism
CENTROID	n pl. -S the center of mass of an object
CENTRUM	n pl. -TRUMS or -TRA the body of a vertebra
CENTUM	n pl. -S one hundred

CENTUPLE	*v* -PLED, -PLING, -PLES to increase a hundredfold
CENTURY	*n* pl. -RIES a period of 100 years
CEORL	*n* pl. -S a freeman of low birth **CEORLISH** *adj*
CEP	*n* pl. -S cepe
CEPE	*n* pl. -S a large mushroom
CEPHALAD	*adv* toward the head
CEPHALIC	*adj* pertaining to the head
CEPHALIN	*n* pl. -S a bodily chemical
CEPHEID	*n* pl. -S a giant star
CERAMAL	*n* pl. -S a heat-resistant alloy
CERAMIC	*n* pl. -S an item made of baked clay
CERAMIST	*n* pl. -S one who makes ceramics
CERASTES	*n* pl. CERASTES a venomous snake
CERATE	*n* pl. -S a medicated ointment
CERATED	*adj* covered with wax
CERATIN	*n* pl. -S keratin
CERATOID	*adj* hornlike
CERCARIA	*n* pl. -IAE or -IAS a parasitic worm
CERCIS	*n* pl. -CISES a shrub
CERCUS	*n* pl. CERCI a sensory appendage of an insect
CERE	*v* CERED, CERING, CERES to wrap in a waxy cloth
CEREAL	*n* pl. -S a food made from grain
CEREBRAL	*n* pl. -S a kind of consonant
CEREBRUM	*n* pl. -BRUMS or -BRA a part of the brain **CEREBRIC** *adj*
CERED	past tense of cere
CEREMENT	*n* pl. -S a waxy cloth
CEREMONY	*n* pl. -NIES a formal observance
CEREUS	*n* pl. -ES a tall cactus
CERIA	*n* pl. -S a chemical compound
CERIC	*adj* containing cerium
CERING	present participle of cere
CERIPH	*n* pl. -S serif
CERISE	*n* pl. -S a red color
CERITE	*n* pl. -S a mineral
CERIUM	*n* pl. -S a metallic element
CERMET	*n* pl. -S ceramal
CERNUOUS	*adj* drooping or nodding
CERO	*n* pl. CEROS a large food fish
CEROTIC	*adj* pertaining to beeswax
CEROTYPE	*n* pl. -S a process of engraving using wax
CEROUS	*adj* pertaining to cerium
CERTAIN	*adj* -TAINER, -TAINEST absolutely confident
CERTES	*adv* in truth
CERTIFY	*v* -FIED, -FYING, -FIES to confirm
CERULEAN	*n* pl. -S a blue color
CERUMEN	*n* pl. -S a waxy secretion of the ear
CERUSE	*n* pl. -S a lead compound
CERUSITE	*n* pl. -S a lead ore
CERVELAS	*n* pl. -ES cervelat
CERVELAT	*n* pl. -S a smoked sausage
CERVICAL	*adj* pertaining to the cervix
CERVID	*adj* of the deer family
CERVINE	*adj* pertaining to deer
CERVIX	*n* pl. -VICES or -VIXES the neck
CESAREAN	*n* pl. -S a method of child delivery
CESARIAN	*n* pl. -S cesarean
CESIUM	*n* pl. -S a metallic element
CESS	*v* -ED, -ING, -ES to tax or assess
CESSION	*n* pl. -S the act of ceding
CESSPIT	*n* pl. -S a cesspool
CESSPOOL	*n* pl. -S a covered well or pit for sewage
CESTA	*n* pl. -S a basket used in jai alai
CESTI	pl. of cestus
CESTODE	*n* pl. -S a tapeworm
CESTOID	*n* pl. -S cestode
CESTOS	*n* pl. -TOI cestus
CESTUS	*n* pl. -TI a belt or girdle
CESTUS	*n* pl. -ES a hand covering for ancient Roman boxers
CESURA	*n* pl. -RAS or -RAE caesura
CETACEAN	*n* pl. -S an aquatic mammal
CETANE	*n* pl. -S a diesel fuel
CETE	*n* pl. -S a group of badgers
CETOLOGY	*n* pl. -GIES the study of whales
CEVICHE	*n* pl. -S seviche
CHABLIS	*n* pl. CHABLIS a dry white wine
CHABOUK	*n* pl. -S a type of whip
CHABUK	*n* pl. -S chabouk
CHACMA	*n* pl. -S a large baboon

CHACONNE	*n* pl. -S an ancient dance	**CHALKY**	*adj* CHALKIER, CHALKIEST resembling chalk
CHAD	*n* pl. -S a scrap of paper **CHADLESS** *adj*	**CHALLA**	*n* pl. -S challah
CHADAR	*n* pl. -DARS or -DRI chador	**CHALLAH**	*n* pl. -LAHS, -LOTH, or -LOT a kind of bread
CHADARIM	a pl. of cheder	**CHALLIE**	*n* pl. -S challis
CHADOR	*n* pl. -DORS or -DRI a large shawl	**CHALLIES**	pl. of chally
CHAETA	*n* pl. -TAE a bristle or seta **CHAETAL** *adj*	**CHALLIS**	*n* pl. -LISES a light fabric
		CHALLOT	a pl. of challah
CHAFE	*v* CHAFED, CHAFING, CHAFES to warm by rubbing	**CHALLOTH**	a pl. of challah
CHAFER	*n* pl. -S a large beetle	**CHALLY**	*n* pl. -LIES challis
CHAFF	*v* -ED, -ING, -S to poke fun at	**CHALONE**	*n* pl. -S a hormone
CHAFFER	*v* -ED, -ING, -S to bargain or haggle	**CHALOT**	a pl. of chalah
		CHALOTH	a pl. of chalah
CHAFFY	*adj* CHAFFIER, CHAFFIEST worthless	**CHALUTZ**	*n* pl. -LUTZIM halutz
CHAFING	present participle of chafe	**CHAM**	*n* pl. -S a khan
CHAGRIN	*v* -GRINED, -GRINING, -GRINS or -GRINNED, -GRINNING, -GRINS to humiliate	**CHAMADE**	*n* pl. -S a signal made with a drum
		CHAMBER	*v* -ED, -ING, -S to put in a chamber (a room)
CHAIN	*v* -ED, -ING, -S to bind with a chain (a series of connected rings)	**CHAMBRAY**	*n* pl. -BRAYS a fine fabric
		CHAMFER	*v* -ED, -ING, -S to groove
CHAINE	*n* pl. -S a series of ballet turns	**CHAMFRON**	*n* pl. -S armor for a horse's head
CHAINMAN	*n* pl. -MEN a surveyor's assistant who uses a measuring chain	**CHAMISE**	*n* pl. -S chamiso
		CHAMISO	*n* pl. -SOS a flowering shrub
CHAINSAW	*v* -SAWED, -SAWING, -SAWS to cut with a chain saw	**CHAMMY**	*v* -MIED, -MYING, -MIES to chamois
CHAIR	*v* -ED, -ING, -S to install in office	**CHAMOIS**	*n* pl. -OIX a soft leather
CHAIRMAN	*n* pl. -MEN the presiding officer of a meeting	**CHAMOIS**	*v* -ED, -ING, -ES to prepare leather like chamois
CHAIRMAN	*v* -MANED, -MANING, -MANS or -MANNED, -MANNING, -MANS to act as chairman of	**CHAMP**	*v* -ED, -ING, -S to chew noisily
		CHAMPAC	*n* pl. -S champak
CHAISE	*n* pl. -S a light carriage	**CHAMPAK**	*n* pl. -S an East Indian tree
CHAKRA	*n* pl. -S a body center in yoga	**CHAMPER**	*n* pl. -S one that champs
CHALAH	*n* pl. -LAHS, -LOTH or -LOT challah	**CHAMPION**	*v* -ED, -ING, -S to defend or support
CHALAZA	*n* pl. -ZAS or -ZAE a band of tissue in an egg **CHALAZAL** *adj*	**CHAMPY**	*adj* broken up by the trampling of beasts
CHALAZIA	*n/pl* tumors of the eyelid	**CHANCE**	*v* CHANCED, CHANCING, CHANCES to risk
CHALCID	*n* pl. -S a tiny fly	**CHANCEL**	*n* pl. -S an area around a church altar
CHALDRON	*n* pl. -S a unit of dry measure		
CHALEH	*n* pl. -S challah	**CHANCERY**	*n* pl. -CERIES a court of public record
CHALET	*n* pl. -S a Swiss cottage	**CHANCIER**	comparative of chancy
CHALICE	*n* pl. -S a drinking cup **CHALICED** *adj*	**CHANCIEST**	superlative of chancy
		CHANCILY	*adv* in a chancy manner
CHALK	*v* -ED, -ING, -S to mark with chalk (a soft limestone)	**CHANCING**	present participle of chance

CHANCRE	*n* pl. -S a hard-based sore
CHANCY	*adj* CHANCIER, CHANCIEST risky
CHANDLER	*n* pl. -S a dealer in provisions
CHANFRON	*n* pl. -S chamfron
CHANG	*n* pl. -S a cattie
CHANGE	*v* CHANGED, CHANGING, CHANGES to make different
CHANGER	*n* pl. -S one that changes
CHANNEL	*v* -NELED, -NELING, -NELS or -NELLED, -NELLING, -NELS to direct along some desired course
CHANSON	*n* pl. -S a song
CHANT	*v* -ED, -ING, -S to sing
CHANTAGE	*n* pl. -S blackmail
CHANTER	*n* pl. -S one that chants
CHANTEY	*n* pl. -TEYS a sailor's song
CHANTIES	pl. of chanty
CHANTOR	*n* pl. -S chanter
CHANTRY	*n* pl. -TRIES an endowment given to a church
CHANTY	*n* pl. -TIES chantey
CHAO	*n* pl. CHAO a monetary unit of Vietnam
CHAOS	*n* pl. -ES a state of total disorder; a confused mass **CHAOTIC** *adj*
CHAP	*v* CHAPPED or CHAPT, CHAPPING, CHAPS to split, crack, or redden
CHAPATI	*n* pl. -S an unleavened bread of India
CHAPATTI	*n* pl. -S chapati
CHAPBOOK	*n* pl. -S a small book of popular tales
CHAPE	*n* pl. -S a part of a scabbard
CHAPEAU	*n* pl. -PEAUX or -PEAUS a hat
CHAPEL	*n* pl. -S a place of worship
CHAPERON	*v* -ED, -ING, -S to accompany
CHAPITER	*n* pl. -S the capital of a column
CHAPLAIN	*n* pl. -S a clergyman for a chapel
CHAPLET	*n* pl. -S a wreath for the head
CHAPMAN	*n* pl. -MEN a peddler
CHAPPATI	*n* pl. -S chapati
CHAPPED	a past tense of chap
CHAPPING	present participle of chap
CHAPT	a past tense of chap
CHAPTER	*v* -ED, -ING, -S to divide a book into chapters (main sections)
CHAQUETA	*n* pl. -S a jacket worn by cowboys
CHAR	*v* CHARRED, CHARRING, CHARS to burn slightly
CHARACID	*n* pl. -S characin
CHARACIN	*n* pl. -S a tropical fish
CHARADE	*n* pl. -S a word represented by pantomime
CHARAS	*n* pl. -ES hashish
CHARCOAL	*v* -ED, -ING, -S to blacken with charcoal (a dark, porous carbon)
CHARD	*n* pl. -S a variety of beet
CHARE	*v* CHARED, CHARING, CHARES to do small jobs
CHARGE	*v* CHARGED, CHARGING, CHARGES to accuse formally
CHARGER	*n* pl. -S one that charges
CHARIER	comparative of chary
CHARIEST	superlative of chary
CHARILY	*adv* in a chary manner
CHARING	present participle of chare
CHARIOT	*v* -ED, -ING, -S to ride in a chariot (a type of cart)
CHARISM	*n* pl. -S charisma
CHARISMA	*n* pl. -MATA a special magnetic appeal
CHARITY	*n* pl. -TIES something given to the needy
CHARK	*v* -ED, -ING, -S to char
CHARKA	*n* pl. -S charkha
CHARKHA	*n* pl. -S a spinning wheel
CHARLADY	*n* pl. -DIES a cleaning woman
CHARLEY	*n* pl. -LEYS charlie
CHARLIE	*n* pl. -LIES a fool
CHARLOCK	*n* pl. -S a troublesome weed
CHARM	*v* -ED, -ING, -S to attract irresistibly
CHARMER	*n* pl. -S one that charms
CHARMING	*adj* -INGER, -INGEST pleasing
CHARNEL	*n* pl. -S a room where corpses are placed
CHARPAI	*n* pl. -S charpoy
CHARPOY	*n* pl. -POYS a bed used in India
CHARQUI	*n* pl. -S a type of meat **CHARQUID** *adj*
CHARR	*n* pl. -S a small-scaled trout
CHARRED	past tense of char
CHARRIER	comparative of charry

CHARRIEST	superlative of charry
CHARRING	present participle of char
CHARRO	*n* pl. -ROS a cowboy
CHARRY	*adj* -RIER, -RIEST resembling charcoal
CHART	*v* -ED, -ING, -S to map out
CHARTER	*v* -ED, -ING, -S to lease or hire
CHARTIST	*n* pl. -S a stock market specialist
CHARY	*adj* CHARIER, CHARIEST cautious
CHASE	*v* CHASED, CHASING, CHASES to pursue
CHASER	*n* pl. -S one that chases
CHASING	*n* pl. -S a design engraved on metal
CHASM	*n* pl. -S a deep cleft in the earth **CHASMAL, CHASMED, CHASMIC, CHASMY** *adj*
CHASSE	*v* CHASSED, CHASSEING, CHASSES to perform a dance movement
CHASSEUR	*n* pl. -S a cavalry soldier
CHASSIS	*n* pl. CHASSIS the frame of a car
CHASTE	*adj* CHASTER, CHASTEST morally pure **CHASTELY** *adv*
CHASTEN	*v* -ED, -ING, -S to chastise
CHASTISE	*v* -TISED, -TISING, -TISES to discipline by punishment
CHASTITY	*n* pl. -TIES moral purity
CHASUBLE	*n* pl. -S a sleeveless vestment
CHAT	*v* CHATTED, CHATTING, CHATS to converse informally
CHATCHKA	*n* pl. -S a knickknack
CHATCHKE	*n* pl. -S chatchka
CHATEAU	*n* pl. -TEAUX or -TEAUS a large country house
CHATTED	past tense of chat
CHATTEL	*n* pl. -S a slave
CHATTER	*v* -ED, -ING, -S to talk rapidly and trivially **CHATTERY** *adj*
CHATTING	present participle of chat
CHATTY	*adj* -TIER, -TIEST talkative **CHATTILY** *adv*
CHAUFER	*n* pl. -S chauffer
CHAUFFER	*n* pl. -S a small furnace
CHAUNT	*v* -ED, -ING, -S to chant
CHAUNTER	*n* pl. -S one that chaunts
CHAUSSES	*n/pl* medieval armor
CHAW	*v* -ED, -ING, -S to chew
CHAWER	*n* pl. -S one that chaws
CHAY	*n* pl. CHAYS the root of an East Indian herb
CHAYOTE	*n* pl. -S a tropical vine
CHAZAN	*n* pl. -ZANS or -ZANIM a cantor
CHAZZAN	*n* pl. -ZANS or -ZANIM chazan
CHAZZEN	*n* pl. -ZENS or -ZENIM chazan
CHEAP	*adj* CHEAPER, CHEAPEST inexpensive
CHEAP	*n* pl. -S a market
CHEAPEN	*v* -ED, -ING, -S to make cheap
CHEAPIE	*n* pl. -S one that is cheap
CHEAPISH	*adj* somewhat cheap
CHEAPLY	*adv* in a cheap manner
CHEAPO	*n* pl. CHEAPOS a cheapie
CHEAT	*v* -ED, -ING, -S to defraud
CHEATER	*n* pl. -S one that cheats
CHEBEC	*n* pl. -S a small bird
CHECHAKO	*n* pl. -KOS a newcomer
CHECK	*v* -ED, -ING, -S to inspect
CHECKER	*v* -ED, -ING, -S to mark with squares
CHECKOFF	*n* pl. -S a method of collecting union dues
CHECKOUT	*n* pl. -S a test of a machine
CHECKROW	*v* -ED, -ING, -S to plant in rows which divide the land into squares
CHECKUP	*n* pl. -S an examination
CHEDDAR	*n* pl. -S a type of cheese
CHEDDITE	*n* pl. -S chedite
CHEDER	*n* pl. CHADARIM or CHEDERS heder
CHEDITE	*n* pl. -S an explosive
CHEEK	*v* -ED, -ING, -S to speak impudently to
CHEEKFUL	*n* pl. -S the amount held in one's cheek
CHEEKY	*adj* CHEEKIER, CHEEKIEST impudent **CHEEKILY** *adv*
CHEEP	*v* -ED, -ING, -S to chirp
CHEEPER	*n* pl. -S one that cheeps
CHEER	*v* -ED, -ING, -S to applaud with shouts of approval
CHEERER	*n* pl. -S one that cheers
CHEERFUL	*adj* -FULLER, -FULLEST full of spirits
CHEERIER	comparative of cheery
CHEERIEST	superlative of cheery

CHEERILY *adv* in a cheery manner

CHEERIO *n* pl. -IOS a greeting

CHEERLED past tense of cheerlead

CHEERLY *adv* cheerily

CHEERO *n* pl. CHEEROS cheerio

CHEERY *adj* CHEERIER, CHEERIEST cheerful

CHEESE *v* CHEESED, CHEESING, CHEESES to stop

CHEESY *adj* CHEESIER, CHEESIEST resembling cheese (a food made from milk curds) **CHEESILY** *adv*

CHEETAH *n* pl. -S a swift-running wildcat

CHEF *v* CHEFFED, CHEFFING, CHEFS to work as a chef (a chief cook)

CHEFDOM *n* pl. -S the status of a chef

CHEGOE *n* pl. -S chigoe

CHELA *n* pl. -LAE a pincerlike claw

CHELA *n* pl. -S a pupil of a guru

CHELATE *v* -LATED, -LATING, -LATES to combine a metal ion with a compound

CHELATOR *n* pl. -S one that chelates

CHELIPED *n* pl. -S a claw-bearing leg

CHELOID *n* pl. -S keloid

CHEMIC *n* pl. -S a chemist

CHEMICAL *n* pl. -S a substance obtained by a process of chemistry

CHEMISE *n* pl. -S a loose dress

CHEMISM *n* pl. -S chemical attraction

CHEMIST *n* pl. -S one versed in chemistry

CHEMO *n* pl. -S treatment (as of disease) with chemical agents

CHEMURGY *n* pl. -GIES a branch of applied chemistry

CHENILLE *n* pl. -S a soft fabric

CHENOPOD *n* pl. -S a flowering plant

CHEQUE *n* pl. -S a written order directing a bank to pay money

CHEQUER *v* -ED, -ING, -S to checker

CHERISH *v* -ED, -ING, -ES to hold dear

CHEROOT *n* pl. -S a square-cut cigar

CHERRY *n* pl. -RIES a fruit

CHERT *n* pl. -S a compact rock

CHERTY *adj* CHERTIER, CHERTIEST resembling chert

CHERUB *n* pl. -UBS or -UBIM or -UBIMS an angel **CHERUBIC** *adj*

CHERVIL *n* pl. -S an aromatic herb

CHESS *n* pl. -ES a weed

CHESSMAN *n* pl. -MEN one of the pieces used in chess (a board game for two players)

CHEST *n* pl. -S a part of the body **CHESTED** *adj*

CHESTFUL *n* pl. -S as much as a chest or box can hold

CHESTNUT *n* pl. -S an edible nut

CHESTY *adj* CHESTIER, CHESTIEST proud

CHETAH *n* pl. -S cheetah

CHETH *n* pl. -S heth

CHETRUM *n* pl. -S a monetary unit of Bhutan

CHEVALET *n* pl. -S a part of a stringed instrument

CHEVERON *n* pl. -S chevron

CHEVIED past tense of chevy

CHEVIES present 3d person sing. of chevy

CHEVIOT *n* pl. -S a coarse fabric

CHEVRE *n* pl. -S a cheese made from goat's milk

CHEVRON *n* pl. -S a V-shaped pattern

CHEVY *v* CHEVIED, CHEVYING, CHEVIES to chase about

CHEW *v* -ED, -ING, -S to crush or grind with the teeth **CHEWABLE** *adj*

CHEWER *n* pl. -S one that chews

CHEWINK *n* pl. -S a common finch

CHEWY *adj* CHEWIER, CHEWIEST not easily chewed

CHEZ *prep* at the home of

CHI *n* pl. -S a Greek letter

CHIA *n* pl. -S a Mexican herb .

CHIAO *n* pl. CHIAO a monetary unit of China

CHIASM *n* pl. -S chiasma

CHIASMA *n* pl. -MATA or -MAS an anatomical junction **CHIASMAL, CHIASMIC** *adj*

CHIASMUS *n* pl. -MI a reversal of word order between parallel phrases **CHIASTIC** *adj*

CHIAUS *n* pl. -ES a Turkish messenger

CHIBOUK *n* pl. -S a tobacco pipe

CHIC *n* pl. -S elegance

CHIC *adj* CHICER, CHICEST smartly stylish

CHICANE *v* -CANED, -CANING, -CANES to trick

CHICANER	*n* pl. -S one that chicanes
CHICANO	*n* pl. -NOS an American of Mexican descent
CHICCORY	*n* pl. -RIES chicory
CHICHI	*n* pl. -S elaborate ornamentation
CHICK	*n* pl. -S a young bird
CHICKEE	*n* pl. -S a stilt house of the Seminole Indians
CHICKEN	*v* -ED, -ING, -S to lose one's nerve
CHICKORY	*n* pl. -RIES chicory
CHICKPEA	*n* pl. -S an Asian herb
CHICLE	*n* pl. -S a tree gum
CHICLY	*adv* in an elegant manner
CHICNESS	*n* pl. -ES elegance
CHICO	*n* pl. -COS a prickly shrub
CHICORY	*n* pl. -RIES a perennial herb
CHIDE	*v* CHIDED or CHID, CHIDDEN, CHIDING, CHIDES to scold
CHIDER	*n* pl. -S one that chides
CHIEF	*adj* CHIEFER, CHIEFEST highest in authority
CHIEF	*n* pl. -S the person highest in authority
CHIEFDOM	*n* pl. -S the domain of a chief
CHIEFLY	*adv* above all
CHIEL	*n* pl. -S chield
CHIELD	*n* pl. -S a young man
CHIFFON	*n* pl. -S a sheer fabric
CHIGETAI	*n* pl. -S a wild ass
CHIGGER	*n* pl. -S a parasitic mite
CHIGNON	*n* pl. -S a woman's hairdo
CHIGOE	*n* pl. -S a tropical flea
CHILD	*n* pl. CHILDREN a young person
CHILDBED	*n* pl. -S the state of a woman giving birth
CHILDE	*n* pl. -S a youth of noble birth
CHILDING	*adj* pregnant
CHILDISH	*adj* resembling a child
CHILDLY	*adj* -LIER, -LIEST resembling a child
CHILDREN	pl. of child
CHILE	*n* pl. -S chili
CHILI	*n* pl. -ES a hot pepper
CHILIAD	*n* pl. -S a group of one thousand
CHILIASM	*n* pl. -S a religious doctrine
CHILIAST	*n* pl. -S a supporter of chiliasm

CHILIDOG	*n* pl. -S a hot dog topped with chili
CHILL	*v* -ED, -ING, -S to make cold
CHILL	*adj* CHILLER, CHILLEST cool
CHILLER	*n* pl. -S one that chills
CHILLI	*n* pl. -ES chili
CHILLUM	*n* pl. -S a part of a water pipe
CHILLY	*adj* CHILLIER, CHILLIEST cool **CHILLILY** *adv*
CHILOPOD	*n* pl. -S a multi-legged insect
CHIMAERA	*n* pl. -S a marine fish
CHIMAR	*n* pl. -S chimere
CHIMB	*n* pl. -S the rim of a cask
CHIMBLEY	*n* pl. -BLEYS chimley
CHIMBLY	*n* pl. -BLIES chimley
CHIME	*v* CHIMED, CHIMING, CHIMES to ring harmoniously
CHIMER	*n* pl. -S one that chimes
CHIMERA	*n* pl. -S an imaginary monster
CHIMERE	*n* pl. -S a bishop's robe
CHIMERIC	*adj* imaginary; unreal
CHIMING	present participle of chime
CHIMLA	*n* pl. -S chimley
CHIMLEY	*n* pl. -LEYS a chimney
CHIMNEY	*n* pl. -NEYS a flue
CHIMP	*n* pl. -S a chimpanzee
CHIN	*v* CHINNED, CHINNING, CHINS to hold with the chin (the lower part of the face)
CHINA	*n* pl. -S fine porcelain ware
CHINBONE	*n* pl. -S the lower jaw
CHINCH	*n* pl. -ES a bedbug
CHINCHY	*adj* CHINCHIER, CHINCHIEST stingy
CHINE	*v* CHINED, CHINING, CHINES to cut through the backbone of
CHINK	*v* -ED, -ING, -S to fill cracks or fissures in
CHINKY	*adj* CHINKIER, CHINKIEST full of cracks
CHINLESS	*adj* lacking a chin
CHINNED	past tense of chin
CHINNING	present participle of chin
CHINO	*n* pl. -NOS a strong fabric
CHINONE	*n* pl. -S quinone
CHINOOK	*n* pl. -S a warm wind
CHINTS	*n* pl. -ES chintz

CHINTZ	*n* pl. -ES a cotton fabric
CHINTZY	*adj* CHINTZIER, CHINTZIEST gaudy; cheap
CHIP	*v* CHIPPED, CHIPPING, CHIPS to break a small piece from
CHIPMUCK	*n* pl. -S a chipmunk
CHIPMUNK	*n* pl. -S a small rodent
CHIPPED	past tense of chip
CHIPPER	*v* -ED, -ING, -S to chirp
CHIPPIE	*n* pl. -S chippy
CHIPPING	present participle of chip
CHIPPY	*n* pl. -PIES a prostitute
CHIPPY	*adj* -PIER, -PIEST belligerent
CHIRAL	*adj* pertaining to an asymmetrical molecule
CHIRK	*v* -ED, -ING, -S to make a shrill noise
CHIRK	*adj* CHIRKER, CHIRKEST cheerful
CHIRM	*v* -ED, -ING, -S to chirp
CHIRO	*n* pl. -ROS a marine fish
CHIRP	*v* -ED, -ING, -S to utter a short, shrill sound
CHIRPER	*n* pl. -S one that chirps
CHIRPY	*adj* CHIRPIER, CHIRPIEST cheerful **CHIRPILY** *adv*
CHIRR	*v* -ED, -ING, -S to make a harsh, vibrant sound
CHIRRE	*v* CHIRRED, CHIRRING, CHIRRES to chirr
CHIRRUP	*v* -ED, -ING, -S to chirp repeatedly **CHIRRUPY** *adj*
CHISEL	*v* -ELED, -ELING, -ELS or -ELLED, -ELLING, -ELS to use a chisel (a cutting tool)
CHISELER	*n* pl. -S one that chisels
CHIT	*n* pl. -S a short letter
CHITAL	*n* pl. CHITAL an Asian deer
CHITCHAT	*v* -CHATTED, -CHATTING, -CHATS to indulge in small talk
CHITIN	*n* pl. -S the main component of insect shells
CHITLIN	*n* pl. -S chitling
CHITLING	*n* pl. -S a part of the small intestine of swine
CHITON	*n* pl. -S a tunic worn in ancient Greece
CHITOSAN	*n* pl. -S a compound derived from chitin
CHITTER	*v* -ED, -ING, -S to twitter
CHITTY	*n* pl. -TIES a chit
CHIVALRY	*n* pl. -RIES knightly behavior and skill
CHIVAREE	*v* -REED, -REEING, -REES to perform a mock serenade
CHIVARI	*v* -RIED, -RIING, -RIES to chivaree
CHIVE	*n* pl. -S an herb used as a seasoning
CHIVVY	*v* -VIED, -VYING, -VIES to chevy
CHIVY	*v* CHIVIED, CHIVYING, CHIVIES to chevy
CHLAMYS	*n* pl. -MYSES or -MYDES a garment worn in ancient Greece
CHLOASMA	*n* pl. -MATA a skin discoloration
CHLORAL	*n* pl. -S a chemical compound
CHLORATE	*n* pl. -S a chemical salt
CHLORDAN	*n* pl. -S a toxic compound of chlorine
CHLORIC	*adj* pertaining to chlorine
CHLORID	*n* pl. -S chloride
CHLORIDE	*n* pl. -S a chlorine compound
CHLORIN	*n* pl. -S chlorine
CHLORINE	*n* pl. -S a gaseous element
CHLORITE	*n* pl. -S a mineral group
CHLOROUS	*adj* pertaining to chlorine
CHOANA	*n* pl. -NAE a funnel-shaped opening
CHOCK	*v* -ED, -ING, -S to secure with a wedge of wood or metal
CHOCKFUL	*adj* full to the limit
CHOICE	*n* pl. -S one that is chosen
CHOICE	*adj* CHOICER, CHOICEST of fine quality **CHOICELY** *adv*
CHOIR	*v* -ED, -ING, -S to sing in unison
CHOIRBOY	*n* pl. -BOYS a boy who sings in a choir (a body of church singers)
CHOKE	*v* CHOKED, CHOKING, CHOKES to impede the breathing of
CHOKER	*n* pl. -S one that chokes
CHOKEY	*adj* CHOKIER, CHOKIEST choky
CHOKING	present participle of choke
CHOKY	*adj* CHOKIER, CHOKIEST tending to cause choking
CHOLATE	*n* pl. -S a chemical salt
CHOLENT	*n* pl. -S a traditional Jewish stew
CHOLER	*n* pl. -S anger
CHOLERA	*n* pl. -S an acute disease

CHOLERIC	*adj* bad-tempered		**CHORIAMB**	*n* pl. -S a type of metrical foot
CHOLINE	*n* pl. -S a B vitamin		**CHORIC**	*adj* pertaining to a chorus
CHOLLA	*n* pl. -S a treelike cactus		**CHORINE**	*n* pl. -S a chorus girl
CHOLO	*n* pl. -LOS a pachuco		**CHORING**	present participle of chore
CHOMP	*v* -ED, -ING, -S to champ		**CHORIOID**	*n* pl. -S choroid
CHOMPER	*n* pl. -S one that chomps		**CHORION**	*n* pl. -S an embryonic membrane
CHON	*n* pl. CHON a monetary unit of South Korea		**CHORIZO**	*n* pl. -ZOS a highly seasoned sausage
CHOOK	*n* pl. -S a chicken		**CHOROID**	*n* pl. -S a membrane of the eye
CHOOSE	*v* CHOSE, CHOSEN, CHOOSING, CHOOSES to take by preference		**CHORTLE**	*v* -TLED, -TLING, -TLES to chuckle with glee
CHOOSER	*n* pl. -S one that chooses		**CHORTLER**	*n* pl. -S one that chortles
CHOOSEY	*adj* CHOOSIER, CHOOSIEST choosy		**CHORUS**	*v* -RUSED, -RUSING, -RUSES or -RUSSED, -RUSSING, -RUSSES to sing in unison
CHOOSING	present participle of choose		**CHOSE**	*n* pl. -S an item of personal property
CHOOSY	*adj* CHOOSIER, CHOOSIEST hard to please		**CHOSEN**	past participle of choose
CHOP	*v* CHOPPED, CHOPPING, CHOPS to sever with a sharp tool		**CHOTT**	*n* pl. -S a saline lake
			CHOUGH	*n* pl. -S a crow-like bird
CHOPIN	*n* pl. -S chopine		**CHOUSE**	*v* CHOUSED, CHOUSING, CHOUSES to swindle
CHOPINE	*n* pl. -S a type of shoe		**CHOUSER**	*n* pl. -S one that chouses
CHOPPED	past tense of chop		**CHOUSH**	*n* pl. -ES chiaus
CHOPPER	*v* -ED, -ING, -S to travel by helicopter		**CHOUSING**	present participle of chouse
CHOPPING	present participle of chop		**CHOW**	*v* -ED, -ING, -S to eat
CHOPPY	*adj* CHOPPIER, CHOPPIEST full of short, rough waves **CHOPPILY** *adv*		**CHOWCHOW**	*n* pl. -S a relish of mixed pickles in mustard
CHORAGUS	*n* pl. -GI or -GUSES the leader of a chorus or choir **CHORAGIC** *adj*		**CHOWDER**	*v* -ED, -ING, -S to make a thick soup of
CHORAL	*n* pl. -S chorale		**CHOWSE**	*v* CHOWSED, CHOWSING, CHOWSES to chouse
CHORALE	*n* pl. -S a hymn that is sung in unison		**CHOWTIME**	*n* pl. -S mealtime
CHORALLY	*adv* harmoniously		**CHRESARD**	*n* pl. -S the available water of the soil
CHORD	*v* -ED, -ING, -S to play a chord (a combination of three or more musical tones)		**CHRISM**	*n* pl. -S a consecrated oil **CHRISMAL** *adj*
CHORDAL	*adj* pertaining to a chord		**CHRISMON**	*n* pl. -MA or -MONS a Christian monogram
CHORDATE	*n* pl. -S any of a large phylum of animals		**CHRISOM**	*n* pl. -S chrism
CHORE	*v* CHORED, CHORING, CHORES to do small jobs		**CHRISTEN**	*v* -ED, -ING, -S to baptise
			CHRISTIE	*n* pl. -S christy
CHOREA	*n* pl. -S a nervous disorder **CHOREAL, CHOREIC** *adj*		**CHRISTY**	*n* pl. -TIES a skiing turn
			CHROMA	*n* pl. -S the purity of a color
CHOREGUS	*n* pl. -GI or -GUSES choragus		**CHROMATE**	*n* pl. -S a chemical salt
CHOREMAN	*n* pl. -MEN a menial worker		**CHROME**	*v* CHROMED, CHROMING, CHROMES to plate with chromium
CHOREOID	*adj* resembling chorea			
CHORIAL	*adj* pertaining to the chorion		**CHROMIC**	*adj* pertaining to chromium

CHROMIDE	*n* pl. -S a tropical fish
CHROMING	*n* pl. -S a chromium ore
CHROMITE	*n* pl. -S a chromium ore
CHROMIUM	*n* pl. -S a metallic element
CHROMIZE	*v* -MIZED, -MIZING, -MIZES to chrome
CHROMO	*n* pl. -MOS a type of color picture
CHROMOUS	*adj* pertaining to chromium
CHROMYL	*n* pl. -S a bivalent radical
CHRONAXY	*n* pl. -AXIES the time required to excite a nerve cell electrically
CHRONIC	*n* pl. -S one that suffers from a long-lasting disease
CHRONON	*n* pl. -S a hypothetical unit of time
CHTHONIC	*adj* pertaining to the gods of the underworld
CHUB	*n* pl. -S a freshwater fish
CHUBASCO	*n* pl. -COS a violent thunderstorm
CHUBBY	*adj* -BIER, -BIEST plump **CHUBBILY** *adv*
CHUCK	*v* -ED, -ING, -S to throw
CHUCKIES	pl. of chucky
CHUCKLE	*v* -LED, -LING, -LES to laugh quietly
CHUCKLER	*n* pl. -S one that chuckles
CHUCKY	*n* pl. CHUCKIES a little chick
CHUDDAH	*n* pl. -S chuddar
CHUDDAR	*n* pl. -S a large, square shawl
CHUDDER	*n* pl. -S chuddar
CHUFA	*n* pl. -S a European sedge
CHUFF	*adj* CHUFFER, CHUFFEST gruff
CHUFF	*v* -ED, -ING, -S to chug
CHUFFY	*adj* -FIER, -FIEST plump
CHUG	*v* CHUGGED, CHUGGING, CHUGS to move with a dull explosive sound
CHUGALUG	*v* -LUGGED, -LUGGING, -LUGS to drink without pause
CHUGGER	*n* pl. -S one that chugs
CHUKAR	*n* pl. -S a game bird
CHUKKA	*n* pl. -S a type of boot
CHUKKAR	*n* pl. -S a chukker
CHUKKER	*n* pl. -S a period of play in polo
CHUM	*v* CHUMMED, CHUMMING, CHUMS to be close friends with someone
CHUMMY	*adj* -MIER, -MIEST friendly **CHUMMILY** *adv*
CHUMP	*v* -ED, -ING, -S to munch
CHUMSHIP	*n* pl. -S friendship
CHUNK	*v* -ED, -ING, -S to make a dull explosive sound
CHUNKY	*adj* CHUNKIER, CHUNKIEST stocky **CHUNKILY** *adv*
CHUNTER	*v* -ED, -ING, -S to mutter
CHURCH	*v* -ED, -ING, -ES to bring to church (a building for Christian worship)
CHURCHLY	*adj* -LIER, -LIEST pertaining to a church
CHURCHY	*adj* CHURCHIER, CHURCHIEST churchly
CHURL	*n* pl. -S a rude person **CHURLISH** *adj*
CHURN	*v* -ED, -ING, -S to stir briskly in order to make butter
CHURNER	*n* pl. -S one that churns
CHURNING	*n* pl. -S the butter churned at one time
CHURR	*v* -ED, -ING, -S to make a vibrant sound
CHUTE	*v* CHUTED, CHUTING, CHUTES to convey by chute (a vertical passage)
CHUTIST	*n* pl. -S a parachutist
CHUTNEE	*n* pl. -S chutney
CHUTNEY	*n* pl. -NEYS a sweet and sour sauce
CHUTZPA	*n* pl. -S chutzpah
CHUTZPAH	*n* pl. -S supreme self-confidence
CHYLE	*n* pl. -S a digestive fluid **CHYLOUS** *adj*
CHYME	*n* pl. -S semi-digested food
CHYMIC	*n* pl. -S chemic
CHYMIST	*n* pl. -S chemist
CHYMOSIN	*n* pl. -S rennin
CHYMOUS	*adj* pertaining to chyme
CIAO	*interj* — used as an expression of greeting and farewell
CIBOL	*n* pl. -S a variety of onion
CIBORIUM	*n* pl. -RIA a vessel for holding holy bread
CIBOULE	*n* pl. -S cibol
CICADA	*n* pl. -DAS or -DAE a winged insect
CICALA	*n* pl. -LAS or -LE cicada

CICATRIX   *n* pl. -TRICES or -TRIXES scar tissue

CICELY   *n* pl. -LIES a fragrant herb

CICERO   *n* pl. -ROS a unit of measure in printing

CICERONE   *n* pl. -NES or -NI a tour guide

CICHLID   *n* pl. -LIDS or -LIDAE a tropical fish

CICISBEO   *n* pl. -BEI or -BEOS a lover of a married woman

CICOREE   *n* pl. -S a perennial herb

CIDER   *n* pl. -S the juice pressed from apples

CIGAR   *n* pl. -S a roll of tobacco leaf for smoking

CIGARET   *n* pl. -S a narrow roll of finely cut tobacco for smoking

CILANTRO   *n* pl. -TROS an herb used in cooking

CILIA   pl. of cilium

CILIARY   *adj* pertaining to cilia

CILIATE   *n* pl. -S one of a class of ciliated protozoans

CILIATED   *adj* having cilia

CILICE   *n* pl. -S a coarse cloth

CILIUM   *n* pl. CILIA a short, hairlike projection

CIMBALOM   *n* pl. -S a Hungarian dulcimer

CIMEX   *n* pl. -MICES a bedbug

CINCH   *v* -ED, -ING, -ES to girth

CINCHONA   *n* pl. -S a Peruvian tree

CINCTURE   *v* -TURED, -TURING, -TURES to gird or encircle

CINDER   *v* -ED, -ING, -S to reduce to cinders (ashes)

CINDERY   *adj* containing cinders

CINE   *n* pl. -S a motion picture

CINEAST   *n* pl. -S a devotee of motion pictures

CINEASTE   *n* pl. -S cineast

CINEMA   *n* pl. -S a motion-picture theater

CINEOL   *n* pl. -S a liquid used as an antiseptic

CINEOLE   *n* pl. -S cineol

CINERARY   *adj* used for cremated ashes

CINERIN   *n* pl. -S a compound used in insecticides

CINGULUM   *n* pl. -LA an anatomical band or girdle

CINNABAR   *n* pl. -S the principal ore of mercury

CINNAMON   *n* pl. -S a spice obtained from tree bark **CINNAMIC** *adj*

CINNAMYL   *n* pl. -S a chemical used to make soap

CINQUAIN   *n* pl. -S a stanza of five lines

CINQUE   *n* pl. -S the number five

CION   *n* pl. -S a cutting from a plant or tree

CIOPPINO   *n* pl. -NOS a spicy fish stew

CIPHER   *v* -ED, -ING, -S to solve problems in arithmetic

CIPHONY   *n* pl. -NIES the electronic scrambling of voice transmissions

CIPOLIN   *n* pl. -S a type of marble

CIRCA   *prep* about; around

CIRCLE   *v* -CLED, -CLING, -CLES to move or revolve around

CIRCLER   *n* pl. -S one that circles

CIRCLET   *n* pl. -S a small ring or ring-shaped object

CIRCLING   present participle of circle

CIRCUIT   *v* -ED, -ING, -S to move around

CIRCUITY   *n* pl. -ITIES lack of straightforwardness

CIRCULAR   *n* pl. -S a leaflet intended for wide distribution

CIRCUS   *n* pl. -ES a public entertainment **CIRCUSY** *adj*

CIRE   *n* pl. -S a highly glazed finish for fabrics

CIRQUE   *n* pl. -S a deep, steep-walled basin on a mountain

CIRRATE   *adj* having cirri

CIRRI   pl. of cirrus

CIRRIPED   *n* pl. -S any of an order of crustaceans

CIRROSE   *adj* cirrous

CIRROUS   *adj* having cirri

CIRRUS   *n* pl. -RI a tendril or similar part

CIRSOID   *adj* varicose

CIS   *adj* having certain atoms on the same side of the molecule

CISCO   *n* pl. -COS or -COES a freshwater fish

CISLUNAR   *adj* situated between the earth and the moon

CISSOID   *n* pl. -S a type of geometric curve

CISSY   *n* pl. -SIES sissy

CIST	*n* pl. -S a prehistoric stone coffin
CISTERN	*n* pl. -S a water tank
CISTERNA	*n* pl. -NAE a fluid-containing sac
CISTRON	*n* pl. -S a segment of DNA
CISTUS	*n* pl. -ES a flowering shrub
CITABLE	*adj* citeable
CITADEL	*n* pl. -S a fortress or stronghold
CITATION	*n* pl. -S the act of citing **CITATORY** *adj*
CITATOR	*n* pl. -S one that cites
CITE	*v* CITED, CITING, CITES to quote as an authority or example
CITEABLE	*adj* suitable for citation
CITER	*n* pl. -S one that cites
CITHARA	*n* pl. -S an ancient stringed instrument
CITHER	*n* pl. -S cittern
CITHERN	*n* pl. -S cittern
CITHREN	*n* pl. -S cittern
CITIED	*adj* having cities
CITIES	pl. of city
CITIFY	*v* -FIED, -FYING, -FIES to urbanize
CITING	present participle of cite
CITIZEN	*n* pl. -S a resident of a city or town
CITOLA	*n* pl. -S a cittern
CITOLE	*n* pl. -S citola
CITRAL	*n* pl. -S a lemon flavoring
CITRATE	*n* pl. -S a salt of citric acid **CITRATED** *adj*
CITREOUS	*adj* having a lemonlike color
CITRIC	*adj* derived from citrus fruits
CITRIN	*n* pl. -S a citric vitamin
CITRINE	*n* pl. -S a variety of quartz
CITRININ	*n* pl. -S an antibiotic
CITRON	*n* pl. -S a lemonlike fruit
CITROUS	*adj* pertaining to a citrus tree
CITRUS	*n* pl. -ES any of a genus of tropical, fruit-bearing trees **CITRUSY** *adj*
CITTERN	*n* pl. -S a pear-shaped guitar
CITY	*n* pl. CITIES a large town
CITYFIED	*adj* having the customs and manners of city people
CITYWARD	*adv* toward the city
CITYWIDE	*adj* including all parts of a city
CIVET	*n* pl. -S a catlike mammal
CIVIC	*adj* pertaining to a city
CIVICISM	*n* pl. -S a system of government based upon individual rights
CIVICS	*n/pl* the science of civic affairs
CIVIE	*n* pl. -S civvy
CIVIL	*adj* pertaining to citizens
CIVILIAN	*n* pl. -S a nonmilitary person
CIVILISE	*v* -LISED, -LISING, -LISES to civilize
CIVILITY	*n* pl. -TIES courtesy; politeness
CIVILIZE	*v* -LIZED, -LIZING, -LIZES to bring out of savagery
CIVILLY	*adv* politely
CIVISM	*n* pl. -S good citizenship
CIVVY	*n* pl. -VIES a civilian
CLABBER	*v* -ED, -ING, -S to curdle
CLACH	*n* pl. -S clachan
CLACHAN	*n* pl. -S a hamlet
CLACK	*v* -ED, -ING, -S to make an abrupt, dry sound
CLACKER	*n* pl. -S one that clacks
CLAD	*v* CLAD, CLADDING, CLADS to coat one metal over another
CLADDING	*n* pl. -S something that overlays
CLADE	*n* pl. -S a group of biological taxa
CLADIST	*n* pl. -S a taxonomist who uses clades in classifying life-forms
CLADODE	*n* pl. -S a leaflike part of a stem
CLAG	*v* CLAGGED, CLAGGING, CLAGS to clog
CLAIM	*v* -ED, -ING, -S to demand as one's due
CLAIMANT	*n* pl. -S one that asserts a right or title
CLAIMER	*n* pl. -S one that claims
CLAM	*v* CLAMMED, CLAMMING, CLAMS to dig for clams (bivalve mollusks)
CLAMANT	*adj* noisy
CLAMBAKE	*n* pl. -S a beach picnic
CLAMBER	*v* -ED, -ING, -S to climb awkwardly
CLAMMED	past tense of clam
CLAMMER	*n* pl. -S one that clams
CLAMMING	present participle of clam
CLAMMY	*adj* CLAMMIER, CLAMMIEST cold and damp **CLAMMILY** *adv*

CLAMOR	*v* -ED, -ING, -S to make loud outcries
CLAMORER	*n* pl. -S one that clamors
CLAMOUR	*v* -ED, -ING, -S to clamor
CLAMP	*v* -ED, -ING, -S to fasten with a clamp (a securing device)
CLAMPER	*n* pl. -S a device worn on shoes to prevent slipping on ice
CLAMWORM	*n* pl. -S a marine worm
CLAN	*n* pl. -S a united group of families
CLANG	*v* -ED, -ING, -S to ring loudly
CLANGER	*n* pl. -S a blunder
CLANGOR	*v* -ED, -ING, -S to clang repeatedly
CLANGOUR	*v* -ED, -ING, -S to clangor
CLANK	*v* -ED, -ING, -S to make a sharp, metallic sound
CLANNISH	*adj* characteristic of a clan
CLANSMAN	*n* pl. -MEN a member of a clan
CLAP	*v* CLAPPED or CLAPT, CLAPPING, CLAPS to strike one palm against the other
CLAPPER	*n* pl. -S one that claps
CLAPTRAP	*n* pl. -S pretentious language
CLAQUE	*n* pl. -S a group of hired applauders
CLAQUER	*n* pl. -S claqueur
CLAQUEUR	*n* pl. -S a member of a claque
CLARENCE	*n* pl. -S a closed carriage
CLARET	*n* pl. -S a dry red wine
CLARIES	pl. of clary
CLARIFY	*v* -FIED, -FYING, -FIES to make clear
CLARINET	*n* pl. -S a woodwind instrument
CLARION	*v* -ED, -ING, -S to proclaim by blowing a medieval trumpet
CLARITY	*n* pl. -TIES the state of being clear
CLARKIA	*n* pl. -S an annual herb
CLARO	*n* pl. -ROS or -ROES a mild cigar
CLARY	*n* pl. CLARIES an aromatic herb
CLASH	*v* -ED, -ING, -ES to conflict or disagree
CLASHER	*n* pl. -S one that clashes
CLASP	*v* CLASPED or CLASPT, CLASPING, CLASPS to embrace tightly
CLASPER	*n* pl. -S one that clasps
CLASS	*v* -ED, -ING, -ES to classify
CLASSER	*n* pl. -S one that classes
CLASSES	pl. of classis
CLASSIC	*n* pl. -S a work of enduring excellence
CLASSICO	*adj* made from grapes grown in a certain part of Italy
CLASSIER	comparative of classy
CLASSIEST	superlative of classy
CLASSIFY	*v* -FIED, -FYING, -FIES to arrange according to characteristics
CLASSILY	*adj* in a classy manner
CLASSIS	*n* pl. CLASSES a governing body in certain churches
CLASSISM	*n* pl. -S discrimination based on social class
CLASSIST	*n* pl. -S an advocate of classism
CLASSY	*adj* CLASSIER, CLASSIEST stylish; elegant
CLAST	*n* pl. -S a fragment of rock
CLASTIC	*n* pl. -S a rock made up of other rocks
CLATTER	*v* -ED, -ING, -S to move with a rattling noise
CLATTERY	*adj* having a rattling noise
CLAUCHT	a past tense of cleek
CLAUGHT	*v* -ED, -ING, -S to clutch
CLAUSE	*n* pl. -S a distinct part of a composition **CLAUSAL** *adj*
CLAUSTRA	*n/pl* basal ganglia in the brain
CLAVATE	*adj* shaped like a club
CLAVE	*n* pl. -S one of a pair of percussion sticks
CLAVER	*v* -ED, -ING, -S to gossip
CLAVI	pl. of clavus
CLAVICLE	*n* pl. -S a bone of the shoulder
CLAVIER	*n* pl. -S a keyboard instrument
CLAVUS	*n* pl. -VI a horny thickening of the skin
CLAW	*v* -ED, -ING, -S to scratch with claws (sharp, curved toenails)
CLAWER	*n* pl. -S one that claws
CLAWLESS	*adj* having no claws
CLAWLIKE	*adj* resembling a claw
CLAXON	*n* pl. -S klaxon
CLAY	*v* -ED, -ING, -S to treat with clay (a fine-grained, earthy material)
CLAYBANK	*n* pl. -S a yellow-brown color
CLAYEY	*adj* CLAYIER, CLAYIEST resembling clay

CLAYISH *adj* resembling or containing clay

CLAYLIKE *adj* resembling clay

CLAYMORE *n* pl. -S a type of sword

CLAYPAN *n* pl. -S a shallow natural depression

CLAYWARE *n* pl. -S pottery

CLEAN *adj* CLEANER, CLEANEST free from dirt or stain

CLEAN *v* -ED, -ING, -S to rid of dirt or stain

CLEANER *n* pl. -S one that cleans

CLEANLY *adj* -LIER, -LIEST habitually clean

CLEANSE *v* CLEANSED, CLEANSING, CLEANSES to clean

CLEANSER *n* pl. -S one that cleanses

CLEANUP *n* pl. -S an act of cleaning

CLEAR *adj* CLEARER, CLEAREST clean and pure

CLEAR *v* -ED, -ING, -S to remove obstructions

CLEARER *n* pl. -S one that clears

CLEARING *n* pl. -S an open space

CLEARLY *adv* in a clear manner

CLEAT *v* -ED, -ING, -S to strengthen with a strip of wood or iron

CLEAVAGE *n* pl. -S the act of cleaving

CLEAVE *v* CLEAVED, CLEFT, CLOVE or CLAVE, CLOVEN, CLEAVING, CLEAVES to split or divide

CLEAVER *n* pl. -S a heavy knife

CLEEK *v* CLAUCHT or CLEEKED, CLEEKING, CLEEKS to clutch

CLEF *n* pl. -S a musical symbol

CLEFT *v* -ED, -ING, -S to insert a scion into the stock of a plant

CLEIDOIC *adj* enclosed in a shell

CLEMATIS *n* pl. -TISES a flowering vine

CLEMENCY *n* pl. -CIES mercy

CLEMENT *adj* merciful

CLENCH *v* -ED, -ING, -ES to grasp firmly

CLENCHER *n* pl. -S one that clenches

CLEOME *n* pl. -S a tropical plant

CLEPE *v* CLEPED or CLEPT, CLEPING, CLEPES to call by name

CLERGY *n* pl. -GIES the body of persons ordained for religious service

CLERIC *n* pl. -S a member of the clergy

CLERICAL *n* pl. -S a cleric

CLERID *n* pl. -S a predatory beetle

CLERIHEW *n* pl. -S a humorous poem

CLERISY *n* pl. -SIES the well-educated class

CLERK *v* -ED, -ING, -S to serve as a clerk (an office worker)

CLERKDOM *n* pl. -S the status or function of a clerk

CLERKISH *adj* resembling or suitable to a clerk

CLERKLY *adj* -LIER, -LIEST pertaining to a clerk

CLEVEITE *n* pl. -S a radioactive mineral

CLEVER *adj* -ERER, -EREST mentally keen **CLEVERLY** *adv*

CLEVIS *n* pl. -ISES a metal fastening device

CLEW *v* -ED, -ING, -S to roll into a ball

CLICHE *n* pl. -S a trite expression **CLICHED** *adj*

CLICK *v* -ED, -ING, -S to make a short, sharp sound

CLICKER *n* pl. -S one that clicks

CLIENT *n* pl. -S a customer **CLIENTAL** *adj*

CLIFF *n* pl. -S a high, steep face of rock

CLIFFY *adj* CLIFFIER, CLIFFIEST abounding in cliffs

CLIFT *n* pl. -S cliff

CLIMATE *n* pl. -S the weather conditions characteristic of an area **CLIMATAL, CLIMATIC** *adj*

CLIMAX *v* -ED, -ING, -ES to reach a high or dramatic point

CLIMB *v* CLIMBED or CLOMB, CLIMBING, CLIMBS to ascend

CLIMBER *n* pl. -S one that climbs

CLIME *n* pl. -S climate

CLINAL *adj* pertaining to a cline

CLINALLY *adv* in a clinal manner

CLINCH *v* -ED, -ING, -ES to settle a matter decisively

CLINCHER *n* pl. -S a decisive fact or remark

CLINE *n* pl. -S a series of changes within a species

CLING *v* CLUNG, CLINGING, CLINGS to adhere closely

CLING *v* -ED, -ING, -S to make a high-pitched ringing sound

CLINGER *n* pl. -S one that clings

CLINGY	*adj* CLINGIER, CLINGIEST adhesive		**CLOMB**	a past tense of climb
CLINIC	*n* pl. -S a medical facility **CLINICAL** *adj*		**CLOMP**	*v* -ED, -ING, -S to walk heavily and clumsily
CLINK	*v* -ED, -ING, -S to make a soft, sharp, ringing sound		**CLON**	*n* pl. -S a group of asexually derived organisms **CLONAL** *adj* **CLONALLY** *adv*
CLINKER	*v* -ED, -ING, -S to form fused residue in burning		**CLONE**	*v* CLONED, CLONING, CLONES to reproduce by asexual means
CLIP	*v* CLIPPED or CLIPT, CLIPPING, CLIPS to trim by cutting		**CLONER**	*n* pl. -S one that clones
CLIPPER	*n* pl. -S one that clips		**CLONIC**	*adj* pertaining to clonus
CLIPPING	*n* pl. -S something that is clipped out or off		**CLONING**	*n* pl. -S a technique for reproducing by asexual means
CLIPT	a past participle of clip		**CLONISM**	*n* pl. -S the condition of having clonus
CLIQUE	*v* CLIQUED, CLIQUING, CLIQUES to form a clique (an exclusive group of persons)		**CLONK**	*v* -ED, -ING, -S to make a dull thumping sound
CLIQUEY	*adj* CLIQUIER, CLIQUIEST inclined to form cliques		**CLONUS**	*n* pl. -ES a form of muscular spasm
CLIQUISH	*adj* cliquey		**CLOOT**	*n* pl. -S a cloven hoof
CLIQUY	*adj* CLIQUIER, CLIQUIEST cliquey		**CLOP**	*v* CLOPPED, CLOPPING, CLOPS to make the sound of a hoof striking pavement
CLITELLA	*n/pl* regions in the body walls of certain annelids		**CLOQUE**	*n* pl. -S a fabric with an embossed design
CLITIC	*n* pl. -S a word pronounced as part of a neighboring word		**CLOSE**	*adj* CLOSER, CLOSEST near **CLOSELY** *adv*
CLITORIS	*n* pl. -RISES or -RIDES a sex organ **CLITORAL, CLITORIC** *adj*		**CLOSE**	*v* CLOSED, CLOSING, CLOSES to block against entry or passage **CLOSABLE** *adj*
CLIVERS	*n* pl. CLIVERS an annual herb		**CLOSEOUT**	*n* pl. -S a clearance sale
CLIVIA	*n* pl. -S a flowering plant		**CLOSER**	*n* pl. -S one that closes
CLOACA	*n* pl. -ACAE or -ACAS a sewer **CLOACAL** *adj*		**CLOSEST**	superlative of close
CLOAK	*v* -ED, -ING, -S to conceal		**CLOSET**	*v* -ED, -ING, -S to enclose in a private room
CLOBBER	*v* -ED, -ING, -S to trounce		**CLOSING**	*n* pl. -S a concluding part
CLOCHARD	*n* pl. -S a vagrant		**CLOSURE**	*v* -SURED, -SURING, -SURES to cloture
CLOCHE	*n* pl. -S a bell-shaped hat		**CLOT**	*v* CLOTTED, CLOTTING, CLOTS to form into a clot (a thick mass)
CLOCK	*v* -ED, -ING, -S to time with a stopwatch			
CLOCKER	*n* pl. -S one that clocks		**CLOTH**	*n* pl. -S fabric
CLOD	*n* pl. -S a dolt **CLODDISH** *adj*		**CLOTHE**	*v* CLOTHED or CLAD, CLOTHING, CLOTHES to provide with clothing
CLODDY	*adj* -DIER, -DIEST lumpy			
CLODPATE	*n* pl. -S a stupid person		**CLOTHIER**	*n* pl. -S one who makes or sells clothing
CLODPOLE	*n* pl. -S clodpate			
CLODPOLL	*n* pl. -S clodpate		**CLOTHING**	*n* pl. -S wearing apparel
CLOG	*v* CLOGGED, CLOGGING, CLOGS to block up or obstruct		**CLOTTED**	past tense of clot
CLOGGER	*n* pl. -S one that clogs		**CLOTTING**	present participle of clot
CLOGGY	*adj* -GIER, -GIEST clogging or able to clog		**CLOTTY**	*adj* tending to clot
CLOISTER	*v* -ED, -ING, -S to seclude			

CLOTURE *v* -TURED, -TURING, -TURES to end a debate by calling for a vote

CLOUD *v* -ED, -ING, -S to cover with clouds (masses of visible vapor)

CLOUDLET *n* pl. -S a small cloud

CLOUDY *adj* CLOUDIER, CLOUDIEST overcast with clouds **CLOUDILY** *adv*

CLOUGH *n* pl. -S a ravine

CLOUR *v* -ED, -ING, -S to knock or bump

CLOUT *v* -ED, -ING, -S to hit with the hand

CLOUTER *n* pl. -S one that clouts

CLOVE *n* pl. -S a spice

CLOVEN *adj* split; divided

CLOVER *n* pl. -S a plant

CLOWDER *n* pl. -S a group of cats

CLOWN *v* -ED, -ING, -S to act like a clown (a humorous performer)

CLOWNERY *n* pl. -ERIES clownish behavior

CLOWNISH *adj* resembling or befitting a clown

CLOY *v* -ED, -ING, -S to gratify beyond desire

CLOZE *n* pl. -S a test of reading comprehension

CLUB *v* CLUBBED, CLUBBING, CLUBS to form a club (an organized group of persons)

CLUBABLE *adj* sociable

CLUBBER *n* pl. -S a member of a club

CLUBBING present participle of club

CLUBBISH *adj* clubby

CLUBBY *adj* -BIER, -BIEST characteristic of a club

CLUBFOOT *n* pl. -FEET a deformed foot

CLUBHAND *n* pl. -S a deformed hand

CLUBHAUL *v* -ED, -ING, -S to put a vessel about

CLUBMAN *n* pl. -MEN a male member of a club

CLUBROOM *n* pl. -S a room for a club's meetings

CLUBROOT *n* pl. -S a plant disease

CLUCK *v* -ED, -ING, -S to make the sound of a hen

CLUE *v* CLUED, CLUEING or CLUING, CLUES to give guiding information

CLUELESS *adj* hopelessly confused or ignorant

CLUMBER *n* pl. -S a stocky spaniel

CLUMP *v* -ED, -ING, -S to form into a thick mass

CLUMPISH *adj* resembling a clump (a thick mass)

CLUMPY *adj* CLUMPIER, CLUMPIEST lumpy

CLUMSY *adj* -SIER, -SIEST awkward **CLUMSILY** *adv*

CLUNG past tense of cling

CLUNK *v* -ED, -ING, -S to thump

CLUNKER *n* pl. -S a jalopy

CLUNKY *adj* CLUNKIER, CLUNKIEST clumsy in style

CLUPEID *n* pl. -S a fish of the herring family

CLUPEOID *n* pl. -S a clupeid

CLUSTER *v* -ED, -ING, -S to form into a cluster (a group of similar objects)

CLUSTERY *adj* pertaining to a cluster

CLUTCH *v* -ED, -ING, -ES to grasp and hold tightly

CLUTCHY *adj* tending to clutch

CLUTTER *v* -ED, -ING, -S to pile in a disorderly state

CLUTTERY *adj* characterized by disorder

CLYPEUS *n* pl. CLYPEI a shield-like structure **CLYPEAL, CLYPEATE** *adj*

CLYSTER *n* pl. -S an enema

COACH *v* -ED, -ING, -ES to tutor or train

COACHER *n* pl. -S one that coaches

COACHMAN *n* pl. -MEN one who drives a coach or carriage

COACT *v* -ED, -ING, -S to act together

COACTION *n* pl. -S joint action

COACTIVE *adj* mutually active

COACTOR *n* pl. -S a fellow actor in a production

COADMIRE *v* -MIRED, -MIRING, -MIRES to admire together

COADMIT *v* -MITTED, -MITTING, -MITS to admit several things equally

COAEVAL *n* pl. -S coeval

COAGENCY *n* pl. -CIES a joint agency

COAGENT *n* pl. -S a person, force, or other agent working together with another

COAGULUM *n* pl. -LA or -LUMS a clot

COAL *v* -ED, -ING, -S to supply with coal (a carbon fuel)

COALA *n* pl. -S koala

COALBIN *n* pl. -S a bin for storing coal

COALBOX *n* pl. -ES a box for storing coal

COALER *n* pl. -S one that supplies coal

COALESCE *v* -ALESCED, -ALESCING, -ALESCES to blend

COALFISH *n* pl. -ES a blackish fish

COALHOLE *n* pl. -S a compartment for storing coal

COALIER comparative of coaly

COALIEST superlative of coaly

COALIFY *v* -FIED, -FYING, -FIES to convert into coal

COALLESS *adj* lacking coal

COALPIT *n* pl. -S a pit from which coal is obtained

COALSACK *n* pl. -S a dark region of the Milky Way

COALSHED *n* pl. -S a shed for storing coal

COALY *adj* COALIER, COALIEST containing coal

COALYARD *n* pl. -S a yard for storing coal

COAMING *n* pl. -S a raised border

COANCHOR *v* -ED, -ING, -S to present televised news reports jointly

COANNEX *v* -ED, -ING, -ES to annex jointly

COAPPEAR *v* -ED, -ING, -S to appear together or at the same time

COAPT *v* -ED, -ING, -S to fit together and make fast

COARSE *adj* COARSER, COARSEST rough **COARSELY** *adv*

COARSEN *v* -ED, -ING, -S to make coarse

COASSIST *v* -ED, -ING, -S to assist jointly

COASSUME *v* -SUMED, -SUMING, -SUMES to assume together

COAST *v* -ED, -ING, -S to slide down a hill

COASTAL *adj* pertaining to or located near a seashore

COASTER *n* pl. -S a sled

COASTING *n* pl. -S coastal trade

COAT *v* -ED, -ING, -S to cover with a coat (an outer garment)

COATEE *n* pl. -S a small coat

COATER *n* pl. -S one that coats

COATI *n* pl. -S a tropical mammal

COATING *n* pl. -S a covering layer

COATLESS *adj* lacking a coat

COATRACK *n* pl. -S a rack or stand for coats

COATROOM *n* pl. -S a room for storing coats

COATTAIL *n* pl. -S the back lower portion of a coat

COATTEND *v* -ED, -ING, -S to attend together

COATTEST *v* -ED, -ING, -S to attest jointly

COAUTHOR *v* -ED, -ING, -S to write together

COAX *v* -ED, -ING, -ES to cajole

COAXAL *adj* coaxial

COAXER *n* pl. -S one that coaxes

COAXIAL *adj* having a common axis

COB *n* pl. -S a corncob

COBALT *n* pl. -S a metallic element **COBALTIC** *adj*

COBB *n* pl. -S a sea gull

COBBER *n* pl. -S a comrade

COBBIER comparative of cobby

COBBIEST superlative of cobby

COBBLE *v* -BLED, -BLING, -BLES to mend

COBBLER *n* pl. -S a mender of shoes

COBBY *adj* -BIER, -BIEST stocky

COBIA *n* pl. -S a large game fish

COBLE *n* pl. -S a small fishing boat

COBNUT *n* pl. -S an edible nut

COBRA *n* pl. -S a venomous snake

COBWEB *v* -WEBBED, -WEBBING, -WEBS to cover with cobwebs (spider webs)

COBWEBBY *adj* -BIER, -BIEST covered with cobwebs

COCA *n* pl. -S a South American shrub

COCAIN *n* pl. -S cocaine

COCAINE *n* pl. -S a narcotic alkaloid

COCCAL *adj* pertaining to a coccus

COCCI pl. of coccus

COCCIC *adj* coccal

COCCID *n* pl. -S an insect

COCCIDIA *n/pl* parasitic protozoans

COCCOID *n* pl. -S a spherical cell or body

COCCUS	*n* pl. COCCI a spherical bacterium **COCCOUS** *adj*
COCCYX	*n* pl. -CYGES or -CYXES a bone of the spine
COCHAIR	*v* -ED, -ING, -S to serve jointly as chairman of
COCHIN	*n* pl. -S a large domestic chicken
COCHLEA	*n* pl. -CHLEAE or -CHLEAS a part of the ear **COCHLEAR** *adj*
COCINERA	*n* pl. -S a cook
COCK	*v* -ED, -ING, -S to tilt to one side
COCKADE	*n* pl. -S an ornament worn on a hat **COCKADED** *adj*
COCKAPOO	*n* pl. -POOS a hybrid between a cocker spaniel and a poodle
COCKATOO	*n* pl. -TOOS a parrot
COCKBILL	*v* -ED, -ING, -S to raise the yardarm on a ship
COCKBOAT	*n* pl. -S a small boat
COCKCROW	*n* pl. -S daybreak
COCKER	*v* -ED, -ING, -S to pamper
COCKEREL	*n* pl. -S a young rooster
COCKEYE	*n* pl. -S a squinting eye **COCKEYED** *adj*
COCKIER	comparative of cocky
COCKIEST	superlative of cocky
COCKILY	*adv* in a cocky manner
COCKISH	*adj* cocky
COCKLE	*v* -LED, -LING, -LES to wrinkle or pucker
COCKLIKE	*adj* resembling a rooster
COCKLOFT	*n* pl. -S a small attic
COCKNEY	*n* pl. -NEYS a resident of the East End of London
COCKPIT	*n* pl. -S a pilot's compartment in certain airplanes
COCKSHUT	*n* pl. -S the close of day
COCKSHY	*n* pl. -SHIES a target in a throwing contest
COCKSPUR	*n* pl. -S a thorny plant
COCKSURE	*adj* certain
COCKTAIL	*v* -ED, -ING, -S to drink alcoholic beverages
COCKUP	*n* pl. -S a turned-up part of something
COCKY	*adj* COCKIER, COCKIEST arrogantly self-confident
COCO	*n* pl. -COS a tall palm tree
COCOA	*n* pl. -S chocolate
COCOANUT	*n* pl. -S coconut
COCOBOLA	*n* pl. -S cocobolo
COCOBOLO	*n* pl. -LOS a tropical tree
COCOMAT	*n* pl. -S a matting made from coir
COCONUT	*n* pl. -S the fruit of the coco
COCOON	*v* -ED, -ING, -S to wrap or envelop tightly
COCOTTE	*n* pl. -S a prostitute
COCOYAM	*n* pl. -S a tropical plant having edible rootstocks
COCREATE	*v* -ATED, -ATING, -ATES to create together
COD	*v* CODDED, CODDING, CODS to fool
CODA	*n* pl. -S a passage at the end of a musical composition
CODABLE	*adj* capable of being coded
CODDED	past tense of cod
CODDER	*n* pl. -S a cod fisherman
CODDING	present participle of cod
CODDLE	*v* -DLED, -DLING, -DLES to pamper
CODDLER	*n* pl. -S one that coddles
CODE	*v* CODED, CODING, CODES to convert into symbols
CODEBOOK	*n* pl. -S a book listing words and their coded equivalents
CODEBTOR	*n* pl. -S one that shares a debt
CODEC	*n* pl. -S an integrated circuit
CODED	past tense of code
CODEIA	*n* pl. -S codeine
CODEIN	*n* pl. -S codeine
CODEINA	*n* pl. -S codeine
CODEINE	*n* pl. -S a narcotic alkaloid
CODELESS	*adj* being without a set of laws
CODEN	*n* pl. -S a coding classification
CODER	*n* pl. -S one that codes
CODERIVE	*v* -RIVED, -RIVING, -RIVES to derive jointly
CODESIGN	*v* -ED, -ING, -S to design jointly
CODEX	*n* pl. -DICES an ancient manuscript
CODFISH	*n* pl. -ES a marine food fish
CODGER	*n* pl. -S an old man
CODICES	pl. of codex
CODICIL	*n* pl. -S a supplement to a will
CODIFIER	*n* pl. -S one that codifies
CODIFY	*v* -FIED, -FYING, -FIES to arrange or systematize

CODING	present participle of code
CODIRECT	v -ED, -ING, -S to direct jointly
CODLIN	n pl. -S codling
CODLING	n pl. -S an unripe apple
CODON	n pl. -S a triplet of nucleotides (basic components of DNA)
CODPIECE	n pl. -S a cover for the crotch in men's breeches
CODRIVE	v -DROVE, -DRIVEN, -DRIVING, -DRIVES to work as a codriver
CODRIVER	n pl. -S one who takes turns driving a vehicle
COED	n pl. -S a female student
COEDIT	v -ED, -ING, -S to edit with another person
COEDITOR	n pl. -S one that coedits
COEFFECT	n pl. -S an accompanying effect
COELIAC	adj celiac
COELOM	n pl. -LOMS or -LOMATA a body cavity in some animals **COELOMIC** adj
COELOME	n pl. -S coelom
COEMBODY	v -BODIED, -BODYING, -BODIES to embody jointly
COEMPLOY	v -ED, -ING, -S to employ together
COEMPT	v -ED, -ING, -S to buy up the entire supply of a product
COENACT	v -ED, -ING, -S to enact jointly or at the same time
COENAMOR	v -ED, -ING, -S to inflame with mutual love
COENDURE	v -DURED, -DURING, -DURES to endure together
COENURE	n pl. -S coenurus
COENURUS	n pl. -RI a tapeworm larva
COENZYME	n pl. -S a substance necessary for the functioning of certain enzymes
COEQUAL	n pl. -S one who is equal with another
COEQUATE	v -QUATED, -QUATING, -QUATES to equate with something else
COERCE	v -ERCED, -ERCING, -ERCES to compel by force or threat
COERCER	n pl. -S one that coerces
COERCION	n pl. -S the act of coercing
COERCIVE	adj serving to coerce
COERECT	v -ED, -ING, -S to erect together

COESITE	n pl. -S a type of silica
COEVAL	n pl. -S one of the same era or period as another
COEVALLY	adv contemporarily
COEVOLVE	v -VOLVED, -VOLVING, -VOLVES to evolve together
COEXERT	v -ED, -ING, -S to exert jointly
COEXIST	v -ED, -ING, -S to exist together
COEXTEND	v -ED, -ING, -S to extend through the same space or time as another
COFACTOR	n pl. -S a coenzyme
COFF	v COFT, COFFING, COFFS to buy
COFFEE	n pl. -S an aromatic, mildly stimulating beverage
COFFER	v -ED, -ING, -S to put in a strongbox
COFFIN	v -ED, -ING, -S to put in a coffin (a burial case)
COFFLE	v -FLED, -FLING, -FLES to chain slaves together
COFFRET	n pl. -S a small strongbox
COFOUND	v -ED, -ING, -S to found jointly
COFT	past tense of coff
COG	v COGGED, COGGING, COGS to cheat at dice
COGENCY	n pl. -CIES the state of being cogent
COGENT	adj convincing **COGENTLY** adv
COGGED	past tense of cog
COGGING	present participle of cog
COGITATE	v -TATED, -TATING, -TATES to ponder
COGITO	n pl. -TOS a philosophical principle
COGNAC	n pl. -S a brandy
COGNATE	n pl. -S one that is related to another
COGNISE	v -NISED, -NISING, -NISES to cognize
COGNIZE	v -NIZED, -NIZING, -NIZES to become aware of in one's mind
COGNIZER	n pl. -S one that cognizes
COGNOMEN	n pl. -MENS or -MINA a family name
COGNOVIT	n pl. -S a written admission of liability
COGON	n pl. -S a tall tropical grass

COGWAY *n* pl. -WAYS a railway operating on steep slopes

COGWHEEL *n* pl. -S a toothed wheel

COHABIT *v* -ED, -ING, -S to live together as man and wife while unmarried

COHEAD *v* -ED, -ING, -S to head jointly

COHEIR *n* pl. -S a joint heir

COHERE *v* -HERED, -HERING, -HERES to stick together

COHERENT *adj* sticking together

COHERER *n* pl. -S a device used to detect radio waves

COHERING present participle of cohere

COHESION *n* pl. -S the act or state of cohering **COHESIVE** *adj*

COHO *n* pl. -HOS a small salmon

COHOBATE *v* -BATED, -BATING, -BATES to distill again

COHOG *n* pl. -S a quahog

COHOLDER *n* pl. -S an athlete who holds a record with another

COHORT *n* pl. -S a companion or associate

COHOSH *n* pl. -ES a medicinal plant

COHOST *v* -ED, -ING, -S to host jointly

COHUNE *n* pl. -S a palm tree

COIF *v* -ED, -ING, -S to style the hair

COIFFE *v* COIFFED, COIFFING, COIFFES to coif

COIFFEUR *n* pl. -S a male hairdresser

COIFFURE *v* -FURED, -FURING, -FURES to coif

COIGN *v* -ED, -ING, -S to quoin

COIGNE *v* COIGNED, COIGNING, COIGNES to quoin

COIL *v* -ED, -ING, -S to wind in even rings

COILER *n* pl. -S one that coils

COIN *v* -ED, -ING, -S to make coins (metal currency) **COINABLE** *adj*

COINAGE *n* pl. -S the act of making coins

COINCIDE *v* -CIDED, -CIDING, -CIDES to be in the same place

COINER *n* pl. -S one that coins

COINFER *v* -FERRED, -FERRING, -FERS to infer jointly

COINHERE *v* -HERED, -HERING, -HERES to inhere jointly

COINMATE *n* pl. -S a fellow inmate

COINSURE *v* -SURED, -SURING, -SURES to insure with another

COINTER *v* -TERRED, -TERRING, -TERS to bury together

COINVENT *v* -ED, -ING, -S to invent together

COIR *n* pl. -S a fiber obtained from coconut husks

COISTREL *n* pl. -S a knave

COISTRIL *n* pl. -S coistrel

COITION *n* pl. -S coitus

COITUS *n* pl. -ES sexual intercourse **COITAL** *adj* **COITALLY** *adv*

COJOIN *v* -ED, -ING, -S to join together

COKE *v* COKED, COKING, COKES to change into a carbon fuel

COKEHEAD *n* pl. -S a cocaine addict

COL *n* pl. -S a depression between two mountains

COLA *n* pl. -S a carbonated beverage

COLANDER *n* pl. -S a kitchen utensil for draining off liquids

COLD *adj* COLDER, COLDEST having little or no warmth

COLD *n* pl. -S the relative lack of heat; a chill

COLDCOCK *v* -ED, -ING, -S to knock unconscious

COLDISH *adj* somewhat cold

COLDLY *adv* in a cold manner

COLDNESS *n* pl. -ES the state of being cold

COLE *n* pl. -S a plant of the cabbage family

COLEAD *v* -LED, -LEADING, -LEADS to lead jointly

COLEADER *n* pl. -S one that coleads

COLESEED *n* pl. -S colza

COLESLAW *n* pl. -S a salad made of shredded raw cabbage

COLESSEE *n* pl. -S a joint lessee

COLESSOR *n* pl. -S a joint lessor

COLEUS *n* pl. -ES a tropical plant

COLEWORT *n* pl. -S cole

COLIC *n* pl. -S acute abdominal pain

COLICIN *n* pl. -S an antibacterial substance

COLICINE *n* pl. -S colicin

COLICKY *adj* pertaining to or associated with colic

COLIES pl. of coly

COLIFORM *n* pl. -S a bacillus of the colon

COLIN *n* pl. -S the bobwhite

COLINEAR *adj* lying in the same straight line

COLISEUM *n* pl. -S a large structure for public entertainment

COLISTIN *n* pl. -S an antibiotic

COLITIS *n* pl. -TISES inflammation of the colon **COLITIC** *adj*

COLLAGE *v* -LAGED, -LAGING, -LAGES to arrange materials in a collage (a kind of artistic composition)

COLLAGEN *n* pl. -S a protein

COLLAPSE *v* -LAPSED, -LAPSING, -LAPSES to crumble suddenly

COLLAR *v* -ED, -ING, -S to provide with a collar (something worn around the neck)

COLLARD *n* pl. -S a variety of kale

COLLARET *n* pl. -S a small collar

COLLATE *v* -LATED, -LATING, -LATES to compare critically

COLLATOR *n* pl. -S one that collates

COLLECT *v* -ED, -ING, -S to bring together in a group

COLLEEN *n* pl. -S an Irish girl

COLLEGE *n* pl. -S a school of higher learning

COLLEGER *n* pl. -S a student supported by funds from his college

COLLEGIA *n/pl* soviet executive councils

COLLET *v* -ED, -ING, -S to set a gem in a rim or ring

COLLIDE *v* -LIDED, -LIDING, -LIDES to come together with violent impact

COLLIDER *n* pl. -S a type of particle accelerator

COLLIE *n* pl. -S a large dog

COLLIED past tense of colly

COLLIER *n* pl. -S a coal miner

COLLIERY *n* pl. -LIERIES a coal mine

COLLIES present 3d person sing. of colly

COLLINS *n* pl. -ES an alcoholic beverage

COLLOGUE *v* -LOGUED, -LOGUING, -LOGUES to conspire

COLLOID *n* pl. -S a type of chemical suspension

COLLOP *n* pl. -S a small portion of meat

COLLOQUY *n* pl. -QUIES a conversation

COLLUDE *v* -LUDED, -LUDING, -LUDES to conspire

COLLUDER *n* pl. -S one that colludes

COLLUVIA *n/pl* rock debris

COLLY *v* -LIED, -LYING, -LIES to blacken with coal dust

COLLYRIA *n/pl* medicinal lotions

COLOBOMA *n* pl. -MATA a lesion of the eye

COLOBUS *n* pl. -BI a long-tailed monkey

COLOCATE *v* -CATED, -CATING, -CATES to place two or more housing units in close proximity

COLOG *n* pl. -S the logarithm of the reciprocal of a number

COLOGNE *n* pl. -S a scented liquid **COLOGNED** *adj*

COLON *n* pl. -S a section of the large intestine

COLON *n* pl. -ES a monetary unit of Costa Rica

COLONE *n* pl. -S colon

COLONEL *n* pl. -S a military officer

COLONI pl. of colonus

COLONIAL *n* pl. -S a citizen of a colony

COLONIC *n* pl. -S irrigation of the colon

COLONIES pl. of colony

COLONISE *v* -NISED, -NISING, -NISES to colonize

COLONIST *n* pl. -S one who settles a colony

COLONIZE *v* -NIZED, -NIZING, -NIZES to establish a colony

COLONUS *n* pl. -NI a freeborn serf

COLONY *n* pl. -NIES a group of emigrants living in a new land

COLOPHON *n* pl. -S an inscription placed at the end of a book

COLOR *v* -ED, -ING, -S to give color (a visual attribute of objects) to

COLORADO *adj* of medium strength and color — used of cigars

COLORANT *n* pl. -S a pigment or dye

COLORED *adj* having color

COLORER *n* pl. -S one that colors

COLORFUL *adj* full of color

COLORING *n* pl. -S appearance in regard to color

COLORISM *n* pl. -S coloring

COLORIST *n* pl. -S a person skilled in the use of color

COLORIZE *v* -IZED, -IZING, -IZES to give color to a black-and-white film

COLORMAN	*n* pl. -MEN a sportscaster who provides commentary during a game
COLOSSAL	*adj* gigantic
COLOSSUS	*n* pl. -LOSSI or -LOSSUSES a gigantic statue
COLOTOMY	*n* pl. -MIES a surgical incision of the colon
COLOUR	*v* -ED, -ING, -S to color
COLOURER	*n* pl. -S colorer
COLPITIS	*n* pl. -TISES a vaginal inflammation
COLT	*n* pl. -S a young male horse **COLTISH** *adj*
COLTER	*n* pl. -S a blade on a plow
COLUBRID	*n* pl. -S any of a large family of snakes
COLUGO	*n* pl. -GOS a small mammal
COLUMBIC	*adj* pertaining to niobium
COLUMEL	*n* pl. -S a small column-like anatomical part
COLUMN	*n* pl. -S a vertical cylindrical support **COLUMNAL, COLUMNAR, COLUMNED** *adj*
COLURE	*n* pl. -S an astronomical circle
COLY	*n* pl. COLIES an African bird
COLZA	*n* pl. -S a plant of the cabbage family
COMA	*n* pl. -S a condition of prolonged unconsciousness
COMA	*n* pl. -MAE a tuft of silky hairs
COMAKE	*v* -MADE, -MAKING, -MAKES to serve as comaker for another's loan
COMAKER	*n* pl. -S one who assumes financial responsibility for another's default
COMAL	*adj* comose
COMANAGE	*v* -AGED, -AGING, -AGES to manage jointly
COMATE	*n* pl. -S a companion
COMATIC	*adj* having blurred vision as a result of coma
COMATIK	*n* pl. -S komatik
COMATOSE	*adj* affected with coma
COMATULA	*n* pl. -LAE a marine animal
COMB	*v* -ED, -ING, -S to arrange or clean with a comb (a toothed instrument)
COMBAT	*v* -BATED, -BATING, -BATS or -BATTED, -BATTING, -BATS to fight against
COMBATER	*n* pl. -S one that combats
COMBE	*n* pl. -S a narrow valley
COMBER	*n* pl. -S one that combs
COMBINE	*v* -BINED, -BINING, -BINES to blend
COMBINER	*n* pl. -S one that combines
COMBINGS	*n/pl* hair removed by a comb
COMBINING	present participle of combine
COMBLIKE	*adj* resembling a comb
COMBO	*n* pl. -BOS a small jazz band
COMBUST	*v* -ED, -ING, -S to burn
COME	*v* CAME, COMING, COMES or COMETH to move toward something or someone
COMEBACK	*n* pl. -S a return to former prosperity
COMEDIAN	*n* pl. -S a humorous entertainer
COMEDIC	*adj* pertaining to comedy
COMEDIES	pl. of comedy
COMEDO	*n* pl. -DOS or -DONES a skin blemish
COMEDOWN	*n* pl. -S a drop in status
COMEDY	*n* pl. -DIES a humorous play, movie, or other work
COMELY	*adj* -LIER, -LIEST pleasing to look at **COMELILY** *adv*
COMEMBER	*n* pl. -S one that shares membership
COMER	*n* pl. -S one showing great promise
COMET	*n* pl. -S a celestial body **COMETARY** *adj*
COMETH	a present 3d person sing. of come
COMETHER	*n* pl. -S an affair or matter
COMETIC	*adj* pertaining to a comet
COMFIER	comparative of comfy
COMFIEST	superlative of comfy
COMFIT	*n* pl. -S a candy
COMFORT	*v* -ED, -ING, -S to soothe in time of grief
COMFREY	*n* pl. -FREYS a coarse herb
COMFY	*adj* -FIER, -FIEST comfortable
COMIC	*n* pl. -S a comedian
COMICAL	*adj* funny
COMING	*n* pl. -S arrival

COMINGLE	*v* -GLED, -GLING, -GLES to blend thoroughly
COMITIA	*n* pl. COMITIA a public assembly in ancient Rome **COMITIAL** *adj*
COMITY	*n* pl. -TIES civility
COMIX	*n/pl* comic books or strips
COMMA	*n* pl. -MAS or -MATA a fragment of a few words or feet in ancient prosody
COMMAND	*v* -ED, -ING, -S to direct with authority
COMMANDO	*n* pl. -DOES or -DOS a military unit
COMMATA	a pl. of comma
COMMENCE	*v* -MENCED, -MENCING, -MENCES to begin
COMMEND	*v* -ED, -ING, -S to praise
COMMENT	*v* -ED, -ING, -S to remark
COMMERCE	*v* -MERCED, -MERCING, -MERCES to commune
COMMIE	*n* pl. -S a Communist
COMMIES	pl. of commy
COMMIT	*v* -MITTED, -MITTING, -MITS to do, perform, or perpetrate
COMMIX	*v* -MIXED or -MIXT, -MIXING, -MIXES to mix together
COMMODE	*n* pl. -S a cabinet
COMMON	*adj* -MONER, -MONEST ordinary
COMMON	*n* pl. -S a tract of publicly used land
COMMONER	*n* pl. -S one of the common people
COMMONLY	*adv* in a common manner
COMMOVE	*v* -MOVED, -MOVING, -MOVES to move violently
COMMUNAL	*adj* belonging to a community; public
COMMUNE	*v* -MUNED, -MUNING, -MUNES to converse intimately
COMMUTE	*v* -MUTED, -MUTING, -MUTES to exchange
COMMUTER	*n* pl. -S one that commutes
COMMY	*n* pl. -MIES commie
COMOSE	*adj* bearing a tuft of silky hairs
COMOUS	*adj* comose
COMP	*v* -ED, -ING, -S to play a jazz accompaniment
COMPACT	*adj* -PACTER, -PACTEST closely and firmly united
COMPACT	*v* -ED, -ING, -S to pack closely together
COMPADRE	*n* pl. -S a close friend
COMPANY	*v* -NIED, -NYING, -NIES to associate with
COMPARE	*v* -PARED, -PARING, -PARES to represent as similar
COMPARER	*n* pl. -S one that compares
COMPART	*v* -ED, -ING, -S to divide into parts
COMPASS	*v* -ED, -ING, -ES to go around
COMPEER	*v* -ED, -ING, -S to equal or match
COMPEL	*v* -PELLED, -PELLING, -PELS to urge forcefully
COMPEND	*n* pl. -S a brief summary
COMPERE	*v* -PERED, -PERING, -PERES to act as master of ceremonies
COMPETE	*v* -PETED, -PETING, -PETES to vie
COMPILE	*v* -PILED, -PILING, -PILES to collect into a volume
COMPILER	*n* pl. -S one that compiles
COMPLAIN	*v* -ED, -ING, -S to express discontent
COMPLEAT	*adj* highly skilled
COMPLECT	*v* -ED, -ING, -S to weave together
COMPLETE	*adj* -PLETER, -PLETEST having all necessary parts
COMPLETE	*v* -PLETED, -PLETING, -PLETES to bring to an end
COMPLEX	*adj* -PLEXER, -PLEXEST complicated
COMPLEX	*v* -ED, -ING, -ES to make complex
COMPLICE	*n* pl. -S an associate
COMPLIED	past tense of comply
COMPLIER	*n* pl. -S one that complies
COMPLIES	present 3d person sing. of comply
COMPLIN	*n* pl. -S compline
COMPLINE	*n* pl. -S the last liturgical prayer of the day
COMPLOT	*v* -PLOTTED, -PLOTTING, -PLOTS to conspire
COMPLY	*v* -PLIED, -PLYING, -PLIES to obey
COMPO	*n* pl. -POS a mixed substance
COMPONE	*adj* compony
COMPONY	*adj* composed of squares of alternating colors

COMPORT v -ED, -ING, -S to conduct oneself in a certain way

COMPOSE v -POSED, -POSING, -POSES to form the substance of

COMPOSER n pl. -S one that writes music

COMPOST v -ED, -ING, -S to fertilize

COMPOTE n pl. -S fruit stewed in syrup

COMPOUND v -ED, -ING, -S to add to

COMPRESS v -ED, -ING, -ES to compact

COMPRISE v -PRISED, -PRISING, -PRISES to include or contain

COMPRIZE v -PRIZED, -PRIZING, -PRIZES to comprise

COMPT v -ED, -ING, -S to count

COMPUTE v -PUTED, -PUTING, -PUTES to calculate

COMPUTER n pl. -S a machine that computes automatically

COMRADE n pl. -S a close friend

COMTE n pl. -S a French nobleman

CON v CONNED, CONNING, CONS to study carefully

CONATION n pl. -S the inclination to act purposefully **CONATIVE** adj

CONATUS n pl. CONATUS an effort

CONCAVE v -CAVED, -CAVING, -CAVES to make concave (curving inward)

CONCEAL v -ED, -ING, -S to keep from sight or discovery

CONCEDE v -CEDED, -CEDING, -CEDES to acknowledge as true

CONCEDER n pl. -S one that concedes

CONCEIT v -ED, -ING, -S to imagine

CONCEIVE v -CEIVED, -CEIVING, -CEIVES to understand

CONCENT n pl. -S harmony

CONCEPT n pl. -S a general idea

CONCERN v -ED, -ING, -S to be of interest to

CONCERT v -ED, -ING, -S to plan

CONCERTO n pl. -TOS or -TI a musical composition

CONCH n pl. -S or -ES a marine mollusk

CONCHA n pl. -CHAE an anatomical shell-like structure **CONCHAL** adj

CONCHIE n pl. -S conchy

CONCHOID n pl. -S a type of geometric curve

CONCHY n pl. -CHIES a conscientious objector

CONCISE adj -CISER, -CISEST succinct

CONCLAVE n pl. -S a secret meeting

CONCLUDE v -CLUDED, -CLUDING, -CLUDES to finish

CONCOCT v -ED, -ING, -S to prepare by combining ingredients

CONCORD n pl. -S a state of agreement

CONCRETE v -CRETED, -CRETING, -CRETES to solidify

CONCUR v -CURRED, -CURRING, -CURS to agree

CONCUSS v -ED, -ING, -ES to injure the brain by a violent blow

CONDEMN v -ED, -ING, -S to criticize severely

CONDENSE v -DENSED, -DENSING, -DENSES to compress

CONDIGN adj deserved; appropriate

CONDO n pl. -DOS or -DOES an individually owned unit in a multiunit structure

CONDOLE v -DOLED, -DOLING, -DOLES to mourn

CONDOLER n pl. -S one that condoles

CONDOM n pl. -S a prophylactic

CONDONE v -DONED, -DONING, -DONES to forgive or overlook

CONDONER n pl. -S one that condones

CONDOR n pl. -S or -ES a coin of Chile

CONDUCE v -DUCED, -DUCING, -DUCES to contribute to a result

CONDUCER n pl. -S one that conduces

CONDUCT v -ED, -ING, -S to lead or guide

CONDUIT n pl. -S a channel or pipe for conveying fluids

CONDYLE n pl. -S a protuberance on a bone **CONDYLAR** adj

CONE v CONED, CONING, CONES to shape like a cone (a geometric solid)

CONELRAD n pl. -S a system of defense in the event of air attack

CONENOSE n pl. -S a bloodsucking insect

CONEPATE n pl. -S a skunk

CONEPATL n pl. -S conepate

CONEY n pl. -NEYS cony

CONFAB v -FABBED, -FABBING, -FABS to chat

CONFECT v -ED, -ING, -S to prepare from various ingredients

CONFER *v* -FERRED, -FERRING, -FERS to bestow

CONFEREE *n* pl. -S one upon whom something is conferred

CONFERVA *n* pl. -VAE or -VAS a freshwater alga

CONFESS *v* -ED, -ING, -ES to acknowledge or disclose

CONFETTO *n* pl. -TI a bonbon

CONFIDE *v* -FIDED, -FIDING, -FIDES to reveal in trust or confidence

CONFIDER *n* pl. -S one that confides

CONFINE *v* -FINED, -FINING, -FINES to shut within an enclosure

CONFINER *n* pl. -S one that confines

CONFIRM *v* -ED, -ING, -S to assure the validity of

CONFIT *n* pl. -S meat cooked and preserved in its own fat

CONFLATE *v* -FLATED, -FLATING, -FLATES to blend

CONFLICT *v* -ED, -ING, -S to come into opposition

CONFLUX *n* pl. -ES a flowing together of streams

CONFOCAL *adj* having the same focus or foci

CONFORM *v* -ED, -ING, -S to become the same or similar

CONFOUND *v* -ED, -ING, -S to confuse

CONFRERE *n* pl. -S a colleague

CONFRONT *v* -ED, -ING, -S to face defiantly

CONFUSE *v* -FUSED, -FUSING, -FUSES to mix up mentally

CONFUTE *v* -FUTED, -FUTING, -FUTES to disprove

CONFUTER *n* pl. -S one that confutes

CONGA *v* -ED, -ING, -S to perform a conga (Latin American dance)

CONGE *n* pl. -S permission to depart

CONGEAL *v* -ED, -ING, -S to change from a fluid to a solid

CONGEE *v* -GEED, -GEEING, -GEES to bow politely

CONGENER *n* pl. -S one of the same kind or class

CONGER *n* pl. -S a marine eel

CONGEST *v* -ED, -ING, -S to fill to excess

CONGIUS *n* pl. -GII an ancient unit of measure

CONGLOBE *v* -GLOBED, -GLOBING, -GLOBES to become a globule

CONGO *n* pl. -GOS congou

CONGO *n* pl. -GOES an eellike amphibian

CONGOU *n* pl. -S a Chinese tea

CONGRATS *n/pl* congratulations

CONGRESS *v* -ED, -ING, -ES to assemble together

CONI pl. of conus

CONIC *n* pl. -S a geometric curve

CONICAL *adj* shaped like a cone

CONICITY *n* pl. -TIES the state of being conical

CONIDIUM *n* pl. -NIDIA a fungus spore **CONIDIAL, CONIDIAN** *adj*

CONIES pl. of cony

CONIFER *n* pl. -S an evergreen tree

CONIINE *n* pl. -S a poisonous alkaloid

CONIN *n* pl. -S coniine

CONINE *n* pl. -S coniine

CONING present participle of cone

CONIOSIS *n* pl. -OSES an infection caused by the inhalation of dust

CONIUM *n* pl. -S a poisonous herb

CONJOIN *v* -ED, -ING, -S to join together **CONJOINT** *adj*

CONJUGAL *adj* pertaining to marriage

CONJUNCT *n* pl. -S one that is joined with another

CONJURE *v* -JURED, -JURING, -JURES to summon a spirit

CONJURER *n* pl. -S a sorcerer

CONJUROR *n* pl. -S conjurer

CONK *v* -ED, -ING, -S to hit on the head

CONKER *n* pl. -S a chestnut used in a British game

CONKY *adj* full of a tree fungus

CONN *v* -ED, -ING, -S to direct the steering of a ship

CONNATE *adj* innate

CONNECT *v* -ED, -ING, -S to join together

CONNED past tense of con

CONNER *n* pl. -S one that cons

CONNING present participle of con

CONNIVE *v* -NIVED, -NIVING, -NIVES to feign ignorance of wrongdoing

CONNIVER *n* pl. -S one that connives

CONNOTE *v* -NOTED, -NOTING, -NOTES to imply another meaning besides the literal one

CONODONT *n* pl. -S a fossil

CONOID *n* pl. -S a geometric solid
CONOIDAL *adj*

CONQUER *v* -ED, -ING, -S to overcome by force

CONQUEST *n* pl. -S the act of conquering

CONQUIAN *n* pl. -S a card game

CONSENT *v* -ED, -ING, -S to permit or approve

CONSERVE *v* -SERVED, -SERVING, -SERVES to protect from loss or depletion

CONSIDER *v* -ED, -ING, -S to think about

CONSIGN *v* -ED, -ING, -S to give over to another's care

CONSIST *v* -ED, -ING, -S to be made up or composed

CONSOL *n* pl. -S a government bond

CONSOLE *v* -SOLED, -SOLING, -SOLES to comfort

CONSOLER *n* pl. -S one that consoles

CONSOMME *n* pl. -S a clear soup

CONSORT *v* -ED, -ING, -S to keep company

CONSPIRE *v* -SPIRED, -SPIRING, -SPIRES to plan secretly with another

CONSTANT *n* pl. -S something that does not vary

CONSTRUE *v* -STRUED, -STRUING, -STRUES to interpret

CONSUL *n* pl. -S an official serving abroad
CONSULAR *adj*

CONSULT *v* -ED, -ING, -S to ask an opinion of

CONSUME *v* -SUMED, -SUMING, -SUMES to use up

CONSUMER *n* pl. -S one that consumes

CONTACT *v* -ED, -ING, -S to communicate with

CONTAGIA *n/pl* causative agents of infectious diseases

CONTAIN *v* -ED, -ING, -S to hold within

CONTE *n* pl. -S a short story

CONTEMN *v* -ED, -ING, -S to scorn

CONTEMPT *n* pl. -S the feeling of one who views something as mean, vile, or worthless

CONTEND *v* -ED, -ING, -S to vie

CONTENT *v* -ED, -ING, -S to satisfy

CONTEST *v* -ED, -ING, -S to compete for

CONTEXT *n* pl. -S the part of a discourse in which a particular word or phrase appears

CONTINUA *n/pl* mathematical sets

CONTINUE *v* -UED, -UING, -UES to go on with

CONTINUO *n* pl. -UOS a type of instrumental part

CONTO *n* pl. -TOS a Portuguese money of account

CONTORT *v* -ED, -ING, -S to twist out of shape

CONTOUR *v* -ED, -ING, -S to make the outline of

CONTRA *n* pl. -S a Nicaraguan revolutionary

CONTRACT *v* -ED, -ING, -S to decrease in size or volume

CONTRAIL *n* pl. -S a visible trail of water vapor from an aircraft

CONTRARY *n* pl. -TRARIES an opposite

CONTRAST *v* -ED, -ING, -S to place in opposition to set off differences

CONTRITE *adj* deeply sorry for one's sins

CONTRIVE *v* -TRIVED, -TRIVING, -TRIVES to devise

CONTROL *v* -TROLLED, -TROLLING, -TROLS to exercise authority over

CONTUSE *v* -TUSED, -TUSING, -TUSES to bruise

CONUS *n* pl. CONI an anatomical part in mammals

CONVECT *v* -ED, -ING, -S to transfer heat by a process of circulation

CONVENE *v* -VENED, -VENING, -VENES to assemble

CONVENER *n* pl. -S one that convenes

CONVENOR *n* pl. -S convener

CONVENT *v* -ED, -ING, -S to convene

CONVERGE *v* -VERGED, -VERGING, -VERGES to come together

CONVERSE *v* -VERSED, -VERSING, -VERSES to speak together

CONVERT *v* -ED, -ING, -S to change into another form

CONVEX *n* pl. -ES a surface or body that is convex (curving outward)

CONVEXLY *adv* in a convex manner

CONVEY *v* -ED, -ING, -S to transport

CONVEYER *n* pl. -S one that conveys

CONVEYOR	*n* pl. -S conveyer
CONVICT	*v* -ED, -ING, -S to prove guilty
CONVINCE	*v* -VINCED, -VINCING, -VINCES to cause to believe something
CONVOKE	*v* -VOKED, -VOKING, -VOKES to cause to assemble
CONVOKER	*n* pl. -S one that convokes
CONVOLVE	*v* -VOLVED, -VOLVING, -VOLVES to roll together
CONVOY	*v* -ED, -ING, -S to escort
CONVULSE	*v* -VULSED, -VULSING, -VULSES to shake violently
CONY	*n* pl. CONIES a rabbit
COO	*v* COOED, COOING, COOS to make the sound of a dove
COOCH	*n* pl. -ES a sinuous dance
COOCOO	*adj* crazy
COOEE	*v* COOEED, COOEEING, COOEES to cry out shrilly
COOER	*n* pl. -S one that coos
COOEY	*v* -EYED, -EYING, -EYS to cooee
COOF	*n* pl. -S a dolt
COOINGLY	*adv* in the manner of cooing doves; affectionately
COOK	*v* -ED, -ING, -S to prepare food by heating **COOKABLE** *adj*
COOKBOOK	*n* pl. -S a book of recipes
COOKER	*n* pl. -S one that cooks
COOKERY	*n* pl. -ERIES the art of cooking
COOKEY	*n* pl. -EYS cookie
COOKIE	*n* pl. -S a small, flat cake
COOKING	*n* pl. -S the act of one that cooks
COOKLESS	*adj* having no person that cooks
COOKOUT	*n* pl. -S a meal eaten and prepared outdoors
COOKSHOP	*n* pl. -S a shop that sells cooked food
COOKTOP	*n* pl. -S a counter-top cooking apparatus
COOKWARE	*n* pl. -S utensils used in cooking
COOKY	*n* pl. COOKIES cookie
COOL	*adj* COOLER, COOLEST moderately cold
COOL	*v* -ED, -ING, -S to make less warm
COOLANT	*n* pl. -S a fluid used to cool engines
COOLDOWN	*n* pl. -S a gradual return of physiological functions to normal levels after strenuous exercise
COOLER	*n* pl. -S something that cools
COOLIE	*n* pl. -S an Oriental laborer
COOLIES	pl. of cooly
COOLISH	*adj* somewhat cool
COOLLY	*adv* in a cool manner
COOLNESS	*n* pl. -ES the state of being cool
COOLTH	*n* pl. -S coolness
COOLY	*n* pl. COOLIES coolie
COOMB	*n* pl. -S combe
COOMBE	*n* pl. -S combe
COON	*n* pl. -S a raccoon
COONCAN	*n* pl. -S conquian
COONSKIN	*n* pl. -S the pelt of a raccoon
COONTIE	*n* pl. -S a tropical plant
COOP	*v* -ED, -ING, -S to confine
COOPER	*v* -ED, -ING, -S to make or mend barrels
COOPERY	*n* pl. -ERIES the trade of coopering
COOPT	*v* -ED, -ING, -S to elect or appoint
COOPTION	*n* pl. -S the act of coopting
COOT	*n* pl. -S an aquatic bird
COOTER	*n* pl. -S a turtle
COOTIE	*n* pl. -S a body louse
COP	*v* COPPED, COPPING, COPS to steal
COPAIBA	*n* pl. -S a resin
COPAL	*n* pl. -S a resin
COPALM	*n* pl. -S a hardwood tree
COPARENT	*n* pl. -S a fellow parent
COPASTOR	*n* pl. -S one that shares the duties of a pastor
COPATRON	*n* pl. -S a fellow patron
COPE	*v* COPED, COPING, COPES to contend or strive
COPECK	*n* pl. -S kopeck
COPEMATE	*n* pl. -S an antagonist
COPEN	*n* pl. -S a blue color
COPEPOD	*n* pl. -S a minute crustacean
COPER	*n* pl. -S a horse dealer
COPIED	past tense of copy
COPIER	*n* pl. -S one that copies
COPIES	present 3d person sing. of copy

COPIHUE	*n* pl. -S a climbing vine	**COQUET**	*v* -QUETTED, -QUETTING, -QUETS to flirt
COPILOT	*n* pl. -S an assistant pilot	**COQUETRY**	*n* pl. -TRIES flirtatious behavior
COPING	*n* pl. -S the top part of a wall	**COQUETTE**	*v* -QUETTED, -QUETTING, -QUETTES to coquet
COPIOUS	*adj* abundant		
COPLANAR	*adj* lying in the same plane	**COQUILLE**	*n* pl. -S a cooking utensil
COPLOT	*v* -PLOTTED, -PLOTTING, -PLOTS to plot together	**COQUINA**	*n* pl. -S a small marine clam
COPPED	past tense of cop	**COQUITO**	*n* pl. -TOS a palm tree
COPPER	*v* -ED, -ING, -S to cover with copper (a metallic element)	**COR**	*interj* — used to express surprise, admiration, or irritation
COPPERAH	*n* pl. -S copra	**CORACLE**	*n* pl. -S a small boat
COPPERAS	*n* pl. -ES a compound used in making inks	**CORACOID**	*n* pl. -S a bone of the shoulder girdle
COPPERY	*adj* resembling copper	**CORAL**	*n* pl. -S a mass of marine animal skeletons
COPPICE	*v* -PICED, -PICING, -PICES to cause to grow in the form of a coppice (a thicket)	**CORANTO**	*n* pl. -TOS or -TOES courante
		CORBAN	*n* pl. -S an offering to God
COPPING	present participle of cop	**CORBEIL**	*n* pl. -S a sculptured fruit basket
COPPRA	*n* pl. -S copra	**CORBEL**	*v* -BELED, -BELING, -BELS or -BELLED, -BELLING, -BELS to provide a wall with a bracket
COPRA	*n* pl. -S dried coconut meat		
COPRAH	*n* pl. -S copra		
COPREMIA	*n* pl. -S a form of blood poisoning **COPREMIC** *adj*	**CORBIE**	*n* pl. -S a raven or crow
		CORBINA	*n* pl. -S a food and game fish
COPRINCE	*n* pl. -S one of two princes ruling jointly	**CORBY**	*n* pl. CORBIES corbie
		CORD	*v* -ED, -ING, -S to fasten with a cord (a thin rope)
COPSE	*n* pl. -S a coppice		
COPTER	*n* pl. -S a helicopter	**CORDAGE**	*n* pl. -S the amount of wood in an area
COPULA	*n* pl. -LAS or -LAE something that links **COPULAR** *adj*		
		CORDATE	*adj* heart-shaped
COPULATE	*v* -LATED, -LATING, -LATES to engage in coitus	**CORDELLE**	*v* -DELLED, -DELLING, -DELLES to tow a boat with a cordelle (a towrope)
COPURIFY	*v* -FIED, -FYING, -FIES to become purified with another substance		
		CORDER	*n* pl. -S one that cords
		CORDIAL	*n* pl. -S a liqueur
COPY	*v* COPIED, COPYING, COPIES to imitate	**CORDING**	*n* pl. -S the ribbed surface of cloth
COPYBOOK	*n* pl. -S a book used in teaching penmanship	**CORDITE**	*n* pl. -S an explosive powder
COPYBOY	*n* pl. -BOYS an office boy	**CORDLESS**	*adj* having no cord
COPYCAT	*v* -CATTED, -CATTING, -CATS to imitate	**CORDLIKE**	*adj* resembling a cord
		CORDOBA	*n* pl. -S a monetary unit of Nicaragua
COPYDESK	*n* pl. -S an editor's desk in a newspaper office		
		CORDON	*v* -ED, -ING, -S to form a barrier around
COPYEDIT	*v* -ED, -ING, -S to prepare copy for the printer		
		CORDOVAN	*n* pl. -S a fine leather
COPYHOLD	*n* pl. -S a type of ownership of land	**CORDUROY**	*v* -ED, -ING, -S to build a type of road
COPYIST	*n* pl. -S an imitator	**CORDWAIN**	*n* pl. -S cordovan
COPYREAD	*v* -READ, -READING, -READS to copyedit	**CORDWOOD**	*n* pl. -S wood used for fuel

CORE	*v* CORED, CORING, CORES to remove the core (the central part) of
COREDEEM	*v* -ED, -ING, -S to redeem jointly
COREIGN	*n* pl. -S a joint reign
CORELATE	*v* -LATED, -LATING, -LATES to place into mutual or reciprocal relation
CORELESS	*adj* having no core
COREMIUM	*n* pl. -MIA an organ of certain fungi
CORER	*n* pl. -S a utensil for coring apples
CORF	*n* pl. CORVES a wagon used in a mine
CORGI	*n* pl. -S a short-legged dog
CORING	present participle of core
CORIUM	*n* pl. -RIA a skin layer
CORK	*v* -ED, -ING, -S to stop up
CORKAGE	*n* pl. -S a charge for wine in a restaurant
CORKER	*n* pl. -S one that corks
CORKIER	comparative of corky
CORKIEST	superlative of corky
CORKLIKE	*adj* resembling cork (a porous tree bark)
CORKWOOD	*n* pl. -S a small tree
CORKY	*adj* CORKIER, CORKIEST corklike
CORM	*n* pl. -S a stem of certain plants **CORMLIKE, CORMOID, CORMOUS** *adj*
CORMEL	*n* pl. -S a small corm
CORN	*v* -ED, -ING, -S to preserve with salt
CORNBALL	*n* pl. -S a hick
CORNCAKE	*n* pl. -S a cake made of cornmeal
CORNCOB	*n* pl. -S the woody core of an ear of corn
CORNCRIB	*n* pl. -S a building in which corn is stored
CORNEA	*n* pl. -S a part of the eye **CORNEAL** *adj*
CORNEL	*n* pl. -S a hardwood tree or shrub
CORNEOUS	*adj* of a hornlike texture
CORNER	*v* -ED, -ING, -S to gain control of
CORNET	*n* pl. -S a trumpetlike instrument
CORNETCY	*n* -CIES a rank in the British cavalry
CORNFED	*adj* fed on corn
CORNHUSK	*n* pl. -S the husk covering an ear of corn
CORNICE	*v* -NICED, -NICING, -NICES to decorate with a molding
CORNICHE	*n* pl. -S a road built along a cliff
CORNICLE	*n* pl. -S a part of an aphid
CORNIER	comparative of corny
CORNIEST	superlative of corny
CORNILY	*adv* in a corny manner
CORNMEAL	*n* pl. -S meal made from corn
CORNPONE	*n* pl. -S a bread made with cornmeal
CORNROW	*v* -ED, -ING, -S to braid hair tightly in rows close to the scalp
CORNU	*n* pl. -NUA a hornlike bone formation **CORNUAL** *adj*
CORNUS	*n* pl. -ES a cornel
CORNUTE	*adj* horn-shaped
CORNUTED	*adj* cornute
CORNUTO	*n* pl. -TOS the husband of an unfaithful wife
CORNY	*adj* CORNIER, CORNIEST trite
CORODY	*n* pl. -DIES an allowance of food or clothes
COROLLA	*n* pl. -S a protective covering of a flower
CORONA	*n* pl. -NAS or -NAE a luminous circle around a celestial body
CORONACH	*n* pl. -S a dirge
CORONAL	*n* pl. -S a wreath worn on the head
CORONARY	*n* pl. -NARIES an artery supplying blood to the heart
CORONATE	*v* -NATED, -NATING, -NATES to crown
CORONEL	*n* pl. -S coronal
CORONER	*n* pl. -S an officer who investigates questionable deaths
CORONET	*n* pl. -S a small crown
CORONOID	*adj* crown-shaped
COROTATE	*v* -TATED, -TATING, -TATES to rotate together
CORPORA	pl. of corpus
CORPORAL	*n* pl. -S a military rank
CORPS	*n* pl. CORPS a military unit
CORPSE	*n* pl. -S a dead body
CORPSMAN	*n* pl. -MEN an enlisted man trained in first aid

CORPUS *n* pl. -PORA a human or animal body

CORRADE *v* -RADED, -RADING, -RADES to erode

CORRAL *v* -RALLED, -RALLING, -RALS to place livestock in a corral (an enclosure)

CORRECT *v* -ED, -ING, -S to make free from error

CORRECT *adj* -RECTER, -RECTEST free from error

CORRIDA *n* pl. -S a bullfight

CORRIDOR *n* pl. -S a narrow hallway

CORRIE *n* pl. -S a cirque

CORRIVAL *n* pl. -S a rival or opponent

CORRODE *v* -RODED, -RODING, -RODES to eat away gradually

CORRODY *n* pl. -DIES corody

CORRUPT *adj* -RUPTER, -RUPTEST dishonest and venal

CORRUPT *v* -ED, -ING, -S to subvert the honesty or integrity of

CORSAC *n* pl. -S an Asian fox

CORSAGE *n* pl. -S a small bouquet of flowers

CORSAIR *n* pl. -S a pirate

CORSE *n* pl. -S a corpse

CORSELET *n* pl. -S a piece of body armor

CORSET *v* -ED, -ING, -S to fit with a corset (a supporting undergarment)

CORSETRY *n* pl. -RIES the work of making corsets

CORSLET *n* pl. -S corselet

CORTEGE *n* pl. -S a retinue

CORTEX *n* pl. -TICES or -TEXES the outer layer of an organ **CORTICAL** *adj*

CORTIN *n* pl. -S a hormone

CORTISOL *n* pl. -S a hormone

CORULER *n* pl. -S one that rules jointly

CORUNDUM *n* pl. -S a hard mineral

CORVEE *n* pl. -S an obligation to perform feudal service

CORVES pl. of corf

CORVET *n* pl. -S corvette

CORVETTE *n* pl. -S a small, swift warship

CORVINA *n* pl. -S corbina

CORVINE *adj* pertaining or belonging to the crow family of birds

CORY *n* pl. CORY a former monetary unit of Guinea

CORYBANT *n* pl. -BANTS or -BANTES a reveler

CORYMB *n* pl. -S a flower cluster **CORYMBED** *adj*

CORYPHEE *n* pl. -S a ballet dancer

CORYZA *n* pl. -S a head cold **CORYZAL** *adj*

COS *n* pl. -ES a variety of lettuce

COSCRIPT *v* -ED, -ING, -S to collaborate in preparing a script for

COSEC *n* pl. -S cosecant

COSECANT *n* pl. -S a trigonometric function of an angle

COSET *n* pl. -S a mathematical subset

COSEY *n* pl. -SEYS a cozy

COSH *v* -ED, -ING, -ES to bludgeon

COSHER *v* -ED, -ING, -S to coddle

COSIE *n* pl. -S a cozy

COSIED past tense of cosy

COSIER comparative of cosy

COSIES present 3d person sing. of cosy

COSIEST superlative of cosy

COSIGN *v* -ED, -ING, -S to sign jointly

COSIGNER *n* pl. -S one that cosigns

COSILY *adv* in a cosy manner

COSINE *n* pl. -S a trigonometric function of an angle

COSINESS *n* pl. -ES coziness

COSMETIC *n* pl. -S a beauty preparation

COSMIC *adj* pertaining to the cosmos

COSMICAL *adj* cosmic

COSMISM *n* pl. -S a philosophical theory

COSMIST *n* pl. -S a supporter of cosmism

COSMOS *n* pl. -ES the universe regarded as an orderly system

COSS *n* pl. COSS kos

COSSACK *n* pl. -S a Russian cavalryman

COSSET *v* -ED, -ING, -S to fondle

COST *v* COST or COSTED, COSTING, COSTS to estimate a price for production of

COSTA *n* pl. -TAE a rib **COSTAL** *adj*

COSTAR *v* -STARRED, -STARRING, -STARS to star with another actor

COSTARD *n* pl. -S a large cooking apple

COSTATE *adj* having a rib or ribs

COSTER *n* pl. -S a hawker of fruit or vegetables

COSTIVE *adj* constipated

COSTLESS *adj* free of charge

COSTLY *adj* -LIER, -LIEST expensive

COSTMARY *n* pl. -MARIES an herb used in salads

COSTREL *n* pl. -S a flask

COSTUME *v* -TUMED, -TUMING, -TUMES to supply with a costume (a style of dress)

COSTUMER *n* pl. -S one that costumes

COSTUMEY *adj* of or pertaining to a costume

COSTUMING present participle of costume

COSY *v* COSIED, COSYING, COSIES cozy

COSY *adj* COSIER, COSIEST cozy

COT *n* pl. -S a light, narrow bed

COTAN *n* pl. -S a trigonometric function of an angle

COTE *v* COTED, COTING, COTES to pass by

COTEAU *n* pl. -TEAUX the higher ground of a region

COTENANT *n* pl. -S one who is a tenant with another in the same place

COTERIE *n* pl. -S a clique

COTHURN *n* pl. -S a buskin worn by ancient Roman actors

COTHURNI *n/pl* cothurns

COTIDAL *adj* indicating coincidence of the tides

COTILLON *n* pl. -S a ballroom dance

COTING present participle of cote

COTQUEAN *n* pl. -S a vulgar woman

COTTA *n* pl. -TAE or -TAS a short surplice

COTTAGE *n* pl. -S a small house **COTTAGEY** *adj*

COTTAGER *n* pl. -S one that lives in a cottage

COTTAR *n* pl. -S a tenant farmer

COTTER *n* pl. -S a pin or wedge used for fastening parts together **COTTERED** *adj*

COTTIER *n* pl. -S cottar

COTTON *v* -ED, -ING, -S to take a liking

COTTONY *adj* resembling cotton (a soft, fibrous material)

COTYLOID *adj* cup-shaped

COTYPE *n* pl. -S a taxonomic type

COUCH *v* -ED, -ING, -ES to put into words

COUCHANT *adj* lying down

COUCHER *n* pl. -S one that couches

COUCHING *n* pl. -S a form of embroidery

COUDE *adj* pertaining to a type of telescope

COUGAR *n* pl. -S a mountain lion

COUGH *v* -ED, -ING, -S to expel air from the lungs noisily

COUGHER *n* pl. -S one that coughs

COULD past tense of can

COULDEST a past 2d person sing. of can

COULDST a past 2d person sing. of can

COULEE *n* pl. -S a small ravine

COULIS *n* pl. -LISES a thick sauce of pureed vegetable or fruit

COULISSE *n* pl. -S a side scene of a theatre stage

COULOIR *n* pl. -S a deep gorge or gully

COULOMB *n* pl. -S an electrical measure

COULTER *n* pl. -S colter

COUMARIN *n* pl. -S a chemical compound **COUMARIC** *adj*

COUMAROU *n* pl. -S the seed of a tropical tree

COUNCIL *n* pl. -S a group of persons appointed for a certain function

COUNSEL *v* -SELED, -SELING, -SELS or -SELLED, -SELLING, -SELS to advise

COUNT *v* -ED, -ING, -S to list or mention the units of one by one to ascertain the total

COUNTER *v* -ED, -ING, -S to oppose

COUNTESS *n* pl. -ES a noblewoman

COUNTIAN *n* pl. -S a resident of a county

COUNTRY *n* pl. -TRIES the territory of a nation

COUNTY *n* pl. -TIES an administrative division of a state

COUP *v* -ED, -ING, -S to overturn

COUPE *n* pl. -S an automobile with two doors

COUPLE *v* -PLED, -PLING, -PLES to unite in pairs

COUPLER *n* pl. -S one that couples

COUPLET *n* pl. -S a pair of successive lines of verse

COUPLING	*n* pl. -S a joining device
COUPON	*n* pl. -S a certificate entitling the holder to certain benefits
COURAGE	*n* pl. -S the quality that enables one to face danger fearlessly; spirit
COURANT	*n* pl. -S courante
COURANTE	*n* pl. -S an old, lively dance
COURANTO	*n* pl. -TOS or -TOES courante
COURIER	*n* pl. -S a messenger
COURLAN	*n* pl. -S a wading bird
COURSE	*v* COURSED, COURSING, COURSES to cause hounds to chase game
COURSER	*n* pl. -S one that courses
COURSING	*n* pl. -S the pursuit of game by hounds
COURT	*v* -ED, -ING, -S to woo
COURTER	*n* pl. -S one that courts
COURTESY	*v* -SIED, -SYING, -SIES to curtsy
COURTIER	*n* pl. -S one who attends a royal court
COURTLY	*adj* -LIER, -LIEST stately
COUSCOUS	*n* pl. -ES a North African cereal
COUSIN	*n* pl. -S a child of one's aunt or uncle **COUSINLY** *adj*
COUSINRY	*n* pl. -RIES cousins collectively
COUTEAU	*n* pl. -TEAUX a knife
COUTER	*n* pl. -S a piece of armor for the elbow
COUTH	*adj* COUTHER, COUTHEST sophisticated
COUTH	*n* pl. -S refinement
COUTHIE	*adj* COUTHIER, COUTHIEST friendly
COUTURE	*n* pl. -S the business of dressmaking
COUVADE	*n* pl. -S a primitive birth ritual
COVALENT	*adj* sharing electron pairs
COVE	*v* COVED, COVING, COVES to curve over or inward
COVEN	*n* pl. -S a group of witches
COVENANT	*v* -ED, -ING, -S to enter into a binding agreement
COVER	*v* -ED, -ING, -S to place something over or upon
COVERAGE	*n* pl. -S the extent to which something is covered
COVERALL	*n* pl. -S a one-piece work garment
COVERER	*n* pl. -S one that covers
COVERING	*n* pl. -S something that covers
COVERLET	*n* pl. -S a bed covering
COVERLID	*n* pl. -S a coverlet
COVERT	*n* pl. -S a hiding place
COVERTLY	*adv* secretly
COVERUP	*n* pl. -S something used to conceal improper activity
COVET	*v* -ED, -ING, -S to desire greatly
COVETER	*n* pl. -S one that covets
COVETOUS	*adj* excessively desirous
COVEY	*n* pl. -EYS a flock of birds
COVIN	*n* pl. -S a conspiracy to defraud
COVING	*n* pl. -S a concave molding
COW	*n* pl. -S or KINE a farm animal
COW	*v* -ED, -ING, -S to intimidate
COWAGE	*n* pl. -S a tropical vine
COWARD	*n* pl. -S one who lacks courage
COWARDLY	*adj* lacking courage
COWBANE	*n* pl. -S a poisonous plant
COWBELL	*n* pl. -S a bell around a cow's neck
COWBERRY	*n* pl. -RIES a pasture shrub
COWBIND	*n* pl. -S a species of bryony
COWBIRD	*n* pl. -S a blackbird
COWBOY	*n* pl. -BOYS a ranch worker
COWEDLY	*adv* in a cowed manner
COWER	*v* -ED, -ING, -S to cringe
COWFISH	*n* pl. -ES an aquatic mammal
COWFLAP	*n* pl. -S cowflop
COWFLOP	*n* pl. -S a cowpat
COWGIRL	*n* pl. -S a female ranch worker
COWHAGE	*n* pl. -S cowage
COWHAND	*n* pl. -S a cowboy
COWHERB	*n* pl. -S an annual herb
COWHERD	*n* pl. -S one who tends cattle
COWHIDE	*v* -HIDED, -HIDING, -HIDES to flog with a leather whip
COWIER	comparative of cowy
COWIEST	superlative of cowy
COWINNER	*n* pl. -S one of two or more winners
COWL	*v* -ED, -ING, -S to cover with a hood
COWLICK	*n* pl. -S a lock of unruly hair

COWLING   *n* pl. -S a covering for an aircraft engine

COWMAN   *n* pl. -MEN one who owns cattle

COWORKER   *n* pl. -S a fellow worker

COWPAT   *n* pl. -S a dropping of cow dung

COWPEA   *n* pl. -S a black-eyed pea

COWPIE   *n* pl. -S a cowpat

COWPLOP   *n* pl. -S a cowpat

COWPOKE   *n* pl. -S a cowboy

COWPOX   *n* pl. -ES a cattle disease

COWRIE   *n* pl. -S cowry

COWRITE   *v* -WROTE, -WRITTEN, -WRITING, -WRITES to collaborate in writing

COWRY   *n* pl. -RIES a glossy seashell

COWSHED   *n* pl. -S a shelter for cows

COWSKIN   *n* pl. -S the hide of a cow

COWSLIP   *n* pl. -S a flowering plant

COWY   *adj* COWIER, COWIEST suggestive of a cow

COX   *v* -ED, -ING, -ES to coxswain

COXA   *n* pl. COXAE the hip or hip joint **COXAL** *adj*

COXALGIA   *n* pl. -S pain in the hip **COXALGIC** *adj*

COXALGY   *n* pl. -GIES coxalgia

COXCOMB   *n* pl. -S a conceited dandy

COXITIS   *n* pl. COXITIDES inflammation of the hip joint

COXSWAIN   *v* -ED, -ING, -S to steer a racing rowboat

COY   *adj* COYER, COYEST shy

COY   *v* -ED, -ING, -S to caress

COYDOG   *n* pl. -S a hybrid between a coyote and a wild dog

COYISH   *adj* somewhat coy

COYLY   *adv* in a coy manner

COYNESS   *n* pl. -ES the state of being coy

COYOTE   *n* pl. -S a small wolf

COYPOU   *n* pl. -S a coypu

COYPU   *n* pl. -S an aquatic rodent

COZ   *n* pl. COZES or COZZES a cousin

COZEN   *v* -ED, -ING, -S to deceive

COZENAGE   *n* pl. -S the practice of cozening

COZENER   *n* pl. -S one that cozens

COZEY   *n* pl. -ZEYS a cover for a teapot

COZIE   *n* pl. -S a cozey

COZIED   past tense of cozy

COZIER   comparative of cozy

COZIES   present 3d person sing. of cozy

COZIEST   superlative of cozy

COZINESS   *n* pl. -ES the state of being cozy

COZY   *v* COZIED, COZYING, COZIES to attempt to get on friendly terms

COZY   *adj* COZIER, COZIEST snug and comfortable **COZILY** *adv*

COZZES   a pl. of coz

CRAAL   *v* -ED, -ING, -S to kraal

CRAB   *v* CRABBED, CRABBING, CRABS to complain

CRABBER   *n* pl. -S one that crabs

CRABBY   *adj* -BIER, -BIEST grumpy **CRABBILY** *adv*

CRABMEAT   *n* pl. -S the edible part of a crab

CRABWISE   *adv* sideways

CRACK   *v* -ED, -ING, -S to break without dividing into parts

CRACKER   *n* pl. -S a thin, crisp biscuit

CRACKING   *n* pl. -S a chemical process

CRACKLE   *v* -LED, -LING, -LES to make a succession of snapping sounds

CRACKLY   *adj* -LIER, -LIEST brittle

CRACKNEL   *n* pl. -S a hard, crisp biscuit

CRACKPOT   *n* pl. -S an eccentric person

CRACKUP   *n* pl. -S a collision

CRACKY   *interj* — used to express surprise

CRADLE   *v* -DLED, -DLING, -DLES to nurture during infancy

CRADLER   *n* pl. -S one that cradles

CRAFT   *v* -ED, -ING, -S to make by hand

CRAFTY   *adj* CRAFTIER, CRAFTIEST skillful in deceiving **CRAFTILY** *adv*

CRAG   *n* pl. -S a large jagged rock **CRAGGED** *adj*

CRAGGY   *adj* -GIER, -GIEST full of crags **CRAGGILY** *adv*

CRAGSMAN   *n* pl. -MEN one who climbs crags

CRAKE   *n* pl. -S a small, harsh-voiced bird

CRAM   *v* CRAMMED, CRAMMING, CRAMS to fill or pack tightly

CRAMBE   *n* pl. -S an annual herb

CRAMBO   *n* pl. -BOS or -BOES a word game

CRAMMED	past tense of cram	**CRASES**	pl. of crasis
CRAMMER	n pl. -S one that crams	**CRASH**	v -ED, -ING, -ES to collide noisily
CRAMMING	present participle of cram	**CRASHER**	n pl. -S one that crashes
CRAMOISY	n pl. -SIES crimson cloth	**CRASIS**	n pl. CRASES a vowel contraction
CRAMP	v -ED, -ING, -S to restrain or confine	**CRASS**	adj CRASSER, CRASSEST grossly vulgar or stupid **CRASSLY** adv
CRAMPIT	n pl. -S a piece of equipment used in curling		
CRAMPON	n pl. -S a device for raising heavy objects	**CRATCH**	n pl. -ES a manger
		CRATE	v CRATED, CRATING, CRATES to put in a packing box
CRAMPOON	n pl. -S crampon		
CRANCH	v -ED, -ING, -ES to craunch	**CRATER**	v -ED, -ING, -S to form cavities in a surface
CRANE	v CRANED, CRANING, CRANES to stretch out one's neck	**CRATON**	n pl. -S a part of the earth's crust **CRATONIC** adj
CRANIA	a pl. of cranium	**CRAUNCH**	v -ED, -ING, -ES to crunch
CRANIAL	adj pertaining to the skull	**CRAVAT**	n pl. -S a necktie
CRANIATE	n pl. -S one that has a skull	**CRAVE**	v CRAVED, CRAVING, CRAVES to desire greatly
CRANING	present participle of crane		
CRANIUM	n pl. -NIUMS or -NIA the skull	**CRAVEN**	v -ED, -ING, -S to make cowardly
CRANK	v -ED, -ING, -S to start manually	**CRAVENLY**	adv in a cowardly manner
CRANK	adj CRANKER, CRANKEST lively	**CRAVER**	n pl. -S one that craves
		CRAVING	n pl. -S a great desire
CRANKIER	comparative of cranky	**CRAW**	n pl. -S the stomach of an animal
CRANKIEST	superlative of cranky	**CRAWDAD**	n pl. -S a crayfish
CRANKILY	adv in a cranky manner	**CRAWFISH**	v -ED, -ING, -ES to back out or retreat
CRANKISH	adj eccentric		
CRANKLE	v -KLED, -KLING, -KLES to crinkle	**CRAWL**	v -ED, -ING, -S to move with the body on or near the ground
CRANKLY	adv in a crank manner	**CRAWLER**	n pl. -S one that crawls
CRANKOUS	adj cranky	**CRAWLWAY**	n pl. -WAYS a small, low tunnel
CRANKPIN	n pl. -S the handle of a crank	**CRAWLY**	adj CRAWLIER, CRAWLIEST creepy
CRANKY	adj CRANKIER, CRANKIEST grumpy		
		CRAYFISH	n pl. -ES a crustacean
CRANNIED	adj having crannies	**CRAYON**	v -ED, -ING, -S to use a drawing implement
CRANNIES	pl. of cranny		
CRANNOG	n pl. -S an artificial island	**CRAZE**	v CRAZED, CRAZING, CRAZES to make insane
CRANNOGE	n pl. -S crannog		
CRANNY	n pl. -NIES a crevice **CRANNIED** adj	**CRAZY**	adj -ZIER, -ZIEST insane **CRAZILY** adv
CRAP	v CRAPPED, CRAPPING, CRAPS to throw a 2, 3, or 12 in a dice game	**CRAZY**	n pl. -ZIES a crazy person
		CREAK	v -ED, -ING, -S to squeak
CRAPE	v CRAPED, CRAPING, CRAPES to crepe	**CREAKY**	adj CREAKIER, CREAKIEST creaking **CREAKILY** adv
CRAPPIE	n pl. -S an edible fish	**CREAM**	v -ED, -ING, -S to form cream (a part of milk)
CRAPPING	present participle of crap		
CRAPPY	adj -PIER, -PIEST markedly inferior in quality	**CREAMER**	n pl. -S a cream pitcher
		CREAMERY	n pl. -ERIES a dairy

CREAMY	*adj* CREAMIER, CREAMIEST rich in cream **CREAMILY** *adv*
CREASE	*v* CREASED, CREASING, CREASES to make a fold or wrinkle in
CREASER	*n* pl. -S one that creases
CREASY	*adj* CREASIER, CREASIEST having folds or wrinkles
CREATE	*v* -ATED, -ATING, -ATES to cause to exist
CREATIN	*n* pl. -S creatine
CREATINE	*n* pl. -S a chemical compound
CREATION	*n* pl. -S something created
CREATIVE	*adj* having the ability to create
CREATOR	*n* pl. -S one that creates
CREATURE	*n* pl. -S a living being
CRECHE	*n* pl. -S a day nursery
CREDAL	*adj* pertaining to a creed
CREDENCE	*n* pl. -S belief
CREDENDA	*n/pl* articles of faith
CREDENT	*adj* believing
CREDENZA	*n* pl. -S a piece of furniture
CREDIBLE	*adj* believable **CREDIBLY** *adv*
CREDIT	*v* -ED, -ING, -S to accept as true
CREDITOR	*n* pl. -S one to whom money is owed
CREDO	*n* pl. -DOS a creed
CREED	*n* pl. -S a statement of belief **CREEDAL** *adj*
CREEK	*n* pl. -S a watercourse smaller than a river
CREEL	*v* -ED, -ING, -S to put fish in a creel (a fish basket)
CREEP	*v* CREPT, CREEPING, CREEPS to crawl
CREEPAGE	*n* pl. -S gradual movement
CREEPER	*n* pl. -S one that creeps
CREEPIE	*n* pl. -S a low stool
CREEPY	*adj* CREEPIER, CREEPIEST repugnant **CREEPILY** *adv*
CREESE	*n* pl. -S kris
CREESH	*v* -ED, -ING, -ES to grease
CREMAINS	*n/pl* the ashes of a cremated body
CREMATE	*v* -MATED, -MATING, -MATES to reduce to ashes by burning
CREMATOR	*n* pl. -S one that cremates
CREME	*n* pl. -S cream
CRENATE	*adj* having an edge with rounded projections
CRENATED	*adj* crenate
CRENEL	*v* -ELED, -ELING, -ELS or -ELLED, -ELLING, -ELS to provide with crenelles
CRENELLE	*n* pl. -S a rounded projection
CREODONT	*n* pl. -S an extinct carnivore
CREOLE	*n* pl. -S a type of mixed language
CREOLISE	*v* -ISED, -ISING, -ISES to creolize
CREOLIZE	*v* -IZED, -IZING, -IZES to cause a language to become a creole
CREOSOL	*n* pl. -S a chemical compound
CREOSOTE	*v* -SOTED, -SOTING, -SOTES to treat with a wood preservative
CREPE	*v* CREPED, CREPING, CREPES to frizz the hair
CREPEY	*adj* CREPIER, CREPIEST crinkly
CREPON	*n* pl. -S a crinkled fabric
CREPT	past tense of creep
CREPY	*adj* CREPIER, CREPIEST crepey
CRESCENT	*n* pl. -S the figure of the moon in its first or last quarter
CRESCIVE	*adj* increasing
CRESOL	*n* pl. -S a chemical disinfectant
CRESS	*n* pl. -ES a plant used in salads
CRESSET	*n* pl. -S a metal cup for burning oil
CREST	*v* -ED, -ING, -S to reach a crest (a peak)
CRESTAL	*adj* pertaining to a crest (a peak)
CRESTING	*n* pl. -S a decorative coping
CRESYL	*n* pl. -S tolyl
CRESYLIC	*adj* pertaining to cresol
CRETIC	*n* pl. -S a type of metrical foot
CRETIN	*n* pl. -S an idiot
CRETONNE	*n* pl. -S a heavy fabric
CREVALLE	*n* pl. -S a food and game fish
CREVASSE	*v* -VASSED, -VASSING, -VASSES to fissure
CREVICE	*n* pl. -S a cleft **CREVICED** *adj*
CREW	*v* -ED, -ING, -S to serve aboard a ship
CREWEL	*n* pl. -S a woolen yarn
CREWLESS	*adj* without any crewmen
CREWMAN	*n* pl. -MEN one who serves on a ship

CREWMATE *n* pl. -S a fellow crewman

CREWNECK *n* pl. -S a sweater with a collarless neckline

CRIB *v* CRIBBED, CRIBBING, CRIBS to confine closely

CRIBBAGE *n* pl. -S a card game

CRIBBER *n* pl. -S one that cribs

CRIBBING *n* pl. -S a supporting framework

CRIBBLED *adj* covered with dots

CRIBROUS *adj* pierced with small holes

CRIBWORK *n* pl. -S a framework of logs

CRICETID *n* pl. -S a small rodent

CRICK *v* -ED, -ING, -S to cause a spasm of the neck

CRICKET *v* -ED, -ING, -S to play cricket (a ball game)

CRICKEY *interj* — used as a mild oath

CRICOID *n* pl. -S a cartilage of the larynx

CRIED past tense of cry

CRIER *n* pl. -S one that cries

CRIES present 3d person sing. of cry

CRIKEY *interj* — used as a mild oath

CRIME *n* pl. -S a violation of the law

CRIMINAL *n* pl. -S one who has committed a crime

CRIMMER *n* pl. -S krimmer

CRIMP *v* -ED, -ING, -S to pleat

CRIMPER *n* pl. -S one that crimps

CRIMPLE *v* -PLED, -PLING, -PLES to wrinkle

CRIMPY *adj* CRIMPIER, CRIMPIEST wavy

CRIMSON *v* -ED, -ING, -S to make crimson (a red color)

CRINGE *v* CRINGED, CRINGING, CRINGES to shrink in fear

CRINGER *n* pl. -S one that cringes

CRINGLE *n* pl. -S a small loop of rope

CRINITE *n* pl. -S a fossil crinoid

CRINKLE *v* -KLED, -KLING, -KLES to wrinkle

CRINKLY *adj* -KLIER, -KLIEST crinkled

CRINOID *n* pl. -S a marine animal

CRINUM *n* pl. -S a tropical herb

CRIOLLO *n* pl. -LLOS a person of Spanish ancestry

CRIPE *interj* — used as a mild oath

CRIPES *interj* — used as a mild oath

CRIPPLE *v* -PLED, -PLING, -PLES to disable or impair

CRIPPLER *n* pl. -S one that cripples

CRIS *n* pl. -ES kris

CRISIS *n* pl. CRISES a crucial turning point **CRISIC** *adj*

CRISP *adj* CRISPER, CRISPEST brittle

CRISP *v* -ED, -ING, -S to make crisp

CRISPATE *adj* curled

CRISPEN *v* -ED, -ING, -S to make crisp

CRISPER *n* pl. -S one that crisps

CRISPLY *adv* in a crisp manner

CRISPY *adj* CRISPIER, CRISPIEST crisp **CRISPILY** *adv*

CRISSUM *n* pl. CRISSA a region of feathers on a bird **CRISSAL** *adj*

CRISTA *n* pl. -TAE a part of a cell

CRISTATE *adj* having a projection on the head

CRITERIA *n/pl* standards of judgment

CRITIC *n* pl. -S one who judges the merits of something **CRITICAL** *adj*

CRITIQUE *v* -TIQUED, -TIQUING, -TIQUES to judge as a critic

CRITTER *n* pl. -S a creature

CRITTUR *n* pl. -S critter

CROAK *v* -ED, -ING, -S to utter a low, hoarse sound

CROAKER *n* pl. -S one that croaks

CROAKY *adj* CROAKIER, CROAKIEST low and hoarse **CROAKILY** *adv*

CROC *n* pl. -S a crocodile

CROCEIN *n* pl. -S a red dye

CROCEINE *n* pl. -S crocein

CROCHET *v* -ED, -ING, -S to do a type of needlework

CROCI a pl. of crocus

CROCINE *adj* pertaining to the crocus

CROCK *v* -ED, -ING, -S to stain or soil

CROCKERY *n* pl. -ERIES pottery

CROCKET *n* pl. -S an architectural ornament

CROCOITE *n* pl. -S a mineral

CROCUS *n* pl. -CUSES or -CI a flowering plant

CROFT *n* pl. -S a small tenant farm

CROFTER *n* pl. -S a tenant farmer

CROJIK	*n* pl. -S a triangular sail
CROMLECH	*n* pl. -S a dolmen
CRONE	*n* pl. -S a withered old woman
CRONY	*n* pl. CRONIES a close friend
CRONYISM	*n* pl. -S a kind of political favoritism
CROOK	*v* -ED, -ING, -S to bend
CROOKED	*adj* -EDER, -EDEST dishonest
CROOKERY	*n* pl. -ERIES crooked activity
CROON	*v* -ED, -ING, -S to sing softly
CROONER	*n* pl. -S one that croons
CROP	*v* CROPPED, CROPPING, CROPS to cut off short
CROPLAND	*n* pl. -S farmland
CROPLESS	*adj* being without crops (agricultural produce)
CROPPED	past tense of crop
CROPPER	*n* pl. -S one that crops
CROPPIE	*n* pl. -S crappie
CROPPING	present participle of crop
CROQUET	*v* -ED, -ING, -S to drive a ball away in a certain game
CROQUIS	*n* pl. CROQUIS a sketch
CRORE	*n* pl. -S a monetary unit of India
CROSIER	*n* pl. -S a bishop's staff
CROSS	*v* -ED, -ING, -ES to intersect
CROSS	*adj* CROSSER, CROSSEST ill-tempered
CROSSARM	*n* pl. -S a horizontal bar
CROSSBAR	*v* -BARRED, -BARRING, -BARS to fasten with crossarms
CROSSBOW	*n* pl. -S a kind of weapon
CROSSCUT	*v* -CUT, -CUTTING, -CUTS to cut across
CROSSE	*n* pl. -S a lacrosse stick
CROSSER	*n* pl. -S one that crosses
CROSSING	*n* pl. -S an intersection
CROSSLET	*n* pl. -S a heraldic symbol
CROSSLY	*adv* in a cross manner
CROSSTIE	*n* pl. -S a transverse beam
CROSSWAY	*n* pl. -WAYS a road that crosses another road
CROTCH	*n* pl. -ES an angle formed by two diverging parts **CROTCHED** *adj*
CROTCHET	*n* pl. -S a small hook
CROTON	*n* pl. -S a tropical plant
CROUCH	*v* -ED, -ING, -ES to stoop

CROUP	*n* pl. -S a disease of the throat
CROUPE	*n* pl. -S the rump of certain animals
CROUPIER	*n* pl. -S an attendant in a casino
CROUPOUS	*adj* pertaining to croup
CROUPY	*adj* CROUPIER, CROUPIEST affected with croup **CROUPILY** *adv*
CROUSE	*adj* lively **CROUSELY** *adv*
CROUTON	*n* pl. -S a small cube of toasted bread
CROW	*v* -ED, -ING, -S to boast
CROWBAR	*v* -BARRED, -BARRING, -BARS to use a steel bar as a lever
CROWD	*v* -ED, -ING, -S to press into an insufficient space
CROWDER	*n* pl. -S one that crowds
CROWDIE	*n* pl. -S crowdy
CROWDY	*n* pl. -DIES porridge
CROWER	*n* pl. -S one that crows
CROWFOOT	*n* pl. -FOOTS or -FEET a flowering plant
CROWN	*v* -ED, -ING, -S to supply with a crown (a royal headpiece)
CROWNER	*n* pl. -S a coroner
CROWNET	*n* pl. -S a coronet
CROWSTEP	*n* pl. -S a step on top of a wall
CROZE	*n* pl. -S a tool used in barrel-making
CROZER	*n* pl. -S a croze
CROZIER	*n* pl. -S crosier
CRUCES	a pl. of crux
CRUCIAL	*adj* of supreme importance
CRUCIAN	*n* pl. -S a European fish
CRUCIATE	*adj* cross-shaped
CRUCIBLE	*n* pl. -S a heat-resistant vessel
CRUCIFER	*n* pl. -S one who carries a cross
CRUCIFIX	*n* pl. -ES a cross bearing an image of Christ
CRUCIFY	*v* -FIED, -FYING, -FIES to put to death on a cross
CRUCK	*n* pl. -S a curved roof timber
CRUD	*v* CRUDDED, CRUDDING, CRUDS to curd
CRUDDY	*adj* -DIER, -DIEST filthy; contemptible
CRUDE	*adj* CRUDER, CRUDEST unrefined **CRUDELY** *adv*
CRUDE	*n* pl. -S unrefined petroleum

CRUDITES	*n/pl* pieces of raw vegetables served with a dip
CRUDITY	*n* pl. -TIES the state of being crude
CRUEL	*adj* CRUELER, CRUELEST or CRUELLER, CRUELLEST indifferent to the pain of others **CRUELLY** *adv*
CRUELTY	*n* pl. -TIES a cruel act
CRUET	*n* pl. -S a glass bottle
CRUISE	*v* CRUISED, CRUISING, CRUISES to sail about touching at several ports
CRUISER	*n* pl. -S a boat that cruises
CRUISING	*n* pl. -S the act of driving around in search of fun
CRULLER	*n* pl. -S a small sweet cake
CRUMB	*v* -ED, -ING, -S to break into crumbs (small pieces)
CRUMBER	*n* pl. -S one that crumbs
CRUMBIER	comparative of crumby
CRUMBIEST	superlative of crumby
CRUMBLE	*v* -BLED, -BLING, -BLES to break into small pieces
CRUMBLY	*adj* -BLIER, -BLIEST easily crumbled
CRUMBUM	*n* pl. -S a despicable person
CRUMBY	*adj* CRUMBIER, CRUMBIEST full of crumbs
CRUMHORN	*n* pl. -S a double-reed woodwind instrument
CRUMMIE	*n* pl. -S a cow with crooked horns
CRUMMY	*adj* -MIER, -MIEST of little or no value
CRUMP	*v* -ED, -ING, -S to crunch
CRUMPET	*n* pl. -S a small cake cooked on a griddle
CRUMPLE	*v* -PLED, -PLING, -PLES to wrinkle
CRUMPLY	*adj* -PLIER, -PLIEST easily wrinkled
CRUNCH	*v* -ED, -ING, -ES to chew with a crackling sound
CRUNCHER	*n* pl. -S one that crunches
CRUNCHY	*adj* CRUNCHIER, CRUNCHIEST crisp
CRUNODE	*n* pl. -S a point at which a curve crosses itself **CRUNODAL** *adj*
CRUOR	*n* pl. -S clotted blood
CRUPPER	*n* pl. -S the rump of a horse
CRURAL	*adj* pertaining to the thigh or leg
CRUS	*n* pl. CRURA a part of the leg
CRUSADE	*v* -SADED, -SADING, -SADES to engage in a holy war
CRUSADER	*n* pl. -S one that crusades
CRUSADO	*n* pl. -DOES or -DOS an old Portuguese coin
CRUSE	*n* pl. -S a small bottle
CRUSET	*n* pl. -S a melting pot
CRUSH	*v* -ED, -ING, -ES to press or squeeze out of shape
CRUSHER	*n* pl. -S one that crushes
CRUSILY	*adj* covered with crosslets
CRUST	*v* -ED, -ING, -S to form a crust (a hardened outer surface)
CRUSTAL	*adj* pertaining to the earth's crust
CRUSTOSE	*adj* forming a thin, brittle crust
CRUSTY	*adj* CRUSTIER, CRUSTIEST surly **CRUSTILY** *adv*
CRUTCH	*v* -ED, -ING, -ES to prop up or support
CRUX	*n* pl. CRUXES or CRUCES a basic or decisive point
CRUZADO	*n* pl. -DOES or -DOS crusado
CRUZEIRO	*n* pl. -ROS a monetary unit of Brazil
CRWTH	*n* pl. -S an ancient stringed musical instrument
CRY	*v* CRIED, CRYING, CRIES to weep **CRYINGLY** *adv*
CRYBABY	*n* pl. -BIES a person who cries easily
CRYOGEN	*n* pl. -S a substance for producing low temperatures
CRYOGENY	*n* pl. -NIES a branch of physics
CRYOLITE	*n* pl. -S a mineral
CRYONICS	*n/pl* the practice of freezing dead bodies for future revival **CRYONIC** *adj*
CRYOSTAT	*n* pl. -S a refrigerating device
CRYOTRON	*n* pl. -S an electronic device
CRYPT	*n* pl. -S a burial vault **CRYPTAL** *adj*
CRYPTIC	*adj* mysterious
CRYPTO	*n* pl. -TOS one who belongs secretly to a group
CRYSTAL	*n* pl. -S a transparent mineral
CTENIDIA	*n/pl* comblike anatomical structures
CTENOID	*adj* comblike

CUB — *n* pl. -S the young of certain animals

CUBAGE — *n* pl. -S cubature

CUBATURE — *n* pl. -S cubical content

CUBBISH — *adj* resembling a cub

CUBBY — *n* pl. -BIES a small, enclosed space

CUBE — *v* CUBED, CUBING, CUBES to form into a cube (a regular solid)

CUBEB — *n* pl. -S a woody vine

CUBER — *n* pl. -S one that cubes

CUBIC — *n* pl. -S a mathematical equation or expression

CUBICAL — *adj* shaped like a cube

CUBICITY — *n* pl. -TIES the state of being cubical

CUBICLE — *n* pl. -S a small chamber

CUBICLY — *adv* in the form of a cube

CUBICULA — *n/pl* burial chambers

CUBIFORM — *adj* shaped like a cube

CUBING — present participle of cube

CUBISM — *n* pl. -S a style of art **CUBISTIC** *adj*

CUBIST — *n* pl. -S an adherent of cubism

CUBIT — *n* pl. -S an ancient measure of length **CUBITAL** *adj*

CUBOID — *n* pl. -S a bone of the foot **CUBOIDAL** *adj*

CUCKOLD — *v* -ED, -ING, -S to make a cuckold (a cornuto) of

CUCKOO — *v* -ED, -ING, -S to repeat monotonously

CUCUMBER — *n* pl. -S a garden vegetable

CUCURBIT — *n* pl. -S a gourd

CUD — *n* pl. -S a portion of food to be chewed again

CUDBEAR — *n* pl. -S a red dye

CUDDIE — *n* pl. -S cuddy

CUDDIES — pl. of cuddy

CUDDLE — *v* -DLED, -DLING, -DLES to hug tenderly

CUDDLER — *n* pl. -S one that cuddles

CUDDLY — *adj* -DLIER, -DLIEST fit for cuddling

CUDDY — *n* pl. -DIES a donkey

CUDGEL — *v* -ELED, -ELING, -ELS or -ELLED, -ELLING, -ELS to beat with a heavy club

CUDGELER — *n* pl. -S one that cudgels

CUDWEED — *n* pl. -S a perennial herb

CUE — *v* CUED, CUING or CUEING, CUES to give a signal to an actor

CUESTA — *n* pl. -S a type of land elevation

CUFF — *v* -ED, -ING, -S to furnish with a cuff (a part of a sleeve)

CUFFLESS — *adj* having no cuff

CUIF — *n* pl. -S coof

CUING — a present participle of cue

CUIRASS — *v* -ED, -ING, -ES to cover with a type of armor

CUISH — *n* pl. -ES cuisse

CUISINE — *n* pl. -S a style of cooking

CUISSE — *n* pl. -S a piece of armor for the thigh

CUITTLE — *v* -TLED, -TLING, -TLES to coax

CUKE — *n* pl. -S a cucumber

CULCH — *n* pl. -ES an oyster bed

CULET — *n* pl. -S a piece of armor for the lower back

CULEX — *n* pl. CULICES a mosquito

CULICID — *n* pl. -S a culicine

CULICINE — *n* pl. -S a mosquito

CULINARY — *adj* pertaining to cookery

CULL — *v* -ED, -ING, -S to select from others

CULLAY — *n* pl. -LAYS quillai

CULLER — *n* pl. -S one that culls

CULLET — *n* pl. -S broken glass gathered for remelting

CULLIED — past tense of cully

CULLIES — present 3d person sing. of cully

CULLION — *n* pl. -S a vile fellow

CULLIS — *n* pl. -LISES a gutter in a roof

CULLY — *v* -LIED, -LYING, -LIES to trick

CULM — *v* -ED, -ING, -S to form a hollow stem

CULOTTE — *n* pl. -S a divided skirt

CULPA — *n* pl. -PAE negligence for which one is liable

CULPABLE — *adj* deserving blame or censure **CULPABLY** *adv*

CULPRIT — *n* pl. -S one that is guilty

CULT — *n* pl. -S a group of zealous devotees

CULTCH — *n* pl. -ES culch

CULTI — a pl. of cultus

CULTIC — *adj* pertaining to a cult

CULTIGEN	*n* pl. -S a cultivar
CULTISH	*adj* pertaining to a cult
CULTISM	*n* pl. -S devotion to a cult
CULTIST	*n* pl. -S a member of a cult
CULTIVAR	*n* pl. -S a variety of plant originating under cultivation
CULTLIKE	*adj* resembling a cult
CULTRATE	*adj* sharp-edged and pointed
CULTURAL	*adj* produced by breeding
CULTURE	*v* -TURED, -TURING, -TURES to make fit for raising crops
CULTUS	*n* pl. -TUSES or -TI a cult
CULVER	*n* pl. -S a pigeon
CULVERIN	*n* pl. -S a medieval musket
CULVERT	*n* pl. -S a conduit
CUM	*prep* together with
CUMARIN	*n* pl. -S coumarin
CUMBER	*v* -ED, -ING, -S to hinder
CUMBERER	*n* pl. -S one that cumbers
CUMBROUS	*adj* unwieldy
CUMIN	*n* pl. -S a plant used in cooking
CUMMER	*n* pl. -S a godmother
CUMMIN	*n* pl. -S cumin
CUMQUAT	*n* pl. -S kumquat
CUMSHAW	*n* pl. -S a gift
CUMULATE	*v* -LATED, -LATING, -LATES to heap
CUMULUS	*n* pl. -LI a type of cloud **CUMULOUS** *adj*
CUNDUM	*n* pl. -S condom
CUNEAL	*adj* cuneate
CUNEATE	*adj* wedge-shaped; triangular
CUNEATED	*adj* cuneate
CUNEATIC	*adj* cuneate
CUNIFORM	*n* pl. -S wedge-shaped writing characters
CUNNER	*n* pl. -S a marine fish
CUNNING	*adj* -NINGER, -NINGEST crafty
CUNNING	*n* pl. -S skill in deception
CUP	*v* CUPPED, CUPPING, CUPS to place in a cup (a small, open container)
CUPBOARD	*n* pl. -S a cabinet
CUPCAKE	*n* pl. -S a small cake
CUPEL	*v* -PELED, -PELING, -PELS or -PELLED, -PELLING, -PELS to refine gold or silver in a cuplike vessel
CUPELER	*n* pl. -S cupeller
CUPELLER	*n* pl. -S one that cupels
CUPFUL	*n* pl. CUPFULS or CUPSFUL as much as a cup can hold
CUPID	*n* pl. -S a naked, winged representation of the Roman god of love
CUPIDITY	*n* pl. -TIES greed; lust
CUPLIKE	*adj* resembling a cup
CUPOLA	*v* -ED, -ING, -S to shape like a dome
CUPPA	*n* pl. -S a cup of tea
CUPPED	past tense of cup
CUPPER	*n* pl. -S one that performs cupping
CUPPING	*n* pl. -S an archaic medical process
CUPPY	*adj* -PIER, -PIEST cuplike
CUPREOUS	*adj* containing copper
CUPRIC	*adj* containing copper
CUPRITE	*n* pl. -S an ore of copper
CUPROUS	*adj* containing copper
CUPRUM	*n* pl. -S copper
CUPSFUL	a pl. of cupful
CUPULA	*n* pl. -LAE a cup-shaped anatomical structure
CUPULAR	*adj* cupulate
CUPULATE	*adj* cup-shaped
CUPULE	*n* pl. -S a cup-shaped anatomical structure
CUR	*n* pl. -S a mongrel dog
CURABLE	*adj* capable of being cured **CURABLY** *adv*
CURACAO	*n* pl. -S a type of liqueur
CURACOA	*n* pl. -S curacao
CURACY	*n* pl. -CIES the office of a curate
CURAGH	*n* pl. -S currach
CURARA	*n* pl. -S curare
CURARE	*n* pl. -S an arrow poison
CURARI	*n* pl. -S curare
CURARINE	*n* pl. -S a poisonous alkaloid
CURARIZE	*v* -RIZED, -RIZING, -RIZES to poison with curare
CURASSOW	*n* pl. -S a turkey-like bird

CURATE	v -RATED, -RATING, -RATES to act as curator of
CURATIVE	n pl. -S something that cures
CURATOR	n pl. -S a museum manager
CURB	v -ED, -ING, -S to restrain **CURBABLE** adj
CURBER	n pl. -S one that curbs
CURBING	n pl. -S a concrete border along a street
CURBSIDE	n pl. -S the side of a pavement bordered by a curbing
CURCH	n pl. -ES a kerchief
CURCULIO	n pl. -LIOS a weevil
CURCUMA	n pl. -S a tropical plant
CURD	v -ED, -ING, -S to curdle
CURDIER	comparative of curdy
CURDIEST	superlative of curdy
CURDLE	v -DLED, -DLING, -DLES to congeal
CURDLER	n pl. -S one that curdles
CURDY	adj CURDIER, CURDIEST curdled
CURE	v CURED, CURING, CURES to restore to health
CURELESS	adj not curable
CURER	n pl. -S one that cures
CURET	n pl. -S a surgical instrument
CURETTE	v -RETTED, -RETTING, -RETTES to treat with a curet
CURF	n pl. -S an incision made by a cutting tool
CURFEW	n pl. -S a regulation concerning the hours which one may keep
CURIA	n pl. -RIAE a court of justice **CURIAL** adj
CURIE	n pl. -S a unit of radioactivity
CURING	present participle of cure
CURIO	n pl. -RIOS an unusual art object
CURIOSA	n/pl pornographic books
CURIOUS	adj -OUSER, -OUSEST eager for information
CURITE	n pl. -S a radioactive mineral
CURIUM	n pl. -S a radioactive element
CURL	v -ED, -ING, -S to form into ringlets
CURLER	n pl. -S one that curls
CURLEW	n pl. -S a shore bird
CURLICUE	v -CUED, -CUING, -CUES to decorate with curlicues (fancy spiral figures)
CURLING	n pl. -S a game played on ice
CURLY	adj CURLIER, CURLIEST tending to curl **CURLILY** adv
CURLYCUE	n pl. -S curlicue
CURN	n pl. -S grain
CURR	v -ED, -ING, -S to purr
CURRACH	n pl. -S a coracle
CURRAGH	n pl. -S currach
CURRAN	n pl. -S curn
CURRANT	n pl. -S an edible berry
CURRENCY	n pl. -CIES money
CURRENT	n pl. -S a continuous flow
CURRICLE	n pl. -S a light carriage
CURRIE	v -RIED, -RYING, -RIES to prepare food a certain way
CURRIED	past tense of curry
CURRIER	n pl. -S one that curries leather
CURRIERY	n pl. -ERIES the shop of a currier
CURRISH	adj resembling a cur
CURRY	v -RIED, -RYING, -RIES to prepare leather for use or sale
CURRYING	present participle of currie
CURSE	v CURSED or CURST, CURSING, CURSES to wish evil upon
CURSED	adj CURSEDER, CURSEDEST wicked **CURSEDLY** adv
CURSER	n pl. -S one that curses
CURSING	present participle of curse
CURSIVE	n pl. -S a style of print
CURSOR	n pl. -S a light indicator on a computer display
CURSORY	adj hasty and superficial
CURST	a past tense of curse
CURT	adj CURTER, CURTEST abrupt
CURTAIL	v -ED, -ING, -S to cut short
CURTAIN	v -ED, -ING, -S to provide with a hanging piece of fabric
CURTAL	n pl. -S an animal with a clipped tail
CURTALAX	n pl. -ES a cutlass
CURTATE	adj shortened
CURTESY	n pl. -SIES a type of legal tenure
CURTLY	adv in a curt manner
CURTNESS	n pl. -ES the quality of being curt

CURTSEY	*v* -ED, -ING, -S to curtsy
CURTSY	*v* -SIED, -SYING, -SIES to bow politely
CURULE	*adj* of the highest rank
CURVE	*v* CURVED, CURVING, CURVES to deviate from straightness **CURVEDLY** *adv*
CURVET	*v* -VETED, -VETING, -VETS or -VETTED, -VETTING, -VETS to prance
CURVEY	*adj* CURVIER, CURVIEST curvy
CURVING	present participle of curve
CURVY	*adj* CURVIER, CURVIEST curved
CUSCUS	*n* pl. -ES an arboreal mammal
CUSEC	*n* pl. -S a volumetric unit of flow of liquids
CUSHAT	*n* pl. -S a pigeon
CUSHAW	*n* pl. -S a variety of squash
CUSHIER	comparative of cushy
CUSHIEST	superlative of cushy
CUSHILY	*adv* in a cushy manner
CUSHION	*v* -ED, -ING, -S to pad with soft material
CUSHIONY	*adj* soft
CUSHY	*adj* CUSHIER, CUSHIEST easy
CUSK	*n* pl. -S a marine food fish
CUSP	*n* pl. -S a pointed end **CUSPATE, CUSPATED, CUSPED** *adj*
CUSPID	*n* pl. -S a pointed tooth
CUSPIDAL	*adj* having a cusp
CUSPIDOR	*n* pl. -S a spittoon
CUSPIS	*n* pl. -PIDES a cusp
CUSS	*v* -ED, -ING, -ES to curse
CUSSEDLY	*adv* in a cranky manner
CUSSER	*n* pl. -S one that cusses
CUSSO	*n* pl. -SOS an Ethiopian tree
CUSSWORD	*n* pl. -S a profane or obscene word
CUSTARD	*n* pl. -S a thick, soft dessert **CUSTARDY** *adj*
CUSTODES	pl. of custos
CUSTODY	*n* pl. -DIES guardianship
CUSTOM	*n* pl. -S a habitual practice
CUSTOMER	*n* pl. -S one who buys something
CUSTOS	*n* pl. -TODES a guardian or keeper
CUSTUMAL	*n* pl. -S a written record of laws and customs
CUT	*v* CUT, CUTTING, CUTS to divide into parts with a sharp-edged instrument
CUTAWAY	*n* pl. -AWAYS a type of coat
CUTBACK	*n* pl. -S a reduction
CUTBANK	*n* pl. -S a steep stream bank
CUTCH	*n* pl. -ES catechu
CUTCHERY	*n* pl. -CHERIES a judicial office in India
CUTDOWN	*n* pl. -S a reduction
CUTE	*adj* CUTER, CUTEST pleasingly attractive **CUTELY** *adv*
CUTENESS	*n* pl. -ES the quality of being cute
CUTES	a pl. of cutis
CUTESIE	*adj* -SIER, -SIEST cutesy
CUTEST	superlative of cute
CUTESY	*adj* -SIER, -SIEST self-consciously cute
CUTEY	*n* pl. -TEYS cutie
CUTGRASS	*n* pl. -ES a swamp grass
CUTICLE	*n* pl. -S the epidermis
CUTICULA	*n* pl. -LAE the outer hard covering of an insect
CUTIE	*n* pl. -S a cute person
CUTIN	*n* pl. -S a waxy substance found on plants
CUTINISE	*v* -ISED, -ISING, -ISES to cutinize
CUTINIZE	*v* -IZED, -IZING, -IZES to become coated with cutin
CUTIS	*n* pl. -TES or -TISES the corium
CUTLAS	*n* pl. -ES cutlass
CUTLASS	*n* pl. -ES a short sword
CUTLER	*n* pl. -S one who sells and repairs cutting tools
CUTLERY	*n* pl. -LERIES the occupation of a cutler
CUTLET	*n* pl. -S a slice of meat
CUTLINE	*n* pl. -S a caption
CUTOFF	*n* pl. -S the point at which something terminates
CUTOUT	*n* pl. -S something cut out
CUTOVER	*n* pl. -S land cleared of trees
CUTPURSE	*n* pl. -S a pickpocket
CUTTABLE	*adj* capable of being cut
CUTTAGE	*n* pl. -S a means of plant propagation

CUTTER	*n* pl. -S one that cuts
CUTTIES	pl. of cutty
CUTTING	*n* pl. -S a section cut from a plant
CUTTLE	*v* -TLED, -TLING, -TLES to fold cloth in a particular fashion
CUTTY	*n* pl. -TIES a thickset girl
CUTUP	*n* pl. -S a mischievous person
CUTWATER	*n* pl. -S the front part of a ship's prow
CUTWORK	*n* pl. -S a type of embroidery
CUTWORM	*n* pl. -S a caterpillar
CUVETTE	*n* pl. -S a small tube or vessel
CWM	*n* pl. -S a cirque
CYAN	*n* pl. -S a blue color
CYANAMID	*n* pl. -S a chemical compound
CYANATE	*n* pl. -S a chemical salt
CYANIC	*adj* blue or bluish
CYANID	*n* pl. -S a compound of cyanogen
CYANIDE	*v* -NIDED, -NIDING, -NIDES to treat an ore with cyanid
CYANIN	*n* pl. -S cyanine
CYANINE	*n* pl. -S a blue dye
CYANITE	*n* pl. -S a mineral **CYANITIC** *adj*
CYANO	*adj* pertaining to cyanogen
CYANOGEN	*n* pl. -S a reactive compound of carbon and nitrogen
CYANOSIS	*n* pl. -NOSES bluish discoloration of the skin **CYANOSED, CYANOTIC** *adj*
CYBORG	*n* pl. -S a human linked to a mechanical device for life support
CYCAD	*n* pl. -S a tropical plant
CYCAS	*n* pl. -ES a tropical plant
CYCASIN	*n* pl. -S a sugar derivative
CYCLAMEN	*n* pl. -S a flowering plant
CYCLASE	*n* pl. -S an enzyme
CYCLE	*v* -CLED, -CLING, -CLES to ride a bicycle
CYCLECAR	*n* pl. -S a type of motor vehicle
CYCLER	*n* pl. -S a cyclist
CYCLERY	*n* pl. -RIES a bicycle shop
CYCLIC	*adj* moving in complete circles **CYCLICLY** *adv*
CYCLICAL	*n* pl. -S a stock whose earnings fluctuate widely with variations in the economy
CYCLING	*n* pl. -S the act of riding a bicycle
CYCLIST	*n* pl. -S one who rides a bicycle

CYCLITOL	*n* pl. -S a chemical compound
CYCLIZE	*v* -CLIZED, -CLIZING, -CLIZES to form one or more rings in a chemical compound
CYCLO	*n* pl. -CLOS a three-wheeled motor vehicle
CYCLOID	*n* pl. -S a geometric curve
CYCLONE	*n* pl. -S a rotating system of winds **CYCLONAL, CYCLONIC** *adj*
CYCLOPS	*n* pl. CYCLOPS a freshwater animal
CYCLOSIS	*n* pl. -CLOSES the circulation of protoplasm within a cell
CYDER	*n* pl. -S cider
CYESIS	*n* pl. CYESES pregnancy
CYGNET	*n* pl. -S a young swan
CYLINDER	*v* -ED, -ING, -S to furnish with a cylinder (a chamber in an engine)
CYLIX	*n* pl. CYLICES kylix
CYMA	*n* pl. -MAS or -MAE a curved molding
CYMAR	*n* pl. -S a simar
CYMATIUM	*n* pl. -TIA a cyma
CYMBAL	*n* pl. -S a percussion instrument
CYMBALER	*n* pl. -S one that plays the cymbals
CYMBALOM	*n* pl. -S cimbalom
CYMBIDIA	*n/pl* tropical orchids
CYMBLING	*n* pl. -S cymling
CYME	*n* pl. -S a flower cluster
CYMENE	*n* pl. -S a hydrocarbon
CYMLIN	*n* pl. -S cymling
CYMLING	*n* pl. -S a variety of squash
CYMOGENE	*n* pl. -S a volatile compound
CYMOID	*adj* resembling a cyma
CYMOL	*n* pl. -S cymene
CYMOSE	*adj* resembling a cyme **CYMOSELY** *adv*
CYMOUS	*adj* cymose
CYNIC	*n* pl. -S a cynical person
CYNICAL	*adj* distrusting the motives of others
CYNICISM	*n* pl. -S cynical quality
CYNOSURE	*n* pl. -S a center of attraction
CYPHER	*v* -ED, -ING, -S to cipher
CYPRES	*n* pl. -ES a legal doctrine
CYPRESS	*n* pl. -ES a thin fabric

CYPRIAN	*n* pl. -S a prostitute
CYPRINID	*n* pl. -S a small freshwater fish
CYPRUS	*n* pl. -ES cypress
CYPSELA	*n* pl. -LAE an achene in certain plants
CYST	*n* pl. -S a sac
CYSTEIN	*n* pl. -S cysteine
CYSTEINE	*n* pl. -S an amino acid
CYSTIC	*adj* pertaining to a cyst
CYSTINE	*n* pl. -S an amino acid
CYSTITIS	*n* pl. -TITIDES inflammation of the urinary bladder
CYSTOID	*n* pl. -S a cyst-like structure
CYTASTER	*n* pl. -S a structure formed in a cell during mitosis
CYTIDINE	*n* pl. -S a compound containing cytosine
CYTOGENY	*n* pl. -NIES the formation of cells
CYTOKINE	*n* pl. -S a kind of substance secreted by cells of the immune system
CYTOLOGY	*n* pl. -GIES a study of cells
CYTON	*n* pl. -S the body of a nerve cell
CYTOSINE	*n* pl. -S a component of DNA and RNA
CYTOSOL	*n* pl. -S the fluid portion of cell material
CZAR	*n* pl. -S an emperor or king
CZARDAS	*n* pl. CZARDAS a Hungarian dance
CZARDOM	*n* pl. -S the domain of a czar
CZAREVNA	*n* pl. -S the daughter of a czar
CZARINA	*n* pl. -S the wife of a czar
CZARISM	*n* pl. -S autocratic government
CZARIST	*n* pl. -S a supporter of czarism
CZARITZA	*n* pl. -S a czarina

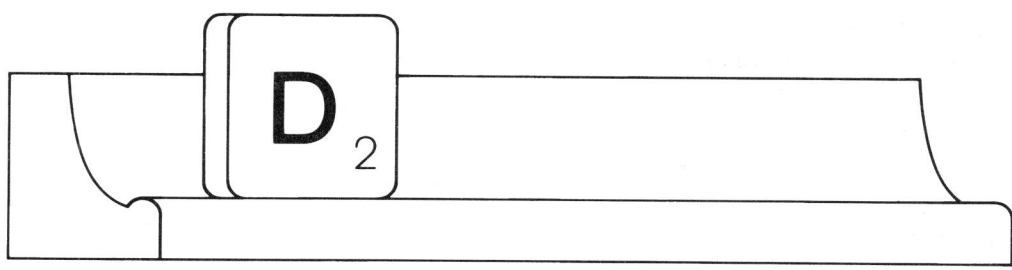

DAB	*v* DABBED, DABBING, DABS to touch lightly	**DAFT**	*adj* DAFTER, DAFTEST insane **DAFTLY** *adv*
DABBER	*n* pl. -S one that dabs	**DAFTNESS**	*n* pl. -ES the quality of being daft
DABBLE	*v* -BLED, -BLING, -BLES to involve oneself in a superficial interest	**DAG**	*n* pl. -S a hanging end or shred
		DAGGA	*n* pl. -S marijuana
DABBLER	*n* pl. -S one that dabbles	**DAGGER**	*v* -ED, -ING, -S to stab with a small knife
DABBLING	*n* pl. -S a superficial interest	**DAGGLE**	*v* -GLED, -GLING, -GLES to drag in mud
DABCHICK	*n* pl. -S a small grebe		
DABSTER	*n* pl. -S a dabbler	**DAGLOCK**	*n* pl. -S a dirty or tangled lock of wool
DACE	*n* pl. -S a freshwater fish		
DACHA	*n* pl. -S a Russian cottage	**DAGOBA**	*n* pl. -S a Buddhist shrine
DACKER	*v* -ED, -ING, -S to waver	**DAGWOOD**	*n* pl. -S a large sandwich
DACOIT	*n* pl. -S a bandit in India	**DAH**	*n* pl. -S a dash in Morse code
DACOITY	*n* pl. -COITIES robbery by dacoits	**DAHABEAH**	*n* pl. -S a large passenger boat
		DAHABIAH	*n* pl. -S dahabeah
DACTYL	*n* pl. -S a type of metrical foot	**DAHABIEH**	*n* pl. -S dahabeah
DACTYLIC	*n* pl. -S a verse consisting of dactyls	**DAHABIYA**	*n* pl. -S dahabeah
		DAHL	*n* pl. -S dal
DACTYLUS	*n* pl. -LI a leg joint of certain insects	**DAHLIA**	*n* pl. -S a flowering plant
		DAHOON	*n* pl. -S an evergreen tree
DAD	*n* pl. -S father	**DAIKER**	*v* -ED, -ING, -S to dacker
DADA	*n* pl. -S an artistic and literary movement	**DAIKON**	*n* pl. -S a Japanese radish
		DAILY	*n* pl. -LIES a newspaper published every weekday
DADAISM	*n* pl. -S the dada movement		
DADAIST	*n* pl. -S a follower of dadaism	**DAIMEN**	*adj* occasional
DADDLE	*v* -DLED, -DLING, -DLES to diddle	**DAIMIO**	*n* pl. -MIOS a former Japanese nobleman
DADDY	*n* pl. -DIES father	**DAIMON**	*n* pl. -S or -ES an attendant spirit **DAIMONIC** *adj*
DADO	*v* -ED, -ING, -ES or -S to set into a groove		
		DAIMYO	*n* pl. -MYOS daimio
DAEDAL	*adj* skillful	**DAINTY**	*n* pl. -TIES something delicious
DAEMON	*n* pl. -S demon **DAEMONIC** *adj*	**DAINTY**	*adj* -TIER, -TIEST delicately pretty **DAINTILY** *adv*
DAFF	*v* -ED, -ING, -S to thrust aside		
		DAIQUIRI	*n* pl. -S a cocktail
DAFFODIL	*n* pl. -S a flowering plant	**DAIRY**	*n* pl. DAIRIES an establishment dealing in milk products
DAFFY	*adj* -FIER, -FIEST silly **DAFFILY** *adv*		
		DAIRYING	*n* pl. -S the business of a dairy

DAIRYMAN *n* pl. -MEN a man who works in or owns a dairy

DAIS *n* pl. -ISES a raised platform

DAISHIKI *n* pl. -S dashiki

DAISY *n* pl. -SIES a flowering plant **DAISIED** *adj*

DAK *n* pl. -S transportation by relays of men and horses

DAKERHEN *n* pl. -S a European bird

DAKOIT *n* pl. -S dacoit

DAKOITY *n* pl. -TIES dacoity

DAL *n* pl. -S a dish of lentils and spices in India

DALAPON *n* pl. -S an herbicide used on unwanted grasses

DALASI *n* pl. DALASI or DALASIS a unit of Gambian currency

DALE *n* pl. -S a valley

DALEDH *n* pl. -S daleth

DALESMAN *n* pl. -MEN one living in a dale

DALETH *n* pl. -S a Hebrew letter

DALLES *n/pl* rapids

DALLIER *n* pl. -S one that dallies

DALLY *v* -LIED, -LYING, -LIES to waste time

DALMATIC *n* pl. -S a wide-sleeved vestment

DALTON *n* pl. -S a unit of atomic mass

DALTONIC *adj* pertaining to a form of color blindness

DAM *v* DAMMED, DAMMING, DAMS to build a barrier to obstruct the flow of water

DAMAGE *v* -AGED, -AGING, -AGES to injure

DAMAGER *n* pl. -S one that damages

DAMAN *n* pl. -S a small mammal

DAMAR *n* pl. -S dammar

DAMASK *v* -ED, -ING, -S to weave with elaborate design

DAME *n* pl. -S a matron

DAMEWORT *n* pl. -S a flowering plant

DAMMAR *n* pl. -S a hard resin

DAMMED past tense of dam

DAMMER *n* pl. -S dammar

DAMMING present participle of dam

DAMN *v* -ED, -ING, -S to curse

DAMNABLE *adj* detestable **DAMNABLY** *adv*

DAMNDEST *n* pl. -S utmost

DAMNED *adj* DAMNEDER, DAMNEDEST or DAMNDEST damnable

DAMNER *n* pl. -S one that damns

DAMNIFY *v* -FIED, -FYING, -FIES to cause loss or damage to

DAMOSEL *n* pl. -S damsel

DAMOZEL *n* pl. -S damsel

DAMP *adj* DAMPER, DAMPEST moist

DAMP *v* -ED, -ING, -S to lessen in intensity

DAMPEN *v* -ED, -ING, -S to moisten

DAMPENER *n* pl. -S one that dampens

DAMPER *n* pl. -S one that damps

DAMPING *n* pl. -S the ability of a device to prevent instability

DAMPISH *adj* somewhat damp

DAMPLY *adv* in a damp manner

DAMPNESS *n* pl. -ES the state of being damp

DAMSEL *n* pl. -S a maiden

DAMSON *n* pl. -S a small purple plum

DANCE *v* DANCED, DANCING, DANCES to move rhythmically to music

DANCER *n* pl. -S one that dances

DANDER *v* -ED, -ING, -S to stroll

DANDIER comparative of dandy

DANDIES pl. of dandy

DANDIEST superlative of dandy

DANDIFY *v* -FIED, -FYING, -FIES to cause to resemble a dandy

DANDILY *adv* in a dandy manner

DANDLE *v* -DLED, -DLING, -DLES to fondle

DANDLER *n* pl. -S one that dandles

DANDRIFF *n* pl. -S dandruff

DANDRUFF *n* pl. -S a scurf that forms on the scalp

DANDY *adj* -DIER, -DIEST fine

DANDY *n* pl. -DIES a man who is overly concerned about his appearance

DANDYISH *adj* suggestive of a dandy

DANDYISM *n* pl. -S the style or conduct of a dandy

DANEGELD *n* pl. -S an annual tax in medieval England

DANEWEED *n* pl. -S a danewort

DANEWORT *n* pl. -S a flowering plant

DANG *v* -ED, -ING, -S to damn

DANGER *v* -ED, -ING, -S to endanger

DANGLE	*v* -GLED, -GLING, -GLES to hang loosely
DANGLER	*n* pl. -S one that dangles
DANIO	*n* pl. -NIOS an aquarium fish
DANISH	*n* pl. DANISH a pastry of raised dough
DANK	*adj* DANKER, DANKEST unpleasantly damp **DANKLY** *adv*
DANKNESS	*n* pl. -ES the state of being dank
DANSEUR	*n* pl. -S a male ballet dancer
DANSEUSE	*n* pl. -S a female ballet dancer
DAP	*v* DAPPED, DAPPING, DAPS to dip lightly or quickly into water
DAPHNE	*n* pl. -S a flowering shrub
DAPHNIA	*n* pl. -S a minute crustacean
DAPPED	past tense of dap
DAPPER	*adj* -PERER, -PEREST looking neat and trim **DAPPERLY** *adv*
DAPPING	present participle of dap
DAPPLE	*v* -PLED, -PLING, -PLES to mark with spots
DAPSONE	*n* pl. -S a medicinal substance
DARB	*n* pl. -S something considered extraordinary
DARBIES	*n/pl* handcuffs
DARE	*v* DARED or DURST, DARING, DARES to have the necessary courage
DAREFUL	*adj* brave
DARER	*n* pl. -S one that dares
DARESAY	*v* to venture to say — DARESAY is the only form of this verb; it is not conjugated
DARIC	*n* pl. -S an ancient Persian coin
DARING	*n* pl. -S bravery
DARINGLY	*adv* in a brave manner
DARIOLE	*n* pl. -S a type of pastry filled with cream, custard, or jelly
DARK	*adj* DARKER, DARKEST having little or no light
DARK	*v* -ED, -ING, -S to darken
DARKEN	*v* -ED, -ING, -S to make dark
DARKENER	*n* pl. -S one that darkens
DARKISH	*adj* somewhat dark
DARKLE	*v* -KLED, -KLING, -KLES to become dark
DARKLY	*adv* -LIER, -LIEST in a dark manner
DARKNESS	*n* pl. -ES the state of being dark
DARKROOM	*n* pl. -S a room in which film is processed
DARKSOME	*adj* dark
DARLING	*n* pl. -S a much-loved person
DARN	*v* -ED, -ING, -S to mend with interlacing stitches
DARNDEST	*n* pl. -S damndest
DARNED	*adj* DARNEDER, DARNEDEST or DARNDEST damned
DARNEL	*n* pl. -S an annual grass
DARNER	*n* pl. -S one that darns
DARNING	*n* pl. -S things to be darned
DARSHAN	*n* pl. -S a Hindu blessing
DART	*v* -ED, -ING, -S to move suddenly or swiftly
DARTER	*n* pl. -S one that darts
DARTLE	*v* -TLED, -TLING, -TLES to dart repeatedly
DASH	*v* -ED, -ING, -ES to strike violently
DASHEEN	*n* pl. -S a tropical plant
DASHER	*n* pl. -S one that dashes
DASHI	*n* pl. -S a fish broth
DASHIER	comparative of dashy
DASHIEST	superlative of dashy
DASHIKI	*n* pl. -S an African tunic
DASHPOT	*n* pl. -S a shock absorber
DASHY	*adj* DASHIER, DASHIEST stylish
DASSIE	*n* pl. -S a hyrax
DASTARD	*n* pl. -S a base coward
DASYURE	*n* pl. -S a flesh-eating mammal
DATA	a pl. of datum
DATABANK	*n* pl. -S a database
DATABASE	*n* pl. -S a collection of data in a computer
DATABLE	*adj* capable of being dated
DATARY	*n* pl. -RIES a cardinal in the Roman Catholic Church
DATCHA	*n* pl. -S dacha
DATE	*v* DATED, DATING, DATES to determine or record the date of **DATEABLE** *adj*
DATEDLY	*adv* in an old-fashioned manner
DATELESS	*adj* having no date
DATELINE	*v* -LINED, -LINING, -LINES to provide a news story with its date and place of origin
DATER	*n* pl. -S one that dates

DATING	present participle of date
DATIVE	*n* pl. -S a grammatical case **DATIVAL** *adj* **DATIVELY** *adv*
DATO	*n* pl. -TOS datto
DATTO	*n* pl. -TOS a Philippine tribal chief
DATUM	*n* pl. -TA or -TUMS something used as a basis for calculating
DATURA	*n* pl. -S a flowering plant **DATURIC** *adj*
DAUB	*v* -ED, -ING, -S to smear
DAUBE	*n* pl. -S a braised meat stew
DAUBER	*n* pl. -S one that daubs
DAUBERY	*n* pl. -ERIES a bad or inexpert painting
DAUBRY	*n* pl. -RIES daubery
DAUBY	*adj* **DAUBIER, DAUBIEST** smeary
DAUGHTER	*n* pl. -S a female child
DAUNDER	*v* -ED, -ING, -S to dander
DAUNT	*v* -ED, -ING, -S to intimidate
DAUNTER	*n* pl. -S one that daunts
DAUPHIN	*n* pl. -S the eldest son of a French king
DAUPHINE	*n* pl. -S the wife of a dauphin
DAUT	*v* -ED, -ING, -S to fondle
DAUTIE	*n* pl. -S a small pet
DAVEN	*v* -ED, -ING, -S to utter Jewish prayers
DAVIT	*n* pl. -S a hoisting device on a ship
DAVY	*n* pl. -VIES a safety lamp
DAW	*v* **DAWED, DAWEN, DAWING, DAWS** to dawn
DAWDLE	*v* -DLED, -DLING, -DLES to waste time
DAWDLER	*n* pl. -S one that dawdles
DAWEN	past participle of daw
DAWK	*n* pl. -S dak
DAWN	*v* -ED, -ING, -S to begin to grow light in the morning
DAWNLIKE	*adj* suggestive of daybreak
DAWT	*v* -ED, -ING, -S to daut
DAWTIE	*n* pl. -S dautie
DAY	*n* pl. DAYS the time between sunrise and sunset
DAYBED	*n* pl. -S a couch that can be converted into a bed
DAYBOOK	*n* pl. -S a diary

DAYBREAK	*n* pl. -S the first appearance of light in the morning
DAYDREAM	*v* -DREAMED or -DREAMT, -DREAMING, -DREAMS to fantasize
DAYFLY	*n* pl. -FLIES a mayfly
DAYGLOW	*n* pl. -S airglow seen during the day
DAYLIGHT	*v* -LIGHTED or -LIT, -LIGHTING, -LIGHTS to illuminate with the light of day
DAYLILY	*n* pl. -LILIES a flowering plant
DAYLONG	*adj* lasting all day
DAYMARE	*n* pl. -S a nightmarish fantasy experienced while awake
DAYROOM	*n* pl. -S a room for reading and recreation
DAYSIDE	*n* pl. -S the sun side of a planet or the moon
DAYSMAN	*n* pl. -MEN an arbiter
DAYSTAR	*n* pl. -S a planet visible in the east just before sunrise
DAYTIME	*n* pl. -S day
DAYWORK	*n* pl. -S work done on a daily basis
DAZE	*v* **DAZED, DAZING, DAZES** to stun **DAZEDLY** *adv*
DAZZLE	*v* -ZLED, -ZLING, -ZLES to blind by bright light
DAZZLER	*n* pl. -S one that dazzles
DE	*prep* of; from — used in names
DEACON	*v* -ED, -ING, -S to read a hymn aloud
DEACONRY	*n* pl. -RIES a clerical office
DEAD	*adj* **DEADER, DEADEST** deprived of life
DEAD	*n* pl. -S the period of greatest intensity
DEADBEAT	*n* pl. -S a loafer
DEADBOLT	*n* pl. -S a lock for a door
DEADEN	*v* -ED, -ING, -S to diminish the sensitivity or vigor of
DEADENER	*n* pl. -S one that deadens
DEADEYE	*n* pl. -S an expert marksman
DEADFALL	*n* pl. -S a type of animal trap
DEADHEAD	*v* -ED, -ING, -S to travel without freight
DEADLIER	comparative of deadly
DEADLIEST	superlative of deadly

DEADLIFT   *v* -ED, -ING, -S to execute a type of lift in weight lifting

DEADLINE   *n* pl. -S a time limit

DEADLOCK   *v* -ED, -ING, -S to come to a standstill

DEADLY   *adj* -LIER, -LIEST fatal

DEADNESS   *n* pl. -ES the state of being dead

DEADPAN   *v* -PANNED, -PANNING, -PANS to act without emotion

DEADWOOD   *n* pl. -S a reinforcement in a ship's keel

DEAERATE   *v* -ATED, -ATING, -ATES to remove air or gas from

DEAF   *adj* DEAFER, DEAFEST lacking the sense of hearing

DEAFEN   *v* -ED, -ING, -S to make deaf

DEAFISH   *adj* somewhat deaf

DEAFLY   *adv* in a deaf manner

DEAFNESS   *n* pl. -ES the state of being deaf

DEAIR   *v* -ED, -ING, -S to remove air from

DEAL   *v* DEALT, DEALING, DEALS to trade or do business

DEALATE   *n* pl. -S an insect divested of its wings **DEALATED** *adj*

DEALER   *n* pl. -S one that deals

DEALFISH   *n* pl. -ES a marine fish

DEALING   *n* pl. -S a business transaction

DEALT   past tense of deal

DEAN   *v* -ED, -ING, -S to serve as dean (the head of a faculty)

DEANERY   *n* pl. -ERIES the office of a dean

DEANSHIP   *n* pl. -S deanery

DEAR   *adj* DEARER, DEAREST greatly loved

DEAR   *n* pl. -S a loved one

DEARIE   *n* pl. -S deary

DEARIES   pl. of deary

DEARLY   *adv* in a dear manner

DEARNESS   *n* pl. -ES the state of being dear

DEARTH   *n* pl. -S scarcity

DEARY   *n* pl. DEARIES darling

DEASH   *v* -ED, -ING, -ES to remove ash from

DEASIL   *adv* clockwise

DEATH   *n* pl. -S the end of life

DEATHBED   *n* pl. -S the bed on which a person dies

DEATHCUP   *n* pl. -S a poisonous mushroom

DEATHFUL   *adj* fatal

DEATHLY   *adj* fatal

DEATHY   *adj* deathly

DEAVE   *v* DEAVED, DEAVING, DEAVES to deafen

DEB   *n* pl. -S a debutante

DEBACLE   *n* pl. -S a sudden collapse

DEBAR   *v* -BARRED, -BARRING, -BARS to exclude

DEBARK   *v* -ED, -ING, -S to unload from a ship

DEBASE   *v* -BASED, -BASING, -BASES to lower in character, quality, or value

DEBASER   *n* pl. -S one that debases

DEBATE   *v* -BATED, -BATING, -BATES to argue about

DEBATER   *n* pl. -S one that debates

DEBAUCH   *v* -ED, -ING, -ES to corrupt

DEBEAK   *v* -ED, -ING, -S to remove the tip of the upper beak of

DEBILITY   *n* pl. -TIES weakness

DEBIT   *v* -ED, -ING, -S to charge with a debt

DEBONAIR   *adj* suave

DEBONE   *v* -BONED, -BONING, -BONES to remove the bones from

DEBONER   *n* pl. -S a bone remover

DEBOUCH   *v* -ED, -ING, -ES to march into the open

DEBOUCHE   *n* pl. -S an opening for the passage of troops

DEBRIDE   *v* -BRIDED, -BRIDING, -BRIDES to remove dead tissue surgically

DEBRIEF   *v* -ED, -ING, -S to question after a mission

DEBRIS   *n* pl. DEBRIS fragments or scattered remains

DEBRUISE   *v* -BRUISED, -BRUISING, -BRUISES to cross a coat of arms

DEBT   *n* pl. -S something that is owed **DEBTLESS** *adj*

DEBTOR   *n* pl. -S one who owes something to another

DEBUG   *v* -BUGGED, -BUGGING, -BUGS to remove bugs from

DEBUGGER   *n* pl. -S one that debugs

DEBUNK   *v* -ED, -ING, -S to expose the sham or falseness of

DEBUNKER *n* pl. -S one that debunks

DEBUT *v* -ED, -ING, -S to make one's first public appearance

DEBUTANT *n* pl. -S one who is debuting

DEBYE *n* pl. -S a unit of measure for electric dipole moments

DECADE *n* pl. -S a period of ten years **DECADAL** *adj*

DECADENT *n* pl. -S one in a state of mental or moral decay

DECAF *n* pl. -S decaffeinated coffee

DECAGON *n* pl. -S a ten-sided polygon

DECAGRAM *n* pl. -S dekagram

DECAL *n* pl. -S a picture or design made to be transferred from specially prepared paper

DECALOG *n* pl. -S the Ten Commandments

DECAMP *v* -ED, -ING, -S to depart from a camping ground

DECANAL *adj* pertaining to a dean

DECANE *n* pl. -S a hydrocarbon

DECANT *v* -ED, -ING, -S to pour from one container into another

DECANTER *n* pl. -S a decorative bottle

DECAPOD *n* pl. -S a ten-legged crustacean

DECARE *n* pl. -S dekare

DECAY *v* -ED, -ING, -S to decompose

DECAYER *n* pl. -S one that decays

DECEASE *v* -CEASED, -CEASING, -CEASES to die

DECEDENT *n* pl. -S a deceased person

DECEIT *n* pl. -S the act of deceiving

DECEIVE *v* -CEIVED, -CEIVING, -CEIVES to mislead by falsehood

DECEIVER *n* pl. -S one that deceives

DECEMVIR *n* pl. -VIRS or -VIRI one of a body of ten Roman magistrates

DECENARY *n* pl. -RIES a tithing

DECENCY *n* pl. -CIES the state of being decent

DECENNIA *n/pl* decades

DECENT *adj* -CENTER -CENTEST conforming to recognized standards of propriety **DECENTLY** *adv*

DECENTER *v* -ED, -ING, -S to put out of center

DECENTRE *v* -TRED, -TRING, -TRES to decenter

DECERN *v* -ED, -ING, -S to decree by judicial sentence

DECIARE *n* pl. -S a metric unit of area

DECIBEL *n* pl. -S a unit of sound intensity

DECIDE *v* -CIDED, -CIDING, -CIDES to make a choice or judgment

DECIDER *n* pl. -S one that decides

DECIDUA *n* pl. -UAS or -UAE a mucous membrane of the uterus **DECIDUAL** *adj*

DECIGRAM *n* pl. -S one tenth of a gram

DECILE *n* pl. -S a statistical interval

DECIMAL *n* pl. -S a fraction whose denominator is some power of ten

DECIMATE *v* -MATED, -MATING, -MATES to destroy a large part of

DECIPHER *v* -ED, -ING, -S to decode

DECISION *v* -ED, -ING, -S to win a victory over a boxing opponent on points

DECISIVE *adj* conclusive

DECK *v* -ED, -ING, -S to adorn

DECKEL *n* pl. -S deckle

DECKER *n* pl. -S something having a specified number of levels, floors, or layers

DECKHAND *n* pl. -S a seaman who performs manual duties

DECKING *n* pl. -S material for a ship's deck

DECKLE *n* pl. -S a frame used in making paper by hand

DECLAIM *v* -ED, -ING, -S to speak formally

DECLARE *v* -CLARED, -CLARING, -CLARES to make known clearly

DECLARER *n* pl. -S one that declares

DECLASS *v* -ED, -ING, -ES to lower in status

DECLASSE *adj* lowered in status

DECLAW *v* -CLAWED, -CLAWING, -CLAWS to surgically remove the claws of

DECLINE *v* -CLINED, -CLINING, -CLINES to refuse

DECLINER *n* pl. -S one that declines

DECO *n* pl. DECOS a decorative style

DECOCT *v* -ED, -ING, -S to extract the flavor of by boiling

DECODE *v* -CODED, -CODING, -CODES to convert a coded message into plain language

DECODER *n* pl. -S one that decodes

DECOLOR *v* -ED, -ING, -S to deprive of color

DECOLOUR *v* -ED, -ING, -S to decolor

DECOR	*n* pl. -S style or mode of decoration
DECORATE	*v* -RATED, -RATING, -RATES to adorn
DECOROUS	*adj* proper
DECORUM	*n* pl. -S conformity to social conventions
DECOUPLE	*v* -PLED, -PLING, -PLES to disconnect
DECOY	*v* -ED, -ING, -S to lure into a trap
DECOYER	*n* pl. -S one that decoys
DECREASE	*v* -CREASED, -CREASING, -CREASES to diminish
DECREE	*v* -CREED, -CREEING, -CREES to order or establish by law or edict
DECREER	*n* pl. -S one that decrees
DECREPIT	*adj* worn out by long use
DECRETAL	*n* pl. -S a papal edict
DECRIAL	*n* pl. -S the act of decrying
DECRIED	past tense of decry
DECRIER	*n* pl. -S one that decries
DECROWN	*v* -ED, -ING, -S to deprive of a crown; depose
DECRY	*v* -CRIED, -CRYING, -CRIES to denounce
DECRYPT	*v* -ED, -ING, -S to decode
DECUMAN	*adj* extremely large
DECUPLE	*v* -PLED, -PLING, -PLES to increase tenfold
DECURIES	pl. of decury
DECURION	*n* pl. -S a commander of a decury
DECURVE	*v* -CURVED, -CURVING, -CURVES to curve downward
DECURY	*n* pl. -RIES a group of ten soldiers in ancient Rome
DEDAL	*adj* daedal
DEDANS	*n* pl. DEDANS a gallery for tennis spectators
DEDICATE	*v* -CATED, -CATING, -CATES to set apart for some special use
DEDUCE	*v* -DUCED, -DUCING, -DUCES to infer
DEDUCT	*v* -ED, -ING, -S to subtract
DEE	*n* pl. -S the letter D
DEED	*v* -ED, -ING, -S to transfer by deed (a legal document)
DEEDLESS	*adj* being without deeds
DEEDY	*adj* DEEDIER, DEEDIEST industrious
DEEJAY	*n* pl. -JAYS a disc jockey
DEEM	*v* -ED, -ING, -S to hold as an opinion
DEEMSTER	*n* pl. -S a judicial officer of the Isle of Man
DEEP	*adj* DEEPER, DEEPEST extending far down from a surface
DEEP	*n* pl. -S a place or thing of great depth
DEEPEN	*v* -ED, -ING, -S to make deep
DEEPENER	*n* pl. -S one that deepens
DEEPLY	*adv* at or to a great depth
DEEPNESS	*n* pl. -ES the quality of being deep
DEER	*n* pl. -S a ruminant mammal **DEERLIKE** *adj*
DEERFLY	*n* pl. -FLIES a bloodsucking fly
DEERSKIN	*n* pl. -S the skin of a deer
DEERWEED	*n* pl. -S a bushlike herb
DEERYARD	*n* pl. -S an area where deer herd in winter
DEET	*n* pl. -S an insect repellent
DEEWAN	*n* pl. -S dewan
DEFACE	*v* -FACED, -FACING, -FACES to mar the appearance of
DEFACER	*n* pl. -S one that defaces
DEFAME	*v* -FAMED, -FAMING, -FAMES to attack the good name of
DEFAMER	*n* pl. -S one that defames
DEFANG	*v* -ED, -ING, -S to make harmless
DEFAT	*v* -FATTED, -FATTING, -FATS to remove fat from
DEFAULT	*v* -ED, -ING, -S to fail to do something required
DEFEAT	*v* -ED, -ING, -S to win victory over
DEFEATER	*n* pl. -S one that defeats
DEFECATE	*v* -CATED, -CATING, -CATES to discharge feces
DEFECT	*v* -ED, -ING, -S to desert an allegiance
DEFECTOR	*n* pl. -S one that defects
DEFENCE	*n* pl. -S something that defends
DEFEND	*v* -ED, -ING, -S to protect
DEFENDER	*n* pl. -S one that defends
DEFENSE	*v* -FENSED, -FENSING, -FENSES to guard against a specific attack

DEFER	*v* -FERRED, -FERRING, -FERS to postpone
DEFERENT	*n* pl. -S an imaginary circle around the earth
DEFERRAL	*n* pl. -S the act of deferring
DEFERRED	past tense of defer
DEFERRER	*n* pl. -S one that defers
DEFERRING	present participle of defer
DEFI	*n* pl. -S a challenge
DEFIANCE	*n* pl. -S bold opposition
DEFIANT	*adj* showing defiance
DEFICIT	*n* pl. -S a shortage
DEFIED	past tense of defy
DEFIER	*n* pl. -S one that defies
DEFIES	present 3d person sing. of defy
DEFILADE	*v* -LADED, -LADING, -LADES to shield from enemy fire
DEFILE	*v* -FILED, -FILING, -FILES to make dirty
DEFILER	*n* pl. -S one that defiles
DEFINE	*v* -FINED, -FINING, -FINES to state the meaning of
DEFINER	*n* pl. -S one that defines
DEFINITE	*adj* known for certain
DEFLATE	*v* -FLATED, -FLATING, -FLATES to release the air or gas from
DEFLATER	*n* pl. -S one that deflates
DEFLATOR	*n* pl. -S one that deflates
DEFLEA	*v* -ED, -ING, -S to rid of fleas
DEFLECT	*v* -ED, -ING, -S to turn aside
DEFLEXED	*adj* bent downward
DEFLOWER	*v* -ED, -ING, -S to deprive of flowers
DEFOAM	*v* -ED, -ING, -S to remove foam from
DEFOAMER	*n* pl. -S one that defoams
DEFOCUS	*v* -CUSED, -CUSING, -CUSES or -CUSSED, -CUSSING, -CUSSES to cause to go out of focus
DEFOG	*v* -FOGGED, -FOGGING, -FOGS to remove fog from
DEFOGGER	*n* pl. -S one that defogs
DEFORCE	*v* -FORCED, -FORCING, -FORCES to withhold by force
DEFOREST	*v* -ED, -ING, -S to clear of forests
DEFORM	*v* -ED, -ING, -S to spoil the form of
DEFORMER	*n* pl. -S one that deforms
DEFRAUD	*v* -ED, -ING, -S to swindle
DEFRAY	*v* -ED, -ING, -S to pay
DEFRAYAL	*n* pl. -S the act of defraying
DEFRAYER	*n* pl. -S one that defrays
DEFROCK	*v* -ED, -ING, -S to unfrock
DEFROST	*v* -ED, -ING, -S to remove frost from
DEFT	*adj* DEFTER, DEFTEST skillful **DEFTLY** *adv*
DEFTNESS	*n* pl. -ES the quality of being deft
DEFUNCT	*adj* deceased
DEFUND	*v* -ED, -ING, -S to withdraw funding from
DEFUSE	*v* -FUSED, -FUSING, -FUSES to remove the fuse from
DEFUZE	*v* -FUZED, -FUZING, -FUZES to defuse
DEFY	*v* -FIED, -FYING, -FIES to resist openly and boldly
DEGAGE	*adj* free and relaxed in manner
DEGAME	*n* pl. -S a tropical tree
DEGAMI	*n* pl. -S degame
DEGAS	*v* -GASSED, -GASSING, -GASSES or -GASES to remove gas from
DEGASSER	*n* pl. -S one that degasses
DEGAUSS	*v* -ED, -ING, -ES to demagnetize
DEGERM	*v* -ED, -ING, -S to remove germs from
DEGLAZE	*v* -GLAZED, -GLAZING, -GLAZES to remove the glaze from
DEGRADE	*v* -GRADED, -GRADING, -GRADES to debase
DEGRADER	*n* pl. -S one that degrades
DEGREASE	*v* -GREASED, -GREASING, -GREASES to remove the grease from
DEGREE	*n* pl. -S one of a series of stages **DEGREED** *adj*
DEGUM	*v* -GUMMED, -GUMMING, -GUMS to free from gum
DEGUST	*v* -ED, -ING, -S to taste with pleasure
DEHISCE	*v* -HISCED, -HISCING, -HISCES to split open
DEHORN	*v* -ED, -ING, -S to deprive of horns
DEHORNER	*n* pl. -S one that dehorns
DEHORT	*v* -ED, -ING, -S to try to dissuade

DEICE   *v* -ICED, -ICING, -ICES to free from ice

DEICER   *n* pl. -S one that deices

DEICIDE   *n* pl. -S the killing of a god **DEICIDAL** *adj*

DEICING   present participle of deice

DEICTIC   *adj* proving directly

DEIFIC   *adj* godlike

DEIFICAL   *adj* deific

DEIFIED   past tense of deify

DEIFIER   *n* pl. -S one that deifies

DEIFORM   *adj* having the form of a god

DEIFY   *v* -FIED, -FYING, -FIES to make a god of

DEIGN   *v* -ED, -ING, -S to lower oneself to do something

DEIL   *n* pl. -S the devil

DEIONIZE   *v* -IZED, -IZING, -IZES to remove ions from

DEISM   *n* pl. -S a religious philosophy

DEIST   *n* pl. -S an adherent of deism **DEISTIC** *adj*

DEITY   *n* pl. -TIES a god or goddess

DEIXIS   *n* pl. DEIXISES the specifying function of some words

DEJECT   *v* -ED, -ING, -S to depress or discourage

DEJECTA   *n/pl* excrements

DEJEUNER   *n* pl. -S a late breakfast

DEKAGRAM   *n* pl. -S a measure equal to ten grams

DEKARE   *n* pl. -S a measure equal to ten ares

DEKE   *v* DEKED, DEKING, DEKES to feint in hockey

DEKKO   *n* pl. -KOS a look

DEL   *n* pl. -S an operator in differential calculus

DELAINE   *n* pl. -S a wool fabric

DELATE   *v* -LATED, -LATING, -LATES to accuse

DELATION   *n* pl. -S the act of delating

DELATOR   *n* pl. -S one that delates

DELAY   *v* -ED, -ING, -S to put off to a later time

DELAYER   *n* pl. -S one that delays

DELE   *v* DELED, DELEING, DELES to delete

DELEAD   *v* -ED, -ING, -S to remove lead from

DELEAVE   *v* -LEAVED, -LEAVING, -LEAVES to separate the copies of

DELEGACY   *n* pl. -CIES the act of delegating

DELEGATE   *v* -GATED, -GATING, -GATES to appoint as one's representative

DELETE   *v* -LETED, -LETING, -LETES to remove written or printed matter

DELETION   *n* pl. -S the act of deleting

DELF   *n* pl. -S delft

DELFT   *n* pl. -S an earthenware

DELI   *n* pl. DELIS a delicatessen

DELICACY   *n* pl. -CIES a choice food

DELICATE   *n* pl. -S a delicacy

DELICT   *n* pl. -S an offense against civil law

DELIGHT   *v* -ED, -ING, -S to give great pleasure to

DELIME   *v* -LIMED, -LIMING, -LIMES to free from lime

DELIMIT   *v* -ED, -ING, -S to mark the boundaries of

DELIRIUM   *n* pl. -IUMS or -IA wild frenzy

DELIST   *v* -ED, -ING, -S to remove from a list

DELIVER   *v* -ED, -ING, -S to take to the intended recipient

DELIVERY   *n* pl. -ERIES the act of delivering

DELL   *n* pl. -S a small, wooded valley

DELLY   *n* pl. DELLIES deli

DELOUSE   *v* -LOUSED, -LOUSING, -LOUSES to remove lice from

DELOUSER   *n* pl. -S one that gets rid of lice

DELPHIC   *adj* ambiguous

DELTA   *n* pl. -S an alluvial deposit at the mouth of a river **DELTAIC, DELTIC** *adj*

DELTOID   *n* pl. -S a shoulder muscle

DELUDE   *v* -LUDED, -LUDING, -LUDES to mislead the mind or judgment of

DELUDER   *n* pl. -S one that deludes

DELUGE   *v* -UGED, -UGING, -UGES to flood

DELUSION   *n* pl. -S the act of deluding

DELUSIVE   *adj* tending to delude

DELUSORY   *adj* delusive

DELUSTER   *v* -ED, -ING, -S to lessen the sheen of

DELUXE *adj* of special elegance or luxury

DELVE *v* DELVED, DELVING, DELVES to search in depth

DELVER *n* pl. -S one that delves

DEMAGOG *v* -ED, -ING, -S to behave like a demagog (a leader who appeals to emotions and prejudices)

DEMAGOGY *n* pl. -GOGIES the rule of a demagog

DEMAND *v* -ED, -ING, -S to ask for with authority

DEMANDER *n* pl. -S one that demands

DEMARCHE *n* pl. -S a procedure

DEMARK *v* -ED, -ING, -S to delimit

DEMAST *v* -ED, -ING, -S to strip masts from

DEME *n* pl. -S a Greek district

DEMEAN *v* -ED, -ING, -S to conduct oneself in a particular manner

DEMEANOR *n* pl. -S the manner in which one conducts oneself

DEMENT *v* -ED, -ING, -S to make insane

DEMENTIA *n* pl. -S mental illness

DEMERARA *n* pl. -S a coarse light-brown sugar

DEMERGE *v* -MERGED, -MERGING, -MERGES to remove a division from a corporation

DEMERGER *v* -ED, -ING, -S to demerge

DEMERIT *v* -ED, -ING, -S to lower in rank or status

DEMERSAL *adj* found at the bottom of the sea

DEMESNE *n* pl. -S the legal possession of land as one's own

DEMETON *n* pl. -S an insecticide

DEMIES pl. of demy

DEMIGOD *n* pl. -S a lesser god

DEMIJOHN *n* pl. -S a narrow-necked jug

DEMILUNE *n* pl. -S a half-moon

DEMIREP *n* pl. -S a prostitute

DEMISE *v* -MISED, -MISING, -MISES to bequeath

DEMIT *v* -MITTED, -MITTING, -MITS to resign

DEMIURGE *n* pl. -S a magistrate of ancient Greece

DEMIVOLT *n* pl. -S a half turn made by a horse

DEMO *n* pl. DEMOS a demonstration

DEMOB *v* -MOBBED, -MOBBING, -MOBS to discharge from military service

DEMOCRAT *n* pl. -S one who believes in political and social equality

DEMODE *adj* demoded

DEMODED *adj* out-of-date

DEMOLISH *v* -ED, -ING, -ES to destroy

DEMON *n* pl. -S an evil spirit

DEMONESS *n* pl. -ES a female demon

DEMONIAC *n* pl. -S one regarded as possessed by a demon

DEMONIAN *adj* demonic

DEMONIC *adj* characteristic of a demon

DEMONISE *v* -ISED, -ISING, -ISES to demonize

DEMONISM *n* pl. -S belief in demons

DEMONIST *n* pl. -S one who believes in demons

DEMONIZE *v* -IZED, -IZING, -IZES to make a demon of

DEMOS *n* pl. -ES the people of an ancient Greek state

DEMOTE *v* -MOTED, -MOTING, -MOTES to lower in rank or grade

DEMOTIC *adj* pertaining to a simplified form of ancient Egyptian writing

DEMOTICS *n/pl* the study of people in society

DEMOTING present participle of demote

DEMOTION *n* pl. -S the act of demoting

DEMOTIST *n* pl. -S a student of demotic writings

DEMOUNT *v* -ED, -ING, -S to remove from a mounting

DEMPSTER *n* pl. -S a deemster

DEMUR *v* -MURRED, -MURRING, -MURS to object

DEMURE *adj* -MURER, -MUREST shy and modest **DEMURELY** *adv*

DEMURRAL *n* pl. -S the act of demurring

DEMURRED past tense of demur

DEMURRER *n* pl. -S one that demurs

DEMURRING present participle of demur

DEMY *n* pl. -MIES a size of paper

DEN *v* DENNED, DENNING, DENS to live in a lair

DENARIUS *n* pl. DENARII a coin of ancient Rome

DENARY *adj* containing ten

DENATURE   *v* -TURED, -TURING, -TURES to deprive of natural qualities

DENAZIFY   *v* -FIED, -FYING, -FIES to rid of Nazism

DENDRITE   *n* pl. -S a branched part of a nerve cell

DENDROID   *adj* shaped like a tree

DENDRON   *n* pl. -S a dendrite

DENE   *n* pl. -S a valley

DENGUE   *n* pl. -S a tropical disease

DENIABLE   *adj* capable of being denied **DENIABLY** *adv*

DENIAL   *n* pl. -S the act of denying

DENIED   past tense of deny

DENIER   *n* pl. -S one that denies

DENIES   present 3d person sing. of deny

DENIM   *n* pl. -S a durable fabric

DENIZEN   *v* -ED, -ING, -S to make a citizen of

DENNED   past tense of den

DENNING   present participle of den

DENOTE   *v* -NOTED, -NOTING, -NOTES to indicate **DENOTIVE** *adj*

DENOUNCE   *v* -NOUNCED, -NOUNCING, -NOUNCES to condemn openly

DENSE   *adj* DENSER, DENSEST compact **DENSELY** *adv*

DENSIFY   *v* -FIED, -FYING, -FIES to make denser

DENSITY   *n* pl. -TIES the state of being dense

DENT   *v* -ED, -ING, -S to make a depression in

DENTAL   *n* pl. -S a dentally produced sound

DENTALIA   *n/pl* mollusks with long, tapering shells

DENTALLY   *adv* with the tip of the tongue against the upper front teeth

DENTATE   *adj* having teeth

DENTATED   *adj* dentate

DENTICLE   *n* pl. -S a small tooth

DENTIL   *n* pl. -S a small rectangular block **DENTILED** *adj*

DENTIN   *n* pl. -S the hard substance forming the body of a tooth **DENTINAL** *adj*

DENTINE   *n* pl. -S dentin

DENTIST   *n* pl. -S one who treats the teeth

DENTOID   *adj* resembling a tooth

DENTURE   *n* pl. -S a set of teeth **DENTURAL** *adj*

DENUDATE   *v* -DATED, -DATING, -DATES to denude

DENUDE   *v* -NUDED, -NUDING, -NUDES to strip of all covering

DENUDER   *n* pl. -S one that denudes

DENY   *v* -NIED, -NYING, -NIES to declare to be untrue

DEODAND   *n* pl. -S property forfeited to the crown under a former English law

DEODAR   *n* pl. -S an East Indian cedar

DEODARA   *n* pl. -S deodar

DEONTIC   *adj* pertaining to moral obligation

DEORBIT   *v* -ED, -ING, -S to come out of an orbit

DEOXY   *adj* having less oxygen than the compound from which it is derived

DEPAINT   *v* -ED, -ING, -S to depict

DEPART   *v* -ED, -ING, -S to go away

DEPARTEE   *n* pl. -S one that departs

DEPEND   *v* -ED, -ING, -S to rely

DEPERM   *v* -ED, -ING, -S to demagnetize

DEPICT   *v* -ED, -ING, -S to portray

DEPICTER   *n* pl. -S one that depicts

DEPICTOR   *n* pl. -S depicter

DEPILATE   *v* -LATED, -LATING, -LATES to remove hair from

DEPLANE   *v* -PLANED, -PLANING, -PLANES to get off an airplane

DEPLETE   *v* -PLETED, -PLETING, -PLETES to lessen or exhaust the supply of

DEPLORE   *v* -PLORED, -PLORING, -PLORES to regret strongly

DEPLORER   *n* pl. -S one that deplores

DEPLOY   *v* -ED, -ING, -S to position troops for battle

DEPLUME   *v* -PLUMED, -PLUMING, -PLUMES to deprive of feathers

DEPOLISH   *v* -ED, -ING, -ES to remove the gloss or polish of

DEPONE   *v* -PONED, -PONING, -PONES to testify under oath

DEPONENT   *n* pl. -S one that depones

DEPORT   *v* -ED, -ING, -S to expel from a country

DEPORTEE   *n* pl. -S one who is deported

DEPOSAL   *n* pl. -S the act of deposing

DEPOSE   v -POSED, -POSING, -POSES to remove from office

DEPOSER   n pl. -S one that deposes

DEPOSIT   v -ED, -ING, -S to place

DEPOT   n pl. -S a railroad or bus station

DEPRAVE   v -PRAVED, -PRAVING, -PRAVES to corrupt in morals

DEPRAVER   n pl. -S one that depraves

DEPRESS   v -ED, -ING, -ES to make sad

DEPRIVAL   n pl. -S the act of depriving

DEPRIVE   v -PRIVED, -PRIVING, -PRIVES to take something away from

DEPRIVER   n pl. -S one that deprives

DEPSIDE   n pl. -S an aromatic compound

DEPTH   n pl. -S deepness

DEPURATE   v -RATED, -RATING, -RATES to free from impurities

DEPUTE   v -PUTED, -PUTING, -PUTES to delegate

DEPUTIZE   v -TIZED, -TIZING, -TIZES to appoint as a deputy

DEPUTY   n pl. -TIES one appointed to act for another

DERAIGN   v -ED, -ING, -S to dispute a claim

DERAIL   v -ED, -ING, -S to run off the rails of a track

DERANGE   v -RANGED, -RANGING, -RANGES to disorder

DERAT   v -RATTED, -RATTING, -RATS to rid of rats

DERATE   v -RATED, -RATING, -RATES to lower the rated capability of

DERAY   n pl. -RAYS disorderly revelry

DERBY   n pl. -BIES a type of hat

DERE   adj dire

DERELICT   n pl. -S something abandoned

DERIDE   v -RIDED, -RIDING, -RIDES to ridicule

DERIDER   n pl. -S one that derides

DERINGER   n pl. -S a short-barreled pistol

DERISION   n pl. -S the act of deriding

DERISIVE   adj expressing derision

DERISORY   adj derisive

DERIVATE   n pl. -S something derived

DERIVE   v -RIVED, -RIVING, -RIVES to obtain or receive from a source

DERIVER   n pl. -S one that derives

DERM   n pl. -S derma

DERMA   n pl. -S a layer of the skin **DERMAL** adj

DERMIS   n pl. -MISES derma **DERMIC** adj

DERMOID   n pl. -S a cystic tumor

DERNIER   adj last

DEROGATE   v -GATED, -GATING, -GATES to detract

DERRICK   n pl. -S a hoisting apparatus

DERRIERE   n pl. -S the buttocks

DERRIS   n pl. -RISES a climbing plant

DERRY   n pl. -RIES a meaningless word used in the chorus of old songs

DERVISH   n pl. -ES a member of a Muslim religious order

DESALT   v -ED, -ING, -S to remove the salt from

DESALTER   n pl. -S one that desalts

DESAND   v -ED, -ING, -S to remove sand from

DESCANT   v -ED, -ING, -S to sing a counterpoint to a melody

DESCEND   v -ED, -ING, -S to come or go down

DESCENT   n pl. -S the act of descending

DESCRIBE   v -SCRIBED, -SCRIBING, -SCRIBES to give a verbal account of

DESCRIER   n pl. -S one that descries

DESCRY   v -SCRIED, -SCRYING, -SCRIES to discern

DESELECT   v -ED, -ING, -S to dismiss from a training program

DESERT   v -ED, -ING, -S to abandon

DESERTER   n pl. -S one that deserts

DESERTIC   adj arid and barren

DESERVE   v -SERVED, -SERVING, -SERVES to be entitled to or worthy of

DESERVER   n pl. -S one that deserves

DESEX   v -ED, -ING, -ES to castrate or spay

DESIGN   v -ED, -ING, -S to conceive and plan out

DESIGNEE   n pl. -S one who is designated

DESIGNER   n pl. -S one that designs

DESILVER   v -ED, -ING, -S to remove the silver from

DESINENT   adj terminating

DESIRE   v -SIRED, -SIRING, -SIRES to wish for

DESIRER *n* pl. -S one that desires

DESIROUS *adj* desiring

DESIST *v* -ED, -ING, -S to cease doing something

DESK *n* pl. -S a writing table

DESKMAN *n* pl. -MEN one who works at a desk

DESKTOP *n* pl. -S the top of a desk

DESMAN *n* pl. -S an aquatic mammal

DESMID *n* pl. -S a freshwater alga

DESMOID *n* pl. -S a very hard tumor

DESOLATE *v* -LATED, -LATING, -LATES to lay waste

DESORB *v* -ED, -ING, -S to remove by the reverse of absorption

DESOXY *adj* deoxy

DESPAIR *v* -ED, -ING, -S to lose all hope

DESPATCH *v* -ED, -ING, -ES to dispatch

DESPISE *v* -SPISED, -SPISING, -SPISES to loathe

DESPISER *n* pl. -S one that despises

DESPITE *v* -SPITED, -SPITING, -SPITES to treat with contempt

DESPOIL *v* -ED, -ING, -S to plunder

DESPOND *v* -ED, -ING, -S to lose spirit or hope

DESPOT *n* pl. -S a tyrant **DESPOTIC** *adj*

DESSERT *n* pl. -S something served as the last course of a meal

DESTAIN *v* -ED, -ING, -S to remove stain from

DESTINE *v* -TINED, -TINING, -TINES to determine beforehand

DESTINY *n* pl. -NIES the fate or fortune to which one is destined

DESTRIER *n* pl. -S a war horse

DESTROY *v* -ED, -ING, -S to damage beyond repair or renewal

DESTRUCT *v* -ED, -ING, -S to destroy

DESUGAR *v* -ED, -ING, -S to remove sugar from

DESULFUR *v* -ED, -ING, -S to free from sulfur

DETACH *v* -ED, -ING, -ES to unfasten and separate

DETACHER *n* pl. -S one that detaches

DETAIL *v* -ED, -ING, -S to report with complete particulars

DETAILER *n* pl. -S one that details

DETAIN *v* -ED, -ING, -S to hold in custody

DETAINEE *n* pl. -S one who is detained

DETAINER *n* pl. -S the unlawful withholding of another's property

DETASSEL *v* -SELED, -SELING, -SELS or -SELLED, -SELLING, -SELS to remove tassels from

DETECT *v* -ED, -ING, -S to discover or perceive

DETECTER *n* pl. -S detector

DETECTOR *n* pl. -S one that detects

DETENT *n* pl. -S a locking or unlocking mechanism

DETENTE *n* pl. -S an easing of international tension

DETER *v* -TERRED, -TERRING, -TERS to stop from proceeding

DETERGE *v* -TERGED, -TERGING, -TERGES to cleanse

DETERGER *n* pl. -S one that deterges

DETERRED past tense of deter

DETERRER *n* pl. -S one that deters

DETERRING present participle of deter

DETEST *v* -ED, -ING, -S to dislike intensely

DETESTER *n* pl. -S one that detests

DETHRONE *v* -THRONED, -THRONING, -THRONES to remove from a throne

DETICK *v* -ED, -ING, -S to remove ticks from

DETICKER *n* pl. -S one that deticks

DETINUE *n* pl. -S an action to recover property wrongfully detained

DETONATE *v* -NATED, -NATING, -NATES to cause to explode

DETOUR *v* -ED, -ING, -S to take an indirect route

DETOX *v* -ED, -ING, -ES to detoxify

DETOXIFY *v* -FIED, -FYING, -FIES to remove a toxin from

DETRACT *v* -ED, -ING, -S to take away

DETRAIN *v* -ED, -ING, -S to get off a railroad train

DETRITUS *n* pl. DETRITUS particles of rock **DETRITAL** *adj*

DETRUDE *v* -TRUDED, -TRUDING, -TRUDES to thrust out

DEUCE *v* DEUCED, DEUCING, DEUCES to bring a tennis score to a tie

DEUCEDLY *adv* extremely

DEUTERIC *adj* pertaining to heavy hydrogen

DEUTERON *n* pl. -S an atomic particle

DEUTZIA *n* pl. -S an ornamental shrub

DEV *n* pl. -S deva

DEVA *n* pl. -S a Hindu god

DEVALUE *v* -UED, -UING, -UES to lessen the worth of

DEVEIN *v* -ED, -ING, -S to remove the dorsal vein from

DEVEL *v* -ED, -ING, -S to strike forcibly

DEVELOP *v* -ED, -ING, -S to bring to a more advanced or effective state

DEVELOPE *v* -OPED, -OPING, -OPES to develop

DEVERBAL *adj* derived from a verb

DEVEST *v* -ED, -ING, -S to divest

DEVIANCE *n* pl. -S the behavior of a deviant

DEVIANCY *n* pl. -CIES deviance

DEVIANT *n* pl. -S one that deviates from a norm

DEVIATE *v* -ATED, -ATING, -ATES to turn aside from a course or norm

DEVIATOR *n* pl. -S one that deviates

DEVICE *n* pl. -S something devised or constructed for a specific purpose

DEVIL *v* -ILED, -ILING, -ILS or -ILLED, -ILLING, -ILS to prepare food with pungent seasoning

DEVILISH *adj* fiendish

DEVILKIN *n* pl. -S a small demon

DEVILLED a past tense of devil

DEVILLING a present participle of devil

DEVILRY *n* pl. -RIES deviltry

DEVILTRY *n* pl. -TRIES mischief

DEVIOUS *adj* indirect

DEVISAL *n* pl. -S the act of devising

DEVISE *v* -VISED, -VISING, -VISES to form in the mind

DEVISEE *n* pl. -S one to whom a will is made

DEVISER *n* pl. -S one that devises

DEVISING present participle of devise

DEVISOR *n* pl. -S one who makes a will

DEVOICE *v* -VOICED, -VOICING, -VOICES to unvoice

DEVOID *adj* completely lacking

DEVOIR *n* pl. -S an act of civility or respect

DEVOLVE *v* -VOLVED, -VOLVING, -VOLVES to transfer from one person to another

DEVON *n* pl. -S one of a breed of small, hardy cattle

DEVOTE *v* -VOTED, -VOTING, -VOTES to give oneself wholly to

DEVOTEE *n* pl. -S an ardent follower or supporter

DEVOTION *n* pl. -S the act of devoting

DEVOUR *v* -ED, -ING, -S to eat up voraciously

DEVOURER *n* pl. -S one that devours

DEVOUT *adj* -VOUTER, -VOUTEST pious **DEVOUTLY** *adv*

DEW *v* -ED, -ING, -S to wet with dew (condensed moisture)

DEWAN *n* pl. -S an official in India

DEWAR *n* pl. -S a double-walled flask

DEWATER *v* -ED, -ING, -S to remove water from

DEWAX *v* -ED, -ING, -ES to remove wax from

DEWBERRY *n* pl. -RIES an edible berry

DEWCLAW *n* pl. -S a vestigial toe

DEWDROP *n* pl. -S a drop of dew

DEWFALL *n* pl. -S the formation of dew

DEWIER comparative of dewy

DEWIEST superlative of dewy

DEWILY *adv* in a dewy manner

DEWINESS *n* pl. -ES the state of being dewy

DEWLAP *n* pl. -S a fold of loose skin under the neck

DEWLESS *adj* having no dew

DEWOOL *v* -ED, -ING, -S to remove the wool from

DEWORM *v* -ED, -ING, -S to rid of worms

DEWORMER *n* pl. -S one that deworms

DEWY *adj* DEWIER, DEWIEST moist with dew

DEX *n* pl. -ES a sulfate used as a central nervous system stimulant

DEXIE *n* pl. -S a tablet of dex

DEXIES pl. of dexy

DEXTER *adj* situated on the right

DEXTRAL *adj* pertaining to the right

DEXTRAN *n* pl. -S a substance used as a blood plasma substitute

DEXTRIN	*n* pl. -S a substance used as an adhesive
DEXTRINE	*n* pl. -S dextrin
DEXTRO	*adj* turning to the right
DEXTROSE	*n* pl. -S a form of glucose
DEXTROUS	*adj* adroit
DEXY	*n* pl. DEXIES dexie
DEY	*n* pl. DEYS a former North African ruler
DEZINC	*v* -ZINCKED, -ZINCKING, -ZINCS or -ZINCED, -ZINCING, -ZINCS to remove zinc from
DHAK	*n* pl. -S an Asian tree
DHAL	*n* pl. -S dal
DHARMA	*n* pl. -S conformity to Hindu law **DHARMIC** *adj*
DHARNA	*n* pl. -S a form of protest in India
DHOBI	*n* pl. -S a person who does laundry in India
DHOLE	*n* pl. -S a wild dog of India
DHOOLY	*n* pl. -LIES dooly
DHOORA	*n* pl. -S durra
DHOOTI	*n* pl. -S dhoti
DHOOTIE	*n* pl. -S dhoti
DHOTI	*n* pl. -S a loincloth worn by Hindu men
DHOURRA	*n* pl. -S durra
DHOW	*n* pl. -S an Arabian sailing vessel
DHURNA	*n* pl. -S dharna
DHURRIE	*n* pl. -S a cotton rug made in India
DHUTI	*n* pl. -S dhoti
DIABASE	*n* pl. -S an igneous rock **DIABASIC** *adj*
DIABETES	*n* pl. DIABETES a metabolic disorder
DIABETIC	*n* pl. -S one who has diabetes
DIABLERY	*n* pl. -RIES sorcery
DIABOLIC	*adj* devilish
DIABOLO	*n* pl. -LOS a game requiring manual dexterity
DIACETYL	*n* pl. -S biacetyl
DIACID	*n* pl. -S a type of acid **DIACIDIC** *adj*
DIACONAL	*adj* pertaining to a deacon
DIADEM	*v* -ED, -ING, -S to adorn with a crown
DIAGNOSE	*v* -NOSED, -NOSING, -NOSES to recognize a disease by its signs and symptoms
DIAGONAL	*n* pl. -S an oblique line
DIAGRAM	*v* -GRAMED, -GRAMING, -GRAMS or -GRAMMED, -GRAMMING, -GRAMS to illustrate by a diagram (a graphic design)
DIAGRAPH	*n* pl. -S a drawing device
DIAL	*v* DIALED, DIALING, DIALS or DIALLED, DIALLING, DIALS to manipulate a calibrated disk
DIALECT	*n* pl. -S a regional variety of a language
DIALER	*n* pl. -S one that dials
DIALING	*n* pl. -S the measurement of time by sundials
DIALIST	*n* pl. -S a dialer
DIALLAGE	*n* pl. -S a mineral
DIALLED	a past tense of dial
DIALLEL	*adj* pertaining to a genetic crossing
DIALLER	*n* pl. -S dialer
DIALLING	*n* pl. -S dialing
DIALLIST	*n* pl. -S dialist
DIALOG	*v* -ED, -ING, -S to dialogue
DIALOGER	*n* pl. -S one that dialogs
DIALOGIC	*adj* conversational
DIALOGUE	*v* -LOGUED, -LOGUING, -LOGUES to carry on a conversation
DIALYSE	*v* -LYSED, -LYSING, -LYSES to dialyze
DIALYSER	*n* pl. -S dialyzer
DIALYSIS	*n* pl. -YSES the separation of substances in a solution by diffusion through a membrane
DIALYTIC	*adj* pertaining to dialysis
DIALYZE	*v* -LYZED, -LYZING, -LYZES to subject to dialysis
DIALYZER	*n* pl. -S an apparatus used for dialysis
DIAMANTE	*n* pl. -S a sparkling decoration
DIAMETER	*n* pl. -S a straight line passing through the center of a circle and ending at the periphery
DIAMIDE	*n* pl. -S a chemical compound
DIAMIN	*n* pl. -S diamine
DIAMINE	*n* pl. -S a chemical compound

DIAMOND	*v* -ED, -ING, -S to adorn with diamonds (precious gems)
DIANTHUS	*n* pl. -ES an ornamental herb
DIAPASON	*n* pl. -S a burst of harmonious sound
DIAPAUSE	*v* -PAUSED, -PAUSING, -PAUSES to undergo dormancy
DIAPER	*v* -ED, -ING, -S to put a diaper (a baby's breechcloth) on
DIAPHONE	*n* pl. -S a low-pitched foghorn
DIAPHONY	*n* pl. -NIES organum
DIAPIR	*n* pl. -S a bend in a layer of rock **DIAPIRIC** *adj*
DIAPSID	*adj* pertaining to a type of reptile
DIARCHY	*n* pl. -CHIES a government with two rulers **DIARCHIC** *adj*
DIARIES	pl. of diary
DIARIST	*n* pl. -S one who keeps a diary
DIARRHEA	*n* pl. -S an intestinal disorder
DIARY	*n* pl. -RIES a personal journal
DIASPORA	*n* pl. -S migration
DIASPORE	*n* pl. -S a mineral
DIASTASE	*n* pl. -S an enzyme
DIASTEM	*n* pl. -S an interruption in the deposition of sediment
DIASTEMA	*n* pl. -MATA a space between teeth
DIASTER	*n* pl. -S a stage in mitosis **DIASTRAL** *adj*
DIASTOLE	*n* pl. -S the normal rhythmical dilation of the heart
DIATOM	*n* pl. -S any of a class of algae
DIATOMIC	*adj* composed of two atoms
DIATONIC	*adj* pertaining to a type of musical scale
DIATRIBE	*n* pl. -S a bitter and abusive criticism
DIATRON	*n* pl. -S a circuitry design that uses diodes
DIAZEPAM	*n* pl. -S a tranquilizer
DIAZIN	*n* pl. -S diazine
DIAZINE	*n* pl. -S a chemical compound
DIAZINON	*n* pl. -S an insecticide
DIAZO	*adj* containing a certain chemical group
DIAZOLE	*n* pl. -S a chemical compound
DIB	*v* DIBBED, DIBBING, DIBS to fish by letting the bait bob lightly on the water
DIBASIC	*adj* having two replaceable hydrogen atoms
DIBBER	*n* pl. -S a planting implement
DIBBING	present participle of dib
DIBBLE	*v* -BLED, -BLING, -BLES to dib
DIBBLER	*n* pl. -S one that dibbles
DIBBUK	*n* pl. -BUKS or -BUKIM dybbuk
DICAST	*n* pl. -S a judge of ancient Athens **DICASTIC** *adj*
DICE	*v* DICED, DICING, DICES to cut into small cubes
DICENTRA	*n* pl. -S a perennial herb
DICER	*n* pl. -S a device that dices food
DICEY	*adj* DICIER, DICIEST dangerous
DICHASIA	*n/pl* flower clusters
DICHOTIC	*adj* affecting the two ears differently
DICHROIC	*adj* having two colors
DICIER	comparative of dicey
DICIEST	superlative of dicey
DICING	present participle of dice
DICK	*n* pl. -S a detective
DICKENS	*n* pl. -ES devil
DICKER	*v* -ED, -ING, -S to bargain
DICKEY	*n* pl. -EYS a blouse front
DICKIE	*n* pl. -S dickey
DICKY	*n* pl. DICKIES dickey
DICKY	*adj* DICKIER, DICKIEST poor in condition
DICLINY	*n* pl. -NIES the state of having stamens and pistils in separate flowers
DICOT	*n* pl. -S a plant with two seed leaves
DICOTYL	*n* pl. -S dicot
DICROTAL	*adj* dicrotic
DICROTIC	*adj* having a double pulse beat
DICTA	a pl. of dictum
DICTATE	*v* -TATED, -TATING, -TATES to read aloud for recording
DICTATOR	*n* pl. -S one that dictates
DICTIER	comparative of dicty
DICTIEST	superlative of dicty
DICTION	*n* pl. -S choice and use of words in speech or writing
DICTUM	*n* pl. -TA or -TUMS an authoritative statement
DICTY	*adj* -TIER, -TIEST snobbish

DICYCLIC   *adj* having two maxima of population each year

DICYCLY   *n* pl. -CLIES the state of being dicyclic

DID   a past tense of do

DIDACT   *n* pl. -S a didactic person

DIDACTIC   *adj* instructive

DIDACTYL   *adj* having two digits at the end of each limb

DIDAPPER   *n* pl. -S a dabchick

DIDDLE   *v* -DLED, -DLING, -DLES to swindle

DIDDLER   *n* pl. -S one that diddles

DIDDLEY   *n* pl. -DLEYS diddly

DIDDLY   *n* pl. -DLIES the least amount

DIDIE   *n* pl. -S didy

DIDIES   pl. of didy

DIDO   *n* pl. -DOS or -DOES a mischievous act

DIDST   a past tense of do

DIDY   *n* pl. -DIES a diaper

DIDYMIUM   *n* pl. -S a mixture of rare-earth elements

DIDYMOUS   *adj* occurring in pairs

DIDYNAMY   *n* pl. -MIES the state of having four stamens in pairs of unequal length

DIE   *v* DIED, DYING, DIES to cease living

DIE   *v* DIED, DIEING, DIES to cut with a die (a device for shaping material)

DIEBACK   *n* pl. -S a gradual dying of plant shoots

DIECIOUS   *adj* dioicous

DIED   past tense of die

DIEHARD   *n* pl. -S a stubborn person

DIEL   *adj* involving a full day

DIELDRIN   *n* pl. -S an insecticide

DIEMAKER   *n* pl. -S one that makes dies

DIENE   *n* pl. -S a chemical compound

DIERESIS   *n* pl. DIERESES the separation of two vowels into two syllables **DIERETIC** *adj*

DIESEL   *v* -ED, -ING, -S to continue running after the ignition is turned off

DIESIS   *n* pl. DIESES a reference mark in printing

DIESTER   *n* pl. -S a type of chemical compound

DIESTOCK   *n* pl. -S a frame for holding dies

DIESTRUM   *n* pl. -S diestrus

DIESTRUS   *n* pl. -ES a period of sexual inactivity

DIET   *v* -ED, -ING, -S to regulate one's daily sustenance

DIETARY   *n* pl. -ETARIES a system of dieting

DIETER   *n* pl. -S one that diets

DIETETIC   *adj* pertaining to diet

DIETHER   *n* pl. -S a chemical compound

DIFFER   *v* -ED, -ING, -S to be unlike

DIFFRACT   *v* -ED, -ING, -S to separate into parts

DIFFUSE   *v* -FUSED, -FUSING, -FUSES to spread widely or thinly

DIFFUSER   *n* pl. -S one that diffuses

DIFFUSOR   *n* pl. -S diffuser

DIG   *v* DUG or DIGGED, DIGGING, DIGS to break up, turn over, or remove earth

DIGAMIES   pl. of digamy

DIGAMIST   *n* pl. -S one who practices digamy

DIGAMMA   *n* pl. -S a Greek letter

DIGAMY   *n* pl. -MIES a second legal marriage **DIGAMOUS** *adj*

DIGEST   *v* -ED, -ING, -S to render food usable for the body

DIGESTER   *n* pl. -S an apparatus in which substances are softened or decomposed

DIGESTOR   *n* pl. -S digester

DIGGED   a past tense of dig

DIGGER   *n* pl. -S one that digs

DIGGING   present participle of dig

DIGGINGS   *n/pl* an excavation site

DIGHT   *v* -ED, -ING, -S to adorn

DIGIT   *n* pl. -S a finger or toe

DIGITAL   *n* pl. -S a piano key

DIGITATE   *adj* having digits

DIGITIZE   *v* -TIZED, -TIZING, -TIZES to put data into digital notation

DIGLOT   *n* pl. -S a bilingual book or edition

DIGNIFY   *v* -FIED, -FYING, -FIES to add dignity to

DIGNITY   *n* pl. -TIES stateliness and nobility of manner

DIGOXIN   *n* pl. -S a drug to improve heart function

DIGRAPH   *n* pl. -S a pair of letters representing a single speech sound

DIGRESS   *v* -ED, -ING, -ES to stray from the main topic

DIHEDRAL   *n* pl. -S a dihedron

DIHEDRON   *n* pl. -S a figure formed by two intersecting planes

DIHYBRID   *n* pl. -S an offspring of parents differing in two pairs of genes

DIHYDRIC   *adj* containing two hydroxyl radicals

DIKDIK   *n* pl. -S a small antelope

DIKE   *v* DIKED, DIKING, DIKES to furnish with an embankment

DIKER   *n* pl. -S one that dikes

DIKTAT   *n* pl. -S a harsh settlement imposed on a defeated nation

DILATANT   *n* pl. -S a dilator

DILATATE   *adj* dilated

DILATE   *v* -LATED, -LATING, -LATES to make wider or larger

DILATER   *n* pl. -S dilator

DILATION   *n* pl. -S the act of dilating

DILATIVE   *adj* tending to dilate

DILATOR   *n* pl. -S one that dilates

DILATORY   *adj* tending to delay

DILDO   *n* pl. -DOS an object used as a penis substitute

DILDOE   *n* pl. -S dildo

DILEMMA   *n* pl. -S a perplexing situation **DILEMMIC** *adj*

DILIGENT   *adj* persevering

DILL   *n* pl. -S an annual herb

DILLED   *adj* flavored with dill

DILLY   *n* pl. DILLIES something remarkable

DILUENT   *n* pl. -S a diluting substance

DILUTE   *v* -LUTED, -LUTING, -LUTES to thin or reduce the concentration of

DILUTER   *n* pl. -S one that dilutes

DILUTION   *n* pl. -S the act of diluting

DILUTIVE   *adj* tending to dilute

DILUTOR   *n* pl. -S diluter

DILUVIA   a pl. of diluvium

DILUVIAL   *adj* pertaining to a flood

DILUVIAN   *adj* diluvial

DILUVION   *n* pl. -S diluvium

DILUVIUM   *n* pl. -VIA or -VIUMS coarse rock material deposited by glaciers

DIM   *adj* DIMMER, DIMMEST obscure

DIM   *v* DIMMED, DIMMING, DIMS to make dim

DIME   *n* pl. -S a coin of the United States

DIMER   *n* pl. -S a molecule composed of two identical molecules

DIMERIC   *adj* dimerous

DIMERISM   *n* pl. -S the state of being dimerous

DIMERIZE   *v* -IZED, -IZING, -IZES to form a dimer

DIMEROUS   *adj* composed of two parts

DIMETER   *n* pl. -S a verse of two metrical feet

DIMETHYL   *n* pl. -S ethane

DIMETRIC   *adj* pertaining to a type of crystal system

DIMINISH   *v* -ED, -ING, -ES to lessen

DIMITY   *n* pl. -TIES a cotton fabric

DIMLY   *adv* in a dim manner

DIMMABLE   *adj* capable of being dimmed

DIMMED   past tense of dim

DIMMER   *n* pl. -S a device for varying the intensity of illumination

DIMMEST   superlative of dim

DIMMING   present participle of dim

DIMNESS   *n* pl. -ES the state of being dim

DIMORPH   *n* pl. -S either of two distinct forms

DIMOUT   *n* pl. -S a condition of partial darkness

DIMPLE   *v* -PLED, -PLING, -PLES to mark with indentations

DIMPLY   *adj* -PLIER, -PLIEST dimpled

DIMWIT   *n* pl. -S a dunce

DIN   *v* DINNED, DINNING, DINS to make a loud noise

DINAR   *n* pl. -S an ancient gold coin of Muslim areas

DINDLE   *v* -DLED, -DLING, -DLES to tingle

DINE	*v* DINED, DINING, DINES to eat dinner
DINER	*n* pl. -S one that dines
DINERIC	*adj* pertaining to the interface between two immiscible liquids
DINERO	*n* pl. -ROS a former silver coin of Peru
DINETTE	*n* pl. -S a small dining room
DING	*v* -ED, -ING, -S to ring
DINGBAT	*n* pl. -S a typographical ornament
DINGDONG	*v* -ED, -ING, -S to make a ringing sound
DINGE	*n* pl. -S the condition of being dingy
DINGER	*n* pl. -S a home run
DINGEY	*n* pl. -GEYS dinghy
DINGHY	*n* pl. -GHIES a small boat
DINGIER	comparative of dingy
DINGIES	pl. of dingy
DINGIEST	superlative of dingy
DINGILY	*adv* in a dingy manner
DINGLE	*n* pl. -S a dell
DINGO	*n* pl. -GOES a wild dog of Australia
DINGUS	*n* pl. -ES a doodad
DINGY	*n* pl. -GIES dinghy
DINGY	*adj* -GIER, -GIEST grimy
DINING	present participle of dine
DINITRO	*adj* containing two nitro groups
DINK	*v* -ED, -ING, -S to adorn
DINKEY	*n* pl. -KEYS a small locomotive
DINKIER	comparative of dinky
DINKIES	pl. of dinky
DINKIEST	superlative of dinky
DINKLY	*adv* neatly
DINKUM	*n* pl. -S the truth
DINKY	*n* pl. -KIES dinkey
DINKY	*adj* -KIER, -KIEST small
DINNED	past tense of din
DINNER	*n* pl. -S the main meal of the day
DINNING	present participle of din
DINOSAUR	*n* pl. -S one of a group of extinct reptiles
DINT	*v* -ED, -ING, -S to dent
DIOBOL	*n* pl. -S a coin of ancient Greece
DIOBOLON	*n* pl. -S diobol

DIOCESAN	*n* pl. -S a bishop
DIOCESE	*n* pl. -S an ecclesiastical district
DIODE	*n* pl. -S a type of electron tube
DIOECISM	*n* pl. -S the state of being dioicous
DIOECY	*n* pl. DIOECIES dioecism
DIOICOUS	*adj* unisexual
DIOL	*n* pl. -S a chemical compound
DIOLEFIN	*n* pl. -S a hydrocarbon
DIOPSIDE	*n* pl. -S a mineral
DIOPTASE	*n* pl. -S a mineral
DIOPTER	*n* pl. -S a measure of refractive power **DIOPTRAL** *adj*
DIOPTRE	*n* pl. -S diopter
DIOPTRIC	*adj* aiding the vision by refraction
DIORAMA	*n* pl. -S a three-dimensional exhibit **DIORAMIC** *adj*
DIORITE	*n* pl. -S an igneous rock **DIORITIC** *adj*
DIOXAN	*n* pl. -S dioxane
DIOXANE	*n* pl. -S a flammable liquid
DIOXID	*n* pl. -S dioxide
DIOXIDE	*n* pl. -S a type of oxide
DIOXIN	*n* pl. -S a toxic solid hydrocarbon
DIP	*v* DIPPED or DIPT, DIPPING, DIPS to immerse briefly
DIPHASE	*adj* having two phases
DIPHASIC	*adj* diphase
DIPHENYL	*n* pl. -S biphenyl
DIPLEGIA	*n* pl. -S paralysis of the same part on both sides of the body
DIPLEX	*adj* pertaining to the simultaneous transmission or reception of two radio signals
DIPLEXER	*n* pl. -S a coupling device
DIPLOE	*n* pl. -S a bony tissue of the cranium **DIPLOIC** *adj*
DIPLOID	*n* pl. -S a cell having the basic chromosome number doubled
DIPLOIDY	*n* pl. -DIES the condition of being a diploid
DIPLOMA	*n* pl. -MAS or -MATA a certificate of an academic degree
DIPLOMA	*v* -ED, -ING, -S to furnish with a diploma
DIPLOMAT	*n* pl. -S a governmental official
DIPLONT	*n* pl. -S an organism having a particular chromosomal structure

DIPLOPIA	*n* pl. -S double vision **DIPLOPIC** *adj*
DIPLOPOD	*n* pl. -S a multi-legged insect
DIPLOSIS	*n* pl. -LOSES a method of chromosome formation
DIPNET	*v* -NETTED, -NETTING, -NETS to scoop fish with a type of net
DIPNOAN	*n* pl. -S a lungfish
DIPODY	*n* pl. -DIES a dimeter **DIPODIC** *adj*
DIPOLE	*n* pl. -S a pair of equal and opposite electric charges **DIPOLAR** *adj*
DIPPABLE	*adj* capable of being dipped
DIPPED	a past tense of dip
DIPPER	*n* pl. -S one that dips
DIPPING	present participle of dip
DIPPY	*adj* -PIER, -PIEST foolish
DIPSAS	*n* pl. DIPSADES a fabled serpent
DIPSO	*n* pl. -SOS a person who craves alcoholic liquors
DIPSTICK	*n* pl. -S a measuring rod
DIPT	a past tense of dip
DIPTERA	pl. of dipteron
DIPTERAL	*adj* having two rows or columns
DIPTERAN	*n* pl. -S a two-winged fly
DIPTERON	*n* pl. -TERA dipteran
DIPTYCA	*n* pl. -S diptych
DIPTYCH	*n* pl. -S an ancient writing tablet
DIQUAT	*n* pl. -S an herbicide
DIRDUM	*n* pl. -S blame
DIRE	*adj* DIRER, DIREST disastrous
DIRECT	*v* -ED, -ING, -S to control or conduct the affairs of
DIRECT	*adj* -RECTER, -RECTEST straightforward **DIRECTLY** *adv*
DIRECTOR	*n* pl. -S one that directs
DIREFUL	*adj* dreadful
DIRELY	*adv* in a dire manner
DIRENESS	*n* pl. -ES the state of being dire
DIRER	comparative of dire
DIREST	superlative of dire
DIRGE	*n* pl. -S a funeral song **DIRGEFUL** *adj*
DIRHAM	*n* pl. -S a monetary unit of Morocco
DIRIMENT	*adj* nullifying
DIRK	*v* -ED, -ING, -S to stab with a small knife
DIRL	*v* -ED, -ING, -S to tremble
DIRNDL	*n* pl. -S a woman's dress
DIRT	*n* pl. -S earth or soil
DIRTBAG	*n* pl. -S a dirty or contemptible person
DIRTY	*adj* DIRTIER, DIRTIEST unclean **DIRTILY** *adv*
DIRTY	*v* DIRTIED, DIRTYING, DIRTIES to make dirty
DIS	*v* DISSED, DISSING, DISSES to insult or criticize
DISABLE	*v* -ABLED, -ABLING, -ABLES to render incapable or unable
DISABUSE	*v* -ABUSED, -ABUSING, -ABUSES to free from false or mistaken ideas
DISAGREE	*v* -AGREED, -AGREEING, -AGREES to differ in opinion
DISALLOW	*v* -ED, -ING, -S to refuse to allow
DISANNUL	*v* -NULLED, -NULLING, -NULS to annul
DISARM	*v* -ED, -ING, -S to deprive of weapons
DISARMER	*n* pl. -S one that disarms
DISARRAY	*v* -ED, -ING, -S to disorder
DISASTER	*n* pl. -S a calamity
DISAVOW	*v* -ED, -ING, -S to disclaim responsibility for
DISBAND	*v* -ED, -ING, -S to break up
DISBAR	*v* -BARRED, -BARRING, -BARS to expel from the legal profession
DISBOSOM	*v* -ED, -ING, -S to confess
DISBOUND	*adj* not having a binding
DISBOWEL	*v* -ELED, -ELING, -ELS or -ELLED, -ELLING, -ELS to remove the intestines of
DISBUD	*v* -BUDDED, -BUDDING, -BUDS to remove buds from
DISBURSE	*v* -BURSED, -BURSING, -BURSES to pay out
DISC	*v* -ED, -ING, -S to disk
DISCANT	*v* -ED, -ING, -S to descant
DISCARD	*v* -ED, -ING, -S to throw away
DISCASE	*v* -CASED, -CASING, -CASES to remove the case of
DISCEPT	*v* -ED, -ING, -S to debate
DISCERN	*v* -ED, -ING, -S to perceive
DISCI	a pl. of discus

DISCIPLE *v* -PLED, -PLING, -PLES to cause to become a follower

DISCLAIM *v* -ED, -ING, -S to renounce any claim to or connection with

DISCLIKE *adj* disklike

DISCLOSE *v* -CLOSED, -CLOSING, -CLOSES to reveal

DISCO *v* -ED, -ING, -S to dance at a discotheque

DISCOID *n* pl. -S a disk

DISCOLOR *v* -ED, -ING, -S to alter the color of

DISCORD *v* -ED, -ING, -S to disagree

DISCOUNT *v* -ED, -ING, -S to reduce the price of

DISCOVER *v* -ED, -ING, -S to gain sight or knowledge of

DISCREET *adj* -CREETER, -CREETEST tactful

DISCRETE *adj* separate

DISCROWN *v* -ED, -ING, -S to deprive of a crown

DISCUS *n* pl. -CUSES or -CI a disk hurled in athletic competition

DISCUSS *v* -ED, -ING, -ES to talk over or write about

DISDAIN *v* -ED, -ING, -S to scorn

DISEASE *v* -EASED, -EASING, -EASES to make unhealthy

DISENDOW *v* -ED, -ING, -S to deprive of endowment

DISEUSE *n* pl. -S a female entertainer

DISFAVOR *v* -ED, -ING, -S to regard with disapproval

DISFROCK *v* -ED, -ING, -S to unfrock

DISGORGE *v* -GORGED, -GORGING, -GORGES to vomit

DISGRACE *v* -GRACED, -GRACING, -GRACES to bring shame or discredit upon

DISGUISE *v* -GUISED, -GUISING, -GUISES to alter the appearance of

DISGUST *v* -ED, -ING, -S to cause nausea or loathing in

DISH *v* -ED, -ING, -ES to put into a dish (a concave vessel)

DISHELM *v* -ED, -ING, -S to deprive of a helmet

DISHERIT *v* -ED, -ING, -S to deprive of an inheritance

DISHEVEL *v* -ELED, -ELING, -ELS or -ELLED, -ELLING, -ELS to make messy

DISHFUL *n* pl. -S as much as a dish can hold

DISHIER comparative of dishy

DISHIEST superlative of dishy

DISHLIKE *adj* resembling a dish

DISHONOR *v* -ED, -ING, -S to deprive of honor

DISHPAN *n* pl. -S a pan for washing dishes

DISHRAG *n* pl. -S a cloth for washing dishes

DISHWARE *n* pl. -S tableware used in serving food

DISHY *adj* DISHIER, DISHIEST attractive

DISINTER *v* -TERRED, -TERRING, -TERS to exhume

DISJECT *v* -ED, -ING, -S to disperse

DISJOIN *v* -ED, -ING, -S to separate

DISJOINT *v* -ED, -ING, -S to put out of order

DISJUNCT *n* pl. -S an alternative in a logical disjunction

DISK *v* -ED, -ING, -S to break up land with a type of farm implement

DISKETTE *n* pl. -S a floppy disk for a computer

DISKLIKE *adj* resembling a disk (a flat, circular plate)

DISLIKE *v* -LIKED, -LIKING, -LIKES to regard with aversion

DISLIKER *n* pl. -S one that dislikes

DISLIMN *v* -ED, -ING, -S to make dim

DISLODGE *v* -LODGED, -LODGING, -LODGES to remove from a firm position

DISLOYAL *adj* not loyal

DISMAL *n* pl. -S a track of swampy land

DISMAL *adj* -MALER, -MALEST cheerless and depressing **DISMALLY** *adv*

DISMAST *v* -ED, -ING, -S to remove the mast of

DISMAY *v* -ED, -ING, -S to deprive of courage or resolution

DISME *n* pl. -S a former coin of the United States

DISMISS *v* -ED, -ING, -ES to permit or cause to leave

DISMOUNT   *v* -ED, -ING, -S to get down from an elevated position

DISOBEY   *v* -ED, -ING, -S to fail to obey

DISOMIC   *adj* having a number of chromosomes duplicated

DISORDER   *v* -ED, -ING, -S to put out of order

DISOWN   *v* -ED, -ING, -S to deny the ownership of

DISPART   *v* -ED, -ING, -S to separate

DISPATCH   *v* -ED, -ING, -ES to send off with speed

DISPEL   *v* -PELLED, -PELLING, -PELS to drive off in various directions

DISPEND   *v* -ED, -ING, -S to squander

DISPENSE   *v* -PENSED, -PENSING, -PENSES to distribute

DISPERSE   *v* -PERSED, -PERSING, -PERSES to scatter

DISPIRIT   *v* -ED, -ING, -S to lower in spirit

DISPLACE   *v* -PLACED, -PLACING, -PLACES to remove from the usual or proper place

DISPLANT   *v* -ED, -ING, -S to dislodge

DISPLAY   *v* -ED, -ING, -S to make evident or obvious

DISPLODE   *v* -PLODED, -PLODING, -PLODES to explode

DISPLUME   *v* -PLUMED, -PLUMING, -PLUMES to deplume

DISPORT   *v* -ED, -ING, -S to amuse oneself

DISPOSAL   *n* pl. -S the act of disposing

DISPOSE   *v* -POSED, -POSING, -POSES to put in place

DISPOSER   *n* pl. -S one that disposes

DISPREAD   *v* -SPREAD, -SPREADING, -SPREADS to spread out

DISPRIZE   *v* -PRIZED, -PRIZING, -PRIZES to disdain

DISPROOF   *n* pl. -S the act of disproving

DISPROVE   *v* -PROVED, -PROVEN, -PROVING, -PROVES to refute

DISPUTE   *v* -PUTED, -PUTING, -PUTES to argue about

DISPUTER   *n* pl. -S one that disputes

DISQUIET   *v* -ED, -ING, -S to deprive of quiet, rest, or peace

DISRATE   *v* -RATED, -RATING, -RATES to lower in rating or rank

DISROBE   *v* -ROBED, -ROBING, -ROBES to undress

DISROBER   *n* pl. -S one that disrobes

DISROOT   *v* -ED, -ING, -S to uproot

DISRUPT   *v* -ED, -ING, -S to throw into confusion

DISS   *v* -ED, -ING, -ES to dis

DISSAVE   *v* -SAVED, -SAVING, -SAVES to use savings for current expenses

DISSEAT   *v* -ED, -ING, -S to unseat

DISSECT   *v* -ED, -ING, -S to cut apart for scientific examination

DISSED   past tense of dis

DISSEISE   *v* -SEISED, -SEISING, -SEISES to deprive

DISSEIZE   *v* -SEIZED, -SEIZING, -SEIZES to disseise

DISSENT   *v* -ED, -ING, -S to disagree

DISSERT   *v* -ED, -ING, -S to discuss in a learned or formal manner

DISSERVE   *v* -SERVED, -SERVING, -SERVES to treat badly

DISSES   present 3d person sing. of dis

DISSEVER   *v* -ED, -ING, -S to sever

DISSING   present participle of dis

DISSOLVE   *v* -SOLVED, -SOLVING, -SOLVES to make into a solution

DISSUADE   *v* -SUADED, -SUADING, -SUADES to persuade not to do something

DISTAFF   *n* pl. -TAFFS or -TAVES a type of staff

DISTAIN   *v* -ED, -ING, -S to stain

DISTAL   *adj* located far from the point of origin **DISTALLY** *adv*

DISTANCE   *v* -TANCED, -TANCING, -TANCES to leave behind

DISTANT   *adj* far off or apart

DISTASTE   *v* -TASTED, -TASTING, -TASTES to dislike

DISTAVES   a pl. of distaff

DISTEND   *v* -ED, -ING, -S to swell

DISTENT   *adj* distended

DISTICH   *n* pl. -S a couplet

DISTIL   *v* -TILLED, -TILLING, -TILS to distill

DISTILL   *v* -ED, -ING, -S to extract by vaporization and condensation

DISTINCT   *adj* -TINCTER, -TINCTEST clearly different

DISTOME   *n* pl. -S a parasitic flatworm

DISTORT   *v* -ED, -ING, -S to put out of shape

DISTRACT   *v* -ED, -ING, -S to divert the attention of

DISTRAIN   *v* -ED, -ING, -S to seize and hold property as security

DISTRAIT   *adj* absentminded

DISTRESS   *v* -ED, -ING, -ES to cause anxiety or suffering to

DISTRICT   *v* -ED, -ING, -S to divide into localities

DISTRUST   *v* -ED, -ING, -S to have no trust in

DISTURB   *v* -ED, -ING, -S to interrupt the quiet, rest, or peace of

DISULFID   *n* pl. -S a chemical compound

DISUNION   *n* pl. -S the state of being disunited

DISUNITE   *v* -UNITED, -UNITING, -UNITES to separate

DISUNITY   *n* pl. -TIES lack of unity

DISUSE   *v* -USED, -USING, -USES to stop using

DISVALUE   *v* -UED, -UING, -UES to treat as of little value

DISYOKE   *v* -YOKED, -YOKING, -YOKES to free from a yoke

DIT   *n* pl. -S a dot in Morse code

DITA   *n* pl. -S a Philippine tree

DITCH   *v* -ED, -ING, -ES to dig a long, narrow excavation in the ground

DITCHER   *n* pl. -S one that ditches

DITE   *n* pl. -S a small amount

DITHEISM   *n* pl. -S belief in two coequal gods

DITHEIST   *n* pl. -S an adherent of ditheism

DITHER   *v* -ED, -ING, -S to act nervously or indecisively

DITHERER   *n* pl. -S one that dithers

DITHERY   *adj* nervously excited

DITHIOL   *adj* containing two chemical groups both of which include sulfur and hydrogen

DITSY   *adj* -SIER, -SIEST silly, eccentric

DITTANY   *n* pl. -NIES a perennial herb

DITTO   *v* -ED, -ING, -S to repeat

DITTY   *n* pl. -TIES a short, simple song

DITZ   *n* pl. -ES a ditsy person

DITZY   *adj* -ZIER, -ZIEST ditsy

DIURESIS   *n* pl. DIURESES excessive discharge of urine

DIURETIC   *n* pl. -S a drug which increases urinary discharge

DIURNAL   *n* pl. -S a diary

DIURON   *n* pl. -S an herbicide

DIVA   *n* pl. -S a distinguished female operatic singer

DIVAGATE   *v* -GATED, -GATING, -GATES to wander

DIVALENT   *adj* having a valence of two

DIVAN   *n* pl. -S a sofa or couch

DIVE   *v* DIVED or DOVE, DIVING, DIVES to plunge headfirst into water

DIVEBOMB   *v* -ED, -ING, -S to drop bombs on a target from a diving airplane

DIVER   *n* pl. -S one that dives

DIVERGE   *v* -VERGED, -VERGING, -VERGES to move in different directions from a common point

DIVERSE   *adj* different

DIVERT   *v* -ED, -ING, -S to turn aside

DIVERTER   *n* pl. -S one that diverts

DIVEST   *v* -ED, -ING, -S to strip or deprive of anything

DIVIDE   *v* -VIDED, -VIDING, -VIDES to separate into parts, areas, or groups

DIVIDEND   *n* pl. -S a quantity to be divided

DIVIDER   *n* pl. -S one that divides

DIVIDING   present participle of divide

DIVIDUAL   *adj* capable of being divided

DIVINE   *v* -VINED, -VINING, -VINES to foretell by occult means

DIVINE   *adj* -VINER, -VINEST pertaining to or characteristic of a god **DIVINELY** *adv*

DIVINER   *n* pl. -S one that divines

DIVING   present participle of dive

DIVINING   present participle of divine

DIVINISE   *v* -NISED, -NISING, -NISES to divinize

DIVINITY   *n* pl. -TIES the state of being divine

DIVINIZE   *v* -NIZED, -NIZING, -NIZES to make divine

DIVISION   *n* pl. -S the act of dividing

DIVISIVE   *adj* causing disunity or dissension

DIVISOR   *n* pl. -S a number by which a dividend is divided

DIVORCE	v -VORCED, -VORCING, -VORCES to terminate the marriage contract between	**DOC**	n pl. -S doctor
		DOCENT	n pl. -S a college or university lecturer
DIVORCEE	n pl. -S a divorced woman	**DOCETIC**	adj pertaining to a religious doctrine
DIVORCER	n pl. -S one that divorces		
DIVORCING	present participle of divorce	**DOCILE**	adj easily trained **DOCILELY** adv
DIVOT	n pl. -S a piece of turf	**DOCILITY**	n pl. -TIES the quality of being docile
DIVULGE	v -VULGED, -VULGING, -VULGES to reveal		
		DOCK	v -ED, -ING, -S to bring into a dock (a wharf)
DIVULGER	n pl. -S one that divulges		
DIVVY	v -VIED, -VYING, -VIES to divide	**DOCKAGE**	n pl. -S a charge for the use of a dock
DIWAN	n pl. -S dewan	**DOCKER**	n pl. -S a dock worker
DIXIT	n pl. -S a statement	**DOCKET**	v -ED, -ING, -S to supply with an identifying statement
DIZEN	v -ED, -ING, -S to dress in fine clothes		
		DOCKHAND	n pl. -S a docker
DIZYGOUS	adj developed from two fertilized ova	**DOCKLAND**	n pl. -S the part of a port occupied by docks
DIZZY	adj -ZIER, -ZIEST having a sensation of whirling **DIZZILY** adv	**DOCKSIDE**	n pl. -S the area adjacent to a dock
DIZZY	v -ZIED, -ZYING, -ZIES to make dizzy	**DOCKYARD**	n pl. -S a shipyard
		DOCTOR	v -ED, -ING, -S to treat medically
DJEBEL	n pl. -S jebel	**DOCTORAL**	adj pertaining to a doctor
DJELLABA	n pl. -S a long hooded garment	**DOCTRINE**	n pl. -S a belief or set of beliefs taught or advocated
DJIN	n pl. -S jinni		
DJINN	n pl. -S jinni	**DOCUMENT**	v -ED, -ING, -S to support by conclusive information or evidence
DJINNI	n pl. DJINN jinni		
DJINNY	n pl. DJINN jinni		
DO	v DID or DIDST, DONE, DOING, present sing. 2d person DO, DOEST or DOST, 3d person DOES, DOETH or DOTH to begin and carry through to completion	**DODDER**	v -ED, -ING, -S to totter
		DODDERER	n pl. -S one that dodders
		DODDERY	adj feeble
		DODGE	v DODGED, DODGING, DODGES to evade
DO	n pl. DOS the first tone of the diatonic musical scale		
		DODGEM	n pl. -S an amusement park ride
DOABLE	adj able to be done	**DODGER**	n pl. -S one that dodges
DOAT	v -ED, -ING, -S to dote	**DODGERY**	n pl. -ERIES evasion
DOBBER	n pl. -S a float for a fishing line	**DODGING**	present participle of dodge
DOBBIN	n pl. -S a farm horse	**DODGY**	adj DODGIER, DODGIEST evasive
DOBBY	n pl. -BIES a fool		
DOBIE	n pl. -S adobe	**DODO**	n pl. -DOES or -DOS an extinct flightless bird
DOBIES	pl. of doby		
DOBLA	n pl. -S a former gold coin of Spain	**DODOISM**	n pl. -S a stupid remark
		DOE	n pl. -S a female deer
DOBLON	n pl. -S or -ES a former gold coin of Spain and Spanish America	**DOER**	n pl. -S one that does something
		DOES	a present 3d person sing. of do
DOBRA	n pl. -S a former gold coin of Portugal	**DOESKIN**	n pl. -S the skin of a doe
		DOEST	a present 2d person sing. of do
DOBSON	n pl. -S an aquatic insect larva	**DOETH**	a present 3d person sing. of do
DOBY	n pl. -BIES dobie	**DOFF**	v -ED, -ING, -S to take off

DOFFER	*n* pl. -S one that doffs
DOG	*v* DOGGED, DOGGING, DOGS to follow after like a dog (a domesticated, carnivorous mammal)
DOGBANE	*n* pl. -S a perennial herb
DOGBERRY	*n* pl. -RIES a wild berry
DOGCART	*n* pl. -S a one-horse carriage
DOGDOM	*n* pl. -S the world of dogs
DOGE	*n* pl. -S the chief magistrate in the former republics of Venice and Genoa
DOGEAR	*v* -ED, -ING, -S to turn down a corner of a page
DOGEDOM	*n* pl. -S the domain of a doge
DOGESHIP	*n* pl. -S the office of a doge
DOGEY	*n* pl. -GEYS dogie
DOGFACE	*n* pl. -S a soldier in the U.S. Army
DOGFIGHT	*v* -FOUGHT, -FIGHTING, -FIGHTS to engage in an aerial battle
DOGFISH	*n* pl. -ES a small shark
DOGGED	past tense of dog
DOGGEDLY	*adv* stubbornly
DOGGER	*n* pl. -S a fishing vessel
DOGGEREL	*n* pl. -S trivial, awkwardly written verse
DOGGERY	*n* pl. -GERIES surly behavior
DOGGIE	*n* pl. -S doggy
DOGGIER	comparative of doggy
DOGGIES	pl. of doggy
DOGGIEST	superlative of doggy
DOGGING	present participle of dog
DOGGISH	*adj* doglike
DOGGO	*adv* in hiding
DOGGONE	*v* -GONED, -GONING, -GONES to damn
DOGGONE	*adj* -GONER, -GONEST damned
DOGGONED	*adj* -GONEDER, -GONEDEST damned
DOGGONING	present participle of doggone
DOGGREL	*n* pl. -S doggerel
DOGGY	*n* pl. -GIES a small dog
DOGGY	*adj* -GIER, -GIEST resembling or suggestive of a dog
DOGHOUSE	*n* pl. -S a shelter for a dog
DOGIE	*n* pl. -S a stray calf
DOGIES	pl. of dogy
DOGLEG	*v* -LEGGED, -LEGGING, -LEGS to move along a bent course
DOGLIKE	*adj* resembling a dog
DOGMA	*n* pl. -MAS or -MATA a principle or belief put forth as authoritative **DOGMATIC** *adj*
DOGNAP	*v* -NAPED, -NAPING, -NAPS or -NAPPED, -NAPPING, -NAPS to steal a dog
DOGNAPER	*n* pl. -S one that dognaps
DOGSBODY	*n* pl. -BODIES a menial worker
DOGSLED	*v* -SLEDDED, -SLEDDING, -SLEDS to move on a sled drawn by dogs
DOGTOOTH	*n* pl. -TEETH a cuspid
DOGTROT	*v* -TROTTED, -TROTTING, -TROTS to move at a steady trot
DOGVANE	*n* pl. -S a small vane
DOGWATCH	*n* pl. -ES a short period of watch duty on a ship
DOGWOOD	*n* pl. -S a tree
DOGY	*n* pl. -GIES dogie
DOILED	*adj* dazed
DOILY	*n* pl. -LIES a small napkin
DOING	*n* pl. -S an action
DOIT	*n* pl. -S a former Dutch coin
DOITED	*adj* old and feeble
DOJO	*n* pl. -JOS a school that teaches judo or karate
DOL	*n* pl. -S a unit of pain intensity
DOLCE	*n* pl. -CI a soft-toned organ stop
DOLDRUMS	*n/pl* a slump or slack period
DOLE	*v* DOLED, DOLING, DOLES to distribute in small portions
DOLEFUL	*adj* -FULLER, -FULLEST mournful
DOLERITE	*n* pl. -S a variety of basalt
DOLESOME	*adj* doleful
DOLING	present participle of dole
DOLL	*v* -ED, -ING, -S to dress stylishly
DOLLAR	*n* pl. -S a monetary unit of the United States
DOLLIED	past tense of dolly
DOLLIES	present 3d person sing. of dolly
DOLLISH	*adj* pretty
DOLLOP	*v* -ED, -ING, -S to dispense in small amounts
DOLLY	*v* -LIED, -LYING, -LIES to move on a wheeled platform

DOLMA	*n* pl. -MAS or -MADES a stuffed grape leaf
DOLMAN	*n* pl. -S a Turkish robe
DOLMEN	*n* pl. -S a prehistoric monument
DOLOMITE	*n* pl. -S a mineral
DOLOR	*n* pl. -S grief
DOLOROSO	*adj* having a mournful musical quality
DOLOROUS	*adj* mournful
DOLOUR	*n* pl. -S dolor
DOLPHIN	*n* pl. -S a marine mammal
DOLT	*n* pl. -S a stupid person **DOLTISH** *adj*
DOM	*n* pl. -S a title given to certain monks
DOMAIN	*n* pl. -S an area of control
DOMAL	*adj* domical
DOME	*v* DOMED, DOMING, DOMES to cover with a dome (a rounded roof)
DOMELIKE	*adj* resembling a dome
DOMESDAY	*n* pl. -DAYS doomsday
DOMESTIC	*n* pl. -S a household servant
DOMIC	*adj* domical
DOMICAL	*adj* shaped like a dome
DOMICIL	*v* -ED, -ING, -S to domicile
DOMICILE	*v* -CILED, -CILING, -CILES to establish in a residence
DOMINANT	*n* pl. -S a controlling genetic character
DOMINATE	*v* -NATED, -NATING, -NATES to control
DOMINE	*n* pl. -S master
DOMINEER	*v* -ED, -ING, -S to tyrannize
DOMING	present participle of dome
DOMINICK	*n* pl. -S one of an American breed of chickens
DOMINIE	*n* pl. -S a clergyman
DOMINION	*n* pl. -S supreme authority
DOMINIUM	*n* pl. -S the right of ownership and control of property
DOMINO	*n* pl. -NOES or -NOS a small mask
DON	*v* DONNED, DONNING, DONS to put on
DONA	*n* pl. -S a Spanish lady
DONATE	*v* -NATED, -NATING, -NATES to contribute
DONATION	*n* pl. -S something donated
DONATIVE	*n* pl. -S a donation
DONATOR	*n* pl. -S a donor
DONE	past participle of do
DONEE	*n* pl. -S a recipient of a gift
DONENESS	*n* pl. -ES the state of being cooked enough
DONG	*n* pl. -S a deep sound like that of a large bell
DONGA	*n* pl. -S a gully in a veldt
DONGOLA	*n* pl. -S a type of leather
DONJON	*n* pl. -S the main tower of a castle
DONKEY	*n* pl. -KEYS the domestic ass
DONNA	*n* pl. DONNAS or DONNE an Italian lady
DONNED	past tense of don
DONNEE	*n* pl. -S the set of assumptions upon which a story proceeds
DONNERD	*adj* donnered
DONNERED	*adj* dazed
DONNERT	*adj* donnered
DONNIKER	*n* pl. -S a bathroom or privy
DONNING	present participle of don
DONNISH	*adj* scholarly
DONOR	*n* pl. -S one that donates
DONSIE	*adj* unlucky
DONSY	*adj* donsie
DONUT	*n* pl. -S doughnut
DONZEL	*n* pl. -S a young squire
DOODAD	*n* pl. -S an article whose name is unknown or forgotten
DOODLE	*v* -DLED, -DLING, -DLES to draw or scribble aimlessly
DOODLER	*n* pl. -S one that doodles
DOOFUS	*n* pl. -ES a stupid or foolish person
DOOLEE	*n* pl. -S a stretcher for the sick or wounded
DOOLIE	*n* pl. -S doolee
DOOLY	*n* pl. -LIES doolee
DOOM	*v* -ED, -ING, -S to destine to an unhappy fate
DOOMFUL	*adj* ominous
DOOMSDAY	*n* pl. -DAYS judgment day
DOOMSTER	*n* pl. -S a judge
DOOMY	*adj* doomful **DOOMILY** *adv*
DOOR	*n* pl. -S a movable barrier at an entranceway

DOORBELL	*n* pl. -S a bell at a door
DOORJAMB	*n* pl. -S a vertical piece at the side of a doorway
DOORKNOB	*n* pl. -S a handle for opening a door
DOORLESS	*adj* having no door
DOORMAN	*n* pl. -MEN the door attendant of a building
DOORMAT	*n* pl. -S a mat placed in front of a door
DOORNAIL	*n* pl. -S a large-headed nail
DOORPOST	*n* pl. -S a doorjamb
DOORSILL	*n* pl. -S the sill of a door
DOORSTEP	*n* pl. -S a step leading to a door
DOORSTOP	*n* pl. -S an object used for holding a door open
DOORWAY	*n* pl. -WAYS the entranceway to a room or building
DOORYARD	*n* pl. -S a yard in front of a house
DOOZER	*n* pl. -S an extraordinary one of its kind
DOOZIE	*n* pl. -S doozy
DOOZY	*n* pl. -ZIES doozer
DOPA	*n* pl. -S a drug to treat Parkinson's disease
DOPAMINE	*n* pl. -S a form of dopa used to stimulate the heart
DOPANT	*n* pl. -S an impurity added to a pure substance
DOPE	*v* DOPED, DOPING, DOPES to give a narcotic to
DOPEHEAD	*n* pl. -S a drug addict
DOPER	*n* pl. -S one that dopes
DOPESTER	*n* pl. -S one who predicts the outcomes of contests
DOPEY	*adj* DOPIER, DOPIEST lethargic; stupid
DOPIER	comparative of dopy
DOPIEST	superlative of dopy
DOPINESS	*n* pl. -ES the state of being dopey
DOPING	present participle of dope
DOPY	*adj* DOPIER, DOPIEST dopey
DOR	*n* pl. -S a black European beetle
DORADO	*n* pl. -DOS a marine fish
DORBUG	*n* pl. -S a dor
DORE	*adj* gilded
DORHAWK	*n* pl. -S a nocturnal bird
DORIES	pl. of dory

DORK	*n* pl. -S a stupid or foolish person
DORKY	*adj* DORKIER, DORKIEST stupid, foolish
DORM	*n* pl. -S a dormitory
DORMANCY	*n* pl. -CIES the state of being dormant
DORMANT	*adj* lying asleep
DORMER	*n* pl. -S a type of window
DORMICE	pl. of dormouse
DORMIE	*adj* being ahead by as many holes in golf as remain to be played
DORMIENT	*adj* dormant
DORMIN	*n* pl. -S a plant hormone
DORMOUSE	*n* pl. -MICE a small rodent
DORMY	*adj* dormie
DORNECK	*n* pl. -S dornick
DORNICK	*n* pl. -S a heavy linen fabric
DORNOCK	*n* pl. -S dornick
DORP	*n* pl. -S a village
DORPER	*n* pl. -S one of a breed of mutton-producing sheep
DORR	*n* pl. -S dor
DORSA	pl. of dorsum
DORSAD	*adv* dorsally
DORSAL	*n* pl. -S a dorsally located anatomical part
DORSALLY	*adv* toward the back
DORSEL	*n* pl. -S a dossal
DORSER	*n* pl. -S dosser
DORSUM	*n* pl. -SA the back
DORTY	*adj* sullen
DORY	*n* pl. -RIES a flat-bottomed boat
DOSAGE	*n* pl. -S the amount of medicine to be given
DOSE	*v* DOSED, DOSING, DOSES to give a specified quantity of medicine to
DOSER	*n* pl. -S one that doses
DOSS	*v* -ED, -ING, -ES to sleep in any convenient place
DOSSAL	*n* pl. -S an ornamental cloth hung behind an altar
DOSSEL	*n* pl. -S dossal
DOSSER	*n* pl. -S a basket carried on the back
DOSSERET	*n* pl. -S a block resting on the capital of a column

DOSSIER	*n* pl. -S a file of papers on a single subject
DOSSIL	*n* pl. -S a cloth roll for wiping ink
DOST	a present 2d person sing. of do
DOT	*v* DOTTED, DOTTING, DOTS to cover with dots (tiny round marks)
DOTAGE	*n* pl. -S a state of senility
DOTAL	*adj* pertaining to a dowry
DOTARD	*n* pl. -S a senile person **DOTARDLY** *adj*
DOTATION	*n* pl. -S an endowment
DOTE	*v* DOTED, DOTING, DOTES to show excessive affection
DOTER	*n* pl. -S one that dotes
DOTH	a present 3d person sing. of do
DOTIER	comparative of doty
DOTIEST	superlative of doty
DOTING	present participle of dote
DOTINGLY	*adv* in an excessively affectionate manner
DOTTED	past tense of dot
DOTTEL	*n* pl. -S dottle
DOTTER	*n* pl. -S one that dots
DOTTEREL	*n* pl. -S a shore bird
DOTTIER	comparative of dotty
DOTTIEST	superlative of dotty
DOTTILY	*adv* in a dotty manner
DOTTING	present participle of dot
DOTTLE	*n* pl. -S a mass of half-burnt pipe tobacco
DOTTREL	*n* pl. -S dotterel
DOTTY	*adj* -TIER, -TIEST crazy
DOTY	*adj* DOTIER, DOTIEST stained by decay
DOUBLE	*v* -BLED, -BLING, -BLES to make twice as great
DOUBLER	*n* pl. -S one that doubles
DOUBLET	*n* pl. -S a close-fitting jacket
DOUBLING	present participle of double
DOUBLOON	*n* pl. -S a former Spanish gold coin
DOUBLURE	*n* pl. -S the lining of a book cover
DOUBLY	*adv* to twice the degree
DOUBT	*v* -ED, -ING, -S to be uncertain about
DOUBTER	*n* pl. -S one that doubts
DOUBTFUL	*adj* uncertain
DOUCE	*adj* sedate **DOUCELY** *adv*
DOUCEUR	*n* pl. -S a gratuity
DOUCHE	*v* DOUCHED, DOUCHING, DOUCHES to cleanse with a jet of water
DOUGH	*n* pl. -S a flour mixture
DOUGHBOY	*n* pl. -BOYS an infantryman
DOUGHIER	comparative of doughy
DOUGHIEST	superlative of doughy
DOUGHNUT	*n* pl. -S a ring-shaped cake
DOUGHT	a past tense of dow
DOUGHTY	*adj* -TIER, -TIEST courageous
DOUGHY	*adj* DOUGHIER, DOUGHIEST resembling dough
DOUM	*n* pl. -S an African palm tree
DOUMA	*n* pl. -S duma
DOUPIONI	*n* pl. -S a silk yarn
DOUR	*adj* DOURER, DOUREST sullen
DOURA	*n* pl. -S durra
DOURAH	*n* pl. -S durra
DOURINE	*n* pl. -S a disease of horses
DOURLY	*adv* in a dour manner
DOURNESS	*n* pl. -ES the state of being dour
DOUSE	*v* DOUSED, DOUSING, DOUSES to plunge into water
DOUSER	*n* pl. -S one that douses
DOUX	*adj* very sweet — used of champagne
DOUZEPER	*n* pl. -S one of twelve legendary knights
DOVE	*n* pl. -S a bird of the pigeon family
DOVECOT	*n* pl. -S dovecote
DOVECOTE	*n* pl. -S a roost for domesticated pigeons
DOVEKEY	*n* pl. -KEYS dovekie
DOVEKIE	*n* pl. -S a seabird
DOVELIKE	*adj* resembling or suggestive of a dove
DOVEN	*v* -ED, -ING, -S to daven
DOVETAIL	*v* -ED, -ING, -S to fit together closely
DOVISH	*adj* not warlike
DOW	*v* DOWED or DOUGHT, DOWING, DOWS to prosper
DOWABLE	*adj* entitled to an endowment
DOWAGER	*n* pl. -S a dignified elderly woman

DOWDY *adj* DOWDIER, DOWDIEST lacking in stylishness or neatness **DOWDILY** *adv* **DOWDYISH** *adj*

DOWDY *n* pl. DOWDIES a dowdy woman

DOWEL *v* -ELED, -ELING, -ELS or -ELLED, -ELLING, -ELS to fasten with wooden pins

DOWER *v* -ED, -ING, -S to provide with a dowry

DOWERY *n* pl. -ERIES dowry

DOWIE *adj* dreary

DOWN *v* -ED, -ING, -S to cause to fall

DOWNBEAT *n* pl. -S the first beat of a musical measure

DOWNCAST *n* pl. -S an overthrow or ruin

DOWNCOME *n* pl. -S downfall

DOWNER *n* pl. -S a depressant drug

DOWNFALL *n* pl. -S a sudden fall

DOWNHAUL *n* pl. -S a rope for hauling down sails

DOWNHILL *n* pl. -S a downward slope

DOWNIER comparative of downy

DOWNIEST superlative of downy

DOWNLAND *n* pl. -S a rolling treeless upland

DOWNLINK *n* pl. -S a communications channel from a spacecraft

DOWNLOAD *v* -ED, -ING, -S to transfer data from a large computer to a smaller one

DOWNPIPE *n* pl. -S a pipe for draining water from a roof

DOWNPLAY *v* -ED, -ING, -S to de-emphasize

DOWNPOUR *n* pl. -S a heavy rain

DOWNSIDE *n* pl. -S a negative aspect

DOWNSIZE *v* -SIZED, -SIZING, -SIZES to produce in a smaller size

DOWNTICK *n* pl. -S a stock market transaction

DOWNTIME *n* pl. -S the time when a machine or factory is inactive

DOWNTOWN *n* pl. -S the business district of a city

DOWNTROD *adj* oppressed

DOWNTURN *n* pl. -S a downward turn

DOWNWARD *adv* from a higher to a lower place

DOWNWASH *n* pl. -ES a downward deflection of air

DOWNWIND *adv* in the direction that the wind blows

DOWNY *adj* DOWNIER, DOWNIEST soft

DOWRY *n* pl. -RIES the money or property a wife brings to her husband at marriage

DOWSABEL *n* pl. -S a sweetheart

DOWSE *v* DOWSED, DOWSING, DOWSES to search for underground water with a divining rod

DOWSER *n* pl. -S one that dowses

DOXIE *n* pl. -S doxy

DOXOLOGY *n* pl. -GIES a hymn or verse of praise to God

DOXY *n* pl. DOXIES a doctrine

DOYEN *n* pl. -S the senior member of a group

DOYENNE *n* pl. -S a female doyen

DOYLEY *n* pl. -LEYS doily

DOYLY *n* pl. -LIES doily

DOZE *v* DOZED, DOZING, DOZES to sleep lightly

DOZEN *v* -ED, -ING, -S to stun

DOZENTH *n* pl. -S twelfth

DOZER *n* pl. -S one that dozes

DOZIER comparative of dozy

DOZIEST superlative of dozy

DOZILY *adv* in a dozy manner

DOZINESS *n* pl. -ES the state of being dozy

DOZING present participle of doze

DOZY *adj* DOZIER, DOZIEST drowsy

DRAB *adj* DRABBER, DRABBEST cheerless

DRAB *v* DRABBED, DRABBING, DRABS to consort with prostitutes

DRABBET *n* pl. -S a coarse linen fabric

DRABBLE *v* -BLED, -BLING, -BLES to draggle

DRABLY *adv* in a drab manner

DRABNESS *n* pl. -ES the quality of being drab

DRACAENA *n* pl. -S a tropical plant

DRACHM *n* pl. -S a unit of weight

DRACHMA *n* pl. -MAS, -MAE or -MAI a monetary unit of Greece

DRACONIC *adj* pertaining to a dragon

DRAFF *n* pl. -S the damp remains of malt after brewing

DRAFFISH *adj* draffy

DRAFFY   *adj* DRAFFIER, DRAFFIEST worthless

DRAFT   *v* -ED, -ING, -S to conscript for military service

DRAFTEE   *n* pl. -S one that is drafted

DRAFTER   *n* pl. -S one that drafts

DRAFTING   *n* pl. -S mechanical drawing

DRAFTY   *adj* DRAFTIER, DRAFTIEST having or exposed to currents of air **DRAFTILY** *adv*

DRAG   *v* DRAGGED, DRAGGING, DRAGS to pull along the ground

DRAGEE   *n* pl. -S a sugarcoated candy

DRAGGER   *n* pl. -S one that drags

DRAGGIER   comparative of draggy

DRAGGIEST   superlative of draggy

DRAGGING   present participle of drag

DRAGGLE   *v* -GLED, -GLING, -GLES to make wet and dirty

DRAGGY   *adj* -GIER, -GIEST sluggish

DRAGLINE   *n* pl. -S a line used for dragging

DRAGNET   *n* pl. -S a net for trawling

DRAGOMAN   *n* pl. -MANS or -MEN an interpreter in Near Eastern countries

DRAGON   *n* pl. -S a mythical, serpentlike monster

DRAGONET   *n* pl. -S a marine fish

DRAGOON   *v* -ED, -ING, -S to harass by the use of troops

DRAGROPE   *n* pl. -S a rope used for dragging

DRAGSTER   *n* pl. -S a vehicle used in drag racing

DRAIL   *n* pl. -S a heavy fishhook

DRAIN   *v* -ED, -ING, -S to draw off a liquid

DRAINAGE   *n* pl. -S the act of draining

DRAINER   *n* pl. -S one that drains

DRAKE   *n* pl. -S a male duck

DRAM   *v* DRAMMED, DRAMMING, DRAMS to tipple

DRAMA   *n* pl. -S a composition written for theatrical performance

DRAMATIC   *adj* pertaining to drama

DRAMEDY   *n* pl. -DIES a sitcom having dramatic scenes

DRAMMED   past tense of dram

DRAMMING   present participle of dram

DRAMMOCK   *n* pl. -S raw oatmeal mixed with cold water

DRAMSHOP   *n* pl. -S a barroom

DRANK   past tense of drink

DRAPE   *v* DRAPED, DRAPING, DRAPES to arrange in graceful folds **DRAPABLE** *adj*

DRAPER   *n* pl. -S a dealer in cloth

DRAPERY   *n* pl. -ERIES cloth arranged in graceful folds

DRAPEY   *adj* characterized by graceful folds

DRAPING   present participle of drape

DRASTIC   *adj* extremely severe

DRAT   *v* DRATTED, DRATTING, DRATS to damn

DRAUGHT   *v* -ED, -ING, -S to draft

DRAUGHTY   *adj* DRAUGHTIER, DRAUGHTIEST drafty

DRAVE   a past tense of drive

DRAW   *v* DREW, DRAWN, DRAWING, DRAWS to move by pulling **DRAWABLE** *adj*

DRAWBACK   *n* pl. -S a hindrance

DRAWBAR   *n* pl. -S a railroad coupler

DRAWBORE   *n* pl. -S a hole for joining a mortise and tenon

DRAWDOWN   *n* pl. -S a lowering of a water level

DRAWEE   *n* pl. -S the person on whom a bill of exchange is drawn

DRAWER   *n* pl. -S one that draws

DRAWING   *n* pl. -S a portrayal in lines of a form or figure

DRAWL   *v* -ED, -ING, -S to speak slowly with vowels greatly prolonged

DRAWLER   *n* pl. -S one that drawls

DRAWLY   *adj* DRAWLIER, DRAWLIEST marked by drawling

DRAWN   past participle of draw

DRAWTUBE   *n* pl. -S a tube that slides within another tube

DRAY   *v* -ED, -ING, -S to transport by dray (a low, strong cart)

DRAYAGE   *n* pl. -S transportation by dray

DRAYMAN   *n* pl. -MEN one who drives a dray

DREAD   *v* -ED, -ING, -S to fear greatly

DREADFUL   *n* pl. -S a publication containing sensational material

DREAM	*v* DREAMED or DREAMT, DREAMING, DREAMS to have a dream (a series of images occurring during sleep)
DREAMER	*n* pl. -S one that dreams
DREAMFUL	*adj* dreamy
DREAMT	a past tense of dream
DREAMY	*adj* DREAMIER, DREAMIEST full of dreams **DREAMILY** *adv*
DREAR	*n* pl. -S the state of being dreary
DREARY	*adj* DREARIER, DREARIEST dismal **DREARILY** *adv*
DREARY	*n* pl. DREARIES a dismal person
DRECK	*n* pl. -S rubbish **DRECKY** *adj*
DREDGE	*v* DREDGED, DREDGING, DREDGES to clear with a dredge (a machine for scooping mud)
DREDGER	*n* pl. -S one that dredges
DREDGING	*n* pl. -S matter that is dredged up
DREE	*v* DREED, DREEING, DREES to suffer
DREG	*n* pl. -S the sediment of liquors **DREGGISH** *adj*
DREGGY	*adj* -GIER, -GIEST full of dregs
DREICH	*adj* dreary
DREIDEL	*n* pl. -S a spinning toy
DREIDL	*n* pl. -S dreidel
DREIGH	*adj* dreich
DREK	*n* pl. -S dreck
DRENCH	*v* -ED, -ING, -ES to wet thoroughly
DRENCHER	*n* pl. -S one that drenches
DRESS	*v* DRESSED or DREST, DRESSING, DRESSES to put clothes on
DRESSAGE	*n* pl. -S the training of a horse in obedience and deportment
DRESSER	*n* pl. -S one that dresses
DRESSING	*n* pl. -S material applied to cover a wound
DRESSY	*adj* DRESSIER, DRESSIEST stylish **DRESSILY** *adv*
DREST	a past tense of dress
DREW	past tense of draw
DRIB	*v* DRIBBED, DRIBBING, DRIBS to drip
DRIBBLE	*v* -BLED, -BLING, -BLES to drivel
DRIBBLER	*n* pl. -S one that dribbles
DRIBBLET	*n* pl. -S driblet
DRIBBLING	present participle of dribble
DRIBBLY	*adj* tending to dribble
DRIBLET	*n* pl. -S a small drop of liquid
DRIED	past tense of dry
DRIEGH	*adj* dreary
DRIER	*n* pl. -S one that dries
DRIES	present 3d person sing. of dry
DRIEST	a superlative of dry
DRIFT	*v* -ED, -ING, -S to move along in a current
DRIFTAGE	*n* pl. -S the act of drifting
DRIFTER	*n* pl. -S one that drifts
DRIFTPIN	*n* pl. -S a metal rod for securing timbers
DRIFTY	*adj* DRIFTIER, DRIFTIEST full of drifts (masses of wind-driven snow)
DRILL	*v* -ED, -ING, -S to bore a hole in
DRILLER	*n* pl. -S one that drills
DRILLING	*n* pl. -S a heavy twilled cotton fabric
DRILY	*adv* dryly
DRINK	*v* DRANK, DRUNK, DRINKING, DRINKS to swallow liquid
DRINKER	*n* pl. -S one that drinks
DRIP	*v* DRIPPED or DRIPT, DRIPPING, DRIPS to fall in drops
DRIPLESS	*adj* designed not to drip
DRIPPER	*n* pl. -S something from which a liquid drips
DRIPPING	*n* pl. -S juice drawn from meat during cooking
DRIPPY	*adj* -PIER, -PIEST very wet
DRIPT	a past tense of drip
DRIVE	*v* DROVE or DRAVE, DRIVEN, DRIVING, DRIVES to urge or propel forward **DRIVABLE** *adj*
DRIVEL	*v* -ELED, -ELING, -ELS or -ELLED, -ELLING, -ELS to let saliva flow from the mouth
DRIVELER	*n* pl. -S one that drivels
DRIVEN	past participle of drive
DRIVER	*n* pl. -S one that drives
DRIVEWAY	*n* pl. -WAYS a private road providing access to a building
DRIVING	*n* pl. -S management of a motor vehicle
DRIZZLE	*v* -ZLED, -ZLING, -ZLES to rain lightly

DRIZZLY	*adj* -ZLIER, -ZLIEST characterized by light rain	**DROUGHT**	*n* pl. -S a dry period
DROGUE	*n* pl. -S a sea anchor	**DROUGHTY**	*adj* DROUGHTIER, DROUGHTIEST dry
DROIT	*n* pl. -S a legal right	**DROUK**	*v* -ED, -ING, -S to drench
DROLL	*adj* DROLLER, DROLLEST comical	**DROUTH**	*n* pl. -S drought
DROLL	*v* -ED, -ING, -S to jest	**DROUTHY**	*adj* DROUTHIER, DROUTHIEST droughty
DROLLERY	*n* pl. -ERIES something droll	**DROVE**	*v* DROVED, DROVING, DROVES to drive cattle or sheep
DROLLY	*adv* in a droll manner	**DROVER**	*n* pl. -S a driver of cattle or sheep
DROMON	*n* pl. -S dromond		
DROMOND	*n* pl. -S a large fast-sailing medieval galley	**DROWN**	*v* -ED, -ING, -S to suffocate in water
DRONE	*v* DRONED, DRONING, DRONES to make a continuous low sound	**DROWND**	*v* -ED, -ING, -S to drown
		DROWNER	*n* pl. -S one that drowns
DRONER	*n* pl. -S one that drones	**DROWSE**	*v* DROWSED, DROWSING, DROWSES to doze
DRONGO	*n* pl. -GOS a tropical bird	**DROWSY**	*adj* DROWSIER, DROWSIEST sleepy **DROWSILY** *adv*
DRONING	present participle of drone		
DRONISH	*adj* habitually lazy	**DRUB**	*v* DRUBBED, DRUBBING, DRUBS to beat severely
DROOL	*v* -ED, -ING, -S to drivel		
DROOP	*v* -ED, -ING, -S to hang downward	**DRUBBER**	*n* pl. -S one that drubs
		DRUBBING	*n* pl. -S a severe beating
DROOPY	*adj* DROOPIER, DROOPIEST drooping **DROOPILY** *adv*	**DRUDGE**	*v* DRUDGED, DRUDGING, DRUDGES to do hard, menial, or tedious work
DROP	*v* DROPPED or DROPT, DROPPING, DROPS to fall in drops (globules)	**DRUDGER**	*n* pl. -S one that drudges
		DRUDGERY	*n* pl. -ERIES hard, menial, or tedious work
DROPHEAD	*n* pl. -S a convertible car		
DROPKICK	*n* pl. -S a type of kick in football	**DRUDGING**	present participle of drudge
DROPLET	*n* pl. -S a tiny drop	**DRUG**	*v* DRUGGED, DRUGGING, DRUGS to affect with a drug (a medicinal substance)
DROPOUT	*n* pl. -S one who quits school prematurely		
DROPPED	a past tense of drop	**DRUGGET**	*n* pl. -S a coarse woolen fabric
DROPPER	*n* pl. -S a tube for dispensing liquid in drops	**DRUGGIE**	*n* pl. -S a drug addict
		DRUGGIST	*n* pl. -S a pharmacist
DROPPING	*n* pl. -S something that has been dropped	**DRUGGY**	*adj* -GIER, -GIEST affected by drugs
DROPSHOT	*n* pl. -S a type of shot in tennis	**DRUID**	*n* pl. -S one of an ancient Celtic order of priests **DRUIDIC** *adj*
DROPSY	*n* pl. -SIES an excessive accumulation of serous fluid **DROPSIED** *adj*	**DRUIDESS**	*n* pl. -ES a female druid
		DRUIDISM	*n* pl. -S the religious system of the druids
DROPT	a past tense of drop		
DROPWORT	*n* pl. -S a perennial herb	**DRUM**	*v* DRUMMED, DRUMMING, DRUMS to beat a drum (a percussion instrument)
DROSERA	*n* pl. -S a sundew		
DROSHKY	*n* pl. -KIES an open carriage		
DROSKY	*n* pl. -KIES droshky	**DRUMBEAT**	*n* pl. -S the sound of a drum
DROSS	*n* pl. -ES waste matter	**DRUMBLE**	*v* -BLED, -BLING, -BLES to move slowly
DROSSY	*adj* DROSSIER, DROSSIEST worthless	**DRUMFIRE**	*n* pl. -S heavy, continuous gunfire

DRUMFISH	*n* pl. -ES a fish that makes a drumming sound
DRUMHEAD	*n* pl. -S the material stretched over the end of a drum
DRUMLIER	comparative of drumly
DRUMLIEST	superlative of drumly
DRUMLIKE	*adj* resembling the head of a drum
DRUMLIN	*n* pl. -S a long hill of glacial drift
DRUMLY	*adj* -LIER, -LIEST dark and gloomy
DRUMMED	past tense of drum
DRUMMER	*n* pl. -S one that drums
DRUMMING	present participle of drum
DRUMROLL	*n* pl. -S a roll played on a drum
DRUNK	*adj* DRUNKER, DRUNKEST intoxicated
DRUNK	*n* pl. -S a drunken person
DRUNKARD	*n* pl. -S one who is habitually drunk
DRUNKEN	*adj* drunk
DRUPE	*n* pl. -S a fleshy fruit
DRUPELET	*n* pl. -S a small drupe
DRUSE	*n* pl. -S a crust of small crystals lining a rock cavity
DRUTHERS	*n/pl* one's preference
DRY	*adj* DRIER, DRIEST or DRYER, DRYEST having no moisture
DRY	*v* DRIED, DRYING, DRIES to make dry **DRYABLE** *adj*
DRY	*n* pl. DRYS a prohibitionist
DRYAD	*n* pl. -S or -ES a nymph of the woods **DRYADIC** *adj*
DRYER	*n* pl. -S drier
DRYISH	*adj* somewhat dry
DRYLAND	*adj* relating to an arid region
DRYLOT	*n* pl. -S an enclosure for livestock
DRYLY	*adv* in a dry manner
DRYNESS	*n* pl. -ES the state of being dry
DRYPOINT	*n* pl. -S a method of engraving
DRYSTONE	*adj* constructed of stone without mortar
DRYWALL	*n* pl. -S board used instead of plaster in walls
DUAD	*n* pl. -S a pair
DUAL	*n* pl. -S a linguistic form
DUALISM	*n* pl. -S a philosophical theory
DUALIST	*n* pl. -S an adherent of dualism

DUALITY	*n* pl. -TIES the state of being twofold
DUALIZE	*v* -IZED, -IZING, -IZES to make twofold
DUALLY	*adv* in two ways
DUB	*v* DUBBED, DUBBING, DUBS to confer knighthood on
DUBBER	*n* pl. -S one that dubs
DUBBIN	*n* pl. -S material for softening and waterproofing leather
DUBBING	*n* pl. -S dubbin
DUBIETY	*n* pl. -ETIES the state of being dubious
DUBIOUS	*adj* doubtful
DUBONNET	*n* pl. -S a red color
DUCAL	*adj* pertaining to a duke (a high-ranking nobleman) **DUCALLY** *adv*
DUCAT	*n* pl. -S any of several gold coins formerly used in Europe
DUCE	*n* pl. DUCES or DUCI a leader
DUCHESS	*n* pl. -ES the wife or widow of a duke
DUCHY	*n* pl. DUCHIES the domain of a duke
DUCI	a pl. of duce
DUCK	*v* -ED, -ING, -S to lower quickly
DUCKBILL	*n* pl. -S a platypus
DUCKER	*n* pl. -S one that ducks
DUCKIE	*adj* ducky
DUCKIER	comparative of ducky
DUCKIES	pl. of ducky
DUCKIEST	superlative of ducky
DUCKLING	*n* pl. -S a young duck
DUCKPIN	*n* pl. -S a type of bowling pin
DUCKTAIL	*n* pl. -S a style of haircut
DUCKWALK	*v* -ED, -ING, -S to walk in a squatting position
DUCKWEED	*n* pl. -S an aquatic plant
DUCKY	*adj* DUCKIER, DUCKIEST excellent
DUCKY	*n* pl. DUCKIES a darling
DUCT	*v* -ED, -ING, -S to convey through a duct (a tubular passage)
DUCTAL	*adj* made up of ducts
DUCTILE	*adj* easily molded or shaped
DUCTING	*n* pl. -S a system of ducts
DUCTLESS	*adj* being without a duct

DUCTULE	*n* pl. -S a small duct	**DUKE**	*v* DUKED, DUKING, DUKES to fight
DUCTWORK	*n* pl. -S a system of ducts	**DUKEDOM**	*n* pl. -S a duchy
DUD	*n* pl. -S a bomb that fails to explode	**DULCET**	*n* pl. -S a soft-toned organ stop
DUDDIE	*adj* ragged	**DULCETLY**	*adv* melodiously
DUDDY	*adj* duddie	**DULCIANA**	*n* pl. -S a soft-toned organ stop
DUDE	*v* DUDED, DUDING, DUDES to dress up in flashy clothes	**DULCIFY**	*v* -FIED, -FYING, -FIES to sweeten
DUDEEN	*n* pl. -S a short tobacco pipe	**DULCIMER**	*n* pl. -S a stringed instrument
DUDGEON	*n* pl. -S a feeling of resentment	**DULCINEA**	*n* pl. -S a sweetheart
DUDING	present participle of dude	**DULIA**	*n* pl. -S veneration of saints
DUDISH	*adj* resembling a dude (a dandy)	**DULL**	*adj* DULLER, DULLEST mentally slow
DUDISHLY	*adv* in the manner of a dude	**DULL**	*v* -ED, -ING, -S to make less sharp
DUE	*n* pl. -S something that is owed	**DULLARD**	*n* pl. -S a dolt
DUECENTO	*n* pl. -TOS the thirteenth century	**DULLISH**	*adj* somewhat dull
DUEL	*v* DUELED, DUELING, DUELS or DUELLED, DUELLING, DUELS to fight formally	**DULLNESS**	*n* pl. -ES the state of being dull
DUELER	*n* pl. -S one that duels	**DULLY**	*adv* in a dull manner
DUELIST	*n* pl. -S a dueler	**DULNESS**	*n* pl. -ES dullness
DUELLED	a past tense of duel	**DULSE**	*n* pl. -S an edible seaweed
DUELLER	*n* pl. -S dueler	**DULY**	*adv* rightfully
DUELLI	a pl. of duello	**DUMA**	*n* pl. -S a Russian council
DUELLING	a present participle of duel	**DUMB**	*adj* DUMBER, DUMBEST incapable of speech
DUELLIST	*n* pl. -S duelist	**DUMB**	*v* -ED, -ING, -S to make silent
DUELLO	*n* pl. -LOS or -LI the art of dueling; a duel	**DUMBBELL**	*n* pl. -S a weight lifted for muscular exercise
DUENDE	*n* pl. -S charisma	**DUMBCANE**	*n* pl. -S a tropical plant
DUENESS	*n* pl. -ES the state of being owed	**DUMBHEAD**	*n* pl. -S a stupid person
DUENNA	*n* pl. -S a governess	**DUMBLY**	*adv* in a dumb manner
DUET	*v* DUETTED, DUETTING, DUETS to perform a duet (a musical composition for two)	**DUMBNESS**	*n* pl. -ES the state of being dumb
		DUMDUM	*n* pl. -S a type of bullet
DUETTIST	*n* pl. -S a participant in a duet	**DUMFOUND**	*v* -ED, -ING, -S to astonish
DUFF	*n* pl. -S a thick pudding	**DUMKA**	*n* pl. -KY a Slavic folk ballad
DUFFEL	*n* pl. -S a coarse woolen fabric	**DUMMKOPF**	*n* pl. -S a dolt
DUFFER	*n* pl. -S a clumsy person	**DUMMY**	*v* -MIED, -MYING, -MIES to make a representation of
DUFFLE	*n* pl. -S duffel	**DUMP**	*v* -ED, -ING, -S to let fall heavily
DUG	*n* pl. -S the teat or udder of a female mammal	**DUMPCART**	*n* pl. -S a type of cart
DUGONG	*n* pl. -S an aquatic mammal	**DUMPER**	*n* pl. -S one that dumps
DUGOUT	*n* pl. -S a canoe made by hollowing out a log	**DUMPIER**	comparative of dumpy
		DUMPIEST	superlative of dumpy
DUI	a pl. of duo	**DUMPILY**	*adv* in a dumpy manner
DUIKER	*n* pl. -S a small antelope	**DUMPING**	*n* pl. -S the selling of large quantities of goods at below the market price
DUIT	*n* pl. -S doit		

DUMPISH	*adj* sad
DUMPLING	*n* pl. -S a ball of dough cooked with stew or soup
DUMPY	*adj* DUMPIER, DUMPIEST short and thick
DUN	*v* DUNNED, DUNNING, DUNS to make demands upon for payment of a debt
DUN	*adj* DUNNER, DUNNEST of a dull brown color
DUNAM	*n* pl. -S a unit of land measure in Israel
DUNCE	*n* pl. -S a stupid person **DUNCICAL, DUNCISH** *adj*
DUNCH	*n* pl. -ES a push
DUNE	*n* pl. -S a hill of sand **DUNELIKE** *adj*
DUNELAND	*n* pl. -S an area having many dunes
DUNG	*v* -ED, -ING, -S to fertilize with manure
DUNGAREE	*n* pl. -S a coarse cotton fabric
DUNGEON	*v* -ED, -ING, -S to confine in a dungeon (an underground prison)
DUNGHILL	*n* pl. -S a heap of manure
DUNGY	*adj* DUNGIER, DUNGIEST filthy
DUNITE	*n* pl. -S an igneous rock **DUNITIC** *adj*
DUNK	*v* -ED, -ING, -S to dip into liquid
DUNKER	*n* pl. -S one that dunks
DUNLIN	*n* pl. -S a wading bird
DUNNAGE	*n* pl. -S packing material used to protect cargo
DUNNED	past tense of dun
DUNNER	comparative of dun
DUNNESS	*n* pl. -ES the state of being dun
DUNNEST	superlative of dun
DUNNING	present participle of dun
DUNNITE	*n* pl. -S an explosive
DUNT	*v* -ED, -ING, -S to strike with a heavy blow
DUO	*n* pl. DUOS or DUI an instrumental duet
DUODENUM	*n* pl. -DENA or -DENUMS the first portion of the small intestine **DUODENAL** *adj*
DUOLOG	*n* pl. -S duologue
DUOLOGUE	*n* pl. -S a conversation between two persons
DUOMO	*n* pl. -MOS or -MI a cathedral
DUOPOLY	*n* pl. -LIES the market condition existing when there are two sellers only
DUOPSONY	*n* pl. -NIES the market condition existing when there are two buyers only
DUOTONE	*n* pl. -S an illustration in two tones
DUP	*v* DUPPED, DUPPING, DUPS to open
DUPE	*v* DUPED, DUPING, DUPES to deceive **DUPABLE** *adj*
DUPER	*n* pl. -S one that dupes
DUPERY	*n* pl. -ERIES the act of duping
DUPING	present participle of dupe
DUPLE	*adj* having two parts or elements
DUPLEX	*v* -ED, -ING, -ES to make duple
DUPLEXER	*n* pl. -S an electronic switching device
DUPPED	past tense of dup
DUPPING	present participle of dup
DURA	*n* pl. -S durra
DURABLE	*adj* able to withstand wear or decay **DURABLY** *adv*
DURABLES	*n/pl* durable goods
DURAL	*adj* of the dura mater (a brain membrane)
DURAMEN	*n* pl. -S the central wood of a tree
DURANCE	*n* pl. -S restraint by or as if by physical force
DURATION	*n* pl. -S continuance in time
DURATIVE	*n* pl. -S a type of verb
DURBAR	*n* pl. -S the court of a native ruler in India
DURE	*v* DURED, DURING, DURES to endure
DURESS	*n* pl. -ES compulsion by threat
DURIAN	*n* pl. -S an East Indian tree
DURING	*prep* throughout the duration of
DURION	*n* pl. -S durian
DURMAST	*n* pl. -S a European oak
DURN	*v* -ED, -ING, -S to damn
DURNED	*adj* DURNEDER, DURNEDEST or DURNDEST damned
DURO	*n* pl. -ROS a Spanish silver dollar
DUROC	*n* pl. -S a large red hog
DURR	*n* pl. -S durra
DURRA	*n* pl. -S a cereal grain
DURRIE	*n* pl. -S dhurrie

DURST	a past tense of dare
DURUM	n pl. -S a kind of wheat
DUSK	v -ED, -ING, -S to become dark
DUSKISH	adj dusky
DUSKY	adj DUSKIER, DUSKIEST somewhat dark **DUSKILY** adv
DUST	v -ED, -ING, -S to make free of dust (minute particles of matter)
DUSTBIN	n pl. -S a trash can
DUSTER	n pl. -S one that dusts
DUSTHEAP	n pl. -S a pile of trash
DUSTIER	comparative of dusty
DUSTIEST	superlative of dusty
DUSTILY	adv in a dusty manner
DUSTLESS	adj being without dust
DUSTLIKE	adj resembling dust
DUSTMAN	n pl. -MEN a trashman
DUSTOFF	n pl. -S a military helicopter for evacuating the wounded
DUSTPAN	n pl. -S a pan for holding swept dust
DUSTRAG	n pl. -S a rag used for dusting
DUSTUP	n pl. -S an argument
DUSTY	adj DUSTIER, DUSTIEST full of dust
DUTCH	adv with each person paying for himself
DUTCHMAN	n pl. -MEN something used to hide structural defects
DUTEOUS	adj dutiful
DUTIABLE	adj subject to import tax
DUTIFUL	adj obedient
DUTY	n pl. -TIES a moral or legal obligation
DUUMVIR	n pl. -VIRS or -VIRI a magistrate of ancient Rome
DUVET	n pl. -S a down-filled bed covering
DUVETINE	n pl. -S duvetyn
DUVETYN	n pl. -S a soft fabric
DUVETYNE	n pl. -S duvetyn
DUXELLES	n pl. DUXELLES a garnish or sauce with minced mushrooms
DWARF	adj DWARFER, DWARFEST extremely small
DWARF	n pl. DWARFS or DWARVES an extremely small person
DWARF	v -ED, -ING, -S to cause to appear small
DWARFISH	adj resembling a dwarf
DWARFISM	n pl. -S a condition of stunted growth
DWARVES	a pl. of dwarf
DWEEB	n pl. -S an unattractive or inept person
DWELL	v DWELT or DWELLED, DWELLING, DWELLS to reside
DWELLER	n pl. -S one that dwells
DWELLING	n pl. -S a place of residence
DWELT	a past tense of dwell
DWINDLE	v -DLED, -DLING, -DLES to decrease steadily
DWINE	v DWINED, DWINING, DWINES to pine or waste away
DYABLE	adj dyeable
DYAD	n pl. -S a pair of units
DYADIC	n pl. -S a sum of mathematical dyads
DYARCHY	n pl. -CHIES diarchy **DYARCHIC** adj
DYBBUK	n pl. -BUKS or -BUKIM a wandering soul in Jewish folklore
DYE	v DYED, DYEING, DYES to treat with a dye (a coloring matter)
DYEABLE	adj capable of being dyed
DYEING	n pl. -S something colored with a dye
DYER	n pl. -S one that dyes
DYESTUFF	n pl. -S a dye
DYEWEED	n pl. -S a shrub that yields a yellow dye
DYEWOOD	n pl. -S a wood from which a dye is extracted
DYING	n pl. -S a passing out of existence
DYKE	v DYKED, DYKING, DYKES to dike
DYNAMIC	n pl. -S a physical force
DYNAMISM	n pl. -S a theory that explains the universe in terms of force or energy
DYNAMIST	n pl. -S an adherent of dynamism
DYNAMITE	v -MITED, -MITING, -MITES to blow up with a powerful explosive
DYNAMO	n pl. -MOS a generator
DYNAST	n pl. -S a ruler
DYNASTY	n pl. -TIES a succession of rulers from the same line of descent **DYNASTIC** adj

DYNATRON *n* pl. -S a type of electron tube

DYNE *n* pl. -S a unit of force

DYNEIN *n* pl. DYNEIN an enzyme involved in cell movement

DYNEL *n* pl. -S a synthetic fiber

DYNODE *n* pl. -S a type of electrode

DYSGENIC *adj* causing the deterioration of hereditary qualities

DYSLEXIA *n* pl. -S impairment of the ability to read

DYSLEXIC *n* pl. -S one who is affected with dyslexia

DYSPEPSY *n* pl. -SIES indigestion

DYSPNEA *n* pl. -S labored breathing **DYSPNEAL, DYSPNEIC** *adj*

DYSPNOEA *n* pl. -S dyspnea **DYSPNOIC** *adj*

DYSTAXIA *n* pl. -S a form of muscular tremor

DYSTOCIA *n* pl. -S difficult labor and delivery in childbirth

DYSTONIA *n* pl. -S a condition of disordered tonicity of muscle tissue **DYSTONIC** *adj*

DYSTOPIA *n* pl. -S a wretched place

DYSURIA *n* pl. -S painful urination **DYSURIC** *adj*

DYVOUR *n* pl. -S one who is bankrupt

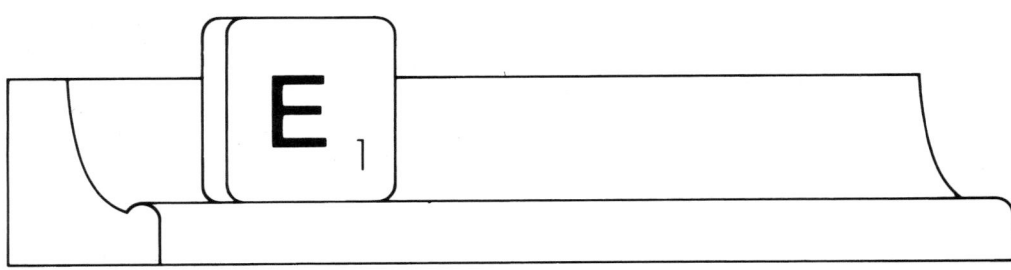

EACH	*adj* being one of two or more distinct individuals
EAGER	*adj* -GERER, -GEREST impatiently longing **EAGERLY** *adv*
EAGER	*n* pl. -S eagre
EAGLE	*n* pl. -S a large bird of prey
EAGLET	*n* pl. -S a young eagle
EAGRE	*n* pl. -S a tidal flood
EANLING	*n* pl. -S yeanling
EAR	*v* -ED, -ING, -S to form the fruiting head of a cereal
EARACHE	*n* pl. -S a pain in the ear (an organ of hearing)
EARDROP	*n* pl. -S an earring
EARDRUM	*n* pl. -S the tympanic membrane
EARED	*adj* having ears
EARFLAP	*n* pl. -S a part of a cap designed to cover the ears
EARFUL	*n* pl. -S a flow of information
EARING	*n* pl. -S a line on a ship
EARL	*n* pl. -S a British nobleman
EARLAP	*n* pl. -S an earflap
EARLDOM	*n* pl. -S the rank of an earl
EARLESS	*adj* lacking ears
EARLIER	comparative of early
EARLIEST	superlative of early
EARLOBE	*n* pl. -S a part of the ear
EARLOCK	*n* pl. -S a curl of hair by the ear
EARLSHIP	*n* pl. -S earldom
EARLY	*adv* -LIER, -LIEST near the beginning of a period of time or a series of events
EARMARK	*v* -ED, -ING, -S to designate for a specific use
EARMUFF	*n* pl. -S one of a pair of ear coverings
EARN	*v* -ED, -ING, -S to gain or deserve for one's labor or service
EARNER	*n* pl. -S one that earns
EARNEST	*n* pl. -S a down payment
EARNINGS	*n/pl* something earned
EARPHONE	*n* pl. -S a listening device worn over the ear
EARPIECE	*n* pl. -S an earphone
EARPLUG	*n* pl. -S a plug for the ear
EARRING	*n* pl. -S an ornament for the earlobe
EARSHOT	*n* pl. -S the range within which sound can be heard
EARSTONE	*n* pl. -S an otolith
EARTH	*v* -ED, -ING, -S to cover with earth (soil)
EARTHEN	*adj* made of earth
EARTHIER	comparative of earthy
EARTHIEST	superlative of earthy
EARTHILY	*adv* in an earthy manner
EARTHLY	*adj* -LIER, -LIEST worldly
EARTHMAN	*n* pl. -MEN a person from the planet earth
EARTHNUT	*n* pl. -S a European herb
EARTHPEA	*n* pl. -S a twining plant
EARTHSET	*n* pl. -S the setting of the earth as seen from the moon
EARTHY	*adj* EARTHIER, EARTHIEST composed of, resembling, or suggestive of earth
EARWAX	*n* pl. -ES cerumen
EARWIG	*v* -WIGGED, -WIGGING, -WIGS to insinuate against in secret
EARWORM	*n* pl. -S a bollworm
EASE	*v* EASED, EASING, EASES to give rest or relief to
EASEFUL	*adj* restful
EASEL	*n* pl. -S a three-legged frame
EASEMENT	*n* pl. -S relief
EASIER	comparative of easy

EASIES	pl. of easy
EASIEST	superlative of easy
EASILY	*adv* without difficulty
EASINESS	*n* pl. -ES the state of being easy
EASING	present participle of ease
EAST	*n* pl. -S a cardinal point of the compass
EASTER	*n* pl. -S a wind or storm from the east
EASTERLY	*n* pl. -LIES a wind from the east
EASTERN	*adj* being to, toward, or in the east
EASTING	*n* pl. -S a movement toward the east
EASTWARD	*n* pl. -S a direction toward the east
EASY	*adj* EASIER, EASIEST not difficult
EASY	*n* pl. EASIES a communications code word for the letter E
EAT	*v* ATE or ET, EATEN, EATING, EATS to consume food
EATABLE	*n* pl. -S an edible
EATER	*n* pl. -S one that eats
EATERY	*n* pl. -ERIES a lunchroom
EATH	*adj* easy
EATING	*n* pl. -S the act of consuming food
EAU	*n* pl. EAUX water
EAVE	*n* pl. -S the lower projecting edge of a roof **EAVED** *adj*
EBB	*v* -ED, -ING, -S to recede
EBBET	*n* pl. -S a common green newt
EBON	*n* pl. -S ebony
EBONIES	pl. of ebony
EBONISE	*v* -ISED, -ISING, -ISES to ebonize
EBONITE	*n* pl. -S a hard rubber
EBONIZE	*v* -IZED, -IZING, -IZES to stain black in imitation of ebony
EBONY	*n* pl. -NIES a hard, heavy wood
ECARTE	*n* pl. -S a card game
ECAUDATE	*adj* having no tail
ECBOLIC	*n* pl. -S a type of drug
ECCLESIA	*n* pl. -SIAE an assembly in ancient Greece
ECCRINE	*adj* producing secretions externally
ECDYSIS	*n* pl. -DYSES the shedding of an outer layer of skin **ECDYSIAL** *adj*
ECDYSON	*n* pl. -S ecdysone
ECDYSONE	*n* pl. -S an insect hormone
ECESIS	*n* pl. -SISES the establishment of a plant or animal in a new environment
ECHARD	*n* pl. -S the water in the soil not available to plants
ECHE	*v* ECHED, ECHING, ECHES to increase
ECHELLE	*n* pl. -S a device for spreading light into its component colors
ECHELON	*v* -ED, -ING, -S to group in a particular formation
ECHIDNA	*n* pl. -NAS or -NAE a spiny anteater
ECHINATE	*adj* spiny
ECHING	present participle of eche
ECHINOID	*n* pl. -S a spiny marine animal
ECHINUS	*n* pl. -NI echinoid
ECHO	*v* -ED, -ING, -ES to produce an echo
ECHO	*n* pl. ECHOES or ECHOS a repetition of sound by reflection of sound waves
ECHOER	*n* pl. -S one that echoes
ECHOEY	*adj* full of echoes
ECHOGRAM	*n* pl. -S a record produced by a device that uses ultrasonic waves
ECHOIC	*adj* resembling an echo
ECHOISM	*n* pl. -S the formation of words in imitation of sounds
ECHOLESS	*adj* producing no echo
ECLAIR	*n* pl. -S a type of pastry
ECLAT	*n* pl. -S brilliance
ECLECTIC	*n* pl. -S one who draws his beliefs from various sources
ECLIPSE	*v* ECLIPSED, ECLIPSING, ECLIPSES to obscure
ECLIPSIS	*n* pl. ECLIPSES or ECLIPSISES an ellipsis
ECLIPTIC	*n* pl. -S an astronomical plane
ECLOGITE	*n* pl. -S a type of rock
ECLOGUE	*n* pl. -S a pastoral poem
ECLOSION	*n* pl. -S the emergence of an insect larva from an egg
ECOCIDE	*n* pl. -S the destruction of the natural environment **ECOCIDAL** *adj*

ECOFREAK	*n* pl. -S a zealous environmentalist
ECOLOGY	*n* pl. -GIES an environmental science **ECOLOGIC** *adj*
ECONOBOX	*n* pl. -ES a small economical car
ECONOMIC	*adj* pertaining to financial matters
ECONOMY	*n* pl. -MIES thrift
ECOTONE	*n* pl. -S a type of ecological zone **ECOTONAL** *adj*
ECOTYPE	*n* pl. -S a subspecies adapted to specific environmental conditions **ECOTYPIC** *adj*
ECRASEUR	*n* pl. -S a surgical instrument
ECRU	*n* pl. -S a yellowish brown color
ECSTASY	*n* pl. -SIES a state of exaltation
ECSTATIC	*n* pl. -S one that is subject to ecstasies
ECTASIS	*n* pl. -TASES the lengthening of a usually short syllable **ECTATIC** *adj*
ECTHYMA	*n* pl. -MATA a virus disease
ECTODERM	*n* pl. -S the outermost germ layer of an embryo
ECTOMERE	*n* pl. -S a cell that develops into ectoderm
ECTOPIA	*n* pl. -S congenital displacement of parts or organs **ECTOPIC** *adj*
ECTOSARC	*n* pl. -S the outermost layer of protoplasm of certain protozoans
ECTOZOAN	*n* pl. -S ectozoon
ECTOZOON	*n* pl. -ZOA a parasite on the body of an animal
ECTYPE	*n* pl. -S a copy **ECTYPAL** *adj*
ECU	*n* pl. -S an old French coin
ECUMENIC	*adj* universal
ECZEMA	*n* pl. -S a skin disease
ED	*n* pl. ED education
EDACIOUS	*adj* voracious
EDACITY	*n* pl. -TIES gluttony
EDAPHIC	*adj* pertaining to the soil
EDDO	*n* pl. -DOES a tropical plant
EDDY	*v* -DIED, -DYING, -DIES to move against the main current
EDEMA	*n* pl. -MAS or -MATA an excessive accumulation of serous fluid
EDENIC	*adj* pertaining to a paradise
EDENTATE	*n* pl. -S a toothless mammal
EDGE	*v* EDGED, EDGING, EDGES to provide with an edge (a bounding or dividing line)
EDGELESS	*adj* lacking an edge
EDGER	*n* pl. -S a tool used to trim a lawn's edge
EDGEWAYS	*adv* edgewise
EDGEWISE	*adv* sideways
EDGIER	comparative of edgy
EDGIEST	superlative of edgy
EDGILY	*adv* in an edgy manner
EDGINESS	*n* pl. -ES the state of being edgy
EDGING	*n* pl. -S something that forms or serves as an edge
EDGY	*adj* EDGIER, EDGIEST tense, nervous, or irritable
EDH	*n* pl. -S an Old English letter
EDIBLE	*n* pl. -S something fit to be eaten
EDICT	*n* pl. -S an authoritative order having the force of law **EDICTAL** *adj*
EDIFICE	*n* pl. -S a building
EDIFIER	*n* pl. -S one that edifies
EDIFY	*v* -FIED, -FYING, -FIES to enlighten
EDILE	*n* pl. -S aedile
EDIT	*v* -ED, -ING, -S to correct and prepare for publication **EDITABLE** *adj*
EDITION	*n* pl. -S a particular series of printed material
EDITOR	*n* pl. -S one that edits
EDITRESS	*n* pl. -ES a female editor
EDUCABLE	*n* pl. -S a mildly retarded person
EDUCATE	*v* -CATED, -CATING, -CATES to teach
EDUCATOR	*n* pl. -S one that educates
EDUCE	*v* EDUCED, EDUCING, EDUCES to draw forth or bring out **EDUCIBLE** *adj*
EDUCT	*n* pl. -S something educed
EDUCTION	*n* pl. -S the act of educing **EDUCTIVE** *adj*
EDUCTOR	*n* pl. -S one that educes
EEL	*n* pl. -S a snakelike fish
EELGRASS	*n* pl. -ES an aquatic plant
EELIER	comparative of eely
EELIEST	superlative of eely
EELLIKE	*adj* resembling an eel

EELPOUT   *n* pl. -S a marine fish

EELWORM   *n* pl. -S a small roundworm

EELY   *adj* EELIER, EELIEST resembling an eel

EERIE   *adj* -RIER, -RIEST weird **EERILY** *adv*

EERINESS   *n* pl. -ES the state of being eerie

EERY   *adj* -RIER, -RIEST eerie

EF   *n* pl. -S the letter F

EFF   *n* pl. -S ef

EFFABLE   *adj* capable of being uttered or expressed

EFFACE   *v* -FACED, -FACING, -FACES to rub or wipe out

EFFACER   *n* pl. -S one that effaces

EFFECT   *v* -ED, -ING, -S to bring about

EFFECTER   *n* pl. -S effector

EFFECTOR   *n* pl. -S a bodily organ that responds to a nerve impulse

EFFENDI   *n* pl. -S a Turkish title of respect

EFFERENT   *n* pl. -S an organ or part conveying nervous impulses to an effector

EFFETE   *adj* exhausted of vigor or energy **EFFETELY** *adv*

EFFICACY   *n* pl. -CIES effectiveness

EFFIGIAL   *adj* resembling an effigy

EFFIGY   *n* pl. -GIES a likeness or representation

EFFLUENT   *n* pl. -S an outflow

EFFLUVIA   *n/pl* byproducts in the form of waste

EFFLUX   *n* pl. -ES an outflow

EFFORT   *n* pl. -S a deliberate exertion

EFFULGE   *v* -FULGED, -FULGING, -FULGES to shine forth

EFFUSE   *v* -FUSED, -FUSING, -FUSES to pour forth

EFFUSION   *n* pl. -S an outpouring of emotion

EFFUSIVE   *adj* pouring forth

EFT   *n* pl. -S a newt

EFTSOON   *adv* soon afterward

EFTSOONS   *adv* eftsoon

EGAD   *interj* — used as a mild oath

EGADS   *interj* egad

EGAL   *adj* equal

EGALITE   *n* pl. -S equality

EGER   *n* pl. -S eagre

EGEST   *v* -ED, -ING, -S to discharge from the body

EGESTA   *n/pl* egested matter

EGESTION   *n* pl. -S the act of egesting **EGESTIVE** *adj*

EGG   *v* -ED, -ING, -S to incite or urge

EGGAR   *n* pl. -S egger

EGGCUP   *n* pl. -S a cup from which an egg is eaten

EGGER   *n* pl. -S a kind of moth

EGGHEAD   *n* pl. -S an intellectual

EGGLESS   *adj* lacking eggs

EGGNOG   *n* pl. -S a beverage

EGGPLANT   *n* pl. -S a perennial herb yielding edible fruit

EGGSHELL   *n* pl. -S the hard exterior of a bird's egg

EGGY   *adj* containing eggs

EGIS   *n* pl. EGISES aegis

EGLATERE   *n* pl. -S a wild rose

EGLOMISE   *adj* made of glass with a painted picture on the back

EGO   *n* pl. EGOS the conscious self

EGOISM   *n* pl. -S extreme devotion to self-interest

EGOIST   *n* pl. -S one who practices egoism **EGOISTIC** *adj*

EGOLESS   *adj* not characterized by egoism

EGOMANIA   *n* pl. -S extreme egotism

EGOTISM   *n* pl. -S self-conceit

EGOTIST   *n* pl. -S a conceited person

EGRESS   *v* -ED, -ING, -ES to go out

EGRET   *n* pl. -S a wading bird

EGYPTIAN   *n* pl. -S a typeface with squared serifs

EH   *interj* — used to express doubt or surprise

EIDE   pl. of eidos

EIDER   *n* pl. -S a large sea duck

EIDETIC   *adj* pertaining to vivid recall

EIDOLIC   *adj* pertaining to an eidolon

EIDOLON   *n* pl. -LONS or -LA a phantom

EIDOS   *n* pl. EIDE an essence

EIGHT   *n* pl. -S a number

EIGHTEEN   *n* pl. -S a number

EIGHTH   *n* pl. -S one of eight equal parts

EIGHTHLY   *adv* in the eighth place

EIGHTVO	*n* pl. -VOS octavo
EIGHTY	*n* pl. EIGHTIES a number
EIKON	*n* pl. -S or -ES icon
EINKORN	*n* pl. -S a variety of wheat
EINSTEIN	*n* pl. -S a very intelligent person
EIRENIC	*adj* irenic
EISWEIN	*n* pl. -S a sweet German wine
EITHER	*adj* being one or the other
EJECT	*v* -ED, -ING, -S to throw out forcibly
EJECTA	*n/pl* ejected material
EJECTION	*n* pl. -S the act of ejecting
EJECTIVE	*n* pl. -S a sound produced with air compressed above the closed glottis
EJECTOR	*n* pl. -S one that ejects
EKE	*v* EKED, EKING, EKES to supplement with great effort
EKISTICS	*n/pl* a science dealing with human habitats **EKISTIC** *adj*
EKPWELE	*n* pl. -S a former monetary unit of Equatorial Guinea
EKTEXINE	*n* pl. -S an outer layer of the exine
EKUELE	*n* pl. EKUELE ekpwele
EL	*n* pl. -S an elevated railroad or train
ELAIN	*n* pl. -S olein
ELAN	*n* pl. -S enthusiasm
ELAND	*n* pl. -S a large antelope
ELAPHINE	*adj* pertaining to a genus of deer
ELAPID	*n* pl. -S a venomous snake
ELAPINE	*adj* pertaining to a family of snakes
ELAPSE	*v* ELAPSED, ELAPSING, ELAPSES to pass away
ELASTASE	*n* pl. -S an enzyme
ELASTIC	*n* pl. -S a stretchable material
ELASTIN	*n* pl. -S a bodily protein
ELATE	*v* ELATED, ELATING, ELATES to raise the spirits of **ELATEDLY** *adv*
ELATER	*n* pl. -S a click beetle
ELATERID	*n* pl. -S an elater
ELATERIN	*n* pl. -S a chemical compound
ELATING	present participle of elate
ELATION	*n* pl. -S a feeling of great joy
ELATIVE	*n* pl. -S an adjectival form in some languages
ELBOW	*v* -ED, -ING, -S to jostle
ELD	*n* pl. -S old age
ELDER	*n* pl. -S an older person
ELDERLY	*n* pl. -LIES a rather old person
ELDEST	*adj* oldest
ELDRESS	*n* pl. -ES a female elder (a church officer)
ELDRICH	*adj* eldritch
ELDRITCH	*adj* weird
ELECT	*v* -ED, -ING, -S to select by vote for an office
ELECTEE	*n* pl. -S a person who has been elected
ELECTION	*n* pl. -S the act of electing
ELECTIVE	*n* pl. -S an optional course of study
ELECTOR	*n* pl. -S one that elects
ELECTRET	*n* pl. -S a type of nonconductor
ELECTRIC	*n* pl. -S something run by electricity
ELECTRO	*v* -ED, -ING, -S to make a metallic copy of a page of type for printing
ELECTRON	*n* pl. -S an elementary particle
ELECTRUM	*n* pl. -S an alloy of gold and silver
ELEGANCE	*n* pl. -S tasteful opulence
ELEGANCY	*n* pl. -CIES elegance
ELEGANT	*adj* tastefully opulent
ELEGIAC	*n* pl. -S a type of verse
ELEGIES	pl. of elegy
ELEGISE	*v* -GISED, -GISING, -GISES to elegize
ELEGIST	*n* pl. -S one that writes elegies
ELEGIT	*n* pl. -S a type of judicial writ
ELEGIZE	*v* -GIZED, -GIZING, -GIZES to write an elegy
ELEGY	*n* pl. -GIES a mournful poem for one who is dead
ELEMENT	*n* pl. -S a substance that cannot be separated into simpler substances by chemical means
ELEMI	*n* pl. -S a fragrant resin
ELENCHUS	*n* pl. -CHI a logical refutation **ELENCHIC, ELENCTIC** *adj*
ELEPHANT	*n* pl. -S a large mammal
ELEVATE	*v* -VATED, -VATING, -VATES to raise

ELEVATED	*n* pl. -S a railway that operates on a raised structure	**ELOPE**	*v* ELOPED, ELOPING, ELOPES to run off secretly to be married
ELEVATOR	*n* pl. -S one that elevates	**ELOPER**	*n* pl. -S one that elopes
ELEVEN	*n* pl. -S a number	**ELOQUENT**	*adj* fluent and convincing in speech
ELEVENTH	*n* pl. -S one of eleven equal parts		
ELEVON	*n* pl. -S a type of airplane control surface	**ELSE**	*adv* in a different place, time, or way
ELF	*n* pl. ELVES a small, often mischievous fairy **ELFLIKE** *adj*	**ELUANT**	*n* pl. -S a solvent
		ELUATE	*n* pl. -S the material obtained by eluting
ELFIN	*n* pl. -S an elf	**ELUDE**	*v* ELUDED, ELUDING, ELUDES to evade
ELFISH	*adj* resembling an elf **ELFISHLY** *adv*		
ELFLOCK	*n* pl. -S a lock of tangled hair	**ELUDER**	*n* pl. -S one that eludes
ELHI	*adj* pertaining to school grades 1 through 12	**ELUENT**	*n* pl. -S eluant
		ELUSION	*n* pl. -S the act of eluding
ELICIT	*v* -ED, -ING, -S to educe	**ELUSIVE**	*adj* tending to elude
ELICITOR	*n* pl. -S one that elicits	**ELUSORY**	*adj* elusive
ELIDE	*v* ELIDED, ELIDING, ELIDES to omit **ELIDIBLE** *adj*	**ELUTE**	*v* ELUTED, ELUTING, ELUTES to remove by means of a solvent
ELIGIBLE	*n* pl. -S one that is qualified to be chosen	**ELUTION**	*n* pl. -S the act of eluting
		ELUVIA	a pl. of eluvium
ELIGIBLY	*adv* in a qualified manner	**ELUVIAL**	*adj* pertaining to an eluvium
ELINT	*n* pl. -S the gathering of intelligence by electronic devices	**ELUVIATE**	*v* -ATED, -ATING, -ATES to undergo a transfer of materials in the soil
ELISION	*n* pl. -S the act of eliding	**ELUVIUM**	*n* pl. -VIA or -VIUMS a soil deposit
ELITE	*n* pl. -S a socially superior group		
ELITISM	*n* pl. -S belief in rule by an elite	**ELVER**	*n* pl. -S a young eel
ELITIST	*n* pl. -S an adherent of elitism	**ELVES**	pl. of elf
ELIXIR	*n* pl. -S a medicinal beverage	**ELVISH**	*adj* elfish **ELVISHLY** *adv*
ELK	*n* pl. -S a large deer	**ELYSIAN**	*adj* delightful
ELKHOUND	*n* pl. -S a hunting dog	**ELYTRON**	*n* pl. -TRA a hardened forewing of certain insects **ELYTROID, ELYTROUS** *adj*
ELL	*n* pl. -S the letter L		
ELLIPSE	*n* pl. -S a type of plane curve		
ELLIPSIS	*n* pl. -LIPSES an omission of a word or words in a sentence	**ELYTRUM**	*n* pl. -TRA elytron
		EM	*n* pl. -S the letter M
ELLIPTIC	*adj* having the shape of an ellipse	**EMACIATE**	*v* -ATED, -ATING, -ATES to make thin
ELM	*n* pl. -S a deciduous tree	**EMANATE**	*v* -NATED, -NATING, -NATES to send forth
ELMY	*adj* -MIER, -MIEST abounding in elms		
		EMANATOR	*n* pl. -S one that emanates
ELODEA	*n* pl. -S an aquatic herb	**EMBALM**	*v* -ED, -ING, -S to treat so as to protect from decay
ELOIGN	*v* -ED, -ING, -S to remove to a distant place		
		EMBALMER	*n* pl. -S one that embalms
ELOIGNER	*n* pl. -S one that eloigns	**EMBANK**	*v* -ED, -ING, -S to confine or protect with a raised structure
ELOIN	*v* -ED, -ING, -S to eloign		
ELOINER	*n* pl. -S one that eloins	**EMBAR**	*v* -BARRED, -BARRING, -BARS to imprison
ELONGATE	*v* -GATED, -GATING, -GATES to lengthen		
		EMBARGO	*v* -ED, -ING, -ES to restrain trade by a governmental order

EMBARK   *v* -ED, -ING, -S to make a start

EMBARRED   past tense of embar

EMBARRING   present participle of embar

EMBASSY   *n* pl. -SIES the headquarters of an ambassador

EMBATTLE   *v* -TLED, -TLING, -TLES to prepare for battle

EMBAY   *v* -ED, -ING, -S to enclose in a bay

EMBED   *v* -BEDDED, -BEDDING, -BEDS to fix firmly into a surrounding mass

EMBER   *n* pl. -S a glowing fragment from a fire

EMBEZZLE   *v* -ZLED, -ZLING, -ZLES to appropriate fraudulently to one's own use

EMBITTER   *v* -ED, -ING, -S to make bitter

EMBLAZE   *v* -BLAZED, -BLAZING, -BLAZES to set on fire

EMBLAZER   *n* pl. -S one that emblazes

EMBLAZON   *v* -ED, -ING, -S to decorate with brilliant colors

EMBLEM   *v* -ED, -ING, -S to represent with an emblem (a graphical symbol)

EMBODIER   *n* pl. -S one that embodies

EMBODY   *v* -BODIED, -BODYING, -BODIES to provide with a body

EMBOLDEN   *v* -ED, -ING, -S to instill with courage

EMBOLI   pl. of embolus

EMBOLIES   pl. of emboly

EMBOLISM   *n* pl. -S the obstruction of a blood vessel by an embolus **EMBOLIC** *adj*

EMBOLUS   *n* pl. -LI an abnormal particle circulating in the blood

EMBOLY   *n* pl. -LIES a phase of embryonic growth

EMBORDER   *v* -ED, -ING, -S to provide with a border

EMBOSK   *v* -ED, -ING, -S to conceal with foliage

EMBOSOM   *v* -ED, -ING, -S to embrace

EMBOSS   *v* -ED, -ING, -ES to decorate with raised designs

EMBOSSER   *n* pl. -S one that embosses

EMBOW   *v* -ED, -ING, -S to arch

EMBOWEL   *v* -ELED, -ELING, -ELS or -ELLED, -ELLING, -ELS to disbowel

EMBOWER   *v* -ED, -ING, -S to surround with foliage

EMBRACE   *v* -BRACED, -BRACING, -BRACES to hug

EMBRACER   *n* pl. -S one that embraces

EMBROIL   *v* -ED, -ING, -S to involve in conflict

EMBROWN   *v* -ED, -ING, -S to make brown

EMBRUE   *v* -BRUED, -BRUING, -BRUES to imbrue

EMBRUTE   *v* -BRUTED, -BRUTING, -BRUTES to imbrute

EMBRYO   *n* pl. -BRYOS an organism in its early stages of development

EMBRYOID   *n* pl. -S a mass of tissue that resembles an embryo

EMBRYON   *n* pl. -S an embryo

EMCEE   *v* -CEED, -CEEING, -CEES to serve as master of ceremonies

EME   *n* pl. -S an uncle

EMEER   *n* pl. -S emir

EMEERATE   *n* pl. -S emirate

EMEND   *v* -ED, -ING, -S to correct

EMENDATE   *v* -DATED, -DATING, -DATES to emend

EMENDER   *n* pl. -S one that emends

EMERALD   *n* pl. -S a green gem

EMERGE   *v* EMERGED, EMERGING, EMERGES to come out into view

EMERGENT   *n* pl. -S a type of aquatic plant

EMERIES   pl. of emery

EMERITA   *n* pl. -TAE a retired woman who retains an honorary title

EMERITUS   *n* pl. -TI a retired person who retains an honorary title

EMEROD   *n* pl. -S a tumor

EMEROID   *n* pl. -S emerod

EMERSED   *adj* standing out of water

EMERSION   *n* pl. -S the act of emerging

EMERY   *n* pl. -ERIES a granular corundum

EMESIS   *n* pl. EMESES the act of vomiting

EMETIC   *n* pl. -S a substance which induces vomiting

EMETIN   *n* pl. -S emetine

EMETINE   *n* pl. -S an alkaloid

EMEU   *n* pl. -S emu

EMEUTE   *n* pl. -S a riot

EMF	*n* pl. -S a difference in electric potential
EMIC	*adj* relating to a type of linguistic analysis
EMIGRANT	*n* pl. -S one that emigrates
EMIGRATE	*v* -GRATED, -GRATING, -GRATES to leave one country or region to settle in another
EMIGRE	*n* pl. -S an emigrant
EMINENCE	*n* pl. -S high station or rank
EMINENCY	*n* pl. -CIES eminence
EMINENT	*adj* of high station or rank
EMIR	*n* pl. -S an Arab chieftain or prince
EMIRATE	*n* pl. -S the rank of an emir
EMISSARY	*n* pl. -SARIES a person sent on a mission
EMISSION	*n* pl. -S the act of emitting **EMISSIVE** *adj*
EMIT	*v* EMITTED, EMITTING, EMITS to send forth
EMITTER	*n* pl. -S one that emits
EMMER	*n* pl. -S a type of wheat
EMMET	*n* pl. -S an ant
EMODIN	*n* pl. -S a chemical compound
EMOTE	*v* EMOTED, EMOTING, EMOTES to express emotion in an exaggerated manner
EMOTER	*n* pl. -S one that emotes
EMOTION	*n* pl. -S an affective state of consciousness
EMOTIVE	*adj* pertaining to emotion
EMPALE	*v* -PALED, -PALING, -PALES to impale
EMPALER	*n* pl. -S one that empales
EMPANADA	*n* pl. -S a pastry turnover
EMPANEL	*v* -ELED, -ELING, -ELS or -ELLED, -ELLING, -ELS to impanel
EMPATHY	*n* pl. -THIES imaginative identification with another's thoughts and feelings **EMPATHIC** *adj*
EMPEROR	*n* pl. -S the ruler of an empire
EMPERY	*n* pl. -PERIES absolute dominion
EMPHASIS	*n* pl. -PHASES special significance imparted to something
EMPHATIC	*adj* strongly expressive
EMPIRE	*n* pl. -S a major political unit
EMPIRIC	*n* pl. -S one who relies on practical experience
EMPLACE	*v* -PLACED, -PLACING, -PLACES to position
EMPLANE	*v* -PLANED, -PLANING, -PLANES to enplane
EMPLOY	*v* -ED -ING, -S to hire
EMPLOYE	*n* pl. -S employee
EMPLOYEE	*n* pl. -S a person who is employed
EMPLOYER	*n* pl. -S one that employs
EMPOISON	*v* -ED, -ING, -S to embitter
EMPORIUM	*n* pl. -RIUMS or -RIA a trading or market center
EMPOWER	*v* -ED, -ING, -S to give legal power to
EMPRESS	*n* pl. -ES a female ruler of an empire
EMPRISE	*n* pl. -S an adventurous undertaking
EMPRIZE	*n* pl. -S emprise
EMPTIED	past tense of empty
EMPTIER	*n* pl. -S one that empties
EMPTIES	present 3d person sing. of empty
EMPTIEST	superlative of empty
EMPTILY	*adv* in an empty manner
EMPTINGS	*n/pl* emptins
EMPTINS	*n/pl* a liquid leavening
EMPTY	*adj* -TIER, -TIEST containing nothing
EMPTY	*v* -TIED, -TYING, -TIES to remove the contents of
EMPURPLE	*v* -PLED, -PLING, -PLES to tinge with purple
EMPYEMA	*n* pl. -EMATA or -EMAS a collection of pus in a body cavity **EMPYEMIC** *adj*
EMPYREAL	*adj* pertaining to the sky
EMPYREAN	*n* pl. -S the highest heaven
EMU	*n* pl. -S a large, flightless bird
EMULATE	*v* -LATED, -LATING, -LATES to try to equal or surpass
EMULATOR	*n* pl. -S one that emulates
EMULOUS	*adj* eager to equal or surpass another
EMULSIFY	*v* -FIED, -FYING, -FIES to make into an emulsion
EMULSION	*n* pl. -S a type of liquid mixture **EMULSIVE** *adj*

EMULSOID *n* pl. -S a liquid dispersed in another liquid

EMYD *n* pl. -S a freshwater tortoise

EMYDE *n* pl. -S emyd

EN *n* pl. -S the letter N

ENABLE *v* -BLED, -BLING, -BLES to make possible

ENABLER *n* pl. -S one that enables

ENACT *v* -ED, -ING, -S to make into a law

ENACTIVE *adj* having the power to enact

ENACTOR *n* pl. -S one that enacts

ENACTORY *adj* pertaining to the enactment of law

ENAMEL *v* -ELED, -ELING, -ELS or -ELLED, -ELLING, -ELS to cover with a hard, glossy surface

ENAMELER *n* pl. -S one that enamels

ENAMINE *n* pl. -S a type of amine

ENAMOR *v* -ED, -ING, -S to inspire with love

ENAMOUR *v* -ED, -ING, -S to enamor

ENATE *n* pl. -S a relative on the mother's side **ENATIC** *adj*

ENATION *n* pl. -S an outgrowth from the surface of an organ

ENCAENIA *n/pl* annual university ceremonies

ENCAGE *v* -CAGED, -CAGING, -CAGES to confine in a cage

ENCAMP *v* -ED, -ING, -S to set up a camp

ENCASE *v* -CASED, -CASING, -CASES to enclose in a case

ENCASH *v* -ED, -ING, -ES to cash

ENCEINTE *n* pl. -S an encircling fortification

ENCHAIN *v* -ED, -ING, -S to bind with chains

ENCHANT *v* -ED, -ING, -S to delight

ENCHASE *v* -CHASED, -CHASING, -CHASES to place in an ornamental setting

ENCHASER *n* pl. -S one that enchases

ENCHORIC *adj* belonging to a particular country

ENCINA *n* pl. -S an evergreen oak **ENCINAL** *adj*

ENCIPHER *v* -ED, -ING, -S to write in characters of hidden meaning

ENCIRCLE *v* -CLED, -CLING, -CLES to form a circle around

ENCLASP *v* -ED, -ING, -S to embrace

ENCLAVE *n* pl. -S a territorial unit enclosed within foreign territory

ENCLITIC *n* pl. -S a word pronounced as part of the preceding word

ENCLOSE *v* -CLOSED, -CLOSING, -CLOSES to close in on all sides

ENCLOSER *n* pl. -S one that encloses

ENCODE *v* -CODED, -CODING, -CODES to put into code

ENCODER *n* pl. -S one that encodes

ENCOMIUM *n* pl. -MIUMS or -MIA a eulogy

ENCORE *v* -CORED, -CORING, -CORES to call for the reappearance of a performer

ENCROACH *v* -ED, -ING, -ES to advance beyond the proper limits

ENCRUST *v* -ED, -ING, -S to cover with a crust

ENCRYPT *v* -ED, -ING, -S to encipher

ENCUMBER *v* -ED, -ING, -S to hinder in action or movement

ENCYCLIC *n* pl. -S a letter addressed by the pope to the bishops of the world

ENCYST *v* -ED, -ING, -S to enclose in a cyst

END *v* -ED, -ING, -S to terminate

ENDAMAGE *v* -AGED, -AGING, -AGES to damage

ENDAMEBA *n* pl. -BAS or -BAE a parasitic ameba

ENDANGER *v* -ED, -ING, -S to imperil

ENDARCH *adj* formed from the center outward

ENDARCHY *n* pl. -CHIES the condition of being endarch

ENDBRAIN *n* pl. -S a part of the brain

ENDEAR *v* -ED, -ING, -S to make dear or beloved

ENDEAVOR *v* -ED, -ING, -S to make an effort

ENDEMIAL *adj* peculiar to a country or people

ENDEMIC *n* pl. -S an endemial disease

ENDEMISM *n* pl. -S the state of being endemial

ENDER *n* pl. -S one that ends something

ENDERMIC *adj* acting by absorption through the skin

ENDEXINE *n* pl. -S an inner layer of the exine

ENDGAME   *n* pl. -S the last stage of a chess game

ENDING   *n* pl. -S a termination

ENDITE   *v* -DITED, -DITING, -DITES to indite

ENDIVE   *n* pl. -S an herb cultivated as a salad plant

ENDLEAF   *n* pl. -LEAVES an endpaper

ENDLESS   *adj* enduring forever

ENDLONG   *adv* lengthwise

ENDMOST   *adj* farthest

ENDNOTE   *n* pl. -S a note placed at the end of the text

ENDOCARP   *n* pl. -S the inner layer of a pericarp

ENDOCAST   *n* pl. -S a cast of the cranial cavity

ENDODERM   *n* pl. -S the innermost germ layer of an embryo

ENDOGAMY   *n* pl. -MIES marriage within a particular group

ENDOGEN   *n* pl. -S a type of plant

ENDOGENY   *n* pl. -NIES growth from within

ENDOPOD   *n* pl. -S a branch of a crustacean limb

ENDORSE   *v* -DORSED, -DORSING, -DORSES to sign the back of a negotiable document

ENDORSEE   *n* pl. -S one to whom a document is transferred by endorsement

ENDORSER   *n* pl. -S one that endorses

ENDORSING   present participle of endorse

ENDORSOR   *n* pl. -S endorser

ENDOSARC   *n* pl. -S a portion of a cell

ENDOSMOS   *n* pl. -ES a form of osmosis

ENDOSOME   *n* pl. -S a cellular particle

ENDOSTEA   *n/pl* bone membranes

ENDOW   *v* -ED, -ING, -S to provide with something

ENDOWER   *n* pl. -S one that endows

ENDOZOIC   *adj* involving passage through an animal

ENDPAPER   *n* pl. -S a sheet of paper used in bookbinding

ENDPLATE   *n* pl. -S a type of nerve terminal

ENDPOINT   *n* pl. -S either of two points that mark the end of a line segment

ENDRIN   *n* pl. -S an insecticide

ENDUE   *v* -DUED, -DUING, -DUES to provide with some quality or gift

ENDURE   *v* -DURED, -DURING, -DURES to last

ENDURO   *n* pl. -DUROS a long race

ENDWAYS   *adv* endwise

ENDWISE   *adv* lengthwise

ENEMA   *n* pl. -MAS or -MATA a liquid injected into the rectum

ENEMY   *n* pl. -MIES one that is antagonistic toward another

ENERGID   *n* pl. -S a nucleus and the body of cytoplasm with which it interacts

ENERGIES   pl. of energy

ENERGISE   *v* -GISED, -GISING, -GISES to energize

ENERGIZE   *v* -GIZED, -GIZING, -GIZES to give energy to

ENERGY   *n* -GIES the capacity for vigorous activity

ENERVATE   *v* -VATED, -VATING, -VATES to deprive of strength or vitality

ENFACE   *v* -FACED, -FACING, -FACES to write on the front of

ENFEEBLE   *v* -BLED, -BLING, -BLES to make feeble

ENFEOFF   *v* -ED, -ING, -S to invest with a feudal estate

ENFETTER   *v* -ED, -ING, -S to enchain

ENFEVER   *v* -ED, -ING, -S to fever

ENFILADE   *v* -LADED, -LADING, -LADES to direct heavy gunfire along the length of

ENFLAME   *v* -FLAMED, -FLAMING, -FLAMES to inflame

ENFOLD   *v* -ED, -ING, -S to envelop

ENFOLDER   *n* pl. -S one that enfolds

ENFORCE   *v* -FORCED, -FORCING, -FORCES to compel obedience to

ENFORCER   *n* pl. -S one that enforces

ENFRAME   *v* -FRAMED, -FRAMING, -FRAMES to frame

ENG   *n* pl. -S a phonetic symbol

ENGAGE   *v* -GAGED, -GAGING, -GAGES to employ

ENGAGER   *n* pl. -S one that engages

ENGENDER   *v* -ED, -ING, -S to bring into existence

ENGILD   *v* -ED, -ING, -S to brighten

ENGINE   *v* -GINED, -GINING, -GINES to equip with machinery

ENGINEER *v* -ED, -ING, -S to carry through or manage by contrivance

ENGINERY *n* pl. -RIES machinery

ENGINING present participle of engine

ENGINOUS *adj* ingenious

ENGIRD *v* -GIRT or -GIRDED, -GIRDING, -GIRDS to gird

ENGIRDLE *v* -DLED, -DLING, -DLES to engird

ENGLISH *v* -ED, -ING, -ES to cause a billiard ball to spin around its vertical axis

ENGLUT *v* -GLUTTED, -GLUTTING, -GLUTS to gulp down

ENGORGE *v* -GORGED, -GORGING, -GORGES to fill with blood

ENGRAFT *v* -ED, -ING, -S to graft for propagation

ENGRAIL *v* -ED, -ING, -S to ornament the edge of with curved indentations

ENGRAIN *v* -ED, -ING, -S to ingrain

ENGRAM *n* pl. -S the durable mark caused by a stimulus upon protoplasm

ENGRAMME *n* pl. -S engram

ENGRAVE *v* -GRAVED, -GRAVING, -GRAVES to form by incision

ENGRAVER *n* pl. -S one that engraves

ENGROSS *v* -ED, -ING, -ES to occupy completely

ENGULF *v* -ED, -ING, -S to surround completely

ENHALO *v* -ED, -ING, -ES or -S to surround with a halo

ENHANCE *v* -HANCED, -HANCING, -HANCES to raise to a higher degree

ENHANCER *n* pl. -S one that enhances

ENIGMA *n* pl. -MAS or -MATA something that is hard to understand or explain

ENISLE *v* -ISLED, -ISLING, -ISLES to isolate

ENJAMBED *adj* marked by the continuation of a sentence from one line of a poem to the next

ENJOIN *v* -ED, -ING, -S to command

ENJOINER *n* pl. -S one that enjoins

ENJOY *v* -ED, -ING, -S to receive pleasure from

ENJOYER *n* pl. -S one that enjoys

ENKINDLE *v* -DLED, -DLING, -DLES to set on fire

ENLACE *v* -LACED, -LACING, -LACES to bind with laces

ENLARGE *v* -LARGED, -LARGING, -LARGES to make or become larger

ENLARGER *n* pl. -S a device used to enlarge photographs

ENLIST *v* -ED, -ING, -S to engage for military service

ENLISTEE *n* pl. -S one that is enlisted

ENLISTER *n* pl. -S one that enlists

ENLIVEN *v* -ED, -ING, -S to make lively

ENMESH *v* -ED, -ING, -ES to ensnare or entangle in a net

ENMITY *n* pl. -TIES hostility

ENNEAD *n* pl. -S a group of nine **ENNEADIC** *adj*

ENNEAGON *n* pl. -S a nonagon

ENNOBLE *v* -BLED, -BLING, -BLES to make noble

ENNOBLER *n* pl. -S one that ennobles

ENNUI *n* pl. -S a feeling of weariness and discontent

ENNUYE *adj* oppressed with ennui

ENNUYEE *adj* ennuye

ENOKI *n* pl. -S a small mushroom

ENOL *n* pl. -S a chemical compound **ENOLIC** *adj*

ENOLASE *n* pl. -S an enzyme

ENOLOGY *n* pl. -GIES oenology

ENORM *adj* enormous

ENORMITY *n* pl. -TIES great wickedness

ENORMOUS *adj* huge

ENOSIS *n* pl. -SISES union

ENOUGH *n* pl. -S a sufficient supply

ENOUNCE *v* ENOUNCED, ENOUNCING, ENOUNCES to announce

ENOW *n* pl. -S enough

ENPLANE *v* -PLANED, -PLANING, -PLANES to board an airplane

ENQUIRE *v* -QUIRED, -QUIRING, -QUIRES to inquire

ENQUIRY *n* pl. -RIES inquiry

ENRAGE *v* -RAGED, -RAGING, -RAGES to make very angry

ENRAPT *adj* rapt

ENRAVISH *v* -ED, -ING, -ES to delight greatly

ENRICH *v* -ED, -ING, -ES to add desirable elements to

ENRICHER *n* pl. -S one that enriches

ENROBE *v* -ROBED, -ROBING, -ROBES to dress

ENROBER *n* pl. -S one that enrobes

ENROL *v* -ROLLED, -ROLLING, -ROLS to enroll

ENROLL *v* -ED, -ING, -S to enter the name of in a register, record, or roll

ENROLLEE *n* pl. -S one that is enrolled

ENROLLER *n* pl. -S one that enrolls

ENROLLING present participle of enrol

ENROOT *v* -ED, -ING, -S to implant

ENS *n* pl. ENTIA an entity

ENSAMPLE *n* pl. -S an example

ENSCONCE *v* -SCONCED, -SCONCING, -SCONCES to settle securely or comfortably

ENSCROLL *v* -ED, -ING, -S to write on a scroll

ENSEMBLE *n* pl. -S a group of complementary parts

ENSERF *v* -ED, -ING, -S to make a serf of

ENSHEATH *v* -ED, -ING, -S to enclose in a sheath

ENSHRINE *v* -SHRINED, -SHRINING, -SHRINES to place in a shrine

ENSHROUD *v* -ED, -ING, -S to conceal

ENSIFORM *adj* sword-shaped

ENSIGN *n* pl. -S a navy officer

ENSIGNCY *n* pl. -CIES the rank of an ensign

ENSILAGE *v* -LAGED, -LAGING, -LAGES to ensile

ENSILE *v* -SILED, -SILING, -SILES to store in a silo

ENSKY *v* -SKIED or -SKYED, -SKYING, -SKIES to raise to the skies

ENSLAVE *v* -SLAVED, -SLAVING, -SLAVES to make a slave of

ENSLAVER *n* pl. -S one that enslaves

ENSNARE *v* -SNARED, -SNARING, -SNARES to trap

ENSNARER *n* pl. -S one that ensnares

ENSNARL *v* -ED, -ING, -S to tangle

ENSORCEL *v* -ED, -ING, -S to bewitch

ENSOUL *v* -ED, -ING, -S to endow with a soul

ENSPHERE *v* -SPHERED, -SPHERING, -SPHERES to enclose in a sphere

ENSUE *v* -SUED, -SUING, -SUES to occur afterward or as a result

ENSURE *v* -SURED, -SURING, -SURES to make certain

ENSURER *n* pl. -S one that ensures

ENSWATHE *v* -SWATHED, -SWATHING, -SWATHES to swathe

ENTAIL *v* -ED, -ING, -S to restrict the inheritance of to a specified line of heirs

ENTAILER *n* pl. -S one that entails

ENTAMEBA *n* pl. -BAE or -BAS endameba

ENTANGLE *v* -TANGLED, -TANGLING, -TANGLES to tangle

ENTASIA *n* pl. -S spasmodic contraction of a muscle

ENTASIS *n* pl. -TASES a slight convexity in a column **ENTASTIC** *adj*

ENTELLUS *n* pl. -ES a hanuman

ENTENTE *n* pl. -S an agreement between nations

ENTER *v* -ED, -ING, -S to come or go into

ENTERA a pl. of enteron

ENTERAL *adj* enteric

ENTERER *n* pl. -S one that enters

ENTERIC *adj* pertaining to the enteron

ENTERON *n* pl. -TERONS or -TERA the alimentary canal

ENTHALPY *n* pl. -PIES a thermodynamic measure of heat

ENTHETIC *adj* introduced from outside

ENTHRAL *v* -THRALLED, -THRALLING, -THRALS to enthrall

ENTHRALL *v* -ED, -ING, -S to charm

ENTHRONE *v* -THRONED, -THRONING, -THRONES to place on a throne

ENTHUSE *v* -THUSED, -THUSING, -THUSES to show enthusiasm

ENTIA pl. of ens

ENTICE *v* -TICED, -TICING, -TICES to allure

ENTICER *n* pl. -S one that entices

ENTIRE *n* pl. -S the whole of something

ENTIRELY *adv* completely

ENTIRETY *n* pl. -TIES completeness

ENTITLE *v* -TLED, -TLING, -TLES to give a title to

ENTITY *n* pl. -TIES something that has a real existence

ENTODERM	*n* pl. -S endoderm
ENTOIL	*v* -ED, -ING, -S to entrap
ENTOMB	*v* -ED, -ING, -S to place in a tomb
ENTOPIC	*adj* situated in the normal place
ENTOZOA	a pl. of entozoan and pl. of entozoon
ENTOZOAL	*adj* entozoic
ENTOZOAN	*n* pl. -ZOANS or -ZOA an entozoic parasite
ENTOZOIC	*adj* living within an animal
ENTOZOON	*n* pl. -ZOA entozoan
ENTRAILS	*n/pl* the internal organs
ENTRAIN	*v* -ED, -ING, -S to board a train
ENTRANCE	*v* -TRANCED, -TRANCING, -TRANCES to fill with delight or wonder
ENTRANT	*n* pl. -S one that enters
ENTRAP	*v* -TRAPPED, -TRAPPING, -TRAPS to trap
ENTREAT	*v* -ED, -ING, -S to ask for earnestly
ENTREATY	*n* pl. -TREATIES an earnest request
ENTREE	*n* pl. -S the principal dish of a meal
ENTRENCH	*v* -ED, -ING, -ES to establish firmly
ENTREPOT	*n* pl. -S a warehouse
ENTRESOL	*n* pl. -S a mezzanine
ENTRIES	pl. of entry
ENTROPY	*n* pl. -PIES a thermodynamic measure of disorder **ENTROPIC** *adj*
ENTRUST	*v* -ED, -ING, -S to give over for safekeeping
ENTRY	*n* pl. -TRIES a place of entrance
ENTRYWAY	*n* pl. -WAYS a passage serving as an entrance
ENTWINE	*v* -TWINED, -TWINING, -TWINES to twine around
ENTWIST	*v* -ED, -ING, -S to twist together
ENURE	*v* -URED, -URING, -URES to inure
ENURESIS	*n* pl. -SISES involuntary urination
ENURETIC	*n* pl. -S one who is affected with enuresis
ENVELOP	*v* -ED, -ING, -S to cover completely
ENVELOPE	*n* pl. -S a paper container
ENVENOM	*v* -ED, -ING, -S to put venom into
ENVIABLE	*adj* desirable **ENVIABLY** *adv*
ENVIED	past tense of envy
ENVIER	*n* pl. -S one that envies
ENVIES	present 3d person sing. of envy
ENVIOUS	*adj* resentful and desirous of another's possessions or qualities
ENVIRON	*v* -ED, -ING, -S to encircle
ENVISAGE	*v* -AGED, -AGING, -AGES to form a mental image of
ENVISION	*v* -ED, -ING, -S to envisage
ENVOI	*n* pl. -S the closing of a poem or prose work
ENVOY	*n* pl. -VOYS a representative
ENVY	*v* -VIED, -VYING, -VIES to be envious of
ENWHEEL	*v* -ED, -ING, -S to encircle
ENWIND	*v* -WOUND, -WINDING, -WINDS to wind around
ENWOMB	*v* -ED, -ING, -S to enclose as if in a womb
ENWRAP	*v* -WRAPPED, -WRAPPING, -WRAPS to envelop
ENZOOTIC	*n* pl. -S a type of animal disease
ENZYM	*n* pl. -S enzyme
ENZYME	*n* pl. -S a complex protein **ENZYMIC** *adj*
EOBIONT	*n* pl. -S a type of basic organism
EOHIPPUS	*n* pl. -ES an extinct horse
EOLIAN	*adj* pertaining to the wind
EOLIPILE	*n* pl. -S a type of engine
EOLITH	*n* pl. -S a prehistoric stone tool **EOLITHIC** *adj*
EOLOPILE	*n* pl. -S eolipile
EON	*n* pl. -S an indefinitely long period of time
EONIAN	*adj* everlasting
EONISM	*n* pl. -S adoption of the dress and mannerisms of the opposite sex
EOSIN	*n* pl. -S a red dye **EOSINIC** *adj*
EOSINE	*n* pl. -S eosin
EPACT	*n* pl. -S the difference between the lengths of the solar and lunar years
EPARCH	*n* pl. -S the head of an eparchy
EPARCHY	*n* pl. -CHIES a district of modern Greece
EPAULET	*n* pl. -S a shoulder ornament

EPAZOTE	*n* pl. -S an herb of the goosefoot family
EPEE	*n* pl. -S a type of sword
EPEEIST	*n* pl. -S one who fences with an epee
EPEIRIC	*adj* pertaining to vertical movement of the earth's crust
EPENDYMA	*n* pl. -S a membrane lining certain body cavities
EPERGNE	*n* pl. -S an ornamental dish
EPHA	*n* pl. -S ephah
EPHAH	*n* pl. -S a Hebrew unit of dry measure
EPHEBE	*n* pl. -S ephebus **EPHEBIC** *adj*
EPHEBOS	*n* pl. -BOI ephebus
EPHEBUS	*n* pl. -BI a young man of ancient Greece
EPHEDRA	*n* pl. -S a desert shrub
EPHEDRIN	*n* pl. -S an alkaloid used to treat allergies
EPHEMERA	*n* pl. -ERAS or -ERAE something of very short life or duration
EPHOD	*n* pl. -S an ancient Hebrew vestment
EPHOR	*n* pl. -ORS or -ORI a magistrate of ancient Greece **EPHORAL** *adj*
EPHORATE	*n* pl. -S the office of ephor
EPIBLAST	*n* pl. -S the ectoderm
EPIBOLY	*n* pl. -LIES the growth of one part around another **EPIBOLIC** *adj*
EPIC	*n* pl. -S a long narrative poem **EPICAL** *adj* **EPICALLY** *adv*
EPICALYX	*n* pl. -LYXES or -LYCES a set of bracts close to and resembling a calyx
EPICARP	*n* pl. -S the outer layer of a pericarp
EPICEDIA	*n/pl* funeral songs
EPICENE	*n* pl. -S one having both male and female characteristics
EPICLIKE	*adj* resembling an epic
EPICOTYL	*n* pl. -S a part of a plant embryo
EPICURE	*n* pl. -S a gourmet
EPICYCLE	*n* pl. -S a circle that rolls on the circumference of another circle
EPIDEMIC	*n* pl. -S a rapid spread of a disease
EPIDERM	*n* pl. -S the outer layer of skin
EPIDOTE	*n* pl. -S a mineral **EPIDOTIC** *adj*
EPIDURAL	*adj* situated on the membrane that encloses the brain
EPIFAUNA	*n* pl. -FAUNAE or -FAUNAS fauna living on a hard sea floor
EPIFOCAL	*adj* pertaining to the point of origin of an earthquake
EPIGEAL	*adj* epigeous
EPIGEAN	*adj* epigeous
EPIGEIC	*adj* epigeous
EPIGENE	*adj* occurring near the surface of the earth
EPIGENIC	*adj* pertaining to change in the mineral character of a rock
EPIGEOUS	*adj* growing on or close to the ground
EPIGON	*n* pl. -S epigone
EPIGONE	*n* pl. -S an inferior imitator **EPIGONIC** *adj*
EPIGONUS	*n* pl. -NI epigone
EPIGRAM	*n* pl. -S a brief, witty remark
EPIGRAPH	*n* pl. -S an engraved inscription
EPIGYNY	*n* pl. -NIES the state of having floral organs near the top of the ovary
EPILEPSY	*n* pl. -SIES a disorder of the nervous system
EPILOG	*n* pl. -S a concluding section
EPILOGUE	*v* -LOGUED, -LOGUING, -LOGUES to provide with a concluding section
EPIMER	*n* pl. -S a type of sugar compound **EPIMERIC** *adj*
EPIMERE	*n* pl. -S a part of an embryo
EPIMYSIA	*n/pl* muscle sheaths
EPINAOS	*n* pl. -NAOI a rear vestibule
EPINASTY	*n* pl. -TIES a downward bending of plant parts
EPIPHANY	*n* pl. -NIES an appearance of a deity
EPIPHYTE	*n* pl. -S a plant growing upon another plant
EPISCIA	*n* pl. -S a tropical herb
EPISCOPE	*n* pl. -S a type of projector
EPISODE	*n* pl. -S an incident in the course of a continuous experience **EPISODIC** *adj*
EPISOME	*n* pl. -S a genetic determinant **EPISOMAL** *adj*
EPISTASY	*n* pl. -SIES a suppression of genetic effect
EPISTLE	*n* pl. -S a long or formal letter

EPISTLER *n* pl. -S one that writes epistles

EPISTOME *n* pl. -S a structure covering the mouth of various invertebrates

EPISTYLE *n* pl. -S a part of a classical building

EPITAPH *n* pl. -S an inscription on a tomb

EPITASIS *n* pl. -ASES the main part of a classical drama

EPITAXY *n* pl. -TAXIES a type of crystalline growth **EPITAXIC** *adj*

EPITHET *n* pl. -S a term used to characterize a person or thing

EPITOME *n* pl. -S a typical or ideal example **EPITOMIC** *adj*

EPITOPE *n* pl. -S a region on the surface of an antigen

EPIZOA pl. of epizoon

EPIZOIC *adj* living on the body of an animal

EPIZOISM *n* pl. -S the state of being epizoic

EPIZOITE *n* pl. -S an epizoic organism

EPIZOON *n* pl. -ZOA an epizoic parasite

EPIZOOTY *n* pl. -TIES a type of animal disease

EPOCH *n* pl. -S a particular period of time **EPOCHAL** *adj*

EPODE *n* pl. -S a type of poem

EPONYM *n* pl. -S the person for whom something is named **EPONYMIC** *adj*

EPONYMY *n* pl. -MIES the derivation of an eponymic name

EPOPEE *n* pl. -S an epic poem

EPOPOEIA *n* pl. -S epopee

EPOS *n* pl. -ES an epic poem

EPOXIDE *n* pl. -S an epoxy compound

EPOXY *v* EPOXIED or EPOXYED, EPOXYING, EPOXIES to glue with epoxy (a type of resin)

EPSILON *n* pl. -S a Greek letter

EQUABLE *adj* not changing or varying greatly **EQUABLY** *adv*

EQUAL *adj* having the same capability, quantity, or effect as another

EQUAL *v* EQUALED, EQUALING, EQUALS or EQUALLED, EQUALLING, EQUALS to be equal to

EQUALISE *v* -ISED, -ISING, -ISES to equalize

EQUALITY *n* pl. -TIES the state of being equal

EQUALIZE *v* -IZED, -IZING, -IZES to make equal

EQUALLED a past tense of equal

EQUALLING a past participle of equal

EQUALLY *adv* in an equal manner

EQUATE *v* EQUATED, EQUATING, EQUATES to make equal

EQUATION *n* pl. -S the act of equating

EQUATOR *n* pl. -S a great circle of spherical celestial bodies

EQUERRY *n* pl. -RIES an officer in charge of the care of horses

EQUID *n* pl. -S an animal of the horse family

EQUINE *n* pl. -S a horse

EQUINELY *adv* in a horselike manner

EQUINITY *n* pl. -TIES the state of being like a horse

EQUINOX *n* pl. -ES a point on the celestial sphere

EQUIP *v* EQUIPPED, EQUIPPING, EQUIPS to provide with whatever is needed

EQUIPAGE *n* pl. -S a carriage

EQUIPPER *n* pl. -S one that equips

EQUIPPING present participle of equip

EQUISETA *n/pl* rushlike plants

EQUITANT *adj* overlapping

EQUITES *n/pl* a privileged military class of ancient Rome

EQUITY *n* pl. -TIES fairness or impartiality

EQUIVOKE *n* pl. -S a play on words

ER *interj* — used to express hesitation

ERA *n* pl. -S an epoch

ERADIATE *v* -ATED, -ATING, -ATES to radiate

ERASE *v* ERASED, ERASING, ERASES to rub or scrape out **ERASABLE** *adj*

ERASER *n* pl. -S one that erases

ERASION *n* pl. -S an erasure

ERASURE *n* pl. -S the act of erasing

ERBIUM *n* pl. -S a metallic element

ERE *prep* previous to; before

ERECT *v* -ED, -ING, -S to build

ERECTER *n* pl. -S erector

ERECTILE *adj* capable of being raised upright

ERECTION *n* pl. -S the act of erecting

ERECTIVE *adj* tending to erect

ERECTLY *adv* in an upright manner

ERECTOR *n* pl. -S one that erects

ERELONG *adv* soon

EREMITE *n* pl. -S a hermit **EREMITIC** *adj*

EREMURUS *n* pl. -URI a perennial herb

ERENOW *adv* before this time

EREPSIN *n* pl. -S a mixture of enzymes in the small intestine

ERETHISM *n* pl. -S abnormal irritability **ERETHIC** *adj*

EREWHILE *adv* some time ago

ERG *n* pl. -S a unit of work or energy

ERGASTIC *adj* constituting the nonliving by-products of protoplasmic activity

ERGATE *n* pl. -S a worker ant

ERGATIVE *adj* pertaining to a type of language

ERGO *conj* therefore

ERGODIC *adj* pertaining to the probability that any state will recur

ERGOT *n* pl. -S a fungus **ERGOTIC** *adj*

ERGOTISM *n* pl. -S poisoning produced by eating ergot-infected grain

ERICA *n* pl. -S a shrub of the heath family

ERICOID *adj* resembling heath

ERIGERON *n* pl. -S an herb

ERINGO *n* pl. -GOES or -GOS eryngo

ERISTIC *n* pl. -S an expert in debate

ERLKING *n* pl. -S an evil spirit of Germanic folklore

ERMINE *n* pl. -S the fur of certain weasels **ERMINED** *adj*

ERN *n* pl. -S erne

ERNE *n* pl. -S a sea eagle

ERODE *v* ERODED, ERODING, ERODES to wear away by constant friction

ERODENT *adj* erosive

ERODIBLE *adj* erosible

ERODING present participle of erode

EROGENIC *adj* arousing sexual desire

EROS *n* pl. -ES sexual desire

EROSE *adj* uneven **EROSELY** *adv*

EROSIBLE *adj* capable of being eroded

EROSION *n* pl. -S the act of eroding

EROSIVE *adj* causing erosion

EROTIC *n* pl. -S an amatory poem **EROTICAL** *adj*

EROTICA *n/pl* literature or art dealing with sexual love

EROTISM *n* pl. -S sexual excitement

EROTIZE *v* -TIZED, -TIZING, -TIZES to give a sexual meaning to

ERR *v* -ED, -ING, -S to make a mistake

ERRANCY *n* pl. -CIES an instance of erring

ERRAND *n* pl. -S a short trip made for a particular purpose

ERRANT *n* pl. -S a wanderer

ERRANTLY *adv* in a wandering manner

ERRANTRY *n* pl. -RIES the state of wandering

ERRATA *n* pl. -S a list of printing errors

ERRATIC *n* pl. -S an eccentric person

ERRATUM *n* pl. -TA a printing error

ERRHINE *n* pl. -S a substance that promotes nasal discharge

ERRINGLY *adv* in a mistaken manner

ERROR *n* pl. -S a mistake

ERS *n* pl. -ES ervil

ERSATZ *n* pl. -ES a substitute

ERST *adv* formerly

ERUCT *v* -ED, -ING, -S to belch

ERUCTATE *v* -TATED, -TATING, -TATES to eruct

ERUDITE *adj* scholarly

ERUGO *n* pl. -GOS aerugo

ERUMPENT *adj* bursting forth

ERUPT *v* -ED, -ING, -S to burst forth

ERUPTION *n* pl. -S the act of erupting

ERUPTIVE *n* pl. -S a type of rock

ERVIL *n* pl. -S a European vetch

ERYNGO *n* pl. -GOES or -GOS a medicinal herb

ERYTHEMA *n* pl. -S a redness of the skin

ERYTHRON *n* pl. -S a bodily organ consisting of the red blood cells

ES *n* pl. ESES ess

ESCALADE *v* -LADED, -LADING, -LADES to enter by means of ladders

ESCALATE   v -LATED, -LATING, -LATES to increase

ESCALLOP   v -ED, -ING, -S to scallop

ESCALOP   v -ED, -ING, -S to escallop

ESCAPADE   n pl. -S a reckless adventure

ESCAPE   v -CAPED, -CAPING, -CAPES to get away

ESCAPEE   n pl. -S one that has escaped

ESCAPER   n pl. -S one that escapes

ESCAPING   present participle of escape

ESCAPISM   n pl. -S the avoidance of reality by diversion of the mind

ESCAPIST   n pl. -S one given to escapism

ESCAR   n pl. -S esker

ESCARGOT   n pl. -S an edible snail

ESCAROLE   n pl. -S a variety of endive

ESCARP   v -ED, -ING, -S to cause to slope steeply

ESCHALOT   n pl. -S a shallot

ESCHAR   n pl. -S a hard, dry scab

ESCHEAT   v -ED, -ING, -S to confiscate

ESCHEW   v -ED, -ING, -S to avoid

ESCHEWAL   n pl. -S the act of eschewing

ESCOLAR   n pl. -S a food fish

ESCORT   v -ED, -ING, -S to accompany

ESCOT   v -ED, -ING, -S to provide support for

ESCROW   v -ED, -ING, -S to place in the custody of a third party

ESCUAGE   n pl. -S scutage

ESCUDO   n pl. -DOS a monetary unit of Portugal

ESCULENT   n pl. -S something that is edible

ESERINE   n pl. -S a toxic alkaloid

ESKAR   n pl. -S esker

ESKER   n pl. -S a narrow ridge of gravel and sand

ESOPHAGI   n/pl tubes connecting the mouth to the stomach

ESOTERIC   adj designed for a select few

ESPALIER   v -ED, -ING, -S to furnish with a trellis

ESPANOL   n pl. -ES a native of Spain

ESPARTO   n pl. -TOS a perennial grass

ESPECIAL   adj special

ESPIAL   n pl. -S the act of espying

ESPIED   past tense of espy

ESPIEGLE   adj playful

ESPIES   present 3d person sing. of espy

ESPOUSAL   n pl. -S a marriage ceremony

ESPOUSE   v -POUSED, -POUSING, -POUSES to marry

ESPOUSER   n pl. -S one that espouses

ESPRESSO   n pl. -SOS a strong coffee

ESPRIT   n pl. -S spirit

ESPY   v -PIED, -PYING, -PIES to catch sight of

ESQUIRE   v -QUIRED, -QUIRING, -QUIRES to escort

ESS   n pl. -ES the letter S

ESSAY   v -ED, -ING, -S to try

ESSAYER   n pl. -S one that essays

ESSAYIST   n pl. -S a writer of essays (prose compositions)

ESSENCE   n pl. -S a fundamental nature or quality

ESSOIN   n pl. -S an excuse

ESSONITE   n pl. -S a variety of garnet

ESTANCIA   n pl. -S a cattle ranch

ESTATE   v -TATED, -TATING, -TATES to provide with landed property

ESTEEM   v -ED, -ING, -S to have a high opinion of

ESTER   n pl. -S a type of chemical compound

ESTERASE   n pl. -S a type of enzyme

ESTERIFY   v -FIED, -FYING, -FIES to convert into an ester

ESTHESIA   n pl. -S the ability to receive sensation

ESTHESIS   n pl. -THESISES or -THESES esthesia

ESTHETE   n pl. -S a person who appreciates beauty

ESTHETIC   n pl. -S a conception of beauty

ESTIMATE   v -MATED, -MATING, -MATES to make an approximate judgment of

ESTIVAL   adj pertaining to summer

ESTIVATE   v -VATED, -VATING, -VATES to spend the summer

ESTOP   v -TOPPED, -TOPPING, -TOPS to impede by estoppel

ESTOPPEL   n pl. -S a legal restraint preventing a person from contradicting his own previous statement

ESTOVERS	*n/pl* necessities allowed by law
ESTRAGON	*n* pl. -S tarragon
ESTRAL	*adj* estrous
ESTRANGE	*v* -TRANGED, -TRANGING, -TRANGES to alienate
ESTRAY	*v* -ED, -ING, -S to stray
ESTREAT	*v* -ED, -ING, -S to copy from court records for use in prosecution
ESTRIN	*n* pl. -S estrone
ESTRIOL	*n* pl. -S an estrogen
ESTROGEN	*n* pl. -S a female sex hormone promoting or producing estrus
ESTRONE	*n* pl. -S an estrogen
ESTROUS	*adj* pertaining to estrus
ESTRUAL	*adj* estrous
ESTRUM	*n* pl. -S estrus
ESTRUS	*n* pl. -ES the period of heat in female mammals
ESTUARY	*n* pl. -ARIES an inlet of the sea at a river's lower end
ESURIENT	*adj* greedy
ET	a past tense of eat
ETA	*n* pl. -S a Greek letter
ETAGERE	*n* pl. -S an ornamental stand
ETALON	*n* pl. -S an optical instrument
ETAMIN	*n* pl. -S etamine
ETAMINE	*n* pl. -S a loosely woven fabric
ETAPE	*n* pl. -S a warehouse
ETATISM	*n* pl. -S state socialism **ETATIST** *adj*
ETCETERA	*n* pl. -S a number of additional items
ETCH	*v* -ED, -ING, -ES to engrave with acid
ETCHANT	*n* pl. -S a substance used in etching
ETCHER	*n* pl. -S one that etches
ETCHING	*n* pl. -S an etched design
ETERNAL	*n* pl. -S something lasting forever
ETERNE	*adj* everlasting
ETERNISE	*v* -NISED, -NISING, -NISES to eternize
ETERNITY	*n* pl. -TIES infinite time
ETERNIZE	*v* -NIZED, -NIZING, -NIZES to make everlasting
ETESIAN	*n* pl. -S an annually recurring wind
ETH	*n* pl. -S edh
ETHANE	*n* pl. -S a gaseous hydrocarbon
ETHANOL	*n* pl. -S an alcohol
ETHENE	*n* pl. -S ethylene
ETHEPHON	*n* pl. -S a synthetic plant growth regulator
ETHER	*n* pl. -S a volatile liquid used as an anesthetic **ETHERIC** *adj*
ETHEREAL	*adj* airy
ETHERIFY	*v* -FIED, -FYING, -FIES to convert into ether
ETHERISH	*adj* resembling ether
ETHERIZE	*v* -IZED, -IZING, -IZES to treat with ether
ETHIC	*n* pl. -S a body of moral principles
ETHICAL	*n* pl. -S a drug sold by prescription only
ETHICIAN	*n* pl. -S an ethicist
ETHICIST	*n* pl. -S a specialist in ethics
ETHICIZE	*v* -CIZED, -CIZING, -CIZES to make ethical
ETHINYL	*n* pl. -S ethynyl
ETHION	*n* pl. -S a pesticide
ETHMOID	*n* pl. -S a bone of the nasal cavity
ETHNARCH	*n* pl. -S the ruler of a people or province
ETHNIC	*n* pl. -S a member of a particular ethnos **ETHNICAL** *adj*
ETHNOS	*n* pl. -ES a group of people who share a common and distinctive culture
ETHOLOGY	*n* pl. -GIES the study of animal behavior
ETHOS	*n* pl. -ES the fundamental character of a culture
ETHOXY	*n* pl. -OXIES ethoxyl
ETHOXYL	*n* pl. -S a univalent chemical radical
ETHYL	*n* pl. -S a univalent chemical radical
ETHYLATE	*v* -ATED, -ATING, -ATES to introduce the ethyl group into
ETHYLENE	*n* pl. -S a flammable gas
ETHYLIC	*adj* pertaining to ethyl
ETHYNE	*n* pl. -S a flammable gas
ETHYNYL	*n* pl. -S a univalent chemical radical

ETIC	*adj* relating to a type of linguistic analysis
ETIOLATE	*v* -LATED, -LATING, -LATES to whiten
ETIOLOGY	*n* pl. -GIES the study of the causes of diseases
ETNA	*n* pl. -S a container for heating liquids
ETOILE	*n* pl. -S a star
ETOUFFEE	*n* pl. -S a Cajun stew
ETUDE	*n* pl. -S a piece of music for the practice of a point of technique
ETUI	*n* pl. -S a case for holding small articles
ETWEE	*n* pl. -S etui
ETYMON	*n* pl. -MA or -MONS the earliest known form of a word
EUCAINE	*n* pl. -S an anesthetic
EUCALYPT	*n* pl. -S an evergreen tree
EUCHARIS	*n* pl. -RISES a flowering plant
EUCHRE	*v* -CHRED, -CHRING, -CHRES to prevent from winning three tricks in euchre (a card game)
EUCLASE	*n* pl. -S a mineral
EUCRITE	*n* pl. -S a type of meteorite **EUCRITIC** *adj*
EUDAEMON	*n* pl. -S eudemon
EUDEMON	*n* pl. -S a good spirit
EUGENIA	*n* pl. -S a tropical evergreen tree
EUGENICS	*n/pl* the science of hereditary improvement **EUGENIC** *adj*
EUGENIST	*n* pl. -S a student of eugenics
EUGENOL	*n* pl. -S an aromatic liquid
EUGLENA	*n* pl. -S a freshwater protozoan
EULACHAN	*n* pl. -S eulachon
EULACHON	*n* pl. -S a marine food fish
EULOGIA	*n* pl. -GIAE holy bread
EULOGIA	*n* pl. -S a blessing
EULOGIES	pl. of eulogy
EULOGISE	*v* -GISED, -GISING, -GISES to eulogize
EULOGIST	*n* pl. -S one that eulogizes
EULOGIUM	*n* pl. -GIA or -GIUMS a eulogy
EULOGIZE	*v* -GIZED, -GIZING, -GIZES to praise highly
EULOGY	*n* pl. -GIES a formal expression of high praise
EUNUCH	*n* pl. -S a castrated man
EUONYMUS	*n* pl. -ES any of a genus of shrubs or small trees
EUPATRID	*n* pl. -RIDS or -RIDAE an aristocrat of ancient Athens
EUPEPSIA	*n* pl. -S good digestion **EUPEPTIC** *adj*
EUPEPSY	*n* pl. -SIES eupepsia
EUPHENIC	*adj* dealing with biological improvement
EUPHONY	*n* pl. -NIES pleasant sound **EUPHONIC** *adj*
EUPHORIA	*n* pl. -S a feeling of well-being **EUPHORIC** *adj*
EUPHOTIC	*adj* pertaining to the upper layer of a body of water
EUPHRASY	*n* pl. -SIES an annual herb
EUPHROE	*n* pl. -S a device used to adjust a shipboard awning
EUPHUISM	*n* pl. -S an artificially elegant style of speech or writing
EUPHUIST	*n* pl. -S one given to euphuism
EUPLOID	*n* pl. -S a cell having three or more identical genomes
EUPLOIDY	*n* pl. -DIES the state of being a euploid
EUPNEA	*n* pl. -S normal breathing **EUPNEIC** *adj*
EUPNOEA	*n* pl. -S eupnea **EUPNOEIC** *adj*
EUREKA	*interj* — used to express triumph upon discovering something
EURIPUS	*n* pl. -PI a swift sea channel
EURO	*n* pl. EUROS a large kangaroo
EUROKY	*n* pl. -KIES the ability of an organism to live under variable conditions **EUROKOUS** *adj*
EUROPIUM	*n* pl. -S a metallic element
EURYBATH	*n* pl. -S an organism that can live in a wide range of water depths
EURYOKY	*n* pl. -KIES euroky
EURYTHMY	*n* pl. -MIES harmony of movement or structure
EUSTACY	*n* pl. -CIES a worldwide change in sea level **EUSTATIC** *adj*
EUSTELE	*n* pl. -S a plant part
EUTAXY	*n* pl. -TAXIES good order
EUTECTIC	*n* pl. -S an alloy that has the lowest possible melting point
EUTROPHY	*n* pl. -PHIES healthful nutrition
EUXENITE	*n* pl. -S a mineral
EVACUANT	*n* pl. -S a cathartic medicine

EVACUATE	*v* -ATED, -ATING, -ATES to remove from a dangerous area
EVACUEE	*n* pl. -S one that is evacuated
EVADE	*v* EVADED, EVADING, EVADES to escape or avoid by cleverness or deceit **EVADABLE, EVADIBLE** *adj*
EVADER	*n* pl. -S one that evades
EVALUATE	*v* -ATED, -ATING, -ATES to determine the value of
EVANESCE	*v* -NESCED, -NESCING, -NESCES to fade away
EVANGEL	*n* pl. -S a preacher of the gospel
EVANISH	*v* -ED, -ING, -ES to vanish
EVASION	*n* pl. -S the act of evading
EVASIVE	*adj* tending to evade
EVE	*n* pl. -S evening
EVECTION	*n* pl. -S irregularity in the moon's motion
EVEN	*adj* EVENER, EVENEST flat and smooth
EVEN	*v* -ED, -ING, -S to make even
EVENER	*n* pl. -S one that evens
EVENFALL	*n* pl. -S twilight
EVENING	*n* pl. -S the latter part of the day and early part of the night
EVENLY	*adv* in an even manner
EVENNESS	*n* pl. -ES the state of being even
EVENSONG	*n* pl. -S an evening prayer service
EVENT	*n* pl. -S something that occurs
EVENTFUL	*adj* momentous
EVENTIDE	*n* pl. -S evening
EVENTUAL	*adj* occurring at a later time
EVER	*adv* at all times
EVERMORE	*adv* forever
EVERSION	*n* pl -S the act of everting
EVERT	*v* -ED, -ING, -S to turn outward or inside out
EVERTOR	*n* pl. -S a muscle that turns a part outward
EVERY	*adj* each without exception
EVERYDAY	*adj* ordinary
EVERYMAN	*n* pl. -MEN the typical or ordinary man
EVERYONE	*pron* every person
EVERYWAY	*adv* in every way
EVICT	*v* -ED, -ING, -S to expel by legal process
EVICTEE	*n* pl. -S one that is evicted
EVICTION	*n* pl. -S the act of evicting
EVICTOR	*n* pl. -S one that evicts
EVIDENCE	*v* -DENCED, -DENCING, -DENCES to indicate clearly
EVIDENT	*adj* clear to the vision or understanding
EVIL	*adj* EVILER, EVILEST or EVILLER, EVILLEST morally bad
EVIL	*n* pl. -S something that is evil
EVILDOER	*n* pl. -S one that does evil
EVILLER	a comparative of evil
EVILLEST	a superlative of evil
EVILLY	*adv* in an evil manner
EVILNESS	*n* pl. -ES the quality of being evil
EVINCE	*v* EVINCED, EVINCING, EVINCES to show clearly **EVINCIVE** *adj*
EVITE	*v* EVITED, EVITING, EVITES to avoid **EVITABLE** *adj*
EVOCABLE	*adj* capable of being evoked
EVOCATOR	*n* pl. -S one that evokes
EVOKE	*v* EVOKED, EVOKING, EVOKES to call forth
EVOKER	*n* pl. -S an evocator
EVOLUTE	*n* pl. -S a type of geometric curve
EVOLVE	*v* EVOLVED, EVOLVING, EVOLVES to develop
EVOLVER	*n* pl. -S one that evolves
EVONYMUS	*n* pl. -ES euonymus
EVULSION	*n* pl. -S the act of pulling out
EVZONE	*n* pl. -S a Greek soldier
EWE	*n* pl. -S a female sheep
EWER	*n* pl. -S a large pitcher
EX	*n* pl. -ES the letter X
EXACT	*adj* -ACTER, -ACTEST precise
EXACT	*v* -ED, -ING, -S to force the payment or yielding of
EXACTA	*n* pl. -S a type of horse racing bet
EXACTER	*n* pl. -S one that exacts
EXACTION	*n* pl. -S the act of exacting
EXACTLY	*adv* in an exact manner
EXACTOR	*n* pl. -S exacter
EXALT	*v* -ED, -ING, -S to raise
EXALTER	*n* pl. -S one that exalts
EXAM	*n* pl. -S an examination
EXAMEN	*n* pl. -S a critical study

EXAMINE	v -INED, -INING, -INES to inspect
EXAMINEE	n pl. -S one that is taking an examination
EXAMINER	n pl. -S one that examines
EXAMINING	present participle of examine
EXAMPLE	v -PLED, -PLING, -PLES to show by representation
EXANTHEM	n pl. -S a skin eruption
EXARCH	n pl. -S the ruler of a province in the Byzantine Empire **EXARCHAL** adj
EXARCHY	n pl. -CHIES the domain of an exarch
EXCAVATE	v -VATED, -VATING, -VATES to dig out
EXCEED	v -ED, -ING, -S to go beyond
EXCEEDER	n pl. -S one that exceeds
EXCEL	v -CELLED, -CELLING, -CELS to surpass others
EXCEPT	v -ED, -ING, -S to leave out
EXCERPT	v -ED, -ING, -S to pick out a passage from for quoting
EXCESS	v -ED, -ING, -ES to eliminate the position of
EXCHANGE	v -CHANGED, -CHANGING, -CHANGES to give and receive reciprocally
EXCIDE	v -CIDED, -CIDING, -CIDES to excise
EXCIMER	n pl. -S a dimer that exists in an excited state
EXCIPLE	n pl. -S a rim around the hymenium of various lichens
EXCISE	v -CISED, -CISING, -CISES to remove by cutting out
EXCISION	n pl. -S the act of excising
EXCITANT	n pl. -S a stimulant
EXCITE	v -CITED, -CITING, -CITES to arouse the emotions of
EXCITER	n pl. -S one that excites
EXCITON	n pl. -S a phenomenon occurring in an excited crystal
EXCITOR	n pl. -S exciter
EXCLAIM	v -ED, -ING, -S to cry out suddenly
EXCLAVE	n pl. -S a portion of a country which is isolated in foreign territory
EXCLUDE	v -CLUDED, -CLUDING, -CLUDES to shut out
EXCLUDER	n pl. -S one that excludes
EXCRETA	n/pl excreted matter **EXCRETAL** adj
EXCRETE	v -CRETED, -CRETING, -CRETES to separate and eliminate from an organic body
EXCRETER	n pl. -S one that excretes
EXCURSUS	n pl. -ES a long appended exposition of a topic
EXCUSE	v -CUSED, -CUSING, -CUSES to apologize for
EXCUSER	n pl. -S one that excuses
EXEC	n pl. -S an executive officer
EXECRATE	v -CRATED, -CRATING, -CRATES to curse
EXECUTE	v -CUTED, -CUTING, -CUTES to carry out
EXECUTER	n pl. -S executor
EXECUTOR	n pl. -S one that executes
EXEDRA	n pl. -DRAE a curved outdoor bench
EXEGESIS	n pl. -GESES critical explanation or analysis **EXEGETIC** adj
EXEGETE	n pl. -S one skilled in exegesis
EXEMPLAR	n pl. -S one that is worthy of being copied
EXEMPLUM	n pl. -PLA an example
EXEMPT	v -ED, -ING, -S to free from an obligation required of others
EXEQUY	n pl. -QUIES a funeral procession **EXEQUIAL** adj
EXERCISE	v -CISED, -CISING, -CISES to make use of
EXERGUE	n pl. -S a space on a coin **EXERGUAL** adj
EXERT	v -ED, -ING, -S to put into action
EXERTION	n pl. -S the act of exerting
EXERTIVE	adj tending to exert
EXEUNT	v they leave the stage — used as a stage direction
EXHALANT	n pl. -S something that exhales
EXHALE	v -HALED, -HALING, -HALES to expel air or vapor
EXHALENT	n pl. -S exhalant
EXHAUST	v -ED, -ING, -S to use up
EXHIBIT	v -ED, -ING, -S to present for public viewing
EXHORT	v -ED, -ING, -S to advise urgently
EXHORTER	n pl. -S one that exhorts

EXHUME	*v* -HUMED, -HUMING, -HUMES to dig out of the earth
EXHUMER	*n* pl. -S one that exhumes
EXIGENCE	*n* pl. -S exigency
EXIGENCY	*n* pl. -CIES urgency
EXIGENT	*adj* urgent
EXIGIBLE	*adj* liable to be demanded
EXIGUITY	*n* pl. -ITIES the state of being exiguous
EXIGUOUS	*adj* meager
EXILE	*v* -ILED, -ILING, -ILES to banish from one's own country
EXILIAN	*adj* exilic
EXILIC	*adj* pertaining to exile (banishment from one's own country)
EXILING	present participle of exile
EXIMIOUS	*adj* excellent
EXINE	*n* pl. -S the outer layer of certain spores
EXIST	*v* -ED, -ING, -S to be
EXISTENT	*n* pl. -S something that exists
EXIT	*v* -ED, -ING, -S to go out
EXITLESS	*adj* lacking a way out
EXOCARP	*n* pl. -S the epicarp
EXOCRINE	*n* pl. -S an external secretion
EXODERM	*n* pl. -S the ectoderm
EXODOS	*n* pl. -DOI a concluding dramatic scene
EXODUS	*n* pl. -ES a movement away
EXOERGIC	*adj* releasing energy
EXOGAMY	*n* pl. -MIES marriage outside of a particular group **EXOGAMIC** *adj*
EXOGEN	*n* pl. -S a type of plant
EXON	*n* pl. -S a sequence in the genetic code **EXONIC** *adj*
EXONUMIA	*n/pl* numismatic items other than coins or paper money
EXORABLE	*adj* persuadable
EXORCISE	*v* -CISED, -CISING, -CISES to free of an evil spirit
EXORCISM	*n* pl. -S the act of exorcising
EXORCIST	*n* pl. -S one who practices exorcism
EXORCIZE	*v* -CIZED, -CIZING, -CIZES to exorcise
EXORDIUM	*n* pl. -DIUMS or -DIA a beginning **EXORDIAL** *adj*
EXOSMOSE	*n* pl. -S a form of osmosis **EXOSMIC** *adj*
EXOSPORE	*n* pl. -S the outer coat of a spore
EXOTERIC	*adj* suitable for the public
EXOTIC	*n* pl. -S something from another part of the world
EXOTICA	*n/pl* things excitingly different or unusual
EXOTISM	*n* pl. -S an exotic
EXOTOXIN	*n* pl. -S an excreted toxin **EXOTOXIC** *adj*
EXPAND	*v* -ED, -ING, -S to increase in size or volume
EXPANDER	*n* pl. -S one that expands
EXPANDOR	*n* pl. -S a type of transducer
EXPANSE	*n* pl. -S a wide, continuous area
EXPAT	*n* pl. -S an expatriate person
EXPECT	*v* -ED, -ING, -S to anticipate
EXPEDITE	*v* -DITED, -DITING, -DITES to speed up the progress of
EXPEL	*v* -PELLED, -PELLING, -PELS to force out
EXPELLEE	*n* pl. -S a deportee
EXPELLER	*n* pl. -S one that expels
EXPELLING	present participle of expel
EXPEND	*v* -ED, -ING, -S to use up
EXPENDER	*n* pl. -S one that expends
EXPENSE	*v* -PENSED, -PENSING, -PENSES to charge with costs
EXPERT	*v* -ED, -ING, -S to serve as an authority
EXPERTLY	*adv* skillfully
EXPIABLE	*adj* capable of being expiated
EXPIATE	*v* -ATED, -ATING, -ATES to atone for
EXPIATOR	*n* pl. -S one that expiates
EXPIRE	*v* -PIRED, -PIRING, -PIRES to come to an end
EXPIRER	*n* pl. -S one that expires
EXPIRY	*n* pl. -RIES a termination
EXPLAIN	*v* -ED, -ING, -S to make plain or understandable
EXPLANT	*v* -ED, -ING, -S to remove from the natural site of growth and place in a medium
EXPLICIT	*n* pl. -S a statement formerly used at the close of a book
EXPLODE	*v* -PLODED, -PLODING, -PLODES to blow up

EXPLODER

EXPLODER *n* pl. -S one that explodes

EXPLOIT *v* -ED, -ING, -S to take advantage of

EXPLORE *v* -PLORED, -PLORING, -PLORES to travel through for the purpose of discovery

EXPLORER *n* pl. -S one that explores

EXPO *n* pl. -POS a public exhibition

EXPONENT *n* pl. -S one who expounds

EXPORT *v* -ED, -ING, -S to send to other countries for commercial purposes

EXPORTER *n* pl. -S one that exports

EXPOSAL *n* pl. -S an exposure

EXPOSE *v* -POSED, -POSING, -POSES to lay open to view

EXPOSER *n* pl. -S one that exposes

EXPOSIT *v* -ED, -ING, -S to expound

EXPOSURE *n* pl. -S the act of exposing

EXPOUND *v* -ED, -ING, -S to explain in detail

EXPRESS *v* -ED, -ING, -ES to set forth in words

EXPRESSO *n* pl. -SOS espresso

EXPULSE *v* -PULSED, -PULSING, -PULSES to expel

EXPUNGE *v* -PUNGED, -PUNGING, -PUNGES to delete

EXPUNGER *n* pl. -S one that expunges

EXSCIND *v* -ED, -ING, -S to cut out

EXSECANT *n* pl. -S a trigonometric function of an angle

EXSECT *v* -ED, -ING, -S to cut out

EXSERT *v* -ED, -ING, -S to thrust out

EXTANT *adj* still in existence

EXTEND *v* -ED, -ING, -S to stretch out to full length

EXTENDER *n* pl. -S a substance added to another substance

EXTENSOR *n* pl. -S a muscle that extends a limb

EXTENT *n* pl. -S the range over which something extends

EXTERIOR *n* pl. -S a part or surface that is outside

EXTERN *n* pl. -S a nonresident of an institution

EXTERNAL *n* pl. -S an exterior

EXTERNE *n* pl. -S extern

EXTINCT *v* -ED, -ING, -S to extinguish

EXTOL *v* -TOLLED, -TOLLING, -TOLS to praise highly

EXTOLL *v* -ED, -ING, -S to extol

EXTOLLER *n* pl. -S one that extols

EXTOLLING present participle of extol

EXTORT *v* -ED, -ING, -S to obtain from a person by violence or intimidation

EXTORTER *n* pl. -S one that extorts

EXTRA *n* pl. -S something additional

EXTRACT *v* -ED, -ING, -S to pull or draw out

EXTRADOS *n* pl. -ES the outer curve of an arch

EXTREMA pl. of extremum

EXTREME *adj* -TREMER, -TREMEST existing in a very high degree

EXTREME *n* pl. -S the highest degree

EXTREMUM *n* pl. -MA a maximum or a minimum of a mathematical function

EXTRORSE *adj* facing outward

EXTRUDE *v* -TRUDED, -TRUDING, -TRUDES to force, thrust, or push out

EXTRUDER *n* pl. -S one that extrudes

EXTUBATE *v* -BATED, -BATING, -BATES to remove a tube from

EXUDATE *n* pl. -S an exuded substance

EXUDE *v* -UDED, -UDING, -UDES to ooze forth

EXULT *v* -ED, -ING, -S to rejoice greatly

EXULTANT *adj* exulting

EXURB *n* pl. -S a residential area lying beyond the suburbs of a city **EXURBAN** *adj*

EXURBIA *n* pl. -S an exurb

EXUVIATE *v* -ATED, -ATING, -ATES to molt

EXUVIUM *n* pl. -VIAE or -VIA the molted covering of an animal **EXUVIAL** *adj*

EYAS *n* pl. -ES a young hawk

EYE *v* EYED, EYING or EYEING, EYES to watch closely **EYEABLE** *adj*

EYE *n* pl. EYES, EYEN or EYNE the organ of sight

EYEBALL *v* -ED, -ING, -S to eye

EYEBAR *n* pl. -S a metal bar with a loop at one or both ends

EYEBEAM *n* pl. -S a glance

EYEBOLT	*n* pl. -S a type of bolt or screw	**EYER**	*n* pl. -S one that eyes
EYEBROW	*n* pl. -S the ridge over the eye	**EYESHADE**	*n* pl. -S a visor for shading the eyes
EYECUP	*n* pl. -S a cup used for applying lotions to the eyes	**EYESHOT**	*n* pl. -S the range of vision
EYED	past tense of eye	**EYESIGHT**	*n* pl. -S the ability to see
EYEDNESS	*n* pl. -ES preference for the use of one eye over the other	**EYESOME**	*adj* pleasant to look at
EYEDROPS	*n/pl* a medicated solution for the eyes applied in drops	**EYESORE**	*n* pl. -S something offensive to the sight
EYEFUL	*n* pl. -S a complete view	**EYESPOT**	*n* pl. -S a simple visual organ of lower animals
EYEGLASS	*n* pl. -ES a lens used to aid vision	**EYESTALK**	*n* pl. -S a stalklike structure with an eye at its tip
EYEHOLE	*n* pl. -S a small opening	**EYESTONE**	*n* pl. -S a disk used to remove foreign matter from the eye
EYEHOOK	*n* pl. -S a type of hook		
EYELASH	*n* pl. -ES a hair growing on the edge of an eyelid	**EYETOOTH**	*n* pl. -TEETH a cuspid
EYELESS	*adj* lacking eyes	**EYEWASH**	*n* pl. -ES an eye lotion
EYELET	*v* -LETTED, -LETTING, -LETS to make a small hole in	**EYEWATER**	*n* pl. -S an eyewash
		EYEWEAR	*n* pl. EYEWEAR a device worn on or over the eyes
EYELID	*n* pl. -S the lid of skin that can be closed over an eyeball	**EYEWINK**	*n* pl. -S a wink of the eye
EYELIKE	*adj* resembling an eye	**EYING**	a present participle of eye
EYELINER	*n* pl. -S makeup for the eyes	**EYNE**	a pl. of eye
EYEN	a pl. of eye	**EYRA**	*n* pl. -S a wild cat of tropical America
EYEPIECE	*n* pl. -S the lens or lens group nearest the eye in an optical instrument	**EYRE**	*n* pl. -S a journey
		EYRIE	*n* pl. -S aerie
EYEPOINT	*n* pl. -S the point at which an eye is placed in using an optical instrument	**EYRIR**	*n* pl. AURAR a monetary unit of Iceland
		EYRY	*n* pl. -RIES aerie

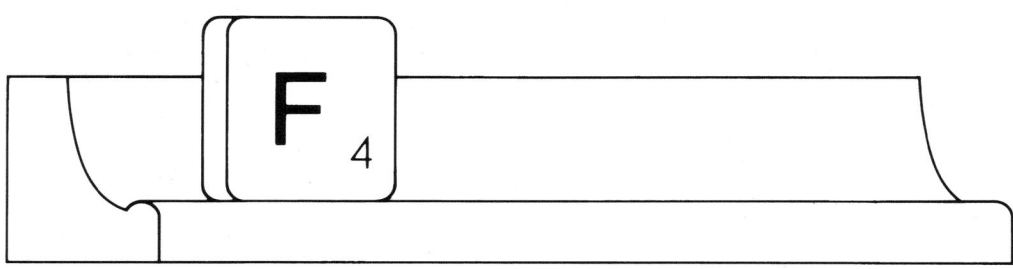

FA	*n* pl. -S the fourth tone of the diatonic musical scale
FABLE	*v* -BLED, -BLING, -BLES to compose or tell fictitious tales
FABLER	*n* pl. -S one that fables
FABLIAU	*n* pl. -AUX a short metrical tale popular in medieval France
FABLING	present participle of fable
FABRIC	*n* pl. -S a woven, felted, or knitted material
FABULAR	*adj* legendary
FABULIST	*n* pl. -S a liar
FABULOUS	*adj* almost unbelievable
FACADE	*n* pl. -S the front of a building
FACE	*v* FACED, FACING, FACES to oppose or meet defiantly **FACEABLE** *adj*
FACEDOWN	*adv* with the front part down
FACELESS	*adj* lacking personal distinction or identity
FACER	*n* pl. -S one that faces
FACET	*v* -ETED, -ETING, -ETS or -ETTED, -ETTING, -ETS to cut small plane surfaces on
FACETE	*adj* witty **FACETELY** *adv*
FACETIAE	*n/pl* witty sayings or writings
FACETTED	a past tense of facet
FACETTING	a present participle of facet
FACEUP	*adv* with the front part up
FACIA	*n* pl. -S fascia
FACIAL	*n* pl. -S a treatment for the face
FACIALLY	*adv* with respect to the face
FACIEND	*n* pl. -S a number to be multiplied by another
FACIES	*n* pl. FACIES general appearance
FACILE	*adj* easily achieved or performed **FACILELY** *adv*
FACILITY	*n* pl. -TIES the quality of being facile
FACING	*n* pl. -S a lining at the edge of a garment
FACT	*n* pl. -S something known with certainty **FACTFUL** *adj*
FACTION	*n* pl. -S a clique within a larger group
FACTIOUS	*adj* promoting dissension
FACTOID	*n* pl. -S a brief news item
FACTOR	*v* -ED, -ING, -S to express as a product of two or more quantities
FACTORY	*n* pl. -RIES a building or group of buildings in which goods are manufactured
FACTOTUM	*n* pl. -S a person employed to do many kinds of work
FACTUAL	*adj* pertaining to facts
FACTURE	*n* pl. -S the act of making something
FACULA	*n* pl. -LAE an unusually bright spot on the sun's surface **FACULAR** *adj*
FACULTY	*n* pl. -TIES an inherent power or ability
FAD	*n* pl. -S a practice or interest that enjoys brief popularity
FADABLE	*adj* capable of fading
FADDIER	comparative of faddy
FADDIEST	superlative of faddy
FADDISH	*adj* inclined to take up fads
FADDISM	*n* pl. -S inclination to take up fads
FADDIST	*n* pl. -S a faddish person
FADDY	*adj* -DIER, -DIEST faddish
FADE	*v* FADED, FADING, FADES to lose color or brightness **FADEDLY** *adv*
FADEAWAY	*n* pl. -AWAYS a type of pitch in baseball
FADELESS	*adj* not fading

FADER	*n* pl. -S one that fades
FADGE	*v* FADGED, FADGING, FADGES to succeed
FADING	*n* pl. -S an Irish dance
FADO	*n* pl. -DOS a Portuguese folk song
FAECES	*n/pl* feces **FAECAL** *adj*
FAENA	*n* pl. -S a series of passes made by a matador in a bullfight
FAERIE	*n* pl. -S a fairy
FAERY	*n* pl. -ERIES faerie
FAG	*v* FAGGED, FAGGING, FAGS to make weary by hard work
FAGGOT	*v* -ED, -ING, -S to fagot
FAGIN	*n* pl. -S a person who instructs others in crime
FAGOT	*v* -ED, -ING, -S to bind together into a bundle
FAGOTER	*n* pl. -S one that fagots
FAGOTING	*n* pl. -S a type of embroidery
FAHLBAND	*n* pl. -S a band or stratum of rock impregnated with metallic sulfides
FAIENCE	*n* pl. -S a variety of glazed pottery
FAIL	*v* -ED, -ING, -S to be unsuccessful in an attempt
FAILING	*n* pl. -S a minor fault or weakness
FAILLE	*n* pl. -S a woven fabric
FAILURE	*n* pl. -S the act of failing
FAIN	*adj* FAINER, FAINEST glad
FAINEANT	*n* pl. -S a lazy person
FAINT	*v* -ED, -ING, -S to lose consciousness
FAINT	*adj* FAINTER, FAINTEST lacking strength or vigor
FAINTER	*n* pl. -S one that faints
FAINTISH	*adj* somewhat faint
FAINTLY	*adv* in a faint manner
FAIR	*adj* FAIRER, FAIREST free from bias, dishonesty, or injustice
FAIR	*v* -ED, -ING, -S to make smooth
FAIRIES	pl. of fairy
FAIRING	*n* pl. -S a structure on an aircraft serving to reduce drag
FAIRISH	*adj* moderately good
FAIRLEAD	*n* pl. -S a device used to hold a ship's rigging in place
FAIRLY	*adv* in a fair manner

FAIRNESS	*n* pl. -ES the quality of being fair
FAIRWAY	*n* pl. -WAYS the mowed part of a golf course between tee and green
FAIRY	*n* pl. FAIRIES an imaginary supernatural being
FAIRYISM	*n* pl. -S the quality of being like a fairy
FAITH	*v* -ED, -ING, -S to believe or trust
FAITHFUL	*n* pl. -S a loyal follower or member
FAITOUR	*n* pl. -S an impostor
FAJITA	*n* pl. -S marinated and grilled beef, chicken, or shrimp served with a flour tortilla
FAKE	*v* FAKED, FAKING, FAKES to contrive and present as genuine
FAKEER	*n* pl. -S fakir
FAKER	*n* pl. -S one that fakes
FAKERY	*n* pl. -ERIES the practice of faking
FAKEY	*adj* not genuine; phony
FAKING	present participle of fake
FAKIR	*n* pl. -S a Hindu ascetic
FALAFEL	*n* pl. FALAFEL ground spiced vegetables formed into patties
FALBALA	*n* pl. -S a trimming for a woman's garment
FALCATE	*adj* curved and tapering to a point
FALCATED	*adj* falcate
FALCES	pl. of falx
FALCHION	*n* pl. -S a broad-bladed sword
FALCON	*n* pl. -S a bird of prey
FALCONER	*n* pl. -S one that hunts with hawks
FALCONET	*n* pl. -S a small falcon
FALCONRY	*n* pl. -RIES the sport of hunting with falcons
FALDERAL	*n* pl. -S nonsense
FALDEROL	*n* pl. -S falderal
FALL	*v* FELL, FALLEN, FALLING, FALLS to descend under the force of gravity
FALLACY	*n* pl. -CIES a false idea
FALLAL	*n* pl. -S a showy article of dress
FALLAWAY	*n* pl. -AWAYS a shot in basketball
FALLBACK	*n* pl. -S an act of retreating
FALLEN	past participle of fall

FALLER	*n* pl. -S one that falls	**FANCIFUL**	*adj* unrealistic
FALLFISH	*n* pl. -ES a freshwater fish	**FANCIFY**	*v* -FIED, -FYING, -FIES to make fancy
FALLIBLE	*adj* capable of erring **FALLIBLY** *adv*	**FANCY**	*adj* -CIER, -CIEST ornamental **FANCILY** *adv*
FALLOFF	*n* pl. -S a decline in quantity or quality	**FANCY**	*v* -CIED, -CYING, -CIES to take a liking to
FALLOUT	*n* pl. -S radioactive debris resulting from a nuclear explosion	**FANDANGO**	*n* pl. -GOS a lively Spanish dance
FALLOW	*v* -ED, -ING, -S to plow and leave unseeded	**FANDOM**	*n* pl. -S an aggregate of enthusiastic devotees
FALSE	*adj* FALSER, FALSEST contrary to truth or fact **FALSELY** *adv*	**FANE**	*n* pl. -S a temple
FALSETTO	*n* pl. -TOS an artificially high voice	**FANEGA**	*n* pl. -S a Spanish unit of dry measure
FALSIE	*n* pl. -S a pad worn within a brassiere	**FANEGADA**	*n* pl. -S a Spanish unit of area
FALSIFY	*v* -FIED, -FYING, -FIES to represent falsely	**FANFARE**	*n* pl. -S a short, lively musical flourish
FALSITY	*n* pl. -TIES something false	**FANFARON**	*n* pl. -S a braggart
FALTBOAT	*n* pl. -S a collapsible boat resembling a kayak	**FANFOLD**	*v* -ED, -ING, -S to fold paper like a fan
FALTER	*v* -ED, -ING, -S to hesitate	**FANG**	*n* pl. -S a long, pointed tooth **FANGED, FANGLESS, FANGLIKE** *adj*
FALTERER	*n* pl. -S one that falters		
FALX	*n* pl. FALCES a sickle-shaped structure	**FANGA**	*n* pl. -S fanega
		FANION	*n* pl. -S a small flag
FAME	*v* FAMED, FAMING, FAMES to make famous	**FANJET**	*n* pl. -S a type of jet engine
FAMELESS	*adj* not famous	**FANLIGHT**	*n* pl. -S a type of window
FAMILIAL	*adj* pertaining to a family	**FANLIKE**	*adj* resembling a fan
FAMILIAR	*n* pl. -S a close friend or associate	**FANNED**	past tense of fan
		FANNER	*n* pl. -S one that fans
FAMILISM	*n* pl. -S a social structure in which the family takes precedence over the individual	**FANNING**	present participle of fan
		FANNY	*n* pl. -NIES the buttocks
FAMILY	*n* pl. -LIES a group of persons related by blood or marriage	**FANO**	*n* pl. FANOS a fanon
		FANON	*n* pl. -S a cape worn by the pope
FAMINE	*n* pl. -S a widespread scarcity of food	**FANTAIL**	*n* pl. -S a fan-shaped tail or end
		FANTASIA	*n* pl. -S a free-form musical composition
FAMING	present participle of fame		
FAMISH	*v* -ED, -ING, -ES to suffer extreme hunger	**FANTASIE**	*n* pl. -S a fantasia
		FANTASIED	past tense of fantasy
FAMOUS	*adj* well-known **FAMOUSLY** *adv*	**FANTASIES**	present 3d person sing. of fantasy
FAMULUS	*n* pl. -LI a servant or attendant	**FANTASM**	*n* pl. -S phantasm
FAN	*v* FANNED, FANNING, FANS to cool or refresh with a fan (a device for putting air into motion)	**FANTAST**	*n* pl. -S an impractical person
		FANTASY	*v* -SIED, -SYING, -SIES to imagine
FANATIC	*n* pl. -S a zealot		
FANCIED	past tense of fancy	**FANTOD**	*n* pl. -S an emotional outburst
FANCIER	*n* pl. -S one that has a special liking for something	**FANTOM**	*n* pl. -S phantom
FANCIES	present 3d person sing. of fancy	**FANUM**	*n* pl. -S fanon

FANWISE	*adj* spread out like an open fan
FANWORT	*n* pl. -S an aquatic plant
FANZINE	*n* pl. -S a magazine written by and for enthusiastic devotees
FAQIR	*n* pl. -S fakir
FAQUIR	*n* pl. -S fakir
FAR	*adv* FARTHER, FARTHEST or FURTHER, FURTHEST at or to a great distance
FARAD	*n* pl. -S a unit of electrical capacitance
FARADAIC	*adj* faradic
FARADAY	*n* pl. -DAYS a unit of electricity
FARADIC	*adj* pertaining to a type of electric current
FARADISE	*v* -DISED, -DISING, -DISES to faradize
FARADISM	*n* pl. -S the use of faradic current for therapeutic purposes
FARADIZE	*v* -DIZED, -DIZING, -DIZES to treat by faradism
FARAWAY	*adj* distant
FARCE	*v* FARCED, FARCING, FARCES to fill out with witty material
FARCER	*n* pl. -S farceur
FARCEUR	*n* pl. -S a joker
FARCI	*adj* stuffed with finely chopped meat
FARCICAL	*adj* absurd
FARCIE	*adj* farci
FARCING	present participle of farce
FARCY	*n* pl. -CIES a disease of horses
FARD	*v* -ED, -ING, -S to apply cosmetics to
FARDEL	*n* pl. -S a bundle
FARE	*v* FARED, FARING, FARES to get along
FARER	*n* pl. -S a traveler
FAREWELL	*v* -ED, -ING, -S to say goodby
FARFAL	*n* pl. -S farfel
FARFEL	*n* pl. -S noodles in the form of small pellets or granules
FARINA	*n* pl. -S a fine meal made from cereal grain
FARING	present participle of fare
FARINHA	*n* pl. -S a meal made from the root of the cassava
FARINOSE	*adj* resembling farina
FARL	*n* pl. -S a thin oatmeal cake

FARLE	*n* pl. -S farl
FARM	*v* -ED, -ING, -S to manage and cultivate as a farm (a tract of land devoted to agriculture) **FARMABLE** *adj*
FARMER	*n* pl. -S one that farms
FARMHAND	*n* pl. -S a farm laborer
FARMING	*n* pl. -S the business of operating a farm
FARMLAND	*n* pl. -S cultivated land
FARMWIFE	*n* pl. -WIVES a farmer's wife
FARMWORK	*n* pl. -S labor done on a farm
FARMYARD	*n* pl. -S an area surrounded by farm buildings
FARNESOL	*n* pl. -S an alcohol used in perfumes
FARNESS	*n* pl. -ES the state of being far off or apart
FARO	*n* pl. FAROS a card game
FAROUCHE	*adj* sullenly shy
FARRAGO	*n* pl. -GOES a confused mixture
FARRIER	*n* pl. -S one that shoes horses
FARRIERY	*n* pl. -ERIES the trade of a farrier
FARROW	*v* -ED, -ING, -S to give birth to a litter of pigs
FARSIDE	*n* pl. -S the farther side
FARTHER	a comparative of far
FARTHEST	a superlative of far
FARTHING	*n* pl. -S a former British coin
FASCES	*n* pl. FASCES an ancient Roman symbol of power
FASCIA	*n* pl. -CIAE or -CIAS a broad and distinct band of color **FASCIAL, FASCIATE** *adj*
FASCICLE	*n* pl. -S a small bundle
FASCINE	*n* pl. -S a bundle of sticks used in building fortifications
FASCISM	*n* pl. -S an oppressive political system
FASCIST	*n* pl. -S an advocate of fascism
FASH	*v* -ED, -ING, -ES to annoy
FASHION	*v* -ED, -ING, -S to give a particular shape or form to
FASHIOUS	*adj* annoying
FAST	*adj* FASTER, FASTEST moving or able to move quickly
FAST	*v* -ED, -ING, -S to abstain from eating
FASTBACK	*n* pl. -S a type of automobile roof

FASTBALL	*n* pl. -S a type of pitch in baseball
FASTEN	*v* -ED, -ING, -S to secure
FASTENER	*n* pl. -S one that fastens
FASTING	*n* pl. -S abstention from eating
FASTNESS	*n* pl. -ES the quality of being fast
FASTUOUS	*adj* arrogant
FAT	*adj* FATTER, FATTEST having an abundance of flesh
FAT	*v* FATTED, FATTING, FATS to make fat
FATAL	*adj* causing or capable of causing death
FATALISM	*n* pl. -S the doctrine that all events are predetermined
FATALIST	*n* pl. -S a believer in fatalism
FATALITY	*n* pl. -TIES a death resulting from an unexpected occurrence
FATALLY	*adv* in a fatal manner
FATBACK	*n* pl. -S a marine fish
FATBIRD	*n* pl. -S a wading bird
FATE	*v* FATED, FATING, FATES to destine
FATEFUL	*adj* decisively important
FATHEAD	*n* pl. -S a dolt
FATHER	*v* -ED, -ING, -S to cause to exist
FATHERLY	*adj* paternal
FATHOM	*v* -ED, -ING, -S to understand
FATIDIC	*adj* pertaining to prophecy
FATIGUE	*v* -TIGUED, -TIGUING, -TIGUES to weary
FATING	present participle of fate
FATLESS	*adj* having no fat
FATLIKE	*adj* resembling fat
FATLING	*n* pl. -S a young animal fattened for slaughter
FATLY	*adv* in the manner of one that is fat
FATNESS	*n* pl. -ES the state of being fat
FATSTOCK	*n* pl. -S livestock that is fat and ready for market
FATTED	past tense of fat
FATTEN	*v* -ED, -ING, -S to make fat
FATTENER	*n* pl. -S one that fattens
FATTER	comparative of fat
FATTEST	superlative of fat
FATTIER	comparative of fatty
FATTIES	pl. of fatty
FATTIEST	superlative of fatty
FATTILY	*adv* in a fatty manner
FATTING	present participle of fat
FATTISH	*adj* somewhat fat
FATTY	*adj* -TIER, -TIEST greasy; oily
FATTY	*n* pl. -TIES one that is fat
FATUITY	*n* pl. -ITIES something foolish or stupid
FATUOUS	*adj* smugly stupid
FATWA	*n* pl. -S an Islamic legal decree
FATWOOD	*n* pl. -S wood used for kindling
FAUBOURG	*n* pl. -S a suburb
FAUCAL	*n* pl. -S a sound produced in the fauces
FAUCES	*n/pl* the passage from the mouth to the pharynx
FAUCET	*n* pl. -S a device for controlling the flow of liquid from a pipe
FAUCIAL	*adj* pertaining to the fauces
FAUGH	*interj* — used to express disgust
FAULD	*n* pl. -S a piece of armor below the breastplate
FAULT	*v* -ED, -ING, -S to criticize
FAULTY	*adj* FAULTIER, FAULTIEST imperfect **FAULTILY** *adv*
FAUN	*n* pl. -S a woodland deity of Roman mythology **FAUNLIKE** *adj*
FAUNA	*n* pl. -NAS or -NAE the animal life of a particular region **FAUNAL** *adj* **FAUNALLY** *adv*
FAUTEUIL	*n* pl. -S an armchair
FAUVE	*n* pl. -S a fauvist
FAUVISM	*n* pl. -S a movement in painting
FAUVIST	*n* pl. -S an advocate of fauvism
FAUX	*adj* not genuine; fake
FAVA	*n* pl. -S the edible seed of a climbing vine
FAVE	*n* pl. -S a favorite
FAVELA	*n* pl. -S a slum area
FAVELLA	*n* pl. -S favela
FAVISM	*n* pl. -S an acute anemia
FAVONIAN	*adj* pertaining to the west wind
FAVOR	*v* -ED, -ING, -S to regard with approval
FAVORER	*n* pl. -S one that favors
FAVORITE	*n* pl. -S a person or thing preferred above all others
FAVOUR	*v* -ED, -ING, -S to favor

FAVOURER	*n* pl. -S favorer
FAVUS	*n* pl. -ES a skin disease
FAWN	*v* -ED, -ING, -S to seek notice or favor by servile demeanor
FAWNER	*n* pl. -S one that fawns
FAWNLIKE	*adj* resembling a young deer
FAWNY	*adj* FAWNIER, FAWNIEST of a yellowish-brown color
FAX	*v* -ED, -ING, -ES to transmit and reproduce by electronic means
FAY	*v* -ED, -ING, -S to join closely
FAYALITE	*n* pl. -S a mineral
FAZE	*v* FAZED, FAZING, FAZES to disturb the composure of
FAZENDA	*n* pl. -S a Brazilian plantation
FEAL	*adj* loyal
FEALTY	*n* pl. -TIES loyalty
FEAR	*v* -ED, -ING, -S to be afraid of
FEARER	*n* pl. -S one that fears
FEARFUL	*adj* -FULLER, -FULLEST afraid
FEARLESS	*adj* unafraid
FEARSOME	*adj* frightening
FEASANCE	*n* pl. -S the performance of a condition, obligation, or duty
FEASE	*v* FEASED, FEASING, FEASES to faze
FEASIBLE	*adj* capable of being done **FEASIBLY** *adv*
FEAST	*v* -ED, -ING, -S to eat sumptuously
FEASTER	*n* pl. -S one that feasts
FEASTFUL	*adj* festive
FEAT	*n* pl. -S a notable act or achievement
FEAT	*adj* FEATER, FEATEST skillful
FEATHER	*v* -ED, -ING, -S to cover with feathers (horny structures that form the principal covering of birds)
FEATHERY	*adj* -ERIER, -ERIEST resembling feathers
FEATLY	*adj* -LIER, -LIEST graceful
FEATURE	*v* -TURED, -TURING, -TURES to give special prominence to
FEAZE	*v* FEAZED, FEAZING, FEAZES to faze
FEBRIFIC	*adj* feverish
FEBRILE	*adj* feverish
FECAL	*adj* pertaining to feces
FECES	*n/pl* bodily waste discharged through the anus
FECIAL	*n* pl. -S fetial
FECK	*n* pl. -S value
FECKLESS	*adj* worthless
FECKLY	*adv* almost
FECULA	*n* pl. -LAE fecal matter
FECULENT	*adj* foul with impurities
FECUND	*adj* fruitful
FED	*n* pl. -S a federal agent
FEDAYEE	*n* pl. -YEEN an Arab commando
FEDERACY	*n* pl. -CIES an alliance
FEDERAL	*n* pl. -S a supporter of a type of central government
FEDERATE	*v* -ATED, -ATING, -ATES to unite in an alliance
FEDORA	*n* pl. -S a type of hat
FEE	*v* FEED, FEEING, FEES to pay a fee (a fixed charge) to
FEEBLE	*adj* -BLER, -BLEST weak **FEEBLY** *adv*
FEEBLISH	*adj* somewhat feeble
FEED	*v* FED, FEEDING, FEEDS to give food to **FEEDABLE** *adj*
FEEDBACK	*n* pl. -S the return of a portion of the output to the input
FEEDBAG	*n* pl. -S a bag for feeding horses
FEEDBOX	*n* pl. -ES a box for animal feed
FEEDER	*n* pl. -S one that feeds
FEEDHOLE	*n* pl. -S one of a series of holes in paper tape
FEEDLOT	*n* pl. -S a plot of land on which livestock is fattened
FEEL	*v* FELT, FEELING, FEELS to perceive through the sense of touch
FEELER	*n* pl. -S a tactile organ
FEELESS	*adj* requiring no fee
FEELING	*n* pl. -S the function or power of perceiving by touch
FEET	pl. of foot **FEETLESS** *adj*
FEEZE	*v* FEEZED, FEEZING, FEEZES to faze
FEH	*n* pl. -S peh
FEIGN	*v* -ED, -ING, -S to pretend
FEIGNER	*n* pl. -S one that feigns
FEIJOA	*n* pl. -S a green edible fruit
FEINT	*v* -ED, -ING, -S to make a deceptive movement

FEIRIE	*adj* nimble
FEIST	*n* pl. -S a small dog of mixed breed
FEISTY	*adj* FEISTIER, FEISTIEST full of nervous energy
FELAFEL	*n* pl. FELAFEL falafel
FELDSHER	*n* pl. -S a medical worker in Russia
FELDSPAR	*n* pl. -S a mineral
FELICITY	*n* pl. -TIES happiness
FELID	*n* pl. -S a feline
FELINE	*n* pl. -S an animal of the cat family
FELINELY	*adv* in a catlike manner
FELINITY	*n* pl. -TIES the quality of being catlike
FELL	*v* -ED, -ING, -S to cause to fall
FELL	*adj* FELLER, FELLEST cruel
FELLA	*n* pl. -S a man or boy
FELLABLE	*adj* capable of being felled
FELLAH	*n* pl. -LAHS, -LAHIN, or -LAHEEN a peasant or laborer in Arab countries
FELLATE	*v* -LATED, -LATING, -LATES to perform fellatio
FELLATIO	*n* pl. -TIOS oral stimulation of the penis
FELLATOR	*n* pl. -S one that fellates
FELLER	*n* pl. -S one that fells
FELLIES	pl. of felly
FELLNESS	*n* pl. -ES extreme cruelty
FELLOE	*n* pl. -S the rim of a wheel
FELLOW	*v* -ED, -ING, -S to produce an equal to
FELLOWLY	*adj* friendly
FELLY	*n* pl. -LIES a felloe
FELON	*n* pl. -S a person who has committed a felony
FELONRY	*n* pl. -RIES the whole class of felons
FELONY	*n* pl. -NIES a grave crime
FELSITE	*n* pl. -S an igneous rock **FELSITIC** *adj*
FELSPAR	*n* pl. -S feldspar
FELSTONE	*n* pl. -S felsite
FELT	*v* -ED, -ING, -S to mat together
FELTING	*n* pl. -S felted material
FELTLIKE	*adj* like a cloth made from wool
FELUCCA	*n* pl. -S a swift sailing vessel
FELWORT	*n* pl. -S a flowering plant
FEM	*n* pl. -S a passive homosexual
FEMALE	*n* pl. -S an individual that bears young or produces ova
FEME	*n* pl. -S a wife
FEMINACY	*n* pl. -CIES the state of being a female
FEMINIE	*n/pl* women collectively
FEMININE	*n* pl. -S a word or form having feminine gender
FEMINISE	*v* -NISED, -NISING, -NISES to feminize
FEMINISM	*n* pl. -S a doctrine advocating rights for women equal to those of men
FEMINIST	*n* pl. -S a supporter of feminism
FEMINITY	*n* pl. -TIES the quality of being womanly
FEMINIZE	*v* -NIZED, -NIZING, -NIZES to make womanly
FEMME	*n* pl. -S a woman
FEMORAL	*adj* pertaining to the femur
FEMUR	*n* pl. -MURS or -MORA a bone of the leg
FEN	*n* pl. -S a marsh
FENAGLE	*v* -GLED, -GLING, -GLES to finagle
FENCE	*v* FENCED, FENCING, FENCES to practice the art of fencing
FENCER	*n* pl. -S one that fences
FENCEROW	*n* pl. -S the land occupied by a fence
FENCIBLE	*n* pl. -S a soldier enlisted for home service only
FENCING	*n* pl. -S the art of using a sword in attack and defense
FEND	*v* -ED, -ING, -S to ward off
FENDER	*n* pl. -S a metal guard over the wheel of a motor vehicle **FENDERED** *adj*
FENESTRA	*n* pl. -TRAE a small anatomical opening
FENLAND	*n* pl. -S marshy ground
FENNEC	*n* pl. -S an African fox
FENNEL	*n* pl. -S a perennial herb
FENNY	*adj* marshy
FENTHION	*n* pl. -S an insecticide
FENURON	*n* pl. -S an herbicide
FEOD	*n* pl. -S a fief

FEODARY	*n* pl. -RIES a vassal	**FERRIED**	past tense of ferry
FEOFF	*v* -ED, -ING, -S to grant a fief to	**FERRIES**	present 3d person sing. of ferry
FEOFFEE	*n* pl. -S one to whom a fief is granted	**FERRITE**	*n* pl. -S a magnetic substance **FERRITIC** *adj*
FEOFFER	*n* pl. -S one that grants a fief to another	**FERRITIN**	*n* pl. -S a protein that contains iron
FEOFFOR	*n* pl. -S feoffer	**FERROUS**	*adj* pertaining to iron
FER	*prep* for	**FERRULE**	*v* -RULED, -RULING, -RULES to furnish with a metal ring or cap to prevent splitting
FERACITY	*n* pl. -TIES the state of being fruitful		
FERAL	*adj* wild	**FERRUM**	*n* pl. -S iron
FERBAM	*n* pl. -S a fungicide	**FERRY**	*v* -RIED, -RYING, -RIES to transport by ferry (a type of boat)
FERE	*n* pl. -S a companion		
FERETORY	*n* pl. -RIES a receptacle in which sacred relics are kept	**FERRYMAN**	*n* pl. -MEN one who operates a ferry
FERIA	*n* pl. -RIAS or -RIAE a weekday of a church calendar on which no feast is celebrated **FERIAL** *adj*	**FERTILE**	*adj* capable of reproducing
		FERULA	*n* pl. -LAE or -LAS a flat piece of wood
FERINE	*adj* feral	**FERULE**	*v* -ULED, -ULING, -ULES to ferrule
FERITY	*n* pl. -TIES wildness		
FERLIE	*n* pl. -S a strange sight	**FERVENCY**	*n* pl. -CIES fervor
FERLY	*n* pl. -LIES ferlie	**FERVENT**	*adj* marked by fervor
FERMATA	*n* pl. -TAS or -TE the sustaining of a musical note, chord, or rest beyond its written time value	**FERVID**	*adj* fervent **FERVIDLY** *adv*
		FERVOR	*n* pl. -S great warmth or intensity
		FERVOUR	*n* pl. -S fervor
FERMENT	*v* -ED, -ING, -S to undergo a type of chemical reaction	**FESCUE**	*n* pl. -S a perennial grass
		FESS	*v* -ED, -ING, -ES to confess
FERMI	*n* pl. -S a unit of length	**FESSE**	*n* pl. -S a horizontal band across the middle of a heraldic shield
FERMION	*n* pl. -S a type of atomic particle		
FERMIUM	*n* pl. -S a radioactive element	**FESSWISE**	*adv* horizontally
FERN	*n* pl. -S a flowerless vascular plant **FERNLESS, FERNLIKE** *adj*	**FESTAL**	*adj* festive **FESTALLY** *adv*
		FESTER	*v* -ED, -ING, -S to generate pus
FERNERY	*n* pl. -ERIES a place in which ferns are grown	**FESTIVAL**	*n* pl. -S a day or time of celebration
FERNY	*adj* FERNIER, FERNIEST abounding in ferns	**FESTIVE**	*adj* of or befitting a festival
		FESTOON	*v* -ED, -ING, -S to hang decorative chains or strips on
FEROCITY	*n* pl. -TIES fierceness		
FERRATE	*n* pl. -S a chemical salt	**FET**	*v* FETTED, FETTING, FETS to fetch
FERREL	*v* -RELED, -RELING, -RELS or -RELLED, -RELLING, -RELS ferrule		
		FETA	*n* pl. -S a Greek cheese
		FETAL	*adj* pertaining to a fetus
FERREOUS	*adj* containing iron	**FETATION**	*n* pl. -S the development of a fetus
FERRET	*v* -ED, -ING, -S to search out by careful investigation		
		FETCH	*v* -ED, -ING, -ES to go after and bring back
FERRETER	*n* pl. -S one that ferrets		
FERRETY	*adj* suggestive of a ferret (a polecat)	**FETCHER**	*n* pl. -S one that fetches
		FETE	*v* FETED, FETING, FETES to honor with a celebration
FERRIAGE	*n* pl. -S transportation by ferry		
FERRIC	*adj* pertaining to iron	**FETERITA**	*n* pl. -S a cereal grass

FETIAL   *n* pl. -S a priest of ancient Rome

FETIALIS   *n* pl. -LES fetial

FETICH   *n* pl. -ES fetish

FETICIDE   *n* pl. -S the killing of a fetus

FETID   *adj* having an offensive odor **FETIDLY** *adv*

FETING   present participle of fete

FETISH   *n* pl. -ES an object believed to have magical power

FETLOCK   *n* pl. -S a joint of a horse's leg

FETOLOGY   *n* pl. -GIES the branch of medicine dealing with the fetus

FETOR   *n* pl. -S an offensive odor

FETTED   past tense of fet

FETTER   *v* -ED, -ING, -S to shackle

FETTERER   *n* pl. -S one that fetters

FETTING   present participle of fet

FETTLE   *v* -TLED, -TLING, -TLES to cover the hearth of with fettling

FETTLING   *n* pl. -S loose material thrown on the hearth of a furnace to protect it

FETUS   *n* pl. -ES the unborn organism carried within the womb in the later stages of its development

FEU   *v* -ED, -ING, -S to grant land to under Scottish feudal law

FEUAR   *n* pl. -S one granted land under Scottish feudal law

FEUD   *v* -ED, -ING, -S to engage in a feud (a bitter, continuous hostility)

FEUDAL   *adj* pertaining to a political and economic system of medieval Europe **FEUDALLY** *adv*

FEUDARY   *n* pl. -RIES a vassal

FEUDIST   *n* pl. -S one that feuds

FEVER   *v* -ED, -ING, -S to affect with fever (abnormal elevation of the body temperature)

FEVERFEW   *n* pl. -S a perennial herb

FEVERISH   *adj* having a fever

FEVEROUS   *adj* feverish

FEW   *adj* FEWER, FEWEST amounting to or consisting of a small number

FEWNESS   *n* pl. -ES the state of being few

FEWTRILS   *n/pl* things of little value

FEY   *adj* FEYER, FEYEST crazy **FEYLY** *adv*

FEYNESS   *n* pl. -ES the state of being fey

FEZ   *n* pl. FEZZES or FEZES a brimless cap worn by men in the Near East **FEZZED** *adj*

FIACRE   *n* pl. -S a small carriage

FIANCE   *n* pl. -S a man engaged to be married

FIANCEE   *n* pl. -S a woman engaged to be married

FIAR   *n* pl. -S the holder of a type of absolute ownership of land under Scottish law

FIASCO   *n* pl. -COES or -CHI a wine bottle

FIASCO   *n* pl. -COES or -COS a complete failure

FIAT   *n* pl. -S an authoritative order

FIB   *v* FIBBED, FIBBING, FIBS to tell a trivial lie

FIBBER   *n* pl. -S one that fibs

FIBER   *n* pl. -S a thread or threadlike object or structure **FIBERED** *adj*

FIBERIZE   *v* -IZED, -IZING, -IZES to break into fibers

FIBRANNE   *n* pl. -S a fabric made of spun-rayon yarn

FIBRE   *n* pl. -S fiber

FIBRIL   *n* pl. -S a small fiber

FIBRILLA   *n* pl. -LAE a fibril

FIBRIN   *n* pl. -S an insoluble protein

FIBROID   *n* pl. -S a fibroma

FIBROIN   *n* pl. -S an insoluble protein

FIBROMA   *n* pl. -MAS or -MATA a benign tumor composed of fibrous tissue

FIBROSIS   *n* pl. -BROSES the development of excess fibrous tissue in a bodily organ **FIBROTIC** *adj*

FIBROUS   *adj* containing, consisting of, or resembling fibers

FIBULA   *n* pl. -LAE or -LAS a bone of the leg **FIBULAR** *adj*

FICE   *n* pl. -S a feist

FICHE   *n* pl. -S a sheet of microfilm

FICHU   *n* pl. -S a woman's scarf

FICIN   *n* pl. -S an enzyme

FICKLE   *adj* -LER, -LEST not constant or loyal **FICKLY** *adv*

FICO   *n* pl. -COES something of little worth

FICTILE   *adj* moldable

FICTION   *n* pl. -S a literary work whose content is produced by the imagination

FICTIVE	*adj* imaginary
FICUS	*n* pl. -ES a tropical tree
FID	*n* pl. -S a square bar used as a support for a topmast
FIDDLE	*v* -DLED, -DLING, -DLES to play a violin
FIDDLER	*n* pl. -S one that fiddles
FIDDLY	*adj* intricately difficult to handle
FIDEISM	*n* pl. -S reliance on faith rather than reason
FIDEIST	*n* pl. -S a believer in fideism
FIDELITY	*n* pl. -TIES loyalty
FIDGE	*v* FIDGED, FIDGING, FIDGES to fidget
FIDGET	*v* -ED, -ING, -S to move nervously or restlessly
FIDGETER	*n* pl. -S one that fidgets
FIDGETY	*adj* nervously restless
FIDGING	present participle of fidge
FIDO	*n* pl. -DOS a defective coin
FIDUCIAL	*adj* based on faith or trust
FIE	*interj* — used to express disapproval
FIEF	*n* pl. -S a feudal estate
FIEFDOM	*n* pl. -S a fief
FIELD	*v* -ED, -ING, -S to play as a fielder
FIELDER	*n* pl. -S one that catches or picks up a ball in play
FIEND	*n* pl. -S a demon
FIENDISH	*adj* extremely wicked or cruel
FIERCE	*adj* FIERCER, FIERCEST violently hostile or aggressive **FIERCELY** *adv*
FIERY	*adj* -ERIER, -ERIEST intensely hot **FIERILY** *adv*
FIESTA	*n* pl. -S a festival
FIFE	*v* FIFED, FIFING, FIFES to play a fife (a high-pitched flute)
FIFER	*n* pl. -S one that plays a fife
FIFTEEN	*n* pl. -S a number
FIFTH	*n* pl. -S one of five equal parts
FIFTHLY	*adv* in the fifth place
FIFTIETH	*n* pl. -S one of fifty equal parts
FIFTY	*n* pl. -TIES a number
FIFTYISH	*adj* being about fifty years old
FIG	*v* FIGGED, FIGGING, FIGS to adorn
FIGEATER	*n* pl. -S a large beetle
FIGHT	*v* FOUGHT, FIGHTING, FIGHTS to attempt to defeat an adversary
FIGHTER	*n* pl. -S one that fights
FIGHTING	*n* pl. -S the act of one that fights
FIGMENT	*n* pl. -S a product of mental invention
FIGULINE	*n* pl. -S a piece of pottery
FIGURAL	*adj* consisting of human or animal form
FIGURANT	*n* pl. -S a ballet dancer who dances only in groups
FIGURATE	*adj* having a definite shape
FIGURE	*v* -URED, -URING, -URES to compute
FIGURER	*n* pl. -S one that figures
FIGURINE	*n* pl. -S a small statue
FIGURING	present participle of figure
FIGWORT	*n* pl. -S a flowering plant
FIL	*n* pl. -S a coin of Iraq and Jordan
FILA	pl. of filum
FILAGREE	*v* -GREED, -GREEING, -GREES to filigree
FILAMENT	*n* pl. -S a very thin thread or threadlike structure
FILAR	*adj* pertaining to a thread
FILAREE	*n* pl. -S a European weed
FILARIA	*n* pl. -IAE a parasitic worm **FILARIAL, FILARIAN** *adj*
FILARIID	*n* pl. -S filaria
FILATURE	*n* pl. -S the reeling of silk from cocoons
FILBERT	*n* pl. -S the edible nut of a European shrub
FILCH	*v* -ED, -ING, -ES to steal
FILCHER	*n* pl. -S one that filches
FILE	*v* FILED, FILING, FILES to arrange in order for future reference **FILEABLE** *adj*
FILEFISH	*n* pl. -ES a marine fish
FILEMOT	*adj* of a brownish yellow color
FILER	*n* pl. -S one that files
FILET	*v* -ED, -ING, -S to fillet
FILIAL	*adj* pertaining to a son or daughter **FILIALLY** *adv*
FILIATE	*v* -ATED, -ATING, -ATES to bring into close association
FILIBEG	*n* pl. -S a pleated skirt worn by Scottish Highlanders

FILICIDE	*n* pl. -S the killing of one's child
FILIFORM	*adj* shaped like a filament
FILIGREE	*v* -GREED, -GREEING, -GREES to adorn with intricate ornamental work
FILING	*n* pl. -S a particle removed by a file
FILISTER	*n* pl. -S a groove on a window frame
FILL	*v* -ED, -ING, -S to put as much as can be held into
FILLE	*n* pl. -S a girl
FILLER	*n* pl. -S one that fills
FILLET	*v* -ED, -ING, -S to cut boneless slices from
FILLIES	pl. of filly
FILLING	*n* pl. -S that which is used to fill something
FILLIP	*v* -ED, -ING, -S to strike sharply
FILLO	*n* pl. -LOS phyllo
FILLY	*n* pl. -LIES a young female horse
FILM	*v* -ED, -ING, -S to make a motion picture **FILMABLE** *adj*
FILMCARD	*n* pl. -S a fiche
FILMDOM	*n* pl. -S the motion-picture industry
FILMER	*n* pl. -S one that films
FILMGOER	*n* pl. -S one that goes to see motion pictures
FILMIC	*adj* pertaining to motion pictures
FILMIER	comparative of filmy
FILMIEST	superlative of filmy
FILMILY	*adv* in a filmy manner
FILMLAND	*n* pl. -S filmdom
FILMSET	*v* -SET, -SETTING, -SETS to photoset
FILMY	*adj* FILMIER, FILMIEST resembling or covered with film; hazy
FILO	*n* pl. -LOS phyllo
FILOSE	*adj* resembling a thread
FILTER	*v* -ED, -ING, -S to pass through a filter (a device for removing suspended matter)
FILTERER	*n* pl. -S one that filters
FILTH	*n* pl. -S foul or dirty matter
FILTHY	*adj* FILTHIER, FILTHIEST offensively dirty **FILTHILY** *adv*
FILTRATE	*v* -TRATED, -TRATING, -TRATES to filter
FILUM	*n* pl. -LA a threadlike anatomical structure
FIMBLE	*n* pl. -S the male hemp plant
FIMBRIA	*n* pl. -BRIAE a fringe or fringe-like structure **FIMBRIAL** *adj*
FIN	*v* FINNED, FINNING, FINS to equip with fins (external paddle-like structures)
FINABLE	*adj* subject to the payment of a fine
FINAGLE	*v* -GLED, -GLING, -GLES to obtain by trickery
FINAGLER	*n* pl. -S one that finagles
FINAL	*n* pl. -S the last examination of an academic course
FINALE	*n* pl. -S a close or termination of something
FINALIS	*n* pl. -LES a type of tone in medieval music
FINALISE	*v* -ISED, -ISING, -ISES finalize
FINALISM	*n* pl. -S the doctrine that all events are determined by ultimate purposes
FINALIST	*n* pl. -S a contestant who reaches the last part of a competition
FINALITY	*n* pl. -TIES the state of being conclusive
FINALIZE	*v* -IZED, -IZING, -IZES to put into finished form
FINALLY	*adv* at the end
FINANCE	*v* -NANCED, -NANCING, -NANCES to supply the money for
FINBACK	*n* pl. -S the rorqual
FINCH	*n* pl. -ES a small bird
FIND	*v* FOUND, FINDING, FINDS to come upon after a search **FINDABLE** *adj*
FINDER	*n* pl. -S one that finds
FINDING	*n* pl. -S something that is found
FINE	*adj* FINER, FINEST excellent
FINE	*v* FINED, FINING, FINES to subject to a fine (a monetary penalty)
FINEABLE	*adj* finable
FINELY	*adv* in a fine manner
FINENESS	*n* pl. -ES the quality of being fine
FINER	comparative of fine
FINERY	*n* pl. -ERIES elaborate adornment
FINESPUN	*adj* developed with extreme care

FINESSE	*v* -NESSED, -NESSING, -NESSES to bring about by adroit maneuvering
FINEST	superlative of fine
FINFISH	*n* pl. -ES a true fish
FINFOOT	*n* pl. -S an aquatic bird
FINGER	*v* -ED, -ING, -S to touch with the fingers (the terminating members of the hand)
FINGERER	*n* pl. -S one that fingers
FINIAL	*n* pl. -S a crowning ornament **FINIALED** *adj*
FINICAL	*adj* finicky
FINICKIN	*adj* finicky
FINICKY	*adj* -ICKIER, -ICKIEST difficult to please
FINIKIN	*adj* finicky
FINIKING	*adj* finicky
FINING	*n* pl. -S the clarifying of wines
FINIS	*n* pl. -NISES the end
FINISH	*v* -ED, -ING, -ES to bring to an end
FINISHER	*n* pl. -S one that finishes
FINITE	*n* pl. -S something that is finite (having definite limits)
FINITELY	*adv* to a finite extent
FINITUDE	*n* pl. -S the state of being finite
FINK	*v* -ED, -ING, -S to inform to the police
FINLESS	*adj* having no fins
FINLIKE	*adj* resembling a fin
FINMARK	*n* pl. -S a monetary unit of Finland
FINNED	past tense of fin
FINNICKY	*adj* -NICKIER, -NICKIEST finicky
FINNIER	comparative of finny
FINNIEST	superlative of finny
FINNING	present participle of fin
FINNMARK	*n* pl. -S finmark
FINNY	*adj* -NIER, -NIEST having or characterized by fins
FINO	*n* pl. -NOS a very dry sherry
FINOCHIO	*n* pl. -CHIOS a perennial herb
FIORD	*n* pl. -S fjord
FIPPLE	*n* pl. -S a plug of wood at the mouth of certain wind instruments
FIQUE	*n* pl. -S a tropical plant
FIR	*n* pl. -S an evergreen tree

FIRE	*v* FIRED, FIRING, FIRES to project by discharging from a gun **FIREABLE** *adj*
FIREARM	*n* pl. -S a weapon from which a shot is discharged by gunpowder
FIREBACK	*n* pl. -S a cast-iron plate along the back of a fireplace
FIREBALL	*n* pl. -S a luminous meteor
FIREBASE	*n* pl. -S a military base from which fire is directed against the enemy
FIREBIRD	*n* pl. -S a brightly colored bird
FIREBOAT	*n* pl. -S a boat equipped with fire-fighting apparatus
FIREBOMB	*v* -ED, -ING, -S to attack with incendiary bombs
FIREBOX	*n* pl. -ES a chamber in which fuel is burned
FIREBRAT	*n* pl. -S a small, wingless insect
FIREBUG	*n* pl. -S an arsonist
FIRECLAY	*n* pl. -CLAYS a heat-resistant clay
FIRED	past tense of fire
FIREDAMP	*n* pl. -S a combustible gas
FIREDOG	*n* pl. -S an andiron
FIREFANG	*v* -ED, -ING, -S to decompose by oxidation
FIREFLY	*n* pl. -FLIES a luminous insect
FIREHALL	*n* pl. -S a fire station
FIRELESS	*adj* having no fire
FIRELIT	*adj* lighted by firelight
FIRELOCK	*n* pl. -S a type of gun
FIREMAN	*n* pl. -MEN a man employed to extinguish fires
FIREPAN	*n* pl. -S an open pan for holding live coals
FIREPINK	*n* pl. -S a flowering plant
FIREPLUG	*n* pl. -S a hydrant
FIREPOT	*n* pl. -S a clay pot filled with burning items
FIRER	*n* pl. -S one that fires
FIREROOM	*n* pl. -S a room containing a ship's boilers
FIRESIDE	*n* pl. -S the area immediately surrounding a fireplace
FIRETRAP	*n* pl. -S a building that is likely to catch on fire
FIREWEED	*n* pl. -S a perennial herb
FIREWOOD	*n* pl. -S wood used as fuel

FIREWORK   *n* pl. -S a device for producing a striking display of light or a loud noise

FIREWORM   *n* pl. -S a glowworm

FIRING   *n* pl. -S the process of maturing ceramic products by heat

FIRKIN   *n* pl. -S a British unit of capacity

FIRM   *adj* FIRMER, FIRMEST unyielding to pressure

FIRM   *v* -ED, -ING, -S to make firm

FIRMAN   *n* pl. -S an edict issued by a Middle Eastern sovereign

FIRMER   *n* pl. -S a woodworking tool

FIRMLY   *adv* in a firm manner

FIRMNESS   *n* pl. -ES the state of being firm

FIRMWARE   *n* pl. -S computer programs permanently stored on a microchip

FIRN   *n* pl. -S neve

FIRRY   *adj* abounding in firs

FIRST   *n* pl. -S something that precedes all others

FIRSTLY   *adv* before all others

FIRTH   *n* pl. -S an inlet of the sea

FISC   *n* pl. -S a state or royal treasury

FISCAL   *n* pl. -S a public prosecutor

FISCALLY   *adv* with regard to financial matters

FISH   *v* -ED, -ING, -ES to catch or try to catch fish (cold-blooded aquatic vertebrates)

FISHABLE   *adj* suitable for fishing

FISHBOLT   *n* pl. -S a type of bolt

FISHBONE   *n* pl. -S a bone of a fish

FISHBOWL   *n* pl. -S a bowl in which live fish are kept

FISHER   *n* pl. -S one that fishes

FISHERY   *n* pl. -ERIES a place for catching fish

FISHEYE   *n* pl. -S a suspicious stare

FISHGIG   *n* pl. -S a pronged implement for spearing fish

FISHHOOK   *n* pl. -S a barbed hook for catching fish

FISHIER   comparative of fishy

FISHIEST   superlative of fishy

FISHILY   *adv* in a fishy manner

FISHING   *n* pl. -S the occupation or pastime of catching fish

FISHLESS   *adj* having no fish

FISHLIKE   *adj* resembling a fish

FISHLINE   *n* pl. -S a line used in fishing

FISHMEAL   *n* pl. -S ground dried fish

FISHNET   *n* pl. -S a net for catching fish

FISHPOLE   *n* pl. -S a fishing rod

FISHPOND   *n* pl. -S a pond abounding in edible fish

FISHTAIL   *v* -ED, -ING, -S to have the rear end of a moving vehicle slide from side to side

FISHWAY   *n* pl. -WAYS a device for enabling fish to pass around a dam

FISHWIFE   *n* pl. -WIVES a woman who sells fish

FISHWORM   *n* pl. -S a worm used as bait

FISHY   *adj* FISHIER, FISHIEST of or resembling fish

FISSATE   *adj* deeply split

FISSILE   *adj* capable of being split

FISSION   *v* -ED, -ING, -S to split into parts

FISSIPED   *n* pl. -S a mammal that has separated toes

FISSURE   *v* -SURED, -SURING, -SURES to split

FIST   *v* -ED, -ING, -S to strike with the fist (the hand closed tightly)

FISTFUL   *n* pl. -S a handful

FISTIC   *adj* pertaining to pugilism

FISTNOTE   *n* pl. -S a part of a text to which attention is drawn by an index mark

FISTULA   *n* pl. -LAE or -LAS a duct formed by the imperfect closing of a wound **FISTULAR** *adj*

FIT   *adj* FITTER, FITTEST healthy

FIT   *v* FITTED, FITTING, FITS to bring to a required form and size

FITCH   *n* pl. -ES a polecat

FITCHEE   *adj* fitchy

FITCHET   *n* pl. -S a fitch

FITCHEW   *n* pl. -S a fitch

FITCHY   *adj* having the arms ending in a point — used of a heraldic cross

FITFUL   *adj* recurring irregularly **FITFULLY** *adv*

FITLY   *adv* in a fit manner

FITMENT   *n* pl. -S equipment

FITNESS   *n* pl. -ES the state of being fit

FITTABLE	*adj* capable of being fitted
FITTED	past tense of fit
FITTER	*n* pl. -S one that fits
FITTEST	superlative of fit
FITTING	*n* pl. -S a small often standardized accessory part
FIVE	*n* pl. -S a number
FIVEFOLD	*adj* five times as great
FIVEPINS	*n/pl* a bowling game
FIVER	*n* pl. -S a five-dollar bill
FIX	*v* FIXED or FIXT, FIXING, FIXES to repair **FIXABLE** *adj*
FIXATE	*v* -ATED, -ATING, -ATES to make stable or stationary
FIXATIF	*n* pl. -S fixative
FIXATION	*n* pl. -S the act of fixating
FIXATIVE	*n* pl. -S a substance for preserving paintings or drawings
FIXEDLY	*adv* firmly
FIXER	*n* pl. -S one that fixes
FIXINGS	*n/pl* accompaniments to the main dish of a meal
FIXIT	*adj* involved with fixing things
FIXITY	*n* pl. -TIES stability
FIXT	a past tense of fix
FIXTURE	*n* pl. -S a permanent part or appendage of a house
FIXURE	*n* pl. -S firmness
FIZ	*n* pl. FIZZES a hissing or sputtering sound
FIZGIG	*n* pl. -S fishgig
FIZZ	*v* -ED, -ING, -ES to make a hissing or sputtering sound
FIZZER	*n* pl. -S one that fizzes
FIZZES	pl. of fiz
FIZZLE	*v* -ZLED, -ZLING, -ZLES to fizz
FIZZY	*adj* FIZZIER, FIZZIEST fizzing
FJELD	*n* pl. -S a high, barren plateau
FJORD	*n* pl. -S a narrow inlet of the sea between steep cliffs
FLAB	*n* pl. -S flabby body tissue
FLABBY	*adj* -BIER, -BIEST flaccid **FLABBILY** *adv*
FLABELLA	*n/pl* fan-shaped anatomical structures
FLACCID	*adj* lacking firmness
FLACK	*v* -ED, -ING, -S to work as a press agent
FLACKERY	*n* pl. -ERIES publicity
FLACON	*n* pl. -S a small stoppered bottle
FLAG	*v* FLAGGED, FLAGGING, FLAGS to mark with a flag (a piece of cloth used as a symbol)
FLAGELLA	*n/pl* long, slender plant shoots
FLAGGER	*n* pl. -S one that flags
FLAGGING	*n* pl. -S a type of pavement
FLAGGY	*adj* -GIER, -GIEST drooping
FLAGLESS	*adj* having no flag
FLAGMAN	*n* pl. -MEN one who carries a flag
FLAGON	*n* pl. -S a large bulging bottle
FLAGPOLE	*n* pl. -S a pole on which a flag is displayed
FLAGRANT	*adj* extremely conspicuous
FLAGSHIP	*n* pl. -S a ship bearing the flag of a fleet
FLAIL	*v* -ED, -ING, -S to swing freely
FLAIR	*n* pl. -S a natural aptitude
FLAK	*n* pl. FLAK antiaircraft fire
FLAKE	*v* FLAKED, FLAKING, FLAKES to peel off in flakes (flat, thin pieces)
FLAKER	*n* pl. -S one that flakes
FLAKEY	*adj* FLAKIER, FLAKIEST flaky
FLAKY	*adj* FLAKIER, FLAKIEST resembling flakes **FLAKILY** *adv*
FLAM	*v* FLAMMED, FLAMMING, FLAMS to deceive
FLAMBE	*v* -BEED, -BEING, -BES to douse with a liqueur and ignite
FLAMBEAU	*n* pl. -BEAUX or -BEAUS a flaming torch
FLAMBEE	*adj* flaming
FLAME	*v* FLAMED, FLAMING, FLAMES to burn brightly
FLAMEN	*n* pl. -MENS or -MINES a priest of ancient Rome
FLAMENCO	*n* pl. -COS a strongly rhythmic style of dancing
FLAMEOUT	*n* pl. -S a failure of a jet engine in flight
FLAMER	*n* pl. -S one that flames
FLAMIER	comparative of flamy
FLAMIEST	superlative of flamy
FLAMINES	a pl. of flamen
FLAMING	present participle of flame
FLAMINGO	*n* pl. -GOS or -GOES a wading bird

FLAMMED	past tense of flam	**FLATCAR**	n pl. -S a railroad car without sides or roof
FLAMMING	present participle of flam	**FLATFISH**	n pl. -ES any of an order of marine fishes
FLAMY	adj FLAMIER, FLAMIEST flaming		
FLAN	n pl. -S or -ES a type of custard	**FLATFOOT**	n pl. -FEET a foot condition
FLANCARD	n pl. -S a piece of armor for the side of a horse	**FLATFOOT**	v -ED, -ING, -S to walk with a dragging gait
FLANERIE	n pl. -S idleness	**FLATHEAD**	n pl. -S a marine food fish
FLANEUR	n pl. -S an idler	**FLATIRON**	n pl. -S a device for pressing clothes
FLANGE	v FLANGED, FLANGING, FLANGES to provide with a protecting rim	**FLATLAND**	n pl. -S land lacking significant variation in elevation
FLANGER	n pl. -S one that flanges	**FLATLET**	n pl. -S a type of apartment
FLANK	v -ED, -ING, -S to be located at the side of	**FLATLING**	adv with a flat side or edge
		FLATLONG	adv flatling
FLANKEN	n/pl beef cut from the sides that is boiled with vegetables	**FLATLY**	adv in a flat manner
FLANKER	n pl. -S one that flanks	**FLATMATE**	n pl. -S one with whom an apartment is shared
FLANNEL	v -NELED, -NELING, -NELS or -NELLED, -NELLING, -NELS to cover with flannel (a soft fabric)	**FLATNESS**	n pl. -ES the state of being flat
		FLATTED	past tense of flat
FLAP	v FLAPPED, FLAPPING, FLAPS to wave up and down	**FLATTEN**	v -ED, -ING, -S to make or become flat
FLAPJACK	n pl. -S a pancake	**FLATTER**	v -ED, -ING, -S to praise excessively
FLAPLESS	adj having no flap (a flat appendage)	**FLATTERY**	n pl. -TERIES the act of flattering
FLAPPED	past tense of flap	**FLATTEST**	superlative of flat
FLAPPER	n pl. -S one that flaps	**FLATTING**	present participle of flat
FLAPPING	present participle of flap	**FLATTISH**	adj somewhat flat
FLAPPY	adj -PIER, -PIEST flapping	**FLATTOP**	n pl. -S an aircraft carrier
FLARE	v FLARED, FLARING, FLARES to burn with a bright, wavering light	**FLATUS**	n pl. -ES intestinal gas
		FLATWARE	n pl. -S tableware that is fairly flat
FLASH	v -ED, -ING, -ES to send forth a sudden burst of light	**FLATWASH**	n pl. -ES flatwork
FLASHER	n pl. -S one that flashes	**FLATWAYS**	adv flatwise
FLASHGUN	n pl. -S a photographic apparatus	**FLATWISE**	adv with the flat side in a particular position
FLASHING	n pl. -S sheet metal used in waterproofing a roof	**FLATWORK**	n pl. -S laundry that can be ironed mechanically
FLASHY	adj FLASHIER, FLASHIEST gaudy **FLASHILY** adv	**FLATWORM**	n pl. -S a flat-bodied worm
FLASK	n pl. -S a narrow-necked container	**FLAUNT**	v -ED, -ING, -S to exhibit in a gaudy manner
FLASKET	n pl. -S a small flask	**FLAUNTER**	n pl. -S one that flaunts
FLAT	adj FLATTER, FLATTEST having a smooth or even surface	**FLAUNTY**	adj FLAUNTIER, FLAUNTIEST gaudy
FLAT	v FLATTED, FLATTING, FLATS to flatten	**FLAUTIST**	n pl. -S flutist
FLATBED	n pl. -S a type of truck or trailer	**FLAVANOL**	n pl. -S flavonol
FLATBOAT	n pl. -S a flat-bottomed boat	**FLAVIN**	n pl. -S a yellow pigment
FLATCAP	n pl. -S a type of hat	**FLAVINE**	n pl. -S flavin

FLAVONE   *n* pl. -S a chemical compound

FLAVONOL   *n* pl. -S a derivative of flavone

FLAVOR   *v* -ED, -ING, -S to give flavor (distinctive taste) to

FLAVORER   *n* pl. -S one that flavors

FLAVORY   *adj* full of flavor

FLAVOUR   *v* -ED, -ING, -S to flavor

FLAVOURY   *adj* flavory

FLAW   *v* -ED, -ING, -S to produce a flaw (an imperfection) in

FLAWLESS   *adj* having no flaw

FLAWY   *adj* FLAWIER, FLAWIEST full of flaws

FLAX   *n* pl. -ES an annual herb

FLAXEN   *adj* of a pale yellow color

FLAXSEED   *n* pl. -S the seed of flax

FLAXY   *adj* FLAXIER, FLAXIEST flaxen

FLAY   *v* -ED, -ING, -S to strip off the skin of

FLAYER   *n* pl. -S one that flays

FLEA   *n* pl. -S a parasitic insect

FLEABAG   *n* pl. -S an inferior hotel

FLEABANE   *n* pl. -S a flowering plant

FLEABITE   *n* pl. -S the bite of a flea

FLEAM   *n* pl. -S a surgical instrument

FLEAPIT   *n* pl. -S a run-down movie theater

FLEAWORT   *n* pl. -S a European herb

FLECHE   *n* pl. -S a steeple

FLECK   *v* -ED, -ING, -S to mark with flecks (tiny streaks or spots)

FLECKY   *adj* flecked

FLECTION   *n* pl. -S the act of bending

FLED   past tense of flee

FLEDGE   *v* FLEDGED, FLEDGING, FLEDGES to furnish with feathers

FLEDGY   *adj* FLEDGIER, FLEDGIEST covered with feathers

FLEE   *v* FLED, FLEEING, FLEES to run away

FLEECE   *v* FLEECED, FLEECING, FLEECES to remove the coat of wool from

FLEECER   *n* pl. -S one that fleeces

FLEECH   *v* -ED, -ING, -ES to coax

FLEECING   present participle of fleece

FLEECY   *adj* FLEECIER, FLEECIEST woolly **FLEECILY** *adv*

FLEER   *v* -ED, -ING, -S to deride

FLEET   *adj* FLEETER, FLEETEST swift **FLEETLY** *adv*

FLEET   *v* -ED, -ING, -S to move swiftly

FLEISHIG   *adj* made of meat or meat products

FLEMISH   *v* -ED, -ING, -ES to coil rope in a certain manner

FLENCH   *v* -ED, -ING, -ES to flense

FLENSE   *v* FLENSED, FLENSING, FLENSES to strip the blubber or skin from

FLENSER   *n* pl. -S one that flenses

FLESH   *v* -ED, -ING, -ES to plunge into the flesh (soft body tissue)

FLESHER   *n* pl. -S one that removes flesh from animal hides

FLESHIER   comparative of fleshy

FLESHIEST   superlative of fleshy

FLESHING   *n* pl. -S the distribution of the lean and fat on an animal

FLESHLY   *adj* -LIER, -LIEST pertaining to the body

FLESHPOT   *n* pl. -S a pot for cooking meat

FLESHY   *adj* FLESHIER, FLESHIEST having much flesh

FLETCH   *v* -ED, -ING, -ES to fledge

FLETCHER   *n* pl. -S one that makes arrows

FLEURY   *adj* having the arms terminating in three leaves — used of a heraldic cross

FLEW   *n* pl. -S a fishing net

FLEX   *v* -ED, -ING, -ES to bend

FLEXAGON   *n* pl. -S a folded paper construction

FLEXIBLE   *adj* capable of being bent **FLEXIBLY** *adv*

FLEXILE   *adj* flexible

FLEXION   *n* pl. -S flection

FLEXOR   *n* pl. -S a muscle that serves to bend a bodily part

FLEXTIME   *n* pl. -S a system that allows flexible working hours

FLEXUOSE   *adj* flexuous

FLEXUOUS   *adj* winding

FLEXURE   *n* pl. -S the act of bending **FLEXURAL** *adj*

FLEY   *v* -ED, -ING, -S to frighten

FLIC   *n* pl. -S a Parisian policeman

FLICHTER   *v* -ED, -ING, -S to flicker

FLICK   *v* -ED, -ING, -S to strike with a quick, light blow

FLICKER   *v* -ED, -ING, -S to move waveringly

FLICKERY   *adj* flickering

FLIED   a past tense of fly

FLIER   *n* pl. -S one that flies

FLIES   present 3d person sing. of fly

FLIEST   superlative of fly

FLIGHT   *v* -ED, -ING, -S to fly in a flock

FLIGHTY   *adj* FLIGHTIER, FLIGHTIEST fickle

FLIMFLAM   *v* -FLAMMED, -FLAMMING, -FLAMS to swindle

FLIMSY   *adj* -SIER, -SIEST lacking solidity or strength **FLIMSILY** *adv*

FLIMSY   *n* pl. -SIES a thin paper

FLINCH   *v* -ED, -ING, -ES to shrink back involuntarily

FLINCHER   *n* pl. -S one that flinches

FLINDER   *n* pl. -S a small fragment

FLING   *v* FLUNG, FLINGING, FLINGS to throw with force

FLINGER   *n* pl. -S one that flings

FLINKITE   *n* pl. -S a mineral

FLINT   *v* -ED, -ING, -S to provide with flint (a spark-producing rock)

FLINTY   *adj* FLINTIER, FLINTIEST resembling flint **FLINTILY** *adv*

FLIP   *v* FLIPPED, FLIPPING, FLIPS to throw with a brisk motion

FLIP   *adj* FLIPPER, FLIPPEST flippant

FLIPPANT   *adj* impudent

FLIPPED   past tense of flip

FLIPPER   *n* pl. -S a broad, flat limb adapted for swimming

FLIPPEST   superlative of flip

FLIPPING   present participle of flip

FLIPPY   *adj* flaring at the bottom

FLIRT   *v* -ED, -ING, -S to behave amorously without serious intent

FLIRTER   *n* pl. -S one that flirts

FLIRTY   *adj* FLIRTIER, FLIRTIEST given to flirting

FLIT   *v* FLITTED, FLITTING, FLITS to move lightly and swiftly

FLITCH   *v* -ED, -ING, -ES to cut into strips

FLITE   *v* FLITED, FLITING, FLITES to quarrel

FLITTED   past tense of flit

FLITTER   *v* -ED, -ING, -S to flutter

FLITTING   present participle of flit

FLIVVER   *n* pl. -S an old, battered car

FLOAT   *v* -ED, -ING, -S to rest or remain on the surface of a liquid

FLOATAGE   *n* pl. -S flotage

FLOATEL   *n* pl. -S a houseboat used as a hotel

FLOATER   *n* pl. -S one that floats

FLOATY   *adj* FLOATIER, FLOATIEST tending to float

FLOC   *v* FLOCCED, FLOCCING, FLOCS to aggregate into floccules

FLOCCI   pl. of floccus

FLOCCOSE   *adj* having woolly tufts

FLOCCULE   *n* pl. -S a tuft-like mass

FLOCCULI   *n/pl* small, loosely aggregated masses

FLOCCUS   *n* pl. FLOCCI a floccule

FLOCK   *v* -ED, -ING, -S to gather or move in a crowd

FLOCKING   *n* pl. -S a velvety design in short fibers on cloth or paper

FLOCKY   *adj* FLOCKIER, FLOCKIEST woolly

FLOE   *n* pl. -S a large mass of floating ice

FLOG   *v* FLOGGED, FLOGGING, FLOGS to beat with a whip or rod

FLOGGER   *n* pl. -S one that flogs

FLOGGING   *n* pl. -S a whipping

FLOKATI   *n* pl. -S a Greek handwoven rug

FLONG   *n* pl. -S a sheet of a certain type of paper

FLOOD   *v* -ED, -ING, -S to inundate

FLOODER   *n* pl. -S one that floods

FLOODLIT   *adj* illuminated by floodlights

FLOODWAY   *n* pl. -WAYS an overflow channel

FLOOEY   *adj* awry

FLOOIE   *adj* flooey

FLOOR   *v* -ED, -ING, -S to provide with a floor (the level base of a room)

FLOORAGE   *n* pl. -S floor space

FLOORER   *n* pl. -S one that floors

FLOORING   *n* pl. -S a floor

FLOOSIE   *n* pl. -S floozy

FLOOSY	*n* pl. -SIES floozy
FLOOZIE	*n* pl. -S floozy
FLOOZY	*n* pl. -ZIES a prostitute
FLOP	*v* FLOPPED, FLOPPING, FLOPS to fall heavily and noisily
FLOPOVER	*n* pl. -S a defect in television reception
FLOPPER	*n* pl. -S one that flops
FLOPPING	present participle of flop
FLOPPY	*n* pl. -PIES a type of computer disk
FLOPPY	*adj* -PIER, -PIEST soft and flexible **FLOPPILY** *adv*
FLORA	*n* pl. -RAS or -RAE the plant life of a particular region
FLORAL	*n* pl. -S a design having flowers
FLORALLY	*adv* in a manner like that of a flower
FLORENCE	*n* pl. -S florin
FLORET	*n* pl. -S a small flower
FLORID	*adj* ruddy **FLORIDLY** *adv*
FLORIGEN	*n* pl. -S a plant hormone
FLORIN	*n* pl. -S a former gold coin of Europe
FLORIST	*n* pl. -S a grower or seller of flowers
FLORUIT	*n* pl. -S a period of flourishing
FLOSS	*v* -ED, -ING, -ES to clean between the teeth with a thread
FLOSSIE	*n* pl. -S a floozy
FLOSSY	*adj* FLOSSIER, FLOSSIEST resembling floss (a soft, light fiber) **FLOSSILY** *adv*
FLOTA	*n* pl. -S a fleet of Spanish ships
FLOTAGE	*n* pl. -S the act of floating
FLOTILLA	*n* pl. -S a fleet of ships
FLOTSAM	*n* pl. -S floating wreckage of a ship or its cargo
FLOUNCE	*v* FLOUNCED, FLOUNCING, FLOUNCES to move with exaggerated motions
FLOUNCY	*adj* FLOUNCIER, FLOUNCIEST flouncing
FLOUNDER	*v* -ED, -ING, -S to struggle clumsily
FLOUR	*v* -ED, -ING, -S to cover with flour (a finely ground meal of grain)
FLOURISH	*v* -ED, -ING, -ES to thrive
FLOURY	*adj* resembling flour
FLOUT	*v* -ED, -ING, -S to treat with contempt
FLOUTER	*n* pl. -S one that flouts
FLOW	*v* -ED, -ING, -S to move steadily and smoothly along
FLOWAGE	*n* pl. -S the act of flowing
FLOWER	*v* -ED, -ING, -S to put forth flowers (reproductive structures of seed-bearing plants)
FLOWERER	*n* pl. -S a plant that flowers at a certain time
FLOWERET	*n* pl. -S a floret
FLOWERY	*adj* -ERIER, -ERIEST abounding in flowers
FLOWN	a past participle of fly
FLU	*n* pl. -S a virus disease
FLUB	*v* FLUBBED, FLUBBING, FLUBS to bungle
FLUBBER	*n* pl. -S one that flubs
FLUBDUB	*n* pl. -S pretentious nonsense
FLUE	*n* pl. -S an enclosed passageway for directing a current **FLUED** *adj*
FLUENCY	*n* pl. -CIES the quality of being fluent
FLUENT	*adj* spoken or written with effortless ease **FLUENTLY** *adv*
FLUERICS	*n/pl* fluidics **FLUERIC** *adj*
FLUFF	*v* -ED, -ING, -S to make fluffy
FLUFFY	*adj* FLUFFIER, FLUFFIEST light and soft **FLUFFILY** *adv*
FLUID	*n* pl. -S a substance that tends to flow **FLUIDAL** *adj*
FLUIDICS	*n/pl* a branch of mechanical engineering **FLUIDIC** *adj*
FLUIDISE	*v* -ISED, -ISING, -ISES to fluidize
FLUIDITY	*n* pl. -TIES the quality of being able to flow
FLUIDIZE	*v* -IZED, -IZING, -IZES to cause to flow like a fluid
FLUIDLY	*adv* with fluidity
FLUIDRAM	*n* pl. -S a unit of liquid capacity
FLUKE	*v* FLUKED, FLUKING, FLUKES to obtain by chance
FLUKEY	*adj* FLUKIER, FLUKIEST fluky
FLUKY	*adj* FLUKIER, FLUKIEST happening by or depending on chance
FLUME	*v* FLUMED, FLUMING, FLUMES to convey by means of an artificial water channel
FLUMMERY	*n* pl. -MERIES a sweet dessert

FLUMMOX	v -ED, -ING, -ES to confuse
FLUMP	v -ED, -ING, -S to fall heavily
FLUNG	past tense of fling
FLUNK	v -ED, -ING, -S to fail an examination or course
FLUNKER	n pl. -S one that flunks
FLUNKEY	n pl. -KEYS flunky
FLUNKY	n pl. -KIES a servile follower
FLUOR	n pl. -S fluorite **FLUORIC** adj
FLUORENE	n pl. -S a chemical compound
FLUORID	n pl. -S fluoride
FLUORIDE	n pl. -S a compound of fluorine
FLUORIN	n pl. -S fluorine
FLUORINE	n pl. -S a gaseous element
FLUORITE	n pl. -S a mineral
FLURRY	v -RIED, -RYING, -RIES to confuse
FLUSH	adj FLUSHER, FLUSHEST ruddy
FLUSH	v -ED, -ING, -ES to blush
FLUSHER	n pl. -S one that flushes
FLUSTER	v -ED, -ING, -S to put into a state of nervous confusion
FLUTE	v FLUTED, FLUTING, FLUTES to play on a flute (a woodwind instrument)
FLUTER	n pl. -S a flutist
FLUTEY	adj FLUTIER, FLUTIEST fluty
FLUTIER	comparative of fluty
FLUTIEST	superlative of fluty
FLUTING	n pl. -S a series of parallel grooves
FLUTIST	n pl. -S one who plays the flute
FLUTTER	v -ED, -ING, -S to wave rapidly and irregularly
FLUTTERY	adj marked by fluttering
FLUTY	adj FLUTIER, FLUTIEST resembling a flute in sound
FLUVIAL	adj pertaining to a river
FLUX	v -ED, -ING, -ES to melt
FLUXGATE	n pl. -S a device to measure a magnetic field
FLUXION	n pl. -S the act of flowing
FLUYT	n pl. -S a type of ship
FLY	v FLEW, FLOWN, FLYING, FLIES to move through the air
FLY	v FLIED, FLYING, FLIES to hit a ball high into the air in baseball
FLY	adj FLIER, FLIEST clever

FLYABLE	adj suitable for flying
FLYAWAY	n pl. -AWAYS one that is elusive
FLYBELT	n pl. -S an area infested with tsetse flies
FLYBLOW	v -BLEW, -BLOWN, -BLOWING, -BLOWS to taint
FLYBOAT	n pl. -S a small, fast boat
FLYBOY	n pl. -BOYS a pilot in an air force
FLYBY	n pl. -BYS a flight of aircraft close to a specified place
FLYER	n pl. -S flier
FLYING	n pl. -S the operation of an aircraft
FLYLEAF	n pl. -LEAVES a blank leaf at the beginning or end of a book
FLYLESS	adj free of flies (winged insects)
FLYMAN	n pl. -MEN a stage worker in a theater
FLYOFF	n pl. -S a competitive testing of model aircraft
FLYOVER	n pl. -S a flight of aircraft over a specific location
FLYPAPER	n pl. -S paper designed to catch or kill flies
FLYPAST	n pl. -S a flyby
FLYSCH	n pl. -ES a sandstone deposit
FLYSPECK	v -ED, -ING, -S to mark with minute spots
FLYTE	v FLYTED, FLYTING, FLYTES to flite
FLYTIER	n pl. -S a maker of fishing flies
FLYTING	n pl. -S a dispute in verse form
FLYTRAP	n pl. -S a trap for catching flies
FLYWAY	n pl. -WAYS an established air route of migratory birds
FLYWHEEL	n pl. -S a heavy disk used in machinery
FOAL	v -ED, -ING, -S to give birth to a horse
FOAM	v -ED, -ING, -S to form foam (a light, bubbly, gas and liquid mass) **FOAMABLE** adj
FOAMER	n pl. -S one that foams
FOAMIER	comparative of foamy
FOAMIEST	superlative of foamy
FOAMILY	adv in a foamy manner
FOAMLESS	adj being without foam
FOAMLIKE	adj resembling foam
FOAMY	adj FOAMIER, FOAMIEST covered with foam

FOB	v FOBBED, FOBBING, FOBS to deceive
FOCACCIA	n pl. -S a flat Italian bread
FOCAL	adj pertaining to a focus
FOCALISE	v -ISED, -ISING, -ISES to focalize
FOCALIZE	v -IZED, -IZING, -IZES to focus
FOCALLY	adv with regard to focus
FOCUS	n pl. -CUSES or -CI a point at which rays converge or from which they diverge
FOCUS	v -CUSED, -CUSING, -CUSES or -CUSSED, -CUSSING, -CUSSES to bring to a focus
FOCUSER	n pl. -S one that focuses
FODDER	v -ED, -ING, -S to feed with coarse food
FODGEL	adj plump
FOE	n pl. -S an enemy
FOEHN	n pl. -S a warm, dry wind
FOEMAN	n pl. -MEN an enemy in war
FOETAL	adj fetal
FOETID	adj fetid
FOETOR	n pl. -S fetor
FOETUS	n pl. -ES fetus
FOG	v FOGGED, FOGGING, FOGS to cover with fog (condensed water vapor near the earth's surface)
FOGBOUND	adj surrounded by fog
FOGBOW	n pl. -S a nebulous arc of light sometimes seen in a fog
FOGDOG	n pl. -S a fogbow
FOGEY	n pl. -GEYS fogy
FOGFRUIT	n pl. -S a flowering plant
FOGGAGE	n pl. -S a second growth of grass
FOGGED	past tense of fog
FOGGER	n pl. -S one that fogs
FOGGING	present participle of fog
FOGGY	adj -GIER, -GIEST filled with fog **FOGGILY** adv
FOGHORN	n pl. -S a horn sounded in a fog
FOGIE	n pl. -S fogy
FOGLESS	adj having no fog
FOGY	n pl. -GIES an old-fashioned person **FOGYISH** adj
FOGYISM	n pl. -S old-fashioned behavior
FOH	interj faugh
FOHN	n pl. -S foehn
FOIBLE	n pl. -S a minor weakness
FOIL	v -ED, -ING, -S to prevent the success of **FOILABLE** adj
FOILSMAN	n pl. -MEN a fencer
FOIN	v -ED, -ING, -S to thrust with a pointed weapon
FOISON	n pl. -S strength
FOIST	v -ED, -ING, -S to force upon slyly
FOLACIN	n pl. -S a B vitamin
FOLATE	n pl. -S folacin
FOLD	v -ED, -ING, -S to lay one part over another part of **FOLDABLE** adj
FOLDAWAY	adj designed to fold out of the way
FOLDBOAT	n pl. -S a faltboat
FOLDER	n pl. -S one that folds
FOLDEROL	n pl. -S falderal
FOLDOUT	n pl. -S a gatefold
FOLIA	a pl. of folium
FOLIAGE	n pl. -S the growth of leaves of a plant **FOLIAGED** adj
FOLIAR	adj pertaining to a leaf
FOLIATE	v -ATED, -ATING, -ATES to hammer into thin plates
FOLIO	v -ED, -ING, -S to number the pages of
FOLIOSE	adj having leaves
FOLIOUS	adj foliose
FOLIUM	n pl. -LIA or -LIUMS a thin layer
FOLK	n pl. -S a people or tribe
FOLKIE	n pl. -S a performer of folk music
FOLKISH	adj characteristic of the common people
FOLKLIFE	n pl. -LIVES the traditions, skills, and products of a people
FOLKLIKE	adj folkish
FOLKLORE	n pl. -S the lore of a people
FOLKMOOT	n pl. -S a general assembly of the people in early England
FOLKMOT	n pl. -S folkmoot
FOLKMOTE	n pl. -S folkmoot
FOLKSY	adj FOLKSIER, FOLKSIEST friendly **FOLKSILY** adv
FOLKTALE	n pl. -S a tale forming part of the oral tradition of a people
FOLKWAY	n pl. -WAYS a traditional custom of a people

FOLKY	_n_ pl. FOLKIES folkie
FOLLES	pl. of follis
FOLLICLE	_n_ pl. -S a small bodily cavity
FOLLIES	pl. of folly
FOLLIS	_n_ pl. -LES a coin of ancient Rome
FOLLOW	_v_ -ED, -ING, -S to come or go after
FOLLOWER	_n_ pl. -S one that follows
FOLLY	_n_ pl. -LIES a foolish idea or action
FOMENT	_v_ -ED, -ING, -S to promote the development of
FOMENTER	_n_ pl. -S one that foments
FOMITE	_n_ pl. -S an inanimate object that serves to transmit infectious organisms
FON	_n_ pl. -S foehn
FOND	_adj_ FONDER, FONDEST having an affection
FOND	_v_ -ED, -ING, -S to display affection
FONDANT	_n_ pl. -S a soft, creamy candy
FONDLE	_v_ -DLED, -DLING, -DLES to caress
FONDLER	_n_ pl. -S one that fondles
FONDLING	_n_ pl. -S one that is fondled
FONDLY	_adv_ in a fond manner
FONDNESS	_n_ pl. -ES affection
FONDU	_n_ pl. -S fondue
FONDUE	_n_ pl. -S a dish of melted cheese
FONT	_n_ pl. -S a receptacle for the water used in baptism **FONTAL** _adj_
FONTANEL	_n_ pl. -S a space in the fetal and infantile skull
FONTINA	_n_ pl. -S an Italian cheese
FOOD	_n_ pl. -S a substance taken into the body to maintain life and growth **FOODLESS** _adj_
FOODIE	_n_ pl. -S an enthusiast of foods and their preparation
FOODWAYS	_n/pl_ the eating habits of a people
FOOFARAW	_n_ pl. -S excessive ornamentation
FOOL	_v_ -ED, -ING, -S to deceive
FOOLERY	_n_ pl. -ERIES foolish behavior or speech
FOOLFISH	_n_ pl. -ES a marine fish
FOOLISH	_adj_ -ISHER, -ISHEST lacking good sense or judgment
FOOLSCAP	_n_ pl. -S a paper size
FOOT	_n_ pl. FEET the terminal part of the leg on which the body stands and moves
FOOT	_v_ -ED, -ING, -S to walk
FOOTAGE	_n_ pl. -S a length or quantity expressed in feet
FOOTBALL	_n_ pl. -S a type of ball
FOOTBATH	_n_ pl. -S a bath for the feet
FOOTBOY	_n_ pl. -BOYS a serving boy
FOOTER	_n_ pl. -S one that walks
FOOTFALL	_n_ pl. -S the sound of a footstep
FOOTGEAR	_n_ pl. -S footwear
FOOTHILL	_n_ pl. -S a low hill at the foot of higher hills
FOOTHOLD	_n_ pl. -S a secure support for the feet
FOOTIE	_n_ pl. -S footsie
FOOTIER	comparative of footy
FOOTIEST	superlative of footy
FOOTING	_n_ pl. -S a foothold
FOOTLE	_v_ -TLED, -TLING, -TLES to waste time
FOOTLER	_n_ pl. -S one that footles
FOOTLESS	_adj_ having no feet
FOOTLIKE	_adj_ resembling a foot
FOOTLING	present participle of footle
FOOTMAN	_n_ pl. -MEN a male servant
FOOTMARK	_n_ pl. -S a mark left by the foot on a surface
FOOTNOTE	_v_ -NOTED, -NOTING, -NOTES to furnish with explanatory notes
FOOTPACE	_n_ pl. -S a walking pace
FOOTPAD	_n_ pl. -S one who robs a pedestrian
FOOTPATH	_n_ pl. -S a path for pedestrians
FOOTRACE	_n_ pl. -S a race run on foot
FOOTREST	_n_ pl. -S a support for the feet
FOOTROPE	_n_ pl. -S a rope used in sailing
FOOTSIE	_n_ pl. -S a flirting game played with the feet
FOOTSLOG	_v_ -SLOGGED, -SLOGGING, -SLOGS to march through mud
FOOTSORE	_adj_ having sore or tired feet
FOOTSTEP	_n_ pl. -S a step with the foot
FOOTSY	_n_ pl. -SIES footsie
FOOTWALL	_n_ pl. -S the layer of rock beneath a vein of ore

FOOTWAY   *n* pl. -WAYS a footpath

FOOTWEAR   *n* pl. FOOTWEAR wearing apparel for the feet

FOOTWORK   *n* pl. -S the use of the feet

FOOTWORN   *adj* footsore

FOOTY   *adj* -TIER, -TIEST paltry

FOOZLE   *v* -ZLED, -ZLING, -ZLES to bungle

FOOZLER   *n* pl. -S one that foozles

FOP   *v* FOPPED, FOPPING, FOPS to deceive

FOPPERY   *n* pl. -PERIES foppish behavior

FOPPISH   *adj* characteristic of a dandy

FOR   *prep* directed or sent to

FORA   a pl. of forum

FORAGE   *v* -AGED, -AGING, -AGES to search about

FORAGER   *n* pl. -S one that forages

FORAM   *n* pl. -S a marine rhizopod

FORAMEN   *n* pl. -MINA or -MENS a small anatomical opening

FORAY   *v* -ED, -ING, -S to raid

FORAYER   *n* pl. -S one that forays

FORB   *n* pl. -S an herb other than grass

FORBAD   a past tense of forbid

FORBADE   a past tense of forbid

FORBEAR   *v* -BORE, -BORNE, -BEARING, -BEARS to refrain from

FORBID   *v* -BADE or -BAD, -BIDDEN, -BIDDING, -BIDS to command not to do something

FORBIDAL   *n* pl. -S the act of forbidding

FORBODE   *v* -BODED, -BODING, -BODES to forebode

FORBORE   past tense of forbear

FORBORNE   past participle of forbear

FORBY   *prep* close by

FORBYE   *prep* forby

FORCE   *v* FORCED, FORCING, FORCES to overcome resistance by the exertion of strength **FORCEDLY** *adv*

FORCEFUL   *adj* strong

FORCEPS   *n* pl. -CIPES an instrument for seizing and holding objects

FORCER   *n* pl. -S one that forces

FORCIBLE   *adj* effected by force **FORCIBLY**

FORCING   present participle of force

FORCIPES   pl. of forceps

FORD   *v* -ED, -ING, -S to cross by wading **FORDABLE** *adj*

FORDLESS   *adj* unable to be forded

FORDO   *v* -DID, -DONE, -DOING, -DOES to destroy

FORE   *n* pl. -S the front part of something

FOREARM   *v* -ED, -ING, -S to arm in advance

FOREBAY   *n* pl. -BAYS a reservoir from which water is taken to run equipment

FOREBEAR   *n* pl. -S an ancestor

FOREBODE   *v* -BODED, -BODING, -BODES to indicate in advance

FOREBODY   *n* pl. -BODIES the forward part of a ship

FOREBOOM   *n* pl. -S the boom of a ship's foremast

FOREBY   *prep* forby

FOREBYE   *prep* forby

FORECAST   *v* -ED, -ING, -S to estimate or calculate in advance

FOREDATE   *v* -DATED, -DATING, -DATES to antedate

FOREDECK   *n* pl. -S the forward part of a ship's deck

FOREDO   *v* -DID, -DONE, -DOING, -DOES to fordo

FOREDOOM   *v* -ED, -ING, -S to doom in advance

FOREFACE   *n* pl. -S the front part of the head of a quadruped

FOREFEEL   *v* -FELT, -FEELING, -FEELS to have a premonition of

FOREFEND   *v* -ED, -ING, -S to forfend

FOREFOOT   *n* pl. -FEET one of the front feet of an animal

FOREGO   *v* -WENT, -GONE, -GOING, -GOES to go before

FOREGOER   *n* pl. -S one that foregoes

FOREGUT   *n* pl. -S the front part of the embryonic alimentary canal

FOREHAND   *n* pl. -S a type of tennis stroke

FOREHEAD   *n* pl. -S the part of the face above the eyes

FOREHOOF   *n* pl. -HOOFS or -HOOVES the hoof of a forefoot

FOREIGN   *adj* situated outside a place or country

FOREKNOW *v* -KNEW, -KNOWN, -KNOWING, -KNOWS to know in advance

FORELADY *n* pl. -DIES a woman who supervises workers

FORELAND *n* pl. -S a projecting mass of land

FORELEG *n* pl. -S one of the front legs of an animal

FORELIMB *n* pl. -S a foreleg

FORELOCK *v* -ED, -ING, -S to fasten with a linchpin

FOREMAN *n* pl. -MEN a man who supervises workers

FOREMAST *n* pl. -S the forward mast of a ship

FOREMILK *n* pl. -S the milk secreted immediately after childbirth

FOREMOST *adj* first in position

FORENAME *n* pl. -S a first name

FORENOON *n* pl. -S the period of daylight before noon

FORENSIC *n* pl -S an argumentative exercise

FOREPART *n* pl. -S the front part

FOREPAST *adj* already in the past

FOREPAW *n* pl. -S the paw of a foreleg

FOREPEAK *n* pl. -S the forward part of a ship's hold

FOREPLAY *n* pl. -PLAYS erotic stimulation preceding sexual intercourse

FORERANK *n* pl. -S the first rank

FORERUN *v* -RAN, -RUNNING, -RUNS to run in advance of

FORESAID *adj* previously said

FORESAIL *n* pl. -S the lowest sail on a foremast

FORESEE *v* -SAW, -SEEN, -SEEING, -SEES to see in advance

FORESEER *n* pl. -S one that foresees

FORESHOW *v* -SHOWED, -SHOWN, -SHOWING, -SHOWS to show in advance

FORESIDE *n* pl. -S the front side

FORESKIN *n* pl. -S the prepuce

FOREST *v* -ED, -ING, -S to convert into a forest (a densely wooded area)

FORESTAL *adj* of or pertaining to a forest

FORESTAY *n* pl. -STAYS a wire or rope used to support a foremast

FORESTER *n* pl. -S one skilled in forestry

FORESTRY *n* pl. -RIES the science of planting and managing forests

FORETELL *v* -TOLD, -TELLING, -TELLS to tell of or about in advance

FORETIME *n* pl. -S the past

FORETOP *n* pl. -S a forelock

FOREVER *n* pl. -S an indefinite length of time

FOREWARN *v* -ED, -ING, -S to warn in advance

FOREWENT past tense of forego

FOREWING *n* pl. -S an anterior wing of an insect

FOREWORD *n* pl. -S an introductory statement

FOREWORN *adj* forworn

FOREYARD *n* pl. -S the lowest yard on a foremast

FORFEIT *v* -ED, -ING, -S to lose as a penalty

FORFEND *v* -ED, -ING, -S to protect

FORGAT a past tense of forget

FORGAVE past tense of forgive

FORGE *v* FORGED, FORGING, FORGES to fashion or reproduce for fraudulent purposes

FORGER *n* pl. -S one that forges

FORGERY *n* pl. -ERIES the act of forging

FORGET *v* -GOT or -GAT, -GOTTEN, -GETTING, -GETS to fail to remember

FORGING *n* pl. -S a forgery

FORGIVE *v* -GAVE, -GIVEN, -GIVING, -GIVES to pardon

FORGIVER *n* pl. -S one that forgives

FORGO *v* -WENT, -GONE, -GOING, -GOES to refrain from

FORGOER *n* pl. -S one that forgoes

FORGOT a past tense of forget

FORGOTTEN past participle of forget

FORINT *n* pl. -S a monetary unit of Hungary

FORJUDGE *v* -JUDGED, -JUDGING, -JUDGES to deprive by judgment of a court

FORK *v* -ED, -ING, -S to work with a fork (a pronged implement) **FORKEDLY** *adv*

FORKBALL *n* pl. -S a breaking pitch in baseball

FORKER *n* pl. -S one that forks

FORKFUL   *n* pl. FORKFULS or FORKSFUL as much as a fork will hold

FORKIER   comparative of forky

FORKIEST   superlative of forky

FORKLESS   *adj* having no fork

FORKLIFT   *v* -ED, -ING, -S to raise or transport by means of a forklift (a machine with projecting prongs)

FORKLIKE   *adj* resembling a fork

FORKSFUL   a pl. of forkful

FORKY   *adj* FORKIER, FORKIEST resembling a fork

FORLORN   *adj* -LORNER, -LORNEST dreary

FORM   *v* -ED, -ING, -S to produce **FORMABLE** *adj*

FORMAL   *n* pl. -S a social event that requires evening dress

FORMALIN   *n* pl. -S an aqueous solution of formaldehyde

FORMALLY   *adv* in a prescribed or customary manner

FORMANT   *n* pl. -S a characteristic component of the quality of a speech sound

FORMAT   *v* -MATTED, -MATTING, -MATS to produce in a specified style

FORMATE   *n* pl. -S a chemical salt

FORME   *n* pl. -S an assemblage of printing type secured in a metal frame

FORMEE   *adj* having the arms narrow at the center and expanding toward the ends — used of a heraldic cross

FORMER   *n* pl. -S one that forms

FORMERLY   *adv* previously

FORMFUL   *adj* exhibiting good form

FORMIC   *adj* pertaining to ants

FORMLESS   *adj* lacking structure

FORMOL   *n* pl. -S formalin

FORMULA   *n* pl. -LAS or -LAE an exact method for doing something

FORMWORK   *n* pl. -S a set of forms to hold concrete until it sets

FORMYL   *n* pl. -S a univalent chemical radical

FORNIX   *n* pl. -NICES an arched anatomical structure **FORNICAL** *adj*

FORRADER   *adv* further ahead

FORRIT   *adv* toward the front

FORSAKE   *v* -SOOK, -SAKEN, -SAKING, -SAKES to quit or leave entirely

FORSAKER   *n* pl. -S one that forsakes

FORSOOTH   *adv* in truth

FORSPENT   *adj* worn out

FORSWEAR   *v* -SWORE, -SWORN, -SWEARING, -SWEARS to deny under oath

FORT   *n* pl. -S a fortified enclosure or structure

FORTE   *n* pl. -S a strong point

FORTES   pl. of fortis

FORTH   *adv* onward in time, place, or order

FORTIES   pl. of forty

FORTIETH   *n* pl. -S one of forty equal parts

FORTIFY   *v* -FIED, -FYING, -FIES to strengthen against attack

FORTIS   *n* pl. -TES a consonant pronounced with relatively strong release of breath

FORTRESS   *v* -ED, -ING, -ES to fortify

FORTUITY   *n* pl. -ITIES an accidental occurrence

FORTUNE   *v* -TUNED, -TUNING, -TUNES to endow with wealth

FORTY   *n* pl. -TIES a number

FORTYISH   *adj* being about forty years old

FORUM   *n* pl. -RUMS or -RA a public meeting place

FORWARD   *adj* -WARDER, -WARDEST being at a point in advance

FORWARD   *v* -ED, -ING, -S to help onward

FORWENT   past tense of forgo

FORWHY   *adv* for what reason

FORWORN   *adj* worn out

FORZANDO   *n* pl. -DOS sforzato

FOSS   *n* pl. -ES fosse

FOSSA   *n* pl. -SAE an anatomical depression **FOSSATE** *adj*

FOSSA   *n* pl. -S a catlike mammal

FOSSE   *n* pl. -S a ditch

FOSSETTE   *n* pl. -S a small fossa

FOSSICK   *v* -ED, -ING, -S to search for gold

FOSSIL   *n* pl. -S the remains of an animal or plant preserved in the earth's crust

FOSTER   *v* -ED, -ING, -S to promote the growth of

FOSTERER   *n* pl. -S one that fosters

FOU	*adj* drunk
FOUETTE	*n* pl. -S a movement in ballet
FOUGHT	past tense of fight
FOUGHTEN	*adj* exhausted especially from fighting
FOUL	*adj* FOULER, FOULEST offensive to the senses
FOUL	*v* -ED, -ING, -S to make foul
FOULARD	*n* pl. -S a soft fabric
FOULING	*n* pl. -S a deposit or crust
FOULLY	*adv* in a foul manner
FOULNESS	*n* pl. -ES the state of being foul
FOUND	*v* -ED, -ING, -S to establish
FOUNDER	*v* -ED, -ING, -S to become disabled
FOUNDRY	*n* pl. -RIES an establishment in which metal is cast
FOUNT	*n* pl. -S a fountain
FOUNTAIN	*v* -ED, -ING, -S to flow like a fountain (a spring of water)
FOUR	*n* pl. -S a number
FOURCHEE	*adj* having the end of each arm forked — used of a heraldic cross
FOURFOLD	*adj* four times as great
FOURGON	*n* pl. -S a wagon for carrying baggage
FOURPLEX	*n* pl. -ES quadplex
FOURSOME	*n* pl. -S a group of four
FOURTEEN	*n* pl. -S a number
FOURTH	*n* pl. -S one of four equal parts
FOURTHLY	*adv* in the fourth place
FOVEA	*n* pl. -VEAE or -VEAS a shallow anatomical depression **FOVEAL, FOVEATE, FOVEATED** *adj*
FOVEOLA	*n* pl. -LAE or -LAS a small fovea **FOVEOLAR** *adj*
FOVEOLE	*n* pl. -S a foveola
FOVEOLET	*n* pl. -S a foveola
FOWL	*v* -ED, -ING, -S to hunt birds
FOWLER	*n* pl. -S one that fowls
FOWLING	*n* pl. -S the hunting of birds
FOWLPOX	*n* pl. -ES a virus disease of poultry
FOX	*v* -ED, -ING, -ES to outwit
FOXFIRE	*n* pl. -S a glow produced by certain fungi on decaying wood
FOXFISH	*n* pl. -ES a large shark
FOXGLOVE	*n* pl. -S a flowering plant
FOXHOLE	*n* pl. -S a small pit used for cover in a battle area
FOXHOUND	*n* pl. -S a hunting dog
FOXHUNT	*v* -ED, -ING, -S to hunt with hounds for a fox
FOXIER	comparative of foxy
FOXIEST	superlative of foxy
FOXILY	*adv* in a foxy manner
FOXINESS	*n* pl. -ES the state of being foxy
FOXING	*n* pl. -S a piece of material used to cover the upper portion of a shoe
FOXLIKE	*adj* resembling a fox (a carnivorous mammal)
FOXSKIN	*n* pl. -S the skin of a fox
FOXTAIL	*n* pl. -S the tail of a fox
FOXTROT	*v* -TROTTED, -TROTTING, -TROTS to dance the fox trot (a dance for couples)
FOXY	*adj* FOXIER, FOXIEST crafty
FOY	*n* pl. FOYS a farewell feast or gift
FOYER	*n* pl. -S an entrance room or hall
FOZINESS	*n* pl. -ES the state of being fozy
FOZY	*adj* -ZIER, -ZIEST too ripe
FRABJOUS	*adj* splendid
FRACAS	*n* pl. -ES a brawl
FRACTAL	*n* pl. -S a complex geometric curve
FRACTED	*adj* broken
FRACTI	pl. of fractus
FRACTION	*v* -ED, -ING, -S to divide into portions
FRACTUR	*n* pl. -S fraktur
FRACTURE	*v* -TURED, -TURING, -TURES to break
FRACTUS	*n* pl. -TI a ragged cloud
FRAE	*prep* from
FRAENUM	*n* pl. -NA or -NUMS frenum
FRAG	*v* FRAGGED, FRAGGING, FRAGS to injure with a type of grenade
FRAGGING	*n* pl. -S the act of one that frags
FRAGILE	*adj* easily broken or damaged
FRAGMENT	*v* -ED, -ING, -S to break into pieces
FRAGRANT	*adj* having a pleasant odor
FRAIL	*adj* FRAILER, FRAILEST fragile **FRAILLY** *adv*

FRAIL	*n* pl. -S a basket for holding dried fruits	**FREAKY**	*adj* FREAKIER, FREAKIEST freakish
FRAILTY	*n* pl. -TIES a weakness of character	**FRECKLE**	*v* -LED, -LING, -LES to mark with freckles (small, brownish spots)
FRAISE	*n* pl. -S a barrier of pointed stakes	**FRECKLY**	*adj* -LIER, -LIEST marked with freckles
FRAKTUR	*n* pl. -S a style of type	**FREE**	*adj* FREER, FREEST not subject to restriction or control
FRAME	*v* FRAMED, FRAMING, FRAMES to construct by putting together the various parts **FRAMABLE** *adj*	**FREE**	*v* FREED, FREEING, FREES to make free
FRAMER	*n* pl. -S one that frames	**FREEBASE**	*v* -BASED, -BASING, -BASES to use a form of cocaine that is inhaled
FRAMING	*n* pl. -S framework		
FRANC	*n* pl. -S a monetary unit of France	**FREEBEE**	*n* pl. -S freebie
FRANCIUM	*n* pl. -S a radioactive element	**FREEBIE**	*n* pl. -S something given or received without charge
FRANK	*adj* FRANKER, FRANKEST honest and unreserved in speech	**FREEBOOT**	*v* -ED, -ING, -S to plunder
		FREEBORN	*adj* born free
FRANK	*v* -ED, -ING, -S to mark (a piece of mail) for free delivery	**FREED**	past tense of free
FRANKER	*n* pl. -S one that franks	**FREEDMAN**	*n* pl. -MEN a man who has been freed from slavery
FRANKLIN	*n* pl. -S a medieval English landowner	**FREEDOM**	*n* pl. -S the state of being free
FRANKLY	*adv* in a frank manner	**FREEFORM**	*adj* having a free flowing design or shape
FRANTIC	*adj* wildly excited	**FREEHAND**	*adj* drawn by hand without mechanical aids
FRAP	*v* FRAPPED, FRAPPING, FRAPS to bind firmly	**FREEHOLD**	*n* pl. -S a form of tenure of real property
FRAPPE	*n* pl. -S a partly frozen drink		
FRASS	*n* pl. -ES debris made by insects	**FREELOAD**	*v* -ED, -ING, -S to live at the expense of others
FRAT	*n* pl. -S a college fraternity	**FREELY**	*adv* in a free manner
FRATER	*n* pl. -S a comrade	**FREEMAN**	*n* pl. -MEN one who is free
FRAUD	*n* pl. -S trickery	**FREENESS**	*n* pl. -ES freedom
FRAUGHT	*v* -ED, -ING, -S to load down	**FREER**	*n* pl. -S one that frees
FRAULEIN	*n* pl. -S a German governess	**FREESIA**	*n* pl. -S an African herb
FRAY	*v* -ED, -ING, -S to wear off by rubbing	**FREEST**	superlative of free
FRAYING	*n* pl. -S something worn off by rubbing	**FREEWAY**	*n* pl. -WAYS an express highway
		FREEWILL	*adj* voluntary
FRAZIL	*n* pl. -S tiny ice crystals formed in supercooled waters	**FREEZE**	*v* FROZE, FROZEN, FREEZING, FREEZES to become hardened into a solid body by loss of heat
FRAZZLE	*v* -ZLED, -ZLING, -ZLES to fray		
FREAK	*v* -ED, -ING, -S to streak with color	**FREEZER**	*n* pl. -S an apparatus for freezing food
FREAKIER	comparative of freaky	**FREIGHT**	*v* -ED, -ING, -S to load with goods for transportation
FREAKIEST	superlative of freaky	**FREMD**	*adj* strange
FREAKILY	*adv* in a freaky manner	**FREMITUS**	*n* pl. -ES a palpable vibration
FREAKISH	*adj* unusual	**FRENA**	a pl. of frenum
FREAKOUT	*n* pl. -S an event marked by wild excitement	**FRENCH**	*v* -ED, -ING, -ES to cut into thin strips before cooking

FRENETIC	*n* pl. -S a frantic person	**FRIED**	past tense of fry
FRENULUM	*n* pl. -LA or -LUMS a frenum	**FRIEND**	*v* -ED, -ING, -S to enter into a warm association with
FRENUM	*n* pl. -NA or -NUMS a connecting fold of membrane	**FRIENDLY**	*adj* -LIER, -LIEST inclined to approve, help, or support
FRENZILY	*adv* in a frantic manner	**FRIENDLY**	*n* pl. -LIES one who is friendly
FRENZY	*v* -ZIED, -ZYING, -ZIES to make frantic	**FRIER**	*n* pl. -S fryer
FREQUENT	*adj* -QUENTER, -QUENTEST occurring again and again	**FRIES**	present 3d person sing. of fry
		FRIEZE	*n* pl. -S a coarse woolen fabric
FREQUENT	*v* -ED, -ING, -S to be in or at often	**FRIGATE**	*n* pl. -S a sailing vessel
		FRIGHT	*v* -ED, -ING, -S to frighten
FRERE	*n* pl. -S brother	**FRIGHTEN**	*v* -ED, -ING, -S to make afraid
FRESCO	*v* -ED, -ING, -ES or -S to paint on a surface of plaster	**FRIGID**	*adj* very cold **FRIGIDLY** *adv*
FRESCOER	*n* pl. -S one that frescoes	**FRIJOL**	*n* pl. -ES a bean used as food
FRESH	*adj* FRESHER, FRESHEST new	**FRIJOLE**	*n* pl. -S frijol
FRESH	*v* -ED, -ING, -ES to freshen	**FRILL**	*v* -ED, -ING, -S to provide with a frill (an ornamental ruffled edge)
FRESHEN	*v* -ED, -ING, -S to make or become fresh	**FRILLER**	*n* pl. -S one that frills
FRESHET	*n* pl. -S a sudden overflow of a stream	**FRILLING**	*n* pl. -S an arrangement of frills
		FRILLY	*adj* FRILLIER, FRILLIEST having frills
FRESHLY	*adv* in a fresh manner	**FRINGE**	*v* FRINGED, FRINGING, FRINGES to provide with a fringe (an ornamental border)
FRESHMAN	*n* pl. -MEN a first-year student		
FRESNEL	*n* pl. -S a unit of frequency		
FRET	*v* FRETTED, FRETTING, FRETS to worry	**FRINGY**	*adj* FRINGIER, FRINGIEST resembling a fringe
FRETFUL	*adj* inclined to fret	**FRIPPERY**	*n* pl. -PERIES excessive ornamentation
FRETLESS	*adj* having no fretwork		
FRETSAW	*n* pl. -S a narrow-bladed saw	**FRISE**	*n* pl. -S frieze
FRETSOME	*adj* fretful	**FRISETTE**	*n* pl. -S frizette
FRETTED	past tense of fret	**FRISEUR**	*n* pl. -S a hairdresser
FRETTER	*n* pl. -S one that frets	**FRISK**	*v* -ED, -ING, -S to move or leap about playfully
FRETTING	present participle of fret	**FRISKER**	*n* pl. -S one that frisks
FRETTY	*adj* -TIER, -TIEST fretful	**FRISKET**	*n* pl. -S a frame used to protect paper in a printing press
FRETWORK	*n* pl. -S ornamental work consisting of interlacing parts		
FRIABLE	*adj* easily crumbled	**FRISKY**	*adj* FRISKIER, FRISKIEST lively and playful **FRISKILY** *adv*
FRIAR	*n* pl. -S a member of a religious order **FRIARLY** *adj*	**FRISSON**	*n* pl. -S a shudder
FRIARY	*n* pl. -ARIES a monastery of friars	**FRIT**	*v* FRITTED, FRITTING, FRITS to fuse into a vitreous substance
FRIBBLE	*v* -BLED, -BLING, -BLES to act foolishly	**FRITH**	*n* pl. -S firth
		FRITT	*v* -ED, -ING, -S to frit
FRIBBLER	*n* pl. -S one that fribbles	**FRITTATA**	*n* pl. -S an unfolded omelet with chopped vegetables or meat
FRICANDO	*n* pl. -DOES a roasted loin of veal		
FRICTION	*n* pl. -S the rubbing of one body against another	**FRITTED**	past tense of frit
		FRITTER	*v* -ED, -ING, -S to squander little by little
FRIDGE	*n* pl. -S a refrigerator	**FRITTING**	present participle of frit

FRITZ	*n* pl. -ES a nonfunctioning state
FRIVOL	*v* -OLED, -OLING, -OLS or -OLLED, -OLLING, -OLS to behave playfully
FRIVOLER	*n* pl. -S one that frivols
FRIZ	*v* -ED, -ING, -ES to frizz
FRIZER	*n* pl. -S frizzer
FRIZETTE	*n* pl. -S a frizzed fringe of hair
FRIZZ	*v* -ED, -ING, -ES to form into small, tight curls
FRIZZER	*n* pl. -S one that frizzes
FRIZZIER	comparative of frizzy
FRIZZIEST	superlative of frizzy
FRIZZILY	*adv* in a frizzy manner
FRIZZLE	*v* -ZLED, -ZLING, -ZLES to frizz
FRIZZLER	*n* pl. -S one that frizzles
FRIZZLY	*adj* -ZLIER, -ZLIEST frizzy
FRIZZY	*adj* FRIZZIER, FRIZZIEST tightly curled
FRO	*adv* away
FROCK	*v* -ED, -ING, -S to clothe in a long, loose outer garment
FROE	*n* pl. -S a cleaving tool
FROG	*v* FROGGED, FROGGING, FROGS to hunt frogs (web-footed, tailless amphibians)
FROGEYE	*n* pl. -S a plant disease **FROGEYED** *adj*
FROGFISH	*n* pl. -ES a marine fish
FROGGED	past tense of frog
FROGGING	present participle of frog
FROGGY	*adj* -GIER, -GIEST abounding in frogs
FROGLIKE	*adj* resembling a frog
FROGMAN	*n* pl. -MEN a person equipped for extended periods of underwater swimming
FROLIC	*v* -ICKED, -ICKING, -ICS to play and run about merrily **FROLICKY** *adj*
FROM	*prep* starting at
FROMAGE	*n* pl. -S cheese
FROMENTY	*n* pl. -TIES frumenty
FROND	*n* pl. -S a type of leaf **FRONDED, FRONDOSE** *adj*
FRONDEUR	*n* pl. -S a rebel
FRONS	*n* pl. FRONTES the upper anterior portion of an insect's head
FRONT	*v* -ED, -ING, -S to provide with a front (a forward part)
FRONT	*adj* FRONTER articulated at the front of the oral passage
FRONTAGE	*n* pl. -S the front of a building or lot
FRONTAL	*n* pl. -S a bone of the skull
FRONTES	pl. of frons
FRONTIER	*n* pl. -S a border between two countries
FRONTLET	*n* pl. -S a decorative band worn across the forehead
FRONTON	*n* pl. -S a jai alai arena
FRORE	*adj* frozen
FROSH	*n* pl. FROSH a freshman
FROST	*v* -ED, -ING, -S to cover with frost (a deposit of minute ice crystals)
FROSTBIT	*adj* injured by extreme cold
FROSTED	*n* pl. -S a type of milk shake
FROSTING	*n* pl. -S icing
FROSTY	*adj* FROSTIER, FROSTIEST covered with frost **FROSTILY** *adv*
FROTH	*v* -ED, -ING, -S to foam
FROTHY	*adj* FROTHIER, FROTHIEST foamy **FROTHILY** *adv*
FROTTAGE	*n* pl. -S masturbation by rubbing against another person
FROTTEUR	*n* pl. -S one who practices frottage
FROUFROU	*n* pl. -S a rustling sound
FROUNCE	*v* FROUNCED, FROUNCING, FROUNCES to pleat
FROUZY	*adj* -ZIER, -ZIEST frowzy
FROW	*n* pl. -S froe
FROWARD	*adj* disobedient
FROWN	*v* -ED, -ING, -S to contract the brow in displeasure
FROWNER	*n* pl. -S one that frowns
FROWST	*v* -ED, -ING, -S to lounge in a stuffy room
FROWSTY	*adj* -TIER, -TIEST musty
FROWSY	*adj* -SIER, -SIEST frowzy
FROWZY	*adj* -ZIER, -ZIEST unkempt **FROWZILY** *adv*
FROZE	past tense of freeze
FROZEN	*adj* very cold **FROZENLY** *adv*
FRUCTIFY	*v* -FIED, -FYING, -FIES to bear fruit

FRUCTOSE *n* pl. -S a sugar found in various fruits

FRUG *v* FRUGGED, FRUGGING, FRUGS to perform a type of vigorous dance

FRUGAL *adj* thrifty **FRUGALLY** *adv*

FRUIT *v* -ED, -ING, -S to bear fruit (usually edible reproductive bodies of a seed plant)

FRUITAGE *n* pl. -S the process of bearing fruit

FRUITER *n* pl. -S one that grows or sells fruit

FRUITFUL *adj* -FULLER, -FULLEST producing abundantly

FRUITIER comparative of fruity

FRUITIEST superlative of fruity

FRUITION *n* pl. -S the accomplishment of something desired

FRUITLET *n* pl. -S a small fruit

FRUITY *adj* FRUITIER, FRUITIEST suggestive of fruit **FRUITILY** *adv*

FRUMENTY *n* pl. -TIES a dish of wheat boiled in milk and sweetened with sugar

FRUMP *n* pl. -S a dowdy woman **FRUMPISH** *adj*

FRUMPY *adj* FRUMPIER, FRUMPIEST dowdy **FRUMPILY** *adv*

FRUSTULE *n* pl. -S the shell of a diatom

FRUSTUM *n* pl. -TA or -TUMS a part of a conical solid

FRY *v* FRIED, FRYING, FRIES to cook over direct heat in hot fat or oil

FRYER *n* pl. -S one that fries

FRYPAN *n* pl. -S a pan for frying food

FUB *v* FUBBED, FUBBING, FUBS to fob

FUBSY *adj* FUBSIER, FUBSIEST chubby and somewhat squat

FUCHSIA *n* pl. -S a flowering shrub

FUCHSIN *n* pl. -S a red dye

FUCHSINE *n* pl. -S fuchsin

FUCI a pl. of fucus

FUCOID *n* pl. -S a brown seaweed **FUCOIDAL** *adj*

FUCOSE *n* pl. -S a type of sugar

FUCOUS *adj* of or pertaining to fucoids

FUCUS *n* pl. -CI or -CUSES any of a genus of brown algae

FUD *n* pl. -S an old-fashioned person

FUDDLE *v* -DLED, -DLING, -DLES to confuse

FUDGE *v* FUDGED, FUDGING, FUDGES to falsify

FUEHRER *n* pl. -S fuhrer

FUEL *v* -ELED, -ELING, -ELS or -ELLED, -ELLING, -ELS to provide with fuel (material used to produce energy)

FUELER *n* pl. -S one that fuels

FUELLER *n* pl. -S fueler

FUELLING a present participle of fuel

FUELWOOD *n* pl. -S firewood

FUG *v* FUGGED, FUGGING, FUGS to make stuffy and odorous

FUGACITY *n* pl. -TIES lack of enduring qualities

FUGAL *adj* being in the style of a fugue **FUGALLY** *adv*

FUGATO *n* pl. -TOS a fugal composition

FUGGED past tense of fug

FUGGING present participle of fug

FUGGY *adj* -GIER, -GIEST stuffy and odorous **FUGGILY** *adv*

FUGIO *n* pl. -GIOS a former coin of the United States

FUGITIVE *n* pl. -S one who flees

FUGLE *v* -GLED, -GLING, -GLES to lead

FUGLEMAN *n* pl. -MEN a leader

FUGU *n* pl. -S a toxin-containing fish

FUGUE *v* FUGUED, FUGUING, FUGUES to compose a fugue (a type of musical composition)

FUGUIST *n* pl. -S one who composes fugues

FUHRER *n* pl. -S a leader

FUJI *n* pl. -S a silk fabric

FULCRUM *n* pl. -CRUMS or -CRA a support for a lever

FULFIL *v* -FILLED, -FILLING, -FILS to fulfill

FULFILL *v* -ED, -ING, -S to bring about the accomplishment of

FULGENT *adj* shining brightly

FULGID *adj* fulgent

FULHAM *n* pl. -S a loaded die

FULL *adj* FULLER, FULLEST filled completely

FULL *v* -ED, -ING, -S to shrink and thicken, as cloth

FULLAM   *n* pl. -S fulham

FULLBACK   *n* pl. -S an offensive back in football

FULLER   *v* -ED, -ING, -S to groove with a type of hammer

FULLERY   *n* pl. -ERIES a place for fulling cloth

FULLFACE   *n* pl. -S a heavy-faced type

FULLNESS   *n* pl. -ES the state of being full

FULLY   *adv* in a full manner

FULMAR   *n* pl. -S an arctic seabird

FULMINE   *v* -MINED, -MINING, -MINES to explode loudly

FULMINIC   *adj* highly explosive

FULNESS   *n* pl. -ES fullness

FULSOME   *adj* repulsive

FULVOUS   *adj* of a brownish yellow color

FUMARASE   *n* pl. -S an enzyme

FUMARATE   *n* pl. -S a chemical salt

FUMARIC   *adj* pertaining to a certain acid

FUMAROLE   *n* pl. -S a hole from which volcanic vapors issue

FUMATORY   *n* pl. -RIES a fumigation chamber

FUMBLE   *v* -BLED, -BLING, -BLES to handle clumsily

FUMBLER   *n* pl. -S one that fumbles

FUME   *v* FUMED, FUMING, FUMES to give off fumes (gaseous exhalations)

FUMELESS   *adj* having no fumes

FUMELIKE   *adj* resembling fumes

FUMER   *n* pl. -S one that fumes

FUMET   *n* pl. -S the odor of meat while cooking

FUMETTE   *n* pl. -S fumet

FUMIER   comparative of fumy

FUMIEST   superlative of fumy

FUMIGANT   *n* pl. -S a substance used in fumigating

FUMIGATE   *v* -GATED, -GATING, -GATES to subject to fumes in order to destroy pests

FUMING   present participle of fume

FUMINGLY   *adv* angrily

FUMITORY   *n* pl. -RIES a climbing plant

FUMULUS   *n* pl. -LI a thin cloud

FUMY   *adj* FUMIER, FUMIEST producing or full of fumes

FUN   *v* FUNNED, FUNNING, FUNS to act playfully

FUN   *adj* FUNNER, FUNNEST providing enjoyment

FUNCTION   *v* -ED, -ING, -S to be in action

FUNCTOR   *n* pl. -S one that functions

FUND   *v* -ED, -ING, -S to provide money for

FUNDUS   *n* pl. -DI the inner basal surface of a bodily organ **FUNDIC** *adj*

FUNERAL   *n* pl. -S a ceremony held for a dead person

FUNERARY   *adj* pertaining to a funeral

FUNEREAL   *adj* funerary

FUNEST   *adj* portending death or evil

FUNFAIR   *n* pl. -S an amusement park

FUNGAL   *n* pl. -S a fungus

FUNGI   a pl. of fungus

FUNGIBLE   *n* pl. -S something that may be exchanged for an equivalent unit of the same class

FUNGIC   *adj* fungous

FUNGO   *n* pl. -GOES a fly ball hit to a fielder for practice in baseball

FUNGOID   *n* pl. -S a growth resembling a fungus

FUNGOUS   *adj* pertaining to a fungus

FUNGUS   *n* pl. -GI or -GUSES any of a major group of lower plants

FUNICLE   *n* pl. -S a cordlike anatomical structure

FUNICULI   *n/pl* funicles

FUNK   *v* -ED, -ING, -S to shrink back in fear

FUNKER   *n* pl. -S one that funks

FUNKIA   *n* pl. -S a flowering plant

FUNKY   *adj* FUNKIER, FUNKIEST having an offensive odor

FUNNED   past tense of fun

FUNNEL   *v* -NELED, -NELING, -NELS or -NELLED, -NELLING, -NELS to pass through a funnel (a cone-shaped utensil)

FUNNER   comparative of fun

FUNNEST   superlative of fun

FUNNING   present participle of fun

FUNNY   *adj* -NIER, -NIEST causing laughter or amusement **FUNNILY** *adv*

FUNNY   *n* pl. -NIES a comic strip

FUNNYMAN   *n* pl. -MEN a comedian

FUR   *v* FURRED, FURRING, FURS to cover with fur (a dressed animal pelt)

FURAN   *n* pl. -S a flammable liquid

FURANE   *n* pl. -S furan

FURANOSE   *n* pl. -S a type of sugar

FURBELOW   *v* -ED, -ING, -S to decorate with ruffles

FURBISH   *v* -ED, -ING, -ES to polish

FURCATE   *v* -CATED, -CATING, -CATES to divide into branches

FURCRAEA   *n* pl. -S a tropical plant

FURCULA   *n* pl. -LAE a forked bone **FURCULAR** *adj*

FURCULUM   *n* pl. -LA a furcula

FURFUR   *n* pl. -ES dandruff

FURFURAL   *n* pl. -S a chemical compound

FURFURAN   *n* pl. -S furan

FURIBUND   *adj* furious

FURIES   pl. of fury

FURIOSO   *adv* with great force — used as a musical direction

FURIOUS   *adj* extremely angry

FURL   *v* -ED, -ING, -S to roll up **FURLABLE** *adj*

FURLER   *n* pl. -S one that furls

FURLESS   *adj* having no fur

FURLONG   *n* pl. -S a unit of distance

FURLOUGH   *v* -ED, -ING, -S to grant a leave of absence to

FURMENTY   *n* pl. -TIES frumenty

FURMETY   *n* pl. -TIES frumenty

FURMITY   *n* pl. -TIES frumenty

FURNACE   *v* -NACED, -NACING, -NACES to subject to heat

FURNISH   *v* -ED, -ING, -ES to equip

FUROR   *n* pl. -S an uproar

FURORE   *n* pl. -S furor

FURRED   past tense of fur

FURRIER   *n* pl. -S one that deals in furs

FURRIERY   *n* pl. -ERIES the business of a furrier

FURRIEST   superlative of furry

FURRILY   *adv* in a furry manner

FURRINER   *n* pl. -S a foreigner

FURRING   *n* pl. -S a trimming or lining of fur

FURROW   *v* -ED, -ING, -S to make furrows (narrow depressions) in

FURROWER   *n* pl. -S one that furrows

FURROWY   *adj* marked by furrows

FURRY   *adj* -RIER, -RIEST covered with fur

FURTHER   *v* -ED, -ING, -S to help forward

FURTHEST   a superlative of far

FURTIVE   *adj* stealthy

FURUNCLE   *n* pl. -S a painful swelling of the skin

FURY   *n* pl. -RIES violent anger

FURZE   *n* pl. -S a spiny shrub

FURZY   *adj* FURZIER, FURZIEST abounding in furze

FUSAIN   *n* pl. -S a fine charcoal used in drawing

FUSCOUS   *adj* of a dusky color

FUSE   *v* FUSED, FUSING, FUSES to equip with a fuse (a detonating device)

FUSEE   *n* pl. -S a large-headed friction match

FUSEL   *n* pl. -S an oily liquid

FUSELAGE   *n* pl. -S the body of an airplane

FUSELESS   *adj* lacking a fuse

FUSIBLE   *adj* capable of being melted **FUSIBLY** *adv*

FUSIFORM   *adj* tapering toward each end

FUSIL   *n* pl. -S a type of musket

FUSILE   *adj* formed by melting

FUSILEER   *n* pl. -S fusilier

FUSILIER   *n* pl. -S a soldier armed with a fusil

FUSILLI   *n* pl. -S spiral-shaped pasta

FUSING   present participle of fuse

FUSION   *n* pl. -S the act of melting together

FUSS   *v* -ED, -ING, -ES to be overly concerned with small details

FUSSER   *n* pl. -S one that fusses

FUSSPOT   *n* pl. -S a fusser

FUSSY   *adj* FUSSIER, FUSSIEST overly concerned with small details **FUSSILY** *adv*

FUSTIAN   *n* pl. -S a cotton fabric

FUSTIC   *n* pl. -S a tropical tree

FUSTY   *adj* -TIER, -TIEST musty **FUSTILY** *adv*

FUTHARC	*n* pl. -S futhark
FUTHARK	*n* pl. -S an ancient alphabet
FUTHORC	*n* pl. -S futhark
FUTHORK	*n* pl. -S futhark
FUTILE	*adj* having no useful result **FUTILELY** *adv*
FUTILITY	*n* pl. -TIES the quality of being futile
FUTON	*n* pl. -S a cotton filled mattress for use as a bed
FUTTOCK	*n* pl. -S a curved timber in the frame of a wooden ship
FUTURE	*n* pl. -S the time yet to come **FUTURAL** *adj*
FUTURISM	*n* pl. -S an artistic and literary movement
FUTURIST	*n* pl. -S an advocate of futurism
FUTURITY	*n* pl. -TIES the future
FUTZ	*v* -ED, -ING, -ES to spend time aimlessly
FUZE	*v* FUZED, FUZING, FUZES to fuse
FUZEE	*n* pl. -S fusee
FUZIL	*n* pl. -S fusil
FUZING	present participle of fuze
FUZZ	*v* -ED, -ING, -ES to become fuzzy
FUZZY	*adj* FUZZIER, FUZZIEST blurry **FUZZILY** *adv*
FYCE	*n* pl. -S feist
FYKE	*n* pl. -S a bag-shaped fishnet
FYLFOT	*n* pl. -S a swastika
FYTTE	*n* pl. -S a division of a poem or song

GAB	*v* GABBED, GABBING, GABS to chatter	**GADI**	*n* pl. -S gaddi
		GADID	*n* pl. -S gadoid
GABBARD	*n* pl. -S a barge	**GADOID**	*n* pl. -S a type of fish
GABBART	*n* pl. -S gabbard	**GADROON**	*v* -ED, -ING, -S to decorate with bands of fluted or reeded molding
GABBED	past tense of gab		
GABBER	*n* pl. -S one that gabs	**GADWALL**	*n* pl. -S a wild duck
GABBIER	comparative of gabby	**GADZOOKS**	*interj* — used as a mild oath
GABBIEST	superlative of gabby	**GAE**	*v* GAED, GANE or GAEN, GAEING or GAUN, GAES to go
GABBING	present participle of gab		
GABBLE	*v* -BLED, -BLING, -BLES to jabber	**GAFF**	*v* -ED, -ING, -S to catch a fish with a sharp hook
GABBLER	*n* pl. -S one that gabbles	**GAFFE**	*n* pl. -S a social blunder
GABBRO	*n* pl. -BROS a type of rock **GABBROIC, GABBROID** *adj*	**GAFFER**	*n* pl. -S an old man
		GAG	*v* GAGGED, GAGGING, GAGS to stop up the mouth
GABBY	*adj* -BIER, -BIEST talkative		
GABELLE	*n* pl. -S a tax on salt **GABELLED** *adj*	**GAGA**	*adj* crazy
		GAGAKU	*n* pl. -S ancient court music of Japan
GABFEST	*n* pl. -S an informal gathering for general talk		
		GAGE	*v* GAGED, GAGING, GAGES to pledge as security
GABIES	pl. of gaby		
GABION	*n* pl. -S a type of basket	**GAGER**	*n* pl. -S gauger
GABLE	*v* -BLED, -BLING, -BLES to form a triangular section of a wall	**GAGGED**	past tense of gag
		GAGGER	*n* pl. -S one that gags
GABOON	*n* pl. -S a spittoon	**GAGGING**	present participle of gag
GABY	*n* pl. -BIES a dolt	**GAGGLE**	*v* -GLED, -GLING, -GLES to cackle
GAD	*v* GADDED, GADDING, GADS to roam about restlessly		
		GAGING	present participle of gage
GADABOUT	*n* pl. -S one that gads about	**GAGMAN**	*n* pl. -MEN one who writes jokes
GADARENE	*adj* headlong	**GAGSTER**	*n* pl. -S a gagman
GADDED	past tense of gad	**GAHNITE**	*n* pl. -S a mineral
GADDER	*n* pl. -S one that gads about	**GAIETY**	*n* pl. -ETIES festive activity
GADDI	*n* pl. -S a hassock	**GAIJIN**	*n* pl. GAIJIN a foreigner in Japan
GADDING	present participle of gad	**GAILY**	*adv* in a gay manner
GADFLY	*n* pl. -FLIES a biting fly	**GAIN**	*v* -ED, -ING, -S to acquire **GAINABLE** *adj*
GADGET	*n* pl. -S a mechanical device **GADGETY** *adj*		
		GAINER	*n* pl. -S one that gains
GADGETRY	*n* pl. -RIES the devising or constructing of gadgets	**GAINFUL**	*adj* profitable

GAINLESS *adj* profitless

GAINLY *adj* -LIER, -LIEST graceful

GAINSAY *v* -SAID, -SAYING, -SAYS to deny

GAINST *prep* against

GAIT *v* -ED, -ING, -S to train a horse to move in a particular way

GAITER *n* pl. -S a covering for the lower leg

GAL *n* pl. -S a girl

GALA *n* pl. -S a celebration

GALABIA *n* pl. -S djellaba

GALABIEH *n* pl. -S djellaba

GALABIYA *n* pl. -S djellaba

GALACTIC *adj* pertaining to a galaxy

GALAGO *n* pl. -GOS a small primate

GALAH *n* pl. -S a cockatoo

GALANGAL *n* pl. -S a medicinal plant

GALATEA *n* pl. -S a strong cotton fabric

GALAVANT *v* -ED, -ING, -S to gad about

GALAX *n* pl. -ES an evergreen herb

GALAXY *n* pl. -AXIES a large system of celestial bodies

GALBANUM *n* pl. -S a gum resin

GALE *n* pl. -S a strong wind

GALEA *n* pl. -LEAE or -LEAS a helmet-shaped anatomical part **GALEATE, GALEATED** *adj*

GALENA *n* pl. -S the principal ore of lead **GALENIC** *adj*

GALENITE *n* pl. -S galena

GALERE *n* pl. -S a group of people having a common quality

GALILEE *n* pl. -S a type of porch

GALIOT *n* pl. -S galliot

GALIPOT *n* pl. -S a type of turpentine

GALIVANT *v* -ED, -ING, -S to gad about

GALL *v* -ED, -ING, -S to vex or irritate

GALLANT *v* -ED, -ING, -S to court a woman

GALLATE *n* pl. -S a chemical salt

GALLEASS *n* pl. -ES a large war galley

GALLEIN *n* pl. -S a green dye

GALLEON *n* pl. -S a large sailing vessel

GALLERIA *n* pl. -S a roofed promenade or court

GALLERY *v* -LERIED, -LERYING, -LERIES to provide with a long covered area

GALLET *v* -ED, -ING, -S to fill in mortar joints with stone chips

GALLETA *n* pl. -S a perennial grass

GALLEY *n* pl. -LEYS a long, low medieval ship

GALLFLY *n* pl. -FLIES a small insect

GALLIARD *n* pl. -S a lively dance

GALLIASS *n* pl. -ES galleass

GALLIC *adj* containing gallium

GALLICAN *adj* pertaining to a French religious movement

GALLIED past tense of gally

GALLIES present 3d person sing. of gally

GALLIOT *n* pl. -S a small galley

GALLIPOT *n* pl. -S a small earthen jar

GALLIUM *n* pl. -S a metallic element

GALLNUT *n* pl. -S an abnormal swelling of plant tissue

GALLON *n* pl. -S a unit of liquid measure

GALLOON *n* pl. -S an ornamental braid

GALLOOT *n* pl. -S galoot

GALLOP *v* -ED, -ING, -S to ride a horse at full speed

GALLOPER *n* pl. -S one that gallops

GALLOUS *adj* containing gallium

GALLOWS *n* pl. -ES a structure used for hanging a condemned person

GALLUS *n* pl. -ES a suspender for trousers **GALLUSED** *adj*

GALLY *v* -LIED, -LYING, -LIES to frighten

GALOOT *n* pl. -S an awkward or uncouth person

GALOP *v* -ED, -ING, -S to dance a galop (a lively round dance)

GALOPADE *n* pl. -S a lively round dance

GALORE *n* pl. -S abundance

GALOSH *n* pl. -ES an overshoe **GALOSHED** *adj*

GALOSHE *n* pl. -S galosh

GALUMPH *v* -ED, -ING, -S to move clumsily

GALVANIC *adj* pertaining to a direct electric current

GALYAC *n* pl. -S galyak

GALYAK *n* pl. -S a fur made from lambskin

GAM *v* GAMMED, GAMMING, GAMS to visit socially

GAMA *n* pl. -S a pasture grass

GAMASHES	*n/pl* boots worn by horseback riders
GAMAY	*n* pl. -MAYS a red grape
GAMB	*n* pl. -S a leg
GAMBA	*n* pl. -S a bass viol
GAMBADE	*n* pl. -S a gambado
GAMBADO	*n* pl. -DOES or -DOS a leap made by a horse
GAMBE	*n* pl. -S gamb
GAMBESON	*n* pl. -S a medieval coat
GAMBIA	*n* pl. -S gambier
GAMBIER	*n* pl. -S an extract obtained from an Asian vine
GAMBIR	*n* pl. -S gambier
GAMBIT	*n* pl. -S a type of chess opening
GAMBLE	*v* -BLED, -BLING, -BLES to play a game of chance for money or valuables
GAMBLER	*n* pl. -S one that gambles
GAMBOGE	*n* pl. -S a gum resin
GAMBOL	*v* -BOLED, -BOLING, -BOLS or -BOLLED, -BOLLING, -BOLS to leap about playfully
GAMBREL	*n* pl. -S a part of a horse's leg
GAMBUSIA	*n* pl. -S a small fish
GAME	*adj* GAMER, GAMEST plucky
GAME	*v* GAMED, GAMING, GAMES to gamble
GAMECOCK	*n* pl. -S a rooster trained for fighting
GAMELAN	*n* pl. -S a type of orchestra
GAMELIKE	*adj* similar to a game (a contest governed by a set of rules)
GAMELY	*adv* in a game manner
GAMENESS	*n* pl. -ES the quality of being game
GAMER	*n* pl. -S an avid game player
GAMESMAN	*n* pl. -MEN one who plays games
GAMESOME	*adj* playful
GAMEST	superlative of game
GAMESTER	*n* pl. -S a gambler
GAMETE	*n* pl. -S a mature reproductive cell **GAMETIC** *adj*
GAMEY	*adj* GAMIER, GAMIEST gamy
GAMIC	*adj* requiring fertilization
GAMIER	comparative of gamy
GAMIEST	superlative of gamy
GAMILY	*adv* in a game manner
GAMIN	*n* pl. -S an urchin
GAMINE	*n* pl. -S a tomboy
GAMINESS	*n* pl. -ES the quality of being gamy
GAMING	*n* pl. -S the practice of gambling
GAMMA	*n* pl. -S a Greek letter
GAMMADIA	*n/pl* Greek ornamental designs
GAMMED	past tense of gam
GAMMER	*n* pl. -S an old woman
GAMMIER	comparative of gammy
GAMMIEST	superlative of gammy
GAMMING	present participle of gam
GAMMON	*v* -ED, -ING, -S to mislead by deceptive talk
GAMMONER	*n* pl. -S one that gammons
GAMMY	*adj* -MIER, -MIEST lame
GAMODEME	*n* pl. -S a somewhat isolated breeding community of organisms
GAMP	*n* pl. -S a large umbrella
GAMUT	*n* pl. -S an entire range
GAMY	*adj* GAMIER, GAMIEST plucky
GAN	past tense of gin
GANACHE	*n* pl. -S creamy chocolate mixture
GANDER	*v* -ED, -ING, -S to wander
GANE	a past participle of gae
GANEF	*n* pl. -S a thief
GANEV	*n* pl. -S ganef
GANG	*v* -ED, -ING, -S to form into a gang (a group)
GANGER	*n* pl. -S a foreman of a gang of laborers
GANGLAND	*n* pl. -S the criminal underworld
GANGLIA	a pl. of ganglion
GANGLIAL	*adj* gangliar
GANGLIAR	*adj* pertaining to a ganglion
GANGLIER	comparative of gangly
GANGLIEST	superlative of gangly
GANGLING	*adj* awkwardly tall and lanky
GANGLION	*n* pl. -GLIA or -GLIONS a group of nerve cells
GANGLY	*adj* -GLIER, -GLIEST gangling
GANGPLOW	*n* pl. -S an agricultural implement
GANGREL	*n* pl. -S a vagabond
GANGRENE	*v* -GRENED, -GRENING, -GRENES to suffer the loss of tissue in part of the body

GANGSTER *n* pl. -S a member of a criminal gang

GANGUE *n* pl. -S the worthless rock in which valuable minerals are found

GANGWAY *n* pl. -WAYS a passageway

GANISTER *n* pl. -S a type of rock

GANJA *n* pl. -S cannabis used for smoking

GANJAH *n* pl. -S ganja

GANNET *n* pl. -S a large seabird

GANOF *n* pl. -S ganef

GANOID *n* pl. -S a type of fish

GANTLET *v* -ED, -ING, -S to overlap railroad tracks

GANTLINE *n* pl. -S a rope on a ship

GANTLOPE *n* pl. -S a former military punishment

GANTRY *n* pl. -TRIES a structure for supporting railroad signals

GANYMEDE *n* pl. -S a youth who serves liquors

GAOL *v* -ED, -ING, -S to jail

GAOLER *n* pl. -S jailer

GAP *v* GAPPED, GAPPING, GAPS to make an opening in

GAPE *v* GAPED, GAPING, GAPES to stare with open mouth

GAPER *n* pl. -S one that gapes

GAPESEED *n* pl. -S something that causes wonder

GAPEWORM *n* pl. -S a worm that causes a disease of young birds

GAPING present participle of gape

GAPINGLY *adv* in a gaping manner

GAPOSIS *n* pl. -SISES a gap in a row of buttons or snaps

GAPPED past tense of gap

GAPPING present participle of gap

GAPPY *adj* -PIER, -PIEST having openings

GAPY *adj* infested with gapeworms

GAR *v* GARRED, GARRING, GARS to cause or compel

GARAGE *v* -RAGED, -RAGING, -RAGES to put in a garage (a car shelter)

GARB *v* -ED, -ING, -S to clothe

GARBAGE *n* pl. -S food waste

GARBANZO *n* pl. -ZOS a chickpea

GARBLE *v* -BLED, -BLING, -BLES to distort the meaning of

GARBLER *n* pl. -S one that garbles

GARBLESS *adj* being without clothing

GARBOARD *n* pl. -S a plank on a ship's bottom

GARBOIL *n* pl. -S turmoil

GARCON *n* pl. -S a waiter

GARDANT *adj* turned directly toward the observer — used of a heraldic animal

GARDEN *v* -ED, -ING, -S to cultivate a plot of ground

GARDENER *n* pl. -S one that gardens

GARDENIA *n* pl. -S a tropical shrub or tree

GARDYLOO *interj* — used as a warning cry

GARFISH *n* pl. -ES a freshwater fish

GARGANEY *n* pl. -NEYS a small duck

GARGET *n* pl. -S mastitis of domestic animals **GARGETY** *adj*

GARGLE *v* -GLED, -GLING, -GLES to rinse the mouth or throat

GARGLER *n* pl. -S one that gargles

GARGOYLE *n* pl. -S an ornamental figure

GARIGUE *n* pl. -S a low scrubland

GARISH *adj* gaudy **GARISHLY** *adv*

GARLAND *v* -ED, -ING, -S to deck with wreaths of flowers

GARLIC *n* pl. -S an herb used in cooking **GARLICKY** *adj*

GARMENT *v* -ED, -ING, -S to clothe

GARNER *v* -ED, -ING, -S to gather and store

GARNET *n* pl. -S a mineral

GARNI *adj* garnished

GARNISH *v* -ED, -ING, -ES to decorate

GAROTE *v* -ROTED, -ROTING, -ROTES to garrote

GAROTTE *v* -ROTTED, -ROTTING, -ROTTES to garrote

GAROTTER *n* pl. -S one that garottes

GARPIKE *n* pl. -S a garfish

GARRED past tense of gar

GARRET *n* pl. -S an attic

GARRING present participle of gar

GARRISON *v* -ED, -ING, -S to assign to a military post

GARRON *n* pl. -S a small, sturdy horse

GARROTE *v* -ROTED, -ROTING, -ROTES to execute by strangling

GARROTER *n* pl. -S one that garrotes

GARROTTE *v* -ROTTED, -ROTTING, -ROTTES to garrote

GARTER *v* -ED, -ING, -S to fasten with an elastic band

GARTH *n* pl. -S a yard or garden

GARVEY *n* pl. -VEYS a small scow

GAS *v* GASSED, GASSING, GASES or GASSES to supply with gas (a substance capable of indefinite expansion)

GASALIER *n* pl. -S gaselier

GASBAG *n* pl. -S a bag for holding gas

GASCON *n* pl. -S a boaster

GASELIER *n* pl. -S a gaslight chandelier

GASEOUS *adj* pertaining to gas

GASH *v* -ED, -ING, -ES to make a long deep cut in

GASH *adj* GASHER, GASHEST knowing

GASHOUSE *n* pl. -S a gasworks

GASIFIED past tense of gasify

GASIFIER *n* pl. -S one that gasifies

GASIFORM *adj* having the form of gas

GASIFY *v* -IFIED, -IFYING, -IFIES to convert into gas

GASKET *n* pl. -S packing for making something fluid-tight

GASKIN *n* pl. -S a part of a horse's leg

GASKING *n* pl. -S a gasket

GASLESS *adj* having no gas

GASLIGHT *n* pl. -S light made by burning gas

GASLIT *adj* illuminated by gaslight

GASMAN *n* pl. -MEN an employee of a gas company

GASOGENE *n* pl. -S gazogene

GASOHOL *n* pl. -S a fuel mixture of gasoline and ethyl alcohol

GASOLENE *n* pl. -S gasoline

GASOLIER *n* pl. -S gaselier

GASOLINE *n* pl. -S a liquid fuel

GASP *v* -ED, -ING, -S to breathe convulsively

GASPER *n* pl. -S a cigarette

GASSED past tense of gas

GASSER *n* pl. -S one that gasses

GASSES a present 3d person sing. of gas

GASSING *n* pl. -S a poisoning by noxious gas

GASSY *adj* -SIER, -SIEST containing gas **GASSILY** *adv*

GAST *v* -ED, -ING, -S to scare

GASTER *n* pl. -S the enlarged part of the abdomen in some insects

GASTIGHT *adj* not allowing gas to escape or enter

GASTNESS *n* pl. -ES fright

GASTRAEA *n* pl. -S a type of metazoan

GASTRAL *adj* pertaining to the stomach

GASTREA *n* pl. -S gastraea

GASTRIC *adj* pertaining to the stomach

GASTRIN *n* pl. -S a hormone

GASTRULA *n* pl. -LAS or -LAE a metazoan embryo

GASWORKS *n* pl. GASWORKS a factory where gas is produced

GAT *n* pl. -S a pistol

GATE *v* GATED, GATING, GATES to supply with a gate (a movable barrier)

GATEAU *n* pl. -TEAUX a rich layer cake

GATEFOLD *n* pl. -S a folded insert in a book or magazine

GATELESS *adj* lacking a gate

GATELIKE *adj* resembling a gate

GATEMAN *n* pl. -MEN a person in charge of a gate

GATEPOST *n* pl. -S a post from which a gate is hung

GATEWAY *n* pl. -WAYS a passage that may be closed by a gate

GATHER *v* -ED, -ING, -S to bring together into one place or group

GATHERER *n* pl. -S one that gathers

GATING present participle of gate

GATOR *n* pl. -S an alligator

GAUCHE *adj* GAUCHER, GAUCHEST lacking social grace **GAUCHELY** *adv*

GAUCHO *n* pl. -CHOS a cowboy of the South American pampas

GAUD *n* pl. -S a showy ornament

GAUDERY *n* pl. -ERIES finery

GAUDY *adj* GAUDIER, GAUDIEST tastelessly showy **GAUDILY** *adv*

GAUDY *n* pl. -DIES a festival

GAUFFER	*v* -ED, -ING, -S to goffer
GAUGE	*v* GAUGED, GAUGING, GAUGES to measure precisely
GAUGER	*n* pl. -S one that gauges
GAULT	*n* pl. -S a heavy, thick clay soil
GAUM	*v* -ED, -ING, -S to smear
GAUN	present participle of gae
GAUNT	*adj* GAUNTER, GAUNTEST emaciated **GAUNTLY** *adv*
GAUNTLET	*v* -ED, -ING, -S to gantlet
GAUNTRY	*n* pl. -TRIES gantry
GAUR	*n* pl. -S a wild ox
GAUSS	*n* pl. -ES a unit of magnetic induction
GAUZE	*n* pl. -S a transparent fabric
GAUZY	*adj* GAUZIER, GAUZIEST resembling gauze **GAUZILY** *adv*
GAVAGE	*n* pl. -S introduction of material into the stomach by a tube
GAVE	past tense of give
GAVEL	*v* -ELED, -ELING, -ELS or -ELLED, -ELLING, -ELS to signal for attention or order by use of a gavel (a small mallet)
GAVELOCK	*n* pl. -S a crowbar
GAVIAL	*n* pl. -S a large reptile
GAVOT	*n* pl. -S a French dance
GAVOTTE	*v* -VOTTED, -VOTTING, -VOTTES to dance a gavot
GAWK	*v* -ED, -ING, -S to stare stupidly
GAWKER	*n* pl. -S one that gawks
GAWKIER	comparative of gawky
GAWKIES	pl. of gawky
GAWKISH	*adj* gawky
GAWKY	*adj* GAWKIER, GAWKIEST awkward **GAWKILY** *adv*
GAWKY	*n* pl. GAWKIES an awkward person
GAWP	*v* -ED, -ING, -S to stare stupidly
GAWPER	*n* pl. -S one that gawps
GAWSIE	*adj* well-fed and healthy looking
GAWSY	*adj* gawsie
GAY	*adj* GAYER, GAYEST merry
GAY	*n* pl. GAYS a homosexual
GAYAL	*n* pl. -S a domesticated ox
GAYETY	*n* pl. -ETIES gaiety
GAYLY	*adv* in a gay manner
GAYNESS	*n* pl. -ES gaiety
GAYWINGS	*n* pl. GAYWINGS a perennial herb
GAZABO	*n* pl. -BOS or -BOES a fellow
GAZANIA	*n* pl. -S a South African herb
GAZAR	*n* pl. -S silky sheer fabric
GAZE	*v* GAZED, GAZING, GAZES to look intently
GAZEBO	*n* pl. -BOS or -BOES a roofed structure open on the sides
GAZELLE	*n* pl. -S a small antelope
GAZER	*n* pl. -S one that gazes
GAZETTE	*v* -ZETTED, -ZETTING, -ZETTES to announce in an official journal
GAZING	present participle of gaze
GAZOGENE	*n* pl. -S an apparatus for carbonating liquids
GAZPACHO	*n* pl. -CHOS a cold, spicy soup
GAZUMP	*v* -ED, -ING, -S to cheat by raising the price originally agreed upon
GAZUMPER	*n* pl. -S one that gazumps
GEAR	*v* -ED, -ING, -S to provide with gears (toothed machine parts)
GEARBOX	*n* pl. -ES an automotive transmission
GEARCASE	*n* pl. -S a casing for gears
GEARING	*n* pl. -S a system of gears
GEARLESS	*adj* being without gears
GECK	*v* -ED, -ING, -S to mock
GECKO	*n* pl. GECKOS or GECKOES a small lizard
GED	*n* pl. -S a food fish
GEE	*v* GEED, GEEING, GEES to turn to the right
GEEGAW	*n* pl. -S gewgaw
GEEK	*n* pl. -S a carnival performer
GEEKY	*adj* GEEKIER, GEEKIEST socially awkward or unappealing
GEEPOUND	*n* pl. -S a unit of mass
GEESE	pl. of goose
GEEST	*n* pl. -S old alluvial matter
GEEZ	*interj* jeez
GEEZER	*n* pl. -S an eccentric man
GEISHA	*n* pl. -S a Japanese girl trained to entertain
GEL	*v* GELLED, GELLING, GELS to become like jelly **GELABLE** *adj*
GELADA	*n* pl. -S a baboon
GELANT	*n* pl. -S gellant

GELATE	*v* -ATED, -ATING, -ATES to gel
GELATI	a pl. of gelato
GELATIN	*n* pl. -S a glutinous substance
GELATINE	*n* pl. -S gelatin
GELATING	present participle of gelate
GELATION	*n* pl. -S the process of gelling
GELATO	*n* pl. -TI or -TOS Italian ice cream
GELD	*v* -ED, -ING, -S to castrate
GELDER	*n* pl. -S one that gelds
GELDING	*n* pl. -S a castrated animal
GELEE	*n* pl. -S a cosmetic gel
GELID	*adj* icy **GELIDLY** *adv*
GELIDITY	*n* pl. -TIES iciness
GELLANT	*n* pl. -S a substance used to produce gelling
GELLED	past tense of gel
GELLING	present participle of gel
GELSEMIA	*n/pl* medicinal plant roots
GELT	*n* pl. -S money
GEM	*v* GEMMED, GEMMING, GEMS to adorn with gems (precious stones)
GEMINAL	*adj* of or pertaining to two substituents on the same atom
GEMINATE	*v* -NATED, -NATING, -NATES to arrange in pairs
GEMLIKE	*adj* resembling a gem
GEMMA	*n* pl. -MAE an asexual reproductive structure
GEMMATE	*v* -MATED, -MATING, -MATES to produce gemmae
GEMMED	past tense of gem
GEMMIER	comparative of gemmy
GEMMIEST	superlative of gemmy
GEMMILY	*adv* in a manner suggesting a gem
GEMMING	present participle of gem
GEMMULE	*n* pl. -S a small gemma
GEMMY	*adj* -MIER, -MIEST resembling a gem
GEMOLOGY	*n* pl. -GIES the science of gems
GEMOT	*n* pl. -S a public meeting in Anglo-Saxon England
GEMOTE	*n* pl. -S gemot
GEMSBOK	*n* pl. -S a large antelope
GEMSBUCK	*n* pl. -S gemsbok
GEMSTONE	*n* pl. -S a precious stone

GEN	*n* pl. -S information obtained from study
GENDARME	*n* pl. -S a policeman
GENDER	*v* -ED, -ING, -S to engender
GENE	*n* pl. -S a hereditary unit
GENERA	a pl. of genus
GENERAL	*n* pl. -S a military officer
GENERATE	*v* -ATED, -ATING, -ATES to bring into existence
GENERIC	*n* pl. -S a type of drug
GENEROUS	*adj* willing to give
GENESIS	*n* pl. GENESES an origin
GENET	*n* pl. -S a carnivorous mammal
GENETIC	*adj* pertaining to genetics
GENETICS	*n/pl* the science of heredity
GENETTE	*n* pl. -S genet
GENEVA	*n* pl. -S a liquor
GENIAL	*adj* having a pleasant or friendly manner **GENIALLY** *adv*
GENIC	*adj* pertaining to genes
GENIE	*n* pl. -S jinni
GENII	a pl. of genius
GENIP	*n* pl. -S a tropical tree
GENIPAP	*n* pl. -S a tropical tree
GENITAL	*adj* pertaining to reproduction
GENITALS	*n/pl* the sexual organs
GENITIVE	*n* pl. -S a grammatical case
GENITOR	*n* pl. -S a male parent
GENITURE	*n* pl. -S birth
GENIUS	*n* pl. GENIUSES or GENII an exceptional natural aptitude
GENOA	*n* pl. -S a triangular sail
GENOCIDE	*n* pl. -S the deliberate extermination of a national or racial group
GENOISE	*n* pl. -S a rich spongecake
GENOM	*n* pl. -S genome
GENOME	*n* pl. -S a haploid set of chromosomes **GENOMIC** *adj*
GENOTYPE	*n* pl. -S the genetic constitution of an organism
GENRE	*n* pl. -S a type or kind
GENRO	*n* pl. -ROS a group of elder statesmen in Japan
GENS	*n* pl. GENTES a type of clan
GENSENG	*n* pl. -S ginseng
GENT	*n* pl. -S a gentleman

GENTEEL	*adj* -TEELER, -TEELEST well-bred or refined
GENTES	pl. of gens
GENTIAN	*n* pl. -S a flowering plant
GENTIL	*adj* kind
GENTILE	*n* pl. -S a non-Jewish person
GENTLE	*adj* -TLER, -TLEST mild **GENTLY** *adv*
GENTLE	*v* -TLED, -TLING, -TLES to tame
GENTOO	*n* pl. -TOOS a gray-backed penguin
GENTRICE	*n* pl. -S good breeding
GENTRIFY	*v* -FIED, -FYING, -FIES to renew a decayed urban area so as to attract middle-class residents
GENTRY	*n* pl. -TRIES people of high social class
GENU	*n* pl. GENUA the knee
GENUINE	*adj* authentic
GENUS	*n* pl. GENERA or GENUSES a kind, sort, or class
GEODE	*n* pl. -S a type of rock
GEODESIC	*n* pl. -S a geometric line
GEODESY	*n* pl. -SIES geographical surveying
GEODETIC	*adj* pertaining to geodesy
GEODIC	*adj* of or pertaining to a geode
GEODUCK	*n* pl. -S a large, edible clam
GEOGNOSY	*n* pl. -SIES a branch of geology
GEOID	*n* pl. -S a hypothetical surface of the earth **GEOIDAL** *adj*
GEOLOGER	*n* pl. -S a specialist in geology
GEOLOGY	*n* pl. -GIES the science that deals with the origin and structure of the earth **GEOLOGIC** *adj*
GEOMANCY	*n* pl. -CIES a method of foretelling the future by geographical features
GEOMETER	*n* pl. -S a specialist in geometry
GEOMETRY	*n* pl. -TRIES a branch of mathematics
GEOPHAGY	*n* pl. -GIES the practice of eating earthy substances
GEOPHONE	*n* pl. -S a device that detects vibrations in the earth
GEOPHYTE	*n* pl. -S a plant having underground buds
GEOPONIC	*adj* pertaining to farming
GEOPROBE	*n* pl. -S a spacecraft for exploring space near the earth
GEORGIC	*n* pl. -S a poem about farming
GEOTAXIS	*n* pl. -TAXES the movement of an organism in response to gravity
GERAH	*n* pl. -S a Hebrew unit of weight
GERANIAL	*n* pl. -S citral
GERANIOL	*n* pl. -S an alcohol used in perfumes
GERANIUM	*n* pl. -S a flowering plant
GERARDIA	*n* pl. -S an herb
GERBERA	*n* pl. -S an herb
GERBIL	*n* pl. -S a burrowing rodent
GERBILLE	*n* pl. -S gerbil
GERENT	*n* pl. -S a ruler or manager
GERENUK	*n* pl. -S a long-necked antelope
GERM	*n* pl. -S a microorganism that causes disease
GERMAN	*n* pl. -S an elaborate dance
GERMANE	*adj* relevant
GERMANIC	*adj* containing germanium (a metallic element)
GERMEN	*n* pl. -MENS or -MINA something that serves as an origin
GERMFREE	*adj* free from germs
GERMIER	comparative of germy
GERMIEST	superlative of germy
GERMINA	a pl. of germen
GERMINAL	*adj* being in the earliest stage of development
GERMY	*adj* GERMIER, GERMIEST full of germs
GERONTIC	*adj* pertaining to old age
GERUND	*n* pl. -S a verbal noun
GESNERIA	*adj* designating a type of flowering plant
GESSO	*n* pl. -SOES a plaster mixture
GESSOED	*adj* having gesso as a coating
GEST	*n* pl. -S a feat
GESTALT	*n* pl. -STALTS or -STALTEN a unified whole
GESTAPO	*n* pl. -POS a secret-police organization
GESTATE	*v* -TATED, -TATING, -TATES to carry in the uterus during pregnancy
GESTE	*n* pl. -S gest
GESTIC	*adj* pertaining to bodily motion
GESTICAL	*adj* gestic

GESTURAL *adj* pertaining to or consisting of gestures (expressive bodily motions)

GESTURE *v* -TURED, -TURING, -TURES to express by bodily motion

GESTURER *n* pl. -S one that gestures

GET *v* GOT, GOTTEN, GETTING, GETS to obtain or acquire **GETABLE, GETTABLE** *adj*

GET *n* pl. GITTIN a divorce by Jewish law

GETA *n* pl. -S a Japanese wooden clog

GETAWAY *n* pl. -AWAYS an escape

GETTER *v* -ED, -ING, -S to purify with a chemically active substance

GETTING present participle of get

GETUP *n* pl. -S a costume

GEUM *n* pl. -S a perennial herb

GEWGAW *n* pl. -S a showy trinket

GEY *adv* very

GEYSER *n* pl. -S a spring that ejects jets of hot water and steam

GHARIAL *n* pl. -S a large reptile

GHARRI *n* pl. -S gharry

GHARRY *n* pl. -RIES a carriage used in India

GHAST *adj* ghastly

GHASTFUL *adj* frightful

GHASTLY *adj* -LIER, -LIEST terrifying

GHAT *n* pl. -S a passage to a river

GHAUT *n* pl. -S ghat

GHAZI *n* pl. -S or -ES a Muslim war hero

GHEE *n* pl. -S a kind of liquid butter

GHERAO *v* -ED, -ING, -ES to coerce by physical means

GHERKIN *n* pl. -S a small cucumber

GHETTO *v* -ED, -ING, -S or -ES to isolate in a slum

GHI *n* pl. -S ghee

GHIBLI *n* pl. -S a hot desert wind

GHILLIE *n* pl. -S a type of shoe

GHOST *v* -ED, -ING, -S to haunt

GHOSTING *n* pl. -S a false image on a television screen

GHOSTLY *adj* -LIER, -LIEST spectral

GHOSTY *adj* GHOSTIER, GHOSTIEST ghostly

GHOUL *n* pl. -S a demon **GHOULISH** *adj*

GHOULIE *n* pl. -S a ghoul

GHYLL *n* pl. -S a ravine

GIANT *n* pl. -S a person or thing of great size

GIANTESS *n* pl. -ES a female giant

GIANTISM *n* pl. -S the condition of being a giant

GIAOUR *n* pl. -S a non-Muslim

GIB *v* GIBBED, GIBBING, GIBS to fasten with a wedge of wood or metal

GIBBER *v* -ED, -ING, -S to jabber

GIBBET *v* -BETED, -BETING, -BETS or -BETTED, -BETTING, -BETS to execute by hanging

GIBBING present participle of gib

GIBBON *n* pl. -S an arboreal ape

GIBBOSE *adj* gibbous

GIBBOUS *adj* irregularly rounded

GIBBSITE *n* pl. -S a mineral

GIBE *v* GIBED, GIBING, GIBES to jeer **GIBINGLY** *adv*

GIBER *n* pl. -S one that gibes

GIBLET *n* pl. -S an edible part of a fowl

GIBSON *n* pl. -S a martini served with a tiny onion

GID *n* pl. -S a disease of sheep

GIDDAP *interj* — used as a command to a horse to go faster

GIDDY *adj* -DIER, -DIEST dizzy **GIDDILY** *adv*

GIDDY *v* -DIED, -DYING, -DIES to make giddy

GIDDYAP *interj* giddap

GIDDYUP *interj* giddap

GIE *v* GIED, GIEN, GIEING, GIES to give

GIFT *v* -ED, -ING, -S to present with a gift (something given without charge)

GIFTEDLY *adv* in a talented manner

GIFTLESS *adj* being without a gift

GIFTWARE *n* pl. -S wares suitable for gifts

GIG *v* GIGGED, GIGGING, GIGS to catch fish with a pronged spear

GIGA *n* pl. GIGHE a gigue

GIGABIT *n* pl. -S a unit of information

GIGABYTE *n* pl. -S 1,073,741,824 bytes

GIGANTIC *adj* huge

GIGAS	*adj* pertaining to variations in plant development
GIGATON	*n* pl. -S a unit of weight
GIGAWATT	*n* pl. -S a unit of power
GIGGED	past tense of gig
GIGGING	present participle of gig
GIGGLE	*v* -GLED, -GLING, -GLES to laugh in a silly manner
GIGGLER	*n* pl. -S one that giggles
GIGGLY	*adj* -GLIER, -GLIEST tending to giggle
GIGHE	pl. of giga
GIGLET	*n* pl. -S a playful girl
GIGLOT	*n* pl. -S giglet
GIGOLO	*n* pl. -LOS a man supported financially by a woman
GIGOT	*n* pl. -S a leg of lamb
GIGUE	*n* pl. -S a lively dance
GILBERT	*n* pl. -S a unit of magnetomotive force
GILD	*v* GILDED or GILT, GILDING, GILDS to cover with a thin layer of gold
GILDER	*n* pl. -S one that gilds
GILDHALL	*n* pl. -S a town hall
GILDING	*n* pl. -S the application of gilt
GILL	*v* -ED, -ING, -S to catch fish with a type of net
GILLER	*n* pl. -S one that gills
GILLIE	*n* pl. -S ghillie
GILLNET	*v* -NETTED, -NETTING, -NETS to gill
GILLY	*v* -LIED, -LYING, -LIES to transport on a type of wagon
GILT	*n* pl. -S the gold with which something is gilded
GILTHEAD	*n* pl. -S a marine fish
GIMBAL	*v* -BALED, -BALING, -BALS or -BALLED, -BALLING, -BALS to support on a set of rings
GIMCRACK	*n* pl. -S a gewgaw
GIMEL	*n* pl. -S a Hebrew letter
GIMLET	*v* -ED, -ING, -S to pierce with a boring tool
GIMMAL	*n* pl. -S a pair of interlocked rings
GIMME	*n* pl. -S something easily won
GIMMICK	*v* -ED, -ING, -S to provide with a gimmick (a novel or tricky feature)
GIMMICKY	*adj* having or being like a gimmick
GIMMIE	*n* pl. -MIES an easy golf putt conceded to an opponent
GIMP	*v* -ED, -ING, -S to limp
GIMPIER	comparative of gimpy
GIMPIEST	superlative of gimpy
GIMPY	*adj* GIMPIER, GIMPIEST limping
GIN	*v* GINNED, GINNING, GINS to remove seeds from cotton
GIN	*v* GAN, GUNNEN, GINNING, GINS to begin
GINGAL	*n* pl. -S jingal
GINGALL	*n* pl. -S jingal
GINGELEY	*n* pl. -LEYS gingelly
GINGELI	*n* pl. -S gingelly
GINGELIES	pl. of gingely
GINGELLI	*n* pl. -S gingelly
GINGELLY	*n* pl. -LIES the sesame seed or its oil
GINGELY	*n* pl. -LIES gingelly
GINGER	*v* -ED, -ING, -S to flavor with ginger (a pungent spice)
GINGERLY	*adv* in a careful manner
GINGERY	*adj* having the characteristics of ginger
GINGHAM	*n* pl. -S a cotton fabric
GINGILI	*n* pl. -LIS gingelly
GINGILLI	*n* pl. -S gingelly
GINGIVA	*n* pl. -VAE the fleshy tissue that surrounds the teeth **GINGIVAL** *adj*
GINGKO	*n* pl. -KOES ginkgo
GINK	*n* pl. -S a fellow
GINKGO	*n* pl. -GOES or -GOS an ornamental tree
GINNED	past tense of gin
GINNER	*n* pl. -S one that gins cotton
GINNING	*n* pl. -S cotton as it comes from a gin
GINNY	*adj* GINNIER, GINNIEST affected with gin (a strong liquor)
GINSENG	*n* pl. -S a perennial herb
GIP	*v* GIPPED, GIPPING, GIPS to gyp
GIPON	*n* pl. -S jupon
GIPPER	*n* pl. -S one that gips
GIPPING	present participle of gip

GIPSY	*v* -SIED, -SYING, -SIES to gypsy
GIRAFFE	*n* pl. -S a long-necked mammal
GIRASOL	*n* pl. -S a variety of opal
GIRASOLE	*n* pl. -S girasol
GIRD	*v* GIRDED or GIRT, GIRDING, GIRDS to surround
GIRDER	*n* pl. -S a horizontal support
GIRDLE	*v* -DLED, -DLING, -DLES to encircle with a belt
GIRDLER	*n* pl. -S one that girdles
GIRL	*n* pl. -S a female child
GIRLHOOD	*n* pl. -S the state of being a girl
GIRLIE	*adj* featuring scantily clothed women
GIRLISH	*adj* of, pertaining to, or having the characteristics of a girl
GIRLY	*adj* girlie
GIRN	*v* -ED, -ING, -S to snarl
GIRO	*n* pl. -ROS an autogiro
GIRON	*n* pl. -S gyron
GIROSOL	*n* pl. -S girasol
GIRSH	*n* pl. -ES qursh
GIRT	*v* -ED, -ING, -S to gird
GIRTH	*v* -ED, -ING, -S to encircle
GISARME	*n* pl. -S a medieval weapon
GISMO	*n* pl. -MOS a gadget
GIST	*n* pl. -S the main point
GIT	*n* pl. -S a foolish person
GITANO	*n* pl. -NOS a Spanish gypsy
GITTERN	*n* pl. -S a medieval guitar
GITTIN	pl. of get
GIVE	*v* GAVE, GIVEN, GIVING, GIVES to transfer freely to another's possession **GIVEABLE** *adj*
GIVEAWAY	*n* pl. -AWAYS something given away free of charge
GIVEBACK	*n* pl. -S a worker's benefit given back to management
GIVEN	*n* pl. -S something assigned as a basis for a calculation
GIVER	*n* pl. -S one that gives
GIVING	present participle of give
GIZMO	*n* pl. -MOS gismo
GIZZARD	*n* pl. -S a digestive organ
GJETOST	*n* pl. -S a hard brown cheese
GLABELLA	*n* pl. -BELLAE the smooth area between the eyebrows
GLABRATE	*adj* glabrous
GLABROUS	*adj* smooth
GLACE	*v* -CEED, -CEING, -CES to cover with icing
GLACIAL	*adj* of or pertaining to glaciers
GLACIATE	*v* -ATED, -ATING, -ATES to cover with glaciers
GLACIER	*n* pl. -S a huge mass of ice
GLACIS	*n* pl. -CISES a slope
GLAD	*adj* GLADDER, GLADDEST feeling pleasure
GLAD	*v* GLADDED, GLADDING, GLADS to gladden
GLADDEN	*v* -ED, -ING, -S to make glad
GLADDER	comparative of glad
GLADDEST	superlative of glad
GLADDING	present participle of glad
GLADE	*n* pl. -S an open space in a forest
GLADIATE	*adj* shaped like a sword
GLADIER	comparative of glady
GLADIEST	superlative of glady
GLADIOLA	*n* pl. -S a flowering plant
GLADIOLI	*n/pl* segments of the sternum
GLADLY	*adv* -LIER, -LIEST in a glad manner
GLADNESS	*n* pl. -ES the state of being glad
GLADSOME	*adj* -SOMER, -SOMEST glad
GLADY	*adj* GLADIER, GLADIEST having glades
GLAIKET	*adj* glaikit
GLAIKIT	*adj* foolish
GLAIR	*v* -ED, -ING, -S to coat with egg white
GLAIRE	*v* GLAIRED, GLAIRING, GLAIRES to glair
GLAIRY	*adj* GLAIRIER, GLAIRIEST resembling egg white
GLAIVE	*n* pl. -S a sword **GLAIVED** *adj*
GLAMOR	*n* pl. -S alluring attractiveness
GLAMOUR	*v* -ED, -ING, -S to bewitch
GLANCE	*v* GLANCED, GLANCING, GLANCES to look quickly
GLANCER	*n* pl. -S one that glances
GLAND	*n* pl. -S a secreting organ
GLANDERS	*n/pl* a disease of horses
GLANDULE	*n* pl. -S a small gland
GLANS	*n* pl. GLANDES the tip of the penis or clitoris

GLARE	v GLARED, GLARING, GLARES to shine with a harshly brilliant light	**GLEEMAN**	n pl. -MEN a minstrel
		GLEESOME	adj gleeful
GLARY	adj GLARIER, GLARIEST glaring	**GLEET**	v -ED, -ING, -S to discharge mucus from the urethra
GLASNOST	n pl. -S a Soviet policy of open political discussion	**GLEETY**	adj GLEETIER, GLEETIEST resembling mucus
GLASS	v -ED, -ING, -ES to encase in glass (a transparent substance)	**GLEG**	adj alert **GLEGLY** adv
GLASSFUL	n pl. -FULS as much as a drinking glass will hold	**GLEGNESS**	n pl. -ES alertness
GLASSIE	n pl. -S a type of playing marble	**GLEN**	n pl. -S a small valley **GLENLIKE** adj
GLASSIER	comparative of glassy	**GLENOID**	adj having the shallow or slightly cupped form of a bone socket
GLASSIEST	superlative of glassy	**GLEY**	n pl. GLEYS a clay soil layer **GLEYED** adj
GLASSILY	adv in a glassy manner		
GLASSINE	n pl. -S a type of paper	**GLEYING**	n pl. -S development of gley
GLASSMAN	n pl. -MEN a glazier	**GLIA**	n pl. -S supporting tissue that binds nerve tissue
GLASSY	adj GLASSIER, GLASSIEST resembling glass	**GLIADIN**	n pl. -S a simple protein
GLAUCOMA	n pl. -S a disease of the eye	**GLIADINE**	n pl. -S gliadin
GLAUCOUS	adj bluish green	**GLIAL**	adj pertaining to the supporting tissue of the central nervous system
GLAZE	v GLAZED, GLAZING, GLAZES to fit windows with glass panes		
GLAZER	n pl. -S a glazier	**GLIB**	adj GLIBBER, GLIBBEST fluent **GLIBLY** adv
GLAZIER	n pl. -S one that glazes	**GLIBNESS**	n pl. -ES the quality of being glib
GLAZIERY	n pl. -ZIERIES the work of a glazier	**GLIDE**	v GLIDED, GLIDING, GLIDES to move effortlessly
GLAZING	n pl. -S glaziery	**GLIDER**	n pl. -S a type of aircraft
GLAZY	adj GLAZIER, GLAZIEST covered with a smooth, glossy coating	**GLIFF**	n pl. -S a brief moment
		GLIM	n pl. -S a light or lamp
GLEAM	v -ED, -ING, -S to shine with a soft radiance	**GLIME**	v GLIMED, GLIMING, GLIMES to glance slyly
GLEAMER	n pl. -S one that gleams	**GLIMMER**	v -ED, -ING, -S to shine faintly or unsteadily
GLEAMY	adj GLEAMIER, GLEAMIEST gleaming	**GLIMPSE**	v GLIMPSED, GLIMPSING, GLIMPSES to see for an instant
GLEAN	v -ED, -ING, -S to gather little by little		
		GLIMPSER	n pl. -S one that glimpses
GLEANER	n pl. -S one that gleans	**GLINT**	v -ED, -ING, -S to glitter
GLEANING	n pl. -S something that is gleaned	**GLIOMA**	n pl. -MAS or -MATA a type of tumor
GLEBA	n pl. -BAE a spore-bearing mass of some fungi	**GLISSADE**	v -SADED, -SADING, -SADES to perform a gliding dance step
GLEBE	n pl. -S the soil or earth	**GLISTEN**	v -ED, -ING, -S to shine by reflection
GLED	n pl. -S glede		
GLEDE	n pl. -S a bird of prey	**GLISTER**	v -ED, -ING, -S to glisten
GLEE	n pl. -S an unaccompanied song	**GLITCH**	n pl. -ES a malfunction
GLEED	n pl. -S a glowing coal	**GLITCHY**	adj characterized by glitches
GLEEFUL	adj merry	**GLITTER**	v -ED, -ING, -S to sparkle
GLEEK	v -ED, -ING, -S to gibe	**GLITTERY**	adj glittering

GLITZ	*n* pl. -ES gaudy showiness
GLITZY	*adj* GLITZIER, GLITZIEST showy
GLOAM	*n* pl. -S twilight
GLOAMING	*n* pl. -S twilight
GLOAT	*v* -ED, -ING, -S to regard with great or excessive satisfaction
GLOATER	*n* pl. -S one that gloats
GLOB	*n* pl. -S a rounded mass
GLOBAL	*adj* spherical **GLOBALLY** *adv*
GLOBATE	*adj* spherical
GLOBATED	*adj* spherical
GLOBBY	*adj* -BIER, -BIEST full of globs
GLOBE	*v* GLOBED, GLOBING, GLOBES to form into a perfectly round body
GLOBIN	*n* pl. -S a simple protein
GLOBOID	*n* pl. -S a spheroid
GLOBOSE	*adj* spherical
GLOBOUS	*adj* spherical
GLOBULAR	*adj* spherical
GLOBULE	*n* pl. -S a small spherical mass
GLOBULIN	*n* pl. -S a simple protein
GLOCHID	*n* pl. -S a barbed hair on some plants
GLOGG	*n* pl. -S an alcoholic beverage
GLOM	*v* GLOMMED, GLOMMING, GLOMS to steal
GLOMUS	*n* pl. -MERA a type of vascular tuft
GLONOIN	*n* pl. -S nitroglycerin
GLOOM	*v* -ED, -ING, -S to become dark
GLOOMFUL	*adj* gloomy
GLOOMING	*n* pl. -S gloaming
GLOOMY	*adj* GLOOMIER, GLOOMIEST dismally dark **GLOOMILY** *adv*
GLOP	*v* GLOPPED, GLOPPING, GLOPS to cover with glop (a messy mass or mixture)
GLOPPY	*adj* being or resembling glop
GLORIA	*n* pl. -S a halo
GLORIED	past tense of glory
GLORIES	present 3d person sing. of glory
GLORIFY	*v* -FIED, -FYING, -FIES to bestow honor or praise on
GLORIOLE	*n* pl. -S a halo
GLORIOUS	*adj* magnificent
GLORY	*v* -RIED, -RYING, -RIES to rejoice proudly
GLOSS	*v* -ED, -ING, -ES to make lustrous
GLOSSA	*n* pl. -SAE or -SAS the tongue **GLOSSAL** *adj*
GLOSSARY	*n* pl. -RIES a list of terms and their definitions
GLOSSEME	*n* pl. -S the smallest linguistic unit that signals a meaning
GLOSSER	*n* pl. -S one that glosses
GLOSSIER	comparative of glossy
GLOSSIES	pl. of glossy
GLOSSINA	*n* pl. -S a tsetse fly
GLOSSY	*adj* GLOSSIER, GLOSSIEST lustrous **GLOSSILY** *adv*
GLOSSY	*n* pl. GLOSSIES a type of photograph
GLOST	*n* pl. -S pottery that has been coated with a glassy surface
GLOTTIS	*n* pl. -TISES or -TIDES the opening between the vocal cords **GLOTTAL, GLOTTIC** *adj*
GLOUT	*v* -ED, -ING, -S to scowl
GLOVE	*v* GLOVED, GLOVING, GLOVES to furnish with gloves (hand coverings)
GLOVER	*n* pl. -S a maker or seller of gloves
GLOW	*v* -ED, -ING, -S to emit light and heat
GLOWER	*v* -ED, -ING, -S to scowl
GLOWFLY	*n* pl. -FLIES a firefly
GLOWWORM	*n* pl. -S a luminous insect
GLOXINIA	*n* pl. -S a tropical plant
GLOZE	*v* GLOZED, GLOZING, GLOZES to explain away
GLUCAGON	*n* pl. -S a hormone
GLUCAN	*n* pl. -S a polymer of glucose
GLUCINUM	*n* pl. -S a metallic element **GLUCINIC** *adj*
GLUCOSE	*n* pl. -S a sugar **GLUCOSIC** *adj*
GLUE	*v* GLUED, GLUING or GLUEING, GLUES to fasten with glue (an adhesive substance)
GLUELIKE	*adj* resembling glue
GLUEPOT	*n* pl. -S a pot for melting glue
GLUER	*n* pl. -S one that glues
GLUEY	*adj* GLUIER, GLUIEST resembling glue **GLUILY** *adv*
GLUG	*v* GLUGGED, GLUGGING, GLUGS to make a gurgling sound

GLUING	present participle of glue
GLUM	*adj* GLUMMER, GLUMMEST being in low spirits **GLUMLY** *adv*
GLUME	*n* pl. -S a bract on grassy plants
GLUMNESS	*n* pl. -ES the state of being glum
GLUMPY	*adj* GLUMPIER, GLUMPIEST glum **GLUMPILY** *adv*
GLUNCH	*v* -ED, -ING, -ES to frown
GLUON	*n* pl. -S a hypothetical massless particle binding quarks together
GLUT	*v* GLUTTED, GLUTTING, GLUTS to feed or fill to excess
GLUTEAL	*adj* of or pertaining to the buttock muscles
GLUTEI	pl. of gluteus
GLUTELIN	*n* pl. -S a plant protein
GLUTEN	*n* pl. -S a tough elastic plant protein substance
GLUTEUS	*n* pl. -TEI a buttock muscle
GLUTTED	past tense of glut
GLUTTING	present participle of glut
GLUTTON	*n* pl. -S a person who eats to excess
GLUTTONY	*n* pl. -TONIES excessive eating
GLYCAN	*n* pl. -S a carbohydrate
GLYCERIN	*n* pl. -S a glycerol **GLYCERIC** *adj*
GLYCEROL	*n* pl. -S a syrupy alcohol
GLYCERYL	*n* pl. -S a radical derived from glycerol
GLYCIN	*n* pl. -S a compound used in photography
GLYCINE	*n* pl. -S an amino acid
GLYCOGEN	*n* pl. -S a carbohydrate
GLYCOL	*n* pl. -S an alcohol **GLYCOLIC** *adj*
GLYCONIC	*n* pl. -S a type of verse line
GLYCOSYL	*n* pl. -S a radical derived from glucose
GLYCYL	*n* pl. -S a radical derived from glycine
GLYPH	*n* pl. -S an ornamental groove **GLYPHIC** *adj*
GLYPTIC	*n* pl. -S the art or process of engraving on gems
GNAR	*v* GNARRED, GNARRING, GNARS to snarl
GNARL	*v* -ED, -ING, -S to twist into a state of deformity
GNARLY	*adj* GNARLIER, GNARLIEST gnarled
GNARR	*v* -ED, -ING, -S to gnar
GNARRED	past tense of gnar
GNARRING	present participle of gnar
GNASH	*v* -ED, -ING, -ES to grind the teeth together
GNAT	*n* pl. -S a small winged insect
GNATHAL	*adj* gnathic
GNATHIC	*adj* of or pertaining to the jaw
GNATHION	*n* pl. -S the tip of the chin
GNATHITE	*n* pl. -S a jawlike appendage of an insect
GNATLIKE	*adj* resembling a gnat
GNATTY	*adj* -TIER, -TIEST infested with gnats
GNAW	*v* GNAWED, GNAWN, GNAWING, GNAWS to wear away by persistent biting **GNAWABLE** *adj*
GNAWER	*n* pl. -S one that gnaws
GNAWING	*n* pl. -S a persistent dull pain
GNAWN	a past participle of gnaw
GNEISS	*n* pl. -ES a type of rock **GNEISSIC** *adj*
GNOCCHI	*n/pl* dumplings made of pasta
GNOME	*n* pl. -S a dwarf
GNOMIC	*adj* resembling or containing aphorisms
GNOMICAL	*adj* gnomic
GNOMISH	*adj* resembling a gnome
GNOMIST	*n* pl. -S a writer of aphorisms
GNOMON	*n* pl. -S a part of a sundial **GNOMONIC** *adj*
GNOSIS	*n* pl. GNOSES mystical knowledge
GNOSTIC	*adj* possessing knowledge
GNU	*n* pl. -S a large antelope
GO	*v* WENT, GONE, GOING, GOES to move along
GOA	*n* pl. -S an Asian gazelle
GOAD	*v* -ED, -ING, -S to drive animals with a goad (a pointed stick)
GOADLIKE	*adj* resembling a goad
GOAL	*v* -ED, -ING, -S to score a goal (a point-scoring play in some games)
GOALIE	*n* pl. -S a player who defends against goals
GOALLESS	*adj* having no goal

GOALPOST *n* pl. -S a post that marks a boundary of the scoring area in some games

GOALWARD *adv* toward a goal (a point-scoring area)

GOANNA *n* pl. -S a large monitor lizard

GOAT *n* pl. -S a horned mammal

GOATEE *n* pl. -S a small pointed beard **GOATEED** *adj*

GOATFISH *n* pl. -ES a tropical fish

GOATHERD *n* pl. -S one who tends goats

GOATISH *adj* resembling a goat

GOATLIKE *adj* goatish

GOATSKIN *n* pl. -S the hide of a goat

GOB *v* GOBBED, GOBBING, GOBS to fill a mine pit with waste material

GOBAN *n* pl. -S gobang

GOBANG *n* pl. -S a Japanese game

GOBBED past tense of gob

GOBBET *n* pl. -S a piece of raw meat

GOBBING present participle of gob

GOBBLE *v* -BLED, -BLING, -BLES to eat hastily

GOBBLER *n* pl. -S a male turkey

GOBIES pl. of goby

GOBIOID *n* pl. -S a fish of the goby family

GOBLET *n* pl. -S a drinking vessel

GOBLIN *n* pl. -S an evil or mischievous creature

GOBO *n* pl. -BOS or -BOES a device used to shield a microphone from extraneous sounds

GOBONEE *adj* gobony

GOBONY *adj* compony

GOBY *n* pl. GOBIES a small fish

GOD *v* GODDED, GODDING, GODS to treat as a god (a supernatural being)

GODCHILD *n* pl. -CHILDREN one whom a person sponsors at baptism

GODDAM *v* -DAMMED, -DAMMING, -DAMS goddamn

GODDAMN *v* -ED, -ING, -S to damn

GODDED past tense of god

GODDESS *n* pl. -ES a female god

GODDING present participle of god

GODET *n* pl. -S insert of cloth in a seam

GODHEAD *n* pl. -S godhood

GODHOOD *n* pl. -S the state of being a god

GODLESS *adj* worshiping no god

GODLIER comparative of godly

GODLIEST superlative of godly

GODLIKE *adj* divine

GODLING *n* pl. -S a lesser god

GODLY *adj* -LIER, -LIEST pious **GODLILY** *adv*

GODOWN *n* pl. -S an oriental warehouse

GODROON *n* pl. -S gadroon

GODSEND *n* pl. -S an unexpected boon

GODSHIP *n* pl. -S the rank of a god

GODSON *n* pl. -S a male godchild

GODWIT *n* pl. -S a wading bird

GOER *n* pl. -S one that goes

GOETHITE *n* pl. -S an ore of iron

GOFER *n* pl. -S an employee who runs errands

GOFFER *v* -ED, -ING, -S to press ridges or pleats into

GOGGLE *v* -GLED, -GLING, -GLES to stare with wide eyes

GOGGLER *n* pl. -S one that goggles

GOGGLY *adj* -GLIER, -GLIEST wide-eyed

GOGLET *n* pl. -S a long-necked jar

GOGO *n* pl. -GOS a discotheque

GOING *n* pl. -S an advance toward an objective

GOITER *n* pl. -S an enlargement of the thyroid gland **GOITROUS** *adj*

GOITRE *n* pl. -S goiter

GOLCONDA *n* pl. -S a source of great wealth

GOLD *n* pl. -S a precious metallic element

GOLD *adj* GOLDER, GOLDEST golden

GOLDARN *n* pl. -S an expression of anger

GOLDBUG *n* pl. -S a gold beetle

GOLDEN *adj* -ENER, -ENEST of the color of gold **GOLDENLY** *adv*

GOLDEYE *n* pl. -S a freshwater fish

GOLDFISH *n* pl. -ES a freshwater fish

GOLDURN *n* pl. -S goldarn

GOLEM *n* pl. -S a legendary creature

GOLF *v* -ED, -ING, -S to play golf (a type of ball game)

GOLFER *n* pl. -S one that golfs

GOLFING *n* pl. -S the game of golf

GOLGOTHA	*n* pl. -S a place of burial	**GOODBY**	*n* pl. -BYS goodbye
GOLIARD	*n* pl. -S a wandering student	**GOODBYE**	*n* pl. -S a concluding remark or gesture at parting
GOLLIWOG	*n* pl. -S a grotesque doll	**GOODIE**	*n* pl. -S goody
GOLLY	*interj* — used as a mild oath	**GOODIES**	pl. of goody
GOLLYWOG	*n* pl. -S golliwog	**GOODISH**	*adj* somewhat good
GOLOSH	*n* pl. -ES galosh	**GOODLY**	*adj* -LIER, -LIEST of pleasing appearance
GOLOSHE	*n* pl. -S galosh		
GOMBO	*n* pl. -BOS gumbo	**GOODMAN**	*n* pl. -MEN the master of a household
GOMBROON	*n* pl. -S a kind of Persian pottery		
GOMERAL	*n* pl. -S a fool	**GOODNESS**	*n* pl. -ES the state of being good
GOMEREL	*n* pl. -S gomeral	**GOODWIFE**	*n* pl. -WIVES the mistress of a household
GOMERIL	*n* pl. -S gomeral		
GOMUTI	*n* pl. -S a palm tree	**GOODWILL**	*n* pl. -S an attitude of friendliness
GONAD	*n* pl. -S a sex gland **GONADAL, GONADIAL, GONADIC** *adj*	**GOODY**	*n* pl. GOODIES a desirable food
		GOOEY	*adj* GOOIER, GOOIEST sticky or viscid
GONDOLA	*n* pl. -S a long, narrow boat		
GONE	*adj* departed	**GOOF**	*v* -ED, -ING, -S to blunder
GONEF	*n* pl. -S ganef	**GOOFBALL**	*n* pl. -S a sleeping pill
GONENESS	*n* pl. -ES a state of exhaustion	**GOOFY**	*adj* GOOFIER, GOOFIEST silly **GOOFILY** *adv*
GONER	*n* pl. -S one who is in a hopeless situation		
		GOOGLY	*n* pl. -GLIES a type of bowled ball in cricket
GONFALON	*n* pl. -S a banner		
GONFANON	*n* pl. -S gonfalon	**GOOGOL**	*n* pl. -S an enormous number
GONG	*v* -ED, -ING, -S to make the sound of a gong (a disk-shaped percussion instrument)	**GOOIER**	comparative of gooey
		GOOIEST	superlative of gooey
		GOOK	*n* pl. -S goo **GOOKY** *adj*
GONGLIKE	*adj* resembling a gong	**GOOMBAH**	*n* pl. -S an older man who is a friend
GONIA	pl. of gonion and of gonium		
GONIDIUM	*n* pl. -IA an asexual reproductive cell **GONIDIAL, GONIDIC** *adj*	**GOOMBAY**	*n* pl. -BAYS calypso music of the Bahamas
		GOON	*n* pl. -S a hired thug
GONIF	*n* pl. -S ganef	**GOONEY**	*n* pl. -NEYS an albatross
GONIFF	*n* pl. -S ganef	**GOONIE**	*n* pl. -S gooney
GONION	*n* pl. -NIA a part of the lower jaw	**GOONY**	*n* pl. -NIES gooney
GONIUM	*n* pl. -NIA an immature reproductive cell	**GOOP**	*n* pl. -S goo, gunk
		GOOPY	*adj* GOOPIER, GOOPIEST sticky, gooey
GONOCYTE	*n* pl. -S a cell that produces gametes		
		GOORAL	*n* pl. -S goral
GONOF	*n* pl. -S ganef	**GOOSE**	*n* pl. GEESE a swimming bird
GONOPH	*n* pl. -S ganef	**GOOSE**	*v* GOOSED, GOOSING, GOOSES to poke between the buttocks
GONOPORE	*n* pl. -S a genital pore		
GONZO	*adj* bizarre		
GOO	*n* pl. GOOS a sticky or viscid substance	**GOOSEY**	*adj* GOOSIER, GOOSIEST goosy
		GOOSY	*adj* GOOSIER, GOOSIEST resembling a goose
GOOBER	*n* pl. -S a peanut		
GOOD	*adj* BETTER, BEST having positive or desirable qualities	**GOPHER**	*n* pl. -S a burrowing rodent
GOOD	*n* pl. -S something that is good	**GOR**	*interj* — used as a mild oath

GORAL	*n* pl. -S a goat antelope
GORBELLY	*n* pl. -LIES a potbelly
GORBLIMY	*interj* blimey
GORCOCK	*n* pl. -S the male red grouse
GORE	*v* GORED, GORING, GORES to pierce with a horn or tusk
GORGE	*v* GORGED, GORGING, GORGES to stuff with food **GORGEDLY** *adv*
GORGEOUS	*adj* beautiful
GORGER	*n* pl. -S one that gorges
GORGERIN	*n* pl. -S a part of a column
GORGET	*n* pl. -S a piece of armor for the throat **GORGETED** *adj*
GORGING	present participle of gorge
GORGON	*n* pl. -S an ugly woman
GORHEN	*n* pl. -S the female red grouse
GORIER	comparative of gory
GORIEST	superlative of gory
GORILLA	*n* pl. -S a large ape
GORILY	*adv* in a gory manner
GORINESS	*n* pl. -ES the state of being gory
GORING	present participle of gore
GORMAND	*n* pl. -S gourmand
GORMLESS	*adj* stupid
GORP	*n* pl. -S a snack for quick energy
GORSE	*n* pl. -S furze
GORSY	*adj* GORSIER, GORSIEST abounding in gorse
GORY	*adj* GORIER, GORIEST bloody
GOSH	*interj* — used as an exclamation of surprise
GOSHAWK	*n* pl. -S a large hawk
GOSLING	*n* pl. -S a young goose
GOSPEL	*n* pl. -S the message concerning Christ, the kingdom of God, and salvation
GOSPELER	*n* pl. -S one that teaches the gospel
GOSPORT	*n* pl. -S a communication device in an airplane
GOSSAMER	*n* pl. -S a fine film of cobwebs
GOSSAN	*n* pl. -S a type of decomposed rock
GOSSIP	*v* -SIPED, -SIPING, -SIPS or -SIPPED, -SIPPING, -SIPS to talk idly about the affairs of others
GOSSIPER	*n* pl. -S one that gossips
GOSSIPRY	*n* pl. -RIES the practice of gossiping
GOSSIPY	*adj* inclined to gossip
GOSSOON	*n* pl. -S a boy
GOSSYPOL	*n* pl. -S a toxic pigment
GOT	past tense of get
GOTHIC	*n* pl. -S a style of printing
GOTHITE	*n* pl. -S goethite
GOTTEN	past participle of get
GOUACHE	*n* pl. -S a method of painting
GOUGE	*v* GOUGED, GOUGING, GOUGES to cut or scoop out
GOUGER	*n* pl. -S one that gouges
GOULASH	*n* pl. -ES a beef stew
GOURAMI	*n* pl. -S or -ES a food fish
GOURD	*n* pl. -S a hard-shelled fruit
GOURDE	*n* pl. -S a monetary unit of Haiti
GOURMAND	*n* pl. -S one who loves to eat
GOURMET	*n* pl. -S a connoisseur of fine food and drink
GOUT	*n* pl. -S a metabolic disease
GOUTY	*adj* GOUTIER, GOUTIEST affected with gout **GOUTILY** *adv*
GOVERN	*v* -ED, -ING, -S to rule or direct
GOVERNOR	*n* pl. -S one that governs
GOWAN	*n* pl. -S a daisy **GOWANED, GOWANY** *adj*
GOWD	*n* pl. -S gold
GOWK	*n* pl. -S a fool
GOWN	*v* -ED, -ING, -S to dress in a gown (a long, loose outer garment)
GOWNSMAN	*n* pl. -MEN a professional or academic person
GOX	*n* pl. -ES gaseous oxygen
GRAAL	*n* pl. -S grail
GRAB	*v* GRABBED, GRABBING, GRABS to grasp suddenly
GRABBER	*n* pl. -S one that grabs
GRABBIER	comparative of grabby
GRABBIEST	superlative of grabby
GRABBING	present participle of grab
GRABBLE	*v* -BLED, -BLING, -BLES to grope
GRABBLER	*n* pl. -S one that grabbles
GRABBY	*adj* -BIER, -BIEST tending to grab

GRABEN   *n* pl. -S a depression of the earth's crust

GRACE   *v* GRACED, GRACING, GRACES to give beauty to

GRACEFUL   *adj* -FULLER, -FULLEST having beauty of form or movement

GRACILE   *adj* gracefully slender

GRACILIS   *n* pl. -LES a thigh muscle

GRACING   present participle of grace

GRACIOSO   *n* pl. -SOS a clown in Spanish comedy

GRACIOUS   *adj* marked by kindness and courtesy

GRACKLE   *n* pl. -S a blackbird

GRAD   *n* pl. -S a graduate

GRADATE   *v* -DATED, -DATING, -DATES to change by degrees

GRADE   *v* GRADED, GRADING, GRADES to arrange in steps or degrees **GRADABLE** *adj*

GRADER   *n* pl. -S one that grades

GRADIENT   *n* pl. -S a rate of inclination

GRADIN   *n* pl. -S gradine

GRADINE   *n* pl. -S one of a series of steps

GRADING   present participle of grade

GRADUAL   *n* pl. -S a hymn sung in alternate parts

GRADUAND   *n* pl. -S one who is about to graduate

GRADUATE   *v* -ATED, -ATING, -ATES to receive an academic degree or diploma

GRADUS   *n* pl. -ES a dictionary of prosody

GRAECIZE   *v* -CIZED, -CIZING, -CIZES to grecize

GRAFFITO   *n* pl. -TI an inscription or drawing made on a rock or wall

GRAFT   *v* -ED, -ING, -S to unite with a growing plant by insertion

GRAFTAGE   *n* pl. -S the process of grafting

GRAFTER   *n* pl. -S one that grafts

GRAHAM   *n* pl. -S whole-wheat flour

GRAIL   *n* pl. -S the object of a long quest

GRAIN   *v* -ED, -ING, -S to form into small particles

GRAINER   *n* pl. -S one that grains

GRAINY   *adj* GRAINIER, GRAINIEST granular

GRAM   pl. -S a unit of mass and weight

GRAMA   *n* pl. -S a pasture grass

GRAMARY   *n* pl. -RIES gramarye

GRAMARYE   *n* pl. -S occult learning; magic

GRAMERCY   *n* pl. -CIES an expression of gratitude

GRAMMAR   *n* pl. -S the study of the formal features of a language

GRAMME   *n* pl. -S gram

GRAMP   *n* pl. -S grandfather

GRAMPUS   *n* pl. -ES a marine mammal

GRAN   *n* pl. -S a grandmother

GRANA   pl. of granum

GRANARY   *n* pl. -RIES a storehouse for grain

GRAND   *adj* GRANDER, GRANDEST large and impressive

GRAND   *n* pl. -S a type of piano

GRANDAD   *n* pl. -S granddad

GRANDAM   *n* pl. -S a grandmother

GRANDAME   *n* pl. -S grandam

GRANDDAD   *n* pl. -S a grandfather

GRANDDAM   *n* pl. -S the female parent of an animal with offspring

GRANDEE   *n* pl. -S man of high social position

GRANDEUR   *n* pl. -S the state of being grand

GRANDKID   *n* pl. -S the child of one's son or daughter

GRANDLY   *adv* in a grand manner

GRANDMA   *n* pl. -S a grandmother

GRANDPA   *n* pl. -S a grandfather

GRANDSIR   *n* pl. -S a grandfather

GRANDSON   *n* pl. -S a son of one's son or daughter

GRANGE   *n* pl. -S a farm

GRANGER   *n* pl. -S a farmer

GRANITA   *n* pl. -S an iced dessert

GRANITE   *n* pl. -S a type of rock **GRANITIC** *adj*

GRANNIE   *n* pl. -S granny

GRANNY   *n* pl. -NIES a grandmother

GRANOLA   *n* pl. -S a breakfast cereal

GRANT   *v* -ED, -ING, -S to bestow upon

GRANTEE   *n* pl. -S one to whom something is granted

GRANTER   *n* pl. -S one that grants

GRANTOR   *n* pl. -S granter

GRANULAR   *adj* composed of granules

GRANULE	*n* pl. -S a small particle
GRANUM	*n* pl. GRANA a part of a plant chloroplast
GRAPE	*n* pl. -S an edible berry
GRAPERY	*n* pl. -ERIES a vinery
GRAPEY	*adj* GRAPIER, GRAPIEST grapy
GRAPH	*v* -ED, -ING, -S to represent by means of a diagram
GRAPHEME	*n* pl. -S a unit of a writing system
GRAPHIC	*n* pl. -S a product of the art of representation
GRAPHITE	*n* pl. -S a variety of carbon
GRAPIER	comparative of grapy
GRAPIEST	superlative of grapy
GRAPLIN	*n* pl. -S a grapnel
GRAPLINE	*n* pl. -S graplin
GRAPNEL	*n* pl. -S a type of anchor
GRAPPA	*n* pl. -S an Italian brandy
GRAPPLE	*v* -PLED, -PLING, -PLES to struggle or contend
GRAPPLER	*n* pl. -S one that grapples
GRAPY	*adj* GRAPIER, GRAPIEST resembling grapes
GRASP	*v* -ED, -ING, -S to seize firmly with the hand
GRASPER	*n* pl. -S one that grasps
GRASS	*v* -ED, -ING, -ES to cover with grass (herbaceous plants)
GRASSY	*adj* GRASSIER, GRASSIEST of, resembling, or pertaining to grass **GRASSILY** *adv*
GRAT	past tense of greet (to weep)
GRATE	*v* GRATED, GRATING, GRATES to reduce to shreds by rubbing
GRATEFUL	*adj* -FULLER, -FULLEST deeply thankful
GRATER	*n* pl. -S one that grates
GRATIFY	*v* -FIED, -FYING, -FIES to satisfy
GRATIN	*n* pl. -S a type of food crust
GRATINE	*adj* covered with a crust
GRATINEE	*v* -NEED, -NEEING, -NEES to cook food that is covered with a crust
GRATING	*n* pl. -S a network of bars covering an opening
GRATIS	*adj* free of charge
GRATUITY	*n* pl. -ITIES a gift of money
GRAUPEL	*n* pl. -S granular snow pellets
GRAVAMEN	*n* pl. -MENS or -MINA the most serious part of an accusation
GRAVE	*adj* GRAVER, GRAVEST extremely serious
GRAVE	*v* GRAVED, GRAVEN, GRAVING, GRAVES to engrave
GRAVEL	*v* -ELED, -ELING, -ELS or -ELLED, -ELLING, -ELS to pave with gravel (a mixture of rock fragments)
GRAVELLY	*adj* containing gravel
GRAVELY	*adv* in a grave manner
GRAVEN	past participle of grave
GRAVER	*n* pl. -S an engraver
GRAVEST	superlative of grave
GRAVID	*adj* pregnant **GRAVIDLY** *adv*
GRAVIDA	*n* pl. -DAS or -DAE a pregnant woman
GRAVIES	pl. of gravy
GRAVING	present participle of grave
GRAVITAS	*n* pl. -ES reserved, dignified behavior
GRAVITON	*n* pl. -S a hypothetical particle
GRAVITY	*n* pl. -TIES the force of attraction toward the earth's center
GRAVLAKS	*n* pl. GRAVLAKS gravlax
GRAVLAX	*n* pl. GRAVLAX cured salmon
GRAVURE	*n* pl. -S a printing process
GRAVY	*n* pl. -VIES a sauce of the fat and juices from cooked meat
GRAY	*adj* GRAYER, GRAYEST of a color between white and black
GRAY	*v* -ED, -ING, -S to make gray
GRAYBACK	*n* pl. -S a gray bird
GRAYFISH	*n* pl. -ES a dogfish
GRAYISH	*adj* somewhat gray
GRAYLAG	*n* pl. -S a wild goose
GRAYLING	*n* pl. -S a food fish
GRAYLY	*adv* in a gray manner
GRAYMAIL	*n* pl. -S pressure on an official to reveal sensitive information
GRAYNESS	*n* pl. -ES the state of being gray
GRAYOUT	*n* pl. -S a temporary blurring of vision
GRAZE	*v* GRAZED, GRAZING, GRAZES to feed on growing grass **GRAZABLE** *adj*
GRAZER	*n* pl. -S one that grazes
GRAZIER	*n* pl. -S one that grazes cattle
GRAZING	*n* pl. -S land used for the feeding of animals

GRAZIOSO	*adj* graceful in style
GREASE	*v* GREASED, GREASING, GREASES to smear with grease (a lubricating substance)
GREASER	*n* pl. -S one that greases
GREASY	*adj* GREASIER, GREASIEST containing or resembling grease **GREASILY** *adv*
GREAT	*adj* GREATER, GREATEST large
GREAT	*n* pl. -S a distinguished or outstanding person
GREATEN	*v* -ED, -ING, -S to make greater
GREATLY	*adv* in a great manner
GREAVE	*n* pl. -S a piece of armor for the leg **GREAVED** *adj*
GREBE	*n* pl. -S a diving bird
GRECIZE	*v* -CIZED, -CIZING, -CIZES to provide with a Greek style
GREE	*v* GREED, GREEING, GREES to agree
GREED	*n* pl. -S excessive desire for gain or wealth
GREEDY	*adj* GREEDIER, GREEDIEST marked by greed **GREEDILY** *adv*
GREEGREE	*n* pl. -S grigri
GREEK	*n* pl. GREEK something unintelligible
GREEN	*adj* GREENER, GREENEST of the color of growing foliage
GREEN	*v* -ED, -ING, -S to become green
GREENBUG	*n* pl. -S a green aphid
GREENERY	*n* pl. -ERIES green vegetation
GREENFLY	*n* pl. -FLIES a green aphid
GREENIE	*n* pl. -S an amphetamine pill
GREENIER	comparative of greeny
GREENIEST	superlative of greeny
GREENING	*n* pl. -S a variety of apple
GREENISH	*adj* somewhat green
GREENLET	*n* pl. -S a vireo
GREENLY	*adv* in a green manner
GREENTH	*n* pl. -S verdure
GREENWAY	*n* pl. -WAYS piece of undeveloped land in a city
GREENY	*adj* GREENIER, GREENIEST somewhat green
GREET	*v* -ED, -ING, -S to address in a friendly and courteous way
GREET	*v* GRAT, GRUTTEN, GREETING, GREETS to weep
GREETER	*n* pl. -S one that greets
GREETING	*n* pl. -S a salutation
GREGO	*n* pl. -GOS a hooded coat
GREIGE	*n* pl. -S fabric in a gray state
GREISEN	*n* pl. -S a type of rock
GREMIAL	*n* pl. -S a lap cloth used by a bishop during a service
GREMLIN	*n* pl. -S a mischievous creature
GREMMIE	*n* pl. -S an inexperienced surfer
GREMMY	*n* pl. -MIES gremmie
GRENADE	*n* pl. -S an explosive device
GREW	past tense of grow
GREWSOME	*adj* -SOMER, -SOMEST gruesome
GREY	*adj* GREYER, GREYEST gray
GREY	*v* -ED, -ING, -S to gray
GREYHEN	*n* pl. -S the female black grouse
GREYISH	*adj* grayish
GREYLAG	*n* pl. -S graylag
GREYLY	*adv* grayly
GREYNESS	*n* pl. -ES grayness
GRIBBLE	*n* pl. -S a marine isopod
GRID	*n* pl. -S a grating
GRIDDER	*n* pl. -S a football player
GRIDDLE	*v* -DLED, -DLING, -DLES to cook on a flat pan
GRIDE	*v* GRIDED, GRIDING, GRIDES to scrape harshly
GRIDIRON	*n* pl. -S a grate for broiling food
GRIDLOCK	*v* -ED, -ING, -S to bring to a standstill
GRIEF	*n* pl. -S intense mental distress
GRIEVANT	*n* pl. -S one that submits a complaint for arbitration
GRIEVE	*v* GRIEVED, GRIEVING, GRIEVES to feel grief
GRIEVER	*n* pl. -S one that grieves
GRIEVOUS	*adj* causing grief
GRIFF	*n* pl. -S griffe
GRIFFE	*n* pl. -S the offspring of a black person and a mulatto
GRIFFIN	*n* pl. -S a mythological creature
GRIFFON	*n* pl. -S griffin
GRIFT	*v* -ED, -ING, -S to swindle
GRIFTER	*n* pl. -S a swindler
GRIG	*n* pl. -S a lively person
GRIGRI	*n* pl. -S a fetish or amulet

GRILL	*v* -ED, -ING, -S to broil on a gridiron
GRILLADE	*n* pl. -S a dish of grilled meat
GRILLAGE	*n* pl. -S a framework of timber
GRILLE	*n* pl. -S a grating
GRILLER	*n* pl. -S one that grills
GRILSE	*n* pl. -S a young salmon
GRIM	*adj* GRIMMER, GRIMMEST stern and unrelenting
GRIMACE	*v* -MACED, -MACING, -MACES to contort the facial features
GRIMACER	*n* pl. -S one that grimaces
GRIME	*v* GRIMED, GRIMING, GRIMES to make dirty
GRIMIER	comparative of grimy
GRIMIEST	superlative of grimy
GRIMILY	*adv* in a grimy manner
GRIMING	present participle of grime
GRIMLY	*adv* in a grim manner
GRIMMER	comparative of grim
GRIMMEST	superlative of grim
GRIMNESS	*n* pl. -ES the quality of being grim
GRIMY	*adj* GRIMIER, GRIMIEST dirty
GRIN	*v* GRINNED, GRINNING, GRINS to smile broadly
GRINCH	*n* pl. -ES one who spoils the fun of others
GRIND	*v* GROUND or GRINDED, GRINDING, GRINDS to wear, smooth, or sharpen by friction
GRINDER	*n* pl. -S one that grinds
GRINDERY	*n* pl. -ERIES a place where tools are ground
GRINNED	past tense of grin
GRINNER	*n* pl. -S one that grins
GRINNING	present participle of grin
GRIOT	*n* pl. -S a tribal entertainer in West Africa
GRIP	*v* GRIPPED or GRIPT, GRIPPING, GRIPS to grasp
GRIPE	*v* GRIPED, GRIPING, GRIPES to grasp
GRIPER	*n* pl. -S one that gripes
GRIPEY	*adj* GRIPIER, GRIPIEST gripy
GRIPIER	comparative of gripy
GRIPIEST	superlative of gripy
GRIPING	present participle of gripe
GRIPMAN	*n* pl. -MEN a cable car operator

GRIPPE	*n* pl. -S a virus disease
GRIPPED	a past tense of grip
GRIPPER	*n* pl. -S one that grips
GRIPPIER	comparative of grippy
GRIPPIEST	superlative of grippy
GRIPPING	present participle of grip
GRIPPLE	*adj* greedy
GRIPPY	*adj* GRIPPIER, GRIPPIEST affected with the grippe
GRIPSACK	*n* pl. -S a valise
GRIPT	a past tense of grip
GRIPY	*adj* GRIPIER, GRIPIEST causing sharp pains in the bowels
GRISEOUS	*adj* grayish
GRISETTE	*n* pl. -S a young French working-class girl
GRISKIN	*n* pl. -S the lean part of a loin of pork
GRISLY	*adj* -LIER, -LIEST horrifying
GRISON	*n* pl. -S a carnivorous mammal
GRIST	*n* pl. -S grain for grinding
GRISTLE	*n* pl. -S the tough part of meat
GRISTLY	*adj* -TLIER, -TLIEST containing gristle
GRIT	*v* GRITTED, GRITTING, GRITS to press the teeth together
GRITH	*n* pl. -S sanctuary for a limited period of time
GRITTY	*adj* -TIER, -TIEST plucky **GRITTILY** *adv*
GRIVET	*n* pl. -S a small monkey
GRIZZLE	*v* -ZLED, -ZLING, -ZLES to complain
GRIZZLER	*n* pl. -S one that grizzles
GRIZZLY	*adj* -ZLIER, -ZLIEST grayish
GRIZZLY	*n* pl. -ZLIES a large bear
GROAN	*v* -ED, -ING, -S to utter a low, mournful sound
GROANER	*n* pl. -S one that groans
GROAT	*n* pl. -S an old English coin
GROCER	*n* pl. -S a dealer in foodstuffs and household supplies
GROCERY	*n* pl. -CERIES a grocer's store
GROG	*n* pl. -S a mixture of liquor and water
GROGGERY	*n* pl. -GERIES a barroom
GROGGY	*adj* -GIER, -GIEST dazed **GROGGILY** *adv*

GROGRAM   n pl. -S a coarse silk fabric

GROGSHOP   n pl. -S a groggery

GROIN   v -ED, -ING, -S to build with intersecting arches

GROMMET   n pl. -S a reinforcing ring of metal

GROMWELL   n pl. -S an herb

GROOM   v -ED, -ING, -S to clean and care for

GROOMER   n pl. -S one that grooms

GROOVE   v GROOVED, GROOVING, GROOVES to form a groove (a long, narrow depression)

GROOVER   n pl. -S one that grooves

GROOVY   adj GROOVIER, GROOVIEST marvelous

GROPE   v GROPED, GROPING, GROPES to feel about with the hands

GROPER   n pl. -S one that gropes

GROSBEAK   n pl. -S a finch

GROSCHEN   n pl. GROSCHEN an Austrian coin

GROSS   adj GROSSER, GROSSEST flagrant

GROSS   v -ED, -ING, -ES to earn exclusive of deductions

GROSSER   n pl. -S a product yielding a large volume of business

GROSSLY   adv in a gross manner

GROSZ   n pl. GROSZY a Polish coin

GROSZE   n pl. GROSZY grosz

GROT   n pl. -S a grotto

GROTTO   n pl. -TOES or -TOS a cave

GROTTY   adj -TIER, -TIEST wretched

GROUCH   v -ED, -ING, -ES to complain

GROUCHY   adj GROUCHIER, GROUCHIEST ill-tempered

GROUND   v -ED, -ING, -S to place on a foundation

GROUNDER   n pl. -S a type of batted baseball

GROUP   v -ED, -ING, -S to arrange in a group (an assemblage of persons or things)

GROUPER   n pl. -S a food fish

GROUPIE   n pl. -S a female follower of rock groups

GROUPING   n pl. -S a set of objects

GROUPOID   n pl. -S a type of mathematical set

GROUSE   v GROUSED, GROUSING, GROUSES to complain

GROUSER   n pl. -S one that grouses

GROUT   v -ED, -ING, -S to fill with a thin mortar

GROUTER   n pl. -S one that grouts

GROUTY   adj GROUTIER, GROUTIEST surly

GROVE   n pl. -S a small forested area **GROVED** adj

GROVEL   v -ELED, -ELING, -ELS or -ELLED, -ELLING, -ELS to crawl in an abject manner

GROVELER   n pl. -S one that grovels

GROW   v GREW, GROWN, GROWING, GROWS to cultivate **GROWABLE** adj

GROWER   n pl. -S one that grows

GROWL   v -ED, -ING, -S to utter a deep, harsh sound

GROWLER   n pl. -S one that growls

GROWLY   adj GROWLIER, GROWLIEST deep and harsh in speech

GROWN   adj mature

GROWNUP   n pl. -S a mature person

GROWTH   n pl. -S development

GROWTHY   adj GROWTHIER, GROWTHIEST fast-growing

GROYNE   n pl. -S a structure built to protect a shore from erosion

GRUB   v GRUBBED, GRUBBING, GRUBS to dig

GRUBBER   n pl. -S one that grubs

GRUBBY   adj -BIER, -BIEST dirty **GRUBBILY** adv

GRUBWORM   n pl. -S the larva of some insects

GRUDGE   v GRUDGED, GRUDGING, GRUDGES to be unwilling to give or admit

GRUDGER   n pl. -S one that grudges

GRUE   n pl. -S a shudder of fear

GRUEL   v -ELED, -ELING, -ELS or -ELLED, -ELLING, -ELS to disable by hard work

GRUELER   n pl. -S one that gruels

GRUELING   n pl. -S an exhausting experience

GRUELLED   a past tense of gruel

GRUELLER   n pl. -S grueler

GRUELLING   present participle of gruel

GRUESOME	*adj* -SOMER, -SOMEST repugnant
GRUFF	*adj* GRUFFER, GRUFFEST low and harsh in speech
GRUFF	*v* -ED, -ING, -S to utter in a gruff voice
GRUFFIER	comparative of gruffy
GRUFFIEST	superlative of gruffy
GRUFFILY	*adv* in a gruffy manner
GRUFFISH	*adj* somewhat gruff
GRUFFLY	*adv* in a gruff manner
GRUFFY	*adj* GRUFFIER, GRUFFIEST gruff
GRUGRU	*n* pl. -S a palm tree
GRUIFORM	*adj* designating an order of birds
GRUM	*adj* GRUMMER, GRUMMEST morose
GRUMBLE	*v* -BLED, -BLING, -BLES to mutter in discontent **GRUMBLY** *adj*
GRUMBLER	*n* pl. -S one that grumbles
GRUME	*n* pl. -S a thick, viscid substance
GRUMMER	comparative of grum
GRUMMEST	superlative of grum
GRUMMET	*n* pl. -S grommet
GRUMOSE	*adj* grumous
GRUMOUS	*adj* consisting of clustered grains
GRUMP	*v* -ED, -ING, -S to complain
GRUMPHIE	*n* pl. -S a pig
GRUMPHY	*n* pl. GRUMPHIES grumphie
GRUMPISH	*adj* grumpy
GRUMPY	*adj* GRUMPIER, GRUMPIEST ill-tempered **GRUMPILY** *adv*
GRUNGE	*n* pl. -S dirt
GRUNGY	*adj* -GIER, -GIEST dirty
GRUNION	*n* pl. -S a small food fish
GRUNT	*v* -ED, -ING, -S to utter a deep, guttural sound
GRUNTER	*n* pl. -S one that grunts
GRUNTLE	*v* -TLED, -TLING, -TLES to put in a good humor
GRUSHIE	*adj* thriving
GRUTCH	*v* -ED, -ING, -ES to grudge
GRUTTEN	past participle of greet (to weep)
GRUYERE	*n* pl. -S a Swiss cheese
GRYPHON	*n* pl. -S griffin
GUACHARO	*n* pl. -ROS or -ROES a tropical bird
GUACO	*n* pl. -COS a tropical plant
GUAIAC	*n* pl. -S guaiacum
GUAIACOL	*n* pl. -S a chemical compound
GUAIACUM	*n* pl. -S a medicinal resin
GUAIOCUM	*n* pl. -S guaiacum
GUAN	*n* pl. -S a large bird
GUANACO	*n* pl. -COS a South American mammal
GUANASE	*n* pl. -S an enzyme
GUANAY	*n* pl. -NAYS a Peruvian cormorant
GUANIDIN	*n* pl. -S a chemical compound
GUANIN	*n* pl. -S guanine
GUANINE	*n* pl. -S a chemical compound
GUANO	*n* pl. -NOS the accumulated excrement of sea birds
GUAR	*n* pl. -S a drought-tolerant legume
GUARANI	*n* pl. -NIS or -NIES a monetary unit of Paraguay
GUARANTY	*v* -TIED, -TYING, -TIES to assume responsibility for the quality of
GUARD	*v* -ED, -ING, -S to protect
GUARDANT	*n* pl. -S a guardian
GUARDER	*n* pl. -S one that guards
GUARDIAN	*n* pl. -S one that guards
GUAVA	*n* pl. -S a tropical shrub
GUAYULE	*n* pl. -S a shrub that is a source of rubber
GUCK	*n* pl. -S a messy substance
GUDE	*n* pl. -S good
GUDGEON	*v* -ED, -ING, -S to dupe
GUENON	*n* pl. -S a long-tailed monkey
GUERDON	*v* -ED, -ING, -S to reward
GUERIDON	*n* pl. -S a small stand or table
GUERILLA	*n* pl. -S a member of a small independent band of soldiers
GUERNSEY	*n* pl. -SEYS a woolen shirt
GUESS	*v* -ED, -ING, -ES to form an opinion from little or no evidence
GUESSER	*n* pl. -S one that guesses
GUEST	*v* -ED, -ING, -S to appear as a visitor
GUFF	*n* pl. -S foolish talk
GUFFAW	*v* -ED, -ING, -S to laugh loudly
GUGGLE	*v* -GLED, -GLING, -GLES to gurgle

GUGLET *n* pl. -S goglet

GUID *n* pl. -S good

GUIDANCE *n* pl. -S advice

GUIDE *v* GUIDED, GUIDING, GUIDES to show the way to **GUIDABLE** *adj*

GUIDER *n* pl. -S one that guides

GUIDEWAY *n* pl. -WAYS a track for controlling the line of motion of something

GUIDON *n* pl. -S a small flag

GUILD *n* pl. -S an association of people of the same trade

GUILDER *n* pl. -S a monetary unit of the Netherlands

GUILE *v* GUILED, GUILING, GUILES to beguile

GUILEFUL *adj* cunning

GUILT *n* pl. -S the fact of having committed an offense

GUILTY *adj* GUILTIER, GUILTIEST worthy of blame for an offense **GUILTILY** *adv*

GUIMPE *n* pl. -S a short blouse

GUINEA *n* pl. -S a former British coin

GUIPURE *n* pl. -S a type of lace

GUIRO *n* pl. -ROS a percussion instrument

GUISARD *n* pl. -S a masker

GUISE *v* GUISED, GUISING, GUISES to disguise

GUITAR *n* pl. -S a stringed musical instrument

GUITGUIT *n* pl. -S a tropical American bird

GUL *n* pl. -S a design in oriental carpets

GULAG *n* pl. -S a forced-labor camp

GULAR *adj* of or pertaining to the throat

GULCH *n* pl. -ES a deep, narrow ravine

GULDEN *n* pl. -S a guilder

GULES *n* pl. GULES the color red

GULF *v* -ED, -ING, -S to swallow up

GULFIER comparative of gulfy

GULFIEST superlative of gulfy

GULFLIKE *adj* resembling a deep chasm

GULFWEED *n* pl. -S a brownish seaweed

GULFY *adj* GULFIER, GULFIEST full of whirlpools

GULL *v* -ED, -ING, -S to deceive

GULLABLE *adj* gullible **GULLABLY** *adv*

GULLET *n* pl. -S the throat

GULLEY *n* pl. -LEYS a ravine

GULLIBLE *adj* easily deceived **GULLIBLY** *adv*

GULLY *v* -LIED, -LYING, -LIES to form ravines by the action of water

GULOSITY *n* pl. -TIES gluttony

GULP *v* -ED, -ING, -S to swallow rapidly

GULPER *n* pl. -S one that gulps

GULPY *adj* GULPIER, GULPIEST marked by gulping

GUM *v* GUMMED, GUMMING, GUMS to smear, seal, or clog with gum (a sticky, viscid substance)

GUMBO *n* pl. -BOS the okra plant

GUMBOIL *n* pl. -S an abscess in the gum

GUMBOOT *n* pl. -S a rubber boot

GUMBOTIL *n* pl. -S a sticky clay

GUMDROP *n* pl. -S a chewy candy

GUMLESS *adj* having no gum

GUMLIKE *adj* resembling gum

GUMMA *n* pl. -MAS or -MATA a soft tumor

GUMMED past tense of gum

GUMMER *n* pl. -S one that gums

GUMMIER comparative of gummy

GUMMIEST superlative of gummy

GUMMING present participle of gum

GUMMITE *n* pl. -S a mixture of various minerals

GUMMOSE *adj* gummy

GUMMOSIS *n* pl. -MOSES a disease of plants

GUMMOUS *adj* gummy

GUMMY *adj* -MIER, -MIEST resembling gum

GUMPTION *n* pl. -S shrewdness

GUMSHOE *v* -SHOED, -SHOEING, -SHOES to investigate stealthily

GUMTREE *n* pl. -S a tree that yields gum

GUMWEED *n* pl. -S a plant covered with a gummy substance

GUMWOOD *n* pl. -S the wood of a gumtree

GUN *v* GUNNED, GUNNING, GUNS to shoot with a gun (a portable firearm)

GUNBOAT *n* pl. -S an armed vessel

GUNDOG *n* pl. -S a hunting dog

GUNFIGHT	*v* -FOUGHT, -FIGHTING, -FIGHTS to fight with guns
GUNFIRE	*n* pl. -S the firing of guns
GUNFLINT	*n* pl. -S the flint in a flintlock
GUNFOUGHT	past tense of gunfight
GUNITE	*n* pl. -S a mixture of cement, sand, and water
GUNK	*n* pl. -S filthy, sticky, or greasy matter **GUNKY** *adj*
GUNKHOLE	*v* -HOLED, -HOLING, -HOLES to make a series of short boat trips
GUNLESS	*adj* having no gun
GUNLOCK	*n* pl. -S the mechanism which ignites the charge of a gun
GUNMAN	*n* pl. -MEN one who is armed with a gun
GUNMETAL	*n* pl. -S a dark gray color
GUNNED	past tense of gun
GUNNEL	*n* pl. -S a marine fish
GUNNEN	past participle of gin
GUNNER	*n* pl. -S one that operates a gun
GUNNERY	*n* pl. -NERIES the use of guns
GUNNING	*n* pl. -S the sport of hunting with a gun
GUNNY	*n* pl. -NIES a coarse fabric
GUNNYBAG	*n* pl. -S a bag made of gunny
GUNPAPER	*n* pl. -S a type of explosive paper
GUNPLAY	*n* pl. -PLAYS the shooting of guns
GUNPOINT	*n* pl. -S the point or aim of a gun
GUNROOM	*n* pl. -S a room on a British warship
GUNSEL	*n* pl. -S a gunman
GUNSHIP	*n* pl. -S an armed helicopter
GUNSHOT	*n* pl. -S a projectile fired from a gun
GUNSMITH	*n* pl. -S one who makes or repairs firearms
GUNSTOCK	*n* pl. -S the rear wooden part of a rifle
GUNWALE	*n* pl. -S the upper edge of a ship's side
GUPPY	*n* pl. -PIES a small, tropical fish
GURGE	*v* GURGED, GURGING, GURGES to swirl
GURGLE	*v* -GLED, -GLING, -GLES to flow unevenly
GURGLET	*n* pl. -S goglet
GURNARD	*n* pl. -S a marine fish
GURNET	*n* pl. -S a gurnard
GURNEY	*n* pl. -NEYS a wheeled cot
GURRY	*n* pl. -RIES fish offal
GURSH	*n* pl. -ES qursh
GURU	*n* pl. -S a Hindu spiritual teacher
GURUSHIP	*n* pl. -S the office of a guru
GUSH	*v* -ED, -ING, -ES to flow forth forcefully
GUSHER	*n* pl. -S a gushing oil well
GUSHY	*adj* GUSHIER, GUSHIEST overly sentimental **GUSHILY** *adv*
GUSSET	*v* -ED, -ING, -S to furnish with a reinforcing piece of material
GUSSIE	*v* -SIED, -SYING, -SIES gussy
GUSSY	*v* -SIED, -SYING, -SIES to dress up in fine or showy clothes
GUST	*v* -ED, -ING, -S to blow in gusts (sudden blasts of wind)
GUSTABLE	*n* pl. -S a savory food
GUSTIER	comparative of gusty
GUSTIEST	superlative of gusty
GUSTILY	*adv* in a gusty manner
GUSTLESS	*adj* having no gusts
GUSTO	*n* pl. -TOES vigorous enjoyment
GUSTY	*adj* GUSTIER, GUSTIEST blowing in gusts
GUT	*v* GUTTED, GUTTING, GUTS to remove the guts (intestines) of
GUTLESS	*adj* lacking courage
GUTLIKE	*adj* resembling guts
GUTSILY	*adv* in a gutsy manner
GUTSY	*adj* GUTSIER, GUTSIEST brave
GUTTA	*n* pl. -TAE a drop of liquid
GUTTATE	*adj* resembling a drop
GUTTATED	*adj* guttate
GUTTED	past tense of gut
GUTTER	*v* -ED, -ING, -S to form channels for draining off water
GUTTERY	*adj* marked by extreme vulgarity or indecency
GUTTIER	comparative of gutty
GUTTIEST	superlative of gutty
GUTTING	present participle of gut
GUTTLE	*v* -TLED, -TLING, -TLES to eat rapidly
GUTTLER	*n* pl. -S one that guttles
GUTTURAL	*n* pl. -S a throaty sound

GUTTY	*adj* -TIER, -TIEST marked by courage
GUV	*n* pl. -S a governor
GUY	*v* -ED, -ING, -S to ridicule
GUYLINE	*n* pl. -S a rope, chain, or wire used as a brace
GUYOT	*n* pl. -S a flat-topped seamount
GUZZLE	*v* -ZLED, -ZLING, -ZLES to drink rapidly
GUZZLER	*n* pl. -S one that guzzles
GWEDUC	*n* pl. -S geoduck
GWEDUCK	*n* pl. -S geoduck
GYBE	*v* GYBED, GYBING, GYBES to shift from side to side while sailing
GYM	*n* pl. -S a room for athletic activities
GYMKHANA	*n* pl. -S an athletic meet
GYMNASIA	*n/pl* gyms
GYMNAST	*n* pl. -S one who is skilled in physical exercises
GYNAECEA	*n/pl* gynecia
GYNAECIA	*n/pl* gynecia
GYNANDRY	*n* pl. -DRIES the condition of having both male and female sexual organs
GYNARCHY	*n* pl. -CHIES government by women
GYNECIC	*adj* pertaining to women
GYNECIUM	*n* pl. -CIA the pistil of a flower
GYNECOID	*adj* resembling a woman
GYNIATRY	*n* pl. -TRIES the treatment of women's diseases
GYNOECIA	*n/pl* gynecia
GYP	*v* GYPPED, GYPPING, GYPS to swindle

GYPLURE	*n* pl. -S a synthetic attractant to trap gypsy moths
GYPPER	*n* pl. -S one that gyps
GYPSEIAN	*adj* of or pertaining to gypsies
GYPSEOUS	*adj* containing gypsum
GYPSTER	*n* pl. -S one that gyps
GYPSUM	*n* pl. -S a mineral
GYPSY	*v* -SIED, -SYING, -SIES to live like a gypsy (a wanderer)
GYPSYDOM	*n* pl. -S the realm of gypsies
GYPSYISH	*adj* resembling a gypsy
GYPSYISM	*n* pl. -S the mode of life of gypsies
GYRAL	*adj* gyratory **GYRALLY** *adv*
GYRASE	*n* pl. -S an enzyme
GYRATE	*v* -RATED, -RATING, -RATES to revolve or rotate
GYRATION	*n* pl. -S the act of gyrating
GYRATOR	*n* pl. -S one that gyrates
GYRATORY	*adj* moving in a circle or spiral
GYRE	*v* GYRED, GYRING, GYRES to move in a circle or spiral
GYRENE	*n* pl. -S a marine
GYRI	pl. of gyrus
GYRING	present participle of gyre
GYRO	*n* pl. -ROS a gyroscope
GYROIDAL	*adj* spiral in arrangement
GYRON	*n* pl. -S a heraldic design
GYROSE	*adj* marked with wavy lines
GYROSTAT	*n* pl. -S a type of stabilizing device
GYRUS	*n* pl. -RI a ridge in the brain
GYVE	*v* GYVED, GYVING, GYVES to shackle

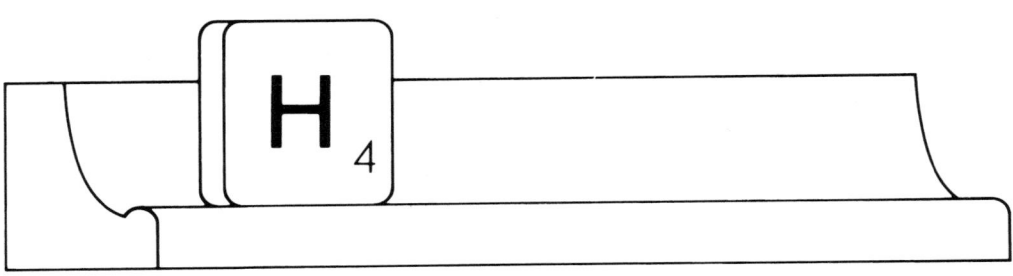

HA	*n* pl. -S a sound of surprise
HAAF	*n* pl. -S a deep-sea fishing ground
HAAR	*n* pl. -S a fog
HABANERA	*n* pl. -S a Cuban dance
HABDALAH	*n* pl. -S a Jewish ceremony
HABILE	*adj* skillful
HABIT	*v* -ED, -ING, -S to clothe or dress
HABITAN	*n* pl. -S a French settler
HABITANT	*n* pl. -S an inhabitant
HABITAT	*n* pl. -S the natural environment of an organism
HABITUAL	*adj* occurring frequently or constantly
HABITUDE	*n* pl. -S a usual course of action
HABITUE	*n* pl. -S a frequent customer
HABITUS	*n* pl. HABITUS bodily build and constitution
HABOOB	*n* pl. -S a violent sandstorm
HABU	*n* pl. -S a poisonous snake
HACEK	*n* pl. -S a mark placed over a letter to modify it
HACHURE	*v* -CHURED, -CHURING, -CHURES to make a hatching on a map
HACIENDA	*n* pl. -S an estate
HACK	*v* -ED, -ING, -S to cut or chop roughly
HACKBUT	*n* pl. -S a type of gun
HACKEE	*n* pl. -S a chipmunk
HACKER	*n* pl. -S one that hacks
HACKIE	*n* pl. -S a taxicab driver
HACKLE	*v* -LED, -LING, -LES to hack
HACKLER	*n* pl. -S one that hackles
HACKLY	*adj* -LIER, -LIEST jagged
HACKMAN	*n* pl. -MEN a hackie
HACKNEY	*v* -NEYED, -NEYING, -NEYS to make common
HACKSAW	*n* pl. -S a type of saw
HACKWORK	*n* pl. -S artistic work done according to formula
HAD	a past tense of have
HADAL	*adj* pertaining to deep parts of the ocean
HADARIM	a pl. of heder
HADDEST	a past 2d person sing. of have
HADDOCK	*n* pl. -S a food fish
HADE	*v* HADED, HADING, HADES to incline
HADITH	*n* pl. HADITH or HADITHS a record of the sayings of Muhammed
HADJ	*n* pl. -ES a pilgrimage to Mecca
HADJEE	*n* pl. -S hadji
HADJI	*n* pl. -S one who has made a hadj
HADRON	*n* pl. -S an elementary particle **HADRONIC** *adj*
HADST	a past 2d person sing. of have
HAE	*v* HAED, HAEN, HAEING, HAES to have
HAEM	*n* pl. -S heme
HAEMAL	*adj* hemal
HAEMATAL	*adj* hemal
HAEMATIC	*n* pl. -S hematic
HAEMATIN	*n* pl. -S hematin
HAEMIC	*adj* hemic
HAEMIN	*n* pl. -S hemin
HAEMOID	*adj* hemoid
HAEN	past participle of hae
HAERES	*n* pl. -REDES heres
HAET	*n* pl. -S a small amount
HAFFET	*n* pl. -S the cheekbone and temple

HAFFIT	*n* pl. -S haffet
HAFIZ	*n* pl. HAFIS a Muslim who knows the Koran by heart
HAFNIUM	*n* pl. -S a metallic element
HAFT	*v* -ED, -ING, -S to supply with a handle
HAFTARA	*n* pl. -RAS, -ROT or -ROTH haphtara
HAFTARAH	*n* pl. -RAHS, -ROT or -ROTH haphtara
HAFTER	*n* pl. -S one that hafts
HAFTORAH	*n* pl. -RAHS, -ROT or -ROTH haphtara
HAG	*v* HAGGED, HAGGING, HAGS to hack
HAGADIC	*adj* haggadic
HAGADIST	*n* pl. -S a haggadic scholar
HAGBERRY	*n* pl. -RIES a small cherry
HAGBORN	*adj* born of a witch
HAGBUSH	*n* pl. -ES a large tree
HAGBUT	*n* pl. -S hackbut
HAGDON	*n* pl. -S a seabird
HAGFISH	*n* pl. -ES an eellike fish
HAGGADA	*n* pl. -DAS, -DOT or -DOTH haggadah
HAGGADAH	*n* pl. -DAHS, -DOT or -DOTH a biblical narrative **HAGGADIC** *adj*
HAGGARD	*n* pl. -S an adult hawk
HAGGED	past tense of hag
HAGGING	present participle of hag
HAGGIS	*n* pl. -GISES a Scottish dish
HAGGISH	*adj* resembling a hag
HAGGLE	*v* -GLED, -GLING, -GLES to bargain
HAGGLER	*n* pl. -S one that haggles
HAGRIDE	*v* -RODE, -RIDDEN, -RIDING, -RIDES to harass
HAH	*n* pl. -S ha
HAHA	*n* pl. -S a fence set in a ditch
HAHNIUM	*n* pl. -S a radioactive element
HAIK	*n* pl. HAIKS or HAIKA an outer garment worn by Arabs
HAIKU	*n* pl. HAIKU a Japanese poem
HAIL	*v* -ED, -ING, -S to welcome
HAILER	*n* pl. -S one that hails
HAIR	*n* pl. -S a threadlike growth
HAIRBALL	*n* pl. -S a ball of hair
HAIRBAND	*n* pl. -S a headband

HAIRCAP	*n* pl. -S a hat
HAIRCUT	*n* pl. -S a cutting of the hair
HAIRDO	*n* pl. -DOS a style of wearing the hair
HAIRED	*adj* having hair
HAIRIER	comparative of hairy
HAIRIEST	superlative of hairy
HAIRLESS	*adj* having no hair
HAIRLIKE	*adj* resembling a hair
HAIRLINE	*n* pl. -S a very thin line
HAIRLOCK	*n* pl. -S a lock of hair
HAIRNET	*n* pl. -S a net worn to keep the hair in place
HAIRPIN	*n* pl. -S a hair fastener
HAIRWORK	*n* pl. -S the making of articles from hair
HAIRWORM	*n* pl. -S a parasitic worm
HAIRY	*adj* HAIRIER, HAIRIEST covered with hair
HAJ	*n* pl. -ES hadj
HAJI	*n* pl. -S hadji
HAJJ	*n* pl. -ES hadj
HAJJI	*n* pl. -S hadji
HAKE	*n* pl. -S a marine fish
HAKEEM	*n* pl. -S hakim
HAKIM	*n* pl. -S a Muslim physician
HALACHA	*n* pl. -CHAS or -CHOT halakah
HALAKAH	*n* pl. -KAHS or -KOTH the legal part of the Talmud
HALAKHA	*n* pl. -KHAS or -KHOT halakah
HALAKIC	*adj* pertaining to the halakah
HALAKIST	*n* pl. -S a halakic writer
HALAKOTH	a pl. of halakah
HALALA	*n* pl. -S a Saudi Arabian coin
HALALAH	*n* pl. -S halala
HALATION	*n* pl. -S a blurring of light in photographs
HALAVAH	*n* pl. -S halvah
HALAZONE	*n* pl. -S a disinfectant for drinking water
HALBERD	*n* pl. -S an axlike weapon of the 15th and 16th centuries
HALBERT	*n* pl. -S halberd
HALCYON	*n* pl. -S a mythical bird
HALE	*adj* HALER, HALEST healthy
HALE	*v* HALED, HALING, HALES to compel to go

HALENESS	*n* pl. -ES the state of being hale	**HALOLIKE**	*adj* resembling a halo
HALER	*n* pl. -LERS or -LERU a coin of the Czech Republic	**HALT**	*v* -ED, -ING, -S to stop
HALEST	superlative of hale	**HALTER**	*v* -ED, -ING, -S to put restraint upon
HALF	*n* pl. HALVES one of two equal parts	**HALTERE**	*n* pl. -S a pair of wings of an insect
HALFBACK	*n* pl. -S a football player	**HALTLESS**	*adj* not hesitant
HALFBEAK	*n* pl. -S a marine fish	**HALUTZ**	*n* pl. -LUTZIM an Israeli farmer
HALFLIFE	*n* pl. -LIVES a measure of radioactive decay	**HALVA**	*n* pl. -S halvah
HALFNESS	*n* pl. -ES the state of being half	**HALVAH**	*n* pl. -S a Turkish confection
HALFTIME	*n* pl. -S an intermission in a football game	**HALVE**	*v* HALVED, HALVING, HALVES to divide into two equal parts
HALFTONE	*n* pl. -S a shade between light and dark	**HALVERS**	*n* pl. HALVERS half shares
HALFWAY	*adj* being in the middle	**HALVES**	pl. of half
HALIBUT	*n* pl. -S a flatfish	**HALVING**	present participle of halve
HALID	*n* pl. -S halide	**HALYARD**	*n* pl. -S a line used to hoist a sail
HALIDE	*n* pl. -S a chemical compound	**HAM**	*v* HAMMED, HAMMING, HAMS to overact
HALIDOM	*n* pl. -S something holy	**HAMADA**	*n* pl. -S hammada
HALIDOME	*n* pl. -S halidom	**HAMAL**	*n* pl. -S a porter in eastern countries
HALING	present participle of hale	**HAMARTIA**	*n* pl. -S a defect of character
HALITE	*n* pl. -S a mineral	**HAMATE**	*n* pl. -S a wrist bone
HALITUS	*n* pl. -ES an exhalation	**HAMAUL**	*n* pl. -S hamal
HALL	*n* pl. -S a large room for assembly	**HAMBONE**	*v* -BONED, -BONING, -BONES to overact
HALLAH	*n* pl. -LAHS, -LOTH or -LOT challah	**HAMBURG**	*n* pl. -S a patty of ground beef
HALLEL	*n* pl. -S a chant of praise	**HAME**	*n* pl. -S a part of a horse collar
HALLIARD	*n* pl. -S halyard	**HAMLET**	*n* pl. -S a small town
HALLMARK	*v* -ED, -ING, -S to mark with an official stamp	**HAMMADA**	*n* pl. -S a desert plateau of bedrock
HALLO	*v* -ED, -ING, -S or -ES to shout	**HAMMAL**	*n* pl. -S hamal
HALLOA	*v* -ED, -ING, -S to hallo	**HAMMED**	past tense of ham
HALLOO	*v* -ED, -ING, -S to hallo	**HAMMER**	*v* -ED, -ING, -S to strike repeatedly
HALLOT	a pl. of hallah	**HAMMERER**	*n* pl. -S one that hammers
HALLOTH	a pl. of hallah	**HAMMIER**	comparative of hammy
HALLOW	*v* -ED, -ING, -S to make holy	**HAMMIEST**	superlative of hammy
HALLOWER	*n* pl. -S one that hallows	**HAMMILY**	*adv* in a hammy manner
HALLUX	*n* pl. -LUCES the big toe	**HAMMING**	present participle of ham
HALLWAY	*n* pl. -WAYS a hall	**HAMMOCK**	*n* pl. -S a hanging cot
HALM	*n* pl. -S haulm	**HAMMY**	*adj* -MIER, -MIEST overly theatrical
HALMA	*n* pl. -S a board game	**HAMPER**	*v* -ED, -ING, -S to hinder
HALO	*v* -ED, -ING, -ES or -S to form a halo (a ring of light)	**HAMPERER**	*n* pl. -S one that hampers
HALOGEN	*n* pl. -S a nonmetallic element	**HAMSTER**	*n* pl. -S a burrowing rodent
HALOID	*n* pl. -S a chemical salt		

HAMULUS   *n* pl. -LI a small hook **HAMULAR, HAMULATE, HAMULOSE, HAMULOUS** *adj*

HAMZA   *n* pl. -S an Arabic diacritical mark

HAMZAH   *n* pl. -S hamza

HANAPER   *n* pl. -S a wicker receptacle

HANCE   *n* pl. -S a side of an arch

HAND   *v* -ED, -ING, -S to present with the hand (the end of the forearm)

HANDBAG   *n* pl. -S a small carrying bag

HANDBALL   *n* pl. -S a small rubber ball

HANDBELL   *n* pl. -S a small bell with a handle

HANDBILL   *n* pl. -S a circular

HANDBOOK   *n* pl. -S a manual

HANDCAR   *n* pl. -S a hand-operated railroad car

HANDCART   *n* pl. -S a cart pushed by hand

HANDCUFF   *v* -ED, -ING, -S to fetter with restraining cuffs

HANDFAST   *v* -ED, -ING, -S to grip securely

HANDFUL   *n* pl. HANDFULS or HANDSFUL as much as the hand can hold

HANDGRIP   *n* pl. -S a grip by the hand or hands

HANDGUN   *n* pl. -S a small firearm

HANDHELD   *n* pl. -S something held in the hand

HANDHOLD   *n* pl. -S a handgrip

HANDICAP   *v* -CAPPED, -CAPPING, -CAPS to hinder

HANDIER   comparative of handy

HANDIEST   superlative of handy

HANDILY   *adv* in a handy manner

HANDLE   *v* -DLED, -DLING, -DLES to touch with the hands

HANDLER   *n* pl. -S one that handles

HANDLESS   *adj* having no hands

HANDLIKE   *adj* resembling a hand

HANDLING   *n* pl. -S the manner in which something is handled

HANDLIST   *n* pl. -S a reference list

HANDLOOM   *n* pl. -S a manually operated loom

HANDMADE   *adj* made by hand

HANDMAID   *n* pl. -S a female servant

HANDOFF   *n* pl. -S a play in football

HANDOUT   *n* pl. -S something given out free

HANDOVER   *n* pl. -S an instance of giving up control

HANDPICK   *v* -ED, -ING, -S to choose carefully

HANDRAIL   *n* pl. -S a railing used for support

HANDSAW   *n* pl. -S a saw used manually

HANDSEL   *v* -SELED, -SELING, -SELS or -SELLED, -SELLING, -SELS to give a gift to

HANDSET   *n* pl. -S a type of telephone

HANDSEWN   *adj* sewn by hand

HANDSFUL   a pl. of handful

HANDSOME   *adj* -SOMER, -SOMEST attractive

HANDWORK   *n* pl. -S manual labor

HANDWRIT   *adj* written by hand

HANDY   *adj* HANDIER, HANDIEST convenient for handling

HANDYMAN   *n* pl. -MEN a man who does odd jobs

HANG   *v* HUNG or HANGED, HANGING, HANGS to attach from above only **HANGABLE** *adj*

HANGAR   *v* -ED, -ING, -S to place in an aircraft shelter

HANGBIRD   *n* pl. -S a type of bird

HANGDOG   *n* pl. -S a sneaky person

HANGER   *n* pl. -S one that hangs

HANGFIRE   *n* pl. -S a delay in detonation

HANGING   *n* pl. -S an execution by strangling with a suspended noose

HANGMAN   *n* pl. -MEN an executioner

HANGNAIL   *n* pl. -S an agnail

HANGNEST   *n* pl. -S a hangbird

HANGOUT   *n* pl. -S a place often visited

HANGOVER   *n* pl. -S the physical effects following a drinking binge

HANGTAG   *n* pl. -S a type of tag used commercially

HANGUL   *n* the Korean alphabetic script

HANGUP   *n* pl. -S an inhibition or obsession

HANIWA   *n/pl* Japanese clay sculptures

HANK   *v* -ED, -ING, -S to fasten a sail

HANKER   *v* -ED, -ING, -S to long for

HANKERER   *n* pl. -S one that hankers

HANKIE   *n* pl. -S hanky

HANKY   *n* pl. -KIES a handkerchief

HANSA   *n* pl. -S hanse

HANSE   *n* pl. -S a guild of merchants

HANSEL	*v* -SELED, -SELING, -SELS or -SELLED, -SELLING, -SELS to handsel
HANSOM	*n* pl. -S a light carriage
HANT	*v* -ED, -ING, -S to haunt
HANTLE	*n* pl. -S a large amount
HANUMAN	*n* pl. -S an East Indian monkey
HAO	*n* pl. HAO a monetary unit of Vietnam
HAP	*v* HAPPED, HAPPING, HAPS to happen
HAPAX	*n* pl. -ES a word that occurs only once
HAPHTARA	*n* pl. -RAS, -ROT or -ROTH a biblical selection
HAPLESS	*adj* luckless
HAPLITE	*n* pl. -S aplite
HAPLOID	*n* pl. -S a cell having only one set of chromosomes
HAPLOIDY	*n* pl. -DIES the state of being a haploid
HAPLONT	*n* pl. -S an organism having a particular chromosomal structure
HAPLOPIA	*n* pl. -S normal vision
HAPLOSIS	*n* pl. -LOSES the halving of the chromosome number
HAPLY	*adv* by chance
HAPPED	past tense of hap
HAPPEN	*v* -ED, -ING, -S to occur
HAPPING	present participle of hap
HAPPY	*adj* -PIER, -PIEST marked by joy **HAPPILY** *adv*
HAPTEN	*n* pl. -S a substance similar to an antigen **HAPTENIC** *adj*
HAPTENE	*n* pl. -S hapten
HAPTIC	*adj* pertaining to the sense of touch
HAPTICAL	*adj* haptic
HARANGUE	*v* -RANGUED, -RANGUING, -RANGUES to deliver a tirade to
HARASS	*v* -ED, -ING, -ES to bother persistently
HARASSER	*n* pl. -S one that harasses
HARBOR	*v* -ED, -ING, -S to shelter
HARBORER	*n* pl. -S one that harbors
HARBOUR	*v* -ED, -ING, -S to harbor
HARD	*adj* HARDER, HARDEST firm and unyielding
HARDBACK	*n* pl. -S a hardcover book
HARDBALL	*n* pl. -S baseball
HARDBOOT	*n* pl. -S a horseman
HARDCASE	*adj* tough
HARDCORE	*adj* unyielding
HARDEDGE	*n* pl. -S a geometric painting
HARDEN	*v* -ED, -ING, -S to make hard
HARDENER	*n* pl. -S one that hardens
HARDHACK	*n* pl. -S a woody plant
HARDHAT	*n* pl. -S a conservative
HARDHEAD	*n* pl. -S a practical person
HARDIER	comparative of hardy
HARDIES	pl. of hardy
HARDIEST	superlative of hardy
HARDILY	*adv* in a hardy manner
HARDLINE	*adj* unyielding
HARDLY	*adv* scarcely
HARDNESS	*n* pl. -ES the state of being hard
HARDNOSE	*n* pl. -S a stubborn person
HARDPAN	*n* pl. -S a layer of hard subsoil
HARDS	*n/pl* the coarse refuse of flax
HARDSET	*adj* rigid
HARDSHIP	*n* pl. -S a difficult, painful condition
HARDTACK	*n* pl. -S a hard biscuit
HARDTOP	*n* pl. -S a type of car
HARDWARE	*n* pl. -S metal goods
HARDWIRE	*v* -WIRED, -WIRING, -WIRES to permanently connect electronic components
HARDWOOD	*n* pl. -S the hard, compact wood of various trees
HARDY	*adj* -DIER, -DIEST very sturdy
HARDY	*n* pl. -DIES a blacksmith's chisel
HARE	*v* HARED, HARING, HARES to run
HAREBELL	*n* pl. -S a perennial herb
HAREEM	*n* pl. -S harem
HARELIKE	*adj* resembling a hare (a long-eared mammal)
HARELIP	*n* pl. -S a deformity of the upper lip
HAREM	*n* pl. -S the section of a Muslim household reserved for women
HARIANA	*n* pl. -S a breed of cattle
HARICOT	*n* pl. -S the seed of various string beans
HARIJAN	*n* pl. -S an outcaste in India

HARING	present participle of hare
HARK	v -ED, -ING, -S to listen to
HARKEN	v -ED, -ING, -S to hearken
HARKENER	n pl. -S one that harkens
HARL	n pl. -S a herl
HARLOT	n pl. -S a prostitute
HARLOTRY	n pl. -RIES prostitution
HARM	v -ED, -ING, -S to injure
HARMER	n pl. -S one that harms
HARMFUL	adj capable of harming
HARMIN	n pl. -S harmine
HARMINE	n pl. -S an alkaloid used as a stimulant
HARMLESS	adj not harmful
HARMONIC	n pl. -S an overtone
HARMONY	n pl. -NIES agreement
HARNESS	v -ED, -ING, -ES to put tackle on a draft animal
HARP	v -ED, -ING, -S to play on a harp (a type of stringed musical instrument)
HARPER	n pl. -S a harpist
HARPIES	pl. of harpy
HARPIN	n pl. -S harping
HARPING	n pl. -S a wooden plank used in shipbuilding
HARPIST	n pl. -S one that plays the harp
HARPOON	v -ED, -ING, -S to strike with a harpoon
HARPY	n pl. -PIES a shrewish person
HARRIDAN	n pl. -S a haggard woman
HARRIED	past tense of harry
HARRIER	n pl. -S a hunting dog
HARRIES	present 3d person sing. of harry
HARROW	v -ED, -ING, -S to break up and level soil
HARROWER	n pl. -S one that harrows
HARRUMPH	v -ED, -ING, -S to make a guttural sound
HARRY	v -RIED, -RYING, -RIES to pillage
HARSH	adj HARSHER, HARSHEST severe **HARSHLY** adv
HARSHEN	v -ED, -ING, -S to make harsh
HARSLET	n pl. -S haslet
HART	n pl. -S a male deer
HARTAL	n pl. -S a stoppage of work

HARUMPH	v -ED, -ING, -S harrumph
HARUSPEX	n pl. -PICES a soothsayer of ancient Rome
HARVEST	v -ED, -ING, -S to gather a crop
HAS	a present 3d person sing. of have
HASH	v -ED, -ING, -ES to mince
HASHEESH	n pl. -ES hashish
HASHHEAD	n pl. -S a hashish addict
HASHISH	n pl. -ES a mild narcotic
HASLET	n pl. -S the edible viscera of an animal
HASP	v -ED, -ING, -S to fasten with a clasp
HASSEL	n pl. -S an argument
HASSLE	v -SLED, -SLING, -SLES to argue
HASSOCK	n pl. -S a footstool
HAST	a present 2d person sing. of have
HASTATE	adj triangular
HASTE	v HASTED, HASTING, HASTES to hasten
HASTEFUL	adj hasty
HASTEN	v -ED, -ING, -S to hurry
HASTENER	n pl. -S one that hastens
HASTING	present participle of haste
HASTY	adj HASTIER, HASTIEST speedy **HASTILY** adv
HAT	v HATTED, HATTING, HATS to provide with a hat (a covering for the head)
HATABLE	adj hateable
HATBAND	n pl. -S a band worn on a hat
HATBOX	n pl. -ES a box for a hat
HATCH	v -ED, -ING, -ES to bring forth young from an egg
HATCHECK	adj pertaining to the checking of hats
HATCHEL	v -ELED, -ELING, -ELS or -ELLED, -ELLING, -ELS to separate flax fibers with a comb
HATCHER	n pl. -S one that hatches
HATCHERY	n pl. -ERIES a place for hatching eggs
HATCHET	n pl. -S a small ax
HATCHING	n pl. -S a series of lines used to show shading
HATCHWAY	n pl. -WAYS an opening in the deck of a ship

HATE	*v* HATED, HATING, HATES to despise
HATEABLE	*adj* meriting hatred
HATEFUL	*adj* detestable
HATER	*n* pl. -S one that hates
HATFUL	*n* pl. HATSFUL or HATFULS as much as a hat can hold
HATH	a present 3d person sing. of have
HATING	present participle of hate
HATLESS	*adj* lacking a hat
HATLIKE	*adj* resembling a hat
HATMAKER	*n* pl. -S one that makes hats
HATPIN	*n* pl. -S a pin for securing a hat
HATRACK	*n* pl. -S a rack for hats
HATRED	*n* pl. -S intense dislike or aversion
HATSFUL	a pl. of hatful
HATTED	past tense of hat
HATTER	*n* pl. -S a hatmaker
HATTERIA	*n* pl. -S a reptile
HATTING	present participle of hat
HAUBERK	*n* pl. -S a coat of armor
HAUGH	*n* pl. -S a low-lying meadow
HAUGHTY	*adj* -TIER, -TIEST arrogant
HAUL	*v* -ED, -ING, -S to pull with force
HAULAGE	*n* pl. -S the act of hauling
HAULER	*n* pl. -S one that hauls
HAULIER	*n* pl. -S hauler
HAULM	*n* pl. -S a plant stem
HAULMY	*adj* HAULMIER, HAULMIEST having haulms
HAULYARD	*n* pl. -S halyard
HAUNCH	*n* pl. -ES the hindquarter **HAUNCHED** *adj*
HAUNT	*v* -ED, -ING, -S to visit frequently
HAUNTER	*n* pl. -S one that haunts
HAUSEN	*n* pl. -S a Russian sturgeon
HAUSFRAU	*n* pl. -FRAUS or -FRAUEN a housewife
HAUT	*adj* haute
HAUTBOIS	*n* pl. HAUTBOIS hautboy
HAUTBOY	*n* pl. -BOYS an oboe
HAUTE	*adj* high-class
HAUTEUR	*n* pl. -S haughty manner or spirit
HAVARTI	*n* pl. -S a Danish cheese
HAVDALAH	*n* pl. -S habdalah

HAVE	*v* past 2d person sing. HAD, HADDEST or HADST, present participle HAVING, present 2d person sing. HAVE or HAST, 3d person sing. HAS or HATH to be in possession of
HAVE	*n* pl. -S a wealthy person
HAVELOCK	*n* pl. -S a covering for a cap
HAVEN	*v* -ED, -ING, -S to shelter
HAVER	*v* -ED, -ING, -S to hem and haw
HAVEREL	*n* pl. -S a fool
HAVING	present participle of have
HAVIOR	*n* pl. -S behavior
HAVIOUR	*n* pl. -S havior
HAVOC	*v* -OCKED, -OCKING, -OCS to destroy
HAVOCKER	*n* pl. -S one that havocs
HAW	*v* -ED, -ING, -S to turn left
HAWFINCH	*n* pl. -ES a Eurasian finch
HAWK	*v* -ED, -ING, -S to peddle
HAWKBILL	*n* pl. -S a sea turtle
HAWKER	*n* pl. -S one that hawks
HAWKEY	*n* pl. -EYS a hawkie
HAWKEYED	*adj* having keen sight
HAWKIE	*n* pl. -S a white-faced cow
HAWKING	*n* pl. -S falconry
HAWKISH	*adj* warlike
HAWKLIKE	*adj* resembling a hawk (a bird of prey)
HAWKMOTH	*n* pl. -S a large moth
HAWKNOSE	*n* pl. -S a large, curved nose
HAWKSHAW	*n* pl. -S a detective
HAWKWEED	*n* pl. -S a weedlike herb
HAWSE	*n* pl. -S a part of a ship's bow
HAWSER	*n* pl. -S a mooring rope
HAWTHORN	*n* pl. -S a thorny shrub
HAY	*v* -ED, -ING, -S to convert into hay (grass, cut and dried for fodder)
HAYCOCK	*n* pl. -S a pile of hay
HAYER	*n* pl. -S one that hays
HAYFIELD	*n* pl. -S a field where grasses for hay are grown
HAYFORK	*n* pl. -S a tool for pitching hay
HAYING	*n* pl. -S the season for harvesting hay
HAYLAGE	*n* pl. -S a type of hay
HAYLOFT	*n* pl. -S a loft for hay storage

HAYMAKER	*n* pl. -S one that makes hay
HAYMOW	*n* pl. -S a hayloft
HAYRACK	*n* pl. -S a frame used in hauling hay
HAYRICK	*n* pl. -S a haystack
HAYRIDE	*n* pl. -S a wagon ride
HAYSEED	*n* pl. -S a bumpkin
HAYSTACK	*n* pl. -S a pile of hay
HAYWARD	*n* pl. -S an officer who tends cattle
HAYWIRE	*n* pl. -S wire used in baling hay
HAZAN	*n* pl. -ZANIM or -ZANS a cantor
HAZARD	*v* -ED, -ING, -S to venture
HAZE	*v* HAZED, HAZING, HAZES to subject to a humiliating initiation
HAZEL	*n* pl. -S a shrub
HAZELHEN	*n* pl. -S a European grouse
HAZELLY	*adj* yellowish brown
HAZELNUT	*n* pl. -S an edible nut
HAZER	*n* pl. -S one that hazes
HAZIER	comparative of hazy
HAZIEST	superlative of hazy
HAZILY	*adv* in a hazy manner
HAZINESS	*n* pl. -ES the state of being hazy
HAZING	*n* pl. -S an attempt to embarrass or ridicule
HAZY	*adj* HAZIER, HAZIEST unclear
HAZZAN	*n* pl. HAZZANIM or HAZZANS hazan
HE	*n* pl. -S a male person
HEAD	*v* -ED, -ING, -S to be chief of
HEADACHE	*n* pl. -S a pain inside the head
HEADACHY	*adj* -ACHIER, -ACHIEST having a headache
HEADBAND	*n* pl. -S a band worn on the head
HEADER	*n* pl. -S a grain harvester
HEADFISH	*n* pl. -ES a marine fish
HEADGATE	*n* pl. -S a gate to control the flow of water
HEADGEAR	*n* pl. -S a covering for the head
HEADHUNT	*v* -ED, -ING, -S to seek out, decapitate, and preserve the heads of enemies
HEADIER	comparative of heady
HEADIEST	superlative of heady
HEADILY	*adv* in a heady manner
HEADING	*n* pl. -S a title

HEADLAMP	*n* pl. -S a light on the front of a car
HEADLAND	*n* pl. -S a cliff
HEADLESS	*adj* lacking a head
HEADLINE	*v* -LINED, -LINING, -LINES to provide with a title
HEADLOCK	*n* pl. -S a wrestling hold
HEADLONG	*adj* rash; impetuous
HEADMAN	*n* pl. -MEN a foreman
HEADMOST	*adj* foremost
HEADNOTE	*n* pl. -S a prefixed note
HEADPIN	*n* pl. -S a bowling pin
HEADRACE	*n* pl. -S a water channel
HEADREST	*n* pl. -S a support for the head
HEADROOM	*n* pl. -S clear vertical space
HEADSAIL	*n* pl. -S a type of sail
HEADSET	*n* pl. -S a pair of earphones
HEADSHIP	*n* pl. -S the position of a leader
HEADSMAN	*n* pl. -MEN an executioner
HEADSTAY	*n* pl. -STAYS a support for a ship's foremast
HEADWAY	*n* pl. -WAYS forward movement
HEADWIND	*n* pl. -S an oncoming wind
HEADWORD	*n* pl. -S a word put at the beginning
HEADWORK	*n* pl. -S mental work
HEADY	*adj* HEADIER, HEADIEST intoxicating
HEAL	*v* -ED, -ING, -S to make sound or whole **HEALABLE** *adj*
HEALER	*n* pl. -S one that heals
HEALTH	*n* pl. -S the physical condition of an organism
HEALTHY	*adj* HEALTHIER, HEALTHIEST having good health
HEAP	*v* -ED, -ING, -S to pile up
HEAR	*v* HEARD, HEARING, HEARS to perceive by the ear **HEARABLE** *adj*
HEARER	*n* pl. -S one that hears
HEARING	*n* pl. -S a preliminary examination
HEARKEN	*v* -ED, -ING, -S to listen to
HEARSAY	*n* pl. -SAYS secondhand information
HEARSE	*v* HEARSED, HEARSING, HEARSES to transport in a hearse (a vehicle for conveying corpses)

HEART   *v* -ED, -ING, -S to hearten

HEARTEN   *v* -ED, -ING, -S to give courage to

HEARTH   *n* pl. -S the floor of a fireplace

HEARTY   *adj* HEARTIER, HEARTIEST very friendly **HEARTILY** *adv*

HEARTY   *n* pl. HEARTIES a comrade

HEAT   *v* HEATED or HET, HEATING, HEATS to make hot **HEATABLE** *adj*

HEATEDLY   *adv* in an inflamed or excited manner

HEATER   *n* pl. -S an apparatus for heating

HEATH   *n* pl. -S an evergreen shrub

HEATHEN   *n* pl. -S an uncivilized person

HEATHER   *n* pl. -S an evergreen shrub **HEATHERY** *adj*

HEATHY   *adj* HEATHIER, HEATHIEST abounding in heath

HEATLESS   *adj* having no warmth

HEAUME   *n* pl. -S a medieval helmet

HEAVE   *v* HEAVED or HOVE, HEAVING, HEAVES to lift forcefully

HEAVEN   *n* pl. -S the sky

HEAVENLY   *adj* -LIER, -LIEST full of beauty and peace

HEAVER   *n* pl. -S one that heaves

HEAVIER   comparative of heavy

HEAVIES   pl. of heavy

HEAVING   present participle of heave

HEAVY   *adj* HEAVIER, HEAVIEST having much weight **HEAVILY** *adv*

HEAVY   *n* pl. HEAVIES a villain

HEAVYSET   *adj* solidly built; stocky

HEBDOMAD   *n* pl. -S the number seven

HEBETATE   *v* -TATED, -TATING, -TATES to make dull

HEBETIC   *adj* pertaining to puberty

HEBETUDE   *n* pl. -S mental dullness

HEBRAIZE   *v* -IZED, -IZING, -IZES to make Hebrew

HECATOMB   *n* pl. -S a great sacrifice or slaughter

HECK   *n* pl. -S hell

HECKLE   *v* -LED, -LING, -LES to harass a speaker

HECKLER   *n* pl. -S one that heckles

HECTARE   *n* pl. -S a unit of area

HECTIC   *adj* filled with turmoil **HECTICLY** *adv*

HECTICAL   *adj* hectic

HECTOR   *v* -ED, -ING, -S to bully

HEDDLE   *n* pl. -S a part of a loom

HEDER   *n* pl. HEDERS or HADARIM a Jewish school

HEDGE   *v* HEDGED, HEDGING, HEDGES to surround with a hedge (a dense row of shrubs)

HEDGEHOG   *n* pl. -S a small mammal

HEDGEHOP   *v* -HOPPED, -HOPPING, -HOPS to fly near the ground

HEDGEPIG   *n* pl. -S a hedgehog

HEDGER   *n* pl. -S one that hedges

HEDGEROW   *n* pl. -S a row of bushes

HEDGING   present participle of hedge

HEDGY   *adj* HEDGIER, HEDGIEST abounding in hedges

HEDONIC   *adj* pertaining to pleasure

HEDONICS   *n/pl* a branch of psychology

HEDONISM   *n* pl. -S the pursuit of pleasure

HEDONIST   *n* pl. -S a follower of hedonism

HEED   *v* -ED, -ING, -S to pay attention to

HEEDER   *n* pl. -S one that heeds

HEEDFUL   *adj* paying close attention

HEEDLESS   *adj* paying little or no attention

HEEHAW   *v* -ED, -ING, -S to guffaw

HEEL   *v* -ED, -ING, -S to supply with a heel (the raised part of a shoe)

HEELBALL   *n* pl. -S a composition used for polishing

HEELER   *n* pl. -S one that puts heels on shoes

HEELING   *n* pl. -S the act of inclining laterally

HEELLESS   *adj* lacking heels

HEELPOST   *n* pl. -S a post fitted to the end of something

HEELTAP   *n* pl. -S material put on the heel of a shoe

HEEZE   *v* HEEZED, HEEZING, HEEZES to hoist

HEFT   *v* -ED, -ING, -S to lift up

HEFTER   *n* pl. -S one that hefts

HEFTY   *adj* HEFTIER, HEFTIEST heavy **HEFTILY** *adv*

HEGARI   *n* pl. -S a grain

HEGEMONY	*n* pl. -NIES great authority	**HELIUM**	*n* pl. -S a gaseous element
HEGIRA	*n* pl. -S an exodus	**HELIX**	*n* pl. -LIXES or -LICES something spiral in form
HEGUMEN	*n* pl. -S the head of a monastery		
HEGUMENE	*n* pl. -S the head of a nunnery	**HELL**	*v* -ED, -ING, -S to behave raucously
HEGUMENY	*n* pl. -NIES the office of a hegumen	**HELLBENT**	*adj* stubbornly determined
HEH	*n* pl. -S a Hebrew letter	**HELLBOX**	*n* pl. -ES a printer's receptacle
HEIFER	*n* pl. -S a young cow	**HELLCAT**	*n* pl. -S a shrewish person
HEIGH	*interj* — used to attract attention	**HELLER**	*n* pl. -S a hellion
HEIGHT	*n* pl. -S the highest point	**HELLERI**	*n* pl. -ES a tropical fish
HEIGHTEN	*v* -ED, -ING, -S to raise	**HELLERY**	*n* pl. -LERIES rough play
HEIGHTH	*n* pl. -S height	**HELLFIRE**	*n* pl. -S the torment of hell
HEIL	*v* -ED, -ING, -S to salute	**HELLHOLE**	*n* pl. -S a horrible place
HEIMISH	*adj* homelike	**HELLION**	*n* pl. -S a troublesome person
HEINIE	*n* pl. -S the buttocks	**HELLISH**	*adj* horrible
HEINOUS	*adj* very wicked	**HELLKITE**	*n* pl. -S a cruel person
HEIR	*v* -ED, -ING, -S to inherit	**HELLO**	*v* -ED, -ING, -ES or -S to greet
HEIRDOM	*n* pl. -S heirship	**HELLUVA**	*adj* disagreeable
HEIRESS	*n* pl. -ES a female inheritor	**HELM**	*v* -ED, -ING, -S to steer a ship
HEIRLESS	*adj* having no inheritors	**HELMET**	*v* -ED, -ING, -S to supply with a helmet (a protective covering for the head)
HEIRLOOM	*n* pl. -S an inherited possession		
HEIRSHIP	*n* pl. -S the right to inheritance		
HEISHI	*n/pl* tiny beads made from shells	**HELMINTH**	*n* pl. -S a worm
HEIST	*v* -ED, -ING, -S to steal	**HELMLESS**	*adj* lacking a helm (a steering system)
HEISTER	*n* pl. -S one that heists		
HEJIRA	*n* pl. -S hegira	**HELMSMAN**	*n* pl. -MEN one that steers a ship
HEKTARE	*n* pl. -S hectare	**HELO**	*n* pl. HELOS a helicopter
HELD	past tense of hold	**HELOT**	*n* pl. -S a slave or serf
HELIAC	*adj* heliacal	**HELOTAGE**	*n* pl. -S helotism
HELIACAL	*adj* pertaining to the sun	**HELOTISM**	*n* pl. -S slavery or serfdom
HELIAST	*n* pl. -S an Athenian judge	**HELOTRY**	*n* pl. -RIES helotism
HELICAL	*adj* shaped like a helix	**HELP**	*v* HELPED or HOLP, HELPED or HOLPEN, HELPING, HELPS to give assistance to **HELPABLE** *adj*
HELICES	*a* pl. of helix		
HELICITY	*n* pl. -TIES a component of a particle's spin		
		HELPER	*n* pl. -S one that helps
HELICOID	*n* pl. -S a type of geometrical surface	**HELPFUL**	*adj* being of service or assistance
HELICON	*n* pl. -S a large bass tuba	**HELPING**	*n* pl. -S a portion of food
HELICOPT	*v* -ED, -ING, -S to travel by helicopter	**HELPLESS**	*adj* defenseless
		HELPMATE	*n* pl. -S a helpful companion
HELILIFT	*v* -ED, -ING, -S to transport by helicopter	**HELPMEET**	*n* pl. -S a helpmate
		HELVE	*v* HELVED, HELVING, HELVES to provide with a handle
HELIO	*n* pl. -LIOS a signaling mirror		
HELIPAD	*n* pl. -S a heliport	**HEM**	*v* HEMMED, HEMMING, HEMS to provide with an edge
HELIPORT	*n* pl. -S an airport for helicopters		
HELISTOP	*n* pl. -S a heliport	**HEMAGOG**	*n* pl. -S an agent that promotes blood flow

HEMAL	*adj* pertaining to the blood
HEMATAL	*adj* hemal
HEMATEIN	*n* pl. -S a chemical compound
HEMATIC	*n* pl. -S a medicine for a blood disease
HEMATIN	*n* pl. -S heme
HEMATINE	*n* pl. -S hematin
HEMATITE	*n* pl. -S an ore of iron
HEMATOID	*adj* resembling blood
HEMATOMA	*n* pl. -MAS or -MATA a swelling filled with blood
HEME	*n* pl. -S a component of hemoglobin
HEMIC	*adj* hemal
HEMIN	*n* pl. -S a chloride of heme
HEMIOLA	*n* pl. -S a rhythmic alteration in music
HEMIOLIA	*n* pl. -S hemiola
HEMIPTER	*n* pl. -S an insect
HEMLINE	*n* pl. -S the bottom edge of a garment
HEMLOCK	*n* pl. -S a poisonous herb
HEMMED	past tense of hem
HEMMER	*n* pl. -S one that hems
HEMMING	present participle of hem
HEMOCOEL	*n* pl. -S a body cavity
HEMOCYTE	*n* pl. -S a blood cell
HEMOID	*adj* hemal
HEMOLYZE	*v* -LYZED, -LYZING, -LYZES to break down red blood cells
HEMOSTAT	*n* pl. -S an instrument for reducing bleeding
HEMP	*n* pl. -S a tall herb
HEMPEN	*adj* made of hemp
HEMPIE	*adj* HEMPIER, HEMPIEST hempy
HEMPIER	comparative of hempy
HEMPIEST	superlative of hempy
HEMPLIKE	*adj* resembling hemp
HEMPSEED	*n* pl. -S the seed of hemp
HEMPWEED	*n* pl. -S a climbing plant
HEMPY	*adj* HEMPIER, HEMPIEST mischievous
HEN	*n* pl. -S a female chicken
HENBANE	*n* pl. -S a poisonous herb
HENBIT	*n* pl. -S a perennial herb
HENCE	*adv* consequently

HENCHMAN	*n* pl. -MEN an unscrupulous supporter
HENCOOP	*n* pl. -S a cage for hens
HENEQUEN	*n* pl. -S a fiber used to make ropes
HENEQUIN	*n* pl. -S henequen
HENHOUSE	*n* pl. -S a shelter for poultry
HENIQUEN	*n* pl. -S henequen
HENLIKE	*adj* resembling a hen
HENNA	*v* -ED, -ING, -S to dye with a reddish coloring
HENNERY	*n* pl. -NERIES a poultry farm
HENPECK	*v* -ED, -ING, -S to dominate by nagging
HENRY	*n* pl. -RIES or -RYS a unit of inductance
HENT	*v* -ED, -ING, -S to grasp
HEP	*adj* hip
HEPARIN	*n* pl. -S a biochemical
HEPATIC	*n* pl. -S a drug acting on the liver
HEPATICA	*n* pl. -CAS or -CAE a perennial herb
HEPATIZE	*v* -TIZED, -TIZING, -TIZES to convert tissue into a firm mass
HEPATOMA	*n* pl. -MAS or -MATA a tumor of the liver
HEPCAT	*n* pl. -S a jazz enthusiast
HEPTAD	*n* pl. -S a group of seven
HEPTAGON	*n* pl. -S a seven-sided polygon
HEPTANE	*n* pl. -S a hydrocarbon used as a solvent
HEPTARCH	*n* pl. -S one of a group of seven rulers
HEPTOSE	*n* pl. -S a chemical compound
HER	*pron* the objective or possessive case of the pronoun she
HERALD	*v* -ED, -ING, -S to proclaim
HERALDIC	*adj* pertaining to heraldry
HERALDRY	*n* pl. -RIES the art or science of armorial bearings
HERB	*n* pl. -S a flowering plant with a nonwoody stem
HERBAGE	*n* pl. -S nonwoody plant life
HERBAL	*n* pl. -S a book about herbs and plants
HERBARIA	*n/pl* collections of dried plants
HERBED	*adj* flavored with herbs
HERBIER	comparative of herby
HERBIEST	superlative of herby

HERBLESS	*adj* lacking herbs
HERBLIKE	*adj* resembling an herb
HERBY	*adj* HERBIER, HERBIEST abounding in herbs
HERCULES	*n* pl. -LESES any man of great size and strength
HERD	*v* -ED, -ING, -S to bring together in a herd (a group of animals)
HERDER	*n* pl. -S one who tends a herd
HERDIC	*n* pl. -S a type of carriage
HERDLIKE	*adj* resembling a herd
HERDMAN	*n* pl. -MEN herdsman
HERDSMAN	*n* pl. -MEN a herder
HERE	*n* pl. -S this place
HEREAT	*adv* at this time
HEREAWAY	*adv* in this vicinity
HEREBY	*adv* by this means
HEREDES	pl. of heres
HEREDITY	*n* pl. -TIES the genetic transmission of characteristics
HEREIN	*adv* in this
HEREINTO	*adv* into this place
HEREOF	*adv* of this
HEREON	*adv* on this
HERES	*n* pl. HEREDES an heir
HERESY	*n* pl. -SIES a belief contrary to a church doctrine
HERETIC	*n* pl. -S one that upholds heresy
HERETO	*adv* to this matter
HERETRIX	*n* pl. -TRIXES or -TRICES heritrix
HEREUNTO	*adv* hereto
HEREUPON	*adv* immediately following this
HEREWITH	*adv* along with this
HERIOT	*n* pl. -S a feudal tribute or payment
HERITAGE	*n* pl. -S something that is inherited
HERITOR	*n* pl. -S one that inherits
HERITRIX	*n* pl. -TRIXES or -TRICES a female heritor
HERL	*n* pl. -S a feathered fishing lure
HERM	*n* pl. -S a type of statue
HERMA	*n* pl. -MAE or -MAI a herm **HERMAEAN** *adj*
HERMETIC	*adj* airtight
HERMIT	*n* pl. -S a recluse **HERMITIC** *adj*
HERMITRY	*n* pl. -RIES the state of being a hermit
HERN	*n* pl. -S a heron
HERNIA	*n* pl. -NIAS or -NIAE the protrusion of an organ through its surrounding wall **HERNIAL** *adj*
HERNIATE	*v* -ATED, -ATING, -ATES to protrude through an abnormal bodily opening
HERO	*n* pl. -ROES or -ROS a hoagie
HEROIC	*n* pl. -S an epic verse
HEROICAL	*adj* courageous; noble
HEROIN	*n* pl. -S an addictive narcotic
HEROINE	*n* pl. -S a brave woman
HEROISM	*n* pl. -S heroic behavior
HEROIZE	*v* -IZED, -IZING, -IZES to make heroic
HERON	*n* pl. -S a wading bird
HERONRY	*n* pl. -RIES a place where herons breed
HERPES	*n* pl. HERPES a skin infection **HERPETIC** *adj*
HERRING	*n* pl. -S a food fish
HERRY	*v* -RIED, -RYING, -RIES to harry
HERS	*pron* the possessive case of the pronoun she
HERSELF	*pron* a form of the 3d person sing. feminine pronoun
HERSTORY	*n* pl. -RIES history with a feminist viewpoint
HERTZ	*n* pl. -ES a unit of frequency
HESITANT	*adj* tending to hesitate
HESITATE	*v* -TATED, -TATING, -TATES to hold back in uncertainty
HESSIAN	*n* pl. -S a coarse cloth
HESSITE	*n* pl. -S a mineral
HEST	*n* pl. -S a command
HET	*n* pl. -S heth
HETAERA	*n* pl. -RAE or -RAS a concubine **HETAERIC** *adj*
HETAIRA	*n* pl. -RAI or -RAS hetaera
HETERO	*n* pl. -EROS a heterosexual
HETH	*n* pl. -S a Hebrew letter
HETMAN	*n* pl. -S a cossack leader
HEUCH	*n* pl. -S heugh
HEUGH	*n* pl. -S a steep cliff
HEW	*v* HEWED, HEWN, HEWING, HEWS to cut with an ax **HEWABLE** *adj*

HEWER	*n* pl. -S one that hews
HEX	*v* -ED, -ING, -ES to cast an evil spell upon
HEXAD	*n* pl. -S a group of six **HEXADIC** *adj*
HEXADE	*n* pl. -S hexad
HEXAGON	*n* pl. -S a polygon having six sides
HEXAGRAM	*n* pl. -S a six-pointed star
HEXAMINE	*n* pl. -S a chemical compound
HEXANE	*n* pl. -S a volatile liquid
HEXAPLA	*n* pl. -S an edition in which six texts are set in parallel columns **HEXAPLAR** *adj*
HEXAPOD	*n* pl. -S a six-legged insect
HEXAPODY	*n* pl. -DIES a line of verse with six feet
HEXARCHY	*n* pl. -CHIES a group of six separate states
HEXER	*n* pl. -S one that hexes
HEXEREI	*n* pl. -S witchcraft
HEXONE	*n* pl. -S a hydrocarbon solvent
HEXOSAN	*n* pl. -S a carbohydrate
HEXOSE	*n* pl. -S a simple sugar
HEXYL	*n* pl. -S a hydrocarbon radical
HEY	*interj* — used to attract attention
HEYDAY	*n* pl. -DAYS the period of one's greatest success
HEYDEY	*n* pl. -DEYS heyday
HI	*interj* — used as a greeting
HIATUS	*n* pl. -ES a gap or missing section **HIATAL** *adj*
HIBACHI	*n* pl. -S a cooking device
HIBERNAL	*adj* pertaining to winter
HIBISCUS	*n* pl. -ES a tropical plant
HIC	*interj* — used to represent a hiccup
HICCOUGH	*v* -ED, -ING, -S to hiccup
HICCUP	*v* -CUPED, -CUPING, -CUPS or -CUPPED, -CUPPING, -CUPS to make a peculiar-sounding, spasmodic inhalation
HICK	*n* pl. -S a rural person **HICKISH** *adj*
HICKEY	*n* pl. HICKEYS or HICKIES a gadget
HICKORY	*n* pl. -RIES a hardwood tree
HID	a past tense of hide
HIDABLE	*adj* able to be hidden
HIDALGO	*n* pl. -GOS a minor Spanish nobleman
HIDDEN	*adj* concealed; obscure **HIDDENLY** *adv*
HIDE	*v* HID, HIDDEN, HIDING, HIDES to conceal
HIDE	*v* HIDED, HIDING, HIDES to flog
HIDEAWAY	*n* pl. -AWAYS a hideout
HIDELESS	*adj* lacking a skin
HIDEOUS	*adj* very ugly
HIDEOUT	*n* pl. -S a place of refuge
HIDER	*n* pl. -S one that hides
HIDING	*n* pl. -S a beating
HIDROSIS	*n* pl. -DROSES abnormal perspiration
HIDROTIC	*n* pl. -S a drug that induces perspiration
HIE	*v* HIED, HIEING or HYING, HIES to hurry
HIEMAL	*adj* pertaining to winter
HIERARCH	*n* pl. -S a religious leader
HIERATIC	*adj* pertaining to priests
HIGGLE	*v* -GLED, -GLING, -GLES to haggle
HIGGLER	*n* pl. -S one that higgles
HIGH	*adj* HIGHER, HIGHEST reaching far upward
HIGH	*n* pl. -S a high level
HIGHBALL	*v* -ED, -ING, -S to go at full speed
HIGHBORN	*adj* of noble birth
HIGHBOY	*n* pl. -BOYS a tall chest of drawers
HIGHBRED	*adj* highborn
HIGHBROW	*n* pl. -S a person who has superior tastes
HIGHBUSH	*adj* forming a tall bush
HIGHJACK	*v* -ED, -ING, -S to hijack
HIGHLAND	*n* pl. -S an elevated region
HIGHLIFE	*n* pl. -S the lifestyle of fashionable society
HIGHLY	*adv* to a high degree
HIGHNESS	*n* pl. -ES the state of being high
HIGHROAD	*n* pl. -S a highway
HIGHSPOT	*n* pl. -S an event of major importance
HIGHT	*v* -ED, -ING, -S to command
HIGHTAIL	*v* -ED, -ING, -S to retreat rapidly

HIGHTH   *n* pl. -S height

HIGHWAY   *n* pl. -WAYS a main road

HIJACK   *v* -ED, -ING, -S to seize a vehicle while in transit

HIJACKER   *n* pl. -S one that hijacks

HIJINKS   *n/pl* mischievous fun

HIKE   *v* HIKED, HIKING, HIKES to walk a long distance

HIKER   *n* pl. -S one that hikes

HILA   pl. of hilum

HILAR   *adj* pertaining to a hilum

HILARITY   *n* pl. -TIES noisy merriment

HILDING   *n* pl. -S a vile person

HILI   pl. of hilus

HILL   *v* -ED, -ING, -S to form into a hill (a rounded elevation)

HILLER   *n* pl. -S one that hills

HILLIER   comparative of hilly

HILLIEST   superlative of hilly

HILLO   *v* -ED, -ING, -S or -ES to hallo

HILLOA   *v* -ED, -ING, -S to hallo

HILLOCK   *n* pl. -S a small hill **HILLOCKY** *adj*

HILLSIDE   *n* pl. -S the side of a hill

HILLTOP   *n* pl. -S the top of a hill

HILLY   *adj* HILLIER, HILLIEST abounding in hills

HILT   *v* -ED, -ING, -S to provide with a hilt (a handle for a weapon)

HILTLESS   *adj* having no hilt

HILUM   *n* pl. HILA a small opening in a bodily organ

HILUS   *n* pl. HILI hilum

HIM   *pron* the objective case of the pronoun he

HIMATION   *n* pl. -MATIA or -MATIONS a loose outer garment

HIMSELF   *pron* a form of the 3d person sing. masculine pronoun

HIN   *n* pl. -S a Hebrew unit of liquid measure

HIND   *n* pl. -S a female red deer

HINDER   *v* -ED, -ING, -S to impede

HINDERER   *n* pl. -S one that hinders

HINDGUT   *n* pl. -S the rear part of the alimentary canal

HINDMOST   *adj* farthest to the rear

HINGE   *v* HINGED, HINGING, HINGES to attach a jointed device

HINGER   *n* pl. -S one that hinges

HINNY   *v* -NIED, -NYING, -NIES to whinny

HINT   *v* -ED, -ING, -S to suggest indirectly

HINTER   *n* pl. -S one that hints

HIP   *v* HIPPED, HIPPING, HIPS to build a type of roof

HIP   *adj* HIPPER, HIPPEST aware of the most current styles and trends

HIPBONE   *n* pl. -S a pelvic bone

HIPLESS   *adj* lacking a hip (the pelvic joint)

HIPLIKE   *adj* suggestive of a hip

HIPLINE   *n* pl. -S the distance around the hips

HIPNESS   *n* pl. -ES the state of being hip

HIPPARCH   *n* pl. -S a cavalry commander in ancient Greece

HIPPED   past tense of hip

HIPPER   comparative of hip

HIPPEST   superlative of hip

HIPPIE   *n* pl. -S a nonconformist

HIPPIER   comparative of hippy

HIPPIEST   superlative of hippy

HIPPING   present participle of hip

HIPPISH   *adj* depressed; sad

HIPPO   *n* pl. -POS a hippopotamus

HIPPY   *adj* -PIER, -PIEST having big hips

HIPSHOT   *adj* lame; awkward

HIPSTER   *n* pl. -S one that is hip

HIRABLE   *adj* available for hire

HIRAGANA   *n* pl. -S a Japanese cursive script

HIRCINE   *adj* pertaining to a goat

HIRE   *v* HIRED, HIRING, HIRES to engage the services of for payment **HIREABLE** *adj*

HIRELING   *n* pl. -S one that works for money only

HIRER   *n* pl. -S one that hires

HIRING   present participle of hire

HIRPLE   *v* -PLED, -PLING, -PLES to limp

HIRSEL   *v* -SELED, -SELING, -SELS or -SELLED, -SELLING, -SELS to herd sheep

HIRSLE   *v* -SLED, -SLING, -SLES to slide along

HIRSUTE   *adj* hairy

HIRUDIN   *n* pl. -S an anticoagulant

HIS   *pron* the possessive form of the pronoun he

HISN   *pron* his

HISPID   *adj* covered with stiff hairs

HISS   *v* -ED, -ING, -ES to make a sibilant sound

HISSELF   *pron* himself

HISSER   *n* pl. -S one that hisses

HISSING   *n* pl. -S an object of scorn

HISSY   *n* pl. HISSIES a tantrum

HIST   *v* -ED, -ING, -S to hoist

HISTAMIN   *n* pl. -S an amine released in allergic reactions

HISTIDIN   *n* pl. -S an amino acid

HISTOGEN   *n* pl. -S interior plant tissue

HISTOID   *adj* pertaining to connective tissue

HISTONE   *n* pl. -S a simple protein

HISTORIC   *adj* important in history

HISTORY   *n* pl. -RIES a chronological record of past events

HIT   *v* HIT, HITTING, HITS to strike forcibly

HITCH   *v* -ED, -ING, -ES to fasten with a knot or hook

HITCHER   *n* pl. -S one that hitches

HITHER   *adv* toward this place

HITHERTO   *adv* up to now

HITLESS   *adj* being without a hit

HITTER   *n* pl. -S one that hits

HITTING   present participle of hit

HIVE   *v* HIVED, HIVING, HIVES to cause to enter a hive (a bee's nest)

HIVELESS   *adj* lacking a hive

HIZZONER   *n* pl. -S — used as a title for a mayor

HM   *interj* hmm

HMM   *interj* — used to express thoughtful consideration

HO   *interj* — used to express surprise

HOACTZIN   *n* pl. -S or -ES hoatzin

HOAGIE   *n* pl. -S a long sandwich

HOAGY   *n* pl. -GIES hoagie

HOAR   *n* pl. -S a white coating

HOARD   *v* -ED, -ING, -S to gather and store away

HOARDER   *n* pl. -S one that hoards

HOARDING   *n* pl. -S something hoarded

HOARIER   comparative of hoary

HOARIEST   superlative of hoary

HOARILY   *adv* in a hoary manner

HOARSE   *adj* HOARSER, HOARSEST low and rough in sound **HOARSELY** *adv*

HOARSEN   *v* -ED, -ING, -S to make hoarse

HOARY   *adj* HOARIER, HOARIEST white with age

HOATZIN   *n* pl. -S or -ES a tropical bird

HOAX   *v* -ED, -ING, -ES to deceive

HOAXER   *n* pl. -S one that hoaxes

HOB   *v* HOBBED, HOBBING, HOBS to furnish with hobnails

HOBBIES   pl. of hobby

HOBBIT   *n* pl. -S a fictitious creature that lives underground

HOBBLE   *v* -BLED, -BLING, -BLES to limp

HOBBLER   *n* pl. -S one that hobbles

HOBBY   *n* pl. -BIES a recreational pastime

HOBBYIST   *n* pl. -S one that pursues a hobby

HOBLIKE   *adj* suggestive of an elf

HOBNAIL   *v* -ED, -ING, -S to put hobnails (short nails with a broad head) on a shoe sole

HOBNOB   *v* -NOBBED, -NOBBING, -NOBS to associate in a friendly way

HOBO   *v* -ED, -ING, -S or -ES to live like a hobo (a vagrant or tramp)

HOBOISM   *n* pl. -S the state of being a hobo

HOCK   *v* -ED, -ING, -S to pawn

HOCKER   *n* pl. -S one that hocks

HOCKEY   *n* pl. -EYS a game played on ice

HOCKSHOP   *n* pl. -S a pawnshop

HOCUS   *v* -CUSED, -CUSING, -CUSES or -CUSSED, -CUSSING, -CUSSES to deceive or cheat

HOD   *n* pl. -S a portable trough

HODAD   *n* pl. -S a nonsurfer

HODADDY   *n* pl. -DIES hodad

HODDEN   *n* pl. -S a coarse cloth

HODDIN   *n* pl. -S hodden

HOE	*v* HOED, HOEING, HOES to use a hoe (a gardening tool)
HOECAKE	*n* pl. -S a cornmeal cake
HOEDOWN	*n* pl. -S a square dance
HOELIKE	*adj* resembling a hoe
HOER	*n* pl. -S one that hoes
HOG	*v* HOGGED, HOGGING, HOGS to take more than one's share
HOGAN	*n* pl. -S a Navaho Indian dwelling
HOGBACK	*n* pl. -S a sharp ridge
HOGFISH	*n* pl. -ES a tropical fish
HOGG	*n* pl. -S a young sheep
HOGGED	past tense of hog
HOGGER	*n* pl. -S one that hogs
HOGGET	*n* pl. -S a young unshorn sheep
HOGGING	present participle of hog
HOGGISH	*adj* coarsely selfish
HOGLIKE	*adj* hoggish
HOGMANAY	*n* pl. -NAYS a Scottish celebration
HOGMANE	*n* pl. -S hogmanay
HOGMENAY	*n* pl. -NAYS hogmanay
HOGNOSE	*n* pl. -S a nonvenomous snake
HOGNUT	*n* pl. -S a hickory nut
HOGSHEAD	*n* pl. -S a large cask
HOGTIE	*v* -TIED, -TIEING or -TYING, -TIES to tie together the legs of
HOGWASH	*n* pl. -ES meaningless talk
HOGWEED	*n* pl. -S a coarse plant
HOICK	*v* -ED, -ING, -S to change directions abruptly
HOIDEN	*v* -ED, -ING, -S to hoyden
HOISE	*v* HOISED, HOISING, HOISES to hoist
HOIST	*v* -ED, -ING, -S to haul up by some mechanical means
HOISTER	*n* pl. -S one that hoists
HOKE	*v* HOKED, HOKING, HOKES to give false value to
HOKEY	*adj* HOKIER, HOKIEST false; contrived **HOKILY** *adv*
HOKINESS	*n* pl. -ES the state of being hokey
HOKKU	*n* pl. HOKKU haiku
HOKUM	*n* pl. -S nonsense
HOKYPOKY	*n* pl. -KIES trickery
HOLARD	*n* pl. -S the total quantity of water in the soil
HOLD	*v* HELD, HOLDEN, HOLDING, HOLDS to maintain possession of **HOLDABLE** *adj*
HOLDALL	*n* pl. -S a carrying case
HOLDBACK	*n* pl. -S a restraining device
HOLDEN	a past participle of hold
HOLDER	*n* pl. -S one that holds
HOLDFAST	*n* pl. -S a fastening device
HOLDING	*n* pl. -S something held
HOLDOUT	*n* pl. -S one who delays signing a contract
HOLDOVER	*n* pl. -S something left over
HOLDUP	*n* pl. -S a delay
HOLE	*v* HOLED, HOLING, HOLES to make a hole (a cavity in a solid)
HOLELESS	*adj* lacking a hole
HOLEY	*adj* full of holes
HOLIBUT	*n* pl. -S halibut
HOLIDAY	*v* -ED, -ING, -S to take a vacation
HOLIER	comparative of holy
HOLIES	pl. of holy
HOLIEST	superlative of holy
HOLILY	*adv* in a holy manner
HOLINESS	*n* pl. -ES the state of being holy
HOLING	present participle of hole
HOLISM	*n* pl. -S a philosophical theory
HOLIST	*n* pl. -S one who adheres to the theory of holism **HOLISTIC** *adj*
HOLK	*v* -ED, -ING, -S to howk
HOLLA	*v* -ED, -ING, -S to hallo
HOLLAND	*n* pl. -S a cotton fabric
HOLLER	*v* -ED, -ING, -S to yell
HOLLIES	pl. of holly
HOLLO	*v* -ED, -ING, -S or -ES to hallo
HOLLOA	*v* -ED, -ING, -S to hallo
HOLLOO	*v* -ED, -ING, -S to hallo
HOLLOW	*adj* -LOWER, -LOWEST not solid **HOLLOWLY** *adv*
HOLLOW	*v* -ED, -ING, -S to make hollow
HOLLY	*n* pl. -LIES a tree
HOLM	*n* pl. -S an island in a river
HOLMIUM	*n* pl. -S a metallic element **HOLMIC** *adj*
HOLOGAMY	*n* pl. -MIES the state of having gametes of the same size and form as other cells

HOLOGRAM *n* pl. -S a three-dimensional photograph

HOLOGYNY *n* pl. -NIES a trait transmitted solely in the female line

HOLOTYPE *n* pl. -S an animal or plant specimen

HOLOZOIC *adj* eating solid foods

HOLP a past tense of help

HOLPEN a past participle of help

HOLS *n/pl* a vacation

HOLSTEIN *n* pl. -S a breed of cattle

HOLSTER *n* pl. -S a case for a pistol

HOLT *n* pl. -S a grove

HOLY *adj* -LIER, -LIEST having a divine nature or origin

HOLY *n* pl. -LIES a holy place

HOLYDAY *n* pl. -DAYS a religious holiday

HOLYTIDE *n* pl. -S a time of religious observance

HOMAGE *v* -AGED, -AGING, -AGES to pay tribute to

HOMAGER *n* pl. -S a feudal vassal

HOMBRE *n* pl. -S a fellow

HOMBURG *n* pl. -S a felt hat

HOME *v* HOMED, HOMING, HOMES to return to one's home (place of residence)

HOMEBODY *n* pl. -BODIES one who likes to stay at home

HOMEBOY *n* pl. -BOYS a boy or man from one's neighborhood

HOMEBRED *n* pl. -S a native athlete

HOMED past tense of home

HOMELAND *n* pl. -S one's native land

HOMELESS *adj* lacking a home

HOMELIKE *adj* suggestive of a home

HOMELY *adj* -LIER, -LIEST unattractive

HOMEMADE *adj* made at home

HOMEOBOX *n* pl. -ES a short DNA sequence

HOMEOTIC *adj* being a gene producing a shift in development

HOMEPORT *v* -ED, -ING, -S to assign a ship to a port

HOMER *v* -ED, -ING, -S to hit a home run

HOMEROOM *n* pl. -S the classroom where pupils report before classes begin

HOMESICK *adj* longing for home

HOMESITE *n* pl. -S a location for a house

HOMESPUN *n* pl. -S a loosely woven fabric

HOMESTAY *n* pl. -STAYS a period during which a visitor in a foreign country lives with a local family

HOMETOWN *n* pl. -S the town of one's birth or residence

HOMEWARD *adv* toward home

HOMEWORK *n* pl. -S work done at home

HOMEY *adj* HOMIER, HOMIEST homelike

HOMICIDE *n* pl. -S the killing of one person by another

HOMIER comparative of homy

HOMIEST superlative of homy

HOMILIST *n* pl. -S one that delivers a homily

HOMILY *n* pl. -LIES a sermon

HOMINES a pl. of homo

HOMINESS *n* pl. -ES the quality of being homey

HOMING present participle of home

HOMINIAN *n* pl. -S a hominid

HOMINID *n* pl. -S a manlike creature

HOMINIES pl. of hominy

HOMININE *adj* characteristic of man

HOMINIZE *v* -NIZED, -NIZING, -NIZES to alter the environment to conform with evolving man

HOMINOID *n* pl. -S a manlike animal

HOMINY *n* pl. -NIES hulled, dried corn

HOMMOCK *n* pl. -S a ridge in an ice field

HOMMOS *n* pl. -ES hummus

HOMO *n* pl. HOMINES or HOMOS a member of the genus that includes modern man

HOMOGAMY *n* pl. -MIES the bearing of sexually similar flowers

HOMOGENY *n* pl. -NIES correspondence in form or structure

HOMOGONY *n* pl. -NIES the condition of having flowers with uniform stamens and pistils

HOMOLOG *n* pl. -S something that exhibits homology

HOMOLOGY *n* pl. -GIES similarity in structure

HOMONYM *n* pl. -S a namesake

HOMONYMY *n* pl. -MIES the condition of having the same name

HOMOSEX *n* pl. -ES homosexuality

HOMY *adj* HOMIER, HOMIEST homey

HON	*n* pl. -S a honeybun
HONAN	*n* pl. -S a fine silk
HONCHO	*v* -ED, -ING, -S to take charge of
HONDA	*n* pl. -S a part of a lariat
HONDLE	*v* -DLED, -DLING, -DLES to haggle
HONE	*v* HONED, HONING, HONES to sharpen
HONER	*n* pl. -S one that hones
HONEST	*adj* -ESTER, -ESTEST truthful **HONESTLY** *adv*
HONESTY	*n* pl. -TIES truthfulness
HONEWORT	*n* pl. -S a perennial herb
HONEY	*v* HONEYED or HONIED, HONEYING, HONEYS to sweeten with honey (a sweet, viscid fluid)
HONEYBEE	*n* pl. -S a type of bee
HONEYBUN	*n* pl. -S a sweetheart
HONEYDEW	*n* pl. -S a sweet fluid
HONEYFUL	*adj* containing much honey
HONG	*n* pl. -S a Chinese factory
HONIED	a past tense of honey
HONING	present participle of hone
HONK	*v* -ED, -ING, -S to emit a cry like that of a goose
HONKER	*n* pl. -S one that honks
HONOR	*v* -ED, -ING, -S to respect
HONORAND	*n* pl. -S an honoree
HONORARY	*n* pl. -ARIES an honor society
HONOREE	*n* pl. -S one that receives an honor
HONORER	*n* pl. -S one that honors
HONOUR	*v* -ED, -ING, -S to honor
HONOURER	*n* pl. -S honorer
HOOCH	*n* pl. -ES cheap whiskey
HOOD	*v* -ED, -ING, -S to furnish with a hood (a covering for the head)
HOODIE	*n* pl. -S a gray crow of Europe
HOODIER	comparative of hoody
HOODIEST	superlative of hoody
HOODLESS	*adj* lacking a hood
HOODLIKE	*adj* resembling a hood
HOODLUM	*n* pl. -S a thug
HOODOO	*v* -ED, -ING, -S to jinx
HOODWINK	*v* -ED, -ING, -S to trick
HOODY	*adj* HOODIER, HOODIEST resembling a hoodlum
HOOEY	*n* pl. -EYS nonsense
HOOF	*v* -ED, -ING, -S to dance
HOOF	*n* pl. HOOVES or HOOFS the hard covering on the feet of certain animals
HOOFBEAT	*n* pl. -S the sound of hooves striking the ground
HOOFER	*n* pl. -S a professional dancer
HOOFLESS	*adj* lacking hooves
HOOFLIKE	*adj* resembling a hoof
HOOK	*v* -ED, -ING, -S to catch with a hook (a bent piece of metal)
HOOKA	*n* pl. -S hookah
HOOKAH	*n* pl. -S a water pipe
HOOKER	*n* pl. -S a prostitute
HOOKEY	*n* pl. -EYS hooky
HOOKIER	comparative of hooky
HOOKIES	pl. of hooky
HOOKIEST	superlative of hooky
HOOKLESS	*adj* lacking a hook
HOOKLET	*n* pl. -S a small hook
HOOKLIKE	*adj* resembling a hook
HOOKNOSE	*n* pl. -S an aquiline nose
HOOKUP	*n* pl. -S an electrical assemblage
HOOKWORM	*n* pl. -S a parasitic worm
HOOKY	*n* pl. HOOKIES truancy
HOOKY	*adj* HOOKIER, HOOKIEST full of hooks
HOOLIE	*adj* easy; slow
HOOLIGAN	*n* pl. -S a hoodlum
HOOLY	*adj* hoolie
HOOP	*v* -ED, -ING, -S to fasten with a hoop (a circular band of metal)
HOOPER	*n* pl. -S one that hoops
HOOPLA	*n* pl. -S commotion
HOOPLESS	*adj* lacking a hoop
HOOPLIKE	*adj* suggestive of a hoop
HOOPOE	*n* pl. -S a European bird
HOOPOO	*n* pl. -POOS hoopoe
HOOPSTER	*n* pl. -S a basketball player
HOORAH	*v* -ED, -ING, -S to hurrah
HOORAY	*v* -ED, -ING, -S to hurrah
HOOSEGOW	*n* pl. -S a jail
HOOSGOW	*n* pl. -S hoosegow
HOOT	*v* -ED, -ING, -S to cry like an owl
HOOTCH	*n* pl. -ES hooch
HOOTER	*n* pl. -S one that hoots

HOOTY   *adj* HOOTIER, HOOTIEST sounding like the cry of an owl

HOOVED   *adj* having hooves

HOOVES   a pl. of hoof

HOP   *v* HOPPED, HOPPING, HOPS to move by jumping on one foot

HOPE   *v* HOPED, HOPING, HOPES to have a desire or expectation

HOPEFUL   *n* pl. -S one that aspires

HOPELESS   *adj* despairing

HOPER   *n* pl. -S one that hopes

HOPHEAD   *n* pl. -S a drug addict

HOPING   present participle of hope

HOPLITE   *n* pl. -S a foot soldier of ancient Greece **HOPLITIC** *adj*

HOPPED   past tense of hop

HOPPER   *n* pl. -S one that hops

HOPPING   *n* pl. -S a going from one place to another of the same kind

HOPPLE   *v* -PLED, -PLING, -PLES to hobble

HOPPY   *adj* -PIER, -PIEST having the taste of hops (catkins of a particular vine)

HOPSACK   *n* pl. -S a coarse fabric

HOPTOAD   *n* pl. -S a toad

HORA   *n* pl. -S an Israeli dance

HORAH   *n* pl. -S hora

HORAL   *adj* hourly

HORARY   *adj* hourly

HORDE   *v* HORDED, HORDING, HORDES to gather in a large group

HORDEIN   *n* pl. -S a simple protein

HORIZON   *n* pl. -S the line where the sky seems to meet the earth

HORMONE   *n* pl. -S a secretion of the endocrine organs **HORMONAL, HORMONIC** *adj*

HORN   *v* -ED, -ING, -S to form a horn (a hard, bonelike projection of the head)

HORNBEAM   *n* pl. -S a small tree

HORNBILL   *n* pl. -S a large-billed bird

HORNBOOK   *n* pl. -S a primer

HORNET   *n* pl. -S a stinging insect

HORNFELS   *n* pl. HORNFELS a silicate rock

HORNIER   comparative of horny

HORNIEST   superlative of horny

HORNILY   *adv* in a horny manner

HORNIST   *n* pl. -S a French horn player

HORNITO   *n* pl. -TOS a mound of volcanic matter

HORNLESS   *adj* lacking a horn

HORNLIKE   *adj* resembling a horn

HORNPIPE   *n* pl. -S a musical instrument

HORNPOUT   *n* pl. -S a catfish

HORNTAIL   *n* pl. -S a wasplike insect

HORNWORM   *n* pl. -S the larva of a hawkmoth

HORNWORT   *n* pl. -S an aquatic herb

HORNY   *adj* HORNIER, HORNIEST hornlike in hardness

HOROLOGE   *n* pl. -S a timepiece

HOROLOGY   *n* pl. -GIES the science of measuring time

HORRENT   *adj* bristling; standing erect

HORRIBLE   *n* pl. -S something that causes horror

HORRIBLY   *adv* dreadfully

HORRID   *adj* repulsive **HORRIDLY** *adv*

HORRIFIC   *adj* causing horror

HORRIFY   *v* -FIED, -FYING, -FIES to cause to feel horror

HORROR   *n* pl. -S a feeling of intense fear or repugnance

HORSE   *v* HORSED, HORSING, HORSES to provide with a horse (a large, hoofed mammal)

HORSECAR   *n* pl. -S a streetcar drawn by a horse

HORSEFLY   *n* pl. -FLIES a large fly

HORSEMAN   *n* pl. -MEN one who rides a horse

HORSEPOX   *n* pl. -ES a skin disease of horses

HORSEY   *adj* HORSIER, HORSIEST horsy

HORSIER   comparative of horsy

HORSIEST   superlative of horsy

HORSILY   *adv* in a horsy manner

HORSING   present participle of horse

HORST   *n* pl. -S a portion of the earth's crust

HORSTE   *n* pl. -S horst

HORSY   *adj* HORSIER, HORSIEST resembling a horse

HOSANNA   *v* -ED, -ING, -S to praise

HOSANNAH   *interj* — used to express praise to God

HOSE	v HOSED, HOSING, HOSES to spray with water
HOSE	n pl. HOSEN stockings or socks
HOSEL	n pl. -S a part of a golf club
HOSEPIPE	n pl. -S a flexible tube for conveying fluids
HOSIER	n pl. -S one that makes hose
HOSIERY	n pl. -SIERIES hose
HOSING	present participle of hose
HOSPICE	n pl. -S a shelter
HOSPITAL	n pl. -S a medical institution
HOSPITIA	n/pl places of shelter
HOSPODAR	n pl. -S a governor of a region under Turkish rule
HOST	v -ED, -ING, -S to entertain socially
HOSTA	n pl. -S a plantain lily
HOSTAGE	n pl. -S a person held as security
HOSTEL	v -TELED, -TELING, -TELS or -TELLED, -TELLING, -TELS to stay at inns overnight while traveling
HOSTELER	n pl. -S an innkeeper
HOSTELRY	n pl. -RIES an inn
HOSTESS	v -ED, -ING, -ES to act as a hostess (a woman who entertains socially)
HOSTILE	n pl. -S an unfriendly person
HOSTLER	n pl. -S a person who tends horses or mules
HOSTLY	adj pertaining to one who hosts
HOT	adj HOTTER, HOTTEST having a high temperature
HOT	v HOTTED, HOTTING, HOTS to heat
HOTBED	n pl. -S a bed of rich soil
HOTBLOOD	n pl. -S a thoroughbred horse
HOTBOX	n pl. -ES an overheated bearing of a railroad car
HOTCAKE	n pl. -S a pancake
HOTCH	v -ED, -ING, -ES to wiggle
HOTCHPOT	n pl. -S the combining of properties in order to divide them equally among heirs
HOTDOG	v -DOGGED, -DOGGING, -DOGS to perform showily
HOTEL	n pl. -S a public lodging
HOTELDOM	n pl. -S hotels and hotel workers
HOTELIER	n pl. -S a hotel manager
HOTELMAN	n pl. -MEN a hotelier
HOTFOOT	v -FOOTED, -FOOTING, -FOOTS to hurry
HOTHEAD	n pl. -S a quick-tempered person
HOTHOUSE	n pl. -S a heated greenhouse
HOTLINE	n pl. -S a direct communications system for immediate contact
HOTLY	adv in a hot manner
HOTNESS	n pl. -ES the state of being hot
HOTPRESS	v -ED, -ING, -ES to subject to heat and pressure
HOTROD	n pl. -S a car modified for high speeds
HOTSHOT	n pl. -S a showily skillful person
HOTSPUR	n pl. -S a hothead
HOTTED	past tense of hot
HOTTER	comparative of hot
HOTTEST	superlative of hot
HOTTING	present participle of hot
HOTTISH	adj somewhat hot
HOUDAH	n pl. -S howdah
HOUND	v -ED, -ING, -S to pursue relentlessly
HOUNDER	n pl. -S one that hounds
HOUR	n pl. -S a period of sixty minutes
HOURI	n pl. -S a beautiful maiden in Muslim belief
HOURLY	adj occurring every hour
HOUSE	v HOUSED, HOUSING, HOUSES to lodge in a house (a building in which people live)
HOUSEBOY	n pl. -BOYS a male servant
HOUSEFLY	n pl. -FLIES a common fly
HOUSEFUL	n pl. -S as much as a house will hold
HOUSEL	v -SELED, -SELING, -SELS or -SELLED, -SELLING, -SELS to administer the Eucharist to
HOUSEMAN	n pl. -MEN a male servant
HOUSER	n pl. -S one who organizes housing projects
HOUSESIT	v -SAT, -SITTING, -SITS to occupy a dwelling while the tenants are away
HOUSETOP	n pl. -S the roof of a house
HOUSING	n pl. -S any dwelling place
HOVE	a past tense of heave
HOVEL	v -ELED, -ELING, -ELS or -ELLED, -ELLING, -ELS to live in a small, miserable dwelling

HOVER   v -ED, -ING, -S to hang suspended in the air

HOVERER   n pl. -S something that hovers

HOW   n pl. -S a method of doing something

HOWBEIT   adv nevertheless

HOWDAH   n pl. -S a seat on an elephant or camel for riders

HOWDIE   n pl. -S a midwife

HOWDY   v -DIED, -DYING, -DIES to greet with the words "how do you do"

HOWE   n pl. -S a valley

HOWEVER   adv nevertheless

HOWF   n pl. -S a place frequently visited

HOWFF   n pl. -S howf

HOWITZER   n pl. -S a short cannon

HOWK   v -ED, -ING, -S to dig

HOWL   v -ED, -ING, -S to cry like a dog

HOWLER   n pl. -S one that howls

HOWLET   n pl. -S an owl

HOY   n pl. HOYS a heavy barge or scow

HOYA   n pl. -S a flowering plant

HOYDEN   v -ED, -ING, -S to act like a tomboy

HOYLE   n pl. -S a rule book

HUARACHE   n pl. -S a flat-heeled sandal

HUARACHO   n pl. -CHOS huarache

HUB   n pl. -S the center of a wheel

HUBBLY   adj having an uneven surface

HUBBUB   n pl. -S an uproar

HUBBY   n pl. -BIES a husband

HUBCAP   n pl. -S a covering for the hub of a wheel

HUBRIS   n pl. -BRISES arrogance

HUCK   n pl. -S a durable fabric

HUCKLE   n pl. -S the hip

HUCKSTER   v -ED, -ING, -S to peddle

HUDDLE   v -DLED, -DLING, -DLES to crowd together

HUDDLER   n pl. -S one that huddles

HUE   n pl. -S color **HUED, HUELESS** adj

HUFF   v -ED, -ING, -S to breathe heavily

HUFFISH   adj sulky

HUFFY   adj HUFFIER, HUFFIEST easily offended **HUFFILY** adv

HUG   v HUGGED, HUGGING, HUGS to clasp tightly in the arms

HUGE   adj HUGER, HUGEST very large **HUGELY** adv

HUGENESS   n pl. -ES the quality of being huge

HUGEOUS   adj huge

HUGER   comparative of huge

HUGEST   superlative of huge

HUGGABLE   adj cuddlesome

HUGGED   past tense of hug

HUGGER   n pl. -S one that hugs

HUGGING   present participle of hug

HUH   interj — used to express surprise

HUIC   interj — used to encourage hunting hounds

HUIPIL   n pl. -S or -ES an embroidered blouse or dress of Mexico

HUISACHE   n pl. -S a flowering plant

HULA   n pl. -S a Hawaiian dance

HULK   v -ED, -ING, -S to appear impressively large

HULKY   adj HULKIER, HULKIEST massive

HULL   v -ED, -ING, -S to remove the shell from a seed

HULLER   n pl. -S one that hulls

HULLO   v -ED, -ING, -S or -ES to hallo

HULLOA   v -ED, -ING, -S to hallo

HUM   v HUMMED, HUMMING, HUMS to sing without opening the lips or saying words

HUMAN   n pl. -S a person

HUMANE   adj -MANER, -MANEST compassionate **HUMANELY** adv

HUMANISE   v -ISED, -ISING, -ISES to humanize

HUMANISM   n pl. -S the quality of being human

HUMANIST   n pl. -S one who studies human nature

HUMANITY   n pl. -TIES the human race

HUMANIZE   v -IZED, -IZING, -IZES to make human

HUMANLY   adv in a human manner

HUMANOID   n pl. -S something having human form

HUMATE   n pl. -S a chemical salt

HUMBLE   adj -BLER, -BLEST modest

HUMBLE	v -BLED, -BLING, -BLES to reduce the pride of	**HUN**	n pl. -S a barbarous, destructive person
HUMBLER	n pl. -S one that humbles	**HUNCH**	v -ED, -ING, -ES to arch forward
HUMBLEST	superlative of humble	**HUNDRED**	n pl. -S a number
HUMBLING	present participle of humble	**HUNG**	a past tense of hang
HUMBLY	adv in a humble manner	**HUNGER**	v -ED, -ING, -S to crave
HUMBUG	v -BUGGED, -BUGGING, -BUGS to deceive	**HUNGOVER**	adj suffering from a hangover
HUMDRUM	n pl. -S a dull, boring person	**HUNGRY**	adj -GRIER, -GRIEST wanting food **HUNGRILY** adv
HUMERAL	n pl. -S a bone of the shoulder	**HUNH**	interj — used to ask for a repetition of an utterance
HUMERUS	n pl. -MERI the large bone of the upper arm	**HUNK**	n pl. -S a large piece
HUMIC	adj derived from humus	**HUNKER**	v -ED, -ING, -S to squat
HUMID	adj having much humidity	**HUNKY**	adj HUNKIER, HUNKIEST muscular and attractive
HUMIDIFY	v -FIED, -FYING, -FIES to make humid	**HUNNISH**	adj resembling a hun
HUMIDITY	n pl. -TIES moisture of the air	**HUNT**	v -ED, -ING, -S to pursue for food or sport **HUNTABLE** adj **HUNTEDLY** adv
HUMIDLY	adv in a humid manner		
HUMIDOR	n pl. -S a cigar case	**HUNTER**	n pl. -S one that hunts
HUMIFIED	adj converted into humus	**HUNTING**	n pl. -S an instance of searching
HUMILITY	n pl. -TIES the quality of being humble	**HUNTRESS**	n pl. -ES a female hunter
		HUNTSMAN	n pl. -MEN a hunter
HUMMABLE	adj capable of being hummed	**HUP**	interj — used to mark a marching cadence
HUMMED	past tense of hum		
HUMMER	n pl. -S one that hums	**HURDIES**	n/pl the buttocks
HUMMING	present participle of hum	**HURDLE**	v -DLED, -DLING, -DLES to jump over
HUMMOCK	v -ED, -ING, -S to form into hummocks (small rounded hills)		
		HURDLER	n pl. -S one that hurdles
HUMMOCKY	adj abounding in hummocks	**HURDS**	n/pl hards
HUMMUS	n pl. -ES a paste of pureed chickpeas and tahini	**HURL**	v -ED, -ING, -S to throw with great force
HUMOR	v -ED, -ING, -S to indulge	**HURLER**	n pl. -S one that hurls
HUMORAL	adj pertaining to bodily fluids	**HURLEY**	n pl. -LEYS hurling
HUMORFUL	adj humorous	**HURLING**	n pl. -S an Irish game
HUMORIST	n pl. -S a humorous writer or entertainer	**HURLY**	n pl. -LIES commotion
		HURRAH	v -ED, -ING, -S to cheer
HUMOROUS	adj funny; witty	**HURRAY**	v -ED, -ING, -S to hurrah
HUMOUR	v -ED, -ING, -S to humor	**HURRIER**	n pl. -S one that hurries
HUMP	v -ED, -ING, -S to arch into a hump (a rounded protuberance)	**HURRY**	v -RIED, -RYING, -RIES to move swiftly
HUMPBACK	n pl. -S a humped back	**HURST**	n pl. -S a small hill
HUMPH	v -ED, -ING, -S to utter a grunt	**HURT**	v HURT, HURTING, HURTS to injure
HUMPLESS	adj lacking a hump		
HUMPY	adj HUMPIER, HUMPIEST full of humps	**HURTER**	n pl. -S one that hurts
		HURTFUL	adj causing injury
HUMUS	n pl. -ES decomposed organic matter	**HURTLE**	v -TLED, -TLING, -TLES to rush violently
HUMVEE	n pl. -S a type of motor vehicle		

HURTLESS *adj* harmless

HUSBAND *v* -ED, -ING, -S to spend wisely

HUSH *v* -ED, -ING, -ES to quiet **HUSHEDLY** *adv*

HUSHABY *v* go to sleep — used imperatively to soothe a child

HUSHFUL *adj* quiet

HUSK *v* -ED, -ING, -S to remove the husk (the outer covering) from

HUSKER *n* pl. -S one that husks

HUSKIER comparative of husky

HUSKIES pl. of husky

HUSKIEST superlative of husky

HUSKILY *adv* in a husky manner

HUSKING *n* pl. -S a gathering of families to husk corn

HUSKLIKE *adj* resembling a husk

HUSKY *adj* -KIER, -KIEST hoarse

HUSKY *n* pl. -KIES an Eskimo dog

HUSSAR *n* pl. -S a cavalry soldier

HUSSY *n* pl. -SIES a lewd woman

HUSTINGS *n* pl. HUSTINGS a British court

HUSTLE *v* -TLED, -TLING, -TLES to hurry

HUSTLER *n* pl. -S one that hustles

HUSWIFE *n* pl. -WIFES or -WIVES a sewing kit

HUT *v* HUTTED, HUTTING, HUTS to live in a hut (a simple shelter)

HUTCH *v* -ED, -ING, -ES to store away

HUTLIKE *adj* resembling a hut

HUTMENT *n* pl. -S a group of huts

HUTTED past tense of hut

HUTTING present participle of hut

HUTZPA *n* pl. -S chutzpah

HUTZPAH *n* pl. -S chutzpah

HUZZA *v* -ED, -ING, -S to cheer

HUZZAH *v* -ED, -ING, -S to huzza

HWAN *n* pl. HWAN a monetary unit of South Korea

HYACINTH *n* pl. -S a flowering plant

HYAENA *n* pl. -S hyena **HYAENIC** *adj*

HYALIN *n* pl. -S hyaline

HYALINE *n* pl. -S a transparent substance

HYALITE *n* pl. -S a colorless opal

HYALOGEN *n* pl. -S a substance found in animal cells

HYALOID *n* pl. -S a membrane of the eye

HYBRID *n* pl. -S the offspring of genetically dissimilar parents

HYBRIS *n* pl. -BRISES hubris

HYDATID *n* pl. -S a cyst caused by a tapeworm

HYDRA *n* pl. -DRAS or -DRAE a freshwater polyp

HYDRACID *n* pl. -S an acid

HYDRAGOG *n* pl. -S a purgative causing watery discharges

HYDRANT *n* pl. -S an outlet from a water main

HYDRANTH *n* pl. -S the oral opening of a hydra

HYDRASE *n* pl. -S an enzyme

HYDRATE *v* -DRATED, -DRATING, -DRATES to combine with water

HYDRATOR *n* pl. -S one that hydrates

HYDRIA *n* pl. -DRIAE a water jar

HYDRIC *adj* pertaining to moisture

HYDRID *n* pl. -S hydride

HYDRIDE *n* pl. -S a chemical compound

HYDRO *n* pl. -DROS electricity produced by waterpower

HYDROGEL *n* pl. -S a colloid

HYDROGEN *n* pl. -S a gaseous element

HYDROID *n* pl. -S a polyp

HYDROMEL *n* pl. -S a mixture of honey and water

HYDRONIC *adj* pertaining to heating and cooling by water

HYDROPIC *adj* affected with hydropsy

HYDROPS *n* pl. -ES hydropsy

HYDROPSY *n* pl. -SIES dropsy

HYDROSKI *n* pl. -S a plate attached to a seaplane to facilitate takeoffs and landings

HYDROSOL *n* pl. -S an aqueous solution of a colloid

HYDROUS *adj* containing water

HYDROXY *adj* containing hydroxyl

HYDROXYL *n* pl. -S the radical or group containing oxygen and hydrogen

HYENA *n* pl. -S a wolflike mammal **HYENIC, HYENINE, HYENOID** *adj*

HYETAL *adj* pertaining to rain

HYGEIST *n* pl. -S an expert in hygiene

HYGIEIST *n* pl. -S hygeist

HYGIENE	*n* pl. -S the science of health **HYGIENIC** *adj*
HYING	present participle of hie
HYLA	*n* pl. -S a tree frog
HYLOZOIC	*adj* pertaining to the doctrine that life and matter are inseparable
HYMEN	*n* pl. -S a vaginal membrane **HYMENAL** *adj*
HYMENEAL	*n* pl. -S a wedding song or poem
HYMENIUM	*n* pl. -NIA or -NIUMS a layer in certain fungi **HYMENIAL** *adj*
HYMN	*v* -ED, -ING, -S to sing a hymn (a song of praise to God)
HYMNAL	*n* pl. -S a book of hymns
HYMNARY	*n* pl. -RIES a hymnal
HYMNBOOK	*n* pl. -S a hymnal
HYMNIST	*n* pl. -S one who composes hymns
HYMNLESS	*adj* lacking a hymn
HYMNLIKE	*adj* resembling a hymn
HYMNODY	*n* pl. -DIES the singing of hymns
HYOID	*n* pl. -S a bone of the tongue **HYOIDAL, HYOIDEAN** *adj*
HYOSCINE	*n* pl. -S a sedative
HYP	*n* pl. -S hypochondria
HYPE	*v* HYPED, HYPING, HYPES to promote extravagantly
HYPER	*adj* very excitable
HYPERGOL	*n* pl. -S a rocket fuel
HYPERON	*n* pl. -S an atomic particle
HYPEROPE	*n* pl. -S a farsighted person
HYPHA	*n* pl. -PHAE a threadlike element of a fungus **HYPHAL** *adj*
HYPHEMIA	*n* pl. -S deficiency of blood
HYPHEN	*v* -ED, -ING, -S to connect words or syllables with a hyphen (a mark of punctuation)
HYPING	present participle of hype
HYPNIC	*adj* pertaining to sleep
HYPNOID	*adj* pertaining to hypnosis or sleep
HYPNOSIS	*n* pl. -NOSES an artificially induced state resembling sleep
HYPNOTIC	*n* pl. -S a sleep-inducing drug
HYPO	*v* -ED, -ING, -S to inject with a hypodermic needle
HYPOACID	*adj* having a lower than normal degree of acidity
HYPODERM	*n* pl. -S a skin layer
HYPOGEA	pl. of hypogeum
HYPOGEAL	*adj* underground
HYPOGEAN	*adj* hypogeal
HYPOGENE	*adj* formed underground
HYPOGEUM	*n* pl. -GEA an underground chamber
HYPOGYNY	*n* pl. -NIES the condition of having flowers with organs situated below the ovary
HYPONEA	*n* pl. -S hyponoia
HYPONOIA	*n* pl. -S dulled mental activity
HYPOPNEA	*n* pl. -S abnormally shallow breathing
HYPOPYON	*n* pl. -S an accumulation of pus in the eye
HYPOTHEC	*n* pl. -S a type of mortgage
HYPOXIA	*n* pl. -S a deficiency of oxygen in body tissue **HYPOXIC** *adj*
HYRACOID	*n* pl. -S a hyrax
HYRAX	*n* pl. -RAXES or -RACES a small, harelike mammal
HYSON	*n* pl. -S a Chinese tea
HYSSOP	*n* pl. -S a medicinal herb
HYSTERIA	*n* pl. -S uncontrollable excitement or fear
HYSTERIC	*n* pl. -S one who is subject to fits of hysteria
HYTE	*adj* insane

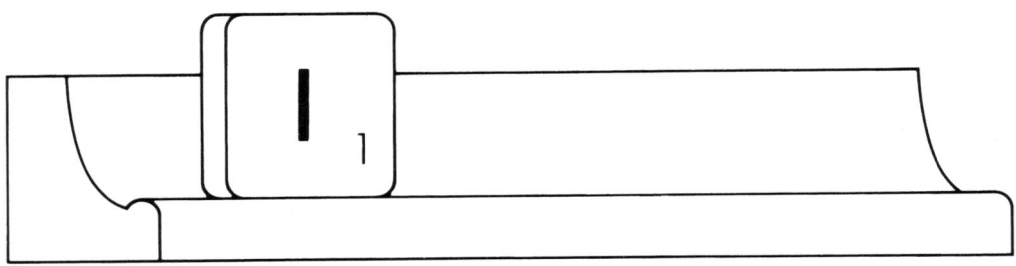

IAMB	*n* pl. -S a type of metrical foot	**ICICLE**	*n* pl. -S a hanging spike of ice **ICICLED** *adj*
IAMBIC	*n* pl. -S an iamb	**ICIER**	comparative of icy
IAMBUS	*n* pl. -BUSES or -BI an iamb	**ICIEST**	superlative of icy
IATRIC	*adj* pertaining to medicine	**ICILY**	*adv* in an icy manner
IATRICAL	*adj* iatric	**ICINESS**	*n* pl. -ES the state of being icy
IBEX	*n* pl. IBEXES or IBICES a wild goat	**ICING**	*n* pl. -S a sweet mixture for covering cakes
IBIDEM	*adv* in the same place	**ICK**	*interj* — used to express disgust
IBIS	*n* pl. IBISES a wading bird	**ICKER**	*n* pl. -S a head of grain
IBOGAINE	*n* pl. -S an alkaloid used as an antidepressant	**ICKINESS**	*n* pl. -ES the state of being icky
ICE	*v* ICED, ICING, ICES to cover with ice (frozen water)	**ICKY**	*adj* ICKIER, ICKIEST repulsive **ICKILY** *adv*
ICEBERG	*n* pl. -S a large floating body of ice	**ICON**	*n* pl. -S or -ES a representation **ICONIC, ICONICAL** *adj*
ICEBLINK	*n* pl. -S a glare over an ice field	**ICTERIC**	*n* pl. -S a remedy for icterus
ICEBOAT	*n* pl. -S a vehicle that sails on ice	**ICTERUS**	*n* pl. -ES a diseased condition of the liver
ICEBOUND	*adj* surrounded by ice	**ICTUS**	*n* pl. -ES a recurring stress or beat in a poetical form **ICTIC** *adj*
ICEBOX	*n* pl. -ES a cabinet for cooling food	**ICY**	*adj* ICIER, ICIEST covered with ice
ICECAP	*n* pl. -S a covering of ice and snow	**ID**	*n* pl. -S a part of the psyche
ICED	past tense of ice	**IDEA**	*n* pl. -S a conception existing in the mind **IDEALESS** *adj*
ICEFALL	*n* pl. -S a kind of frozen waterfall	**IDEAL**	*n* pl. -S a standard of perfection
ICEHOUSE	*n* pl. -S a building for storing ice	**IDEALISE**	*v* -ISED, -ISING, -ISES to idealize
ICEKHANA	*n* pl. -S an automotive event held on a frozen lake	**IDEALISM**	*n* pl. -S the pursuit of noble goals
ICELESS	*adj* having no ice	**IDEALIST**	*n* pl. -S an adherent of idealism
ICELIKE	*adj* resembling ice	**IDEALITY**	*n* pl. -TIES the state of being perfect; something idealized
ICEMAN	*n* pl. -MEN a man who supplies ice	**IDEALIZE**	*v* -IZED, -IZING, -IZES to regard as perfect
ICH	*n* pl. ICHS a disease of certain fishes	**IDEALLY**	*adv* perfectly
ICHNITE	*n* pl. -S a fossil footprint	**IDEALOGY**	*n* pl. -GIES ideology
ICHOR	*n* pl. -S a watery discharge from a wound **ICHOROUS** *adj*	**IDEATE**	*v* -ATED, -ATING, -ATES to form an idea
ICHTHYIC	*adj* pertaining to fishes		

IDEATION	*n* pl. -S the act of ideating
IDEATIVE	*adj* pertaining to ideation
IDEM	*adj* the same
IDENTIC	*adj* identical
IDENTIFY	*v* -FIED, -FYING, -FIES to establish the identity of
IDENTITY	*n* pl. -TIES the essential character of a person or thing
IDEOGRAM	*n* pl. -S a type of written symbol
IDEOLOGY	*n* pl. -GIES a systematic body of ideas
IDES	*n* pl. IDES a certain day in the ancient Roman calendar
IDIOCY	*n* pl. -CIES the condition of being an idiot
IDIOLECT	*n* pl. -S one's speech pattern
IDIOM	*n* pl. -S an expression peculiar to a language
IDIOT	*n* pl. -S a mentally deficient person **IDIOTIC** *adj*
IDIOTISM	*n* pl. -S idiocy
IDLE	*adj* IDLER, IDLEST inactive
IDLE	*v* IDLED, IDLING, IDLES to pass time idly
IDLENESS	*n* pl. -ES the state of being idle
IDLER	*n* pl. -S one that idles
IDLESSE	*n* pl. -S idleness
IDLEST	superlative of idle
IDLING	present participle of idle
IDLY	*adv* in an idle manner
IDOCRASE	*n* pl. -S a mineral
IDOL	*n* pl. -S an object of worship
IDOLATER	*n* pl. -S one that worships idols
IDOLATOR	*n* pl. -S idolater
IDOLATRY	*n* pl. -TRIES the worship of idols
IDOLISE	*v* -ISED, -ISING, -ISES to idolize
IDOLISER	*n* pl. -S one that idolises
IDOLISM	*n* pl. -S idolatry
IDOLIZE	*v* -IZED, -IZING, -IZES to worship
IDOLIZER	*n* pl. -S one that idolizes
IDONEITY	*n* pl. -TIES the state of being idoneous
IDONEOUS	*adj* suitable
IDYL	*n* pl. -S a poem or prose work depicting scenes of rural simplicity
IDYLIST	*n* pl. -S a writer of idyls

IDYLL	*n* pl. -S idyl **IDYLLIC** *adj*
IDYLLIST	*n* pl. -S idylist
IF	*n* pl. -S a possibility
IFF	*conj* if and only if
IFFINESS	*n* pl. -ES the state of being iffy
IFFY	*adj* IFFIER, IFFIEST full of uncertainty
IGLOO	*n* pl. -LOOS an Eskimo dwelling
IGLU	*n* pl. -S igloo
IGNATIA	*n* pl. -S a medicinal seed
IGNEOUS	*adj* pertaining to fire
IGNIFY	*v* -FIED, -FYING, -FIES to burn
IGNITE	*v* -NITED, -NITING, -NITES to set on fire
IGNITER	*n* pl. -S one that ignites
IGNITION	*n* pl. -S the act of igniting
IGNITOR	*n* pl. -S igniter
IGNITRON	*n* pl. -S a type of rectifier tube
IGNOBLE	*adj* of low character **IGNOBLY** *adv*
IGNOMINY	*n* pl. -NIES disgrace or dishonor
IGNORAMI	*n/pl* utterly ignorant persons
IGNORANT	*adj* having no knowledge
IGNORE	*v* -NORED, -NORING, -NORES to refuse to notice
IGNORER	*n* pl. -S one that ignores
IGUANA	*n* pl. -S a tropical lizard
IGUANIAN	*n* pl. -S a lizard related to the iguana
IHRAM	*n* pl. -S the garb worn by Muslim pilgrims
IKAT	*n* pl. -S a fabric of tie-dyed yarns
IKEBANA	*n* pl. -S the Japanese art of flower arranging
IKON	*n* pl. -S icon
ILEA	pl. of ileum
ILEAC	*adj* pertaining to the ileum
ILEAL	*adj* ileac
ILEITIS	*n* pl. ILEITIDES inflammation of the ileum
ILEUM	*n* pl. ILEA a part of the small intestine
ILEUS	*n* pl. -ES intestinal obstruction
ILEX	*n* pl. -ES a holly
ILIA	pl. of ilium
ILIAC	*adj* pertaining to the ilium
ILIAD	*n* pl. -S a long poem
ILIAL	*adj* iliac

ILIUM	*n* pl. ILIA a bone of the peivis
ILK	*n* pl. -S a class or kind
ILKA	*adj* each
ILL	*n* pl. -S an evil
ILL	*adj* ILLER, ILLEST not well
ILLATION	*n* pl. -S the act of inferring
ILLATIVE	*n* pl. -S a word or phrase introducing an inference
ILLEGAL	*n* pl. -S a person who enters a country without authorization
ILLICIT	*adj* not permitted
ILLINIUM	*n* pl. -S a radioactive element
ILLIQUID	*adj* not being cash
ILLITE	*n* pl. -S a group of minerals **ILLITIC** *adj*
ILLNESS	*n* pl. -ES sickness
ILLOGIC	*n* pl. -S absence of logic
ILLUME	*v* -LUMED, -LUMING, -LUMES to illuminate
ILLUMINE	*v* -MINED, -MINING, -MINES to illuminate
ILLUSION	*n* pl. -S a false perception
ILLUSIVE	*adj* illusory
ILLUSORY	*adj* based on illusion
ILLUVIUM	*n* pl. -VIA or -VIUMS a type of material accumulated in soil **ILLUVIAL** *adj*
ILLY	*adv* badly
ILMENITE	*n* pl. -S a mineral
IMAGE	*v* -AGED, -AGING, -AGES to imagine
IMAGER	*n* pl. -S one that images
IMAGERY	*n* pl. -ERIES mental pictures
IMAGINAL	*adj* pertaining to an imago
IMAGINE	*v* -INED, -INING, -INES to form a mental picture of
IMAGINER	*n* pl. -S one that imagines
IMAGING	*n* pl. -S the action of producing a visible representation
IMAGINING	present participle of imagine
IMAGISM	*n* pl. -S a movement in poetry
IMAGIST	*n* pl. -S an adherent of imagism
IMAGO	*n* pl. -GOES or -GOS an adult insect
IMAM	*n* pl. -S a Muslim priest
IMAMATE	*n* pl. -S the office of an imam
IMARET	*n* pl. -S a Turkish inn
IMAUM	*n* pl. -S imam
IMBALM	*v* -ED, -ING, -S to embalm

IMBALMER	*n* pl. -S embalmer
IMBARK	*v* -ED, -ING, -S to embark
IMBECILE	*n* pl. -S a mentally deficient person
IMBED	*v* -BEDDED, -BEDDING, -BEDS to embed
IMBIBE	*v* -BIBED, -BIBING, -BIBES to drink
IMBIBER	*n* pl. -S one that imbibes
IMBITTER	*v* -ED, -ING, -S to embitter
IMBLAZE	*v* -BLAZED, -BLAZING, -BLAZES to emblaze
IMBODY	*v* -BODIED, -BODYING, -BODIES to embody
IMBOLDEN	*v* -ED, -ING, -S to embolden
IMBOSOM	*v* -ED, -ING, -S to embosom
IMBOWER	*v* -ED, -ING, -S to embower
IMBROWN	*v* -ED, -ING, -S to embrown
IMBRUE	*v* -BRUED, -BRUING, -BRUES to stain
IMBRUTE	*v* -BRUTED, -BRUTING, -BRUTES to make brutal
IMBUE	*v* -BUED, -BUING, -BUES to make thoroughly wet
IMID	*n* pl. -S imide
IMIDE	*n* pl. -S a chemical compound **IMIDIC** *adj*
IMIDO	*adj* containing an imide
IMINE	*n* pl. -S a chemical compound
IMINO	*adj* containing an imine
IMITABLE	*adj* capable of being imitated
IMITATE	*v* -TATED, -TATING, -TATES to behave in the same way as
IMITATOR	*n* pl. -S one that imitates
IMMANE	*adj* great in size
IMMANENT	*adj* existing within
IMMATURE	*n* pl. -S an individual that is not fully grown or developed
IMMENSE	*adj* -MENSER, -MENSEST great in size
IMMERGE	*v* -MERGED, -MERGING, -MERGES to immerse
IMMERSE	*v* -MERSED, -MERSING, -MERSES to plunge into a liquid
IMMESH	*v* -ED, -ING, -ES to enmesh
IMMIES	pl. of immy
IMMINENT	*adj* ready to take place
IMMINGLE	*v* -GLED, -GLING, -GLES to blend

IMMIX   *v* -ED, -ING, -ES to mix in

IMMOBILE   *adj* incapable of being moved

IMMODEST   *adj* not modest

IMMOLATE   *v* -LATED, -LATING, -LATES to kill as a sacrifice

IMMORAL   *adj* contrary to established morality

IMMORTAL   *n* pl. -S one who is not subject to death

IMMOTILE   *adj* lacking mobility

IMMUNE   *n* pl. -S one who is protected from a disease

IMMUNISE   *v* -NISED, -NISING, -NISES to immunize

IMMUNITY   *n* pl. -TIES the state of being protected from a disease

IMMUNIZE   *v* -NIZED, -NIZING, -NIZES to protect from a disease

IMMURE   *v* -MURED, -MURING, -MURES to imprison

IMMY   *n* pl. -MIES a type of playing marble

IMP   *v* -ED, -ING, -S to graft feathers onto a bird's wing

IMPACT   *v* -ED, -ING, -S to pack firmly together

IMPACTER   *n* pl. -S one that impacts

IMPACTOR   *n* pl. -S impacter

IMPAINT   *v* -ED, -ING, -S to paint or depict

IMPAIR   *v* -ED, -ING, -S to make worse

IMPAIRER   *n* pl. -S one that impairs

IMPALA   *n* pl. -S an African antelope

IMPALE   *v* -PALED, -PALING, -PALES to pierce with a pointed object

IMPALER   *n* pl. -S one that impales

IMPANEL   *v* -ELED, -ELING, -ELS or -ELLED, -ELLING, -ELS to enter on a list for jury duty

IMPARITY   *n* pl. -TIES lack of equality

IMPARK   *v* -ED, -ING, -S to confine in a park

IMPART   *v* -ED, -ING, -S to make known

IMPARTER   *n* pl. -S one that imparts

IMPASSE   *n* pl. -S a road or passage having no exit

IMPASTE   *v* -PASTED, -PASTING, -PASTES to make into a paste

IMPASTO   *n* pl. -TOS a painting technique

IMPAVID   *adj* brave

IMPAWN   *v* -ED, -ING, -S to pawn

IMPEACH   *v* -ED, -ING, -ES to charge with misconduct in office

IMPEARL   *v* -ED, -ING, -S to make pearly

IMPEDE   *v* -PEDED, -PEDING, -PEDES to obstruct the progress of

IMPEDER   *n* pl. -S one that impedes

IMPEL   *v* -PELLED, -PELLING, -PELS to force into action

IMPELLER   *n* pl. -S one that impels

IMPELLOR   *n* pl. -S impeller

IMPEND   *v* -ED, -ING, -S to be imminent

IMPERIA   a pl. of imperium

IMPERIAL   *n* pl. -S an emperor or empress

IMPERIL   *v* -ILED, -ILING, -ILS or -ILLED, -ILLING, -ILS to place in jeopardy

IMPERIUM   *n* pl. -RIUMS or -RIA absolute power

IMPETIGO   *n* pl. -GOS a skin disease

IMPETUS   *n* pl. -ES an impelling force

IMPHEE   *n* pl. -S an African grass

IMPI   *n* pl. -S a body of warriors

IMPIETY   *n* pl. -TIES lack of piety

IMPING   *n* pl. -S the process of grafting

IMPINGE   *v* -PINGED, -PINGING, -PINGES to collide

IMPINGER   *n* pl. -S one that impinges

IMPIOUS   *adj* not pious

IMPISH   *adj* mischievous **IMPISHLY** *adv*

IMPLANT   *v* -ED, -ING, -S to set securely

IMPLEAD   *v* -ED, -ING, -S to sue in a court of law

IMPLEDGE   *v* -PLEDGED, -PLEDGING, -PLEDGES to pawn

IMPLICIT   *adj* implied

IMPLIED   past tense of imply

IMPLIES   present 3d person sing. of imply

IMPLODE   *v* -PLODED, -PLODING, -PLODES to collapse inward

IMPLORE   *v* -PLORED, -PLORING, -PLORES to beg for urgently

IMPLORER   *n* pl. -S one that implores

IMPLY   *v* -PLIED, -PLYING, -PLIES to indicate or suggest indirectly

IMPOLICY   *n* pl. -CIES an unwise course of action

IMPOLITE   *adj* not polite

IMPONE   *v* -PONED, -PONING, -PONES to wager

IMPOROUS	*adj* extremely dense	**INACTION**	*n* pl. -S lack of action
IMPORT	*v* -ED, -ING, -S to bring into a country from abroad	**INACTIVE**	*adj* not active
IMPORTER	*n* pl. -S one that imports	**INANE**	*adj* INANER, INANEST nonsensical **INANELY** *adv*
IMPOSE	*v* -POSED, -POSING, -POSES to establish as compulsory	**INANE**	*n* pl. -S empty space
IMPOSER	*n* pl. -S one that imposes	**INANITY**	*n* pl. -TIES something that is inane
IMPOST	*v* -ED, -ING, -S to determine customs duties	**INAPT**	*adj* not apt **INAPTLY** *adv*
IMPOSTER	*n* pl. -S impostor	**INARABLE**	*adj* not arable
IMPOSTOR	*n* pl. -S one that poses as another for deceptive purposes	**INARCH**	*v* -ED, -ING, -ES to graft with in a certain way
IMPOTENT	*n* pl. -S one that is powerless	**INARM**	*v* -ED, -ING, -S to encircle with the arms
IMPOUND	*v* -ED, -ING, -S to seize and retain in legal custody	**INBEING**	*n* pl. -S the state of being inherent
IMPOWER	*v* -ED, -ING, -S to empower	**INBOARD**	*n* pl. -S a type of boat motor
IMPREGN	*v* -ED, -ING, -S to make pregnant	**INBORN**	*adj* existing in one from birth
IMPRESA	*n* pl. -S a type of emblem	**INBOUND**	*v* -ED, -ING, -S to put a basketball in play from out of bounds
IMPRESE	*n* pl. -S impresa		
IMPRESS	*v* -ED, -ING, -ES to affect strongly	**INBOUNDS**	*adj* being within certain boundaries
IMPREST	*n* pl. -S a loan or advance of money	**INBRED**	*n* pl. -S a product of inbreeding
IMPRIMIS	*adv* in the first place	**INBREED**	*v* -BRED, -BREEDING, -BREEDS to breed closely related stock
IMPRINT	*v* -ED, -ING, -S to produce a mark by pressure		
IMPRISON	*v* -ED, -ING, -S to confine	**INBUILT**	*adj* forming an integral part of a structure
IMPROPER	*adj* not proper	**INBURST**	*n* pl. -S the act of bursting inward
IMPROV	*n* pl. -S improvisation	**INBY**	*adv* inward
IMPROVE	*v* -PROVED, -PROVING, -PROVES to make better	**INBYE**	*adv* inby
IMPROVER	*n* pl. -S one that improves	**INCAGE**	*v* -CAGED, -CAGING, -CAGES to encage
IMPUDENT	*adj* offensively bold or disrespectful	**INCANT**	*v* -ED, -ING, -S to utter ritually
IMPUGN	*v* -ED, -ING, -S to make insinuations against	**INCASE**	*v* -CASED, -CASING, -CASES to encase
IMPUGNER	*n* pl. -S one that impugns	**INCENSE**	*v* -CENSED, -CENSING, -CENSES to make angry
IMPULSE	*v* -PULSED, -PULSING, -PULSES to give impetus to	**INCENTER**	*n* pl. -S the point where the three lines bisecting the angles of a triangle meet
IMPUNITY	*n* pl. -TIES exemption from penalty		
IMPURE	*adj* not pure **IMPURELY** *adv*	**INCEPT**	*v* -ED, -ING, -S to take in
IMPURITY	*n* pl. -TIES something that is impure	**INCEPTOR**	*n* pl. -S one that incepts
		INCEST	*n* pl. -S sexual intercourse between closely related persons
IMPUTE	*v* -PUTED, -PUTING, -PUTES to credit to a person or a cause	**INCH**	*v* -ED, -ING, -ES to move very slowly
IMPUTER	*n* pl. -S one that imputes	**INCHMEAL**	*adv* little by little
IN	*v* INNED, INNING, INS to harvest	**INCHOATE**	*adj* being in an early stage
		INCHWORM	*n* pl. -S a type of worm

INCIDENT   *n* pl. -S an event

INCIPIT   *n* pl. -S the opening words of a text

INCISAL   *adj* being the cutting edge of a tooth

INCISE   *v* -CISED, -CISING, -CISES to cut into

INCISION   *n* pl. -S the act of incising

INCISIVE   *adj* penetrating

INCISOR   *n* pl. -S a cutting tooth

INCISORY   *adj* adapted for cutting

INCISURE   *n* pl. -S a notch or cleft of a body part

INCITANT   *n* pl. -S something that incites

INCITE   *v* -CITED, -CITING, -CITES to arouse to action

INCITER   *n* pl. -S one that incites

INCIVIL   *adj* discourteous

INCLASP   *v* -ED, -ING, -S to enclasp

INCLINE   *v* -CLINED, -CLINING, -CLINES to slant

INCLINER   *n* pl. -S one that inclines

INCLIP   *v* -CLIPPED, -CLIPPING, -CLIPS to clasp

INCLOSE   *v* -CLOSED, -CLOSING, -CLOSES to enclose

INCLOSER   *n* pl. -S one that incloses

INCLUDE   *v* -CLUDED, -CLUDING, -CLUDES to have as a part

INCOG   *n* pl. -S a disguised person

INCOME   *n* pl. -S a sum of money earned regularly

INCOMER   *n* pl. -S one that comes in

INCOMING   *n* pl. -S an arrival

INCONNU   *n* pl. -S a large food fish

INCONY   *adj* pretty

INCORPSE   *v* -CORPSED, -CORPSING, -CORPSES to become combined with

INCREASE   *v* -CREASED, -CREASING, -CREASES to make or become greater

INCREATE   *adj* not created

INCROSS   *v* -ED, -ING, -ES to inbreed

INCRUST   *v* -ED, -ING, -S to encrust

INCUBATE   *v* -BATED, -BATING, -BATES to warm eggs for hatching

INCUBUS   *n* pl. -BI or -BUSES a demon

INCUDAL   *adj* pertaining to the incus

INCUDATE   *adj* incudal

INCUDES   pl. of incus

INCULT   *adj* uncultivated

INCUMBER   *v* -ED, -ING, -S to encumber

INCUR   *v* -CURRED, -CURRING, -CURS to bring upon oneself

INCURVE   *v* -CURVED, -CURVING, -CURVES to curve inward

INCUS   *n* pl. INCUDES a bone in the middle ear

INCUSE   *v* -CUSED, -CUSING, -CUSES to mark by stamping

INDABA   *n* pl. -S a meeting of South African tribes

INDAGATE   *v* -GATED, -GATING, -GATES to investigate

INDAMIN   *n* pl. -S indamine

INDAMINE   *n* pl. -S a chemical compound

INDEBTED   *adj* beholden

INDECENT   *adj* -CENTER, -CENTEST not decent

INDEED   *adv* in truth

INDENE   *n* pl. -S a hydrocarbon

INDENT   *v* -ED, -ING, -S to cut or tear irregularly

INDENTER   *n* pl. -S one that indents

INDENTOR   *n* pl. -S indenter

INDEVOUT   *adj* not devout

INDEX   *n* pl. INDEXES or INDICES a type of reference guide at the end of a book

INDEX   *v* -ED, -ING, -ES to provide with an index

INDEXER   *n* pl. -S one that indexes

INDEXING   *n* pl. -S the linking of wages and prices to cost-of-living levels

INDICAN   *n* pl. -S a chemical compound

INDICANT   *n* pl. -S something that indicates

INDICATE   *v* -CATED, -CATING, -CATES to point out

INDICES   a pl. of index

INDICIA   *n* pl. -S a distinctive mark

INDICIUM   *n* pl. -S an indicia

INDICT   *v* -ED, -ING, -S to charge with a crime

INDICTEE   *n* pl. -S one that is indicted

INDICTER   *n* pl. -S one that indicts

INDICTOR   *n* pl. -S indicter

INDIE   *n* pl. -S a person who is independent

INDIGEN   *n* pl. -S indigene

INDIGENE   *n* pl. -S a native

INDIGENT   *n* pl. -S a needy person

INDIGN   *adj* disgraceful **INDIGNLY** *adv*

INDIGO   *n* pl. -GOS or -GOES a blue dye

INDIGOID   *n* pl. -S a blue dye

INDIRECT   *adj* not direct

INDITE   *v* -DITED, -DITING, -DITES to write or compose

INDITER   *n* pl. -S one that indites

INDIUM   *n* pl. -S a metallic element

INDOCILE   *adj* not docile

INDOL   *n* pl. -S indole

INDOLE   *n* pl. -S a chemical compound

INDOLENT   *adj* lazy

INDOOR   *adj* pertaining to the interior of a building

INDOORS   *adv* in or into a house

INDORSE   *v* -DORSED, -DORSING, -DORSES to endorse

INDORSEE   *n* pl. -S endorsee

INDORSER   *n* pl. -S endorser

INDORSING   present participle of indorse

INDORSOR   *n* pl. -S endorsor

INDOW   *v* -ED, -ING, -S to endow

INDOXYL   *n* pl. -S a chemical compound

INDRAFT   *n* pl. -S an inward flow or current

INDRAWN   *adj* drawn in

INDRI   *n* pl. -S a short-tailed lemur

INDUCE   *v* -DUCED, -DUCING, -DUCES to influence into doing something

INDUCER   *n* pl. -S one that induces

INDUCT   *v* -ED, -ING, -S to bring into military service

INDUCTEE   *n* pl. -S one that is inducted

INDUCTOR   *n* pl. -S one that inducts

INDUE   *v* -DUED, -DUING, -DUES to endue

INDULGE   *v* -DULGED, -DULGING, -DULGES to yield to the desire of

INDULGER   *n* pl. -S one that indulges

INDULIN   *n* pl. -S induline

INDULINE   *n* pl. -S a blue dye

INDULT   *n* pl. -S a privilege granted by the pope

INDURATE   *v* -RATED, -RATING, -RATES to make hard

INDUSIUM   *n* pl. -SIA an enclosing membrane **INDUSIAL** *adj*

INDUSTRY   *n* pl. -TRIES a group of productive enterprises

INDWELL   *v* -DWELT, -DWELLING, -DWELLS to live within

INEARTH   *v* -ED, -ING, -S to bury

INEDIBLE   *adj* not fit to be eaten

INEDITA   *n/pl* unpublished literary works

INEDITED   *adj* not published

INEPT   *adj* not suitable **INEPTLY** *adv*

INEQUITY   *n* pl. -TIES unfairness

INERRANT   *adj* free from error

INERT   *n* pl. -S something that lacks active properties

INERTIA   *n* pl. -TIAS or -TIAE the tendency of a body to resist acceleration **INERTIAL** *adj*

INERTLY   *adv* inactively

INEXACT   *adj* not exact

INEXPERT   *n* pl. -S a novice

INFALL   *n* pl. -S movement under the influence of gravity toward a celestial object

INFAMOUS   *adj* having a vile reputation

INFAMY   *n* pl. -MIES the state of being infamous

INFANCY   *n* pl. -CIES the state of being an infant

INFANT   *n* pl. -S a child in the earliest stages of life

INFANTA   *n* pl. -S a daughter of a Spanish or Portuguese monarch

INFANTE   *n* pl. -S a younger son of a Spanish or Portuguese monarch

INFANTRY   *n* pl. -TRIES a branch of the army composed of foot soldiers

INFARCT   *n* pl. -S an area of dead or dying tissue

INFARE   *n* pl. -S a reception for newlyweds

INFAUNA   *n* pl. -NAS or -NAE fauna living on a soft sea floor **INFAUNAL** *adj*

INFECT   *v* -ED, -ING, -S to contaminate with disease-producing germs

INFECTER   *n* pl. -S one that infects

INFECTOR   *n* pl. -S infecter

INFECUND   *adj* barren

INFEOFF	*v* -ED, -ING, -S to enfeoff
INFER	*v* -FERRED, -FERRING, -FERS to reach or derive by reasoning
INFERIOR	*n* pl. -S one of lesser rank
INFERNAL	*adj* pertaining to hell
INFERNO	*n* pl. -NOS a place that resembles or suggests hell
INFERRED	past tense of infer
INFERRER	*n* pl. -S one that infers
INFERRING	present participle of infer
INFEST	*v* -ED, -ING, -S to overrun in large numbers
INFESTER	*n* pl. -S one that infests
INFIDEL	*n* pl. -S one who has no religious faith
INFIELD	*n* pl. -S a part of a baseball field
INFIGHT	*v* -FOUGHT, -FIGHTING, -FIGHTS to contend with others within the same group
INFINITE	*n* pl. -S something that has no limits
INFINITY	*n* pl. -TIES the state of having no limits
INFIRM	*v* -ED, -ING, -S to weaken or destroy the validity of
INFIRMLY	*adv* in a feeble manner
INFIX	*v* -ED, -ING, -ES to implant
INFIXION	*n* pl. -S the act of infixing
INFLAME	*v* -FLAMED, -FLAMING, -FLAMES to set on fire
INFLAMER	*n* pl. -S one that inflames
INFLATE	*v* -FLATED, -FLATING, -FLATES to cause to expand by filling with gas or air
INFLATER	*n* pl. -S one that inflates
INFLATOR	*n* pl. -S inflater
INFLECT	*v* -ED, -ING, -S to bend
INFLEXED	*adj* bent inward
INFLICT	*v* -ED, -ING, -S to cause to be endured; impose
INFLIGHT	*adj* done during an air voyage
INFLOW	*n* pl. -S the act of flowing in
INFLUENT	*n* pl. -S a tributary
INFLUX	*n* pl. -ES a flowing in
INFO	*n* pl. -FOS information
INFOLD	*v* -ED, -ING, -S to fold inward
INFOLDER	*n* pl. -S one that infolds
INFORM	*v* -ED, -ING, -S to supply with information
INFORMAL	*adj* marked by the absence of formality or ceremony
INFORMER	*n* pl. -S one that informs
INFOUGHT	past tense of infight
INFRA	*adv* below
INFRACT	*v* -ED, -ING, -S to break a legal rule
INFRARED	*n* pl. -S a part of the invisible spectrum
INFRINGE	*v* -FRINGED, -FRINGING, -FRINGES to violate an oath or a law
INFRUGAL	*adj* not frugal
INFUSE	*v* -FUSED, -FUSING, -FUSES to permeate with something
INFUSER	*n* pl. -S one that infuses
INFUSION	*n* pl. -S the act of infusing
INFUSIVE	*adj* capable of infusing
INGATE	*n* pl. -S a channel by which molten metal enters a mold
INGATHER	*v* -ED, -ING, -S to gather in
INGENUE	*n* pl. -S a naive young woman
INGEST	*v* -ED, -ING, -S to take into the body
INGESTA	*n/pl* ingested material
INGLE	*n* pl. -S a fire
INGOING	*adj* entering
INGOT	*v* -ED, -ING, -S to shape into a convenient form for storage
INGRAFT	*v* -ED, -ING, -S to engraft
INGRAIN	*v* -ED, -ING, -S to impress firmly on the mind
INGRATE	*n* pl. -S an ungrateful person
INGRESS	*n* pl. -ES the act of entering
INGROUP	*n* pl. -S a group united by common interests
INGROWN	*adj* grown into the flesh
INGROWTH	*n* pl. -S growth inward
INGUINAL	*adj* pertaining to the groin
INGULF	*v* -ED, -ING, -S to engulf
INHABIT	*v* -ED, -ING, -S to live in
INHALANT	*n* pl. -S something that is inhaled
INHALE	*v* -HALED, -HALING, -HALES to take into the lungs
INHALER	*n* pl. -S one that inhales
INHAUL	*n* pl. -S a line for bringing in a sail
INHAULER	*n* pl. -S an inhaul

INHERE	*v* -HERED, -HERING, -HERES to be inherent	**INKPOT**	*n* pl. -S an inkwell
INHERENT	*adj* existing in something as an essential characteristic	**INKSTAND**	*n* pl. -S an inkwell
		INKSTONE	*n* pl. -S a stone on which dry ink and water are mixed
INHERIT	*v* -ED, -ING, -S to receive by legal succession	**INKWELL**	*n* pl. -S a small container for ink
INHESION	*n* pl. -S the state of inhering	**INKWOOD**	*n* pl. -S an evergreen tree
INHIBIN	*n* pl. -S a human hormone	**INKY**	*adj* INKIER, INKIEST resembling ink
INHIBIT	*v* -ED, -ING, -S to restrain or hold back	**INLACE**	*v* -LACED, -LACING, -LACES to enlace
INHUMAN	*adj* lacking desirable human qualities	**INLAID**	past tense of inlay
INHUMANE	*adj* not humane	**INLAND**	*n* pl. -S the interior of a region
INHUME	*v* -HUMED, -HUMING, -HUMES to bury	**INLANDER**	*n* pl. -S one living in the interior of a region
INHUMER	*n* pl. -S one that inhumes	**INLAY**	*v* -LAID, -LAYING, -LAYS to set into a surface
INIMICAL	*adj* unfriendly	**INLAYER**	*n* pl. -S one that inlays
INION	*n* pl. INIA a part of the skull	**INLET**	*v* -LET, -LETTING, -LETS to insert
INIQUITY	*n* pl. -TIES a gross injustice		
INITIAL	*v* -TIALED, -TIALING, -TIALS or -TIALLED, -TIALLING, -TIALS to mark with the first letters of one's name	**INLIER**	*n* pl. -S a type of rock formation
		INLY	*adv* inwardly
		INMATE	*n* pl. -S one who is confined to an institution
INITIATE	*v* -ATED, -ATING, -ATES to originate	**INMESH**	*v* -ED, -ING, -ES to enmesh
INJECT	*v* -ED, -ING, -S to force a fluid into	**INMOST**	*adj* farthest within
		INN	*v* -ED, -ING, -S to put up at an inn (a public lodging house)
INJECTOR	*n* pl. -S one that injects		
INJURE	*v* -JURED, -JURING, -JURES to do or cause injury to	**INNARDS**	*n/pl* the internal organs
		INNATE	*adj* inborn **INNATELY** *adv*
INJURER	*n* pl. -S one that injures	**INNED**	past tense of in
INJURY	*n* pl. -RIES harm inflicted or suffered	**INNER**	*n* pl. -S something that is within
		INNERLY	*adv* inwardly
INK	*v* -ED, -ING, -S to mark with ink (a colored fluid used for writing)	**INNERVE**	*v* -NERVED, -NERVING, -NERVES to stimulate
INKBERRY	*n* pl. -RIES a small shrub	**INNING**	*n* pl. -S a division of a baseball game
INKBLOT	*n* pl. -S a blotted pattern of spilled ink		
		INNLESS	*adj* having no inns
INKER	*n* pl. -S one that inks	**INNOCENT**	*adj* -CENTER, -CENTEST free from guilt or sin
INKHORN	*n* pl. -S a small container for ink		
INKIER	comparative of inky	**INNOCENT**	*n* pl. -S an innocent person
INKIEST	superlative of inky	**INNOVATE**	*v* -VATED, -VATING, -VATES to introduce something new
INKINESS	*n* pl. -ES the state of being inky		
INKJET	*adj* being a high-speed printing process using jets of ink	**INNUENDO**	*v* -ED, -ING, -S or -ES to make a derogatory implication
INKLE	*n* pl. -S a tape used for trimming	**INOCULUM**	*n* pl. -LA or -LUMS the material used in an inoculation
INKLESS	*adj* being without ink		
INKLIKE	*adj* resembling ink	**INOSITE**	*n* pl. -S inositol
INKLING	*n* pl. -S a slight suggestion	**INOSITOL**	*n* pl. -S an alcohol found in plant and animal tissue

INPHASE	*adj* having matching electrical phases
INPOUR	*v* -ED, -ING, -S to pour in
INPUT	*v* -PUTTED, -PUTTING, -PUTS to enter data into a computer
INQUEST	*n* pl. -S a legal inquiry
INQUIET	*v* -ED, -ING, -S to disturb
INQUIRE	*v* -QUIRED, -QUIRING, -QUIRES to ask about
INQUIRER	*n* pl. -S one that inquires
INQUIRY	*n* pl. -RIES a question
INRO	*n* pl. INRO a Japanese ornamental container
INROAD	*n* pl. -S a hostile invasion
INRUSH	*n* pl. -ES a rushing in
INSANE	*adj* -SANER, -SANEST mentally unsound **INSANELY** *adv*
INSANITY	*n* pl. -TIES the state of being insane; something utterly foolish
INSCAPE	*n* pl. -S the inner essential quality of something
INSCRIBE	*v* -SCRIBED, -SCRIBING, -SCRIBES to write or engrave as a lasting record
INSCROLL	*v* -ED, -ING, -S to enscroll
INSCULP	*v* -ED, -ING, -S to engrave
INSEAM	*n* pl. -S an inner seam
INSECT	*n* pl. -S any of a class of small invertebrate animals
INSECTAN	*adj* pertaining to insects
INSECURE	*adj* unsafe
INSERT	*v* -ED, -ING, -S to put in
INSERTER	*n* pl. -S one that inserts
INSET	*v* -SETTED, -SETTING, -SETS to insert
INSETTER	*n* pl. -S one that inserts
INSHEATH	*v* -ED, -ING, -S to ensheath
INSHORE	*adj* near the shore
INSHRINE	*v* -SHRINED, -SHRINING, -SHRINES to enshrine
INSIDE	*n* pl. -S something that lies within
INSIDER	*n* pl. -S an accepted member of a clique
INSIGHT	*n* pl. -S a perception of the inner nature of things
INSIGNE	*n* pl. INSIGNIA an insignia
INSIGNIA	*n* pl. -S an emblem of authority or honor
INSIPID	*adj* dull and uninteresting
INSIST	*v* -ED, -ING, -S to be resolute on some matter
INSISTER	*n* pl. -S one that insists
INSNARE	*v* -SNARED, -SNARING, -SNARES to ensnare
INSNARER	*n* pl. -S ensnarer
INSOFAR	*adv* to such an extent
INSOLATE	*v* -LATED, -LATING, -LATES to expose to sunlight
INSOLE	*n* pl. -S the inner sole of a boot or shoe
INSOLENT	*n* pl. -S an extremely rude person
INSOMNIA	*n* pl. -S chronic inability to sleep
INSOMUCH	*adv* to such a degree
INSOUL	*v* -ED, -ING, -S to ensoul
INSPAN	*v* -SPANNED, -SPANNING, -SPANS to harness or yoke to a vehicle
INSPECT	*v* -ED, -ING, -S to look carefully at or over
INSPHERE	*v* -SPHERED, -SPHERING, -SPHERES to ensphere
INSPIRE	*v* -SPIRED, -SPIRING, -SPIRES to animate the mind or emotions of
INSPIRER	*n* pl. -S one that inspires
INSPIRIT	*v* -ED, -ING, -S to fill with spirit or life
INSTABLE	*adj* unstable
INSTAL	*v* -STALLED, -STALLING, -STALS to install
INSTALL	*v* -ED, -ING, -S to place in position for use
INSTANCE	*v* -STANCED, -STANCING, -STANCES to cite as an example
INSTANCY	*n* pl. -CIES urgency
INSTANT	*n* pl. -S a very short time
INSTAR	*v* -STARRED, -STARRING, -STARS to adorn with stars
INSTATE	*v* -STATED, -STATING, -STATES to place in office
INSTEAD	*adv* as a substitute or equivalent
INSTEP	*n* pl. -S a part of the foot
INSTIL	*v* -STILLED, -STILLING, -STILS to instill
INSTILL	*v* -ED, -ING, -S to infuse slowly
INSTINCT	*n* pl. -S an inborn behavioral pattern
INSTROKE	*n* pl. -S an inward stroke

INSTRUCT v -ED, -ING, -S to supply with knowledge

INSULANT n pl. -S an insulating material

INSULAR n pl. -S an islander

INSULATE v -LATED, -LATING, -LATES to separate with nonconducting material

INSULIN n pl. -S a hormone

INSULT v -ED, -ING, -S to treat offensively

INSULTER n pl. -S one that insults

INSURANT n pl. -S one who is insured

INSURE v -SURED, -SURING, -SURES to guarantee against loss

INSURED n pl. -S one who is insured

INSURER n pl. -S one that insures

INSURING present participle of insure

INSWATHE v -SWATHED, -SWATHING, -SWATHES to enswathe

INSWEPT adj narrowed in front

INTACT adj not damaged in any way

INTAGLIO n pl. -GLIOS or -GLI an incised or sunken design

INTAGLIO v -ED, -ING, -S to engrave in intaglio

INTAKE n pl. -S the act of taking in

INTARSIA n pl. -S a decorative technique

INTEGER n pl. -S a whole number

INTEGRAL n pl. -S a total unit

INTEND v -ED, -ING, -S to have as a specific aim or purpose

INTENDED n pl. -S one's spouse to-be

INTENDER n pl. -S one that intends

INTENSE adj -TENSER, -TENSEST existing in an extreme degree

INTENT n pl. -S a purpose

INTENTLY adv in an unwavering manner

INTER v -TERRED, -TERRING, -TERS to bury

INTERACT v -ED, -ING, -S to act on each other

INTERAGE adj including persons of various ages

INTERBED v -BEDDED, -BEDDING, -BEDS to insert between other layers

INTERCOM n pl. -S a type of communication system

INTERCUT v -CUT, -CUTTING, -CUTS to alternate camera shots

INTEREST v -ED, -ING, -S to engage the attention of

INTERIM n pl. -S an interval

INTERIOR n pl. -S the inside

INTERLAP v -LAPPED, -LAPPING, -LAPS to lap one over another

INTERLAY v -LAID, -LAYING, -LAYS to place between

INTERMIT v -MITTED, -MITTING, -MITS to stop temporarily

INTERMIX v -ED, -ING, -ES to mix together

INTERN v -ED, -ING, -S to confine during a war

INTERNAL n pl. -S an inner attribute

INTERNE n pl. -S a recent medical school graduate on a hospital staff

INTERNEE n pl. -S one who has been interned

INTERRED past tense of inter

INTERREX n pl. -REGES a type of sovereign

INTERRING present participle of inter

INTERROW adj existing between rows

INTERSEX n pl. -ES a person having characteristics of both sexes

INTERTIE n pl. -S a type of electrical connection

INTERVAL n pl. -S a space of time between periods or events

INTERWAR adj happening between wars

INTHRAL v -THRALLED, -THRALLING, -THRALS to enthrall

INTHRALL v -ED, -ING, -S to enthrall

INTHRONE v -THRONED, -THRONING, -THRONES to enthrone

INTI n pl. -S a monetary unit of Peru

INTIMA n pl. -MAE or -MAS the innermost layer of an organ **INTIMAL** adj

INTIMACY n pl. -CIES the state of being closely associated

INTIMATE v -MATED, -MATING, -MATES to make known indirectly

INTIME adj cozy

INTIMIST n pl. -S a writer or artist who deals with deep personal experiences

INTINE n pl. -S the inner wall of a spore

INTITLE v -TLED, -TLING, -TLES to entitle

INTITULE v -ULED, -ULING, -ULES to entitle

INTO	*prep* to the inside of
INTOMB	*v* -ED, -ING, -S to entomb
INTONATE	*v* -NATED, -NATING, -NATES to intone
INTONE	*v* -TONED, -TONING, -TONES to speak in a singing voice
INTONER	*n* pl. -S one that intones
INTORT	*v* -ED, -ING, -S to twist inward
INTOWN	*adj* located in the center of a city
INTRADAY	*adj* occurring within a single day
INTRADOS	*n* pl. -ES the inner curve of an arch
INTRANT	*n* pl. -S an entrant
INTREAT	*v* -ED, -ING, -S to entreat
INTRENCH	*v* -ED, -ING, -ES to entrench
INTREPID	*adj* fearless
INTRIGUE	*v* -TRIGUED, -TRIGUING, -TRIGUES to arouse the curiosity of
INTRO	*n* pl. -TROS an introduction
INTROFY	*v* -FIED, -FYING, -FIES to increase the wetting properties of
INTROIT	*n* pl. -S music sung at the beginning of a worship service
INTROMIT	*v* -MITTED, -MITTING, -MITS to put in
INTRON	*n* pl. -S an intervening sequence in the genetic code
INTRORSE	*adj* facing inward
INTRUDE	*v* -TRUDED, -TRUDING, -TRUDES to thrust or force oneself in
INTRUDER	*n* pl. -S one that intrudes
INTRUST	*v* -ED, -ING, -S to entrust
INTUBATE	*v* -BATED, -BATING, -BATES to insert a tube into
INTUIT	*v* -ED, -ING, -S to know without conscious reasoning
INTURN	*n* pl. -S a turning inward **INTURNED** *adj*
INTWINE	*v* -TWINED, -TWINING, -TWINES to entwine
INTWIST	*v* -ED, -ING, -S to entwist
INULASE	*n* pl. -S an enzyme
INULIN	*n* pl. -S a chemical compound
INUNDANT	*adj* inundating
INUNDATE	*v* -DATED, -DATING, -DATES to overwhelm with water
INURBANE	*adj* not urbane
INURE	*v* -URED, -URING, -URES to accustom to accept something undesirable
INURN	*v* -ED, -ING, -S to put in an urn
INUTILE	*adj* useless
INVADE	*v* -VADED, -VADING, -VADES to enter for conquest or plunder
INVADER	*n* pl. -S one that invades
INVALID	*v* -ED, -ING, -S to disable physically
INVAR	*n* pl. -S an iron-nickel alloy
INVASION	*n* pl. -S the act of invading **INVASIVE** *adj*
INVECTED	*adj* edged by convex curves
INVEIGH	*v* -ED, -ING, -S to protest angrily
INVEIGLE	*v* -GLED, -GLING, -GLES to induce by guile or flattery
INVENT	*v* -ED, -ING, -S to devise originally
INVENTER	*n* pl. -S inventor
INVENTOR	*n* pl. -S one that invents
INVERITY	*n* pl. -TIES lack of truth
INVERSE	*n* pl. -S something that is opposite
INVERT	*v* -ED, -ING, -S to turn upside down
INVERTER	*n* pl. -S one that inverts
INVERTOR	*n* pl. -S a type of electrical device
INVEST	*v* -ED, -ING, -S to commit something of value for future profit
INVESTOR	*n* pl. -S one that invests
INVIABLE	*adj* not viable **INVIABLY** *adv*
INVIRILE	*adj* not virile
INVISCID	*adj* not viscid
INVITAL	*adj* not vital
INVITE	*v* -VITED, -VITING, -VITES to request the presence of
INVITEE	*n* pl. -S one that is invited
INVITER	*n* pl. -S one that invites
INVITING	present participle of invite
INVOCATE	*v* -CATED, -CATING, -CATES to invoke
INVOICE	*v* -VOICED, -VOICING, -VOICES to bill
INVOKE	*v* -VOKED, -VOKING, -VOKES to appeal to for aid
INVOKER	*n* pl. -S one that invokes

INVOLUTE	v -LUTED, -LUTING, -LUTES to roll or curl up	**IONIZER**	n pl. -S one that ionizes
INVOLVE	v -VOLVED, -VOLVING, -VOLVES to contain or include as a part	**IONOGEN**	n pl. -S a compound capable of forming ions
		IONOMER	n pl. -S a type of plastic
INVOLVER	n pl. -S one that involves	**IONONE**	n pl. -S a chemical compound
INWALL	v -ED, -ING, -S to surround with a wall	**IOTA**	n pl. -S a Greek letter
INWARD	adv toward the inside	**IOTACISM**	n pl. -S excessive use of the letter iota
INWARDLY	adv on the inside	**IPECAC**	n pl. -S a medicinal plant
INWARDS	adv inward	**IPOMOEA**	n pl. -S a flowering plant
INWEAVE	v -WOVE or -WEAVED, -WOVEN, -WEAVING, -WEAVES to weave together	**IRACUND**	adj easily angered
		IRADE	n pl. -S a decree of a Muslim ruler
INWIND	v -WOUND, -WINDING, -WINDS to enwind	**IRATE**	adj IRATER, IRATEST angry **IRATELY** adv
INWRAP	v -WRAPPED, -WRAPPING, -WRAPS to enwrap	**IRE**	v IRED, IRING, IRES to anger
IODATE	v -DATED, -DATING, -DATES to iodize	**IREFUL**	adj angry **IREFULLY** adv
		IRELESS	adj not angry
IODATION	n pl. -S the act of iodating	**IRENIC**	adj peaceful in purpose
IODIC	adj pertaining to iodine	**IRENICAL**	adj irenic
IODID	n pl. -S iodide	**IRENICS**	n/pl a branch of theology
IODIDE	n pl. -S a compound of iodine	**IRID**	n pl. -S a plant of the iris family
IODIN	n pl. -S iodine	**IRIDES**	a pl. of iris
IODINATE	v -ATED, -ATING, -ATES to iodize	**IRIDIC**	adj pertaining to iridium
		IRIDIUM	n pl. -S a metallic element
IODINE	n pl. -S a nonmetallic element	**IRING**	present participle of ire
IODISE	v -DISED, -DISING, -DISES iodize	**IRIS**	n pl. IRISES or IRIDES a part of the eye
IODISM	n pl. -S iodine poisoning	**IRIS**	v -ED, -ING, -ES to give the form of a rainbow to
IODIZE	v -DIZED, -DIZING, -DIZES to treat with iodine	**IRITIS**	n pl. -TISES inflammation of the iris **IRITIC** adj
IODIZER	n pl. -S one that iodizes		
IODOFORM	n pl. -S an iodine compound	**IRK**	v -ED, -ING, -S to annoy or weary
IODOPHOR	n pl. -S an iodine compound	**IRKSOME**	adj tending to irk
IODOPSIN	n pl. -S a pigment in the retina	**IROKO**	n pl. -KOS a large African tree
IODOUS	adj pertaining to iodine	**IRON**	v -ED, -ING, -S to furnish with iron (a metallic element)
IOLITE	n pl. -S a mineral		
ION	n pl. -S an electrically charged atom	**IRONBARK**	n pl. -S a timber tree
		IRONCLAD	n pl. -S an armored warship
IONIC	n pl. -S a style of type	**IRONE**	n pl. -S an aromatic oil
IONICITY	n pl. -TIES the state of existing as or like an ion	**IRONER**	n pl. -S a machine for pressing clothes
IONISE	v -ISED, -ISING, -ISES to ionize	**IRONIC**	adj pertaining to irony
IONIUM	n pl. -S an isotope of thorium	**IRONICAL**	adj ironic
IONIZE	v -IZED, -IZING, -IZES to convert into ions	**IRONIES**	pl. of irony

IRONING   *n* pl. -S clothes pressed or to be pressed

IRONIST   *n* pl. -S one who uses irony

IRONIZE   *v* -NIZED, -NIZING, -NIZES to mix with nutritional iron

IRONLIKE   *adj* resembling iron

IRONNESS   *n* pl. -ES the state of being iron

IRONSIDE   *n* pl. -S a man of great strength

IRONWARE   *n* pl. -S articles made of iron

IRONWEED   *n* pl. -S a shrub

IRONWOOD   *n* pl. -S a hardwood tree

IRONWORK   *n* pl. -S objects made of iron

IRONY   *n* pl. -NIES the use of words to express the opposite of what is literally said

IRREAL   *adj* not real

IRRIGATE   *v* -GATED, -GATING, -GATES to supply with water by artificial means

IRRITANT   *n* pl. -S something that irritates

IRRITATE   *v* -TATED, -TATING, -TATES to excite to impatience or anger

IRRUPT   *v* -ED, -ING, -S to rush in forcibly

IS   present 3d person sing. of be

ISAGOGE   *n* pl. -S a type of introduction to a branch of study

ISAGOGIC   *n* pl. -S a branch of theology

ISARITHM   *n* pl. -S an isopleth

ISATIN   *n* pl. -S a chemical compound **ISATINIC** *adj*

ISATINE   *n* pl. -S isatin

ISBA   *n* pl. -S a Russian log hut

ISCHEMIA   *n* pl. -S a type of anemia **ISCHEMIC** *adj*

ISCHIUM   *n* pl. -CHIA a pelvic bone **ISCHIAL** *adj*

ISLAND   *v* -ED, -ING, -S to make into an island (a land area entirely surrounded by water)

ISLANDER   *n* pl. -S one that lives on an island

ISLE   *v* ISLED, ISLING, ISLES to place on an isle (a small island)

ISLELESS   *adj* lacking an isle

ISLET   *n* pl. -S a small island

ISLING   present participle of isle

ISM   *n* pl. -S a distinctive theory or doctrine

ISOBAR   *n* pl. -S a type of atom **ISOBARIC** *adj*

ISOBARE   *n* pl. -S isobar

ISOBATH   *n* pl. -S a line on a map connecting points of equal water depth

ISOCHEIM   *n* pl. -S a type of isotherm

ISOCHIME   *n* pl. -S isocheim

ISOCHOR   *n* pl. -S isochore

ISOCHORE   *n* pl. -S a curve used to show a relationship between pressure and temperature

ISOCHRON   *n* pl. -S a line on a chart connecting points representing the same time

ISOCLINE   *n* pl. -S a type of rock formation

ISOCRACY   *n* pl. -CIES a form of government

ISODOSE   *adj* pertaining to zones that receive equal doses of radiation

ISOGAMY   *n* pl. -MIES the fusion of two similar gametes

ISOGENIC   *adj* genetically similar

ISOGENY   *n* pl. -NIES the state of being of similar origin

ISOGLOSS   *n* pl. -ES a line on a map between linguistically varied areas

ISOGON   *n* pl. -S a polygon having equal angles

ISOGONAL   *n* pl. -S isogone

ISOGONE   *n* pl. -S a line on a map used to show characteristics of the earth's magnetic field

ISOGONIC   *n* pl. -S isogone

ISOGONY   *n* pl. -NIES an equivalent relative growth of parts

ISOGRAFT   *v* -ED, -ING, -S to transplant from one individual to another of the same species

ISOGRAM   *n* pl. -S a line on a map connecting points of equal value

ISOGRAPH   *n* pl. -S a line on a map indicating areas that are linguistically similar

ISOGRIV   *n* pl. -S a line drawn on a map such that all points have equal grid variation

ISOHEL   *n* pl. -S a line on a map connecting points receiving equal sunshine

ISOHYET   *n* pl. -S a line on a map connecting points having equal rainfall

ISOLABLE	*adj* capable of being isolated
ISOLATE	*v* -LATED, -LATING, -LATES to set apart from others
ISOLATOR	*n* pl. -S one that isolates
ISOLEAD	*n* pl. -S a line on a ballistic graph
ISOLINE	*n* pl. -S an isogram
ISOLOG	*n* pl. -S isologue
ISOLOGUE	*n* pl. -S a type of chemical compound
ISOMER	*n* pl. -S a type of chemical compound **ISOMERIC** *adj*
ISOMETRY	*n* pl. -TRIES equality of measure
ISOMORPH	*n* pl. -S something similar to something else in form
ISONOMY	*n* pl. -MIES equality of civil rights **ISONOMIC** *adj*
ISOPACH	*n* pl. -S an isogram connecting points of equal thickness
ISOPHOTE	*n* pl. -S a curve on a chart joining points of equal light intensity
ISOPLETH	*n* pl. -S a type of isogram
ISOPOD	*n* pl. -S a kind of crustacean
ISOPODAN	*n* pl. -S an isopod
ISOPRENE	*n* pl. -S a volatile liquid
ISOSPIN	*n* pl. -S a type of quantum number
ISOSPORY	*n* pl. -RIES the condition of producing sexual or asexual spores of but one kind
ISOSTASY	*n* pl. -SIES the state of balance in the earth's crust
ISOTACH	*n* pl. -S a line on a map connecting points of equal wind velocity
ISOTHERE	*n* pl. -S a type of isotherm
ISOTHERM	*n* pl. -S a line on a map connecting points of equal mean temperature
ISOTONE	*n* pl. -S a type of atom
ISOTONIC	*adj* of equal tension
ISOTOPE	*n* pl. -S a form of an element **ISOTOPIC** *adj*
ISOTOPY	*n* pl. -PIES the state of being an isotope
ISOTROPY	*n* pl. -PIES the state of being identical in all directions
ISOTYPE	*n* pl. -S a type of diagram **ISOTYPIC** *adj*
ISOZYME	*n* pl. -S a type of enzyme **ISOZYMIC** *adj*
ISSEI	*n* pl. -S a Japanese immigrant to the United States
ISSUABLE	*adj* authorized for issuing **ISSUABLY** *adv*
ISSUANCE	*n* pl. -S the act of issuing
ISSUANT	*adj* coming forth
ISSUE	*v* -SUED, -SUING, -SUES to come forth
ISSUER	*n* pl. -S one that issues
ISTHMI	a pl. of isthmus
ISTHMIAN	*n* pl. -S a native of an isthmus
ISTHMIC	*adj* pertaining to an isthmus
ISTHMOID	*adj* isthmic
ISTHMUS	*n* pl. -MUSES or -MI a strip of land connecting two larger land masses
ISTLE	*n* pl. -S a strong fiber
IT	*pron* the 3d person sing. neuter pronoun
ITALIC	*n* pl. -S a style of print
ITCH	*v* -ED, -ING, -ES to have an uneasy or tingling skin sensation
ITCHING	*n* pl. -S an uneasy or tingling skin sensation
ITCHY	*adj* ITCHIER, ITCHIEST causing an itching sensation **ITCHILY** *adv*
ITEM	*v* -ED, -ING, -S to itemize
ITEMISE	*v* -ISED, -ISING, -ISES itemize
ITEMIZE	*v* -IZED, -IZING, -IZES to set down the particulars of
ITEMIZER	*n* pl. -S one that itemizes
ITERANCE	*n* pl. -S repetition
ITERANT	*adj* repeating
ITERATE	*v* -ATED, -ATING, -ATES to repeat
ITERUM	*adv* again; once more
ITHER	*adj* other
ITS	*pron* the possessive form of the pronoun it
ITSELF	*pron* a reflexive form of the pronoun it
IVIED	*adj* covered with ivy
IVORY	*n* pl. -RIES a hard white substance found in elephant tusks
IVY	*n* pl. IVIES a climbing vine **IVYLIKE** *adj*
IWIS	*adv* certainly
IXIA	*n* pl. -S a flowering plant

IXODID *n* pl. -S a bloodsucking insect

IXORA *n* pl. -S a flowering plant

IXTLE *n* pl. -S istle

IZAR *n* pl. -S an outer garment worn by Muslim women

IZZARD *n* pl. -S the letter Z

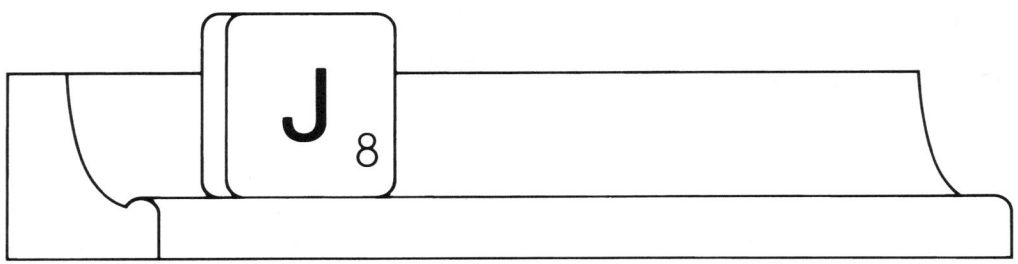

JAB	*v* JABBED, JABBING, JABS to poke sharply	**JACQUARD**	*n* pl. -S a fabric of intricate weave
JABBER	*v* -ED, -ING, -S to talk rapidly	**JACULATE**	*v* -LATED, -LATING, -LATES to throw
JABBERER	*n* pl. -S one that jabbers	**JADE**	*v* JADED, JADING, JADES to weary **JADEDLY** *adv*
JABBING	present participle of jab		
JABIRU	*n* pl. -S a wading bird	**JADEITE**	*n* pl. -S a mineral **JADITIC** *adj*
JABOT	*n* pl. -S a decoration on a shirt	**JADISH**	*adj* worn-out **JADISHLY** *adv*
JACAL	*n* pl. -ES or -S a hut	**JAEGER**	*n* pl. -S a hunter
JACAMAR	*n* pl. -S a tropical bird	**JAG**	*v* JAGGED, JAGGING, JAGS to cut unevenly
JACANA	*n* pl. -S a wading bird		
JACINTH	*n* pl. -S a variety of zircon	**JAGER**	*n* pl. -S jaeger
JACINTHE	*n* pl. -S an orange color	**JAGG**	*v* -ED, -ING, -S to jag
JACK	*v* -ED, -ING, -S to raise with a type of lever	**JAGGARY**	*n* pl. -RIES jaggery
		JAGGED	*adj* -GEDER, -GEDEST having a sharply uneven edge or surface **JAGGEDLY** *adv*
JACKAL	*n* pl. -S a doglike mammal		
JACKAROO	*n* pl. -ROOS jackeroo	**JAGGER**	*n* pl. -S one that jags
JACKASS	*n* pl. -ES a male donkey	**JAGGERY**	*n* pl. -GERIES a coarse, dark sugar
JACKBOOT	*n* pl. -S a heavy boot		
JACKDAW	*n* pl. -S a crowlike bird	**JAGGHERY**	*n* pl. -GHERIES jaggery
JACKER	*n* pl. -S one that jacks	**JAGGING**	present participle of jag
JACKEROO	*n* pl. -ROOS an inexperienced ranch hand	**JAGGY**	*adj* -GIER, -GIEST jagged
		JAGLESS	*adj* smooth and even
JACKET	*v* -ED, -ING, -S to provide with a jacket (a short coat)	**JAGRA**	*n* pl. -S jaggery
		JAGUAR	*n* pl. -S a large feline animal
JACKFISH	*n* pl. -ES a food fish	**JAIL**	*v* -ED, -ING, -S to put in jail (a place of confinement)
JACKIES	pl. of jacky		
JACKLEG	*n* pl. -S an unskilled worker	**JAILBAIT**	*n* pl. JAILBAIT a girl under the age of consent with whom sexual intercourse constitutes statutory rape
JACKPOT	*n* pl. -S a top prize or reward		
JACKROLL	*v* -ED, -ING, -S to rob a drunken or sleeping person		
		JAILBIRD	*n* pl. -S a prisoner
JACKSTAY	*n* pl. -STAYS a rope on a ship	**JAILER**	*n* pl. -S a keeper of a jail
JACKY	*n* pl. JACKIES a sailor	**JAILOR**	*n* pl. -S jailer
JACOBIN	*n* pl. -S a pigeon	**JAKE**	*adj* all right; fine
JACOBUS	*n* pl. -ES an old English coin	**JAKES**	*n/pl* an outhouse
JACONET	*n* pl. -S a cotton cloth		

JALAP	*n* pl. -S a Mexican plant **JALAPIC** *adj*
JALAPENO	*n* pl. -NOS a hot pepper
JALAPIN	*n* pl. -S a medicinal substance contained in jalap
JALOP	*n* pl. -S jalap
JALOPPY	*n* pl. -PIES jalopy
JALOPY	*n* pl. -LOPIES a decrepit car
JALOUSIE	*n* pl. -S a type of window
JAM	*v* JAMMED, JAMMING, JAMS to force together tightly
JAMB	*v* -ED, -ING, -S to jam
JAMBE	*n* pl. -S a jambeau
JAMBEAU	*n* pl. -BEAUX a piece of armor for the leg
JAMBOREE	*n* pl. -S a noisy celebration
JAMMED	past tense of jam
JAMMER	*n* pl. -S one that jams
JAMMIES	*n/pl* pajamas
JAMMING	present participle of jam
JAMMY	*adj* -MIER, -MIEST sticky with jam (boiled fruit and sugar)
JANE	*n* pl. -S a girl or woman
JANGLE	*v* -GLED, -GLING, -GLES to make a harsh, metallic sound
JANGLER	*n* pl. -S one that jangles
JANGLY	*adj* -GLIER, -GLIEST jangling
JANIFORM	*adj* hypocritical
JANISARY	*n* pl. -SARIES janizary
JANITOR	*n* pl. -S a maintenance man
JANIZARY	*n* pl. -ZARIES a Turkish soldier
JANTY	*adj* jaunty
JAPAN	*v* -PANNED, -PANNING, -PANS to coat with a glossy, black lacquer
JAPANIZE	*v* -NIZED, -NIZING, -NIZES to make Japanese
JAPANNER	*n* pl. -S one that japans
JAPANNING	present participle of japan
JAPE	*v* JAPED, JAPING, JAPES to mock
JAPER	*n* pl. -S one that japes
JAPERY	*n* pl. -ERIES mockery
JAPING	present participle of jape
JAPINGLY	*adv* in a japing manner
JAPONICA	*n* pl. -S an Asian shrub
JAR	*v* JARRED, JARRING, JARS to cause to shake
JARFUL	*n* pl. JARFULS or JARSFUL the quantity held by a jar (a cylindrical container)
JARGON	*v* -ED, -ING, -S to speak or write an obscure and often pretentious kind of language
JARGONEL	*n* pl. -S a variety of pear
JARGOON	*n* pl. -S a variety of zircon
JARHEAD	*n* pl. -S a marine soldier
JARINA	*n* pl. -S the hard seed of a palm tree
JARL	*n* pl. -S a Scandinavian nobleman
JARLDOM	*n* pl. -S the domain of a jarl
JAROSITE	*n* pl. -S a mineral
JAROVIZE	*v* -VIZED, -VIZING, -VIZES to hasten the flowering of a plant
JARRAH	*n* pl. -S an evergreen tree
JARRED	past tense of jar
JARRING	present participle of jar
JARSFUL	a pl. of jarful
JARVEY	*n* pl. -VEYS the driver of a carriage for hire
JASMIN	*n* pl. -S jasmine
JASMINE	*n* pl. -S a climbing shrub
JASPER	*n* pl. -S a variety of quartz **JASPERY** *adj*
JASSID	*n* pl. -S any of a family of plant pests
JATO	*n* pl. -TOS a takeoff aided by jet propulsion
JAUK	*v* -ED, -ING, -S to dawdle
JAUNCE	*v* JAUNCED, JAUNCING, JAUNCES to prance
JAUNDICE	*v* -DICED, -DICING, -DICES to prejudice unfavorably
JAUNT	*v* -ED, -ING, -S to make a pleasure trip
JAUNTY	*adj* -TIER, -TIEST having a lively and self-confident manner **JAUNTILY** *adv*
JAUP	*v* -ED, -ING, -S to splash
JAVA	*n* pl. -S coffee
JAVELIN	*v* -ED, -ING, -S to pierce with a javelin (a light spear)
JAVELINA	*n* pl. -S a peccary
JAW	*v* -ED, -ING, -S to jabber
JAWAN	*n* pl. -S a soldier of India
JAWBONE	*v* -BONED, -BONING, -BONES to attempt to convince

JAWBONER	*n* pl. -S one that jawbones
JAWLIKE	*adj* resembling the jaw (the framework of the mouth)
JAWLINE	*n* pl. -S the outline of the lower jaw
JAY	*n* pl. JAYS a corvine bird
JAYBIRD	*n* pl. -S a jay
JAYGEE	*n* pl. -S a military officer
JAYVEE	*n* pl. -S a junior varsity player
JAYWALK	*v* -ED, -ING, -S to cross a street recklessly
JAZZ	*v* -ED, -ING, -ES to enliven
JAZZER	*n* pl. -S one that jazzes
JAZZLIKE	*adj* resembling a type of music
JAZZMAN	*n* pl. -MEN a type of musician
JAZZY	*adj* JAZZIER, JAZZIEST lively **JAZZILY** *adv*
JEALOUS	*adj* resentful of another's advantages
JEALOUSY	*n* pl. -SIES a jealous feeling
JEAN	*n* pl. -S a durable cotton fabric
JEBEL	*n* pl. -S a mountain
JEE	*v* JEED, JEEING, JEES to gee
JEEP	*v* -ED, -ING, -S to travel by a small type of motor vehicle
JEEPERS	*interj* — used as a mild oath
JEEPNEY	*n* pl. -NEYS a Philippine jitney
JEER	*v* -ED, -ING, -S to mock
JEERER	*n* pl. -S one that jeers
JEEZ	*interj* — used as a mild oath
JEFE	*n* pl. -S a chief
JEHAD	*n* pl. -S jihad
JEHU	*n* pl. -S a fast driver
JEJUNA	pl. of jejunum
JEJUNAL	*adj* pertaining to the jejunum
JEJUNE	*adj* uninteresting; childish **JEJUNELY** *adv*
JEJUNITY	*n* pl. -TIES something that is jejune
JEJUNUM	*n* pl. -NA a part of the small intestine
JELL	*v* -ED, -ING, -S to congeal
JELLABA	*n* pl. -S djellaba
JELLIFY	*v* -FIED, -FYING, -FIES to jelly
JELLY	*v* -LIED, -LYING, -LIES to make into a jelly (a soft, semisolid substance)
JELUTONG	*n* pl. -S a tropical tree
JEMADAR	*n* pl. -S an officer in the army of India
JEMIDAR	*n* pl. -S jemadar
JEMMY	*v* -MIED, -MYING, -MIES to jimmy
JENNET	*n* pl. -S a small horse
JENNY	*n* pl. -NIES a female donkey
JEON	*n* pl. JEON a monetary unit of South Korea
JEOPARD	*v* -ED, -ING, -S to imperil
JEOPARDY	*n* pl. -DIES risk of loss or injury
JERBOA	*n* pl. -S a small rodent
JEREED	*n* pl. -S a wooden javelin
JEREMIAD	*n* pl. -S a tale of woe
JERID	*n* pl. -S jereed
JERK	*v* -ED, -ING, -S to move with a sharp, sudden motion
JERKER	*n* pl. -S one that jerks
JERKIES	pl. of jerky
JERKIN	*n* pl. -S a sleeveless jacket
JERKY	*adj* JERKIER, JERKIEST characterized by jerking movements **JERKILY** *adv*
JERKY	*n* pl. -KIES dried meat
JEROBOAM	*n* pl. -S a wine bottle
JERREED	*n* pl. -S jereed
JERRICAN	*n* pl. -S jerrycan
JERRID	*n* pl. -S jereed
JERRY	*n* pl. -RIES a German soldier
JERRYCAN	*n* pl. -S a fuel container
JERSEY	*n* pl. -SEYS a close-fitting knitted shirt **JERSEYED** *adj*
JESS	*v* -ED, -ING, -ES to fasten straps around the legs of a hawk
JESSANT	*adj* shooting forth
JESSE	*v* JESSED, JESSING, JESSES to jess
JEST	*v* -ED, -ING, -S to joke
JESTER	*n* pl. -S one that jests
JESTFUL	*adj* tending to jest
JESTING	*n* pl. -S the act of one who jests
JET	*v* JETTED, JETTING, JETS to spurt forth in a stream
JETBEAD	*n* pl. -S an ornamental shrub
JETE	*n* pl. -S a ballet leap
JETLIKE	*adj* resembling a jet airplane
JETLINER	*n* pl. -S a type of aircraft

JETON	*n* pl. -S jetton
JETPORT	*n* pl. -S a type of airport
JETSAM	*n* pl. -S goods cast overboard
JETSOM	*n* pl. -S jetsam
JETTED	past tense of jet
JETTIED	past tense of jetty
JETTIER	comparative of jetty
JETTIES	present 3d person sing. of jetty
JETTIEST	superlative of jetty
JETTING	present participle of jet
JETTISON	*v* -ED, -ING, -S to cast overboard
JETTON	*n* pl. -S a piece used in counting
JETTY	*v* -TIED, -TYING, -TIES to jut
JETTY	*adj* -TIER, -TIEST having the color jet black
JEU	*n* pl. JEUX a game
JEWEL	*v* -ELED, -ELING, -ELS or -ELLED, -ELLING, -ELS to adorn or equip with jewels (precious stones)
JEWELER	*n* pl. -S a dealer or maker of jewelry
JEWELLER	*n* pl. -S jeweler
JEWELLING	a present participle of jewel
JEWELRY	*n* pl. -RIES an article or articles for personal adornment
JEWFISH	*n* pl. -ES a large marine fish
JEZAIL	*n* pl. -S a type of firearm
JEZEBEL	*n* pl. -S a scheming, wicked woman
JIAO	*n* pl. JIAO chiao
JIB	*v* JIBBED, JIBBING, JIBS to refuse to proceed further
JIBB	*v* -ED, -ING, -S to shift from side to side while sailing
JIBBER	*n* pl. -S a horse that jibs
JIBBING	present participle of jib
JIBBOOM	*n* pl. -S a ship's spar
JIBE	*v* JIBED, JIBING, JIBES to gibe **JIBINGLY** *adv*
JIBER	*n* pl. -S one that jibes
JICAMA	*n* pl. -S a tropical plant with edible roots
JIFF	*n* pl. -S jiffy
JIFFY	*n* pl. -FIES a short time
JIG	*v* JIGGED, JIGGING, JIGS to bob
JIGGER	*v* -ED, -ING, -S to jerk up and down
JIGGERED	*adj* damned
JIGGING	present participle of jig
JIGGLE	*v* -GLED, -GLING, -GLES to shake lightly
JIGGLY	*adj* -GLIER, -GLIEST unsteady
JIGSAW	*v* -SAWED, -SAWN, -SAWING, -SAWS to cut with a type of saw
JIHAD	*n* pl. -S a Muslim holy war
JILL	*n* pl. -S a unit of liquid measure
JILLION	*n* pl. -S a very large number
JILT	*v* -ED, -ING, -S to reject a lover
JILTER	*n* pl. -S one that jilts
JIMINY	*interj* — used to express surprise
JIMJAMS	*n/pl* violent delirium
JIMMINY	*interj* jiminy
JIMMY	*v* -MIED, -MYING, -MIES to pry open with a crowbar
JIMP	*adj* JIMPER, JIMPEST natty **JIMPLY** *adv*
JIMPY	*adj* jimp
JIN	*n* pl. -S jinn
JINGAL	*n* pl. -S a heavy musket
JINGALL	*n* pl. -S jingal
JINGKO	*n* pl. -KOES ginkgo
JINGLE	*v* -GLED, -GLING, -GLES to make a tinkling sound
JINGLER	*n* pl. -S one that jingles
JINGLY	*adj* -GLIER, -GLIEST jingling
JINGO	*n* pl. -GOES a zealous patriot **JINGOISH** *adj*
JINGOISM	*n* pl. -S the spirit or policy of jingoes
JINGOIST	*n* pl. -S a jingo
JINK	*v* -ED, -ING, -S to move quickly out of the way
JINKER	*n* pl. -S one that jinks
JINN	*n* pl. -S a supernatural being in Muslim mythology
JINNEE	*n* pl. JINN jinn
JINNI	*n* pl. JINN jinn
JINX	*v* -ED, -ING, -ES to bring bad luck to
JIPIJAPA	*n* pl. -S a tropical plant
JITNEY	*n* pl. -NEYS a small bus
JITTER	*v* -ED, -ING, -S to fidget

JITTERY	*adj* -TERIER, -TERIEST extremely nervous
JIUJITSU	*n* pl. -S jujitsu
JIUJUTSU	*n* pl. -S jujitsu
JIVE	*v* JIVED, JIVING, JIVES to play jazz or swing music
JIVEASS	*adj* insincere, phony
JIVER	*n* pl. -S one that jives
JIVEY	*adj* JIVIER, JIVIEST jazzy, lively
JNANA	*n* pl. -S knowledge acquired through meditation
JO	*n* pl. JOES a sweetheart
JOANNES	*n* pl. JOANNES johannes
JOB	*v* JOBBED, JOBBING, JOBS to work by the piece
JOBBER	*n* pl. -S a pieceworker
JOBBERY	*n* pl. -BERIES corruption in public office
JOBBING	present participle of job
JOBLESS	*adj* having no job
JOBNAME	*n* pl. -S a computer code for a job instruction
JOCK	*n* pl. -S an athletic supporter
JOCKETTE	*n* pl. -S a woman who rides horses in races
JOCKEY	*v* -EYED, -EYING, -EYS to maneuver for an advantage
JOCKO	*n* pl. JOCKOS a monkey
JOCOSE	*adj* humorous **JOCOSELY** *adv*
JOCOSITY	*n* pl. -TIES the state of being jocose
JOCULAR	*adj* given to joking
JOCUND	*adj* cheerful **JOCUNDLY** *adv*
JODHPUR	*n* pl. -S a type of boot
JOE	*n* pl. -S a fellow
JOEY	*n* pl. -EYS a young kangaroo
JOG	*v* JOGGED, JOGGING, JOGS to run at a slow, steady pace
JOGGER	*n* pl. -S one that jogs
JOGGING	*n* pl. -S the practice of running at a slow, steady pace
JOGGLE	*v* -GLED, -GLING, -GLES to shake slightly
JOGGLER	*n* pl. -S one that joggles
JOHANNES	*n* pl. JOHANNES a Portuguese coin
JOHN	*n* pl. -S a toilet
JOHNBOAT	*n* pl. -S a narrow square-ended boat
JOHNNY	*n* pl. -NIES a sleeveless hospital gown
JOIN	*v* -ED, -ING, -S to unite **JOINABLE** *adj*
JOINDER	*n* pl. -S a joining of parties in a lawsuit
JOINER	*n* pl. -S a carpenter
JOINERY	*n* pl. -ERIES the trade of a joiner
JOINING	*n* pl. -S a juncture
JOINT	*v* -ED, -ING, -S to fit together by means of a junction
JOINTER	*n* pl. -S one that joints
JOINTLY	*adv* together
JOINTURE	*v* -TURED, -TURING, -TURES to set aside property as an inheritance
JOIST	*v* -ED, -ING, -S to support with horizontal beams
JOJOBA	*n* pl. -S a small tree
JOKE	*v* JOKED, JOKING, JOKES to say something amusing
JOKER	*n* pl. -S one that jokes
JOKESTER	*n* pl. -S a practical joker
JOKEY	*adj* JOKIER, JOKIEST amusing **JOKILY** *adv*
JOKIER	comparative of jokey
JOKIEST	superlative of jokey
JOKINESS	*n* pl. -ES the state of being jokey
JOKING	present participle of joke
JOKINGLY	*adv* in a joking manner
JOKY	*adj* JOKIER, JOKIEST jokey
JOLE	*n* pl. -S jowl
JOLLIED	past tense of jolly
JOLLIER	comparative of jolly
JOLLIES	present 3d person sing. of jolly
JOLLIEST	superlative of jolly
JOLLIFY	*v* -FIED, -FYING, -FIES to make jolly
JOLLITY	*n* pl. -TIES mirth
JOLLY	*adj* -LIER, -LIEST cheerful **JOLLILY** *adv*
JOLLY	*v* -LIED, -LYING, -LIES to put in a good humor for one's own purposes
JOLT	*v* -ED, -ING, -S to jar or shake roughly
JOLTER	*n* pl. -S one that jolts
JOLTY	*adj* JOLTIER, JOLTIEST marked by a jolting motion **JOLTILY** *adv*

JONES	*n* pl. JONESES a drug addiction
JONGLEUR	*n* pl. -S a minstrel
JONQUIL	*n* pl. -S a perennial herb
JORAM	*n* pl. -S jorum
JORDAN	*n* pl. -S a type of container
JORUM	*n* pl. -S a large drinking bowl
JOSEPH	*n* pl. -S a woman's long cloak
JOSH	*v* -ED, -ING, -ES to tease
JOSHER	*n* pl. -S one that joshes
JOSS	*n* pl. -ES a Chinese idol
JOSTLE	*v* -TLED, -TLING, -TLES to bump or push roughly
JOSTLER	*n* pl. -S one that jostles
JOT	*v* JOTTED, JOTTING, JOTS to write down quickly
JOTA	*n* pl. -S a Spanish dance
JOTTER	*n* pl. -S one that jots
JOTTING	*n* pl. -S a brief note
JOTTY	*adj* written down quickly
JOUAL	*n* pl. -S a dialect of Canadian French
JOUK	*v* -ED, -ING, -S to dodge
JOULE	*n* pl. -S a unit of energy
JOUNCE	*v* JOUNCED, JOUNCING, JOUNCES to move roughly up and down
JOUNCY	*adj* JOUNCIER, JOUNCIEST marked by a jouncing motion
JOURNAL	*n* pl. -S a record of daily events
JOURNEY	*v* -ED, -ING, -S to travel
JOUST	*v* -ED, -ING, -S to engage in personal combat
JOUSTER	*n* pl. -S one that jousts
JOVIAL	*adj* good-humored **JOVIALLY** *adv*
JOVIALTY	*n* pl. -TIES the quality or state of being jovial
JOW	*v* -ED, -ING, -S to toll
JOWAR	*n* pl. -S a durra grown in India
JOWL	*n* pl. -S the fleshy part under the lower jaw **JOWLED** *adj*
JOWLY	*adj* JOWLIER, JOWLIEST having prominent jowls
JOY	*v* -ED, -ING, -S to rejoice
JOYANCE	*n* pl. -S gladness
JOYFUL	*adj* -FULLER, -FULLEST happy **JOYFULLY** *adv*
JOYLESS	*adj* being without gladness
JOYOUS	*adj* joyful **JOYOUSLY** *adv*
JOYPOP	*v* -POPPED, -POPPING, -POPS to use habit-forming drugs occasionally
JOYRIDE	*v* -RODE, -RIDDEN, -RIDING, -RIDES to take an automobile ride for pleasure
JOYRIDER	*n* pl. -S one that joyrides
JOYSTICK	*n* pl. -S the control stick in an airplane
JUBA	*n* pl. -S a lively dance
JUBBAH	*n* pl. -S a loose outer garment
JUBE	*n* pl. -S a platform in a church
JUBHAH	*n* pl. -S jubbah
JUBILANT	*adj* exultant
JUBILATE	*v* -LATED, -LATING, -LATES to exult
JUBILE	*n* pl. -S jubilee
JUBILEE	*n* pl. -S a celebration
JUDAS	*n* pl. -ES a peephole
JUDDER	*v* -ED, -ING, -S to vibrate
JUDGE	*v* JUDGED, JUDGING, JUDGES to decide on critically
JUDGER	*n* pl. -S one that judges
JUDGMENT	*n* pl. -S an authoritative opinion
JUDICIAL	*adj* pertaining to courts of law
JUDO	*n* pl. -DOS a form of jujitsu
JUDOIST	*n* pl. -S one skilled in judo
JUDOKA	*n* pl. -S a judoist
JUG	*v* JUGGED, JUGGING, JUGS to put into a jug (a large, deep container with a narrow mouth and a handle)
JUGA	a pl. of jugum
JUGAL	*adj* pertaining to the cheek or cheekbone
JUGATE	*adj* occurring in pairs
JUGFUL	*n* pl. JUGFULS or JUGSFUL as much as a jug will hold
JUGGED	past tense of jug
JUGGING	present participle of jug
JUGGLE	*v* -GLED, -GLING, -GLES to perform feats of manual dexterity
JUGGLER	*n* pl. -S one that juggles
JUGGLERY	*n* pl. -GLERIES the art of a juggler
JUGGLING	*n* pl. -S jugglery
JUGHEAD	*n* pl. -S a dolt
JUGSFUL	a pl. of jugful

JUGULA	pl. of jugulum
JUGULAR	*n* pl. -S a vein of the neck
JUGULATE	*v* -LATED, -LATING, -LATES to suppress a disease by extreme measures
JUGULUM	*n* pl. -LA a part of a bird's neck
JUGUM	*n* pl. -GA or -GUMS a pair of the opposite leaflets of a pinnate leaf
JUICE	*v* JUICED, JUICING, JUICES to extract the juice (the liquid part of a fruit or vegetable) from
JUICER	*n* pl. -S a juice extractor
JUICY	*adj* JUICIER, JUICIEST full of juice **JUICILY** *adv*
JUJITSU	*n* pl. -S a Japanese art of self-defense
JUJU	*n* pl. -S an object regarded as having magical power
JUJUBE	*n* pl. -S a fruit-flavored candy
JUJUISM	*n* pl. -S the system of beliefs connected with jujus
JUJUIST	*n* pl. -S a follower of jujuism
JUJUTSU	*n* pl. -S jujitsu
JUKE	*v* JUKED, JUKING, JUKES to fake out of position
JUKEBOX	*n* pl. -ES a coin-operated phonograph
JULEP	*n* pl. -S a sweet drink
JULIENNE	*v* -ENNED, -ENNING, -ENNES to cut food into long thin strips
JUMBAL	*n* pl. -S a ring-shaped cookie
JUMBLE	*v* -BLED, -BLING, -BLES to mix in a disordered manner
JUMBLER	*n* pl. -S one that jumbles
JUMBO	*n* pl. -BOS a very large specimen of its kind
JUMBUCK	*n* pl. -S a sheep
JUMP	*v* -ED, -ING, -S to spring off the ground
JUMPER	*n* pl. -S one that jumps
JUMPOFF	*n* pl. -S a starting point
JUMPSUIT	*n* pl. -S a one-piece garment
JUMPY	*adj* JUMPIER, JUMPIEST nervous **JUMPILY** *adv*
JUN	*n* pl. JUN a coin of North Korea
JUNCO	*n* pl. -COS or -COES a small finch
JUNCTION	*n* pl. -S a place where things join
JUNCTURE	*n* pl. -S the act of joining
JUNGLE	*n* pl. -S land covered with dense tropical vegetation **JUNGLED** *adj*
JUNGLY	*adj* -GLIER, -GLIEST resembling a jungle
JUNIOR	*n* pl. -S a person who is younger than another
JUNIPER	*n* pl. -S an evergreen tree
JUNK	*v* -ED, -ING, -S to discard as trash
JUNKER	*n* pl. -S something ready for junking
JUNKET	*v* -ED, -ING, -S to banquet
JUNKETER	*n* pl. -S one that junkets
JUNKIE	*n* pl. -S a drug addict
JUNKMAN	*n* pl. -MEN one who buys and sells junk
JUNKY	*adj* JUNKIER, JUNKIEST worthless
JUNKYARD	*n* pl. -S a place where junk is stored
JUNTA	*n* pl. -S a political or governmental council
JUNTO	*n* pl. -TOS a political faction
JUPE	*n* pl. -S a woman's jacket
JUPON	*n* pl. -S a tunic
JURA	pl. of jus
JURAL	*adj* pertaining to law **JURALLY** *adv*
JURANT	*n* pl. -S one that takes an oath
JURAT	*n* pl. -S a statement on an affidavit
JURATORY	*adj* pertaining to an oath
JUREL	*n* pl. -S a food fish
JURIDIC	*adj* pertaining to the law
JURIST	*n* pl. -S one versed in the law **JURISTIC** *adj*
JUROR	*n* pl. -S a member of a jury
JURY	*v* -RIED, -RYING, -RIES to select material for exhibition
JURYMAN	*n* pl. -MEN a juror
JUS	*n* pl. JURA a legal right
JUSSIVE	*n* pl. -S a word used to express command
JUST	*v* -ED, -ING, -S to joust
JUST	*adj* JUSTER, JUSTEST acting in conformity with what is morally good
JUSTER	*n* pl. -S jouster
JUSTICE	*n* pl. -S a judge

JUSTIFY	*v* -FIED, -FYING, -FIES to show to be just, right, or valid
JUSTLE	*v* -TLED, -TLING, -TLES to jostle
JUSTLY	*adv* in a just manner
JUSTNESS	*n* pl. -ES the quality of being just

JUT	*v* JUTTED, JUTTING, JUTS to protrude
JUTE	*n* pl. -S a strong, coarse fiber
JUTTY	*v* -TIED, -TYING, -TIES to jut
JUVENAL	*n* pl. -S a young bird's plumage
JUVENILE	*n* pl. -S a young person

KA	*n* pl. -S the spiritual self of a human being in Egyptian religion
KAAS	*n* pl. KAAS kas
KAB	*n* pl. -S an ancient Hebrew unit of measure
KABAB	*n* pl. -S kabob
KABAKA	*n* pl. -S a Ugandan emperor
KABALA	*n* pl. -S cabala
KABAR	*n* pl. -S caber
KABAYA	*n* pl. -S a cotton jacket
KABBALA	*n* pl. -S cabala
KABBALAH	*n* pl. -S cabala
KABELJOU	*n* pl. -S a large food fish
KABIKI	*n* pl. -S a tropical tree
KABOB	*n* pl. -S cubes of meat cooked on a skewer
KABUKI	*n* pl. -S a form of Japanese theater
KACHINA	*n* pl. -S an ancestral spirit
KADDISH	*n* pl. -DISHIM a Jewish prayer
KADI	*n* pl. -S cadi
KAE	*n* pl. -S a bird resembling a crow
KAF	*n* pl. -S kaph
KAFFIR	*n* pl. -S kafir
KAFFIYEH	*n* pl. -S a large, square kerchief
KAFIR	*n* pl. -S a cereal grass
KAFTAN	*n* pl. -S caftan
KAGU	*n* pl. -S a flightless bird
KAHUNA	*n* pl. -S a medicine man
KAIAK	*n* pl. -S kayak
KAIF	*n* pl. -S kef
KAIL	*n* pl. -S kale
KAILYARD	*n* pl. -S kaleyard
KAIN	*n* pl. -S a tax paid in produce or livestock
KAINIT	*n* pl. -S kainite
KAINITE	*n* pl. -S a mineral salt
KAISER	*n* pl. -S an emperor
KAISERIN	*n* pl. -S a kaiser's wife
KAJEPUT	*n* pl. -S cajuput
KAKA	*n* pl. -S a parrot
KAKAPO	*n* pl. -POS a flightless parrot
KAKEMONO	*n* pl. -NOS a Japanese scroll
KAKI	*n* pl. -S a Japanese tree
KAKIEMON	*n* pl. -S a Japanese porcelain
KALAM	*n* pl. -S a type of Muslim theology
KALE	*n* pl. -S a variety of cabbage
KALENDS	*n* pl. KALENDS calends
KALEWIFE	*n* pl. -WIVES a female vegetable vendor
KALEYARD	*n* pl. -S a kitchen garden
KALIAN	*n* pl. -S a hookah
KALIF	*n* pl. -S caliph
KALIFATE	*n* pl. -S califate
KALIMBA	*n* pl. -S an African musical instrument
KALIPH	*n* pl. -S caliph
KALIUM	*n* pl. -S potassium
KALLIDIN	*n* pl. -S a hormone
KALMIA	*n* pl. -S an evergreen shrub
KALONG	*n* pl. -S a fruit-eating bat
KALPA	*n* pl. -S a period of time in Hindu religion
KALPAK	*n* pl. -S calpac
KALYPTRA	*n* pl. -S a thin veil
KAMAAINA	*n* pl. -S a longtime resident of Hawaii
KAMACITE	*n* pl. -S an alloy of nickel and iron
KAMALA	*n* pl. -S an Asian tree
KAME	*n* pl. -S a mound of detrital material

KAMI	*n* pl. KAMI a sacred power or force
KAMIK	*n* pl. -S a type of boot
KAMIKAZE	*n* pl. -S a plane to be flown in a suicide crash on a target
KAMPONG	*n* pl. -S a small village
KAMSEEN	*n* pl. -S khamsin
KAMSIN	*n* pl. -S khamsin
KANA	*n* pl. -S the Japanese syllabic script
KANBAN	*n* pl. -S a manufacturing strategy wherein parts are delivered only as needed
KANE	*n* pl. -S kain
KANGAROO	*n* pl. -ROOS an Australian mammal
KANJI	*n* pl. -S a system of Japanese writing
KANTAR	*n* pl. -S a unit of weight
KANTELE	*n* pl. -S a type of harp
KAOLIANG	*n* pl. -S an Asian sorghum
KAOLIN	*n* pl. -S a fine white clay **KAOLINIC** *adj*
KAOLINE	*n* pl. -S kaolin
KAON	*n* pl. -S a type of meson
KAPA	*n* pl. -S a coarse cloth
KAPH	*n* pl. -S a Hebrew letter
KAPOK	*n* pl. -S a mass of silky fibers
KAPPA	*n* pl. -S a Greek letter
KAPUT	*adj* ruined
KAPUTT	*adj* kaput
KARAKUL	*n* pl. -S an Asian sheep
KARAOKE	*n* pl. -S a musical device to which a user sings along
KARAT	*n* pl. -S a unit of quality for gold
KARATE	*n* pl. -S a Japanese art of self-defense
KARMA	*n* pl. -S the force generated by a person's actions **KARMIC** *adj*
KARN	*n* pl. -S cairn
KAROO	*n* pl. -ROOS karroo
KAROSS	*n* pl. -ES an African garment
KARROO	*n* pl. -ROOS a dry plateau
KARST	*n* pl. -S a limestone region **KARSTIC** *adj*
KART	*n* pl. -S a small motor vehicle
KARTING	*n* pl. -S the sport of racing karts
KARYOTIN	*n* pl. -S the nuclear material of a cell
KAS	*n* pl. KAS a large cupboard
KASBAH	*n* pl. -S casbah
KASHA	*n* pl. -S a cooked cereal
KASHER	*v* -ED, -ING, -S to kosher
KASHMIR	*n* pl. -S cashmere
KASHRUT	*n* pl. -S kashruth
KASHRUTH	*n* pl. -S the Jewish dietary laws
KAT	*n* pl. -S an evergreen shrub
KATA	*n* pl. -S an exercise of set movements
KATAKANA	*n* pl. -S a Japanese syllabic symbol
KATCHINA	*n* pl. -S kachina
KATCINA	*n* pl. -S kachina
KATHODE	*n* pl. -S cathode **KATHODAL, KATHODIC** *adj*
KATION	*n* pl. -S cation
KATYDID	*n* pl. -S a grasshopper
KAURI	*n* pl. -S a timber tree
KAURY	*n* pl. -RIES kauri
KAVA	*n* pl. -S a tropical shrub
KAVAKAVA	*n* pl. -S kava
KAVASS	*n* pl. -ES a Turkish policeman
KAY	*n* pl. KAYS the letter K
KAYAK	*v* -ED, -ING, -S to travel in a kayak (an Eskimo canoe)
KAYAKER	*n* pl. -S one that rides in a kayak
KAYAKING	*n* pl. -S the act or skill of managing a kayak
KAYLES	*n/pl* a British game
KAYO	*v* -ED, -ING, -S or -ES to knock out
KAZACHOK	*n* pl. -ZACHKI a Russian folk dance
KAZATSKI	*n* pl. -ES kazachok
KAZATSKY	*n* pl. -SKIES kazachok
KAZOO	*n* pl. -ZOOS a toy musical instrument
KBAR	*n* pl. -S a kilobar
KEA	*n* pl. -S a parrot
KEBAB	*n* pl. -S kabob
KEBAR	*n* pl. -S caber
KEBBIE	*n* pl. -S a rough walking stick
KEBBOCK	*n* pl. -S kebbuck
KEBBUCK	*n* pl. -S a whole cheese

KEBLAH	*n* pl. -S kiblah
KEBOB	*n* pl. -S kabob
KECK	*v* -ED, -ING, -S to retch
KECKLE	*v* -LED, -LING, -LES to wind with rope to prevent chafing
KEDDAH	*n* pl. -S an enclosure for elephants
KEDGE	*v* KEDGED, KEDGING, KEDGES to move a vessel with the use of an anchor
KEDGEREE	*n* pl. -S a food in India
KEEF	*n* pl. -S kef
KEEK	*v* -ED, -ING, -S to peep
KEEL	*v* -ED, -ING, -S to capsize
KEELAGE	*n* pl. -S the amount paid to keep a boat in a harbor
KEELBOAT	*n* pl. -S a freight boat
KEELHALE	*v* -HALED, -HALING, -HALES to keelhaul
KEELHAUL	*v* -ED, -ING, -S to rebuke severely
KEELLESS	*adj* having no keel (the main structural part of a ship)
KEELSON	*n* pl. -S a beam in a ship
KEEN	*adj* KEENER, KEENEST enthusiastic
KEEN	*v* -ED, -ING, -S to wail loudly over the dead
KEENER	*n* pl. -S one that keens
KEENLY	*adv* in a keen manner
KEENNESS	*n* pl. -ES sharpness
KEEP	*v* KEPT, KEEPING, KEEPS to continue to possess **KEEPABLE** *adj*
KEEPER	*n* pl. -S one that keeps
KEEPING	*n* pl. -S custody
KEEPSAKE	*n* pl. -S a memento
KEESHOND	*n* pl. -HONDS or -HONDEN a small, heavy-coated dog
KEESTER	*n* pl. -S keister
KEET	*n* pl. -S a young guinea fowl
KEEVE	*n* pl. -S a tub or vat
KEF	*n* pl. -S hemp smoked to produce euphoria
KEFFIYEH	*n* pl. -S kaffiyeh
KEFIR	*n* pl. -S a fermented beverage made from cow's milk
KEG	*n* pl. -S a small barrel
KEGELER	*n* pl. -S kegler
KEGLER	*n* pl. -S a bowler
KEGLING	*n* pl. -S bowling
KEIR	*n* pl. -S kier
KEISTER	*n* pl. -S the buttocks
KEITLOA	*n* pl. -S a rhinoceros
KELEP	*n* pl. -S a stinging ant
KELIM	*n* pl. -S kilim
KELLY	*n* pl. -LIES a bright green color
KELOID	*n* pl. -S a scar caused by excessive growth of fibrous tissue **KELOIDAL** *adj*
KELP	*v* -ED, -ING, -S to burn a type of seaweed
KELPIE	*n* pl. -S a water sprite
KELPY	*n* pl. -PIES kelpie
KELSON	*n* pl. -S keelson
KELTER	*n* pl. -S kilter
KELVIN	*n* pl. -S a unit of temperature
KEMP	*n* pl. -S a champion
KEMPT	*adj* neatly kept
KEN	*v* KENNED or KENT, KENNING, KENS to know
KENAF	*n* pl. -S an East Indian plant
KENCH	*n* pl. -ES a bin for salting fish
KENDO	*n* pl. -DOS a Japanese sport
KENNED	a past tense of ken
KENNEL	*v* -NELED, -NELING, -NELS or -NELLED, -NELLING, -NELS to keep in a shelter for dogs
KENNING	*n* pl. -S a metaphorical compound word or phrase
KENO	*n* pl. -NOS a game of chance
KENOSIS	*n* pl. -SISES the incarnation of Christ **KENOTIC** *adj*
KENOTRON	*n* pl. -S a type of diode
KENT	a past tense of ken
KEP	*v* KEPPED, KEPPEN or KIPPEN, KEPPING, KEPS to catch
KEPHALIN	*n* pl. -S cephalin
KEPI	*n* pl. -S a type of cap
KEPPED	past tense of kep
KEPPEN	a past participle of kep
KEPPING	present participle of kep
KEPT	past tense of keep
KERAMIC	*n* pl. -S ceramic
KERATIN	*n* pl. -S a fibrous protein
KERATOID	*adj* horny

KERATOMA   *n* pl. -MAS or -MATA a skin disease

KERATOSE   *adj* of or resembling horny tissue

KERB   *v* -ED, -ING, -S to provide with curbing

KERCHIEF   *n* pl. -CHIEFS or -CHIEVES a cloth worn as a head covering

KERCHOO   *interj* ahchoo

KERF   *v* -ED, -ING, -S to make an incision with a cutting tool

KERMES   *n* pl. KERMES a red dye

KERMESS   *n* pl. -ES kermis

KERMESSE   *n* pl. -S kermis

KERMIS   *n* pl. -MISES a local outdoor festival

KERN   *v* -ED, -ING, -S to be formed with a projecting typeface

KERNE   *n* pl. -S a medieval foot soldier

KERNEL   *v* -NELED, -NELING, -NELS or -NELLED, -NELLING, -NELS to envelop as a kernel (the inner part of a nut)

KERNITE   *n* pl. -S a mineral

KEROGEN   *n* pl. -S a substance found in shale

KEROSENE   *n* pl. -S a fuel oil

KEROSINE   *n* pl. -S kerosene

KERPLUNK   *v* -ED, -ING, -S to fall or drop with a heavy sound

KERRIA   *n* pl. -S a Chinese shrub

KERRY   *n* pl. -RIES one of an Irish breed of cattle

KERSEY   *n* pl. -SEYS a woolen cloth

KERYGMA   *n* pl. -MATA the preaching of the gospel

KESTREL   *n* pl. -S a small falcon

KETCH   *n* pl. -ES a sailing vessel

KETCHUP   *n* pl. -S a spicy tomato sauce

KETENE   *n* pl. -S a toxic gas

KETO   *adj* of or pertaining to ketone

KETOL   *n* pl. -S a chemical compound

KETONE   *n* pl. -S a type of chemical compound **KETONIC** *adj*

KETOSE   *n* pl. -S a simple sugar

KETOSIS   *n* pl. -TOSES a buildup of ketones in the body **KETOTIC** *adj*

KETTLE   *n* pl. -S a vessel for boiling liquids

KEVEL   *n* pl. -S a belaying cleat or peg

KEVIL   *n* pl. -S kevel

KEX   *n* pl. -ES a dry, hollow stalk

KEY   *v* -ED, -ING, -S to provide with a key (a device used to turn the bolt in a lock)

KEYBOARD   *v* -ED, -ING, -S to operate a machine by means of a keyset

KEYCARD   *n* pl. -S a coded card for operating a device

KEYHOLE   *n* pl. -S a hole for a key

KEYLESS   *adj* being without a key

KEYNOTE   *v* -NOTED, -NOTING, -NOTES to deliver the main speech at a function

KEYNOTER   *n* pl. -S one that keynotes

KEYPAD   *n* pl. -S a small keyboard

KEYPUNCH   *v* -ED, -ING, -ES to perforate with a machine

KEYSET   *n* pl. -S a system of finger levers

KEYSTER   *n* pl. -S keister

KEYSTONE   *n* pl. -S the central stone of an arch

KEYWAY   *n* pl. -WAYS a slot for a key

KEYWORD   *n* pl. -S a significant word

KHADDAR   *n* pl. -S a cotton cloth

KHADI   *n* pl. -S khaddar

KHAF   *n* pl. -S kaph

KHAKI   *n* pl. -S a durable cloth

KHALIF   *n* pl. -S caliph

KHALIFA   *n* pl. -S caliph

KHAMSEEN   *n* pl. -S khamsin

KHAMSIN   *n* pl. -S a hot, dry wind

KHAN   *n* pl. -S an Asian ruler

KHANATE   *n* pl. -S the domain of a khan

KHAPH   *n* pl. -S kaph

KHAT   *n* pl. -S kat

KHAZEN   *n* pl. -ZENS or -ZENIM hazzan

KHEDA   *n* pl. -S keddah

KHEDAH   *n* pl. -S keddah

KHEDIVE   *n* pl. -S a Turkish viceroy **KHEDIVAL** *adj*

KHET   *n* pl. -S heth

KHETH   *n* pl. -S heth

KHI   *n* pl. -S chi

KHIRKAH   *n* pl. -S a patchwork garment

KHOUM   *n* pl. -S a monetary unit of Mauritania

KIANG	*n* pl. -S a wild ass
KIAUGH	*n* pl. -S trouble; worry
KIBBE	*n* pl. -S a Near Eastern dish of ground lamb and bulgur
KIBBEH	*n* pl. -S kibbe
KIBBI	*n* pl. -S kibbe
KIBBITZ	*v* -ED, -ING, -ES kibitz
KIBBLE	*v* -BLED, -BLING, -BLES to grind coarsely
KIBBUTZ	*n* pl. -BUTZIM a collective farm in Israel
KIBE	*n* pl. -S a sore caused by exposure to cold
KIBEI	*n* pl. -S one born in America of immigrant Japanese parents and educated in Japan
KIBITZ	*v* -ED, -ING, -ES to meddle
KIBITZER	*n* pl. -S one that kibitzes
KIBLA	*n* pl. -S kiblah
KIBLAH	*n* pl. -S the direction toward which Muslims face while praying
KIBOSH	*v* -ED, -ING, -ES to stop
KICK	*v* -ED, -ING, -S to strike out with the foot or feet **KICKABLE** *adj*
KICKBACK	*n* pl. -S a strong reaction
KICKBALL	*n* pl. -S baseball using an inflated ball that is kicked
KICKER	*n* pl. -S one that kicks
KICKIER	comparative of kicky
KICKIEST	superlative of kicky
KICKOFF	*n* pl. -S the kick that begins play in football
KICKSHAW	*n* pl. -S a trifle or trinket
KICKUP	*n* pl. -S a noisy argument
KICKY	*adj* KICKIER, KICKIEST exciting
KID	*v* KIDDED, KIDDING, KIDS to tease
KIDDER	*n* pl. -S one that kids
KIDDIE	*n* pl. -S a small child
KIDDIES	pl. of kiddy
KIDDING	present participle of kid
KIDDISH	*adj* childish
KIDDO	*n* pl. -DOS or -DOES — used as a form of familiar address
KIDDUSH	*n* pl. -ES a Jewish prayer
KIDDY	*n* pl. -DIES kiddie
KIDLIKE	*adj* resembling a child
KIDNAP	*v* -NAPED, -NAPING, -NAPS or -NAPPED, -NAPPING, -NAPS to take a person by force and often for ransom
KIDNAPEE	*n* pl. -S one that is kidnaped
KIDNAPER	*n* pl. -S one that kidnaps
KIDNAPPER	*n* pl. -S kidnaper
KIDNAPPING	present participle of kidnap
KIDNEY	*n* pl. -NEYS a bodily organ
KIDSKIN	*n* pl. -S a type of leather
KIDVID	*n* pl. -S television programs for children
KIEF	*n* pl. -S kef
KIELBASA	*n* pl. -BASAS, -BASI, or -BASY a smoked sausage
KIER	*n* pl. -S a vat for boiling and dyeing fabrics
KIESTER	*n* pl. -S keister
KIF	*n* pl. -S kef
KILIM	*n* pl. -S an oriental tapestry
KILL	*v* -ED, -ING, -S to cause to die
KILLDEE	*n* pl. -S killdeer
KILLDEER	*n* pl. -S a wading bird
KILLER	*n* pl. -S one that kills
KILLICK	*n* pl. -S a small anchor
KILLIE	*n* pl. -S a freshwater fish
KILLING	*n* pl. -S a sudden notable success
KILLJOY	*n* pl. -JOYS one who spoils the fun of others
KILLOCK	*n* pl. -S killick
KILN	*v* -ED, -ING, -S to bake in a type of oven
KILO	*n* pl. KILOS a kilogram or kilometer
KILOBAR	*n* pl. -S a unit of atmospheric pressure
KILOBASE	*n* pl. -S unit of measure of a nucleic-acid chain
KILOBAUD	*n* pl. -S a unit of data transmission speed
KILOBIT	*n* pl. -S a unit of computer information
KILOBYTE	*n* pl. -S 1,024 bytes
KILOGRAM	*n* pl. -S a unit of mass and weight
KILOMOLE	*n* pl. -S one thousand moles
KILORAD	*n* pl. -S a unit of nuclear radiation
KILOTON	*n* pl. -S a unit of weight

KILOVOLT	*n* pl. -S a unit of electromotive force
KILOWATT	*n* pl. -S a unit of power
KILT	*v* -ED, -ING, -S to make creases or pleats in
KILTER	*n* pl. -S good condition
KILTIE	*n* pl. -S one who wears a kilt (a type of skirt)
KILTING	*n* pl. -S an arrangement of kilt pleats
KILTY	*n* pl. KILTIES kiltie
KIMCHEE	*n* pl. -S kimchi
KIMCHI	*n* pl. -S a spicy Korean dish of pickled cabbage
KIMONO	*n* pl. -NOS a loose robe **KIMONOED** *adj*
KIN	*n* pl. -S a group of persons of common ancestry
KINA	*n* pl. -S a monetary unit of Papua New Guinea
KINASE	*n* pl. -S an enzyme
KIND	*adj* KINDER, KINDEST having a gentle, giving nature
KIND	*n* pl. -S a class of similar or related objects or individuals
KINDLE	*v* -DLED, -DLING, -DLES to cause to burn
KINDLER	*n* pl. -S one that kindles
KINDLESS	*adj* lacking kindness
KINDLING	*n* pl. -S material that is easily ignited
KINDLY	*adj* -LIER, -LIEST kind
KINDNESS	*n* pl. -ES the quality of being kind
KINDRED	*n* pl. -S a natural grouping
KINE	*n* pl. -S a type of television tube
KINEMA	*n* pl. -S cinema
KINESIC	*adj* pertaining to kinesics
KINESICS	*n/pl* the study of body motion in relation to communication
KINESIS	*n* pl. -NESES a type of movement
KINETIC	*adj* pertaining to motion
KINETICS	*n/pl* a branch of science dealing with motion
KINETIN	*n* pl. -S a substance that increases plant growth
KINFOLK	*n/pl* relatives
KINFOLKS	*n/pl* kinfolk
KING	*v* -ED, -ING, -S to reign as king (a male monarch)
KINGBIRD	*n* pl. -S an American bird
KINGBOLT	*n* pl. -S a kingpin
KINGCUP	*n* pl. -S a marsh plant
KINGDOM	*n* pl. -S the area ruled by a king
KINGFISH	*n* pl. -ES a marine food fish
KINGHOOD	*n* pl. -S the office of a king
KINGLESS	*adj* having no king
KINGLET	*n* pl. -S a king who rules over a small area
KINGLIKE	*adj* resembling a king
KINGLY	*adj* -LIER, -LIEST of or befitting a king
KINGPIN	*n* pl. -S a central bolt connecting an axle to a vehicle
KINGPOST	*n* pl. -S a supporting structure of a roof
KINGSHIP	*n* pl. -S the power or position of a king
KINGSIDE	*n* pl. -S a part of a chessboard
KINGWOOD	*n* pl. -S a hardwood tree
KININ	*n* pl. -S a hormone
KINK	*v* -ED, -ING, -S to form a tight curl or bend in
KINKAJOU	*n* pl. -S an arboreal mammal
KINKY	*adj* KINKIER, KINKIEST tightly curled **KINKILY** *adv*
KINO	*n* pl. -NOS a gum resin
KINSFOLK	*n/pl* kinfolk
KINSHIP	*n* pl. -S relationship
KINSMAN	*n* pl. -MEN a male relative
KIOSK	*n* pl. -S an open booth
KIP	*v* KIPPED, KIPPING, KIPS to sleep
KIPPEN	a past participle of kep
KIPPER	*v* -ED, -ING, -S to cure fish by salting and smoking
KIPPERER	*n* pl. -S one that kippers
KIPPING	present participle of kip
KIPSKIN	*n* pl. -S an animal hide that has not been tanned
KIR	*n* pl. -S an alcoholic beverage
KIRIGAMI	*n* pl. -S the Japanese art of folding paper
KIRK	*n* pl. -S a church
KIRKMAN	*n* pl. -MEN a member of a church
KIRMESS	*n* pl. -ES kermis
KIRN	*v* -ED, -ING, -S to churn
KIRSCH	*n* pl. -ES a kind of brandy

KIRTLE | *n* pl. -S a man's tunic or coat **KIRTLED** *adj*

KISHKA | *n* pl. -S kishke

KISHKE | *n* pl. -S a sausage

KISMAT | *n* pl. -S kismet

KISMET | *n* pl. -S destiny **KISMETIC** *adj*

KISS | *v* -ED, -ING, -ES to touch with the lips as a sign of affection **KISSABLE** *adj* **KISSABLY** *adv*

KISSER | *n* pl. -S one that kisses

KISSY | *adj* inclined to kiss

KIST | *n* pl. -S a chest, box, or coffin

KISTFUL | *n* pl. -S as much as a kist can hold

KIT | *v* KITTED, KITTING, KITS to equip

KITCHEN | *n* pl. -S a room where food is cooked

KITE | *v* KITED, KITING, KITES to obtain money or credit fraudulently

KITELIKE | *adj* resembling a kite (a light, covered frame flown in the wind)

KITER | *n* pl. -S one that kites

KITH | *n* pl. -S one's friends and neighbors

KITHARA | *n* pl. -S cithara

KITHE | *v* KITHED, KITHING, KITHES to make known

KITING | present participle of kite

KITLING | *n* pl. -S a young animal

KITSCH | *n* pl. -ES faddish art or literature **KITSCHY** *adj*

KITTED | past tense of kit

KITTEL | *n* pl. KITTEL a Jewish ceremonial robe

KITTEN | *v* -ED, -ING, -ES to bear kittens (young cats)

KITTIES | pl. of kitty

KITTING | present participle of kit

KITTLE | *v* -TLED, -TLING, -TLES to tickle

KITTLE | *adj* -TLER, -TLEST ticklish

KITTY | *n* pl. -TIES a kitten or cat

KIVA | *n* pl. -S an underground ceremonial chamber

KIWI | *n* pl. -S a flightless bird

KLATCH | *n* pl. -ES a social gathering

KLATSCH | *n* pl. -ES klatch

KLAVERN | *n* pl. -S a local branch of the Ku Klux Klan

KLAXON | *n* pl. -S a low-pitched horn

KLEAGLE | *n* pl. -S an official in the Ku Klux Klan

KLEPHT | *n* pl. -S a Greek guerrilla **KLEPHTIC** *adj*

KLEZMER | *n* pl. -MORIM a Jewish folk musician

KLISTER | *n* pl. -S a wax for skis

KLONG | *n* pl. -S a canal

KLOOF | *n* pl. -S a ravine

KLUDGE | *n* pl. -S a system composed of ill-fitting components

KLUGE | *n* pl. -S kludge

KLUTZ | *n* pl. -ES a clumsy person

KLUTZY | *adj* KLUTZIER, KLUTZIEST clumsy

KLYSTRON | *n* pl. -S a type of electron tube

KNACK | *v* -ED, -ING, -S to strike sharply

KNACKER | *n* pl. -S one that buys old livestock

KNACKERY | *n* pl. -ERIES the place of business of a knacker

KNAP | *v* KNAPPED, KNAPPING, KNAPS to strike sharply

KNAPPER | *n* pl. -S one that knaps

KNAPSACK | *n* pl. -S a bag carried on the back

KNAPWEED | *n* pl. -S a meadow plant

KNAR | *n* pl. -S a bump on a tree **KNARRED, KNARRY** *adj*

KNAUR | *n* pl. -S knar

KNAVE | *n* pl. -S a dishonest person **KNAVISH** *adj*

KNAVERY | *n* pl. -ERIES trickery

KNAWEL | *n* pl. -S a Eurasian plant

KNEAD | *v* -ED, -ING, -S to work into a uniform mixture with the hands

KNEADER | *n* pl. -S one that kneads

KNEE | *v* KNEED, KNEEING, KNEES to strike with the knee (a joint of the leg)

KNEECAP | *v* -CAPPED, -CAPPING, -CAPS to maim by shooting in the kneecap (a bone at the front of the knee)

KNEEHOLE | *n* pl. -S a space for the knees

KNEEL | *v* KNELT or KNEELED, KNEELING, KNEELS to rest on the knees

KNEELER | *n* pl. -S one that kneels

KNEEPAD	*n* pl. -S a covering for a knee		**KNOTTED**	past tense of knot
KNEEPAN	*n* pl. -S the kneecap		**KNOTTER**	*n* pl. -S one that knots
KNEESOCK	*n* pl. -S a sock reaching up to the knee		**KNOTTING**	*n* pl. -S a fringe made of knotted threads
KNELL	*v* -ED, -ING, -S to sound a bell		**KNOTTY**	*adj* -TIER, -TIEST full of knots **KNOTTILY** *adv*
KNELT	a past tense of kneel		**KNOTWEED**	*n* pl. -S a common weed
KNESSET	*n* pl. -S the Israeli parliament		**KNOUT**	*v* -ED, -ING, -S to flog with a leather whip
KNEW	past tense of know			
KNICKERS	*n/pl* loose-fitting pants gathered at the knee		**KNOW**	*v* KNEW, KNOWN, KNOWING, KNOWS to have a true understanding of **KNOWABLE** *adj*
KNIFE	*n* pl. KNIVES a sharp-edged instrument used for cutting			
KNIFE	*v* KNIFED, KNIFING, KNIFES to cut with a knife		**KNOWER**	*n* pl. -S one that knows
			KNOWING	*adj* -INGER, -INGEST astute
KNIFER	*n* pl. -S one that knifes		**KNOWING**	*n* pl. -S knowledge
KNIGHT	*v* -ED, -ING, -S to make a knight (a medieval gentleman-soldier) of		**KNOWN**	*n* pl. -S a mathematical quantity whose value is given
KNIGHTLY	*adj* of or befitting a knight		**KNUBBY**	*adj* -BIER, -BIEST nubby
KNISH	*n* pl. -ES dough stuffed with filling and fried		**KNUCKLE**	*v* -LED, -LING, -LES to hit with the knuckles (the joints of the fingers)
KNIT	*v* KNITTED, KNITTING, KNITS to make a fabric or garment by joining loops of yarn			
			KNUCKLER	*n* pl. -S a type of baseball pitch
KNITTER	*n* pl. -S one that knits		**KNUCKLY**	*adj* -LIER, -LIEST having prominent knuckles
KNITTING	*n* pl. -S work done by a knitter			
KNITWEAR	*n* pl. KNITWEAR knitted clothing		**KNUR**	*n* pl. -S a bump on a tree
KNIVES	pl. of knife		**KNURL**	*v* -ED, -ING, -S to make grooves or ridges in
KNOB	*n* pl. -S a rounded protuberance **KNOBBED, KNOBLIKE** *adj*		**KNURLY**	*adj* KNURLIER, KNURLIEST gnarly
KNOBBLY	*adj* -BLIER, -BLIEST having very small knobs		**KOA**	*n* pl. -S a timber tree
			KOALA	*n* pl. -S an Australian mammal
KNOBBY	*adj* -BIER, -BIEST full of knobs		**KOAN**	*n* pl. -S a paradox meditated on by Buddhist monks
KNOCK	*v* -ED, -ING, -S to strike sharply			
KNOCKER	*n* pl. -S one that knocks		**KOB**	*n* pl. -S a reddish brown antelope
KNOCKOFF	*n* pl. -S a copy that sells for less than the original		**KOBO**	*n* pl. KOBO a monetary unit of Nigeria
KNOCKOUT	*n* pl. -S a blow that induces unconsciousness		**KOBOLD**	*n* pl. -S an elf
			KOEL	*n* pl. -S an Australian bird
KNOLL	*v* -ED, -ING, -S to knell		**KOHL**	*n* pl. -S a type of eye makeup
KNOLLER	*n* pl. -S one that knolls		**KOHLRABI**	*n* pl. -ES a variety of cabbage
KNOLLY	*adj* hilly		**KOI**	*n* pl. KOI a large and colorful fish
KNOP	*n* pl. -S a knob **KNOPPED** *adj*		**KOINE**	*n* pl. -S a type of dialect
KNOSP	*n* pl. -S a knob		**KOKANEE**	*n* pl. -S a food fish
KNOT	*v* KNOTTED, KNOTTING, KNOTS to tie in a knot (a closed loop)		**KOLA**	*n* pl. -S cola
			KOLACKY	*n* pl. KOLACKY a kind of pastry
KNOTHOLE	*n* pl. -S a hole in a plank		**KOLBASI**	*n* pl. -S kielbasa
KNOTLESS	*adj* having no knots		**KOLBASSI**	*n* pl. -S kielbasa
KNOTLIKE	*adj* resembling a knot		**KOLHOZ**	*n* pl. -HOZY or -HOZES kolkhoz

KOLINSKI	*n* pl. -ES kolinsky
KOLINSKY	*n* pl. -SKIES an Asian mink
KOLKHOS	*n* pl. -KHOSY or -KHOSES kolkhoz
KOLKHOZ	*n* pl. -KHOZY or -KHOZES a collective farm in Russia
KOLKOZ	*n* pl. -KOZY or -KOZES kolkhoz
KOLO	*n* pl. -LOS a European folk dance
KOMATIK	*n* pl. -S an Eskimo sledge
KOMONDOR	*n* pl. -DORS, -DOROK, or -DOROCK a large, shaggy-coated dog
KONK	*v* -ED, -ING, -S conk
KOODOO	*n* pl. -DOOS kudu
KOOK	*n* pl. -S an eccentric person
KOOKIE	*adj* KOOKIER, KOOKIEST kooky
KOOKY	*adj* KOOKIER, KOOKIEST eccentric
KOP	*n* pl. -S a hill
KOPECK	*n* pl. -S a Russian coin
KOPEK	*n* pl. -S kopeck
KOPH	*n* pl. -S a Hebrew letter
KOPJE	*n* pl. -S a small hill
KOPPA	*n* pl. -S a Greek letter
KOPPIE	*n* pl. -S kopje
KOR	*n* pl. -S a Hebrew unit of measure
KORAT	*n* pl. -S a cat having a silver-blue coat
KORE	*n* pl. -RAI an ancient Greek statue of a young woman
KORUNA	*n* pl. KORUNAS, KORUNY, or KORUN a monetary unit of the Czech Republic
KOS	*n* pl. KOS a land measure in India
KOSHER	*v* -ED, -ING, -S to make fit to be eaten according to Jewish dietary laws
KOSS	*n* pl. KOSS kos
KOTO	*n* pl. -TOS a musical instrument
KOTOW	*v* -ED, -ING, -S to kowtow
KOTOWER	*n* pl. -S one that kotows
KOUMIS	*n* pl. -MISES koumiss
KOUMISS	*n* pl. -ES a beverage made from camel's milk
KOUMYS	*n* pl. -ES koumiss
KOUMYSS	*n* pl. -ES koumiss
KOUPREY	*n* pl. -PREYS a short-haired ox
KOUROS	*n* pl. -ROI an ancient Greek statue of a young man
KOUSSO	*n* pl. -SOS cusso
KOWTOW	*v* -ED, -ING, -S to behave in a servile manner
KOWTOWER	*n* pl. -S one that kowtows
KRAAL	*v* -ED, -ING, -S to pen in a type of enclosure
KRAFT	*n* pl. -S a strong paper
KRAIT	*n* pl. -S a venomous snake
KRAKEN	*n* pl. -S a legendary sea monster
KRATER	*n* pl. -S a type of vase
KRAUT	*n* pl. -S sauerkraut
KREEP	*n* pl. -S a basaltic lunar rock
KREMLIN	*n* pl. -S a Russian citadel
KREPLACH	*n* pl. KREPLACH dumplings filled with ground meat or cheese
KREUTZER	*n* pl. -S a former monetary unit of Austria
KREUZER	*n* pl. -S kreutzer
KRILL	*n* pl. -S an aggregate of small marine crustaceans
KRIMMER	*n* pl. -S a kind of fur
KRIS	*n* pl. -ES a short sword
KRONA	*n* pl. KRONUR a monetary unit of Iceland
KRONA	*n* pl. KRONOR a monetary unit of Sweden
KRONE	*n* pl. KRONER a monetary unit of Denmark
KRONE	*n* pl. KRONEN a former monetary unit of Austria
KRONOR	pl. of krona
KRONUR	pl. of krona
KROON	*n* pl. KROONS or KROONI a former monetary unit of Estonia
KRUBI	*n* pl. -S a tropical plant
KRUBUT	*n* pl. -S krubi
KRULLER	*n* pl. -S cruller
KRUMHORN	*n* pl. -S crumhorn
KRYOLITE	*n* pl. -S cryolite
KRYOLITH	*n* pl. -S cryolite
KRYPTON	*n* pl. -S a gaseous element
KUCHEN	*n* pl. KUCHEN a coffee cake
KUDO	*n* pl. -DOS award; honor
KUDU	*n* pl. -S a large antelope
KUDZU	*n* pl. -S an Asian vine
KUE	*n* pl. -S the letter Q

KUGEL   *n* pl. -S a baked pudding of potatoes or noodles

KUKRI   *n* pl. -S a long, curved knife of Nepal

KULAK   *n* pl. -LAKS or -LAKI a rich Russian peasant

KULTUR   *n* pl. -S culture; civilization

KUMISS   *n* pl. -ES koumiss

KUMMEL   *n* pl. -S a type of liqueur

KUMQUAT   *n* pl. -S a citrus fruit

KUMYS   *n* pl. -ES koumiss

KUNZITE   *n* pl. -S a mineral

KURBASH   *v* -ED, -ING, -ES to flog with a leather whip

KURGAN   *n* pl. -S a mound of earth over a grave

KURTA   *n* pl. -S a shirt worn in India

KURTOSIS   *n* pl. -SISES the relative degree of curvature in a statistical curve

KURU   *n* pl. -S a disease of the nervous system

KUSSO   *n* pl. -SOS cusso

KUVASZ   *n* pl. -VASZOK a large dog having a white coat

KVAS   *n* pl. -ES kvass

KVASS   *n* pl. -ES a Russian beer

KVETCH   *v* -ED, -ING, -ES to complain

KVETCHY   *adj* KVETCHIER, KVETCHIEST habitually complaining

KWACHA   *n* pl. KWACHA a monetary unit of Zambia

KWANZA   *n* pl. -S a monetary unit of Angola

KYACK   *n* pl. -S a packsack

KYAK   *n* pl. -S a kayak (an Eskimo canoe)

KYANISE   *v* -ISED, -ISING, -ISES to kyanize

KYANITE   *n* pl. -S cyanite

KYANIZE   *v* -IZED, -IZING, -IZES to treat wood with a type of preservative

KYAR   *n* pl. -S coir

KYAT   *n* pl. -S a monetary unit of Myanmar

KYBOSH   *v* -ED, -ING, -ES to kibosh

KYLIX   *n* pl. -LIKES a drinking vessel

KYMOGRAM   *n* pl. -S a record of fluid pressure

KYPHOSIS   *n* pl. -PHOSES abnormal curvature of the spine **KYPHOTIC** *adj*

KYRIE   *n* pl. -S a religious petition for mercy

KYTE   *n* pl. -S the stomach

KYTHE   *v* KYTHED, KYTHING, KYTHES to kithe

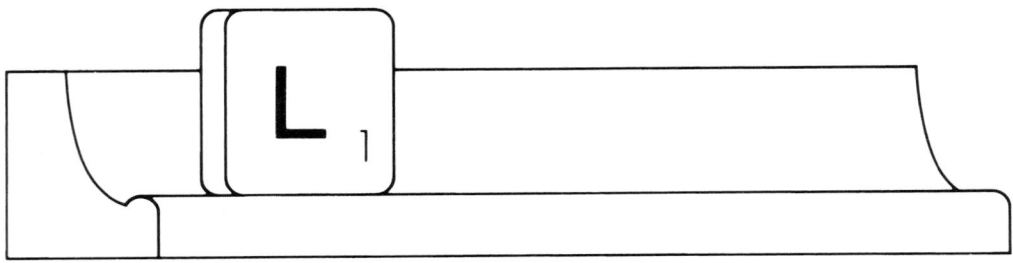

LA	*n* pl. -S the sixth tone of the diatonic musical scale	**LABRADOR**	*n* pl. -S a hunting dog
LAAGER	*v* -ED, -ING, -S to form a defensive encampment	**LABRET**	*n* pl. -S an ornament worn in a perforation of the lip
LAARI	*n* pl. LAARI a monetary unit of the Maldives	**LABROID**	*n* pl. -S a marine fish
		LABRUM	*n* pl. -BRA or -BRUMS a lip or liplike structure
LAB	*n* pl. -S a laboratory	**LABRUSCA**	*adj* designating a fox grape
LABARUM	*n* pl. -RA or -RUMS an ecclesiastical banner	**LABURNUM**	*n* pl. -S an ornamental tree
LABDANUM	*n* pl. -S a fragrant resin	**LAC**	*n* pl. -S a resinous substance secreted by certain insects
LABEL	*v* -BELED, -BELING, -BELS or -BELLED, -BELLING, -BELS to describe or designate	**LACE**	*v* LACED, LACING, LACES to fasten by means of a lace (a cord for drawing together two edges)
LABELER	*n* pl. -S one that labels	**LACELESS**	*adj* lacking lace
LABELLA	pl. of labellum	**LACELIKE**	*adj* resembling lace
LABELLED	a past tense of label	**LACER**	*n* pl. -S one that laces
LABELLER	*n* pl. -S labeler	**LACERATE**	*v* -ATED, -ATING, -ATES to tear roughly
LABELLING	a present participle of label	**LACERTID**	*n* pl. -S a type of lizard
LABELLUM	*n* pl. -LA the lower petal of an orchid	**LACEWING**	*n* pl. -S a winged insect
LABIA	pl. of labium	**LACEWOOD**	*n* pl. -S an Australian tree
LABIAL	*n* pl. -S a labially produced sound	**LACEWORK**	*n* pl. -S a delicate openwork fabric
LABIALLY	*adv* by means of the lips	**LACEY**	*adj* LACIER, LACIEST lacy
LABIATE	*n* pl. -S a labiated plant	**LACHES**	*n* pl. LACHES undue delay in asserting a legal right
LABIATED	*adj* having corollas that are divided into two liplike parts	**LACIER**	comparative of lacy
		LACIEST	superlative of lacy
LABILE	*adj* likely to change	**LACILY**	*adv* in a lacy manner
LABILITY	*n* pl. -TIES the state of being labile	**LACINESS**	*n* pl. -ES the quality of being lacy
LABIUM	*n* pl. -BIA a fold of the vulva	**LACING**	*n* pl. -S a contrasting marginal band of color
LABOR	*v* -ED, -ING, -S to work	**LACK**	*v* -ED, -ING, -S to be without
LABORER	*n* pl. -S one that labors	**LACKADAY**	*interj* — used to express regret
LABORITE	*n* pl. -S a supporter of labor interests	**LACKER**	*v* -ED, -ING, -S to lacquer
LABOUR	*v* -ED, -ING, -S to labor	**LACKEY**	*v* -ED, -ING, -S to act in a servile manner
LABOURER	*n* pl. -S laborer		
LABRA	a pl. of labrum	**LACONIC**	*adj* using a minimum of words

LACONISM *n* pl. -S brevity of expression

LACQUER *v* -ED, -ING, -S to coat with a glossy substance

LACQUEY *v* -ED, -ING, -S to lackey

LACRIMAL *n* pl. -S a type of vase

LACROSSE *n* pl. -S a type of ball game

LACTAM *n* pl. -S a chemical compound

LACTARY *adj* pertaining to milk

LACTASE *n* pl. -S an enzyme

LACTATE *v* -TATED, -TATING, -TATES to secrete milk

LACTEAL *n* pl. -S a lymphatic vessel

LACTEAN *adj* lacteous

LACTEOUS *adj* resembling milk

LACTIC *adj* derived from milk

LACTONE *n* pl. -S any of a group of esters **LACTONIC** *adj*

LACTOSE *n* pl. -S a lactic sugar

LACUNA *n* pl. -NAE or -NAS an empty space or missing part **LACUNAL, LACUNARY, LACUNATE** *adj*

LACUNAR *n* pl. -NARS or -NARIA a ceiling with recessed panels

LACUNE *n* pl. -S lacuna

LACUNOSE *adj* marked by shallow depressions

LACY *adj* LACIER, LACIEST resembling lacework

LAD *n* pl. -S a boy or youth

LADANUM *n* pl. -S labdanum

LADDER *v* -ED, -ING, -S to cause a run in a stocking

LADDIE *n* pl. -S a lad

LADE *v* LADED, LADEN, LADING, LADES to load with a cargo

LADEN *v* -ED, -ING, -S to lade

LADER *n* pl. -S one that lades

LADIES pl. of lady

LADING *n* pl. -S cargo; freight

LADINO *n* pl. -NOS a fast-growing clover

LADLE *v* -DLED, -DLING, -DLES to lift out with a ladle (a type of spoon)

LADLEFUL *n* pl. -S as much as a ladle will hold

LADLER *n* pl. -S one that ladles

LADLING present participle of ladle

LADRON *n* pl. -S ladrone

LADRONE *n* pl. -S a thief

LADY *n* pl. -DIES a woman of refinement and gentle manners

LADYBIRD *n* pl. -S a ladybug

LADYBUG *n* pl. -S a small beetle

LADYFISH *n* pl. -ES a bonefish

LADYHOOD *n* pl. -S the state of being a lady

LADYISH *adj* somewhat ladylike

LADYKIN *n* pl. -S a small lady

LADYLIKE *adj* resembling or suitable to a lady

LADYLOVE *n* pl. -S a sweetheart

LADYPALM *n* pl. -S a palm tree

LADYSHIP *n* pl. -S the condition of being a lady

LAETRILE *n* pl. -S a drug derived from apricot pits

LAEVO *adj* levo

LAG *v* LAGGED, LAGGING, LAGS to stay or fall behind

LAGAN *n* pl. -S goods thrown into the sea with a buoy attached to enable recovery

LAGEND *n* pl. -S lagan

LAGER *v* -ED, -ING, -S to laager

LAGGARD *n* pl. -S one that lags

LAGGED past tense of lag

LAGGER *n* pl. -S a laggard

LAGGING *n* pl. -S an insulating material

LAGNAPPE *n* pl. -S a small gift given to a customer with his purchase

LAGOON *n* pl. -S a shallow body of water **LAGOONAL** *adj*

LAGUNA *n* pl. -S lagoon

LAGUNE *n* pl. -S lagoon

LAHAR *n* pl. -S a flowing mass of volcanic debris

LAIC *n* pl. -S a layman **LAICAL** *adj* **LAICALLY** *adv*

LAICH *n* pl. -S laigh

LAICISE *v* -ICISED, -ICISING, -ICISES to laicize

LAICISM *n* pl. -S a political system free from clerical control

LAICIZE *v* -ICIZED, -ICIZING, -ICIZES to free from clerical control

LAID a past tense of lay

LAIGH *n* pl. -S a lowland

LAIN past participle of lie

LAIR *v* -ED, -ING, -S to live in a lair (a wild animal's resting or dwelling place)

LAIRD *n* pl. -S the owner of a landed estate **LAIRDLY** *adj*

LAITANCE *n* pl. -S a milky deposit on the surface of fresh concrete

LAITH *adj* loath **LAITHLY** *adv*

LAITY *n* pl. -ITIES the nonclerical membership of a religious faith

LAKE *n* pl. -S a sizable inland body of water **LAKELIKE** *adj*

LAKED *adj* subjected to the process of laking

LAKEPORT *n* pl. -S a city located on the shore of a lake

LAKER *n* pl. -S a lake fish

LAKESIDE *n* pl. -S the land along the edge of a lake

LAKH *n* pl. -S the sum of one hundred thousand

LAKING *n* pl. -S the reddening of blood plasma by the release of hemoglobin from the red corpuscles

LAKY *adj* LAKIER, LAKIEST of the color of blood

LALL *v* -ED, -ING, -S to articulate the letter *r* as *l*

LALLAN *n* pl. -S a lowland

LALLAND *n* pl. -S a lowland

LALLYGAG *v* -GAGGED, -GAGGING, -GAGS to dawdle

LAM *v* LAMMED, LAMMING, LAMS to flee hastily

LAMA *n* pl. -S a Buddhist monk

LAMASERY *n* pl. -SERIES a monastery of lamas

LAMB *v* -ED, -ING, -S to give birth to a lamb (a young sheep)

LAMBAST *v* -ED, -ING, -S to lambaste

LAMBASTE *v* -BASTED, -BASTING, -BASTES to beat severely

LAMBDA *n* pl. -S a Greek letter **LAMBDOID** *adj*

LAMBENCY *n* pl. -CIES the quality or an instance of being lambent

LAMBENT *adj* flickering lightly and gently over a surface

LAMBER *n* pl. -S a ewe that is lambing

LAMBERT *n* pl. -S a unit of brightness

LAMBIE *n* pl. -S a lambkin

LAMBIER comparative of lamby

LAMBIEST superlative of lamby

LAMBKILL *n* pl. -S an evergreen shrub

LAMBKIN *n* pl. -S a small lamb

LAMBLIKE *adj* resembling a lamb

LAMBSKIN *n* pl. -S the skin of a lamb

LAMBY *adj* LAMBIER, LAMBIEST resembling a lamb

LAME *adj* LAMER, LAMEST physically disabled

LAME *v* LAMED, LAMING, LAMES to make lame

LAMED *n* pl. -S a Hebrew letter

LAMEDH *n* pl. -S lamed

LAMELLA *n* pl. -LAE or -LAS a thin plate, scale, or membrane **LAMELLAR** *adj*

LAMELY *adv* in a lame manner

LAMENESS *n* pl. -ES the state of being lame

LAMENT *v* -ED, -ING, -S to express sorrow or regret for

LAMENTER *n* pl. -S one that laments

LAMER comparative of lame

LAMEST superlative of lame

LAMIA *n* pl. -MIAS or -MIAE a female demon

LAMINA *n* pl. -NAE or -NAS a thin plate, scale, or layer **LAMINAL, LAMINAR, LAMINARY** *adj*

LAMINATE *v* -NATED, -NATING, -NATES to compress into a thin plate

LAMING present participle of lame

LAMINOSE *adj* composed of laminae

LAMINOUS *adj* laminose

LAMISTER *n* pl. -S lamster

LAMMED past tense of lam

LAMMING present participle of lam

LAMP *v* -ED, -ING, -S to look at

LAMPAD *n* pl. -S a candlestick

LAMPAS *n* pl. -ES inflammation of the roof of a horse's mouth

LAMPERS *n* pl. -ES lampas

LAMPION *n* pl. -S a type of light-generating device

LAMPOON *v* -ED, -ING, -S to ridicule in a satirical composition

LAMPPOST *n* pl. -S a post supporting a streetlight

LAMPREY *n* pl. -PREYS an eellike fish

LAMPYRID	*n* pl. -S any of a family of beetles
LAMSTER	*n* pl. -S a fugitive
LANAI	*n* pl. -S a veranda
LANATE	*adj* covered with wool
LANATED	*adj* lanate
LANCE	*v* LANCED, LANCING, LANCES to pierce with a lance (a spearlike weapon)
LANCELET	*n* pl. -S a small marine organism
LANCER	*n* pl. -S a cavalryman armed with a lance
LANCET	*n* pl. -S a narrow, pointed arch **LANCETED** *adj*
LANCIERS	*n* pl. LANCIERS a French dance
LANCING	present participle of lance
LAND	*v* -ED, -ING, -S to set down upon land (solid ground)
LANDAU	*n* pl. -S a type of carriage
LANDER	*n* pl. -S one that lands
LANDFALL	*n* pl. -S a sighting or approach to land
LANDFILL	*n* pl. -S a system of waste disposal
LANDFORM	*n* pl. -S a natural feature of the earth's surface
LANDGRAB	*n* pl. -S a swift and often fraudulent seizure of land
LANDING	*n* pl. -S a place for discharging or taking on passengers or cargo
LANDLADY	*n* pl. -DIES a female landlord
LANDLER	*n* pl. -S a slow Austrian dance
LANDLESS	*adj* owning no land
LANDLINE	*n* pl. -S a line of communication on land
LANDLORD	*n* pl. -S one who owns and rents out real estate
LANDMAN	*n* pl. -MEN one who lives and works on land
LANDMARK	*n* pl. -S an object that marks a boundary line
LANDMASS	*n* pl. -ES a large area of land
LANDMEN	pl. of landman
LANDSIDE	*n* pl. -S a part of a plow
LANDSKIP	*n* pl. -S landscape
LANDSLEIT	pl. of landsman
LANDSLID	past tense of landslide (to win an election by an overwhelming majority)
LANDSLIP	*n* pl. -S the fall of a mass of earth
LANDSMAN	*n* pl. LANDSLEIT a fellow Jew coming from one's own section of Eastern Europe
LANDSMAN	*n* pl. -MEN landman
LANDWARD	*adv* toward the land
LANE	*n* pl. -S a narrow passageway
LANELY	*adj* lonely
LANEWAY	*n* pl. -WAYS a lane
LANG	*adj* long
LANGLAUF	*n* pl. -S a cross-country ski run
LANGLEY	*n* pl. -LEYS a unit of illumination
LANGRAGE	*n* pl. -S a shot formerly used in naval warfare
LANGREL	*n* pl. -S langrage
LANGSHAN	*n* pl. -S any of a breed of large domestic fowl
LANGSYNE	*n* pl. -S time long past
LANGUAGE	*n* pl. -S a body of words and systems serving as a means of communication
LANGUE	*n* pl. -S a type of language
LANGUET	*n* pl. -S a tonguelike part
LANGUID	*adj* lacking in vigor or vitality
LANGUISH	*v* -ED, -ING, -ES to lose vigor or vitality
LANGUOR	*n* pl. -S the state of being languid
LANGUR	*n* pl. -S an Asian monkey
LANIARD	*n* pl. -S lanyard
LANIARY	*n* pl. -ARIES a cuspid
LANITAL	*n* pl. -S a woollike fiber
LANK	*adj* LANKER, LANKEST long and slender **LANKLY** *adv*
LANKNESS	*n* pl. -ES the state of being lank
LANKY	*adj* LANKIER, LANKIEST ungracefully tall and thin **LANKILY** *adv*
LANNER	*n* pl. -S a falcon of Europe and Asia
LANNERET	*n* pl. -S a male lanner
LANOLIN	*n* pl. -S a fatty substance obtained from wool
LANOLINE	*n* pl. -S lanolin
LANOSE	*adj* lanate
LANOSITY	*n* pl. -TIES the state of being lanose
LANTANA	*n* pl. -S a tropical shrub
LANTERN	*n* pl. -S a protective case for a light
LANTHORN	*n* pl. -S a lantern

LANUGO   *n* pl. -GOS fine, soft hair

LANYARD   *n* pl. -S a fastening rope on a ship

LAP   *v* LAPPED, LAPPING, LAPS to fold over or around something

LAPBOARD   *n* pl. -S a flat board used as a table or desk

LAPDOG   *n* pl. -S a small dog

LAPEL   *n* pl. -S an extension of the collar of a garment **LAPELED, LAPELLED** *adj*

LAPFUL   *n* pl. -S as much as the lap can hold

LAPIDARY   *n* pl. -DARIES one who works with precious stones

LAPIDATE   *v* -DATED, -DATING, -DATES to hurl stones at

LAPIDES   pl. of lapis

LAPIDIFY   *v* -FIED, -FYING, -FIES to turn to stone

LAPIDIST   *n* pl. -S a lapidary

LAPILLUS   *n* pl. -LI a small fragment of lava

LAPIN   *n* pl. -S a rabbit

LAPIS   *n* pl. LAPIDES a stone

LAPIS   *n* pl. -PISES a mineral

LAPPED   past tense of lap

LAPPER   *v* -ED, -ING, -S to lopper

LAPPET   *n* pl. -S a decorative flap on a garment **LAPPETED** *adj*

LAPPING   present participle of lap

LAPSE   *v* LAPSED, LAPSING, LAPSES to fall from a previous standard **LAPSABLE, LAPSIBLE** *adj*

LAPSER   *n* pl. -S one that lapses

LAPSUS   *n* pl. LAPSUS a mistake

LAPTOP   *n* pl. -S a small computer for use on one's lap

LAPWING   *n* pl. -S a shore bird

LAR   *n* pl. -ES or -S a tutelary god or spirit of an ancient Roman household

LARBOARD   *n* pl. -S the left-hand side of a ship

LARCENER   *n* pl. -S one that commits larceny

LARCENY   *n* pl. -NIES the felonious taking and removal of another's personal goods

LARCH   *n* pl. -ES a coniferous tree

LARD   *v* -ED, -ING, -S to coat with lard (the melted fat of hogs)

LARDER   *n* pl. -S a place where food is stored

LARDIER   comparative of lardy

LARDIEST   superlative of lardy

LARDLIKE   *adj* resembling lard

LARDON   *n* pl. -S a thin slice of bacon or pork

LARDOON   *n* pl. -S lardon

LARDY   *adj* LARDIER, LARDIEST resembling lard

LAREE   *n* pl. -S lari

LARES   a pl. of lar

LARGANDO   *adj* becoming gradually slower — used as a musical direction

LARGE   *adj* LARGER, LARGEST of considerable size or quantity **LARGELY** *adv*

LARGE   *n* pl. -S generosity

LARGESS   *n* pl. -ES generosity

LARGESSE   *n* pl. -S largess

LARGEST   superlative of large

LARGISH   *adj* somewhat large

LARGO   *n* pl. -GOS a slow musical movement

LARI   *n* pl. -S a monetary unit of Maldives

LARIAT   *v* -ED, -ING, -S to lasso

LARINE   *adj* resembling a gull

LARK   *v* -ED, -ING, -S to behave playfully

LARKER   *n* pl. -S one that larks

LARKIER   comparative of larky

LARKIEST   superlative of larky

LARKISH   *adj* playful

LARKSOME   *adj* playful

LARKSPUR   *n* pl. -S a flowering plant

LARKY   *adj* LARKIER, LARKIEST playful

LARRIGAN   *n* pl. -S a type of moccasin

LARRIKIN   *n* pl. -S a rowdy

LARRUP   *v* -ED, -ING, -S to beat or thrash

LARRUPER   *n* pl. -S one that larrups

LARUM   *n* pl. -S an alarm

LARVA   *n* pl. -VAE or -VAS the immature form of various insects and animals when newly hatched **LARVAL** *adj*

LARYNX   *n* pl. LARYNGES or LARYNXES an organ of the respiratory tract **LARYNGAL** *adj*

LASAGNA	*n* pl. -S an Italian baked dish		**LATER**	comparative of late
LASAGNE	*n* pl. -S lasagna		**LATERAD**	*adv* toward the side
LASCAR	*n* pl. -S an East Indian sailor		**LATERAL**	*v* -ED, -ING, -S to throw a sideward pass in football
LASE	*v* LASED, LASING, LASES to function as a laser		**LATERITE**	*n* pl. -S a type of soil
LASER	*n* pl. -S a device that amplifies light waves		**LATERIZE**	*v* -IZED, -IZING, -IZES to convert to laterite
LASH	*v* -ED, -ING, -ES to strike with a whip		**LATEST**	*n* pl. -S the most recent development
LASHER	*n* pl. -S one that lashes		**LATEWOOD**	*n* pl. -S a part of an annual ring of wood
LASHING	*n* pl. -S a flogging		**LATEX**	*n* pl. LATICES or LATEXES a milky liquid of certain plants
LASHINS	*n/pl* an abundance			
LASHKAR	*n* pl. -S lascar		**LATH**	*v* -ED, -ING, -S to cover with laths (thin strips of wood)
LASING	present participle of lase		**LATHE**	*v* LATHED, LATHING, LATHES to cut or shape on a type of machine
LASS	*n* pl. -ES a young woman			
LASSIE	*n* pl. -S a lass		**LATHER**	*v* -ED, -ING, -S to cover with lather (a light foam)
LASSO	*v* -ED, -ING, -S or -ES to catch with a lasso (a long rope with a running noose)		**LATHERER**	*n* pl. -S one that lathers
			LATHERY	*adj* covered with lather
LASSOER	*n* pl. -S one that lassos		**LATHI**	*n* pl. -S a heavy stick of bamboo and iron in India
LAST	*v* -ED, -ING, -S to continue in existence		**LATHIER**	comparative of lathy
LASTER	*n* pl. -S one that lasts		**LATHIEST**	superlative of lathy
LASTING	*n* pl. -S a durable fabric		**LATHING**	*n* pl. -S work made of or using laths
LASTLY	*adv* in conclusion			
LAT	*n* pl. LATS or LATI a former monetary unit of Latvia		**LATHWORK**	*n* pl. -S lathing
			LATHY	*adj* LATHIER, LATHIEST long and slender
LATAKIA	*n* pl. -S a variety of Turkish tobacco		**LATI**	a pl. of lat
LATCH	*v* -ED, -ING, -ES to close with a type of fastening device		**LATICES**	a pl. of latex
			LATIGO	*n* pl. -GOS or -GOES a strap used to fasten a saddle
LATCHET	*n* pl. -S a thong used to fasten a shoe			
LATCHKEY	*n* pl. -KEYS a key for opening a latched door		**LATINITY**	*n* pl. -TIES a manner of writing or speaking Latin
LATE	*adj* LATER, LATEST coming or occurring after the expected time		**LATINIZE**	*v* -IZED, -IZING, -IZES to translate into Latin
LATED	*adj* belated		**LATINO**	*n* pl. -NOS a Latin American
LATEEN	*n* pl. -S a sailing vessel		**LATISH**	*adj* somewhat late
LATEENER	*n* pl. -S a lateen		**LATITUDE**	*n* pl. -S freedom from narrow restrictions
LATELY	*adv* not long ago			
LATEN	*v* -ED, -ING, -S to become late		**LATKE**	*n* pl. -S a potato pancake
LATENCY	*n* pl. -CIES the state of being present but not manifest		**LATOSOL**	*n* pl. -S a tropical soil
			LATRIA	*n* pl. -S the supreme worship given to God only, in Roman Catholicism
LATENESS	*n* pl. -ES the state of being late			
LATENT	*n* pl. -S a barely visible fingerprint that can be developed for study		**LATRINE**	*n* pl. -S a type of toilet
			LATTE	*n* pl. -S espresso coffee with milk
LATENTLY	*adv* dormantly		**LATTEN**	*n* pl. -S a brass-like alloy

LATTER *adj* being the second mentioned of two

LATTERLY *adv* lately

LATTICE *v* -TICED, -TICING, -TICES to form a structure consisting of interlaced strips of material

LATTIN *n* pl. -S latten

LAUAN *n* pl. -S a Philippine timber

LAUD *v* -ED, -ING, -S to praise

LAUDABLE *adj* worthy of praise **LAUDABLY** *adv*

LAUDANUM *n* pl. -S a type of opium preparation

LAUDATOR *n* pl. -S a lauder

LAUDER *n* pl. -S one that lauds

LAUGH *v* -ED, -ING, -S to express emotion, typically mirth, by a series of inarticulate sounds

LAUGHER *n* pl. -S one that laughs

LAUGHING *n* pl. -S laughter

LAUGHTER *n* pl. -S the act or sound of one that laughs

LAUNCE *n* pl. -S a marine fish

LAUNCH *v* -ED, -ING, -ES to set in motion

LAUNCHER *n* pl. -S a launching device

LAUNDER *v* -ED, -ING, -S to wash clothes

LAUNDRY *n* pl. -DRIES a collection of clothes to be washed

LAURA *n* pl. -RAS or -RAE a type of monastery

LAUREATE *v* -ATED, -ATING, -ATES to laurel

LAUREL *v* -RELED, -RELING, -RELS or -RELLED, -RELLING, -RELS to crown with a wreath of evergreen leaves

LAUWINE *n* pl. -S an avalanche

LAV *n* pl. -S a lavatory

LAVA *n* pl. -S molten rock that issues from a volcano

LAVABO *n* pl. -BOES or -BOS a ceremonial washing in certain Christian churches

LAVAGE *n* pl. -S a washing

LAVALAVA *n* pl. -S a Polynesian garment

LAVALIER *n* pl. -S a pendant worn on a chain around the neck

LAVALIKE *adj* resembling lava

LAVATION *n* pl. -S the acting of washing

LAVATORY *n* pl. -RIES a room equipped with washing and toilet facilities

LAVE *v* LAVED, LAVING, LAVES to wash

LAVEER *v* -ED, -ING, -S to sail against the wind

LAVENDER *v* -ED, -ING, -S to sprinkle with a type of perfume

LAVER *n* pl. -S a vessel used for ancient Hebrew ceremonial washings

LAVEROCK *n* pl. -S a songbird

LAVING present participle of lave

LAVISH *adj* -ISHER, -ISHEST expending or giving in great amounts **LAVISHLY** *adv*

LAVISH *v* -ED, -ING, -ES to expend or give in great amounts

LAVISHER *n* pl. -S one that lavishes

LAVROCK *n* pl. -S laverock

LAW *v* -ED, -ING, -S to take a complaint to court for settlement

LAWBOOK *n* pl. -S a book containing or dealing with laws

LAWFUL *adj* allowed by law (the body of rules governing the affairs of a community) **LAWFULLY** *adv*

LAWGIVER *n* pl. -S one who institutes a legal system

LAWINE *n* pl. -S lauwine

LAWING *n* pl. -S a bill for food or drink in a tavern

LAWLESS *adj* having no system of laws

LAWLIKE *adj* being like the law

LAWMAKER *n* pl. -S a legislator

LAWMAN *n* pl. -MEN a law-enforcement officer

LAWN *n* pl. -S an area of grass-covered land **LAWNY** *adj*

LAWSUIT *n* pl. -S a legal action

LAWYER *v* -ED, -ING, -S to work as a member of the legal profession

LAWYERLY *adj* befitting a member of the legal profession

LAX *adj* LAXER, LAXEST not strict or stringent

LAXATION *n* pl. -S the act of relaxing

LAXATIVE *n* pl. -S a drug that stimulates evacuation of the bowels

LAXITY *n* pl. -ITIES the state of being lax

LAXLY *adv* in a lax manner

LAXNESS *n* pl. -ES laxity

LAY v LAID or LAYED, LAYING, LAYS to deposit as a wager

LAYABOUT n pl. -S a lazy person

LAYAWAY n pl. -AWAYS an item that has been reserved with a down payment

LAYER v -ED, -ING, -S to form a layer (a single thickness, coating, or covering)

LAYERAGE n pl. -S a method of plant propagation

LAYERING n pl. -S layerage

LAYETTE n pl. -S an outfit of clothing and equipment for a newborn child

LAYMAN n pl. -MEN a member of the laity

LAYOFF n pl. -S the suspension or dismissal of employees

LAYOUT n pl. -S an arrangement or plan

LAYOVER n pl. -S a stopover

LAYUP n pl. -S a shot in basketball

LAYWOMAN n pl. -WOMEN a female member of the laity

LAZAR n pl. -S a beggar afflicted with a loathsome disease

LAZARET n pl. -S a hospital treating contagious diseases

LAZE v LAZED, LAZING, LAZES to pass time lazily

LAZIED past tense of lazy

LAZIER comparative of lazy

LAZIES present 3d person sing. of lazy

LAZIEST superlative of lazy

LAZILY adv in a lazy manner

LAZINESS n pl. -ES the state of being lazy

LAZING present participle of laze

LAZULI n pl. -S a mineral

LAZULITE n pl. -S a mineral

LAZURITE n pl. -S a mineral

LAZY adj LAZIER, LAZIEST disinclined toward work or exertion

LAZY v LAZIED, LAZYING, LAZIES to move or lie lazily

LAZYISH adj somewhat lazy

LEA n pl. -S a meadow

LEACH v -ED, -ING, -ES to subject to the filtering action of a liquid

LEACHATE n pl. -S a solution obtained by leaching

LEACHER n pl. -S one that leaches

LEACHY adj LEACHIER, LEACHIEST porous

LEAD v LED, LEADING, LEADS to show the way to by going in advance

LEAD v -ED, -ING, -S to cover with lead (a heavy metallic element)

LEADEN adj oppressively heavy **LEADENLY** adv

LEADER n pl. -S one that leads or guides

LEADIER comparative of leady

LEADIEST superlative of leady

LEADING n pl. -S a covering or border of lead

LEADLESS adj having no lead

LEADMAN n pl. -MEN a worker in charge of other workers

LEADOFF n pl. -S an opening play or move

LEADSMAN n pl. -MEN a seaman who measures the depth of water

LEADWORK n pl. -S something made of lead

LEADWORT n pl. -S a tropical plant

LEADY adj LEADIER, LEADIEST resembling lead

LEAF n pl. LEAVES a usually green, flattened organ of vascular plants

LEAF v -ED, -ING, -S to turn pages rapidly

LEAFAGE n pl. -S foliage

LEAFIER comparative of leafy

LEAFIEST superlative of leafy

LEAFLESS adj having no leaves

LEAFLET v -LETED, -LETING, -LETS or -LETTED, -LETTING, -LETS to distribute printed sheets of paper

LEAFLIKE adj resembling a leaf

LEAFWORM n pl. -S a moth larva that feeds on leaves

LEAFY adj LEAFIER, LEAFIEST covered with leaves

LEAGUE v LEAGUED, LEAGUING, LEAGUES to come together for a common purpose

LEAGUER v -ED, -ING, -S to besiege

LEAK v -ED, -ING, -S to permit the escape of something through a breach or flaw

LEAKAGE n pl. -S the act or an instance of leaking

LEAKER n pl. -S one that leaks

LEAKLESS adj designed not to leak

LEAKY   adj LEAKIER, LEAKIEST tending to leak **LEAKILY** adv

LEAL   adj loyal **LEALLY** adv

LEALTY   n pl. -TIES loyalty

LEAN   v LEANED or LEANT, LEANING, LEANS to deviate from a vertical position

LEAN   adj LEANER, LEANEST having little fat **LEANLY** adv

LEANER   n pl. -S one that leans

LEANING   n pl. -S a tendency

LEANNESS   n pl. -ES the state of being lean

LEANT   a past tense of lean

LEAP   v LEAPED or LEAPT or LEPT, LEAPING, LEAPS to spring off the ground

LEAPER   n pl. -S one that leaps

LEAPFROG   v -FROGGED, -FROGGING, -FROGS to jump over with the legs wide apart

LEAPT   a past tense of leap

LEAR   n pl. -S learning

LEARIER   comparative of leary

LEARIEST   superlative of leary

LEARN   v LEARNED or LEARNT, LEARNING, LEARNS to gain knowledge by experience, instruction, or study

LEARNER   n pl. -S one that learns

LEARNING   n pl. -S acquired knowledge

LEARNT   a past tense of learn

LEARY   adj LEARIER, LEARIEST leery

LEASE   v LEASED, LEASING, LEASES to grant temporary use of in exchange for rent **LEASABLE** adj

LEASER   n pl. -S one that leases

LEASH   v -ED, -ING, -ES to restrain an animal with a line or thong

LEASING   n pl. -S a falsehood

LEAST   n pl. -S something that is smallest in size or degree

LEATHER   v -ED, -ING, -S to cover with leather (the dressed or tanned hide of an animal)

LEATHERN   adj made of leather

LEATHERY   adj resembling leather

LEAVE   v LEFT, LEAVING, LEAVES to go away from

LEAVED   adj having a leaf or leaves

LEAVEN   v -ED, -ING, -S to produce fermentation in

LEAVER   n pl. -S one that leaves

LEAVES   pl. of leaf

LEAVING   n pl. -S a leftover

LEAVY   adj LEAVIER, LEAVIEST leafy

LEBEN   n pl. -S a type of liquid food

LECH   v -ED, -ING, -ES to engage in lechery

LECHAYIM   n pl. -S lehayim

LECHER   v -ED, -ING, -S to engage in lechery

LECHERY   n pl. -ERIES excessive sexual indulgence

LECHWE   n pl. -S an African antelope

LECITHIN   n pl. -S any of a group of fatty substances found in plant and animal tissues

LECTERN   n pl. -S a reading desk

LECTIN   n pl. -S a protein that binds to a sugar molecule

LECTION   n pl. -S a portion of sacred writing read in a church service

LECTOR   n pl. -S a reader of the lessons in a church service

LECTURE   v -TURED, -TURING, -TURES to expound on a specific subject

LECTURER   n pl. -S one that lectures

LECYTHIS   adj designating a family of tropical shrubs

LECYTHUS   n pl. -THI lekythos

LED   past tense of lead

LEDGE   n pl. -S a narrow, shelflike projection

LEDGER   n pl. -S an account book of final entry

LEDGY   adj LEDGIER, LEDGIEST abounding in ledges

LEE   n pl. -S shelter from the wind

LEEBOARD   n pl. -S a board attached to a sailing vessel to prevent leeway

LEECH   v -ED, -ING, -ES to cling to and feed upon or drain

LEEK   n pl. -S an herb used in cookery

LEER   v -ED, -ING, -S to look with a sideways glance

LEERY   adj LEERIER, LEERIEST suspicious **LEERILY** adv

LEET   n pl. -S a former English court for petty offenses

LEEWARD   n pl. -S the direction toward which the wind is blowing

LEEWAY   *n* pl. -WAYS the lateral drift of a ship

LEFT   *adj* LEFTER, LEFTEST pertaining to the side of the body to the north when one faces east

LEFT   *n* pl. -S the left side or hand

LEFTIES   pl. of lefty

LEFTISH   *adj* inclined to be a leftist

LEFTISM   *n* pl. -S a liberal political philosophy

LEFTIST   *n* pl. -S an advocate of leftism

LEFTOVER   *n* pl. -S an unused or unconsumed portion

LEFTWARD   *adv* toward the left

LEFTWING   *adj* favoring leftism

LEFTY   *n* pl. LEFTIES a left-handed person

LEG   *v* LEGGED, LEGGING, LEGS to move with the legs (appendages that serve as a means of support and locomotion)

LEGACY   *n* pl. -CIES something bequeathed

LEGAL   *n* pl. -S an authorized investment that may be made by investors such as savings banks

LEGALESE   *n* pl. -S the specialized language of lawyers

LEGALISE   *v* -ISED, -ISING, -ISES to legalize

LEGALISM   *n* pl. -S strict conformity to the law

LEGALIST   *n* pl. -S an adherent of legalism

LEGALITY   *n* pl. -TIES the condition of being lawful

LEGALIZE   *v* -IZED, -IZING, -IZES to make lawful

LEGALLY   *adv* in a lawful manner

LEGATE   *v* -GATED, -GATING, -GATES to bequeath

LEGATEE   *n* pl. -S the inheritor of a legacy

LEGATINE   *adj* pertaining to an official envoy

LEGATING   present participle of legate

LEGATION   *n* pl. -S the sending of an official envoy

LEGATO   *n* pl. -TOS a smooth and flowing musical style

LEGATOR   *n* pl. -S one that legates

LEGEND   *n* pl. -S an unverified story from earlier times

LEGENDRY   *n* pl. -RIES a collection of legends

LEGER   *n* pl. -S fishing bait made to lie on the bottom

LEGERITY   *n* pl. -TIES quickness of the mind or body

LEGES   pl. of lex

LEGGED   past tense of leg

LEGGIER   comparative of leggy

LEGGIERO   *adv* in a light or graceful manner — used as a musical direction

LEGGIEST   superlative of leggy

LEGGIN   *n* pl. -S legging

LEGGING   *n* pl. -S a covering for the leg

LEGGY   *adj* -GIER, -GIEST having long legs

LEGHORN   *n* pl. -S a smooth, plaited straw

LEGIBLE   *adj* capable of being read **LEGIBLY** *adv*

LEGION   *n* pl. -S a large military force

LEGIST   *n* pl. -S one learned or skilled in the law

LEGIT   *n* pl. -S legitimate drama

LEGLESS   *adj* having no legs

LEGLIKE   *adj* resembling a leg

LEGMAN   *n* pl. -MEN a newspaperman assigned to gather information

LEGONG   *n* pl. -S a Balinese dance

LEGROOM   *n* pl. -S space in which to extend the legs

LEGUME   *n* pl. -S a type of plant

LEGUMIN   *n* pl. -S a plant protein

LEGWORK   *n* pl. -S work that involves extensive walking

LEHAYIM   *n* pl. -S a traditional Jewish toast

LEHR   *n* pl. -S a type of oven

LEHUA   *n* pl. -S a tropical tree

LEI   *n* pl. -S a wreath of flowers

LEISTER   *v* -ED, -ING, -S to spear with a three-pronged fishing implement

LEISURE   *n* pl. -S freedom from the demands of work or duty **LEISURED** *adj*

LEK   *n* pl. LEKS or LEKE or LEKU a monetary unit of Albania

LEKVAR   *n* pl. -S a prune butter

LEKYTHOS   *n* pl. -THOI an oil jar used in ancient Greece

LEKYTHUS   *n* pl. -THI lekythos

LEMAN   *n* pl. -S a lover

LEMMA   *n* pl. -MAS or -MATA a type of proposition in logic

LEMMING   *n* pl. -S a mouselike rodent

LEMNISCI   *n/pl* bands of nerve fibers

LEMON   *n* pl. -S a citrus fruit **LEMONISH, LEMONY** *adj*

LEMONADE   *n* pl. -S a beverage

LEMPIRA   *n* pl. -S a monetary unit of Honduras

LEMUR   *n* pl. -S an arboreal mammal related to the monkeys

LEMURES   *n/pl* the ghosts of the dead in ancient Roman religion

LEMURINE   *adj* pertaining to a lemur

LEMUROID   *n* pl. -S a lemur

LEND   *v* LENT, LENDING, LENDS to give the temporary use of **LENDABLE** *adj*

LENDER   *n* pl. -S one that lends

LENES   pl. of lenis

LENGTH   *n* pl. -S the longer or longest dimension of an object

LENGTHEN   *v* -ED, -ING, -S to make or become longer

LENGTHY   *adj* LENGTHIER, LENGTHIEST very long

LENIENCE   *n* pl. -S leniency

LENIENCY   *n* pl. -CIES the quality of being lenient

LENIENT   *adj* gently tolerant

LENIS   *n* pl. LENES a speech sound pronounced with little or no aspiration

LENITION   *n* pl. -S a change in articulation

LENITIVE   *n* pl. -S a soothing medicine

LENITY   *n* pl. -TIES leniency

LENO   *n* pl. -NOS a style of weaving

LENS   *n* pl. -ES a piece of transparent material used in changing the convergence of light rays **LENSLESS** *adj*

LENS   *v* -ED, -ING, -ES to make a film of

LENSE   *n* pl. -S lens

LENSMAN   *n* pl. -MEN a photographer

LENT   past tense of lend

LENTANDO   *adv* becoming slower — used as a musical direction

LENTEN   *adj* meager

LENTIC   *adj* pertaining to still water

LENTICEL   *n* pl. -S a mass of cells on a plant stem

LENTIGO   *n* pl. -TIGINES a freckle

LENTIL   *n* pl. -S a Eurasian annual plant

LENTISK   *n* pl. -S an evergreen tree

LENTO   *n* pl. -TOS a slow musical movement

LENTOID   *adj* lens-shaped

LEONE   *n* pl. -S a monetary unit of Sierra Leone

LEONINE   *adj* pertaining to a lion

LEOPARD   *n* pl. -S a large, carnivorous feline mammal

LEOTARD   *n* pl. -S a close-fitting garment

LEPER   *n* pl. -S one affected with leprosy

LEPIDOTE   *n* pl. -S a flowering shrub

LEPORID   *n* pl. -RIDS or -RIDAE a gnawing mammal

LEPORINE   *adj* resembling a rabbit or hare

LEPROSE   *adj* leprous

LEPROSY   *n* pl. -SIES a chronic disease characterized by skin lesions and deformities

LEPROTIC   *adj* leprous

LEPROUS   *adj* affected with leprosy

LEPT   a past tense of leap

LEPTON   *n* pl. -TA a monetary unit of Greece

LEPTON   *n* pl. -S a subatomic particle **LEPTONIC** *adj*

LESBIAN   *n* pl. -S a female homosexual

LESION   *n* pl. -S an abnormal change in the structure of an organ or tissue **LESIONED** *adj*

LESS   *adj* LESSER, LEAST not as great in quantity or degree

LESSEE   *n* pl. -S one to whom a lease is granted

LESSEN   *v* -ED, -ING, -S to make or become less

LESSER   *adj* not as large or important

LESSON   *v* -ED, -ING, -S to instruct

LESSOR   *n* pl. -S one that grants a lease

LEST   *conj* for fear that

LET   *v* LETTED, LETTING, LETS to hinder

LETCH   *v* -ED, -ING, -ES lech

LETDOWN   *n* pl. -S a decrease

LETHAL *n* pl. -S a death-causing genetic defect

LETHALLY *adv* in a deadly manner

LETHARGY *n* pl. -GIES drowsiness; sluggishness

LETHE *n* pl. -S forgetfulness **LETHEAN** *adj*

LETTED past tense of let

LETTER *v* -ED, -ING, -S to mark with letters (written symbols representing speech sounds)

LETTERER *n* pl. -S one that letters

LETTING present participle of let

LETTUCE *n* pl. -S an herb cultivated as a salad plant

LETUP *n* pl. -S a lessening or relaxation

LEU *n* pl. LEI a monetary unit of Romania

LEUCEMIA *n* pl. -S leukemia **LEUCEMIC** *adj*

LEUCIN *n* pl. -S leucine

LEUCINE *n* pl. -S an amino acid

LEUCITE *n* pl. -S a mineral **LEUCITIC** *adj*

LEUCOMA *n* pl. -S leukoma

LEUD *n* pl. -S or -ES a feudal vassal

LEUKEMIA *n* pl. -S a disease of the blood-forming organs

LEUKEMIC *n* pl. -S one affected with leukemia

LEUKOMA *n* pl. -S an opacity of the cornea

LEUKON *n* pl. -S a bodily organ consisting of the white blood cells

LEUKOSIS *n* pl. -KOSES leukemia **LEUKOTIC** *adj*

LEV *n* pl. LEVA a monetary unit of Bulgaria

LEVANT *v* -ED, -ING, -S to avoid a debt

LEVANTER *n* pl. -S an easterly Mediterranean wind

LEVATOR *n* pl. -ES or -S a muscle that raises an organ or part

LEVEE *v* LEVEED, LEVEEING, LEVEES to provide with an embankment

LEVEL *v* -ELED, -ELING, -ELS or -ELLED, -ELLING, -ELS to make even

LEVELER *n* pl. -S one that levels

LEVELLER *n* pl. -S leveler

LEVELLING a present participle of level

LEVELLY *adv* in an even manner

LEVER *v* -ED, -ING, -S to move with a lever (a rigid body used to lift weight)

LEVERAGE *v* -AGED, -AGING, -AGES to provide with a type of economic advantage

LEVERET *n* pl. -S a young hare

LEVIABLE *adj* liable to be levied

LEVIED past tense of levy

LEVIER *n* pl. -S one that levies

LEVIES present 3d person sing. of levy

LEVIGATE *v* -GATED, -GATING, -GATES to reduce to a fine powder

LEVIN *n* pl. -S lightning

LEVIRATE *n* pl. -S the custom of marrying the widow of one's brother

LEVITATE *v* -TATED, -TATING, -TATES to rise and float in the air

LEVITY *n* pl. -TIES conduct characterized by a lack of seriousness

LEVO *adj* turning toward the left

LEVODOPA *n* pl. -S a form of dopa

LEVOGYRE *adj* turning toward the left

LEVULIN *n* pl. -S a chemical compound

LEVULOSE *n* pl. -S a very sweet sugar

LEVY *v* LEVIED, LEVYING, LEVIES to impose or collect by legal authority

LEWD *adj* LEWDER, LEWDEST obscene **LEWDLY** *adv*

LEWDNESS *n* pl. -ES the state of being lewd

LEWIS *n* pl. -ISES a hoisting device

LEWISITE *n* pl. -S a vesicant liquid

LEWISSON *n* pl. -S lewis

LEX *n* pl. LEGES law

LEXEME *n* pl. -S a linguistic unit **LEXEMIC** *adj*

LEXICAL *adj* pertaining to the words of a language

LEXICON *n* pl. -CA or -CONS a dictionary

LEXIS *n* pl. LEXES the vocabulary of a language, a group, or a subject field

LEY *n* pl. LEYS lea

LI *n* pl. -S a Chinese unit of distance

LIABLE *adj* subject or susceptible to something possible or likely

LIAISE *v* LIAISED, LIAISING, LIAISES to establish liaison

LIAISON *n* pl. -S a means for maintaining communication

LIANA *n* pl. -S a tropical vine

LIANE *n* pl. -S liana

LIANG *n* pl. -S a Chinese unit of weight

LIANOID *adj* pertaining to a liana

LIAR *n* pl. -S one that speaks falsely

LIARD *n* pl. -S a former silver coin of France

LIB *n* pl. -S liberation

LIBATION *n* pl. -S a ceremonial pouring of a liquid

LIBECCIO *n* pl. -CIOS a southwest wind

LIBEL *v* -BELED, -BELING, -BELS or -BELLED, -BELLING, -BELS to make or publish a defamatory statement about

LIBELANT *n* pl. -S a plaintiff in a type of lawsuit

LIBELEE *n* pl. -S a defendant in a type of lawsuit

LIBELER *n* pl. -S one that libels

LIBELIST *n* pl. -S a libeler

LIBELLED a past tense of libel

LIBELLEE *n* pl. -S libelee

LIBELLER *n* pl. -S libeler

LIBELLING a present participle of libel

LIBELOUS *adj* defamatory

LIBER *n* pl. LIBRI or LIBERS a book of public records

LIBERAL *n* pl. -S a person favorable to progress or reform

LIBERATE *v* -ATED, -ATING, -ATES to set free

LIBERTY *n* pl. -TIES the state of being free

LIBIDO *n* pl. -DOS the energy derived from instinctual biological drives

LIBLAB *n* pl. -S a person supporting a coalition of liberal and labor groups

LIBRA *n* pl. -BRAE an ancient Roman unit of weight

LIBRA *n* pl. -S a former gold coin of Peru

LIBRARY *n* pl. -BRARIES a place where literary materials are kept for reading and reference

LIBRATE *v* -BRATED, -BRATING, -BRATES to move from side to side

LIBRETTO *n* pl. -TOS or -TI the text of an opera

LIBRI a pl. of liber

LICE pl. of louse

LICENCE *v* -CENCED, -CENCING, -CENCES to license

LICENCEE *n* pl. -S licensee

LICENCER *n* pl. -S licenser

LICENSE *v* -CENSED, -CENSING, -CENSES to issue or grant authoritative permission to

LICENSEE *n* pl. -S one that is licensed

LICENSER *n* pl. -S one that licenses

LICENSOR *n* pl. -S licenser

LICENTE a pl. of sente

LICH *n* pl. -ES a corpse

LICHEE *n* pl. -S litchi

LICHEN *v* -ED, -ING, -S to cover with lichens (flowerless plants)

LICHENIN *n* pl. -S a chemical compound

LICHI *n* pl. -S litchi

LICHT *v* -ED, -ING, -S to light

LICHTLY *adv* lightly

LICIT *adj* lawful **LICITLY** *adv*

LICK *v* -ED, -ING, -S to pass the tongue over the surface of

LICKER *n* pl. -S one that licks

LICKING *n* pl. -S a thrashing or beating

LICKSPIT *n* pl. -S a fawning person

LICORICE *n* pl. -S a perennial herb

LICTOR *n* pl. -S a magistrate's attendant in ancient Rome

LID *v* LIDDED, LIDDING, LIDS to provide with a lid (a movable cover)

LIDAR *n* pl. -S an electronic locating device

LIDLESS *adj* having no lid

LIDO *n* pl. -DOS a fashionable beach resort

LIE *v* LIED, LYING, LIES to speak falsely

LIE *v* LAY, LAIN, LYING, LIES to be in or get into a horizontal position

LIED *n* pl. LIEDER a German song

LIEF *adj* LIEFER, LIEFEST willing **LIEFLY** *adv*

LIEGE *n* pl. -S a feudal lord

LIEGEMAN *n* pl. -MEN a feudal vassal

LIEN   *n* pl. -S a legal right to hold or sell a debtor's property

LIENABLE   *adj* capable of being subjected to a lien

LIENAL   *adj* pertaining to the spleen

LIENTERY   *n* pl. -TERIES a form of diarrhea

LIER   *n* pl. -S one that lies or reclines

LIERNE   *n* pl. -S a connecting part in Gothic vaulting

LIEU   *n* pl. -S place; stead

LIEVE   *adv* LIEVER, LIEVEST gladly

LIFE   *n* pl. LIVES the quality that distinguishes animals and plants from inanimate matter

LIFEBOAT   *n* pl. -S a small rescue boat

LIFEFUL   *adj* full of life

LIFELESS   *adj* having no life

LIFELIKE   *adj* resembling a living thing

LIFELINE   *n* pl. -S a rope used to aid a person in distress

LIFELONG   *adj* lasting for a lifetime

LIFER   *n* pl. -S a prisoner serving a life sentence

LIFETIME   *n* pl. -S the period of living existence

LIFEWAY   *n* pl. -WAYS a way of living

LIFEWORK   *n* pl. -S the major work of one's lifetime

LIFT   *v* -ED, -ING, -S to move to a higher position **LIFTABLE** *adj*

LIFTER   *n* pl. -S one that lifts

LIFTGATE   *n* pl. -S a rear panel on a station wagon that opens upward

LIFTMAN   *n* pl. -MEN an elevator operator

LIFTOFF   *n* pl. -S the vertical takeoff of a rocket

LIGAMENT   *n* pl. -S a band of firm, fibrous tissue

LIGAN   *n* pl. -S lagan

LIGAND   *n* pl. -S a type of ion or molecule

LIGASE   *n* pl. -S an enzyme

LIGATE   *v* -GATED, -GATING, -GATES to bind

LIGATION   *n* pl. -S the act of ligating **LIGATIVE** *adj*

LIGATURE   *v* -TURED, -TURING, -TURES to ligate

LIGER   *n* pl. -S the offspring of a male lion and a female tiger

LIGHT   *adj* LIGHTER, LIGHTEST having little weight

LIGHT   *v* LIGHTED or LIT, LIGHTING, LIGHTS to illuminate

LIGHTEN   *v* -ED, -ING, -S to reduce the weight of

LIGHTER   *v* -ED, -ING, -S to convey in a type of barge

LIGHTFUL   *adj* brightly illuminated

LIGHTING   *n* pl. -S illumination

LIGHTISH   *adj* somewhat light

LIGHTLY   *adv* to a moderate degree

LIGNEOUS   *adj* of or resembling wood

LIGNIFY   *v* -FIED, -FYING, -FIES to convert into wood

LIGNIN   *n* pl. -S an essential part of woody tissue

LIGNITE   *n* pl. -S a type of coal **LIGNITIC** *adj*

LIGROIN   *n* pl. -S a flammable liquid

LIGROINE   *n* pl. -S ligroin

LIGULA   *n* pl. -LAE or -LAS a strap-shaped organ or part **LIGULAR, LIGULATE, LIGULOID** *adj*

LIGULE   *n* pl. -S a strap-shaped plant part

LIGURE   *n* pl. -S a precious stone

LIKABLE   *adj* pleasant

LIKE   *v* LIKED, LIKING, LIKES to find pleasant

LIKE   *adj* LIKER, LIKEST possessing the same or almost the same characteristics

LIKEABLE   *adj* likable

LIKED   past tense of like

LIKELY   *adj* -LIER, -LIEST probable

LIKEN   *v* -ED, -ING, -S to represent as similar

LIKENESS   *n* pl. -ES a pictorial representation

LIKER   *n* pl. -S one that likes

LIKEST   superlative of like

LIKEWISE   *adv* in a similar manner

LIKING   *n* pl. -S a feeling of attraction or affection

LIKUTA   *n* pl. MAKUTA a monetary unit of Zaire

LILAC   *n* pl. -S a flowering shrub

LILIED   *adj* covered with lilies

LILIES   pl. of lily

LILLIPUT	*n* pl. -S a very small person	**LIMIT**	*v* -ED, -ING, -S to restrict
LILT	*v* -ED, -ING, -S to sing or speak rhythmically	**LIMITARY**	*adj* limiting
LILY	*n* pl. LILIES a flowering plant **LILYLIKE** *adj*	**LIMITED**	*n* pl. -S a train or bus making few stops
		LIMITER	*n* pl. -S one that limits
LIMA	*n* pl. -S the edible seed of a tropical American plant	**LIMITES**	pl. of limes
LIMACINE	*adj* resembling a type of mollusk	**LIMMER**	*n* pl. -S a scoundrel
LIMACON	*n* pl. -S a type of geometric curve	**LIMN**	*v* -ED, -ING, -S to depict by painting or drawing
LIMAN	*n* pl. -S a lagoon	**LIMNER**	*n* pl. -S one that limns
LIMB	*v* -ED, -ING, -S to cut off the arms or legs of	**LIMNETIC**	*adj* pertaining to the open water of a lake or pond
LIMBA	*n* pl. -S an African tree	**LIMNIC**	*adj* limnetic
LIMBATE	*adj* having an edge of a different color	**LIMO**	*n* pl. LIMOS a limousine
LIMBECK	*n* pl. -S alembic	**LIMONENE**	*n* pl. -S a chemical compound
LIMBER	*adj* -BERER, -BEREST flexible **LIMBERLY** *adv*	**LIMONITE**	*n* pl. -S a major ore of iron
		LIMP	*v* -ED, -ING, -S to walk lamely
LIMBER	*v* -ED, -ING, -S to make flexible	**LIMP**	*adj* LIMPER, LIMPEST lacking rigidity
LIMBI	a pl. of limbus	**LIMPA**	*n* pl. -S rye bread made with molasses
LIMBIC	*adj* pertaining to a system of the brain		
LIMBIER	comparative of limby	**LIMPER**	*n* pl. -S one that limps
LIMBIEST	superlative of limby	**LIMPET**	*n* pl. -S a type of mollusk
LIMBLESS	*adj* having no arms or legs	**LIMPID**	*adj* transparent **LIMPIDLY** *adv*
LIMBO	*n* pl. -BOS a condition of oblivion or neglect	**LIMPKIN**	*n* pl. -S a wading bird
		LIMPLY	*adv* in a limp manner
LIMBUS	*n* pl. -BUSES or -BI a distinctive border	**LIMPNESS**	*n* pl. -ES the state of being limp
		LIMPSEY	*adj* -SIER, -SIEST limpsy
LIMBY	*adj* LIMBIER, LIMBIEST having many large branches	**LIMPSY**	*adj* -SIER, -SIEST lacking strength or vigor
LIME	*v* LIMED, LIMING, LIMES to treat with lime (a calcium compound)	**LIMULOID**	*n* pl. -S a horseshoe crab
		LIMULUS	*n* pl. -LI a horseshoe crab
LIMEADE	*n* pl. -S a beverage	**LIMY**	*adj* LIMIER, LIMIEST resembling or containing lime
LIMEKILN	*n* pl. -S a furnace in which shells are burned to produce lime		
		LIN	*n* pl. -S linn
LIMELESS	*adj* having no lime	**LINABLE**	*adj* lineable
LIMEN	*n* pl. -MENS or -MINA a sensory threshold	**LINAC**	*n* pl. -S a device for imparting high velocities to charged particles
LIMERICK	*n* pl. -S a humorous verse		
LIMES	*n* pl. LIMITES a fortified boundary	**LINAGE**	*n* pl. -S the number of lines of printed material
LIMEY	*n* pl. -EYS a British sailor	**LINALOL**	*n* pl. -S linalool
LIMIER	comparative of limy	**LINALOOL**	*n* pl. -S a fragrant alcohol
LIMIEST	superlative of limy	**LINCHPIN**	*n* pl. -S a locking pin inserted in the end of a shaft
LIMINA	a pl. of limen		
LIMINAL	*adj* pertaining to the limen	**LINDANE**	*n* pl. -S an insecticide
LIMINESS	*n* pl. -ES the state of being limy	**LINDEN**	*n* pl. -S a tall forest tree
LIMING	present participle of lime	**LINDY**	*n* pl. -DIES a lively dance

LINE	*v* LINED, LINING, LINES to mark with lines (slender, continuous marks)
LINEABLE	*adj* lying in a straight line
LINEAGE	*n* pl. -S direct descent from an ancestor
LINEAL	*adj* being directly descended from an ancestor **LINEALLY** *adv*
LINEAR	*adj* of or resembling a straight line **LINEARLY** *adv*
LINEATE	*adj* marked with lines
LINEATED	*adj* lineate
LINEBRED	*adj* produced by interbreeding within a particular line of descent
LINECUT	*n* pl. -S a type of printing plate
LINED	past tense of line
LINELESS	*adj* having no lines
LINELIKE	*adj* resembling a line
LINEMAN	*n* pl. -MEN one who installs or repairs telephone wires
LINEN	*n* pl. -S a fabric woven from the fibers of flax **LINENY** *adj*
LINER	*n* pl. -S a commercial ship or airplane
LINESMAN	*n* pl. -MEN a football official
LINEUP	*n* pl. -S a row of persons
LINEY	*adj* LINIER, LINIEST liny
LING	*n* pl. -S a heath plant
LINGA	*n* pl. -S lingam
LINGAM	*n* pl. -S a Hindu phallic symbol
LINGCOD	*n* pl. -S a marine food fish
LINGER	*v* -ED, -ING, -S to delay leaving
LINGERER	*n* pl. -S one that lingers
LINGERIE	*n* pl. -S women's underwear
LINGIER	comparative of lingy
LINGIEST	superlative of lingy
LINGO	*n* pl. -GOES strange or incomprehensible language
LINGUA	*n* pl. -GUAE the tongue or a tonguelike part
LINGUAL	*n* pl. -S a sound articulated with the tongue
LINGUINE	*n* pl. -S linguini
LINGUINI	*n* pl. -S a type of pasta
LINGUIST	*n* pl. -S a person skilled in several languages
LINGY	*adj* LINGIER, LINGIEST covered with heaths
LINIER	comparative of liney and liny
LINIEST	superlative of liney and liny
LINIMENT	*n* pl. -S a medicinal liquid
LININ	*n* pl. -S a substance in the nucleus of a cell
LINING	*n* pl. -S an inner layer
LINK	*v* -ED, -ING, -S to connect **LINKABLE** *adj*
LINKAGE	*n* pl. -S the act of linking
LINKBOY	*n* pl. -BOYS a man or boy hired to carry a torch to light the way along dark streets
LINKER	*n* pl. -S one that links
LINKMAN	*n* pl. -MEN a linkboy
LINKSMAN	*n* pl. -MEN a golfer
LINKUP	*n* pl. -S something that serves as a linking device
LINKWORK	*n* pl. -S something composed of interlocking rings
LINKY	*adj* full of interlocking rings
LINN	*n* pl. -S a waterfall
LINNET	*n* pl. -S a European songbird
LINO	*n* pl. -NOS linoleum
LINOCUT	*n* pl. -S a print made from a design cut into linoleum
LINOLEUM	*n* pl. -S a durable material used as a floor covering
LINSANG	*n* pl. -S a carnivorous mammal
LINSEED	*n* pl. -S flaxseed
LINSEY	*n* pl. -SEYS a coarse fabric
LINSTOCK	*n* pl. -S a stick having one end divided to hold a match
LINT	*n* pl. -S an accumulation of bits of fiber
LINTEL	*n* pl. -S a horizontal supporting beam
LINTER	*n* pl. -S a machine for removing fibers from cotton seeds
LINTIER	comparative of linty
LINTIEST	superlative of linty
LINTLESS	*adj* free from lint
LINTOL	*n* pl. -S lintel
LINTY	*adj* LINTIER, LINTIEST covered with lint
LINUM	*n* pl. -S a plant of the flax family
LINURON	*n* pl. -S a herbicide
LINY	*adj* LINIER, LINIEST resembling a line
LION	*n* pl. -S a large, carnivorous feline mammal

LIONESS	*n* pl. -ES a female lion
LIONFISH	*n* pl. -ES a tropical fish
LIONISE	*v* -ISED, -ISING, -ISES to lionize
LIONISER	*n* pl. -S one that lionises
LIONIZE	*v* -IZED, -IZING, -IZES to treat or regard as a celebrity
LIONIZER	*n* pl. -S one that lionizes
LIONLIKE	*adj* resembling a lion
LIP	*v* LIPPED, LIPPING, LIPS to touch with the lips (the folds of flesh around the mouth)
LIPASE	*n* pl. -S an enzyme
LIPID	*n* pl. -S any of a class of fatty substances **LIPIDIC** *adj*
LIPIDE	*n* pl. -S lipid
LIPIN	*n* pl. -S a lipid
LIPLESS	*adj* having no lips
LIPLIKE	*adj* resembling a lip
LIPOCYTE	*n* pl. -S a fat-producing cell
LIPOID	*n* pl. -S a lipid **LIPOIDAL** *adj*
LIPOMA	*n* pl. -MAS or -MATA a tumor of fatty tissue
LIPOSOME	*n* pl. -S a microscopic globule composed of lipids
LIPPED	past tense of lip
LIPPEN	*v* -ED, -ING, -S to trust
LIPPER	*v* -ED, -ING, -S to ripple
LIPPING	*n* pl. -S a liplike outgrowth of bone
LIPPY	*adj* -PIER, -PIEST impudent
LIPSTICK	*n* pl. -S a cosmetic used to color the lips
LIQUATE	*v* -QUATED, -QUATING, -QUATES to purify metal by heating
LIQUEFY	*v* -FIED, -FYING, -FIES to make or become liquid
LIQUEUR	*n* pl. -S a sweetened alcoholic beverage
LIQUID	*n* pl. -S a substance that flows freely
LIQUIDLY	*adv* in a free-flowing manner
LIQUIFY	*v* -FIED, -FYING, -FIES to liquefy
LIQUOR	*v* -ED, -ING, -S to intoxicate with liquor (an alcoholic beverage)
LIRA	*n* pl. LIRI a monetary unit of Malta
LIRA	*n* pl. LIRE or LIRAS a monetary unit of Italy
LIRA	*n* pl. LIROTH or LIROT a former monetary unit of Israel
LIRIPIPE	*n* pl. -S a long scarf
LISENTE	a pl. of sente
LISLE	*n* pl. -S a fine, tightly twisted cotton thread
LISP	*v* -ED, -ING, -S to pronounce the letters *s* and *z* imperfectly
LISPER	*n* pl. -S one that lisps
LISSOM	*adj* lissome **LISSOMLY** *adv*
LISSOME	*adj* lithe
LIST	*v* -ED, -ING, -S to write down in a particular order **LISTABLE** *adj*
LISTEE	*n* pl. -S one that is on a list
LISTEL	*n* pl. -S a narrow molding
LISTEN	*v* -ED, -ING, -S to make conscious use of the sense of hearing
LISTENER	*n* pl. -S one that listens
LISTER	*n* pl. -S a type of plow
LISTING	*n* pl. -S something that is listed
LISTLESS	*adj* languid
LIT	*n* pl. -S the litas
LITANY	*n* pl. -NIES a ceremonial form of prayer
LITAS	*n* pl. LITAI or LITU a former monetary unit of Lithuania
LITCHI	*n* pl. -S the edible fruit of a Chinese tree
LITE	*adj* lower in calories or having less of some ingredient
LITER	*n* pl. -S a unit of capacity
LITERACY	*n* pl. -CIES the ability to read and write
LITERAL	*n* pl. -S a small error in printing or writing
LITERARY	*adj* of, pertaining to, or having the characteristics of books and writings
LITERATE	*n* pl. -S one who can read and write
LITERATI	*n/pl* scholars collectively
LITHARGE	*n* pl. -S a monoxide of lead
LITHE	*adj* LITHER, LITHEST bending easily **LITHELY** *adv*
LITHEMIA	*n* pl. -S an excess of uric acid in the blood **LITHEMIC** *adj*
LITHIA	*n* pl. -S an oxide of lithium
LITHIC	*adj* pertaining to lithium
LITHIFY	*v* -FIED, -FYING, -FIES to petrify

LITHIUM	*n* pl. -S a metallic element
LITHO	*v* -ED, -ING, -S to make prints by lithography
LITHOID	*adj* resembling stone
LITHOSOL	*n* pl. -S a type of soil
LITIGANT	*n* pl. -S one who is engaged in a lawsuit
LITIGATE	*v* -GATED, -GATING, -GATES to subject to legal proceedings
LITMUS	*n* pl. -ES a blue coloring matter
LITORAL	*adj* pertaining to a coastal region
LITOTES	*n* pl. LITOTES a figure of speech in which an assertion is made by the negation of its opposite **LITOTIC** *adj*
LITRE	*n* pl. -S liter
LITTEN	*adj* lighted
LITTER	*v* -ED, -ING, -S to scatter rubbish about
LITTERER	*n* pl. -S one that litters
LITTERY	*adj* covered with rubbish
LITTLE	*adj* -TLER, -TLEST small
LITTLE	*n* pl. -S a small amount
LITTLISH	*adj* somewhat little
LITTORAL	*n* pl. -S a coastal region
LITU	a pl. of litas
LITURGY	*n* pl. -GIES a prescribed system of public worship **LITURGIC** *adj*
LIVABLE	*adj* suitable for living in
LIVE	*v* LIVED, LIVING, LIVES to function as an animal or plant
LIVE	*adj* LIVER, LIVEST having life
LIVEABLE	*adj* livable
LIVELONG	*adj* long in passing
LIVELY	*adj* -LIER, -LIEST full of energy **LIVELILY** *adv*
LIVEN	*v* -ED, -ING, -S to make lively
LIVENER	*n* pl. -S one that livens
LIVENESS	*n* pl. -ES the state of being live
LIVER	*n* pl. -S a secreting organ
LIVERIED	*adj* wearing a livery
LIVERISH	*adj* having a liver disorder
LIVERY	*n* pl. -ERIES a uniform worn by servants
LIVES	pl. of life
LIVEST	superlative of live
LIVETRAP	*v* -TRAPPED, -TRAPPING, -TRAPS to capture in a type of animal trap
LIVID	*adj* having the skin abnormally discolored **LIVIDLY** *adv*
LIVIDITY	*n* pl. -TIES the state of being livid
LIVIER	*n* pl. -S livyer
LIVING	*n* pl. -S a means of subsistence
LIVINGLY	*adv* realistically
LIVRE	*n* pl. -S a former monetary unit of France
LIVYER	*n* pl. -S a permanent resident of Newfoundland
LIXIVIUM	*n* pl. -IA or -IUMS a solution obtained by leaching **LIXIVIAL** *adj*
LIZARD	*n* pl. -S any of a suborder of reptiles
LLAMA	*n* pl. -S a ruminant mammal
LLANO	*n* pl. -NOS an open, grassy plain
LO	*interj* — used to attract attention or to express surprise
LOACH	*n* pl. -ES a freshwater fish
LOAD	*v* -ED, -ING, -S to place in or on a means of conveyance
LOADER	*n* pl. -S one that loads
LOADING	*n* pl. -S a burden
LOADSTAR	*n* pl. -S lodestar
LOAF	*n* pl. LOAVES a shaped mass of bread
LOAF	*v* -ED, -ING, -S to pass time idly
LOAFER	*n* pl. -S one that loafs
LOAM	*v* -ED, -ING, -S to cover with loam (a type of soil)
LOAMLESS	*adj* having no loam
LOAMY	*adj* LOAMIER, LOAMIEST resembling loam
LOAN	*v* -ED, -ING, -S to lend **LOANABLE** *adj*
LOANER	*n* pl. -S one that loans
LOANING	*n* pl. -S a lane
LOANWORD	*n* pl. -S a word taken from another language
LOATH	*adj* unwilling
LOATHE	*v* LOATHED, LOATHING, LOATHES to detest greatly
LOATHER	*n* pl. -S one that loathes
LOATHFUL	*adj* repulsive
LOATHING	*n* pl. -S extreme dislike

LOATHLY	*adj* repulsive
LOAVES	pl. of loaf
LOB	*v* LOBBED, LOBBING, LOBS to throw or hit in a high arc
LOBAR	*adj* pertaining to a lobe
LOBATE	*adj* having lobes **LOBATELY** *adv*
LOBATED	*adj* lobate
LOBATION	*n* pl. -S the formation of lobes
LOBBED	past tense of lob
LOBBER	*n* pl. -S one that lobs
LOBBING	present participle of lob
LOBBY	*v* -BIED, -BYING, -BIES to attempt to influence legislators
LOBBYER	*n* pl. -S a lobbyist
LOBBYGOW	*n* pl. -S an errand boy
LOBBYISM	*n* pl. -S the practice of lobbying
LOBBYIST	*n* pl. -S one who lobbies
LOBE	*n* pl. -S a rounded, projecting anatomical part **LOBED** *adj*
LOBEFIN	*n* pl. -S a bony fish
LOBELIA	*n* pl. -S a flowering plant
LOBELINE	*n* pl. -S a poisonous alkaloid
LOBLOLLY	*n* pl. -LIES a pine tree
LOBO	*n* pl. -BOS the timber wolf
LOBOTOMY	*n* pl. -MIES a type of surgical operation
LOBSTER	*v* -ED, -ING, -S to fish for lobsters (marine crustaceans)
LOBSTICK	*n* pl. -S a tree with its lower branches trimmed
LOBULE	*n* pl. -S a small lobe **LOBULAR, LOBULATE, LOBULOSE** *adj*
LOBWORM	*n* pl. -S a lugworm
LOCA	a pl. of locus
LOCAL	*n* pl. -S a train or bus making all stops
LOCALE	*n* pl. -S a locality
LOCALISE	*v* -ISED, -ISING, -ISES to localize
LOCALISM	*n* pl. -S a custom or mannerism peculiar to a locality
LOCALIST	*n* pl. -S one who is strongly concerned with the matters of a locality
LOCALITE	*n* pl. -S a resident of a locality
LOCALITY	*n* pl. -TIES an area or neighborhood
LOCALIZE	*v* -IZED, -IZING, -IZES to confine to a particular area
LOCALLY	*adv* in a particular area
LOCATE	*v* -CATED, -CATING, -CATES to determine the position of
LOCATER	*n* pl. -S one that locates
LOCATION	*n* pl. -S the place where something is at a given moment
LOCATIVE	*n* pl. -S a type of grammatical case
LOCATOR	*n* pl. -S locater
LOCH	*n* pl. -S a lake
LOCHAN	*n* pl. -S a small lake
LOCHIA	*n* pl. LOCHIA a vaginal discharge following childbirth **LOCHIAL** *adj*
LOCI	a pl. of locus
LOCK	*v* -ED, -ING, -S to secure by means of a mechanical fastening device **LOCKABLE** *adj*
LOCKAGE	*n* pl. -S a toll on a ship passing through a canal
LOCKBOX	*n* pl. -ES a box that locks
LOCKDOWN	*n* pl. -S the confinement of prisoners to their cells
LOCKER	*n* pl. -S an enclosure that may be locked
LOCKET	*n* pl. -S a small ornamental case
LOCKJAW	*n* pl. -S a form of tetanus
LOCKNUT	*n* pl. -S a nut which keeps another from loosening
LOCKOUT	*n* pl. -S a closing of a business to coerce employees to agree to terms
LOCKRAM	*n* pl. -S a coarse, linen fabric
LOCKSTEP	*n* pl. -S a mode of marching in close file
LOCKUP	*n* pl. -S a jail
LOCO	*n* pl. -COS or -COES locoweed
LOCO	*v* -ED, -ING, -S to poison with locoweed
LOCOFOCO	*n* pl. -COS a type of friction match
LOCOISM	*n* pl. -S a disease of livestock
LOCOMOTE	*v* -MOTED, -MOTING, -MOTES to move about
LOCOWEED	*n* pl. -S a plant that causes poisoning when eaten by livestock
LOCULAR	*adj* having or divided into loculi
LOCULATE	*adj* locular
LOCULE	*n* pl. -S loculus **LOCULED** *adj*

LOCULUS	*n* pl. -LI a small, cell-like chamber
LOCUM	*n* pl. -S a temporary substitute
LOCUS	*n* pl. LOCI or LOCA a place
LOCUST	*n* pl. -S a migratory grasshopper
LOCUSTA	*n* pl. -TAE a spikelet **LOCUSTAL** *adj*
LOCUTION	*n* pl. -S a particular form of expression
LOCUTORY	*n* pl. -RIES a room in a monastery
LODE	*n* pl. -S a deposit of ore
LODEN	*n* pl. -S a thick, woolen fabric
LODESTAR	*n* pl. -S a star used as a point of reference
LODGE	*v* LODGED, LODGING, LODGES to furnish with temporary quarters
LODGER	*n* pl. -S one that resides in rented quarters
LODGING	*n* pl. -S a temporary place to live
LODGMENT	*n* pl. -S a lodging
LODICULE	*n* pl. -S a scale at the base of the ovary of a grass
LOESS	*n* pl. -ES a soil deposit **LOESSAL, LOESSIAL** *adj*
LOFT	*v* -ED, -ING, -S to store in a loft (an upper room)
LOFTER	*n* pl. -S a type of golf club
LOFTIER	comparative of lofty
LOFTIEST	superlative of lofty
LOFTILY	*adv* in a lofty manner
LOFTLESS	*adj* having no loft
LOFTLIKE	*adj* resembling a loft
LOFTY	*adj* LOFTIER, LOFTIEST extending high in the air
LOG	*v* LOGGED, LOGGING, LOGS to cut down trees for timber
LOGAN	*n* pl. -S a stone balanced to permit easy movement
LOGANIA	*adj* designating a family of flowering plants
LOGBOOK	*n* pl. -S a record book of a ship or aircraft
LOGE	*n* pl. -S a small compartment
LOGGATS	*n/pl* loggets
LOGGED	past tense of log
LOGGER	*n* pl. -S one that logs
LOGGETS	*n/pl* an old English throwing game
LOGGIA	*n* pl. -GIAS or -GIE an open gallery
LOGGING	*n* pl. -S the business of cutting down trees for timber
LOGGY	*adj* -GIER, -GIEST logy
LOGIA	a pl. of logion
LOGIC	*n* pl. -S the science of reasoning
LOGICAL	*adj* pertaining to logic
LOGICIAN	*n* pl. -S one who is skilled in logic
LOGICISE	*v* -CISED, -CISING, -CISES to logicize
LOGICIZE	*v* -CIZED, -CIZING, -CIZES to reason
LOGIER	comparative of logy
LOGIEST	superlative of logy
LOGILY	*adv* in a logy manner
LOGINESS	*n* pl. -ES the state of being logy
LOGION	*n* pl. -GIA or -GIONS a saying attributed to Jesus
LOGISTIC	*n* pl. -S symbolic logic
LOGJAM	*n* pl. -S a tangled mass of logs
LOGO	*n* pl. LOGOS an identifying symbol
LOGOGRAM	*n* pl. -S a symbol used to represent an entire word
LOGOMACH	*n* pl. -S one given to arguing about words
LOGOS	*n* pl. LOGOI the rational principle that governs the universe in ancient Greek philosophy
LOGOTYPE	*n* pl. -S a piece of type bearing a syllable, word, or words
LOGOTYPY	*n* pl. -TYPIES the use of logotypes
LOGROLL	*v* -ED, -ING, -S to obtain passage of by exchanging political favors
LOGWAY	*n* pl. -WAYS a ramp used in logging
LOGWOOD	*n* pl. -S a tropical tree
LOGY	*adj* -GIER, -GIEST sluggish
LOIN	*n* pl. -S a part of the side and back between the ribs and the hipbone
LOITER	*v* -ED, -ING, -S to stand idly about
LOITERER	*n* pl. -S one that loiters
LOLL	*v* -ED, -ING, -S to lounge
LOLLER	*n* pl. -S one that lolls
LOLLIES	pl. of lolly

LOLLIPOP	*n* pl. -S a piece of candy on the end of a stick	**LONGTIME**	*adj* of long duration
LOLLOP	*v* -ED, -ING, -S to loll	**LONGUEUR**	*n* pl. -S a dull and tedious section
LOLLY	*n* pl. -LIES a lollipop	**LONGWAYS**	*adv* longwise
LOLLYGAG	*v* -GAGGED, -GAGGING, -GAGS to lallygag	**LONGWISE**	*adv* lengthwise
LOLLYPOP	*n* pl. -S lollipop	**LOO**	*v* -ED, -ING, -S to subject to a forfeit at loo (a card game)
LOMEIN	*n* pl. -S a Chinese dish of noodles, meat, and vegetables	**LOOBY**	*n* pl. -BIES a large, awkward person
LOMENT	*n* pl. -S a type of plant pod	**LOOEY**	*n* pl. -EYS looie
LOMENTUM	*n* pl. -TA or -TUMS loment	**LOOF**	*n* pl. -S the palm of the hand
LONE	*adj* having no companions	**LOOFA**	*n* pl. -S loofah
LONELY	*adj* -LIER, -LIEST sad from lack of companionship **LONELILY** *adv*	**LOOFAH**	*n* pl. -S a tropical vine
LONENESS	*n* pl. -ES the state of being lone	**LOOIE**	*n* pl. -S a lieutenant of the armed forces
LONER	*n* pl. -S one that avoids others	**LOOK**	*v* -ED, -ING, -S to use one's eyes in seeing
LONESOME	*n* pl. -S self	**LOOKDOWN**	*n* pl. -S a marine fish
LONG	*adj* LONGER, LONGEST extending for a considerable distance	**LOOKER**	*n* pl. -S one that looks
LONG	*v* -ED, -ING, -S to desire strongly	**LOOKOUT**	*n* pl. -S one engaged in keeping watch
LONGAN	*n* pl. -S the edible fruit of a Chinese tree	**LOOKUP**	*n* pl. -S the process of looking something up
LONGBOAT	*n* pl. -S the largest boat carried by a sailing vessel	**LOOM**	*v* -ED, -ING, -S to appear in an enlarged and indistinct form
LONGBOW	*n* pl. -S a type of archery bow	**LOON**	*n* pl. -S a diving waterfowl
LONGE	*v* LONGED, LONGEING, LONGES to guide a horse by means of a long rope	**LOONEY**	*adj* -NIER, -NIEST loony
		LOONEY	*n* pl. -EYS loony
LONGER	*n* pl. -S one that longs	**LOONY**	*adj* -NIER, -NIEST crazy
LONGERON	*n* pl. -S a longitudinal support of an airplane	**LOONY**	*n* pl. -NIES a loony person
LONGHAIR	*n* pl. -S an intellectual	**LOOP**	*v* -ED, -ING, -S to form loops (circular or oval openings)
LONGHAND	*n* pl. -S ordinary handwriting	**LOOPER**	*n* pl. -S one that loops
LONGHEAD	*n* pl. -S a person having a long skull	**LOOPHOLE**	*v* -HOLED, -HOLING, -HOLES to make small openings in
LONGHORN	*n* pl. -S one of a breed of long-horned cattle	**LOOPY**	*adj* LOOPIER, LOOPIEST full of loops
LONGIES	*n/pl* long underwear	**LOOSE**	*adj* LOOSER, LOOSEST not firm, taut, or rigid **LOOSELY** *adv*
LONGING	*n* pl. -S a strong desire	**LOOSE**	*v* LOOSED, LOOSING, LOOSES to set free
LONGISH	*adj* somewhat long	**LOOSEN**	*v* -ED, -ING, -S to make looser
LONGLEAF	*n* pl. -LEAVES an evergreen tree	**LOOSENER**	*n* pl. -S one that loosens
LONGLINE	*n* pl. -S a type of fishing line	**LOOSER**	comparative of loose
LONGLY	*adv* for a considerable distance	**LOOSEST**	superlative of loose
LONGNESS	*n* pl. -ES the state of being long	**LOOSING**	present participle of loose
LONGSHIP	*n* pl. -S a medieval ship	**LOOT**	*v* -ED, -ING, -S to plunder
LONGSOME	*adj* tediously long	**LOOTER**	*n* pl. -S one that loots
LONGSPUR	*n* pl. -S a long-clawed finch		

LOP	*v* LOPPED, LOPPING, LOPS to cut off branches or twigs from
LOPE	*v* LOPED, LOPING, LOPES to run with a steady, easy gait
LOPER	*n* pl. -S one that lopes
LOPPED	past tense of lop
LOPPER	*v* -ED, -ING, -S to curdle
LOPPING	present participle of lop
LOPPY	*adj* -PIER, -PIEST hanging limply
LOPSIDED	*adj* leaning to one side
LOPSTICK	*n* pl. -S lobstick
LOQUAT	*n* pl. -S a small yellow fruit
LORAL	*adj* pertaining to the space between the eye and bill of a bird
LORAN	*n* pl. -S a type of navigational system
LORD	*v* -ED, -ING, -S to invest with the power of a lord (a person having dominion over others)
LORDING	*n* pl. -S a lordling
LORDLESS	*adj* having no lord
LORDLIER	comparative of lordly
LORDLIEST	superlative of lordly
LORDLIKE	*adj* lordly
LORDLING	*n* pl. -S a young or unimportant lord
LORDLY	*adj* -LIER, -LIEST of or befitting a lord
LORDOMA	*n* pl. -S lordosis
LORDOSIS	*n* pl. -DOSES a curvature of the spinal column **LORDOTIC** *adj*
LORDSHIP	*n* pl. -S the power of a lord
LORE	*n* pl. -S traditional knowledge or belief
LOREAL	*adj* loral
LORGNON	*n* pl. -S a pair of eyeglasses with a handle
LORICA	*n* pl. -CAE a protective covering or shell
LORICATE	*n* pl. -S an animal having a lorica
LORIES	pl. of lory
LORIKEET	*n* pl. -S a small parrot
LORIMER	*n* pl. -S a maker of implements for harnesses and saddles
LORINER	*n* pl. -S lorimer
LORIS	*n* pl. -RISES an Asian lemur
LORN	*adj* abandoned
LORNNESS	*n* pl. -ES the state of being lorn

LORRY	*n* pl. -RIES a type of wagon or truck
LORY	*n* pl. -RIES a small parrot
LOSE	*v* LOST, LOSING, LOSES to come to be without and be unable to find **LOSABLE** *adj*
LOSEL	*n* pl. -S a worthless person
LOSER	*n* pl. -S one that loses
LOSING	*n* pl. -S a loss
LOSINGLY	*adv* in a manner characterized by defeat
LOSS	*n* pl. -ES the act of one that loses
LOSSY	*adj* causing dissipation of electrical energy
LOST	*adj* not to be found or recovered
LOSTNESS	*n* pl. -ES the state of being lost
LOT	*v* LOTTED, LOTTING, LOTS to distribute proportionately
LOTA	*n* pl. -S lotah
LOTAH	*n* pl. -S a small water vessel used in India
LOTH	*adj* loath
LOTHARIO	*n* pl. -IOS a seducer of women
LOTHSOME	*adj* repulsive
LOTI	*n* pl. MALOTI a monetary unit of Lesotho
LOTIC	*adj* pertaining to moving water
LOTION	*n* pl. -S a liquid preparation for external application
LOTOS	*n* pl. -ES lotus
LOTTE	*n* pl. -S a monkfish
LOTTED	past tense of lot
LOTTERY	*n* pl. -TERIES a type of gambling game
LOTTING	present participle of lot
LOTTO	*n* pl. -TOS a game of chance
LOTUS	*n* pl. -ES an aquatic plant
LOUCHE	*adj* not reputable
LOUD	*adj* LOUDER, LOUDEST strongly audible
LOUDEN	*v* -ED, -ING, -S to make or become louder
LOUDISH	*adj* somewhat loud
LOUDLY	*adv* -LIER, -LIEST in a loud manner
LOUDNESS	*n* pl. -ES the quality of being loud
LOUGH	*n* pl. -S a lake
LOUIE	*n* pl. -S looie

LOUIS — *n* pl. LOUIS a former gold coin of France

LOUNGE — *v* LOUNGED, LOUNGING, LOUNGES to recline or lean in a relaxed, lazy manner

LOUNGER — *n* pl. -S one that lounges

LOUNGY — *adj* suitable for lounging

LOUP — *v* LOUPED, LOUPEN, LOUPING, LOUPS to leap

LOUPE — *n* pl. -S a small magnifying glass

LOUR — *v* -ED, -ING, -S to lower

LOURY — *adj* lowery

LOUSE — *n* pl. LICE a parasitic insect

LOUSE — *v* LOUSED, LOUSING, LOUSES to spoil or bungle

LOUSY — *adj* LOUSIER, LOUSIEST mean or contemptible **LOUSILY** *adv*

LOUT — *v* -ED, -ING, -S to bow in respect

LOUTISH — *adj* clumsy

LOUVER — *n* pl. -S a type of window **LOUVERED** *adj*

LOUVRE — *n* pl. -S louver **LOUVRED** *adj*

LOVABLE — *adj* having qualities that attract love **LOVABLY** *adv*

LOVAGE — *n* pl. -S a perennial herb

LOVAT — *n* pl. -S a chiefly green color mixture in fabrics

LOVE — *v* LOVED, LOVING, LOVES to feel great affection for

LOVEABLE — *adj* lovable **LOVEABLY** *adv*

LOVEBIRD — *n* pl. -S a small parrot

LOVEBUG — *n* pl. -S a small black fly that swarms along highways

LOVED — past tense of love

LOVELESS — *adj* feeling no love

LOVELIER — comparative of lovely

LOVELIES — pl. of lovely

LOVELIEST — superlative of lovely

LOVELILY — *adv* in a lovely manner

LOVELOCK — *n* pl. -S a lock of hair hanging separately

LOVELORN — *adj* not loved

LOVELY — *adj* -LIER, -LIEST beautiful

LOVELY — *n* pl. -LIES a beautiful woman

LOVER — *n* pl. -S one that loves another **LOVERLY** *adj*

LOVESICK — *adj* languishing with love

LOVESOME — *adj* lovely

LOVEVINE — *n* pl. -S a twining herb

LOVING — *adj* affectionate

LOVINGLY — *adv* in a loving manner

LOW — *adj* LOWER, LOWEST having relatively little upward extension

LOW — *v* -ED, -ING, -S to utter the sound characteristic of cattle

LOWBALL — *v* -ED, -ING, -S to give a customer a deceptively low price

LOWBORN — *adj* of humble birth

LOWBOY — *n* pl. -BOYS a low chest of drawers

LOWBRED — *adj* lowborn

LOWBROW — *n* pl. -S an uncultivated person

LOWDOWN — *n* pl. -S the whole truth

LOWE — *v* LOWED, LOWING, LOWES to blaze

LOWER — *v* -ED, -ING, -S to appear dark and threatening

LOWERY — *adj* dark and threatening

LOWING — *n* pl. -S the sound characteristic of cattle

LOWISH — *adj* somewhat low

LOWLAND — *n* pl. -S an area of land lying lower than the adjacent country

LOWLIFE — *n* pl. -LIFES or -LIVES a despicable person

LOWLIFER — *n* pl. -S a lowlife

LOWLIGHT — *n* pl. -S an unpleasant event, detail, or part

LOWLY — *adj* -LIER, -LIEST low in position or rank

LOWN — *adj* peaceful

LOWNESS — *n* pl. -ES the state of being low

LOWRIDER — *n* pl. -S a car having a lowered suspension

LOWSE — *adj* loose

LOX — *v* -ED, -ING, -ES to supply with lox (liquid oxygen)

LOYAL — *adj* -ALER, -ALEST faithful to one's allegiance

LOYALISM — *n* pl. -S loyalty

LOYALIST — *n* pl. -S one who is loyal

LOYALLY — *adv* in a loyal manner

LOYALTY — *n* pl. -TIES the state of being loyal

LOZENGE — *n* pl. -S a small, often medicated candy

LUAU — *n* pl. -S a Hawaiian feast

LUBBER   n pl. -S a clumsy person **LUBBERLY** adj

LUBE   n pl. -S a lubricant

LUBRIC   adj slippery

LUBRICAL   adj lubric

LUCARNE   n pl. -S a type of window

LUCE   n pl. -S a freshwater fish

LUCENCE   n pl. -S lucency

LUCENCY   n pl. -CIES the quality of being lucent

LUCENT   adj giving off light **LUCENTLY** adv

LUCERN   n pl. -S lucerne

LUCERNE   n pl. -S alfalfa

LUCES   a pl. of lux

LUCID   adj easily understood **LUCIDLY** adv

LUCIDITY   n pl. -TIES the quality of being lucid

LUCIFER   n pl. -S a friction match

LUCK   v -ED, -ING, -S to succeed by chance or good fortune

LUCKIE   n pl. -S an old woman

LUCKLESS   adj unlucky

LUCKY   adj LUCKIER, LUCKIEST having good fortune **LUCKILY** adv

LUCRE   n pl. -S monetary gain

LUCULENT   adj lucid

LUDE   n pl. -S a methaqualone pill

LUDIC   adj aimlessly playful

LUES   n pl. LUES syphilis

LUETIC   n pl. -S one infected with syphilis

LUFF   v -ED, -ING, -S to steer a sailing vessel nearer into the wind

LUFFA   n pl. -S loofah

LUG   v LUGGED, LUGGING, LUGS to carry or pull with effort

LUGE   v LUGED, LUGEING, LUGES to race on a luge (a small sled)

LUGER   n pl. -S one that luges

LUGGAGE   n pl. -S articles containing a traveler's belongings

LUGGED   past tense of lug

LUGGER   n pl. -S a small sailing vessel

LUGGIE   n pl. -S a small wooden dish or pail

LUGGING   present participle of lug

LUGSAIL   n pl. -S a type of sail

LUGWORM   n pl. -S a burrowing marine worm

LUKEWARM   adj moderately warm

LULL   v -ED, -ING, -S to cause to sleep or rest

LULLABY   v -BIED, -BYING, -BIES to lull with a soothing song

LULU   n pl. -S something remarkable

LUM   n pl. -S a chimney

LUMBAGO   n pl. -GOS pain in the lower back

LUMBAR   n pl. -S an anatomical part situated near the loins

LUMBER   v -ED, -ING, -S to cut down and prepare timber for market

LUMBERER   n pl. -S one that lumbers

LUMEN   n pl. -MENS or -MINA the inner passage of a tubular organ **LUMENAL, LUMINAL** adj

LUMINARY   n pl. -NARIES a body that gives light

LUMINISM   n pl. -S a style of painting

LUMINIST   n pl. -S a painter who uses the effects of light

LUMINOUS   adj giving off light

LUMMOX   n pl. -ES a clumsy person

LUMP   v -ED, -ING, -S to make into lumps (shapeless masses)

LUMPEN   n pl. -S an uprooted individual

LUMPER   n pl. -S a laborer employed to load and unload ships

LUMPFISH   n pl. -ES a marine fish

LUMPISH   adj stupid

LUMPY   adj LUMPIER, LUMPIEST full of lumps **LUMPILY** adv

LUNA   n pl. -S an alchemical designation for silver

LUNACY   n pl. -CIES insanity

LUNAR   n pl. -S an observation of the moon taken for navigational purposes

LUNARIAN   n pl. -S a supposed inhabitant of the moon

LUNATE   adj crescent-shaped **LUNATELY** adv

LUNATED   adj lunate

LUNATIC   n pl. -S an insane person

LUNATION   n pl. -S the interval between two successive new moons

LUNCH   v -ED, -ING, -ES to eat a noonday meal

LUNCHEON   n pl. -S a noonday meal

LUNCHER	*n* pl. -S one that lunches
LUNE	*n* pl. -S a crescent-shaped figure
LUNET	*n* pl. -S lunette
LUNETTE	*n* pl. -S a crescent-shaped object
LUNG	*n* pl. -S a respiratory organ
LUNGAN	*n* pl. -S longan
LUNGE	*v* LUNGED, LUNGING, LUNGES to make a forceful forward movement
LUNGEE	*n* pl. -S lungi
LUNGER	*n* pl. -S one that lunges
LUNGFISH	*n* pl. -ES a type of fish
LUNGFUL	*n* pl. -S as much as the lungs can hold
LUNGI	*n* pl. -S a loincloth worn by men in India
LUNGING	present participle of lunge
LUNGWORM	*n* pl. -S a parasitic worm
LUNGWORT	*n* pl. -S a European herb
LUNGYI	*n* pl. -S lungi
LUNIER	comparative of luny
LUNIES	pl. of luny
LUNIEST	superlative of luny
LUNK	*n* pl. -S a lunkhead
LUNKER	*n* pl. -S a large game fish
LUNKHEAD	*n* pl. -S a stupid person
LUNT	*v* -ED, -ING, -S to emit smoke
LUNULA	*n* pl. -LAE a small crescent-shaped structure **LUNULAR, LUNULATE** *adj*
LUNULE	*n* pl. -S lunula
LUNY	*adj* -NIER, -NIEST loony
LUNY	*n* pl. -NIES a loony
LUPANAR	*n* pl. -S a brothel
LUPIN	*n* pl. -S lupine
LUPINE	*n* pl. -S a flowering plant
LUPOUS	*adj* pertaining to lupus
LUPULIN	*n* pl. -S a medicinal powder obtained from the hop plant
LUPUS	*n* pl. -ES a skin disease
LURCH	*v* -ED, -ING, -ES to sway abruptly
LURCHER	*n* pl. -S one that lurks or prowls
LURDAN	*n* pl. -S a lazy or stupid person
LURDANE	*n* pl. -S lurdan
LURE	*v* LURED, LURING, LURES to attract with something desirable
LURER	*n* pl. -S one that lures
LURID	*adj* causing shock or horror **LURIDLY** *adv*
LURING	present participle of lure
LURK	*v* -ED, -ING, -S to wait in concealment
LURKER	*n* pl. -S one that lurks
LUSCIOUS	*adj* having a very pleasing taste or smell
LUSH	*adj* LUSHER, LUSHEST abounding in vegetation **LUSHLY** *adv*
LUSH	*v* -ED, -ING, -ES to drink to excess
LUSHNESS	*n* pl. -ES the state of being lush
LUST	*v* -ED, -ING, -S to have an intense desire
LUSTER	*v* -ED, -ING, -S to make or become lustrous
LUSTFUL	*adj* marked by excessive sexual desire
LUSTIER	comparative of lusty
LUSTIEST	superlative of lusty
LUSTILY	*adv* in a lusty manner
LUSTRA	a pl. of lustrum
LUSTRAL	*adj* pertaining to a lustrum
LUSTRATE	*v* -TRATED, -TRATING, -TRATES to purify ceremonially
LUSTRE	*v* -TRED, -TRING, -TRES to luster
LUSTRING	*n* pl. -S a glossy silk fabric
LUSTROUS	*adj* reflecting light evenly and efficiently
LUSTRUM	*n* pl. -TRUMS or -TRA a ceremonial purification of the population in ancient Rome
LUSTY	*adj* LUSTIER, LUSTIEST full of vigor
LUSUS	*n* pl. -ES an abnormality
LUTANIST	*n* pl. -S one who plays the lute
LUTE	*v* LUTED, LUTING, LUTES to play a lute (a stringed musical instrument)
LUTEA	pl. of luteum
LUTEAL	*adj* pertaining to the luteum
LUTECIUM	*n* pl. -S lutetium
LUTED	past tense of lute
LUTEFISK	*n* pl. -S dried codfish
LUTEIN	*n* pl. -S a yellow pigment
LUTENIST	*n* pl. -S lutanist

LUTEOLIN   *n* pl. -S a yellow pigment

LUTEOUS   *adj* light to moderate greenish yellow in color

LUTETIUM   *n* pl. -S a metallic element

LUTEUM   *n* pl. -TEA a hormone-secreting body

LUTHERN   *n* pl. -S a type of window

LUTHIER   *n* pl. -S one who makes stringed instruments

LUTING   *n* pl. -S a substance used as a sealant

LUTIST   *n* pl. -S a lutanist

LUTZ   *n* pl. -ES a jump in figure skating

LUV   *n* pl. -S a sweetheart

LUX   *n* pl. LUXES or LUCES a unit of illumination

LUXATE   *v* -ATED, -ATING, -ATES to put out of joint

LUXATION   *n* pl. -S the act of luxating

LUXE   *n* pl. -S luxury

LUXURY   *n* pl. -RIES free indulgence in that which affords pleasure or comfort

LWEI   *n* pl. -S a monetary unit of Angola

LYARD   *adj* streaked with gray

LYART   *adj* lyard

LYASE   *n* pl. -S an enzyme

LYCEE   *n* pl. -S a French secondary school

LYCEUM   *n* pl. -CEUMS or -CEA a hall for public lectures or discussions

LYCHEE   *n* pl. -S litchi

LYCHNIS   *n* pl. -NISES a flowering plant

LYCOPENE   *n* pl. -S a red pigment

LYCOPOD   *n* pl. -S an evergreen plant

LYDDITE   *n* pl. -S an explosive

LYE   *n* pl. -S a solution used in making soap

LYING   *n* pl. -S the act of telling lies

LYINGLY   *adv* falsely

LYMPH   *n* pl. -S a body fluid containing white blood cells **LYMPHOID** *adj*

LYMPHOMA   *n* pl. -MAS or -MATA a type of tumor

LYNCEAN   *adj* of or resembling a lynx

LYNCH   *v* -ED, -ING, -ES to put to death without legal sanction

LYNCHER   *n* pl. -S one that lynches

LYNCHING   *n* pl. -S the act of one who lynches

LYNCHPIN   *n* pl. -S linchpin

LYNX   *n* pl. -ES a short-tailed wildcat

LYOPHILE   *adj* pertaining to a type of colloid

LYRATE   *adj* having the shape of a lyre **LYRATELY** *adv*

LYRATED   *adj* lyrate

LYRE   *n* pl. -S an ancient harp-like instrument

LYREBIRD   *n* pl. -S an Australian bird

LYRIC   *n* pl. -S a lyrical poem

LYRICAL   *adj* having the form of a song

LYRICISE   *v* -CISED, -CISING, -CISES to lyricize

LYRICISM   *n* pl. -S the quality of being lyrics

LYRICIST   *n* pl. -S one who writes the words for songs

LYRICIZE   *v* -CIZED, -CIZING, -CIZES to write lyrics

LYRIFORM   *adj* lyrate

LYRISM   *n* pl. -S lyricism

LYRIST   *n* pl. -S one who plays the lyre

LYSATE   *n* pl. -S a product of lysis

LYSE   *v* LYSED, LYSING, LYSES to cause to undergo lysis

LYSIN   *n* pl. -S a substance capable of disintegrating blood cells or bacteria

LYSINE   *n* pl. -S an amino acid

LYSING   present participle of lyse

LYSIS   *n* pl. LYSES the disintegration of cells by lysins

LYSOGEN   *n* pl. -S a type of antigen

LYSOGENY   *n* pl. -NIES the state of being like a lysogen

LYSOSOME   *n* pl. -S a saclike part of a cell

LYSOZYME   *n* pl. -S an enzyme

LYSSA   *n* pl. -S rabies

LYTIC   *adj* pertaining to lysis

LYTTA   *n* pl. -TAE or -TAS a fibrous band in the tongue of certain carnivorous mammals

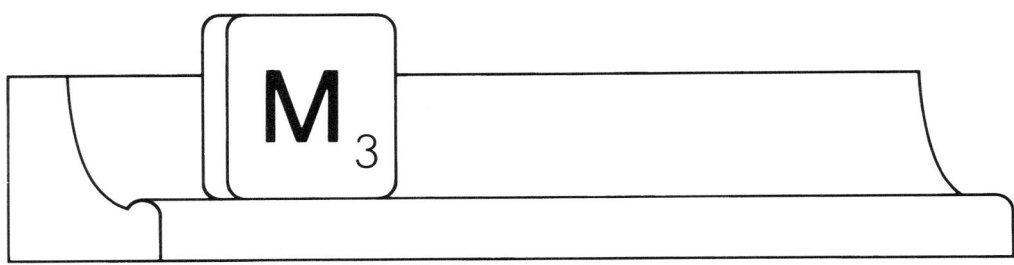

MA	*n* pl. -S mother
MAAR	*n* pl. -S a volcanic crater
MABE	*n* pl. -S a cultured pearl
MAC	*n* pl. -S a raincoat
MACABER	*adj* macabre
MACABRE	*adj* gruesome
MACACO	*n* pl. -COS a lemur
MACADAM	*n* pl. -S a type of pavement
MACAQUE	*n* pl. -S a short-tailed monkey
MACARONI	*n* pl. -NIS or -NIES a tubular pasta
MACAROON	*n* pl. -S a type of cookie
MACAW	*n* pl. -S a large parrot
MACCABAW	*n* pl. -S maccaboy
MACCABOY	*n* pl. -BOYS a type of snuff
MACCHIA	*n* pl. -CHIE a dense growth of small trees and shrubs
MACCOBOY	*n* pl. -BOYS maccaboy
MACE	*v* MACED, MACING, MACES to attack with a clublike weapon
MACER	*n* pl. -S an official who carries a ceremonial staff
MACERATE	*v* -ATED, -ATING, -ATES to soften by soaking in liquid
MACH	*n* pl. -S a number indicating the ratio of the speed of a body to the speed of sound
MACHE	*n* pl. -S a European herb
MACHETE	*n* pl. -S a large, heavy knife
MACHINE	*v* -CHINED, -CHINING, -CHINES to process by machine (a mechanical device)
MACHISMO	*n* pl. -MOS strong masculinity
MACHO	*n* pl. -CHOS a person who exhibits machismo
MACHREE	*n* pl. -S dear
MACHZOR	*n* pl. -ZORIM or -ZORS mahzor
MACING	present participle of mace
MACK	*n* pl. -S mac
MACKEREL	*n* pl. -S a marine food fish
MACKINAW	*n* pl. -S a woolen fabric
MACKLE	*v* -LED, -LING, -LES to blur in printing
MACLE	*n* pl. -S a spot or discoloration in a mineral **MACLED** *adj*
MACON	*n* pl. -S a red or white French wine
MACRAME	*n* pl. -S a trimming of knotted thread or cord
MACRO	*n* pl. -ROS a type of computer instruction
MACRON	*n* pl. -S a symbol placed over a vowel to show that it has a long sound
MACRURAL	*adj* pertaining to macruran
MACRURAN	*n* pl. -S any of a suborder of crustaceans
MACULA	*n* pl. -LAE or -LAS a spot **MACULAR** *adj*
MACULATE	*v* -LATED, -LATING, -LATES to mark with spots
MACULE	*v* -ULED, -ULING, -ULES to mackle
MACUMBA	*n* pl. -S a religion practiced in Brazil
MAD	*adj* MADDER, MADDEST insane
MAD	*v* MADDED, MADDING, MADS to madden
MADAM	*n* pl. -S a woman who manages a brothel
MADAME	*n* pl. -S madam
MADAME	*n* pl. MESDAMES the French title of respect for a married woman
MADCAP	*n* pl. -S an impulsive person
MADDED	past tense of mad
MADDEN	*v* -ED, -ING, -S to make or become mad
MADDER	*n* pl. -S a perennial herb

MADDEST	superlative of mad
MADDING	present participle of mad
MADDISH	*adj* somewhat mad
MADE	past tense of make
MADEIRA	*n* pl. -S a white wine
MADHOUSE	*n* pl. -S an insane asylum
MADLY	*adv* in a mad manner
MADMAN	*n* pl. -MEN a man who is insane
MADNESS	*n* pl. -ES the state of being mad
MADONNA	*n* pl. -S a former Italian title of respect for a woman
MADRAS	*n* pl. -ES a cotton fabric
MADRE	*n* pl. -S mother
MADRIGAL	*n* pl. -S a short lyric poem
MADRONA	*n* pl. -S an evergreen tree
MADRONE	*n* pl. -S madrona
MADRONO	*n* pl. -NOS madrona
MADURO	*n* pl. -ROS a dark-colored, relatively strong cigar
MADWOMAN	*n* pl. -WOMEN a woman who is insane
MADWORT	*n* pl. -S a flowering plant
MADZOON	*n* pl. -S matzoon
MAE	*n* pl. -S more
MAENAD	*n* pl. -S or -ES a female participant in ancient Greek orgies **MAENADIC** *adj*
MAESTOSO	*n* pl. -SOS a stately musical passage
MAESTRO	*n* pl. -STROS or -STRI a master of an art
MAFFIA	*n* pl. -S mafia
MAFFICK	*v* -ED, -ING, -S to celebrate boisterously
MAFIA	*n* pl. -S a secret criminal organization
MAFIC	*adj* pertaining to minerals rich in magnesium and iron
MAFIOSO	*n* pl. -SI a member of the mafia
MAFTIR	*n* pl. -S the concluding section of a parashah
MAG	*n* pl. -S a magazine
MAGAZINE	*n* pl. -S a type of periodical publication
MAGDALEN	*n* pl. -S a reformed prostitute
MAGE	*n* pl. -S a magician
MAGENTA	*n* pl. -S a purplish red dye

MAGGOT	*n* pl. -S the legless larva of certain insects **MAGGOTY** *adj*
MAGI	pl. of magus
MAGIAN	*n* pl. -S a magus
MAGIC	*v* -ICKED, -ICKING, -ICS to affect by magic (sorcery)
MAGICAL	*adj* resembling magic
MAGICIAN	*n* pl. -S one skilled in magic
MAGICKED	past tense of magic
MAGICKING	present participle of magic
MAGILP	*n* pl. -S megilp
MAGISTER	*n* pl. -S a master or teacher
MAGLEV	*n* pl. -S a train using magnets to move above the tracks
MAGMA	*n* pl. -MAS or -MATA the molten matter from which igneous rock is formed **MAGMATIC** *adj*
MAGNATE	*n* pl. -S a powerful or influential person
MAGNESIA	*n* pl. -S a medicinal compound **MAGNESIC** *adj*
MAGNET	*n* pl. -S a body that possesses the property of attracting iron
MAGNETIC	*n* pl. -S a magnet
MAGNETO	*n* pl. -TOS a type of electric generator
MAGNETON	*n* pl. -S a unit of magnetic moment
MAGNIFIC	*adj* magnificent
MAGNIFY	*v* -FIED, -FYING, -FIES to increase the perceived size of
MAGNOLIA	*n* pl. -S a flowering shrub or tree
MAGNUM	*n* pl. -S a large wine bottle
MAGOT	*n* pl. -S a tailless ape
MAGPIE	*n* pl. -S a corvine bird
MAGUEY	*n* pl. -GUEYS a tropical plant
MAGUS	*n* pl. -GI a magician
MAHARAJA	*n* pl. -S a king or prince in India
MAHARANI	*n* pl. -S the wife of a maharaja
MAHATMA	*n* pl. -S a Hindu sage
MAHIMAHI	*n* pl. MAHIMAHI a food fish in Hawaii
MAHJONG	*n* pl. -S a game of Chinese origin
MAHJONGG	*n* pl. -S mahjong
MAHOE	*n* pl. -S a tropical tree
MAHOGANY	*n* pl. -NIES a tropical tree
MAHONIA	*n* pl. -S a flowering shrub

MAHOUT *n* pl. -S the keeper and driver of an elephant

MAHUANG *n* pl. -S an Asian plant

MAHZOR *n* pl. -ZORIM or -ZORS a Jewish prayer book

MAID *n* pl. -S a maiden **MAIDISH** *adj*

MAIDEN *n* pl. -S a young unmarried woman **MAIDENLY** *adj*

MAIDHOOD *n* pl. -S the state of being a maiden

MAIEUTIC *adj* pertaining to a method of eliciting knowledge

MAIGRE *adj* containing neither flesh nor its juices

MAIHEM *n* pl. -S mayhem

MAIL *v* -ED, -ING, -S to send by a governmental postal system **MAILABLE** *adj*

MAILBAG *n* pl. -S a bag for carrying mail (postal material)

MAILBOX *n* pl. -ES a box for depositing mail

MAILE *n* pl. -S a Pacific island vine

MAILER *n* pl. -S one that mails

MAILING *n* pl. -S a rented farm

MAILL *n* pl. -S a payment

MAILLESS *adj* having no armor

MAILLOT *n* pl. -S a woman's one-piece bathing suit

MAILMAN *n* pl. -MEN a man who carries and delivers mail

MAIM *v* -ED, -ING, -S to injure so as to cause lasting damage

MAIMER *n* pl. -S one that maims

MAIN *n* pl. -S the principal part

MAINLAND *n* pl. -S a principal land mass

MAINLINE *v* -LINED, -LINING, -LINES to inject a narcotic into a major vein

MAINLY *adv* for the most part

MAINMAST *n* pl. -S the principal mast of a vessel

MAINSAIL *n* pl. -S the principal sail of a vessel

MAINSTAY *n* pl. -STAYS a principal support

MAINTAIN *v* -ED, -ING, -S to keep in proper condition

MAINTOP *n* pl. -S a platform at the head of a mainmast

MAIOLICA *n* pl. -S majolica

MAIR *n* pl. -S more

MAIST *n* pl. -S most

MAIZE *n* pl. -S an American cereal grass

MAJAGUA *n* pl. -S a tropical tree

MAJESTIC *adj* having majesty

MAJESTY *n* pl. -TIES regal dignity

MAJOLICA *n* pl. -S a type of pottery

MAJOR *v* -ED, -ING, -S to pursue a specific principal course of study

MAJORITY *n* pl. -TIES the greater number or part

MAJORLY *adv* mainly

MAKAR *n* pl. -S a poet

MAKE *v* MADE, MAKING, MAKES to cause to exist **MAKABLE**, **MAKEABLE** *adj*

MAKEBATE *n* pl. -S one that encourages quarrels

MAKEFAST *n* pl. -S an object to which a boat is tied

MAKEOVER *n* pl. -S a changing of appearance

MAKER *n* pl. -S one that makes

MAKEUP *n* pl. -S the way in which the parts or ingredients of something are put together

MAKIMONO *n* pl. -NOS a Japanese ornamental scroll

MAKING *n* pl. -S material from which something can be developed

MAKO *n* pl. -KOS a large shark

MAKUTA pl. of likuta

MALACCA *n* pl. -S the cane of an Asian rattan palm

MALADY *n* pl. -DIES an illness

MALAISE *n* pl. -S a feeling of vague discomfort

MALAMUTE *n* pl. -S an Alaskan sled dog

MALANGA *n* pl. -S a yautia

MALAPERT *n* pl. -S an impudent person

MALAPROP *n* pl. -S a humorous misuse of a word

MALAR *n* pl. -S the cheekbone

MALARIA *n* pl. -S an infectious disease **MALARIAL**, **MALARIAN** *adj*

MALARKEY *n* pl. -KEYS nonsense

MALARKY *n* pl. -KIES malarkey

MALAROMA *n* pl. -S a malodor

MALATE *n* pl. -S a chemical salt

MALE   *n* pl. -S an individual that begets young by fertilizing the female

MALEATE   *n* pl. -S a chemical salt

MALEDICT   *v* -ED, -ING, -S to curse

MALEFIC   *adj* producing or causing evil

MALEMIUT   *n* pl. -S malamute

MALEMUTE   *n* pl. -S malamute

MALENESS   *n* pl. -ES the quality of being a male

MALFED   *adj* badly fed

MALGRE   *prep* in spite of

MALIC   *adj* pertaining to apples

MALICE   *n* pl. -S a desire to injure another

MALIGN   *v* -ED, -ING, -S to speak evil of

MALIGNER   *n* pl. -S one that maligns

MALIGNLY   *adv* in an evil manner

MALIHINI   *n* pl. -S a newcomer to Hawaii

MALINE   *n* pl. -S a delicate net used for veils

MALINGER   *v* -ED, -ING, -S to feign illness in order to avoid duty or work

MALISON   *n* pl. -S a curse

MALKIN   *n* pl. -S an untidy woman

MALL   *v* -ED, -ING, -S to maul

MALLARD   *n* pl. -S a wild duck

MALLEE   *n* pl. -S an evergreen tree

MALLEI   pl. of malleus

MALLEOLI   *n/pl* bony protuberances of the ankle

MALLET   *n* pl. -S a type of hammer

MALLEUS   *n* pl. -LEI a bone of the middle ear

MALLOW   *n* pl. -S a flowering plant

MALM   *n* pl. -S a soft, friable limestone

MALMSEY   *n* pl. -SEYS a white wine

MALMY   *adj* MALMIER, MALMIEST resembling malm

MALODOR   *n* pl. -S an offensive odor

MALOTI   pl. of loti

MALPOSED   *adj* being in the wrong position

MALT   *v* -ED, -ING, -S to treat or combine with malt (germinated grain)

MALTASE   *n* pl. -S an enzyme

MALTED   *n* pl. -S a sweet beverage

MALTHA   *n* pl. -S a natural tar

MALTIER   comparative of malty

MALTIEST   superlative of malty

MALTOL   *n* pl. -S a chemical compound

MALTOSE   *n* pl. -S a type of sugar

MALTREAT   *v* -ED, -ING, -S to treat badly

MALTSTER   *n* pl. -S one that makes malt

MALTY   *adj* MALTIER, MALTIEST resembling malt

MALVASIA   *n* pl. -S malmsey

MAMA   *n* pl. -S mother

MAMALIGA   *n* pl. -S a cornmeal porridge

MAMBA   *n* pl. -S a venomous snake

MAMBO   *v* -ED, -ING, -ES or -S to perform a ballroom dance

MAMELUKE   *n* pl. -S a slave in Muslim countries

MAMEY   *n* pl. -MEYS or -MEYES a tropical tree

MAMIE   *n* pl. -S mamey

MAMLUK   *n* pl. -S mameluke

MAMMA   *n* pl. -S mama

MAMMA   *n* pl. -MAE a milk-secreting organ

MAMMAL   *n* pl. -S any of a class of warm-blooded vertebrates

MAMMARY   *adj* pertaining to the mammae

MAMMATE   *adj* having mammae

MAMMATUS   *n* pl. -TI a type of cloud

MAMMEE   *n* pl. -S mamey

MAMMER   *v* -ED, -ING, -S to hesitate

MAMMET   *n* pl. -S maumet

MAMMEY   *n* pl. -MEYS mamey

MAMMIE   *n* pl. -S mammy

MAMMIES   pl. of mammy

MAMMILLA   *n* pl. -LAE a nipple

MAMMITIS   *n* pl. -MITIDES mastitis

MAMMOCK   *v* -ED, -ING, -S to shred

MAMMON   *n* pl. -S material wealth

MAMMOTH   *n* pl. -S an extinct elephant

MAMMY   *n* pl. -MIES mother

MAN   *n* pl. MEN an adult human male

MAN   *v* MANNED, MANNING, MANS to supply with men

MANA   *n* pl. -S a supernatural force in certain Pacific island religions

MANACLE   *v* -CLED, -CLING, -CLES to handcuff

MANAGE   *v* -AGED, -AGING, -AGES to control or direct

MANAGER	*n* pl. -S one that manages
MANAKIN	*n* pl. -S a tropical bird
MANANA	*n* pl. -S tomorrow
MANATEE	*n* pl. -S an aquatic mammal **MANATOID** *adj*
MANCHE	*n* pl. -S a heraldic design
MANCHET	*n* pl. -S a small loaf of fine white bread
MANCIPLE	*n* pl. -S an officer authorized to purchase provisions
MANDALA	*n* pl. -S a Hindu or Buddhist graphic symbol of the universe **MANDALIC** *adj*
MANDAMUS	*v* -ED, -ING, -ES to command by means of writ issued by a superior court
MANDARIN	*n* pl. -S a citrus fruit
MANDATE	*v* -DATED, -DATING, -DATES to authorize or decree
MANDATOR	*n* pl. -S one that mandates
MANDIBLE	*n* pl. -S the bone of the lower jaw
MANDIOCA	*n* pl. -S manioc
MANDOLA	*n* pl. -S an ancient lute
MANDOLIN	*n* pl. -S a stringed musical instrument
MANDRAKE	*n* pl. -S a European herb
MANDREL	*n* pl. -S a shaft on which a tool is mounted
MANDRIL	*n* pl. -S mandrel
MANDRILL	*n* pl. -S a large baboon
MANE	*n* pl. -S the long hair growing on and about the neck of some animals **MANED, MANELESS** *adj*
MANEGE	*n* pl. -S the art of training and riding horses
MANEUVER	*v* -ED, -ING, -S to change the position of for a specific purpose
MANFUL	*adj* courageous **MANFULLY** *adv*
MANGABEY	*n* pl. -BEYS a long-tailed monkey
MANGABY	*n* pl. -BIES mangabey
MANGANIC	*adj* containing manganese (a metallic element)
MANGE	*n* pl. -S a skin disease of domestic animals
MANGEL	*n* pl. -S a variety of beet
MANGER	*n* pl. -S a trough or box from which horses or cattle eat
MANGEY	*adj* MANGIER, MANGIEST mangy
MANGIER	comparative of mangy
MANGIEST	superlative of mangy
MANGILY	*adv* in a mangy manner
MANGLE	*v* -GLED, -GLING, -GLES to cut, slash, or crush so as to disfigure
MANGLER	*n* pl. -S one that mangles
MANGO	*n* pl. -GOES or -GOS an edible tropical fruit
MANGOLD	*n* pl. -S mangel
MANGONEL	*n* pl. -S a medieval military device for hurling stones
MANGROVE	*n* pl. -S a tropical tree or shrub
MANGY	*adj* MANGIER, MANGIEST affected with mange
MANHOLE	*n* pl. -S a hole providing entrance to an underground or enclosed structure
MANHOOD	*n* pl. -S the state of being a man
MANHUNT	*n* pl. -S an intensive search for a person
MANIA	*n* pl. -S an excessive interest or enthusiasm
MANIAC	*n* pl. -S an insane person **MANIACAL** *adj*
MANIC	*n* pl. -S one that is affected with mania
MANICURE	*v* -CURED, -CURING, -CURES to trim and polish the fingernails of
MANIFEST	*v* -ED, -ING, -S to show clearly
MANIFOLD	*v* -ED, -ING, -S to make several copies of
MANIHOT	*n* pl. -S a tropical plant
MANIKIN	*n* pl. -S an anatomical model of the human body
MANILA	*n* pl. -S a strong paper
MANILLA	*n* pl. -S manila
MANILLE	*n* pl. -S the second highest trump in certain card games
MANIOC	*n* pl. -S a tropical plant
MANIOCA	*n* pl. -S manioc
MANIPLE	*n* pl. -S a silk band worn on the left arm as a vestment
MANITO	*n* pl. -TOS manitou
MANITOU	*n* pl. -S an Algonquian Indian deity
MANITU	*n* pl. -S manitou
MANKIND	*n* pl. MANKIND the human race
MANLESS	*adj* destitute of men
MANLIKE	*adj* resembling a man

MANLY   *adj* -LIER, -LIEST having the qualities of a man **MANLILY** *adv*

MANMADE   *adj* made by man

MANNA   *n* pl. -S divinely supplied food

MANNAN   *n* pl. -S a type of sugar

MANNED   past tense of man

MANNER   *n* pl. -S a way of acting **MANNERED** *adj*

MANNERLY   *adj* polite

MANNIKIN   *n* pl. -S manikin

MANNING   present participle of man

MANNISH   *adj* resembling or characteristic of a man

MANNITE   *n* pl. -S mannitol **MANNITIC** *adj*

MANNITOL   *n* pl. -S an alcohol

MANNOSE   *n* pl. -S a type of sugar

MANO   *n* pl. -NOS a stone used for grinding foods

MANOR   *n* pl. -S a landed estate or territorial unit **MANORIAL** *adj*

MANPACK   *adj* designed to be carried by one person

MANPOWER   *n* pl. -S the number of men available for service

MANQUE   *adj* frustrated in the fulfillment of one's aspirations

MANROPE   *n* pl. -S a rope used as a handrail

MANSARD   *n* pl. -S a type of roof

MANSE   *n* pl. -S a clergyman's house

MANSION   *n* pl. -S a large, impressive house

MANTA   *n* pl. -S a cotton fabric

MANTEAU   *n* pl. -TEAUS or -TEAUX a loose cloak

MANTEL   *n* pl. -S a shelf above a fireplace

MANTELET   *n* pl. -S a mobile screen used to protect soldiers

MANTES   a pl. of mantis

MANTIC   *adj* having powers of prophecy

MANTID   *n* pl. -S mantis

MANTILLA   *n* pl. -S a woman's scarf

MANTIS   *n* pl. -TISES or -TES a predatory insect

MANTISSA   *n* pl. -S the decimal part of a logarithm

MANTLE   *v* -TLED, -TLING, -TLES to cloak

MANTLET   *n* pl. -S mantelet

MANTLING   *n* pl. -S an ornamental cloth

MANTRA   *n* pl. -S a mystical formula of prayer or incantation in Hinduism **MANTRIC** *adj*

MANTRAP   *n* pl. -S a trap for catching men

MANTUA   *n* pl. -S a woman's gown

MANUAL   *n* pl. -S a small reference book

MANUALLY   *adv* by means of the hands

MANUARY   *adj* involving the hands

MANUBRIA   *n/pl* handle-shaped anatomical parts

MANUMIT   *v* -MITTED, -MITTING, -MITS to free from slavery

MANURE   *v* -NURED, -NURING, -NURES to fertilize with manure (animal excrement)

MANURER   *n* pl. -S one that manures

MANURIAL   *adj* of or pertaining to manure

MANURING   present participle of manure

MANUS   *n* pl. MANUS the end of the forelimb in vertebrates

MANWARD   *adv* toward man

MANWARDS   *adv* manward

MANWISE   *adv* in a manner characteristic of man

MANY   *adj* MORE, MOST consisting of or amounting to a large number

MANYFOLD   *adv* by many times

MAP   *v* MAPPED, MAPPING, MAPS to delineate on a map (a representation of a region)

MAPLE   *n* pl. -S a hardwood tree

MAPLIKE   *adj* resembling a map

MAPMAKER   *n* pl. -S one that makes maps

MAPPABLE   *adj* capable of being mapped

MAPPED   past tense of map

MAPPER   *n* pl. -S one that maps

MAPPING   *n* pl. -S a mathematical correspondence

MAQUETTE   *n* pl. -S a small preliminary model

MAQUI   *n* pl. -S maquis

MAQUIS   *n* pl. MAQUIS a thick underbrush

MAR   *v* MARRED, MARRING, MARS to detract from the perfection or wholeness of

MARABOU   *n* pl. -S an African stork

MARABOUT   *n* pl. -S a marabou

MARACA   *n* pl. -S a percussion instrument

MARANTA   *n* pl. -S a tropical plant

MARASCA *n* pl. -S a wild cherry

MARASMUS *n* pl. -ES a wasting away of the body **MARASMIC** *adj*

MARATHON *n* pl. -S a long-distance race

MARAUD *v* -ED, -ING, -S to rove in search of booty

MARAUDER *n* pl. -S one that marauds

MARAVEDI *n* pl. -S a former coin of Spain

MARBLE *v* -BLED, -BLING, -BLES to give a mottled appearance to

MARBLER *n* pl. -S one that marbles

MARBLING *n* pl. -S an intermixture of fat and lean in meat

MARBLY *adj* -BLIER, -BLIEST mottled

MARC *n* pl. -S the residue remaining after a fruit has been pressed

MARCATO *adv* with strong accentuation — used as a musical direction

MARCEL *v* -CELLED, -CELLING, -CELS to make a deep, soft wave in the hair

MARCH *v* -ED, -ING, -ES to walk in a formal military manner

MARCHEN *n* pl. MARCHEN a folktale

MARCHER *n* pl. -S one that marches

MARCHESA *n* pl. -CHESE the wife or widow of a marchese

MARCHESE *n* pl. -CHESI an Italian nobleman

MARE *n* pl. -S a mature female horse

MARE *n* pl. -RIA a dark area on the surface of the moon or Mars

MAREMMA *n* pl. -REMME a marshy coastal region

MARENGO *adj* served with a sauce of mushrooms, tomatoes, oil, and wine

MARGARIC *adj* pearly

MARGARIN *n* pl. -S a butter substitute

MARGAY *n* pl. -GAYS a small American wildcat

MARGE *n* pl. -S a margin

MARGENT *v* -ED, -ING, -S to margin

MARGIN *v* -ED, -ING, -S to provide with a margin (a border)

MARGINAL *adj* of or pertaining to a margin

MARGRAVE *n* pl. -S the military governor of a medieval German border province

MARIA pl. of mare

MARIACHI *n* pl. -S a Mexican musical band

MARIGOLD *n* pl. -S a flowering plant

MARIMBA *n* pl. -S a percussion instrument

MARINA *n* pl. -S a docking area for small boats

MARINADE *v* -NADED, -NADING, -NADES to marinate

MARINARA *n* pl. -S a seasoned tomato sauce

MARINATE *v* -NATED, -NATING, -NATES to soak in a seasoned liquid before cooking

MARINE *n* pl. -S a soldier trained for service at sea and on land

MARINER *n* pl. -S a sailor

MARIPOSA *n* pl. -S a flowering plant

MARISH *n* pl. -ES a marsh

MARITAL *adj* pertaining to marriage

MARITIME *adj* pertaining to navigation or commerce on the sea

MARJORAM *n* pl. -S fragrant herb

MARK *v* -ED, -ING, -S to make a visible impression on

MARKDOWN *n* pl. -S a reduction in price

MARKEDLY *adv* in an evident manner

MARKER *n* pl. -S one that marks

MARKET *v* -ED, -ING, -S to offer for sale

MARKETER *n* pl. -S one that markets

MARKHOOR *n* pl. -S markhor

MARKHOR *n* pl. -S a wild goat

MARKING *n* pl. -S a pattern of marks

MARKKA *n* pl. -KAA or -KAS a monetary unit of Finland

MARKSMAN *n* pl. -MEN a person skillful at hitting a target

MARKUP *n* pl. -S an increase in price

MARL *v* -ED, -ING, -S to fertilize with marl (an earthy deposit containing lime, clay, and sand)

MARLIER comparative of marly

MARLIEST superlative of marly

MARLIN *n* pl. -S a marine game fish

MARLINE *n* pl. -S a rope used on a ship

MARLING *n* pl. -S marline

MARLITE *n* pl. -S a type of marl **MARLITIC** *adj*

MARLY *adj* MARLIER, MARLIEST abounding with marl

MARMITE *n* pl. -S a large soup kettle

MARMOSET *n* pl. -S a small monkey

MARMOT *n* pl. -S a burrowing rodent

MAROCAIN *n* pl. -S a light crinkled fabric

MAROON *v* -ED, -ING, -S to abandon in an isolated place

MARPLOT *n* pl. -S one that ruins a plan by meddling

MARQUE *n* pl. -S reprisal

MARQUEE *n* pl. -S a rooflike structure projecting over an entrance

MARQUESS *n* pl. -ES marquis

MARQUIS *n* pl. -ES a European nobleman

MARQUISE *n* pl. -S the wife or widow of a marquis

MARRAM *n* pl. -S a beach grass

MARRANO *n* pl. -NOS a Jew in Spain who professed Christianity to avoid persecution

MARRED past tense of mar

MARRER *n* pl. -S one that mars

MARRIAGE *n* pl. -S the legal union of a man and woman

MARRIED *n* pl. -S one who has entered into marriage

MARRIER *n* pl. -S one that marries

MARRIES present 3d person sing. of marry

MARRING present participle of mar

MARRON *n* pl. -S a variety of chestnut

MARROW *v* -ED, -ING, -S to marry

MARROWY *adj* pithy

MARRY *v* -RIED, -RYING, -RIES to enter into marriage

MARSALA *n* pl. -S a Sicilian wine

MARSE *n* pl. -S master

MARSH *n* pl. -ES a tract of low, wet land

MARSHAL *v* -ED, -ING, -S to put in proper order

MARSHALL *v* -ED, -ING, -S to marshal

MARSHY *adj* MARSHIER, MARSHIEST resembling a marsh

MARSUPIA *n/pl* abdominal pouches of certain mammals

MART *v* -ED, -ING, -S to market

MARTAGON *n* pl. -S a flowering plant

MARTELLO *n* pl. -LOS a circular fort

MARTEN *n* pl. -S a carnivorous mammal

MARTIAL *adj* pertaining to war

MARTIAN *n* pl. -S a supposed inhabitant of the planet Mars

MARTIN *n* pl. -S a small bird

MARTINET *n* pl. -S one who demands rigid adherence to rules

MARTINI *n* pl. -S an alcoholic beverage

MARTLET *n* pl. -S a martin

MARTYR *v* -ED, -ING, -S to put to death for adhering to a belief

MARTYRLY *adj* resembling a martyr

MARTYRY *n* pl. -TYRIES a shrine erected in honor of a martyred person

MARVEL *v* -VELED, -VELING, -VELS or -VELLED, -VELLING, -VELS to be filled with wonder or astonishment

MARVY *adj* marvelous

MARYJANE *n* pl. -S marijuana

MARZIPAN *n* pl. -S an almond candy

MASCARA *v* -ED, -ING, -S to color the eyelashes or eyebrows with a cosmetic

MASCON *n* pl. -S a concentration of dense mass beneath the moon's surface

MASCOT *n* pl. -S a person, animal, or object believed to bring good luck

MASER *n* pl. -S a device for amplifying electrical impulses

MASH *v* -ED, -ING, -ES to reduce to a pulpy mass

MASHER *n* pl. -S one that mashes

MASHIE *n* pl. -S a golf club

MASHY *n* pl. MASHIES mashie

MASJID *n* pl. -S a mosque

MASK *v* -ED, -ING, -S to cover with a mask (a covering used to disguise the face) **MASKABLE** *adj*

MASKEG *n* pl. -S muskeg

MASKER *n* pl. -S one that wears a mask

MASKING *n* pl. -S a piece of scenery used to conceal parts of a stage from the audience

MASKLIKE *adj* suggestive of a mask

MASON *v* -ED, -ING, -S to build with stone or brick

MASONIC *adj* pertaining to masonry

MASONRY *n* pl. -RIES a structure built of stone or brick

MASQUE *n* pl. -S a dramatic entertainment formerly popular in England

MASQUER *n* pl. -S masker

MASS	*v* -ED, -ING, -ES to assemble in a mass (a body of coherent matter)
MASSA	*n* pl. -S master
MASSACRE	*v* -CRED, -CRING, -CRES to kill indiscriminately
MASSAGE	*v* -SAGED, -SAGING, -SAGES to manipulate parts of the body for remedial or hygienic purposes
MASSAGER	*n* pl. -S one that massages
MASSCULT	*n* pl. -S culture as popularized by the mass media
MASSE	*n* pl. -S a type of shot in billiards
MASSEDLY	*adv* in a massed manner
MASSETER	*n* pl. -S a muscle that raises the lower jaw
MASSEUR	*n* pl. -S a man who massages
MASSEUSE	*n* pl. -S a woman who massages
MASSICOT	*n* pl. -S a yellow pigment
MASSIER	comparative of massy
MASSIEST	superlative of massy
MASSIF	*n* pl. -S a principal mountain mass
MASSIVE	*adj* of considerable size
MASSLESS	*adj* having no mass
MASSY	*adj* MASSIER, MASSIEST massive
MAST	*v* -ED, -ING, -S to provide with a mast (a long pole on a ship that supports the sails and rigging)
MASTABA	*n* pl. -S an ancient Egyptian tomb
MASTABAH	*n* pl. -S mastaba
MASTER	*v* -ED, -ING, -S to become skilled in
MASTERLY	*adj* very skillful
MASTERY	*n* pl. -TERIES superior knowledge or skill
MASTHEAD	*v* -ED, -ING, -S to raise to the top of a mast
MASTIC	*n* pl. -S an aromatic resin
MASTICHE	*n* pl. -S mastic
MASTIFF	*n* pl. -S a large, short-haired dog
MASTITIS	*n* pl. -TITIDES inflammation of the breast **MASTITIC** *adj*
MASTIX	*n* pl. -ES mastic
MASTLESS	*adj* having no mast
MASTLIKE	*adj* resembling a mast
MASTODON	*n* pl. -S an extinct elephant-like mammal

MASTOID	*n* pl. -S the rear portion of the temporal bone
MASURIUM	*n* pl. -S a metallic element
MAT	*v* MATTED, MATTING, MATS to pack down into a dense mass
MATADOR	*n* pl. -S the bullfighter who kills the bull in a bullfight
MATAMBALA	a pl. of tambala
MATCH	*v* -ED, -ING, -ES to set in competition or opposition
MATCHBOX	*n* pl. -ES a small box
MATCHER	*n* pl. -S one that matches
MATCHUP	*n* pl. -S a setting of two players against each other
MATE	*v* MATED, MATING, MATES to join as mates (partners in a union)
MATELESS	*adj* having no mate
MATELOT	*n* pl. -S a sailor
MATELOTE	*n* pl. -S a fish stew
MATER	*n* pl. -TERS or -TRES mother
MATERIAL	*n* pl. -S the substance of which anything is or may be composed
MATERIEL	*n* pl. -S the aggregate of equipment and supplies used by an organization
MATERNAL	*adj* pertaining to a mother
MATESHIP	*n* pl. -S the state of being a mate
MATEY	*n* pl. -EYS a friend
MATH	*n* pl. -S mathematics
MATILDA	*n* pl. -S a hobo's bundle
MATIN	*n* pl. -S a morning song, as of birds
MATINAL	*adj* pertaining to the morning
MATINEE	*n* pl. -S a daytime performance
MATINESS	*n* pl. -ES friendliness
MATING	*n* pl. -S the period during which a seasonal-breeding animal can mate
MATLESS	*adj* having no mats (small floor coverings)
MATRASS	*n* pl. -ES a long-necked glass vessel
MATRES	a pl. of mater
MATRIX	*n* pl. -TRICES or -TRIXES something within which something else originates or develops
MATRON	*n* pl. -S a married woman of established social position **MATRONAL, MATRONLY** *adj*

MATSAH *n* pl. -S matzo

MATT *v* -ED, -ING, -S to matte

MATTE *v* MATTED, MATTING, MATTES to produce a dull finish on

MATTED past tense of mat, matt, and matte

MATTEDLY *adv* in a tangled manner

MATTER *v* -ED, -ING, -S to be of importance

MATTERY *adj* producing pus

MATTIN *n* pl. -S matin

MATTING *n* pl. -S a woven fabric used as a floor covering

MATTOCK *n* pl. -S a digging tool

MATTOID *n* pl. -S a mentally unbalanced person

MATTRASS *n* pl. -ES matrass

MATTRESS *n* pl. -ES a large pad filled with resilient material used on or as a bed

MATURATE *v* -RATED, -RATING, -RATES to mature

MATURE *adj* -TURER, -TUREST fully developed **MATURELY** *adv*

MATURE *v* -TURED, -TURING, -TURES to make or become mature

MATURITY *n* pl. -TIES the state of being mature

MATZA *n* pl. -S matzo

MATZAH *n* pl. -S matzo

MATZO *n* pl. -ZOS, -ZOT, or -ZOTH an unleavened bread

MATZOH *n* pl. -S matzo

MATZOON *n* pl. -S a food made from milk

MATZOT a pl. of matzo

MATZOTH a pl. of matzo

MAUD *n* pl. -S a Scottish gray and black plaid

MAUDLIN *adj* excessively emotional

MAUGER *prep* maugre

MAUGRE *prep* in spite of

MAUL *v* -ED, -ING, -S to injure by beating

MAULER *n* pl. -S one that mauls

MAUMET *n* pl. -S an idol

MAUMETRY *n* pl. -RIES idolatry

MAUN *v* must — MAUN is the only form of this verb; it cannot be conjugated

MAUND *n* pl. -S an Asian unit of weight

MAUNDER *v* -ED, -ING, -S to talk incoherently

MAUNDY *n* pl. -DIES the religious ceremony of washing the feet of the poor

MAUSOLEA *n/pl* large, stately tombs

MAUT *n* pl. -S malt

MAUVE *n* pl. -S a purple color

MAVEN *n* pl. -S mavin

MAVERICK *n* pl. -S an unbranded range animal

MAVIE *n* pl. -S mavis

MAVIN *n* pl. -S an expert

MAVIS *n* pl. -VISES a songbird

MAW *v* MAWED, MAWN, MAWING, MAWS to mow

MAWKISH *adj* offensively sentimental

MAX *n* pl. -ES maximum

MAXI *n* pl. -S a long skirt or coat

MAXICOAT *n* pl. -S a long coat

MAXILLA *n* pl. -LAE or -LAS the upper jaw or jawbone

MAXIM *n* pl. -S a brief statement of a general truth or principle

MAXIMA a pl. of maximum

MAXIMAL *n* pl. -S an element of a mathematical set that is followed by no other

MAXIMIN *n* pl. -S the maximum of a set of minima

MAXIMISE *v* -MISED, -MISING, -MISES to maximize

MAXIMITE *n* pl. -S a powerful explosive

MAXIMIZE *v* -MIZED, -MIZING, -MIZES to make as great as possible

MAXIMUM *n* pl. -MUMS or -MA the greatest possible amount, quantity, or degree

MAXIXE *n* pl. -S a Brazilian dance

MAXWELL *n* pl. -S a unit of magnetic flux

MAY *v* present 2d person sing. MAY, MAYEST, or MAYST, past tense MIGHT — used as an auxiliary to express permission

MAY *v* -ED, -ING, -S to gather flowers in the spring

MAYA *n* pl. -S the power to produce illusions, in Hindu philosophy **MAYAN** *adj*

MAYAPPLE *n* pl. -S a perennial herb

MAYBE	*n* pl. -S an uncertainty
MAYBUSH	*n* pl. -ES a flowering shrub
MAYDAY	*n* pl. -DAYS a radio distress call
MAYEST	a present 2d person sing. of may
MAYFLY	*n* pl. -FLIES a winged insect
MAYHAP	*adv* maybe
MAYHEM	*n* pl. -S the offense of willfully maiming a person
MAYING	*n* pl. -S the gathering of spring flowers
MAYO	*n* pl. -YOS mayonnaise
MAYOR	*n* pl. -S the chief executive official of a city or borough **MAYORAL** *adj*
MAYORESS	*n* pl. -ES a female mayor
MAYPOLE	*n* pl. -S a decorated pole used in a spring celebration
MAYPOP	*n* pl. -S a flowering vine
MAYST	a present 2d person sing. of may
MAYVIN	*n* pl. -S mavin
MAYWEED	*n* pl. -S a malodorous weed
MAZAEDIA	*n/pl* spore-producing organs of certain lichens
MAZARD	*n* pl. -S the head or face
MAZE	*v* MAZED, MAZING, MAZES to bewilder **MAZEDLY** *adv*
MAZELIKE	*adj* mazy
MAZER	*n* pl. -S a large drinking bowl
MAZIER	comparative of mazy
MAZIEST	superlative of mazy
MAZILY	*adv* in a mazy manner
MAZINESS	*n* pl. -ES the quality of being mazy
MAZING	present participle of maze
MAZOURKA	*n* pl. -S mazurka
MAZUMA	*n* pl. -S money
MAZURKA	*n* pl. -S a Polish dance
MAZY	*adj* MAZIER, MAZIEST full of confusing turns and passages
MAZZARD	*n* pl. -S a wild cherry
MBIRA	*n* pl. -S an African musical instrument
ME	*pron* the objective case of the pronoun I
MEAD	*n* pl. -S an alcoholic beverage
MEADOW	*n* pl. -S a tract of grassland **MEADOWY** *adj*
MEAGER	*adj* deficient in quantity or quality **MEAGERLY** *adv*
MEAGRE	*adj* meager **MEAGRELY** *adv*
MEAL	*n* pl. -S the food served and eaten in one sitting
MEALIE	*n* pl. -S an ear of corn
MEALIER	comparative of mealy
MEALIEST	superlative of mealy
MEALLESS	*adj* lacking a meal
MEALTIME	*n* pl. -S the usual time for a meal
MEALWORM	*n* pl. -S the destructive larva of certain beetles
MEALY	*adj* MEALIER, MEALIEST soft, dry, and friable
MEALYBUG	*n* pl. -S a destructive insect
MEAN	*v* MEANT, MEANING, MEANS to intend
MEAN	*adj* MEANER, MEANEST inferior in grade, quality, or character
MEANDER	*v* -ED, -ING, -S to wander
MEANER	*n* pl. -S one that means
MEANIE	*n* pl. -S a nasty person
MEANIES	pl. of meany
MEANING	*n* pl. -S something that one intends to convey by language
MEANLY	*adv* in a mean manner
MEANNESS	*n* pl. -ES the state of being mean
MEANT	past tense of mean
MEANTIME	*n* pl. -S the intervening time
MEANY	*n* pl. MEANIES meanie
MEASLE	*n* pl. -S a tapeworm larva **MEASLED** *adj*
MEASLY	*adj* -SLIER, -SLIEST meager
MEASURE	*v* -SURED, -SURING, -SURES to ascertain the dimensions, quantity, or capacity of
MEASURER	*n* pl. -S one that measures
MEAT	*n* pl. -S animal flesh used as food **MEATED** *adj*
MEATAL	*adj* pertaining to a meatus
MEATBALL	*n* pl. -S a small ball of chopped meat
MEATHEAD	*n* pl. -S a dolt
MEATIER	comparative of meaty
MEATIEST	superlative of meaty
MEATILY	*adv* in a meaty manner
MEATLESS	*adj* having no meat

MEATLOAF   *n* pl. -LOAVES a baked loaf of ground meat

MEATMAN   *n* pl. -MEN a vendor of meat

MEATUS   *n* pl. -ES a natural body passage

MEATY   *adj* MEATIER, MEATIEST full of meat

MECCA   *n* pl. -S a place visited by many people

MECHANIC   *n* pl. -S a person who works with machines

MECONIUM   *n* pl. -S the first fecal excretion of a newborn child

MED   *adj* medical

MEDAKA   *n* pl. -S a Japanese fish

MEDAL   *v* -ALED, -ALING, -ALS or -ALLED, -ALLING, -ALS to honor with a medal (a commemorative piece of metal)

MEDALIST   *n* pl. -S a person to whom a medal has been awarded

MEDALLIC   *adj* of or pertaining to a medal

MEDALLING   a present participle of medal

MEDDLE   *v* -DLED, -DLING, -DLES to interest oneself in what is not one's concern

MEDDLER   *n* pl. -S one that meddles

MEDEVAC   *v* -VACKED, -VACKING, -VACS to evacuate the wounded from a battlefield by helicopter

MEDFLY   *n* pl. -FLIES a Mediterranean fruit fly

MEDIA   *n* pl. -DIAE the middle layer of a blood or lymph vessel

MEDIA   *n* pl. -S a channel of communication

MEDIACY   *n* pl. -CIES the act of mediating

MEDIAD   *adv* toward the middle of a body or part

MEDIAE   pl. of media

MEDIAL   *n* pl. -S a sound, syllable, or letter in the middle of a word

MEDIALLY   *adv* in a central manner

MEDIAN   *n* pl. -S a central part

MEDIANLY   *adv* medially

MEDIANT   *n* pl. -S a type of musical tone

MEDIATE   *v* -ATED, -ATING, -ATES to act between disputing parties in order to bring about a settlement

MEDIATOR   *n* pl. -S one that mediates

MEDIC   *n* pl. -S one engaged in medical work

MEDICAID   *n* pl. -S a type of governmental health program

MEDICAL   *n* pl. -S a physical examination

MEDICARE   *n* pl. -S a type of governmental health program

MEDICATE   *v* -CATED, -CATING, -CATES to treat with medicine

MEDICINE   *v* -CINED, -CINING, -CINES to administer medicine (a substance used in the treatment of disease) to

MEDICK   *n* pl. -S a flowering plant

MEDICO   *n* pl. -COS a doctor or medical student

MEDIEVAL   *n* pl. -S a person belonging to the Middle Ages

MEDII   pl. of medius

MEDINA   *n* pl. -S the native quarter of a North African city

MEDIOCRE   *adj* neither good nor bad

MEDITATE   *v* -TATED, -TATING, -TATES to ponder

MEDIUM   *n* pl. -DIA or -DIUMS a surrounding environment in which something functions and thrives

MEDIUS   *n* pl. -DII the middle finger

MEDLAR   *n* pl. -S a Eurasian tree

MEDLEY   *n* pl. -LEYS a mixture

MEDULLA   *n* pl. -LAS or -LAE the central tissue in the stems of certain plants **MEDULLAR** *adj*

MEDUSA   *n* pl. -SAE or -SAS a jellyfish **MEDUSAL** *adj*

MEDUSAN   *n* pl. -S medusa

MEDUSOID   *n* pl. -S medusa

MEED   *n* pl. -S a deserved reward

MEEK   *adj* MEEKER, MEEKEST lacking in spirit and courage **MEEKLY** *adv*

MEEKNESS   *n* pl. -ES the quality of being meek

MEERKAT   *n* pl. -S an African mongoose

MEET   *v* MET, MEETING, MEETS to come into the company or presence of

MEETER   *n* pl. -S one that meets

MEETING   *n* pl. -S an assembly for a common purpose

MEETLY   *adv* suitably

MEETNESS   *n* pl. -ES suitability

MEGABAR   *n* pl. -S a unit of pressure

MEGABIT *n* pl. -S a unit of computer information

MEGABUCK *n* pl. -S one million dollars

MEGABYTE *n* pl. -S 1,048,576 bytes

MEGACITY *n* pl. -CITIES a very large city

MEGADEAL *n* pl. -S a business deal involving a lot of money

MEGADOSE *n* pl. -S an abnormally large dose

MEGADYNE *n* pl. -S a unit of force

MEGAHIT *n* pl. -S something extremely successful

MEGALITH *n* pl. -S a huge stone used in prehistoric monuments

MEGALOPS *n* pl. -LOPSES a larval stage of most crabs

MEGAPOD *n* pl. -S megapode

MEGAPODE *n* pl. -S a large-footed bird

MEGASS *n* pl. -ES a bagasse

MEGASSE *n* pl. -S megass

MEGASTAR *n* pl. -S an extremely successful performer

MEGATON *n* pl. -S a unit of explosive force

MEGAVOLT *n* pl. -S a unit of electromotive force

MEGAWATT *n* pl. -S a unit of power

MEGILLAH *n* pl. -S a long, involved story

MEGILP *n* pl. -S a substance with which pigments are mixed in painting

MEGILPH *n* pl. -S megilp

MEGOHM *n* pl. -S a unit of electrical resistance

MEGRIM *n* pl. -S a migraine

MEIKLE *adj* large

MEINIE *n* pl. -S meiny

MEINY *n* pl. -NIES a retinue

MEIOSIS *n* pl. -OSES a type of cell division **MEIOTIC** *adj*

MEL *n* pl. -S honey

MELAMED *n* pl. -LAMDIM a teacher in a Jewish school

MELAMINE *n* pl. -S a chemical compound

MELANGE *n* pl. -S a mixture

MELANIAN *adj* pertaining to dark pigmentation

MELANIC *n* pl. -S one who is affected with melanism

MELANIN *n* pl. -S a dark pigment

MELANISM *n* pl. -S abnormally dark pigmentation of the skin

MELANIST *n* pl. -S a melanic

MELANITE *n* pl. -S a black variety of garnet

MELANIZE *v* -NIZED, -NIZING, -NIZES to make dark

MELANOID *n* pl. -S a dark pigment

MELANOMA *n* pl. -MAS or -MATA a darkly pigmented tumor

MELANOUS *adj* having dark skin and hair

MELD *v* -ED, -ING, -S to blend

MELDER *n* pl. -S the amount of grain ground at one time

MELEE *n* pl. -S a confused struggle

MELIC *adj* pertaining to song

MELILITE *n* pl. -S a mineral group

MELILOT *n* pl. -S a flowering plant

MELINITE *n* pl. -S a powerful explosive

MELISMA *n* pl. -MAS or -MATA melodic embellishment

MELL *v* -ED, -ING, -S to mix

MELLIFIC *adj* producing honey

MELLOW *adj* -LOWER, -LOWEST soft and full-flavored from ripeness **MELLOWLY** *adv*

MELLOW *v* -ED, -ING, -S to make or become mellow

MELODEON *n* pl. -S a musical instrument

MELODIA *n* pl. -S a type of organ stop

MELODIC *adj* pertaining to melody

MELODICA *n* pl. -S a harmonica with a small keyboard at one end

MELODIES pl. of melody

MELODISE *v* -DISED, -DISING, -DISES to melodize

MELODIST *n* pl. -S a composer of melodies

MELODIZE *v* -DIZED, -DIZING, -DIZES to compose a melody

MELODY *n* pl. -DIES an agreeable succession of musical sounds

MELOID *n* pl. -S a type of beetle

MELON *n* pl. -S any of various gourds

MELT *v* -ED, -ING, -S to change from a solid to a liquid state by heat **MELTABLE** *adj*

MELTAGE *n* pl. -S the process of melting

MELTDOWN *n* pl. -S the melting of the core of a nuclear reactor

MELTER *n* pl. -S one that melts

MELTON *n* pl. -S a heavy woolen fabric

MEM *n* pl. -S a Hebrew letter

MEMBER *n* pl. -S a distinct part of a whole **MEMBERED** *adj*

MEMBRANE *n* pl. -S a thin, pliable layer of tissue

MEMENTO *n* pl. -TOS or -TOES something that serves as a reminder of the past

MEMO *n* pl. MEMOS a note designating something to be remembered

MEMOIR *n* pl. -S a biography

MEMORIAL *n* pl. -S something that serves as a remembrance of a person or event

MEMORISE *v* -ISED, -ISING, -ISES memorize

MEMORIZE *v* -RIZED, -RIZING, -RIZES to commit to memory

MEMORY *n* pl. -RIES the mental faculty of retaining and recalling past experience

MEMSAHIB *n* pl. -S a European woman living in colonial India

MEN pl. of man

MENACE *v* -ACED, -ACING, -ACES to threaten

MENACER *n* pl. -S one that menaces

MENAD *n* pl. -S maenad

MENAGE *n* pl. -S a household

MENARCHE *n* pl. -S the first occurrence of menstruation

MENAZON *n* pl. -S an insecticide

MEND *v* -ED, -ING, -S to repair **MENDABLE** *adj*

MENDER *n* pl. -S one that mends

MENDIGO *n* pl. -GOS a freshwater fish

MENDING *n* pl. -S an accumulation of articles to be mended

MENFOLK *n/pl* the men of a family or community

MENFOLKS *n/pl* menfolk

MENHADEN *n* pl. -S a marine fish

MENHIR *n* pl. -S a prehistoric monument

MENIAL *n* pl. -S a domestic servant

MENIALLY *adv* in a servile manner

MENINX *n* pl. -NINGES any of the membranes enclosing the brain and spinal cord

MENISCUS *n* pl. -CI or -CUSES a crescent-shaped body **MENISCAL** *adj*

MENO *adv* less — used as a musical direction

MENOLOGY *n* pl. -GIES an ecclesiastical calendar

MENORAH *n* pl. -S a candleholder used in Jewish worship

MENSA *n* pl. -SAS or -SAE the grinding surface of a tooth

MENSAL *adj* pertaining to or used at the table

MENSCH *n* pl. MENSCHES or MENSCHEN an admirable person

MENSE *v* MENSED, MENSING, MENSES to do honor to

MENSEFUL *adj* proper

MENSTRUA *n/pl* solvents

MENSURAL *adj* pertaining to measure

MENSWEAR *n* pl. MENSWEAR clothing for men

MENTA pl. of mentum

MENTAL *adj* pertaining to the mind **MENTALLY** *adv*

MENTHENE *n* pl. -S a liquid hydrocarbon

MENTHOL *n* pl. -S an alcohol

MENTION *v* -ED, -ING, -S to refer to in a casual manner

MENTOR *v* -ED, -ING, -S to serve as a friend and teacher to

MENTUM *n* pl. -TA the chin

MENU *n* pl. -S a list of the dishes available in a restaurant

MEOU *v* -ED, -ING, -S meow

MEOW *v* -ED, -ING, -S to make the crying sound of a cat

MEPHITIS *n* pl. -TISES an offensive odor **MEPHITIC** *adj*

MERCAPTO *adj* containing a particular chemical group

MERCER *n* pl. -S a dealer in textiles

MERCERY *n* pl. -CERIES a mercer's shop

MERCHANT *v* -ED, -ING, -S to buy and sell goods for profit

MERCIES pl. of mercy

MERCIFUL *adj* full of mercy

MERCURY *n* pl. -RIES a metallic element **MERCURIC** *adj*

MERCY *n* pl. -CIES compassion shown to an offender or enemy

MERE *n* pl. -S a pond or lake

MERE *adj* MERER, MEREST being nothing more than **MERELY** *adv*

MERENGUE *n* pl. -S a ballroom dance

MERGE	*v* MERGED, MERGING, MERGES to combine
MERGENCE	*n* pl. -S the act of merging
MERGER	*n* pl. -S the union of two or more businesses into a single enterprise
MERGING	present participle of merge
MERIDIAN	*n* pl. -S a circle around the earth passing through both poles
MERINGUE	*n* pl. -S a topping for pastries
MERINO	*n* pl. -NOS a fine wool
MERISIS	*n* pl. MERISES growth
MERISTEM	*n* pl. -S formative plant tissue
MERISTIC	*adj* made up of segments
MERIT	*v* -ED, -ING, -S to earn
MERK	*n* pl. -S a former coin of Scotland
MERL	*n* pl. -S merle
MERLE	*n* pl. -S a blackbird
MERLIN	*n* pl. -S a European falcon
MERLON	*n* pl. -S the solid part of an indented parapet
MERLOT	*n* pl. -S a dry red wine
MERMAID	*n* pl. -S a legendary marine creature
MERMAN	*n* pl. -MEN a legendary marine creature
MEROPIA	*n* pl. -S partial blindness **MEROPIC** *adj*
MERRY	*adj* -RIER, -RIEST cheerful **MERRILY** *adv*
MESA	*n* pl. -S a land formation having a flat top and steep sides
MESALLY	*adv* medially
MESARCH	*adj* originating in a mesic habitat
MESCAL	*n* pl. -S a cactus
MESDAMES	pl. of madame
MESEEMS	*v* past tense MESEEMED present 3d person sing. MESEEMETH it seems to me — MESEEMS is an impersonal verb and is used only in the 3d person sing.
MESH	*v* -ED, -ING, -ES to entangle
MESHIER	comparative of meshy
MESHIEST	superlative of meshy
MESHUGA	*adj* crazy
MESHUGAH	*adj* meshuga
MESHUGGA	*adj* meshuga
MESHUGGE	*adj* meshuga

MESHWORK	*n* pl. -S a network
MESHY	*adj* MESHIER, MESHIEST netty
MESIAL	*adj* situated in the middle **MESIALLY** *adv*
MESIAN	*adj* mesial
MESIC	*adj* characterized by a medium supply of moisture
MESMERIC	*adj* pertaining to hypnotism
MESNALTY	*n* pl. -TIES a type of feudal estate
MESNE	*n* pl. -S a feudal lord holding land from a superior
MESOCARP	*n* pl. -S the middle layer of a pericarp
MESODERM	*n* pl. -S the middle germ layer of an embryo
MESOGLEA	*n* pl. -S a gelatinous material in sponges
MESOMERE	*n* pl. -S an embryonic segment
MESON	*n* pl. -S a subatomic particle **MESONIC** *adj*
MESOPHYL	*n* pl. -S the soft tissue of a leaf
MESOSOME	*n* pl. -S a specialized cellular part
MESOTRON	*n* pl. -S a meson
MESQUIT	*n* pl. -S mesquite
MESQUITE	*n* pl. -S a spiny tree or shrub
MESS	*v* -ED, -ING, -ES to make dirty or untidy
MESSAGE	*v* -SAGED, -SAGING, -SAGES to send as a message (an oral, written, or signaled communication)
MESSAN	*n* pl. -S a lapdog
MESSIAH	*n* pl. -S an expected liberator
MESSIER	comparative of messy
MESSIEST	superlative of messy
MESSIEURS	pl. of monsieur
MESSILY	*adv* in a messy manner
MESSMAN	*n* pl. -MEN a serviceman who works in a dining facility
MESSMATE	*n* pl. -S a person with whom one eats regularly
MESSUAGE	*n* pl. -S a dwelling house with its adjacent buildings and land
MESSY	*adj* MESSIER, MESSIEST dirty or untidy
MESTEE	*n* pl. -S mustee
MESTESO	*n* pl. -SOS or -SOES mestizo
MESTINO	*n* pl. -NOS or -NOES mestizo

MESTIZA   *n* pl. -S a female mestizo

MESTIZO   *n* pl. -ZOS or -ZOES a person of mixed ancestry

MET   past tense of meet

META   *adj* pertaining to positions in a benzene ring separated by one carbon atom

METAGE   *n* pl. -S an official measurement of weight or contents

METAL   *v* -ALED, -ALING, -ALS or -ALLED, -ALLING, -ALS to cover with metal (any of various ductile, fusible, and lustrous substances)

METALISE   *v* -ISED, -ISING, -ISES to metalize

METALIST   *n* pl. -S one who works with metals

METALIZE   *v* -IZED, -IZING, -IZES to treat with metal

METALLED   a past tense of metal

METALLIC   *n* pl. -S a fabric or yarn made of or coated with metal

METALLING   a present participle of metal

METAMER   *n* pl. -S a type of chemical compound

METAMERE   *n* pl. -S a somite

METAPHOR   *n* pl. -S a type of figure of speech

METATE   *n* pl. -S a stone used for grinding grains

METAZOAN   *n* pl. -S any of a major division of multicellular animals **METAZOAL, METAZOIC** *adj*

METAZOON   *n* pl. -ZOA a metazoan

METE   *v* METED, METING, METES to distribute by measure

METEOR   *n* pl. -S a small celestial body that enters the earth's atmosphere **METEORIC** *adj*

METEPA   *n* pl. -S a chemical compound

METER   *v* -ED, -ING, -S to measure by mechanical means

METERAGE   *n* pl. -S the process of metering

METH   *n* pl. -S a stimulant drug

METHADON   *n* pl. -S a narcotic drug

METHANE   *n* pl. -S a flammable gas

METHANOL   *n* pl. -S a toxic alcohol

METHINKS   *v* past tense METHOUGHT it seems to me — METHINKS is an impersonal verb and is used only in the 3d person sing.

METHOD   *n* pl. -S a means of procedure

METHODIC   *adj* systematic

METHOUGHT   past tense of methinks

METHOXY   *adj* containing a certain chemical group

METHOXYL   *adj* methoxy

METHYL   *n* pl. -S a univalent radical **METHYLIC** *adj*

METHYLAL   *n* pl. -S a flammable liquid

METICAL   *n* pl. -CAIS or -CALS a monetary unit of Mozambique

METIER   *n* pl. -S a vocation

METING   present participle of mete

METIS   *n* pl. METIS a person of mixed ancestry

METISSE   *n* pl. -S a female metis

METONYM   *n* pl. -S a word used in metonymy

METONYMY   *n* pl. -MIES a type of figure of speech

METOPE   *n* pl. -PES or -PAE a space between two triglyphs

METOPIC   *adj* pertaining to the forehead

METOPON   *n* pl. -S a narcotic drug

METRE   *v* -TRED, -TRING, -TRES to meter

METRIC   *n* pl. -S a standard of measurement

METRICAL   *adj* pertaining to or composed in a system of arranged and measured rhythm

METRIFY   *v* -FIED, -FYING, -FIES to compose in metrical form

METRING   present participle of metre

METRIST   *n* pl. -S one who metrifies

METRITIS   *n* pl. -TISES inflammation of the uterus

METRO   *n* pl. -ROS a subway

METTLE   *n* pl. -S quality of character **METTLED** *adj*

METUMP   *n* pl. -S a tumpline

MEUNIERE   *adj* cooked in browned butter

MEW   *v* -ED, -ING, -S to confine

MEWL   *v* -ED, -ING, -S to whimper

MEWLER   *n* pl. -S one that mewls

MEZCAL   *n* pl. -S mescal

MEZE   *n* pl. -S a Greek or Middle Eastern appetizer

MEZEREON   *n* pl. -S a flowering shrub

MEZEREUM   *n* pl. -S mezereon

MEZQUIT	*n* pl. -S mesquite
MEZQUITE	*n* pl. -S mesquite
MEZUZA	*n* pl. -S mezuzah
MEZUZAH	*n* pl. -ZAHS, -ZOT, or -ZOTH a Judaic scroll
MEZZO	*n* pl. -ZOS a female voice of a full, deep quality
MHO	*n* pl. MHOS a unit of electrical conductance
MI	*n* pl. -S the third tone of the diatonic musical scale
MIAOU	*v* -ED, -ING, -S to meow
MIAOW	*v* -ED, -ING, -S to meow
MIASM	*n* pl. -S miasma
MIASMA	*n* pl. -MAS or -MATA a noxious vapor **MIASMAL, MIASMIC** *adj*
MIAUL	*v* -ED, -ING, -S to meow
MIB	*n* pl. -S a type of playing marble
MICA	*n* pl. -S a mineral
MICAWBER	*n* pl. -S a person who remains hopeful despite adversity
MICE	pl. of mouse
MICELL	*n* pl. -S micelle
MICELLA	*n* pl. -LAE micelle
MICELLE	*n* pl. -S a coherent strand or structure in a fiber **MICELLAR** *adj*
MICHE	*v* MICHED, MICHING, MICHES to skulk
MICKEY	*n* pl. -EYS a drugged drink
MICKLE	*adj* -LER, -LEST large
MICKLE	*n* pl. -S a large amount
MICRA	a pl. of micron
MICRIFY	*v* -FIED, -FYING, -FIES to make small
MICRO	*n* pl. -CROS a very small computer
MICROBAR	*n* pl. -S a unit of atmospheric pressure
MICROBE	*n* pl. -S a minute life form **MICROBIC** *adj*
MICROBUS	*n* pl. -BUSES or -BUSSES a small bus
MICRODOT	*n* pl. -S a copy of printed matter reduced to the size of a dot
MICROHM	*n* pl. -S a unit of electrical resistance
MICROLUX	*n* pl. -LUXES or -LUCES a unit of illumination
MICROMHO	*n* pl. -S a unit of electrical conductance

MICRON	*n* pl. -CRONS or -CRA a unit of length
MICRURGY	*n* pl. -GIES the use of minute tools under high magnification
MID	*n* pl. -S the middle
MIDAIR	*n* pl. -S a region in the middle of the air
MIDBRAIN	*n* pl. -S the middle region of the brain
MIDCULT	*n* pl. -S middle-class culture
MIDDAY	*n* pl. -DAYS the middle of the day
MIDDEN	*n* pl. -S a dunghill
MIDDIES	pl. of middy
MIDDLE	*v* -DLED, -DLING, -DLES to place in the middle (the area or point equidistant from extremes or limits)
MIDDLER	*n* pl. -S a student in an intermediate grade
MIDDLING	*n* pl. -S a cut of pork
MIDDY	*n* pl. -DIES a loosely fitting blouse
MIDFIELD	*n* pl. -S the middle portion of a playing field
MIDGE	*n* pl. -S a small winged insect
MIDGET	*n* pl. -S a very small person
MIDGUT	*n* pl. -S the middle part of the embryonic digestive tract
MIDI	*n* pl. -S a skirt or coat that extends to the middle of the calf
MIDIRON	*n* pl. -S a golf club
MIDLAND	*n* pl. -S the middle part of a country
MIDLEG	*n* pl. -S the middle of the leg
MIDLIFE	*n* pl. -LIVES middle age
MIDLINE	*n* pl. -S a median line
MIDMONTH	*n* pl. -S the middle of the month
MIDMOST	*n* pl. -S a part exactly in the middle
MIDNIGHT	*n* pl. -S the middle of the night
MIDNOON	*n* pl. -S midday
MIDPOINT	*n* pl. -S a point at the middle
MIDRANGE	*n* pl. -S the middle of a range
MIDRASH	*n* pl. -RASHIM or -RASHOTH an early Jewish interpretation of a biblical text
MIDRIB	*n* pl. -S the central vein of a leaf
MIDRIFF	*n* pl. -S the middle part of the body

MIDSHIP   *adv* pertaining to the middle of a ship

MIDSHIPS   *adv* toward the middle of a ship

MIDSIZE   *adj* of intermediate size

MIDSIZED   *adj* midsize

MIDSOLE   *n* pl. -S a middle layer of the sole of a shoe

MIDSPACE   *n* pl. -S the middle of a space

MIDST   *n* pl. -S the middle

MIDSTORY   *n* pl. -RIES the middle of a story

MIDTERM   *n* pl. -S an examination given in the middle of an academic semester

MIDTOWN   *n* pl. -S the central part of a city

MIDWATCH   *n* pl. -ES a watch on a ship between midnight and 4 A.M.

MIDWAY   *n* pl. -WAYS an avenue at a fair or carnival for concessions and amusements

MIDWEEK   *n* pl. -S the middle of the week

MIDWIFE   *v* -WIFED, -WIFING, -WIFES or -WIVED, -WIVING, -WIVES to assist a woman in childbirth

MIDYEAR   *n* pl. -S the middle of the year

MIEN   *n* pl. -S demeanor

MIFF   *v* -ED, -ING, -S to annoy

MIFFY   *adj* MIFFIER, MIFFIEST easily annoyed

MIG   *n* pl. -S a type of playing marble

MIGG   *n* pl. -S mig

MIGGLE   *n* pl. -S a mig

MIGHT   *n* pl. -S strength

MIGHTY   *adj* MIGHTIER, MIGHTIEST strong **MIGHTILY** *adv*

MIGNON   *n* pl. -S a cut of beef

MIGNONNE   *adj* daintily small

MIGRAINE   *n* pl. -S a severe headache

MIGRANT   *n* pl. -S one that migrates

MIGRATE   *v* -GRATED, -GRATING, -GRATES to move from one region to another

MIGRATOR   *n* pl. -S a migrant

MIHRAB   *n* pl. -S a niche in a mosque

MIJNHEER   *n* pl. -S mynheer

MIKADO   *n* pl. -DOS an emperor of Japan

MIKE   *v* MIKED, MIKING, MIKES to amplify or record by use of a microphone

MIKRON   *n* pl. -KRONS or -KRA micron

MIKVAH   *n* pl. -VAHS or -VOTH a place for ritual bathing by Orthodox Jews

MIKVEH   *n* pl. -S mikvah

MIL   *n* pl. -S a unit of length

MILADI   *n* pl. -S milady

MILADY   *n* pl. -DIES an English gentlewoman

MILAGE   *n* pl. -S mileage

MILCH   *adj* giving milk

MILCHIG   *adj* made of or derived from milk

MILD   *adj* MILDER, MILDEST not harsh or rough

MILDEN   *v* -ED, -ING, -S to make or become mild

MILDEW   *v* -ED, -ING, -S to affect with mildew (a whitish growth produced by fungi)

MILDEWY   *adj* affected with or resembling mildew

MILDLY   *adv* in a mild manner

MILDNESS   *n* pl. -ES the quality of being mild

MILE   *n* pl. -S a unit of distance

MILEAGE   *n* pl. -S total distance expressed in miles

MILEPOST   *n* pl. -S a post indicating distance in miles

MILER   *n* pl. -S one that runs a mile race

MILESIMO   *n* pl. -MOS a former monetary unit of Chile

MILFOIL   *n* pl. -S a perennial herb

MILIA   pl. of milium

MILIARIA   *n* pl. -S a skin disease

MILIARY   *adj* made up of many small projections

MILIEU   *n* pl. -LIEUS or -LIEUX environment

MILITANT   *n* pl. -S a person who is aggressively engaged in a cause

MILITARY   *n* pl. -TARIES armed forces

MILITATE   *v* -TATED, -TATING, -TATES to have influence or effect

MILITIA   *n* pl. -S a citizen army

MILIUM   *n* pl. -IA a small, whitish lump in the skin

MILK   *v* -ED, -ING, -S to draw milk (a whitish, nutritious liquid) from the udder of

MILKER   *n* pl. -S one that milks

MILKFISH   *n* pl. -ES a marine food fish

MILKIER   comparative of milky

MILKIEST	superlative of milky	**MILLIPED**	*n* pl. -S a multi-legged arthropod
MILKILY	*adv* in a milky manner	**MILLIREM**	*n* pl. -S a quantity of ionizing radiation
MILKMAID	*n* pl. -S a woman who milks cows		
MILKMAN	*n* pl. -MEN a man who sells or delivers milk	**MILLPOND**	*n* pl. -S a pond for supplying water to run a mill wheel (a type of waterwheel)
MILKSHED	*n* pl. -S a region supplying milk to a particular community	**MILLRACE**	*n* pl. -S the current of water that drives a mill wheel
MILKSOP	*n* pl. -S an effeminate man	**MILLRUN**	*n* pl. -S a millrace
MILKWEED	*n* pl. -S a plant that secretes a milky juice	**MILLWORK**	*n* pl. -S woodwork produced by milling
MILKWOOD	*n* pl. -S a tropical tree	**MILNEB**	*n* pl. -S a fungicide
MILKWORT	*n* pl. -S a flowering plant	**MILO**	*n* pl. -LOS a cereal grass
MILKY	*adj* MILKIER, MILKIEST resembling or suggestive of milk	**MILORD**	*n* pl. -S an English gentleman
MILL	*v* -ED, -ING, -S to grind by mechanical means **MILLABLE** *adj*	**MILPA**	*n* pl. -S a field that is cleared from a jungle for farming purposes
MILLAGE	*n* pl. -S a type of monetary rate	**MILREIS**	*n* pl. MILREIS a former monetary unit of Portugal
MILLCAKE	*n* pl. -S a residue from pressed linseed	**MILT**	*v* -ED, -ING, -S to impregnate with milt (fish sperm)
MILLDAM	*n* pl. -S a dam built to form a millpond	**MILTER**	*n* pl. -S a male fish at breeding time
MILLE	*n* pl. -S a thousand	**MILTY**	*adj* MILTIER, MILTIEST full of milt
MILLEPED	*n* pl. -S milliped		
MILLER	*n* pl. -S one that mills	**MIM**	*adj* primly demure
MILLET	*n* pl. -S a cereal grass	**MIMBAR**	*n* pl. -S a pulpit in a mosque
MILLIARD	*n* pl. -S a billion	**MIME**	*v* MIMED, MIMING, MIMES to mimic
MILLIARE	*n* pl. -S a unit of area		
MILLIARY	*n* pl. -ARIES an ancient Roman milestone	**MIMEO**	*v* -ED, -ING, -S to make copies of by use of a mimeograph
MILLIBAR	*n* pl. -S a unit of atmospheric pressure	**MIMER**	*n* pl. -S one that mimes
MILLIEME	*n* pl. -S unit of value of Egypt and Sudan	**MIMESIS**	*n* pl. -SISES mimicry **MIMETIC** *adj*
		MIMETITE	*n* pl. -S an ore of lead
MILLIER	*n* pl. -S a unit of weight	**MIMIC**	*v* -ICKED, -ICKING, -ICS to imitate closely
MILLIGAL	*n* pl. -S a unit of acceleration		
MILLILUX	*n* pl. -LUXES or -LUCES a unit of illumination	**MIMICAL**	*adj* of the nature of mimicry
		MIMICKER	*n* pl. -S one that mimics
MILLIME	*n* pl. -S a coin of Tunisia	**MIMICKING**	present participle of mimic
MILLIMHO	*n* pl. -MHOS a unit of electrical conductance	**MIMICRY**	*n* pl. -RIES an instance of mimicking
MILLINE	*n* pl. -S a unit of advertising space	**MIMING**	present participle of mime
		MIMOSA	*n* pl. -S a tropical plant
MILLINER	*n* pl. -S one who makes or sells women's hats	**MINA**	*n* pl. -NAS or -NAE an ancient unit of weight and value
MILLING	*n* pl. -S a corrugated edge on a coin	**MINABLE**	*adj* capable of being mined
MILLIOHM	*n* pl. -S a unit of electrical resistance	**MINACITY**	*n* pl. -TIES the state of being threatening
MILLION	*n* pl. -S a number	**MINAE**	a pl. of mina

MINARET   *n* pl. -S a slender tower attached to a mosque

MINATORY   *adj* threatening

MINCE   *v* MINCED, MINCING, MINCES to cut into very small pieces

MINCER   *n* pl. -S one that minces

MINCY   *adj* MINCIER, MINCIEST affectedly dainty

MIND   *v* -ED, -ING, -S to heed

MINDER   *n* pl. -S one that minds

MINDFUL   *adj* heedful

MINDLESS   *adj* lacking intelligence

MINDSET   *n* pl. -S a fixed mental attitude

MINE   *v* MINED, MINING, MINES to dig into for valuable materials

MINEABLE   *adj* minable

MINER   *n* pl. -S one that mines

MINERAL   *n* pl. -S a naturally occurring inorganic substance having a characteristic set of physical properties

MINGIER   comparative of mingy

MINGIEST   superlative of mingy

MINGLE   *v* -GLED, -GLING, -GLES to mix together

MINGLER   *n* pl. -S one that mingles

MINGY   *adj* -GIER, -GIEST mean and stingy

MINI   *n* pl. -S something distinctively smaller than others of its kind

MINIBIKE   *n* pl. -S a small motorcycle

MINIBUS   *n* pl. -BUSES or -BUSSES a small bus

MINICAB   *n* pl. -S a small taxicab

MINICAMP   *n* pl. -S a short training camp for football players

MINICAR   *n* pl. -S a small automobile

MINIFY   *v* -FIED, -FYING, -FIES to make small or smaller

MINIKIN   *n* pl. -S a small or dainty creature

MINILAB   *n* pl. -S a retail outlet offering rapid on-site film development

MINIM   *n* pl. -S a unit of liquid measure

MINIMA   a pl. of minimum

MINIMAL   *n* pl. -S an element of a mathematical set that precedes all others

MINIMAX   *n* pl. -ES the minimum of a set of maxima

MINIMILL   *n* pl. -S a small-scale steel mill

MINIMISE   *v* -MISED, -MISING, -MISES to minimize

MINIMIZE   *v* -MIZED, -MIZING, -MIZES to make as small as possible

MINIMUM   *n* pl. -MUMS or -MA the least possible amount, quantity, or degree

MINING   *n* pl. -S the process or business of working mines (excavations in the earth)

MINION   *n* pl. -S a servile follower

MINIPARK   *n* pl. -S a small city park

MINISH   *v* -ED, -ING, -ES to diminish

MINISKI   *n* pl. -S a short ski

MINISTER   *v* -ED, -ING, -S to give aid or service

MINISTRY   *n* pl. -TRIES the act of ministering

MINIUM   *n* pl. -S a red pigment

MINIVAN   *n* pl. -S a small van

MINIVER   *n* pl. -S a white fur

MINK   *n* pl. -S a carnivorous mammal

MINKE   *n* pl. -S a small whale

MINNOW   *n* pl. -S a small fish

MINNY   *n* pl. -NIES minnow

MINOR   *v* -ED, -ING, -S to pursue a specific subordinate course of study

MINORCA   *n* pl. -S any of a breed of large domestic fowls

MINORITY   *n* pl. -TIES the smaller number or part

MINSTER   *n* pl. -S a large or important church

MINSTREL   *n* pl. -S a medieval musician

MINT   *v* -ED, -ING, -S to produce by stamping metal, as coins

MINTAGE   *n* pl. -S the act of minting

MINTER   *n* pl. -S one that mints

MINTY   *adj* MINTIER, MINTIEST having the flavor mint (an aromatic herb)

MINUEND   *n* pl. -S a number from which another is to be subtracted

MINUET   *n* pl. -S a slow, stately dance

MINUS   *n* pl. -ES a negative quantity

MINUTE   *v* -UTED, -UTING, -UTES to make a brief note of

MINUTE   *adj* -NUTER, -NUTEST very small **MINUTELY** *adv*

MINUTIA   *n* pl. -TIAE a small detail **MINUTIAL** *adj*

MINUTING   present participle of minute

MINX   *n* pl. -ES a pert girl **MINXISH** *adj*

MINYAN   *n* pl. -YANS or -YANIM the minimum number required to be present for the conduct of a Jewish service

MIOSIS   *n* pl. -OSES excessive contraction of the pupil of the eye

MIOTIC   *n* pl. -S an agent that causes miosis

MIQUELET   *n* pl. -S a former Spanish or French soldier

MIR   *n* pl. MIRS or MIRI a Russian peasant commune

MIRACLE   *n* pl. -S an event ascribed to supernatural or divine origin

MIRADOR   *n* pl. -S an architectural feature designed to afford an extensive view

MIRAGE   *n* pl. -S a type of optical illusion

MIRE   *v* MIRED, MIRING, MIRES to cause to stick in swampy ground

MIREX   *n* pl. -ES an insecticide

MIRI   a pl. of mir

MIRIER   comparative of miry

MIRIEST   superlative of miry

MIRINESS   *n* pl. -ES the state of being miry

MIRING   present participle of mire

MIRK   *adj* MIRKER, MIRKEST murk

MIRK   *n* pl. -S murk

MIRKY   *adj* MIRKIER, MIRKIEST murky **MIRKILY** *adv*

MIRLITON   *n* pl. -S a chayote

MIRROR   *v* -ED, -ING, -S to reflect an image of

MIRTH   *n* pl. -S spirited gaiety **MIRTHFUL** *adj*

MIRY   *adj* MIRIER, MIRIEST swampy

MIRZA   *n* pl. -S a Persian title of honor

MISACT   *v* -ED, -ING, -S to act badly

MISADAPT   *v* -ED, -ING, -S to adapt wrongly

MISADD   *v* -ED, -ING, -S to add incorrectly

MISAGENT   *n* pl. -S a bad agent

MISAIM   *v* -ED, -ING, -S to aim badly

MISALIGN   *v* -ED, -ING, -S to align improperly

MISALLY   *v* -LIED, -LYING, -LIES to ally badly

MISALTER   *v* -ED, -ING, -S to alter wrongly

MISANDRY   *n* pl. -DRIES hatred of men

MISAPPLY   *v* -PLIED, -PLYING, -PLIES to apply wrongly

MISASSAY   *v* -ED, -ING, -S to attempt unsuccessfully

MISATE   past tense of miseat

MISATONE   *v* -ATONED, -ATONING, -ATONES to atone wrongly

MISAVER   *v* -AVERRED, -AVERRING, -AVERS to speak erroneously

MISAWARD   *v* -ED, -ING, -S to award wrongly

MISBEGIN   *v* -GAN, -GUN, -GINNING, -GINS to begin wrongly

MISBEGOT   *adj* born out of wedlock

MISBIAS   *v* -ASED, -ASING, -ASES or -ASSED, -ASSING, -ASSES to bias wrongly

MISBILL   *v* -ED, -ING, -S to bill wrongly

MISBIND   *v* -BOUND, -BINDING, -BINDS to bind imperfectly

MISBRAND   *v* -ED, -ING, -S to brand incorrectly

MISBUILD   *v* -BUILT, -BUILDING, -BUILDS to build imperfectly

MISCALL   *v* -ED, -ING, -S to call by a wrong name

MISCARRY   *v* -RIED, -RYING, -RIES to be unsuccessful

MISCAST   *v* -CAST, -CASTING, -CASTS to cast in an unsuitable role

MISCHIEF   *n* pl. -S action that causes irritation, harm, or trouble

MISCIBLE   *adj* capable of being mixed

MISCITE   *v* -CITED, -CITING, -CITES to misquote

MISCLAIM   *v* -ED, -ING, -S to claim wrongfully

MISCLASS   *v* -ED, -ING, -ES to put in the wrong class

MISCODE   *v* -CODED, -CODING, -CODES to code wrongly

MISCOIN   *v* -ED, -ING, -S to coin improperly

MISCOLOR   *v* -ED, -ING, -S to color incorrectly

MISCOOK   *v* -ED, -ING, -S to cook badly

MISCOPY   *v* -COPIED, -COPYING, -COPIES to copy incorrectly

MISCOUNT   *v* -ED, -ING, -S to count incorrectly

MISCUE	*v* -CUED, -CUING, -CUES to make a faulty stroke in billiards	**MISFIRE**	*v* -FIRED, -FIRING, -FIRES to fail to fire
MISCUT	*v* -CUT, -CUTTING, -CUTS to cut incorrectly	**MISFIT**	*v* -FITTED, -FITTING, -FITS to fit badly
MISDATE	*v* -DATED, -DATING, -DATES to date incorrectly	**MISFOCUS**	*v* -CUSED, -CUSING, -CUSES or -CUSSED, -CUSSING, -CUSSES to focus badly
MISDEAL	*v* -DEALT, -DEALING, -DEALS to deal cards incorrectly	**MISFORM**	*v* -ED, -ING, -S to misshape
MISDEED	*n* pl. -S an evil act	**MISFRAME**	*v* -FRAMED, -FRAMING, -FRAMES to frame badly
MISDEEM	*v* -ED, -ING, -S to judge unfavorably	**MISGAUGE**	*v* -GAUGED, -GAUGING, -GAUGES to gauge wrongly or inaccurately
MISDIAL	*v* -DIALED, -DIALING, -DIALS or -DIALLED, -DIALLING, -DIALS to dial wrongly	**MISGIVE**	*v* -GAVE, -GIVEN, -GIVING, -GIVES to make doubtful or fearful
MISDO	*v* -DID, -DONE, -DOING, -DOES to do wrongly	**MISGRADE**	*v* -GRADED, -GRADING, -GRADES to grade incorrectly
MISDOER	*n* pl. -S one that misdoes	**MISGRAFT**	*v* -ED, -ING, -S to graft wrongly
MISDOING	*n* pl. -S an instance of doing wrong	**MISGROW**	*v* -GREW, -GROWN, -GROWING, -GROWS to grow abnormally
MISDONE	past participle of misdo		
MISDOUBT	*v* -ED, -ING, -S to doubt	**MISGUESS**	*v* -ED, -ING, -ES to guess wrongly
MISDRAW	*v* -DREW, -DRAWN, -DRAWING, -DRAWS to draw incorrectly	**MISGUIDE**	*v* -GUIDED, -GUIDING, -GUIDES to guide wrongly
MISDRIVE	*v* -DROVE, -DRIVEN, -DRIVING, -DRIVES to drive wrongly or improperly	**MISHAP**	*n* pl. -S an unfortunate accident
		MISHEAR	*v* -HEARD, -HEARING, -HEARS to hear incorrectly
MISE	*n* pl. -S an agreement or settlement	**MISHIT**	*v* -HIT, -HITTING, -HITS to hit poorly
MISEASE	*n* pl. -S discomfort		
MISEAT	*v* -ATE, -EATEN, -EATING, -EATS to eat improperly	**MISHMASH**	*n* pl. -ES a confused mixture
MISEDIT	*v* -ED, -ING, -S to edit incorrectly	**MISHMOSH**	*n* pl. -ES mishmash
MISENROL	*v* -ROLLED, -ROLLING, -ROLS to misenroll	**MISINFER**	*v* -FERRED, -FERRING, -FERS to infer wrongly
MISENROLL	*v* -ED, -ING, -S to enroll improperly	**MISINTER**	*v* -TERRED, -TERRING, -TERS to inter improperly
MISENTER	*v* -ED, -ING, -S to enter erroneously	**MISJOIN**	*v* -ED, -ING, -S to join improperly
MISENTRY	*n* pl. -TRIES an erroneous entry	**MISJUDGE**	*v* -JUDGED, -JUDGING, -JUDGES to judge wrongly
MISER	*n* pl. -S one who hoards money greedily	**MISKAL**	*n* pl. -S an Oriental unit of weight
MISERERE	*n* pl. -S a part of a church seat	**MISKEEP**	*v* -KEPT, -KEEPING, -KEEPS to keep wrongly
MISERLY	*adj* characteristic of a miser	**MISKICK**	*v* -ED, -ING, -S to kick badly
MISERY	*n* pl. -ERIES a state of great suffering	**MISKNOW**	*v* -KNEW, -KNOWN, -KNOWING, -KNOWS to fail to understand or recognize
MISEVENT	*n* pl. -S a mishap		
MISFAITH	*n* pl. -S lack of faith; disbelief	**MISLABEL**	*v* -BELED, -BELING, -BELS or -BELLED, -BELLING, -BELS to label incorrectly or falsely
MISFIELD	*v* -ED, -ING, -S to field badly		
MISFILE	*v* -FILED, -FILING, -FILES to file in the wrong place	**MISLABOR**	*v* -ED, -ING, -S to labor badly
		MISLAIN	past participle of mislie

MISLAY *v* -LAID, -LAYING, -LAYS to put in a forgotten place

MISLAYER *n* pl. -S one that mislays

MISLEAD *v* -LED, -LEADING, -LEADS to lead astray

MISLEARN *v* -LEARNED or -LEARNT, -LEARNING, -LEARNS to learn wrongly

MISLIE *v* -LAY, -LAIN, -LYING, -LIES to lie in a wrong position

MISLIGHT *v* -LIGHTED or -LIT, -LIGHTING, -LIGHTS to lead astray by its light

MISLIKE *v* -LIKED, -LIKING, -LIKES to dislike

MISLIKER *n* pl. -S one that mislikes

MISLIT a past tense of mislight

MISLIVE *v* -LIVED, -LIVING, -LIVES to live a bad life

MISLODGE *v* -LODGED, -LODGING, -LODGES to lodge in a wrong place

MISLYING present participle of mislie

MISMAKE *v* -MADE, -MAKING, -MAKES to make incorrectly

MISMARK *v* -ED, -ING, -S to mark wrongly

MISMATCH *v* -ED, -ING, -ES to match badly

MISMATE *v* -MATED, -MATING, -MATES to mate unsuitably

MISMEET *v* -MET, -MEETING, -MEETS to meet under unfortunate circumstances

MISMOVE *v* -MOVED, -MOVING, -MOVES to move wrongly

MISNAME *v* -NAMED, -NAMING, -NAMES to call by a wrong name

MISNOMER *n* pl. -S a name wrongly used

MISO *n* pl. -SOS a type of food paste

MISOGAMY *n* pl. -MIES a hatred of marriage

MISOGYNY *n* pl. -NIES a hatred of women

MISOLOGY *n* pl. -GIES a hatred of debate or reasoning

MISORDER *v* -ED, -ING, -S to order incorrectly

MISPAGE *v* -PAGED, -PAGING, -PAGES to page incorrectly

MISPAINT *v* -ED, -ING, -S to paint wrongly

MISPARSE *v* -PARSED, -PARSING, -PARSES to parse incorrectly

MISPART *v* -ED, -ING, -S to part badly

MISPATCH *v* -ED, -ING, -ES to patch badly

MISPEN *v* -PENNED, -PENNING, -PENS to write incorrectly

MISPLACE *v* -PLACED, -PLACING, -PLACES to put in a wrong place

MISPLAN *v* -PLANNED, -PLANNING, -PLANS to plan badly

MISPLANT *v* -ED, -ING, -S to plant wrongly

MISPLAY *v* -ED, -ING, -S to make a bad play in a game

MISPLEAD *v* -PLEADED or -PLED, -PLEADING, -PLEADS to plead wrongly or falsely

MISPOINT *v* -ED, -ING, -S to point improperly

MISPOISE *v* -POISED, -POISING, -POISES to poise incorrectly

MISPRICE *v* -PRICED, -PRICING, -PRICES to price incorrectly

MISPRINT *v* -ED, -ING, -S to print incorrectly

MISPRIZE *v* -PRIZED, -PRIZING, -PRIZES to despise

MISQUOTE *v* -QUOTED, -QUOTING, -QUOTES to quote incorrectly

MISRAISE *v* -RAISED, -RAISING, -RAISES to raise wrongly

MISRATE *v* -RATED, -RATING, -RATES to rate incorrectly

MISREAD *v* -READ, -READING, -READS to read incorrectly

MISREFER *v* -FERRED, -FERRING, -FERS to refer incorrectly

MISRELY *v* -LIED, -LYING, -LIES to rely wrongly

MISROUTE *v* -ROUTED, -ROUTING, -ROUTES to route incorrectly

MISRULE *v* -RULED, -RULING, -RULES to rule unwisely or unjustly

MISS *v* -ED, -ING, -ES to fail to make contact with

MISSABLE *adj* able to be missed

MISSAL *n* pl. -S a prayer book

MISSAY *v* -SAID, -SAYING, -SAYS to say incorrectly

MISSEAT *v* -ED, -ING, -S to seat wrongly

MISSEL *n* pl. -S a European thrush

MISSEND *v* -SENT, -SENDING, -SENDS to send incorrectly

MISSENSE *n* pl. -S a form of genetic mutation

MISSET *v* -SET, -SETTING, -SETS to set incorrectly

MISSHAPE   *v* -SHAPED, -SHAPEN, -SHAPING, -SHAPES to shape badly

MISSHOD   *adj* improperly shod

MISSIES   pl. of missy

MISSILE   *n* pl. -S an object or weapon that is thrown or projected

MISSILRY   *n* pl. -RIES the science of designing and operating guided missiles

MISSION   *v* -ED, -ING, -S to send to perform a specific task

MISSIS   *n* pl. -SISES a wife

MISSIVE   *n* pl. -S a written communication

MISSORT   *v* -ED, -ING, -S to sort badly or improperly

MISSOUND   *v* -ED, -ING, -S to sound wrongly

MISSOUT   *n* pl. -S a losing throw of dice

MISSPACE   *v* -SPACED, -SPACING, -SPACES to space incorrectly

MISSPEAK   *v* -SPOKE, -SPOKEN, -SPEAKING, -SPEAKS to speak incorrectly

MISSPELL   *v* -SPELLED or -SPELT, -SPELLING, -SPELLS to spell incorrectly

MISSPEND   *v* -SPENT, -SPENDING, -SPENDS to spend wrongly

MISSPOKE   past tense of misspeak

MISSPOKEN   past participle of misspeak

MISSTART   *v* -ED, -ING, -S to start off badly

MISSTATE   *v* -STATED, -STATING, -STATES to state wrongly

MISSTEER   *v* -ED, -ING, -S to steer wrongly

MISSTEP   *n* pl. -S a false step

MISSTOP   *v* -STOPPED, -STOPPING, -STOPS to stop wrongly

MISSTYLE   *v* -STYLED, -STYLING, -STYLES to style or call wrongly

MISSUIT   *v* -ED, -ING, -S to suit badly

MISSUS   *n* pl. -ES missis

MISSY   *n* pl. MISSIES a young girl

MIST   *v* -ED, -ING, -S to become blurry

MISTAKE   *v* -TOOK or -TEUK, -TAKEN, -TAKING, -TAKES to interpret wrongly

MISTAKER   *n* pl. -S one that mistakes

MISTBOW   *n* pl. -S a fogbow

MISTEACH   *v* -TAUGHT, -TEACHING, -TEACHES to teach wrongly or badly

MISTEND   *v* -ED, -ING, -S to tend to improperly

MISTER   *n* pl. -S sir

MISTERM   *v* -ED, -ING, -S to call by a wrong name

MISTEUK   a past tense of mistake

MISTHINK   *v* -THOUGHT, -THINKING, -THINKS to think wrongly

MISTHROW   *v* -THREW, -THROWN, -THROWING, -THROWS to throw errantly

MISTIER   comparative of misty

MISTIEST   superlative of misty

MISTILY   *adv* in a misty manner

MISTIME   *v* -TIMED, -TIMING, -TIMES to time wrongly

MISTITLE   *v* -TLED, -TLING, -TLES to call by a wrong title

MISTOOK   a past tense of mistake

MISTOUCH   *v* -ED, -ING, -ES to touch improperly

MISTRACE   *v* -TRACED, -TRACING, -TRACES to trace wrongly

MISTRAIN   *v* -ED, -ING, -S to train improperly

MISTRAL   *n* pl. -S a cold, dry wind

MISTREAT   *v* -ED, -ING, -S to treat badly

MISTRESS   *n* pl. -ES a woman in a position of authority

MISTRIAL   *n* pl. -S a trial made invalid because of some error in procedure

MISTRUST   *v* -ED, -ING, -S to distrust

MISTRUTH   *n* pl. -S a lie

MISTRYST   *v* -ED, -ING, -S to fail to keep an appointment with

MISTUNE   *v* -TUNED, -TUNING, -TUNES to tune incorrectly

MISTUTOR   *v* -ED, -ING, -S to instruct or bring up badly

MISTY   *adj* MISTIER, MISTIEST blurry

MISTYPE   *v* -TYPED, -TYPING, -TYPES to type incorrectly

MISUNION   *n* pl. -S a bad union

MISUSAGE   *n* pl. -S incorrect use

MISUSE   *v* -USED, -USING, -USES to use incorrectly

MISUSER   *n* pl. -S one that misuses

MISVALUE   *v* -UED, -UING, -UES to value incorrectly

MISWORD	*v* -ED, -ING, -S to word wrongly
MISWRITE	*v* -WROTE or -WRIT, -WRITTEN, -WRITING, -WRITES to write incorrectly
MISYOKE	*v* -YOKED, -YOKING, -YOKES to yoke improperly
MITE	*n* pl. -S a small arachnid
MITER	*v* -ED, -ING, -S to raise to the rank of a bishop
MITERER	*n* pl. -S one that miters
MITHER	*n* pl. -S mother
MITICIDE	*n* pl. -S a substance used to kill mites
MITIER	comparative of mity
MITIEST	superlative of mity
MITIGATE	*v* -GATED, -GATING, -GATES to make less severe
MITIS	*n* pl. -TISES a type of wrought iron
MITOGEN	*n* pl. -S a substance that induces mitosis
MITOSIS	*n* pl. -TOSES a type of cell division **MITOTIC** *adj*
MITRAL	*adj* pertaining to a valve of the heart
MITRE	*v* -TRED, -TRING, -TRES to miter
MITSVAH	*n* pl. -VAHS or -VOTH mitzvah
MITT	*n* pl. -S a type of baseball glove
MITTEN	*n* pl. -S a type of covering for the hand
MITTIMUS	*n* pl. -ES a warrant committing a person to prison
MITY	*adj* MITIER, MITIEST infested with mites
MITZVAH	*n* pl. -VAHS or -VOTH a commandment of Jewish law
MIX	*v* MIXED or MIXT, MIXING, MIXES to put together into one mass **MIXABLE, MIXIBLE** *adj*
MIXER	*n* pl. -S one that mixes
MIXOLOGY	*n* pl. -GIES the art of making mixed drinks
MIXT	a past tense of mix
MIXTURE	*n* pl. -S something produced by mixing
MIXUP	*n* pl. -S a state of confusion
MIZEN	*n* pl. -S mizzen
MIZZEN	*n* pl. -S a type of sail
MIZZLE	*v* -ZLED, -ZLING, -ZLES to rain in fine droplets
MIZZLY	*adj* characterized by a fine rain
MM	*interj* — used to express assent or satisfaction
MNEMONIC	*n* pl. -S a device to assist the memory
MO	*n* pl. MOS a moment
MOA	*n* pl. -S an extinct flightless bird
MOAN	*v* -ED, -ING, -S to utter a low, mournful sound
MOANER	*n* pl. -S one that moans
MOANFUL	*adj* moaning
MOAT	*v* -ED, -ING, -S to surround with a moat (a water-filled trench)
MOATLIKE	*adj* suggestive of a moat
MOB	*v* MOBBED, MOBBING, MOBS to crowd about
MOBBER	*n* pl. -S one that mobs
MOBBISH	*adj* characteristic of a mob (a disorderly crowd of people)
MOBCAP	*n* pl. -S a woman's cap
MOBILE	*n* pl. -S a form of sculpture
MOBILISE	*v* -LISED, -LISING, -LISES to mobilize
MOBILITY	*n* pl. -TIES the ability to move
MOBILIZE	*v* -LIZED, -LIZING, -LIZES to put into movement
MOBLED	*adj* wrapped in or as if in a hood
MOBOCRAT	*n* pl. -S a supporter of mob rule
MOBSTER	*n* pl. -S a gangster
MOC	*n* pl. -S a moccasin
MOCCASIN	*n* pl. -S a type of shoe
MOCHA	*n* pl. -S a choice, pungent coffee
MOCHILA	*n* pl. -S a leather covering for a saddle
MOCK	*v* -ED, -ING, -S to ridicule **MOCKABLE** *adj*
MOCKER	*n* pl. -S one that mocks
MOCKERY	*n* pl. -ERIES the act of mocking
MOCKUP	*n* pl. -S a full-sized model
MOD	*n* pl. -S one who wears boldly stylish clothes
MODAL	*adj* pertaining to a mode **MODALLY** *adv*
MODALITY	*n* pl. -TIES the state of being modal
MODE	*n* pl. -S a method of doing or acting

MODEL	v -ELED, -ELING, -ELS or -ELLED, -ELLING, -ELS to plan or form after a pattern	**MOG**	v MOGGED, MOGGING, MOGS to move away
MODELER	n pl. -S one that models	**MOGGIE**	n pl. -S moggy
MODELING	n pl. -S the treatment of volume in sculpture	**MOGGY**	n pl. -GIES a cat
		MOGUL	n pl. -S an important person
MODELIST	n pl. -S one who makes models	**MOHAIR**	n pl. -S the long, silky hair of the Angora goat
MODELLED	a past tense of model	**MOHEL**	n pl. -HALIM, -HELIM or -HELS a person who performs Jewish ritual circumcisions
MODELLER	n pl. -S modeler		
MODELLING	a present participle of model		
MODEM	n pl. -S a device for converting signals from one form to another	**MOHUR**	n pl. -S a former gold coin of India
MODERATE	v -ATED, -ATING, -ATES to make less extreme	**MOIDORE**	n pl. -S a former gold coin of Portugal
MODERATO	n pl. -TOS a musical passage played at a medium tempo	**MOIETY**	n pl. -ETIES a half
		MOIL	v -ED, -ING, -S to work hard
MODERN	adj -ERNER, -ERNEST pertaining to present or recent time **MODERNLY** adv	**MOILER**	n pl. -S one that moils
		MOIRA	n pl. -RAI fate or destiny, in ancient Greek religion
MODERN	n pl. -S a person of modern times or views	**MOIRE**	n pl. -S a fabric having a wavy pattern
MODERNE	adj pretentiously modern	**MOIST**	adj MOISTER, MOISTEST slightly wet
MODEST	adj -ESTER, -ESTEST having a moderate regard for oneself **MODESTLY** adv	**MOISTEN**	v -ED, -ING, -S to make or become moist
MODESTY	n pl. -TIES the quality of being modest	**MOISTFUL**	adj moist
MODI	pl. of modus	**MOISTLY**	adv in a moist manner
MODICUM	n pl. -CA or -CUMS a small amount	**MOISTURE**	n pl. -S condensed or diffused liquid
		MOJARRA	n pl. -S a marine fish
MODIFIER	n pl. -S one that modifies	**MOJO**	n pl. -JOS or -JOES a magic charm
MODIFY	v -FIED, -FYING, -FIES to change in form or character		
MODIOLUS	n pl. -LI a bony shaft of the inner ear	**MOKE**	n pl. -S a donkey
		MOL	n pl. -S mole
MODISH	adj stylish **MODISHLY** adv	**MOLA**	n pl. -S a marine fish
MODISTE	n pl. -S a dealer in stylish women's clothing	**MOLAL**	adj pertaining to a mole
		MOLALITY	n pl. -TIES the number of moles of solute per liter of solvent
MODULAR	adj pertaining to a module		
MODULATE	v -LATED, -LATING, -LATES to adjust to a certain proportion	**MOLAR**	n pl. -S a grinding tooth
		MOLARITY	n pl. -TIES the number of moles of solute per liter of solution
MODULE	n pl. -S a standard of measurement		
MODULO	adv with respect to a modulus	**MOLASSES**	n pl. -LASSESES a thick syrup
MODULUS	n pl. -LI a number that produces the same remainder when divided into each of two numbers	**MOLD**	v -ED, -ING, -S to work into a particular shape **MOLDABLE** adj
		MOLDER	v -ED, -ING, -S to turn to dust by natural decay
MODUS	n pl. -DI a mode		
MOFETTE	n pl. -S a noxious emanation from a fissure in the earth	**MOLDIER**	comparative of moldy
		MOLDIEST	superlative of moldy
MOFFETTE	n pl. -S mofette	**MOLDING**	n pl. -S a long, narrow strip used to decorate a surface

MOLDWARP	*n* pl. -S a burrowing mammal
MOLDY	*adj* MOLDIER, MOLDIEST musty
MOLE	*n* pl. -S the quantity of a compound that has a weight equal to the compound's molecular weight
MOLECULE	*n* pl. -S the smallest physical unit of an element
MOLEHILL	*n* pl. -S a small mound of earth
MOLESKIN	*n* pl. -S a cotton fabric
MOLEST	*v* -ED, -ING, -S to disturb or annoy
MOLESTER	*n* pl. -S one that molests
MOLIES	pl. of moly
MOLINE	*adj* having arms forked and curved at the ends — used of a heraldic cross
MOLL	*n* pl. -S a gangster's girlfriend
MOLLAH	*n* pl. -S mullah
MOLLIE	*n* pl. -S a tropical fish
MOLLIES	pl. of molly
MOLLIFY	*v* -FIED, -FYING, -FIES to soothe
MOLLUSC	*n* pl. -S mollusk
MOLLUSK	*n* pl. -S any of a phylum of soft-bodied invertebrates
MOLLY	*n* pl. -LIES mollie
MOLOCH	*n* pl. -S a spiny lizard
MOLT	*v* -ED, -ING, -S to cast off an outer covering
MOLTEN	*adj* made liquid by heat **MOLTENLY** *adv*
MOLTER	*n* pl. -S one that molts
MOLTO	*adv* very — used in musical directions
MOLY	*n* pl. -LIES a wild garlic
MOLYBDIC	*adj* pertaining to a certain metallic element
MOM	*n* pl. -S mother
MOME	*n* pl. -S a fool
MOMENT	*n* pl. -S a brief period of time
MOMENTA	a pl. of momentum
MOMENTLY	*adv* from moment to moment
MOMENTO	*n* pl. -TOS or -TOES memento
MOMENTUM	*n* pl. -TA or -TUMS force of movement
MOMI	a pl. of momus
MOMISM	*n* pl. -S an excessive dependence on mothers
MOMMA	*n* pl. -S mother
MOMMY	*n* pl. -MIES mother
MOMSER	*n* pl. -S a bastard
MOMUS	*n* pl. -MUSES or -MI a carping person
MOMZER	*n* pl. -S momser
MON	*n* pl. MEN man
MONACHAL	*adj* pertaining to monks
MONACID	*n* pl. -S monoacid
MONAD	*n* pl. -S a single-celled organism **MONADAL, MONADIC** *adj*
MONADES	pl. of monas
MONADISM	*n* pl. -S a philosophical doctrine
MONANDRY	*n* pl. -DRIES the condition of having one husband at a time
MONARCH	*n* pl. -S an absolute ruler
MONARCHY	*n* pl. -CHIES rule by a monarch
MONARDA	*n* pl. -S an aromatic herb
MONAS	*n* pl. MONADES a monad
MONASTIC	*n* pl. -S a monk
MONAURAL	*adj* pertaining to sound transmission, recording, or reproduction involving a single transmission path
MONAXIAL	*adj* having one axis
MONAXON	*n* pl. -S a straight spicule in sponges
MONAZITE	*n* pl. -S a mineral
MONDE	*n* pl. -S the world
MONDO	*n* pl. -DOS a rapid question and answer technique employed in Zen Buddhism
MONECIAN	*adj* having both male and female sex organs in the same individual
MONELLIN	*n* pl. -S a protein extracted from a West African red berry
MONERAN	*n* pl. -S a cellular organism that does not have a distinct nucleus
MONETARY	*adj* pertaining to money
MONETISE	*v* -TISED, -TISING, -TISES to monetize
MONETIZE	*v* -TIZED, -TIZING, -TIZES to coin into money
MONEY	*n* pl. MONEYS or MONIES an official medium of exchange and measure of value
MONEYBAG	*n* pl. -S a bag for holding money
MONEYED	*adj* having much money
MONEYER	*n* pl. -S one that coins money

MONEYMAN *n* pl. -MEN a person who invests large sums of money

MONGEESE a pl. of mongoose

MONGER *v* -ED, -ING, -S to peddle

MONGO *n* pl. -GOS mungo

MONGOE *n* pl. -S mungo

MONGOL *n* pl. -S a person affected with a form of mental deficiency

MONGOOSE *n* pl. -GOOSES or -GEESE a carnivorous mammal

MONGREL *n* pl. -S an animal or plant of mixed breed

MONGST *prep* amongst

MONICKER *n* pl. -S moniker

MONIE *adj* many

MONIED *adj* moneyed

MONIES a pl. of money

MONIKER *n* pl. -S a name

MONISH *v* -ED, -ING, -ES to warn

MONISM *n* pl. -S a philosophical theory

MONIST *n* pl. -S an adherent of monism **MONISTIC** *adj*

MONITION *n* pl. -S a warning

MONITIVE *adj* giving warning

MONITOR *v* -ED, -ING, -S to keep track of

MONITORY *n* pl. -RIES a letter of warning

MONK *n* pl. -S a man who is a member of a secluded religious order

MONKERY *n* pl. -ERIES the mode of life of monks

MONKEY *v* -ED, -ING, -S to mimic

MONKFISH *n* pl. -ES a marine fish

MONKHOOD *n* pl. -S the state of being a monk

MONKISH *adj* pertaining to monks

MONO *n* pl. MONOS an infectious disease

MONOACID *n* pl. -S a type of acid

MONOCARP *n* pl. -S a plant that yields fruit only once before dying

MONOCLE *n* pl. -S an eyeglass for one eye **MONOCLED** *adj*

MONOCOT *n* pl. -S a type of seed plant

MONOCRAT *n* pl. -S an autocrat

MONOCYTE *n* pl. -S a type of white blood cell

MONODIST *n* pl. -S one who writes monodies

MONODY *n* pl. -DIES an elegy performed by one person **MONODIC** *adj*

MONOECY *n* pl. -CIES the condition of being monecian

MONOFIL *n* pl. -S a single filament of synthetic fiber

MONOFUEL *n* pl. -S a type of rocket propellant

MONOGAMY *n* pl. -MIES marriage with one person at a time

MONOGENY *n* pl. -NIES asexual reproduction

MONOGERM *adj* being a fruit that produces a single plant

MONOGLOT *n* pl. -S a person speaking or writing only one language

MONOGRAM *v* -GRAMED, -GRAMING, -GRAMS or -GRAMMED, -GRAMMING, -GRAMS to mark with a design of one's initials

MONOGYNY *n* pl. -NIES the condition of having one wife at a time

MONOHULL *n* pl. -S a vessel with a single hull

MONOLITH *n* pl. -S a large block of stone

MONOLOG *n* pl. -S a lengthy speech by one person

MONOLOGY *n* pl. -GIES the act of uttering a monolog

MONOMER *n* pl. -S a type of chemical compound

MONOMIAL *n* pl. -S an algebraic expression consisting of a single term

MONOPODE *n* pl. -S a creature having one foot

MONOPODY *n* pl. -DIES a measure consisting of a single metrical foot

MONOPOLE *n* pl. -S a type of radio antenna

MONOPOLY *n* pl. -LIES exclusive control of a commodity or service in a particular market

MONORAIL *n* pl. -S a single rail serving as a track for a wheeled vehicle

MONOSOME *n* pl. -S an unpaired chromosome

MONOSOMY *n* pl. -MIES a condition of having one unpaired chromosome

MONOTINT *n* pl. -S a painting done in different shades of one color

MONOTONE *n* pl. -S a vocal utterance in one unvaried tone

MONOTONY *n* pl. -NIES tedious sameness

MONOTYPE *n* pl. -S the only representative of its group

MONOXIDE *n* pl. -S a type of oxide

MONS *n* pl. MONTES a protuberance of the body

MONSIEUR	*n* pl. MESSIEURS a French title of courtesy for a man
MONSOON	*n* pl. -S a seasonal wind
MONSTER	*n* pl. -S a strange or terrifying creature
MONSTERA	*n* pl. -S a tropical American plant
MONTAGE	*v* -TAGED, -TAGING, -TAGES to combine into a composite picture
MONTANE	*n* pl. -S the lower vegetation belt of a mountain
MONTE	*n* pl. -S a card game
MONTEITH	*n* pl. -S a large punch bowl
MONTERO	*n* pl. -ROS a type of cap
MONTES	pl. of mons
MONTH	*n* pl. -S a period of approximately 30 days
MONTHLY	*n* pl. -LIES a publication issued once a month
MONUMENT	*n* pl. -S a structure built as a memorial
MONURON	*n* pl. -S an herbicide
MONY	*adj* many
MOO	*v* -ED, -ING, -S to make the deep, moaning sound of a cow
MOOCH	*v* -ED, -ING, -ES to obtain without paying
MOOCHER	*n* pl. -S one that mooches
MOOD	*n* pl. -S a person's emotional state at a particular moment
MOODY	*adj* MOODIER, MOODIEST given to changing moods **MOODILY** *adv*
MOOL	*n* pl. -S soft soil
MOOLA	*n* pl. -S moolah
MOOLAH	*n* pl. -S money
MOOLEY	*n* pl. -EYS muley
MOON	*v* -ED, -ING, -S to spend time idly
MOONBEAM	*n* pl. -S a ray of light from the moon (the earth's natural satellite)
MOONBOW	*n* pl. -S a rainbow formed by light from the moon
MOONCALF	*n* pl. -CALVES a foolish person
MOONDUST	*n* pl. -S dust on the moon
MOONEYE	*n* pl. -S a freshwater fish
MOONFISH	*n* pl. -ES a marine fish
MOONIER	comparative of moony
MOONIEST	superlative of moony
MOONILY	*adv* in a moony manner
MOONISH	*adj* fickle
MOONLESS	*adj* lacking the light of the moon
MOONLET	*n* pl. -S a small satellite
MOONLIKE	*adj* resembling the moon
MOONLIT	*adj* lighted by the moon
MOONPORT	*n* pl. -S a facility for launching spacecraft to the moon
MOONRISE	*n* pl. -S the rising of the moon above the horizon
MOONSAIL	*n* pl. -S a light, square sail
MOONSEED	*n* pl. -S a climbing plant
MOONSET	*n* pl. -S the setting of the moon below the horizon
MOONSHOT	*n* pl. -S the launching of a spacecraft to the moon
MOONWALK	*n* pl. -S an instance of walking on the moon
MOONWARD	*adv* toward the moon
MOONWORT	*n* pl. -S a flowering plant
MOONY	*adj* MOONIER, MOONIEST resembling the moon
MOOR	*v* -ED, -ING, -S to secure a vessel by means of cables
MOORAGE	*n* pl. -S the act of mooring
MOORCOCK	*n* pl. -S the male moorfowl
MOORFOWL	*n* pl. -S a game bird
MOORHEN	*n* pl. -S the female moorfowl
MOORIER	comparative of moory
MOORIEST	superlative of moory
MOORING	*n* pl. -S a place where a vessel may be moored
MOORISH	*adj* marshy
MOORLAND	*n* pl. -S a tract of marshy land
MOORWORT	*n* pl. -S a marsh plant
MOORY	*adj* MOORIER, MOORIEST marshy
MOOSE	*n* pl. MOOSE a ruminant mammal
MOOT	*v* -ED, -ING, -S to bring up for discussion
MOOTER	*n* pl. -S one that moots
MOP	*v* MOPPED, MOPPING, MOPS to wipe with a mop (an implement for cleaning floors)
MOPBOARD	*n* pl. -S a board at the base of a wall

MOPE	v MOPED, MOPING, MOPES to act in a dejected or gloomy manner
MOPED	n pl. -S a type of motorbike
MOPER	n pl. -S one that mopes
MOPERY	n pl. -PERIES an act of dawdling
MOPEY	adj MOPIER, MOPIEST dejected
MOPIER	comparative of mopy
MOPIEST	superlative of mopy
MOPING	present participle of mope
MOPINGLY	adv in a moping manner
MOPISH	adj given to moping **MOPISHLY** adv
MOPOKE	n pl. -S an Australian bird
MOPPED	past tense of mop
MOPPER	n pl. -S one that mops
MOPPET	n pl. -S a child
MOPPING	present participle of mop
MOPY	adj MOPIER, MOPIEST mopey
MOQUETTE	n pl. -S a woolen fabric
MOR	n pl. -S a forest humus
MORA	n pl. -RAE or -RAS a unit of metrical time in prosody
MORAINE	n pl. -S an accumulation of debris deposited by a glacier **MORAINAL, MORAINIC** adj
MORAL	adj pertaining to principles of right and wrong **MORALLY** adv
MORALE	n pl. -S the state of the spirits of an individual or group
MORALISE	v -ISED, -ISING, -ISES to moralize
MORALISM	n pl. -S the practice of moralizing
MORALIST	n pl. -S a teacher of morality
MORALITY	n pl. -TIES conformity to the rules of right conduct
MORALIZE	v -IZED, -IZING, -IZES to explain in a moral sense
MORALS	n/pl rules of conduct with respect to right and wrong
MORASS	n pl. -ES a marsh **MORASSY** adj
MORATORY	adj authorizing delay of payment
MORAY	n pl. -RAYS a tropical eel
MORBID	adj gruesome **MORBIDLY** adv
MORBIFIC	adj causing disease
MORBILLI	n/pl a virus disease
MORCEAU	n pl. -CEAUX a short literary or musical composition
MORDANCY	n pl. -CIES a sarcastic quality
MORDANT	v -ED, -ING, -S to treat with a caustic substance
MORDENT	n pl. -S a melodic embellishment
MORE	n pl. -S a greater amount
MOREEN	n pl. -S a heavy fabric
MOREL	n pl. -S an edible mushroom
MORELLE	n pl. -S a flowering plant
MORELLO	n pl. -LOS a variety of sour cherry
MOREOVER	adv in addition
MORESQUE	n pl. -S an ancient decorative style
MORGAN	n pl. -S a unit of distance between genes
MORGEN	n pl. -S a Dutch unit of land area
MORGUE	n pl. -S a place where dead bodies are kept for identification
MORIBUND	adj being about to die
MORION	n pl. -S a type of helmet
MORN	n pl. -S morning
MORNING	n pl. -S the early part of the day
MOROCCO	n pl. -COS a soft leather
MORON	n pl. -S a mentally deficient person **MORONIC** adj
MORONISM	n pl. -S the condition of being a moron
MORONITY	n pl. -TIES moronism
MOROSE	adj sullen **MOROSELY** adv
MOROSITY	n pl. -TIES the state of being morose
MORPH	n pl. -S a type of phoneme
MORPHEME	n pl. -S a linguistic unit
MORPHIA	n pl. -S morphine
MORPHIC	adj pertaining to form
MORPHIN	n pl. -S morphine
MORPHINE	n pl. -S a narcotic alkaloid
MORPHO	n pl. -PHOS a tropical butterfly
MORRION	n pl. -S morion
MORRIS	n pl. -RISES an English folk dance
MORRO	n pl. -ROS a rounded elevation
MORROW	n pl. -S the next day
MORSE	adj designating a code used in telegraphy
MORSEL	v -SELED, -SELING, -SELS or -SELLED, -SELLING, -SELS to divide into small pieces

MORT   *n* pl. -S a note sounded on a hunting horn to announce the killing of an animal

MORTAL   *n* pl. -S a human being

MORTALLY   *adv* fatally

MORTAR   *v* -ED, -ING, -S to secure with mortar (a type of cement)

MORTARY   *adj* containing or resembling mortar

MORTGAGE   *v* -GAGED, -GAGING, -GAGES to pledge to a creditor as security

MORTICE   *v* -TICED, -TICING, -TICES to mortise

MORTIFY   *v* -FIED, -FYING, -FIES to humiliate

MORTISE   *v* -TISED, -TISING, -TISES to join or fasten securely

MORTISER   *n* pl. -S one that mortises

MORTMAIN   *n* pl. -S perpetual ownership of land

MORTUARY   *n* pl. -ARIES a place where dead bodies are kept until burial

MORULA   *n* pl. -LAE or -LAS an embryonic mass of cells **MORULAR** *adj*

MOSAIC   *v* -ICKED, -ICKING, -ICS to form into a mosaic (a type of inlaid surface decoration)

MOSASAUR   *n* pl. -S an extinct lizard

MOSCHATE   *adj* musky

MOSEY   *v* -ED, -ING, -S to saunter

MOSHAV   *n* pl. -SHAVIM a cooperative settlement of small farms in Israel

MOSK   *n* pl. -S mosque

MOSQUE   *n* pl. -S a Muslim house of worship

MOSQUITO   *n* pl. -TOES or -TOS a winged insect

MOSS   *v* -ED, -ING, -ES to cover with moss (a growth of small, leafy-stemmed plants)

MOSSBACK   *n* pl. -S a large, old fish

MOSSER   *n* pl. -S one that gathers or works with moss

MOSSIER   comparative of mossy

MOSSIEST   superlative of mossy

MOSSLIKE   *adj* resembling moss

MOSSO   *adv* rapidly — used as a musical direction

MOSSY   *adj* MOSSIER, MOSSIEST covered with moss

MOST   *n* pl. -S the greatest amount

MOSTE   past tense of mote

MOSTEST   *n* pl. -S most

MOSTLY   *adv* mainly

MOT   *n* pl. -S a witty saying

MOTE   *v* past tense MOSTE may

MOTE   *n* pl. -S a small particle

MOTEL   *n* pl. -S a roadside hotel

MOTET   *n* pl. -S a type of choral composition

MOTEY   *adj* full of motes

MOTH   *n* pl. -S a winged insect

MOTHBALL   *v* -ED, -ING, -S to put into storage

MOTHER   *v* -ED, -ING, -S to give birth to

MOTHERLY   *adj* maternal

MOTHERY   *adj* slimy

MOTHLIKE   *adj* resembling a moth

MOTHY   *adj* MOTHIER, MOTHIEST full of moths

MOTIF   *n* pl. -S a recurring thematic element in an artistic work **MOTIFIC** *adj*

MOTILE   *n* pl. -S one whose mental imagery consists chiefly of inner feelings of action

MOTILITY   *n* pl. -TIES the ability to move

MOTION   *v* -ED, -ING, -S to signal by a bodily movement

MOTIONAL   *adj* pertaining to movement

MOTIONER   *n* pl. -S one that motions

MOTIVATE   *v* -VATED, -VATING, -VATES to provide with an incentive

MOTIVE   *v* -TIVED, -TIVING, -TIVES to motivate

MOTIVIC   *adj* pertaining to a musical motif

MOTIVITY   *n* pl. -TIES the ability to move

MOTLEY   *adj* -LEYER, -LEYEST or -LIER, -LIEST composed of diverse elements

MOTLEY   *n* pl. -LEYS a garment of various colors

MOTMOT   *n* pl. -S a tropical bird

MOTOR   *v* -ED, -ING, -S to travel by automobile

MOTORBUS   *n* pl. -BUSES or -BUSSES a bus

MOTORCAR   *n* pl. -S an automobile

MOTORDOM   *n* pl. -S the motor vehicle industry

MOTORIC *adj* pertaining to muscular movement

MOTORING *n* pl. -S the recreation of traveling by automobile

MOTORISE *v* -ISED, -ISING, -ISES to motorize

MOTORIST *n* pl. -S one who travels by automobile

MOTORIZE *v* -IZED, -IZING, -IZES to equip with motor vehicles

MOTORMAN *n* pl. -MEN one who operates an electric streetcar or subway train

MOTORWAY *n* pl. -WAYS a type of highway

MOTT *n* pl. -S motte

MOTTE *n* pl. -S a small growth of trees on a prairie

MOTTLE *v* -TLED, -TLING, -TLES to mark with spots or streaks of different colors

MOTTLER *n* pl. -S one that mottles

MOTTO *n* pl. -TOES or -TOS a short expression of a guiding principle

MOUCH *v* -ED, -ING, -ES to mooch

MOUCHOIR *n* pl. -S a small handkerchief

MOUE *n* pl. -S a pouting grimace

MOUFFLON *n* pl. -S mouflon

MOUFLON *n* pl. -S a wild sheep

MOUILLE *adj* pronounced with the front of the tongue against the palate

MOUJIK *n* pl. -S muzhik

MOULAGE *n* pl. -S the making of a cast or mold of a mark for use in a criminal investigation

MOULD *v* -ED, -ING, -S to mold

MOULDER *v* -ED, -ING, -S to molder

MOULDING *n* pl. -S molding

MOULDY *adj* MOULDIER, MOULDIEST moldy

MOULIN *n* pl. -S a vertical cavity in a glacier

MOULT *v* -ED, -ING, -S to molt

MOULTER *n* pl. -S molter

MOUND *v* -ED, -ING, -S to pile

MOUNT *v* -ED, -ING, -S to get up on

MOUNTAIN *n* pl. -S a large, natural elevation of the earth's surface

MOUNTER *n* pl. -S one that mounts

MOUNTING *n* pl. -S something that provides a backing or appropriate setting for something else

MOURN *v* -ED, -ING, -S to feel or express grief or sorrow

MOURNER *n* pl. -S one that mourns

MOURNFUL *adj* -FULLER, -FULLEST expressing grief or sorrow

MOURNING *n* pl. -S an outward sign of grief

MOUSE *n* pl. MICE a small rodent

MOUSE *v* MOUSED, MOUSING, MOUSES to catch mice

MOUSER *n* pl. -S an animal that catches mice

MOUSEY *adj* MOUSIER, MOUSIEST mousy

MOUSIER comparative of mousy

MOUSIEST superlative of mousy

MOUSILY *adv* in a mousy manner

MOUSING *n* pl. -S a wrapping around the shank end of a hook

MOUSSAKA *n* pl. -S a Middle Eastern dish of meat and eggplant

MOUSSE *v* MOUSSED, MOUSSING, MOUSSES to style with mousse (foamy preparation used in styling hair)

MOUSY *adj* MOUSIER, MOUSIEST resembling a mouse

MOUTH *v* -ED, -ING, -S to put into the mouth

MOUTHER *n* pl. -S a speaker

MOUTHFUL *n* pl. -S as much as the mouth can hold

MOUTHY *adj* MOUTHIER, MOUTHIEST very talkative **MOUTHILY** *adv*

MOUTON *n* pl. -S sheepskin processed to resemble seal or beaver

MOVABLE *n* pl. -S something that can be moved

MOVABLY *adv* so as to be capable of being moved

MOVE *v* MOVED, MOVING, MOVES to change from one position to another

MOVEABLE *n* pl. -S movable

MOVEABLY *adv* movably

MOVED past tense of move

MOVELESS *adj* incapable of movement

MOVEMENT *n* pl. -S the act of moving

MOVER *n* pl. -S one that moves

MOVIE *n* pl. -S a motion picture

MOVIEDOM *n* pl. -S filmdom

MOVIEOLA	*n* pl. -S a device for viewing and editing film
MOVING	present participle of move
MOVINGLY	*adv* so as to affect the emotions
MOVIOLA	*n* pl. -S movieola
MOW	*v* MOWED, MOWN, MOWING, MOWS to cut down standing herbage
MOWER	*n* pl. -S one that mows
MOWING	*n* pl. -S the act of cutting down standing herbage
MOXA	*n* pl. -S a Chinese plant
MOXIE	*n* pl. -S spirit or courage
MOZETTA	*n* pl. -TAS or -TE mozzetta
MOZO	*n* pl. -ZOS a manual laborer
MOZZETTA	*n* pl. -TAS or -TE a hooded cape worn by bishops
MRIDANGA	*n* pl. -S a drum of India
MU	*n* pl. -S a Greek letter
MUCH	*n* pl. -ES a great amount
MUCHACHO	*n* pl. -CHOS a young man
MUCHLY	*adv* very much
MUCHNESS	*n* pl. -ES the quality of being great
MUCID	*adj* musty
MUCIDITY	*n* pl. -TIES the state of being mucid
MUCILAGE	*n* pl. -S an adhesive substance
MUCIN	*n* pl. -S a protein secreted by the mucous membranes **MUCINOID, MUCINOUS** *adj*
MUCK	*v* -ED, -ING, -S to fertilize with manure
MUCKER	*n* pl. -S a vulgar person
MUCKIER	comparative of mucky
MUCKIEST	superlative of mucky
MUCKILY	*adv* in a mucky manner
MUCKLE	*n* pl. -S a large amount
MUCKLUCK	*n* pl. -S mukluk
MUCKRAKE	*v* -RAKED, -RAKING, -RAKES to search for and expose corruption
MUCKWORM	*n* pl. -S a worm found in manure
MUCKY	*adj* MUCKIER, MUCKIEST filthy
MUCLUC	*n* pl. -S mukluk
MUCOID	*n* pl. -S a complex protein **MUCOIDAL** *adj*
MUCOR	*n* pl. -S a type of fungus
MUCOSA	*n* pl. -SAE or -SAS a mucous membrane **MUCOSAL** *adj*
MUCOSE	*adj* mucous
MUCOSITY	*n* pl. -TIES the state of being mucous
MUCOUS	*adj* secreting or containing mucus
MUCRO	*n* pl. -CRONES a sharp point at the end of certain plant and animal organs
MUCUS	*n* pl. -ES a viscid bodily fluid
MUD	*v* MUDDED, MUDDING, MUDS to cover with mud (soft, wet earth)
MUDCAP	*v* -CAPPED, -CAPPING, -CAPS to cover an explosive with mud before detonating
MUDCAT	*n* pl. -S a type of catfish
MUDDER	*n* pl. -S a racehorse that runs well on a muddy track
MUDDIED	past tense of muddy
MUDDIER	comparative of muddy
MUDDIES	present 3d person sing. of muddy
MUDDIEST	superlative of muddy
MUDDILY	*adv* in a muddy manner
MUDDING	present participle of mud
MUDDLE	*v* -DLED, -DLING, -DLES to mix in a disordered manner
MUDDLER	*n* pl. -S one that muddles
MUDDLY	*adj* disordered
MUDDY	*adj* -DIER, -DIEST covered or filled with mud
MUDDY	*v* -DIED, -DYING, -DIES to make or become muddy
MUDFISH	*n* pl. -ES a fish found in mud or muddy water
MUDFLAT	*n* pl. -S a level tract alternately covered and left bare by the tide
MUDFLOW	*n* pl. -S a moving mass of mud
MUDGUARD	*n* pl. -S a fender
MUDHOLE	*n* pl. -S a hole or hollow place full of mud
MUDLARK	*n* pl. -S a street urchin
MUDPACK	*n* pl. -S cosmetic paste for the face
MUDPUPPY	*n* pl. -PIES a large salamander
MUDRA	*n* pl. -S a hand gesture in East Indian classical dancing
MUDROCK	*n* pl. -S pelite

MUDROOM	*n* pl. -S a room for shedding muddy clothing or footwear
MUDSILL	*n* pl. -S the lowest supporting timber of a structure
MUDSLIDE	*n* pl. -S a mudflow down a slope
MUDSTONE	*n* pl. -S a type of rock
MUEDDIN	*n* pl. -S muezzin
MUENSTER	*n* pl. -S a mild cheese
MUESLI	*n* pl. -S a breakfast cereal
MUEZZIN	*n* pl. -S a Muslim crier who calls the faithful to prayer
MUFF	*v* -ED, -ING, -S to bungle
MUFFIN	*n* pl. -S a small, round bread
MUFFLE	*v* -FLED, -FLING, -FLES to wrap with something to deaden sound
MUFFLER	*n* pl. -S a device for deadening sound
MUFTI	*n* pl. -S a judge who interprets Muslim religious law
MUG	*v* MUGGED, MUGGING, MUGS to assault with intent to rob
MUGFUL	*n* pl. -S as much as a mug can hold
MUGG	*v* -ED, -ING, -S to make funny faces
MUGGAR	*n* pl. -S mugger
MUGGED	past tense of mug
MUGGEE	*n* pl. -S one who is mugged
MUGGER	*n* pl. -S a large Asian crocodile
MUGGIER	comparative of muggy
MUGGIEST	superlative of muggy
MUGGILY	*adv* in a muggy manner
MUGGING	*n* pl. -S a street assault or beating
MUGGINS	*n* pl. MUGGINS a card game
MUGGUR	*n* pl. -S mugger
MUGGY	*adj* -GIER, -GIEST warm and humid
MUGWORT	*n* pl. -S a flowering plant
MUGWUMP	*n* pl. -S a political independent
MUHLY	*n* pl. MUHLIES a perennial grass
MUJIK	*n* pl. -S muzhik
MUKLUK	*n* pl. -S a soft boot worn by Eskimos
MUKTUK	*n* pl. -S whale skin used for food
MULATTO	*n* pl. -TOES or -TOS the offspring of one white and one black parent

MULBERRY	*n* pl. -RIES a tree bearing an edible, berrylike fruit
MULCH	*v* -ED, -ING, -ES to provide with a protective covering for the soil
MULCT	*v* -ED, -ING, -S to defraud
MULE	*v* MULED, MULING, MULES to strike from dies belonging to two different issues, as a coin
MULETA	*n* pl. -S a red cloth used by a matador
MULETEER	*n* pl. -S one who drives mules (hoofed work animals)
MULEY	*n* pl. -LEYS a hornless cow
MULING	present participle of mule
MULISH	*adj* stubborn **MULISHLY** *adv*
MULL	*v* -ED, -ING, -S to ponder
MULLA	*n* pl. -S mullah
MULLAH	*n* pl. -S a Muslim religious leader or teacher
MULLEIN	*n* pl. -S a Eurasian herb
MULLEN	*n* pl. -S mullein
MULLER	*n* pl. -S a grinding implement
MULLET	*n* pl. -S an edible fish
MULLEY	*n* pl. -LEYS muley
MULLIGAN	*n* pl. -S a stew of various meats and vegetables
MULLION	*v* -ED, -ING, -S to provide with vertical dividing strips
MULLITE	*n* pl. -S a mineral
MULLOCK	*n* pl. -S waste earth or rock from a mine **MULLOCKY** *adj*
MULTIAGE	*adj* including people of various ages
MULTICAR	*adj* owning or involving several cars
MULTIFID	*adj* divided into many parts
MULTIJET	*adj* having more than two jets
MULTIPED	*n* pl. -S an animal having many feet
MULTIPLE	*n* pl. -S the product of a quantity by an integer
MULTIPLY	*v* -PLIED, -PLYING, -PLIES to increase in number
MULTITON	*adj* weighing many tons
MULTIUSE	*adj* having many uses
MULTURE	*n* pl. -S a fee paid to a miller for grinding grain
MUM	*v* MUMMED, MUMMING, MUMS to act in a disguise

MUMBLE	v -BLED, -BLING, -BLES to speak unclearly
MUMBLER	n pl. -S one that mumbles
MUMBLY	adj given to mumbling
MUMM	v -ED, -ING, -S to mum
MUMMED	past tense of mum and mumm
MUMMER	n pl. -S one that mums
MUMMERY	n pl. -MERIES a performance by mummers
MUMMIED	past tense of mummy
MUMMIES	present 3d person sing. of mummy
MUMMIFY	v -FIED, -FYING, -FIES to preserve by embalming
MUMMING	present participle of mum
MUMMY	v -MIED, -MYING, -MIES to mummify
MUMP	v -ED, -ING, -S to beg
MUMPER	n pl. -S one that mumps
MUMU	n pl. -S muumuu
MUN	n pl. -S man; fellow
MUNCH	v -ED, -ING, -ES to chew with a crackling sound
MUNCHER	n pl. -S one that munches
MUNCHIES	n/pl hunger pangs
MUNCHKIN	n pl. -S a small friendly person
MUNDANE	adj ordinary
MUNDUNGO	n pl. -GOS a foul-smelling tobacco
MUNGO	n pl. -GOS a low-quality wool
MUNGOOSE	n pl. -S mongoose
MUNI	n pl. -S a security issued by a state or local government
MUNIMENT	n pl. -S a means of defense
MUNITION	v -ED, -ING, -S to furnish with war materiel
MUNNION	n pl. -S a muntin
MUNSTER	n pl. -S muenster
MUNTIN	n pl. -S a dividing strip for window panes
MUNTING	n pl. -S muntin
MUNTJAC	n pl. -S a small Asian deer
MUNTJAK	n pl. -S muntjac
MUON	n pl. -S a subatomic particle **MUONIC** adj
MUONIUM	n pl. -S an electron and a positive muon bound together
MURA	n pl. -S a Japanese village
MURAENID	n pl. -S a moray
MURAL	n pl. -S a painting applied directly to a wall or ceiling
MURALIST	n pl. -S a painter of murals
MURDER	v -ED, -ING, -S to kill unlawfully with premeditated malice
MURDEREE	n pl. -S one that is murdered
MURDERER	n pl. -S one that murders
MURE	v MURED, MURING, MURES to immure
MUREIN	n pl. -S a type of polymer
MUREX	n pl. -RICES or -REXES a marine mollusk
MURIATE	n pl. -S chloride
MURIATED	adj pickled
MURICATE	adj covered with short, sharp points
MURICES	a pl. of murex
MURID	n pl. -S a murine
MURINE	n pl. -S any of a family of small rodents
MURING	present participle of mure
MURK	adj MURKER, MURKEST dark **MURKLY** adv
MURK	n pl. -S darkness
MURKY	adj MURKIER, MURKIEST dark **MURKILY** adv
MURMUR	v -ED, -ING, -S to speak unclearly
MURMURER	n pl. -S one that murmurs
MURPHY	n pl. -PHIES a potato
MURR	n pl. -S murre
MURRA	n pl. -S a substance used to make fine vases and cups in ancient Rome
MURRAIN	n pl. -S a disease of cattle
MURRE	n pl. -S a diving bird
MURRELET	n pl. -S a small diving bird
MURREY	n pl. -REYS a dark purple color
MURRHA	n pl. -S murra **MURRHINE** adj
MURRINE	adj pertaining to murra
MURRY	n pl. -RIES a moray
MURTHER	v -ED, -ING, -S to murder
MUSCA	n pl. -CAE any of a genus of flies
MUSCADEL	n pl. -S muscatel
MUSCADET	n pl. -S a dry white French wine
MUSCAT	n pl. -S a sweet, white grape

MUSCATEL	*n* pl. -S a wine made from muscat grapes
MUSCID	*n* pl. -S musca
MUSCLE	*v* -CLED, -CLING, -CLES to proceed by force
MUSCLY	*adj* composed of muscle (tissue that produces bodily movement)
MUSCULAR	*adj* pertaining to muscle
MUSE	*v* MUSED, MUSING, MUSES to ponder
MUSEFUL	*adj* pensive
MUSER	*n* pl. -S one that muses
MUSETTE	*n* pl. -S a small bagpipe
MUSEUM	*n* pl. -S a place where objects of lasting interest or value are cared for and exhibited
MUSH	*v* -ED, -ING, -ES to travel over snow with a dog sled
MUSHER	*n* pl. -S one that mushes
MUSHROOM	*v* -ED, -ING, -S to grow or spread rapidly
MUSHY	*adj* MUSHIER, MUSHIEST pulpy **MUSHILY** *adv*
MUSIC	*n* pl. -S vocal or instrumental sounds organized to produce a unified composition
MUSICAL	*n* pl. -S a play in which dialogue is interspersed with songs and dances
MUSICALE	*n* pl. -S a program of music performed at a social gathering
MUSICIAN	*n* pl. -S one who performs or composes music
MUSING	*n* pl. -S contemplation
MUSINGLY	*adv* in a pensive manner
MUSJID	*n* pl. -S a mosque
MUSK	*n* pl. -S a strongly odorous substance secreted by certain animals
MUSKEG	*n* pl. -S a marsh
MUSKET	*n* pl. -S a type of firearm
MUSKETRY	*n* pl. -RIES the technique of firing small arms
MUSKIE	*n* pl. -S a freshwater fish
MUSKIER	comparative of musky
MUSKIEST	superlative of musky
MUSKILY	*adv* in a musky manner
MUSKIT	*n* pl. -S mesquite
MUSKRAT	*n* pl. -S an aquatic rodent
MUSKY	*adj* MUSKIER, MUSKIEST resembling musk
MUSLIN	*n* pl. -S a cotton fabric
MUSPIKE	*n* pl. -S a freshwater fish
MUSQUASH	*n* pl. -ES the muskrat
MUSS	*v* -ED, -ING, -ES to mess
MUSSEL	*n* pl. -S a bivalve mollusk
MUSSY	*adj* MUSSIER, MUSSIEST messy **MUSSILY** *adv*
MUST	*v* -ED, -ING, -S to become musty
MUSTACHE	*n* pl. -S a growth of hair on the upper lip
MUSTANG	*n* pl. -S a wild horse
MUSTARD	*n* pl. -S a pungent seasoning
MUSTARDY	*adj* resembling mustard
MUSTEE	*n* pl. -S an octoroon
MUSTER	*v* -ED, -ING, -S to summon or assemble
MUSTH	*n* pl. -S a state of frenzy occurring in male elephants
MUSTY	*adj* MUSTIER, MUSTIEST having a stale odor **MUSTILY** *adv*
MUT	*n* pl. -S mutt
MUTABLE	*adj* capable of change **MUTABLY** *adv*
MUTAGEN	*n* pl. -S a substance that causes biological mutation
MUTANT	*n* pl. -S something that undergoes mutation
MUTASE	*n* pl. -S an enzyme
MUTATE	*v* -TATED, -TATING, -TATES to undergo mutation
MUTATION	*n* pl. -S the act of changing **MUTATIVE** *adj*
MUTCH	*n* pl. -ES a close-fitting cap
MUTCHKIN	*n* pl. -S a Scottish unit of liquid measure
MUTE	*adj* MUTER, MUTEST characterized by an absence of speech **MUTELY** *adv*
MUTE	*v* MUTED, MUTING, MUTES to deaden the sound of **MUTEDLY** *adv*
MUTENESS	*n* pl. -ES the state of being mute
MUTER	comparative of mute
MUTEST	superlative of mute
MUTICOUS	*adj* lacking a point
MUTILATE	*v* -LATED, -LATING, -LATES to deprive of a limb or other essential part

MUTINE	*v* -TINED, -TINING, -TINES to mutiny
MUTINEER	*v* -ED, -ING, -S to mutiny
MUTING	present participle of mute
MUTINIED	past tense of mutiny
MUTINIES	present 3d person sing. of mutiny
MUTINING	present participle of mutine
MUTINOUS	*adj* disposed to mutiny
MUTINY	*v* -NIED, -NYING, -NIES to revolt against constituted authority
MUTISM	*n* pl. -S muteness
MUTON	*n* pl. -S a unit of nucleic acid
MUTT	*n* pl. -S a mongrel dog
MUTTER	*v* -ED, -ING, -S to speak unclearly
MUTTERER	*n* pl. -S one that mutters
MUTTON	*n* pl. -S the flesh of sheep used as food **MUTTONY** *adj*
MUTUAL	*adj* shared in common **MUTUALLY** *adv*
MUTUEL	*n* pl. -S a system of betting on races
MUTULE	*n* pl. -S an ornamental block used in classical Greek architecture **MUTULAR** *adj*
MUUMUU	*n* pl. -S a long, loose dress
MUZHIK	*n* pl. -S a Russian peasant
MUZJIK	*n* pl. -S muzhik
MUZZIER	comparative of muzzy
MUZZIEST	superlative of muzzy
MUZZILY	*adv* in a muzzy manner
MUZZLE	*v* -ZLED, -ZLING, -ZLES to put a covering over the mouth of to prevent biting or eating
MUZZLER	*n* pl. -S one that muzzles
MUZZY	*adj* -ZIER, -ZIEST confused
MY	*pron* the possessive form of the pronoun I
MYALGIA	*n* pl. -S muscular pain **MYALGIC** *adj*
MYASIS	*n* pl. MYASES myiasis
MYCELE	*n* pl. -S mycelium
MYCELIUM	*n* pl. -LIA the vegetative portion of a fungus **MYCELIAL, MYCELIAN, MYCELOID** *adj*
MYCETOMA	*n* pl. -MAS or -MATA a fungous infection
MYCOLOGY	*n* pl. -GIES the branch of botany dealing with fungi
MYCOSIS	*n* pl. -COSES a disease caused by a fungus **MYCOTIC** *adj*
MYELIN	*n* pl. -S a fatty substance that encases certain nerve fibers **MYELINIC** *adj*
MYELINE	*n* pl. -S myelin
MYELITIS	*n* pl. -LITIDES inflammation of the bone marrow
MYELOID	*adj* pertaining to bone marrow
MYELOMA	*n* pl. -MAS or -MATA a tumor of the bone marrow
MYIASIS	*n* pl. MYIASES infestation of human tissue by fly maggots
MYLONITE	*n* pl. -S a type of rock
MYNA	*n* pl. -S an Asian bird
MYNAH	*n* pl. -S myna
MYNHEER	*n* pl. -S a Dutch title of courtesy for a man
MYOBLAST	*n* pl. -S a cell capable of giving rise to muscle cells
MYOGENIC	*adj* originating in muscle tissue
MYOGRAPH	*n* pl. -S an instrument for recording muscular contractions
MYOID	*adj* resembling muscle
MYOLOGY	*n* pl. -GIES the study of muscles **MYOLOGIC** *adj*
MYOMA	*n* pl. -MAS or -MATA a tumor composed of muscle tissue
MYOPATHY	*n* pl. -THIES a disorder of muscle tissue
MYOPE	*n* pl. -S one who is affected with myopia
MYOPIA	*n* pl. -S a visual defect **MYOPIC** *adj*
MYOPY	*n* pl. -PIES myopia
MYOSCOPE	*n* pl. -S an instrument for observing muscular contractions
MYOSIN	*n* pl. -S a protein found in muscle tissue
MYOSIS	*n* pl. MYOSES miosis
MYOSITIS	*n* pl. -TISES muscular pain from infection
MYOSOTE	*n* pl. -S myosotis
MYOSOTIS	*n* pl. -TISES a flowering plant
MYOTIC	*n* pl. -S miotic
MYOTOME	*n* pl. -S a portion of an embryonic somite
MYOTONIA	*n* pl. -S temporary muscular rigidity **MYOTONIC** *adj*
MYRIAD	*n* pl. -S a very large number

MYRIAPOD	*n* pl. -S a multi-legged arthropod
MYRICA	*n* pl. -S a medicinal tree bark
MYRIOPOD	*n* pl. -S myriapod
MYRMIDON	*n* pl. -S a loyal follower
MYRRH	*n* pl. -S an aromatic gum resin **MYRRHIC** *adj*
MYRTLE	*n* pl. -S an evergreen shrub
MYSELF	*pron* a form of the 1st person sing. pronoun
MYSID	*n* pl. -S a small crustacean
MYSOST	*n* pl. -S a mild cheese
MYSTAGOG	*n* pl. -S a teacher of religious mysteries
MYSTERY	*n* pl. -TERIES something that is not or cannot be known, understood, or explained
MYSTIC	*n* pl. -S one who professes to have had mystical experiences
MYSTICAL	*adj* spiritually significant or symbolic
MYSTICLY	*adv* in a mystical manner
MYSTIFY	*v* -FIED, -FYING, -FIES to perplex
MYSTIQUE	*n* pl. -S an aura of mystery or mystical power surrounding a particular person or thing
MYTH	*n* pl. -S a type of traditional story
MYTHIC	*adj* mythical
MYTHICAL	*adj* based on or described in a myth
MYTHOS	*n* pl. -THOI a myth
MYTHY	*adj* MYTHIER, MYTHIEST resembling myth
MYXEDEMA	*n* pl. -S a disease caused by decreased activity of the thyroid gland
MYXOCYTE	*n* pl. -S a large cell found in mucous tissue
MYXOID	*adj* containing mucus
MYXOMA	*n* pl. -MAS or -MATA a tumor composed of mucous tissue

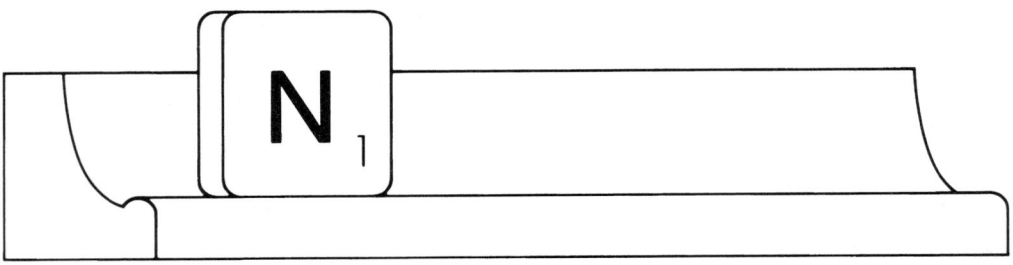

NA	*adv* no; not	**NAH**	*adv* no
NAAN	*n* pl. -S nan	**NAIAD**	*n* pl. -S or -ES a water nymph
NAB	*v* NABBED, NABBING, NABS to capture or arrest	**NAIF**	*n* pl. -S a naive person
NABBER	*n* pl. -S one that nabs	**NAIL**	*v* -ED, -ING, -S to fasten with a nail (a slender piece of metal)
NABE	*n* pl. -S a neighborhood movie theater	**NAILER**	*n* pl. -S one that nails
NABIS	*n* pl. NABIS a group of French artists	**NAILFOLD**	*n* pl. -S a fold of skin around the fingernail
NABOB	*n* pl. -S one who becomes rich and prominent **NABOBISH** *adj*	**NAILHEAD**	*n* pl. -S the top of a nail
		NAILSET	*n* pl. -S a steel rod for driving a nail into something
NABOBERY	*n* pl. -ERIES the state of being a nabob	**NAINSOOK**	*n* pl. -S a cotton fabric
NABOBESS	*n* pl. -ES a female nabob	**NAIRA**	*n* pl. NAIRA a monetary unit of Nigeria
NABOBISM	*n* pl. -S great wealth and luxury	**NAIVE**	*adj* NAIVER, NAIVEST lacking sophistication **NAIVELY** *adv*
NACELLE	*n* pl. -S a shelter on an aircraft		
NACHAS	*n* pl. NACHAS pride in another's accomplishments	**NAIVE**	*n* pl. -S a naive person
		NAIVETE	*n* pl. -S the quality of being naive
NACHES	*n* pl. NACHES nachas	**NAIVETY**	*n* pl. -TIES naivete
NACHO	*n* pl. -CHOS a tortilla chip topped with cheese and a savory mixture and broiled	**NAKED**	*adj* -KEDER, -KEDEST being without clothing or covering **NAKEDLY** *adv*
NACRE	*n* pl. -S the pearly internal layer of certain shells **NACRED, NACREOUS** *adj*	**NALED**	*n* pl. -S an insecticide
		NALOXONE	*n* pl. -S a chemical compound
NADA	*n* pl. -S nothing	**NAM**	a past tense of nim
NADIR	*n* pl. -S a point on the celestial sphere **NADIRAL** *adj*	**NAME**	*v* NAMED, NAMING, NAMES to give a title to **NAMABLE, NAMEABLE** *adj*
NAE	*adv* no; not		
NAETHING	*n* pl. -S nothing	**NAMELESS**	*adj* lacking distinction or fame
NAEVUS	*n* pl. -VI nevus **NAEVOID** *adj*	**NAMELY**	*adv* that is to say
NAG	*v* NAGGED, NAGGING, NAGS to find fault incessantly	**NAMER**	*n* pl. -S one that names
		NAMESAKE	*n* pl. -S one who is named after another
NAGANA	*n* pl. -S a disease of horses in Africa	**NAMETAG**	*n* pl. -S a tag bearing one's name worn for identification
NAGGER	*n* pl. -S one that nags		
NAGGING	present participle of nag	**NAMING**	present participle of name
NAGGY	*adj* -GIER, -GIEST given to nagging	**NAN**	*n* pl. -S a round flat bread
		NANA	*n* pl. -S a grandmother

NANDIN	*n* pl. -S an evergreen shrub	**NARD**	*n* pl. -S a fragrant ointment **NARDINE** *adj*
NANDINA	*n* pl. -S an Asian shrub	**NARES**	pl. of naris
NANISM	*n* pl. -S abnormal smallness	**NARGHILE**	*n* pl. -S a hookah
NANKEEN	*n* pl. -S a cotton fabric	**NARGILE**	*n* pl. -S narghile
NANKIN	*n* pl. -S nankeen	**NARGILEH**	*n* pl. -S narghile
NANNIE	*n* pl. -S nanny	**NARIS**	*n* pl. NARES a nostril **NARIAL,**
NANNY	*n* pl. -NIES a children's nurse		**NARIC, NARINE** *adj*
NANOGRAM	*n* pl. -S a unit of mass and weight	**NARK**	*v* -ED, -ING, -S to spy or inform
NANOWATT	*n* pl. -S a unit of power	**NARKY**	*adj* irritable
NAOS	*n* pl. NAOI an ancient temple	**NARRATE**	*v* -RATED, -RATING, -RATES to tell a story
NAP	*v* NAPPED, NAPPING, NAPS to sleep briefly	**NARRATER**	*n* pl. -S narrator
NAPALM	*v* -ED, -ING, -S to assault with a type of incendiary bomb	**NARRATOR**	*n* pl. -S one that narrates
NAPE	*n* pl. -S the back of the neck	**NARROW**	*adj* -ROWER, -ROWEST of little width **NARROWLY** *adv*
NAPERY	*n* pl. -PERIES table linen	**NARROW**	*v* -ED, -ING, -S to make narrow
NAPHTHA	*n* pl. -S a volatile liquid	**NARTHEX**	*n* pl. -ES a vestibule in a church
NAPHTHOL	*n* pl. -S a chemical compound	**NARWAL**	*n* pl. -S narwhal
NAPHTHYL	*n* pl. -S a radical derived from naphthalene	**NARWHAL**	*n* pl. -S an arctic aquatic mammal
NAPHTOL	*n* pl. -S naphthol	**NARWHALE**	*n* pl. -S narwhal
NAPIFORM	*adj* shaped like a turnip	**NARY**	*adj* not one
NAPKIN	*n* pl. -S a piece of material used to wipe the hands and mouth	**NASAL**	*n* pl. -S a sound uttered through the nose
NAPLESS	*adj* threadbare	**NASALISE**	*v* -ISED, -ISING, -ISES to nasalize
NAPOLEON	*n* pl. -S a type of pastry	**NASALITY**	*n* pl. -TIES the quality or an instance of being produced nasally
NAPPE	*n* pl. -S a type of rock formation		
NAPPED	past tense of nap	**NASALIZE**	*v* -IZED, -IZING, -IZES to produce sounds through the nose
NAPPER	*n* pl. -S one that naps		
NAPPIE	*n* pl. -S a diaper	**NASALLY**	*adv* through the nose
NAPPING	present participle of nap	**NASCENCE**	*n* pl. -S nascency
NAPPY	*adj* -PIER, -PIEST kinky	**NASCENCY**	*n* pl. -CIES birth; origin
NARC	*n* pl. -S an undercover drug agent	**NASCENT**	*adj* coming into existence
NARCEIN	*n* pl. -S narceine	**NASION**	*n* pl. -S a point in the skull **NASIAL** *adj*
NARCEINE	*n* pl. -S an opium derivative	**NASTIC**	*adj* pertaining to an automatic response of plants
NARCISM	*n* pl. -S excessive love of oneself		
NARCISSI	*n/pl* bulbous flowering plants	**NASTY**	*adj* -TIER, -TIEST offensive to the senses **NASTILY** *adv*
NARCIST	*n* pl. -S one given to narcism		
NARCO	*n* pl. -COS narc	**NASTY**	*n* pl. -TIES something that is nasty
NARCOSE	*adj* characterized by stupor		
NARCOSIS	*n* pl. -COSES a drug-induced stupor	**NATAL**	*adj* pertaining to one's birth
		NATALITY	*n* pl. -TIES birth rate
NARCOTIC	*n* pl. -S a drug that dulls the senses	**NATANT**	*adj* floating or swimming **NATANTLY** *adv*

NATATION	*n* pl. -S the act of swimming
NATATORY	*adj* pertaining to swimming
NATCH	*adv* naturally
NATES	*n/pl* the buttocks
NATHLESS	*adv* nevertheless
NATION	*n* pl. -S a politically organized people who share a territory, customs, and history
NATIONAL	*n* pl. -S a citizen of a nation
NATIVE	*n* pl. -S an original inhabitant of an area
NATIVELY	*adv* in an inborn manner
NATIVISM	*n* pl. -S a policy of favoring the interests of native inhabitants
NATIVIST	*n* pl. -S an advocate of nativism
NATIVITY	*n* pl. -TIES the process of being born
NATRIUM	*n* pl. -S sodium
NATRON	*n* pl. -S a chemical compound
NATTER	*v* -ED, -ING, -S to chatter
NATTY	*adj* -TIER, -TIEST neatly dressed **NATTILY** *adv*
NATURAL	*n* pl. -S a type of musical note
NATURE	*n* pl. -S the essential qualities of a person or thing **NATURED** *adj*
NATURISM	*n* pl. -S nudism
NATURIST	*n* pl. -S a nudist
NAUGHT	*n* pl. -S a zero
NAUGHTY	*adj* -TIER, -TIEST disobedient
NAUMACHY	*n* pl. -CHIES a mock sea battle
NAUPLIUS	*n* pl. -PLII a form of certain crustaceans **NAUPLIAL** *adj*
NAUSEA	*n* pl. -S a stomach disturbance
NAUSEANT	*n* pl. -S an agent that induces nausea
NAUSEATE	*v* -ATED, -ATING, -ATES to affect with nausea
NAUSEOUS	*adj* affected with nausea
NAUTCH	*n* pl. -ES a dancing exhibition in India
NAUTICAL	*adj* pertaining to ships
NAUTILUS	*n* pl. -LUSES or -LI a spiral-shelled mollusk
NAVAID	*n* pl. -S a navigational device
NAVAL	*adj* pertaining to ships **NAVALLY** *adv*
NAVAR	*n* pl. -S a system of air navigation
NAVE	*n* pl. -S the main part of a church
NAVEL	*n* pl. -S a depression in the abdomen
NAVETTE	*n* pl. -S a gem cut in a pointed oval form
NAVICERT	*n* pl. -S a document permitting a vessel passage through a naval blockade
NAVIES	pl. of navy
NAVIGATE	*v* -GATED, -GATING, -GATES to plan and control the course of
NAVVY	*n* pl. -VIES a manual laborer
NAVY	*n* pl. -VIES a nation's warships
NAW	*adv* no
NAWAB	*n* pl. -S a nabob
NAY	*n* pl. NAYS a negative vote
NAYSAYER	*n* pl. -S one that denies or opposes something
NAZI	*n* pl. -S a type of fascist
NAZIFY	*v* -FIED, -FYING, -FIES to cause to be like a nazi
NE	*adj* born with the name of
NEAP	*n* pl. -S a tide of lowest range
NEAR	*adj* NEARER, NEAREST situated within a short distance
NEAR	*v* -ED, -ING, -S to approach
NEARBY	*adj* near
NEARLY	*adv* -LIER, -LIEST with close approximation
NEARNESS	*n* pl. -ES the state of being near
NEARSIDE	*n* pl. -S the left side
NEAT	*adj* NEATER, NEATEST being in a state of cleanliness and order
NEAT	*n* pl. -S a bovine
NEATEN	*v* -ED, -ING, -S to make neat
NEATH	*prep* beneath
NEATHERD	*n* pl. -S a cowherd
NEATLY	*adv* in a neat manner
NEATNESS	*n* pl. -ES the state of being neat
NEB	*n* pl. -S the beak of a bird
NEBBISH	*n* pl. -ES a meek person **NEBBISHY** *adj*
NEBULA	*n* pl. -LAS or -LAE a cloud-like interstellar mass **NEBULAR** *adj*
NEBULE	*adj* composed of successive short curves
NEBULISE	*v* -LISED, -LISING, -LISES to nebulize

NEBULIZE *v* -LIZED, -LIZING, -LIZES to reduce to a fine spray

NEBULOSE *adj* nebulous

NEBULOUS *adj* unclear

NEBULY *adj* nebule

NECK *v* -ED, -ING, -S to kiss and caress in lovemaking

NECKBAND *n* pl. -S a band worn around the neck (the part of the body joining the head to the trunk)

NECKER *n* pl. -S one that necks

NECKING *n* pl. -S a small molding near the top of a column

NECKLACE *n* pl. -S an ornament worn around the neck

NECKLESS *adj* having no neck

NECKLIKE *adj* resembling the neck

NECKLINE *n* pl. -S the line formed by the neck opening of a garment

NECKTIE *n* pl. -S a strip of fabric worn around the neck

NECKWEAR *n* pl. NECKWEAR something that is worn around the neck

NECROPSY *v* -SIED, -SYING, -SIES to perform an autopsy on

NECROSE *v* -CROSED, -CROSING, -CROSES to affect with necrosis

NECROSIS *n* pl. -CROSES the death of living tissue **NECROTIC** *adj*

NECTAR *n* pl. -S a delicious drink

NECTARY *n* pl. -TARIES a plant gland

NEE *adj* born with the name of

NEED *v* -ED, -ING, -S to have an urgent or essential use for

NEEDER *n* pl. -S one that needs

NEEDFUL *n* pl. -S something that is needed

NEEDIER comparative of needy

NEEDIEST superlative of needy

NEEDILY *adv* in a needy manner

NEEDLE *v* -DLED, -DLING, -DLES to sew with a slender, pointed instrument

NEEDLER *n* pl. -S one that needles

NEEDLESS *adj* not necessary

NEEDLING *n* pl. -S the act of one who needles

NEEDY *adj* NEEDIER, NEEDIEST in a state of poverty

NEEM *n* pl. -S an East Indian tree

NEEP *n* pl. -S a turnip

NEGATE *v* -GATED, -GATING, -GATES to nullify

NEGATER *n* pl. -S one that negates

NEGATION *n* pl. -S the act of negating

NEGATIVE *v* -TIVED, -TIVING, -TIVES to veto

NEGATON *n* pl. -S negatron

NEGATOR *n* pl. -S negater

NEGATRON *n* pl. -S an electron

NEGLECT *v* -ED, -ING, -S to fail to pay attention to

NEGLIGE *n* pl. -S negligee

NEGLIGEE *n* pl. -S a woman's dressing gown

NEGROID *n* pl. -S member of the black race

NEGRONI *n* pl. -S an alcoholic beverage

NEGUS *n* pl. -ES an alcoholic beverage

NEIF *n* pl. -S nieve

NEIGH *v* -ED, -ING, -S to utter the cry of a horse

NEIGHBOR *v* -ED, -ING, -S to live close to

NEIST *adj* next

NEITHER *adj* not one or the other

NEKTON *n* pl. -S free-swimming marine animals **NEKTONIC** *adj*

NELLIE *n* pl. -S an effeminate male

NELLY *n* pl. -LIES nellie

NELSON *n* pl. -S a wrestling hold

NELUMBO *n* pl. -BOS an aquatic herb

NEMA *n* pl. -S a nematode

NEMATIC *adj* pertaining to a phase of a liquid crystal

NEMATODE *n* pl. -S a kind of worm

NEMESIS *n* pl. NEMESES an unbeatable opponent

NENE *n* pl. NENE a Hawaiian goose

NEOLITH *n* pl. -S an ancient stone implement

NEOLOGY *n* pl. -GIES a new word or phrase **NEOLOGIC** *adj*

NEOMORPH *n* pl. -S a type of biological structure

NEOMYCIN *n* pl. -S an antibiotic drug

NEON *n* pl. -S a gaseous element **NEONED** *adj*

NEONATE *n* pl. -S a newborn child **NEONATAL** *adj*

NEOPHYTE *n* pl. -S a novice

NEOPLASM *n* pl. -S a tumor

NEOPRENE *n* pl. -S a synthetic rubber

NEOTENY *n* pl. -NIES attainment of sexual maturity in the larval stage **NEOTENIC** *adj*

NEOTERIC *n* pl. -S a modern author

NEOTYPE *n* pl. -S a specimen of a species

NEPENTHE *n* pl. -S a drug that induces forgetfulness

NEPHEW *n* pl. -S a son of one's brother or sister

NEPHRIC *adj* renal

NEPHRISM *n* pl. -S ill health caused by a kidney disease

NEPHRITE *n* pl. -S a mineral

NEPHRON *n* pl. -S an excretory unit of a kidney

NEPOTISM *n* pl. -S favoritism shown to a relative **NEPOTIC** *adj*

NEPOTIST *n* pl. -S one who practices nepotism

NERD *n* pl. -S a socially inept person **NERDISH** *adj*

NERDY *adj* NERDIER, NERDIEST socially inept

NEREID *n* pl. -S a sea nymph

NEREIS *n* pl. -REIDES a marine worm

NERITIC *adj* pertaining to shallow water

NEROL *n* pl. -S a fragrant alcohol

NEROLI *n* pl. -S a fragrant oil

NERTS *interj* — used to express defiance

NERTZ *interj* nerts

NERVATE *adj* having veins

NERVE *v* NERVED, NERVING, NERVES to give courage to

NERVIER comparative of nervy

NERVIEST superlative of nervy

NERVILY *adv* in a nervy manner

NERVINE *n* pl. -S a soothing medicine

NERVING *n* pl. -S a type of veterinary operation

NERVOUS *adj* easily excited

NERVULE *n* pl. -S nervure

NERVURE *n* pl. -S a vascular ridge on a leaf

NERVY *adj* NERVIER, NERVIEST impudent

NESCIENT *n* pl. -S one who is ignorant

NESS *n* pl. -ES a headland

NEST *v* -ED, -ING, -S to build a nest (a structure for holding bird eggs)

NESTABLE *adj* capable of being fitted closely within another container

NESTER *n* pl. -S one that nests

NESTLE *v* -TLED, -TLING, -TLES to lie snugly

NESTLER *n* pl. -S one that nestles

NESTLIKE *adj* resembling a nest

NESTLING *n* pl. -S a young bird

NESTOR *n* pl. -S a wise old man

NET *v* NETTED, NETTING, NETS to catch in a net (a type of openwork fabric)

NETHER *adj* situated below

NETLESS *adj* having no net

NETLIKE *adj* resembling a net

NETOP *n* pl. -S friend; companion

NETSUKE *n* pl. -S a button-like fixture on Japanese clothing

NETT *v* -ED, -ING, -S to net

NETTABLE *adj* capable of being netted

NETTED past tense of net, nett

NETTER *n* pl. -S one that nets

NETTIER comparative of netty

NETTIEST superlative of netty

NETTING *n* pl. -S a net

NETTLE *v* -TLED, -TLING, -TLES to make angry

NETTLER *n* pl. -S one that nettles

NETTLY *adj* -TLIER, -TLIEST prickly

NETTY *adj* -TIER, -TIEST resembling a net

NETWORK *v* -ED, -ING, -S to cover with or as if with crossing lines

NEUK *n* pl. -S nook

NEUM *n* pl. -S neume

NEUME *n* pl. -S a sign used in musical notation **NEUMATIC, NEUMIC** *adj*

NEURAL *adj* pertaining to the nervous system **NEURALLY** *adv*

NEURAXON *n* pl. -S a part of a neuron

NEURINE *n* pl. -S a ptomaine poison

NEURITIC *n* pl. -S one affected with neuritis

NEURITIS *n* pl. -RITIDES or -RITISES inflammation of a nerve

NEUROID *adj* resembling a nerve

NEUROMA	*n* pl. -MAS or -MATA a type of tumor
NEURON	*n* pl. -S the basic cellular unit of the nervous system **NEURONAL, NEURONIC** *adj*
NEURONE	*n* pl. -S neuron
NEUROSIS	*n* pl. -ROSES a type of emotional disturbance **NEUROSAL** *adj*
NEUROTIC	*n* pl. -S one affected with a neurosis
NEURULA	*n* pl. -LAE or -LAS a vertebrate embryo
NEUSTON	*n* pl. -S an aggregate of small aquatic organisms
NEUTER	*v* -ED, -ING, -S to castrate
NEUTRAL	*n* pl. -S one that is impartial
NEUTRINO	*n* pl. -NOS a subatomic particle
NEUTRON	*n* pl. -S a subatomic particle
NEVE	*n* pl. -S a granular snow
NEVER	*adv* at no time
NEVUS	*n* pl. -VI a birthmark **NEVOID** *adj*
NEW	*adj* NEWER, NEWEST existing only a short time
NEW	*n* pl. -S something that is new
NEWBORN	*n* pl. -S a recently born infant
NEWCOMER	*n* pl. -S one that has recently arrived
NEWEL	*n* pl. -S a staircase support
NEWFOUND	*adj* newly found
NEWIE	*n* pl. -S something new
NEWISH	*adj* somewhat new
NEWLY	*adv* recently
NEWLYWED	*n* pl. -S a person recently married
NEWMOWN	*adj* recently mown
NEWNESS	*n* pl. -ES the state of being new
NEWS	*n/pl* a report of recent events
NEWSBOY	*n* pl. -BOYS a boy who delivers or sells newspapers
NEWSCAST	*n* pl. -S a news broadcast
NEWSHAWK	*n* pl. -S a newspaper reporter
NEWSIE	*n* pl. -S newsy
NEWSIER	comparative of newsy
NEWSIES	pl. of newsy
NEWSIEST	superlative of newsy
NEWSLESS	*adj* having no news
NEWSMAN	*n* pl. -MEN a news reporter
NEWSPEAK	*n* pl. -S a deliberately ambiguous language
NEWSREEL	*n* pl. -S a short movie presenting current events
NEWSROOM	*n* pl. -S a room where the news is gathered
NEWSY	*adj* NEWSIER, NEWSIEST full of news
NEWSY	*n* pl. NEWSIES a newsboy
NEWT	*n* pl. -S a small salamander
NEWTON	*n* pl. -S a unit of force
NEXT	*adj* coming immediately after; adjoining
NEXTDOOR	*adj* located in the next building or room
NEXUS	*n* pl. -ES a connection or link
NGULTRUM	*n* pl. -S a monetary unit of Bhutan
NGWEE	*n* pl. NGWEE a monetary unit of Zambia
NIACIN	*n* pl. -S a B vitamin
NIB	*v* NIBBED, NIBBING, NIBS to provide with a penpoint
NIBBLE	*v* -BLED, -BLING, -BLES to eat with small bites
NIBBLER	*n* pl. -S one that nibbles
NIBLICK	*n* pl. -S a golf club
NIBLIKE	*adj* resembling a penpoint
NICAD	*n* pl. -S nickel cadmium
NICE	*adj* NICER, NICEST pleasing to the senses **NICELY** *adv*
NICENESS	*n* pl. -ES the quality of being nice
NICETY	*n* pl. -TIES a fine point or distinction
NICHE	*v* NICHED, NICHING, NICHES to place in a receding space or hollow
NICK	*v* -ED, -ING, -S to make a shallow cut in
NICKEL	*v* -ELED, -ELING, -ELS or -ELLED, -ELLING, -ELS to plate with nickel (a metallic element)
NICKELIC	*adj* pertaining to or containing nickel
NICKER	*v* -ED, -ING, -S to neigh
NICKLE	*v* -LED, -LING, -LES nickel
NICKNACK	*n* pl. -S a trinket
NICKNAME	*v* -NAMED, -NAMING, -NAMES to give an alternate name to
NICOL	*n* pl. -S a type of prism

NICOTIN *n* pl. -S nicotine

NICOTINE *n* pl. -S a poisonous alkaloid in tobacco

NICTATE *v* -TATED, -TATING, -TATES to wink

NIDAL *adj* pertaining to a nidus

NIDE *v* NIDED, NIDING, NIDES to nest

NIDERING *n* pl. -S a coward

NIDGET *n* pl. -S an idiot

NIDI a pl. of nidus

NIDIFY *v* -FIED, -FYING, -FIES to nest

NIDING present participle of nide

NIDUS *n* pl. NIDI or NIDUSES a nest or breeding place

NIECE *n* pl. -S a daughter of one's brother or sister

NIELLIST *n* pl. -S one that niellos

NIELLO *n* pl. -LI or -LOS a black metallic substance

NIELLO *v* -ED, -ING, -S to decorate with niello

NIEVE *n* pl. -S the fist or hand

NIFFER *v* -ED, -ING, -S to barter

NIFTY *adj* -TIER, -TIEST stylish; pleasing **NIFTILY** *adv*

NIFTY *n* pl. -TIES something that is nifty

NIGGARD *v* -ED, -ING, -S to act stingily

NIGGLE *v* -GLED, -GLING, -GLES to worry over petty details

NIGGLER *n* pl. -S one that niggles

NIGGLING *n* pl. -S petty or meticulous work

NIGH *adj* NIGHER, NIGHEST near

NIGH *v* -ED, -ING, -S to approach

NIGHNESS *n* pl. -ES the state of being nigh

NIGHT *n* pl. -S the period from sunset to sunrise

NIGHTCAP *n* pl. -S a cap worn to bed

NIGHTIE *n* pl. -S a nightgown

NIGHTIES pl. of nighty

NIGHTJAR *n* pl. -S a nocturnal bird

NIGHTLY *adv* every night; at night

NIGHTY *n* pl. NIGHTIES nightie

NIGRIFY *v* -FIED, -FYING, -FIES to make black

NIGROSIN *n* pl. -S a type of dye

NIHIL *n* pl. -S nothing

NIHILISM *n* pl. -S a doctrine that denies traditional values

NIHILIST *n* pl. -S an adherent of nihilism

NIHILITY *n* pl. -TIES the state of being nothing

NIL *n* pl. -S nothing

NILGAI *n* pl. -S a large antelope

NILGAU *n* pl. -S nilgai

NILGHAI *n* pl. -S nilgai

NILGHAU *n* pl. -S nilgai

NILL *v* -ED, -ING, -S to be unwilling

NIM *v* NAM or NIMMED, NIMMING, NIMS to steal

NIMBLE *adj* -BLER, -BLEST agile **NIMBLY** *adv*

NIMBUS *n* pl. -BI or -BUSES a luminous cloud **NIMBUSED** *adj*

NIMIETY *n* pl. -ETIES excess **NIMIOUS** *adj*

NIMMED past tense of nim

NIMMING present participle of nim

NIMROD *n* pl. -S a hunter

NINE *n* pl. -S a number

NINEBARK *n* pl. -S a flowering shrub

NINEFOLD *adj* nine times as great

NINEPIN *n* pl. -S a wooden pin used in a bowling game

NINETEEN *n* pl. -S a number

NINETY *n* pl. -TIES a number

NINJA *n* pl. -S a feudal Japanese warrior

NINNY *n* pl. -NIES a fool **NINNYISH** *adj*

NINON *n* pl. -S a sheer fabric

NINTH *n* pl. -S one of nine equal parts

NINTHLY *adv* in the ninth place

NIOBATE *n* pl. -S a chemical salt

NIOBIUM *n* pl. -S a metallic element **NIOBIC**, **NIOBOUS** *adj*

NIP *v* NIPPED, NIPPING, NIPS to pinch

NIPA *n* pl. -S a palm tree

NIPPER *n* pl. -S one that nips

NIPPIER comparative of nippy

NIPPIEST superlative of nippy

NIPPILY *adv* in a nippy manner

NIPPING present participle of nip

NIPPLE *n* pl. -S a protuberance on the breast **NIPPLED** *adj*

NIPPY	*adj* -PIER, -PIEST sharp or biting	**NIXIE**	*n* pl. -S a female water sprite
NIRVANA	*n* pl. -S a blessed state in Buddhism **NIRVANIC** *adj*	**NIXY**	*n* pl. NIXIES an undeliverable piece of mail
NISEI	*n* pl. -S one born in America of immigrant Japanese parents	**NIZAM**	*n* pl. -S a former sovereign of India
NISI	*adj* not yet final	**NIZAMATE**	*n* pl. -S the territory of a nizam
NISUS	*n* pl. NISUS an effort	**NO**	*n* pl. NOS or NOES a negative reply
NIT	*n* pl. -S the egg of a parasitic insect	**NOB**	*n* pl. -S a wealthy person
NITE	*n* pl. -S night	**NOBBIER**	comparative of nobby
NITER	*n* pl. -S a chemical salt	**NOBBIEST**	superlative of nobby
NITERIE	*n* pl. -S nitery	**NOBBILY**	*adv* in a nobby manner
NITERY	*n* pl. -ERIES a nightclub	**NOBBLE**	*v* -BLED, -BLING, -BLES to disable a racehorse
NITID	*adj* bright		
NITINOL	*n* pl. -S an alloy of nickel and titanium	**NOBBLER**	*n* pl. -S one that nobbles
		NOBBY	*adj* -BIER, -BIEST elegant
NITON	*n* pl. -S radon	**NOBELIUM**	*n* pl. -S a radioactive element
NITPICK	*v* -ED, -ING, -S to fuss over petty details	**NOBILITY**	*n* pl. -TIES the social class composed of nobles
NITPICKY	*adj* -PICKIER, -PICKIEST tending to nitpick	**NOBLE**	*adj* -BLER, -BLEST possessing qualities of excellence
NITRATE	*v* -TRATED, -TRATING, -TRATES to treat with nitric acid	**NOBLE**	*n* pl. -S a person of high birth, rank, or title
NITRATOR	*n* pl. -S one that nitrates	**NOBLEMAN**	*n* pl. -MEN a noble
NITRE	*n* pl. -S niter	**NOBLER**	comparative of noble
NITRIC	*adj* containing nitrogen	**NOBLESSE**	*n* pl. -S the nobility
NITRID	*n* pl. -S nitride	**NOBLEST**	superlative of noble
NITRIDE	*v* -TRIDED, -TRIDING, -TRIDES to convert into a nitride (a compound of nitrogen)	**NOBLY**	*adv* in a noble manner
		NOBODY	*n* pl. -BODIES an unimportant person
NITRIFY	*v* -FIED, -FYING, -FIES to combine with nitrogen	**NOCENT**	*adj* harmful
NITRIL	*n* pl. -S nitrile	**NOCK**	*v* -ED, -ING, -S to notch a bow or arrow
NITRILE	*n* pl. -S a chemical compound		
NITRITE	*n* pl. -S a salt of nitrous acid	**NOCTUID**	*n* pl. -S a night-flying moth **NOCTUOID** *adj*
NITRO	*n* pl. -TROS a nitrated product	**NOCTULE**	*n* pl. -S a large bat
NITROGEN	*n* pl. -S a gaseous element	**NOCTURN**	*n* pl. -S a religious service
NITROLIC	*adj* pertaining to a class of acids	**NOCTURNE**	*n* pl. -S a musical composition
NITROSO	*adj* containing nitrosyl	**NOCUOUS**	*adj* harmful
NITROSYL	*n* pl. -S a univalent radical	**NOD**	*v* NODDED, NODDING, NODS to briefly lower the head forward
NITROUS	*adj* containing nitrogen		
NITTY	*adj* -TIER, -TIEST full of nits	**NODAL**	*adj* of the nature of a node **NODALLY** *adv*
NITWIT	*n* pl. -S a stupid person		
NIVAL	*adj* pertaining to snow	**NODALITY**	*n* pl. -TIES the state of being nodal
NIVEOUS	*adj* resembling snow		
NIX	*v* -ED, -ING, -ES to veto	**NODDED**	past tense of nod
NIX	*n* pl. NIXES or NIXE a water sprite	**NODDER**	*n* pl. -S one that nods
		NODDIES	pl. of noddy

NODDING present participle of nod

NODDLE *v* -DLED, -DLING, -DLES to nod frequently

NODDY *n* pl. -DIES a fool

NODE *n* pl. -S a swollen enlargement

NODI pl. of nodus

NODICAL *adj* pertaining to an astronomical point

NODOSE *adj* having nodes

NODOSITY *n* pl. -TIES the state of being nodose

NODOUS *adj* nodose

NODULE *n* pl. -S a small node **NODULAR, NODULOSE, NODULOUS** *adj*

NODUS *n* pl. -DI a difficulty

NOEL *n* pl. -S a Christmas carol

NOES a pl. of no

NOESIS *n* pl. -SISES the process of reason

NOETIC *adj* pertaining to reason

NOG *v* NOGGED, NOGGING, NOGS to fill in a space in a wall with bricks

NOGG *n* pl. -S a strong ale

NOGGIN *n* pl. -S a small cup

NOGGING *n* pl. -S a type of masonry

NOH *n* pl. NOH the classical drama of Japan

NOHOW *adv* in no manner

NOIL *n* pl. -S a kind of short fiber **NOILY** *adj*

NOIR *n* pl. -S a bleak type of crime fiction **NOIRISH** *adj*

NOISE *v* NOISED, NOISING, NOISES to spread as a rumor or report

NOISETTE *n* pl. -S a small round piece of meat

NOISOME *adj* disgusting; harmful

NOISY *adj* NOISIER, NOISIEST making loud sounds **NOISILY** *adv*

NOLO *n* pl. -LOS a type of legal plea

NOM *n* pl. -S a name

NOMA *n* pl. -S a severe inflammation of the mouth

NOMAD *n* pl. -S a wanderer **NOMADIC** *adj*

NOMADISM *n* pl. -S the mode of life of a nomad

NOMARCH *n* pl. -S the head of a nome

NOMARCHY *n* pl. -ARCHIES a nome

NOMBLES *n/pl* numbles

NOMBRIL *n* pl. -S a point on a heraldic shield

NOME *n* pl. -S a province of modern Greece

NOMEN *n* pl. -MINA the second name of an ancient Roman

NOMINAL *n* pl. -S a word used as a noun

NOMINATE *v* -NATED, -NATING, -NATES to name as a candidate

NOMINEE *n* pl. -S one that is nominated

NOMISM *n* pl. -S strict adherence to moral law **NOMISTIC** *adj*

NOMOGRAM *n* pl. -S a type of graph

NOMOLOGY *n* pl. -GIES the science of law

NOMOS *n* pl. NOMOI law

NONA *n* pl. -S a virus disease

NONACID *n* pl. -S a substance that is not an acid

NONACTOR *n* pl. -S a person who is not an actor

NONADULT *n* pl. -S a person who is not an adult

NONAGE *n* pl. -S a period of immaturity

NONAGON *n* pl. -S a nine-sided polygon

NONART *n* pl. -S something that is not art

NONBANK *n* pl. -S a business that is not a bank

NONBASIC *adj* not basic

NONBEING *n* pl. -S lack of being

NONBLACK *n* pl. -S one that is not black

NONBODY *n* pl. -BODIES a person's nonphysical nature

NONBOOK *n* pl. -S a book of little literary merit

NONBRAND *adj* lacking a brand name

NONCASH *adj* other than cash

NONCE *n* pl. -S the present occasion

NONCLASS *n* pl. -ES a lack of class

NONCLING *adj* not clinging

NONCOLA *adj* being a drink that is not a cola

NONCOLOR *n* pl. -S a lack of color

NONCOM *n* pl. -S a noncommissioned officer

NONCRIME *n* pl. -S something that is not a crime

NONDAIRY *adj* having no milk products

NONDANCE *n* pl. -S an unrhythmic dance

NONDRUG	*adj* not involving drugs
NONE	*n* pl. -S one of seven canonical daily periods for prayer and devotion
NONEGO	*n* pl. -GOS all that is not part of the ego
NONELECT	*adj* not chosen
NONELITE	*adj* not belonging to an elite group
NONEMPTY	*adj* not empty
NONENTRY	*n* pl. -TRIES the fact of not entering
NONEQUAL	*n* pl. -S one that is not equal
NONESUCH	*n* pl. -ES a person or thing without an equal
NONET	*n* pl. -S a composition for nine instruments or voices
NONEVENT	*n* pl. -S an expected event that does not occur
NONFACT	*n* pl. -S a statement not based on fact
NONFAN	*n* pl. -S a person who is not a fan (an enthusiast)
NONFARM	*adj* not pertaining to the farm
NONFAT	*adj* having no fat solids
NONFATAL	*adj* not fatal
NONFATTY	*adj* not fatty
NONFINAL	*adj* not being the last
NONFLUID	*n* pl. -S a substance that is not a fluid
NONFOCAL	*adj* not focal
NONFOOD	*adj* pertaining to something other than food
NONFUEL	*adj* not used as a fuel
NONGAME	*adj* not hunted for food, sport, or fur
NONGAY	*n* pl. -S a person who is not a homosexual
NONGLARE	*adj* that does not glare
NONGREEN	*adj* not green
NONGUEST	*n* pl. -S one who is not a guest
NONGUILT	*n* pl. -S the absence of guilt
NONHARDY	*adj* not hardy
NONHEME	*adj* not containing iron that is bound like that of heme
NONHERO	*n* pl. -ROES an antihero
NONHOME	*adj* not taking place in the home
NONHUMAN	*adj* not human
NONIDEAL	*adj* not ideal
NONIMAGE	*adj* not having an image
NONIONIC	*adj* not ionic
NONIRON	*adj* not needing to be ironed
NONISSUE	*n* pl. -S a topic that is not controversial
NONJUROR	*n* pl. -S one who refuses to take a required oath
NONJURY	*adj* not involving a jury
NONLABOR	*adj* not pertaining to labor
NONLEAFY	*adj* not having leaves
NONLEGAL	*adj* not legal
NONLIFE	*n* pl. -LIVES the absence of life
NONLOCAL	*n* pl. -S one that is not local
NONMAJOR	*n* pl. -S a student who is not majoring in a specified subject
NONMAN	*n* pl. -MEN a being that is not a man
NONMEAT	*adj* not containing meat
NONMETAL	*n* pl. -S an element that lacks metallic properties
NONMETRO	*adj* not metropolitan
NONMODAL	*adj* not modal
NONMONEY	*adj* not involving money
NONMORAL	*adj* not pertaining to morals
NONMUSIC	*n* pl. -S inferior music
NONNAVAL	*adj* not naval
NONNEWS	*adj* not being news
NONNOVEL	*n* pl. -S a literary work that is not a novel
NONOBESE	*adj* not obese
NONOHMIC	*adj* not measured in ohms
NONOILY	*adj* not oily
NONOWNER	*n* pl. -S one who is not the owner
NONPAGAN	*n* pl. -S one who is not a pagan
NONPAID	*adj* not paid
NONPAPAL	*adj* not papal
NONPAR	*adj* being a stock that has no face value
NONPARTY	*adj* not affiliated with any political party
NONPAST	*n* pl. -S a verb form that lacks an inflection for a past tense
NONPEAK	*adj* being a time when something is not at its highest level
NONPLAY	*n* pl. -PLAYS a theatrical work that is not a play

NONPLUS *v* -PLUSED, -PLUSING, -PLUSES or -PLUSSED, -PLUSSING, -PLUSSES to baffle

NONPOINT *adj* not occurring at a definite single site

NONPOLAR *adj* not polar

NONPOOR *adj* not being poor

NONPRINT *adj* not involving printed material

NONPROS *v* -PROSSED, -PROSSING, -PROSSES to enter a judgment against a plaintiff who fails to prosecute

NONQUOTA *adj* not included in or subject to a quota

NONRATED *adj* not rated

NONRIGID *adj* not rigid

NONRIVAL *n* pl. -S an unimportant rival

NONROYAL *adj* not royal

NONRURAL *adj* not rural

NONSELF *n* pl. -SELVES foreign material in a body

NONSENSE *n* pl. -S behavior or language that is meaningless or absurd

NONSKED *n* pl. -S an airline without scheduled flying times

NONSKID *adj* designed to inhibit skidding

NONSKIER *n* pl. -S one that does not ski

NONSLIP *adj* designed to prevent slipping

NONSOLAR *adj* not solar

NONSOLID *n* pl. -S a substance that is not a solid

NONSTICK *adj* allowing of easy removal of cooked food particles

NONSTOP *adj* making no stops

NONSTORY *n* pl. -RIES an insignificant news story

NONSTYLE *n* pl. -S a style that is not identifiable

NONSUCH *n* pl. -ES nonesuch

NONSUGAR *n* pl. -S a substance that is not a sugar

NONSUIT *v* -ED, -ING, -S to dismiss the lawsuit of

NONTAX *n* pl. -ES a tax of little consequence

NONTIDAL *adj* not tidal

NONTITLE *adj* pertaining to an athletic contest in which a title is not at stake

NONTONAL *adj* lacking tonality

NONTOXIC *adj* not toxic

NONTRUMP *adj* not having a trump

NONTRUTH *n* pl. -S something that is not true

NONUNION *n* pl. -S failure of a broken bone to heal

NONUPLE *n* pl. -S a number nine times as great as another

NONURBAN *adj* not urban

NONUSE *n* pl. -S failure to use

NONUSER *n* pl. -S one that is not a user

NONUSING *adj* not using

NONVALID *adj* not valid

NONVIRAL *adj* not viral

NONVOCAL *adj* not vocal

NONVOTER *n* pl. -S one that does not vote

NONWAR *n* pl. -S a war that is not officially declared

NONWHITE *n* pl. -S a person who is not of the white race

NONWOODY *adj* not woody

NONWORD *n* pl. -S a word that has no meaning

NONWORK *adj* not involving work

NONWOVEN *n* pl. -S a fabric not made by weaving

NONYL *n* pl. -S an alkyl radical

NONZERO *adj* having a value other than zero

NOO *adv* now

NOODGE *v* NOODGED, NOODGING, NOODGES to nag

NOODLE *v* -DLED, -DLING, -DLES to play idly on a musical instrument

NOOK *n* pl. -S a corner, as in a room **NOOKLIKE** *adj*

NOON *n* pl. -S midday

NOONDAY *n* pl. -DAYS noon

NOONING *n* pl. -S a meal eaten at noon

NOONTIDE *n* pl. -S noon

NOONTIME *n* pl. -S noon

NOOSE *v* NOOSED, NOOSING, NOOSES to secure with a type of loop

NOOSER *n* pl. -S one that nooses

NOPAL *n* pl. -S a cactus

NOPE *adv* no

NOR *conj* and not

NORDIC	*adj* pertaining to cross-country ski racing and ski jumping
NORI	*n* pl. -S dried seaweed pressed into sheets
NORIA	*n* pl. -S a type of waterwheel
NORITE	*n* pl. -S a granular rock **NORITIC** *adj*
NORLAND	*n* pl. -S a region in the north
NORM	*n* pl. -S a standard regarded as typical for a specific group
NORMAL	*n* pl. -S the usual or expected state or form
NORMALCY	*n* pl. -CIES conformity with the norm
NORMALLY	*adv* as a rule; usually
NORMANDE	*adj* prepared with foods associated with Normandy
NORMED	*adj* having a norm
NORMLESS	*adj* having no norm
NORTH	*n* pl. -S a point of the compass
NORTHER	*n* pl. -S a wind or storm from the north
NORTHERN	*n* pl. -S a person living in the north
NORTHING	*n* pl. -S movement toward the north
NOSE	*v* NOSED, NOSING, NOSES to sniff with the nose (the organ of smell)
NOSEBAG	*n* pl. -S a feedbag
NOSEBAND	*n* pl. -S a part of a horse's bridle
NOSED	past tense of nose
NOSEDIVE	*n* pl. -S a steep downward plunge
NOSEGAY	*n* pl. -GAYS a bouquet
NOSELESS	*adj* having no nose
NOSELIKE	*adj* resembling a nose
NOSEY	*adj* NOSIER, NOSIEST nosy
NOSH	*v* -ED, -ING, -ES to eat snacks between meals
NOSHER	*n* pl. -S one that noshes
NOSIER	comparative of nosy, nosey
NOSIEST	superlative of nosy, nosey
NOSILY	*adv* in a nosy manner
NOSINESS	*n* pl. -ES the quality of being nosy
NOSING	*n* pl. -S a projecting edge
NOSOLOGY	*n* pl. -GIES a classification of diseases
NOSTOC	*n* pl. -S a freshwater alga
NOSTRIL	*n* pl. -S an external opening of the nose
NOSTRUM	*n* pl. -S a medicine of one's own invention
NOSY	*adj* NOSIER, NOSIEST unduly curious
NOT	*adv* in no way
NOTA	pl. of notum
NOTABLE	*n* pl. -S a person of distinction
NOTABLY	*adv* in a distinguished manner
NOTAL	*adj* pertaining to a notum
NOTARIAL	*adj* pertaining to a notary
NOTARIZE	*v* -RIZED, -RIZING, -RIZES to certify through a notary
NOTARY	*n* pl. -RIES a public officer who certifies documents
NOTATE	*v* -TATED, -TATING, -TATES to put into notation
NOTATION	*n* pl. -S a system of symbols
NOTCH	*v* -ED, -ING, -ES to make an angular cut in
NOTCHER	*n* pl. -S one that notches
NOTE	*v* NOTED, NOTING, NOTES to write down
NOTEBOOK	*n* pl. -S a book in which to write
NOTECASE	*n* pl. -S a billfold
NOTED	past tense of note
NOTEDLY	*adv* in a famous manner
NOTELESS	*adj* undistinguished
NOTEPAD	*n* pl. -S a number of sheets of paper glued together at one end
NOTER	*n* pl. -S one that notes
NOTHER	*adj* different
NOTHING	*n* pl. -S the absence of all quantity or magnitude
NOTICE	*v* -TICED, -TICING, -TICES to become aware of
NOTICER	*n* pl. -S one that notices
NOTIFIER	*n* pl. -S one that notifies
NOTIFY	*v* -FIED, -FYING, -FIES to inform
NOTING	present participle of note
NOTION	*n* pl. -S a general idea **NOTIONAL** *adj*
NOTORNIS	*n* pl. NOTORNIS a flightless bird
NOTTURNO	*n* pl. -NI a nocturne
NOTUM	*n* pl. -TA a part of the thorax of an insect

NOUGAT   *n* pl. -S a chewy candy

NOUGHT   *n* pl. -S naught

NOUMENON   *n* pl. -MENA an object of intellectual intuition **NOUMENAL** *adj*

NOUN   *n* pl. -S a word used to denote the name of something **NOUNAL, NOUNLESS** *adj* **NOUNALLY** *adv*

NOURISH   *v* -ED, -ING, -ES to sustain with food

NOUS   *n* pl. -ES mind, reason, or intellect

NOUVEAU   *adj* newly arrived or developed

NOUVELLE   *adj* pertaining to a form of French cooking

NOVA   *n* pl. -VAS or -VAE a type of star **NOVALIKE** *adj*

NOVATION   *n* pl. -S the substitution of a new legal obligation for an old one

NOVEL   *n* pl. -S a fictional prose narrative

NOVELISE   *v* -ISED, -ISING, -ISES to novelize

NOVELIST   *n* pl. -S a writer of novels

NOVELIZE   *v* -IZED, -IZING, -IZES to put into the form of a novel

NOVELLA   *n* pl. -LAS or -LE a short novel

NOVELLY   *adv* in a new or unusual manner

NOVELTY   *n* pl. -TIES something new or unusual

NOVENA   *n* pl. -NAS or -NAE a religious devotion lasting nine days

NOVERCAL   *adj* pertaining to a stepmother

NOVICE   *n* pl. -S a person new to any field or activity

NOW   *n* pl. -S the present time

NOWADAYS   *adv* in these times

NOWAY   *adv* in no way

NOWAYS   *adv* noway

NOWHERE   *n* pl. -S a nonexistent place

NOWISE   *adv* not at all

NOWNESS   *n* pl. -ES the state of existing at the present time

NOWT   *n* pl. -S naught

NOXIOUS   *adj* harmful to health

NOYADE   *n* pl. -S an execution by drowning

NOZZLE   *n* pl. -S a projecting spout

NTH   *adj* pertaining to an indefinitely large ordinal number

NU   *n* pl. -S a Greek letter

NUANCE   *n* pl. -S a slight variation **NUANCED** *adj*

NUB   *n* pl. -S a protuberance or knob

NUBBIER   comparative of nubby

NUBBIEST   superlative of nubby

NUBBIN   *n* pl. -S an undeveloped fruit

NUBBLE   *n* pl. -S a small nub

NUBBLY   *adj* -BLIER, -BLIEST having nubbles

NUBBY   *adj* -BIER, -BIEST having nubs

NUBIA   *n* pl. -S a woman's scarf

NUBILE   *adj* suitable for marriage

NUBILITY   *n* pl. -TIES the quality of being nubile

NUBILOSE   *adj* nubilous

NUBILOUS   *adj* cloudy

NUCELLUS   *n* pl. -LI the essential part of a plant ovule **NUCELLAR** *adj*

NUCHA   *n* pl. -CHAE the nape of the neck

NUCHAL   *n* pl. -S an anatomical part lying in the region of the nape

NUCLEAL   *adj* nuclear

NUCLEAR   *adj* pertaining to a nucleus

NUCLEASE   *n* pl. -S an enzyme

NUCLEATE   *v* -ATED, -ATING, -ATES to form into a nucleus

NUCLEI   a pl. of nucleus

NUCLEIN   *n* pl. -S a protein found in nuclei

NUCLEOID   *n* pl. -S the DNA-containing area of certain cells

NUCLEOLE   *n* pl. -S a part of a nucleus

NUCLEOLI   *n/pl* nucleoles

NUCLEON   *n* pl. -S a subatomic particle

NUCLEUS   *n* pl. -CLEI or -CLEUSES an essential part of a cell

NUCLIDE   *n* pl. -S a species of atom **NUCLIDIC** *adj*

NUDE   *adj* NUDER, NUDEST being without clothing or covering **NUDELY** *adv*

NUDE   *n* pl. -S a nude figure

NUDENESS   *n* pl. -ES nudity

NUDER   comparative of nude

NUDEST   superlative of nude

NUDGE   *v* NUDGED, NUDGING, NUDGES to push gently

NUDGER   *n* pl. -S one that nudges

NUDICAUL   *adj* having leafless stems

NUDIE _n_ pl. -S a movie featuring nude performers

NUDISM _n_ pl. -S the practice of going nude

NUDIST _n_ pl. -S an advocate of nudism

NUDITY _n_ pl. -TIES the state of being nude

NUDNICK _n_ pl. -S nudnik

NUDNIK _n_ pl. -S an annoying person

NUDZH _v_ -ED, -ING, -ES to noodge

NUGATORY _adj_ having no power

NUGGET _n_ pl. -S a mass of solid matter **NUGGETY** _adj_

NUISANCE _n_ pl. -S a source of annoyance

NUKE _v_ NUKED, NUKING, NUKES to attack with nuclear weapons

NULL _v_ -ED, -ING, -S to reduce to nothing

NULLAH _n_ pl. -S a ravine

NULLIFY _v_ -FIED, -FYING, -FIES to make useless or ineffective

NULLITY _n_ pl. -TIES something of no legal force

NUMB _adj_ NUMBER, NUMBEST lacking sensation

NUMB _v_ -ED, -ING, -S to make numb

NUMBAT _n_ pl. -S a small Australian mammal

NUMBER _v_ -ED, -ING, -S to count

NUMBERER _n_ pl. -S one that numbers

NUMBFISH _n_ pl. -ES a fish capable of emitting electric shocks

NUMBLES _n/pl_ animal entrails

NUMBLY _adv_ in a numb manner

NUMBNESS _n_ pl. -ES the state of being numb

NUMEN _n_ pl. -MINA a deity

NUMERACY _n_ pl. -CIES the ability to understand basic mathematics

NUMERAL _n_ pl. -S a symbol that expresses a number

NUMERARY _adj_ pertaining to numbers

NUMERATE _v_ -ATED, -ATING, -ATES to count

NUMERIC _n_ pl. -S a numeral

NUMEROUS _adj_ many

NUMINA pl. of numen

NUMINOUS _n_ pl. -ES the presence or revelation of the numen

NUMMARY _adj_ pertaining to coins

NUMMULAR _adj_ shaped like a coin

NUMSKULL _n_ pl. -S a dunce

NUN _n_ pl. -S a woman belonging to a religious order

NUNATAK _n_ pl. -S a mountain peak completely surrounded by glacial ice

NUNCHAKU _n_ pl. -S a Japanese weapon

NUNCIO _n_ pl. -CIOS an ambassador from the pope

NUNCLE _n_ pl. -S an uncle

NUNLIKE _adj_ resembling a nun

NUNNERY _n_ pl. -NERIES a religious house for nuns

NUNNISH _adj_ of, pertaining to, or characteristic of a nun

NUPTIAL _n_ pl. -S a wedding

NURD _n_ pl. -S nerd

NURL _v_ -ED, -ING, -S to knurl

NURSE _v_ NURSED, NURSING, NURSES to care for the sick or infirm

NURSER _n_ pl. -S a baby's bottle

NURSERY _n_ pl. -ERIES a room for young children

NURSING _n_ pl. -S the profession of one who nurses

NURSLING _n_ pl. -S an infant

NURTURAL _adj_ pertaining to the process of nurturing

NURTURE _v_ -TURED, -TURING, -TURES to nourish

NURTURER _n_ pl. -S one that nurtures

NUT _v_ NUTTED, NUTTING, NUTS to gather nuts (hard-shelled dry fruits)

NUTANT _adj_ drooping

NUTATE _v_ -TATED, -TATING, -TATES to exhibit nutation

NUTATION _n_ pl. -S an oscillatory movement of the axis of a rotating body

NUTBROWN _adj_ of a dark brown

NUTCASE _n_ pl. -S a crazy person

NUTGALL _n_ pl. -S a gallnut

NUTGRASS _n_ pl. -ES a perennial herb

NUTHATCH _n_ pl. -ES a small bird

NUTHOUSE _n_ pl. -S an insane asylum

NUTLET _n_ pl. -S a small nut

NUTLIKE _adj_ resembling a nut

NUTMEAT _n_ pl. -S the edible kernel of a nut

NUTMEG   *n* pl. -S an aromatic seed used as a spice

NUTPICK   *n* pl. -S a device for extracting the kernels from nuts

NUTRIA   *n* pl. -S the coypu

NUTRIENT   *n* pl. -S a nourishing substance

NUTSEDGE   *n* pl. -S nutgrass

NUTSHELL   *n* pl. -S the shell of a nut

NUTSY   *adj* NUTSIER, NUTSIEST crazy

NUTTED   past tense of nut

NUTTER   *n* pl. -S one that gathers nuts

NUTTING   *n* pl. -S the act of gathering nuts

NUTTY   *adj* -TIER, -TIEST silly; crazy **NUTTILY** *adv*

NUTWOOD   *n* pl. -S a nut-bearing tree

NUZZLE   *v* -ZLED, -ZLING, -ZLES to push with the nose

NUZZLER   *n* pl. -S one that nuzzles

NYALA   *n* pl. -S an antelope

NYLGHAI   *n* pl. -S nilgai

NYLGHAU   *n* pl. -S nilgai

NYLON   *n* pl. -S a synthetic material

NYMPH   *n* pl. -S a female spirit **NYMPHAL, NYMPHEAN** *adj*

NYMPHA   *n* pl. -PHAE a fold of the vulva

NYMPHET   *n* pl. -S a young nymph

NYMPHO   *n* pl. -PHOS a woman obsessed by sexual desire

NYSTATIN   *n* pl. -S an antibiotic

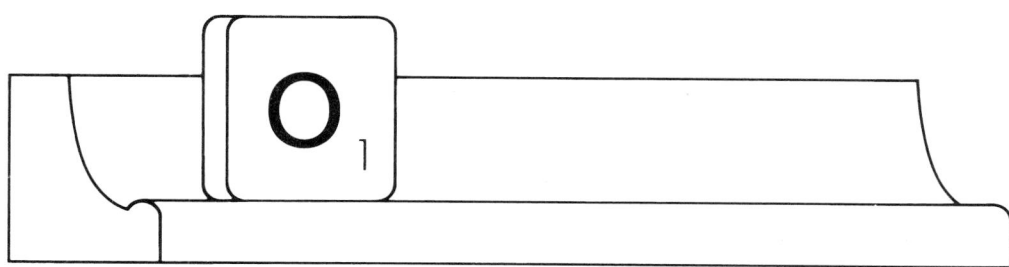

OAF   *n* pl. OAFS or OAVES a clumsy, stupid person **OAFISH** *adj* **OAFISHLY** *adv*

OAK   *n* pl. -S a hardwood tree or shrub **OAKEN, OAKLIKE** *adj*

OAKMOSS   *n* pl. -ES a lichen that grows on oak trees

OAKUM   *n* pl. -S loosely twisted hemp fiber

OAR   *v* -ED, -ING, -S to propel with oars (long, broad-bladed poles)

OARFISH   *n* pl. -ES a marine fish

OARLESS   *adj* having no oars

OARLIKE   *adj* resembling an oar

OARLOCK   *n* pl. -S a device for holding an oar in place

OARSMAN   *n* pl. -MEN a person who rows a boat

OASIS   *n* pl. OASES a green area in a desert region

OAST   *n* pl. -S a type of kiln

OAT   *n* pl. -S a cereal grass

OATCAKE   *n* pl. -S a cake made of oatmeal

OATEN   *adj* pertaining to oats

OATER   *n* pl. -S a cowboy movie

OATH   *n* pl. -S a formal declaration or promise to fulfill a pledge

OATLIKE   *adj* resembling oats

OATMEAL   *n* pl. -S meal made from oats

OAVES   a pl. of oaf

OBCONIC   *adj* conical with the apex below

OBDURACY   *n* pl. -CIES the quality or an instance of being obdurate

OBDURATE   *adj* stubborn

OBE   *n* pl. -S obeah

OBEAH   *n* pl. -S a form of sorcery of African origin

OBEAHISM   *n* pl. -S the use of obeah

OBEDIENT   *adj* obeying or willing to obey

OBEISANT   *adj* showing reverence or respect

OBELI   pl. of obelus

OBELIA   *n* pl. -S a marine hydroid

OBELISE   *v* -LISED, -LISING, -LISES to obelize

OBELISK   *n* pl. -S a four-sided shaft of stone with a pyramidal top

OBELISM   *n* pl. -S the act of obelizing

OBELIZE   *v* -LIZED, -LIZING, -LIZES to mark with an obelus

OBELUS   *n* pl. -LI a symbol used in ancient manuscripts to indicate a doubtful passage

OBESE   *adj* very fat **OBESELY** *adv*

OBESITY   *n* pl. -TIES the state or condition of being obese

OBEY   *v* -ED, -ING, -S to follow the commands or guidance of **OBEYABLE** *adj*

OBEYER   *n* pl. -S one that obeys

OBI   *n* pl. -S obeah

OBIA   *n* pl. -S obeah

OBIISM   *n* pl. -S obeahism

OBIT   *n* pl. -S an obituary

OBITUARY   *n* pl. -ARIES a published notice of a death

OBJECT   *v* -ED, -ING, -S to argue in opposition

OBJECTOR   *n* pl. -S one that objects

OBJET   *n* pl. -S an article of artistic value

OBLAST   *n* pl. -LASTS or -LASTI an administrative division of Russia

OBLATE   *n* pl. -S a layman residing in a monastery

OBLATELY   *adv* elliptically

OBLATION   *n* pl. -S the act of making a religious offering **OBLATORY** *adj*

OBLIGATE	*v* -GATED, -GATING, -GATES to oblige
OBLIGATO	*n* pl. -TI or -TOS an important musical part
OBLIGE	*v* OBLIGED, OBLIGING, OBLIGES to put in one's debt by a favor or service
OBLIGEE	*n* pl. -S one that is obliged
OBLIGER	*n* pl. -S one that obliges
OBLIGING	present participle of oblige
OBLIGOR	*n* pl. -S one who places himself under a legal obligation
OBLIQUE	*v* OBLIQUED, OBLIQUING, OBLIQUES to slant
OBLIVION	*n* pl. -S the state of being forgotten; the act of forgetting
OBLONG	*n* pl. -S something that is oblong (elongated)
OBLONGLY	*adv* in an oblong manner
OBLOQUY	*n* pl. -QUIES abusive language
OBOE	*n* pl. -S a woodwind instrument
OBOIST	*n* pl. -S one who plays the oboe
OBOL	*n* pl. -S a coin of ancient Greece
OBOLE	*n* pl. -S a coin of medieval France
OBOLUS	*n* pl. -LI an obol
OBOVATE	*adj* ovate with the narrow end at the base
OBOVOID	*adj* ovoid with the narrow end at the base
OBSCENE	*adj* -SCENER, -SCENEST indecent
OBSCURE	*adj* -SCURER, -SCUREST dark or indistinct
OBSCURE	*v* -SCURED, -SCURING, -SCURES to make obscure
OBSEQUY	*n* pl. -QUIES a funeral rite
OBSERVE	*v* -SERVED, -SERVING, -SERVES to look attentively
OBSERVER	*n* pl. -S one that observes
OBSESS	*v* -ED, -ING, -ES to dominate the thoughts of
OBSESSOR	*n* pl. -S something that obsesses
OBSIDIAN	*n* pl. -S a volcanic glass
OBSOLETE	*v* -LETED, -LETING, -LETES to make out-of-date
OBSTACLE	*n* pl. -S something that obstructs
OBSTRUCT	*v* -ED, -ING, -S to get in the way of
OBTAIN	*v* -ED, -ING, -S to gain possession of
OBTAINER	*n* pl. -S one that obtains
OBTECT	*adj* covered by a hardened secretion
OBTECTED	*adj* obtect
OBTEST	*v* -ED, -ING, -S to beseech
OBTRUDE	*v* -TRUDED, -TRUDING, -TRUDES to thrust forward
OBTRUDER	*n* pl. -S one that obtrudes
OBTUND	*v* -ED, -ING, -S to deaden
OBTURATE	*v* -RATED, -RATING, -RATES to close or stop up
OBTUSE	*adj* -TUSER, -TUSEST dull **OBTUSELY** *adv*
OBTUSITY	*n* pl. -TIES the state of being obtuse
OBVERSE	*n* pl. -S the side of a coin bearing the main design
OBVERT	*v* -ED, -ING, -S to turn so as to show a different surface
OBVIATE	*v* -ATED, -ATING, -ATES to prevent or eliminate by effective measures **OBVIABLE** *adj*
OBVIATOR	*n* pl. -S one that obviates
OBVIOUS	*adj* easily perceived or understood
OBVOLUTE	*adj* rolled or tuned in
OCA	*n* pl. -S a South American herb
OCARINA	*n* pl. -S a wind instrument
OCCASION	*v* -ED, -ING, -S to cause
OCCIDENT	*n* pl. -S the west
OCCIPUT	*n* pl. -PITA or -PUTS the back part of the skull
OCCLUDE	*v* -CLUDED, -CLUDING, -CLUDES to close or stop up
OCCLUSAL	*adj* pertaining to the biting surface of a tooth
OCCULT	*v* -ED, -ING, -S to conceal
OCCULTER	*n* pl. -S one that occults
OCCULTLY	*adv* secretly
OCCUPANT	*n* pl. -S a resident
OCCUPIER	*n* pl. -S one who occupies
OCCUPY	*v* -PIED, -PYING, -PIES to engage the attention or energies of
OCCUR	*v* -CURRED, -CURRING, -CURS to take place

OCEAN	*n* pl. -S the vast body of salt water that covers most of the earth's surface **OCEANIC** *adj*
OCEANAUT	*n* pl. -S an aquanaut
OCELLAR	*adj* pertaining to an ocellus
OCELLATE	*adj* having ocelli
OCELLUS	*n* pl. -LI a minute simple eye
OCELOT	*n* pl. -S an American wildcat **OCELOID** *adj*
OCHER	*v* -ED, -ING, -S to color with ocher (a red or yellow iron ore used as a pigment)
OCHEROUS	*adj* containing or resembling ocher
OCHERY	*adj* ocherous
OCHONE	*interj* — used to express grief
OCHRE	*v* OCHRED, OCHRING, OCHRES to ocher
OCHREA	*n* pl. -REAE ocrea
OCHREOUS	*adj* ocherous
OCHRING	present participle of ochre
OCHROID	*adj* ocherous
OCHROUS	*adj* ocherous
OCHRY	*adj* ochery
OCKER	*n* pl. -S a boorish person
OCOTILLO	*n* pl. -LOS a Mexican shrub
OCREA	*n* pl. -REAE a sheathing plant part
OCREATE	*adj* having ocreae
OCTAD	*n* pl. -S a group of eight **OCTADIC** *adj*
OCTAGON	*n* pl. -S an eight-sided polygon
OCTAL	*adj* pertaining to a number system with a base of eight
OCTAN	*n* pl. -S a fever recurring every eighth day
OCTANE	*n* pl. -S a liquid hydrocarbon
OCTANGLE	*n* pl. -S an octagon
OCTANOL	*n* pl. -S an alcohol
OCTANT	*n* pl. -S an eighth of a circle **OCTANTAL** *adj*
OCTARCHY	*n* pl. -TARCHIES a government by eight persons
OCTAVE	*n* pl. -S a type of musical interval **OCTAVAL** *adj*
OCTAVO	*n* pl. -VOS a page size
OCTET	*n* pl. -S a group of eight
OCTETTE	*n* pl. -S octet

OCTONARY	*n* pl. -NARIES a stanza of eight lines
OCTOPOD	*n* pl. -S any of an order of eight-armed mollusks
OCTOPUS	*n* pl. -PUSES, -PI, or -PODES a nocturnal octopod
OCTOROON	*n* pl. -S a person of one-eighth black ancestry
OCTROI	*n* pl. -S a tax on certain articles brought into a city
OCTUPLE	*v* -PLED, -PLING, -PLES to multiply by eight
OCTUPLET	*n* pl. -S a group of eight related items
OCTUPLEX	*adj* being eight times as great
OCTUPLING	present participle of octuple
OCTUPLY	*adv* to eight times the degree
OCTYL	*n* pl. -S a univalent radical
OCULAR	*n* pl. -S an eyepiece
OCULARLY	*adv* by means of the eyes or sight
OCULIST	*n* pl. -S a physician who treats diseases of the eye
OCULUS	*n* pl. -LI a circular window
OD	*n* pl. -S a hypothetical force of natural power
ODALISK	*n* pl. -S a female slave in a harem
ODD	*adj* ODDER, ODDEST unusual
ODD	*n* pl. -S one that is odd
ODDBALL	*n* pl. -S an eccentric person
ODDISH	*adj* somewhat odd
ODDITY	*n* pl. -TIES one that is odd
ODDLY	*adv* in an odd manner
ODDMENT	*n* pl. -S a remnant
ODDNESS	*n* pl. -ES the state of being odd
ODE	*n* pl. -S a lyric poem
ODEON	*n* pl. -S odeum
ODEUM	*n* pl. ODEA or ODEUMS a theater or concert hall
ODIC	*adj* pertaining to an ode
ODIOUS	*adj* deserving or causing hatred **ODIOUSLY** *adv*
ODIST	*n* pl. -S one who writes odes
ODIUM	*n* pl. -S hatred
ODOGRAPH	*n* pl. -S an odometer
ODOMETER	*n* pl. -S a device for measuring distance traveled

ODOMETRY	*n* pl. -TRIES the process of using an odometer
ODONATE	*n* pl. -S any of an order of predacious insects
ODONTOID	*n* pl. -S a toothlike vertebral projection
ODOR	*n* pl. -S the property of a substance that affects the sense of smell **ODORED, ODORFUL** *adj*
ODORANT	*n* pl. -S an odorous substance
ODORIZE	*v* -IZED, -IZING, -IZES to make odorous
ODORLESS	*adj* having no odor
ODOROUS	*adj* having an odor
ODOUR	*n* pl. -S odor **ODOURFUL** *adj*
ODYL	*n* pl. -S an od
ODYLE	*n* pl. -S odyl
ODYSSEY	*n* pl. -SEYS a long, wandering journey
OE	*n* pl. -S a whirlwind off the Faeroe islands
OECOLOGY	*n* pl. -GIES ecology
OEDEMA	*n* pl. -MAS or -MATA edema
OEDIPAL	*adj* pertaining to the libidinal feelings in a child toward the parent of the opposite sex
OEDIPEAN	*adj* oedipal
OEILLADE	*n* pl. -S an amorous look
OENOLOGY	*n* pl. -GIES the study of wines
OENOMEL	*n* pl. -S an ancient Greek beverage of wine and honey
OERSTED	*n* pl. -S a unit of magnetic intensity
OESTRIN	*n* pl. -S estrin
OESTRIOL	*n* pl. -S estriol
OESTRONE	*n* pl. -S estrone
OESTROUS	*adj* estrous
OESTRUM	*n* pl. -S estrum
OESTRUS	*n* pl. -ES estrus
OEUVRE	*n* pl. -S a work of art
OF	*prep* coming from
OFF	*v* -ED, -ING, -S to go away
OFFAL	*n* pl. -S waste material
OFFBEAT	*n* pl. -S an unaccented beat in a musical measure
OFFCAST	*n* pl. -S a castoff
OFFCUT	*n* pl. -S something that is cut off
OFFENCE	*n* pl. -S offense

OFFEND	*v* -ED, -ING, -S to commit an offense
OFFENDER	*n* pl. -S one that offends
OFFENSE	*n* pl. -S a violation of a moral or social code
OFFER	*v* -ED, -ING, -S to present for acceptance or rejection
OFFERER	*n* pl. -S one that offers
OFFERING	*n* pl. -S a contribution
OFFEROR	*n* pl. -S offerer
OFFHAND	*adv* without preparation
OFFICE	*n* pl. -S a position of authority
OFFICER	*v* -ED, -ING, -S to furnish with officers (persons holding positions of authority)
OFFICIAL	*n* pl. -S one that holds a position of authority
OFFING	*n* pl. -S the near future
OFFISH	*adj* aloof **OFFISHLY** *adv*
OFFKEY	*adj* pitched higher or lower than the correct musical tone
OFFLOAD	*v* -ED, -ING, -S to unload
OFFPRINT	*v* -ED, -ING, -S to reprint an excerpt
OFFRAMP	*n* pl. -S a road leading off an expressway
OFFSET	*v* -SET, -SETTING, -SETS to compensate for
OFFSHOOT	*n* pl. -S a lateral shoot from a main stem
OFFSHORE	*adv* away from the shore
OFFSIDE	*n* pl. -S an improper football play
OFFSTAGE	*n* pl. -S a part of a stage not visible to the audience
OFFTRACK	*adj* away from a racetrack
OFT	*adv* OFTER, OFTEST often
OFTEN	*adv* -ENER, -ENEST frequently
OFTTIMES	*adv* often
OGAM	*n* pl. -S ogham
OGDOAD	*n* pl. -S a group of eight
OGEE	*n* pl. -S an S-shaped molding
OGHAM	*n* pl. -S an Old Irish alphabet **OGHAMIC** *adj*
OGHAMIST	*n* pl. -S one who writes in ogham
OGIVE	*n* pl. -S a pointed arch **OGIVAL** *adj*
OGLE	*v* OGLED, OGLING, OGLES to stare at
OGLER	*n* pl. -S one that ogles

OGRE	*n* pl. -S a monster
OGREISH	*adj* resembling an ogre
OGREISM	*n* pl. -S the state of being ogreish
OGRESS	*n* pl. -ES a female ogre
OGRISH	*adj* ogreish **OGRISHLY** *adv*
OGRISM	*n* pl. -S ogreism
OH	*v* -ED, -ING, -S to exclaim in surprise, pain, or desire
OHIA	*n* pl. -S lehua
OHM	*n* pl. -S a unit of electrical resistance **OHMIC** *adj*
OHMAGE	*n* pl. -S electrical resistance expressed in ohms
OHMMETER	*n* pl. -S an instrument for measuring ohmage
OHO	*interj* — used to express surprise or exultation
OIDIUM	*n* pl. OIDIA a type of fungus
OIL	*v* -ED, -ING, -S to supply with oil (a greasy liquid used for lubrication, fuel, or illumination)
OILBIRD	*n* pl. -S a tropical bird
OILCAMP	*n* pl. -S a living area for workers at an oil well
OILCAN	*n* pl. -S a can for applying lubricating oil
OILCLOTH	*n* pl. -S a waterproof fabric
OILCUP	*n* pl. -S a closed cup for supplying lubricant
OILER	*n* pl. -S one that oils
OILHOLE	*n* pl. -S a hole through which lubricating oil is injected
OILIER	comparative of oily
OILIEST	superlative of oily
OILILY	*adv* in an oily manner
OILINESS	*n* pl. -ES the state of being oily
OILMAN	*n* pl. -MEN one who owns or operates oil wells
OILPAPER	*n* pl. -S a water-resistant paper
OILPROOF	*adj* impervious to oil
OILSEED	*n* pl. -S a seed from which oil is pressed out
OILSKIN	*n* pl. -S a waterproof fabric
OILSTONE	*n* pl. -S a stone for sharpening tools
OILTIGHT	*adj* being so tight as to prevent the passage of oil
OILWAY	*n* pl. -WAYS a channel for the passage of oil
OILY	*adj* OILIER, OILIEST covered or soaked with oil
OINK	*v* -ED, -ING, -S to utter the natural grunt of a hog
OINOLOGY	*n* pl. -GIES oenology
OINOMEL	*n* pl. -S oenomel
OINTMENT	*n* pl. -S a viscous preparation applied to the skin as a medicine or cosmetic
OITICICA	*n* pl. -S a South American tree
OKA	*n* pl. -S a Turkish unit of weight
OKAPI	*n* pl. -S an African ruminant mammal
OKAY	*v* -ED, -ING, -S to approve
OKE	*n* pl. -S oka
OKEH	*n* pl. -S approval
OKEYDOKE	*adj* perfectly all right
OKRA	*n* pl. -S a tall annual herb
OLD	*adj* OLDER, OLDEST or ELDER, ELDEST living or existing for a relatively long time
OLD	*n* pl. -S an individual of a specified age
OLDEN	*adj* pertaining to a bygone era
OLDIE	*n* pl. -S a popular song of an earlier day
OLDISH	*adj* somewhat old
OLDNESS	*n* pl. -ES the state of being old
OLDSQUAW	*n* pl. -S a sea duck
OLDSTER	*n* pl. -S an old person
OLDSTYLE	*n* pl. -S a style of printing type
OLDWIFE	*n* pl. -WIVES a marine fish
OLDY	*n* pl. OLDIES oldie
OLE	*n* pl. -S a shout of approval
OLEA	pl. of oleum
OLEANDER	*n* pl. -S a flowering shrub
OLEASTER	*n* pl. -S a flowering shrub
OLEATE	*n* pl. -S a chemical salt
OLEFIN	*n* pl. -S an alkene **OLEFINIC** *adj*
OLEFINE	*n* pl. -S olefin
OLEIC	*adj* pertaining to oil
OLEIN	*n* pl. -S the liquid portion of a fat
OLEINE	*n* pl. -S olein
OLEO	*n* pl. OLEOS margarine
OLEUM	*n* pl. OLEA oil
OLEUM	*n* pl. -S a corrosive liquid
OLIBANUM	*n* pl. -S a fragrant resin

OLIGARCH *n* pl. -S a ruler in a government by the few

OLIGOMER *n* pl. -S a type of polymer

OLIGURIA *n* pl. -S reduced excretion of urine

OLIO *n* pl. OLIOS a miscellaneous collection

OLIVARY *adj* shaped like an olive

OLIVE *n* pl. -S the small oval fruit of a Mediterranean tree

OLIVINE *n* pl. -S a mineral **OLIVINIC** *adj*

OLLA *n* pl. -S a wide-mouthed pot or jar

OLOGIST *n* pl. -S an expert in a particular ology

OLOGY *n* pl. -GIES a branch of knowledge

OLOROSO *n* pl. -SOS a dark sherry

OLYMPIAD *n* pl. -S a celebration of the Olympic Games

OM *n* pl. -S a mantra used in contemplation of ultimate reality

OMASUM *n* pl. -SA the third stomach of a ruminant

OMBER *n* pl. -S ombre

OMBRE *n* pl. -S a card game

OMEGA *n* pl. -S a Greek letter

OMELET *n* pl. -S a dish of beaten eggs cooked and folded around a filling

OMELETTE *n* pl. -S omelet

OMEN *v* -ED, -ING, -S to be an omen (a prophetic sign) of

OMENTUM *n* pl. -TA or -TUMS a fold in an abdominal membrane **OMENTAL** *adj*

OMER *n* pl. -S a Hebrew unit of dry measure

OMICRON *n* pl. -S a Greek letter

OMIKRON *n* pl. -S omicron

OMINOUS *adj* portending evil

OMISSION *n* pl. -S something left undone

OMISSIVE *adj* marked by omission

OMIT *v* OMITTED, OMITTING, OMITS to leave out

OMITTER *n* pl. -S one that omits

OMNIARCH *n* pl. -S an almighty ruler

OMNIBUS *n* pl. -ES a bus

OMNIFIC *adj* unlimited in creative power

OMNIFORM *adj* of all forms

OMNIMODE *adj* of all modes

OMNIVORA *n/pl* omnivores

OMNIVORE *n* pl. -S an animal that eats all kinds of food

OMOPHAGY *n* pl. -GIES the eating of raw flesh

OMPHALOS *n* pl. -LI a central point

ON *n* pl. -S the side of the wicket where a batsman stands in cricket

ONAGER *n* pl. -GERS or -GRI a wild ass of central Asia

ONANISM *n* pl. -S coitus deliberately interrupted to prevent insemination

ONANIST *n* pl. -S one who practices onanism

ONBOARD *adj* carried aboard a vehicle

ONCE *n* one single time

ONCIDIUM *n* pl. -S a tropical orchid

ONCOGENE *n* pl. -S a gene that causes a cell to become cancerous

ONCOLOGY *n* pl. -GIES the science of tumors

ONCOMING *n* pl. -S an approach

ONDOGRAM *n* pl. -S a graph of electric wave forms

ONE *n* pl. -S a number

ONEFOLD *adj* constituting a single, undivided whole

ONEIRIC *adj* pertaining to dreams

ONENESS *n* pl. -ES unity

ONEROUS *adj* burdensome or oppressive

ONERY *adj* -ERIER, -ERIEST ornery

ONESELF *pron* a person's self

ONETIME *adj* former

ONGOING *adj* continuing without interruption

ONION *n* pl. -S the edible bulb of a cultivated herb **ONIONY** *adj*

ONIUM *adj* characterized by a complex cation

ONLOOKER *n* pl. -S a spectator

ONLY *adv* with nothing or no one else

ONRUSH *n* pl. -ES a forward rush or flow

ONSET *n* pl. -S a beginning

ONSHORE *adv* toward the shore

ONSIDE *adj* not offside

ONSTAGE *adj* being on a part of the stage visible to the audience

ONSTREAM	*adv* in or into production
ONTIC	*adj* having real being or existence
ONTO	*prep* to a position upon
ONTOGENY	*n* pl. -NIES the development of an individual organism
ONTOLOGY	*n* pl. -GIES the branch of philosophy that deals with being
ONUS	*n* pl. -ES a burden or responsibility
ONWARD	*adv* toward a point ahead or in front
ONWARDS	*adv* onward
ONYX	*n* pl. -ES a variety of quartz
OOCYST	*n* pl. -S a zygote
OOCYTE	*n* pl. -S an egg before maturation
OODLES	*n* pl. OODLES a large amount
OODLINS	*n* pl. OODLINS oodles
OOGAMETE	*n* pl. -S a female gamete of certain protozoa
OOGAMOUS	*adj* having structurally dissimilar gametes
OOGAMY	*n* pl. -MIES the state of being oogamous
OOGENY	*n* pl. -NIES the development of ova
OOGONIUM	*n* pl. -NIA or -NIUMS a female sexual organ in certain algae and fungi **OOGONIAL** *adj*
OOH	*v* -ED, -ING, -S to exclaim in amazement, joy, or surprise
OOLACHAN	*n* pl. -S eulachon
OOLITE	*n* pl. -S a variety of limestone **OOLITIC** *adj*
OOLITH	*n* pl. -S oolite
OOLOGIST	*n* pl. -S an expert in oology
OOLOGY	*n* pl. -GIES the study of birds' eggs **OOLOGIC** *adj*
OOLONG	*n* pl. -S a dark Chinese tea
OOMIAC	*n* pl. -S umiak
OOMIACK	*n* pl. -S umiak
OOMIAK	*n* pl. -S umiak
OOMPAH	*v* -ED, -ING, -S to play a repeated rhythmic bass accompaniment
OOMPH	*n* pl. -S spirited vigor
OOPHYTE	*n* pl. -S a stage of development in certain plants **OOPHYTIC** *adj*
OOPS	*interj* — used to express mild apology, surprise, or dismay

OORALI	*n* pl. -S curare
OORIE	*adj* ourie
OOSPERM	*n* pl. -S a fertilized egg
OOSPHERE	*n* pl. -S an unfertilized egg within an oogonium
OOSPORE	*n* pl. -S a fertilized egg within an oogonium **OOSPORIC** *adj*
OOT	*n* pl. -S out
OOTHECA	*n* pl. -CAE an egg case of certain insects **OOTHECAL** *adj*
OOTID	*n* pl. -S one of the four sections into which a mature ovum divides
OOZE	*v* OOZED, OOZING, OOZES to flow or leak out slowly
OOZINESS	*n* pl. -ES the state of being oozy
OOZY	*adj* OOZIER, OOZIEST containing or resembling soft mud or slime **OOZILY** *adv*
OP	*n* pl. -S a style of abstract art
OPACIFY	*v* -FIED, -FYING, -FIES to make opaque
OPACITY	*n* pl. -TIES something that is opaque
OPAH	*n* pl. -S a marine fish
OPAL	*n* pl. -S a mineral
OPALESCE	*v* -ESCED, -ESCING, -ESCES to emit an iridescent shimmer of colors
OPALINE	*n* pl. -S an opaque white glass
OPAQUE	*adj* OPAQUER, OPAQUEST impervious to light **OPAQUELY** *adv*
OPAQUE	*v* OPAQUED, OPAQUING, OPAQUES to make opaque
OPE	*v* OPED, OPING, OPES to open
OPEN	*adj* OPENER, OPENEST affording unobstructed access, passage, or view
OPEN	*v* -ED, -ING, -S to cause to become open **OPENABLE** *adj*
OPENCAST	*adj* worked from a surface open to the air
OPENER	*n* pl. -S one that opens
OPENING	*n* pl. -S a vacant or unobstructed space
OPENLY	*adv* in an open manner
OPENNESS	*n* pl. -ES the state of being open
OPENWORK	*n* pl. -S ornamental or structural work containing numerous openings
OPERA	*n* pl. -S a form of musical drama

OPERABLE *adj* capable of being used **OPERABLY** *adv*

OPERAND *n* pl. -S a quantity on which a mathematical operation is performed

OPERANT *n* pl. -S one that operates

OPERATE *v* -ATED, -ATING, -ATES to perform a function

OPERATIC *n* pl. -S the technique of staging operas

OPERATOR *n* pl. -S a symbol that represents a mathematical function

OPERCELE *n* pl. -S opercule

OPERCULA *n/pl* opercules

OPERCULE *n* pl. -S an anatomical part that serves as a lid or cover

OPERETTA *n* pl. -S a light musical drama with spoken dialogue

OPERON *n* pl. -S a type of gene cluster

OPEROSE *adj* involving great labor

OPHIDIAN *n* pl. -S a snake

OPHITE *n* pl. -S a green mottled igneous rock **OPHITIC** *adj*

OPIATE *v* -ATED, -ATING, -ATES to treat with opium

OPINE *v* OPINED, OPINING, OPINES to hold or state as an opinion

OPING present participle of ope

OPINION *n* pl. -S a conclusion or judgment one holds to be true

OPIOID *n* pl. -S a peptide that acts like opium

OPIUM *n* pl. -S an addictive narcotic

OPIUMISM *n* pl. -S opium addiction

OPPIDAN *n* pl. -S a townsman

OPPILATE *v* -LATED, -LATING, -LATES to obstruct **OPPILANT** *adj*

OPPONENT *n* pl. -S one that opposes another

OPPOSE *v* -POSED, -POSING, -POSES to be in contention or conflict with

OPPOSER *n* pl. -S one that opposes

OPPOSITE *n* pl. -S one that is radically different from another in some related way

OPPRESS *v* -ED, -ING, -ES to burden by abuse of power or authority

OPPUGN *v* -ED, -ING, -S to assail with argument

OPPUGNER *n* pl. -S one that oppugns

OPSIN *n* pl. -S a type of protein

OPSONIC *adj* pertaining to opsonin

OPSONIFY *v* -FIED, -FYING, -FIES to opsonize

OPSONIN *n* pl. -S an antibody of blood serum

OPSONIZE *v* -NIZED, -NIZING, -NIZES to form opsonins in

OPT *v* -ED, -ING, -S to choose

OPTATIVE *n* pl. -S a mood of verbs that expresses a wish or desire

OPTIC *n* pl. -S an eye

OPTICAL *adj* pertaining to sight

OPTICIAN *n* pl. -S one who makes or deals in optical goods

OPTICIST *n* pl. -S one engaged in the study of light and vision

OPTIMA a pl. of optimum

OPTIMAL *adj* most desirable

OPTIME *n* pl. -S an honor student in mathematics at Cambridge University

OPTIMISE *v* -MISED, -MISING, -MISES to optimize

OPTIMISM *n* pl. -S a disposition to look on the favorable side of things

OPTIMIST *n* pl. -S one who exhibits optimism

OPTIMIZE *v* -MIZED, -MIZING, -MIZES to make as perfect, useful, or effective as possible

OPTIMUM *n* pl. -MA or -MUMS the most favorable condition for obtaining a given result

OPTION *v* -ED, -ING, -S to grant an option (a right to buy or sell something at a specified price within a specified time) on

OPTIONAL *n* pl. -S an elective course of study

OPTIONEE *n* pl. -S one who holds a legal option

OPULENCE *n* pl. -S wealth

OPULENCY *n* pl. -CIES opulence

OPULENT *adj* wealthy

OPUNTIA *n* pl. -S an American cactus

OPUS *n* pl. OPERA or OPUSES a literary of musical work

OPUSCULA *n/pl* opuscules

OPUSCULE *n* pl. -S a minor work

OQUASSA	*n* pl. -S a small lake trout
OR	*n* pl. -S the heraldic color gold
ORA	pl. of os
ORACH	*n* pl. -ES a cultivated plant
ORACHE	*n* pl. -S orach
ORACLE	*n* pl. -S a person through whom a deity is believed to speak **ORACULAR** *adj*
ORAD	*adv* toward the mouth
ORAL	*n* pl. -S an examination requiring spoken answers
ORALISM	*n* pl. -S the use of oral methods of teaching the deaf
ORALIST	*n* pl. -S an advocate of oralism
ORALITY	*n* pl. -TIES the state of being produced orally
ORALLY	*adv* through the mouth
ORANG	*n* pl. -S a large ape
ORANGE	*n* pl. -S a citrus fruit
ORANGERY	*n* pl. -RIES a place where orange trees are cultivated
ORANGEY	*adj* -ANGIER, -ANGIEST orangy
ORANGISH	*adj* of a somewhat orange color
ORANGY	*adj* -ANGIER, -ANGIEST resembling or suggestive of an orange
ORATE	*v* ORATED, ORATING, ORATES to speak formally
ORATION	*n* pl. -S a formal speech
ORATOR	*n* pl. -S one that orates
ORATORIO	*n* pl. -RIOS a type of musical composition
ORATORY	*n* pl. -RIES the art of public speaking
ORATRESS	*n* pl. -ES oratrix
ORATRIX	*n* pl. -TRICES a female orator
ORB	*v* -ED, -ING, -S to form into a circle or sphere
ORBIER	comparative of orby
ORBIEST	superlative of orby
ORBIT	*v* -ED, -ING, -S to move or revolve around
ORBITAL	*n* pl. -S a subdivision of a nuclear shell
ORBITER	*n* pl. -S one that orbits
ORBY	*adj* ORBIER, ORBIEST resembling a circle or sphere
ORC	*n* pl. -S a marine mammal
ORCA	*n* pl. -S orc
ORCEIN	*n* pl. -S a reddish brown dye
ORCHARD	*n* pl. -S an area for the cultivation of fruit trees
ORCHID	*n* pl. -S a flowering plant
ORCHIL	*n* pl. -S a purple dye
ORCHIS	*n* pl. -CHISES an orchid
ORCHITIS	*n* pl. -TISES inflammation of the testicle **ORCHITIC** *adj*
ORCIN	*n* pl. -S orcinol
ORCINOL	*n* pl. -S a chemical compound
ORDAIN	*v* -ED, -ING, -S to invest with holy authority
ORDAINER	*n* pl. -S one that ordains
ORDEAL	*n* pl. -S a severely difficult or painful experience
ORDER	*v* -ED, -ING, -S to give a command or instruction to
ORDERER	*n* pl. -S one that orders
ORDERLY	*n* pl. -LIES a male attendant
ORDINAL	*n* pl. -S a number designating position in a series
ORDINAND	*n* pl. -S a person about to be ordained
ORDINARY	*adj* -NARIER, -NARIEST of a kind to be expected in the normal order of events
ORDINARY	*n* pl. -NARIES something that is ordinary
ORDINATE	*n* pl. -S a particular geometric coordinate
ORDINES	a pl. of ordo
ORDNANCE	*n* pl. -S artillery; a cannon
ORDO	*n* pl. -DINES or -DOS a calendar of religious directions
ORDURE	*n* pl. -S manure
ORE	*n* pl. -S a mineral or rock containing a valuable metal
OREAD	*n* pl. -S a mountain nymph in Greek mythology
ORECTIC	*adj* pertaining to appetites or desires
ORECTIVE	*adj* orectic
OREGANO	*n* pl. -NOS an aromatic herb used as a seasoning
OREIDE	*n* pl. -S oroide
ORFRAY	*n* pl. -FRAYS orphrey
ORGAN	*n* pl. -S a differentiated part of an organism performing a specific function
ORGANA	a pl. of organon and organum

ORGANDIE	*n* pl. -S organdy
ORGANDY	*n* pl. -DIES a cotton fabric
ORGANIC	*n* pl. -S a substance of animal or vegetable origin
ORGANISE	*v* -NISED, -NISING, -NISES to organize
ORGANISM	*n* pl. -S any form of animal or plant life
ORGANIST	*n* pl. -S one who plays the organ (a keyboard musical instrument)
ORGANIZE	*v* -NIZED, -NIZING, -NIZES to form into an orderly whole
ORGANON	*n* pl. -GANA or -GANONS a system of rules for scientific investigation
ORGANUM	*n* pl. -GANA or -GANUMS organon
ORGANZA	*n* pl. -S a sheer fabric
ORGASM	*n* pl. -S the climax of sexual excitement **ORGASMIC, ORGASTIC** *adj*
ORGEAT	*n* pl. -S an almond-flavored syrup
ORGIAC	*adj* of the nature of an orgy
ORGIC	*adj* orgiac
ORGONE	*n* pl. -S a postulated energy pervading the universe
ORGULOUS	*adj* proud
ORGY	*n* pl. -GIES a party marked by unrestrained sexual indulgence
ORIBATID	*n* pl. -S any of a family of eyeless mites
ORIBI	*n* pl. -S an African antelope
ORIEL	*n* pl. -S a type of projecting window
ORIENT	*v* -ED, -ING, -S to adjust in relation to something else
ORIENTAL	*n* pl. -S an inhabitant of an eastern country
ORIFICE	*n* pl. -S a mouth or mouthlike opening
ORIGAMI	*n* pl. -S the Japanese art of paper folding
ORIGAN	*n* pl. -S marjoram
ORIGANUM	*n* pl. -S an aromatic herb
ORIGIN	*n* pl. -S a coming into being
ORIGINAL	*n* pl. -S the first form of something
ORINASAL	*n* pl. -S a sound pronounced through both the mouth and nose
ORIOLE	*n* pl. -S an American songbird
ORISON	*n* pl. -S a prayer
ORLE	*n* pl. -S a heraldic border
ORLOP	*n* pl. -S the lowest deck of a ship
ORMER	*n* pl. -S an abalone
ORMOLU	*n* pl. -S an alloy used to imitate gold
ORNAMENT	*v* -ED, -ING, -S to decorate
ORNATE	*adj* elaborately or excessively ornamented **ORNATELY** *adv*
ORNERY	*adj* -NERIER, -NERIEST stubborn and mean-spirited
ORNIS	*n* pl. ORNITHES avifauna
ORNITHIC	*adj* pertaining to birds
OROGENY	*n* pl. -NIES the process of mountain formation **OROGENIC** *adj*
OROIDE	*n* pl. -S an alloy used to imitate gold
OROLOGY	*n* pl. -GIES the study of mountains
OROMETER	*n* pl. -S a type of barometer
OROTUND	*adj* full and clear in sound
ORPHAN	*v* -ED, -ING, -S to deprive of both parents
ORPHIC	*adj* mystical
ORPHICAL	*adj* orphic
ORPHREY	*n* pl. -PHREYS an ornamental band or border
ORPIMENT	*n* pl. -S a yellow dye
ORPIN	*n* pl. -S orpine
ORPINE	*n* pl. -S a perennial herb
ORRA	*adj* occasional
ORRERY	*n* pl. -RERIES a mechanical model of the solar system
ORRICE	*n* pl. -S orris
ORRIS	*n* pl. -RISES a flowering plant
ORT	*n* pl. -S a scrap of food
ORTHICON	*n* pl. -S a type of television camera tube
ORTHO	*adj* pertaining to reproduction in a photograph of the full range of colors in nature
ORTHODOX	*n* pl. -ES one holding traditional beliefs
ORTHOEPY	*n* pl. -EPIES the study of correct pronunciation
ORTHOSIS	*n* pl. -THOSES an orthotic
ORTHOTIC	*n* pl. -S a brace for weak joints or muscles
ORTOLAN	*n* pl. -S a European bird

ORYX	*n* pl. -ES an African antelope
ORZO	*n* pl. -ZOS rice-shaped pasta
OS	*n* pl. ORA an orifice
OS	*n* pl. OSSA a bone
OS	*n* pl. OSAR an esker
OSCINE	*n* pl. -S any of a family of songbirds **OSCININE** *adj*
OSCITANT	*adj* yawning
OSCULA	pl. of osculum
OSCULANT	*adj* adhering closely
OSCULAR	*adj* pertaining to the mouth
OSCULATE	*v* -LATED, -LATING, -LATES to kiss
OSCULE	*n* pl. -S osculum
OSCULUM	*n* pl. -LA an opening in a sponge
OSE	*n* pl. -S an esker
OSIER	*n* pl. -S a European tree
OSMATIC	*adj* depending mainly on the sense of smell
OSMICS	*n/pl* the study of the sense of smell
OSMIUM	*n* pl. -S a metallic element **OSMIC, OSMIOUS** *adj*
OSMOL	*n* pl. -S a unit of osmotic pressure **OSMOLAL** *adj*
OSMOLAR	*adj* osmotic
OSMOLE	*n* pl. -S osmol
OSMOSE	*v* -MOSED, -MOSING, -MOSES to undergo osmosis
OSMOSIS	*n* pl. -MOSES a form of diffusion of a fluid through a membrane
OSMOTIC	*adj* pertaining to osmosis
OSMOUS	*adj* containing osmium
OSMUND	*n* pl. -S any of a genus of large ferns
OSMUNDA	*n* pl. -S osmund
OSNABURG	*n* pl. -S a cotton fabric
OSPREY	*n* pl. -PREYS an American hawk
OSSA	pl. of os
OSSEIN	*n* pl. -S a protein substance in bone
OSSEOUS	*adj* resembling bone
OSSIA	*conj* or else — used as a musical direction
OSSICLE	*n* pl. -S a small bone
OSSIFIC	*adj* pertaining to the formation of bone
OSSIFIER	*n* pl. -S one that ossifies

OSSIFY	*v* -FIED, -FYING, -FIES to convert into bone
OSSUARY	*n* pl. -ARIES a receptacle for the bones of the dead
OSTEAL	*adj* osseous
OSTEITIS	*n* pl. -ITIDES inflammation of bone **OSTEITIC** *adj*
OSTEOID	*n* pl. -S uncalcified bone matrix
OSTEOMA	*n* pl. -MAS or -MATA a tumor of bone tissue
OSTEOSIS	*n* pl. -OSES or -OSISES the formation of bone
OSTIA	pl. of ostium
OSTIARY	*n* pl. -ARIES a doorkeeper at a church
OSTINATO	*n* pl. -TOS a constantly recurring musical phrase
OSTIOLE	*n* pl. -S a small bodily opening **OSTIOLAR** *adj*
OSTIUM	*n* pl. OSTIA an opening in a bodily organ
OSTLER	*n* pl. -S hostler
OSTMARK	*n* pl. -S a former East German monetary unit
OSTOMY	*n* pl. -MIES a type of surgical operation
OSTOSIS	*n* pl. -TOSES or -TOSISES the formation of bone
OSTRACOD	*n* pl. -S a minute freshwater crustacean
OSTRACON	*n* pl. -CA a fragment containing an inscription
OSTRICH	*n* pl. -ES a large, flightless bird
OTALGIA	*n* pl. -S pain in the ear **OTALGIC** *adj*
OTALGY	*n* pl. -GIES otalgia
OTHER	*n* pl. -S one that remains of two or more
OTIC	*adj* pertaining to the ear
OTIOSE	*adj* lazy **OTIOSELY** *adv*
OTIOSITY	*n* pl. -TIES the state of being otiose
OTITIS	*n* pl. OTITIDES inflammation of the ear **OTITIC** *adj*
OTOCYST	*n* pl. -S an organ of balance in many invertebrates
OTOLITH	*n* pl. -S a hard mass that forms in the inner ear
OTOLOGY	*n* pl. -GIES the science of the ear
OTOSCOPE	*n* pl. -S an instrument for examining the ear

OTOSCOPY _n_ pl. -PIES the use of an otoscope

OTOTOXIC _adj_ adversely affecting hearing or balance

OTTAR _n_ pl. -S attar

OTTAVA _n_ pl. -S an octave

OTTER _n_ pl. -S a carnivorous mammal

OTTO _n_ pl. -TOS attar

OTTOMAN _n_ pl. -S a type of sofa

OUABAIN _n_ pl. -S a cardiac stimulant

OUCH _v_ -ED, -ING, -ES to ornament with ouches (settings for precious stones)

OUD _n_ pl. -S a stringed instrument of northern Africa

OUGHT _v_ -ED, -ING, -S to owe

OUGUIYA _n_ pl. OUGUIYA a monetary unit of Mauritania

OUISTITI _n_ pl. -S a South American monkey

OUNCE _n_ pl. -S a unit of weight

OUPH _n_ pl. -S ouphe

OUPHE _n_ pl. -S an elf

OUR _pron_ a possessive form of the pronoun we

OURANG _n_ pl. -S orang

OURARI _n_ pl. -S curare

OUREBI _n_ pl. -S oribi

OURIE _adj_ shivering with cold

OURS _pron_ a possessive form of the pronoun we

OURSELF _pron_ myself — used in formal or regal contexts

OUSEL _n_ pl. -S ouzel

OUST _v_ -ED, -ING, -S to expel or remove from a position or place

OUSTER _n_ pl. -S the act of ousting

OUT _v_ -ED, -ING, -S to be revealed

OUTACT _v_ -ED, -ING, -S to surpass in acting

OUTADD _v_ -ED, -ING, -S to surpass in adding

OUTAGE _n_ pl. -S a failure or interruption in use or functioning

OUTARGUE _v_ -GUED, -GUING, -GUES to get the better of by arguing

OUTASK _v_ -ED, -ING, -S to surpass in asking

OUTATE past tense of outeat

OUTBACK _n_ pl. -S isolated rural country

OUTBAKE _v_ -BAKED, -BAKING, -BAKES to surpass in baking

OUTBARK _v_ -ED, -ING, -S to surpass in barking

OUTBAWL _v_ -ED, -ING, -S to surpass in bawling

OUTBEAM _v_ -ED, -ING, -S to surpass in beaming

OUTBEG _v_ -BEGGED, -BEGGING, -BEGS to surpass in begging

OUTBID _v_ -BID, -BIDDEN, -BIDDING, -BIDS to bid higher than

OUTBITCH _v_ -ED, -ING, -ES to surpass in bitching

OUTBLAZE _v_ -BLAZED, -BLAZING, -BLAZES to surpass in brilliance of light

OUTBLEAT _v_ -ED, -ING, -S to surpass in bleating

OUTBLESS _v_ -ED, -ING, -ES to surpass in blessing

OUTBLOOM _v_ -ED, -ING, -S to surpass in blooming

OUTBLUFF _v_ -ED, -ING, -S to surpass in bluffing

OUTBLUSH _v_ -ED, -ING, -ES to surpass in blushing

OUTBOARD _n_ pl. -S a type of motor

OUTBOAST _v_ -ED, -ING, -S to surpass in boasting

OUTBOUGHT past tense of outbuy

OUTBOUND _adj_ outward bound

OUTBOX _v_ -ED, -ING, -ES to surpass in boxing

OUTBRAG _v_ -BRAGGED, -BRAGGING, -BRAGS to surpass in bragging

OUTBRAVE _v_ -BRAVED, -BRAVING, -BRAVES to surpass in courage

OUTBRAWL _v_ -ED, -ING, -S to surpass in brawling

OUTBREAK _n_ pl. -S a sudden eruption

OUTBREED _v_ -BRED, -BREEDING, -BREEDS to interbreed relatively unrelated stocks

OUTBRIBE _v_ -BRIBED, -BRIBING, -BRIBES to surpass in bribing

OUTBUILD _v_ -BUILT, -BUILDING, -BUILDS to surpass in building

OUTBULK _v_ -ED, -ING, -S to surpass in bulking

OUTBULLY _v_ -LIED, -LYING, -LIES to surpass in bullying

OUTBURN	v -BURNED or -BURNT, -BURNING, -BURNS to burn longer than
OUTBURST	n pl. -S a sudden and violent outpouring
OUTBUY	v -BOUGHT, -BUYING, -BUYS to surpass in buying
OUTBY	adv outdoors
OUTBYE	adv outby
OUTCAPER	v -ED, -ING, -S to surpass in capering
OUTCAST	n pl. -S one that is cast out
OUTCASTE	n pl. -S a Hindu who has been expelled from his caste
OUTCATCH	v -CAUGHT, -CATCHING, -CATCHES to surpass in catching
OUTCAVIL	v -ILED, -ILING, -ILS or -ILLED, -ILLING, -ILS to surpass in caviling
OUTCHARM	v -ED, -ING, -S to surpass in charming
OUTCHEAT	v -ED, -ING, -S to surpass in cheating
OUTCHIDE	v -CHIDED or -CHID, -CHIDDEN, -CHIDING, -CHIDES to surpass in chiding
OUTCLASS	v -ED, -ING, -ES to surpass so decisively as to appear of a higher class
OUTCLIMB	v -CLIMBED or -CLOMB, -CLIMBING, -CLIMBS to surpass in climbing
OUTCOACH	v -ED, -ING, -ES to surpass in coaching
OUTCOME	n pl. -S a result
OUTCOOK	v -ED, -ING, -S to surpass in cooking
OUTCOUNT	v -ED, -ING, -S to surpass in counting
OUTCRAWL	v -ED, -ING, -S to surpass in crawling
OUTCRIED	past tense of outcry
OUTCRIES	present 3d person sing. of outcry
OUTCROP	v -CROPPED, -CROPPING, -CROPS to protrude above the soil
OUTCROSS	v -ED, -ING, -ES to cross with a relatively unrelated individual
OUTCROW	v -ED, -ING, -S to surpass in crowing
OUTCRY	v -CRIED, -CRYING, -CRIES to cry louder than
OUTCURSE	v -CURSED, -CURSING, -CURSES to surpass in cursing
OUTCURVE	n pl. -S a type of pitch in baseball
OUTDANCE	v -DANCED, -DANCING, -DANCES to surpass in dancing
OUTDARE	v -DARED, -DARING, -DARES to surpass in daring
OUTDATE	v -DATED, -DATING, -DATES to make out-of-date
OUTDO	v -DID, -DONE, -DOING, -DOES to exceed in performance
OUTDODGE	v -DODGED, -DODGING, -DODGES to surpass in dodging
OUTDOER	n pl. -S one that outdoes
OUTDONE	past participle of outdo
OUTDOOR	adj pertaining to the open air
OUTDOORS	adv in the open air
OUTDRAG	v -DRAGGED, -DRAGGING, -DRAGS to surpass in drag racing
OUTDRANK	past tense of outdrink
OUTDRAW	v -DREW, -DRAWN, -DRAWING, -DRAWS to attract a larger audience than
OUTDREAM	v -DREAMED or -DREAMT, -DREAMING, -DREAMS to surpass in dreaming
OUTDRESS	v -ED, -ING, -ES to surpass in dressing
OUTDREW	past tense of outdraw
OUTDRINK	v -DRANK, -DRUNK, -DRINKING, -DRINKS to surpass in drinking
OUTDRIVE	v -DROVE, -DRIVEN, -DRIVING, -DRIVES to drive a golf ball farther than
OUTDROP	v -DROPPED, -DROPPING, -DROPS to surpass in dropping
OUTDRUNK	past participle of outdrink
OUTDUEL	v -DUELED, -DUELING, -DUELS or -DUELLED, -DUELLING, -DUELS to surpass in dueling
OUTEARN	v -ED, -ING, -S to surpass in earning
OUTEAT	v -ATE, -EATEN, -EATING, -EATS to surpass in eating
OUTECHO	v -ED, -ING, -ES to surpass in echoing
OUTER	n pl. -S a part of a target
OUTFABLE	v -BLED, -BLING, -BLES to surpass in fabling

OUTFACE *v* -FACED, -FACING, -FACES to confront unflinchingly

OUTFALL *n* pl. -S the outlet of a body of water

OUTFAST *v* -ED, -ING, -S to surpass in fasting

OUTFAWN *v* -ED, -ING, -S to surpass in fawning

OUTFEAST *v* -ED, -ING, -S to surpass in feasting

OUTFEEL *v* -FELT, -FEELING, -FEELS to surpass in feeling

OUTFIELD *n* pl. -S a part of a baseball field

OUTFIGHT *v* -FOUGHT, -FIGHTING, -FIGHTS to defeat

OUTFIND *v* -FOUND, -FINDING, -FINDS to surpass in finding

OUTFIRE *v* -FIRED, -FIRING, -FIRES to surpass in firing

OUTFISH *v* -ED, -ING, -ES to surpass in fishing

OUTFIT *v* -FITTED, -FITTING, -FITS to equip

OUTFLANK *v* -ED, -ING, -S to gain a tactical advantage over

OUTFLOW *v* -ED, -ING, -S to flow out

OUTFLY *v* -FLEW, -FLOWN, -FLYING, -FLIES to surpass in speed of flight

OUTFOOL *v* -ED, -ING, -S to surpass in fooling

OUTFOOT *v* -ED, -ING, -S to surpass in speed

OUTFOUGHT past tense of outfight

OUTFOUND past tense of outfind

OUTFOX *v* -ED, -ING, -ES to outwit

OUTFROWN *v* -ED, -ING, -S to frown more than

OUTGAIN *v* -ED, -ING, -S to gain more than

OUTGAS *v* -GASSED, -GASSING, -GASSES to remove gas from

OUTGIVE *v* -GAVE, -GIVEN, -GIVING, -GIVES to give more than

OUTGLARE *v* -GLARED, -GLARING, -GLARES to surpass in glaring

OUTGLOW *v* -ED, -ING, -S to surpass in glowing

OUTGNAW *v* -GNAWED, -GNAWN, -GNAWING, -GNAWS to surpass in gnawing

OUTGO *v* -WENT, -GONE, -GOING, -GOES to go beyond

OUTGOING *n* pl. -S a departure

OUTGREW past tense of outgrow

OUTGRIN *v* -GRINNED, -GRINNING, -GRINS to surpass in grinning

OUTGROSS *v* -ED, -ING, -ES to surpass in gross earnings

OUTGROUP *n* pl. -S a group of people outside one's own group

OUTGROW *v* -GREW, -GROWN, -GROWING, -GROWS to grow too large for

OUTGUESS *v* -ED, -ING, -ES to anticipate the actions of

OUTGUIDE *v* -GUIDED, -GUIDING, -GUIDES to surpass in guiding

OUTGUN *v* -GUNNED, -GUNNING, -GUNS to surpass in firepower

OUTGUSH *n* pl. -ES a gushing out

OUTHAUL *n* pl. -S a rope for extending a sail along a spar

OUTHEAR *v* -HEARD, -HEARING, -HEARS to surpass in hearing

OUTHIT *v* -HIT, -HITTING, -HITS to get more hits than

OUTHOMER *v* -ED, -ING, -S to surpass in hitting home runs

OUTHOUSE *n* pl. -S a toilet housed in a small structure

OUTHOWL *v* -ED, -ING, -S to surpass in howling

OUTHUMOR *v* -ED, -ING, -S to surpass in humoring

OUTHUNT *v* -ED, -ING, -S to surpass in hunting

OUTING *n* pl. -S a short pleasure trip

OUTJINX *v* -ED, -ING, -ES to surpass in jinxing

OUTJUMP *v* -ED, -ING, -S to surpass in jumping

OUTJUT *v* -JUTTED, -JUTTING, -JUTS to stick out

OUTKEEP *v* -KEPT, -KEEPING, -KEEPS to surpass in keeping

OUTKICK *v* -ED, -ING, -S to surpass in kicking

OUTKILL *v* -ED, -ING, -S to surpass in killing

OUTKISS *v* -ED, -ING, -ES to surpass in kissing

OUTLAID past tense of outlay

OUTLAIN past participle of outlie

OUTLAND *n* pl. -S a foreign land

OUTLAST   v -ED, -ING, -S to last longer than

OUTLAUGH   v -ED, -ING, -S to surpass in laughing

OUTLAW   v -ED, -ING, -S to prohibit

OUTLAWRY   n pl. -RIES habitual defiance of the law

OUTLAY   v -LAID, -LAYING, -LAYS to pay out

OUTLEAP   v -LEAPED or -LEAPT, -LEAPING, -LEAPS to surpass in leaping

OUTLEARN   v -LEARNED or -LEARNT, -LEARNING, -LEARNS to surpass in learning

OUTLET   n pl. -S a passage for escape or discharge

OUTLIE   v -LAY, -LAIN, -LYING, -LIES to lie beyond

OUTLIER   n pl. -S an outlying area or portion

OUTLINE   v -LINED, -LINING, -LINES to indicate the main features or different parts of

OUTLINER   n pl. -S one that outlines

OUTLIVE   v -LIVED, -LIVING, -LIVES to live longer than

OUTLIVER   n pl. -S one that outlives

OUTLOOK   n pl. -S a point of view

OUTLOVE   v -LOVED, -LOVING, -LOVES to surpass in loving

OUTLYING   present participle of outlie

OUTMAN   v -MANNED, -MANNING, -MANS to surpass in manpower

OUTMARCH   v -ED, -ING, -ES to surpass in marching

OUTMATCH   v -ED, -ING, -ES to outdo

OUTMODE   v -MODED, -MODING, -MODES to outdate

OUTMOST   adj farthest out

OUTMOVE   v -MOVED, -MOVING, -MOVES to move faster or farther than

OUTPACE   v -PACED, -PACING, -PACES to surpass in speed

OUTPAINT   v -ED, -ING, -S to surpass in painting

OUTPASS   v -ED, -ING, -ES to excel in passing a football

OUTPITCH   v -ED, -ING, -ES to surpass in pitching

OUTPITY   v -PITIED, -PITYING, -PITIES to surpass in pitying

OUTPLAN   v -PLANNED, -PLANNING, -PLANS to surpass in planning

OUTPLAY   v -ED, -ING, -S to excel or defeat in a game

OUTPLOD   v -PLODDED, -PLODDING, -PLODS to surpass in plodding

OUTPLOT   v -PLOTTED, -PLOTTING, -PLOTS to surpass in plotting

OUTPOINT   v -ED, -ING, -S to score more points than

OUTPOLL   v -ED, -ING, -S to get more votes than

OUTPORT   n pl. -S a port of export or departure

OUTPOST   n pl. -S a body of troops stationed at a distance from the main body

OUTPOUR   v -ED, -ING, -S to pour out

OUTPOWER   v -ED, -ING, -S to surpass in power

OUTPRAY   v -ED, -ING, -S to surpass in praying

OUTPREEN   v -ED, -ING, -S to surpass in preening

OUTPRESS   v -ED, -ING, -ES to surpass in pressing

OUTPRICE   v -PRICED, -PRICING, -PRICES to surpass in pricing

OUTPULL   v -ED, -ING, -S to attract a larger audience or following than

OUTPUNCH   v -ED, -ING, -ES to surpass in punching

OUTPUSH   v -ED, -ING, -ES to surpass in pushing

OUTPUT   v -PUTTED, -PUTTING, -PUTS to produce

OUTQUOTE   v -QUOTED, -QUOTING, -QUOTES to surpass in quoting

OUTRACE   v -RACED, -RACING, -RACES to run faster or farther than

OUTRAGE   v -RAGED, -RAGING, -RAGES to arouse anger or resentment in

OUTRAISE   v -RAISED, -RAISING, -RAISES to surpass in raising

OUTRAN   past tense of outrun

OUTRANCE   n pl. -S the last extremity

OUTRANG   past tense of outring

OUTRANGE   v -RANGED, -RANGING, -RANGES to surpass in range

OUTRANK   v -ED, -ING, -S to rank higher than

OUTRATE v -RATED, -RATING, -RATES to surpass in a rating

OUTRAVE v -RAVED, -RAVING, -RAVES to surpass in raving

OUTRE adj deviating from what is usual or proper

OUTREACH v -ED, -ING, -ES to reach beyond

OUTREAD v -READ, -READING, -READS to surpass in reading

OUTRIDE v -RODE, -RIDDEN, -RIDING, -RIDES to ride faster or better than

OUTRIDER n pl. -S a mounted attendant who rides before or beside a carriage

OUTRIGHT adj being without limit or reservation

OUTRING v -RANG, -RUNG, -RINGING, -RINGS to ring louder than

OUTRIVAL v -VALED, -VALING, -VALS or -VALLED, -VALLING, -VALS to outdo in a competition or rivalry

OUTROAR v -ED, -ING, -S to roar louder than

OUTROCK v -ED, -ING, -S to surpass in rocking

OUTRODE past tense of outride

OUTROLL v -ED, -ING, -S to roll out

OUTROOT v -ED, -ING, -S to pull up by the roots

OUTROW v -ED, -ING, -S to surpass in rowing

OUTRUN v -RAN, -RUNNING, -RUNS to run faster than

OUTRUNG past participle of outring

OUTRUSH v -ED, -ING, -ES to surpass in rushing

OUTSAIL v -ED, -ING, -S to sail faster than

OUTSANG past tense of outsing

OUTSAT past tense of outsit

OUTSAVOR v -ED, -ING, -S to surpass in a distinctive taste or smell

OUTSAW past tense of outsee

OUTSCOLD v -ED, -ING, -S to surpass in scolding

OUTSCOOP v -ED, -ING, -S to surpass in scooping

OUTSCORE v -SCORED, -SCORING, -SCORES to score more points than

OUTSCORN v -ED, -ING, -S to surpass in scorning

OUTSEE v -SAW, -SEEN, -SEEING, -SEES to see beyond

OUTSELL v -SOLD, -SELLING, -SELLS to sell more than

OUTSERT n pl. -S a folded sheet placed around a folded section of printed matter

OUTSERVE v -SERVED, -SERVING, -SERVES to surpass in serving

OUTSET n pl. -S a beginning

OUTSHAME v -SHAMED, -SHAMING, -SHAMES to surpass in shaming

OUTSHINE v -SHONE or -SHINED, -SHINING, -SHINES to shine brighter than

OUTSHOOT v -SHOT, -SHOOTING, -SHOOTS to shoot better than

OUTSHOUT v -ED, -ING, -S to shout louder than

OUTSIDE n pl. -S the outer side, surface, or part

OUTSIDER n pl. -S one that does not belong to a particular group

OUTSIGHT n pl. -S the power of perceiving external things

OUTSIN v -SINNED, -SINNING, -SINS to surpass in sinning

OUTSING v -SANG, -SUNG, -SINGING, -SINGS to surpass in singing

OUTSIT v -SAT, -SITTING, -SITS to remain sitting or in session longer than

OUTSIZE n pl. -S an unusual size **OUTSIZED** adj

OUTSKATE v -SKATED, -SKATING, -SKATES to surpass in skating

OUTSKIRT n pl. -S an outlying area

OUTSLEEP v -SLEPT, -SLEEPING, -SLEEPS to sleep later than

OUTSLICK v -ED, -ING, -S to get the better of by trickery or cunning

OUTSMART v -ED, -ING, -S to outwit

OUTSMILE v -SMILED, -SMILING, -SMILES to surpass in smiling

OUTSMOKE v -SMOKED, -SMOKING, -SMOKES to surpass in smoking

OUTSNORE v -SNORED, -SNORING, -SNORES to surpass in snoring

OUTSOAR v -ED, -ING, -S to soar beyond

OUTSOLD past tense of outsell

OUTSOLE n pl. -S the outer sole of a boot or shoe

OUTSPAN *v* -SPANNED, -SPANNING, -SPANS to unharness a draft animal

OUTSPEAK *v* -SPOKE, -SPOKEN, -SPEAKING, -SPEAKS to outdo in speaking

OUTSPEED *v* -SPED or -SPEEDED, -SPEEDING, -SPEEDS to go faster than

OUTSPELL *v* -SPELLED or -SPELT, -SPELLING, -SPELLS to surpass in spelling

OUTSPEND *v* -SPENT, -SPENDING, -SPENDS to exceed the limits of in spending

OUTSPOKE past tense of outspeak

OUTSPOKEN past participle of outspeak

OUTSTAND *v* -STOOD, -STANDING, -STANDS to endure beyond

OUTSTARE *v* -STARED, -STARING, -STARES to outface

OUTSTART *v* -ED, -ING, -S to get ahead of at the start

OUTSTATE *v* -STATED, -STATING, -STATES to surpass in stating

OUTSTAY *v* -ED, -ING, -S to surpass in staying power

OUTSTEER *v* -ED, -ING, -S to surpass in steering

OUTSTOOD past tense of outstand

OUTSTRIP *v* -STRIPPED, -STRIPPING, -STRIPS to go faster or farther than

OUTSTUDY *v* -STUDIED, -STUDYING, -STUDIES to surpass in studying

OUTSTUNT *v* -ED, -ING, -S to surpass in stunting

OUTSULK *v* -ED, -ING, -S to surpass in sulking

OUTSUNG past participle of outsing

OUTSWEAR *v* -SWORE or -SWARE, -SWORN, -SWEARING, -SWEARS to surpass in swearing

OUTSWIM *v* -SWAM, -SWUM, -SWIMMING, -SWIMS to swim faster or farther than

OUTTAKE *n* pl. -S a passage outwards

OUTTALK *v* -ED, -ING, -S to surpass in talking

OUTTASK *v* -ED, -ING, -S to surpass in tasking

OUTTELL *v* -TOLD, -TELLING, -TELLS to say openly

OUTTHANK *v* -ED, -ING, -S to surpass in thanking

OUTTHINK *v* -THOUGHT, -THINKING, -THINKS to get the better of by thinking

OUTTHROB *v* -THROBBED, -THROBBING, -THROBS to surpass in throbbing

OUTTHROW *v* -THREW, -THROWN, -THROWING, -THROWS to throw farther or more accurately than

OUTTOLD past tense of outtell

OUTTOWER *v* -ED, -ING, -S to tower above

OUTTRADE *v* -TRADED, -TRADING, -TRADES to get the better of in a trade

OUTTRICK *v* -ED, -ING, -S to get the better of by trickery

OUTTROT *v* -TROTTED, -TROTTING, -TROTS to surpass in trotting

OUTTRUMP *v* -ED, -ING, -S to outplay

OUTTURN *n* pl. -S a quantity produced

OUTVALUE *v* -UED, -UING, -UES to be worth more than

OUTVAUNT *v* -ED, -ING, -S to surpass in vaunting

OUTVIE *v* -VIED, -VYING, -VIES to surpass in a competition

OUTVOICE *v* -VOICED, -VOICING, -VOICES to surpass in loudness of voice

OUTVOTE *v* -VOTED, -VOTING, -VOTES to defeat by a majority of votes

OUTVYING present participle of outvie

OUTWAIT *v* -ED, -ING, -S to exceed in patience

OUTWALK *v* -ED, -ING, -S to surpass in walking

OUTWAR *v* -WARRED, -WARRING, -WARS to surpass in warring

OUTWARD *adv* toward the outside

OUTWARDS *adv* outward

OUTWARRED past tense of outwar

OUT-WARRING present participle of outwar

OUTWASH *n* pl. -ES detritus washed from a glacier

OUTWASTE *v* -WASTED, -WASTING, -WASTES to surpass in wasting

OUTWATCH *v* -ED, -ING, -ES to watch longer than

OUTWEAR *v* -WORE, -WORN, -WEARING, -WEARS to last longer than

OUTWEARY *v* -RIED, -RYING, -RIES to surpass in wearying

OUTWEEP *v* -WEPT, -WEEPING, -WEEPS to weep more than

OUTWEIGH *v* -ED, -ING, -S to weigh more than

OUTWENT past tense of outgo

OUTWEPT past tense of outweep

OUTWHIRL *v* -ED, -ING, -S to surpass in whirling

OUTWILE *v* -WILED, -WILING, -WILES to surpass in wiling

OUTWILL *v* -ED, -ING, -S to surpass in willpower

OUTWIND *v* -ED, -ING, -S to cause to be out of breath

OUTWISH *v* -ED, -ING, -ES to surpass in wishing

OUTWIT *v* -WITTED, -WITTING, -WITS to get the better of by superior cleverness

OUTWORE past tense of outwear

OUTWORK *v* -WORKED or -WROUGHT, -WORKING, -WORKS to work faster or better than

OUTWORN past participle of outwear

OUTWRITE *v* -WROTE or -WRIT, -WRITTEN, -WRITING, -WRITES to write better than

OUT-WROUGHT a past tense of outwork

OUTYELL *v* -ED, -ING, -S to yell louder than

OUTYELP *v* -ED, -ING, -S to surpass in yelping

OUTYIELD *v* -ED, -ING, -S to surpass in yield

OUZEL *n* pl. -S a European bird

OUZO *n* pl. -ZOS a Greek liqueur

OVA pl. of ovum

OVAL *n* pl. -S an oval (egg-shaped) figure or object

OVALITY *n* pl. -TIES ovalness

OVALLY *adv* in the shape of an oval

OVALNESS *n* pl. -ES the state of being oval

OVARIAL *adj* ovarian

OVARIAN *adj* pertaining to an ovary

OVARIES pl. of ovary

OVARIOLE *n* pl. -S one of the tubes of which the ovaries of most insects are composed

OVARITIS *n* pl. -RITIDES inflammation of an ovary

OVARY *n* pl. -RIES a female reproductive gland

OVATE *adj* egg-shaped **OVATELY** *adv*

OVATION *n* pl. -S an expression or demonstration of popular acclaim

OVEN *n* pl. -S an enclosed compartment in which substances are heated **OVENLIKE** *adj*

OVENBIRD *n* pl. -S an American songbird

OVENWARE *n* pl. -S heat-resistant dishes for baking and serving food

OVER *v* -ED, -ING, -S to leap above and to the other side of

OVERABLE *adj* excessively able

OVERACT *v* -ED, -ING, -S to act with exaggeration

OVERAGE *n* pl. -S an amount in excess

OVERAGED *adj* too old to be useful

OVERALL *n* pl. -S a loose outer garment

OVERAPT *adj* excessively apt

OVERARCH *v* -ED, -ING, -ES to form an arch over

OVERARM *adj* done with the arm above the shoulder

OVERATE past tense of overeat

OVERAWE *v* -AWED, -AWING, -AWES to subdue by inspiring awe

OVERBAKE *v* -BAKED, -BAKING, -BAKES to bake too long

OVERBEAR *v* -BORE, -BORNE or -BORN, -BEARING, -BEARS to bring down by superior weight or force

OVERBEAT *v* -BEAT, -BEATEN, -BEATING, -BEATS to beat too much

OVERBED *adj* spanning a bed

OVERBET *v* -BET or -BETTED, -BETTING, -BETS to bet too much

OVERBID *v* -BID, -BID or -BIDDEN, -BIDDING, -BIDS to bid higher than

OVERBIG *adj* too big

OVERBILL *v* -ED, -ING, -S to bill too much

OVERBITE *n* pl. -S a faulty closure of the teeth

OVERBLOW *v* -BLEW, -BLOWN, -BLOWING, -BLOWS to give excessive importance to

OVERBOIL *v* -ED, -ING, -S to boil too long

OVERBOLD *adj* excessively bold or forward

OVERBOOK v -ED, -ING, -S to issue reservations in excess of the space available

OVERBORE past tense of overbear

OVERBORN a past participle of overbear

OVERBORNE a past participle of overbear

OVER-BOUGHT past tense of overbuy

OVERBRED adj bred too finely or to excess

OVERBURN v -BURNED or -BURNT, -BURNING, -BURNS to burn too long

OVERBUSY adj too busy

OVERBUY v -BOUGHT, -BUYING, -BUYS to buy in quantities exceeding need or demand

OVERCALL v -ED, -ING, -S to overbid

OVERCAME past tense of overcome

OVERCAST v -CAST or -CASTED, -CASTING, -CASTS to become cloudy or dark

OVERCOAT n pl. -S a warm coat worn over indoor clothing

OVERCOLD adj too cold

OVERCOME v -CAME, -COMING, -COMES to get the better of

OVERCOOK v -ED, -ING, -S to cook too long

OVERCOOL v -ED, -ING, -S to make too cool

OVERCOY adj too coy

OVERCRAM v -CRAMMED, -CRAMMING, -CRAMS to stuff or cram to excess

OVERCROP v -CROPPED, -CROPPING, -CROPS to exhaust the fertility of by cultivating to excess

OVERCURE v -CURED, -CURING, -CURES to cure too long

OVERCUT v -CUT, -CUTTING, -CUTS to cut too much

OVERDARE v -DARED, -DARING, -DARES to become too daring

OVERDEAR adj too dear; too costly

OVERDECK v -ED, -ING, -S to adorn extravagantly

OVERDO v -DID, -DONE, -DOING, -DOES to do to excess

OVERDOER n pl. -S one that overdoes

OVERDOG n pl. -S one that is dominant or victorious

OVERDOSE v -DOSED, -DOSING, -DOSES to give an excessive dose to

OVERDRAW v -DREW, -DRAWN, -DRAWING, -DRAWS to draw checks on in excess of the balance

OVERDRY v -DRIED, -DRYING, -DRIES to dry too much

OVERDUB v -DUBBED, -DUBBING, -DUBS to add sound to an existing recording

OVERDUE adj not paid when due

OVERDYE v -DYED, -DYEING, -DYES to dye with too much color

OVEREASY adj too easy

OVEREAT v -ATE, -EATEN, -EATING, -EATS to eat to excess

OVEREDIT v -ED, -ING, -S to edit more than necessary

OVERFAR adj too great in distance, extent, or degree

OVERFAST adj too fast

OVERFAT adj too fat

OVERFEAR v -ED, -ING, -S to fear too much

OVERFEED v -FED, -FEEDING, -FEEDS to feed too much

OVERFILL v -ED, -ING, -S to fill to overflowing

OVERFISH v -ED, -ING, -ES to deplete the supply of fish in an area by fishing to excess

OVERFLOW v -FLOWED, -FLOWN, -FLOWING, -FLOWS to flow over the top of

OVERFLY v -FLEW, -FLOWN, -FLYING, -FLIES to fly over

OVERFOND adj too fond or affectionate

OVERFOUL adj too foul

OVERFREE adj too free

OVERFULL adj too full

OVERFUND v -ED, -ING, -S to fund more than required

OVERGILD v -GILDED or -GILT, -GILDING, -GILDS to gild over

OVERGIRD v -GIRDED or -GIRT, -GIRDING, -GIRDS to gird to excess

OVERGLAD adj too glad

OVERGOAD v -ED, -ING, -S to goad too much

OVERGROW v -GREW, -GROWN, -GROWING, -GROWS to grow over

OVERHAND v -ED, -ING, -S to sew with short, vertical stitches

OVERHANG v -HUNG, -HANGING, -HANGS to hang or project over

OVERHARD *adj* too hard

OVERHATE *v* -HATED, -HATING, -HATES to hate to excess

OVERHAUL *v* -ED, -ING, -S to examine carefully for needed repairs

OVERHEAD *n* pl. -S the general cost of running a business

OVERHEAP *v* -ED, -ING, -S to heap up or accumulate to excess

OVERHEAR *v* -HEARD, -HEARING, -HEARS to hear without the speaker's knowledge or intention

OVERHEAT *v* -ED, -ING, -S to heat to excess

OVERHIGH *adj* too high

OVERHOLD *v* -HELD, -HOLDING, -HOLDS to rate too highly

OVERHOLY *adj* too holy

OVERHOPE *v* -HOPED, -HOPING, -HOPES to hope exceedingly

OVERHOT *adj* too hot

OVERHUNG past tense of overhang

OVERHUNT *v* -ED, -ING, -S to deplete the supply of game in an area by hunting to excess

OVERHYPE *v* -HYPED, -HYPING, -HYPES to hype to excess

OVERIDLE *adj* too idle

OVERJOY *v* -ED, -ING, -S to fill with great joy

OVERJUST *adj* too just

OVERKEEN *adj* too keen

OVERKILL *v* -ED, -ING, -S to destroy with more nuclear force than required

OVERKIND *adj* too kind

OVERLADE *v* -LADED, -LADEN, -LADING, -LADES to load with too great a burden

OVERLAID past tense of overlay

OVERLAIN past participle of overlie

OVERLAND *n* pl. -S a train or stagecoach that travels over land

OVERLAP *v* -LAPPED, -LAPPING, -LAPS to extend over and cover a part of

OVERLATE *adj* too late

OVERLAX *adj* too lax

OVERLAY *v* -LAID, -LAYING, -LAYS to lay over

OVERLEAF *adv* on the other side of the page

OVERLEAP *v* -LEAPED or -LEAPT, -LEAPING, -LEAPS to leap over

OVERLEND *v* -LENT, -LENDING, -LENDS to lend too much

OVERLET *v* -LET, -LETTING, -LETS to let to excess

OVERLEWD *adj* too lewd

OVERLIE *v* -LAY, -LAIN, -LYING, -LIES to lie over

OVERLIT a past tense of overlight

OVERLIVE *v* -LIVED, -LIVING, -LIVES to outlive

OVERLOAD *v* -ED, -ING, -S to load to excess

OVERLONG *adj* too long

OVERLOOK *v* -ED, -ING, -S to fail to notice

OVERLORD *v* -ED, -ING, -S to rule tyrannically

OVERLOUD *adj* too loud

OVERLOVE *v* -LOVED, -LOVING, -LOVES to love to excess

OVERLUSH *adj* excessively lush

OVERLY *adv* to an excessive degree

OVERLYING present participle of overlie

OVERMAN *n* pl. -MEN a foreman

OVERMAN *v* -MANNED, -MANNING, -MANS to provide with more men than are needed

OVERMANY *adj* too many

OVERMEEK *adj* excessively meek

OVERMELT *v* -ED, -ING, -S to melt too much

OVERMEN pl. of overman

OVERMILD *adj* too mild

OVERMILK *v* -ED, -ING, -S to milk to excess

OVERMINE *v* -MINED, -MINING, -MINES to mine to excess

OVERMIX *v* -ED, -ING, -ES to mix too much

OVERMUCH *n* pl. -ES an excess

OVERNEAR *adj* too near

OVERNEAT *adj* too neat

OVERNEW *adj* too new

OVERNICE *adj* excessively nice

OVERPASS *v* -PASSED or -PAST, -PASSING, -PASSES to pass over

OVERPAY *v* -PAID, -PAYING, -PAYS to pay too much

OVERPERT *adj* too pert

OVERPLAN *v* -PLANNED, -PLANNING, -PLANS to plan to excess

OVERPLAY *v* -ED, -ING, -S to exaggerate

OVERPLOT   *v* -PLOTTED, -PLOTTING, -PLOTS to devise an overly complex plot for

OVERPLUS   *n* pl. -ES a surplus

OVERPLY   *v* -PLIED, -PLYING, -PLIES to ply to excess; overwork

OVERPUMP   *v* -ED, -ING, -S to pump to excess

OVERRAN   past tense of overrun

OVERRANK   *adj* too luxuriant in growth

OVERRASH   *adj* too rash

OVERRATE   *v* -RATED, -RATING, -RATES to rate too highly

OVERRICH   *adj* too rich

OVERRIDE   *v* -RODE, -RIDDEN, -RIDING, -RIDES to ride over

OVERRIFE   *adj* too rife

OVERRIPE   *adj* too ripe

OVERRODE   past tense of override

OVERRUDE   *adj* excessively rude

OVERRUFF   *v* -ED, -ING, -S to trump with a higher trump card than has already been played

OVERRULE   *v* -RULED, -RULING, -RULES to disallow the arguments of

OVERRUN   *v* -RAN, -RUNNING, -RUNS to spread or swarm over

OVERSAD   *adj* excessively sad

OVERSALE   *n* pl. -S the act of overselling

OVERSALT   *v* -ED, -ING, -S to salt to excess

OVERSAVE   *v* -SAVED, -SAVING, -SAVES to save too much

OVERSAW   past tense of oversee

OVERSEA   *adv* overseas

OVERSEAS   *adv* beyond or across the sea

OVERSEE   *v* -SAW, -SEEN, -SEEING, -SEES to watch over and direct

OVERSEED   *v* -ED, -ING, -S to seed to excess

OVERSEER   *n* pl. -S one that oversees

OVERSELL   *v* -SOLD, -SELLING, -SELLS to sell more of than can be delivered

OVERSET   *v* -SET, -SETTING, -SETS to turn or tip over

OVERSEW   *v* -SEWED, -SEWN, -SEWING, -SEWS to overhand

OVERSHOE   *n* pl. -S a protective outer shoe

OVERSHOT   *n* pl. -S a type of fabric weave

OVERSICK   *adj* too sick

OVERSIDE   *n* pl. -S the other side of a phonograph record

OVERSIZE   *n* pl. -S an unusually large size

OVERSLIP   *v* -SLIPPED or -SLIPT, -SLIPPING, -SLIPS to leave out

OVERSLOW   *adj* too slow

OVERSOAK   *v* -ED, -ING, -S to soak too much

OVERSOFT   *adj* too soft

OVERSOLD   past tense of oversell

OVERSOON   *adv* too soon

OVERSOUL   *n* pl. -S a supreme reality or mind in transcendentalism

OVERSPIN   *n* pl. -S a forward spin imparted to a ball

OVERSTAY   *v* -ED, -ING, -S to stay beyond the limits or duration of

OVERSTEP   *v* -STEPPED, -STEPPING, -STEPS to go beyond

OVERSTIR   *v* -STIRRED, -STIRRING, -STIRS to stir too much

OVERSUDS   *v* -ED, -ING, -ES to form an excessive amount of suds

OVERSUP   *v* -SUPPED, -SUPPING, -SUPS to sup to excess

OVERSURE   *adj* too sure

OVERT   *adj* open to view

OVERTAKE   *v* -TOOK, -TAKEN, -TAKING, -TAKES to catch up with

OVERTALK   *v* -ED, -ING, -S to talk to excess

OVERTAME   *adj* too tame

OVERTART   *adj* too tart

OVERTASK   *v* -ED, -ING, -S to task too severely

OVERTAX   *v* -ED, -ING, -ES to tax too heavily

OVERTHIN   *adj* too thin

OVERTIME   *v* -TIMED, -TIMING, -TIMES to exceed the desired timing for

OVERTIP   *v* -TIPPED, -TIPPING, -TIPS to tip more than what is customary

OVERTIRE   *v* -TIRED, -TIRING, -TIRES to tire excessively

OVERTLY   *adv* in an overt manner

OVERTOIL   *v* -ED, -ING, -S to wear out or exhaust by excessive toil

OVERTONE   *n* pl. -S a higher partial tone

OVERTOOK   past tense of overtake

OVERTOP   *v* -TOPPED, -TOPPING, -TOPS to rise above the top of

OVERTRIM *v* -TRIMMED, -TRIMMING, -TRIMS to trim too much

OVERTURE *v* -TURED, -TURING, -TURES to propose

OVERTURN *v* -ED, -ING, -S to turn over

OVERURGE *v* -URGED, -URGING, -URGES to urge too much

OVERUSE *v* -USED, -USING, -USES to use too much

OVERVIEW *n* pl. -S a summary

OVERVOTE *v* -VOTED, -VOTING, -VOTES to defeat by a majority of votes

OVERWARM *v* -ED, -ING, -S to warm too much

OVERWARY *adj* too wary

OVERWEAK *adj* too weak

OVERWEAR *v* -WORE, -WORN, -WEARING, -WEARS to wear out

OVERWEEN *v* -ED, -ING, -S to be arrogant

OVERWET *v* -WETTED, -WETTING, -WETS to wet too much

OVERWIDE *adj* too wide

OVERWILY *adj* too wily

OVERWIND *v* -WOUND, -WINDING, -WINDS to wind too much, as a watch

OVERWISE *adj* too wise

OVERWORD *n* pl. -S a word or phrase repeated at intervals in a song

OVERWORE past tense of overwear

OVERWORK *v* -WORKED or -WROUGHT, -WORKING, -WORKS to cause to work too hard

OVERWORN past participle of overwear

OVER-WOUND past tense of overwind

OVER-WROUGHT a past tense of overwork

OVERZEAL *n* pl. -S excess of zeal

OVIBOS *n* pl. OVIBOS a wild ox

OVICIDE *n* pl. -S an agent that kills eggs **OVICIDAL** *adj*

OVIDUCT *n* pl. -S a tube through which ova travel from an ovary **OVIDUCAL** *adj*

OVIFORM *adj* shaped like an egg

OVINE *n* pl. -S a sheep or a closely related animal

OVIPARA *n/pl* egg-laying animals

OVIPOSIT *v* -ED, -ING, -S to lay eggs

OVISAC *n* pl. -S a sac containing an ovum or ova

OVOID *n* pl. -S an egg-shaped body **OVOIDAL** *adj*

OVOLO *n* pl. -LI or -LOS a convex molding

OVONIC *n* pl. -S an electronic device

OVULATE *v* -LATED, -LATING, -LATES to produce ova

OVULE *n* pl. -S a rudimentary seed **OVULAR, OVULARY** *adj*

OVUM *n* pl. OVA the female reproductive cell of animals

OW *interj* — used to express sudden pain

OWE *v* OWED, OWING, OWES to be under obligation to pay or repay

OWL *n* pl. -S a nocturnal bird

OWLET *n* pl. -S a young owl

OWLISH *adj* resembling an owl **OWLISHLY** *adv*

OWLLIKE *adj* owlish

OWN *v* -ED, -ING, -S to have as a belonging **OWNABLE** *adj*

OWNER *n* pl. -S one that owns

OWSE *n* pl. OWSEN ox

OX *n* pl. OXEN a hoofed mammal

OX *n* pl. -ES a clumsy person

OXALATE *v* -LATED, -LATING, -LATES to treat with an oxalate (a chemical salt)

OXALIS *n* pl. -ALISES a flowering plant **OXALIC** *adj*

OXAZEPAM *n* pl. -S a tranquilizing drug

OXAZINE *n* pl. -S a chemical compound

OXBLOOD *n* pl. -S a deep red color

OXBOW *n* pl. -S a U-shaped piece of wood in an ox yoke

OXCART *n* pl. -S an ox-drawn cart

OXEN pl. of ox

OXEYE *n* pl. -S a flowering plant

OXFORD *n* pl. -S a type of shoe

OXHEART *n* pl. -S a variety of sweet cherry

OXID *n* pl. -S oxide

OXIDABLE *adj* capable of being oxidized

OXIDANT *n* pl. -S an oxidizing agent

OXIDASE *n* pl. -S an oxidizing enzyme **OXIDASIC** *adj*

OXIDATE   *v* -DATED, -DATING, -DATES to oxidize

OXIDE   *n* pl. -S a binary compound of oxygen with another element or radical **OXIDIC** *adj*

OXIDISE   *v* -DISED, -DISING, -DISES to oxidize

OXIDISER   *n* pl. -S oxidizer

OXIDIZE   *v* -DIZED, -DIZING, -DIZES to combine with oxygen

OXIDIZER   *n* pl. -S an oxidant

OXIM   *n* pl. -S oxime

OXIME   *n* pl. -S a chemical compound

OXLIP   *n* pl. -S a flowering plant

OXO   *adj* containing oxygen

OXPECKER   *n* pl. -S an African bird

OXTAIL   *n* pl. -S the tail of an ox

OXTER   *n* pl. -S the armpit

OXTONGUE   *n* pl. -S a European herb

OXY   *adj* containing oxygen

OXYACID   *n* pl. -S an acid that contains oxygen

OXYGEN   *n* pl. -S a gaseous element **OXYGENIC** *adj*

OXYMORON   *n* pl. -MORA a combination of contradictory or incongruous words

OXYPHIL   *n* pl. -S oxyphile

OXYPHILE   *n* pl. -S an organism that thrives in a relatively acid environment

OXYSALT   *n* pl. -S a salt of an oxyacid

OXYSOME   *n* pl. -S a structural unit of cellular cristae

OXYTOCIC   *n* pl. -S a drug that hastens the process of childbirth

OXYTOCIN   *n* pl. -S a pituitary hormone

OXYTONE   *n* pl. -S a word having heavy stress on the last syllable

OY   *interj* — used to express dismay or pain

OYER   *n* pl. -S a type of legal writ

OYES   *n* pl. OYESSES oyez

OYEZ   *n* pl. OYESSES a cry used to introduce the opening of a court of law

OYSTER   *v* -ED, -ING, -S to gather oysters (edible mollusks)

OYSTERER   *n* pl. -S one that gathers or sells oysters

OZONATE   *v* -ATED, -ATING, -ATES to treat or combine with ozone

OZONE   *n* pl. -S a form of oxygen **OZONIC** *adj*

OZONIDE   *n* pl. -S a compound of ozone

OZONISE   *v* -ISED, -ISING, -ISES to ozonize

OZONIZE   *v* -IZED, -IZING, -IZES to convert into ozone

OZONIZER   *n* pl. -S a device for converting oxygen into ozone

OZONOUS   *adj* pertaining to ozone

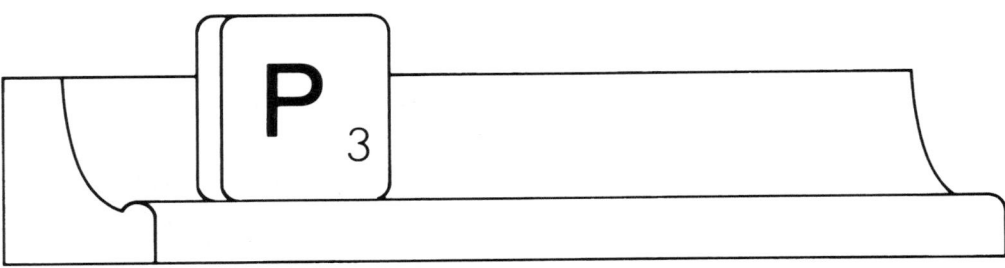

PA	*n* pl. -S a father	**PACKING**	*n* pl. -S material used to pack
PABLUM	*n* pl. -S insipid writing or speech	**PACKLY**	*adv* intimately
PABULUM	*n* pl. -S food **PABULAR** *adj*	**PACKMAN**	*n* pl. -MEN a peddler
PAC	*n* pl. -S a shoe like a moccasin	**PACKNESS**	*n* pl. -ES intimacy
PACA	*n* pl. -S a large rodent	**PACKSACK**	*n* pl. -S a carrying bag to be worn on the back
PACE	*v* PACED, PACING, PACES to walk with a regular step	**PACKWAX**	*n* pl. -ES paxwax
PACER	*n* pl. -S a horse whose gait is a pace	**PACT**	*n* pl. -S an agreement
		PACTION	*n* pl. -S a pact
PACHA	*n* pl. -S pasha	**PAD**	*v* PADDED, PADDING, PADS to line or stuff with soft material
PACHADOM	*n* pl. -S pashadom	**PADAUK**	*n* pl. -S a tropical tree
PACHALIC	*n* pl. -S pashalik	**PADDER**	*n* pl. -S one that pads
PACHINKO	*n* pl. -KOS a Japanese pinball game	**PADDIES**	pl. of paddy
PACHISI	*n* pl. -S a board game of India	**PADDING**	*n* pl. -S material with which to pad
PACHOULI	*n* pl. -S an East Indian herb	**PADDLE**	*v* -DLED, -DLING, -DLES to propel with a broad-bladed implement
PACHUCO	*n* pl. -COS a flashy Mexican-American youth		
PACIFIC	*adj* peaceful	**PADDLER**	*n* pl. -S one that paddles
PACIFIED	past tense of pacify	**PADDLING**	*n* pl. -S the act of one who paddles
PACIFIER	*n* pl. -S one that pacifies		
PACIFIES	present 3d person sing. of pacify	**PADDOCK**	*v* -ED, -ING, -S to confine in an enclosure for horses
PACIFISM	*n* pl. -S opposition to war or violence	**PADDY**	*n* pl. -DIES a rice field
PACIFIST	*n* pl. -S an advocate of pacifism	**PADI**	*n* pl. -S paddy
PACIFY	*v* -FIED, -FYING, -FIES to make peaceful	**PADISHAH**	*n* pl. -S a sovereign
		PADLE	*n* pl. -S a hoe
PACING	present participle of pace	**PADLOCK**	*v* -ED, -ING, -S to secure with a type of lock
PACK	*v* -ED, -ING, -S to put into a receptacle for transportation or storage **PACKABLE** *adj*	**PADNAG**	*n* pl. -S a horse that moves along at an easy pace
PACKAGE	*v* -AGED, -AGING, -AGES to make into a package (a wrapped or boxed object)	**PADOUK**	*n* pl. -S padauk
		PADRE	*n* pl. PADRES or PADRI a Christian clergyman
PACKAGER	*n* pl. -S one that packages	**PADRONE**	*n* pl. -NES or -NI a master
PACKER	*n* pl. -S one that packs	**PADSHAH**	*n* pl. -S padishah
PACKET	*v* -ED, -ING, -S to make into a small package	**PADUASOY**	*n* pl. -SOYS a strong silk fabric

PAEAN	*n* pl. -S a song of joy
PAEANISM	*n* pl. -S the chanting of a paean
PAELLA	*n* pl. -S a saffron-flavored stew
PAEON	*n* pl. -S a metrical foot of four syllables
PAESAN	*n* pl. -S paesano
PAESANO	*n* pl. -NI or -NOS a fellow countryman
PAGAN	*n* pl. -S an irreligious person
PAGANDOM	*n* pl. -S the realm of pagans
PAGANISE	*v* -ISED, -ISING, -ISES to paganize
PAGANISH	*adj* resembling a pagan
PAGANISM	*n* pl. -S an irreligious attitude
PAGANIST	*n* pl. -S a pagan
PAGANIZE	*v* -IZED, -IZING, -IZES to make irreligious
PAGE	*v* PAGED, PAGING, PAGES to summon by calling out the name of
PAGEANT	*n* pl. -S an elaborate public spectacle
PAGEBOY	*n* pl. -BOYS a woman's hairstyle
PAGED	past tense of page
PAGER	*n* pl. -S a beeper
PAGINAL	*adj* pertaining to the pages of a book
PAGINATE	*v* -NATED, -NATING, -NATES to number the pages of
PAGING	*n* pl. -S a transfer of computer pages
PAGOD	*n* pl. -S pagoda
PAGODA	*n* pl. -S a Far Eastern temple
PAGURIAN	*n* pl. -S a hermit crab
PAGURID	*n* pl. -S pagurian
PAH	*interj* — used as an exclamation of disgust
PAHLAVI	*n* pl. -S a former coin of Iran
PAHOEHOE	*n* pl. -S smooth solidified lava
PAID	a past tense of pay
PAIK	*v* -ED, -ING, -S to beat or strike
PAIL	*n* pl. -S a watertight cylindrical container
PAILFUL	*n* pl. PAILFULS or PAILSFUL as much as a pail can hold
PAILLARD	*n* pl. -S a slice of meat pounded thin and grilled
PAIN	*v* -ED, -ING, -S to cause pain (suffering or distress)

PAINCH	*n* pl. -ES paunch
PAINFUL	*adj* -FULLER, -FULLEST causing pain
PAINLESS	*adj* not causing pain
PAINT	*v* -ED, -ING, -S to make a representation of with paints (coloring substances)
PAINTER	*n* pl. -S one that paints
PAINTING	*n* pl. -S a picture made with paints
PAINTY	*adj* PAINTIER, PAINTIEST covered with paint
PAIR	*v* -ED, -ING, -S to arrange in sets of two
PAIRING	*n* pl. -S a matching of two opponents in a tournament
PAISA	*n* pl. PAISE or PAISAS a coin of Pakistan
PAISAN	*n* pl. -S paisano
PAISANA	*n* pl. -S a female compatriot
PAISANO	*n* pl. -NOS a fellow countryman
PAISE	a pl. of paisa
PAISLEY	*n* pl. -LEYS a patterned wool fabric
PAJAMA	*n* pl. -S a garment for sleeping or lounging
PAJAMAED	*adj* wearing pajamas
PAKEHA	*n* pl. -S a person who is not of Maori descent
PAL	*v* PALLED, PALLING, PALS to associate as friends
PALABRA	*n* pl. -S a word
PALACE	*n* pl. -S a royal residence **PALACED** *adj*
PALADIN	*n* pl. -S a knightly champion
PALAIS	*n* pl. PALAIS a palace
PALATAL	*n* pl. -S a bone of the palate
PALATE	*n* pl. -S the roof of the mouth
PALATIAL	*adj* resembling a palace
PALATINE	*n* pl. -S a high officer of an empire
PALAVER	*v* -ED, -ING, -S to chatter
PALAZZO	*n* pl. -ZI an impressive building
PALAZZOS	*n/pl* wide-legged pants for women
PALE	*adj* PALER, PALEST lacking intensity of color
PALE	*v* PALED, PALING, PALES to make or become pale

PALEA   *n* pl. -LEAE a small bract **PALEAL** *adj*

PALEFACE   *n* pl. -S a white person

PALELY   *adv* in a pale manner

PALENESS   *n* pl. -ES the quality of being pale

PALEOSOL   *n* pl. -S a layer of ancient soil

PALER   comparative of pale

PALEST   superlative of pale

PALESTRA   *n* pl. -TRAS or -TRAE a school for athletics in ancient Greece

PALET   *n* pl. -S a palea

PALETOT   *n* pl. -S a loose overcoat

PALETTE   *n* pl. -S a board on which an artist mixes colors

PALEWAYS   *adv* palewise

PALEWISE   *adv* vertically

PALFREY   *n* pl. -FREYS a riding horse

PALIER   comparative of paly

PALIEST   superlative of paly

PALIKAR   *n* pl. -S a Greek soldier

PALIMONY   *n* pl. -NIES an allowance paid to one member of an unmarried couple who have separated

PALING   *n* pl. -S a picket fence

PALINODE   *n* pl. -S a formal retraction

PALISADE   *v* -SADED, -SADING, -SADES to fortify with a heavy fence

PALISH   *adj* somewhat pale

PALL   *v* -ED, -ING, -S to become insipid

PALLADIA   *n/pl* safeguards

PALLADIC   *adj* pertaining to the metallic element palladium

PALLED   past tense of pal

PALLET   *n* pl. -S a bed or mattress of straw

PALLETTE   *n* pl. -S a piece of armor protecting the armpit

PALLIA   a pl. of pallium

PALLIAL   *adj* pertaining to a part of the brain

PALLIATE   *v* -ATED, -ATING, -ATES to conceal the seriousness of

PALLID   *adj* pale **PALLIDLY** *adv*

PALLIER   comparative of pally

PALLIEST   superlative of pally

PALLING   present participle of pal

PALLIUM   *n* pl. -LIA or -LIUMS a cloak worn in ancient Rome

PALLOR   *n* pl. -S paleness

PALLY   *adj* -LIER, -LIEST marked by close friendship

PALM   *v* -ED, -ING, -S to touch with the palm (inner surface) of the hand

PALMAR   *adj* pertaining to the palm

PALMARY   *adj* worthy of praise

PALMATE   *adj* resembling an open hand

PALMATED   *adj* palmate

PALMER   *n* pl. -S a religious pilgrim

PALMETTE   *n* pl. -S a type of ornament

PALMETTO   *n* pl. -TOS or -TOES a tropical tree

PALMIER   comparative of palmy

PALMIEST   superlative of palmy

PALMIST   *n* pl. -S a fortune-teller

PALMITIN   *n* pl. -S a chemical compound

PALMLIKE   *adj* resembling a palm tree

PALMY   *adj* PALMIER, PALMIEST marked by prosperity

PALMYRA   *n* pl. -S a tropical tree

PALOMINO   *n* pl. -NOS a slender-legged horse

PALOOKA   *n* pl. -S an inferior boxer

PALP   *n* pl. -S a palpus

PALPABLE   *adj* capable of being felt **PALPABLY** *adv*

PALPAL   *adj* pertaining to a palpus

PALPATE   *v* -PATED, -PATING, -PATES to examine by touch

PALPATOR   *n* pl. -S one that palpates

PALPEBRA   *n* pl. -BRAE an eyelid

PALPUS   *n* pl. -PI a sensory organ of an arthropod

PALSHIP   *n* pl. -S the relation existing between close friends

PALSY   *v* -SIED, -SYING, -SIES to paralyze

PALTER   *v* -ED, -ING, -S to talk or act insincerely

PALTERER   *n* pl. -S one that palters

PALTRY   *adj* -TRIER, -TRIEST petty **PALTRILY** *adv*

PALUDAL   *adj* pertaining to a marsh

PALUDISM   *n* pl. -S malaria

PALY   *adj* PALIER, PALIEST somewhat pale

PAM	*n* pl. -S the jack of clubs in certain card games	**PANE**	*n* pl. -S a sheet of glass for a window **PANED** *adj*
PAMPA	*n* pl. -S a grassland of South America	**PANEL**	*v* -ELED, -ELING, -ELS or -ELLED, -ELLING, -ELS to decorate with thin sheets of material
PAMPEAN	*n* pl. -S a native of the pampas		
PAMPER	*v* -ED, -ING, -S to treat with extreme or excessive indulgence	**PANELING**	*n* pl. -S material with which to panel
PAMPERER	*n* pl. -S one that pampers	**PANELIST**	*n* pl. -S a member of a discussion or advisory group
PAMPERO	*n* pl. -ROS a cold, dry wind	**PANELLED**	a past tense of panel
PAMPHLET	*n* pl. -S a printed work with a paper cover	**PANELLING**	a present participle of panel
PAN	*v* PANNED, PANNING, PANS to criticize harshly	**PANETELA**	*n* pl. -S panatela
PANACEA	*n* pl. -S a remedy for all diseases or ills **PANACEAN** *adj*	**PANFISH**	*n* pl. -ES any small fish that can be fried whole
PANACHE	*n* pl. -S an ornamental tuft of feathers	**PANFRY**	*v* -FRIED, -FRYING, -FRIES to fry in a frying pan
PANADA	*n* pl. -S a thick sauce	**PANFUL**	*n* pl. -S as much as a pan will hold
PANAMA	*n* pl. -S a lightweight hat	**PANG**	*v* -ED, -ING, -S to cause to have spasms of pain
PANATELA	*n* pl. -S a long, slender cigar		
PANBROIL	*v* -ED, -ING, -S to fry in a pan with little or no fat	**PANGA**	*n* pl. -S a large knife
PANCAKE	*v* -CAKED, -CAKING, -CAKES to land an airplane in a certain manner	**PANGEN**	*n* pl. -S a hypothetical heredity-controlling particle of protoplasm
		PANGENE	*n* pl. -S pangen
PANCETTA	*n* pl. -S unsmoked Italian bacon	**PANGOLIN**	*n* pl. -S a toothless mammal
PANCHAX	*n* pl. -ES a tropical fish	**PANHUMAN**	*adj* pertaining to all humanity
PANCREAS	*n* pl. -ES a large gland	**PANIC**	*v* -ICKED, -ICKING, -ICS to be overwhelmed by fear
PANDA	*n* pl. -S an herbivorous mammal		
PANDANUS	*n* pl. -NI or -NUSES a tropical plant	**PANICKY**	*adj* -ICKIER, -ICKIEST tending to panic
PANDECT	*n* pl. -S a complete body of laws	**PANICLE**	*n* pl. -S a loosely branched flower cluster **PANICLED** *adj*
PANDEMIC	*n* pl. -S a widespread disease	**PANICUM**	*n* pl. -S a grass
PANDER	*v* -ED, -ING, -S to provide gratification for others' desires	**PANIER**	*n* pl. -S pannier
		PANMIXIA	*n* pl. -S random mating within a breeding population
PANDERER	*n* pl. -S one that panders		
PANDIED	past tense of pandy	**PANMIXIS**	*n* pl. -MIXES panmixia
PANDIES	present 3d person sing. of pandy	**PANNE**	*n* pl. -S a lustrous velvet
PANDIT	*n* pl. -S a wise or learned man in India	**PANNED**	past tense of pan
		PANNIER	*n* pl. -S a large basket
PANDOOR	*n* pl. -S pandour	**PANNIKIN**	*n* pl. -S a small saucepan
PANDORA	*n* pl. -S bandore	**PANNING**	present participle of pan
PANDORE	*n* pl. -S bandore	**PANOCHA**	*n* pl. -S a coarse Mexican sugar
PANDOUR	*n* pl. -S a marauding soldier	**PANOCHE**	*n* pl. -S panocha
PANDOWDY	*n* pl. -DIES an apple dessert	**PANOPLY**	*n* pl. -PLIES a suit of armor
PANDURA	*n* pl. -S bandore	**PANOPTIC**	*adj* including everything visible in one view
PANDY	*v* -DIED, -DYING, -DIES to punish by striking the hand		
		PANORAMA	*n* pl. -S a complete view

PANPIPE	*n* pl. -S a musical instrument
PANSOPHY	*n* pl. -PHIES universal knowledge
PANSY	*n* pl. -SIES a flowering plant
PANT	*v* -ED, -ING, -S to breathe quickly and with difficulty
PANTHEON	*n* pl. -S a temple dedicated to all the gods
PANTHER	*n* pl. -S a leopard
PANTIE	*n* pl. -S a woman's or child's undergarment
PANTIES	pl. of panty
PANTILE	*n* pl. -S a roofing tile **PANTILED** *adj*
PANTO	*n* pl. -TOS a pantomime
PANTOFLE	*n* pl. -S a slipper
PANTOUM	*n* pl. -S a verse form
PANTRY	*n* pl. -TRIES a closet or room for storing kitchen utensils
PANTSUIT	*n* pl. -S a type of woman's suit
PANTY	*n* pl. PANTIES pantie
PANZER	*n* pl. -S an armored combat vehicle
PAP	*n* pl. -S a soft food for infants
PAPA	*n* pl. -S a father
PAPACY	*n* pl. -CIES the office of the pope
PAPAIN	*n* pl. -S an enzyme
PAPAL	*adj* pertaining to the pope **PAPALLY** *adv*
PAPAW	*n* pl. -S a fleshy fruit
PAPAYA	*n* pl. -S a melon-like fruit **PAPAYAN** *adj*
PAPER	*v* -ED, -ING, -S to cover or wrap with paper (a thin sheet material made of cellulose pulp)
PAPERBOY	*n* pl. -BOYS a newsboy
PAPERER	*n* pl. -S one that papers
PAPERY	*adj* resembling paper
PAPHIAN	*n* pl. -S a prostitute
PAPILLA	*n* pl. -LAE a nipple-like projection **PAPILLAR** *adj*
PAPILLON	*n* pl. -S a small dog having large ears
PAPOOSE	*n* pl. -S an American Indian baby
PAPPI	a pl. of pappus
PAPPIER	comparative of pappy
PAPPIES	pl. of pappy
PAPPIEST	superlative of pappy
PAPPOOSE	*n* pl. -S papoose
PAPPUS	*n* pl. -PI a tuft of bristles on the achene of certain plants **PAPPOSE, PAPPOUS** *adj*
PAPPY	*adj* -PIER, -PIEST resembling pap
PAPPY	*n* pl. -PIES a father
PAPRICA	*n* pl. -S paprika
PAPRIKA	*n* pl. -S a seasoning made from red peppers
PAPULA	*n* pl. -LAE papule
PAPULE	*n* pl. -S a pimple **PAPULAR, PAPULOSE** *adj*
PAPYRUS	*n* pl. -RUSES or -RI a tall aquatic plant **PAPYRAL, PAPYRIAN, PAPYRINE** *adj*
PAR	*v* PARRED, PARRING, PARS to shoot in a standard number of strokes in golf
PARA	*n* pl. -S a monetary unit of Yugoslavia
PARABLE	*n* pl. -S a simple story conveying a moral or religious lesson
PARABOLA	*n* pl. -S a conic section
PARACHOR	*n* pl. -S a mathematical constant that relates molecular volume to surface tension
PARADE	*v* -RADED, -RADING, -RADES to march in a public procession
PARADER	*n* pl. -S one that parades
PARADIGM	*n* pl. -S a pattern or example
PARADING	present participle of parade
PARADISE	*n* pl. -S a place of extreme beauty or delight
PARADOR	*n* pl. -S a government-owned hotel in Spain
PARADOS	*n* pl. -ES a protective embankment
PARADOX	*n* pl. -ES a statement seemingly contradictory or absurd yet perhaps true
PARADROP	*v* -DROPPED, -DROPPING, -DROPS to deliver by parachute
PARAFFIN	*v* -ED, -ING, -S to coat with a waxy substance
PARAFORM	*n* pl. -S a substance used as an antiseptic
PARAGOGE	*n* pl. -S the addition of a sound or sounds at the end of a word
PARAGON	*v* -ED, -ING, -S to compare with
PARAKEET	*n* pl. -S a small parrot

PARAKITE	*n* pl. -S a parachute kite for towing a person through the air by a motorboat
PARALLAX	*n* pl. -ES an apparent optical displacement of an object
PARALLEL	*v* -LELED, -LELING, -LELS or -LELLED, -LELLING, -LELS to be similar or analogous to
PARALYSE	*v* -LYSED, -LYSING, -LYSES to paralyze
PARALYZE	*v* -LYZED, -LYZING, -LYZES to render incapable of movement
PARAMENT	*n* pl. -MENTS or -MENTA an ornamental vestment
PARAMO	*n* pl. -MOS a plateau region of South America
PARAMOUR	*n* pl. -S an illicit lover
PARANG	*n* pl. -S a heavy knife
PARANOEA	*n* pl. -S paranoia
PARANOIA	*n* pl. -S a mental disorder
PARANOIC	*n* pl. -S a paranoid
PARANOID	*n* pl. -S one affected with paranoia
PARAPET	*n* pl. -S a protective wall
PARAPH	*n* pl. -S a flourish at the end of a signature
PARAQUAT	*n* pl. -S a weed killer
PARAQUET	*n* pl. -S parakeet
PARASANG	*n* pl. -S a Persian unit of distance
PARASHAH	*n* pl. -SHOTH or -SHIOTH a passage in Jewish scripture
PARASITE	*n* pl. -S an organism that lives and feeds on or in another organism
PARASOL	*n* pl. -S a small, light umbrella
PARAVANE	*n* pl. -S an underwater device used to cut cables
PARAWING	*n* pl. -S a winglike parachute
PARAZOAN	*n* pl. -S any of a major division of multicellular animals
PARBOIL	*v* -ED, -ING, -S to cook partially by boiling for a short time
PARCEL	*v* -CELED, -CELING, -CELS or -CELLED, -CELLING, -CELS to divide into parts or shares
PARCENER	*n* pl. -S a joint heir
PARCH	*v* -ED, -ING, -ES to make very dry
PARCHESI	*n* pl. -S pachisi
PARCHISI	*n* pl. -S pachisi
PARD	*n* pl. -S a leopard
PARDAH	*n* pl. -S purdah
PARDEE	*interj* pardi
PARDI	*interj* — used as a mild oath
PARDIE	*interj* pardi
PARDINE	*adj* pertaining to a leopard
PARDNER	*n* pl. -S chum; friend
PARDON	*v* -ED, -ING, -S to release from liability for an offense
PARDONER	*n* pl. -S one that pardons
PARDY	*interj* pardi
PARE	*v* PARED, PARING, PARES to cut off the outer covering of
PARECISM	*n* pl. -S the state of having the male and female sexual organs beside or near each other
PAREIRA	*n* pl. -S a medicinal plant root
PARENT	*v* -ED, -ING, -S to exercise the functions of a parent (a father or mother)
PARENTAL	*adj* pertaining to a parent
PAREO	*n* pl. -REOS pareu
PARER	*n* pl. -S one that pares
PARERGON	*n* pl. -GA a composition derived from a larger work
PARESIS	*n* pl. -RESES partial loss of the ability to move
PARETIC	*n* pl. -S one affected with paresis
PAREU	*n* pl. -S a Polynesian garment
PAREVE	*adj* parve
PARFAIT	*n* pl. -S a frozen dessert
PARFLESH	*n* pl. -ES a rawhide soaked in lye to remove the hair and dried
PARFOCAL	*adj* having lenses with the corresponding focal points in the same plane
PARGE	*v* PARGED, PARGING, PARGES to parget
PARGET	*v* -GETED, -GETING, -GETS or -GETTED, -GETTING, -GETS to cover with plaster
PARGING	*n* pl. -S a thin coat of mortar or plaster for sealing masonry
PARGO	*n* pl. -GOS a food fish
PARHELIA	*n/pl* bright circular spots appearing on a solar halo
PARHELIC	*adj* pertaining to parhelia
PARIAH	*n* pl. -S a social outcast
PARIAN	*n* pl. -S a hard, white porcelain
PARIES	*n* pl. PARIETES the wall of an organ

PARIETAL   *n* pl. -S a bone of the skull

PARING   *n* pl. -S something pared off

PARIS   *n* pl. -ISES a European herb

PARISH   *n* pl. -ES an ecclesiastical district

PARITY   *n* pl. -TIES equality

PARK   *v* -ED, -ING, -S to leave a vehicle in a location for a time

PARKA   *n* pl. -S a hooded garment

PARKER   *n* pl. -S one that parks

PARKING   *n* pl. -S an area in which vehicles may be left

PARKLAND   *n* pl. -S a grassland region with isolated or grouped trees

PARKLIKE   *adj* resembling an outdoor recreational area

PARKWAY   *n* pl. -WAYS a wide highway

PARLANCE   *n* pl. -S a manner of speaking

PARLANDO   *adj* sung in a manner suggestive of speech

PARLANTE   *adj* parlando

PARLAY   *v* -ED, -ING, -S to bet an original wager and its winnings on a subsequent event

PARLE   *v* PARLED, PARLING, PARLES to parley

PARLEY   *v* -LEYED, -LEYING, -LEYS to discuss terms with an enemy

PARLEYER   *n* pl. -S one who parleys

PARLING   present participle of parle

PARLOR   *n* pl. -S a room for the entertainment of visitors

PARLOUR   *n* pl. -S parlor

PARLOUS   *adj* dangerous

PARODIC   *adj* comically imitative

PARODIED   past tense of parody

PARODIES   present 3d person sing. of parody

PARODIST   *n* pl. -S one who parodies

PARODOS   *n* pl. -DOI an ode sung in ancient Greek drama

PARODY   *v* -DIED, -DYING, -DIES to imitate a serious literary work for comic effect

PAROL   *n* pl. -S an utterance

PAROLE   *v* -ROLED, -ROLING, -ROLES to release from prison before completion of the imposed sentence

PAROLEE   *n* pl. -S one who is paroled

PARONYM   *n* pl. -S a word having the same root as another

PAROQUET   *n* pl. -S parakeet

PAROTIC   *adj* situated near the ear

PAROTID   *n* pl. -S a salivary gland

PAROTOID   *n* pl. -S a gland of certain toads and frogs

PAROUS   *adj* having produced offspring

PAROXYSM   *n* pl. -S a sudden fit or attack

PARQUET   *v* -ED, -ING, -S to furnish with a floor of inlaid design

PARR   *n* pl. -S a young salmon

PARRAL   *n* pl. -S parrel

PARRED   past tense of par

PARREL   *n* pl. -S a sliding loop of rope or chain used on a ship

PARRIDGE   *n* pl. -S porridge

PARRIED   past tense of parry

PARRIES   present 3d person sing. of parry

PARRING   present participle of par

PARRITCH   *n* pl. -ES porridge

PARROKET   *n* pl. -S parakeet

PARROT   *v* -ED, -ING, -S to repeat or imitate without thought or understanding

PARROTER   *n* pl. -S one that parrots

PARROTY   *adj* resembling a parrot (a hook-billed tropical bird)

PARRY   *v* -RIED, -RYING, -RIES to ward off a blow

PARSE   *v* PARSED, PARSING, PARSES to describe and analyze grammatically **PARSABLE** *adj*

PARSEC   *n* pl. -S a unit of astronomical distance

PARSER   *n* pl. -S one that parses

PARSING   present participle of parse

PARSLEY   *n* pl. -LEYS a cultivated herb **PARSLEYED, PARSLIED** *adj*

PARSNIP   *n* pl. -S a European herb

PARSON   *n* pl. -S a clergyman **PARSONIC** *adj*

PART   *v* -ED, -ING, -S to divide or break into separate pieces

PARTAKE   *v* -TOOK, -TAKEN, -TAKING, -TAKES to participate

PARTAKER   *n* pl. -S one that partakes

PARTAN   *n* pl. -S an edible crab

PARTERRE   *n* pl. -S a section of a theater

PARTIAL   *n* pl. -S a simple component of a complex tone

PARTIBLE	*adj* divisible
PARTICLE	*n* pl. -S a very small piece or part
PARTIED	past tense of party
PARTIER	*n* pl. -S partyer
PARTIES	present 3d person sing. of party
PARTING	*n* pl. -S a division or separation
PARTISAN	*n* pl. -S a firm supporter of a person, party, or cause
PARTITA	*n* pl. -S a set of related instrumental pieces
PARTITE	*adj* divided into parts
PARTIZAN	*n* pl. -S partisan
PARTLET	*n* pl. -S a woman's garment
PARTLY	*adv* in some measure or degree
PARTNER	*v* -ED, -ING, -S to associate with in some activity of common interest
PARTON	*n* pl. -S a hypothetical atomic particle
PARTOOK	past tense of partake
PARTWAY	*adv* to some extent
PARTY	*v* -TIED, -TYING, -TIES to attend a social gathering
PARTYER	*n* pl. -S one that parties
PARURA	*n* pl. -S parure
PARURE	*n* pl. -S a set of matched jewelry
PARVE	*adj* made without milk or meat
PARVENU	*n* pl. -S one who has suddenly risen above his class
PARVENUE	*adj* characteristic of a parvenu
PARVIS	*n* pl. -VISES an enclosed area in front of a church
PARVISE	*n* pl. -S parvis
PARVO	*n* pl. -VOS a contagious disease of dogs
PARVOLIN	*n* pl. -S an oily liquid obtained from fish
PAS	*n* pl. PAS a dance step
PASCAL	*n* pl. -S a unit of pressure
PASCHAL	*n* pl. -S a candle used in certain religious ceremonies
PASE	*n* pl. -S a movement of a matador's cape
PASEO	*n* pl. -SEOS a leisurely stroll
PASH	*v* -ED, -ING, -ES to strike violently
PASHA	*n* pl. -S a former Turkish high official
PASHADOM	*n* pl. -S the rank of a pasha
PASHALIC	*n* pl. -S pashalik
PASHALIK	*n* pl. -S the territory of a pasha
PASQUIL	*n* pl. -S a satire or lampoon
PASS	*v* -ED, -ING, -ES to go by
PASSABLE	*adj* fairly good or acceptable **PASSABLY** *adv*
PASSADE	*n* pl. -S a turn of a horse backward or forward on the same ground
PASSADO	*n* pl. -DOS or -DOES a forward thrust in fencing
PASSAGE	*v* -SAGED, -SAGING, -SAGES to make a voyage
PASSANT	*adj* walking with the farther forepaw raised — used of a heraldic animal
PASSBAND	*n* pl. -S a frequency band that permits transmission with maximum efficiency
PASSBOOK	*n* pl. -S a bankbook
PASSE	*adj* outmoded
PASSEE	*adj* passe
PASSEL	*n* pl. -S a large quantity or number
PASSER	*n* pl. -S one that passes
PASSERBY	*n* pl. PASSERSBY one who passes by
PASSIBLE	*adj* capable of feeling or suffering
PASSIM	*adv* here and there
PASSING	*n* pl. -S a death
PASSION	*n* pl. -S an intense emotion
PASSIVE	*n* pl. -S a verb form
PASSKEY	*n* pl. -KEYS a key that opens several different locks
PASSLESS	*adj* incapable of being traveled over or through
PASSOVER	*n* pl. -S the lamb eaten at the feast of a Jewish holiday
PASSPORT	*n* pl. -S a document allowing travel from one country to another
PASSUS	*n* pl. -ES a section of a story or poem
PASSWORD	*n* pl. -S a secret word that must be spoken to gain admission
PAST	*n* pl. -S time gone by
PASTA	*n* pl. -S a food made of dough
PASTE	*v* PASTED, PASTING, PASTES to fasten with a sticky mixture
PASTEL	*n* pl. -S a soft, delicate hue
PASTER	*n* pl. -S one that pastes

PASTERN *n* pl. -S a part of a horse's foot

PASTEUP *n* pl. -S a finished copy to be photographed for making a printing plate

PASTICCI *n/pl* pastiches

PASTICHE *n* pl. -S an artistic work made of fragments from various sources

PASTIE *n* pl. -S pasty

PASTIER comparative of pasty

PASTIES pl. of pasty

PASTIEST superlative of pasty

PASTIL *n* pl. -S pastille

PASTILLE *n* pl. -S a lozenge

PASTIME *n* pl. -S a recreational activity

PASTINA *n* pl. -S a type of macaroni

PASTING present participle of paste

PASTIS *n* pl. -TISES a French liqueur

PASTLESS *adj* having no past

PASTNESS *n* pl. -ES the state of being past or gone by

PASTOR *v* -ED, -ING, -S to serve as the spiritual overseer of

PASTORAL *n* pl. -S a literary or artistic work that depicts country life

PASTRAMI *n* pl. -S a highly seasoned smoked beef

PASTROMI *n* pl. -S pastrami

PASTRY *n* pl. -TRIES a sweet baked food

PASTURAL *adj* pertaining to a pasture

PASTURE *v* -TURED, -TURING, -TURES to put in a pasture (a grazing area)

PASTURER *n* pl. -S one that pastures livestock

PASTY *adj* PASTIER, PASTIEST pale and unhealthy in appearance

PASTY *n* pl. PASTIES a meat pie

PAT *v* PATTED, PATTING, PATS to touch lightly

PATACA *n* pl. -S a monetary unit of Macao

PATAGIAL *adj* pertaining to a patagium

PATAGIUM *n* pl. -GIA a wing membrane of a bat

PATAMAR *n* pl. -S a sailing vessel

PATCH *v* -ED, -ING, -ES to mend or cover a hole or weak spot in

PATCHER *n* pl. -S one that patches

PATCHY *adj* PATCHIER, PATCHIEST uneven in quality **PATCHILY** *adv*

PATE *n* pl. -S the top of the head **PATED** *adj*

PATELLA *n* pl. -LAE or -LAS the flat movable bone at the front of the knee **PATELLAR** *adj*

PATEN *n* pl. -S a plate

PATENCY *n* pl. -CIES the state of being obvious

PATENT *v* -ED, -ING, -S to obtain a patent (a government grant protecting the rights of an inventor) on

PATENTEE *n* pl. -S one that holds a patent

PATENTLY *adv* obviously

PATENTOR *n* pl. -S one that grants a patent

PATER *n* pl. -S a father

PATERNAL *adj* pertaining to a father

PATH *n* pl. -S a trodden way or track

PATHETIC *adj* arousing pity

PATHLESS *adj* having no path

PATHOGEN *n* pl. -S any disease-producing organism

PATHOS *n* pl. -ES a quality that arouses feelings of pity or compassion

PATHWAY *n* pl. -WAYS a path

PATIENCE *n* pl. -S the quality of being patient

PATIENT *adj* -TIENTER, -TIENTEST able to endure disagreeable circumstances without complaint

PATIENT *n* pl. -S one who is under medical treatment

PATIN *n* pl. -S paten

PATINA *n* pl. -NAE or -NAS a green film that forms on bronze

PATINATE *v* -NATED, -NATING, -NATES to give a patina to

PATINE *v* -TINED, -TINING, -TINES to cover with a patina

PATINIZE *v* -NIZED, -NIZING, -NIZES to patinate

PATIO *n* pl. -TIOS an outdoor paved area adjoining a house

PATLY *adv* suitably

PATNESS *n* pl. -ES suitability

PATOIS *n* pl. PATOIS a dialect

PATRIOT *n* pl. -S one who loves his country

PATROL *v* -TROLLED, -TROLLING, -TROLS to pass through an area for the purposes of observation or security

PATRON _n_ pl. -S a regular customer **PATRONAL, PATRONLY** _adj_

PATROON _n_ pl. -S a landowner granted manorial rights under old Dutch law

PATSY _n_ pl. -SIES a person who is easily fooled

PATTAMAR _n_ pl. -S patamar

PATTED past tense of pat

PATTEE _adj_ paty

PATTEN _n_ pl. -S a shoe having a thick wooden sole

PATTER _v_ -ED, -ING, -S to talk glibly or rapidly

PATTERER _n_ pl. -S one that patters

PATTERN _v_ -ED, -ING, -S to make according to a prescribed design

PATTIE _n_ pl. -S patty

PATTING present participle of pat

PATTY _n_ pl. -TIES a small, flat cake of chopped food

PATTYPAN _n_ pl. -S a pan in which patties are baked

PATULENT _adj_ patulous

PATULOUS _adj_ spreading; open

PATY _adj_ formee

PATZER _n_ pl. -S an inept chess player

PAUCITY _n_ pl. -TIES smallness of number or quantity

PAUGHTY _adj_ arrogant

PAULDRON _n_ pl. -S a piece of armor for the shoulder

PAULIN _n_ pl. -S a sheet of waterproof material

PAUNCH _n_ pl. -ES the belly or abdomen **PAUNCHED** _adj_

PAUNCHY _adj_ PAUNCHIER, PAUNCHIEST having a protruding belly

PAUPER _v_ -ED, -ING, -S to reduce to poverty

PAUSAL _adj_ pertaining to a break or rest in speaking or writing

PAUSE _v_ PAUSED, PAUSING, PAUSES to stop temporarily

PAUSER _n_ pl. -S one that pauses

PAVAN _n_ pl. -S a slow, stately dance

PAVANE _n_ pl. -S pavan

PAVE _v_ PAVED, PAVING, PAVES to cover with material that forms a firm, level surface

PAVEED _adj_ set close together to conceal a metal base

PAVEMENT _n_ pl. -S a paved surface

PAVER _n_ pl. -S one that paves

PAVID _adj_ timid

PAVILION _v_ -ED, -ING, -S to cover with a large tent

PAVILLON _n_ pl. -S the bell of a wind instrument

PAVIN _n_ pl. -S pavan

PAVING _n_ pl. -S pavement

PAVIOR _n_ pl. -S a paver

PAVIOUR _n_ pl. -S a paver

PAVIS _n_ pl. -ISES a large medieval shield

PAVISE _n_ pl. -S pavis

PAVISER _n_ pl. -S a soldier carrying a pavis

PAVLOVA _n_ pl. -S a meringue dessert

PAVONINE _adj_ resembling a peacock

PAW _v_ -ED, -ING, -S to strike or scrape with a beating motion

PAWER _n_ pl. -S one that paws

PAWKY _adj_ PAWKIER, PAWKIEST sly **PAWKILY** _adv_

PAWL _n_ pl. -S a hinged mechanical part

PAWN _v_ -ED, -ING, -S to give as security for something borrowed **PAWNABLE** _adj_

PAWNAGE _n_ pl. -S an act of pawning

PAWNEE _n_ pl. -S one to whom something is pawned

PAWNER _n_ pl. -S one that pawns something

PAWNOR _n_ pl. -S pawner

PAWNSHOP _n_ pl. -S a place where things are pawned

PAWPAW _n_ pl. -S papaw

PAX _n_ pl. -ES a ceremonial embrace given to signify Christian love and unity

PAXWAX _n_ pl. -ES the nuchal ligament of a quadruped

PAY _v_ PAID or PAYED, PAYING, PAYS to give money or something of value in exchange for goods or services

PAYABLE _adj_ profitable **PAYABLY** _adv_

PAYABLES _n/pl_ accounts payable

PAYBACK   *n* pl. -S a return on an investment equal to the original capital outlay

PAYCHECK   *n* pl. -S a check in payment of wages or salary

PAYDAY   *n* pl. -DAYS the day on which wages are paid

PAYEE   *n* pl. -S one to whom money is paid

PAYER   *n* pl. -S one that pays

PAYGRADE   *n* pl. -S the grade of military personnel according to a base pay scale

PAYLOAD   *n* pl. -S the part of a cargo producing income

PAYMENT   *n* pl. -S something that is paid

PAYNIM   *n* pl. -S a pagan

PAYOFF   *n* pl. -S the act of distributing gains

PAYOLA   *n* pl. -S a secret payment for favors

PAYOR   *n* pl. -S payer

PAYOUT   *n* pl. -S money that is paid out

PAYROLL   *n* pl. -S a list of employees entitled to payment

PAZAZZ   *n* pl. -ES pizazz

PE   *n* pl. -S a Hebrew letter

PEA   *n* pl. -S the edible seed of an annual herb

PEACE   *v* PEACED, PEACING, PEACES to be or become silent

PEACEFUL   *adj* -FULLER, -FULLEST undisturbed; calm

PEACENIK   *n* pl. -S one who demonstrates against a war

PEACH   *v* -ED, -ING, -ES to inform against someone

PEACHER   *n* pl. -S one that peaches

PEACHY   *adj* PEACHIER, PEACHIEST dandy

PEACING   present participle of peace

PEACOAT   *n* pl. -S a heavy woolen jacket

PEACOCK   *v* -ED, -ING, -S to strut vainly

PEACOCKY   *adj* -COCKIER, -COCKIEST flamboyant, showy

PEAFOWL   *n* pl. -S a large pheasant

PEAG   *n* pl. -S wampum

PEAGE   *n* pl. -S peag

PEAHEN   *n* pl. -S a female peafowl

PEAK   *v* -ED, -ING, -S to reach a maximum

PEAKIER   comparative of peaky

PEAKIEST   superlative of peaky

PEAKISH   *adj* somewhat sickly

PEAKLESS   *adj* having no peak (a pointed top)

PEAKLIKE   *adj* resembling a peak

PEAKY   *adj* PEAKIER, PEAKIEST sickly

PEAL   *v* -ED, -ING, -S to ring out

PEALIKE   *adj* resembling a pea

PEAN   *n* pl. -S paean

PEANUT   *n* pl. -S the nutlike seed or pod of an annual vine

PEAR   *n* pl. -S a fleshy fruit

PEARL   *v* -ED, -ING, -S to adorn with pearls (smooth, rounded masses formed in certain mollusks)

PEARLASH   *n* pl. -ES an alkaline compound

PEARLER   *n* pl. -S one that dives for pearls

PEARLITE   *n* pl. -S a cast-iron alloy

PEARLY   *adj* PEARLIER, PEARLIEST resembling a pearl

PEARMAIN   *n* pl. -S a variety of apple

PEART   *adj* PEARTER, PEARTEST lively **PEARTLY** *adv*

PEASANT   *n* pl. -S a person of inferior social rank

PEASCOD   *n* pl. -S peasecod

PEASE   *n* pl. PEASEN or PEASES a pea

PEASECOD   *n* pl. -S a pea pod

PEAT   *n* pl. -S a substance composed of partially decayed vegetable matter

PEATY   *adj* PEATIER, PEATIEST resembling or containing peat

PEAVEY   *n* pl. -VEYS a lever used to move logs

PEAVY   *n* pl. -VIES peavey

PEBBLE   *v* -BLED, -BLING, -BLES to cover with pebbles (small, rounded stones)

PEBBLY   *adj* -BLIER, -BLIEST resembling pebbles

PEC   *n* pl. -S a chest muscle

PECAN   *n* pl. -S a nut-bearing tree

PECCABLE   *adj* liable to sin

PECCANCY   *n* pl. -CIES the state of being peccant

PECCANT	*adj* sinful
PECCARY	*n* pl. -RIES a piglike hoofed mammal
PECCAVI	*n* pl. -S a confession of sin
PECH	*v* -ED, -ING, -S to pant
PECHAN	*n* pl. -S the stomach
PECK	*v* -ED, -ING, -S to strike with the beak or something pointed
PECKER	*n* pl. -S one that pecks
PECKISH	*adj* irritable
PECKY	*adj* PECKIER, PECKIEST marked by decay caused by fungi
PECORINO	*n* pl. -NOS or -NI a hard cheese made from sheep's milk
PECTASE	*n* pl. -S an enzyme
PECTATE	*n* pl. -S a chemical salt
PECTEN	*n* pl. -TENS or -TINES a comblike anatomical part
PECTIN	*n* pl. -S a carbohydrate derivative **PECTIC** *adj*
PECTIZE	*v* -TIZED, -TIZING, -TIZES to change into a jelly
PECTORAL	*n* pl. -S something worn on the breast
PECULATE	*v* -LATED, -LATING, -LATES to embezzle
PECULIAR	*n* pl. -S something belonging exclusively to a person
PECULIUM	*n* pl. -LIA private property
PED	*n* pl. -S a natural soil aggregate
PEDAGOG	*n* pl. -S a teacher
PEDAGOGY	*n* pl. -GIES the work of a teacher
PEDAL	*v* -ALED, -ALING, -ALS or -ALLED, -ALLING, -ALS to operate by means of foot levers
PEDALFER	*n* pl. -S a type of soil
PEDALIER	*n* pl. -S the pedal keyboard of an organ
PEDALLED	a past tense of pedal
PEDALLING	a present participle of pedal
PEDALO	*n* pl. -LOS a paddleboat powered by pedals
PEDANT	*n* pl. -S one who flaunts his knowledge **PEDANTIC** *adj*
PEDANTRY	*n* pl. -RIES ostentatious display of knowledge
PEDATE	*adj* resembling a foot **PEDATELY** *adv*
PEDDLE	*v* -DLED, -DLING, -DLES to travel about selling wares

PEDDLER	*n* pl. -S one that peddles
PEDDLERY	*n* pl. -RIES the trade of a peddler
PEDDLING	present tense of peddle
PEDERAST	*n* pl. -S a man who engages in sexual activities with boys
PEDES	pl. of pes
PEDESTAL	*v* -TALED, -TALING, -TALS or -TALLED, -TALLING, -TALS to provide with an architectural support or base
PEDICAB	*n* pl. -S a passenger vehicle that is pedaled
PEDICEL	*n* pl. -S a slender basal part of an organism
PEDICLE	*n* pl. -S pedicel **PEDICLED** *adj*
PEDICURE	*v* -CURED, -CURING, -CURES to administer a cosmetic treatment to the feet and toenails
PEDIFORM	*adj* shaped like a foot
PEDIGREE	*n* pl. -S a line of ancestors
PEDIMENT	*n* pl. -S a triangular architectural part
PEDIPALP	*n* pl. -S an appendage of an arachnid
PEDLAR	*n* pl. -S peddler
PEDLARY	*n* pl. -LARIES peddlery
PEDLER	*n* pl. -S peddler
PEDLERY	*n* pl. -LERIES peddlery
PEDOCAL	*n* pl. -S a type of soil
PEDOLOGY	*n* pl. -GIES the scientific study of the behavior and development of children
PEDRO	*n* pl. -DROS a card game
PEDUNCLE	*n* pl. -S a flower stalk
PEE	*n* pl. -S the letter P
PEEBEEN	*n* pl. -S a large hardwood evergreen tree
PEEK	*v* -ED, -ING, -S to look furtively or quickly
PEEKABOO	*n* pl. -BOOS a children's game
PEEL	*v* -ED, -ING, -S to strip off an outer covering of **PEELABLE** *adj*
PEELER	*n* pl. -S one that peels
PEELING	*n* pl. -S a piece or strip that has been peeled off
PEEN	*v* -ED, -ING, -S to beat with the non-flat end of a hammerhead
PEEP	*v* -ED, -ING, -S to utter a short, shrill cry
PEEPER	*n* pl. -S one that peeps

PEEPHOLE *n* pl. -S a small opening through which one may look

PEEPSHOW *n* pl. -S an exhibition viewed through a small opening

PEEPUL *n* pl. -S pipal

PEER *v* -ED, -ING, -S to look narrowly or searchingly

PEERAGE *n* pl. -S the rank of a nobleman

PEERESS *n* pl. -ES a noblewoman

PEERIE *n* pl. -S peery

PEERLESS *adj* having no equal

PEERY *n* pl. PEERIES a child's toy

PEESWEEP *n* pl. -S a lapwing

PEETWEET *n* pl. -S a wading bird

PEEVE *v* PEEVED, PEEVING, PEEVES to annoy

PEEVISH *adj* irritable

PEEWEE *n* pl. -S an unusually small person or thing

PEEWIT *n* pl. -S pewit

PEG *v* PEGGED, PEGGING, PEGS to fasten with a peg (a wooden pin)

PEGBOARD *n* pl. -S a board with holes for pegs

PEGBOX *n* pl. -ES a part of a stringed instrument

PEGGED past tense of peg

PEGGING present participle of peg

PEGLESS *adj* lacking a peg

PEGLIKE *adj* resembling a peg

PEH *n* pl. -S pe

PEIGNOIR *n* pl. -S a woman's gown

PEIN *v* -ED, -ING, -S to peen

PEISE *v* PEISED, PEISING, PEISES to weigh

PEKAN *n* pl. -S a carnivorous mammal

PEKE *n* pl. -S a small, long-haired dog

PEKIN *n* pl. -S a silk fabric

PEKOE *n* pl. -S a black tea

PELAGE *n* pl. -S the coat or covering of a mammal **PELAGIAL** *adj*

PELAGIC *adj* oceanic

PELE *n* pl. -S a medieval fortified tower

PELERINE *n* pl. -S a woman's cape

PELF *n* pl. -S money or wealth

PELICAN *n* pl. -S a large, web-footed bird

PELISSE *n* pl. -S a long outer garment

PELITE *n* pl. -S a rock composed of fine fragments **PELITIC** *adj*

PELLAGRA *n* pl. -S a niacin-deficiency disease

PELLET *v* -ED, -ING, -S to strike with pellets (small rounded masses)

PELLETAL *adj* resembling a pellet

PELLICLE *n* pl. -S a thin skin or film

PELLMELL *n* pl. -S a jumbled mass

PELLUCID *adj* transparent

PELMET *n* pl. -S a decorative cornice

PELON *adj* hairless

PELORIA *n* pl. -S abnormal regularity of a flower form **PELORIAN, PELORIC** *adj*

PELORUS *n* pl. -ES a navigational instrument

PELOTA *n* pl. -S a court game of Spanish origin

PELT *v* -ED, -ING, -S to strike repeatedly with blows or missiles

PELTAST *n* pl. -S a soldier of ancient Greece

PELTATE *adj* shaped like a shield

PELTER *v* -ED, -ING, -S to pelt

PELTRY *n* pl. -RIES an animal skin

PELVIC *n* pl. -S a bone of the pelvis

PELVIS *n* pl. -VES or -VISES a part of the skeleton

PEMBINA *n* pl. -S a variety of cranberry

PEMICAN *n* pl. -S pemmican

PEMMICAN *n* pl. -S a food prepared by North American Indians

PEMOLINE *n* pl. -S a drug used as a stimulant

PEMPHIX *n* pl. -ES a skin disease

PEN *v* PENNED, PENNING, PENS to write with a pen (an instrument for writing with fluid ink)

PENAL *adj* pertaining to punishment

PENALISE *v* -ISED, -ISING, -ISES to penalize

PENALITY *n* pl. -TIES liability to punishment

PENALIZE *v* -IZED, -IZING, -IZES to subject to a penalty

PENALLY *adv* in a penal manner

PENALTY *n* pl. -TIES a punishment imposed for violation of a law, rule, or agreement

PENANCE	*v* -ANCED, -ANCING, -ANCES to impose a type of punishment upon
PENANG	*n* pl. -S a cotton fabric
PENATES	*n/pl* the Roman gods of the household
PENCE	a pl. of penny
PENCEL	*n* pl. -S a small flag
PENCHANT	*n* pl. -S a strong liking for something
PENCIL	*v* -CILED, -CILING, -CILS or -CILLED, -CILLING, -CILS to produce by using a pencil (a writing and drawing implement)
PENCILER	*n* pl. -S one that pencils
PEND	*v* -ED, -ING, -S to remain undecided or unsettled
PENDANT	*n* pl. -S a hanging ornament
PENDENCY	*n* pl. -CIES a pending state
PENDENT	*n* pl. -S pendant
PENDULUM	*n* pl. -S a type of free swinging body **PENDULAR** *adj*
PENES	a pl. of penis
PENGO	*n* pl. -GOS a former monetary unit of Hungary
PENGUIN	*n* pl. -S a flightless, aquatic bird
PENICIL	*n* pl. -S a small tuft of hairs
PENIS	*n* pl. -NES or -NISES the male organ of copulation **PENIAL, PENILE** *adj*
PENITENT	*n* pl. -S a person who repents his sins
PENKNIFE	*n* pl. -KNIVES a small pocketknife
PENLIGHT	*n* pl. -S a small flashlight
PENLITE	*n* pl. -S penlight
PENMAN	*n* pl. -MEN an author
PENNA	*n* pl. -NAE any of the feathers that determine a bird's shape
PENNAME	*n* pl. -S a name used by an author instead of his real name
PENNANT	*n* pl. -S a long, narrow flag
PENNATE	*adj* having wings or feathers
PENNATED	*adj* pennate
PENNE	*n* pl. PENNE short tubular pasta
PENNED	past tense of pen
PENNER	*n* pl. -S one that pens
PENNI	*n* pl. -NIA or -NIS a Finnish coin
PENNIES	a pl. of penny
PENNINE	*n* pl. -S a mineral
PENNING	present participle of pen
PENNON	*n* pl. -S a pennant **PENNONED** *adj*
PENNY	*n* pl. PENNIES or PENCE a coin of the United Kingdom
PENOCHE	*n* pl. -S penuche
PENOLOGY	*n* pl. -GIES the science of the punishment of crime
PENONCEL	*n* pl. -S a small pennon
PENPOINT	*n* pl. -S the point of a pen
PENSEE	*n* pl. -S a thought
PENSIL	*n* pl. -S pencel
PENSILE	*adj* hanging loosely
PENSION	*v* -ED, -ING, -S to grant a retirement allowance to
PENSIONE	*n* pl. -S a boarding house
PENSIVE	*adj* engaged in deep thought
PENSTER	*n* pl. -S a writer
PENSTOCK	*n* pl. -S a conduit for conveying water to a waterwheel
PENT	*adj* confined
PENTACLE	*n* pl. -S a five-pointed star
PENTAD	*n* pl. -S a group of five
PENTAGON	*n* pl. -S a five-sided polygon
PENTANE	*n* pl. -S a volatile liquid
PENTANOL	*n* pl. -S an alcohol
PENTARCH	*n* pl. -S one of five joint rulers
PENTENE	*n* pl. -S a liquid hydrocarbon
PENTODE	*n* pl. -S a type of electron tube
PENTOMIC	*adj* made up of five battle groups
PENTOSAN	*n* pl. -S a complex carbohydrate
PENTOSE	*n* pl. -S a sugar having five carbon atoms per molecule
PENTYL	*n* pl. -S amyl
PENUCHE	*n* pl. -S a fudge-like candy
PENUCHI	*n* pl. -S penuche
PENUCHLE	*n* pl. -S pinochle
PENUCKLE	*n* pl. -S pinochle
PENULT	*n* pl. -S the next to last syllable in a word
PENUMBRA	*n* pl. -BRAE or -BRAS a partial shadow
PENURY	*n* pl. -RIES extreme poverty
PEON	*n* pl. -S or -ES an unskilled laborer

PEONAGE   *n* pl. -S the condition of being a peon

PEONISM   *n* pl. -S peonage

PEONY   *n* pl. -NIES a flowering plant

PEOPLE   *v* -PLED, -PLING, -PLES to furnish with inhabitants

PEOPLER   *n* pl. -S one that peoples

PEP   *v* PEPPED, PEPPING, PEPS to fill with energy

PEPERONI   *n* pl. -S a highly seasoned sausage

PEPLOS   *n* pl. -ES a garment worn by women in ancient Greece

PEPLUM   *n* pl. -LUMS or -LA a short section attached to the waistline of a garment **PEPLUMED** *adj*

PEPLUS   *n* pl. -ES peplos

PEPO   *n* pl. -POS a fruit having a fleshy interior and a hard rind

PEPONIDA   *n* pl. -S pepo

PEPONIUM   *n* pl. -S pepo

PEPPED   past tense of pep

PEPPER   *v* -ED, -ING, -S to season with pepper (a pungent condiment)

PEPPERER   *n* pl. -S one that peppers

PEPPERY   *adj* resembling pepper

PEPPING   present participle of pep

PEPPY   *adj* -PIER, -PIEST full of energy **PEPPILY** *adv*

PEPSIN   *n* pl. -S a digestive enzyme of the stomach

PEPSINE   *n* pl. -S pepsin

PEPTIC   *n* pl. -S a substance that promotes digestion

PEPTID   *n* pl. -S peptide

PEPTIDE   *n* pl. -S a combination of amino acids **PEPTIDIC** *adj*

PEPTIZE   *v* -TIZED, -TIZING, -TIZES to increase the colloidal dispersion of

PEPTIZER   *n* pl. -S one that peptizes

PEPTONE   *n* pl. -S a protein compound **PEPTONIC** *adj*

PER   *prep* for each

PERACID   *n* pl. -S a type of acid

PERCALE   *n* pl. -S a cotton fabric

PERCEIVE   *v* -CEIVED, -CEIVING, -CEIVES to become aware of through the senses

PERCENT   *n* pl. -S one part in a hundred

PERCEPT   *n* pl. -S something perceived

PERCH   *v* -ED, -ING, -ES to sit or rest on an elevated place

PERCHER   *n* pl. -S one that perches

PERCOID   *n* pl. -S a spiny-finned fish

PERCUSS   *v* -ED, -ING, -ES to strike with force

PERDIE   *interj* pardi

PERDU   *n* pl. -S a soldier sent on a dangerous mission

PERDUE   *n* pl. -S perdu

PERDURE   *v* -DURED, -DURING, -DURES to continue to exist

PERDY   *interj* pardi

PEREGRIN   *n* pl. -S a swift falcon much used in falconry

PEREION   *n* pl. -REIA the thorax of some crustaceans

PEREON   *n* pl. -REA pereion

PEREOPOD   *n* pl. -S an appendage of the pereion

PERFECT   *adj* -FECTER, -FECTEST lacking fault or defect; of an extreme kind

PERFECT   *v* -ED, -ING, -S to make perfect

PERFECTA   *n* pl. -S a system of betting

PERFECTO   *n* pl. -TOS a medium-sized cigar

PERFIDY   *n* pl. -DIES deliberate breach of faith or trust

PERFORCE   *adv* of necessity

PERFORM   *v* -ED, -ING, -S to begin and carry through to completion

PERFUME   *v* -FUMED, -FUMING, -FUMES to fill with a fragrant odor

PERFUMER   *n* pl. -S one that perfumes

PERFUSE   *v* -FUSED, -FUSING, -FUSES to spread over or through something

PERGOLA   *n* pl. -S a shaded shelter or passageway

PERHAPS   *n* pl. -ES something open to doubt or conjecture

PERI   *n* pl. -S a supernatural being of Persian mythology

PERIANTH   *n* pl. -S an outer covering of a flower

PERIAPT   *n* pl. -S an amulet

PERIBLEM   *n* pl. -S a region of plant tissue

PERICARP   *n* pl. -S the wall of a ripened plant ovary or fruit

PERICOPE   *n* pl. -PES or -PAE a selection from a book

PERIDERM *n* pl. -S an outer layer of plant tissue

PERIDIUM *n* pl. -IA the covering of the spore-bearing organ in many fungi **PERIDIAL** *adj*

PERIDOT *n* pl. -S a mineral

PERIGEE *n* pl. -S the point in the orbit of a celestial body which is nearest to the earth **PERIGEAL, PERIGEAN** *adj*

PERIGON *n* pl. -S an angle equal to 360 degrees

PERIGYNY *n* pl. -NIES the state of being situated on a cuplike organ surrounding the pistil

PERIL *v* -ILED, -ILING, -ILS or -ILLED, -ILLING, -ILS to imperil

PERILLA *n* pl. -S an Asian herb

PERILOUS *adj* dangerous

PERILUNE *n* pl. -S the point in the orbit of a celestial body which is nearest to the moon

PERINEUM *n* pl. -NEA a region of the body at the lower end of the trunk **PERINEAL** *adj*

PERIOD *n* pl. -S a portion of time

PERIODIC *adj* recurring at regular intervals

PERIODID *n* pl. -S an iodide

PERIOTIC *adj* surrounding the ear

PERIPETY *n* pl. -TIES a sudden change in a course of events

PERIPTER *n* pl. -S a structure with a row of columns around all sides

PERIQUE *n* pl. -S a dark tobacco

PERISARC *n* pl. -S a protective covering of certain hydrozoans

PERISH *v* -ED, -ING, -ES to die

PERIWIG *n* pl. -S a wig

PERJURE *v* -JURED, -JURING, -JURES to make a perjurer of

PERJURER *n* pl. -S one guilty of perjury

PERJURY *n* pl. -RIES the willful giving of false testimony under oath in a judicial proceeding

PERK *v* -ED, -ING, -S to carry oneself jauntily

PERKISH *adj* somewhat perky

PERKY *adj* PERKIER, PERKIEST jaunty **PERKILY** *adv*

PERLITE *n* pl. -S a volcanic glass **PERLITIC** *adj*

PERM *v* -ED, -ING, -S to give hair a permanent wave

PERMEANT *adj* that permeates

PERMEASE *n* pl. -S a catalyzing agent

PERMEATE *v* -ATED, -ATING, -ATES to spread through

PERMIT *v* -MITTED, -MITTING, -MITS to allow

PERMUTE *v* -MUTED, -MUTING, -MUTES to change the order of

PERONEAL *adj* pertaining to the fibula

PERORAL *adj* occurring through the mouth

PERORATE *v* -RATED, -RATING, -RATES to make a lengthy speech

PEROXID *n* pl. -S peroxide

PEROXIDE *v* -IDED, -IDING, -IDES to treat with peroxide (a bleaching agent)

PEROXY *adj* containing the bivalent group O_2

PERPEND *v* -ED, -ING, -S to ponder

PERPENT *n* pl. -S a large building stone

PERPLEX *v* -ED, -ING, -ES to make mentally uncertain

PERRON *n* pl. -S an outdoor stairway

PERRY *n* pl. -RIES a beverage of pear juice often fermented

PERSALT *n* pl. -S a chemical salt

PERSE *n* pl. -S a blue color

PERSIST *v* -ED, -ING, -S to continue resolutely in some activity

PERSON *n* pl. -S a human being

PERSONA *n* pl. -NAE a character in a literary work

PERSONA *n* pl. -S the public role that a person assumes

PERSONAL *n* pl. -S a brief, private notice in a newspaper

PERSPIRE *v* -SPIRED, -SPIRING, -SPIRES to give off moisture through the pores of the skin **PERSPIRY** *adj*

PERSUADE *v* -SUADED, -SUADING, -SUADES to cause to do something by means of argument, reasoning, or entreaty

PERT *adj* PERTER, PERTEST impudent **PERTLY** *adv*

PERTAIN *v* -ED, -ING, -S to have reference or relation

PERTNESS *n* pl. -ES the quality of being pert

PERTURB *v* -ED, -ING, -S to disturb greatly

PERUKE *n* pl. -S a wig **PERUKED** *adj*

PERUSAL	*n* pl. -S the act of perusing	**PETCOCK**	*n* pl. -S a small valve or faucet
PERUSE	*v* -RUSED, -RUSING, -RUSES to read	**PETECHIA**	*n* pl. -CHIAE a small hemorrhagic spot on a body surface
PERUSER	*n* pl. -S one that peruses	**PETER**	*v* -ED, -ING, -S to diminish gradually
PERVADE	*v* -VADED, -VADING, -VADES to spread through every part of		
PERVADER	*n* pl. -S one that pervades	**PETIOLAR**	*adj* pertaining to a petiole
PERVERSE	*adj* willfully deviating from desired or expected conduct	**PETIOLE**	*n* pl. -S the stalk of a leaf **PETIOLED** *adj*
PERVERT	*v* -ED, -ING, -S to turn away from the right course of action	**PETIT**	*adj* small; minor
PERVIOUS	*adj* capable of being penetrated	**PETITE**	*n* pl. -S a clothing size for short women
PES	*n* pl. PEDES a foot or footlike part	**PETITION**	*v* -ED, -ING, -S to make a formal request
PESADE	*n* pl. -S the position of a horse when rearing	**PETNAP**	*v* -NAPPED, -NAPPING, -NAPS to steal a pet for profit
PESETA	*n* pl. -S a monetary unit of Spain	**PETRALE**	*n* pl. -S a food fish
PESEWA	*n* pl. -S a monetary unit of Ghana	**PETREL**	*n* pl. -S a small seabird
PESKY	*adj* -KIER, -KIEST annoying **PESKILY** *adv*	**PETRIFY**	*v* -FIED, -FYING, -FIES to convert into stone
PESO	*n* pl. -SOS a monetary unit of various Spanish-speaking countries	**PETROL**	*n* pl. -S gasoline
		PETROLIC	*adj* derived from petroleum
		PETRONEL	*n* pl. -S a portable firearm
PESSARY	*n* pl. -RIES a contraceptive device worn in the vagina	**PETROSAL**	*adj* petrous
		PETROUS	*adj* resembling stone in hardness
PEST	*n* pl. -S an annoying person or thing	**PETSAI**	*n* pl. -S Chinese cabbage
		PETTED	past tense of pet
PESTER	*v* -ED, -ING, -S to bother	**PETTEDLY**	*adv* peevishly
PESTERER	*n* pl. -S one that pesters	**PETTER**	*n* pl. -S one that pets
PESTHOLE	*n* pl. -S a place liable to epidemic disease	**PETTI**	pl. of petto
		PETTIER	comparative of petty
PESTLE	*v* -TLED, -TLING, -TLES to crush with a club-shaped hand tool	**PETTIEST**	superlative of petty
		PETTIFOG	*v* -FOGGED, -FOGGING, -FOGS to quibble
PESTO	*n* pl. -TOS a sauce of basil, garlic, and olive oil	**PETTILY**	*adv* in a petty manner
PESTY	*adj* PESTIER, PESTIEST annoying	**PETTING**	*n* pl. -S amorous caressing and kissing
PET	*v* PETTED, PETTING, PETS to caress with the hand	**PETTISH**	*adj* peevish
		PETTLE	*v* -TLED, -TLING, -TLES to caress
PETAL	*n* pl. -S a leaflike part of a corolla **PETALED, PETALLED** *adj*	**PETTO**	*n* pl. -TI the breast
PETALINE	*adj* resembling a petal	**PETTY**	*adj* -TIER, -TIEST insignificant
PETALODY	*n* pl. -DIES the metamorphosis of various floral organs into petals	**PETULANT**	*adj* peevish
		PETUNIA	*n* pl. -S a tropical herb
PETALOID	*adj* resembling a petal	**PETUNTSE**	*n* pl. -S a mineral
PETALOUS	*adj* having petals	**PETUNTZE**	*n* pl. -S petuntse
PETARD	*n* pl. -S an explosive device	**PEW**	*n* pl. -S a bench in church
PETASOS	*n* pl. -ES petasus	**PEWEE**	*n* pl. -S a small bird
PETASUS	*n* pl. -ES a broad-brimmed hat worn in ancient Greece		

PEWIT   *n* pl. -S the lapwing

PEWTER   *n* pl. -S a tin alloy

PEWTERER   *n* pl. -S one that makes articles of pewter

PEYOTE   *n* pl. -S a cactus

PEYOTL   *n* pl. -S peyote

PEYTRAL   *n* pl. -S a piece of armor for the breast of a horse

PEYTREL   *n* pl. -S peytral

PFENNIG   *n* pl. -NIGS or -NIGE a bronze coin of Germany

PFFT   *interj* — used to express a sudden ending

PFUI   *interj* phooey

PHAETON   *n* pl. -S a light carriage

PHAGE   *n* pl. -S an organism that destroys bacteria

PHALANGE   *n* pl. -S any bone of a finger or toe

PHALANX   *n* pl. -ES a formation of infantry in ancient Greece

PHALLI   a pl. of phallus

PHALLIC   *adj* pertaining to a phallus

PHALLISM   *n* pl. -S worship of the phallus as symbolic of nature's creative power

PHALLIST   *n* pl. -S one who practices phallism

PHALLUS   *n* pl. -LI or -LUSES the penis

PHANTASIED   past tense of phantasy

PHANTASIES   present 3d person sing. of phantasy

PHANTASM   *n* pl. -S a creation of the imagination

PHANTAST   *n* pl. -S fantast

PHANTASY   *v* -SIED, -SYING, -SIES to fantasy

PHANTOM   *n* pl. -S something existing in appearance only

PHARAOH   *n* pl. -S a ruler of ancient Egypt

PHARISEE   *n* pl. -S a hypocritically self-righteous person

PHARMACY   *n* pl. -CIES a drugstore

PHAROS   *n* pl. -ES a lighthouse or beacon to guide seamen

PHARYNX   *n* pl. -YNGES or -YNXES a section of the digestive tract

PHASE   *v* PHASED, PHASING, PHASES to plan or carry out by phases (distinct stages of development) **PHASEAL, PHASIC** *adj*

PHASEOUT   *n* pl. -S a gradual stopping of operations

PHASIS   *n* pl. PHASES a phase

PHASMID   *n* pl. -S a tropical insect

PHAT   *adj* susceptible of easy and rapid typesetting

PHATIC   *adj* sharing feelings rather than ideas

PHEASANT   *n* pl. -S a large, long-tailed bird

PHELLEM   *n* pl. -S a layer of plant cells

PHELONIA   *n/pl* liturgical vestments

PHENATE   *n* pl. -S a salt of carbolic acid

PHENAZIN   *n* pl. -S a chemical compound

PHENETIC   *adj* pertaining to a type of classificatory system

PHENETOL   *n* pl. -S a volatile liquid

PHENIX   *n* pl. -ES phoenix

PHENOL   *n* pl. -S a caustic compound

PHENOLIC   *n* pl. -S a synthetic resin

PHENOM   *n* pl. -S a person of extraordinary ability or promise

PHENOXY   *adj* containing a radical derived from phenol

PHENYL   *n* pl. -S a univalent chemical radical **PHENYLIC** *adj*

PHEW   *interj* — used to express relief, fatigue, or disgust

PHI   *n* pl. -S a Greek letter

PHIAL   *n* pl. -S a vial

PHILABEG   *n* pl. -S filibeg

PHILIBEG   *n* pl. -S filibeg

PHILOMEL   *n* pl. -S a songbird

PHILTER   *v* -ED, -ING, -S to put under the spell of a love potion

PHILTRE   *v* -TRED, -TRING, -TRES to philter

PHILTRUM   *n* pl. -TRA the indentation between the upper lip and the nose

PHIMOSIS   *n* pl. -MOSES the abnormal constriction of the opening of the prepuce **PHIMOTIC** *adj*

PHIZ   *n* pl. -ES a face or facial expression

PHLEGM   *n* pl. -S a thick mucus secreted in the air passages

PHLEGMY   *adj* PHLEGMIER, PHLEGMIEST resembling phlegm

PHLOEM   *n* pl. -S a complex plant tissue

PHLOX   *n* pl. -ES a flowering plant

PHOBIA   *n* pl. -S an obsessive or irrational fear

PHOBIC   *n* pl. -S one affected with a phobia

PHOCINE   *adj* pertaining to seals

PHOEBE   *n* pl. -S a small bird

PHOEBUS   *n* pl. -ES the sun

PHOENIX   *n* pl. -ES a mythical bird

PHON   *n* pl. -S a unit of loudness

PHONAL   *adj* pertaining to speech sounds

PHONATE   *v* -NATED, -NATING, -NATES to produce speech sounds

PHONE   *v* PHONED, PHONING, PHONES to telephone

PHONEME   *n* pl. -S a unit of speech **PHONEMIC** *adj*

PHONETIC   *adj* pertaining to speech sounds

PHONEY   *v* -ED, -ING, -S to phony

PHONEY   *adj* -NIER, -NIEST phony

PHONIC   *adj* pertaining to the nature of sound

PHONICS   *n/pl* the science of sound

PHONIED   past tense of phony

PHONIER   comparative of phoney and phony

PHONIES   present 3d person sing. of phony

PHONIEST   superlative of phoney and phony

PHONILY   *adv* in a phony manner

PHONING   present participle of phone

PHONO   *n* pl. -NOS a record player

PHONON   *n* pl. -S a quantum of vibrational energy

PHONY   *adj* -NIER, -NIEST not genuine or real

PHONY   *v* -NIED, -NYING, -NIES to alter so as to make appear genuine

PHOOEY   *interj* — used as an exclamation of disgust or contempt

PHORATE   *n* pl. -S an insecticide

PHORONID   *n* pl. -S a wormlike marine animal

PHOSGENE   *n* pl. -S a poisonous gas

PHOSPHID   *n* pl. -S a chemical compound

PHOSPHIN   *n* pl. -S a poisonous gas

PHOSPHOR   *n* pl. -S a substance that will emit light when exposed to radiation

PHOT   *n* pl. -S a unit of illumination

PHOTIC   *adj* pertaining to light

PHOTICS   *n/pl* the science of light

PHOTO   *v* -ED, -ING, -S to photograph

PHOTOG   *n* pl. -S one who takes photographs

PHOTOMAP   *v* -MAPPED, -MAPPING, -MAPS to map by means of aerial photography

PHOTON   *n* pl. -S an elementary particle **PHOTONIC** *adj*

PHOTOPIA   *n* pl. -S vision in bright light **PHOTOPIC** *adj*

PHOTOSET   *v* -SET, -SETTING, -SETS to prepare for printing by photographic means

PHPHT   *interj* pht

PHRASAL   *adj* pertaining to a group of two or more associated words

PHRASE   *v* PHRASED, PHRASING, PHRASES to express in words

PHRASING   *n* pl. -S manner or style of verbal expression

PHRATRY   *n* pl. -TRIES a tribal unit among primitive peoples **PHRATRAL, PHRATRIC** *adj*

PHREATIC   *adj* pertaining to underground waters

PHRENIC   *adj* pertaining to the mind

PHRENSY   *v* -SIED, -SYING, -SIES to frenzy

PHT   *interj* — used as an expression of mild anger or annoyance

PHTHALIC   *adj* pertaining to a certain acid

PHTHALIN   *n* pl. -S a chemical compound

PHTHISIC   *n* pl. -S phthisis

PHTHISIS   *n* pl. PHTHISES a disease of the lungs

PHUT   *n* pl. -S a dull, abrupt sound

PHYLA   pl. of phylon and phylum

PHYLAE   pl. of phyle

PHYLAR   *adj* pertaining to a phylum

PHYLAXIS   *n* pl. -AXISES an inhibiting of infection by the body

PHYLE   *n* pl. -LAE a political subdivision in ancient Greece **PHYLIC** *adj*

PHYLESIS   *n* pl. -LESES or -LESISES the course of evolutionary development **PHYLETIC** *adj*

PHYLLARY   *n* pl. -RIES a bract of certain plants

PHYLLITE   *n* pl. -S a foliated rock

PHYLLO   *n* pl. -LOS very thin pastry dough

PHYLLODE   *n* pl. -S a flattened petiole that serves as a leaf

PHYLLOID   *n* pl. -S a leaflike plant part

PHYLLOME	*n* pl. -S a leaf of a plant
PHYLON	*n* pl. -LA a genetically related group
PHYLUM	*n* pl. -LA a taxonomic division
PHYSED	*n* pl. -S physical education
PHYSES	pl. of physis
PHYSIC	*v* -ICKED, -ICKING, -ICS to treat with medicine
PHYSICAL	*n* pl. -S a medical examination of the body
PHYSIQUE	*n* pl. -S the form or structure of the body
PHYSIS	*n* pl. PHYSES the principle of growth or change in nature
PHYTANE	*n* pl. -S a chemical compound
PHYTOID	*adj* resembling a plant
PHYTOL	*n* pl. -S an alcohol
PHYTON	*n* pl. -S a structural unit of a plant **PHYTONIC** *adj*
PI	*n* pl. -S a Greek letter
PI	*v* PIED, PIEING or PIING, PIES to jumble or disorder
PIA	*n* pl. -S a membrane of the brain
PIACULAR	*adj* atoning
PIAFFE	*v* PIAFFED, PIAFFING, PIAFFES to perform a piaffer
PIAFFER	*n* pl. -S a movement in horsemanship
PIAL	*adj* pertaining to a pia
PIAN	*n* pl. -S a tropical disease **PIANIC** *adj*
PIANISM	*n* pl. -S performance on the piano
PIANIST	*n* pl. -S one who plays the piano
PIANO	*n* pl. -NOS a musical instrument
PIASABA	*n* pl. -S piassava
PIASAVA	*n* pl. -S piassava
PIASSABA	*n* pl. -S piassava
PIASSAVA	*n* pl. -S a coarse, stiff fiber
PIASTER	*n* pl. -S a monetary unit of several Arab countries
PIASTRE	*n* pl. -S piaster
PIAZZA	*n* pl. -ZAS or -ZE a public square in an Italian town
PIBAL	*n* pl. -S a small balloon for determining the direction and speed of the wind
PIBROCH	*n* pl. -S a musical piece played on the bagpipe
PIC	*n* pl. -S a photograph
PICA	*n* pl. -S a craving for unnatural food
PICACHO	*n* pl. -CHOS an isolated peak of a hill
PICADOR	*n* pl. -ES or -S a horseman in a bullfight
PICAL	*adj* resembling a pica
PICARA	*n* pl. -S a female picaro
PICARO	*n* pl. -ROS a vagabond
PICAROON	*v* -ED, -ING, -S to act as a pirate
PICAYUNE	*n* pl. -S a former Spanish-American coin
PICCOLO	*n* pl. -LOS a small flute
PICE	*n* pl. PICE a former coin of India and Pakistan
PICEOUS	*adj* glossy-black in color
PICIFORM	*adj* pertaining to an order of birds
PICK	*v* -ED, -ING, -S to select
PICKADIL	*n* pl. -S a type of collar
PICKAX	*v* -ED, -ING, -ES to use a pickax (a tool for breaking hard surfaces)
PICKAXE	*v* -AXED, -AXING, -AXES to pickax
PICKEER	*v* -ED, -ING, -S to skirmish in advance of an army
PICKER	*n* pl. -S one that picks
PICKEREL	*n* pl. -S a freshwater fish
PICKET	*v* -ED, -ING, -S to stand outside of some location, as a business, to publicize one's grievances against it
PICKETER	*n* pl. -S one who pickets
PICKIER	comparative of picky
PICKIEST	superlative of picky
PICKING	*n* pl. -S the act of one that picks
PICKLE	*v* -LED, -LING, -LES to preserve or flavor in a solution of brine or vinegar
PICKLOCK	*n* pl. -S a tool for opening locks
PICKOFF	*n* pl. -S a play in baseball
PICKUP	*n* pl. -S a small truck
PICKWICK	*n* pl. -S a device for raising wicks in oil lamps
PICKY	*adj* PICKIER, PICKIEST fussy
PICLORAM	*n* pl. -S an herbicide
PICNIC	*v* -NICKED, -NICKING, -NICS to go on a picnic (an outdoor excursion with food)

PICNICKY	*adj* pertaining to a picnic	**PIETA**	*n* pl. -S a representation of the Virgin Mary mourning over the body of Christ
PICOGRAM	*n* pl. -S one trillionth of a gram		
PICOLIN	*n* pl. -S picoline	**PIETIES**	pl. of piety
PICOLINE	*n* pl. -S a chemical compound	**PIETISM**	*n* pl. -S piety
PICOMOLE	*n* pl. -S one trillionth of a mole	**PIETIST**	*n* pl. -S a pious person
PICOT	*v* -ED, -ING, -S to edge with ornamental loops	**PIETY**	*n* pl. -TIES the quality or state of being pious
PICOTEE	*n* pl. -S a variety of carnation	**PIFFLE**	*v* -FLED, -FLING, -FLES to babble
PICQUET	*n* pl. -S piquet		
PICRATE	*n* pl. -S a chemical salt **PICRATED** *adj*	**PIG**	*v* PIGGED, PIGGING, PIGS to bear pigs (cloven-hoofed mammals)
PICRIC	*adj* having a very bitter taste	**PIGBOAT**	*n* pl. -S a submarine
PICRITE	*n* pl. -S an igneous rock **PICRITIC** *adj*	**PIGEON**	*n* pl. -S a short-legged bird
PICTURE	*v* -TURED, -TURING, -TURES to make a visual representation of	**PIGFISH**	*n* pl. -ES a marine fish
		PIGGED	past tense of pig
PICUL	*n* pl. -S an Asian unit of weight	**PIGGERY**	*n* pl. -GERIES a pigpen
PIDDLE	*v* -DLED, -DLING, -DLES to waste time	**PIGGIE**	*n* pl. -S piggy
		PIGGIER	comparative of piggy
PIDDLER	*n* pl. -S one that piddles	**PIGGIES**	pl. of piggy
PIDDLY	*adj* insignificant	**PIGGIEST**	superlative of piggy
PIDDOCK	*n* pl. -S a bivalve mollusk	**PIGGIN**	*n* pl. -S a small wooden pail
PIDGIN	*n* pl. -S a mixed language	**PIGGING**	present participle of pig
PIE	*v* PIED, PIEING, PIES to pi	**PIGGISH**	*adj* greedy or dirty
PIEBALD	*n* pl. -S a spotted animal	**PIGGY**	*n* pl. -GIES a small pig
PIECE	*v* PIECED, PIECING, PIECES to join into a whole	**PIGGY**	*adj* -GIER, -GIEST piggish
		PIGLET	*n* pl. -S a small pig
PIECER	*n* pl. -S one that pieces	**PIGLIKE**	*adj* resembling a pig
PIECING	*n* pl. -S material to be sewn together	**PIGMENT**	*v* -ED, -ING, -S to add a coloring matter to
PIECRUST	*n* pl. -S the crust of a pie	**PIGMY**	*n* pl. -MIES pygmy
PIED	past tense of pie	**PIGNOLI**	*n* pl. -S pignolia
PIEDFORT	*n* pl. -S piefort	**PIGNOLIA**	*n* pl. -S the edible seed of nut pines
PIEDMONT	*n* pl. -S an area lying at the foot of a mountain	**PIGNUS**	*n* pl. -NORA property held as security for a debt
PIEFORT	*n* pl. -S an unusually thick coin		
PIEING	a present participle of pi	**PIGNUT**	*n* pl. -S a hickory nut
PIEPLANT	*n* pl. -S a rhubarb	**PIGOUT**	*n* pl. -S an instance of eating to excess
PIER	*n* pl. -S a structure extending from land out over water	**PIGPEN**	*n* pl. -S a place where pigs are kept
PIERCE	*v* PIERCED, PIERCING, PIERCES to cut or pass into or through	**PIGSKIN**	*n* pl. -S the skin of a pig
		PIGSNEY	*n* pl. -NEYS a darling
PIERCER	*n* pl. -S one that pierces	**PIGSTICK**	*v* -ED, -ING, -S to hunt for wild boar
PIEROGI	*n* pl. -ES a small dumpling with a filling		
		PIGSTY	*n* pl. -STIES a pigpen
PIERROT	*n* pl. -S a clown	**PIGTAIL**	*n* pl. -S a tight braid of hair

PIGWEED	*n* pl. -S a weedy plant
PIING	a present participle of pi
PIKA	*n* pl. -S a small mammal
PIKAKE	*n* pl. -S an East Indian vine
PIKE	*v* PIKED, PIKING, PIKES to pierce with a pike (a long spear)
PIKEMAN	*n* pl. -MEN a soldier armed with a pike
PIKER	*n* pl. -S a stingy person
PIKI	*n* pl. -S thin blue cornmeal bread
PIKING	present participle of pike
PILAF	*n* pl. -S a dish made of seasoned rice and often meat
PILAFF	*n* pl. -S pilaf
PILAR	*adj* pertaining to hair
PILASTER	*n* pl. -S a rectangular column
PILAU	*n* pl. -S pilaf
PILAW	*n* pl. -S pilaf
PILCHARD	*n* pl. -S a small marine fish
PILE	*v* PILED, PILING, PILES to lay one upon the other
PILEA	pl. of pileum
PILEATE	*adj* having a pileus
PILEATED	*adj* pileate
PILED	past tense of pile
PILEI	pl. of pileus
PILELESS	*adj* not having a raised surface of yarn
PILEOUS	*adj* pilose
PILEUM	*n* pl. -LEA the top of a bird's head
PILEUP	*n* pl. -S a collision involving several motor vehicles
PILEUS	*n* pl. -LEI the umbrella-shaped portion of a mushroom
PILEWORT	*n* pl. -S a medicinal plant
PILFER	*v* -ED, -ING, -S to steal
PILFERER	*n* pl. -S one that pilfers
PILGRIM	*n* pl. -S a traveler or wanderer
PILI	*n* pl. -S a Philippine tree
PILIFORM	*adj* resembling a hair
PILING	*n* pl. -S a structure of building supports
PILL	*v* -ED, -ING, -S to dose with pills (small, rounded masses of medicine)
PILLAGE	*v* -LAGED, -LAGING, -LAGES to plunder
PILLAGER	*n* pl. -S one that pillages
PILLAR	*v* -ED, -ING, -S to provide with vertical building supports
PILLBOX	*n* pl. -ES a small box for pills
PILLION	*n* pl. -S a pad or cushion for an extra rider on a horse or motorcycle
PILLORY	*v* -RIED, -RYING, -RIES to expose to public ridicule or abuse
PILLOW	*v* -ED, -ING, -S to rest on a pillow (a cushion for the head)
PILLOWY	*adj* resembling a pillow
PILOSE	*adj* covered with hair
PILOSITY	*n* pl. -TIES the state of being pilose
PILOT	*v* -ED, -ING, -S to control the course of
PILOTAGE	*n* pl. -S the act of piloting
PILOTING	*n* pl. -S a branch of navigation
PILOUS	*adj* pilose
PILSENER	*n* pl. -S pilsner
PILSNER	*n* pl. -S a light beer
PILULE	*n* pl. -S a small pill **PILULAR** *adj*
PILUS	*n* pl. -LI a hair or hairlike structure
PILY	*adj* divided into a number of wedge-shaped heraldic designs
PIMA	*n* pl. -S a strong, high-grade cotton
PIMENTO	*n* pl. -TOS pimiento
PIMIENTO	*n* pl. -TOS a sweet pepper
PIMP	*v* -ED, -ING, -S to solicit clients for a prostitute
PIMPLE	*n* pl. -S an inflamed swelling of the skin **PIMPLED** *adj*
PIMPLY	*adj* -PLIER, -PLIEST covered with pimples
PIN	*v* PINNED, PINNING, PINS to fasten with a pin (a slender, pointed piece of metal)
PINA	*n* pl. -S a pineapple
PINAFORE	*n* pl. -S a child's apron
PINANG	*n* pl. -S a palm tree
PINASTER	*n* pl. -S a pine tree
PINATA	*n* pl. -S a pottery jar used in a Mexican game
PINBALL	*n* pl. -S an electric game
PINBONE	*n* pl. -S the hipbone
PINCER	*n* pl. -S one of the two pivoted parts of a grasping tool

PINCH	*v* -ED, -ING, -ES to squeeze between two edges or surfaces
PINCHBUG	*n* pl. -S a large beetle
PINCHECK	*n* pl. -S a fabric design
PINCHER	*n* pl. -S one that pinches
PINDER	*n* pl. -S an official who formerly impounded stray animals
PINDLING	*adj* puny or sickly
PINE	*v* PINED, PINING, PINES to yearn intensely
PINEAL	*n* pl. -S a gland in the brain
PINECONE	*n* pl. -S a cone-shaped fruit of a pine tree
PINED	past tense of pine
PINELAND	*n* pl. -S land forested with pine
PINELIKE	*adj* resembling a pine (an evergreen tree)
PINENE	*n* pl. -S the main constituent of turpentine
PINERY	*n* pl. -ERIES an area where pineapples are grown
PINESAP	*n* pl. -S a fragrant herb
PINETUM	*n* pl. -TA a plantation of pine trees
PINEWOOD	*n* pl. -S the wood of a pine tree
PINEY	*adj* PINIER, PINIEST piny
PINFISH	*n* pl. -ES a small marine fish
PINFOLD	*v* -ED, -ING, -S to confine in an enclosure for stray animals
PING	*v* -ED, -ING, -S to produce a brief, high-pitched sound
PINGER	*n* pl. -S a device for producing pulses of sound
PINGO	*n* pl. -GOS a hill forced up by the effects of frost
PINGRASS	*n* pl. -ES a European weed
PINGUID	*adj* greasy
PINHEAD	*n* pl. -S the head of a pin
PINHOLE	*n* pl. -S a small hole made by a pin
PINIER	comparative of piney and piny
PINIEST	superlative of piney and piny
PINING	present participle of pine
PINION	*v* -ED, -ING, -S to remove or bind the wing feathers of to prevent flight
PINITE	*n* pl. -S a mineral
PINITOL	*n* pl. -S an alcohol
PINK	*adj* PINKER, PINKEST of a pale reddish hue
PINK	*v* -ED, -ING, -S to cut a saw-toothed edge on cloth
PINKEN	*v* -ED, -ING, -S to become pink
PINKER	*n* pl. -S one that pinks
PINKEY	*n* pl. -EYS a ship with a narrow overhanging stern
PINKEYE	*n* pl. -S an inflammation of the eye
PINKIE	*n* pl. -S the little finger
PINKIES	pl. of pinky
PINKING	*n* pl. -S a method of cutting or decorating
PINKISH	*adj* somewhat pink
PINKLY	*adv* with a pink hue
PINKNESS	*n* pl. -ES the state of being pink
PINKO	*n* pl. PINKOS or PINKOES a person who holds somewhat radical political views
PINKROOT	*n* pl. -S a medicinal plant root
PINKY	*n* pl. PINKIES pinkie
PINNA	*n* pl. -NAE or -NAS a feather, wing, or winglike part
PINNACE	*n* pl. -S a small sailing ship
PINNACLE	*v* -CLED, -CLING, -CLES to place on a summit
PINNAE	a pl. of pinna
PINNAL	*adj* pertaining to a pinna
PINNATE	*adj* resembling a feather
PINNATED	*adj* pinnate
PINNED	past tense of pin
PINNER	*n* pl. -S one that pins
PINNIES	pl. of pinny
PINNING	present participle of pin
PINNIPED	*n* pl. -S a mammal with limbs modified into flippers
PINNULA	*n* pl. -LAE pinnule **PINNULAR** *adj*
PINNULE	*n* pl. -S a pinnate part or organ
PINNY	*n* pl. -NIES a pinafore
PINOCHLE	*n* pl. -S a card game
PINOCLE	*n* pl. -S pinochle
PINOLE	*n* pl. -S a finely ground flour
PINON	*n* pl. -S or -ES a pine tree
PINOT	*n* pl. -S a red or white grape
PINPOINT	*v* -ED, -ING, -S to locate precisely

PINPRICK	*v* -ED, -ING, -S to puncture with a pin
PINSCHER	*n* pl. -S a large, short-haired dog
PINT	*n* pl. -S a liquid and dry measure of capacity
PINTA	*n* pl. -S a skin disease
PINTADA	*n* pl. -S pintado
PINTADO	*n* pl. -DOS or -DOES a large food fish
PINTAIL	*n* pl. -S a river duck
PINTANO	*n* pl. -NOS a tropical fish
PINTLE	*n* pl. -S a pin on which something turns
PINTO	*n* pl. -TOS or -TOES a spotted horse
PINTSIZE	*adj* small
PINUP	*n* pl. -S a picture that may be pinned up on a wall
PINWALE	*n* pl. -S a type of fabric
PINWEED	*n* pl. -S a perennial herb
PINWHEEL	*v* -ED, -ING, -S to revolve at the end of a stick
PINWORK	*n* pl. -S a type of embroidery
PINWORM	*n* pl. -S a parasitic worm
PINY	*adj* PINIER, PINIEST suggestive of or covered with pine trees
PINYIN	*n* a system for transliterating Chinese ideograms into the Latin alphabet
PINYON	*n* pl. -S pinon
PIOLET	*n* pl. -S an ice ax
PION	*n* pl. -S a subatomic particle **PIONIC** *adj*
PIONEER	*v* -ED, -ING, -S to take part in the beginnings of
PIOSITY	*n* pl. -TIES an excessive show of piety
PIOUS	*adj* marked by religious reverence **PIOUSLY** *adv*
PIP	*v* PIPPED, PIPPING, PIPS to break through the shell of an egg
PIPAGE	*n* pl. -S a system of pipes
PIPAL	*n* pl. -S a fig tree of India
PIPE	*v* PIPED, PIPING, PIPES to convey by means of a pipe (a hollow cylinder)
PIPEAGE	*n* pl. -S pipage
PIPEFISH	*n* pl. -ES a slender fish
PIPEFUL	*n* pl. -S a quantity sufficient to fill a tobacco pipe

PIPELESS	*adj* having no pipe
PIPELIKE	*adj* resembling a pipe
PIPELINE	*v* -LINED, -LINING, -LINES to convey by a line of pipe
PIPER	*n* pl. -S one that plays on a tubular musical instrument
PIPERINE	*n* pl. -S a chemical compound
PIPESTEM	*n* pl. -S the stem of a tobacco pipe
PIPET	*v* -PETTED, -PETTING, -PETS to pipette
PIPETTE	*v* -PETTED, -PETTING, -PETTES to measure liquid with a calibrated tube
PIPIER	comparative of pipy
PIPIEST	superlative of pipy
PIPINESS	*n* pl. -ES the quality of being pipy
PIPING	*n* pl. -S a system of pipes
PIPINGLY	*adv* shrilly
PIPIT	*n* pl. -S a songbird
PIPKIN	*n* pl. -S a small pot
PIPPED	past tense of pip
PIPPIN	*n* pl. -S any of several varieties of apple
PIPPING	present participle of pip
PIPY	*adj* PIPIER, PIPIEST shrill
PIQUANCE	*n* pl. -S piquancy
PIQUANCY	*n* pl. -CIES the quality of being piquant
PIQUANT	*adj* agreeably sharp in taste
PIQUE	*v* PIQUED, PIQUING, PIQUES to arouse anger or resentment in
PIQUET	*n* pl. -S a card game
PIRACY	*n* pl. -CIES robbery on the high seas
PIRAGUA	*n* pl. -S a dugout canoe
PIRANA	*n* pl. -S piranha
PIRANHA	*n* pl. -S a voracious fish
PIRARUCU	*n* pl. -S a large food fish
PIRATE	*v* -RATED, -RATING, -RATES to commit piracy
PIRATIC	*adj* pertaining to piracy
PIRAYA	*n* pl. -S piranha
PIRIFORM	*adj* pyriform
PIRN	*n* pl. -S a spinning-wheel bobbin
PIROG	*n* pl. -ROGEN, -ROGHI or -ROGI a large Russian pastry
PIROGI	*n* pl. -ES pierogi

PIROGUE   *n* pl. -S piragua

PIROQUE   *n* pl. -S piragua

PIROZHOK   *n* pl. -ROZHKI, -ROSHKI or -ROJKI a small Russian pastry

PISCARY   *n* pl. -RIES a place for fishing

PISCATOR   *n* pl. -S a fisherman

PISCINA   *n* pl. -NAE or -NAS a basin used in certain church ceremonies **PISCINAL** *adj*

PISCINE   *adj* pertaining to fish

PISCO   *n* pl. -COS a Peruvian brandy

PISH   *v* -ED, -ING, -ES to express contempt

PISHOGE   *n* pl. -S pishogue

PISHOGUE   *n* pl. -S an evil spell

PISIFORM   *n* pl. -S a small bone of the wrist

PISMIRE   *n* pl. -S an ant

PISO   *n* pl. -SOS the Philippine peso

PISOLITE   *n* pl. -S a limestone

PISSOIR   *n* pl. -S a public urinal

PISTACHE   *n* pl. -S a shade of green

PISTE   *n* pl. -S a downhill ski trail

PISTIL   *n* pl. -S the seed-bearing organ of flowering plants

PISTOL   *v* -TOLED, -TOLING, -TOLS or -TOLLED, -TOLLING, -TOLS to shoot with a small firearm

PISTOLE   *n* pl. -S a former European gold coin

PISTON   *n* pl. -S a part of an engine

PIT   *v* PITTED, PITTING, PITS to mark with cavities or depressions

PITA   *n* pl. -S a strong fiber

PITAPAT   *v* -PATTED, -PATTING, -PATS to make a repeated tapping sound

PITCH   *v* -ED, -ING, -ES to throw

PITCHER   *n* pl. -S a container for holding and pouring liquids

PITCHIER   comparative of pitchy

PITCHIEST   superlative of pitchy

PITCHILY   *adv* in a very dark manner

PITCHMAN   *n* pl. -MEN a salesman of small wares

PITCHOUT   *n* pl. -S a type of pitch in baseball

PITCHY   *adj* PITCHIER, PITCHIEST tarry

PITEOUS   *adj* pitiful

PITFALL   *n* pl. -S a hidden danger or difficulty

PITH   *v* -ED, -ING, -S to sever the spinal cord of

PITHEAD   *n* pl. -S a mine entrance

PITHLESS   *adj* lacking force

PITHY   *adj* PITHIER, PITHIEST concise **PITHILY** *adv*

PITIABLE   *adj* pitiful **PITIABLY** *adv*

PITIED   past tense of pity

PITIER   *n* pl. -S one that pities

PITIES   present 3d person sing. of pity

PITIFUL   *adj* -FULLER, -FULLEST arousing pity

PITILESS   *adj* having no pity

PITMAN   *n* pl. -MEN a mine worker

PITMAN   *n* pl. -S a connecting rod

PITON   *n* pl. -S a metal spike used in mountain climbing

PITSAW   *n* pl. -S a large saw for cutting logs

PITTANCE   *n* pl. -S a small allowance of money

PITTED   past tense of pit

PITTING   *n* pl. -S an arrangement of cavities or depressions

PITY   *v* PITIED, PITYING, PITIES to feel pity (sorrow aroused by another's misfortune)

PIU   *adv* more — used as a musical direction

PIVOT   *v* -ED, -ING, -S to turn on a shaft or rod

PIVOTAL   *adj* critically important

PIVOTMAN   *n* pl. -MEN a center on a basketball team

PIX   *n* pl. -ES pyx

PIXEL   *n* pl. -S a basic unit of a video image

PIXIE   *n* pl. -S pixy **PIXIEISH** *adj*

PIXINESS   *n* pl. -ES the state of being playfully mischievous

PIXY   *n* pl. PIXIES a playfully mischievous fairy or elf **PIXYISH** *adj*

PIZAZZ   *n* pl. -ES the quality of being exciting or attractive

PIZAZZY   *adj* having pizazz

PIZZA   *n* pl. -S an Italian open pie

PIZZERIA   *n* pl. -S a place where pizzas are made and sold

PIZZLE   *n* pl. -S the penis of an animal

PLACABLE   *adj* capable of being placated **PLACABLY** *adv*

PLACARD   *v* -ED, -ING, -S to publicize by means of posters

PLACATE   *v* -CATED, -CATING, -CATES to soothe or mollify

PLACATER   *n* pl. -S one that placates

PLACE   *v* PLACED, PLACING, PLACES to set in a particular position

PLACEBO   *n* pl. -BOS or -BOES a substance containing no medication that is given for its psychological effect

PLACEMAN   *n* pl. -MEN a political appointee to a public office

PLACENTA   *n* pl. -TAS or -TAE a vascular organ in most mammals

PLACER   *n* pl. -S one that places

PLACET   *n* pl. -S a vote of assent

PLACID   *adj* calm or peaceful **PLACIDLY** *adv*

PLACING   present participle of place

PLACK   *n* pl. -S a former coin of Scotland

PLACKET   *n* pl. -S a slit in a garment

PLACOID   *n* pl. -S a fish having platelike scales

PLAFOND   *n* pl. -S an elaborately decorated ceiling

PLAGAL   *adj* designating a medieval musical mode

PLAGE   *n* pl. -S a bright region on the sun

PLAGIARY   *n* pl. -RIES the act of passing off another's work as one's own

PLAGUE   *v* PLAGUED, PLAGUING, PLAGUES to harass or torment

PLAGUER   *n* pl. -S one that plagues

PLAGUEY   *adj* plaguy

PLAGUING   present participle of plague

PLAGUY   *adj* troublesome **PLAGUILY** *adv*

PLAICE   *n* pl. -S a European flatfish

PLAID   *n* pl. -S a woolen scarf of a checkered pattern **PLAIDED** *adj*

PLAIN   *adj* PLAINER, PLAINEST evident **PLAINLY** *adv*

PLAIN   *v* -ED, -ING, -S to complain

PLAINT   *n* pl. -S a complaint

PLAISTER   *v* -ED, -ING, -S to plaster

PLAIT   *v* -ED, -ING, -S to braid

PLAITER   *n* pl. -S one that plaits

PLAITING   *n* pl. -S something that is plaited

PLAN   *v* PLANNED, PLANNING, PLANS to formulate a plan (a method for achieving an end)

PLANAR   *adj* flat

PLANARIA   *n* pl. -S an aquatic flatworm

PLANATE   *adj* having a flat surface

PLANCH   *n* pl. -ES a plank

PLANCHE   *n* pl. -S planch

PLANCHET   *n* pl. -S a flat piece of metal for stamping into a coin

PLANE   *v* PLANED, PLANING, PLANES to make smooth or even

PLANER   *n* pl. -S one that planes

PLANET   *n* pl. -S a celestial body

PLANFORM   *n* pl. -S the contour of an object as viewed from above

PLANGENT   *adj* resounding loudly

PLANING   present participle of plane

PLANISH   *v* -ED, -ING, -ES to toughen and smooth by hammering lightly

PLANK   *v* -ED, -ING, -S to cover with planks (long, flat pieces of lumber)

PLANKING   *n* pl. -S covering made of planks

PLANKTER   *n* pl. -S any organism that is an element of plankton

PLANKTON   *n* pl. -S the minute animal and plant life of a body of water

PLANLESS   *adj* having no plan

PLANNED   past tense of plan

PLANNER   *n* pl. -S one that plans

PLANNING   *n* pl. -S the establishment of goals or policies

PLANOSOL   *n* pl. -S a type of soil

PLANT   *v* -ED, -ING, -S to place in the ground for growing

PLANTAIN   *n* pl. -S a short-stemmed herb

PLANTAR   *adj* pertaining to the sole of the foot

PLANTER   *n* pl. -S one that plants

PLANTING   *n* pl. -S an area where plants are grown

PLANTLET   *n* pl. -S a small plant

PLANULA   *n* pl. -LAE the free-swimming larva of certain organisms **PLANULAR** *adj*

PLAQUE   *n* pl. -S an ornamental plate or disk

PLASH   *v* -ED, -ING, -ES to weave together

PLASHER   *n* pl. -S one that plashes

PLASHY   *adj* PLASHIER, PLASHIEST marshy

PLASM   *n* pl. -S plasma

PLASMA   *n* pl. -S the liquid part of blood **PLASMIC** *adj*

PLASMID   *n* pl. -S a hereditary structure of a cell

PLASMIN   *n* pl. -S an enzyme

PLASMOID   *n* pl. -S a type of high energy particle

PLASMON   *n* pl. -S a determinant of inheritance believed to exist in cells

PLASTER   *v* -ED, -ING, -S to cover with plaster (a mixture of lime, sand, and water)

PLASTERY   *adj* resembling plaster

PLASTIC   *n* pl. -S any of a group of synthetic or natural moldable materials

PLASTID   *n* pl. -S a structure in plant cells

PLASTRON   *n* pl. -S a part of the shell of a turtle **PLASTRAL** *adj*

PLASTRUM   *n* pl. -S plastron

PLAT   *v* PLATTED, PLATTING, PLATS to plait

PLATAN   *n* pl. -S a large tree

PLATANE   *n* pl. -S platan

PLATE   *v* PLATED, PLATING, PLATES to coat with a thin layer of metal

PLATEAU   *n* pl. -TEAUS or -TEAUX a level stretch of elevated land

PLATEAU   *v* -ED, -ING, -S to reach a period or condition of stability

PLATED   past tense of plate

PLATEFUL   *n* pl. PLATEFULS or PLATESFUL the quantity that fills a plate (a shallow dish)

PLATELET   *n* pl. -S a small, flattened body

PLATEN   *n* pl. -S the roller of a typewriter

PLATER   *n* pl. -S one that plates

PLATESFUL   a pl. of plateful

PLATFORM   *n* pl. -S a raised floor or flat surface

PLATIER   comparative of platy

PLATIES   a pl. of platy

PLATIEST   superlative of platy

PLATINA   *n* pl. -S platinum

PLATING   *n* pl. -S a thin layer of metal

PLATINIC   *adj* pertaining to platinum

PLATINUM   *n* pl. -S a metallic element

PLATONIC   *adj* purely spiritual and free from sensual desire

PLATOON   *v* -ED, -ING, -S to alternate with another player at the same position

PLATTED   past tense of plat

PLATTER   *n* pl. -S a large, shallow dish

PLATTING   present participle of plat

PLATY   *adj* PLATIER, PLATIEST split into thin, flat pieces

PLATY   *n* pl. PLATYS or PLATIES a small tropical fish

PLATYPUS   *n* pl. -PUSES or -PI an aquatic mammal

PLAUDIT   *n* pl. -S an expression of praise

PLAUSIVE   *adj* expressing praise

PLAY   *v* -ED, -ING, -S to engage in amusement or sport **PLAYABLE** *adj*

PLAYA   *n* pl. -S the bottom of a desert basin

PLAYACT   *v* -ED, -ING, -S to take part in a theatrical performance

PLAYBACK   *n* pl. -S the act of replaying a newly made recording

PLAYBILL   *n* pl. -S a program for a theatrical performance

PLAYBOOK   *n* pl. -S a book containing one or more literary works for the stage

PLAYBOY   *n* pl. -BOYS a man devoted to pleasurable activities

PLAYDATE   *n* pl. -S the scheduled date for showing a theatrical production

PLAYDAY   *n* pl. -DAYS a holiday

PLAYDOWN   *n* pl. -S a playoff

PLAYER   *n* pl. -S one that plays

PLAYFUL   *adj* frolicsome

PLAYGIRL   *n* pl. -S a woman devoted to pleasurable activities

PLAYGOER   *n* pl. -S one who attends the theater

PLAYLAND   *n* pl. -S a recreational area

PLAYLESS   *adj* lacking playfulness

PLAYLET   *n* pl. -S a short theatrical performance

PLAYLIKE *adj* resembling a theatrical performance

PLAYLIST *n* pl. -S a list of recordings to be played on the air

PLAYMATE *n* pl. -S a companion in play

PLAYOFF *n* pl. -S a series of games played to determine a championship

PLAYPEN *n* pl. -S an enclosure in which a young child may play

PLAYROOM *n* pl. -S a recreation room

PLAYSUIT *n* pl. -S a sports outfit for women and children

PLAYTIME *n* pl. -S a time for play or amusement

PLAYWEAR *n* pl. PLAYWEAR clothing worn for leisure activities

PLAZA *n* pl. -S a public square

PLEA *n* pl. -S an entreaty

PLEACH *v* -ED, -ING, -ES to weave together

PLEAD *v* PLEADED or PLED, PLEADING, PLEADS to ask for earnestly

PLEADER *n* pl. -S one that pleads

PLEADING *n* pl. -S an allegation in a legal action

PLEASANT *adj* -ANTER, -ANTEST pleasing

PLEASE *v* PLEASED, PLEASING, PLEASES to give enjoyment or satisfaction to

PLEASER *n* pl. -S one that pleases

PLEASURE *v* -SURED, -SURING, -SURES to please

PLEAT *v* -ED, -ING, -S to fold in an even manner

PLEATER *n* pl. -S one that pleats

PLEB *n* pl. -S a commoner

PLEBE *n* pl. -S a freshman at a military or naval academy

PLEBEIAN *n* pl. -S a commoner

PLECTRON *n* pl. -TRONS or -TRA plectrum

PLECTRUM *n* pl. -TRUMS or -TRA an implement used to pluck the strings of a stringed instrument

PLED a past tense of plead

PLEDGE *v* PLEDGED, PLEDGING, PLEDGES to give as security for something borrowed

PLEDGEE *n* pl. -S one to whom something is pledged

PLEDGEOR *n* pl. -S pledger

PLEDGER *n* pl. -S one that pledges something

PLEDGET *n* pl. -S a pad of absorbent cotton

PLEDGING present participle of pledge

PLEDGOR *n* pl. -S pledger

PLEIAD *n* pl. -S or -ES a group of seven illustrious persons

PLENA a pl. of plenum

PLENARY *adj* complete in every respect

PLENCH *n* pl. -ES a tool serving as pliers and a wrench

PLENISH *v* -ED, -ING, -ES to fill up

PLENISM *n* pl. -S the doctrine that space is fully occupied by matter

PLENIST *n* pl. -S an advocate of plenism

PLENTY *n* pl. -TIES a sufficient or abundant amount

PLENUM *n* pl. -NUMS or -NA space considered as fully occupied by matter

PLEONASM *n* pl. -S the use of needless words

PLEOPOD *n* pl. -S an appendage of crustaceans

PLESSOR *n* pl. -S plexor

PLETHORA *n* pl. -S an excess

PLEURA *n* pl. -RAE or -RAS a membrane that envelops the lungs **PLEURAL** *adj*

PLEURISY *n* pl. -SIES inflammation of the pleura

PLEURON *n* pl. -RA a part of a thoracic segment of an insect

PLEUSTON *n* pl. -S aquatic vegetation

PLEW *n* pl. -S a beaver skin

PLEXAL *adj* pertaining to a plexus

PLEXOR *n* pl. -S a small, hammer-like medical instrument

PLEXUS *n* pl. -ES an interlacing of parts

PLIABLE *adj* easily bent **PLIABLY** *adv*

PLIANCY *n* pl. -CIES the quality of being pliant

PLIANT *adj* easily bent **PLIANTLY** *adv*

PLICA *n* pl. -CAE a fold of skin **PLICAL** *adj*

PLICATE *adj* pleated

PLICATED *adj* plicate

PLIE *n* pl. -S a movement in ballet

PLIED past tense of ply

PLIER	*n* pl. -S one that plies	**PLOUGHER**	*n* pl. -S one that ploughs
PLIES	present 3d person sing. of ply	**PLOVER**	*n* pl. -S a shore bird
PLIGHT	*v* -ED, -ING, -S to promise or bind by a solemn pledge	**PLOW**	*v* -ED, -ING, -S to turn up land with a plow (a farm implement) **PLOWABLE** *adj*
PLIGHTER	*n* pl. -S one that plights	**PLOWBACK**	*n* pl. -S a reinvestment of profits in a business
PLIMSOL	*n* pl. -S plimsoll		
PLIMSOLE	*n* pl. -S plimsoll	**PLOWBOY**	*n* pl. -BOYS a boy who leads a plow team
PLIMSOLL	*n* pl. -S a rubber-soled cloth shoe	**PLOWER**	*n* pl. -S one that plows
PLINK	*v* -ED, -ING, -S to shoot at random targets	**PLOWHEAD**	*n* pl. -S the clevis of a plow
PLINKER	*n* pl. -S one that plinks	**PLOWLAND**	*n* pl. -S land suitable for cultivation
PLINTH	*n* pl. -S a stone or slab upon which a column or pedestal rests	**PLOWMAN**	*n* pl. -MEN a man who plows
PLIOTRON	*n* pl. -S a type of vacuum tube	**PLOY**	*v* -ED, -ING, -S to move from a line into column
PLISKIE	*n* pl. -S a practical joke	**PLUCK**	*v* -ED, -ING, -S to pull out or off
PLISKY	*n* pl. -KIES pliskie	**PLUCKER**	*n* pl. -S one that plucks
PLISSE	*n* pl. -S a puckered texture of cloth	**PLUCKY**	*adj* PLUCKIER, PLUCKIEST brave and spirited **PLUCKILY** *adv*
PLOD	*v* PLODDED, PLODDING, PLODS to walk heavily	**PLUG**	*v* PLUGGED, PLUGGING, PLUGS to seal or close with a plug (a piece of material used to fill a hole)
PLODDER	*n* pl. -S one that plods		
PLOIDY	*n* pl. -DIES the extent of repetition of the basic number of chromosomes		
		PLUGGER	*n* pl. -S one that plugs
		PLUGLESS	*adj* having no plug
PLONK	*v* -ED, -ING, -S to plunk	**PLUGOLA**	*n* pl. -S free incidental advertising on radio or television
PLOP	*v* PLOPPED, PLOPPING, PLOPS to drop or fall heavily	**PLUGUGLY**	*n* pl. -LIES a hoodlum
PLOSION	*n* pl. -S a release of breath after the articulation of certain consonants	**PLUM**	*n* pl. -S a fleshy fruit
		PLUMAGE	*n* pl. -S the feathers of a bird **PLUMAGED** *adj*
PLOSIVE	*n* pl. -S a sound produced by plosion	**PLUMATE**	*adj* resembling a feather
PLOT	*v* PLOTTED, PLOTTING, PLOTS to plan secretly	**PLUMB**	*v* -ED, -ING, -S to determine the depth of
PLOTLESS	*adj* planless	**PLUMBAGO**	*n* pl. -GOS graphite
PLOTLINE	*n* pl. -S the main story of a book	**PLUMBER**	*n* pl. -S one who installs and repairs plumbing
PLOTTAGE	*n* pl. -S an area of land		
PLOTTED	past tense of plot	**PLUMBERY**	*n* pl. -ERIES the work of a plumber
PLOTTER	*n* pl. -S one that plots		
PLOTTIER	comparative of plotty	**PLUMBIC**	*adj* containing lead
PLOTTIES	pl. of plotty	**PLUMBING**	*n* pl. -S the pipe system of a building
PLOTTING	present participle of plot		
PLOTTY	*adj* -TIER, -TIEST full of intrigue, as a novel	**PLUMBISM**	*n* pl. -S lead poisoning
		PLUMBOUS	*adj* containing lead
PLOTTY	*n* pl. -TIES a hot, spiced beverage	**PLUMBUM**	*n* pl. -S lead
PLOTZ	*v* -ED, -ING, -ES to be overwhelmed by an emotion	**PLUME**	*v* PLUMED, PLUMING, PLUMES to cover with feathers
PLOUGH	*v* -ED, -ING, -S to plow	**PLUMELET**	*n* pl. -S a small feather

PLUMERIA   *n* pl. -S a flowering shrub

PLUMIER   comparative of plumy

PLUMIEST   superlative of plumy

PLUMING   present participle of plume

PLUMIPED   *n* pl. -S a bird having feathered feet

PLUMLIKE   *adj* resembling a plum

PLUMMET   *v* -ED, -ING, -S to drop straight down

PLUMMY   *adj* -MIER, -MIEST full of plums

PLUMOSE   *adj* having feathers

PLUMP   *adj* PLUMPER, PLUMPEST well-rounded and full in form

PLUMP   *v* -ED, -ING, -S to make plump

PLUMPEN   *v* -ED, -ING, -S to plump

PLUMPER   *n* pl. -S a heavy fall

PLUMPISH   *adj* somewhat plump

PLUMPLY   *adv* in a plump way

PLUMULE   *n* pl. -S the primary bud of a plant embryo **PLUMULAR** *adj*

PLUMY   *adj* PLUMIER, PLUMIEST covered with feathers

PLUNDER   *v* -ED, -ING, -S to rob of goods by force

PLUNGE   *v* PLUNGED, PLUNGING, PLUNGES to throw or thrust suddenly or forcibly into something

PLUNGER   *n* pl. -S one that plunges

PLUNK   *v* -ED, -ING, -S to fall or drop heavily

PLUNKER   *n* pl. -S one that plunks

PLURAL   *n* pl. -S a word that expresses more than one

PLURALLY   *adv* in a manner or form that expresses more than one

PLUS   *n* pl. PLUSES or PLUSSES an additional quantity

PLUSH   *adj* PLUSHER, PLUSHEST luxurious **PLUSHLY** *adv*

PLUSH   *n* pl. -ES a fabric with a long pile

PLUSHY   *adj* PLUSHIER, PLUSHIEST luxurious **PLUSHILY** *adv*

PLUSSAGE   *n* pl. -S an amount over and above another

PLUSSES   a pl. of plus

PLUTEUS   *n* pl. -TEI the larva of a sea urchin

PLUTON   *n* pl. -S a formation of igneous rock **PLUTONIC** *adj*

PLUVIAL   *n* pl. -S a prolonged period of wet climate

PLUVIAN   *adj* characterized by much rain

PLUVIOSE   *adj* pluvious

PLUVIOUS   *adj* pertaining to rain

PLY   *v* PLIED, PLYING, PLIES to supply with or offer repeatedly **PLYINGLY** *adv*

PLYER   *n* pl. -S plier

PLYWOOD   *n* pl. -S a building material

PNEUMA   *n* pl. -S the soul or spirit

POACEOUS   *adj* pertaining to plants of the grass family

POACH   *v* -ED, -ING, -ES to trespass for the purpose of taking game or fish

POACHER   *n* pl. -S one that poaches

POACHY   *adj* POACHIER, POACHIEST swampy

POCHARD   *n* pl. -S a sea duck

POCK   *v* -ED, -ING, -S to mark with pocks (pustules caused by an eruptive disease)

POCKET   *v* -ED, -ING, -S to place in a pouch sewed into a garment

POCKETER   *n* pl. -S one that pockets

POCKMARK   *v* -ED, -ING, -S to mark with scars caused by an eruptive disease

POCKY   *adj* POCKIER, POCKIEST covered with pocks **POCKILY** *adv*

POCO   *adv* a little — used as a musical direction

POCOSIN   *n* pl. -S an upland swamp

POD   *v* PODDED, PODDING, PODS to produce seed vessels

PODAGRA   *n* pl. -S gout in the foot **PODAGRAL, PODAGRIC** *adj*

PODESTA   *n* pl. -S an Italian magistrate

PODGY   *adj* PODGIER, PODGIEST pudgy **PODGILY** *adv*

PODIA   a pl. of podium

PODIATRY   *n* pl. -TRIES the study and treatment of the human foot

PODITE   *n* pl. -S a limb segment of an arthropod **PODITIC** *adj*

PODIUM   *n* pl. -DIUMS or -DIA a small platform

PODLIKE   *adj* resembling a pod (a seed vessel)

PODOCARP	*adj* designating a family of evergreen trees
PODOMERE	*n* pl. -S a podite
PODSOL	*n* pl. -S podzol **PODSOLIC** *adj*
PODZOL	*n* pl. -S an infertile soil **PODZOLIC** *adj*
POECHORE	*n* pl. -S a semiarid region
POEM	*n* pl. -S a composition in verse
POESY	*n* pl. -ESIES poetry
POET	*n* pl. -S one who writes poems
POETESS	*n* pl. -ES a female poet
POETIC	*adj* pertaining to poetry
POETICAL	*adj* poetic
POETICS	*n/pl* poetic theory or practice
POETISE	*v* -ISED, -ISING, -ISES to poetize
POETISER	*n* pl. -S poetizer
POETIZE	*v* -IZED, -IZING, -IZES to write poetry
POETIZER	*n* pl. -S one that poetizes
POETLESS	*adj* lacking a poet
POETLIKE	*adj* resembling a poet
POETRY	*n* pl. -RIES literary work in metrical form
POGEY	*n* pl. -GEYS any form of government relief
POGIES	pl. of pogy
POGONIA	*n* pl. -S a small orchid
POGONIP	*n* pl. -S a dense fog of suspended ice particles
POGROM	*v* -ED, -ING, -S to massacre systematically
POGY	*n* pl. -GIES a marine fish
POH	*interj* — used to express disgust
POI	*n* pl. -S a Hawaiian food
POIGNANT	*adj* emotionally distressing
POILU	*n* pl. -S a French soldier
POIND	*v* -ED, -ING, -S to seize and sell the property of to satisfy a debt
POINT	*v* -ED, -ING, -S to indicate direction with the finger
POINTE	*n* pl. -S a ballet position
POINTER	*n* pl. -S one that points
POINTMAN	*n* pl. -MEN a certain player in hockey
POINTY	*adj* POINTIER, POINTIEST coming to a sharp, tapering end
POISE	*v* POISED, POISING, POISES to hold in a state of equilibrium
POISER	*n* pl. -S one that poises
POISHA	*n* pl. POISHA the paisa of Bangladesh
POISON	*v* -ED, -ING, -S to administer a harmful substance to
POISONER	*n* pl. -S one that poisons
POITREL	*n* pl. -S peytral
POKE	*v* POKED, POKING, POKES to push or prod
POKER	*n* pl. -S one that pokes
POKEROOT	*n* pl. -S pokeweed
POKEWEED	*n* pl. -S a perennial herb
POKEY	*n* pl. -KEYS poky
POKIER	comparative of poky
POKIES	pl. of poky
POKIEST	superlative of poky
POKILY	*adv* in a poky manner
POKINESS	*n* pl. -ES the state of being poky
POKING	present participle of poke
POKY	*n* pl. POKIES a jail
POKY	*adj* POKIER, POKIEST slow
POL	*n* pl. -S a politician
POLAR	*n* pl. -S a straight line related to a point
POLARISE	*v* -ISED, -ISING, -ISES to polarize
POLARITY	*n* pl. -TIES the possession of two opposite qualities
POLARIZE	*v* -IZED, -IZING, -IZES to give polarity to
POLARON	*n* pl. -S a type of electron
POLDER	*n* pl. -S a tract of low land reclaimed from a body of water
POLE	*v* POLED, POLING, POLES to propel with a pole (a long, thin piece of wood or metal)
POLEAX	*v* -ED, -ING, -ES to strike with an axlike weapon
POLEAXE	*v* -AXED, -AXING, -AXES to poleax
POLECAT	*n* pl. -S a carnivorous mammal
POLED	past tense of pole
POLEIS	pl. of polis
POLELESS	*adj* having no pole
POLEMIC	*n* pl. -S a controversial argument
POLEMIST	*n* pl. -S one who engages in polemics

POLEMIZE   *v* -MIZED, -MIZING, -MIZES to engage in polemics

POLENTA   *n* pl. -S a thick mush of cornmeal

POLER   *n* pl. -S one that poles

POLESTAR   *n* pl. -S a guiding principle

POLEWARD   *adv* in the direction of either extremity of the earth's axis

POLEYN   *n* pl. -S a protective piece of leather for the knee

POLICE   *v* -LICED, -LICING, -LICES to make clean or orderly

POLICY   *n* pl. -CIES an action or a procedure considered with reference to prudence or expediency

POLING   present participle of pole

POLIO   *n* pl. -LIOS an infectious virus disease

POLIS   *n* pl. -LEIS an ancient Greek city-state

POLISH   *v* -ED, -ING, -ES to make smooth and lustrous by rubbing

POLISHER   *n* pl. -S one that polishes

POLITE   *adj* -LITER, -LITEST showing consideration for others **POLITELY** *adv*

POLITIC   *adj* shrewd

POLITICK   *v* -ED, -ING, -S to engage in politics

POLITICO   *n* pl. -COS or -COES one who politicks

POLITICS   *n/pl* the art or science of government

POLITY   *n* pl. -TIES a form or system of government

POLKA   *v* -ED, -ING, -S to perform a lively dance

POLL   *v* -ED, -ING, -S to question for the purpose of surveying public opinion

POLLACK   *n* pl. -S a marine food fish

POLLARD   *v* -ED, -ING, -S to cut the top branches of a tree back to the trunk

POLLEE   *n* pl. -S one who is polled

POLLEN   *v* -ED, -ING, -S to convey pollen (the fertilizing element in a seed plant) to

POLLER   *n* pl. -S one that polls

POLLEX   *n* pl. -LICES the innermost digit of the forelimb **POLLICAL** *adj*

POLLINIA   *n/pl* masses of pollen grains

POLLINIC   *adj* pertaining to pollen

POLLIST   *n* pl. -S a poller

POLLIWOG   *n* pl. -S a tadpole

POLLOCK   *n* pl. -S pollack

POLLSTER   *n* pl. -S a poller

POLLUTE   *v* -LUTED, -LUTING, -LUTES to make unclean or impure

POLLUTER   *n* pl. -S one that pollutes

POLLYWOG   *n* pl. -S polliwog

POLO   *n* pl. -LOS a game played on horseback

POLOIST   *n* pl. -S a polo player

POLONIUM   *n* pl. -S a radioactive element

POLTROON   *n* pl. -S a base coward

POLY   *n* pl. POLYS a type of white blood cell

POLYBRID   *n* pl. -S a type of hybrid plant

POLYCOT   *n* pl. -S a type of plant

POLYENE   *n* pl. -S a chemical compound **POLYENIC** *adj*

POLYGALA   *n* pl. -S a flowering plant

POLYGAMY   *n* pl. -MIES the condition of having more than one spouse at the same time

POLYGENE   *n* pl. -S a type of gene

POLYGLOT   *n* pl. -S one that speaks or writes several languages

POLYGON   *n* pl. -S a closed plane figure bounded by straight lines

POLYGONY   *n* pl. -NIES an herb

POLYGYNY   *n* pl. -NIES the condition of having more than one wife at the same time

POLYMATH   *n* pl. -S a person of great and varied learning

POLYMER   *n* pl. -S a complex chemical compound

POLYNYA   *n* pl. -YAS or -YI an area of open water surrounded by sea ice

POLYOMA   *n* pl. -S a type of virus

POLYP   *n* pl. -S an invertebrate

POLYPARY   *n* pl. -ARIES the common supporting structure of a polyp colony

POLYPI   a pl. of polypus

POLYPIDE   *n* pl. -S a polyp

POLYPNEA   *n* pl. -S rapid breathing

POLYPOD   *n* pl. -S a many-footed organism

POLYPODY   *n* pl. -DIES a fern

POLYPOID	*adj* resembling a polyp
POLYPORE	*n* pl. -S a type of fungus
POLYPOUS	*adj* pertaining to a polyp
POLYPUS	*n* pl. -PI or -PUSES a growth protruding from the mucous lining of an organ
POLYSEMY	*n* pl. -MIES diversity of meanings
POLYSOME	*n* pl. -S a cluster of protein particles
POLYTENE	*adj* having chromosomes of a certain type
POLYTENY	*n* pl. -NIES the state of being polytene
POLYTYPE	*n* pl. -S a crystal structure
POLYURIA	*n* pl. -S excessive urination **POLYURIC** *adj*
POLYZOAN	*n* pl. -S a bryozoan
POLYZOIC	*adj* composed of many zooids
POMACE	*n* pl. -S the pulpy residue of crushed fruits
POMADE	*v* -MADED, -MADING, -MADES to apply a perfumed hair dressing to
POMANDER	*n* pl. -S a mixture of aromatic substances
POMATUM	*n* pl. -S a perfumed hair dressing
POME	*n* pl. -S a fleshy fruit with a core
POMELO	*n* pl. -LOS a grapefruit
POMFRET	*n* pl. -S a marine fish
POMMEE	*adj* having arms with knoblike ends — used of a heraldic cross
POMMEL	*v* -MELED, -MELING, -MELS or -MELLED, -MELLING, -MELS to strike with the fists
POMOLOGY	*n* pl. -GIES the study of fruits
POMP	*n* pl. -S stately or splendid display
POMPANO	*n* pl. -NOS a marine food fish
POMPOM	*n* pl. -S an antiaircraft cannon
POMPON	*n* pl. -S an ornamental tuft or ball
POMPOUS	*adj* marked by exaggerated self-importance
PONCE	*v* PONCED, PONCING, PONCES to pimp
PONCHO	*n* pl. -CHOS a type of cloak
POND	*v* -ED, -ING, -S to collect into a pond (a small body of water)
PONDER	*v* -ED, -ING, -S to consider something deeply and thoroughly
PONDERER	*n* pl. -S one that ponders
PONDWEED	*n* pl. -S an aquatic plant
PONE	*n* pl. -S a corn bread
PONENT	*adj* affirmative
PONG	*v* -ED, -ING, -S to stink
PONGEE	*n* pl. -S a type of silk
PONGID	*n* pl. -S an anthropoid ape
PONIARD	*v* -ED, -ING, -S to stab with a dagger
PONIED	past tense of pony
PONIES	present 3d person sing. of pony
PONS	*n* pl. PONTES a band of nerve fibers in the brain
PONTIFEX	*n* pl. -FICES an ancient Roman priest
PONTIFF	*n* pl. -S a pope or bishop
PONTIFIC	*adj* pertaining to a pope or bishop
PONTIFICES	pl. of pontifex
PONTIL	*n* pl. -S a punty
PONTINE	*adj* pertaining to bridges
PONTON	*n* pl. -S pontoon
PONTOON	*n* pl. -S a flat-bottomed boat
PONY	*v* -NIED, -NYING, -NIES to prepare lessons with the aid of a literal translation
PONYTAIL	*n* pl. -S a hairstyle
POOCH	*v* -ED, -ING, -ES to bulge
POOD	*n* pl. -S a Russian unit of weight
POODLE	*n* pl. -S a heavy-coated dog
POOF	*interj* — used to indicate an instantaneous occurrence
POOH	*v* -ED, -ING, -S to express contempt for
POOL	*v* -ED, -ING, -S to combine in a common fund
POOLHALL	*n* pl. -S a poolroom
POOLROOM	*n* pl. -S an establishment for the playing of billiards
POOLSIDE	*n* pl. -S the area surrounding a swimming pool
POON	*n* pl. -S an East Indian tree
POOP	*v* -ED, -ING, -S to tire out
POOR	*adj* POORER, POOREST lacking the means of support
POORI	*n* pl. -S a light, flat wheat cake
POORISH	*adj* somewhat poor
POORLY	*adv* in a poor manner
POORNESS	*n* pl. -ES the state of being poor

POORTITH	*n* pl. -S poverty
POP	*v* POPPED, POPPING, POPS to make a sharp, explosive sound
POPCORN	*n* pl. -S a variety of corn
POPE	*n* pl. -S the head of the Roman Catholic Church **POPELESS, POPELIKE** *adj*
POPEDOM	*n* pl. -S the office of a pope
POPEYED	*adj* having bulging eyes
POPGUN	*n* pl. -S a toy gun
POPINJAY	*n* pl. -JAYS a vain person
POPLAR	*n* pl. -S a fast-growing tree
POPLIN	*n* pl. -S a durable fabric
POPLITIC	*adj* pertaining to the part of the leg behind the knee
POPOVER	*n* pl. -S a very light egg muffin
POPPA	*n* pl. -S papa
POPPED	past tense of pop
POPPER	*n* pl. -S one that pops
POPPET	*n* pl. -S a mechanical valve
POPPIED	*adj* covered with poppies
POPPIES	pl. of poppy
POPPING	present participle of pop
POPPLE	*v* -PLED, -PLING, -PLES to move in a bubbling or rippling manner
POPPY	*n* pl. -PIES a flowering plant
POPSIE	*n* pl. -S popsy
POPSY	*n* pl. -SIES a girlfriend
POPULACE	*n* pl. -S the common people
POPULAR	*adj* liked by many people
POPULATE	*v* -LATED, -LATING, -LATES to inhabit
POPULISM	*n* pl. -S populists' doctrines
POPULIST	*n* pl. -S a member of a party which represents the common people
POPULOUS	*adj* containing many inhabitants
PORCH	*n* pl. -ES a covered structure at the entrance to a building
PORCINE	*adj* pertaining to swine
PORCINO	*n* pl. -NI an edible mushroom
PORE	*v* PORED, PORING, PORES to gaze intently
PORGY	*n* pl. -GIES a marine food fish
PORISM	*n* pl. -S a type of mathematical proposition
PORK	*n* pl. -S the flesh of swine used as food
PORKER	*n* pl. -S a pig
PORKIER	comparative of porky
PORKIES	pl. of porky
PORKIEST	superlative of porky
PORKPIE	*n* pl. -S a man's hat
PORKWOOD	*n* pl. -S a tropical tree
PORKY	*adj* PORKIER, PORKIEST resembling pork
PORKY	*n* pl. -KIES a porcupine
PORN	*n* pl. -S pornography
PORNO	*n* pl. -NOS pornography
PORNY	*adj* PORNIER, PORNIEST pornographic
POROSE	*adj* porous
POROSITY	*n* pl. -TIES the state of being porous
POROUS	*adj* having minute openings **POROUSLY** *adv*
PORPHYRY	*n* pl. -RIES an igneous rock
PORPOISE	*n* pl. -S an aquatic mammal
PORRECT	*adj* extended forward
PORRIDGE	*n* pl. -S a soft food **PORRIDGY** *adj*
PORT	*v* -ED, -ING, -S to shift to the left side
PORTABLE	*n* pl. -S something that can be carried
PORTABLY	*adv* so as to be capable of being carried
PORTAGE	*v* -TAGED, -TAGING, -TAGES to transport from one navigable waterway to another
PORTAL	*n* pl. -S a door, gate, or entrance **PORTALED** *adj*
PORTANCE	*n* pl. -S demeanor
PORTAPAK	*n* pl. -S a portable combined video recorder and camera
PORTEND	*v* -ED, -ING, -S to serve as an omen of
PORTENT	*n* pl. -S an omen
PORTER	*v* -ED, -ING, -S to carry luggage for pay
PORTHOLE	*n* pl. -S a small window in a ship's side
PORTICO	*n* pl. -COS or -COES a type of porch
PORTIERE	*n* pl. -S a curtain for a doorway

PORTION _v_ -ED, -ING, -S to divide into shares for distribution

PORTLESS _adj_ having no place for ships to load or unload

PORTLY _adj_ -LIER, -LIEST rather heavy or fat

PORTRAIT _n_ pl. -S a likeness of a person

PORTRAY _v_ -ED, -ING, -S to represent pictorially

PORTRESS _n_ pl. -ES a female doorkeeper

POSADA _n_ pl. -S an inn

POSE _v_ POSED, POSING, POSES to assume a fixed position

POSER _n_ pl. -S one that poses

POSEUR _n_ pl. -S an affected or insincere person

POSH _adj_ POSHER, POSHEST stylish or elegant **POSHLY** _adv_

POSHNESS _n_ pl. -ES the quality of being posh

POSIES pl. of posy

POSING present participle of pose

POSINGLY _adv_ in a posing manner

POSIT _v_ -ED, -ING, -S to place

POSITION _v_ -ED, -ING, -S to put in a particular location

POSITIVE _adj_ -TIVER, -TIVEST certain

POSITIVE _n_ pl. -S a quantity greater than zero

POSITRON _n_ pl. -S a subatomic particle

POSOLOGY _n_ pl. -GIES a branch of medicine that deals with drug dosages

POSSE _n_ pl. -S a body of men summoned to aid a peace officer

POSSESS _v_ -ED, -ING, -ES to have as property

POSSET _n_ pl. -S a hot, spiced drink

POSSIBLE _adj_ -BLER, -BLEST capable of happening or proving true **POSSIBLY** _adv_

POSSUM _n_ pl. -S opossum

POST _v_ -ED, -ING, -S to affix in a public place

POSTAGE _n_ pl. -S the charge for mailing an item

POSTAL _n_ pl. -S a postcard

POSTALLY _adv_ in a manner pertaining to the mails

POSTANAL _adj_ situated behind the anus

POSTBAG _n_ pl. -S a mailbag

POSTBASE _adj_ following a base word

POSTBOX _n_ pl. -ES a mailbox

POSTBOY _n_ pl. -BOYS a boy who carries mail

POSTBURN _adj_ following a burn

POSTCARD _n_ pl. -S a card for use in the mail

POSTCAVA _n_ pl. -VAE a vein in higher vertebrates

POSTCODE _n_ pl. -S a code of numbers and letters used in a mailing address

POSTCOUP _adj_ following a coup

POSTDATE _v_ -DATED, -DATING, -DATES to give a date later than the actual date to

POSTDIVE _adj_ following a dive

POSTDOC _n_ pl. -S one engaged in postdoctoral study

POSTDRUG _adj_ following the taking of a drug

POSTEEN _n_ pl. -S an Afghan outer garment

POSTER _n_ pl. -S a printed or written notice for posting

POSTERN _n_ pl. -S a rear door or gate

POSTFACE _n_ pl. -S a brief note placed at the end of a publication

POSTFIRE _adj_ following a fire

POSTFIX _v_ -ED, -ING, -ES to affix at the end of something

POSTFORM _v_ -ED, -ING, -S to shape subsequently

POSTGAME _adj_ following a game

POSTHEAT _n_ pl. -S heat applied to a metal after welding

POSTHOLE _n_ pl. -S a hole for a fence post

POSTICHE _n_ pl. -S an imitation

POSTIN _n_ pl. -S posteen

POSTING _n_ pl. -S the act of transferring to a ledger

POSTIQUE _n_ pl. -S postiche

POSTLUDE _n_ pl. -S a closing musical piece

POSTMAN _n_ pl. -MEN a mailman

POSTMARK _v_ -ED, -ING, -S to stamp mail with an official mark

POSTORAL _adj_ situated behind the mouth

POSTPAID _adv_ with the postage prepaid

POSTPONE _v_ -PONED, -PONING, -PONES to put off to a future time

POSTRACE _adj_ following a race

POSTRIOT _adj_ following a riot

POSTSHOW *adj* following a show

POSTSYNC *v* -ED, -ING, -S to add sound to a film after a scene has been photographed

POSTTAX *adj* remaining after taxes

POSTTEEN *adj* occurring after one's teenage years

POSTTEST *n* pl. -S a test given after an instructional program

POSTURAL *adj* pertaining to the position of the body

POSTURE *v* -TURED, -TURING, -TURES to assume a particular position

POSTURER *n* pl. -S one that postures

POSTWAR *adj* occurring or existing after a war

POSY *n* pl. -SIES a flower or bouquet

POT *v* POTTED, POTTING, POTS to put in a pot (a round, fairly deep container)

POTABLE *n* pl. -S a liquid suitable for drinking

POTAGE *n* pl. -S a thick soup

POTAMIC *adj* pertaining to rivers

POTASH *n* pl. -ES an alkaline compound

POTASSIC *adj* pertaining to potassium (a metallic element)

POTATION *n* pl. -S the act of drinking

POTATO *n* pl. -TOES the edible tuber of a cultivated plant

POTATORY *adj* pertaining to drinking

POTBELLY *n* pl. -LIES a protruding abdominal region

POTBOIL *v* -ED, -ING, -S to produce inferior literary or artistic work

POTBOY *n* pl. -BOYS a boy who serves customers in a tavern

POTEEN *n* pl. -S Irish whiskey that is distilled unlawfully

POTENCE *n* pl. -S potency

POTENCY *n* pl. -CIES the quality of being potent

POTENT *adj* powerful **POTENTLY** *adv*

POTFUL *n* pl. -S as much as a pot can hold

POTHEAD *n* pl. -S one who smokes marijuana

POTHEEN *n* pl. -S poteen

POTHER *v* -ED, -ING, -S to trouble

POTHERB *n* pl. -S any herb used as a food or seasoning

POTHOLE *n* pl. -S a deep hole in a road **POTHOLED** *adj*

POTHOOK *n* pl. -S a hook for lifting or hanging pots

POTHOUSE *n* pl. -S a tavern

POTICHE *n* pl. -S a type of vase

POTION *n* pl. -S a magical or medicinal drink

POTLACH *n* pl. -ES a ceremonial feast

POTLACHE *n* pl. -S potlach

POTLATCH *v* -ED, -ING, -ES to hold a ceremonial feast for

POTLIKE *adj* resembling a pot

POTLINE *n* pl. -S a row of electrolytic cells

POTLUCK *n* pl. -S food which is incidentally available

POTMAN *n* pl. -MEN a man who serves customers in a tavern

POTPIE *n* pl. -S a deep-dish pie containing meat and vegetables

POTSHARD *n* pl. -S potsherd

POTSHERD *n* pl. -S a fragment of broken pottery

POTSHOT *v* -SHOT, -SHOTTING, -SHOTS to shoot randomly at

POTSIE *n* pl. -S potsy

POTSTONE *n* pl. -S a variety of steatite

POTSY *n* pl. -SIES a children's game

POTTAGE *n* pl. -S a thick soup

POTTED past tense of pot

POTTEEN *n* pl. -S poteen

POTTER *v* -ED, -ING, -S to putter

POTTERER *n* pl. -S one that potters

POTTERY *n* pl. -TERIES ware molded from clay and hardened by heat

POTTIER comparative of potty

POTTIES pl. of potty

POTTIEST superlative of potty

POTTING present participle of pot

POTTLE *n* pl. -S a drinking vessel

POTTO *n* pl. -TOS a lemur of tropical Africa

POTTY *adj* -TIER, -TIEST of little importance

POTTY *n* pl. -TIES a small toilet seat

POTZER *n* pl. -S patzer

POUCH *v* -ED, -ING, -ES to put in a pouch (a small, flexible receptacle)

POUCHY	*adj* POUCHIER, POUCHIEST resembling a pouch
POUF	*n* pl. -S a loose roll of hair **POUFED** *adj*
POUFF	*n* pl. -S pouf **POUFFED** *adj*
POUFFE	*n* pl. -S pouf
POULARD	*n* pl. -S a spayed hen
POULARDE	*n* pl. -S poulard
POULT	*n* pl. -S a young domestic fowl
POULTER	*n* pl. -S one that deals in poultry
POULTICE	*v* -TICED, -TICING, -TICES to apply a healing substance to
POULTRY	*n* pl. -TRIES domestic fowls kept for eggs or meat
POUNCE	*v* POUNCED, POUNCING, POUNCES to make a sudden assault or approach
POUNCER	*n* pl. -S one that pounces
POUND	*v* -ED, -ING, -S to strike heavily and repeatedly
POUNDAGE	*n* pl. -S the act of impounding
POUNDAL	*n* pl. -S a unit of force
POUNDER	*n* pl. -S one that pounds
POUR	*v* -ED, -ING, -S to cause to flow **POURABLE** *adj*
POURER	*n* pl. -S one that pours
POUSSIE	*n* pl. -S pussy
POUT	*v* -ED, -ING, -S to protrude the lips in ill humor
POUTER	*n* pl. -S one that pouts
POUTFUL	*adj* pouty
POUTY	*adj* POUTIER, POUTIEST tending to pout
POVERTY	*n* pl. -TIES the state of being poor
POW	*n* pl. -S an explosive sound
POWDER	*v* -ED, -ING, -S to reduce to powder (matter in a finely divided state)
POWDERER	*n* pl. -S one that powders
POWDERY	*adj* resembling powder
POWER	*v* -ED, -ING, -S to provide with means of propulsion
POWERFUL	*adj* possessing great force
POWTER	*n* pl. -S a domestic pigeon
POWWOW	*v* -ED, -ING, -S to hold a conference
POX	*v* -ED, -ING, -ES to infect with syphilis
POXVIRUS	*n* pl. -ES a type of virus
POYOU	*n* pl. -S an armadillo of Argentina
POZZOLAN	*n* pl. -S a finely divided material used to make cement
PRAAM	*n* pl. -S pram
PRACTIC	*adj* practical
PRACTICE	*v* -TICED, -TICING, -TICES to perform often so as to acquire skill
PRACTISE	*v* -TISED, -TISING, -TISES to practice
PRAECIPE	*n* pl. -S a legal writ
PRAEDIAL	*adj* pertaining to land
PRAEFECT	*n* pl. -S prefect
PRAELECT	*v* -ED, -ING, -S to prelect
PRAETOR	*n* pl. -S an ancient Roman magistrate
PRAHU	*n* pl. -S prau
PRAIRIE	*n* pl. -S a tract of grassland
PRAISE	*v* PRAISED, PRAISING, PRAISES to express approval or admiration of
PRAISER	*n* pl. -S one that praises
PRALINE	*n* pl. -S a confection made of nuts cooked in sugar
PRAM	*n* pl. -S a flat-bottomed boat
PRANCE	*v* PRANCED, PRANCING, PRANCES to spring forward on the hind legs
PRANCER	*n* pl. -S one that prances
PRANDIAL	*adj* pertaining to a meal
PRANG	*v* -ED, -ING, -S to cause to crash
PRANK	*v* -ED, -ING, -S to adorn gaudily
PRANKISH	*adj* mischievous
PRAO	*n* pl. PRAOS prau
PRASE	*n* pl. -S a mineral
PRAT	*n* pl. -S the buttocks
PRATE	*v* PRATED, PRATING, PRATES to chatter
PRATER	*n* pl. -S one that prates
PRATFALL	*n* pl. -S a fall on the buttocks
PRATING	present participle of prate
PRATIQUE	*n* pl. -S clearance given a ship by the health authority of a port
PRATTLE	*v* -TLED, -TLING, -TLES to babble
PRATTLER	*n* pl. -S one that prattles
PRAU	*n* pl. -S a swift Malaysian sailing vessel

PRAWN	*v* -ED, -ING, -S to fish for prawns (edible shellfish)
PRAWNER	*n* pl. -S one that prawns
PRAXIS	*n* pl. PRAXISES or PRAXES practical use of a theory
PRAY	*v* -ED, -ING, -S to address prayers to
PRAYER	*n* pl. -S a devout petition to a deity
PREACH	*v* -ED, -ING, -ES to advocate or recommend urgently
PREACHER	*n* pl. -S one that preaches
PREACHY	*adj* PREACHIER, PREACHIEST tending to preach
PREACT	*v* -ED, -ING, -S to act beforehand
PREADAPT	*v* -ED, -ING, -S to adapt beforehand
PREADMIT	*v* -MITTED, -MITTING, -MITS to admit beforehand
PREADOPT	*v* -ED, -ING, -S to adopt beforehand
PREADULT	*adj* preceding adulthood
PREAGED	*adj* previously aged
PREALLOT	*v* -LOTTED, -LOTTING, -LOTS to allot beforehand
PREAMBLE	*n* pl. -S an introductory statement
PREAMP	*n* pl. -S an amplifier
PREANAL	*adj* situated in front of the anus
PREARM	*v* -ED, -ING, -S to arm beforehand
PREAUDIT	*n* pl. -S an audit made prior to a final settlement of a transaction
PREAVER	*v* -VERRED, -VERRING, -VERS to aver or assert beforehand
PREAXIAL	*adj* situated in front of an axis
PREBAKE	*v* -BAKED, -BAKING, -BAKES to bake beforehand
PREBASAL	*adj* situated in front of a base
PREBEND	*n* pl. -S a clergyman's stipend
PREBILL	*v* -ED, -ING, -S to bill beforehand
PREBIND	*v* -BOUND, -BINDING, -BINDS to bind beforehand
PREBLESS	*v* -ED, -ING, -ES to bless beforehand
PREBOIL	*v* -ED, -ING, -S to boil beforehand
PREBOOK	*v* -ED, -ING, -S to book beforehand
PREBOOM	*adj* preceding a sudden expansion of business
PREBOUND	past tense of prebind
PRECAST	*v* -CAST, -CASTING, -CASTS to cast before placing into position
PRECAVA	*n* pl. -VAE a vein in higher vertebrates **PRECAVAL** *adj*
PRECEDE	*v* -CEDED, -CEDING, -CEDES to go before
PRECENT	*v* -ED, -ING, -S to lead a church choir in singing
PRECEPT	*n* pl. -S a rule of conduct
PRECESS	*v* -ED, -ING, -ES to rotate with a complex motion
PRECHECK	*v* -ED, -ING, -S to check beforehand
PRECHILL	*v* -ED, -ING, -S to chill beforehand
PRECIEUX	*adj* excessively refined
PRECINCT	*n* pl. -S a subdivision of a city or town
PRECIOUS	*n* pl. -ES a darling
PRECIPE	*n* pl. -S praecipe
PRECIS	*v* -ED, -ING, -ES to make a concise summary of
PRECISE	*adj* -CISER, -CISEST sharply and clearly defined or stated
PRECITED	*adj* previously cited
PRECLEAN	*v* -ED, -ING, -S to clean beforehand
PRECLEAR	*v* -ED, -ING, -S to clear beforehand
PRECLUDE	*v* -CLUDED, -CLUDING, -CLUDES to make impossible by previous action
PRECODE	*v* -CODED, -CODING, -CODES to code beforehand
PRECOOK	*v* -ED, -ING, -S to cook beforehand
PRECOOL	*v* -ED, -ING, -S to cool beforehand
PRECOUP	*adj* preceding a coup
PRECRASH	*adj* preceding a crash
PRECURE	*v* -CURED, -CURING, -CURES to cure beforehand
PRECUT	*v* -CUT, -CUTTING, -CUTS to cut beforehand
PREDATE	*v* -DATED, -DATING, -DATES to date before the actual or a specified time
PREDATOR	*n* pl. -S one that plunders
PREDAWN	*n* pl. -S the time just before dawn
PREDIAL	*adj* praedial

PREDICT   *v* -ED, -ING, -S to tell of or about in advance

PREDIVE   *adj* preceding a dive

PREDRILL   *v* -ED, -ING, -S to drill beforehand

PREDUSK   *n* pl. -S the time just before dusk

PREE   *v* PREED, PREEING, PREES to test by tasting

PREEDIT   *v* -ED, -ING, -S to edit beforehand

PREELECT   *v* -ED, -ING, -S to elect or choose beforehand

PREEMIE   *n* pl. -S an infant born prematurely

PREEMPT   *v* -ED, -ING, -S to acquire by prior right

PREEN   *v* -ED, -ING, -S to smooth or clean with the beak or tongue

PREENACT   *v* -ED, -ING, -S to enact beforehand

PREENER   *n* pl. -S one that preens

PREERECT   *v* -ED, -ING, -S to erect beforehand

PREEXIST   *v* -ED, -ING, -S to exist before

PREFAB   *v* -FABBED, -FABBING, -FABS to construct beforehand

PREFACE   *v* -ACED, -ACING, -ACES to provide with an introductory statement

PREFACER   *n* pl. -S one that prefaces

PREFADE   *v* -FADED, -FADING, -FADES to fade beforehand

PREFECT   *n* pl. -S an ancient Roman official

PREFER   *v* -FERRED, -FERRING, -FERS to hold in higher regard or esteem

PREFIGHT   *adj* preceding a fight

PREFILE   *v* -FILED, -FILING, -FILES to file beforehand

PREFIRE   *v* -FIRED, -FIRING, -FIRES to fire beforehand

PREFIX   *v* -ED, -ING, -ES to add as a prefix (a form affixed to the beginning of a root word)

PREFIXAL   *adj* pertaining to or being a prefix

PREFLAME   *adj* preceding a flame

PREFOCUS   *v* -CUSED, -CUSING, -CUSES or -CUSSED, -CUSSING, -CUSSES to focus beforehand

PREFORM   *v* -ED, -ING, -S to form beforehand

PREFRANK   *v* -ED, -ING, -S to frank beforehand

PREFREEZE   *v* -FROZE, -FROZEN, -FREEZING, -FREEZES to freeze beforehand

PREGAME   *adj* preceding a game

PREGGERS   *adj* pregnant

PREGNANT   *adj* carrying a developing fetus in the uterus

PREHEAT   *v* -ED, -ING, -S to heat beforehand

PREHUMAN   *n* pl. -S a prototype of man

PREJUDGE   *v* -JUDGED, -JUDGING, -JUDGES to judge beforehand

PRELACY   *n* pl. -CIES the office of a prelate

PRELATE   *n* pl. -S a high-ranking clergyman **PRELATIC** *adj*

PRELECT   *v* -ED, -ING, -S to lecture

PRELEGAL   *adj* occurring before the commencement of studies in law

PRELIFE   *n* pl. -LIVES a life conceived as lived before one's earthly life

PRELIM   *n* pl. -S a preliminary match

PRELIMIT   *v* -ED, -ING, -S to limit beforehand

PRELUDE   *v* -LUDED, -LUDING, -LUDES to play a musical introduction

PRELUDER   *n* pl. -S one that preludes

PRELUNCH   *adj* preceding lunch

PREMADE   *adj* made beforehand

PREMAN   *n* pl. -MEN a hypothetical ancestor of man

PREMEAL   *adj* preceding a meal

PREMED   *n* pl. -S a student preparing for the study of medicine

PREMEDIC   *n* pl. -S a premed

PREMEET   *adj* preceding a meet

PREMEN   pl. of preman

PREMIE   *n* pl. -S preemie

PREMIER   *n* pl. -S a prime minister

PREMIERE   *v* -MIERED, -MIERING, -MIERES to present publicly for the first time

PREMISE   *v* -MISED, -MISING, -MISES to state in advance

PREMISS   *n* pl. -ES a proposition in logic

PREMIUM   *n* pl. -S an additional payment

PREMIX   *v* -MIXED or -MIXT, -MIXING, -MIXES to mix before use

PREMOLAR   *n* pl. -S a tooth

PREMOLD   *v* -ED, -ING, -S to mold beforehand

PREMOLT *adj* preceding a molt

PREMORAL *adj* preceding the development of a moral code

PREMORSE *adj* ending abruptly, as if bitten off

PREMUNE *adj* resistant to a disease

PRENAME *n* pl. -S a forename

PRENATAL *adj* prior to birth

PRENOMEN *n* pl. -MENS or -MINA the first name of an ancient Roman

PRENOON *adj* preceding noon

PRENTICE *v* -TICED, -TICING, -TICES to place with an employer for instruction in a trade

PREORDER *v* -ED, -ING, -S to order beforehand

PREP *v* PREPPED, PREPPING, PREPS to attend a preparatory school

PREPACK *v* -ED, -ING, -S to package before retail distribution

PREPAID past tense of prepay

PREPARE *v* -PARED, -PARING, -PARES to put in proper condition or readiness

PREPARER *n* pl. -S one that prepares

PREPASTE *v* -PASTED, -PASTING, -PASTES to paste beforehand

PREPAY *v* -PAID, -PAYING, -PAYS to pay in advance

PREPENSE *adj* planned in advance

PREPILL *adj* preceding the development of a contraceptive pill

PREPLACE *v* -PLACED, -PLACING, -PLACES to place beforehand

PREPLAN *v* -PLANNED, -PLANNING, -PLANS to plan in advance

PREPLANT *adj* occurring before planting

PREPPED past tense of prep

PREPPIE *n* pl. -S one who preps

PREPPING present participle of prep

PREPPY *adj* -PIER, -PIEST associated with the style and behavior of preparatory school students **PREPPILY** *adv*

PREPREG *n* pl. -S reinforcing material already impregnated with a synthetic resin

PREPRICE *v* -PRICED, -PRICING, -PRICES to price beforehand

PREPRINT *v* -ED, -ING, -S to print in advance

PREPUCE *n* pl. -S a fold of skin covering the penis

PREPUNCH *v* -ED, -ING, -ES to punch in advance

PREPUPAL *adj* preceding the pupal stage

PREQUEL *n* pl. -S a book whose story precedes that of an earlier work

PRERACE *adj* preceding a race

PRERENAL *adj* situated in front of the kidney

PRERINSE *n* pl. -S a rinsing beforehand

PRERIOT *adj* preceding a riot

PREROCK *adj* preceding the development of rock music

PRESA *n* pl. -SE a musical symbol

PRESAGE *v* -SAGED, -SAGING, -SAGES to foretell

PRESAGER *n* pl. -S one that presages

PRESALE *adj* preceding a sale

PRESCIND *v* -ED, -ING, -S to consider separately

PRESCORE *v* -SCORED, -SCORING, -SCORES to record the sound of before filming

PRESE pl. of presa

PRESELL *v* -SOLD, -SELLING, -SELLS to promote a product not yet being sold to the public

PRESENCE *n* pl. -S close proximity

PRESENT *v* -ED, -ING, -S to bring into the presence of someone

PRESERVE *v* -SERVED, -SERVING, -SERVES to keep free from harm or danger

PRESET *v* -SET, -SETTING, -SETS to set beforehand

PRESHAPE *v* -SHAPED, -SHAPING, -SHAPES to shape beforehand

PRESHOW *v* -SHOWED, -SHOWN, -SHOWING, -SHOWS to show beforehand

PRESIDE *v* -SIDED, -SIDING, -SIDES to occupy the position of authority

PRESIDER *n* pl. -S one that presides

PRESIDIA *n/pl* Soviet executive committees

PRESIDIO *n* pl. -DIOS a Spanish fort

PRESIFT *v* -ED, -ING, -S to sift beforehand

PRESLEEP *adj* preceding sleep

PRESLICE *v* -SLICED, -SLICING, -SLICES to slice beforehand

PRESOAK *v* -ED, -ING, -S to soak beforehand

PRESOLD	past tense of presell	**PRETREAT**	*v* -ED, -ING, -S to treat beforehand
PRESONG	*adj* preceding a song		
PRESORT	*v* -ED, -ING, -S to sort beforehand	**PRETRIAL**	*n* pl. -S a proceeding that precedes a trial
PRESPLIT	*adj* preceding a split	**PRETRIM**	*v* -TRIMMED, -TRIMMING, -TRIMS to trim beforehand
PRESS	*v* -ED, -ING, -ES to act upon with steady force	**PRETTIED**	past tense of pretty
PRESSER	*n* pl. -S one that presses	**PRETTIER**	comparative of pretty
PRESSING	*n* pl. -S an instance of stamping with a press	**PRETTIES**	present 3d person sing. of pretty
		PRETTIEST	superlative of pretty
PRESSMAN	*n* pl. -MEN a printing press operator	**PRETTIFY**	*v* -FIED, -FYING, -FIES to make pretty
PRESSOR	*n* pl. -S a substance that raises blood pressure	**PRETTY**	*v* -TIED, -TYING, -TIES to make pretty
PRESSRUN	*n* pl. -S a continuous operation of a printing press	**PRETTY**	*adj* -TIER, -TIEST pleasing to the eye **PRETTILY** *adv*
PRESSURE	*v* -SURED, -SURING, -SURES to apply force to	**PRETYPE**	*v* -TYPED, -TYPING, -TYPES to type beforehand
PREST	*n* pl. -S a loan	**PRETZEL**	*n* pl. -S a glazed, salted cracker
PRESTAMP	*v* -ED, -ING, -S to stamp beforehand	**PREUNION**	*n* pl. -S a union beforehand
PRESTER	*n* pl. -S a priest	**PREUNITE**	*v* -UNITED, -UNITING, -UNITES to unite beforehand
PRESTIGE	*n* pl. -S distinction or reputation in the eyes of people	**PREVAIL**	*v* -ED, -ING, -S to triumph
PRESTO	*n* pl. -TOS a musical passage played in rapid tempo	**PREVENT**	*v* -ED, -ING, -S to keep from happening
PRESUME	*v* -SUMED, -SUMING, -SUMES to take for granted	**PREVIEW**	*v* -ED, -ING, -S to view or exhibit in advance
PRESUMER	*n* pl. -S one that presumes	**PREVIOUS**	*adj* coming or occurring before in time or order
PRETAPE	*v* -TAPED, -TAPING, -TAPES to tape beforehand	**PREVISE**	*v* -VISED, -VISING, -VISES to foresee
PRETASTE	*v* -TASTED, -TASTING, -TASTES to taste beforehand	**PREVISOR**	*n* pl. -S one that previses
PRETAX	*adj* existing before provision for taxes	**PREVUE**	*v* -VUED, -VUING, -VUES to preview
PRETEEN	*n* pl. -S a child under the age of thirteen	**PREWAR**	*adj* occurring or existing before a war
PRETENCE	*n* pl. -S pretense	**PREWARM**	*v* -ED, -ING, -S to warm beforehand
PRETEND	*v* -ED, -ING, -S to assume or display a false appearance of	**PREWARN**	*v* -ED, -ING, -S to warn in advance
PRETENSE	*n* pl. -S the act of pretending	**PREWASH**	*v* -ED, -ING, -ES to wash beforehand
PRETERIT	*n* pl. -S a past tense in grammar	**PREWORK**	*adj* preceding work
PRETERM	*adj* pertaining to premature birth	**PREWRAP**	*v* -WRAPPED, -WRAPPING, -WRAPS to wrap beforehand
PRETEST	*v* -ED, -ING, -S to give a preliminary test to	**PREX**	*n* pl. -ES prexy
PRETEXT	*v* -ED, -ING, -S to allege as an excuse	**PREXY**	*n* pl. PREXIES a president
PRETOR	*n* pl. -S praetor	**PREY**	*v* -ED, -ING, -S to seize and devour animals for food
PRETRAIN	*v* -ED, -ING, -S to train beforehand	**PREYER**	*n* pl. -S one that preys

PREZ	*n* pl. -ES a president
PRIAPEAN	*adj* priapic
PRIAPI	a pl. of priapus
PRIAPIC	*adj* phallic
PRIAPISM	*n* pl. -S a persistent erection of the penis
PRIAPUS	*n* pl. -PUSES or -PI a representation of the phallus
PRICE	*v* PRICED, PRICING, PRICES to set a value on
PRICER	*n* pl. -S one that prices
PRICEY	*adj* PRICIER, PRICIEST expensive
PRICIER	comparative of pricey and pricy
PRICIEST	superlative of pricey and pricy
PRICING	present participle of price
PRICK	*v* -ED, -ING, -S to puncture slightly
PRICKER	*n* pl. -S one that pricks
PRICKET	*n* pl. -S a spike for holding a candle upright
PRICKIER	comparative of pricky
PRICKIEST	superlative of pricky
PRICKING	*n* pl. -S a prickly feeling
PRICKLE	*v* -LED, -LING, -LES to prick
PRICKLY	*adj* -LIER, -LIEST having many sharp points
PRICKY	*adj* PRICKIER, PRICKIEST prickly
PRICY	*adj* PRICIER, PRICIEST pricey
PRIDE	*v* PRIDED, PRIDING, PRIDES to feel pride (a feeling of self-esteem)
PRIDEFUL	*adj* full of pride
PRIED	past tense of pry
PRIEDIEU	*n* pl. -DIEUS or -DIEUX a piece of furniture for kneeling on during prayer
PRIER	*n* pl. -S one that pries
PRIES	present 3d person sing. of pry
PRIEST	*v* -ED, -ING, -S to ordain as a priest (one authorized to perform religious rites)
PRIESTLY	*adj* -LIER, -LIEST characteristic of or befitting a priest
PRIG	*v* PRIGGED, PRIGGING, PRIGS to steal
PRIGGERY	*n* pl. -GERIES priggism
PRIGGISH	*adj* marked by priggism
PRIGGISM	*n* pl. -S prim adherence to convention
PRILL	*v* -ED, -ING, -S to convert into pellets
PRIM	*adj* PRIMMER, PRIMMEST formally precise or proper
PRIM	*v* PRIMMED, PRIMMING, PRIMS to give a prim expression to
PRIMA	*n* pl. -S primo
PRIMACY	*n* pl. -CIES the state of being first
PRIMAGE	*n* pl. -S an amount paid as an addition to freight charges
PRIMAL	*adj* being at the beginning or foundation
PRIMARY	*n* pl. -RIES a preliminary election
PRIMATAL	*n* pl. -S a primate
PRIMATE	*n* pl. -S any of an advanced order of mammals
PRIME	*v* PRIMED, PRIMING, PRIMES to make ready
PRIMELY	*adv* excellently
PRIMER	*n* pl. -S a book that covers the basics of a subject
PRIMERO	*n* pl. -ROS a card game
PRIMEVAL	*adj* pertaining to the earliest ages
PRIMI	a pl. of primo
PRIMINE	*n* pl. -S the outer covering of an ovule
PRIMING	*n* pl. -S the act of one that primes
PRIMLY	*adv* in a prim manner
PRIMMED	past tense of prim
PRIMMER	comparative of prim
PRIMMEST	superlative of prim
PRIMMING	present participle of prim
PRIMNESS	*n* pl. -ES the state of being prim
PRIMO	*n* pl. -MOS or -MI the main part in a musical piece
PRIMP	*v* -ED, -ING, -S to dress or adorn carefully
PRIMROSE	*n* pl. -S a perennial herb
PRIMSIE	*adj* prim
PRIMULA	*n* pl. -S primrose
PRIMUS	*n* pl. -ES the head bishop of Scotland
PRINCE	*n* pl. -S a non-reigning male member of a royal family
PRINCELY	*adj* -LIER, -LIEST of or befitting a prince

PRINCESS	*n* pl. -ES a non-reigning female member of a royal family	**PRIVATE**	*adj* -VATER, -VATEST not for public use or knowledge
PRINCIPE	*n* pl. -PI a prince	**PRIVATE**	*n* pl. -S a soldier of lower rank
PRINCOCK	*n* pl. -S a coxcomb	**PRIVET**	*n* pl. -S an ornamental shrub
PRINCOX	*n* pl. -ES princock	**PRIVIER**	comparative of privy
PRINK	*v* -ED, -ING, -S to dress or adorn in a showy manner	**PRIVIES**	pl. of privy
PRINKER	*n* pl. -S one that prinks	**PRIVITY**	*n* pl. -TIES private knowledge
PRINT	*v* -ED, -ING, -S to produce by pressed type on a surface	**PRIVY**	*adj* PRIVIER, PRIVIEST private **PRIVILY** *adv*
PRINTER	*n* pl. -S one that prints	**PRIVY**	*n* pl. PRIVIES an outhouse
PRINTERY	*n* pl. -ERIES a place where printing is done	**PRIZE**	*v* PRIZED, PRIZING, PRIZES to value highly
PRINTING	*n* pl. -S a reproduction from a printing surface	**PRIZER**	*n* pl. -S one who vies for a reward
PRINTOUT	*n* pl. -S the printed output of a computer	**PRO**	*n* pl. PROS an argument or vote in favor of something
PRION	*n* pl. -S a protein particle	**PROA**	*n* pl. -S prau
PRIOR	*n* pl. -S an officer in a monastery	**PROBABLE**	*n* pl. -S something likely to occur or prove true
PRIORATE	*n* pl. -S the office of a prior	**PROBABLY**	*adv* without much doubt
PRIORESS	*n* pl. -ES a nun corresponding in rank to a prior	**PROBAND**	*n* pl. -S one whose reactions or responses are studied
PRIORIES	pl. of priory	**PROBANG**	*n* pl. -S a surgical rod
PRIORITY	*n* pl. -TIES precedence established by importance	**PROBATE**	*v* -BATED, -BATING, -BATES to establish the validity of
PRIORLY	*adv* previously	**PROBE**	*v* PROBED, PROBING, PROBES to investigate or examine thoroughly
PRIORY	*n* pl. -RIES a religious house	**PROBER**	*n* pl. -S one that probes
PRISE	*v* PRISED, PRISING, PRISES to raise or force with a lever	**PROBIT**	*n* pl. -S a unit of statistical probability
PRISERE	*n* pl. -S a succession of vegetational stages	**PROBITY**	*n* pl. -TIES complete and confirmed integrity
PRISM	*n* pl. -S a solid which disperses light into a spectrum	**PROBLEM**	*n* pl. -S a perplexing question or situation
PRISMOID	*n* pl. -S a geometric solid	**PROCAINE**	*n* pl. -S a compound used as a local anesthetic
PRISON	*v* -ED, -ING, -S to imprison	**PROCARP**	*n* pl. -S a female sexual organ in certain algae
PRISONER	*n* pl. -S one that is imprisoned	**PROCEED**	*v* -ED, -ING, -S to go forward or onward
PRISS	*v* -ED, -ING, -ES to act in a prissy manner	**PROCESS**	*v* -ED, -ING, -ES to treat or prepare by a special method
PRISSY	*adj* -SIER, -SIEST excessively or affectedly proper **PRISSILY** *adv*	**PROCHAIN**	*adj* prochein
PRISSY	*n* pl. -SIES one who is prissy	**PROCHEIN**	*adj* nearest in time, relation, or degree
PRISTANE	*n* pl. -S a chemical compound	**PROCLAIM**	*v* -ED, -ING, -S to make known publicly or officially
PRISTINE	*adj* pertaining to the earliest time or state	**PROCTOR**	*v* -ED, -ING, -S to supervise
PRITHEE	*interj* — used to express a wish or request	**PROCURAL**	*n* pl. -S the act of procuring
PRIVACY	*n* pl. -CIES the state of being private		

PROCURE	v -CURED, -CURING, -CURES to obtain by effort
PROCURER	n pl. -S one that procures
PROD	v PRODDED, PRODDING, PRODS to jab with something pointed
PRODDER	n pl. -S one that prods
PRODIGAL	n pl. -S one who spends lavishly and foolishly
PRODIGY	n pl. -GIES a child having exceptional talent or ability
PRODROME	n pl. -DROMES or -DROMATA a sign of impending disease
PRODUCE	v -DUCED, -DUCING, -DUCES to bring into existence
PRODUCER	n pl. -S one that produces
PRODUCT	n pl. -S something produced by labor or effort
PROEM	n pl. -S an introductory statement **PROEMIAL** adj
PROETTE	n pl. -S a female professional athlete
PROF	n pl. -S a professor
PROFANE	v -FANED, -FANING, -FANES to treat with irreverence or abuse
PROFANER	n pl. -S one that profanes
PROFESS	v -ED, -ING, -ES to affirm openly
PROFFER	v -ED, -ING, -S to present for acceptance
PROFILE	v -FILED, -FILING, -FILES to draw an outline of
PROFILER	n pl. -S one that profiles
PROFIT	v -ED, -ING, -S to gain an advantage or benefit
PROFITER	n pl. -S one that profits
PROFOUND	adj -FOUNDER, -FOUNDEST intellectually deep and penetrating
PROFOUND	n pl. -S something that is very deep
PROFUSE	adj pouring forth generously
PROG	v PROGGED, PROGGING, PROGS to prowl about for food or plunder
PROGENY	n pl. -NIES a descendant or offspring
PROGERIA	n pl. -S premature aging
PROGGER	n pl. -S one that progs
PROGGING	present participle of prog
PROGNOSE	v -NOSED, -NOSING, -NOSES to forecast the probable course of a disease
PROGRADE	adj pertaining to the orbital motion of a body
PROGRAM	v -GRAMED, -GRAMING, -GRAMS or -GRAMMED, -GRAMMING, -GRAMS to arrange in a plan of proceedings
PROGRESS	v -ED, -ING, -ES to move forward or onward
PROHIBIT	v -ED, -ING, -S to forbid by authority
PROJECT	v -ED, -ING, -S to extend outward
PROJET	n pl. -S a plan or outline
PROLABOR	adj favoring organized labor
PROLAMIN	n pl. -S a simple protein
PROLAN	n pl. -S a sex hormone
PROLAPSE	v -LAPSED, -LAPSING, -LAPSES to fall or slip out of place
PROLATE	adj extended lengthwise
PROLE	n pl. -S a member of the working class
PROLEG	n pl. -S an abdominal leg of certain insect larvae
PROLIFIC	adj producing abundantly
PROLINE	n pl. -S an amino acid
PROLIX	adj tediously long and wordy **PROLIXLY** adv
PROLOG	v -ED, -ING, -S to prologue
PROLOGUE	v -LOGUED, -LOGUING, -LOGUES to preface
PROLONG	v -ED, -ING, -S to lengthen in duration
PROLONGE	n pl. -S a rope used for pulling a gun carriage
PROM	n pl. -S a formal dance
PROMINE	n pl. -S a substance that promotes growth
PROMISE	v -ISED, -ISING, -ISES to make a declaration of assurance
PROMISEE	n pl. -S one who is promised something
PROMISER	n pl. -S promisor
PROMISING	present participle of promise
PROMISOR	n pl. -S one that promises
PROMO	n pl. -MOS a promotional presentation

PROMOTE	*v* -MOTED, -MOTING, -MOTES to contribute to the progress of
PROMOTER	*n* pl. -S one that promotes
PROMPT	*adj* PROMPTER, PROMPTEST quick to act or respond
PROMPT	*v* -ED, -ING, -S to induce to action
PROMPTER	*n* pl. -S one that prompts
PROMPTLY	*adv* in a prompt manner
PROMULGE	*v* -MULGED, -MULGING, -MULGES to proclaim
PRONATE	*v* -NATED, -NATING, -NATES to turn the palm downward or backward
PRONATOR	*n* pl. -S or -ES a forearm or forelimb muscle
PRONE	*adj* lying with the front or face downward **PRONELY** *adv*
PRONG	*v* -ED, -ING, -S to pierce with a pointed projection
PRONOTUM	*n* pl. -NOTA a hard outer plate of an insect
PRONOUN	*n* pl. -S a word that may be used in place of a noun
PRONTO	*adv* quickly
PROOF	*v* -ED, -ING, -S to examine for errors
PROOFER	*n* pl. -S one that proofs
PROP	*v* PROPPED, PROPPING, PROPS to keep from falling
PROPANE	*n* pl. -S a flammable gas
PROPEL	*v* -PELLED, -PELLING, -PELS to cause to move forward or onward
PROPEND	*v* -ED, -ING, -S to have a tendency toward
PROPENE	*n* pl. -S a flammable gas
PROPENOL	*n* pl. -S a flammable liquid
PROPENSE	*adj* tending toward
PROPENYL	*adj* pertaining to a certain chemical group
PROPER	*adj* -ERER, -EREST suitable **PROPERLY** *adv*
PROPER	*n* pl. -S a portion of the Mass
PROPERTY	*n* pl. -TIES something owned
PROPHAGE	*n* pl. -S a form of virus
PROPHASE	*n* pl. -S the first stage in mitosis
PROPHECY	*n* pl. -CIES a prediction
PROPHESY	*v* -SIED, -SYING, -SIES to predict
PROPHET	*n* pl. -S one who predicts
PROPINE	*v* -PINED, -PINING, -PINES to offer as a gift
PROPJET	*n* pl. -S a type of airplane
PROPMAN	*n* pl. -MEN a man in charge of stage properties
PROPOLIS	*n* pl. -LISES a resinous substance used as a cement by bees
PROPONE	*v* -PONED, -PONING, -PONES to propose
PROPOSAL	*n* pl. -S something that is proposed
PROPOSE	*v* -POSED, -POSING, -POSES to put forward for consideration or acceptance
PROPOSER	*n* pl. -S one that proposes
PROPOUND	*v* -ED, -ING, -S to propose
PROPPED	past tense of prop
PROPPING	present participle of prop
PROPYL	*n* pl. -S a univalent radical **PROPYLIC** *adj*
PROPYLON	*n* pl. -LA an entrance to a temple
PRORATE	*v* -RATED, -RATING, -RATES to divide proportionately
PROROGUE	*v* -ROGUED, -ROGUING, -ROGUES to discontinue a session of
PROSAIC	*adj* pertaining to prose
PROSAISM	*n* pl. -S a prosaic style
PROSAIST	*n* pl. -S a writer of prose
PROSE	*v* PROSED, PROSING, PROSES to write prose (writing without metrical structure)
PROSECT	*v* -ED, -ING, -S to dissect
PROSER	*n* pl. -S a prosaist
PROSIER	comparative of prosy
PROSIEST	superlative of prosy
PROSILY	*adv* in a prosy manner
PROSING	present participle of prose
PROSIT	*interj* — used as a drinking toast
PROSO	*n* pl. -SOS millet
PROSODY	*n* pl. -DIES the study of poetical forms **PROSODIC** *adj*
PROSOMA	*n* pl. -S the front region of the body of an invertebrate **PROSOMAL** *adj*
PROSPECT	*v* -ED, -ING, -S to explore for mineral deposits
PROSPER	*v* -ED, -ING, -S to be successful or fortunate

PROSS   *n* pl. -ES a prostitute

PROSSIE   *n* pl. -S a prostitute

PROST   *interj* prosit

PROSTATE   *n* pl. -S a gland in male mammals

PROSTIE   *n* pl. -S a prostitute

PROSTYLE   *n* pl. -S a building having a row of columns across the front only

PROSY   *adj* PROSIER, PROSIEST prosaic

PROTAMIN   *n* pl. -S a simple protein

PROTASIS   *n* pl. -ASES the introductory part of a classical drama **PROTATIC** *adj*

PROTEA   *n* pl. -S an evergreen shrub

PROTEAN   *n* pl. -S a type of protein

PROTEASE   *n* pl. -S an enzyme

PROTECT   *v* -ED, -ING, -S to keep from harm, attack, or injury

PROTEGE   *n* pl. -S one whose career is promoted by an influential person

PROTEGEE   *n* pl. -S a female protege

PROTEI   pl. of proteus

PROTEID   *n* pl. -S protein

PROTEIDE   *n* pl. -S proteid

PROTEIN   *n* pl. -S a nitrogenous organic compound

PROTEND   *v* -ED, -ING, -S to extend

PROTEOSE   *n* pl. -S a water-soluble protein

PROTEST   *v* -ED, -ING, -S to express strong objection

PROTEUS   *n* pl. -TEI any of a genus of aerobic bacteria

PROTEUS   *n* pl. -ES one that readily changes his appearance or principles

PROTIST   *n* pl. -S any of a group of unicellular organisms

PROTIUM   *n* pl. -S an isotope of hydrogen

PROTOCOL   *v* -COLED, -COLING, -COLS or -COLLED, -COLLING, -COLS to form a preliminary draft of an official document

PROTON   *n* pl. -S a subatomic particle **PROTONIC** *adj*

PROTOPOD   *n* pl. -S a part of a crustacean appendage

PROTOXID   *n* pl. -S an oxide

PROTOZOA   *n/pl* unicellular microscopic organisms

PROTRACT   *v* -ED, -ING, -S to prolong

PROTRUDE   *v* -TRUDED, -TRUDING, -TRUDES to extend beyond the main portion

PROTYL   *n* pl. -S protyle

PROTYLE   *n* pl. -S a hypothetical substance from which all the elements are supposedly derived

PROUD   *adj* PROUDER, PROUDEST having or displaying pride **PROUDLY** *adv*

PROUDFUL   *adj* prideful

PROUNION   *adj* favoring labor unions

PROVE   *v* PROVED, PROVEN, PROVING, PROVES to establish the truth or validity of **PROVABLE** *adj* **PROVABLY** *adv*

PROVENLY   *adv* without doubt

PROVER   *n* pl. -S one that proves

PROVERB   *v* -ED, -ING, -S to make a byword of

PROVIDE   *v* -VIDED, -VIDING, -VIDES to supply

PROVIDER   *n* pl. -S one that provides

PROVINCE   *n* pl. -S an administrative division of a country

PROVING   present participle of prove

PROVIRUS   *n* pl. -ES a form of virus **PROVIRAL** *adj*

PROVISO   *n* pl. -SOS or -SOES a clause in a document introducing a condition or restriction

PROVOKE   *v* -VOKED, -VOKING, -VOKES to incite to anger or resentment

PROVOKER   *n* pl. -S one that provokes

PROVOST   *n* pl. -S a high-ranking university official

PROW   *n* pl. -S the forward part of a ship

PROW   *adj* PROWER, PROWEST brave

PROWAR   *adj* favoring war

PROWESS   *n* pl. -ES exceptional ability

PROWL   *v* -ED, -ING, -S to move about stealthily

PROWLER   *n* pl. -S one that prowls

PROXEMIC   *adj* pertaining to a branch of environmental study

PROXIES   pl. of proxy

PROXIMAL   *adj* located near the point of origin

PROXIMO   *adj* of or occurring in the following month

PROXY	*n* pl. PROXIES a person authorized to act for another
PRUDE	*n* pl. -S a prudish person
PRUDENCE	*n* pl. -S the quality of being prudent
PRUDENT	*adj* having, showing, or exercising good judgment
PRUDERY	*n* pl. -ERIES excessive regard for propriety, modesty, or morality
PRUDISH	*adj* marked by prudery
PRUINOSE	*adj* having a powdery covering
PRUNE	*v* PRUNED, PRUNING, PRUNES to cut off branches or parts from **PRUNABLE** *adj*
PRUNELLA	*n* pl. -S a strong woolen fabric
PRUNELLE	*n* pl. -S a plum-flavored liqueur
PRUNELLO	*n* pl. -LOS prunella
PRUNER	*n* pl. -S one that prunes
PRUNING	present participle of prune
PRUNUS	*n* pl. -ES a flowering tree
PRURIENT	*adj* having lustful thoughts or desires
PRURIGO	*n* pl. -GOS a skin disease
PRURITUS	*n* pl. -ES intense itching **PRURITIC** *adj*
PRUSSIC	*adj* pertaining to a type of acid
PRUTA	*n* pl. PRUTOT prutah
PRUTAH	*n* pl. PRUTOTH a monetary unit of Israel
PRY	*v* PRIED, PRYING, PRIES to inquire impertinently into private matters **PRYINGLY** *adv*
PRYER	*n* pl. -S prier
PRYTHEE	*interj* prithee
PSALM	*v* -ED, -ING, -S to praise in psalms (sacred songs)
PSALMIC	*adj* of or pertaining to a psalm
PSALMIST	*n* pl. -S a writer of psalms
PSALMODY	*n* pl. -DIES the use of psalms in worship
PSALTER	*n* pl. -S a book of psalms
PSALTERY	*n* pl. -TERIES an ancient stringed musical instrument
PSALTRY	*n* pl. -TRIES psaltery
PSAMMITE	*n* pl. -S a fine-grained rock
PSAMMON	*n* pl. -S a group of microorganisms living in waterlogged sands
PSCHENT	*n* pl. -S a crown worn by ancient Egyptian kings
PSEPHITE	*n* pl. -S a rock composed of small pebbles
PSEUD	*n* pl. -S a person pretending to be an intellectual
PSEUDO	*n* pl. PSEUDOS a pseud
PSHAW	*v* -ED, -ING, -S to utter an expression of disapproval
PSI	*n* pl. -S a Greek letter
PSILOCIN	*n* pl. -S a hallucinogenic drug
PSILOSIS	*n* pl. -LOSES a tropical disease **PSILOTIC** *adj*
PSOAS	*n* pl. PSOAI or PSOAE a muscle of the loin **PSOATIC** *adj*
PSOCID	*n* pl. -S a minute winged insect
PSORALEA	*n* pl. -S a plant of the bean family
PSORALEN	*n* pl. -S a drug used to treat psoriasis
PSST	*interj* — used to attract someone's attention
PSYCH	*v* -ED, -ING, -S to put into the proper frame of mind
PSYCHE	*n* pl. -S the mental structure of a person
PSYCHIC	*n* pl. -S one sensitive to extrasensory phenomena
PSYCHO	*n* pl. -CHOS a mentally unstable person
PSYLLA	*n* pl. -S any of various plant lice
PSYLLID	*n* pl. -S psylla
PSYLLIUM	*n* pl. -S the seed of a fleawort
PSYWAR	*n* pl. -S psychological warfare
PTERIN	*n* pl. -S a chemical compound
PTEROPOD	*n* pl. -S a type of mollusk
PTERYGIA	*n/pl* fleshy growths over the cornea
PTERYLA	*n* pl. -LAE a feathered area on the skin of a bird
PTISAN	*n* pl. -S a tea of herbs or barley
PTOMAIN	*n* pl. -S ptomaine
PTOMAINE	*n* pl. -S a compound produced by the decomposition of protein
PTOSIS	*n* pl. PTOSES a drooping of the upper eyelid **PTOTIC** *adj*
PTYALIN	*n* pl. -S a salivary enzyme
PTYALISM	*n* pl. -S an excessive flow of saliva
PUB	*n* pl. -S a tavern
PUBERTY	*n* pl. -TIES a period of sexual maturation **PUBERAL, PUBERTAL** *adj*

PUBES	n pl. PUBES the lower part of the abdomen	**PUFFER**	n pl. -S one that puffs
PUBIC	adj pertaining to the pubes or pubis	**PUFFERY**	n pl. -ERIES excessive public praise
PUBIS	n pl. PUBES the forward portion of either of the hipbones	**PUFFIN**	n pl. -S a sea bird
		PUFFY	adj -FIER, -FIEST swollen **PUFFILY** adv
PUBLIC	n pl. -S the community or the people as a whole	**PUG**	v PUGGED, PUGGING, PUGS to fill in with clay or mortar
PUBLICAN	n pl. -S one who owns or manages a pub	**PUGAREE**	n pl. -S pugree
PUBLICLY	adv by the public	**PUGGAREE**	n pl. -S pugree
PUBLISH	v -ED, -ING, -ES to print and issue to the public	**PUGGED**	past tense of pug
PUCCOON	n pl. -S an herb that yields a red dye	**PUGGIER**	comparative of puggy
		PUGGIEST	superlative of puggy
PUCE	n pl. -S a dark red color	**PUGGING**	present participle of pug
PUCK	n pl. -S a rubber disk used in ice hockey	**PUGGISH**	adj somewhat stubby
		PUGGREE	n pl. -S pugree
PUCKA	adj pukka	**PUGGRY**	n pl. -GRIES pugree
PUCKER	v -ED, -ING, -S to gather into small wrinkles or folds	**PUGGY**	adj -GIER, -GIEST puggish
		PUGH	interj — used to express disgust
PUCKERER	n pl. -S one that puckers	**PUGILISM**	n pl. -S the art or practice of fighting with the fists
PUCKERY	adj -ERIER, -ERIEST having a tendency to pucker	**PUGILIST**	n pl. -S one who fights with his fists
PUCKISH	adj impish		
PUD	n pl. -S pudding	**PUGMARK**	n pl. -S a footprint
PUDDING	n pl. -S a thick, soft dessert	**PUGREE**	n pl. -S a cloth band wrapped around a hat
PUDDLE	v -DLED, -DLING, -DLES to strew with puddles (small pools of water)	**PUISNE**	n pl. -S one of lesser rank
		PUISSANT	adj powerful
PUDDLER	n pl. -S one who subjects iron to puddling	**PUJA**	n pl. -S a Hindu prayer ritual
		PUJAH	n pl. -S puja
PUDDLING	n pl. -S the process of converting pig iron to wrought iron	**PUKE**	v PUKED, PUKING, PUKES to vomit
PUDDLY	adj -DLIER, -DLIEST full of puddles	**PUKKA**	adj genuine
PUDENCY	n pl. -CIES modesty	**PUL**	n pl. PULS or PULI a coin of Afghanistan
PUDENDUM	n pl. -DA the external genital organs of a woman **PUDENDAL** adj	**PULA**	n pl. PULA a monetary unit of Botswana
PUDGY	adj PUDGIER, PUDGIEST short and fat **PUDGILY** adv	**PULE**	v PULED, PULING, PULES to whine
PUDIBUND	adj prudish	**PULER**	n pl. -S one that pules
PUDIC	adj to the pudendum	**PULI**	n pl. -LIK or -LIS a long-haired sheepdog
PUEBLO	n pl. -LOS a communal dwelling of certain Indian tribes	**PULICENE**	adj pertaining to fleas
PUERILE	adj childish	**PULICIDE**	n pl. -S an agent used for destroying fleas
PUFF	v -ED, -ING, -S to blow in short gusts	**PULIK**	a pl. of puli
		PULING	n pl. -S a plaintive cry
PUFFBALL	n pl. -S any of various globular fungi	**PULINGLY**	adv in a whining manner

PULL   *v* -ED, -ING, -S to exert force in order to cause motion toward the force

PULLBACK   *n* pl. -S a restraint or drawback

PULLER   *n* pl. -S one that pulls

PULLET   *n* pl. -S a young hen

PULLEY   *n* pl. -LEYS a device used for lifting weight

PULLMAN   *n* pl. -S a railroad sleeping car

PULLOUT   *n* pl. -S a withdrawal

PULLOVER   *n* pl. -S a garment that is put on by being drawn over the head

PULLUP   *n* pl. -S the act of raising oneself while hanging by the hands

PULMONIC   *adj* pertaining to the lungs

PULMOTOR   *n* pl. -S a respiratory device

PULP   *v* -ED, -ING, -S to reduce to pulp (a soft, moist mass of matter)

PULPAL   *adj* pertaining to pulp **PULPALLY** *adv*

PULPER   *n* pl. -S one that pulps

PULPIER   comparative of pulpy

PULPIEST   superlative of pulpy

PULPILY   *adv* in a pulpy manner

PULPIT   *n* pl. -S a platform in a church **PULPITAL** *adj*

PULPLESS   *adj* having no pulp

PULPOUS   *adj* pulpy

PULPWOOD   *n* pl. -S soft wood used in making paper

PULPY   *adj* PULPIER, PULPIEST resembling pulp

PULQUE   *n* pl. -S a fermented Mexican beverage

PULSANT   *adj* pulsating

PULSAR   *n* pl. -S a celestial source of radio waves

PULSATE   *v* -SATED, -SATING, -SATES to expand and contract rhythmically

PULSATOR   *n* pl. -S something that pulsates

PULSE   *v* PULSED, PULSING, PULSES to pulsate

PULSEJET   *n* pl. -S a type of engine

PULSER   *n* pl. -S a device that causes pulsations

PULSING   present participle of pulse

PULSION   *n* pl. -S propulsion

PULSOJET   *n* pl. -S pulsejet

PULVILLI   *n/pl* pads between the claws of an insect's foot

PULVINUS   *n* pl. -NI a swelling at the base of a leaf **PULVINAR** *adj*

PUMA   *n* pl. -S a cougar

PUMELO   *n* pl. -LOS pomelo

PUMICE   *v* -ICED, -ICING, -ICES to polish with a porous volcanic rock

PUMICER   *n* pl. -S one that pumices

PUMICITE   *n* pl. -S a porous volcanic rock

PUMMEL   *v* -MELED, -MELING, -MELS or -MELLED, -MELLING, -MELS to pommel

PUMMELO   *n* pl. -LOS a shaddock

PUMP   *v* -ED, -ING, -S to cause to flow by means of a pump (a device for moving fluids)

PUMPER   *n* pl. -S one that pumps

PUMPKIN   *n* pl. -S a large, edible fruit

PUMPLESS   *adj* lacking a pump

PUMPLIKE   *adj* resembling a pump

PUN   *v* PUNNED, PUNNING, PUNS to make a pun (a play on words)

PUNA   *n* pl. -S a cold, arid plateau

PUNCH   *v* -ED, -ING, -ES to perforate with a type of tool

PUNCHEON   *n* pl. -S a vertical supporting timber

PUNCHER   *n* pl. -S one that punches

PUNCHY   *adj* PUNCHIER, PUNCHIEST dazed **PUNCHILY** *adv*

PUNCTATE   *adj* covered with dots

PUNCTUAL   *adj* being on time

PUNCTURE   *v* -TURED, -TURING, -TURES to pierce with a pointed object

PUNDIT   *n* pl. -S a Hindu scholar **PUNDITIC** *adj*

PUNDITRY   *n* pl. -RIES the learning of pundits

PUNG   *n* pl. -S a box-shaped sleigh

PUNGENCY   *n* pl. -CIES the state of being pungent

PUNGENT   *adj* sharply affecting the organs of taste or smell

PUNGLE   *v* -GLED, -GLING, -GLES to contribute

PUNIER   comparative of puny

PUNIEST   superlative of puny

PUNILY   *adv* in a puny manner

PUNINESS   *n* pl. -ES the state of being puny

PUNISH   *v* -ED, -ING, -ES to impose a penalty on in requital for wrongdoing

PUNISHER   *n* pl. -S one that punishes

PUNITION   *n* pl. -S the act of punishing; punishment

PUNITIVE   *adj* inflicting punishment

PUNITORY   *adj* punitive

PUNK   *n* pl. -S dry, decayed wood used as tinder

PUNK   *adj* PUNKER, PUNKEST of inferior quality

PUNKA   *n* pl. -S a ceiling fan used in India

PUNKAH   *n* pl. -S punka

PUNKER   *n* pl. -S a punk rock musician

PUNKEY   *n* pl. -KEYS punkie

PUNKIE   *n* pl. -S a biting gnat

PUNKIN   *n* pl. -S pumpkin

PUNKISH   *adj* pertaining to a style inspired by punk rock

PUNKY   *adj* PUNKIER, PUNKIEST resembling punk

PUNNED   past tense of pun

PUNNER   *n* pl. -S a punster

PUNNET   *n* pl. -S a small basket

PUNNING   present participle of pun

PUNNY   *adj* -NIER, -NIEST being or involving a pun

PUNSTER   *n* pl. -S one who is given to punning

PUNT   *v* -ED, -ING, -S to propel through water with a pole

PUNTER   *n* pl. -S one that punts

PUNTO   *n* pl. -TOS a hit or thrust in fencing

PUNTY   *n* pl. -TIES an iron rod used in glassmaking

PUNY   *adj* PUNIER, PUNIEST of inferior size, strength, or significance

PUP   *v* PUPPED, PUPPING, PUPS to give birth to puppies

PUPA   *n* pl. -PAS or -PAE an intermediate stage of a metamorphic insect **PUPAL** *adj*

PUPARIUM   *n* pl. -IA a pupal shell **PUPARIAL** *adj*

PUPATE   *v* -PATED, -PATING, -PATES to pass through the pupal stage

PUPATION   *n* pl. -S the act of pupating

PUPFISH   *n* pl. -ES a small, freshwater fish

PUPIL   *n* pl. -S a student under the close supervision of a teacher

PUPILAGE   *n* pl. -S the state of being a pupil

PUPILAR   *adj* pertaining to a part of the eye

PUPILARY   *adj* pupilar

PUPPED   past tense of pup

PUPPET   *n* pl. -S a small figure, as of a person or animal, manipulated by the hand

PUPPETRY   *n* pl. -RIES the art of making or manipulating puppets

PUPPING   present participle of pup

PUPPY   *n* pl. -PIES a young dog **PUPPYISH** *adj*

PUPPYDOM   *n* pl. -S the world of puppies

PUR   *v* PURRED, PURRING, PURS to purr

PURANA   *n* pl. -S a Hindu scripture **PURANIC** *adj*

PURBLIND   *adj* partially blind

PURCHASE   *v* -CHASED, -CHASING, -CHASES to acquire by the payment of money

PURDA   *n* pl. -S purdah

PURDAH   *n* pl. -S a curtain used in India to seclude women

PURE   *adj* PURER, PUREST free from anything different, inferior, or contaminating

PUREBRED   *n* pl. -S an animal of unmixed stock

PUREE   *v* -REED, -REEING, -REES to reduce to a thick pulp by cooking and sieving

PURELY   *adv* in a pure manner

PURENESS   *n* pl. -ES the quality of being pure

PURER   comparative of pure

PUREST   superlative of pure

PURFLE   *v* -FLED, -FLING, -FLES to decorate the border of

PURFLING   *n* pl. -S an ornamental border

PURGE   *v* PURGED, PURGING, PURGES to purify

PURGER   *n* pl. -S one that purges

PURGING   *n* pl. -S the act of purifying

PURI   *n* pl. -S poori

PURIFIER   *n* pl. -S one that purifies

PURIFY   *v* -FIED, -FYING, -FIES to free from impurities

PURIN	*n* pl. -S purine
PURINE	*n* pl. -S a chemical compound
PURISM	*n* pl. -S strict adherence to traditional correctness
PURIST	*n* pl. -S one who practices purism **PURISTIC** *adj*
PURITAN	*n* pl. -S a rigorously moral or religious person
PURITY	*n* pl. -TIES the quality of being pure
PURL	*v* -ED, -ING, -S to knit with a particular stitch
PURLIEU	*n* pl. -S an outlying or neighboring area
PURLIN	*n* pl. -S a horizontal supporting timber
PURLINE	*n* pl. -S purlin
PURLOIN	*v* -ED, -ING, -S to steal
PURPLE	*adj* -PLER, -PLEST of a color intermediate between red and blue
PURPLE	*v* -PLED, -PLING, -PLES to make purple
PURPLISH	*adj* somewhat purple
PURPLY	*adj* purplish
PURPORT	*v* -ED, -ING, -S to profess or claim
PURPOSE	*v* -POSED, -POSING, -POSES to resolve to perform or accomplish
PURPURA	*n* pl. -S a disease characterized by purple spots on the skin
PURPURE	*n* pl. -S the heraldic color purple
PURPURIC	*adj* pertaining to purpura
PURPURIN	*n* pl. -S a reddish dye
PURR	*v* -ED, -ING, -S to utter a low, vibrant sound
PURRED	past tense of pur and purr
PURRING	present participle of pur and purr
PURSE	*v* PURSED, PURSING, PURSES to pucker
PURSER	*n* pl. -S an officer in charge of a ship's accounts
PURSIER	comparative of pursy
PURSIEST	superlative of pursy
PURSILY	*adv* in a pursy manner
PURSING	present participle of purse
PURSLANE	*n* pl. -S a common garden herb
PURSUANT	*adv* in accordance
PURSUE	*v* -SUED, -SUING, -SUES to follow in order to overtake or capture
PURSUER	*n* pl. -S one that pursues
PURSUIT	*n* pl. -S the act of pursuing
PURSY	*adj* PURSIER, PURSIEST short of breath
PURULENT	*adj* secreting pus
PURVEY	*v* -ED, -ING, -S to supply
PURVEYOR	*n* pl. -S one that purveys
PURVIEW	*n* pl. -S the extent of operation, authority, or concern
PUS	*n* pl. -ES a viscous fluid formed in infected tissue
PUSH	*v* -ED, -ING, -ES to exert force in order to cause motion away from the force
PUSHBALL	*n* pl. -S a type of ball game
PUSHCART	*n* pl. -S a light cart pushed by hand
PUSHDOWN	*n* pl. -S a store of computer data
PUSHER	*n* pl. -S one that pushes
PUSHFUL	*adj* pushy
PUSHIER	comparative of pushy
PUSHIEST	superlative of pushy
PUSHILY	*adv* in a pushy manner
PUSHOVER	*n* pl. -S an easily defeated person or team
PUSHPIN	*n* pl. -S a large-headed pin
PUSHROD	*n* pl. -S a rod for operating the valves in an engine
PUSHUP	*n* pl. -S a type of exercise
PUSHY	*adj* PUSHIER, PUSHIEST offensively aggressive
PUSLEY	*n* pl. -LEYS pussley
PUSLIKE	*adj* resembling pus
PUSS	*n* pl. -ES a cat
PUSSIER	comparative of pussy
PUSSIES	pl. of pussy
PUSSIEST	superlative of pussy
PUSSLEY	*n* pl. -LEYS purslane
PUSSLIKE	*adj* catlike
PUSSLY	*n* pl. -LIES pussley
PUSSY	*n* pl. PUSSIES a cat
PUSSY	*adj* -SIER, -SIEST full of pus
PUSSYCAT	*n* pl. -S a cat

PUSTULE	*n* pl. -S a small elevation of the skin containing pus **PUSTULAR, PUSTULED** *adj*
PUT	*v* PUT, PUTTING, PUTS to place in a particular position
PUTAMEN	*n* pl. -MINA the hard covering of the kernel of certain fruits
PUTATIVE	*adj* generally regarded as such
PUTLOG	*n* pl. -S a horizontal supporting timber
PUTOFF	*n* pl. -S an excuse
PUTON	*n* pl. -S a hoax or deception
PUTOUT	*n* pl. -S an act of causing an out in baseball
PUTREFY	*v* -FIED, -FYING, -FIES to make or become putrid
PUTRID	*adj* being in a decomposed, foul-smelling state **PUTRIDLY** *adv*
PUTSCH	*n* pl. -ES a suddenly executed attempt to overthrow a government
PUTT	*v* -ED, -ING, -S to hit with a light stroke in golf
PUTTEE	*n* pl. -S a strip of cloth wound around the leg
PUTTER	*v* -ED, -ING, -S to occupy oneself in a leisurely or ineffective manner
PUTTERER	*n* pl. -S one that putters
PUTTI	pl. of putto
PUTTIED	past tense of putty
PUTTIER	*n* pl. -S one that putties
PUTTING	present participle of put
PUTTO	*n* pl. -TI an infant boy in art
PUTTY	*v* -TIED, -TYING, -TIES to fill with a type of cement
PUTZ	*v* -ED, -ING, -ES to waste time
PUZZLE	*v* -ZLED, -ZLING, -ZLES to cause uncertainty and indecision in
PUZZLER	*n* pl. -S something that puzzles
PYA	*n* pl. -S a copper coin of Burma
PYAEMIA	*n* pl. -S pyemia **PYAEMIC** *adj*
PYCNIDIA	*n/pl* spore-bearing organs of certain fungi
PYCNOSIS	*n* pl. -NOSES pyknosis
PYCNOTIC	*adj* pyknotic
PYE	*n* pl. -S a book of ecclesiastical rules in the pre-Reformation English church

PYELITIS	*n* pl. -TISES inflammation of the pelvis or the kidney **PYELITIC** *adj*
PYEMIA	*n* pl. -S the presence of pus in the blood **PYEMIC** *adj*
PYGIDIUM	*n* pl. -IA the posterior region of certain invertebrates **PYGIDIAL** *adj*
PYGMY	*n* pl. -MIES a small person **PYGMAEAN, PYGMEAN, PYGMOID, PYGMYISH** *adj*
PYGMYISM	*n* pl. -S a stunted or dwarfish condition
PYIC	*adj* pertaining to pus
PYIN	*n* pl. -S a protein compound contained in pus
PYJAMAS	*n* pl. PYJAMAS pajamas
PYKNIC	*n* pl. -S a person having a broad, stocky build
PYKNOSIS	*n* pl. -NOSES a shrinking and thickening of a cell nucleus
PYKNOTIC	*adj* exhibiting pyknosis
PYLON	*n* pl. -S a tall structure marking an entrance or approach
PYLORUS	*n* pl. -RI or -RUSES the opening between the stomach and the duodenum **PYLORIC** *adj*
PYODERMA	*n* pl. -S a pus-causing skin disease
PYOGENIC	*adj* producing pus
PYOID	*adj* puslike
PYORRHEA	*n* pl. -S a discharge of pus
PYOSIS	*n* pl. -OSES the formation of pus
PYRALID	*n* pl. -S a long-legged moth
PYRAMID	*v* -ED, -ING, -S to raise or increase by adding amounts gradually
PYRAN	*n* pl. -S a chemical compound **PYRANOID** *adj*
PYRANOSE	*n* pl. -S a simple sugar
PYRE	*n* pl. -S a pile of combustible material
PYRENE	*n* pl. -S a putamen
PYRENOID	*n* pl. -S a protein body of certain lower organisms
PYRETIC	*adj* pertaining to fever
PYREXIA	*n* pl. -S fever **PYREXIAL, PYREXIC** *adj*
PYRIC	*adj* pertaining to burning
PYRIDINE	*n* pl. -S a flammable liquid **PYRIDIC** *adj*
PYRIFORM	*adj* pear-shaped

PYRITE   *n* pl. -S a metallic sulfide **PYRITIC, PYRITOUS** *adj*

PYROGEN   *n* pl. -S a substance that produces fever

PYROLA   *n* pl. -S a perennial herb

PYROLIZE   *v* -LIZED, -LIZING, -LIZES to pyrolyze

PYROLOGY   *n* pl. -GIES the scientific examination of materials by heat

PYROLYZE   *v* -LYZED, -LYZING, -LYZES to affect compounds by the application of heat

PYRONE   *n* pl. -S a chemical compound

PYRONINE   *n* pl. -S a dye

PYROPE   *n* pl. -S a variety of garnet

PYROSIS   *n* pl. -SISES heartburn

PYROSTAT   *n* pl. -S a thermostat

PYROXENE   *n* pl. -S any of a group of minerals common in igneous rocks

PYRRHIC   *n* pl. -S a type of metrical foot

PYRROL   *n* pl. -S pyrrole

PYRROLE   *n* pl. -S a chemical compound **PYRROLIC** *adj*

PYRUVATE   *n* pl. -S a chemical salt

PYTHON   *n* pl. -S a large snake **PYTHONIC** *adj*

PYURIA   *n* pl. -S the presence of pus in the urine

PYX   *n* pl. -ES a container in which the eucharistic bread is kept

PYXIDES   pl. of pyxis

PYXIDIUM   *n* pl. -IA a type of seed vessel

PYXIE   *n* pl. -S an evergreen shrub

PYXIS   *n* pl. PYXIDES a pyxidium

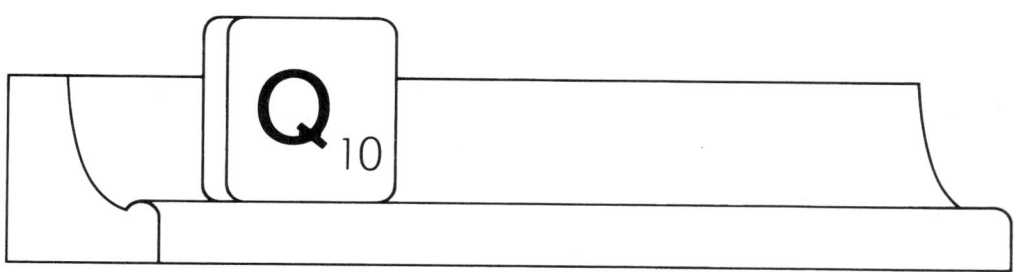

QAID	*n* pl. -S caid
QANAT	*n* pl. -S a system of underground tunnels and wells in the Middle East
QAT	*n* pl. -S kat
QINDAR	*n* pl. -DARS or -DARKA qintar
QINTAR	*n* pl. -S a monetary unit of Albania
QIVIUT	*n* pl. -S the wool of a musk-ox
QOPH	*n* pl. -S koph
QUA	*adv* in the capacity of
QUAALUDE	*n* pl. -S a sedative drug
QUACK	*v* -ED, -ING, -S to utter the characteristic cry of a duck
QUACKERY	*n* pl. -ERIES fraudulent practice
QUACKISH	*adj* fraudulent
QUACKISM	*n* pl. -S quackery
QUAD	*v* QUADDED, QUADDING, QUADS to space out by means of quadrats
QUADPLEX	*n* pl. -ES a building having four units
QUADRANS	*n* pl. -RANTES an ancient Roman coin
QUADRANT	*n* pl. -S a quarter section of a circle
QUADRAT	*n* pl. -S a piece of type metal used for filling spaces
QUADRATE	*v* -RATED, -RATING, -RATES to correspond or agree
QUADRIC	*n* pl. -S a type of geometric surface
QUADRIGA	*n* pl. -GAE a chariot drawn by four horses
QUADROON	*n* pl. -S a person of one-quarter black ancestry
QUAERE	*n* pl. -S a question
QUAESTOR	*n* pl. -S an ancient Roman magistrate

QUAFF	*v* -ED, -ING, -S to drink deeply
QUAFFER	*n* pl. -S one that quaffs
QUAG	*n* pl. -S a quagmire
QUAGGA	*n* pl. -S an extinct zebralike mammal
QUAGGY	*adj* -GIER, -GIEST marshy
QUAGMIRE	*n* pl. -S an area of marshy ground
QUAGMIRY	*adj* -MIRIER, -MIRIEST marshy
QUAHAUG	*n* pl. -S quahog
QUAHOG	*n* pl. -S an edible clam
QUAI	*n* pl. -S quay
QUAICH	*n* pl. -ES or -S a small drinking vessel
QUAIGH	*n* pl. -S quaich
QUAIL	*v* -ED, -ING, -S to cower
QUAINT	*adj* QUAINTER, QUAINTEST pleasingly old-fashioned or unfamiliar **QUAINTLY** *adv*
QUAKE	*v* QUAKED, QUAKING, QUAKES to shake or vibrate
QUAKER	*n* pl. -S one that quakes
QUAKY	*adj* QUAKIER, QUAKIEST tending to quake **QUAKILY** *adv*
QUALE	*n* pl. -LIA a property considered apart from things having the property
QUALIFY	*v* -FIED, -FYING, -FIES to make suitable or capable
QUALITY	*n* pl. -TIES a characteristic or attribute
QUALM	*n* pl. -S a feeling of doubt or misgiving
QUALMISH	*adj* having qualms
QUALMY	*adj* QUALMIER, QUALMIEST qualmish
QUAMASH	*n* pl. -ES camass
QUANDANG	*n* pl. -S quandong
QUANDARY	*n* pl. -RIES a dilemma

QUANDONG	*n* pl. -S an Australian tree
QUANGO	*n* pl. -GOS a public administrative board
QUANT	*v* -ED, -ING, -S to propel through water with a pole
QUANTA	pl. of quantum
QUANTAL	*adj* pertaining to a quantum
QUANTIC	*n* pl. -S a type of mathematical function
QUANTIFY	*v* -FIED, -FYING, -FIES to determine the quantity of
QUANTILE	*n* pl. -S any of the values of a random variable that divides a frequency distribution
QUANTITY	*n* pl. -TIES a specified or indefinite amount or number
QUANTIZE	*v* -TIZED, -TIZING, -TIZES to limit the possible values of to a discrete set
QUANTONG	*n* pl. -S quandong
QUANTUM	*n* pl. -TA a fundamental unit of energy
QUARE	*adj* queer
QUARK	*n* pl. -S a hypothetical atomic particle
QUARREL	*v* -RELED, -RELING, -RELS or -RELLED, -RELLING, -RELS to engage in an angry dispute
QUARRIER	*n* pl. -S one that quarries
QUARRY	*v* -RIED, -RYING, -RIES to dig stone from an excavation
QUART	*n* pl. -S a liquid measure of capacity
QUARTAN	*n* pl. -S a recurrent malarial fever
QUARTE	*n* pl. -S a fencing thrust
QUARTER	*v* -ED, -ING, -S to divide into four equal parts
QUARTERN	*n* pl. -S one-fourth of something
QUARTET	*n* pl. -S a group of four
QUARTIC	*n* pl. -S a type of mathematical function
QUARTILE	*n* pl. -S a portion of a frequency distribution
QUARTO	*n* pl. -TOS the size of a piece of paper cut four from a sheet
QUARTZ	*n* pl. -ES a mineral
QUASAR	*n* pl. -S a distant celestial object emitting strong radio waves
QUASH	*v* -ED, -ING, -ES to suppress completely
QUASHER	*n* pl. -S one that quashes
QUASI	*adj* similar but not exactly the same
QUASS	*n* pl. -ES kvass
QUASSIA	*n* pl. -S a tropical tree
QUASSIN	*n* pl. -S a medicinal compound obtained from the wood of a quassia
QUATE	*adj* quiet
QUATORZE	*n* pl. -S a set of four cards of the same denomination scoring fourteen points
QUATRAIN	*n* pl. -S a stanza of four lines
QUATRE	*n* pl. -S the four at cards or dice
QUAVER	*v* -ED, -ING, -S to quiver
QUAVERER	*n* pl. -S one that quavers
QUAVERY	*adj* quivery
QUAY	*n* pl. QUAYS a wharf **QUAYLIKE** *adj*
QUAYAGE	*n* pl. -S a charge for the use of a quay
QUAYSIDE	*n* pl. -S the area adjacent to a quay
QUEAN	*n* pl. -S a harlot
QUEASY	*adj* -SIER, -SIEST easily nauseated **QUEASILY** *adv*
QUEAZY	*adj* -ZIER, -ZIEST queasy
QUEEN	*v* -ED, -ING, -S to make a queen (a female monarch) of
QUEENDOM	*n* pl. -S the area ruled by a queen
QUEENLY	*adj* -LIER, -LIEST of or befitting a queen
QUEER	*adj* QUEERER, QUEEREST deviating from the expected or normal
QUEER	*v* -ED, -ING, -S to spoil the effect or success of
QUEERISH	*adj* somewhat queer
QUEERLY	*adv* in a queer manner
QUELL	*v* -ED, -ING, -S to suppress
QUELLER	*n* pl. -S one that quells
QUENCH	*v* -ED, -ING, -ES to put out or extinguish
QUENCHER	*n* pl. -S one that quenches
QUENELLE	*n* pl. -S a type of dumpling
QUERCINE	*adj* pertaining to oaks
QUERIDA	*n* pl. -S a female sweetheart
QUERIED	past tense of query
QUERIER	*n* pl. -S a querist

QUERIES	present 3d person sing. of query
QUERIST	*n* pl. -S one who queries
QUERN	*n* pl. -S a hand-turned grain mill
QUERY	*v* -RIED, -RYING, -RIES to question
QUEST	*v* -ED, -ING, -S to make a search
QUESTER	*n* pl. -S one that quests
QUESTION	*v* -ED, -ING, -S to put a question (an inquiry) to
QUESTOR	*n* pl. -S quaestor
QUETZAL	*n* pl. -S or -ES a tropical bird
QUEUE	*v* QUEUED, QUEUING or QUEUEING, QUEUES to line up
QUEUER	*n* pl. -S one that queues
QUEY	*n* pl. QUEYS a young cow
QUEZAL	*n* pl. -S or -ES quetzal
QUIBBLE	*v* -BLED, -BLING, -BLES to argue over trivialities
QUIBBLER	*n* pl. -S one that quibbles
QUICHE	*n* pl. -S a custard-filled pastry
QUICK	*adj* QUICKER, QUICKEST acting or capable of acting with speed
QUICK	*n* pl. -S a sensitive area of flesh
QUICKEN	*v* -ED, -ING, -S to speed up
QUICKIE	*n* pl. -S something done quickly
QUICKLY	*adv* in a quick manner
QUICKSET	*n* pl. -S a plant suitable for hedges
QUID	*n* pl. -S a portion of something to be chewed
QUIDDITY	*n* pl. -TIES the true nature of a thing
QUIDNUNC	*n* pl. -S a nosy person
QUIET	*adj* -ETER, -ETEST making little or no noise
QUIET	*v* -ED, -ING, -S to cause to be quiet
QUIETEN	*v* -ED, -ING, -S to quiet
QUIETER	*n* pl. -S one that quiets
QUIETISM	*n* pl. -S a form of religious mysticism
QUIETIST	*n* pl. -S an advocate of quietism
QUIETLY	*adv* in a quiet manner
QUIETUDE	*n* pl. -S a state of tranquillity
QUIETUS	*n* pl. -ES a final settlement
QUIFF	*n* pl. -S a forelock
QUILL	*v* -ED, -ING, -S to press small ridges in
QUILLAI	*n* pl. -S an evergreen tree
QUILLAIA	*n* pl. -S a quillai
QUILLAJA	*n* pl. -S a quillai
QUILLET	*n* pl. -S a trivial distinction
QUILLING	*n* pl. -S material that is quilled
QUILT	*v* -ED, -ING, -S to stitch together with padding in between
QUILTER	*n* pl. -S one that quilts
QUILTING	*n* pl. -S material that is used for making quilts
QUIN	*n* pl. -S a quintuplet
QUINARY	*n* pl. -RIES a group of five
QUINATE	*adj* arranged in groups of five
QUINCE	*n* pl. -S an apple-like fruit
QUINCUNX	*n* pl. -ES an arrangement of five objects
QUINELA	*n* pl. -S quinella
QUINELLA	*n* pl. -S a type of bet in horse racing
QUINIC	*adj* pertaining to quinine
QUINIELA	*n* pl. -S quinella
QUININ	*n* pl. -S quinine
QUININA	*n* pl. -S quinine
QUININE	*n* pl. -S a medicinal alkaloid
QUINNAT	*n* pl. -S a food fish
QUINOA	*n* pl. -S a weedy plant
QUINOID	*n* pl. -S a chemical compound
QUINOL	*n* pl. -S a chemical compound
QUINOLIN	*n* pl. -S a chemical compound
QUINONE	*n* pl. -S a chemical compound
QUINSY	*n* pl. -SIES an inflammation of the tonsils
QUINT	*n* pl. -S a group of five
QUINTA	*n* pl. -S a country estate in Portugal or Latin America
QUINTAIN	*n* pl. -S an object used as a target in a medieval sport
QUINTAL	*n* pl. -S a unit of weight
QUINTAN	*n* pl. -S a recurrent fever
QUINTAR	*n* pl. -S qintar
QUINTE	*n* pl. -S a position in fencing
QUINTET	*n* pl. -S a group of five
QUINTIC	*n* pl. -S a type of mathematical function
QUINTILE	*n* pl. -S a portion of a frequency distribution
QUINTIN	*n* pl. -S a fine linen

QUIP	*v* QUIPPED, QUIPPING, QUIPS to make witty remarks
QUIPPER	*n* pl. -S one that quips
QUIPPISH	*adj* witty
QUIPPU	*n* pl. -S quipu
QUIPSTER	*n* pl. -S one that quips
QUIPU	*n* pl. -S an ancient calculating device
QUIRE	*v* QUIRED, QUIRING, QUIRES to arrange sheets of paper in sets of twenty-four
QUIRK	*v* -ED, -ING, -S to twist
QUIRKISH	*adj* quirky
QUIRKY	*adj* QUIRKIER, QUIRKIEST peculiar **QUIRKILY** *adv*
QUIRT	*v* -ED, -ING, -S to strike with a riding whip
QUISLING	*n* pl. -S a traitor who aids the invaders of his country
QUIT	*v* QUITTED, QUITTING, QUITS to end one's engagement in or occupation with
QUITCH	*n* pl. -ES a perennial grass
QUITE	*adv* to the fullest extent
QUITRENT	*n* pl. -S a fixed rent due from a socage tenant
QUITTED	past tense of quit
QUITTER	*n* pl. -S one that quits
QUITTING	present participle of quit
QUITTOR	*n* pl. -S an inflammation of an animal's hoof
QUIVER	*v* -ED, -ING, -S to shake with a slight but rapid motion
QUIVERER	*n* pl. -S one that quivers
QUIVERY	*adj* marked by quivering
QUIXOTE	*n* pl. -S a quixotic person
QUIXOTIC	*adj* extremely idealistic
QUIXOTRY	*n* pl. -TRIES quixotic action or thought
QUIZ	*v* QUIZZED, QUIZZING, QUIZZES to test the knowledge of by asking questions
QUIZZER	*n* pl. -S one that quizzes
QUOD	*n* pl. -S a prison
QUOHOG	*n* pl. -S quahog
QUOIN	*v* -ED, -ING, -S to secure with a type of wedge
QUOIT	*v* -ED, -ING, -S to play a throwing game similar to ringtoss
QUOKKA	*n* pl. -S a short-tailed wallaby
QUOMODO	*n* pl. -DOS a means or manner
QUONDAM	*adj* that once was
QUORUM	*n* pl. -S a particularly chosen group
QUOTA	*n* pl. -S a proportional part or share
QUOTE	*v* QUOTED, QUOTING, QUOTES to repeat the words of **QUOTABLE** *adj* **QUOTABLY** *adv*
QUOTER	*n* pl. -S one that quotes
QUOTH	*v* said — QUOTH is the only accepted form of this verb; it cannot be conjugated
QUOTHA	*interj* — used to express surprise or sarcasm
QUOTIENT	*n* pl. -S the number resulting from the division of one number by another
QUOTING	present participle of quote
QURSH	*n* pl. -ES a monetary unit of Saudi Arabia
QURUSH	*n* pl. -ES qursh
QWERTY	*n* pl. -TYS a standard keyboard

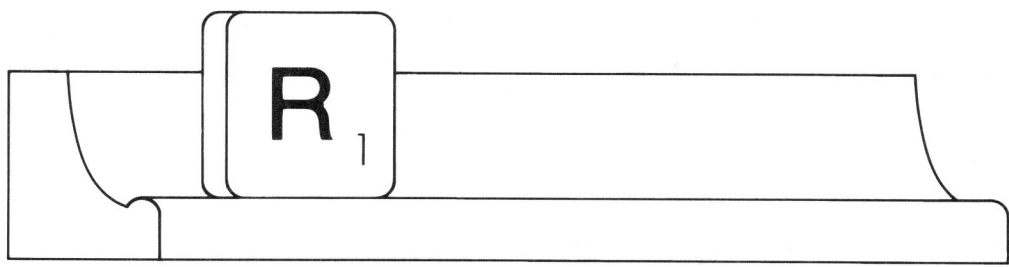

RABAT   *n* pl. -S a dickey attached to a clerical collar

RABATO   *n* pl. -TOS a wide, lace-edged collar

RABBET   *v* -ED, -ING, -S to cut a groove in

RABBI   *n* pl. -S or -ES a Jewish spiritual leader

RABBIN   *n* pl. -S rabbi

RABBINIC   *adj* pertaining to rabbis

RABBIT   *v* -ED, -ING, -S to hunt rabbits (rodent-like mammals)

RABBITER   *n* pl. -S one that rabbits

RABBITRY   *n* pl. -RIES a place where rabbits are kept

RABBITY   *adj* resembling a rabbit

RABBLE   *v* -BLED, -BLING, -BLES to mob

RABBLER   *n* pl. -S an iron bar used in puddling

RABBONI   *n* pl. -S master; teacher — used as a Jewish title of respect

RABIC   *adj* pertaining to rabies

RABID   *adj* affected with rabies **RABIDLY** *adv*

RABIDITY   *n* pl. -TIES the state of being rabid

RABIES   *n* pl. RABIES an infectious virus disease **RABIETIC** *adj*

RACCOON   *n* pl. -S a carnivorous mammal

RACE   *v* RACED, RACING, RACES to compete in a contest of speed

RACEMATE   *n* pl. -S a chemical salt

RACEME   *n* pl. -S a mode of arrangement of flowers along an axis **RACEMED** *adj*

RACEMIC   *adj* pertaining to a racemate

RACEMISM   *n* pl. -S the state of being racemic

RACEMIZE   *v* -MIZED, -MIZING, -MIZES to convert into a racemic compound

RACEMOID   *adj* pertaining to a raceme

RACEMOSE   *adj* having the form of a raceme

RACEMOUS   *adj* racemose

RACER   *n* pl. -S one that races

RACEWAY   *n* pl. -WAYS a channel for conducting water

RACHET   *n* pl. -S ratchet

RACHILLA   *n* pl. -LAE the central stalk of a grass spikelet

RACHIS   *n* pl. -CHISES or -CHIDES the spinal column **RACHIAL** *adj*

RACHITIS   *n* pl. -TIDES rickets **RACHITIC** *adj*

RACIAL   *adj* pertaining to an ethnic group **RACIALLY** *adv*

RACIER   comparative of racy

RACIEST   superlative of racy

RACILY   *adv* in a racy manner

RACINESS   *n* pl. -ES the quality of being racy

RACING   *n* pl. -S the sport of engaging in contests of speed

RACISM   *n* pl. -S a doctrine of racial superiority

RACIST   *n* pl. -S an advocate of racism

RACK   *v* -ED, -ING, -S to place in a type of framework

RACKER   *n* pl. -S one that racks

RACKET   *v* -ED, -ING, -S to make a loud noise

RACKETY   *adj* -ETIER, -ETIEST noisy

RACKFUL   *n* pl. -S as much as a rack can hold

RACKLE   *adj* impetuous; rash

RACKWORK   *n* pl. -S a type of mechanism

RACLETTE   *n* pl. -S a cheese dish

RACON   *n* pl. -S a type of radar transmitter

RACOON   *n* pl. -S raccoon

RACQUET — *n* pl. -S a lightweight implement used in various ball games

RACY — *adj* RACIER, RACIEST bordering on impropriety or indecency

RAD — *v* RADDED, RADDING, RADS to fear

RADAR — *n* pl. -S an electronic locating device

RADDLE — *v* -DLED, -DLING, -DLES to weave together

RADIABLE — *adj* capable of radiating

RADIAL — *n* pl. -S a part diverging from a center

RADIALE — *n* pl. -LIA a bone of the carpus

RADIALLY — *adv* in a diverging manner

RADIAN — *n* pl. -S a unit of angular measure

RADIANCE — *n* pl. -S brightness

RADIANCY — *n* pl. -CIES radiance

RADIANT — *n* pl. -S a point from which rays are emitted

RADIATE — *v* -ATED, -ATING, -ATES to emit rays

RADIATOR — *n* pl. -S a heating device

RADICAL — *n* pl. -S a group of atoms that acts as a unit in chemical compounds

RADICAND — *n* pl. -S a quantity in mathematics

RADICATE — *v* -CATED, -CATING, -CATES to cause to take root

RADICEL — *n* pl. -S a rootlet

RADICES — a pl. of radix

RADICLE — *n* pl. -S a part of a plant embryo

RADII — a pl. of radius

RADIO — *v* -ED, -ING, -S to transmit by radio (an apparatus for wireless communication)

RADIOMAN — *n* pl. -MEN a radio operator or technician

RADISH — *n* pl. -ES a pungent, edible root

RADIUM — *n* pl. -S a radioactive element

RADIUS — *n* pl. -DII or -DIUSES a straight line from the center of a circle to the circumference

RADIX — *n* pl. -DICES or -DIXES the root of a plant

RADOME — *n* pl. -S a domelike device used to shelter a radar antenna

RADON — *n* pl. -S a radioactive element

RADULA — *n* pl. -LAE or -LAS a tonguelike organ of mollusks **RADULAR** *adj*

RADWASTE — *n* pl. -S radioactive waste

RAFF — *n* pl. -S riffraff

RAFFIA — *n* pl. -S a palm tree

RAFFISH — *adj* tawdry

RAFFLE — *v* -FLED, -FLING, -FLES to dispose of by a form of lottery

RAFFLER — *n* pl. -S one that raffles

RAFT — *v* -ED, -ING, -S to transport on a raft (a type of buoyant structure)

RAFTER — *n* pl. -S a supporting beam

RAFTERED — *adj* furnished with rafters

RAFTSMAN — *n* pl. -MEN one who manages a raft

RAG — *v* RAGGED, RAGGING, RAGS to scold

RAGA — *n* pl. -S a Hindu musical form

RAGBAG — *n* pl. -S a bag for storing scraps of cloth

RAGE — *v* RAGED, RAGING, RAGES to act or speak with violent anger

RAGEE — *n* pl. -S ragi

RAGGED — *adj* -GEDER, -GEDEST tattered **RAGGEDLY** *adv*

RAGGEDY — *adj* somewhat ragged

RAGGEE — *n* pl. -S ragi

RAGGIES — pl. of raggy

RAGGING — present participle of rag

RAGGLE — *n* pl. -S a groove cut in masonry

RAGGY — *n* pl. -GIES ragi

RAGI — *n* pl. -S an East Indian cereal grass

RAGING — present participle of rage

RAGINGLY — *adv* in a furious manner

RAGLAN — *n* pl. -S a type of overcoat

RAGMAN — *n* pl. -MEN one who gathers and sells scraps of cloth

RAGOUT — *v* -ED, -ING, -S to make into a highly seasoned stew

RAGTAG — *n* pl. -S riffraff

RAGTIME — *n* pl. -S a style of American dance music

RAGTOP — *n* pl. -S a convertible automobile

RAGWEED — *n* pl. -S a weedy herb

RAGWORT — *n* pl. -S a flowering plant

RAH — *interj* — used to cheer on a team or player

RAIA	*n* pl. -S rayah
RAID	*v* -ED, -ING, -S to make a sudden assault on
RAIDER	*n* pl. -S one that raids
RAIL	*v* -ED, -ING, -S to scold in abusive or insolent language
RAILBIRD	*n* pl. -S a racing enthusiast
RAILBUS	*n* pl. -BUSES or -BUSSES a passenger car equipped for operation on rails
RAILCAR	*n* pl. -S a railroad car
RAILER	*n* pl. -S one that rails
RAILHEAD	*n* pl. -S the end of a railroad line
RAILING	*n* pl. -S a fence-like barrier
RAILLERY	*n* pl. -LERIES good-natured teasing
RAILROAD	*v* -ED, -ING, -S to transport by railroad (a type of road on which locomotives are run)
RAILWAY	*n* pl. -WAYS a railroad
RAIMENT	*n* pl. -S clothing
RAIN	*v* -ED, -ING, -S to fall like rain (drops of water condensed from atmospheric vapor)
RAINBAND	*n* pl. -S a dark band in the solar spectrum
RAINBIRD	*n* pl. -S a type of bird
RAINBOW	*n* pl. -S an arc of spectral colors formed in the sky
RAINCOAT	*n* pl. -S a waterproof coat
RAINDROP	*n* pl. -S a drop of rain
RAINFALL	*n* pl. -S a fall of rain
RAINIER	comparative of rainy
RAINIEST	superlative of rainy
RAINILY	*adv* in a rainy manner
RAINLESS	*adj* having no rain
RAINOUT	*n* pl. -S atomic fallout occurring in precipitation
RAINWASH	*v* -ED, -ING, -ES to wash material downhill by rain
RAINWEAR	*n* pl. -S waterproof clothing
RAINY	*adj* RAINIER, RAINIEST marked by rain
RAISE	*v* RAISED, RAISING, RAISES to move to a higher position **RAISABLE** *adj*
RAISER	*n* pl. -S one that raises
RAISIN	*n* pl. -S a dried grape **RAISINY** *adj*
RAISING	*n* pl. -S an elevation

RAISONNE	*adj* arranged systematically
RAJ	*n* pl. -ES dominion; sovereignty
RAJA	*n* pl. -S rajah
RAJAH	*n* pl. -S a king or prince in India
RAKE	*v* RAKED, RAKING, RAKES to gather with a toothed implement
RAKEE	*n* pl. -S raki
RAKEHELL	*n* pl. -S a man lacking in moral restraint
RAKEOFF	*n* pl. -S a share of profits
RAKER	*n* pl. -S one that rakes
RAKI	*n* pl. -S a Turkish liqueur
RAKING	present participle of rake
RAKISH	*adj* dapper **RAKISHLY** *adv*
RALE	*n* pl. -S an abnormal respiratory sound
RALLIED	past tense of rally
RALLIER	*n* pl. -S one that rallies
RALLINE	*adj* pertaining to a family of marsh birds
RALLY	*v* -LIED, -LYING, -LIES to call together for a common purpose
RALLYE	*n* pl. -S a type of automobile race
RALLYING	*n* pl. -S the sport of driving in rallyes
RALLYIST	*n* pl. -S a participant in a rallye
RALPH	*v* -ED, -ING, -S to vomit
RAM	*v* RAMMED, RAMMING, RAMS to strike with great force
RAMATE	*adj* having branches
RAMBLE	*v* -BLED, -BLING, -BLES to wander
RAMBLER	*n* pl. -S one that rambles
RAMBUTAN	*n* pl. -S the edible fruit of a Malayan tree
RAMEE	*n* pl. -S ramie
RAMEKIN	*n* pl. -S a cheese dish
RAMENTUM	*n* pl. -TA a scale formed on the surface of leaves
RAMEQUIN	*n* pl. -S ramekin
RAMET	*n* pl. -S an independent member of a clone
RAMI	pl. of ramus
RAMIE	*n* pl. -S an Asian shrub
RAMIFORM	*adj* shaped like a branch
RAMIFY	*v* -FIED, -FYING, -FIES to divide into branches
RAMILIE	*n* pl. -S ramillie

RAMILLIE	*n* pl. -S a type of wig
RAMJET	*n* pl. -S a type of engine
RAMMED	past tense of ram
RAMMER	*n* pl. -S one that rams
RAMMIER	comparative of rammy
RAMMIEST	superlative of rammy
RAMMING	present participle of ram
RAMMISH	*adj* resembling a ram (a male sheep)
RAMMY	*adj* -MIER, -MIEST rammish
RAMOSE	*adj* having many branches **RAMOSELY** *adv*
RAMOSITY	*n* pl. -TIES the state of being ramose
RAMOUS	*adj* ramose
RAMP	*v* -ED, -ING, -S to rise or stand on the hind legs
RAMPAGE	*v* -PAGED, -PAGING, -PAGES to move about wildly or violently
RAMPAGER	*n* pl. -S one that rampages
RAMPANCY	*n* pl. -CIES the state of being rampant
RAMPANT	*adj* unrestrained
RAMPART	*v* -ED, -ING, -S to furnish with a fortifying embankment
RAMPIKE	*n* pl. -S a standing dead tree
RAMPION	*n* pl. -S a European plant
RAMPOLE	*n* pl. -S rampike
RAMROD	*v* -RODDED, -RODDING, -RODS to supervise
RAMSHORN	*n* pl. -S a snail used as an aquarium scavenger
RAMSON	*n* pl. -S a broad-leaved garlic
RAMTIL	*n* pl. -S a tropical plant
RAMULOSE	*adj* having many small branches
RAMULOUS	*adj* ramulose
RAMUS	*n* pl. -MI a branch-like part of a structure
RAN	past tense of run and rin
RANCE	*n* pl. -S a variety of marble
RANCH	*v* -ED, -ING, -ES to work on a ranch (an establishment for raising livestock)
RANCHER	*n* pl. -S one that owns or works on a ranch
RANCHERO	*n* pl. -ROS a rancher
RANCHMAN	*n* pl. -MEN a rancher
RANCHO	*n* pl. -CHOS a ranch
RANCID	*adj* having an unpleasant odor or taste **RANCIDLY** *adv*
RANCOR	*n* pl. -S bitter and vindictive enmity **RANCORED** *adj*
RANCOUR	*n* pl. -S rancor
RAND	*n* pl. -S a strip of leather at the heel of a shoe
RANDAN	*n* pl. -S a boat rowed by three persons
RANDIER	comparative of randy
RANDIES	pl. of randy
RANDIEST	superlative of randy
RANDOM	*n* pl. -S a haphazard course
RANDOMLY	*adv* in a haphazard manner
RANDY	*adj* -DIER, -DIEST lustful
RANDY	*n* pl. RANDIES a rude person
RANEE	*n* pl. -S rani
RANG	past tense of ring
RANGE	*v* RANGED, RANGING, RANGES to place in a particular order
RANGER	*n* pl. -S an officer supervising the care of a forest
RANGY	*adj* RANGIER, RANGIEST tall and slender
RANI	*n* pl. -S the wife of a rajah
RANID	*n* pl. -S any of a large family of frogs
RANK	*v* -ED, -ING, -S to determine the relative position of
RANK	*adj* RANKER, RANKEST strong and disagreeable in odor or taste
RANKER	*n* pl. -S an enlisted soldier
RANKING	*n* pl. -S a listing of ranked individuals
RANKISH	*adj* somewhat rank
RANKLE	*v* -KLED, -KLING, -KLES to cause irritation or resentment in
RANKLY	*adv* in a rank manner
RANKNESS	*n* pl. -ES the state of being rank
RANPIKE	*n* pl. -S rampike
RANSACK	*v* -ED, -ING, -S to search thoroughly
RANSOM	*v* -ED, -ING, -S to obtain the release of by paying a demanded price
RANSOMER	*n* pl. -S one that ransoms
RANT	*v* -ED, -ING, -S to speak in a loud or vehement manner
RANTER	*n* pl. -S one that rants

RANULA	*n* pl. -S a cyst formed under the tongue	**RARE**	*adj* RARER, RAREST occurring infrequently
RAP	*v* RAPPED, RAPPING, RAPS to strike sharply	**RARE**	*v* RARED, RARING, RARES to be enthusiastic
RAPACITY	*n* pl. -TIES the quality of being ravenous	**RAREBIT**	*n* pl. -S a cheese dish
		RAREFIER	*n* pl. -S one that rarefies
RAPE	*v* RAPED, RAPING, RAPES to force to submit to sexual intercourse	**RAREFY**	*v* -EFIED, -EFYING, -EFIES to make less dense
RAPER	*n* pl. -S a rapist	**RARELY**	*adv* not often
RAPESEED	*n* pl. -S the seed of a European herb	**RARENESS**	*n* pl. -ES the quality of being rare
		RARER	comparative of rare
RAPHE	*n* pl. RAPHAE or RAPHES a seamlike ridge between two halves of an organ or part	**RARERIPE**	*n* pl. -S a fruit that ripens early
		RAREST	superlative of rare
RAPHIA	*n* pl. -S raffia	**RARIFY**	*v* -FIED, -FYING, -FIES to rarefy
RAPHIDE	*n* pl. -S a needle-shaped crystal occurring in plant cells	**RARING**	*adj* full of enthusiasm
		RARITY	*n* pl. -TIES rareness
RAPHIS	*n* pl. -PHIDES raphide	**RAS**	*n* pl. -ES an Ethiopian prince
RAPID	*adj* -IDER, -IDEST fast-moving **RAPIDLY** *adv*	**RASBORA**	*n* pl. -S a tropical fish
RAPID	*n* pl. -S a fast-moving part of a river	**RASCAL**	*n* pl. -S an unscrupulous or dishonest person
RAPIDITY	*n* pl. -TIES swiftness	**RASCALLY**	*adj* characteristic of a rascal
RAPIER	*n* pl. -S a long, slender sword **RAPIERED** *adj*	**RASE**	*v* RASED, RASING, RASES to raze
RAPINE	*n* pl. -S the taking of property by force	**RASER**	*n* pl. -S one that rases
RAPING	present participle of rape	**RASH**	*adj* RASHER, RASHEST acting without due caution or forethought
RAPINI	*n/pl* rappini		
RAPIST	*n* pl. -S one who rapes	**RASH**	*n* pl. -ES a skin eruption **RASHLIKE** *adj*
RAPPAREE	*n* pl. -S a plunderer		
RAPPED	past tense of rap	**RASHER**	*n* pl. -S a thin slice of meat
RAPPEE	*n* pl. -S a strong snuff	**RASHLY**	*adv* in a rash manner
RAPPEL	*v* -PELED, -PELING, -PELS or -PELLED, -PELLING, -PELS to descend from a steep height by means of a rope	**RASHNESS**	*n* pl. -ES the state of being rash
		RASING	present participle of rase
		RASORIAL	*adj* habitually scratching the ground for food
RAPPEN	*n* pl. RAPPEN a monetary unit of Switzerland	**RASP**	*v* -ED, -ING, -S to rub with something rough
RAPPER	*n* pl. -S one that raps	**RASPER**	*n* pl. -S one that rasps
RAPPING	present participle of rap	**RASPISH**	*adj* irritable
RAPPINI	*n/pl* immature turnip plants	**RASPY**	*adj* RASPIER, RASPIEST rough
RAPPORT	*n* pl. -S a harmonious relationship	**RASSLE**	*v* -SLED, -SLING, -SLES to wrestle
RAPT	*adj* deeply engrossed **RAPTLY** *adv*	**RASTER**	*n* pl. -S the area reproducing images on the picture tube of a television set
RAPTNESS	*n* pl. -ES the state of being rapt		
RAPTOR	*n* pl. -S a bird of prey	**RASURE**	*n* pl. -S erasure
RAPTURE	*v* -TURED, -TURING, -TURES to fill with great joy	**RAT**	*v* RATTED, RATTING, RATS to hunt rats (long-tailed rodents)

RATABLE *adj* capable of being rated **RATABLY** *adv*

RATAFEE *n* pl. -S ratafia

RATAFIA *n* pl. -S an almond-flavored liqueur

RATAL *n* pl. -S an amount on which rates are assessed

RATAN *n* pl. -S rattan

RATANY *n* pl. -NIES rhatany

RATAPLAN *v* -PLANNED, -PLANNING, -PLANS to make a rapidly repeating sound

RATATAT *n* pl. -S a quick, sharp rapping sound

RATBAG *n* pl. -S an eccentric or disagreeable person

RATCH *n* pl. -ES a ratchet

RATCHET *v* -ED, -ING, -S to increase or decrease by small amounts

RATE *v* RATED, RATING, RATES to estimate the value of

RATEABLE *adj* ratable **RATEABLY** *adv*

RATEL *n* pl. -S a carnivorous mammal

RATER *n* pl. -S one that rates

RATFINK *n* pl. -S a contemptible person

RATFISH *n* pl. -ES a marine fish

RATH *adj* rathe

RATHE *adj* appearing or ripening early

RATHER *adv* preferably

RATHOLE *n* pl. -S a hole made by a rat

RATICIDE *n* pl. -S a substance for killing rats

RATIFIER *n* pl. -S one that ratifies

RATIFY *v* -FIED, -FYING, -FIES to approve and sanction formally

RATINE *n* pl. -S a heavy fabric woven loosely

RATING *n* pl. -S relative estimate or evaluation

RATIO *n* pl. -TIOS a proportional relationship

RATION *v* -ED, -ING, -S to distribute in fixed portions

RATIONAL *n* pl. -S a number that can be expressed as a quotient of integers

RATITE *n* pl. -S a flightless bird

RATLIKE *adj* resembling a rat

RATLIN *n* pl. -S ratline

RATLINE *n* pl. -S one of the ropes forming the steps of a ship's rope ladder

RATO *n* pl. -TOS a rocket-assisted airplane takeoff

RATOON *v* -ED, -ING, -S to sprout from a root planted the previous year

RATOONER *n* pl. -S a plant that ratoons

RATSBANE *n* pl. -S rat poison

RATTAIL *n* pl. -S a marine fish

RATTAN *n* pl. -S a palm tree

RATTED past tense of rat

RATTEEN *n* pl. -S a coarse woolen fabric

RATTEN *v* -ED, -ING, -S to harass

RATTENER *n* pl. -S one that rattens

RATTER *n* pl. -S an animal used for catching rats

RATTIER comparative of ratty

RATTIEST superlative of ratty

RATTING present participle of rat

RATTISH *adj* ratlike

RATTLE *v* -TLED, -TLING, -TLES to make a quick succession of short, sharp sounds

RATTLER *n* pl. -S one that rattles

RATTLING *n* pl. -S ratline

RATTLY *adj* tending to rattle

RATTON *n* pl. -S a rat

RATTOON *v* -ED, -ING, -S to ratoon

RATTRAP *n* pl. -S a trap for catching rats

RATTY *adj* -TIER, -TIEST infested with rats

RAUCITY *n* pl. -TIES the state of being raucous

RAUCOUS *adj* loud and unruly

RAUNCH *n* pl. -ES vulgarity

RAUNCHY *adj* -CHIER, -CHIEST slovenly

RAVAGE *v* -AGED, -AGING, -AGES to destroy

RAVAGER *n* pl. -S one that ravages

RAVE *v* RAVED, RAVING, RAVES to speak irrationally or incoherently

RAVEL *v* -ELED, -ELING, -ELS or -ELLED, -ELLING, -ELS to separate the threads of

RAVELER *n* pl. -S one that ravels

RAVELIN *n* pl. -S a type of fortification

RAVELING *n* pl. -S a loose thread

RAVELLED a past tense of ravel

RAVELLER	*n* pl. -S raveler	
RAVELLING	*n* pl. -S raveling	
RAVELLY	*adj* tangled	
RAVEN	*v* -ED, -ING, -S to eat in a ravenous manner	
RAVENER	*n* pl. -S one that ravens	
RAVENING	*n* pl. -S rapacity	
RAVENOUS	*adj* extremely hungry	
RAVER	*n* pl. -S one that raves	
RAVIGOTE	*n* pl. -S a spiced vinegar sauce	
RAVIN	*v* -ED, -ING, -S to raven	
RAVINE	*n* pl. -S a narrow, steep-sided valley	
RAVING	*n* pl. -S irrational, incoherent speech	
RAVINGLY	*adv* in a delirious manner	
RAVIOLI	*n* pl. -S an Italian pasta dish	
RAVISH	*v* -ED, -ING, -ES to seize and carry off by force	
RAVISHER	*n* pl. -S one that ravishes	
RAW	*adj* RAWER, RAWEST uncooked	
RAW	*n* pl. -S a sore or irritated spot	
RAWBONED	*adj* having little flesh	
RAWHIDE	*v* -HIDED, -HIDING, -HIDES to beat with a type of whip	
RAWIN	*n* pl. -S a wind measurement made by tracking a balloon with radar	
RAWISH	*adj* somewhat raw	
RAWLY	*adv* in a raw manner	
RAWNESS	*n* pl. -ES the state of being raw	
RAX	*v* -ED, -ING, -ES to stretch out	
RAY	*v* -ED, -ING, -S to emit rays (narrow beams of light)	
RAYA	*n* pl. -S rayah	
RAYAH	*n* pl. -S a non-Muslim inhabitant of Turkey	
RAYGRASS	*n* pl. -ES ryegrass	
RAYLESS	*adj* having no rays	
RAYLIKE	*adj* resembling a narrow beam of light	
RAYON	*n* pl. -S a synthetic fiber	
RAZE	*v* RAZED, RAZING, RAZES to tear down or demolish	
RAZEE	*v* -ZEED, -ZEEING, -ZEES to make lower by removing the upper deck, as a ship	
RAZER	*n* pl. -S one that razes	

RAZING	present participle of raze	
RAZOR	*v* -ED, -ING, -S to shave or cut with a sharp-edged instrument	
RAZZ	*v* -ED, -ING, -ES to deride	
RE	*n* pl. -S the second tone of the diatonic musical scale	

R₁ E₁ Following is a list of self-explanatory verbs containing the prefix RE- (again):

REABSORB	*v* -ED, -ING, -S
REACCEDE	*v* -CEDED, -CEDING, -CEDES
REACCENT	*v* -ED, -ING, -S
REACCEPT	*v* -ED, -ING, -S
REACCUSE	*v* -CUSED, -CUSING, -CUSES
READAPT	*v* -ED, -ING, -S
READD	*v* -ED, -ING, -S
READDICT	*v* -ED, -ING, -S
READJUST	*v* -ED, -ING, -S
READMIT	*v* -MITTED, -MITTING, -MITS
READOPT	*v* -ED, -ING, -S
READORN	*v* -ED, -ING, -S
REAFFIRM	*v* -ED, -ING, -S
REAFFIX	*v* -ED, -ING, -ES
REALIGN	*v* -ED, -ING, -S
REALLOT	*v* -LOTTED, -LOTTING, -LOTS
REALTER	*v* -ED, -ING, -S
REANNEX	*v* -ED, -ING, -ES
REANOINT	*v* -ED, -ING, -S
REAPPEAR	*v* -ED, -ING, -S
REAPPLY	*v* -PLIED, -PLYING, -PLIES
REARGUE	*v* -GUED, -GUING, -GUES
REARM	*v* -ED, -ING, -S
REAROUSE	*v* -AROUSED, -AROUSING, -AROUSES
REARREST	*v* -ED, -ING, -S
REASCEND	*v* -ED, -ING, -S
REASSAIL	*v* -ED, -ING, -S
REASSERT	*v* -ED, -ING, -S
REASSESS	*v* -ED, -ING, -ES
REASSIGN	*v* -ED, -ING, -S
REASSORT	*v* -ED, -ING, -S
REASSUME	*v* -SUMED, -SUMING, -SUMES
REASSURE	*v* -SURED, -SURING, -SURES
REATTACH	*v* -ED, -ING, -ES
REATTACK	*v* -ED, -ING, -S
REATTAIN	*v* -ED, -ING, -S
REAVAIL	*v* -ED, -ING, -S
REAVOW	*v* -ED, -ING, -S

REAWAKE	v -AWAKED or -AWOKE, -AWOKEN, -AWAKING, -AWAKES
REAWAKEN	v -ED, -ING, -S
REBAIT	v -ED, -ING, -S
REBEGIN	v -GAN, -GUN, -GINNING, -GINS
REBID	v -BID, -BIDDEN, -BIDDING, -BIDS
REBILL	v -ED, -ING, -S
REBIND	v -BOUND, -BINDING, -BINDS
REBLEND	v -ED, -ING, -S
REBLOOM	v -ED, -ING, -S
REBOARD	v -ED, -ING, -S
REBODY	v -BODIED, -BODYING, -BODIES
REBOIL	v -ED, -ING, -S
REBOOK	v -ED, -ING, -S
REBOOT	v -ED, -ING, -S
REBORE	v -BORED, -BORING, -BORES
REBOTTLE	v -TLED, -TLING, -TLES
REBOUGHT	past tense of rebuy
REBOUND	past tense of rebind
REBREED	v -BRED, -BREEDING, -BREEDS
REBUILD	v -BUILT or -BUILDED, -BUILDING, -BUILDS
REBURY	v -BURIED, -BURYING, -BURIES
REBUTTON	v -ED, -ING, -S
REBUY	v -BOUGHT, -BUYING, -BUYS
RECANE	v -CANED, -CANING, -CANES
RECARRY	v -RIED, -RYING, -RIES
RECAST	v -CAST, -CASTING, -CASTS
RECHANGE	v -CHANGED, -CHANGING, -CHANGES
RECHARGE	v -CHARGED, -CHARGING, -CHARGES
RECHART	v -ED, -ING, -S
RECHECK	v -ED, -ING, -S
RECHEW	v -ED, -ING, -S
RECHOOSE	v -CHOSE, -CHOSEN, -CHOOSING, -CHOOSES
RECIRCLE	v -CLED, -CLING, -CLES
RECLAD	a past tense of reclothe
RECLASP	v -ED, -ING, -S
RECLEAN	v -ED, -ING, -S
RECLOTHE	v -CLOTHED or -CLAD, -CLOTHING, -CLOTHES
RECOAL	v -ED, -ING, -S
RECOCK	v -ED, -ING, -S
RECODE	v -CODED, -CODING, -CODES
RECODIFY	v -FIED, -FYING, -FIES
RECOIN	v -ED, -ING, -S
RECOLOR	v -ED, -ING, -S
RECOMB	v -ED, -ING, -S
RECOMMIT	v -MITTED, -MITTING, -MITS
RECOOK	v -ED, -ING, -S
RECOPY	v -COPIED, -COPYING, -COPIES
RECORK	v -ED, -ING, -S
RECOUPLE	v -PLED, -PLING, -PLES
RECRATE	v -CRATED, -CRATING, -CRATES
RECROSS	v -ED, -ING, -ES
RECROWN	v -ED, -ING, -S
RECUT	v -CUT, -CUTTING, -CUTS
REDAMAGE	v -AGED, -AGING, -AGES
REDATE	v -DATED, -DATING, -DATES
REDECIDE	v -CIDED, -CIDING, -CIDES
REDEFEAT	v -ED, -ING, -S
REDEFECT	v -ED, -ING, -S
REDEFINE	v -FINED, -FINING, -FINES
REDEFY	v -FIED, -FYING, -FIES
REDEMAND	v -ED, -ING, -S
REDENY	v -NIED, -NYING, -NIES
REDEPLOY	v -ED, -ING, -S
REDESIGN	v -ED, -ING, -S
REDIAL	v -DIALED, -DIALING, -DIALS or -DIALLED, -DIALLING, -DIALS
REDID	past tense of redo
REDIGEST	v -ED, -ING, -S
REDIP	v -DIPPED or -DIPT, -DIPPING, -DIPS
REDIVIDE	v -VIDED, -VIDING, -VIDES
REDO	v -DID, -DONE, -DOING, -DOES
REDOCK	v -ED, -ING, -S
REDON	v -DONNED, -DONNING, -DONS
REDONE	past participle of redo
REDRAW	v -DREW, -DRAWN, -DRAWING, -DRAWS
REDREAM	v -DREAMED or -DREAMT, -DREAMING, -DREAMS
REDRIED	past tense of redry
REDRIES	present 3d person sing. of redry
REDRILL	v -ED, -ING, -S
REDRIVE	v -DROVE, -DRIVEN, -DRIVING, -DRIVES
REDRY	v -DRIED, -DRYING, -DRIES
REDUB	v -DUBBED, -DUBBING, -DUBS
REDYE	v -DYED, -DYEING, -DYES
REEARN	v -ED, -ING, -S
REECHO	v -ED, -ING, -ES
REEDIT	v -ED, -ING, -S
REEJECT	v -ED, -ING, -S
REELECT	v -ED, -ING, -S
REEMBARK	v -ED, -ING, -S
REEMBODY	v -BODIED, -BODYING, -BODIES
REEMERGE	v -EMERGED, -EMERGING, -EMERGES
REEMIT	v -EMITTED, -EMITTING, -EMITS
REEMPLOY	v -ED, -ING, -S
REENACT	v -ED, -ING, -S
REENDOW	v -ED, -ING, -S
REENGAGE	v -GAGED, -GAGING, -GAGES
REENJOY	v -ED, -ING, -S
REENLIST	v -ED, -ING, -S

REENROLL	*v* -ED, -ING, -S
REENTER	*v* -ED, -ING, -S
REEQUIP	*v* -EQUIPPED, -EQUIPPING, -EQUIPS
REERECT	*v* -ED, -ING, -S
REEVOKE	*v* -EVOKED, -EVOKING, -EVOKES
REEXPEL	*v* -PELLED, -PELLING, -PELS
REEXPORT	*v* -ED, -ING, -S
REEXPOSE	*v* -POSED, -POSING, -POSES
REFALL	*v* -FELL, -FALLEN, -FALLING, -FALLS
REFASTEN	*v* -ED, -ING, -S
REFEED	*v* -FED, -FEEDING, -FEEDS
REFEEL	*v* -FELT, -FEELING, -FEELS
REFELL	past tense of refall
REFENCE	*v* -FENCED, -FENCING, -FENCES
REFIGHT	*v* -FOUGHT, -FIGHTING, -FIGHTS
REFIGURE	*v* -URED, -URING, -URES
REFILE	*v* -FILED, -FILING, -FILES
REFILL	*v* -ED, -ING, -S
REFILM	*v* -ED, -ING, -S
REFILTER	*v* -ED, -ING, -S
REFIND	*v* -FOUND, -FINDING, -FINDS
REFIRE	*v* -FIRED, -FIRING, -FIRES
REFIX	*v* -ED, -ING, -ES
REFLEW	past tense of refly
REFLIES	present 3d person sing. of refly
REFLOAT	*v* -ED, -ING, -S
REFLOOD	*v* -ED, -ING, -S
REFLOW	*v* -ED, -ING, -S
REFLOWER	*v* -ED, -ING, -S
REFLY	*v* -FLEW, -FLOWN, -FLYING, -FLIES
REFOCUS	*v* -CUSED, -CUSING, -CUSES or -CUSSED, -CUSSING, -CUSSES
REFOLD	*v* -ED, -ING, -S
REFORGE	*v* -FORGED, -FORGING, -FORGES
REFORMAT	*v* -MATTED, -MATTING, -MATS
REFOUGHT	past tense of refight
REFOUND	*v* -ED, -ING, -S
REFRAME	*v* -FRAMED, -FRAMING, -FRAMES
REFREEZE	*v* -FROZE, -FROZEN, -FREEZING, -FREEZES
REFRONT	*v* -ED, -ING, -S
REFRY	*v* -FRIED, -FRYING, -FRIES
REFUEL	*v* -ELED, -ELING, -ELS or -ELLED, -ELLING, -ELS
REGAIN	*v* -ED, -ING, -S
REGATHER	*v* -ED, -ING, -S
REGAUGE	*v* -GAUGED, -GAUGING, -GAUGES
REGAVE	past tense of regive
REGEAR	*v* -ED, -ING, -S
REGILD	*v* -GILDED or -GILT, -GILDING, -GILDS
REGIVE	*v* -GAVE, -GIVEN, -GIVING, -GIVES
REGLAZE	*v* -GLAZED, -GLAZING, -GLAZES

REGLOSS	*v* -ED, -ING, -ES
REGLOW	*v* -ED, -ING, -S
REGLUE	*v* -GLUED, -GLUING, -GLUES
REGRADE	*v* -GRADED, -GRADING, -GRADES
REGRAFT	*v* -ED, -ING, -S
REGRANT	*v* -ED, -ING, -S
REGREEN	*v* -ED, -ING, -S
REGREW	past tense of regrow
REGRIND	*v* -GROUND, -GRINDING, -GRINDS
REGROOM	*v* -ED, -ING, -S
REGROOVE	*v* -GROOVED, -GROOVING, -GROOVES
REGROUND	past tense of regrind
REGROUP	*v* -ED, -ING, -S
REGROW	*v* -GREW, -GROWN, -GROWING, -GROWS
REHAMMER	*v* -ED, -ING, -S
REHANDLE	*v* -DLED, -DLING, -DLES
REHANG	*v* -HUNG or -HANGED, -HANGING, -HANGS
REHARDEN	*v* -ED, -ING, -S
REHASH	*v* -ED, -ING, -ES
REHEAR	*v* -HEARD, -HEARING, -HEARS
REHEAT	*v* -ED, -ING, -S
REHEEL	*v* -ED, -ING, -S
REHEM	*v* -HEMMED, -HEMMING, -HEMS
REHINGE	*v* -HINGED, -HINGING, -HINGES
REHIRE	*v* -HIRED, -HIRING, -HIRES
REHUNG	a past tense of rehang
REIGNITE	*v* -NITED, -NITING, -NITES
REIMAGE	*v* -AGED, -AGING, -AGES
REIMPORT	*v* -ED, -ING, -S
REIMPOSE	*v* -POSED, -POSING, -POSES
REINCITE	*v* -CITED, -CITING, -CITES
REINCUR	*v* -CURRED, -CURRING, -CURS
REINDEX	*v* -ED, -ING, -ES
REINDICT	*v* -ED, -ING, -S
REINDUCE	*v* -DUCED, -DUCING, -DUCES
REINDUCT	*v* -ED, -ING, -S
REINFECT	*v* -ED, -ING, -S
REINFORM	*v* -ED, -ING, -S
REINFUSE	*v* -FUSED, -FUSING, -FUSES
REINJECT	*v* -ED, -ING, -S
REINJURE	*v* -JURED, -JURING, -JURES
REINK	*v* -ED, -ING, -S
REINSERT	*v* -ED, -ING, -S
REINSURE	*v* -SURED, -SURING, -SURES
REINTER	*v* -TERRED, -TERRING, -TERS
REINVADE	*v* -VADED, -VADING, -VADES
REINVENT	*v* -ED, -ING, -S
REINVEST	*v* -ED, -ING, -S
REINVITE	*v* -VITED, -VITING, -VITES
REINVOKE	*v* -VOKED, -VOKING, -VOKES
REISSUE	*v* -SUED, -SUING, -SUES

REJACKET	v -ED, -ING, -S
REJOIN	v -ED, -ING, -S
REJUDGE	v -JUDGED, -JUDGING, -JUDGES
REJUGGLE	v -GLED, -GLING, -GLES
REKEY	v -ED, -ING, -S
REKINDLE	v -DLED, -DLING, -DLES
REKNIT	v -KNITTED, -KNITTING, -KNITS
RELABEL	v -BELED, -BELING, -BELS or -BELLED, -BELLING, -BELS
RELACE	v -LACED, -LACING, -LACES
RELAUNCH	v -ED, -ING, -ES
RELAY	v -LAID, -LAYING, -LAYS
RELEARN	v -LEARNED or -LEARNT, -LEARNING, -LEARNS
RELEND	v -LENT, -LENDING, -LENDS
RELET	v -LET, -LETTING, -LETS
RELETTER	v -ED, -ING, -S
RELIGHT	v -LIGHTED or -LIT, -LIGHTING, -LIGHTS
RELINE	v -LINED, -LINING, -LINES
RELINK	v -ED, -ING, -S
RELIST	v -ED, -ING, -S
RELIT	a past tense of relight
RELOAD	v -ED, -ING, -S
RELOAN	v -ED, -ING, -S
RELOCK	v -ED, -ING, -S
RELOOK	v -ED, -ING, -S
REMAIL	v -ED, -ING, -S
REMAKE	v -MADE, -MAKING, -MAKES
REMAP	v -MAPPED, -MAPPING, -MAPS
REMARKET	v -ED, -ING, -S
REMARRY	v -RIED, -RYING, -RIES
REMASTER	v -ED, -ING, -S
REMATCH	v -ED, -ING, -ES
REMATE	v -MATED, -MATING, -MATES
REMEET	v -MET, -MEETING, -MEETS
REMELT	v -ED, -ING, -S
REMEND	v -ED, -ING, -S
REMERGE	v -MERGED, -MERGING, -MERGES
REMET	past tense of remeet
REMIX	v -MIXED or -MIXT, -MIXING, -MIXES
REMODIFY	v -FIED, -FYING, -FIES
REMOLD	v -ED, -ING, -S
REMOUNT	v -ED, -ING, -S
RENAIL	v -ED, -ING, -S
RENAME	v -NAMED, -NAMING, -NAMES
RENEST	v -ED, -ING, -S
RENOTIFY	v -FIED, -FYING, -FIES
RENUMBER	v -ED, -ING, -S
REOBJECT	v -ED, -ING, -S
REOBTAIN	v -ED, -ING, -S
REOCCUPY	v -PIED, -PYING, -PIES
REOCCUR	v -CURRED, -CURRING, -CURS

REOIL	v -ED, -ING, -S
REOPEN	v -ED, -ING, -S
REOPPOSE	v -POSED, -POSING, -POSES
REORDAIN	v -ED, -ING, -S
REORDER	v -ED, -ING, -S
REORIENT	v -ED, -ING, -S
REOUTFIT	v -FITTED, -FITTING, -FITS
REPACIFY	v -FIED, -FYING, -FIES
REPACK	v -ED, -ING, -S
REPAINT	v -ED, -ING, -S
REPANEL	v -ELED, -ELING, -ELS or -ELLED, -ELLING, -ELS
REPAPER	v -ED, -ING, -S
REPARK	v -ED, -ING, -S
REPASS	v -ED, -ING, -ES
REPATCH	v -ED, -ING, -ES
REPAVE	v -PAVED, -PAVING, -PAVES
REPEG	v -PEGGED, -PEGGING, -PEGS
REPEOPLE	v -PLED, -PLING, -PLES
REPERK	v -ED, -ING, -S
REPHRASE	v -PHRASED, -PHRASING, -PHRASES
REPIN	v -PINNED, -PINNING, -PINS
REPLAN	v -PLANNED, -PLANNING, -PLANS
REPLANT	v -ED, -ING, -S
REPLATE	v -PLATED, -PLATING, -PLATES
REPLAY	v -ED, -ING, -S
REPLEAD	v -PLEADED or -PLED, -PLEADING, -PLEADS
REPLEDGE	v -PLEDGED, -PLEDGING, -PLEDGES
REPLOT	v -PLOTTED, -PLOTTING, -PLOTS
REPLUMB	v -ED, -ING, -S
REPLUNGE	v -PLUNGED, -PLUNGING, -PLUNGES
REPOLISH	v -ED, -ING, -ES
REPOLL	v -ED, -ING, -S
REPOT	v -POTTED, -POTTING, -POTS
REPOUR	v -ED, -ING, -S
REPOWER	v -ED, -ING, -S
REPRICE	v -PRICED, -PRICING, -PRICES
REPRINT	v -ED, -ING, -S
REPROBE	v -PROBED, -PROBING, -PROBES
REPUMP	v -ED, -ING, -S
REPURIFY	v -FIED, -FYING, -FIES
REPURSUE	v -SUED, -SUING, -SUES
RERACK	v -ED, -ING, -S
RERAISE	v -RAISED, -RAISING, -RAISES
REREAD	v -READ, -READING, -READS
RERECORD	v -ED, -ING, -S
REREMIND	v -ED, -ING, -S
REREPEAT	v -ED, -ING, -S
REREVIEW	v -ED, -ING, -S
RERIG	v -RIGGED, -RIGGING, -RIGS

RERISE	*v* -ROSE, -RISEN, -RISING, -RISES	**RESOLD**	past tense of resell
REROLL	*v* -ED, -ING, -S	**RESOLDER**	*v* -ED, -ING, -S
REROOF	*v* -ED, -ING, -S	**RESOLE**	*v* -SOLED, -SOLING, -SOLES
REROSE	past tense of rerise	**RESOUGHT**	past tense of reseek
REROUTE	*v* -ROUTED, -ROUTING, -ROUTES	**RESOW**	*v* -SOWED, -SOWN, -SOWING, -SOWS
RESADDLE	*v* -DLED, -DLING, -DLES		
RESAID	past tense of resay	**RESPACE**	*v* -SPACED, -SPACING, -SPACES
RESAIL	*v* -ED, -ING, -S	**RESPADE**	*v* -SPADED, -SPADING, -SPADES
RESALUTE	*v* -LUTED, -LUTING, -LUTES	**RESPEAK**	*v* -SPOKE, -SPOKEN, -SPEAKING, -SPEAKS
RESAMPLE	*v* -PLED, -PLING, -PLES		
RESAW	*v* -SAWED, -SAWN, -SAWING, -SAWS	**RESPELL**	*v* -SPELLED or -SPELT, -SPELLING, -SPELLS
RESAY	*v* -SAID, -SAYING, -SAYS	**RESPLICE**	*v* -SPLICED, -SPLICING, -SPLICES
RESCHOOL	*v* -ED, -ING, -S	**RESPLIT**	*v* -SPLIT, -SPLITTING, -SPLITS
RESCORE	*v* -SCORED, -SCORING, -SCORES	**RESPOKE**	past tense of respeak
RESCREEN	*v* -ED, -ING, -S	**RESPOKEN**	past participle of respeak
RESCULPT	*v* -ED, -ING, -S	**RESPOT**	*v* -SPOTTED, -SPOTTING, -SPOTS
RESEAL	*v* -ED, -ING, -S	**RESPRANG**	a past tense of respring
RESEASON	*v* -ED, -ING, -S	**RESPRAY**	*v* -ED, -ING, -S
RESEAT	*v* -ED, -ING, -S	**RESPREAD**	*v* -SPREAD, -SPREADING, -SPREADS
RESECURE	*v* -CURED, -CURING, -CURES		
RESEE	*v* -SAW, -SEEN, -SEEING, -SEES	**RESPRING**	*v* -SPRANG or -SPRUNG, -SPRINGING, -SPRINGS
RESEED	*v* -ED, -ING, -S		
RESEEK	*v* -SOUGHT, -SEEKING, -SEEKS	**RESPROUT**	*v* -ED, -ING, -S
RESEEN	past participle of resee	**RESTACK**	*v* -ED, -ING, -S
RESEIZE	*v* -SEIZED, -SEIZING, -SEIZES	**RESTAFF**	*v* -ED, -ING, -S
RESELL	*v* -SOLD, -SELLING, -SELLS	**RESTAGE**	*v* -STAGED, -STAGING, -STAGES
RESEND	*v* -SENT, -SENDING, -SENDS	**RESTAMP**	*v* -ED, -ING, -S
RESET	*v* -SET, -SETTING, -SETS	**RESTART**	*v* -ED, -ING, -S
RESETTLE	*v* -TLED, -TLING, -TLES	**RESTATE**	*v* -STATED, -STATING, -STATES
RESEW	*v* -SEWED, -SEWN, -SEWING, -SEWS	**RESTITCH**	*v* -ED, -ING, -ES
		RESTOCK	*v* -ED, -ING, -S
RESHAPE	*v* -SHAPED, -SHAPING, -SHAPES	**RESTOKE**	*v* -STOKED, -STOKING, -STOKES
RESHAVE	*v* -SHAVED, -SHAVEN, -SHAVING, -SHAVES	**RESTRESS**	*v* -ED, -ING, -ES
		RESTRIKE	*v* -STRUCK, -STRICKEN, -STRIKING, -STRIKES
RESHINE	*v* -SHONE or -SHINED, -SHINING, -SHINES		
		RESTRING	*v* -STRUNG, -STRINGING, -STRINGS
RESHIP	*v* -SHIPPED, -SHIPPING, -SHIPS		
RESHOE	*v* -SHOD, -SHOEING, -SHOES	**RESTRIVE**	*v* -STROVE, -STRIVEN, -STRIVING, -STRIVES
RESHONE	a past tense of reshine		
RESHOOT	*v* -SHOT, -SHOOTING, -SHOOTS	**RESTRUCK**	past tense of restrike
RESHOW	*v* -SHOWED, -SHOWN, -SHOWING, -SHOWS	**RESTRUNG**	past tense of restring
		RESTUDY	*v* -STUDIED, -STUDYING, -STUDIES
RESIFT	*v* -ED, -ING, -S	**RESTUFF**	*v* -ED, -ING, -S
RESIGHT	*v* -ED, -ING, -S	**RESTYLE**	*v* -STYLED, -STYLING, -STYLES
RESILVER	*v* -ED, -ING, -S	**RESUBMIT**	*v* -MITTED, -MITTING, -MITS
RESITE	*v* -SITED, -SITING, -SITES	**RESUMMON**	*v* -ED, -ING, -S
RESIZE	*v* -SIZED, -SIZING, -SIZES	**RESUPPLY**	*v* -PLIED, -PLYING, -PLIES
RESKETCH	*v* -ED, -ING, -ES	**RESURVEY**	*v* -ED, -ING, -S
RESLATE	*v* -SLATED, -SLATING, -SLATES	**RETACK**	*v* -ED, -ING, -S
RESMELT	*v* -ED, -ING, -S	**RETACKLE**	*v* -LED, -LING, -LES
RESMOOTH	*v* -ED, -ING, -S	**RETAG**	*v* -TAGGED, -TAGGING, -TAGS
RESOAK	*v* -ED, -ING, -S	**RETAILOR**	*v* -ED, -ING, -S
RESOD	*v* -SODDED, -SODDING, -SODS	**RETAPE**	*v* -TAPED, -TAPING, -TAPES
		RETARGET	*v* -ED, -ING, -S

RETASTE	*v* -TASTED, -TASTING, -TASTES
RETAX	*v* -ED, -ING, -ES
RETEACH	*v* -TAUGHT, -TEACHING, -TEACHES
RETEAM	*v* -ED, -ING, -S
RETEAR	*v* -TORE, -TORN, -TEARING, -TEARS
RETELL	*v* -TOLD, -TELLING, -TELLS
RETEMPER	*v* -ED, -ING, -S
RETEST	*v* -ED, -ING, -S
RETHINK	*v* -THOUGHT, -THINKING, -THINKS
RETHREAD	*v* -ED, -ING, -S
RETIE	*v* -TIED, -TYING, -TIES
RETILE	*v* -TILED, -TILING, -TILES
RETIME	*v* -TIMED, -TIMING, -TIMES
RETINT	*v* -ED, -ING, -S
RETITLE	*v* -TLED, -TLING, -TLES
RETOLD	past tense of retell
RETORE	past tense of retear
RETORN	past participle of retear
RETRACK	*v* -ED, -ING, -S
RETRAIN	*v* -ED, -ING, -S
RETRIM	*v* -TRIMMED, -TRIMMING, -TRIMS
RETRY	*v* -TRIED, -TRYING, -TRIES
RETUNE	*v* -TUNED, -TUNING, -TUNES
RETWIST	*v* -ED, -ING, -S
RETYING	present participle of retie
RETYPE	*v* -TYPED, -TYPING, -TYPES
REUNIFY	*v* -FIED, -FYING, -FIES
REUNITE	*v* -UNITED, -UNITING, -UNITES
REUSE	*v* -USED, -USING, -USES
REUTTER	*v* -ED, -ING, -S
REVALUE	*v* -UED, -UING, -UES
REVERIFY	*v* -FIED, -FYING, -FIES
REVEST	*v* -ED, -ING, -S
REVIEW	*v* -ED, -ING, -S
REVISIT	*v* -ED, -ING, -S
REVOICE	*v* -VOICED, -VOICING, -VOICES
REVOTE	*v* -VOTED, -VOTING, -VOTES
REWAKE	*v* -WAKED or -WOKE, -WOKEN, -WAKING, -WAKES
REWAKEN	*v* -ED, -ING, -S
REWAN	a past tense of rewin
REWARM	*v* -ED, -ING, -S
REWASH	*v* -ED, -ING, -ES
REWAX	*v* -ED, -ING, -ES
REWEAVE	*v* -WOVE or -WEAVED, -WOVEN, -WEAVING, -WEAVES
REWED	*v* -WEDDED, -WEDDING, -WEDS
REWEIGH	*v* -ED, -ING, -S
REWELD	*v* -ED, -ING, -S
REWET	*v* -WETTED, -WETTING, -WETS
REWIDEN	*v* -ED, -ING, -S
REWIN	*v* -WON or -WAN, -WINNING, -WINS

REWIND	*v* -WOUND or -WINDED, -WINDING, -WINDS
REWIRE	*v* -WIRED, -WIRING, -WIRES
REWOKE	a past tense of rewake
REWOKEN	past participle of rewake
REWON	a past tense of rewin
REWORK	*v* -WORKED or -WROUGHT, -WORKING, -WORKS
REWOUND	a past tense of rewind
REWOVE	a past tense of reweave
REWOVEN	past participle of reweave
REWRAP	*v* -WRAPPED, or -WRAPT, -WRAPPING, -WRAPS
REWRITE	*v* -WROTE, -WRITTEN, -WRITING, -WRITES
REWROUGHT	a past tense of rework
REZONE	*v* -ZONED, -ZONING, -ZONES

REACH	*v* -ED, -ING, -ES to stretch out or put forth
REACHER	*n* pl. -S one that reaches
REACT	*v* -ED, -ING, -S to respond to a stimulus
REACTANT	*n* pl. -S one that reacts
REACTION	*n* pl. -S the act of reacting
REACTIVE	*adj* tending to react
REACTOR	*n* pl. -S one that reacts
READ	*v* READ, READING, READS to look at so as to take in the meaning of, as something written or printed **READABLE** *adj* **READABLY** *adv*
READER	*n* pl. -S one that reads
READERLY	*adj* typical of a reader
READIED	past tense of ready
READIER	comparative of ready
READIES	present 3d person sing. of ready
READIEST	superlative of ready
READILY	*adv* in a ready manner
READING	*n* pl. -S material that is read
READOUT	*n* pl. -S a presentation of computer data
READY	*adj* READIER, READIEST prepared
READY	*v* READIED, READYING, READIES to make ready
REAGENT	*n* pl. -S a substance used in a chemical reaction to ascertain the nature or composition of another

REAGIN	n pl. -S a type of antibody **REAGINIC** adj	**REB**	n pl. -S a Confederate soldier
REAL	adj REALER, REALEST having actual existence	**REBAR**	n pl. -S a steel rod for use in reinforced concrete
REAL	n pl. -S or -ES a former monetary unit of Spain	**REBATE**	v -BATED, -BATING, -BATES to deduct or return from a payment or bill
REAL	n pl. REIS a former monetary unit of Portugal and Brazil	**REBATER**	n pl. -S one that rebates
		REBATO	n pl. -TOS rabato
REALGAR	n pl. -S a mineral	**REBBE**	n pl. -S a rabbi
REALIA	n/pl objects used by a teacher to illustrate everyday living	**REBEC**	n pl. -S an ancient stringed instrument
REALISE	v -ISED, -ISING, -ISES to realize	**REBECK**	n pl. -S rebec
REALISER	n pl. -S one that realises	**REBEL**	v -BELLED, -BELLING, -BELS to oppose the established government of one's land
REALISM	n pl. -S concern with fact or reality		
REALIST	n pl. -S one who is concerned with fact or reality	**REBELDOM**	n pl. -S an area controlled by rebels
REALITY	n pl. -TIES something that is real	**REBIRTH**	n pl. -S a new or second birth
REALIZE	v -IZED, -IZING, -IZES to understand completely	**REBOANT**	adj resounding loudly
		REBOP	n pl. -S a type of music
REALIZER	n pl. -S one that realizes	**REBORN**	adj born again
REALLY	adv actually	**REBOUND**	v -ED, -ING, -S to spring back
REALM	n pl. -S a kingdom	**REBOZO**	n pl. -ZOS a long scarf
REALNESS	n pl. -ES the state of being real	**REBRANCH**	v -ED, -ING, -ES to form secondary branches
REALTY	n pl. -TIES property in buildings and land	**REBUFF**	v -ED, -ING, -S to reject or refuse curtly
REAM	v -ED, -ING, -S to enlarge with a reamer		
REAMER	n pl. -S a tool used to enlarge holes	**REBUKE**	v -BUKED, -BUKING, -BUKES to criticize sharply
REAP	v -ED, -ING, -S to cut for harvest **REAPABLE** adj	**REBUKER**	n pl. -S one that rebukes
		REBURIAL	n pl. -S a second burial
REAPER	n pl. -S one that reaps	**REBUS**	n pl. -ES a type of puzzle
REAPHOOK	n pl. -S an implement used in reaping	**REBUT**	v -BUTTED, -BUTTING, -BUTS to refute
REAR	v -ED, -ING, -S to lift upright	**REBUTTAL**	n pl. -S argument or proof that rebuts
REARER	n pl. -S one that rears		
REARMICE	n/pl reremice	**REBUTTER**	n pl. -S one that rebuts
REARMOST	adj coming or situated last	**REBUTTING**	present participle of rebut
REARWARD	n pl. -S the rearmost division of an army	**REC**	n pl. -S recreation
		RECALL	v -ED, -ING, -S to call back
REASCENT	n pl. -S a new or second ascent	**RECALLER**	n pl. -S one that recalls
REASON	v -ED, -ING, -S to derive inferences or conclusions from known or presumed facts	**RECAMIER**	n pl. -S a backless couch
		RECANT	v -ED, -ING, -S to make a formal retraction or disavowal of
REASONER	n pl. -S one that reasons	**RECANTER**	n pl. -S one that recants
REATA	n pl. -S riata	**RECAP**	v -CAPPED, -CAPPING, -CAPS to review by a brief summary
REAVE	v REAVED or REFT, REAVING, REAVES to plunder		
REAVER	n pl. -S one that reaves	**RECCE**	n pl. -S a recon

RECEDE   *v* -CEDED, -CEDING, -CEDES to move back or away

RECEIPT   *v* -ED, -ING, -S to mark as having been paid

RECEIVE   *v* -CEIVED, -CEIVING, -CEIVES to come into possession of

RECEIVER   *n* pl. -S one that receives

RECENCY   *n* pl. -CIES the state of being recent

RECENT   *adj* -CENTER, -CENTEST of or pertaining to a time not long past **RECENTLY** *adv*

RECEPT   *n* pl. -S a type of mental image

RECEPTOR   *n* pl. -S a nerve ending specialized to receive stimuli

RECESS   *v* -ED, -ING, -ES to place in a receding space or hollow

RECHEAT   *n* pl. -S a hunting call

RECIPE   *n* pl. -S a set of instructions for making something

RECISION   *n* pl. -S a cancellation

RECITAL   *n* pl. -S a detailed account

RECITE   *v* -CITED, -CITING, -CITES to declaim or say from memory

RECITER   *n* pl. -S one that recites

RECK   *v* -ED, -ING, -S to be concerned about

RECKLESS   *adj* foolishly heedless of danger

RECKON   *v* -ED, -ING, -S to count or compute

RECKONER   *n* pl. -S one that reckons

RECLAIM   *v* -ED, -ING, -S to make suitable for cultivation or habitation

RECLAME   *n* pl. -S publicity

RECLINE   *v* -CLINED, -CLINING, -CLINES to lean or lie back

RECLINER   *n* pl. -S one that reclines

RECLUSE   *n* pl. -S one who lives in solitude and seclusion

RECOIL   *v* -ED, -ING, -S to draw back in fear or disgust

RECOILER   *n* pl. -S one that recoils

RECON   *n* pl. -S a preliminary survey

RECONVEY   *v* -ED, -ING, -S to convey back to a previous position

RECORD   *v* -ED, -ING, -S to set down for preservation

RECORDER   *n* pl. -S one that records

RECOUNT   *v* -ED, -ING, -S to relate in detail

RECOUP   *v* -ED, -ING, -S to get back the equivalent of

RECOUPE   *adj* divided twice

RECOURSE   *n* pl. -S a turning or applying to someone or something for aid

RECOVER   *v* -ED, -ING, -S to obtain again after losing

RECOVERY   *n* pl. -ERIES an economic upturn

RECREANT   *n* pl. -S a coward

RECREATE   *v* -ATED, -ATING, -ATES to refresh mentally or physically

RECRUIT   *v* -ED, -ING, -S to engage for military service

RECTA   a pl. of rectum

RECTAL   *adj* pertaining to the rectum **RECTALLY** *adv*

RECTI   pl. of rectus

RECTIFY   *v* -FIED, -FYING, -FIES to correct

RECTO   *n* pl. -TOS a right-hand page of a book

RECTOR   *n* pl. -S a clergyman in charge of a parish

RECTORY   *n* pl. -RIES a rector's dwelling

RECTRIX   *n* pl. -TRICES a feather of a bird's tail

RECTUM   *n* pl. -TUMS or -TA the terminal portion of the large intestine

RECTUS   *n* pl. -TI a straight muscle

RECUR   *v* -CURRED, -CURRING, -CURS to happen again

RECURVE   *v* -CURVED, -CURVING, -CURVES to curve backward or downward

RECUSAL   *n* pl. -S the act of recusing

RECUSANT   *n* pl. -S one who refuses to accept established authority

RECUSE   *v* -CUSED, -CUSING, -CUSES to disqualify or challenge as judge in a particular case

RECYCLE   *v* -CLED, -CLING, -CLES to process in order to extract useful materials

RECYCLER   *n* pl. -S one that recycles

RED   *adj* REDDER, REDDEST of the color of blood

RED   *v* REDDED, REDDING, REDS to redd

REDACT   *v* -ED, -ING, -S to prepare for publication

REDACTOR   *n* pl. -S one that redacts

REDAN	*n* -pl. -S A type of fortification	**REDOLENT**	*adj* fragrant
REDARGUE	*v* -GUED, -GUING, -GUES to disprove	**REDOUBLE**	*v* -BLED, -BLING, -BLES to double
REDBAIT	*v* -ED, -ING, -S to denounce as Communist	**REDOUBT**	*n* pl. -S an enclosed fortification
REDBAY	*n* pl. -BAYS a small tree	**REDOUND**	*v* -ED, -ING, -S to have an effect
REDBIRD	*n* pl. -S a bird with red plumage	**REDOUT**	*n* pl. -S a condition in which blood is driven to the head
REDBONE	*n* pl. -S a hunting dog	**REDOWA**	*n* pl. -S a lively dance
REDBRICK	*n* pl. -S a modern British university	**REDOX**	*n* pl. -ES a type of chemical reaction
REDBUD	*n* pl. -S a small tree	**REDPOLL**	*n* pl. -S a small finch
REDBUG	*n* pl. -S a chigger	**REDRAFT**	*v* -ED, -ING, -S to make a revised copy of
REDCAP	*n* pl. -S a porter		
REDCOAT	*n* pl. -S a British soldier during the American Revolution	**REDRAWER**	*n* pl. -S one that redraws
		REDRESS	*v* -ED, -ING, -ES to set right
REDD	*v* -ED, -ING, -S to put in order	**REDROOT**	*n* pl. -S a perennial herb
REDDED	past tense of red and redd	**REDSHANK**	*n* pl. -S a shore bird
REDDEN	*v* -ED, -ING, -S to make or become red	**REDSHIFT**	*n* pl. -S a displacement of the spectrum of a celestial body toward the longer wavelengths
REDDER	*n* pl. -S one that redds		
REDDEST	superlative of red	**REDSHIRT**	*v* -ED, -ING, -S to keep a college athlete out of varsity play in order to extend his eligibility
REDDING	present participle of red and redd		
REDDISH	*adj* somewhat red	**REDSTART**	*n* pl. -S a small songbird
REDDLE	*v* -DLED, -DLING, -DLES to ruddle	**REDTAIL**	*n* pl. -S a type of hawk
		REDTOP	*n* pl. -S a type of grass
REDE	*v* REDED, REDING, REDES to advise	**REDUCE**	*v* -DUCED, -DUCING, -DUCES to diminish
REDEAR	*n* pl. -S a common sunfish	**REDUCER**	*n* pl. -S one that reduces
REDEEM	*v* -ED, -ING, -S to buy back	**REDUCTOR**	*n* pl. -S an apparatus for the reduction of metallic ions in solution
REDEEMER	*n* pl. -S one that redeems		
REDEYE	*n* pl. -S a railroad danger signal		
REDFIN	*n* pl. -S a freshwater fish	**REDUVIID**	*n* pl. -S a bloodsucking insect
REDFISH	*n* pl. -ES an edible rockfish	**REDUX**	*adj* brought back
REDHEAD	*n* pl. -S a person with red hair	**REDWARE**	*n* pl. -S an edible seaweed
REDHORSE	*n* pl. -S a freshwater fish	**REDWING**	*n* pl. -S a European thrush
REDIA	*n* pl. -DIAE or -DIAS the larva of certain flatworms **REDIAL** *adj*	**REDWOOD**	*n* pl. -S a very tall evergreen tree
		REE	*n* pl. -S the female Eurasian sandpiper
REDING	present participle of rede	**REECHY**	*adj* REECHIER, REECHIEST foul, rancid
REDIRECT	*v* -ED, -ING, -S to change the course or direction of		
REDLEG	*n* pl. -S a bird with red legs	**REED**	*v* -ED, -ING, -S to fasten with reeds (the stalks of tall grasses)
REDLINE	*v* -LINED, -LINING, -LINES to withhold loans or insurance from certain neighborhoods		
		REEDBIRD	*n* pl. -S the bobolink
		REEDBUCK	*n* pl. -S an African antelope
REDLY	*adv* with red color	**REEDIER**	comparative of reedy
REDNESS	*n* pl. -ES the state of being red	**REEDIEST**	superlative of reedy
REDO	*n* pl. -DOS something that is done again	**REEDIFY**	*v* -FIED, -FYING, -FIES to rebuild

REEDILY   *adv* with a thin, piping sound

REEDING   *n* pl. -S a convex molding

REEDLIKE   *adj* resembling a reed

REEDLING   *n* pl. -S a marsh bird

REEDMAN   *n* pl. -MEN one who plays a reed instrument

REEDY   *adj* REEDIER, REEDIEST abounding in reeds

REEF   *v* -ED, -ING, -S to reduce the area of a sail **REEFABLE** *adj*

REEFER   *n* pl. -S one that reefs

REEFY   *adj* REEFIER, REEFIEST abounding in ridges of rock

REEK   *v* -ED, -ING, -S to give off a strong, unpleasant odor

REEKER   *n* pl. -S one that reeks

REEKY   *adj* REEKIER, REEKIEST reeking

REEL   *v* -ED, -ING, -S to wind on a type of rotary device **REELABLE** *adj*

REELER   *n* pl. -S one that reels

REENTRY   *n* pl. -TRIES a new or second entry

REEST   *v* -ED, -ING, -S to balk

REEVE   *v* REEVED or ROVE, ROVEN, REEVING, REEVES to fasten by passing through or around something

REF   *v* REFFED, REFFING, REFS to referee

REFACE   *v* -FACED, -FACING, -FACES to repair the outer surface of

REFECT   *v* -ED, -ING, -S to refresh with food and drink

REFEL   *v* -FELLED, -FELLING, -FELS to reject

REFER   *v* -FERRED, -FERRING, -FERS to direct to a source for help or information

REFEREE   *v* -EED, -EEING, -EES to supervise the play in certain sports

REFERENT   *n* pl. -S something referred to

REFERRAL   *n* pl. -S one that is referred

REFERRED   past tense of refer

REFERRER   *n* pl. -S one that refers

REFERRING   present participle of refer

REFFED   past tense of ref

REFFING   present participle of ref

REFINE   *v* -FINED, -FINING, -FINES to free from impurities

REFINER   *n* pl. -S one that refines

REFINERY   *n* pl. -ERIES a place where crude material is refined

REFINING   present participle of refine

REFINISH   *v* -ED, -ING, -ES to give a new surface to

REFIT   *v* -FITTED, -FITTING, -FITS to prepare and equip for additional use

REFLATE   *v* -FLATED, -FLATING, -FLATES to inflate again

REFLECT   *v* -ED, -ING, -S to turn or throw back from a surface

REFLET   *n* pl. -S special brilliance of surface

REFLEX   *v* -ED, -ING, -ES to bend back

REFLEXLY   *adv* in a reflexed manner

REFLUENT   *adj* flowing back

REFLUX   *v* -ED, -ING, -ES to cause to flow back

REFOREST   *v* -ED, -ING, -S to replant with trees

REFORM   *v* -ED, -ING, -S to change to a better state

REFORMER   *n* pl. -S one that reforms

REFRACT   *v* -ED, -ING, -S to deflect in a particular manner, as a ray of light

REFRAIN   *v* -ED, -ING, -S to keep oneself back

REFRESH   *v* -ED, -ING, -ES to restore the well-being and vigor of

REFT   a past tense of reave

REFUGE   *v* -UGED, -UGING, -UGES to give or take shelter

REFUGEE   *n* pl. -S one who flees for safety

REFUGIUM   *n* pl. -GIA a stable area during a period of continental climactic change

REFUND   *v* -ED, -ING, -S to give back

REFUNDER   *n* pl. -S one that refunds

REFUSAL   *n* pl. -S the act of refusing

REFUSE   *v* -FUSED, -FUSING, -FUSES to express oneself as unwilling to accept, do, or comply with

REFUSER   *n* pl. -S one that refuses

REFUSNIK   *n* pl. -S a Soviet citizen who is refused permission to emigrate

REFUTAL   *n* pl. -S the act of refuting

REFUTE   *v* -FUTED, -FUTING, -FUTES to prove to be false or erroneous

REFUTER   *n* pl. -S one that refutes

REG   *n* pl. -S a regulation

REGAINER   *n* pl. -S one that regains

REGAL   *adj* of or befitting a king

REGALE   *v* -GALED, -GALING, -GALES to delight

REGALER   *n* pl. -S one that regales

REGALIA   *n/pl* the rights and privileges of a king

REGALITY   *n* pl. -TIES regal authority

REGALLY   *adv* in a regal manner

REGARD   *v* -ED, -ING, -S to look upon with a particular feeling

REGATTA   *n* pl. -S a boat race

REGELATE   *v* -LATED, -LATING, -LATES to refreeze ice by reducing the pressure

REGENCY   *n* pl. -CIES the office of a regent

REGENT   *n* pl. -S one who rules in the place of a sovereign **REGENTAL** *adj*

REGES   pl. of rex

REGGAE   *n* pl. -S a form of popular Jamaican music

REGICIDE   *n* pl. -S the killing of a king

REGIME   *n* pl. -S a system of government

REGIMEN   *n* pl. -S a systematic plan

REGIMENT   *v* -ED, -ING, -S to form into military units

REGINA   *n* pl. -NAE or -NAS queen **REGINAL** *adj*

REGION   *n* pl. -S an administrative area or division

REGIONAL   *n* pl. -S something that serves as a region

REGISTER   *v* -ED, -ING, -S to record officially

REGISTRY   *n* pl. -TRIES the act of registering

REGIUS   *adj* holding a professorship founded by the sovereign

REGLET   *n* pl. -S a flat, narrow molding

REGMA   *n* pl. -MATA a type of fruit

REGNA   pl. of regnum

REGNAL   *adj* pertaining to a king or his reign

REGNANCY   *n* pl. -CIES the state of being regnant

REGNANT   *adj* reigning

REGNUM   *n* pl. -NA dominion

REGOLITH   *n* pl. -S a layer of loose rock

REGORGE   *v* -GORGED, -GORGING, -GORGES to vomit

REGOSOL   *n* pl. -S a type of soil

REGRATE   *v* -GRATED, -GRATING, -GRATES to buy up in order to sell for a higher price in the same area

REGREET   *v* -ED, -ING, -S to greet in return

REGRESS   *v* -ED, -ING, -ES to go back

REGRET   *v* -GRETTED, -GRETTING, -GRETS to look back upon with sorrow or remorse

REGROWTH   *n* pl. -S a new or second growth

REGULAR   *n* pl. -S an habitual customer

REGULATE   *v* -LATED, -LATING, -LATES to control according to rule

REGULUS   *n* pl. -LI or -LUSES a mass that forms beneath the slag in a furnace **REGULINE** *adj*

REHAB   *v* -HABBED, -HABBING, -HABS to restore to a good condition

REHABBER   *n* pl. -S one that rehabs

REHEARSE   *v* -HEARSED, -HEARSING, -HEARSES to practice in preparation for a public appearance

REHEATER   *n* pl. -S one that reheats

REHOBOAM   *n* pl. -S a wine bottle

REHOUSE   *v* -HOUSED, -HOUSING, -HOUSES to establish in a new housing unit

REI   *n* pl. -S an erroneous English form for a former Portuguese coin

REIF   *n* pl. -S robbery

REIFIER   *n* pl. -S one that reifies

REIFY   *v* -IFIED, -IFYING, -IFIES to regard as real or concrete

REIGN   *v* -ED, -ING, -S to exercise sovereign power

REIN   *v* -ED, -ING, -S to restrain

REINDEER   *n* pl. -S a large deer

REINJURY   *n* pl. -RIES a second injury

REINLESS   *adj* unrestrained

REINSMAN   *n* pl. -MEN a skilled rider of horses

REIS   pl. of real

REISSUER   *n* pl. -S one that reissues

REITBOK   *n* pl. -S the reedbuck

REIVE   *v* REIVED, REIVING, REIVES to plunder

REIVER	*n* pl. -S one that reives
REJECT	*v* -ED, -ING, -S to refuse to accept, consider, or make use of
REJECTEE	*n* pl. -S one that is rejected
REJECTER	*n* pl. -S one that rejects
REJECTOR	*n* pl. -S rejecter
REJIGGER	*v* -ED, -ING, -S to alter
REJOICE	*v* -JOICED, -JOICING, -JOICES to feel joyful
REJOICER	*n* pl. -S one that rejoices
RELAPSE	*v* -LAPSED, -LAPSING, -LAPSES to fall or slip back into a former state
RELAPSER	*n* pl. -S one that relapses
RELATE	*v* -LATED, -LATING, -LATES to give an account of
RELATER	*n* pl. -S one that relates
RELATION	*n* pl. -S a significant association between two or more things
RELATIVE	*n* pl. -S one who is connected with another by blood or marriage
RELATOR	*n* pl. -S relater
RELAX	*v* -ED, -ING, -ES to make less tense or rigid
RELAXANT	*n* pl. -S a drug that relieves muscular tension
RELAXER	*n* pl. -S one that relaxes
RELAXIN	*n* pl. -S a female hormone
RELAY	*v* -ED, -ING, -S to send along by using fresh sets to replace tired ones
RELEASE	*v* -LEASED, -LEASING, -LEASES to set free
RELEASER	*n* pl. -S one that releases
RELEGATE	*v* -GATED, -GATING, -GATES to assign
RELENT	*v* -ED, -ING, -S to become less severe
RELEVANT	*adj* pertaining to the matter at hand
RELEVE	*n* pl. -S a raising onto the toe in ballet
RELIABLE	*n* pl. -S one that can be relied on
RELIABLY	*adv* in a manner that can be relied on
RELIANCE	*n* pl. -S confident or trustful dependence
RELIANT	*adj* showing reliance
RELIC	*n* pl. -S a surviving memorial of something past
RELICT	*n* pl. -S an organism surviving in a changed environment
RELIED	past tense of rely
RELIEF	*n* pl. -S aid in the form of money or necessities
RELIER	*n* pl. -S one that relies
RELIES	present 3d person sing. of rely
RELIEVE	*v* -LIEVED, -LIEVING, -LIEVES to lessen or free from pain or discomfort
RELIEVER	*n* pl. -S one that relieves
RELIEVO	*n* pl. -VOS the projection of figures or forms from a flat background
RELIGION	*n* pl. -S the worship of a god or the supernatural
RELIQUE	*n* pl. -S relic
RELISH	*v* -ED, -ING, -ES to enjoy
RELIVE	*v* -LIVED, -LIVING, -LIVES to experience again
RELOADER	*n* pl. -S one that reloads
RELOCATE	*v* -CATED, -CATING, -CATES to establish in a new place
RELUCENT	*adj* reflecting light
RELUCT	*v* -ED, -ING, -S to show opposition
RELUME	*v* -LUMED, -LUMING, -LUMES to light again
RELUMINE	*v* -MINED, -MINING, -MINES to relume
RELY	*v* -LIED, -LYING, -LIES to place trust or confidence
REM	*n* pl. -S a quantity of ionizing radiation
REMAIN	*v* -ED, -ING, -S to continue in the same state
REMAKER	*n* pl. -S one that remakes
REMAN	*v* -MANNED, -MANNING, -MANS to furnish with a fresh supply of men
REMAND	*v* -ED, -ING, -S to send back
REMANENT	*adj* remaining
REMANNED	past tense of reman
REMANNING	present participle of reman
REMARK	*v* -ED, -ING, -S to say or write briefly or casually
REMARKER	*n* pl. -S one that remarks
REMARQUE	*n* pl. -S a mark made in the margin of an engraved plate
REMEDIAL	*adj* intended to correct something

REMEDY	v -DIED, -DYING, -DIES to relieve or cure
REMEMBER	v -ED, -ING, -S to bring to mind again
REMEX	n pl. REMIGES a flight feather of a bird's wing **REMIGIAL** adj
REMIND	v -ED, -ING, -S to cause to remember
REMINDER	n pl. -S one that reminds
REMINT	v -ED, -ING, -S to melt down and make into new coin
REMISE	v -MISED, -MISING, -MISES to give up a claim to
REMISS	adj careless **REMISSLY** adv
REMIT	v -MITTED, -MITTING, -MITS to send money in payment
REMITTAL	n pl. -S the act of remitting
REMITTER	n pl. -S one that remits
REMITTING	present participle of remit
REMITTOR	n pl. -S remitter
REMNANT	n pl. -S something remaining
REMODEL	v -ELED, -ELING, -ELS or -ELLED, -ELLING, -ELS to make over
REMOLADE	n pl. -S a piquant sauce
REMORA	n pl. -S a type of marine fish **REMORID** adj
REMORSE	n pl. -S deep anguish caused by a sense of guilt
REMOTE	adj -MOTER, -MOTEST situated far away **REMOTELY** adv
REMOTE	n pl. -S a broadcast originating outside a studio
REMOTION	n pl. -S the act of removing
REMOVAL	n pl. -S the act of removing
REMOVE	v -MOVED, -MOVING, -MOVES to take or move away
REMOVER	n pl. -S one that removes
REMUDA	n pl. -S a herd of horses
RENAL	adj pertaining to the kidneys
RENATURE	v -TURED, -TURING, -TURES to restore natural qualities
REND	v RENT or RENDED, RENDING, RENDS to tear apart forcibly
RENDER	v -ED, -ING, -S to cause to be or become
RENDERER	n pl. -S one that renders
RENDIBLE	adj capable of being rent
RENDZINA	n pl. -S a type of soil
RENEGADE	v -GADED, -GADING, -GADES to become a traitor
RENEGADO	n pl. -DOS or -DOES a traitor
RENEGE	v -NEGED, -NEGING, -NEGES to fail to carry out a promise or commitment
RENEGER	n pl. -S one that reneges
RENEW	v -ED, -ING, -S to make new or as if new again
RENEWAL	n pl. -S the act of renewing
RENEWER	n pl. -S one that renews
RENIFORM	adj kidney-shaped
RENIG	v -NIGGED, -NIGGING, -NIGS to renege
RENIN	n pl. -S an enzyme
RENITENT	adj resisting physical pressure
RENMINBI	n pl. RENMINBI currency in the People's Republic of China
RENNASE	n pl. -S rennin
RENNET	n pl. -S a lining membrane in the stomach of certain young animals
RENNIN	n pl. -S an enzyme
RENOGRAM	n pl. -S a photographic depiction of the course of renal excretion
RENOUNCE	v -NOUNCED, -NOUNCING, -NOUNCES to disown
RENOVATE	v -VATED, -VATING, -VATES to make like new
RENOWN	v -ED, -ING, -S to make famous
RENT	v -ED, -ING, -S to obtain temporary use of in return for compensation **RENTABLE** adj
RENTAL	n pl. -S an amount paid or collected as rent
RENTE	n pl. -S annual income under French law
RENTER	n pl. -S one that rents
RENTIER	n pl. -S one that receives a fixed income
RENVOI	n pl. -S the expulsion by a government of an alien
REOFFER	v -ED, -ING, -S to offer for public sale
REOVIRUS	n pl. -ES a type of virus
REP	n pl. -S a cross-ribbed fabric
REPAID	past tense of repay
REPAIR	v -ED, -ING, -S to restore to good condition
REPAIRER	n pl. -S one that repairs

REPAND   adj having a wavy margin
REPANDLY adv

REPARTEE   n pl. -S a quick, witty reply

REPAST   v -ED, -ING, -S to eat or feast

REPAY   v -PAID, -PAYING, -PAYS to pay back

REPEAL   v -ED, -ING, -S to revoke

REPEALER   n pl. -S one that repeals

REPEAT   v -ED, -ING, -S to say or do again

REPEATER   n pl. -S one that repeats

REPEL   v -PELLED, -PELLING, -PELS to drive back

REPELLER   n pl. -S one that repels

REPENT   v -ED, -ING, -S to feel remorse or self-reproach for a past action

REPENTER   n pl. -S one that repents

REPETEND   n pl. -S a phrase or sound that is repeated

REPINE   v -PINED, -PINING, -PINES to express discontent

REPINER   n pl. -S one that repines

REPLACE   v -PLACED, -PLACING, -PLACES to take the place of

REPLACER   n pl. -S one that replaces

REPLETE   adj abundantly supplied

REPLEVIN   v -ED, -ING, -S to replevy

REPLEVY   v -PLEVIED, -PLEVYING, -PLEVIES to regain possession of by legal action

REPLICA   n pl. -S a close copy or reproduction

REPLICON   n pl. -S a section of nucleic acid that replicates as a unit

REPLIER   n pl. -S one that replies

REPLY   v -PLIED, -PLYING, -PLIES to answer

REPO   n pl. -POS something repossessed

REPORT   v -ED, -ING, -S to give an account of

REPORTER   n pl. -S one that reports

REPOSAL   n pl. -S the act of reposing

REPOSE   v -POSED, -POSING, -POSES to lie at rest

REPOSER   n pl. -S one that reposes

REPOSIT   v -ED, -ING, -S to put away

REPOUSSE   n pl. -S a raised design hammered in metal

REPP   n pl. -S rep

REPPED   adj resembling rep

REPRESS   v -ED, -ING, -ES to keep under control

REPRIEVE   v -PRIEVED, -PRIEVING, -PRIEVES to postpone the punishment of

REPRISAL   n pl. -S an act of retaliation

REPRISE   v -PRISED, -PRISING, -PRISES to take back by force

REPRO   n pl. -PROS a trial sheet of printed material suitable for photographic reproduction

REPROACH   v -ED, -ING, -ES to find fault with

REPROOF   n pl. -S criticism for a fault

REPROVAL   n pl. -S reproof

REPROVE   v -PROVED, -PROVING, -PROVES to rebuke

REPROVER   n pl. -S one that reproves

REPTANT   adj creeping or crawling

REPTILE   n pl. -S any of a class of cold-blooded, air-breathing vertebrates

REPUBLIC   n pl. -S a constitutional form of government

REPUGN   v -ED, -ING, -S to oppose

REPULSE   v -PULSED, -PULSING, -PULSES to drive back

REPULSER   n pl. -S one that repulses

REPUTE   v -PUTED, -PUTING, -PUTES to consider to be as specified

REQUEST   v -ED, -ING, -S to express a desire for

REQUIEM   n pl. -S a musical composition for the dead

REQUIN   n pl. -S a voracious shark

REQUIRE   v -QUIRED, -QUIRING, -QUIRES to have need of

REQUIRER   n pl. -S one that requires

REQUITAL   n pl. -S something given in return, compensation, or retaliation

REQUITE   v -QUITED, -QUITING, -QUITES to make equivalent return for

REQUITER   n pl. -S one that requites

RERAN   past tense of rerun

REREDOS   n pl. -ES an ornamental screen behind an altar

REREMICE   n/pl bats (flying mammals)

REREWARD   n pl. -S rearward

REROLLER   n pl. -S one that rerolls

RERUN   *v* -RAN, -RUNNING, -RUNS to present a repetition of a recorded performance

RES   *n* pl. RES a particular thing or matter

RESALE   *n* pl. -S the act of selling again

RESCALE   *v* -SCALED, -SCALING, -SCALES to plan on a new scale

RESCIND   *v* -ED, -ING, -S to annul

RESCRIPT   *n* pl. -S something rewritten

RESCUE   *v* -CUED, -CUING, -CUES to free from danger

RESCUER   *n* pl. -S one that rescues

RESEARCH   *v* -ED, -ING, -ES to investigate thoroughly

RESEAU   *n* pl. -SEAUS or -SEAUX a filter screen for making color films

RESECT   *v* -ED, -ING, -S to excise part of an organ or structure surgically

RESEDA   *n* pl. -S a flowering plant

RESELLER   *n* pl. -S one that resells

RESEMBLE   *v* -BLED, -BLING, -BLES to be similar to

RESENT   *v* -ED, -ING, -S to feel or express annoyance or ill will at

RESERVE   *v* -SERVED, -SERVING, -SERVES to keep back for future use

RESERVER   *n* pl. -S one that reserves

RESETTER   *n* pl. -S one that resets

RESH   *n* pl. -ES a Hebrew letter

RESHAPER   *n* pl. -S one that reshapes something

RESID   *n* pl. -S a type of fuel oil

RESIDE   *v* -SIDED, -SIDING, -SIDES to dwell permanently or continuously

RESIDENT   *n* pl. -S one who resides

RESIDER   *n* pl. -S a resident

RESIDUA   a pl. of residuum

RESIDUAL   *n* pl. -S something left over

RESIDUE   *n* pl. -S something remaining after the removal of a part

RESIDUUM   *n* pl. -SIDUA or -SIDUUMS residue

RESIGN   *v* -ED, -ING, -S to give up one's office or position

RESIGNER   *n* pl. -S one that resigns

RESILE   *v* -SILED, -SILING, -SILES to spring back

RESIN   *v* -ED, -ING, -S to treat with resin (a viscous substance obtained from certain plants)

RESINATE   *v* -ATED, -ATING, -ATES to resin

RESINIFY   *v* -FIED, -FYING, -FIES to convert into resin

RESINOID   *n* pl. -S a resinous substance

RESINOUS   *adj* resembling resin

RESINY   *adj* resinous

RESIST   *v* -ED, -ING, -S to strive against

RESISTER   *n* pl. -S one that resists

RESISTOR   *n* pl. -S a device in an electric circuit

RESOJET   *n* pl. -S a pulsejet

RESOLUTE   *adj* -LUTER, -LUTEST characterized by firmness or determination

RESOLUTE   *n* pl. -S one who is resolute

RESOLVE   *v* -SOLVED, -SOLVING, -SOLVES to make a firm decision about

RESOLVER   *n* pl. -S one that resolves

RESONANT   *n* pl. -S a resounding sound

RESONATE   *v* -NATED, -NATING, -NATES to resound

RESORB   *v* -ED, -ING, -S to absorb again

RESORCIN   *n* pl. -S a chemical compound

RESORT   *v* -ED, -ING, -S to go frequently or habitually

RESORTER   *n* pl. -S one that resorts

RESOUND   *v* -ED, -ING, -S to make a loud, long, or echoing sound

RESOURCE   *n* pl. -S an available supply

RESPECT   *v* -ED, -ING, -S to have a high regard for

RESPIRE   *v* -SPIRED, -SPIRING, -SPIRES to breathe

RESPITE   *v* -SPITED, -SPITING, -SPITES to relieve temporarily

RESPOND   *v* -ED, -ING, -S to say or act in return

RESPONSA   *n/pl* written rabbinic decisions

RESPONSE   *n* pl. -S a reply or reaction

REST   *v* -ED, -ING, -S to refresh oneself by ceasing work or activity

RESTER   *n* pl. -S one that rests

RESTFUL   *adj* -FULLER, -FULLEST tranquil

RESTIVE   *adj* difficult to control

RESTLESS   *adj* unable or disinclined to remain at rest

RESTORAL	*n* pl. -S the act of restoring
RESTORE	*v* -STORED, -STORING, -STORES to bring back to a former or original condition
RESTORER	*n* pl. -S one that restores
RESTRAIN	*v* -ED, -ING, -S to hold back from action
RESTRICT	*v* -ED, -ING, -S to keep within certain boundaries
RESTROOM	*n* pl. -S a room furnished with toilets and sinks
RESULT	*v* -ED, -ING, -S to occur as a consequence
RESUME	*v* -SUMED, -SUMING, -SUMES to take up again after interruption
RESUMER	*n* pl. -S one that resumes
RESUPINE	*adj* lying on the back
RESURGE	*v* -SURGED, -SURGING, -SURGES to rise again
RET	*v* RETTED, RETTING, RETS to soak in order to loosen the fiber from the woody tissue
RETABLE	*n* pl. -S a raised shelf above an altar
RETAIL	*v* -ED, -ING, -S to sell in small quantities
RETAILER	*n* pl. -S one that retails
RETAIN	*v* -ED, -ING, -S to keep possession of
RETAINER	*n* pl. -S one that retains
RETAKE	*v* -TOOK, -TAKEN, -TAKING, -TAKES to take back
RETAKER	*n* pl. -S one that retakes
RETARD	*v* -ED, -ING, -S to slow the progress of
RETARDER	*n* pl. -S one that retards
RETCH	*v* -ED, -ING, -ES to make an effort to vomit
RETE	*n* pl. -TIA an anatomical mesh or network
RETEM	*n* pl. -S a desert shrub
RETENE	*n* pl. -S a chemical compound
RETIA	pl. of rete
RETIAL	*adj* pertaining to a rete
RETIARII	*n/pl* ancient Roman gladiators
RETIARY	*adj* resembling a net
RETICENT	*adj* tending to be silent
RETICLE	*n* pl. -S a network of lines in the eyepiece of an optical instrument
RETICULA	*n/pl* netlike structures
RETICULE	*n* pl. -S a woman's handbag
RETIFORM	*adj* arranged like a net
RETINA	*n* pl. -NAS or -NAE a membrane of the eye
RETINAL	*n* pl. -S retinene
RETINE	*n* pl. -S a substance in cells that retards growth and cell division
RETINENE	*n* pl. -S a pigment in the retina
RETINITE	*n* pl. -S a fossil resin
RETINOID	*n* pl. -S a compound analogous to vitamin A
RETINOL	*n* pl. -S a liquid hydrocarbon
RETINUE	*n* pl. -S a group of attendants **RETINUED** *adj*
RETINULA	*n* pl. -LAE or -LAS a neural receptor of an arthropod's eye
RETIRANT	*n* pl. -S a retiree
RETIRE	*v* -TIRED, -TIRING, -TIRES to go away or withdraw
RETIREE	*n* pl. -S one who has retired from his vocation
RETIRER	*n* pl. -S one that retires
RETIRING	*adj* shy
RETOOK	past tense of retake
RETOOL	*v* -ED, -ING, -S to reequip with tools
RETORT	*v* -ED, -ING, -S to answer back sharply
RETORTER	*n* pl. -S one that retorts
RETOUCH	*v* -ED, -ING, -ES to add new details or touches to
RETRACE	*v* -TRACED, -TRACING, -TRACES to go back over
RETRACT	*v* -ED, -ING, -S to take back
RETRAL	*adj* situated toward the back **RETRALLY** *adv*
RETREAD	*v* -ED, -ING, -S to furnish with a new tread
RETREAT	*v* -ED, -ING, -S to go back or backward
RETRENCH	*v* -ED, -ING, -ES to curtail
RETRIAL	*n* pl. -S a second trial
RETRIEVE	*v* -TRIEVED, -TRIEVING, -TRIEVES to get back
RETRO	*n* pl. -ROS a rocket on a spacecraft that produces thrust in a direction opposite to the line of flight
RETROACT	*v* -ED, -ING, -S to act in return

RETROFIT	*v* -FITTED, -FITTING, -FITS to furnish with new parts not originally available
RETRORSE	*adj* bent backward
RETSINA	*n* pl. -S a resin-flavored Greek wine
RETTED	past tense of ret
RETTING	present participle of ret
RETURN	*v* -ED, -ING, -S to come or go back
RETURNEE	*n* pl. -S one that has returned
RETURNER	*n* pl. -S one that returns
RETUSE	*adj* having a rounded apex with a shallow notch — used of leaves
REUNION	*n* pl. -S a reuniting of persons after separation
REUNITER	*n* pl. -S one that reunites
REUSABLE	*adj* capable of being used again
REV	*v* REVVED, REVVING, REVS to increase the speed of
REVAMP	*v* -ED, -ING, -S to make over
REVAMPER	*n* pl. -S one that revamps
REVANCHE	*n* pl. -S a political policy designed to regain lost territory
REVEAL	*v* -ED, -ING, -S to make known
REVEALER	*n* pl. -S one that reveals
REVEHENT	*adj* carrying back
REVEILLE	*n* pl. -S a morning bugle call
REVEL	*v* -ELED, -ELING, -ELS or -ELLED, -ELLING, -ELS to engage in revelry
REVELER	*n* pl. -S one that revels
REVELLER	*n* pl. -S reveler
REVELLING	present participle of revel
REVELRY	*n* pl. -RIES noisy merrymaking
REVENANT	*n* pl. -S one that returns
REVENGE	*v* -VENGED, -VENGING, -VENGES to inflict injury in return for
REVENGER	*n* pl. -S one that revenges
REVENUE	*n* pl. -S the income of a government **REVENUAL, REVENUED** *adj*
REVENUER	*n* pl. -S a revenue officer
REVERB	*v* -ED, -ING, -S to continue in a series of echoes
REVERE	*v* -VERED, -VERING, -VERES to regard with great respect
REVEREND	*n* pl. -S a clergyman
REVERENT	*adj* deeply respectful
REVERER	*n* pl. -S one that reveres
REVERIE	*n* pl. -S a daydream
REVERIES	pl. of revery
REVERING	present participle of revere
REVERS	*n* pl. REVERS a part of a garment turned back to show the inside
REVERSAL	*n* pl. -S the act of reversing
REVERSE	*v* -VERSED, -VERSING, -VERSES to turn or move in the opposite direction
REVERSER	*n* pl. -S one that reverses
REVERSO	*n* pl. -VERSOS verso
REVERT	*v* -ED, -ING, -S to return to a former state
REVERTER	*n* pl. -S one that reverts
REVERY	*n* pl. -ERIES reverie
REVET	*v* -VETTED, -VETTING, -VETS to face with masonry
REVIEWAL	*n* pl. -S the act of reviewing
REVIEWER	*n* pl. -S one that reviews
REVILE	*v* -VILED, -VILING, -VILES to denounce with abusive language
REVILER	*n* pl. -S one that reviles
REVISAL	*n* pl. -S a revision
REVISE	*v* -VISED, -VISING, -VISES to make a new or improved version of
REVISER	*n* pl. -S one that revises
REVISION	*n* pl. -S a revised version
REVISOR	*n* pl. -S reviser
REVISORY	*adj* pertaining to revision
REVIVAL	*n* pl. -S renewed attention to or interest in something
REVIVE	*v* -VIVED, -VIVING, -VIVES to bring back to life or consciousness
REVIVER	*n* pl. -S one that revives
REVIVIFY	*v* -FIED, -FYING, -FIES to give new life to
REVIVING	present participle of revive
REVOKE	*v* -VOKED, -VOKING, -VOKES to annul by taking back
REVOKER	*n* pl. -S one that revokes
REVOLT	*v* -ED, -ING, -S to rise up against authority
REVOLTER	*n* pl. -S one that revolts
REVOLUTE	*adj* rolled backward or downward

REVOLVE	*v* -VOLVED, -VOLVING, -VOLVES to turn about an axis
REVOLVER	*n* pl. -S a type of handgun
REVUE	*n* pl. -S a type of musical show
REVUIST	*n* pl. -S a writer of revues
REVULSED	*adj* affected with revulsion
REVVED	past tense of rev
REVVING	present participle of rev
REWARD	*v* -ED, -ING, -S to give recompense to for worthy behavior
REWARDER	*n* pl. -S one that rewards
REWINDER	*n* pl. -S one that rewinds
REWORD	*v* -ED, -ING, -S to state again in other words
REWRITER	*n* pl. -S one that rewrites
REX	*n* pl. REGES king
REX	*n* pl. -ES an animal with a single wavy layer of hair
REYNARD	*n* pl. -S a fox
RHABDOM	*n* pl. -S a rodlike structure in the retinula
RHABDOME	*n* pl. -S rhabdom
RHACHIS	*n* pl. -CHISES or -CHIDES rachis
RHAMNOSE	*n* pl. -S a sugar found in plants
RHAMNUS	*n* pl. -ES a thorny tree or shrub
RHAPHE	*n* pl. -PHAE or -PHES raphe
RHAPSODE	*n* pl. -S a reciter of epic poetry in ancient Greece
RHAPSODY	*n* pl. -DIES an exalted expression of feeling
RHATANY	*n* pl. -NIES a South American shrub
RHEA	*n* pl. -S a flightless bird
RHEBOK	*n* pl. -S a large antelope
RHEMATIC	*adj* pertaining to a verb
RHENIUM	*n* pl. -S a metallic element
RHEOBASE	*n* pl. -S the smallest amount of electricity required to stimulate a nerve
RHEOLOGY	*n* pl. -GIES the study of matter in the fluid state
RHEOPHIL	*adj* living in flowing water
RHEOSTAT	*n* pl. -S a resistor used to control electric current
RHESUS	*n* pl. -ES an Asian monkey
RHETOR	*n* pl. -S a teacher of rhetoric
RHETORIC	*n* pl. -S the study of effective speech and writing
RHEUM	*n* pl. -S a watery discharge from the eyes or nose **RHEUMIC** *adj*
RHEUMY	*adj* RHEUMIER, RHEUMIEST marked by rheum
RHINAL	*adj* pertaining to the nose
RHINITIS	*n* pl. RHINITIDES inflammation of the mucous membranes of the nose
RHINO	*n* pl. -NOS a rhinoceros
RHIZOBIA	*n/pl* rod-shaped bacteria
RHIZOID	*n* pl. -S a rootlike structure
RHIZOMA	*n* pl. -MATA rhizome
RHIZOME	*n* pl. -S a rootlike, underground stem **RHIZOMIC** *adj*
RHIZOPOD	*n* pl. -S any of a class of protozoans
RHIZOPUS	*n* pl. -PI or -PUSES any of a genus of mold fungi
RHO	*n* pl. RHOS a Greek letter
RHODAMIN	*n* pl. -S a red dye
RHODIUM	*n* pl. -S a metallic element **RHODIC** *adj*
RHODORA	*n* pl. -S a flowering shrub
RHOMB	*n* pl. -S a rhombus
RHOMBI	a pl. of rhombus
RHOMBIC	*adj* having the shape of a rhombus
RHOMBOID	*n* pl. -S a type of geometric figure
RHOMBUS	*n* pl. -BUSES or -BI a type of geometric figure
RHONCHUS	*n* pl. -CHI a rattling respiratory sound **RHONCHAL** *adj*
RHUBARB	*n* pl. -S a perennial herb
RHUMB	*n* pl. -S a point of the mariner's compass
RHUMBA	*v* -ED, -ING, -S to rumba
RHUS	*n* pl. -ES any of a genus of shrubs and trees
RHYME	*v* RHYMED, RHYMING, RHYMES to compose verse with corresponding terminal sounds
RHYMER	*n* pl. -S one that rhymes
RHYOLITE	*n* pl. -S a volcanic rock
RHYTA	pl. of rhyton
RHYTHM	*n* pl. -S movement or procedure with uniform recurrence of strong and weak elements
RHYTHMIC	*n* pl. -S the science of rhythm
RHYTON	*n* pl. -TONS or -TA an ancient Greek drinking horn

RIA   *n* pl. -S a long, narrow inlet

RIAL   *n* pl. -S a monetary unit of Iran

RIALTO   *n* pl. -TOS a marketplace

RIANT   *adj* cheerful **RIANTLY** *adv*

RIATA   *n* pl. -S a lasso

RIB   *v* RIBBED, RIBBING, RIBS to poke fun at

RIBALD   *n* pl. -S one who uses crude language

RIBALDLY   *adv* crudely

RIBALDRY   *n* pl. -RIES crude language

RIBAND   *n* pl. -S a ribbon

RIBBAND   *n* pl. -S a long, narrow strip used in shipbuilding

RIBBED   past tense of rib

RIBBER   *n* pl. -S one that ribs

RIBBIER   comparative of ribby

RIBBIEST   superlative of ribby

RIBBING   *n* pl. -S the act of one that ribs

RIBBON   *v* -ED, -ING, -S to decorate with ribbons (narrow strips of fine fabric)

RIBBONY   *adj* resembling ribbon

RIBBY   *adj* -BIER, -BIEST marked by prominent ribs (curved bony rods in the body)

RIBES   *n* pl. RIBES a flowering shrub

RIBGRASS   *n* pl. -ES a weedy plant

RIBIER   *n* pl. -S a large, black grape

RIBLESS   *adj* having no ribs

RIBLET   *n* pl. -S the rib end in a breast of lamb or veal

RIBLIKE   *adj* resembling a rib

RIBOSE   *n* pl. -S a pentose sugar

RIBOSOME   *n* pl. -S a particle composed of protein and ribonucleic acid

RIBWORT   *n* pl. -S ribgrass

RICE   *v* RICED, RICING, RICES to press through a ricer

RICEBIRD   *n* pl. -S the bobolink

RICER   *n* pl. -S a kitchen utensil consisting of a container perforated with small holes

RICERCAR   *n* pl. -S an instrumental composition

RICH   *adj* RICHER, RICHEST having wealth

RICHEN   *v* -ED, -ING, -S to make rich

RICHES   *n/pl* wealth

RICHLY   *adv* in a rich manner

RICHNESS   *n* pl. -ES the state of being rich

RICHWEED   *n* pl. -S a flowering plant

RICIN   *n* pl. -S a poisonous protein

RICING   present participle of rice

RICINUS   *n* pl. -ES a large-leaved plant

RICK   *v* -ED, -ING, -S to pile hay in stacks

RICKETS   *n/pl* a disease resulting from vitamin D deficiency

RICKETY   *adj* -ETIER, -ETIEST likely to fall or collapse

RICKEY   *n* pl. -EYS an alcoholic beverage containing lime juice, sugar, and soda water

RICKRACK   *n* pl. -S a flat braid used as a trimming

RICKSHA   *n* pl. -S rickshaw

RICKSHAW   *n* pl. -S a small, two-wheeled passenger vehicle

RICOCHET   *v* -CHETED, -CHETING, -CHETS or -CHETTED, -CHETTING, -CHETS to rebound from a surface

RICOTTA   *n* pl. -S an Italian cheese

RICRAC   *n* pl. -S rickrack

RICTUS   *n* pl. -ES the expanse of the open mouth **RICTAL** *adj*

RID   *v* RID or RIDDED, RIDDING, RIDS to free from something objectionable

RIDABLE   *adj* capable of being ridden

RIDDANCE   *n* pl. -S deliverance

RIDDED   a past tense of rid

RIDDEN   past participle of ride

RIDDER   *n* pl. -S one that rids

RIDDING   present participle of rid

RIDDLE   *v* -DLED, -DLING, -DLES to pierce with many holes

RIDDLER   *n* pl. -S one that riddles

RIDE   *v* RODE, RIDDEN, RIDING, RIDES to sit on, control, and be conveyed by an animal or machine

RIDEABLE   *adj* ridable

RIDENT   *adj* laughing

RIDER   *n* pl. -S one that rides

RIDGE   *v* RIDGED, RIDGING, RIDGES to form into ridges (long, narrow elevations)

RIDGEL	*n* pl. -S a ridgling
RIDGIER	comparative of ridgy
RIDGIEST	superlative of ridgy
RIDGIL	*n* pl. -S a ridgling
RIDGING	present participle of ridge
RIDGLING	*n* pl. -S a male animal with undescended testicles
RIDGY	*adj* RIDGIER, RIDGIEST having ridges
RIDICULE	*v* -CULED, -CULING, -CULES to make fun of
RIDING	*n* pl. -S the act of one that rides
RIDLEY	*n* pl. -LEYS a sea turtle
RIDOTTO	*n* pl. -TOS a public musical entertainment in 18th century England
RIEL	*n* pl. -S a monetary unit of Cambodia
RIESLING	*n* pl. -S a white Rhine wine
RIEVER	*n* pl. -S reaver
RIF	*v* RIFFED, RIFFING, RIFS to dismiss from employment
RIFAMPIN	*n* pl. -S an antibiotic
RIFE	*adj* RIFER, RIFEST abundant **RIFELY** *adv*
RIFENESS	*n* pl. -ES the state of being rife
RIFF	*v* -ED, -ING, -S to riffle
RIFFED	past tense of rif
RIFFING	present participle of rif
RIFFLE	*v* -FLED, -FLING, -FLES to flip through hastily
RIFFLER	*n* pl. -S a filing and scraping tool
RIFFRAFF	*n* pl. -S the disreputable element of society
RIFLE	*v* -FLED, -FLING, -FLES to search through and rob
RIFLEMAN	*n* pl. -MEN a soldier armed with a rifle (a type of firearm)
RIFLER	*n* pl. -S one that rifles
RIFLERY	*n* pl. -RIES the practice of shooting at targets with a rifle
RIFLING	*n* pl. -S the system of grooves in a gun barrel
RIFT	*v* -ED, -ING, -S to form rifts (clefts)
RIFTLESS	*adj* having no rift
RIG	*v* RIGGED, RIGGING, RIGS to put in proper condition for use
RIGADOON	*n* pl. -S a lively dance
RIGATONI	*n* pl. -S a tubular pasta
RIGAUDON	*n* pl. -S rigadoon
RIGGED	past tense of rig
RIGGER	*n* pl. -S one that rigs
RIGGING	*n* pl. -S the system of lines, chains, and tackle used aboard a ship
RIGHT	*adj* RIGHTER, RIGHTEST being in accordance with what is good, proper, or just
RIGHT	*v* -ED, -ING, -S to put in proper order or condition
RIGHTER	*n* pl. -S one that rights
RIGHTFUL	*adj* just or proper
RIGHTIES	pl. of righty
RIGHTISM	*n* pl. -S a conservative political philosophy
RIGHTIST	*n* pl. -S an advocate of rightism
RIGHTLY	*adv* in a right manner
RIGHTO	*interj* — used to express cheerful consent
RIGHTY	*n* pl. RIGHTIES a right-handed person
RIGID	*adj* not flexible
RIGIDIFY	*v* -FIED, -FYING, -FIES to make rigid
RIGIDITY	*n* pl. -TIES the state of being rigid
RIGIDLY	*adv* in a rigid manner
RIGOR	*n* pl. -S strictness or severity
RIGORISM	*n* pl. -S strictness or severity in conduct or attitude
RIGORIST	*n* pl. -S one that professes rigorism
RIGOROUS	*adj* characterized by rigor
RIGOUR	*n* pl. -S rigor
RIKISHA	*n* pl. -S rickshaw
RIKSHAW	*n* pl. -S rickshaw
RILE	*v* RILED, RILING, RILES to anger
RILEY	*adj* angry
RILIEVO	*n* pl. -VI relievo
RILING	present participle of rile
RILL	*v* -ED, -ING, -S to flow like a rill (a small brook)
RILLE	*n* pl. -S a valley on the moon's surface
RILLET	*n* pl. -S a small rill

RIM	*v* RIMMED, RIMMING, RIMS to provide with a rim (an outer edge)
RIME	*v* RIMED, RIMING, RIMES to rhyme
RIMER	*n* pl. -S one that rimes
RIMESTER	*n* pl. -S a rimer
RIMFIRE	*n* pl. -S a cartridge having the primer set in the rim of the shell
RIMIER	comparative of rimy
RIMIEST	superlative of rimy
RIMINESS	*n* pl. -ES the condition of being rimy
RIMING	present participle of rime
RIMLAND	*n* pl. -S an outlying area
RIMLESS	*adj* having no rim
RIMMED	past tense of rim
RIMMER	*n* pl. -S a reamer
RIMMING	present participle of rim
RIMOSE	*adj* marked by cracks **RIMOSELY** *adv*
RIMOSITY	*n* pl. -TIES the state of being rimose
RIMOUS	*adj* rimose
RIMPLE	*v* -PLED, -PLING, -PLES to wrinkle
RIMROCK	*n* pl. -S a type of rock formation
RIMY	*adj* RIMIER, RIMIEST frosty
RIN	*v* RAN, RINNING, RINS to run or melt
RIND	*n* pl. -S a thick and firm outer covering **RINDED** *adj*
RING	*v* -ED, -ING, -S to form a ring (a circular band) around
RING	*v* RANG, RUNG, RINGING, RINGS to give forth a clear, resonant sound
RINGBARK	*v* -ED, -ING, -S to make an encircling cut through the bark of
RINGBOLT	*n* pl. -S a type of eyebolt
RINGBONE	*n* pl. -S a bony growth on a horse's foot
RINGDOVE	*n* pl. -S a European pigeon
RINGENT	*adj* having open liplike parts
RINGER	*n* pl. -S one that rings
RINGGIT	*n* pl. -S a monetary unit of Malaysia
RINGHALS	*n* pl. -ES a venomous snake
RINGLET	*n* pl. -S a small ring
RINGLIKE	*adj* resembling a ring
RINGNECK	*n* pl. -S a bird having a ring of color around the neck
RINGSIDE	*n* pl. -S the area just outside a boxing or wrestling ring (a square enclosure)
RINGTAIL	*n* pl. -S an animal having a tail with ringlike markings
RINGTAW	*n* pl. -S a game of marbles
RINGTOSS	*n* pl. -ES a game in which the object is to toss a ring onto an upright stick
RINGWORM	*n* pl. -S a skin disease
RINK	*n* pl. -S a surface of ice for skating
RINNING	present participle of rin
RINSE	*v* RINSED, RINSING, RINSES to cleanse with clear water **RINSABLE, RINSIBLE** *adj*
RINSER	*n* pl. -S one that rinses
RINSING	*n* pl. -S the act of one that rinses
RIOJA	*n* pl. -S a dry red Spanish wine
RIOT	*v* -ED, -ING, -S to take part in a violent public disturbance
RIOTER	*n* pl. -S one that riots
RIOTOUS	*adj* characterized by rioting
RIP	*v* RIPPED, RIPPING, RIPS to tear or cut apart roughly
RIPARIAN	*adj* pertaining to the bank of a river
RIPCORD	*n* pl. -S a cord pulled to release a parachute
RIPE	*adj* RIPER, RIPEST fully developed **RIPELY** *adv*
RIPE	*v* RIPED, RIPING, RIPES to cleanse
RIPEN	*v* -ED, -ING, -S to become ripe
RIPENER	*n* pl. -S one that ripens
RIPENESS	*n* pl. -ES the state of being ripe
RIPER	comparative of ripe
RIPEST	superlative of ripe
RIPIENO	*n* pl. -NI or -NOS tutti
RIPING	present participle of ripe
RIPOFF	*n* pl. -S an instance of stealing
RIPOST	*v* -ED, -ING, -S to riposte
RIPOSTE	*v* -POSTED, -POSTING, -POSTES to make a return thrust in fencing
RIPPABLE	*adj* capable of being ripped
RIPPED	past tense of rip
RIPPER	*n* pl. -S one that rips

RIPPING	*adj* excellent	**RIVAL**	*v* -VALED, -VALING, -VALS or -VALLED, -VALLING, -VALS to strive to equal or surpass
RIPPLE	*v* -PLED, -PLING, -PLES to form ripples (small waves)	**RIVALRY**	*n* pl. -RIES competition
RIPPLER	*n* pl. -S a toothed tool for cleaning flax fiber	**RIVE**	*v* RIVED, RIVEN, RIVING, RIVES to tear apart
RIPPLET	*n* pl. -S a small ripple	**RIVER**	*n* pl. -S a large, natural stream of water
RIPPLING	present participle of ripple		
RIPPLY	*adj* -PLIER, -PLIEST marked by ripples	**RIVERBED**	*n* pl. -S the area covered or once covered by a river
RIPRAP	*v* -RAPPED, -RAPPING, -RAPS to strengthen with a foundation of broken stones	**RIVERINE**	*adj* pertaining to a river
		RIVET	*v* -ETED, -ETING, -ETS or -ETTED, -ETTING, -ETS to fasten with a type of metal bolt
RIPSAW	*n* pl. -S a type of saw		
RIPSTOP	*n* pl. -S a fabric woven so that small tears do not spread	**RIVETER**	*n* pl. -S one that rivets
		RIVIERA	*n* pl. -S a coastal resort area
RIPTIDE	*n* pl. -S a tide that opposes other tides	**RIVIERE**	*n* pl. -S a necklace of precious stones
RISE	*v* ROSE, RISEN, RISING, RISES to move upward	**RIVING**	present participle of rive
		RIVULET	*n* pl. -S a small stream
RISER	*n* pl. -S one that rises	**RIVULOSE**	*adj* having narrow, winding lines
RISHI	*n* pl. -S a Hindu sage	**RIYAL**	*n* pl. -S a monetary unit of Saudi Arabia
RISIBLE	*adj* inclined to laugh **RISIBLY** *adv*		
		ROACH	*v* -ED, -ING, -ES to cause to arch
RISIBLES	*n/pl* a sense of the ridiculous		
RISING	*n* pl. -S the act of one that rises	**ROAD**	*n* pl. -S an open way for public passage
RISK	*v* -ED, -ING, -S to expose to a risk (a chance of injury or loss)	**ROADBED**	*n* pl. -S the foundation for a railroad track
RISKER	*n* pl. -S one that risks	**ROADEO**	*n* pl. -EOS a competition for truck drivers
RISKLESS	*adj* free of risk		
RISKY	*adj* RISKIER, RISKIEST dangerous **RISKILY** *adv*	**ROADIE**	*n* pl. -S a person who works for traveling entertainers
RISOTTO	*n* pl. -TOS a rice dish	**ROADKILL**	*n* pl. -S an animal that has been killed on a road
RISQUE	*adj* bordering on impropriety or indecency	**ROADLESS**	*adj* having no roads
		ROADSHOW	*n* pl. -S a theatrical show on tour
RISSOLE	*n* pl. -S a small roll filled with meat or fish	**ROADSIDE**	*n* pl. -S the area along the side of a road
RISUS	*n* pl. -ES a grin or laugh		
RITARD	*n* pl. -S a musical passage with a gradual slackening in tempo	**ROADSTER**	*n* pl. -S a light, open automobile
		ROADWAY	*n* pl. -WAYS a road
RITE	*n* pl. -S a ceremonial act or procedure	**ROADWORK**	*n* pl. -S outdoor running as a form of physical conditioning
RITTER	*n* pl. -S a knight	**ROAM**	*v* -ED, -ING, -S to move about without purpose or plan
RITUAL	*n* pl. -S a system of rites		
RITUALLY	*adv* ceremonially	**ROAMER**	*n* pl. -S one that roams
RITZ	*n* pl. -ES pretentious display	**ROAN**	*n* pl. -S an animal having a coat sprinkled with white or gray
RITZY	*adj* RITZIER, RITZIEST elegant **RITZILY** *adv*	**ROAR**	*v* -ED, -ING, -S to utter a loud, deep sound
RIVAGE	*n* pl. -S a coast, shore, or bank	**ROARER**	*n* pl. -S one that roars

ROARING   *n* pl. -S a loud, deep sound

ROAST   *v* -ED, -ING, -S to cook with dry heat

ROASTER   *n* pl. -S one that roasts

ROB   *v* ROBBED, ROBBING, ROBS to take property from illegally

ROBALO   *n* pl. -LOS a marine food fish

ROBAND   *n* pl. -S a piece of yarn used to fasten a sail

ROBBED   past tense of rob

ROBBER   *n* pl. -S one that robs

ROBBERY   *n* pl. -BERIES the act of one who robs

ROBBIN   *n* pl. -S a roband

ROBBING   present participle of rob

ROBE   *v* ROBED, ROBING, ROBES to cover with a robe (a long, loose outer garment)

ROBIN   *n* pl. -S a songbird

ROBLE   *n* pl. -S an oak tree

ROBORANT   *n* pl. -S an invigorating drug

ROBOT   *n* pl. -S a humanlike machine that performs various functions **ROBOTIC** *adj*

ROBOTICS   *n/pl* a field of interest concerned with robots

ROBOTISM   *n* pl. -S the state of being a robot

ROBOTIZE   *v* -IZED, -IZING, -IZES to make automatic

ROBOTRY   *n* pl. -RIES the science of robots

ROBUST   *adj* -BUSTER, -BUSTEST strong and healthy **ROBUSTLY** *adv*

ROBUSTA   *n* pl. -S a coffee grown in Africa

ROC   *n* pl. -S a legendary bird of prey

ROCAILLE   *n* pl. -S rococo

ROCHET   *n* pl. -S a linen vestment

ROCK   *v* -ED, -ING, -S to move back and forth

ROCKABY   *n* pl. -BIES a song used to lull a child to sleep

ROCKABYE   *n* pl. -S rockaby

ROCKAWAY   *n* pl. -WAYS a light carriage

ROCKER   *n* pl. -S a rocking chair

ROCKERY   *n* pl. -ERIES a rock garden

ROCKET   *v* -ED, -ING, -S to convey by means of a rocket (a device propelled by the reaction of escaping gases)

ROCKETER   *n* pl. -S one that designs or launches rockets

ROCKETRY   *n* pl. -RIES the science of rockets

ROCKFALL   *n* pl. -S a mass of fallen rocks

ROCKFISH   *n* pl. -ES a fish living around rocks

ROCKIER   comparative of rocky

ROCKIEST   superlative of rocky

ROCKLESS   *adj* having no rocks

ROCKLIKE   *adj* resembling a rock (a large mass of stone)

ROCKLING   *n* pl. -S a marine fish

ROCKOON   *n* pl. -S a small rocket

ROCKROSE   *n* pl. -S a flowering plant

ROCKWEED   *n* pl. -S a brown seaweed

ROCKWORK   *n* pl. -S a natural mass of rocks

ROCKY   *adj* ROCKIER, ROCKIEST unsteady

ROCOCO   *n* pl. -COS a style of architecture and decoration

ROD   *v* RODDED, RODDING, RODS to provide with a rod (a straight, slender piece of wood, metal, or other material)

RODE   past tense of ride

RODENT   *n* pl. -S a gnawing mammal

RODEO   *v* -ED, -ING, -S to perform cowboy skills in a contest

RODLESS   *adj* having no rod

RODLIKE   *adj* resembling a rod

RODMAN   *n* pl. -MEN a surveyor's assistant

RODSMAN   *n* pl. -MEN rodman

ROE   *n* pl. -S the mass of eggs within a female fish

ROEBUCK   *n* pl. -S the male of a small Eurasian deer

ROENTGEN   *n* pl. -S a unit of radiation dosage

ROGATION   *n* pl. -S the proposal of a law in ancient Rome

ROGATORY   *adj* requesting information

ROGER   *n* pl. -S the pirate flag bearing the skull and crossbones

ROGUE   *v* ROGUED, ROGUEING or ROGUING, ROGUES to defraud

ROGUERY   *n* pl. -ERIES roguish conduct

ROGUISH   *adj* dishonest

ROIL   *v* -ED, -ING, -S to make muddy

ROILY   *adj* ROILIER, ROILIEST muddy

ROISTER   *v* -ED, -ING, -S to revel

ROLAMITE *n* pl. -S a nearly frictionless mechanical device

ROLE *n* pl. -S a part played by an actor

ROLF *v* -ED, -ING, -S to practice a type of massage

ROLFER *n* pl. -S one that rolfs

ROLL *v* -ED, -ING, -S to move along by repeatedly turning over

ROLLAWAY *adj* mounted on rollers

ROLLBACK *n* pl. -S a return to a lower level of prices or wages

ROLLER *n* pl. -S a rotating cylinder

ROLLICK *v* -ED, -ING, -S to frolic

ROLLICKY *adj* given to rollicking

ROLLING *n* pl. -S the act of one that rolls

ROLLMOP *n* pl. -S a fillet of herring

ROLLOUT *n* pl. -S a type of play in football

ROLLOVER *n* pl. -S a motor vehicle accident in which the vehicle overturns

ROLLTOP *adj* having a flexible, sliding cover

ROLLWAY *n* pl. -WAYS an incline for rolling logs

ROM *n* pl. -S a Gypsy man or boy

ROMAINE *n* pl. -S a variety of lettuce

ROMAN *n* pl. -S a metrical narrative of medieval France

ROMANCE *v* -MANCED, -MANCING, -MANCES to woo

ROMANCER *n* pl. -S one that romances

ROMANISE *v* -ISED, -ISING, -ISES to romanize

ROMANIZE *v* -IZED, -IZING, -IZES to write in the Roman alphabet

ROMANO *n* pl. -NOS an Italian cheese

ROMANTIC *n* pl. -S a fanciful person

ROMAUNT *n* pl. -S a long, medieval tale

ROMEO *n* pl. -MEOS a male lover

ROMP *v* -ED, -ING, -S to play boisterously

ROMPER *n* pl. -S one that romps

ROMPISH *adj* inclined to romp

RONDEAU *n* pl. -DEAUX a short poem of fixed form

RONDEL *n* pl. -S a rondeau of 14 lines

RONDELET *n* pl. -S a rondeau of 5 or 7 lines

RONDELLE *n* pl. -S rondel

RONDO *n* pl. -DOS a type of musical composition

RONDURE *n* pl. -S a circle or sphere

RONION *n* pl. -S a mangy animal or person

RONNEL *n* pl. -S an insecticide

RONTGEN *n* pl. -S roentgen

RONYON *n* pl. -S ronion

ROOD *n* pl. -S a crucifix

ROOF *v* -ED, -ING, -S to provide with a roof (the external upper covering of a building)

ROOFER *n* pl. -S one that builds or repairs roofs

ROOFING *n* pl. -S material for a roof

ROOFLESS *adj* having no roof

ROOFLIKE *adj* resembling a roof

ROOFLINE *n* pl. -S the profile of a roof

ROOFTOP *n* pl. -S a roof

ROOFTREE *n* pl. -S a horizontal timber in a roof

ROOK *v* -ED, -ING, -S to swindle

ROOKERY *n* pl. -ERIES a colony of rooks (European crows)

ROOKIE *n* pl. -S a novice

ROOKY *adj* ROOKIER, ROOKIEST abounding in rooks

ROOM *v* -ED, -ING, -S to occupy a room (a walled space within a building)

ROOMER *n* pl. -S a lodger

ROOMETTE *n* pl. -S a small room

ROOMFUL *n* pl. -S as much as a room can hold

ROOMIE *n* pl. -S a roommate

ROOMMATE *n* pl. -S one with whom a room is shared

ROOMY *adj* ROOMIER, ROOMIEST spacious **ROOMILY** *adv*

ROORBACH *n* pl. -S roorback

ROORBACK *n* pl. -S a false story used for political advantage

ROOSE *v* ROOSED, ROOSING, ROOSES to praise

ROOSER *n* pl. -S one that rooses

ROOST *v* -ED, -ING, -S to settle down for rest or sleep

ROOSTER *n* pl. -S a male chicken

ROOT *v* -ED, -ING, -S to put forth a root (an underground portion of a plant)

ROOTAGE *n* pl. -S a system of roots

ROOTER   *n* pl. -S one that gives encouragement or support

ROOTHOLD   *n* pl. -S the embedding of a plant to soil through the growing of roots

ROOTIER   comparative of rooty

ROOTIEST   superlative of rooty

ROOTLESS   *adj* having no roots

ROOTLET   *n* pl. -S a small root

ROOTLIKE   *adj* resembling a root

ROOTY   *adj* ROOTIER, ROOTIEST full of roots

ROPE   *v* ROPED, ROPING, ROPES to bind with a rope (a thick line of twisted fibers) **ROPABLE** *adj*

ROPELIKE   *adj* resembling a rope

ROPER   *n* pl. -S one that ropes

ROPERY   *n* pl. -ERIES a place where ropes are made

ROPEWALK   *n* pl. -S a long path where ropes are made

ROPEWAY   *n* pl. -WAYS an aerial cable used to transport freight

ROPEY   *adj* ROPIER, ROPIEST ropy

ROPIER   comparative of ropy

ROPIEST   superlative of ropy

ROPILY   *adv* in a ropy manner

ROPINESS   *n* pl. -ES the quality of being ropy

ROPING   present participle of rope

ROPY   *adj* ROPIER, ROPIEST resembling a rope or ropes

ROQUE   *n* pl. -S a form of croquet

ROQUET   *v* -ED, -ING, -S to cause one's own ball to hit another in croquet

RORQUAL   *n* pl. -S a large whale

ROSARIAN   *n* pl. -S a cultivator of roses

ROSARIUM   *n* pl. -IA or -IUMS a rose garden

ROSARY   *n* pl. -RIES a series of prayers in the Roman Catholic Church

ROSCOE   *n* pl. -S a pistol

ROSE   *v* ROSED, ROSING, ROSES to make the color of a rose (a reddish flower)

ROSEATE   *adj* rose-colored

ROSEBAY   *n* pl. -BAYS an evergreen shrub

ROSEBUD   *n* pl. -S the bud of a rose

ROSEBUSH   *n* pl. -ES a shrub that bears roses

ROSED   past tense of rose

ROSEFISH   *n* pl. -ES a marine food fish

ROSELIKE   *adj* resembling a rose

ROSELLE   *n* pl. -S a tropical plant

ROSEMARY   *n* pl. -MARIES an evergreen shrub

ROSEOLA   *n* pl. -S a rose-colored skin rash **ROSEOLAR** *adj*

ROSEROOT   *n* pl. -S a perennial herb

ROSERY   *n* pl. -ERIES a place where roses are grown

ROSESLUG   *n* pl. -S a larval sawfly that eats rose leaves

ROSET   *n* pl. -S resin

ROSETTE   *n* pl. -S an ornament resembling a rose

ROSEWOOD   *n* pl. -S a tropical tree

ROSIER   comparative of rosy

ROSIEST   superlative of rosy

ROSILY   *adv* in a rosy manner

ROSIN   *v* -ED, -ING, -S to treat with rosin (a brittle resin)

ROSINESS   *n* pl. -ES the state of being rosy

ROSING   present participle of rose

ROSINOL   *n* pl. -S rosin oil

ROSINOUS   *adj* resembling rosin

ROSINY   *adj* rosinous

ROSOLIO   *n* pl. -LIOS a liqueur made from raisins and brandy

ROSTELLA   *n/pl* small, beaklike structures

ROSTER   *n* pl. -S a list of names

ROSTRA   a pl. of rostrum

ROSTRAL   *adj* pertaining to a rostrum

ROSTRATE   *adj* having a rostrum

ROSTRUM   *n* pl. -TRA or -TRUMS a beaklike process or part

ROSULATE   *adj* arranged in the form of a rosette

ROSY   *adj* ROSIER, ROSIEST rose-colored

ROT   *v* ROTTED, ROTTING, ROTS to decompose

ROTA   *n* pl. -S a roster

ROTARY   *n* pl. -RIES a rotating part or device

ROTATE   *v* -TATED, -TATING, -TATES to turn about an axis

ROTATION   *n* pl. -S the act or an instance of rotating **ROTATIVE** *adj*

ROTATOR   *n* pl. -S one that rotates

ROTATOR	*n* pl. -ES a muscle serving to rotate a part of the body
ROTATORY	*adj* pertaining to rotation
ROTCH	*n* pl. -ES rotche
ROTCHE	*n* pl. -S a seabird
ROTE	*n* pl. -S mechanical routine
ROTENONE	*n* pl. -S an insecticide
ROTGUT	*n* pl. -S inferior liquor
ROTI	*n* pl. -S an unleavened bread
ROTIFER	*n* pl. -S a microscopic aquatic organism
ROTIFORM	*adj* shaped like a wheel
ROTL	*n* pl. ROTLS or ARTAL a unit of weight in Muslim countries
ROTO	*n* pl. -TOS a type of printing process
ROTOR	*n* pl. -S a rotating part of a machine
ROTOTILL	*v* -ED, -ING, -S to till soil with a type of farming implement
ROTTE	*n* pl. -S a medieval stringed instrument
ROTTED	past tense of rot
ROTTEN	*adj* -TENER, -TENEST being in a state of decay **ROTTENLY** *adv*
ROTTER	*n* pl. -S a scoundrel
ROTTING	present participle of rot
ROTUND	*adj* marked by roundness **ROTUNDLY** *adv*
ROTUNDA	*n* pl. -S a round building
ROTURIER	*n* pl. -S a commoner
ROUBLE	*n* pl. -S ruble
ROUCHE	*n* pl. -S ruche
ROUE	*n* pl. -S a lecherous man
ROUEN	*n* pl. -S any of a breed of domestic ducks
ROUGE	*v* ROUGED, ROUGING, ROUGES to color with a red cosmetic
ROUGH	*adj* ROUGHER, ROUGHEST having an uneven surface
ROUGH	*v* -ED, -ING, -S to make rough
ROUGHAGE	*n* pl. -S coarse, bulky food
ROUGHDRY	*v* -DRIED, -DRYING, -DRIES to dry without ironing, as washed clothes
ROUGHEN	*v* -ED, -ING, -S to make rough
ROUGHER	*n* pl. -S one that roughs
ROUGHHEW	*v* -HEWED, -HEWN, -HEWING, -HEWS to shape roughly
ROUGHISH	*adj* somewhat rough
ROUGHLEG	*n* pl. -S a large hawk
ROUGHLY	*adv* in a rough manner
ROUGING	present participle of rouge
ROUILLE	*n* pl. -S a peppery garlic sauce
ROULADE	*n* pl. -S a musical embellishment
ROULEAU	*n* pl. -LEAUX or -LEAUS a roll of coins wrapped in paper
ROULETTE	*v* -LETTED, -LETTING, -LETTES to make tiny slits in
ROUND	*adj* ROUNDER, ROUNDEST shaped like a sphere
ROUND	*v* -ED, -ING, -S to make round
ROUNDEL	*n* pl. -S a round figure or object
ROUNDER	*n* pl. -S a tool for rounding
ROUNDISH	*adj* somewhat round
ROUNDLET	*n* pl. -S a small circle
ROUNDLY	*adv* in a round manner
ROUNDUP	*n* pl. -S the driving together of cattle scattered over a range
ROUP	*v* -ED, -ING, -S to auction
ROUPET	*adj* roupy
ROUPY	*adj* ROUPIER, ROUPIEST hoarse **ROUPILY** *adv*
ROUSE	*v* ROUSED, ROUSING, ROUSES to bring out of a state of sleep or inactivity
ROUSER	*n* pl. -S one that rouses
ROUSSEAU	*n* pl. -S fried pemmican
ROUST	*v* -ED, -ING, -S to arouse and drive out
ROUSTER	*n* pl. -S a wharf laborer and deckhand
ROUT	*v* -ED, -ING, -S to defeat overwhelmingly
ROUTE	*v* ROUTED, ROUTING, ROUTES to send on a particular course
ROUTEMAN	*n* pl. -MEN one who conducts business on a customary course
ROUTER	*n* pl. -S a scooping tool
ROUTEWAY	*n* pl. -WAYS an established course of travel
ROUTH	*n* pl. -S an abundance
ROUTINE	*n* pl. -S a regular course of procedure
ROUTING	present participle of route

ROUX   *n* pl. ROUX a mixture of butter and flour

ROVE   *v* ROVED, ROVING, ROVES to roam

ROVEN   a past participle of reeve

ROVER   *n* pl. -S one that roves

ROVING   *n* pl. -S a roll of textile fibers

ROVINGLY   *adv* in a roving manner

ROW   *v* -ED, -ING, -S to propel by means of oars **ROWABLE** *adj*

ROWAN   *n* pl. -S a Eurasian tree

ROWBOAT   *n* pl. -S a small boat designed to be rowed

ROWDY   *adj* -DIER, -DIEST disorderly in behavior **ROWDILY** *adv*

ROWDY   *n* pl. -DIES a rowdy person

ROWDYISH   *adj* tending to be rowdy

ROWDYISM   *n* pl. -S disorderly behavior

ROWEL   *v* -ELED, -ELING, -ELS or -ELLED, -ELLING, -ELS to prick with a spiked wheel in order to urge forward

ROWEN   *n* pl. -S a second growth of grass

ROWER   *n* pl. -S one that rows

ROWING   *n* pl. -S the sport of racing in light, long, and narrow rowboats

ROWLOCK   *n* pl. -S an oarlock

ROWTH   *n* pl. -S routh

ROYAL   *n* pl. -S a size of printing paper

ROYALISM   *n* pl. -S support of a monarch or monarchy

ROYALIST   *n* pl. -S a supporter of a monarch or monarchy

ROYALLY   *adv* in a kingly manner

ROYALTY   *n* pl. -TIES the status or power of a monarch

ROYSTER   *v* -ED, -ING, -S to roister

ROZZER   *n* pl. -S a policeman

RUANA   *n* pl. -S a woolen poncho

RUB   *v* RUBBED, RUBBING, RUBS to move along the surface of a body with pressure

RUBABOO   *n* pl. -BOOS a type of soup

RUBACE   *n* pl. -S rubasse

RUBAIYAT   *n* pl. RUBAIYAT four-lined stanzas in Persian poetry

RUBASSE   *n* pl. -S a variety of quartz

RUBATO   *n* pl. -TOS a fluctuation of speed within a musical phrase

RUBBABOO   *n* pl. -BOOS rubaboo

RUBBED   past tense of rub

RUBBER   *v* -ED, -ING, -S to stretch one's neck in looking at something

RUBBERY   *adj* resembling rubber (an elastic substance)

RUBBING   *n* pl. -S an image produced by rubbing

RUBBISH   *n* pl. -ES worthless, unwanted matter **RUBBISHY** *adj*

RUBBLE   *v* -BLED, -BLING, -BLES to reduce to rubble (broken pieces)

RUBBLY   *adj* -BLIER, -BLIEST abounding in rubble

RUBDOWN   *n* pl. -S a brisk rubbing of the body

RUBE   *n* pl. -S a rustic

RUBELLA   *n* pl. -S a virus disease

RUBEOLA   *n* pl. -S a virus disease **RUBEOLAR** *adj*

RUBICUND   *adj* ruddy

RUBIDIUM   *n* pl. -S a metallic element **RUBIDIC** *adj*

RUBIED   past tense of ruby

RUBIER   comparative of ruby

RUBIES   present 3d person sing. of ruby

RUBIEST   superlative of ruby

RUBIGO   *n* pl. -GOS red iron oxide

RUBIOUS   *adj* ruby-colored

RUBLE   *n* pl. -S a monetary unit of the Soviet Union

RUBOFF   *n* pl. -S a deep impression made by close contact

RUBOUT   *n* pl. -S an instance of obliterating something

RUBRIC   *n* pl. -S a part of a manuscript or book that appears in red **RUBRICAL** *adj*

RUBUS   *n* pl. RUBUS a plant of the rose family

RUBY   *v* -BIED, -BYING, -BIES to tint with the color of a ruby (a deep-red precious stone)

RUBY   *adj* -BIER, -BIEST of a deep-red color

RUBYLIKE   *adj* resembling a ruby

RUCHE   *n* pl. -S a pleated strip of fine fabric

RUCHED   *adj* trimmed with a ruche

RUCHING   *n* pl. -S a ruche

RUCK	*v* -ED, -ING, -S to wrinkle or crease	**RUG**	*v* RUGGED, RUGGING, RUGS to tear roughly
RUCKLE	*v* -LED, -LING, -LES to ruck	**RUGA**	*n* pl. -GAE an anatomical fold or wrinkle **RUGAL, RUGATE** *adj*
RUCKSACK	*n* pl. -S a knapsack		
RUCKUS	*n* pl. -ES a noisy disturbance	**RUGBY**	*n* pl. -BIES a form of football
RUCTION	*n* pl. -S a ruckus	**RUGGED**	*adj* -GEDER, -GEDEST having an uneven surface **RUGGEDLY** *adv*
RUCTIOUS	*adj* quarrelsome		
RUDD	*n* pl. -S a freshwater fish	**RUGGER**	*n* pl. -S rugby
RUDDER	*n* pl. -S a vertical blade used to direct the course of a vessel	**RUGGING**	present participle of rug
		RUGLIKE	*adj* resembling a rug (a thick fabric used as a floor covering)
RUDDIER	comparative of ruddy		
RUDDIEST	superlative of ruddy	**RUGOLA**	*n* pl. -S arugula
RUDDILY	*adv* in a ruddy manner	**RUGOSA**	*n* pl. -S a flowering plant
RUDDLE	*v* -DLED, -DLING, -DLES to color with a red dye	**RUGOSE**	*adj* full of wrinkles **RUGOSELY** *adv*
RUDDOCK	*n* pl. -S a European bird	**RUGOSITY**	*n* pl. -TIES the state of being rugose
RUDDY	*adj* -DIER, -DIEST having a healthy, reddish color		
		RUGOUS	*adj* rugose
RUDE	*adj* RUDER, RUDEST discourteous or impolite **RUDELY** *adv*	**RUGULOSE**	*adj* having small wrinkles
		RUIN	*v* -ED, -ING, -S to destroy **RUINABLE** *adj*
RUDENESS	*n* pl. -ES the quality of being rude	**RUINATE**	*v* -ATED, -ATING, -ATES to ruin
RUDERAL	*n* pl. -S a plant growing in poor land	**RUINER**	*n* pl. -S one that ruins
		RUING	present participle of rue
RUDESBY	*n* pl. -BIES a rude person	**RUINOUS**	*adj* destructive
RUDEST	superlative of rude	**RULE**	*v* RULED, RULING, RULES to exercise control over **RULABLE** *adj*
RUDIMENT	*n* pl. -S a basic principle or element		
RUE	*v* RUED, RUING, RUES to feel sorrow or remorse for	**RULELESS**	*adj* not restrained or regulated by law
RUEFUL	*adj* feeling sorrow or remorse **RUEFULLY** *adv*	**RULER**	*n* pl. -S one that rules
		RULING	*n* pl. -S an authoritative decision
RUER	*n* pl. -S one that rues	**RULY**	*adj* RULIER, RULIEST orderly
RUFF	*v* -ED, -ING, -S to trump	**RUM**	*n* pl. -S an alcoholic liquor
RUFFE	*n* pl. -S a freshwater fish	**RUM**	*adj* RUMMER, RUMMEST odd
RUFFIAN	*n* pl. -S a tough, lawless person	**RUMAKI**	*n* pl. -S chicken liver wrapped together with water chestnuts in a bacon slice
RUFFLE	*v* -FLED, -FLING, -FLES to destroy the smoothness of		
RUFFLER	*n* pl. -S one that ruffles	**RUMBA**	*v* -ED, -ING, -S to perform a ballroom dance
RUFFLIER	comparative of ruffly		
RUFFLIEST	superlative of ruffly	**RUMBLE**	*v* -BLED, -BLING, -BLES to make a deep, thunderous sound
RUFFLIKE	*adj* resembling a ruff (a pleated collar)		
		RUMBLER	*n* pl. -S one that rumbles
RUFFLING	present participle of ruffle	**RUMBLING**	*n* pl. -S a thunderous sound
RUFFLY	*adj* -FLIER, -FLIEST not smooth	**RUMBLY**	*adj* tending to rumble
RUFIYAA	*n* pl. RUFIYAA a monetary unit of the Maldives	**RUMEN**	*n* pl. -MINA or -MENS a part of the stomach of a ruminant **RUMINAL** *adj*
RUFOUS	*adj* reddish		

RUMINANT   *n* pl. -S a hoofed, even-toed mammal

RUMINATE   *v* -NATED, -NATING, -NATES to chew again

RUMMAGE   *v* -MAGED, -MAGING, -MAGES to search thoroughly through

RUMMAGER   *n* pl. -S one that rummages

RUMMER   *n* pl. -S a large drinking glass

RUMMEST   superlative of rum

RUMMY   *n* pl. -MIES a card game

RUMMY   *adj* -MIER, -MIEST odd

RUMOR   *v* -ED, -ING, -S to spread by hearsay

RUMOUR   *v* -ED, -ING, -S to rumor

RUMP   *n* pl. -S the lower and back part of the trunk **RUMPLESS** *adj*

RUMPLE   *v* -PLED, -PLING, -PLES to wrinkle

RUMPLY   *adj* -PLIER, -PLIEST rumpled

RUMPUS   *n* pl. -ES a noisy disturbance

RUN   *v* RAN, RUNNING, RUNS to move by rapid steps

RUNABOUT   *n* pl. -S a small, open auto

RUNAGATE   *n* pl. -S a deserter

RUNAWAY   *n* pl. -AWAYS one that runs away

RUNBACK   *n* pl. -S a type of run in football

RUNDLE   *n* pl. -S a rung

RUNDLET   *n* pl. -S a small barrel

RUNDOWN   *n* pl. -S a summary

RUNE   *n* pl. -S a letter of an ancient alphabet **RUNELIKE** *adj*

RUNG   *n* pl. -S a crosspiece forming a step of a ladder **RUNGLESS** *adj*

RUNIC   *adj* pertaining to a rune

RUNKLE   *v* -KLED, -KLING, -KLES to wrinkle

RUNLESS   *adj* scoring no runs in baseball

RUNLET   *n* pl. -S a small stream

RUNNEL   *n* pl. -S a small stream

RUNNER   *n* pl. -S one that runs

RUNNING   *n* pl. -S a race

RUNNY   *adj* -NIER, -NIEST tending to drip

RUNOFF   *n* pl. -S rainfall that is not absorbed by the soil

RUNOUT   *n* pl. -S the end of a film strip

RUNOVER   *n* pl. -S matter for publication that exceeds the allotted space

RUNROUND   *n* pl. -S evasive action

RUNT   *n* pl. -S a small person or animal **RUNTISH** *adj*

RUNTY   *adj* RUNTIER, RUNTIEST small

RUNWAY   *n* pl. -WAYS a landing and takeoff strip for aircraft

RUPEE   *n* pl. -S a monetary unit of India

RUPIAH   *n* pl. -S a monetary unit of Indonesia

RUPTURE   *v* -TURED, -TURING, -TURES to burst

RURAL   *adj* pertaining to the country

RURALISE   *v* -ISED, -ISING, -ISES to ruralize

RURALISM   *n* pl. -S the state of being rural

RURALIST   *n* pl. -S one who lives in the country

RURALITE   *n* pl. -S a ruralist

RURALITY   *n* pl. -TIES the state of being rural

RURALIZE   *v* -IZED, -IZING, -IZES to make rural

RURALLY   *adv* in a rural manner

RURBAN   *adj* partially rural and urban

RUSE   *n* pl. -S a deception

RUSH   *v* -ED, -ING, -ES to move swiftly

RUSHEE   *n* pl. -S a college student seeking admission to a fraternity or sorority

RUSHER   *n* pl. -S one that rushes

RUSHIER   comparative of rushy

RUSHIEST   superlative of rushy

RUSHING   *n* pl. -S yardage gained in football by running plays

RUSHLIKE   *adj* resembling a rush (a grasslike marsh plant)

RUSHY   *adj* RUSHIER, RUSHIEST abounding in rushes

RUSINE   *adj* pertaining to a genus of deer

RUSK   *n* pl. -S a sweetened biscuit

RUSSET   *n* pl. -S a reddish or yellowish brown color **RUSSETY** *adj*

RUSSIFY   *v* -FIED, -FYING, -FIES to make Russian

RUST   *v* -ED, -ING, -S to form rust (a reddish coating that forms on iron) **RUSTABLE** *adj*

RUSTIC   *n* pl. -S one who lives in the country

RUSTICAL   *n* pl. -S a rustic

RUSTICLY	*adv* in a rural manner
RUSTIER	comparative of rusty
RUSTIEST	superlative of rusty
RUSTILY	*adv* in a rusty manner
RUSTLE	*v* -TLED, -TLING, -TLES to make a succession of slight, soft sounds
RUSTLER	*n* pl. -S one that rustles
RUSTLESS	*adj* free from rust
RUSTLING	present participle of rustle
RUSTY	*adj* RUSTIER, RUSTIEST covered with rust
RUT	*v* RUTTED, RUTTING, RUTS to make ruts (grooves) in
RUTABAGA	*n* pl. -S a plant having a thick, edible root
RUTH	*n* pl. -S compassion
RUTHENIC	*adj* pertaining to a rare, metallic element
RUTHFUL	*adj* full of compassion
RUTHLESS	*adj* having no compassion
RUTILANT	*adj* having a reddish glow
RUTILE	*n* pl. -S a mineral
RUTIN	*n* pl. -S a chemical compound
RUTTED	past tense of rut
RUTTIER	comparative of rutty
RUTTIEST	superlative of rutty
RUTTILY	*adv* in a rutty manner
RUTTING	present participle of rut
RUTTISH	*adj* lustful
RUTTY	*adj* -TIER, -TIEST marked by ruts
RYA	*n* pl. -S a Scandinavian handwoven rug
RYE	*n* pl. -S a cereal grass
RYEGRASS	*n* pl. -ES a European grass
RYKE	*v* RYKED, RYKING, RYKES to reach
RYND	*n* pl. -S an iron support
RYOKAN	*n* pl. -S a Japanese inn
RYOT	*n* pl. -S a tenant farmer in India

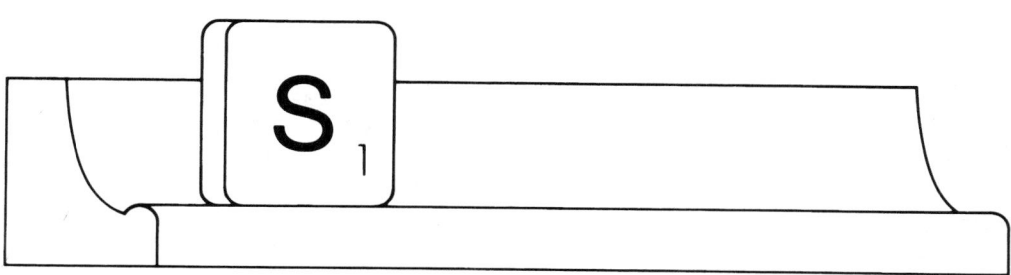

SAB	*v* SABBED, SABBING, SABS to sob
SABATON	*n* pl. -S a piece of armor for the foot
SABAYON	*n* pl. -S a sauce of whipped egg yolks, sugar, and wine
SABBAT	*n* pl. -S an assembly of demons and witches
SABBATH	*n* pl. -S sabbat
SABBATIC	*adj* bringing a period of rest
SABBED	past tense of sab
SABBING	present participle of sab
SABE	*v* SABED, SABEING, SABES to savvy
SABER	*v* -ED, -ING, -S to strike with a saber (a type of sword)
SABIN	*n* pl. -S a unit of sound absorption
SABINE	*n* pl. -S savin
SABIR	*n* pl. -S a French-based pidgin language
SABLE	*n* pl. -S a carnivorous mammal
SABOT	*n* pl. -S a wooden shoe
SABOTAGE	*v* -TAGED, -TAGING, -TAGES to destroy maliciously
SABOTEUR	*n* pl. -S one who sabotages
SABRA	*n* pl. -S a native Israeli
SABRE	*v* -BRED, -BRING, -BRES to saber
SABULOSE	*adj* sabulous
SABULOUS	*adj* sandy
SAC	*n* pl. -S a pouchlike structure in an animal or plant
SACATON	*n* pl. -S a perennial grass
SACBUT	*n* pl. -S sackbut
SACCADE	*n* pl. -S a rapid, jerky movement of the eye **SACCADIC** *adj*
SACCATE	*adj* having a sac
SACCULAR	*adj* resembling a sac
SACCULE	*n* pl. -S a small sac
SACCULUS	*n* pl. -LI saccule
SACHEM	*n* pl. -S a North American Indian chief **SACHEMIC** *adj*
SACHET	*n* pl. -S a small bag containing perfumed powder **SACHETED** *adj*
SACK	*v* -ED, -ING, -S to put into a sack (a large bag)
SACKBUT	*n* pl. -S a medieval trombone
SACKER	*n* pl. -S one that sacks
SACKFUL	*n* pl. SACKFULS or SACKSFUL as much as a sack can hold
SACKING	*n* pl. -S material for making sacks
SACKLIKE	*adj* resembling a sack
SACKSFUL	a pl. of sackful
SACLIKE	*adj* resembling a sac
SACQUE	*n* pl. -S a loose-fitting dress
SACRA	pl. of sacrum
SACRAL	*n* pl. -S a vertebra or nerve situated near the sacrum
SACRARIA	*n/pl* ancient Roman shrines
SACRED	*adj* dedicated to or set apart for the worship of a deity **SACREDLY** *adv*
SACRING	*n* pl. -S the consecration of bread and wine of the Eucharist
SACRIST	*n* pl. -S a person in charge of a sacristy
SACRISTY	*n* pl. -TIES a room in which sacred vessels and vestments are kept
SACRUM	*n* pl. -CRA or -CRUMS a bone of the pelvis
SAD	*adj* SADDER, SADDEST unhappy
SADDEN	*v* -ED, -ING, -S to make sad

SADDHU	*n* pl. -S sadhu
SADDLE	*v* -DLED, -DLING, -DLES to put a saddle (a leather seat for a rider) on
SADDLER	*n* pl. -S one that makes, repairs, or sells saddles
SADDLERY	*n* pl. -DLERIES the shop of a saddler
SADDLING	present participle of saddle
SADE	*n* pl. -S a Hebrew letter
SADHE	*n* pl. -S sade
SADHU	*n* pl. -S a Hindu holy man
SADI	*n* pl. -S sade
SADIRON	*n* pl. -S a heavy flatiron
SADISM	*n* pl. -S a tendency to take delight in inflicting pain
SADIST	*n* pl. -S one marked by sadism **SADISTIC** *adj*
SADLY	*adv* in a sad manner
SADNESS	*n* pl. -ES the state of being sad
SAE	*adv* so
SAFARI	*v* -ED, -ING, -S to go on a hunting expedition
SAFE	*adj* SAFER, SAFEST free from danger **SAFELY** *adv*
SAFE	*n* pl. -S a metal receptacle for storing valuables
SAFENESS	*n* pl. -ES the quality of being safe
SAFER	comparative of safe
SAFEST	superlative of safe
SAFETY	*v* -TIED, -TYING, -TIES to protect against failure, breakage, or accident
SAFFRON	*n* pl. -S a flowering plant
SAFRANIN	*n* pl. -S a red dye
SAFROL	*n* pl. -S safrole
SAFROLE	*n* pl. -S a poisonous liquid
SAG	*v* SAGGED, SAGGING, SAGS to bend or sink downward from weight or pressure
SAGA	*n* pl. -S a medieval Scandinavian narrative
SAGACITY	*n* pl. -TIES wisdom
SAGAMAN	*n* pl. -MEN a writer of sagas
SAGAMORE	*n* pl. -S an Algonquian Indian chief
SAGANASH	*n* pl. -ES a white man — an Algonquian Indian term
SAGBUT	*n* pl. -S sackbut
SAGE	*adj* SAGER, SAGEST wise **SAGELY** *adv*
SAGE	*n* pl. -S an aromatic herb used as seasoning
SAGENESS	*n* pl. -ES wisdom
SAGER	comparative of sage
SAGEST	superlative of sage
SAGGAR	*v* -ED, -ING, -S to bake in a saggar (a protective clay casing)
SAGGARD	*n* pl. -S a saggar
SAGGED	past tense of sag
SAGGER	*v* -ED, -ING, -S to saggar
SAGGING	present participle of sag
SAGGY	*adj* -GIER, -GIEST characterized by sagging
SAGIER	comparative of sagy
SAGIEST	superlative of sagy
SAGITTAL	*adj* resembling an arrow or arrowhead
SAGO	*n* pl. -GOS a tropical tree
SAGUARO	*n* pl. -ROS a tall cactus
SAGUM	*n* pl. -GA a cloak worn by ancient Roman soldiers
SAGY	*adj* SAGIER, SAGIEST flavored with sage
SAHIB	*n* pl. -S sir; master — used as a term of respect in colonial India
SAHIWAL	*n* pl. -S any of a breed of humped dairy cattle
SAHUARO	*n* pl. -ROS saguaro
SAICE	*n* pl. -S syce
SAID	*n* pl. -S sayyid
SAIGA	*n* pl. -S a small antelope
SAIL	*v* -ED, -ING, -S to move across the surface of water by the action of wind **SAILABLE** *adj*
SAILBOAT	*n* pl. -S a boat that sails
SAILER	*n* pl. -S a vessel that sails
SAILFISH	*n* pl. -ES a large marine fish
SAILING	*n* pl. -S the act of one that sails
SAILOR	*n* pl. -S a member of a ship's crew **SAILORLY** *adj*
SAIMIN	*n* pl. -S a Hawaiian noodle soup
SAIN	*v* -ED, -ING, -S to make the sign of the cross on
SAINFOIN	*n* pl. -S a perennial herb
SAINT	*v* -ED, -ING, -S to declare to be a saint (a person of exceptional holiness)

SAINTDOM	*n* pl. -S the condition of being a saint
SAINTLY	*adj* -LIER, -LIEST of or befitting a saint
SAITH	a present 3d person sing. of say
SAITHE	*n* pl. SAITHE a marine food fish
SAIYID	*n* pl. -S sayyid
SAJOU	*n* pl. -S a capuchin
SAKE	*n* pl. -S benefit, interest, or advantage
SAKER	*n* pl. -S a Eurasian falcon
SAKI	*n* pl. -S a Japanese liquor
SAL	*n* pl. -S salt
SALAAM	*v* -ED, -ING, -S to greet with a low bow
SALABLE	*adj* capable of being or fit to be sold **SALABLY** *adv*
SALACITY	*n* pl. -TIES lewdness
SALAD	*n* pl. -S a dish of green, raw vegetables
SALADANG	*n* pl. -S a wild ox
SALAL	*n* pl. -S a small shrub
SALAMI	*n* pl. -S a seasoned sausage
SALARIAT	*n* pl. -S the class of salaried persons
SALARY	*v* -RIED, -RYING, -RIES to pay a periodic, fixed compensation to
SALCHOW	*n* pl. -S a figure-skating jump
SALE	*n* pl. -S the act or an instance of selling
SALEABLE	*adj* salable **SALEABLY** *adv*
SALEP	*n* pl. -S a starchy meal ground from the roots of certain orchids
SALEROOM	*n* pl. -S a room in which goods are displayed for sale
SALESMAN	*n* pl. -MEN a man who sells merchandise
SALIC	*adj* pertaining to a group of igneous rocks
SALICIN	*n* pl. -S a chemical compound
SALICINE	*n* pl. -S salicin
SALIENCE	*n* pl. -S a projecting feature or detail
SALIENCY	*n* pl. -CIES salience
SALIENT	*n* pl. -S the part of a fortification projecting closest to the enemy
SALIFY	*v* -FIED, -FYING, -FIES to combine with a salt
SALINA	*n* pl. -S a pond, marsh, or lake containing salt water
SALINE	*n* pl. -S a salt solution
SALINITY	*n* pl. -TIES a concentration of salt
SALINIZE	*v* -NIZED, -NIZING, -NIZES to treat with salt
SALIVA	*n* pl. -S a fluid secreted by the glands of the mouth **SALIVARY** *adj*
SALIVATE	*v* -VATED, -VATING, -VATES to secrete saliva
SALL	*v* shall — SALL is the only form of this verb; it cannot be conjugated
SALLET	*n* pl. -S a light medieval helmet
SALLIED	past tense of sally
SALLIER	*n* pl. -S one that sallies
SALLIES	present 3d person sing. of sally
SALLOW	*adj* -LOWER, -LOWEST of a sickly yellowish color **SALLOWLY** *adv*
SALLOW	*v* -ED, -ING, -S to make sallow
SALLOWY	*adj* abounding in willow trees
SALLY	*v* -LIED, -LYING, -LIES to rush out suddenly
SALMI	*n* pl. -S a dish of roasted game birds
SALMON	*n* pl. -S a food fish
SALMONID	*n* pl. -S a fish of the salmon family
SALOL	*n* pl. -S a chemical compound
SALON	*n* pl. -S a large room in which guests are received
SALOON	*n* pl. -S a tavern
SALOOP	*n* pl. -S a hot drink made from an infusion of aromatic herbs
SALP	*n* pl. -S salpa
SALPA	*n* pl. -PAE or -PAS a free-swimming tunicate
SALPIAN	*n* pl. -S salpa
SALPID	*n* pl. -S salpa
SALPINX	*n* pl. -PINGES an anatomical tube
SALSA	*n* pl. -S a spicy sauce of tomatoes, onions, and peppers
SALSIFY	*n* pl. -FIES a European herb
SALSILLA	*n* pl. -S a tropical plant
SALT	*v* -ED, -ING, -S to treat with salt (a crystalline compound used as a seasoning and preservative)
SALT	*adj* SALTER, SALTEST salty

SALTANT	*adj* jumping or dancing
SALTBOX	*n* pl. -ES a type of house
SALTBUSH	*n* pl. -ES a salt-tolerant plant
SALTER	*n* pl. -S one that salts
SALTERN	*n* pl. -S a place where salt is produced
SALTIE	*n* pl. -S a deep-sea vessel sailing the Great Lakes
SALTIER	*n* pl. -S saltire
SALTIEST	superlative of salty
SALTILY	*adv* in a salty manner
SALTINE	*n* pl. -S a salted cracker
SALTING	*n* pl. -S land regularly flooded by tides
SALTIRE	*n* pl. -S a heraldic design
SALTISH	*adj* somewhat salty
SALTLESS	*adj* having no salt
SALTLIKE	*adj* resembling salt
SALTNESS	*n* pl. -ES the state of being salty
SALTPAN	*n* pl. -S a large pan for making salt by evaporation
SALTWORK	*n* pl. -S a saltern
SALTWORT	*n* pl. -S a seaside herb
SALTY	*adj* SALTIER, SALTIEST tasting of or containing salt
SALUKI	*n* pl. -S a tall, slender dog
SALUTARY	*adj* producing a beneficial effect
SALUTE	*v* -LUTED, -LUTING, -LUTES to greet with a sign of welcome or respect
SALUTER	*n* pl. -S one that salutes
SALVABLE	*adj* capable of being saved **SALVABLY** *adv*
SALVAGE	*v* -VAGED, -VAGING, -VAGES to save from loss or destruction
SALVAGEE	*n* pl. -S one in whose favor salvage has been effected
SALVAGER	*n* pl. -S one that salvages
SALVAGING	present participle of salvage
SALVE	*v* SALVED, SALVING, SALVES to soothe
SALVER	*n* pl. -S a tray or serving platter
SALVIA	*n* pl. -S a flowering plant
SALVIFIC	*adj* having the power to save
SALVING	present participle of salve
SALVO	*v* -ED, -ING, -S or -ES to discharge firearms simultaneously
SALVOR	*n* pl. -S a salvager
SAMARA	*n* pl. -S a dry, one-seeded fruit
SAMARIUM	*n* pl. -S a metallic element
SAMBA	*v* -ED, -ING, -S to perform a Brazilian dance
SAMBAR	*n* pl. -S a large Asian deer
SAMBHAR	*n* pl. -S sambar
SAMBHUR	*n* pl. -S sambar
SAMBO	*n* pl. -BOS a Latin American of mixed black and Indian ancestry
SAMBUCA	*n* pl. -S an ancient stringed instrument
SAMBUKE	*n* pl. -S sambuca
SAMBUR	*n* pl. -S sambar
SAME	*adj* resembling in every relevant respect
SAMECH	*n* pl. -S samek
SAMEK	*n* pl. -S a Hebrew letter
SAMEKH	*n* pl. -S samek
SAMENESS	*n* pl. -ES lack of change or variety
SAMIEL	*n* pl. -S the simoom
SAMISEN	*n* pl. -S a Japanese stringed instrument
SAMITE	*n* pl. -S a silk fabric
SAMIZDAT	*n* pl. -S a system in the Soviet Union for printing and distributing unauthorized literature
SAMLET	*n* pl. -S a young salmon
SAMOSA	*n* pl. -S a filled pastry turnover
SAMOVAR	*n* pl. -S a metal urn for heating water
SAMP	*n* pl. -S coarsely ground corn
SAMPAN	*n* pl. -S a flat-bottomed Chinese skiff
SAMPHIRE	*n* pl. -S a European herb
SAMPLE	*v* -PLED, -PLING, -PLES to test a representative portion of a whole
SAMPLER	*n* pl. -S one that samples
SAMPLING	*n* pl. -S a small part selected for analysis
SAMSARA	*n* pl. -S the cycle of birth, death, and rebirth in Buddhism
SAMSHU	*n* pl. -S a Chinese liquor
SAMURAI	*n* pl. -S a Japanese warrior
SANATIVE	*adj* having the power to cure or heal
SANCTA	a pl. of sanctum

SANCTIFY   *v* -FIED, -FYING, -FIES to make holy

SANCTION   *v* -ED, -ING, -S to authorize

SANCTITY   *n* pl. -TIES holiness

SANCTUM   *n* pl. -TUMS or -TA a sacred place

SAND   *v* -ED, -ING, -S to cover with sand (a loose, granular rock material)

SANDAL   *v* -DALED, -DALING, -DALS or -DALLED, -DALLING, -DALS to provide with sandals (light, open shoes)

SANDARAC   *n* pl. -S an aromatic resin

SANDBAG   *v* -BAGGED, -BAGGING, -BAGS to surround with bags of sand

SANDBANK   *n* pl. -S a large mass of sand

SANDBAR   *n* pl. -S a ridge of sand formed in a river or sea

SANDBOX   *n* pl. -ES a box containing sand for children to play in

SANDBUR   *n* pl. -S an annual herb

SANDBURR   *n* pl. -S sandbur

SANDDAB   *n* pl. -S a small flatfish

SANDER   *n* pl. -S one that sands

SANDFISH   *n* pl. -ES a marine fish

SANDFLY   *n* pl. -FLIES a biting fly

SANDHI   *n* pl. -S a process of phonetic modification

SANDHOG   *n* pl. -S a worker who digs or works in sand

SANDIER   comparative of sandy

SANDIEST   superlative of sandy

SANDLIKE   *adj* resembling sand

SANDLING   *n* pl. -S a marine fish

SANDLOT   *n* pl. -S a vacant lot

SANDMAN   *n* pl. -MEN a mythical person who makes children sleepy by sprinkling sand in their eyes

SANDPEEP   *n* pl. -S a wading bird

SANDPILE   *n* pl. -S a pile of sand

SANDPIT   *n* pl. -S a pit dug in sandy soil

SANDSHOE   *n* pl. -S a lightweight sneaker

SANDSOAP   *n* pl. -S a type of soap

SANDSPUR   *n* pl. -S a sandbur

SANDWICH   *v* -ED, -ING, -ES to place between two layers or objects

SANDWORM   *n* pl. -S a sand-dwelling worm

SANDWORT   *n* pl. -S a flowering plant

SANDY   *adj* SANDIER, SANDIEST containing or covered with sand

SANE   *adj* SANER, SANEST mentally sound **SANELY** *adv*

SANE   *v* SANED, SANING, SANES to sain

SANENESS   *n* pl. -ES sanity

SANER   comparative of sane

SANEST   superlative of sane

SANG   past tense of sing

SANGA   *n* pl. -S sangar

SANGAR   *n* pl. -S a temporary fortification for two or three men

SANGAREE   *n* pl. -S an alcoholic beverage

SANGER   *n* pl. -S sangar

SANGH   *n* pl. -S an association promoting unity between the different groups in Hinduism

SANGRIA   *n* pl. -S an alcoholic beverage

SANGUINE   *n* pl. -S a red color

SANICLE   *n* pl. -S a medicinal herb

SANIES   *n* pl. SANIES a fluid discharged from wounds **SANIOUS** *adj*

SANING   present participle of sane

SANITARY   *n* pl. -TARIES a public urinal

SANITATE   *v* -TATED, -TATING, -TATES to sanitize

SANITIES   pl. of sanity

SANITISE   *v* -TISED, -TISING, -TISES to sanitize

SANITIZE   *v* -TIZED, -TIZING, -TIZES to guard against infection or disease by cleaning or sterilizing

SANITY   *n* pl. -TIES the state of being sane

SANJAK   *n* pl. -S an administrative district of Turkey

SANK   past tense of sink

SANNOP   *n* pl. -S sannup

SANNUP   *n* pl. -S a married male American Indian

SANNYASI   *n* pl. -S a Hindu monk

SANS   *prep* without

SANSAR   *n* pl. -S sarsar

SANSEI   *n* pl. -S a grandchild of Japanese immigrants to the United States

SANSERIF   *n* pl. -S a typeface without serifs

SANTALIC   *adj* pertaining to sandalwood

SANTALOL   *n* pl. -S sandalwood oil

SANTIMS	*n* pl. -TIMI a former coin of Latvia
SANTIR	*n* pl. -S a Persian dulcimer
SANTO	*n* pl. -TOS a wooden image of a saint
SANTOL	*n* pl. -S a tropical tree
SANTONIN	*n* pl. -S a chemical compound
SANTOUR	*n* pl. -S santir
SANTUR	*n* pl. -S santir
SAP	*v* SAPPED, SAPPING, SAPS to deplete or weaken gradually
SAPAJOU	*n* pl. -S a capuchin
SAPHEAD	*n* pl. -S a foolish, stupid, or gullible person
SAPHENA	*n* pl. -NAE a vein of the leg
SAPID	*adj* pleasant to the taste
SAPIDITY	*n* pl. -TIES the state of being sapid
SAPIENCE	*n* pl. -S wisdom
SAPIENCY	*n* pl. -CIES sapience
SAPIENS	*adj* pertaining to recent man
SAPIENT	*adj* wise
SAPLESS	*adj* lacking vitality
SAPLING	*n* pl. -S a young tree
SAPONIFY	*v* -FIED, -FYING, -FIES to convert into soap
SAPONIN	*n* pl. -S a soapy substance obtained from plants
SAPONINE	*n* pl. -S saponin
SAPONITE	*n* pl. -S a mineral found in veins and cavities of rocks
SAPOR	*n* pl. -S flavor **SAPOROUS** *adj*
SAPOTA	*n* pl. -S an evergreen tree
SAPOTE	*n* pl. -S a tropical American tree
SAPOUR	*n* pl. -S sapor
SAPPED	past tense of sap
SAPPER	*n* pl. -S a military engineer
SAPPHIC	*n* pl. -S a type of verse form
SAPPHIRE	*n* pl. -S a blue gem
SAPPHISM	*n* pl. -S lesbianism
SAPPHIST	*n* pl. -S a lesbian
SAPPING	present participle of sap
SAPPY	*adj* -PIER, -PIEST silly **SAPPILY** *adv*
SAPREMIA	*n* pl. -S a form of blood poisoning **SAPREMIC** *adj*
SAPROBE	*n* pl. -S an organism that derives its nourishment from decaying organic matter **SAPROBIC** *adj*
SAPROPEL	*n* pl. -S mud consisting chiefly of decaying organic matter
SAPSAGO	*n* pl. -GOS a hard green cheese
SAPWOOD	*n* pl. -S the newly formed outer wood of a tree
SARABAND	*n* pl. -S a stately Spanish dance
SARAN	*n* pl. -S a thermoplastic resin
SARAPE	*n* pl. -S serape
SARCASM	*n* pl. -S a sharply mocking or contemptuous remark
SARCENET	*n* pl. -S a silk fabric
SARCOID	*n* pl. -S a disease of horses
SARCOMA	*n* pl. -MAS or -MATA a type of tumor
SARCOUS	*adj* composed of flesh or muscle
SARD	*n* pl. -S a variety of quartz
SARDANA	*n* pl. -S a Spanish folk dance
SARDAR	*n* pl. -S sirdar
SARDINE	*n* pl. -S a small food fish
SARDIUS	*n* pl. -ES sard
SARDONIC	*adj* mocking
SARDONYX	*n* pl. -ES a variety of quartz
SAREE	*n* pl. -S sari
SARGASSO	*n* pl. -GASSOS a brownish seaweed
SARGE	*n* pl. -S sergeant
SARI	*n* pl. -S an outer garment worn by Hindu women
SARIN	*n* pl. -S a toxic gas
SARK	*n* pl. -S a shirt
SARKY	*adj* SARKIER, SARKIEST sarcastic
SARMENT	*n* pl. -S a type of plant stem
SARMENTA	*n/pl* sarments
SAROD	*n* pl. -S a lute of northern India
SARODE	*n* pl. -S sarod
SARODIST	*n* pl. -S one who plays the sarod
SARONG	*n* pl. -S an outer garment worn in the Pacific islands
SAROS	*n* pl. -ES the eclipse cycle of the sun and moon
SARSAR	*n* pl. -S a cold, whistling wind
SARSEN	*n* pl. -S a large sandstone block
SARSENET	*n* pl. -S sarcenet
SARTOR	*n* pl. -S a tailor
SARTORII	*n/pl* flat, narrow thigh muscles

SASH   *v* -ED, -ING, -ES to furnish with a frame in which glass is set

SASHAY   *v* -ED, -ING, -S to flounce

SASHIMI   *n* pl. -S a Japanese dish of sliced raw fish

SASIN   *n* pl. -S an antelope of India

SASS   *v* -ED, -ING, -ES to talk impudently to

SASSABY   *n* pl. -BIES an African antelope

SASSIER   comparative of sassy

SASSIES   pl. of sassy

SASSIEST   superlative of sassy

SASSILY   *adv* in a sassy manner

SASSWOOD   *n* pl. -S an African tree

SASSY   *n* pl. -SIES sasswood

SASSY   *adj* SASSIER, SASSIEST impudent

SASTRUGA   *n* pl. -GI a ridge of snow formed by the wind in polar regions

SAT   past tense of sit

SATANG   *n* pl. -S a monetary unit of Thailand

SATANIC   *adj* extremely evil

SATANISM   *n* pl. -S worship of the powers of evil

SATANIST   *n* pl. -S one who practices satanism

SATARA   *n* pl. -S a woolen fabric

SATAY   *n* pl. -TAYS marinated meat that is skewered and broiled and dipped in peanut sauce

SATCHEL   *n* pl. -S a small carrying bag

SATE   *v* SATED, SATING, SATES to satiate

SATEEN   *n* pl. -S a cotton fabric

SATEM   *adj* pertaining to a group of Indo-European languages

SATI   *n* pl. -S suttee

SATIABLE   *adj* capable of being satiated **SATIABLY** *adv*

SATIATE   *v* -ATED, -ATING, -ATES to satisfy to or beyond capacity

SATIETY   *n* pl. -ETIES the state of being satiated

SATIN   *n* pl. -S a smooth fabric

SATINET   *n* pl. -S a thin satin

SATING   present participle of sate

SATINPOD   *n* pl. -S a flowering plant

SATINY   *adj* resembling satin

SATIRE   *n* pl. -S the use of derisive wit to attack folly or wickedness **SATIRIC** *adj*

SATIRISE   *v* -RISED, -RISING, -RISES to satirize

SATIRIST   *n* pl. -S one who satirizes

SATIRIZE   *v* -RIZED, -RIZING, -RIZES to subject to satire

SATISFY   *v* -FIED, -FYING, -FIES to provide fully with what is desired, expected, or needed

SATORI   *n* pl. -S the illumination of spirit sought by Zen Buddhists

SATRAP   *n* pl. -S a governor of a province in ancient Persia

SATRAPY   *n* pl. -PIES the territory of a satrap

SATSUMA   *n* pl. -S a variety of orange

SATURANT   *n* pl. -S a substance used to saturate

SATURATE   *v* -RATED, -RATING, -RATES to fill completely with something that permeates

SATYR   *n* pl. -S a woodland deity of Greek mythology **SATYRIC** *adj*

SATYRID   *n* pl. -S a brownish butterfly

SAU   *n* pl. SAU xu

SAUCE   *v* SAUCED, SAUCING, SAUCES to season with sauce (a flavorful liquid dressing)

SAUCEBOX   *n* pl. -ES a saucy person

SAUCEPAN   *n* pl. -S a cooking utensil

SAUCER   *n* pl. -S a small, shallow dish

SAUCH   *n* pl. -S saugh

SAUCING   present participle of sauce

SAUCY   *adj* SAUCIER, SAUCIEST impudent **SAUCILY** *adv*

SAUGER   *n* pl. -S a freshwater fish

SAUGH   *n* pl. -S a willow tree **SAUGHY** *adj*

SAUL   *n* pl. -S soul

SAULT   *n* pl. -S a waterfall

SAUNA   *n* pl. -S a Finnish steam bath

SAUNTER   *v* -ED, -ING, -S to walk in a leisurely manner

SAUREL   *n* pl. -S a marine fish

SAURIAN   *n* pl. -S any of a suborder of reptiles

SAUROPOD   *n* pl. -S any of a suborder of large dinosaurs

SAURY   *n* pl. -RIES a marine fish

SAUSAGE	n pl. -S finely chopped and seasoned meat stuffed into a casing
SAUTE	v -TEED or -TED, -TEING, -TES to fry in a small amount of fat
SAUTERNE	n pl. -S a sweet white wine
SAUTOIR	n pl. -S a saltire
SAUTOIRE	n pl. -S sautoir
SAVABLE	adj capable of being saved
SAVAGE	adj -AGER, -AGEST fierce **SAVAGELY** adv
SAVAGE	v -AGED, -AGING, -AGES to attack or treat brutally
SAVAGERY	n pl. -RIES the quality of being savage
SAVAGEST	superlative of savage
SAVAGING	present participle of savage
SAVAGISM	n pl. -S savagery
SAVANNA	n pl. -S a flat, treeless grassland
SAVANNAH	n pl. -S savanna
SAVANT	n pl. -S a man of profound learning
SAVARIN	n pl. -S a yeast cake baked in a ring mold
SAVATE	n pl. -S a pugilistic sport
SAVE	v SAVED, SAVING, SAVES to rescue from danger, injury, or loss **SAVEABLE** adj
SAVELOY	n pl. -LOYS a highly seasoned sausage
SAVER	n pl. -S one that saves
SAVIN	n pl. -S an evergreen shrub
SAVINE	n pl. -S savin
SAVING	n pl. -S the act or an instance of saving
SAVINGLY	adv in a thrifty manner
SAVIOR	n pl. -S one that saves
SAVIOUR	n pl. -S savior
SAVOR	v -ED, -ING, -S to taste or smell with pleasure
SAVORER	n pl. -S one that savors
SAVORIER	comparative of savory
SAVORIES	pl. of savory
SAVOROUS	adj savory
SAVORY	adj -VORIER, -VORIEST pleasant to the taste or smell **SAVORILY** adv
SAVORY	n pl. -VORIES a savory dish served before or after a meal
SAVOUR	v -ED, -ING, -S to savor
SAVOURER	n pl. -S savorer
SAVOURY	adj -VOURIER, -VOURIEST savory
SAVOURY	n pl. -VOURIES a savory
SAVOY	n pl. -VOYS a variety of cabbage
SAVVY	v -VIED, -VYING, -VIES to understand
SAVVY	adj -VIER, -VIEST shrewd
SAW	v SAWED, SAWN, SAWING, SAWS to cut or divide with a saw (a type of cutting tool)
SAWBILL	n pl. -S a tropical bird
SAWBONES	n pl. -BONESES a surgeon
SAWBUCK	n pl. -S a sawhorse
SAWDUST	n pl. -S small particles of wood produced in sawing
SAWER	n pl. -S one that saws
SAWFISH	n pl. -ES a marine fish
SAWFLY	n pl. -FLIES a winged insect
SAWHORSE	n pl. -S a rack used to support a piece of wood being sawed
SAWLIKE	adj resembling a saw
SAWLOG	n pl. -S a log large enough to saw into boards
SAWMILL	n pl. -S a place where logs are sawed
SAWN	a past participle of saw
SAWNEY	n pl. -NEYS a foolish person
SAWTOOTH	n pl. -TEETH a cutting edge on a saw
SAWYER	n pl. -S one that saws wood for a living
SAX	n pl. -ES a saxophone
SAXATILE	adj living or growing among rocks
SAXHORN	n pl. -S a brass wind instrument
SAXONY	n pl. -NIES a woolen fabric
SAXTUBA	n pl. -S a bass saxhorn
SAY	v SAID, SAYING, present sing. 2d person SAY, SAYEST, or SAYST, 3d person SAYS or SAITH to utter **SAYABLE** adj
SAYER	n pl. -S one that says
SAYID	n pl. -S sayyid
SAYING	n pl. -S a maxim
SAYONARA	n pl. -S goodby
SAYST	a present 2d person sing. of say

SAYYID	*n* pl. -S lord; sir — used as a title of respect for a Muslim dignitary
SCAB	*v* SCABBED, SCABBING, SCABS to become covered with a scab (a crust that forms over a healing wound)
SCABBARD	*v* -ED, -ING, -S to put into a sheath, as a sword
SCABBLE	*v* -BLED, -BLING, -BLES to shape roughly
SCABBY	*adj* -BIER, -BIEST covered with scabs **SCABBILY** *adv*
SCABIES	*n* pl. SCABIES a skin disease
SCABIOSA	*n* pl. -S scabious
SCABIOUS	*n* pl. -ES a flowering plant
SCABLAND	*n* pl. -S rocky land with little soil cover
SCABLIKE	*adj* resembling a scab
SCABROUS	*adj* roughened with small projections
SCAD	*n* pl. -S a marine fish
SCAFFOLD	*v* -ED, -ING, -S to provide with a scaffold (a temporary platform for workmen)
SCAG	*n* pl. -S heroin
SCALABLE	*adj* capable of being scaled **SCALABLY** *adv*
SCALADE	*n* pl. -S an act of scaling the walls of a fortification
SCALADO	*n* pl. -DOS scalade
SCALAGE	*n* pl. -S a percentage deduction to compensate for shrinkage
SCALAR	*n* pl. -S a mathematical quantity possessing only magnitude
SCALARE	*n* pl. -S a tropical fish
SCALAWAG	*n* pl. -S a rascal
SCALD	*v* -ED, -ING, -S to burn with hot liquid or steam
SCALDIC	*adj* skaldic
SCALE	*v* SCALED, SCALING, SCALES to climb up or over
SCALENE	*adj* designating a triangle having no two sides equal
SCALENUS	*n* pl. -NI a muscle of the neck
SCALEPAN	*n* pl. -S a pan on a weighing scale
SCALER	*n* pl. -S one that scales
SCALEUP	*n* pl. -S an increase based on a fixed ratio
SCALIER	comparative of scaly
SCALIEST	superlative of scaly
SCALING	present participle of scale
SCALL	*n* pl. -S a scaly eruption of the skin
SCALLION	*n* pl. -S an onion-like plant
SCALLOP	*v* -ED, -ING, -S to bake in a sauce topped with bread crumbs
SCALP	*v* -ED, -ING, -S to remove an upper part from
SCALPEL	*n* pl. -S a small surgical knife
SCALPER	*n* pl. -S one that scalps
SCALY	*adj* SCALIER, SCALIEST peeling off in flakes
SCAM	*v* SCAMMED, SCAMMING, SCAMS to cheat or swindle
SCAMMONY	*n* pl. -NIES a climbing plant
SCAMP	*v* -ED, -ING, -S to perform in a hasty or careless manner
SCAMPER	*v* -ED, -ING, -S to run playfully about
SCAMPI	*n* pl. SCAMPI or SCAMPIES large shrimp used in Italian cooking
SCAMPISH	*adj* rascally
SCAN	*v* SCANNED, SCANNING, SCANS to examine closely
SCANDAL	*v* -DALED, -DALING, -DALS or -DALLED, -DALLING, -DALS to defame
SCANDENT	*adj* climbing, as a plant
SCANDIA	*n* pl. -S an oxide of scandium
SCANDIUM	*n* pl. -S a metallic element **SCANDIC** *adj*
SCANNED	past tense of scan
SCANNER	*n* pl. -S one that scans
SCANNING	*n* pl. -S close examination
SCANSION	*n* pl. -S the analysis of verse into metrical feet and rhythm patterns
SCANT	*adj* SCANTER, SCANTEST meager
SCANT	*v* -ED, -ING, -S to provide with a meager portion
SCANTIER	comparative of scanty
SCANTIES	*n/pl* brief panties for women
SCANTLY	*adv* in a scant manner
SCANTY	*adj* SCANTIER, SCANTIEST meager **SCANTILY** *adv*
SCAPE	*v* SCAPED, SCAPING, SCAPES to escape
SCAPHOID	*n* pl. -S a bone of the wrist
SCAPOSE	*adj* bearing a leafless stalk

SCAPULA	*n* pl. -LAE or -LAS a bone of the shoulder
SCAPULAR	*n* pl. -S a sleeveless outer garment worn by monks
SCAR	*v* SCARRED, SCARRING, SCARS to form a scar (a mark left by the healing of injured tissue)
SCARAB	*n* pl. -S a large, black beetle
SCARCE	*adj* SCARCER, SCARCEST infrequently seen or found
SCARCELY	*adv* by a narrow margin
SCARCITY	*n* pl. -TIES the quality of being scarce
SCARE	*v* SCARED, SCARING, SCARES to frighten
SCARER	*n* pl. -S one that scares
SCAREY	*adj* SCARIER, SCARIEST scary
SCARF	*n* pl. SCARFS or SCARVES a piece of cloth worn for warmth or protection
SCARF	*v* -ED, -ING, -S to cover with a scarf
SCARFPIN	*n* pl. -S a tiepin
SCARIER	comparative of scarey and scary
SCARIEST	superlative of scarey and scary
SCARIFY	*v* -FIED, -FYING, -FIES to make superficial cuts in
SCARILY	*adv* in a scary manner
SCARING	present participle of scare
SCARIOSE	*adj* scarious
SCARIOUS	*adj* thin, dry, and membranous
SCARLESS	*adj* having no scars
SCARLET	*n* pl. -S a red color
SCARP	*v* -ED, -ING, -S to cut or make into a steep slope
SCARPER	*v* -ED, -ING, -S to flee
SCARPH	*v* -ED, -ING, -S to unite by means of a type of joint
SCARRED	past tense of scar
SCARRING	present participle of scar
SCARRY	*adj* -RIER, -RIEST marked with scars
SCART	*v* -ED, -ING, -S to scratch
SCARVES	a pl. of scarf
SCARY	*adj* SCARIER, SCARIEST frightening
SCAT	*v* SCATTED, SCATTING, SCATS to leave hastily
SCATBACK	*n* pl. -S a type of player in football
SCATHE	*v* SCATHED, SCATHING, SCATHES to criticize severely
SCATT	*n* pl. -S a tax
SCATTED	past tense of scat
SCATTER	*v* -ED, -ING, -S to go or send in various directions
SCATTING	present participle of scat
SCATTY	*adj* -TIER, -TIEST crazy
SCAUP	*n* pl. -S a sea duck
SCAUPER	*n* pl. -S an engraving tool
SCAUR	*n* pl. -S a protruding, isolated rock
SCAVENGE	*v* -ENGED, -ENGING, -ENGES to search through rubbish for usable items
SCENA	*n* pl. -S an elaborate composition for a single voice
SCENARIO	*n* pl. -IOS a summary of the plot of a dramatic work
SCEND	*v* -ED, -ING, -S to rise upward, as a ship on a wave
SCENE	*n* pl. -S the place where some action or event occurs
SCENERY	*n* pl. -ERIES a picturesque landscape or view
SCENIC	*adj* pertaining to scenery
SCENICAL	*adj* scenic
SCENT	*v* -ED, -ING, -S to fill with an odor
SCEPTER	*v* -ED, -ING, -S to invest with royal authority
SCEPTIC	*n* pl. -S skeptic
SCEPTRAL	*adj* pertaining to royal authority
SCEPTRE	*v* -TRED, -TRING, -TRES to scepter
SCHAPPE	*n* pl. -S a silk fabric
SCHAV	*n* pl. -S a chilled soup
SCHEDULE	*v* -ULED, -ULING, -ULES to assign to a certain date or time
SCHEMA	*n* pl. -MATA or -MAS a generalized diagram or plan
SCHEME	*v* SCHEMED, SCHEMING, SCHEMES to plan or plot
SCHEMER	*n* pl. -S one that schemes
SCHERZO	*n* pl. -ZOS or -ZI a lively musical movement
SCHILLER	*n* pl. -S a brownish luster occurring on certain minerals
SCHISM	*n* pl. -S a division into opposing parties

SCHIST *n* pl. -S a rock that readily splits into parallel layers

SCHIZIER comparative of schizy

SCHIZIEST superlative of schizy

SCHIZO *n* pl. SCHIZOS a schizoid

SCHIZOID *n* pl. -S a person affected with a type of psychotic disorder

SCHIZONT *n* pl. -S an organism that reproduces by a form of asexual reproduction

SCHIZY *adj* SCHIZIER, SCHIZIEST affected with schizophrenia

SCHIZZY *adj* SCHIZZIER, SCHIZZIEST schizy

SCHLEP *v* SCHLEPPED, SCHLEPPING, SCHLEPS to lug or drag

SCHLEPP *v* -ED, -ING, -S to schlep

SCHLIERE *n* pl. -REN a small streak in an igneous rock

SCHLOCK *n* pl. -S inferior merchandise

SCHLOCKY *adj* of inferior quality

SCHLUMP *v* -ED, -ING, -S to go about lazily or sloppily dressed

SCHMALTZ *n* pl. -ES excessive sentimentality

SCHMALZ *n* pl. -ES schmaltz

SCHMALZY *adj* SCHMALZIER, SCHMALZIEST characterized by schmaltz

SCHMEAR *n* pl. -S an aggregate of related things

SCHMEER *v* -ED, -ING, -S to bribe

SCHMELZE *n* pl. -S a type of decorative glass

SCHMO *n* pl. SCHMOES or SCHMOS a stupid person

SCHMOE *n* pl. -S schmo

SCHMOOS *v* -ED, -ING, -ES to schmooze

SCHMOOSE *v* SCHMOOSED, SCHMOOSING, SCHMOOSES to schmooze

SCHMOOZE *v* SCHMOOZED, SCHMOOZING, SCHMOOZES to gossip

SCHMUCK *n* pl. -S a foolish or clumsy person

SCHNAPPS *n* pl. SCHNAPPS a strong liquor

SCHNAPS *n* pl. SCHNAPS schnapps

SCHNECKE *n* pl. -KEN a sweet roll

SCHNOOK *n* pl. -S an easily deceived person

SCHNOZ *n* pl. SCHNOZZES the nose

SCHNOZZ *n* pl. -ES schnoz

SCHOLAR *n* pl. -S a learned person

SCHOLIUM *n* pl. -LIA or -LIUMS an explanatory marginal note

SCHOOL *v* -ED, -ING, -S to educate in an institution of learning

SCHOONER *n* pl. -S a sailing vessel

SCHORL *n* pl. -S a mineral

SCHRIK *n* pl. -S sudden fright

SCHROD *n* pl. -S scrod

SCHTICK *n* pl. -S shtick

SCHTIK *n* pl. -S shtick

SCHUIT *n* pl. -S a Dutch sailing vessel

SCHUL *n* pl. SCHULN shul

SCHUSS *v* -ED, -ING, -ES to make a fast, straight run in skiing

SCHUSSER *n* pl. -S one that schusses

SCHWA *n* pl. -S a type of vowel sound

SCIAENID *n* pl. -S a carnivorous fish

SCIATIC *n* pl. -S a nerve, vein, or artery situated near the hip

SCIATICA *n* pl. -S a painful disorder of the hip and adjoining areas

SCIENCE *n* pl. -S a department of systematized knowledge

SCILICET *adv* namely

SCILLA *n* pl. -S a flowering plant

SCIMETAR *n* pl. -S scimitar

SCIMITAR *n* pl. -S a curved Oriental sword

SCIMITER *n* pl. -S scimitar

SCINCOID *n* pl. -S one of a family of smooth, short-limbed lizards

SCIOLISM *n* pl. -S superficial knowledge

SCIOLIST *n* pl. -S one whose knowledge is superficial

SCION *n* pl. -S a child or descendant

SCIROCCO *n* pl. -COS sirocco

SCIRRHUS *n* pl. -RHI or -RHUSES a hard tumor

SCISSILE *adj* capable of being cut or split easily

SCISSION *n* pl. -S the act of cutting or splitting

SCISSOR *v* -ED, -ING, -S to cut with a two-bladed cutting implement

SCISSURE *n* pl. -S a lengthwise cut

SCIURID *n* pl. -S a sciurine

SCIURINE   *n* pl. -S a rodent of the squirrel family

SCIUROID   *adj* resembling a squirrel

SCLAFF   *v* -ED, -ING, -S to strike the ground with the club before hitting the ball in golf

SCLAFFER   *n* pl. -S one that sclaffs

SCLERA   *n* pl. -RAS or -RAE the white, fibrous outer coat of the eyeball **SCLERAL** *adj*

SCLEREID   *n* pl. -S a type of plant cell

SCLERITE   *n* pl. -S one of the hard plates forming the outer covering of an arthropod

SCLEROID   *adj* sclerous

SCLEROMA   *n* pl. -MATA a hardened patch of cellular tissue

SCLEROSE   *v* -ROSED, -ROSING, -ROSES to become hard, as tissue

SCLEROUS   *adj* hardened

SCOFF   *v* -ED, -ING, -S to express rude doubt or derision

SCOFFER   *n* pl. -S one that scoffs

SCOFFLAW   *n* pl. -S an habitual law violator

SCOLD   *v* -ED, -ING, -S to rebuke harshly

SCOLDER   *n* pl. -S one that scolds

SCOLDING   *n* pl. -S a harsh reproof

SCOLEX   *n* pl. -LECES or -LICES the knoblike head of a tapeworm

SCOLIOMA   *n* pl. -S abnormal curvature of the spine

SCOLLOP   *v* -ED, -ING, -S to scallop

SCONCE   *v* SCONCED, SCONCING, SCONCES to fine

SCONE   *n* pl. -S a flat, round cake

SCOOP   *v* -ED, -ING, -S to take up with a scoop (a spoonlike utensil)

SCOOPER   *n* pl. -S one that scoops

SCOOPFUL   *n* pl. SCOOPFULS or SCOOPSFUL as much as a scoop will hold

SCOOT   *v* -ED, -ING, -S to go quickly

SCOOTER   *n* pl. -S a two-wheeled vehicle

SCOP   *n* pl. -S an Old English poet

SCOPE   *v* SCOPED, SCOPING, SCOPES to look at in order to evaluate

SCOPULA   *n* pl. -LAE or -LAS a dense tuft of hairs

SCORCH   *v* -ED, -ING, -ES to burn slightly so as to alter the color or taste

SCORCHER   *n* pl. -S one that scorches

SCORE   *v* SCORED, SCORING, SCORES to make a point in a game or contest

SCOREPAD   *n* pl. -S a pad on which scored points are recorded

SCORER   *n* pl. -S one that scores

SCORIA   *n* pl. -RIAE the refuse of a smelted metal or ore

SCORIFY   *v* -FIED, -FYING, -FIES to reduce to scoria

SCORING   present participle of score

SCORN   *v* -ED, -ING, -S to treat or regard with contempt

SCORNER   *n* pl. -S one that scorns

SCORNFUL   *adj* feeling or expressing contempt

SCORPION   *n* pl. -S a stinging arachnid

SCOT   *n* pl. -S a tax

SCOTCH   *v* -ED, -ING, -ES to put a definite end to

SCOTER   *n* pl. -S a sea duck

SCOTIA   *n* pl. -S a concave molding

SCOTOMA   *n* pl. -MAS or -MATA a blind spot in the field of vision

SCOTOPIA   *n* pl. -S vision in dim light **SCOTOPIC** *adj*

SCOTTIE   *n* pl. -S a short-legged terrier

SCOUR   *v* -ED, -ING, -S to cleanse or polish by hard rubbing

SCOURER   *n* pl. -S one that scours

SCOURGE   *v* SCOURGED, SCOURGING, SCOURGES to punish severely

SCOURGER   *n* pl. -S one that scourges

SCOURING   *n* pl. -S material removed by scouring

SCOUSE   *n* pl. -S a type of meat stew

SCOUT   *v* -ED, -ING, -S to observe for the purpose of obtaining information

SCOUTER   *n* pl. -S one that scouts

SCOUTH   *n* pl. -S plenty

SCOUTHER   *v* -ED, -ING, -S to scorch

SCOUTING   *n* pl. -S the act of one that scouts

SCOW   *v* -ED, -ING, -S to transport by scow (a flat-bottomed boat)

SCOWDER   *v* -ED, -ING, -S to scouther

SCOWL   *v* -ED, -ING, -S to frown angrily

SCOWLER   *n* pl. -S one that scowls

SCRABBLE *v* -BLED, -BLING, -BLES to claw or grope about frantically

SCRABBLY *adj* -BLIER, -BLIEST raspy

SCRAG *v* SCRAGGED, SCRAGGING, SCRAGS to wring the neck of

SCRAGGLY *adj* -GLIER, -GLIEST uneven

SCRAGGY *adj* -GIER, -GIEST scrawny

SCRAICH *v* -ED, -ING, -S to utter a shrill cry

SCRAIGH *v* -ED, -ING, -S to scraich

SCRAM *v* SCRAMMED, SCRAMMING, SCRAMS to leave quickly

SCRAMBLE *v* -BLED, -BLING, -BLES to move or climb hurriedly

SCRAMJET *n* pl. -S a type of aircraft engine

SCRANNEL *n* pl. -S a thin person

SCRAP *v* SCRAPPED, SCRAPPING, SCRAPS to discard

SCRAPE *v* SCRAPED, SCRAPING, SCRAPES to rub so as to remove an outer layer

SCRAPER *n* pl. -S one that scrapes

SCRAPIE *n* pl. -S a disease of sheep

SCRAPING *n* pl. -S something scraped off

SCRAPPED past tense of scrap

SCRAPPER *n* pl. -S a fighter

SCRAPPIER comparative of scrappy

SCRAPPIEST superlative of scrappy

SCRAPPING present participle of scrap

SCRAPPLE *n* pl. -S a seasoned mixture of ground meat and cornmeal

SCRAPPY *adj* -PIER, -PIEST marked by fighting spirit

SCRATCH *v* -ED, -ING, -ES to make a thin, shallow cut or mark on

SCRATCHY *adj* SCRATCHIER, SCRATCHIEST made by scratching

SCRAWL *v* -ED, -ING, -S to write hastily or illegibly

SCRAWLER *n* pl. -S one that scrawls

SCRAWLY *adj* SCRAWLIER, SCRAWLIEST written hastily or illegibly

SCRAWNY *adj* -NIER, -NIEST extremely thin

SCREAK *v* -ED, -ING, -S to screech

SCREAKY *adj* screechy

SCREAM *v* -ED, -ING, -S to utter a prolonged, piercing cry

SCREAMER *n* pl. -S one that screams

SCREE *n* pl. -S a mass of rocks at the foot of a slope

SCREECH *v* -ED, -ING, -ES to utter a harsh, shrill cry

SCREECHY *adj* SCREECHIER, SCREECHIEST screeching

SCREED *v* -ED, -ING, -S to shred

SCREEN *v* -ED, -ING, -S to provide with a screen (a device designed to divide, conceal, or protect)

SCREENER *n* pl. -S one that screens

SCREW *v* -ED, -ING, -S to attach with a screw (a type of metal fastener)

SCREWER *n* pl. -S one that screws

SCREWUP *n* pl. -S an instance of bungling

SCREWY *adj* SCREWIER, SCREWIEST crazy

SCRIBAL *adj* pertaining to a public clerk or secretary

SCRIBBLE *v* -BLED, -BLING, -BLES to write hastily or carelessly

SCRIBE *v* SCRIBED, SCRIBING, SCRIBES to mark with a scriber

SCRIBER *n* pl. -S a pointed instrument used for marking off material to be cut

SCRIED past tense of scry

SCRIES present 3d person sing. of scry

SCRIEVE *v* SCRIEVED, SCRIEVING, SCRIEVES to move along swiftly and smoothly

SCRIM *n* pl. -S a cotton fabric

SCRIMP *v* -ED, -ING, -S to be very or overly thrifty

SCRIMPER *n* pl. -S one that scrimps

SCRIMPIT *adj* meager

SCRIMPY *adj* SCRIMPIER, SCRIMPIEST meager

SCRIP *n* pl. -S a small piece of paper

SCRIPT *v* -ED, -ING, -S to prepare a written text for, as a play or motion picture

SCRIPTER *n* pl. -S one that scripts

SCRIVE *v* SCRIVED, SCRIVING, SCRIVES to engrave

SCROD *n* pl. -S a young cod

SCROFULA *n* pl. -S a disease of the lymph glands

SCROGGY *adj* -GIER, -GIEST of stunted growth

SCROLL *v* -ED, -ING, -S to move text across a display screen

SCROOCH *v* -ED, -ING, -ES to crouch

SCROOGE *n* pl. -S a miserly person

SCROOP *v* -ED, -ING, -S to make a harsh, grating sound

SCROOTCH *v* -ED, -ING, -ES to scrooch

SCROTUM *n* pl. -TA or -TUMS the pouch of skin that contains the testes **SCROTAL** *adj*

SCROUGE *v* SCROUGED, SCROUGING, SCROUGES to crowd

SCROUNGE *v* SCROUNGED, SCROUNGING, SCROUNGES to gather by foraging

SCROUNGY *adj* SCROUNGIER, SCROUNGIEST dirty

SCRUB *v* SCRUBBED, SCRUBBING, SCRUBS to rub hard in order to clean

SCRUBBER *n* pl. -S one that scrubs

SCRUBBY *adj* -BIER, -BIEST inferior in size or quality

SCRUFF *n* pl. -S the back of the neck

SCRUFFY *adj* -FIER, -FIEST shabby

SCRUM *v* SCRUMMED, SCRUMMING, SCRUMS to engage in a scrummage (a formation around the ball in rugby)

SCRUNCH *v* -ED, -ING, -ES to crush

SCRUPLE *v* -PLED, -PLING, -PLES to hesitate because of ethical considerations

SCRUTINY *n* pl. -NIES a close examination

SCRY *v* SCRIED, SCRYING, SCRIES to engage in crystal gazing

SCUBA *n* pl. -S an underwater breathing device

SCUD *v* SCUDDED, SCUDDING, SCUDS to run or move swiftly

SCUDO *n* pl. -DI a former Italian coin

SCUFF *v* -ED, -ING, -S to walk without lifting the feet

SCUFFLE *v* -FLED, -FLING, -FLES to struggle in a rough, confused manner

SCUFFLER *n* pl. -S one that scuffles

SCULK *v* -ED, -ING, -S to skulk

SCULKER *n* pl. -S skulker

SCULL *v* -ED, -ING, -S to propel with a type of oar

SCULLER *n* pl. -S one that sculls

SCULLERY *n* pl. -LERIES a room in which kitchen utensils are cleaned and stored

SCULLION *n* pl. -S a kitchen servant who does menial work

SCULP *v* -ED, -ING, -S to sculpt

SCULPIN *n* pl. -S a freshwater fish

SCULPT *v* -ED, -ING, -S to form an image or representation of from solid material

SCULPTOR *n* pl. -S one that sculpts

SCUM *v* SCUMMED, SCUMMING, SCUMS to remove the scum (impure or extraneous matter) from

SCUMBAG *n* pl. -S a dirtbag

SCUMBLE *v* -BLED, -BLING, -BLES to soften the outlines or colors of by rubbing lightly

SCUMLIKE *adj* resembling scum

SCUMMED past tense of scum

SCUMMER *n* pl. -S one that scums

SCUMMING present participle of scum

SCUMMY *adj* -MIER, -MIEST covered with scum

SCUNNER *v* -ED, -ING, -S to feel loathing or disgust

SCUP *n* pl. -S a marine food fish

SCUPPAUG *n* pl. -S scup

SCUPPER *v* -ED, -ING, -S to ambush

SCURF *n* pl. -S scaly or shredded dry skin

SCURFY *adj* SCURFIER, SCURFIEST covered with scurf

SCURRIED past tense of scurry

SCURRIES present 3d person sing. of scurry

SCURRIL *adj* scurrile

SCURRILE *adj* expressed in coarse and abusive language

SCURRY *v* -RIED, -RYING, -RIES to move hurriedly

SCURVY *adj* -VIER, -VIEST base or contemptible **SCURVILY** *adv*

SCURVY *n* pl. -VIES a disease resulting from vitamin C deficiency

SCUT *n* pl. -S a short tail, as of a rabbit

SCUTA pl. of scutum

SCUTAGE *n* pl. -S a tax exacted by a feudal lord in lieu of military service

SCUTATE *adj* shaped like a shield

SCUTCH   *v* -ED, -ING, -ES to separate the woody fiber from by beating

SCUTCHER   *n* pl. -S one that scutches

SCUTE   *n* pl. -S a horny plate or scale

SCUTELLA   *n/pl* small, scutate organs or parts

SCUTTER   *v* -ED, -ING, -S to scurry

SCUTTLE   *v* -TLED, -TLING, -TLES to scurry

SCUTUM   *n* pl. -TA scute

SCUZZY   *adj* -ZIER, -ZIEST dirty or shabby

SCYPHATE   *adj* shaped like a cup

SCYPHUS   *n* pl. -PHI a Greek cup with two handles

SCYTHE   *v* SCYTHED, SCYTHING, SCYTHES to cut with a scythe (a single-bladed cutting implement)

SEA   *n* pl. -S the ocean

SEABAG   *n* pl. -S a bag used by a sailor

SEABEACH   *n* pl. -ES a beach lying along the sea

SEABED   *n* pl. -S a seafloor

SEABIRD   *n* pl. -S a bird frequenting the ocean or seacoast

SEABOARD   *n* pl. -S the seacoast

SEABOOT   *n* pl. -S a waterproof boot

SEABORNE   *adj* carried on or over the sea

SEACOAST   *n* pl. -S land bordering on the sea

SEACOCK   *n* pl. -S a valve in a ship's hull

SEACRAFT   *n* pl. -S skill in sea navigation

SEADOG   *n* pl. -S a fogbow

SEADROME   *n* pl. -S an airport in the sea

SEAFARER   *n* pl. -S a sailor

SEAFLOOR   *n* pl. -S the bottom of a sea

SEAFOOD   *n* pl. -S edible fish or shellfish from the sea

SEAFOWL   *n* pl. -S a seabird

SEAFRONT   *n* pl. -S an area along the edge of the sea

SEAGIRT   *adj* surrounded by the sea

SEAGOING   *adj* designed for use on the sea

SEAGULL   *n* pl. -S a gull frequenting the sea

SEAL   *v* -ED, -ING, -S to close or make secure against access, leakage, or passage **SEALABLE** *adj*

SEALANT   *n* pl. -S a sealing agent

SEALER   *n* pl. -S one that seals

SEALERY   *n* pl. -ERIES the occupation of hunting seals

SEALLIKE   *adj* resembling a seal (an aquatic mammal)

SEALSKIN   *n* pl. -S the skin of a seal

SEAM   *v* -ED, -ING, -S to join with a seam (a line formed by sewing two pieces of fabric together)

SEAMAN   *n* pl. -MEN a sailor **SEAMANLY** *adj*

SEAMARK   *n* pl. -S a landmark serving as a navigational guide to mariners

SEAMER   *n* pl. -S one that seams

SEAMIER   comparative of seamy

SEAMIEST   superlative of seamy

SEAMLESS   *adj* having no seam

SEAMLIKE   *adj* resembling a seam

SEAMOUNT   *n* pl. -S an undersea mountain

SEAMSTER   *n* pl. -S a person whose occupation is sewing

SEAMY   *adj* SEAMIER, SEAMIEST unpleasant

SEANCE   *n* pl. -S a meeting of persons seeking spiritualistic messages

SEAPIECE   *n* pl. -S a seascape

SEAPLANE   *n* pl. -S an airplane designed to take off from or land on the water

SEAPORT   *n* pl. -S a harbor or town accessible to seagoing ships

SEAQUAKE   *n* pl. -S an undersea earthquake

SEAR   *adj* SEARER, SEAREST sere

SEAR   *v* -ED, -ING, -S to burn the surface of

SEARCH   *v* -ED, -ING, -ES to look through or over carefully in order to find something

SEARCHER   *n* pl. -S one that searches

SEAROBIN   *n* pl. -S a marine fish

SEASCAPE   *n* pl. -S a picture of the sea

SEASCOUT   *n* pl. -S a boy scout trained in water activities

SEASHELL   *n* pl. -S the shell of a marine mollusk

SEASHORE   *n* pl. -S land bordering on the sea

SEASICK   *adj* affected with nausea caused by the motion of a vessel at sea

SEASIDE   *n* pl. -S the seashore

SEASON   *v* -ED, -ING, -S to heighten or improve the flavor of by adding savory ingredients

SEASONAL	adj occurring at a certain time of the year
SEASONER	n pl. -S one that seasons
SEAT	v -ED, -ING, -S to place on a seat (something on which one sits)
SEATER	n pl. -S one that seats
SEATING	n pl. -S material for covering seats
SEATLESS	adj having no seat
SEATMATE	n pl. -S one with whom one shares a seat
SEATRAIN	n pl. -S a ship equipped to carry railroad cars
SEATWORK	n pl. -S work done at one's seat
SEAWALL	n pl. -S a wall to protect a shoreline from erosion
SEAWAN	n pl. -S wampum
SEAWANT	n pl. -S seawan
SEAWARD	n pl. -S the direction toward the open sea
SEAWARE	n pl. -S seaweed used as fertilizer
SEAWATER	n pl. -S water from the sea
SEAWAY	n pl. -WAYS the headway made by a ship
SEAWEED	n pl. -S a plant growing in the sea
SEBACIC	adj derived from a certain acid
SEBASIC	adj sebacic
SEBUM	n pl. -S a fatty matter secreted by certain glands of the skin
SEC	n pl. -S secant
SECALOSE	n pl. -S a complex carbohydrate
SECANT	n pl. -S a trigonometric function of an angle
SECANTLY	adv in an intersecting manner
SECATEUR	n pl. -S a pruning tool
SECCO	n pl. -COS the art of painting on dry plaster
SECEDE	v -CEDED, -CEDING, -CEDES to withdraw formally from an alliance or association
SECEDER	n pl. -S one that secedes
SECERN	v -ED, -ING, -S to discern as separate
SECLUDE	v -CLUDED, -CLUDING, -CLUDES to remove or set apart from others
SECOND	v -ED, -ING, -S to give support or encouragement to
SECONDE	n pl. -S a position in fencing
SECONDER	n pl. -S one that seconds
SECONDLY	adv in the next place after the first
SECONDO	n pl. -DI the lower part in a piano duet
SECPAR	n pl. -S a parsec
SECRECY	n pl. -CIES the condition of being secret
SECRET	adj -CRETER, -CRETEST kept from knowledge or view
SECRET	n pl. -S something kept from the knowledge of others
SECRETE	v -CRETED, -CRETING, -CRETES to generate and separate out from cells or bodily fluids
SECRETIN	n pl. -S a hormone
SECRETLY	adv in a secret manner
SECRETOR	n pl. -S one that secretes
SECT	n pl. -S a group of people united by common beliefs or interests
SECTARY	n pl. -RIES a member of a sect
SECTILE	adj capable of being cut smoothly
SECTION	v -ED, -ING, -S to divide into sections (distinct parts)
SECTOR	v -ED, -ING, -S to divide into sectors (sections)
SECTORAL	adj of or pertaining to a sector
SECULAR	n pl. -S a layman
SECUND	adj having the parts or organs arranged on one side only **SECUNDLY** adv
SECUNDUM	adv according to
SECURE	adj -CURER, -CUREST free from danger **SECURELY** adv
SECURE	v -CURED, -CURING, -CURES to make firm or tight
SECURER	n pl. -S one that secures
SECUREST	superlative of secure
SECURING	present participle of secure
SECURITY	n pl. -TIES the state of being secure
SEDAN	n pl. -S a type of automobile
SEDARIM	a pl. of seder
SEDATE	adj -DATER, -DATEST calm **SEDATELY** adv
SEDATE	v -DATED, -DATING, -DATES to administer a sedative to

SEDATION   *n* pl. -S the reduction of stress or excitement by the use of sedatives

SEDATIVE   *n* pl. -S a drug that induces a calm state

SEDER   *n* pl. -DARIM or -DERS a Jewish ceremonial dinner

SEDERUNT   *n* pl. -S a prolonged sitting

SEDGE   *n* pl. -S a marsh plant

SEDGY   *adj* SEDGIER, SEDGIEST abounding in sedge

SEDILE   *n* pl. -LIA one of the seats in a church for the use of the officiating clergy

SEDILIUM   *n* pl. -LIA sedile

SEDIMENT   *v* -ED, -ING, -S to settle to the bottom of a liquid

SEDITION   *n* pl. -S incitement of rebellion against a government

SEDUCE   *v* -DUCED, -DUCING, -DUCES to lead astray **SEDUCIVE** *adj*

SEDUCER   *n* pl. -S one that seduces

SEDULITY   *n* pl. -TIES the state of being sedulous

SEDULOUS   *adj* diligent

SEDUM   *n* pl. -S a flowering plant

SEE   *v* SAW, SEEN, SEEING, SEES to perceive with the eyes **SEEABLE** *adj*

SEECATCH   *n* pl. -CATCHIE an adult male fur seal

SEED   *v* -ED, -ING, -S to plant seeds (propagative plant structures) in

SEEDBED   *n* pl. -S land prepared for seeding

SEEDCAKE   *n* pl. -S a sweet cake containing aromatic seeds

SEEDCASE   *n* pl. -S a pericarp

SEEDER   *n* pl. -S one that seeds

SEEDIER   comparative of seedy

SEEDIEST   superlative of seedy

SEEDILY   *adv* in a seedy manner

SEEDLESS   *adj* having no seeds

SEEDLIKE   *adj* resembling a seed

SEEDLING   *n* pl. -S a young plant

SEEDMAN   *n* pl. -MEN seedsman

SEEDPOD   *n* pl. -S a type of seed vessel

SEEDSMAN   *n* pl. -MEN a dealer in seeds

SEEDTIME   *n* pl. -S the season for sowing seeds

SEEDY   *adj* SEEDIER, SEEDIEST containing seeds; inferior in condition or quality

SEEING   *n* pl. -S the act of one that sees

SEEK   *v* SOUGHT, SEEKING, SEEKS to go in search of

SEEKER   *n* pl. -S one that seeks

SEEL   *v* -ED, -ING, -S to stitch closed the eyes of, as a falcon during training

SEELY   *adj* frail

SEEM   *v* -ED, -ING, -S to give the impression of being

SEEMER   *n* pl. -S one that seems

SEEMING   *n* pl. -S outward appearance

SEEMLY   *adj* -LIER, -LIEST of pleasing appearance

SEEN   past participle of see

SEEP   *v* -ED, -ING, -S to pass slowly through small openings

SEEPAGE   *n* pl. -S the quantity of fluid that has seeped

SEEPY   *adj* SEEPIER, SEEPIEST soaked or oozing with water

SEER   *n* pl. -S a prophet

SEERESS   *n* pl. -ES a female seer

SEESAW   *v* -ED, -ING, -S to move up and down or back and forth

SEETHE   *v* SEETHED, SEETHING, SEETHES to surge or foam as if boiling

SEG   *n* pl. -S one who advocates racial segregation

SEGETAL   *adj* growing in fields of grain

SEGGAR   *n* pl. -S a saggar

SEGMENT   *v* -ED, -ING, -S to divide into sections

SEGNO   *n* pl. -GNI or -GNOS a musical sign

SEGO   *n* pl. -GOS a perennial herb

SEGUE   *v* -GUED, -GUEING, -GUES to proceed without pause from one musical theme to another

SEI   *n* pl. -S a rorqual

SEICENTO   *n* pl. -TOS the seventeenth century

SEICHE   *n* pl. -S an oscillation of the surface of a lake or landlocked sea

SEIDEL   *n* pl. -S a large beer glass

SEIF   *n* pl. -S a long, narrow sand dune

SEIGNEUR *n* pl. -S seignior

SEIGNIOR *n* pl. -S a feudal lord

SEIGNORY *n* pl. -GNORIES the power of a seignior

SEINE *v* SEINED, SEINING, SEINES to catch fish with a large, vertically hanging net

SEINER *n* pl. -S one that seines

SEISE *v* SEISED, SEISING, SEISES to seize **SEISABLE** *adj*

SEISER *n* pl. -S seizer

SEISIN *n* pl. -S seizin

SEISING *n* pl. -S seizing

SEISM *n* pl. -S an earthquake **SEISMAL, SEISMIC** *adj*

SEISMISM *n* pl. -S the natural activity involved in earthquakes

SEISOR *n* pl. -S seizor

SEISURE *n* pl. -S seizure

SEIZE *v* SEIZED, SEIZING, SEIZES to take hold of suddenly and forcibly **SEIZABLE** *adj*

SEIZER *n* pl. -S one that seizes

SEIZIN *n* pl. -S legal possession of land

SEIZING *n* pl. -S the act of one that seizes

SEIZOR *n* pl. -S one that takes seizin

SEIZURE *n* pl. -S the act of seizing

SEJANT *adj* represented in a sitting position — used of a heraldic animal

SEJEANT *adj* sejant

SEL *n* pl. -S self

SELADANG *n* pl. -S saladang

SELAH *n* pl. -S a word of unknown meaning often marking the end of a verse in the Psalms

SELAMLIK *n* pl. -S the portion of a Turkish house reserved for men

SELCOUTH *adj* unusual

SELDOM *adj* infrequent **SELDOMLY** *adv*

SELECT *v* -ED, -ING, -S to choose

SELECTEE *n* pl. -S one that is selected

SELECTLY *adv* by selection

SELECTOR *n* pl. -S one that selects

SELENATE *n* pl. -S a chemical salt

SELENIC *adj* pertaining to selenium

SELENIDE *n* pl. -S a compound of selenium

SELENITE *n* pl. -S a variety of gypsum

SELENIUM *n* pl. -S a nonmetallic element **SELENOUS** *adj*

SELF *n* pl. SELVES the total, essential, or particular being of one person

SELF *v* -ED, -ING, -S to inbreed

SELFDOM *n* pl. -S selfhood

SELFHEAL *n* pl. -S a perennial herb

SELFHOOD *n* pl. -S the state of being an individual person

SELFISH *adj* concerned chiefly or only with oneself

SELFLESS *adj* unselfish

SELFNESS *n* pl. -ES selfhood

SELFSAME *adj* identical

SELFWARD *adv* toward oneself

SELL *v* SOLD, SELLING, SELLS to give up to another for money or other valuable consideration **SELLABLE** *adj*

SELLE *n* pl. -S a saddle

SELLER *n* pl. -S one that sells

SELLOUT *n* pl. -S a performance for which all seats have been sold

SELSYN *n* pl. -S a type of remote-control device

SELTZER *n* pl. -S carbonated mineral water

SELVA *n* pl. -S a tropical rain forest

SELVAGE *n* pl. -S the edge of a woven fabric finished to prevent raveling **SELVAGED** *adj*

SELVEDGE *n* pl. -S selvage

SELVES pl. of self

SEMANTIC *adj* pertaining to meaning

SEMATIC *adj* serving as a warning

SEME *n* pl. -S a type of ornamental pattern

SEMEME *n* pl. -S the meaning of a morpheme **SEMEMIC** *adj*

SEMEN *n* pl. -MINA or -MENS a fluid produced in the male reproductive organs

SEMESTER *n* pl. -S a period constituting half of an academic year

SEMI *n* pl. -S a freight trailer

SEMIARID *adj* characterized by light rainfall

SEMIBALD *adj* partly bald

SEMICOMA *n* pl. -S a coma from which a person can be aroused

SEMIDEAF *adj* partly deaf

SEMIDOME *n* pl. -S a half dome

SEMIDRY *adj* moderately dry

SEMIFIT *adj* conforming somewhat to the lines of the body

SEMIGALA *adj* somewhat gala

SEMIHARD *adj* moderately hard

SEMIHIGH *adj* moderately high

SEMIHOBO *n* pl. -BOS or -BOES a person having some of the characteristics of a hobo

SEMILOG *adj* having one scale logarithmic and the other arithmetic

SEMIMAT *adj* having a slight luster

SEMIMATT *adj* semimat

SEMIMUTE *adj* having partially lost the faculty of speech

SEMINA a pl. of semen

SEMINAL *adj* pertaining to semen

SEMINAR *n* pl. -S an advanced study group at a college or university

SEMINARY *n* pl. -NARIES a school for the training of priests, ministers, or rabbis

SEMINUDE *adj* partly nude

SEMIOSIS *n* pl. -OSES a process in which something functions as a sign to an organism

SEMIOTIC *n* pl. -S a general theory of signs and symbolism

SEMIPRO *n* pl. -PROS one who is engaged in some field or sport for pay on a part-time basis

SEMIRAW *adj* somewhat raw

SEMIS *n* pl. -MISES a coin of ancient Rome

SEMISOFT *adj* moderately soft

SEMITIST *n* pl. -S one who favors Jewish interests

SEMITONE *n* pl. -S a type of musical tone

SEMIWILD *adj* somewhat wild

SEMOLINA *n* pl. -S a granular product of wheat used for pasta

SEMPLE *adj* of humble birth

SEMPLICE *adj* simple — used as a musical direction

SEMPRE *adv* in the same manner throughout — used as a musical direction

SEN *n* pl. SEN a monetary unit of Japan

SENARIUS *n* pl. -NARII a Greek or Latin verse consisting of six metrical feet

SENARY *adj* pertaining to the number six

SENATE *n* pl. -S an assembly having high deliberative and legislative functions

SENATOR *n* pl. -S a member of a senate

SEND *v* SENT, SENDING, SENDS to cause to go **SENDABLE** *adj*

SEND *v* -ED, -ING, -S to scend

SENDAL *n* pl. -S a silk fabric

SENDER *n* pl. -S one that sends

SENDOFF *n* pl. -S a farewell celebration

SENDUP *n* pl. -S a parody

SENE *n* pl. SENE a monetary unit of Western Samoa

SENECA *n* pl. -S senega

SENECIO *n* pl. -CIOS a flowering plant

SENEGA *n* pl. -S a medicinal plant root

SENGI *n* pl. SENGI a monetary unit of Zaire

SENHOR *n* pl. -S or -ES a Portuguese or Brazilian gentleman

SENHORA *n* pl. -S a married Portuguese or Brazilian woman

SENILE *n* pl. -S one who exhibits senility

SENILELY *adv* in a senile manner

SENILITY *n* pl. -TIES mental and physical infirmity due to old age

SENIOR *n* pl. -S a person who is older than another

SENITI *n* pl. SENITI a monetary unit of Tonga

SENNA *n* pl. -S a medicinal plant

SENNET *n* pl. -S a call sounded on a trumpet signaling the entrance or exit of actors

SENNIGHT *n* pl. -S a week

SENNIT *n* pl. -S braided straw used in making hats

SENOPIA *n* pl. -S an improvement of near vision

SENOR *n* pl. -S or -ES a Spanish gentleman

SENORA *n* pl. -S a married Spanish woman

SENORITA *n* pl. -S an unmarried Spanish girl or woman

SENRYU *n* pl. SENRYU a Japanese poem

SENSA	pl. of sensum	**SEPIA**	*n* pl. -S a brown pigment **SEPIC** *adj*
SENSATE	*v* -SATED, -SATING, -SATES to sense	**SEPOY**	*n* pl. -POYS a native of India serving in the British army
SENSE	*v* SENSED, SENSING, SENSES to perceive by the senses (any of certain agencies through which an individual receives impressions of the external world)	**SEPPUKU**	*n* pl. -S a Japanese form of suicide
		SEPSIS	*n* pl. SEPSES bacterial invasion of the body
SENSEFUL	*adj* sensible	**SEPT**	*n* pl. -S a clan
SENSIBLE	*adj* -BLER, -BLEST having or showing good judgment **SENSIBLY** *adv*	**SEPTA**	pl. of septum
		SEPTAL	*adj* pertaining to a septum
SENSIBLE	*n* pl. -S something that can be sensed	**SEPTARIA**	*n/pl* limestone nodules
SENSILLA	*n* pl. -LAE a simple sense organ	**SEPTATE**	*adj* having a septum
SENSING	present participle of sense	**SEPTET**	*n* pl. -S a group of seven
SENSOR	*n* pl. -S a device that receives and responds to a stimulus	**SEPTETTE**	*n* pl. -S septet
		SEPTIC	*n* pl. -S an agent producing sepsis **SEPTICAL** *adj*
SENSORIA	*n/pl* the parts of the brain concerned with the reception and interpretation of sensory stimuli	**SEPTIME**	*n* pl. -S a position in fencing
		SEPTUM	*n* pl. -TA or -TUMS a dividing membrane or partition
SENSORY	*adj* pertaining to the senses or sensation	**SEPTUPLE**	*v* -PLED, -PLING, -PLES to make seven times as great
SENSUAL	*adj* pertaining to the physical senses	**SEQUEL**	*n* pl. -S something that follows and serves as a continuation
SENSUM	*n* pl. -SA an object of perception or sensation	**SEQUELA**	*n* pl. -QUELAE an abnormal condition resulting from a preceding disease
SENSUOUS	*adj* pertaining to or derived from the senses		
SENT	past tense of send (to cause to go)	**SEQUENCE**	*v* -QUENCED, -QUENCING, -QUENCES to arrange in consecutive order
SENTE	*n* pl. LICENTE or LISENTE a monetary unit of Lesotho	**SEQUENCY**	*n* pl. -CIES the following of one thing after another
SENTENCE	*v* -TENCED, -TENCING, -TENCES to declare judicially the extent of punishment to be imposed	**SEQUENT**	*n* pl. -S something that follows
		SEQUIN	*n* pl. -S a shiny ornamental disk **SEQUINED** *adj*
SENTI	*n* pl. SENTI a former monetary unit of Tanzania	**SEQUITUR**	*n* pl. -S the conclusion of an inference
SENTIENT	*n* pl. -S a person or thing capable of sensation	**SEQUOIA**	*n* pl. -S a large evergreen tree
SENTIMO	*n* pl. -MOS a monetary unit of the Philippines	**SER**	*n* pl. -S a unit of weight of India
		SERA	a pl. of serum
SENTINEL	*v* -NELED, -NELING, -NELS or -NELLED, -NELLING, -NELS to stand guard	**SERAC**	*n* pl. -S a large mass of ice broken off of a glacier
		SERAGLIO	*n* pl. -GLIOS a harem
SENTRY	*n* pl. -TRIES one who stands guard	**SERAI**	*n* pl. -S a Turkish palace
		SERAIL	*n* pl. -S a seraglio
SEPAL	*n* pl. -S one of the individual leaves of a calyx **SEPALED, SEPALINE, SEPALLED, SEPALOID, SEPALOUS** *adj*	**SERAL**	*adj* pertaining to a series of ecological changes
SEPARATE	*v* -RATED, -RATING, -RATES to set or keep apart	**SERAPE**	*n* pl. -S a colorful woolen shawl

SERAPH *n* pl. -APHS, -APHIM, or -APHIN a winged celestial being **SERAPHIC** *adj*

SERAPHIM *n* pl. -S seraph

SERDAB *n* pl. -S a chamber within an ancient Egyptian tomb

SERE *adj* SERER, SEREST withered; dry

SERE *v* SERED, SERING, SERES to sear

SEREIN *n* pl. -S a fine rain falling from an apparently clear sky

SERENADE *v* -NADED, -NADING, -NADES to perform an honorific evening song for

SERENATA *n* pl. -TAS or -TE a dramatic cantata

SERENE *adj* SERENER, SERENEST calm; tranquil **SERENELY** *adv*

SERENE *n* pl. -S a serene condition or expanse

SERENITY *n* pl. -TIES the state of being serene

SERER comparative of sere

SEREST superlative of sere

SERF *n* pl. -S a feudal slave

SERFAGE *n* pl. -S serfdom

SERFDOM *n* pl. -S the state of being a serf

SERFHOOD *n* pl. -S serfdom

SERFISH *adj* characteristic of a serf

SERFLIKE *adj* serfish

SERGE *n* pl. -S a twilled fabric

SERGEANT *n* pl. -S a noncommissioned military officer

SERGING *n* pl. -S a process of finishing the raw edges of a fabric

SERIAL *n* pl. -S a literary or dramatic work presented in successive installments

SERIALLY *adv* in the manner or form of a serial

SERIATE *v* -ATED, -ATING, -ATES to put into a series

SERIATIM *adv* serially

SERICIN *n* pl. -S a kind of protein

SERIEMA *n* pl. -S a Brazilian bird

SERIES *n* pl. SERIES an arrangement of one after another

SERIF *n* pl. -S a fine line used to finish off the main stroke of a letter **SERIFED**, **SERIFFED** *adj*

SERIN *n* pl. -S a European finch

SERINE *n* pl. -S an amino acid

SERING present participle of sere

SERINGA *n* pl. -S a Brazilian tree

SERIOUS *adj* thoughtful or subdued in appearance or manner

SERJEANT *n* pl. -S sergeant

SERMON *n* pl. -S a religious discourse **SERMONIC** *adj*

SEROLOGY *n* pl. -GIES the science of serums

SEROSA *n* pl. -SAS or -SAE a thin membrane lining certain bodily cavities **SEROSAL** *adj*

SEROSITY *n* pl. -TIES the quality or state of being serous

SEROTINE *n* pl. -S a European bat

SEROTYPE *n* pl. -S a group of closely related organisms distinguished by a common set of antigens

SEROUS *adj* of or resembling serum

SEROW *n* pl. -S an Asian antelope

SERPENT *n* pl. -S a snake

SERPIGO *n* pl. -GOES or -GINES a spreading skin eruption

SERRANID *n* pl. -S a marine fish

SERRANO *n* pl. -NOS a small hot pepper

SERRATE *v* -RATED, -RATING, -RATES to furnish with toothlike projections

SERRY *v* -RIED, -RYING, -RIES to crowd together

SERUM *n* pl. -RUMS or -RA the watery portion of whole blood **SERUMAL** *adj*

SERVABLE *adj* capable of serving or being served

SERVAL *n* pl. -S an African wildcat

SERVANT *n* pl. -S one that serves others

SERVE *v* SERVED, SERVING, SERVES to work for

SERVER *n* pl. -S one that serves another

SERVICE *v* -VICED, -VICING, -VICES to repair

SERVICER *n* pl. -S one that services

SERVILE *adj* slavishly submissive

SERVING *n* pl. -S a portion of food

SERVITOR *n* pl. -S a male servant

SERVO *n* pl. -VOS an automatic device used to control another mechanism

SESAME	*n* pl. -S an East Indian plant
SESAMOID	*n* pl. -S a nodular mass of bone or cartilage
SESSILE	*adj* permanently attached
SESSION	*n* pl. -S a meeting of a legislative or judicial body for the transaction of business
SESSPOOL	*n* pl. -S cesspool
SESTERCE	*n* pl. -S a coin of ancient Rome
SESTET	*n* pl. -S a stanza of six lines
SESTINA	*n* pl. -S a type of verse form
SESTINE	*n* pl. -S sestina
SET	*v* SET, SETTING, SETS to put in a particular position
SETA	*n* pl. -TAE a coarse, stiff hair **SETAL** *adj*
SETBACK	*n* pl. -S a defeat
SETENANT	*n* pl. -S a postage stamp that differs in design from others in the same sheet
SETIFORM	*adj* having the form of a seta
SETLINE	*n* pl. -S a strong fishing line
SETOFF	*n* pl. -S something that offsets something else
SETON	*n* pl. -S a type of surgical thread
SETOSE	*adj* covered with setae
SETOUS	*adj* setose
SETOUT	*n* pl. -S a display
SETSCREW	*n* pl. -S a type of screw
SETT	*n* pl. -S the burrow of a badger
SETTEE	*n* pl. -S a long seat with a high back
SETTER	*n* pl. -S one that sets
SETTING	*n* pl. -S the scenery used in a dramatic production
SETTLE	*v* -TLED, -TLING, -TLES to place in a desired state or order
SETTLER	*n* pl. -S one that settles
SETTLING	*n* pl. -S sediment
SETTLOR	*n* pl. -S one that makes a legal settlement
SETULOSE	*adj* covered with seta
SETULOUS	*adj* setulose
SETUP	*n* pl. -S the way something is arranged
SEVEN	*n* pl. -S a number
SEVENTH	*n* pl. -S one of seven equal parts
SEVENTY	*n* pl. -TIES a number

SEVER	*v* -ED, -ING, -S to divide or cut into parts
SEVERAL	*n* pl. -S a few persons or things
SEVERE	*adj* -VERER, -VEREST unsparing in the treatment of others **SEVERELY** *adv*
SEVERITY	*n* pl. -TIES the quality or state of being severe
SEVICHE	*n* pl. -S a dish of raw fish
SEVRUGA	*n* pl. -S caviar from the Caspian Sea
SEW	*v* SEWED, SEWN, SEWING, SEWS to mend or fasten with a needle and thread **SEWABLE** *adj*
SEWAGE	*n* pl. -S the waste matter carried off by sewers
SEWAN	*n* pl. -S seawan
SEWAR	*n* pl. -S a medieval servant
SEWER	*v* -ED, -ING, -S to clean or maintain sewers (underground conduits for waste)
SEWERAGE	*n* pl. -S sewage
SEWING	*n* pl. -S material that has been or is to be sewed
SEWN	a past participle of sew
SEX	*v* -ED, -ING, -ES to determine the sex (the property by which organisms are classified according to reproductive functions) of
SEXIER	comparative of sexy
SEXIEST	superlative of sexy
SEXILY	*adv* in a sexy manner
SEXINESS	*n* pl. -ES the quality or state of being sexy
SEXISM	*n* pl. -S prejudice or discrimination against women
SEXIST	*n* pl. -S one that practices sexism
SEXLESS	*adj* lacking sexual characteristics
SEXOLOGY	*n* pl. -GIES the study of human sexual behavior
SEXPOT	*n* pl. -S a sexually attractive woman
SEXT	*n* pl. -S one of seven canonical daily periods for prayer and devotion
SEXTAIN	*n* pl. -S a stanza of six lines
SEXTAN	*n* pl. -S a recurrent malarial fever
SEXTANT	*n* pl. -S an instrument for measuring angular distances
SEXTARII	*n/pl* ancient Roman units of liquid measure
SEXTET	*n* pl. -S a group of six

SEXTETTE	*n* pl. -S sextet
SEXTILE	*n* pl. -S the position of two celestial bodies when they are sixty degrees apart
SEXTO	*n* pl. -TOS sixmo
SEXTON	*n* pl. -S a maintenance worker of a church
SEXTUPLE	*v* -PLED, -PLING, -PLES to make six times as great
SEXTUPLY	*adv* to six times as much or as many
SEXUAL	*adj* pertaining to sex **SEXUALLY** *adv*
SEXY	*adj* SEXIER, SEXIEST arousing sexual desire
SFERICS	*n/pl* an electronic detector of storms
SFORZATO	*n* pl. -TOS the playing of a tone or chord with sudden force
SFUMATO	*n* pl. -TOS a technique used in painting
SH	*interj* — used to urge silence
SHA	*interj* — used to urge silence
SHABBY	*adj* -BIER, -BIEST ragged **SHABBILY** *adv*
SHACK	*n* pl. -S a shanty
SHACKLE	*v* -LED, -LING, -LES to confine with metal fastenings placed around the wrists or ankles
SHACKLER	*n* pl. -S one that shackles
SHACKO	*n* pl. -KOS or -KOES shako
SHAD	*n* pl. -S a food fish
SHADBLOW	*n* pl. -S a shadbush
SHADBUSH	*n* pl. -ES a flowering tree or shrub
SHADCHAN	*n* pl. -CHANIM or -CHANS a Jewish marriage broker
SHADDOCK	*n* pl. -S a citrus fruit
SHADE	*v* SHADED, SHADING, SHADES to screen from light or heat
SHADER	*n* pl. -S one that shades
SHADFLY	*n* pl. -FLIES a winged insect
SHADIER	comparative of shady
SHADIEST	superlative of shady
SHADILY	*adv* in a shady manner
SHADING	*n* pl. -S protection against light or heat
SHADOOF	*n* pl. -S a device used in Egypt for raising water for irrigation
SHADOW	*v* -ED, -ING, -S to make dark or gloomy
SHADOWER	*n* pl. -S one that shadows
SHADOWY	*adj* -OWIER, -OWIEST dark
SHADRACH	*n* pl. -S a mass of unfused material in the hearth of a blast furnace
SHADUF	*n* pl. -S shadoof
SHADY	*adj* SHADIER, SHADIEST shaded
SHAFT	*v* -ED, -ING, -S to push or propel with a pole
SHAFTING	*n* pl. -S a system of rods for transmitting motion or power
SHAG	*v* SHAGGED, SHAGGING, SHAGS to make shaggy
SHAGBARK	*n* pl. -S a hardwood tree
SHAGGY	*adj* -GIER, -GIEST covered with long, coarse hair **SHAGGILY** *adv*
SHAGREEN	*n* pl. -S the rough skin of certain sharks
SHAH	*n* pl. -S an Iranian ruler
SHAHDOM	*n* pl. -S the territory ruled by a shah
SHAIRD	*n* pl. -S shard
SHAIRN	*n* pl. -S sharn
SHAITAN	*n* pl. -S an evil spirit
SHAKE	*v* SHOOK, SHAKEN, SHAKING, SHAKES to move to and fro with short, rapid movements **SHAKABLE** *adj*
SHAKEOUT	*n* pl. -S a minor economic recession
SHAKER	*n* pl. -S one that shakes
SHAKEUP	*n* pl. -S a total reorganization
SHAKIER	comparative of shaky
SHAKIEST	superlative of shaky
SHAKILY	*adv* in a shaky manner
SHAKING	present participle of shake
SHAKO	*n* pl. -KOS or -KOES a type of military hat
SHAKY	*adj* SHAKIER, SHAKIEST shaking
SHALE	*n* pl. -S a fissile rock
SHALED	*adj* having a shell or husk
SHALEY	*adj* SHALIER, SHALIEST shaly
SHALIER	comparative of shaly
SHALIEST	superlative of shaly

SHALL	*v* present sing. 2d person SHALL or SHALT, past sing. 2d person SHOULD, SHOULDST, or SHOULDEST — used as an auxiliary to express futurity, inevitability, or command
SHALLOON	*n* pl. -S a woolen fabric
SHALLOP	*n* pl. -S a small, open boat
SHALLOT	*n* pl. -S a plant resembling an onion
SHALLOW	*adj* -LOWER, -LOWEST having little depth
SHALLOW	*v* -ED, -ING, -S to make shallow
SHALOM	*n* pl. -S a word used as a Jewish greeting or farewell
SHALT	a present 2d person sing. of shall
SHALY	*adj* SHALIER, SHALIEST resembling shale
SHAM	*v* SHAMMED, SHAMMING, SHAMS to feign
SHAMABLE	*adj* capable of being shamed
SHAMAN	*n* pl. -S a medicine man among certain North American Indians **SHAMANIC** *adj*
SHAMAS	*n* pl. -MOSIM shammes
SHAMBLE	*v* -BLED, -BLING, -BLES to walk awkwardly
SHAME	*v* SHAMED, SHAMING, SHAMES to cause to feel a painful sense of guilt or degradation
SHAMEFUL	*adj* disgraceful
SHAMES	*n* pl. -MOSIM shammes
SHAMING	present participle of shame
SHAMMAS	*n* pl. -MASIM shammes
SHAMMASH	*n* pl. -MASHIM shammes
SHAMMED	past tense of sham
SHAMMER	*n* pl. -S one that shams
SHAMMES	*n* pl. -MOSIM a minor official of a synagogue
SHAMMIED	past tense of shammy
SHAMMIES	present 3d person sing. of shammy
SHAMMING	present participle of sham
SHAMMOS	*n* pl. -MOSIM shammes
SHAMMOSIM	pl. of shammes
SHAMMY	*v* -MIED, -MYING, -MIES to chamois
SHAMOIS	*n* pl. SHAMOIS chamois
SHAMOS	*n* pl. -MOSIM shammes

SHAMOSIM	pl. of shames
SHAMOY	*v* -ED, -ING, -S to chamois
SHAMPOO	*v* -ED, -ING, -S to cleanse with a special preparation
SHAMROCK	*n* pl. -S a three-leaved plant
SHAMUS	*n* pl. -ES a private detective
SHANDY	*n* pl. -DIES an alcoholic drink
SHANGHAI	*v* -ED, -ING, -S to kidnap for service aboard a ship
SHANK	*v* -ED, -ING, -S to hit sharply to the right, as a golf ball
SHANNY	*n* pl. -NIES a marine fish
SHANTEY	*n* pl. -TEYS chantey
SHANTI	*n* pl. -S peace
SHANTIES	pl. of shanty
SHANTIH	*n* pl. -S shanti
SHANTUNG	*n* pl. -S a silk fabric
SHANTY	*n* pl. -TIES a small, crudely built dwelling
SHAPE	*v* SHAPED, SHAPEN, SHAPING, SHAPES to give shape (outward form) to **SHAPABLE** *adj*
SHAPELY	*adj* -LIER, -LIEST having a pleasing shape
SHAPER	*n* pl. -S one that shapes
SHAPEUP	*n* pl. -S a system of hiring a work crew
SHAPING	present participle of shape
SHARD	*n* pl. -S a fragment of broken pottery
SHARE	*v* SHARED, SHARING, SHARES to have, get, or use in common with another or others **SHARABLE** *adj*
SHARER	*n* pl. -S one that shares
SHARIF	*n* pl. -S sherif
SHARING	present participle of share
SHARK	*v* -ED, -ING, -S to live by trickery
SHARKER	*n* pl. -S one that sharks
SHARN	*n* pl. -S cow dung **SHARNY** *adj*
SHARP	*adj* SHARPER, SHARPEST suitable for or capable of cutting or piercing
SHARP	*v* -ED, -ING, -S to raise in pitch, as a musical tone
SHARPEN	*v* -ED, -ING, -S to make sharp
SHARPER	*n* pl. -S a swindler
SHARPIE	*n* pl. -S a very alert person
SHARPLY	*adv* in a sharp manner

SHARPY	*n* pl. SHARPIES sharpie	**SHEDDER**	*n* pl. -S one that casts off something
SHASHLIK	*n* pl. -S kabob		
SHASLIK	*n* pl. -S shashlik	**SHEDDING**	present participle of shed
SHATTER	*v* -ED, -ING, -S to break into pieces	**SHEDLIKE**	*adj* resembling a shed
		SHEEN	*v* -ED, -ING, -S to shine
SHAUGH	*n* pl. -S a thicket	**SHEENFUL**	*adj* shining
SHAUL	*v* -ED, -ING, -S to shoal	**SHEENY**	*adj* SHEENIER, SHEENIEST shining
SHAVE	*v* SHAVED, SHAVEN, SHAVING, SHAVES to sever the hair close to the roots **SHAVABLE** *adj*	**SHEEP**	*n* pl. SHEEP a ruminant mammal
		SHEEPCOT	*n* pl. -S an enclosure for sheep
SHAVER	*n* pl. -S one that shaves	**SHEEPDOG**	*n* pl. -S a dog trained to guard and herd sheep
SHAVIE	*n* pl. -S a trick or prank		
SHAVING	*n* pl. -S something shaved off	**SHEEPISH**	*adj* embarrassed
SHAW	*v* SHAWED, SHAWN, SHAWING, SHAWS to show	**SHEEPMAN**	*n* pl. -MEN a person who raises sheep
SHAWL	*v* -ED, -ING, -S to wrap in a shawl (a piece of cloth worn as a covering)	**SHEER**	*v* -ED, -ING, -S to swerve
		SHEER	*adj* SHEERER, SHEEREST of very thin texture **SHEERLY** *adv*
SHAWM	*n* pl. -S an early woodwind instrument	**SHEET**	*v* -ED, -ING, -S to cover with a sheet (a thin, rectangular piece of material)
SHAWN	past participle of shaw		
SHAY	*n* pl. SHAYS a chaise	**SHEETER**	*n* pl. -S one that sheets
SHE	*n* pl. -S a female person	**SHEETFED**	*adj* pertaining to a type of printing press
SHEA	*n* pl. -S an African tree		
SHEAF	*v* -ED, -ING, -S to sheave	**SHEETING**	*n* pl. -S material in the form of sheets
SHEAL	*n* pl. -S shealing		
SHEALING	*n* pl. -S a shepherd's hut	**SHEEVE**	*n* pl. -S a grooved pulley wheel
SHEAR	*v* SHEARED or SHORE, SHORN, SHEARING, SHEARS to cut the hair or wool from	**SHEIK**	*n* pl. -S an Arab chief
		SHEIKDOM	*n* pl. -S the area ruled by a sheik
		SHEIKH	*n* pl. -S sheik
SHEARER	*n* pl. -S one that shears	**SHEILA**	*n* pl. -S a young woman
SHEARING	*n* pl. -S an instance of cutting hair or wool	**SHEITAN**	*n* pl. -S shaitan
		SHEKEL	*n* pl. -S an ancient unit of weight and money
SHEATH	*v* -ED, -ING, -S to sheathe		
SHEATHE	*v* SHEATHED, SHEATHING, SHEATHES to put into a protective case	**SHELDUCK**	*n* pl. -S a European duck
		SHELF	*n* pl. SHELVES a flat rigid structure used to support articles
SHEATHER	*n* pl. -S one that sheathes	**SHELFFUL**	*n* pl. -S as much as a shelf can hold
SHEAVE	*v* SHEAVED, SHEAVING, SHEAVES to gather into a bundle		
		SHELL	*v* -ED, -ING, -S to divest of a shell (a hard outer covering)
SHEBANG	*n* pl. -S a situation, organization, or matter		
		SHELLAC	*v* -LACKED, -LACKING, -LACS to cover with a thin varnish
SHEBEAN	*n* pl. -S shebeen		
SHEBEEN	*n* pl. -S a place where liquor is sold illegally	**SHELLACK**	*v* -ED, -ING, -S to shellac
		SHELLER	*n* pl. -S one that shells
SHED	*v* SHEDDED, SHEDDING, SHEDS to house in a shed (a small, low structure)	**SHELLY**	*adj* SHELLIER, SHELLIEST abounding in seashells
		SHELTA	*n* pl. -S an esoteric jargon of Gaelic
SHEDABLE	*adj* capable of being cast off		

SHELTER   *v* -ED, -ING, -S to provide cover or protection for

SHELTIE   *n* pl. -S a small, shaggy pony

SHELTY   *n* pl. -TIES sheltie

SHELVE   *v* SHELVED, SHELVING, SHELVES to place on a shelf

SHELVER   *n* pl. -S one that shelves

SHELVES   pl. of shelf

SHELVING   *n* pl. -S material for shelves

SHELVY   *adj* SHELVIER, SHELVIEST inclining gradually

SHEND   *v* SHENT, SHENDING, SHENDS to disgrace

SHEOL   *n* pl. -S hell

SHEPHERD   *v* -ED, -ING, -S to watch over carefully

SHEQEL   *n* pl. SHEQALIM shekel

SHERBERT   *n* pl. -S sherbet

SHERBET   *n* pl. -S a frozen fruit-flavored mixture

SHERD   *n* pl. -S shard

SHEREEF   *n* pl. -S sherif

SHERIF   *n* pl. -S an Arab ruler

SHERIFF   *n* pl. -S a law-enforcement officer of a county

SHERLOCK   *n* pl. -S a detective

SHEROOT   *n* pl. -S cheroot

SHERPA   *n* pl. -S a soft fabric for linings

SHERRIS   *n* pl. -RISES sherry

SHERRY   *n* pl. -RIES a fortified wine with a nutty flavor

SHETLAND   *n* pl. -S a wool yarn

SHEUCH   *n* pl. -S sheugh

SHEUGH   *n* pl. -S a ditch

SHEW   *v* SHEWED, SHEWN, SHEWING, SHEWS to show

SHEWER   *n* pl. -S one that shews

SHH   *interj* sh

SHIATSU   *n* pl. -S a massage using finger pressure

SHIATZU   *n* pl. -S shiatsu

SHIBAH   *n* pl. -S shiva

SHICKER   *n* pl. -S a drunkard

SHIED   past tense of shy

SHIEL   *n* pl. -S shieling

SHIELD   *v* -ED, -ING, -S to provide with a protective cover or shelter

SHIELDER   *n* pl. -S one that shields

SHIELING   *n* pl. -S shealing

SHIER   *n* pl. -S a horse having a tendency to shy

SHIES   present 3d person sing. of shy

SHIEST   a superlative of shy

SHIFT   *v* -ED, -ING, -S to move from one position to another

SHIFTER   *n* pl. -S one that shifts

SHIFTY   *adj* SHIFTIER, SHIFTIEST tricky **SHIFTILY** *adv*

SHIGELLA   *n* pl. -LAE or -LAS any of a genus of aerobic bacteria

SHIITAKE   *n* pl. -S a dark Oriental mushroom

SHIKAR   *v* -KARRED, -KARRING, -KARS to hunt

SHIKAREE   *n* pl. -S a big game hunter

SHIKARI   *n* pl. -S shikaree

SHIKARRED   past tense of shikar

SHIKARRING   present participle of shikar

SHIKKER   *n* pl. -S shicker

SHILINGI   *n* pl. SHILINGI a monetary unit of Tanzania

SHILL   *v* -ED, -ING, -S to act as a decoy

SHILLALA   *n* pl. -S a short, thick club

SHILLING   *n* pl. -S a former monetary unit of Great Britain

SHILPIT   *adj* sickly

SHILY   *adv* in a shy manner

SHIM   *v* SHIMMED, SHIMMING, SHIMS to fill out or level by inserting a thin wedge

SHIMMER   *v* -ED, -ING, -S to glimmer

SHIMMERY   *adj* shimmering

SHIMMING   present participle of shim

SHIMMY   *v* -MIED, -MYING, -MIES to vibrate or wobble

SHIN   *v* SHINNED, SHINNING, SHINS to climb by gripping and pulling alternately with the hands and legs

SHINBONE   *n* pl. -S the tibia

SHINDIG   *n* pl. -S an elaborate dance or party

SHINDY   *n* pl. -DYS or -DIES a shindig

SHINE   *v* SHONE or SHINED, SHINING, SHINES to emit light

SHINER   *n* pl. -S one that shines

SHINGLE	v -GLED, -GLING, -GLES to cover with shingles (thin, oblong pieces of building material)	**SHIRR**	v -ED, -ING, -S to draw into three or more parallel rows, as cloth
SHINGLER	n pl. -S one that shingles	**SHIRRING**	n pl. -S a shirred arrangement of cloth
SHINGLY	adj covered with small, loose stones	**SHIRT**	n pl. -S a garment for the upper part of the body
SHINIER	comparative of shiny	**SHIRTING**	n pl. -S fabric used for making shirts
SHINIEST	superlative of shiny		
SHINILY	adv in a shiny manner	**SHIRTY**	adj SHIRTIER, SHIRTIEST angry
SHINING	adj emitting or reflecting light	**SHIST**	n pl. -S schist
SHINLEAF	n pl. -LEAFS or -LEAVES a perennial herb	**SHITAKE**	n pl. -S shiitake
		SHITTAH	n pl. -S a hardwood tree
SHINNED	past of shin	**SHITTIM**	n pl. -S the wood of the shittah
SHINNERY	n pl. -NERIES a dense growth of small trees	**SHIV**	n pl. -S a knife
SHINNEY	v -ED, -ING, -S to play a form of hockey	**SHIVA**	n pl. -S a period of mourning
		SHIVAH	n pl. -S shiva
SHINNING	present participle of shin	**SHIVAREE**	v -REED, -REEING, -REES to chivaree
SHINNY	v -NIED, -NYING, -NIES to shin		
SHINY	adj SHINIER, SHINIEST filled with light	**SHIVE**	n pl. -S a thin fragment
		SHIVER	v -ED, -ING, -S to tremble with fear or cold
SHIP	v SHIPPED, SHIPPING, SHIPS to transport by ship (a vessel suitable for navigation in deep water)	**SHIVERER**	n pl. -S one that shivers
		SHIVERY	adj shivering
SHIPLAP	n pl. -S an overlapping joint used in carpentry	**SHLEMIEL**	n pl. -S an unlucky bungler
		SHLEP	v SHLEPPED, SHLEPPING, SHLEPS to schlep
SHIPLOAD	n pl. -S as much as a ship can carry	**SHLEPP**	v -ED, -ING, -S to schlep
SHIPMAN	n pl. -MEN a sailor	**SHLOCK**	n pl. -S schlock
SHIPMATE	n pl. -S a fellow sailor	**SHLUMP**	v -ED, -ING, -S to schlump
SHIPMENT	n pl. -S something that is shipped	**SHLUMPY**	adj slovenly
SHIPPED	past tense of ship	**SHMALTZ**	n pl. -ES schmaltz
SHIPPEN	n pl. -S a cowshed	**SHMALTZY**	adj SHMALTZIER, SHMALTZIEST schmalzy
SHIPPER	n pl. -S one that ships		
SHIPPING	n pl. -S the business of one that ships	**SHMEAR**	n pl. -S schmear
		SHMO	n pl. SHMOES schmo
SHIPPON	n pl. -S shippen	**SHMOOZE**	v SHMOOZED, SHMOOZING, SHMOOZES to schmooze
SHIPSIDE	n pl. -S the area alongside a ship		
SHIPWAY	n pl. -WAYS a canal deep enough to serve ships	**SHMUCK**	n pl. -S schmuck
		SHNAPS	n pl. SHNAPS schnapps
SHIPWORM	n pl. -S a wormlike mollusk	**SHNOOK**	n pl. -S schnook
SHIPYARD	n pl. -S a place where ships are built or repaired	**SHOAL**	adj SHOALER, SHOALEST shallow
SHIRE	n pl. -S a territorial division of Great Britain	**SHOAL**	v -ED, -ING, -S to become shallow
SHIRK	v -ED, -ING, -S to avoid work or duty	**SHOALY**	adj SHOALIER, SHOALIEST full of shallow areas
SHIRKER	n pl. -S one that shirks	**SHOAT**	n pl. -S a young hog

SHOCK	v -ED, -ING, -S to strike with great surprise, horror, or disgust	**SHOP**	v SHOPPED, SHOPPING, SHOPS to examine goods with intent to buy
SHOCKER	n pl. -S one that shocks	**SHOPBOY**	n pl. -BOYS a salesclerk
SHOD	a past tense of shoe	**SHOPGIRL**	n pl. -S a salesgirl
SHODDEN	a past participle of shoe	**SHOPHAR**	n pl. -PHARS or -PHROTH shofar
SHODDY	adj -DIER, -DIEST of inferior quality **SHODDILY** adv	**SHOPLIFT**	v -ED, -ING, -S to steal goods from a store
SHODDY	n pl. -DIES a low-quality wool	**SHOPMAN**	n pl. -MEN one who owns or operates a small store
SHOE	n pl. SHOES or SHOON a covering for the foot	**SHOPPE**	n pl. -S a small store
SHOE	v SHOD or SHOED, SHODDEN, SHOEING, SHOES to provide with shoes	**SHOPPED**	past tense of shop
		SHOPPER	n pl. -S one that shops
SHOEBILL	n pl. -S a wading bird	**SHOPPING**	n pl. -S the act of one that shops
SHOEHORN	v -ED, -ING, -S to force into a small space	**SHOPTALK**	n pl. -S conversation concerning one's business or occupation
SHOELACE	n pl. -S a lace for fastening a shoe	**SHOPWORN**	adj worn out from being on display in a store
SHOELESS	adj having no shoe	**SHORAN**	n pl. -S a type of navigational system
SHOEPAC	n pl. -S a waterproof boot		
SHOEPACK	n pl. -S shoepac	**SHORE**	v SHORED, SHORING, SHORES to prop with a supporting timber
SHOER	n pl. -S one that shoes horses		
SHOETREE	n pl. -S a device shaped like a foot that is inserted into a shoe to preserve its shape	**SHORING**	n pl. -S a system of supporting timbers
		SHORL	n pl. -S schorl
SHOFAR	n pl. SHOFARS or SHOFROTH a ram's-horn trumpet blown in certain Jewish rituals	**SHORN**	a past participle of shear
		SHORT	adj SHORTER, SHORTEST having little length
SHOG	v SHOGGED, SHOGGING, SHOGS to move along	**SHORT**	v -ED, -ING, -S to cause a type of electrical malfunction in
SHOGUN	n pl. -S a former military leader of Japan **SHOGUNAL** adj	**SHORTAGE**	n pl. -S an insufficient supply or amount
SHOJI	n pl. -S a paper screen used as a partition or door in a Japanese house	**SHORTCUT**	v -CUT, -CUTTING, -CUTS to take a shorter or quicker way
SHOLOM	n pl. -S shalom	**SHORTEN**	v -ED, -ING, -S to make or become shorter
SHONE	a past tense of shine	**SHORTIA**	n pl. -S a perennial herb
SHOO	v -ED, -ING, -S to drive away	**SHORTIE**	n pl. -S shorty
SHOOFLY	n pl. -FLIES a child's rocker	**SHORTIES**	pl. of shorty
SHOOK	n pl. -S a set of parts for assembling a barrel or packing	**SHORTISH**	adj somewhat short
SHOOL	v -ED, -ING, -S to shovel	**SHORTLY**	adv in a short time
SHOON	a pl. of shoe	**SHORTY**	n pl. SHORTIES one that is short
SHOOT	v SHOT, SHOOTING, SHOOTS to hit, wound, or kill with a missile discharged from a weapon	**SHOT**	v SHOTTED, SHOTTING, SHOTS to load with shot (small lead or steel pellets)
SHOOTER	n pl. -S one that shoots		
SHOOTING	n pl. -S the act of one that shoots	**SHOTE**	n pl. -S shoat
SHOOTOUT	n pl. -S a battle fought with handguns or rifles	**SHOTGUN**	v -GUNNED, -GUNNING, -GUNS to shoot with a type of gun

SHOTT	*n* pl. -S chott
SHOTTED	past tense of shot
SHOTTEN	*adj* having spawned — used of a fish
SHOTTING	present participle of shot
SHOULD	past tense of shall
SHOULDER	*v* -ED, -ING, -S to assume the burden or responsibility of
SHOULDEST	a 2d person sing. past tense of shall
SHOULDST	a 2d person sing. past tense of shall
SHOUT	*v* -ED, -ING, -S to utter loudly
SHOUTER	*n* pl. -S one that shouts
SHOVE	*v* SHOVED, SHOVING, SHOVES to push roughly
SHOVEL	*v* -ELED, -ELING, -ELS or -ELLED, -ELLING, -ELS to take up with a shovel (a digging implement)
SHOVELER	*n* pl. -S one that shovels
SHOVER	*n* pl. -S one that shoves
SHOVING	present participle of shove
SHOW	*v* SHOWED, SHOWN, SHOWING, SHOWS to cause or permit to be seen **SHOWABLE** *adj*
SHOWBIZ	*n* pl. -BIZZES show business
SHOWBOAT	*v* -ED, -ING, -S to show off
SHOWCASE	*v* -CASED, -CASING, -CASES to exhibit
SHOWDOWN	*n* pl. -S an event that forces the conclusion of an issue
SHOWER	*v* -ED, -ING, -S to bathe in a spray of water
SHOWERER	*n* pl. -S one that showers
SHOWERY	*adj* abounding with brief periods of rain
SHOWGIRL	*n* pl. -S a chorus girl
SHOWIER	comparative of showy
SHOWIEST	superlative of showy
SHOWILY	*adv* in a showy manner
SHOWING	*n* pl. -S an exhibition or display
SHOWMAN	*n* pl. -MEN a theatrical producer
SHOWN	past participle of show
SHOWOFF	*n* pl. -S one given to pretentious display
SHOWRING	*n* pl. -S a ring where animals are displayed

SHOWROOM	*n* pl. -S a room used for the display of merchandise
SHOWY	*adj* SHOWIER, SHOWIEST making a great or brilliant display
SHOYU	*n* pl. -S soy sauce
SHRANK	past tense of shrink
SHRAPNEL	*n* pl. SHRAPNEL fragments from an exploding bomb, mine, or shell
SHRED	*v* SHREDDED, SHREDDING, SHREDS to tear into small strips
SHREDDER	*n* pl. -S one that shreds
SHREW	*v* -ED, -ING, -S to curse
SHREWD	*adj* SHREWDER, SHREWDEST having keen insight **SHREWDLY** *adv*
SHREWDIE	*n* pl. -S a shrewd person
SHREWISH	*adj* ill-tempered
SHRI	*n* pl. -S sri
SHRIEK	*v* -ED, -ING, -S to utter a shrill cry
SHRIEKER	*n* pl. -S one that shrieks
SHRIEKY	*adj* SHRIEKIER, SHRIEKIEST shrill
SHRIEVAL	*adj* pertaining to a sheriff
SHRIEVE	*v* SHRIEVED, SHRIEVING, SHRIEVES to shrive
SHRIFT	*n* pl. -S the act of shriving
SHRIKE	*n* pl. -S a predatory bird
SHRILL	*adj* SHRILLER, SHRILLEST having a high-pitched and piercing quality **SHRILLY** *adv*
SHRILL	*v* -ED, -ING, -S to utter a shrill sound
SHRIMP	*v* -ED, -ING, -S to catch shrimps (small marine decapods)
SHRIMPER	*n* pl. -S a shrimp fisher
SHRIMPY	*adj* SHRIMPIER, SHRIMPIEST abounding in shrimp
SHRINE	*v* SHRINED, SHRINING, SHRINES to place in a shrine (a receptacle for sacred relics)
SHRINK	*v* SHRANK, SHRUNK or SHRUNKEN, SHRINKING, SHRINKS to contract or draw back
SHRINKER	*n* pl. -S one that shrinks
SHRIVE	*v* SHROVE or SHRIVED, SHRIVEN, SHRIVING, SHRIVES to hear the confession of and grant absolution to

SHRIVEL   v -ELED, -ELING, -ELS or -ELLED, -ELLING, -ELS to contract into wrinkles

SHRIVER   n pl. -S one that shrives

SHRIVING   present participle of shrive

SHROFF   v -ED, -ING, -S to test the genuineness of, as a coin

SHROUD   v -ED, -ING, -S to wrap in burial clothing

SHROVE   a past tense of shrive

SHRUB   n pl. -S a low, woody plant

SHRUBBY   adj -BIER, -BIEST covered with shrubs

SHRUG   v SHRUGGED, SHRUGGING, SHRUGS to raise and contract the shoulders

SHRUNK   a past tense of shrink

SHRUNKEN   a past participle of shrink

SHTETEL   n pl. SHTETLACH or SHTETELS a Jewish village

SHTETL   n pl. SHTETLACH or SHTETLS shtetel

SHTICK   n pl. -S an entertainment routine

SHTIK   n pl. -S shtick

SHUCK   v -ED, -ING, -S to remove the husk or shell from

SHUCKER   n pl. -S one that shucks

SHUCKING   n pl. -S the act of one that shucks

SHUDDER   v -ED, -ING, -S to tremble

SHUDDERY   adj shuddering

SHUFFLE   v -FLED, -FLING, -FLES to walk without lifting the feet

SHUFFLER   n pl. -S one that shuffles

SHUL   n pl. SHULN or SHULS a synagogue

SHUN   v SHUNNED, SHUNNING, SHUNS to avoid

SHUNNER   n pl. -S one that shuns

SHUNPIKE   v -PIKED, -PIKING, -PIKES to travel on side roads to avoid expressways

SHUNT   v -ED, -ING, -S to turn aside

SHUNTER   n pl. -S one that shunts

SHUSH   v -ED, -ING, -ES to silence

SHUT   v SHUT, SHUTTING, SHUTS to close

SHUTDOWN   n pl. -S a temporary closing of an industrial plant

SHUTE   v SHUTED, SHUTING, SHUTES to chute

SHUTEYE   n pl. -S sleep

SHUTOFF   n pl. -S a device that shuts something off

SHUTOUT   n pl. -S a game in which one team fails to score

SHUTTER   v -ED, -ING, -S to provide with shutters (hinged window covers)

SHUTTING   present participle of shut

SHUTTLE   v -TLED, -TLING, -TLES to move or travel back and forth

SHWANPAN   n pl. -S swanpan

SHY   adj SHIER, SHIEST or SHYER, SHYEST timid

SHY   v SHIED, SHYING, SHIES to move suddenly back or aside, as in fear

SHYER   n pl. -S shier

SHYLOCK   v -ED, -ING, -S to lend money at high interest rates

SHYLY   adv in a shy manner

SHYNESS   n pl. -ES the state of being shy

SHYSTER   n pl. -S an unscrupulous lawyer or politician

SI   n pl. -S ti

SIAL   n pl. -S a type of rock formation **SIALIC** adj

SIALID   n pl. -S an alderfly

SIALIDAN   n pl. -S sialid

SIALOID   adj resembling saliva

SIAMANG   n pl. -S a large, black gibbon

SIAMESE   n pl. -S a water pipe with a connection for two hoses

SIB   n pl. -S a sibling

SIBB   n pl. -S sib

SIBILANT   n pl. -S a speech sound produced by the fricative passage of breath through a narrow orifice

SIBILATE   v -LATED, -LATING, -LATES to hiss

SIBLING   n pl. -S one having the same parents as another

SIBYL   n pl. -S a female prophet **SIBYLIC, SIBYLLIC** adj

SIC   v SICCED, SICCING, SICS to urge to attack

SICCAN   adj such

SICE   n pl. -S syce

SICK	*adj* SICKER, SICKEST affected with disease or ill health
SICK	*v* -ED, -ING, -S to sic
SICKBAY	*n* pl. -BAYS a ship's hospital
SICKBED	*n* pl. -S a sick person's bed
SICKEE	*n* pl. -S sickie
SICKEN	*v* -ED, -ING, -S to make sick
SICKENER	*n* pl. -S one that sickens
SICKERLY	*adv* securely
SICKIE	*n* pl. -S an emotionally sick person
SICKISH	*adj* somewhat sick
SICKLE	*v* -LED, -LING, -LES to cut with an agricultural implement having a single blade
SICKLY	*adj* -LIER, -LIEST appearing as if sick **SICKLILY** *adv*
SICKLY	*v* -LIED, -LYING, -LIES to make sickly
SICKNESS	*n* pl. -ES the state of being sick
SICKO	*n* pl. SICKOS sickie
SICKOUT	*n* pl. -S an organized absence of workers claiming to be sick
SICKROOM	*n* pl. -S a room occupied by a sick person
SIDDUR	*n* pl. -DURIM or -DURS a Jewish prayer book
SIDE	*v* SIDED, SIDING, SIDES to agree with or support
SIDEARM	*adj* thrown with a sideways sweep of the arm
SIDEBAND	*n* pl. -S a band of radio frequencies
SIDEBAR	*n* pl. -S a short news story accompanying a major story
SIDECAR	*n* pl. -S a passenger car attached to a motorcycle
SIDED	past tense of side
SIDEHILL	*n* pl. -S a hillside
SIDEKICK	*n* pl. -S a close friend
SIDELINE	*v* -LINED, -LINING, -LINES to put out of action
SIDELING	*adj* sloping
SIDELONG	*adj* directed to one side
SIDEMAN	*n* pl. -MEN a member of a jazz band
SIDEREAL	*adj* pertaining to the stars
SIDERITE	*n* pl. -S a mineral
SIDESHOW	*n* pl. -S a small show offered in addition to a main attraction
SIDESLIP	*v* -SLIPPED, -SLIPPING, -SLIPS to slip to one side
SIDESPIN	*n* pl. -S a type of spin imparted to a ball
SIDESTEP	*v* -STEPPED, -STEPPING, -STEPS to step to one side
SIDEWALK	*n* pl. -S a paved walk for pedestrians
SIDEWALL	*n* pl. -S a side surface of a tire
SIDEWARD	*adv* toward one side
SIDEWAY	*adv* sideways
SIDEWAYS	*adv* toward or from one side
SIDEWISE	*adv* sideways
SIDING	*n* pl. -S material used for surfacing a frame building
SIDLE	*v* -DLED, -DLING, -DLES to move sideways
SIDLER	*n* pl. -S one that sidles
SIEGE	*v* SIEGED, SIEGING, SIEGES to attempt to capture or gain
SIEMENS	*n* pl. SIEMENS a unit of electrical conductance
SIENITE	*n* pl. -S syenite
SIENNA	*n* pl. -S a brown pigment
SIEROZEM	*n* pl. -S a type of soil
SIERRA	*n* pl. -S a mountain range **SIERRAN** *adj*
SIESTA	*n* pl. -S an afternoon nap or rest
SIEUR	*n* pl. -S an old French title of respect for a man
SIEVE	*v* SIEVED, SIEVING, SIEVES to pass through a sieve (a utensil for separating the coarse parts from the fine parts of loose matter)
SIFAKA	*n* pl. -S a lemur of Madagascar
SIFFLEUR	*n* pl. -S an animal that makes a whistling noise
SIFT	*v* -ED, -ING, -S to sieve
SIFTER	*n* pl. -S one that sifts
SIFTING	*n* pl. -S the work of a sifter
SIGANID	*n* pl. -S any of a family of fishes
SIGH	*v* -ED, -ING, -S to let out a sigh (a deep, audible breath)
SIGHER	*n* pl. -S one that sighs
SIGHLESS	*adj* uttering no sigh
SIGHLIKE	*adj* resembling a sigh
SIGHT	*v* -ED, -ING, -S to observe or notice
SIGHTER	*n* pl. -S one that sights

SIGHTING	*n* pl. -S an observation
SIGHTLY	*adj* -LIER, -LIEST pleasing to look at
SIGHTSEE	*v* -SAW, -SEEN, -SEEING, -SEES to visit and view places of interest
SIGIL	*n* pl. -S an official seal
SIGLOS	*n* pl. -LOI an ancient Persian coin
SIGMA	*n* pl. -S a Greek letter **SIGMATE** *adj*
SIGMOID	*n* pl. -S an S-shaped curve in a bodily part
SIGN	*v* -ED, -ING, -S to write one's name on
SIGNAGE	*n* pl. -S a system of signs in a community
SIGNAL	*v* -NALED, -NALING, -NALS or -NALLED, -NALLING, -NALS to notify by a means of communication
SIGNALER	*n* pl. -S one that signals
SIGNALLY	*adv* notably
SIGNEE	*n* pl. -S a signer of a document
SIGNER	*n* pl. -S one that signs
SIGNET	*v* -ED, -ING, -S to mark with an official seal
SIGNIFY	*v* -FIED, -FYING, -FIES to make known
SIGNIOR	*n* pl. -GNIORI or -GNIORS signor
SIGNIORY	*n* pl. -GNIORIES signory
SIGNOR	*n* pl. -GNORI or -GNORS an Italian title of courtesy for a man
SIGNORA	*n* pl. -GNORE or -GNORAS an Italian title of courtesy for a married woman
SIGNORE	*n* pl. -GNORI signor
SIGNORY	*n* pl. -GNORIES seignory
SIGNPOST	*v* -ED, -ING, -S to provide with signposts (posts bearing signs)
SIKE	*n* pl. -S syke
SIKER	*adj* secure
SILAGE	*n* pl. -S fodder that has been preserved in a silo
SILANE	*n* pl. -S a chemical compound
SILD	*n* pl. -S a young herring
SILENCE	*v* -LENCED, -LENCING, -LENCES to make silent
SILENCER	*n* pl. -S one that silences
SILENI	pl. of silenus
SILENT	*adj* -LENTER, -LENTEST making no sound or noise **SILENTLY** *adv*
SILENTS	*n/pl* silent movies
SILENUS	*n* pl. -NI a woodland deity of Greek mythology
SILESIA	*n* pl. -S a cotton fabric
SILEX	*n* pl. -ES silica
SILICA	*n* pl. -S a form of silicon
SILICATE	*n* pl. -S a chemical salt
SILICIC	*adj* pertaining to silicon
SILICIDE	*n* pl. -S a silicon compound
SILICIFY	*v* -FIED, -FYING, -FIES to convert into silica
SILICIUM	*n* pl. -S silicon
SILICLE	*n* pl. -S a short, flat silique
SILICON	*n* pl. -S a nonmetallic element
SILICONE	*n* pl. -S a silicon compound
SILICULA	*n* pl. -LAE a silicle
SILIQUA	*n* pl. -QUAE silique
SILIQUE	*n* pl. -LIQUES a type of seed capsule
SILK	*v* -ED, -ING, -S to cover with silk (a soft, lustrous fabric)
SILKEN	*adj* made of silk
SILKIER	comparative of silky
SILKIES	pl. of silky
SILKIEST	superlative of silky
SILKILY	*adv* in a silky manner
SILKLIKE	*adj* resembling silk
SILKWEED	*n* pl. -S milkweed
SILKWORM	*n* pl. -S a caterpillar that spins a cocoon of silk fibers
SILKY	*adj* SILKIER, SILKIEST resembling silk
SILKY	*n* pl. SILKIES a glossy-coated terrier
SILL	*n* pl. -S the horizontal piece at the base of a window
SILLABUB	*n* pl. -S an alcoholic dessert
SILLER	*n* pl. -S silver
SILLIBUB	*n* pl. -S sillabub
SILLY	*adj* -LIER, -LIEST showing a lack of good sense **SILLILY** *adv*
SILLY	*n* pl. -LIES a silly person
SILO	*v* -ED, -ING, -S to store in a silo (a tall, cylindrical structure)
SILOXANE	*n* pl. -S a chemical compound
SILT	*v* -ED, -ING, -S to fill with silt (a sedimentary material)

SILTY	*adj* SILTIER, SILTIEST full of silt
SILURID	*n* pl. -S any of a family of catfishes
SILUROID	*n* pl. -S a silurid
SILVA	*n* pl. -VAS or -VAE sylva
SILVAN	*n* pl. -S sylvan
SILVER	*v* -ED, -ING, -S to cover with silver (a metallic element)
SILVERER	*n* pl. -S one that silvers
SILVERLY	*adv* with a silvery appearance
SILVERN	*adj* silvery
SILVERY	*adj* resembling silver
SILVEX	*n* pl. -ES an herbicide
SILVICAL	*adj* pertaining to silvics
SILVICS	*n/pl* the study of forest trees
SIM	*n* pl. -S simulation
SIMA	*n* pl. -S an igneous rock
SIMAR	*n* pl. -S a woman's light jacket or robe
SIMARUBA	*n* pl. -S a tropical tree
SIMAZINE	*n* pl. -S an herbicide
SIMIAN	*n* pl. -S an ape or monkey
SIMILAR	*adj* being like but not completely identical to
SIMILE	*n* pl. -S a figure of speech
SIMIOID	*adj* simious
SIMIOUS	*adj* pertaining to simians
SIMITAR	*n* pl. -S scimitar
SIMLIN	*n* pl. -S cymling
SIMMER	*v* -ED, -ING, -S to cook below or just at the boiling point
SIMNEL	*n* pl. -S a crisp bread
SIMOLEON	*n* pl. -S a dollar
SIMONIAC	*n* pl. -S one who practices simony
SIMONIES	pl. of simony
SIMONIST	*n* pl. -S a simoniac
SIMONIZE	*v* -NIZED, -NIZING, -NIZES to polish with wax
SIMONY	*n* pl. -NIES the buying or selling of a church office
SIMOOM	*n* pl. -S a hot, dry desert wind
SIMOON	*n* pl. -S simoom
SIMP	*n* pl. -S a foolish person
SIMPER	*v* -ED, -ING, -S to smile in a silly manner
SIMPERER	*n* pl. -S one that simpers
SIMPLE	*adj* SIMPLER, SIMPLEST not complex or complicated
SIMPLE	*n* pl. -S something that is simple
SIMPLEX	*n* pl. -PLEXES, -PLICES, or -PLICIA a simple word
SIMPLIFY	*v* -FIED, -FYING, -FIES to make simple
SIMPLISM	*n* pl. -S the tendency to oversimplify an issue or problem
SIMPLIST	*n* pl. -S a person given to simplism
SIMPLY	*adv* in a simple manner
SIMULANT	*n* pl. -S one that simulates
SIMULAR	*n* pl. -S a simulant
SIMULATE	*v* -LATED, -LATING, -LATES to take on the appearance of
SIN	*v* SINNED, SINNING, SINS to commit a sin (an offense against religious or moral law)
SINAPISM	*n* pl. -S a pasty mixture applied to an irritated part of the body
SINCE	*adv* from then until now
SINCERE	*adj* -CERER, -CEREST free from hypocrisy or falseness
SINCIPUT	*n* pl. -CIPUTS or -CIPITA the forehead
SINE	*n* pl. -S a trigonometric function of an angle
SINECURE	*n* pl. -S an office or position requiring little or no work
SINEW	*v* -ED, -ING, -S to strengthen
SINEWY	*adj* lean and muscular
SINFONIA	*n* pl. -NIE a symphony
SINFUL	*adj* marked by sin **SINFULLY** *adv*
SING	*v* SANG, SUNG, SINGING, SINGS to utter with musical inflections of the voice **SINGABLE** *adj*
SINGE	*v* SINGED, SINGEING, SINGES to burn slightly
SINGER	*n* pl. -S one that sings
SINGLE	*v* -GLED, -GLING, -GLES to select from a group
SINGLET	*n* pl. -S a man's undershirt or jersey
SINGLY	*adv* without the company of others
SINGSONG	*n* pl. -S monotonous cadence in speaking or reading
SINGULAR	*n* pl. -S a word form that denotes one person or thing

SINH   *n* pl. -S a hyperbolic function of an angle

SINICIZE   *v* -CIZED, -CIZING, -CIZES to modify by Chinese influence

SINISTER   *adj* threatening or portending evil

SINK   *v* SANK, SUNK or SUNKEN, SINKING, SINKS to move to a lower level **SINKABLE** *adj*

SINKAGE   *n* pl. -S the act, process, or degree of sinking

SINKER   *n* pl. -S one that sinks

SINKHOLE   *n* pl. -S a natural depression in a land surface

SINLESS   *adj* free from sin

SINNED   past tense of sin

SINNER   *n* pl. -S one that sins

SINNING   present participle of sin

SINOLOGY   *n* pl. -GIES the study of the Chinese

SINOPIA   *n* pl. -PIAS or -PIE a red pigment

SINSYNE   *adv* since

SINTER   *v* -ED, -ING, -S to make cohesive by the combined action of heat and pressure

SINUATE   *v* -ATED, -ATING, -ATES to curve in and out

SINUOUS   *adj* characterized by curves, bends, or turns

SINUS   *n* pl. -ES a cranial cavity

SINUSOID   *n* pl. -S a mathematical curve

SIP   *v* SIPPED, SIPPING, SIPS to drink in small quantities

SIPE   *v* SIPED, SIPING, SIPES to seep

SIPHON   *v* -ED, -ING, -S to draw off through a siphon (a type of tube)

SIPHONAL   *adj* of or pertaining to a siphon

SIPHONIC   *adj* siphonal

SIPING   present participle of sipe

SIPPED   past tense of sip

SIPPER   *n* pl. -S one that sips

SIPPET   *n* pl. -S a small piece of bread soaked in gravy

SIPPING   present participle of sip

SIR   *n* pl. -S a respectful form of address used to a man

SIRDAR   *n* pl. -S a person of rank in India

SIRE   *v* SIRED, SIRING, SIRES to beget

SIREE   *n* pl. -S sirree

SIREN   *n* pl. -S a device that produces a penetrating warning sound

SIRENIAN   *n* pl. -S any of an order of aquatic mammals

SIRING   present participle of sire

SIRLOIN   *n* pl. -S a cut of beef

SIROCCO   *n* pl. -COS a hot, dry wind

SIRRA   *n* pl. -S sirrah

SIRRAH   *n* pl. -S a form of address used to inferiors

SIRREE   *n* pl. -S sir

SIRUP   *n* pl. -S syrup **SIRUPY** *adj*

SIRVENTE   *n* pl. -S a satirical medieval song or poem

SIS   *n* pl. SISES sister

SISAL   *n* pl. -S a strong fiber used for rope

SISKIN   *n* pl. -S a Eurasian finch

SISSY   *n* pl. -SIES an effeminate man or boy

SISSY   *adj* SISSIER, SISSIEST sissyish

SISSYISH   *adj* resembling a sissy

SISTER   *v* -ED, -ING, -S to treat like a sister (a female sibling)

SISTERLY   *adj* of or resembling a sister

SISTROID   *adj* included between the convex sides of two intersecting curves

SISTRUM   *n* pl. -TRUMS or -TRA an ancient Egyptian percussion instrument

SIT   *v* SAT, SAT or SITTEN, SITTING, SITS to rest on the buttocks

SITAR   *n* pl. -S a lute of India

SITARIST   *n* pl. -S one who plays the sitar

SITCOM   *n* pl. -S a television comedy series with continuing characters

SITE   *v* SITED, SITING, SITES to place in position for operation

SITH   *adv* since

SITHENCE   *adv* since

SITHENS   *adv* since

SITING   present participle of site

SITOLOGY   *n* pl. -GIES the science of nutrition and diet

SITTEN   a past participle of sit

SITTER   *n* pl. -S one that sits

SITTING   *n* pl. -S a meeting or session

SITUATE   *v* -ATED, -ATING, -ATES to place in a certain position

SITUP — *n* pl. -S an exercise in which one moves from a lying to a sitting position

SITUS — *n* pl. -TUSES a position or location

SITZMARK — *n* pl. -S a mark left in the snow by a skier who has fallen backward

SIVER — *n* pl. -S a sewer

SIX — *n* pl. -ES a number

SIXFOLD — *adj* being six times as great as

SIXMO — *n* pl. -MOS a paper size

SIXPENCE — *n* pl. -S a British coin worth six pennies

SIXPENNY — *adj* worth sixpence

SIXTE — *n* pl. -S a fencing parry

SIXTEEN — *n* pl. -S a number

SIXTH — *n* pl. -S one of six equal parts

SIXTHLY — *adv* in the sixth place

SIXTIETH — *n* pl. -S one of sixty equal parts

SIXTY — *n* pl. -TIES a number

SIXTYISH — *adj* being about sixty years old

SIZABLE — *adj* of considerable size **SIZABLY** *adv*

SIZAR — *n* pl. -S a British student who receives financial assistance from his college

SIZE — *v* SIZED, SIZING, SIZES to arrange according to size (physical proportions)

SIZEABLE — *adj* sizable **SIZEABLY** *adv*

SIZER — *n* pl. -S sizar

SIZIER — comparative of sizy

SIZIEST — superlative of sizy

SIZINESS — *n* pl. -ES the quality or state of being sizy

SIZING — *n* pl. -S a substance used as a glaze or filler for porous materials

SIZY — *adj* SIZIER, SIZIEST viscid

SIZZLE — *v* -ZLED, -ZLING, -ZLES to burn or fry with a hissing sound

SIZZLER — *n* pl. -S a very hot day

SJAMBOK — *v* -ED, -ING, -S to strike with a whip used in South Africa

SKA — *n* pl. -S a popular music of Jamaica

SKAG — *n* pl. -S heroin

SKALD — *n* pl. -S an ancient Scandinavian poet **SKALDIC** *adj*

SKAT — *n* pl. -S a card game

SKATE — *v* SKATED, SKATING, SKATES to glide over ice or the ground on skates (shoes fitted with runners or wheels)

SKATER — *n* pl. -S one that skates

SKATING — *n* pl. -S the sport of gliding on skates

SKATOL — *n* pl. -S skatole

SKATOLE — *n* pl. -S a chemical compound

SKEAN — *n* pl. -S a type of dagger

SKEANE — *n* pl. -S a length of yarn wound in a loose coil

SKEE — *v* SKEED, SKEEING, SKEES to ski

SKEEN — *n* pl. -S skean

SKEET — *n* pl. -S the sport of shooting at clay pigeons hurled in the air by spring traps

SKEETER — *n* pl. -S a skeet shooter

SKEG — *n* pl. -S a timber that connects the keel and sternpost of a ship

SKEIGH — *adj* proud

SKEIN — *v* -ED, -ING, -S to wind into long, loose coils

SKELETON — *n* pl. -S the supporting or protective framework of a human or animal body **SKELETAL** *adj*

SKELLUM — *n* pl. -S a rascal

SKELM — *n* pl. -S skellum

SKELP — *v* SKELPED or SKELPIT, SKELPING, SKELPS to slap

SKELTER — *v* -ED, -ING, -S to scurry

SKENE — *n* pl. -S skean

SKEP — *n* pl. -S a beehive

SKEPSIS — *n* pl. -SISES the attitude or outlook of a skeptic

SKEPTIC — *n* pl. -S a person who doubts generally accepted ideas

SKERRY — *n* pl. -RIES a small, rocky island

SKETCH — *v* -ED, -ING, -ES to make a rough, hasty drawing of

SKETCHER — *n* pl. -S one that sketches

SKETCHY — *adj* SKETCHIER, SKETCHIEST lacking in completeness or clearness

SKEW — *v* -ED, -ING, -S to turn aside

SKEWBACK — *n* pl. -S a sloping surface against which the end of an arch rests

SKEWBALD — *n* pl. -S a horse having patches of brown and white

SKEWER *v* -ED, -ING, -S to pierce with a long pin, as meat

SKEWNESS *n* pl. -ES lack of symmetry

SKI *v* -ED, -ING, -S to travel on skis (long, narrow strips of wood or metal)

SKIABLE *adj* capable of being skied over

SKIAGRAM *n* pl. -S a picture made up of shadows or outlines

SKIBOB *n* pl. -S a vehicle used for traveling over snow

SKID *v* SKIDDED, SKIDDING, SKIDS to slide sideways as a result of a loss of traction

SKIDDER *n* pl. -S one that skids

SKIDDOO *v* -ED, -ING, -S to go away

SKIDDY *adj* -DIER, -DIEST likely to cause skidding

SKIDOO *v* -ED, -ING, -S to skiddoo

SKIDWAY *n* pl. -WAYS a platform on which logs are piled for loading or sawing

SKIED past tense of ski and sky

SKIER *n* pl. -S one that skis

SKIES present 3d person sing. of sky

SKIEY *adj* skyey

SKIFF *n* pl. -S a small, open boat

SKIFFLE *v* -FLED, -FLING, -FLES to play a particular style of music

SKIING *n* pl. -S the sport of traveling on skis

SKIJORER *n* pl. -S a skier who is drawn over snow by a horse or vehicle

SKILFUL *adj* skillful

SKILL *n* pl. -S the ability to do something well **SKILLED** *adj*

SKILLESS *adj* having no skill

SKILLET *n* pl. -S a frying pan

SKILLFUL *adj* having skill

SKILLING *n* pl. -S a former coin of Scandinavian countries

SKIM *v* SKIMMED, SKIMMING, SKIMS to remove floating matter from the surface of

SKIMMER *n* pl. -S one that skims

SKIMMING *n* pl. -S something that is skimmed from a liquid

SKIMP *v* -ED, -ING, -S to scrimp

SKIMPY *adj* SKIMPIER, SKIMPIEST scanty **SKIMPILY** *adv*

SKIN *v* SKINNED, SKINNING, SKINS to strip or deprive of skin (the membranous tissue covering the body of an animal)

SKINFUL *n* pl. -S as much as a skin container can hold

SKINHEAD *n* pl. -S one whose hair is cut very short

SKINK *v* -ED, -ING, -S to pour out or serve, as liquor

SKINKER *n* pl. -S one that skinks

SKINLESS *adj* having no skin

SKINLIKE *adj* resembling skin

SKINNED past tense of skin

SKINNER *n* pl. -S one that skins

SKINNING present participle of skin

SKINNY *adj* -NIER, -NIEST very thin

SKINT *adj* having no money

SKIORING *n* pl. -S a form of skiing

SKIP *v* SKIPPED, SKIPPING, SKIPS to move with light springing steps

SKIPJACK *n* pl. -S a marine fish

SKIPLANE *n* pl. -S an airplane designed to take off from or land on snow

SKIPPED past tense of skip

SKIPPER *v* -ED, -ING, -S to act as master or captain of

SKIPPET *n* pl. -S a small box for protecting an official seal

SKIPPING present participle of skip

SKIRL *v* -ED, -ING, -S to produce a shrill sound

SKIRMISH *v* -ED, -ING, -ES to engage in a minor battle

SKIRR *v* -ED, -ING, -S to move rapidly

SKIRRET *n* pl. -S an Asian herb

SKIRT *v* -ED, -ING, -S to go or pass around

SKIRTER *n* pl. -S one that skirts

SKIRTING *n* pl. -S a board at the base of a wall

SKIT *n* pl. -S a short dramatic scene

SKITE *v* SKITED, SKITING, SKITES to move away quickly

SKITTER *v* -ED, -ING, -S to move lightly or rapidly along a surface

SKITTERY *adj* -TERIER, -TERIEST skittish

SKITTISH *adj* easily frightened

SKITTLE *n* pl. -S a wooden pin used in a bowling game

SKIVE	*v* SKIVED, SKIVING, SKIVES to pare
SKIVER	*n* pl. -S one that skives
SKIVVY	*v* -VIED, -VYING, -VIES to work as a female servant
SKIWEAR	*n* pl. SKIWEAR clothing suitable for wear while skiing
SKLENT	*v* -ED, -ING, -S to slant
SKOAL	*v* -ED, -ING, -S to drink to the health of
SKOOKUM	*adj* excellent
SKOSH	*n* pl. -ES a small amount
SKREEGH	*v* -ED, -ING, -S to screech
SKREIGH	*v* -ED, -ING, -S to screech
SKUA	*n* pl. -S a predatory seabird
SKULK	*v* -ED, -ING, -S to move about stealthily
SKULKER	*n* pl. -S one that skulks
SKULL	*n* pl. -S the framework of the head **SKULLED** *adj*
SKULLCAP	*n* pl. -S a close-fitting cap
SKUNK	*v* -ED, -ING, -S to defeat overwhelmingly
SKY	*v* SKIED or SKYED, SKYING, SKIES to hit or throw toward the sky (the upper atmosphere)
SKYBORNE	*adj* airborne
SKYBOX	*n* pl. -ES an enclosure of seats situated high in a stadium
SKYCAP	*n* pl. -S a porter at an airport
SKYDIVE	*v* -DIVED or -DOVE, -DIVING, -DIVES to parachute from an airplane for sport
SKYDIVER	*n* pl. -S one that skydives
SKYEY	*adj* resembling the sky
SKYHOOK	*n* pl. -S a hook conceived as being suspended from the sky
SKYJACK	*v* -ED, -ING, -S to hijack an airplane
SKYLARK	*v* -ED, -ING, -S to frolic
SKYLIGHT	*n* pl. -S a window in a roof or ceiling
SKYLINE	*n* pl. -S the horizon
SKYLIT	*adj* having a skylight
SKYMAN	*n* pl. -MEN an aviator
SKYPHOS	*n* pl. -PHOI a drinking vessel used in ancient Greece
SKYSAIL	*n* pl. -S a type of sail
SKYWALK	*n* pl. -S an elevated walkway between two buildings
SKYWARD	*adv* toward the sky
SKYWARDS	*adv* skyward
SKYWAY	*n* pl. -WAYS an elevated highway
SKYWRITE	*v* -WROTE, -WRITTEN, -WRITING, -WRITES to write in the sky by releasing a visible vapor from an airplane
SLAB	*v* SLABBED, SLABBING, SLABS to cover with slabs (broad, flat pieces of solid material)
SLABBER	*v* -ED, -ING, -S to slobber
SLABBERY	*adj* slobbery
SLABBING	present participle of slab
SLABLIKE	*adj* resembling a slab
SLACK	*adj* SLACKER, SLACKEST not tight or taut
SLACK	*v* -ED, -ING, -S to slacken
SLACKEN	*v* -ED, -ING, -S to make less tight or taut
SLACKER	*n* pl. -S a shirker
SLACKLY	*adv* in a slack manner
SLAG	*v* SLAGGED, SLAGGING, SLAGS to convert into slag (the fused residue of a smelted ore)
SLAGGY	*adj* -GIER, -GIEST resembling slag
SLAIN	past participle of slay
SLAINTE	*interj* — used to toast one's health
SLAKE	*v* SLAKED, SLAKING, SLAKES to quench **SLAKABLE** *adj*
SLAKER	*n* pl. -S one that slakes
SLALOM	*v* -ED, -ING, -S to ski in a zigzag course
SLAM	*v* SLAMMED, SLAMMING, SLAMS to shut forcibly and noisily
SLAMMER	*n* pl. -S a jail
SLANDER	*v* -ED, -ING, -S to defame
SLANG	*v* -ED, -ING, -S to use slang (extremely informal or vulgar language)
SLANGY	*adj* SLANGIER, SLANGIEST being or containing slang **SLANGILY** *adv*
SLANK	a past tense of slink
SLANT	*v* -ED, -ING, -S to deviate from the horizontal or vertical
SLANTY	*adj* deviating from the horizontal or vertical

SLAP	*v* SLAPPED, SLAPPING, SLAPS to strike with the open hand
SLAPDASH	*n* pl. -ES careless work
SLAPJACK	*n* pl. -S a pancake
SLAPPED	past tense of slap
SLAPPER	*n* pl. -S one that slaps
SLAPPING	present participle of slap
SLASH	*v* -ED, -ING, -ES to cut with violent sweeping strokes
SLASHER	*n* pl. -S one that slashes
SLASHING	*n* pl. -S the act of one that slashes
SLAT	*v* SLATTED, SLATTING, SLATS to provide with slats (narrow strips of wood or metal)
SLATCH	*n* pl. -ES a calm between breaking waves
SLATE	*v* SLATED, SLATING, SLATES to cover with slate (a roofing material)
SLATER	*n* pl. -S one that slates
SLATEY	*adj* SLATIER, SLATIEST slaty
SLATHER	*v* -ED, -ING, -S to spread thickly
SLATIER	comparative of slaty
SLATIEST	superlative of slaty
SLATING	*n* pl. -S the act of one that slates
SLATTED	past tense of slat
SLATTERN	*n* pl. -S a slovenly woman
SLATTING	*n* pl. -S material for making slats
SLATY	*adj* SLATIER, SLATIEST resembling slate
SLAVE	*v* SLAVED, SLAVING, SLAVES to work like a slave (one who is owned by another)
SLAVER	*v* -ED, -ING, -S to drool
SLAVERER	*n* pl. -S one that slavers
SLAVERY	*n* pl. -ERIES ownership of one person by another
SLAVEY	*n* pl. -EYS a female servant
SLAVING	present participle of slave
SLAVISH	*adj* pertaining to or characteristic of a slave
SLAW	*n* pl. -S coleslaw
SLAY	*v* SLEW, SLAIN, SLAYING, SLAYS to kill violently
SLAY	*v* SLAYED, SLAIN, SLAYING, SLAYS to amuse overwhelmingly
SLAYER	*n* pl. -S one that slays
SLEAVE	*v* SLEAVED, SLEAVING, SLEAVES to separate into filaments
SLEAZE	*n* pl. -S a sleazy quality
SLEAZO	*adj* sleazy
SLEAZY	*adj* SLEAZIER, SLEAZIEST shoddy **SLEAZILY** *adv*
SLED	*v* SLEDDED, SLEDDING, SLEDS to convey on a sled (a vehicle for carrying people or loads over snow or ice)
SLEDDER	*n* pl. -S one that sleds
SLEDDING	*n* pl. -S the act of one that sleds
SLEDGE	*v* SLEDGED, SLEDGING, SLEDGES to convey on a type of sled
SLEEK	*adj* SLEEKER, SLEEKEST smooth and glossy
SLEEK	*v* -ED, -ING, -S to make sleek
SLEEKEN	*v* -ED, -ING, -S to sleek
SLEEKIER	comparative of sleeky
SLEEKIEST	superlative of sleeky
SLEEKIT	*adj* sleek
SLEEKLY	*adv* in a sleek manner
SLEEKY	*adj* SLEEKIER, SLEEKIEST sleek
SLEEP	*v* SLEPT, SLEEPING, SLEEPS to be in a natural, periodic state of rest
SLEEPER	*n* pl. -S one that sleeps
SLEEPING	*n* pl. -S the act of one that sleeps
SLEEPY	*adj* SLEEPIER, SLEEPIEST ready or inclined to sleep **SLEEPILY** *adv*
SLEET	*v* -ED, -ING, -S to shower sleet (frozen rain)
SLEETY	*adj* SLEETIER, SLEETIEST resembling sleet
SLEEVE	*v* SLEEVED, SLEEVING, SLEEVES to furnish with a sleeve (the part of a garment covering the arm)
SLEIGH	*v* -ED, -ING, -S to ride in a sled
SLEIGHER	*n* pl. -S one that sleighs
SLEIGHT	*n* pl. -S deftness
SLENDER	*adj* -DERER, -DEREST thin
SLEPT	past tense of sleep
SLEUTH	*v* -ED, -ING, -S to act as a detective
SLEW	*v* -ED, -ING, -S to slue

SLICE   *v* SLICED, SLICING, SLICES to cut into thin, flat pieces

SLICER   *n* pl. -S one that slices

SLICK   *adj* SLICKER, SLICKEST smooth and slippery

SLICK   *v* -ED, -ING, -S to make slick

SLICKER   *n* pl. -S an oilskin raincoat

SLICKLY   *adv* in a slick manner

SLIDE   *v* SLID, SLIDDEN, SLIDING, SLIDES to move smoothly along a surface **SLIDABLE** *adj*

SLIDER   *n* pl. -S one that slides

SLIDEWAY   *n* pl. -WAYS a route along which something slides

SLIDING   present participle of slide

SLIER   a comparative of sly

SLIEST   a superlative of sly

SLIGHT   *adj* SLIGHTER, SLIGHTEST small in size or amount **SLIGHTLY** *adv*

SLIGHT   *v* -ED, -ING, -S to treat with disregard

SLILY   *adv* in a sly manner

SLIM   *adj* SLIMMER, SLIMMEST slender

SLIM   *v* SLIMMED, SLIMMING, SLIMS to make slim

SLIME   *v* SLIMED, SLIMING, SLIMES to cover with slime (viscous mud)

SLIMIER   comparative of slimy

SLIMIEST   superlative of slimy

SLIMILY   *adv* in a slimy manner

SLIMING   present participle of slime

SLIMLY   *adv* in a slim manner

SLIMMED   past tense of slim

SLIMMER   *n* pl. -S a dieter

SLIMMEST   superlative of slim

SLIMMING   present participle of slim

SLIMNESS   *n* pl. -ES the state of being slim

SLIMPSY   *adj* -SIER, -SIEST slimsy

SLIMSY   *adj* -SIER, -SIEST flimsy

SLIMY   *adj* SLIMIER, SLIMIEST resembling slime

SLING   *v* SLUNG, SLINGING, SLINGS to throw with a sudden motion

SLINGER   *n* pl. -S one that slings

SLINK   *v* SLUNK or SLANK or SLINKED, SLINKING, SLINKS to move stealthily

SLINKY   *adj* SLINKIER, SLINKIEST stealthy **SLINKILY** *adv*

SLIP   *v* SLIPPED or SLIPT, SLIPPING, SLIPS to slide suddenly and accidentally

SLIPCASE   *n* pl. -S a protective box for a book

SLIPE   *v* SLIPED, SLIPING, SLIPES to peel

SLIPFORM   *v* -ED, -ING, -S to construct with the use of a mold in which concrete is placed to set

SLIPKNOT   *n* pl. -S a type of knot

SLIPLESS   *adj* free from errors

SLIPOUT   *n* pl. -S an insert in a newspaper

SLIPOVER   *n* pl. -S a pullover

SLIPPAGE   *n* pl. -S a falling off from a standard or level

SLIPPED   a past tense of slip

SLIPPER   *n* pl. -S a light, low shoe

SLIPPERY   *adj* -PERIER, -PERIEST causing or tending to cause slipping

SLIPPING   present participle of slip

SLIPPY   *adj* -PIER, -PIEST slippery

SLIPSHOD   *adj* carelessly done or made

SLIPSLOP   *n* pl. -S watery food

SLIPSOLE   *n* pl. -S a thin insole

SLIPT   a past tense of slip

SLIPUP   *n* pl. -S a mistake

SLIPWARE   *n* pl. -S a type of pottery

SLIPWAY   *n* pl. -WAYS an area sloping toward the water in a shipyard

SLIT   *v* SLITTED, SLITTING, SLITS to make a slit (a long, narrow cut) in

SLITHER   *v* -ED, -ING, -S to slide from side to side

SLITHERY   *adj* slippery

SLITLESS   *adj* having no slits

SLITTED   past tense of slit

SLITTER   *n* pl. -S one that slits

SLITTING   present participle of slit

SLIVER   *v* -ED, -ING, -S to cut into long, thin pieces

SLIVERER   *n* pl. -S one that slivers

SLIVOVIC   *n* pl. -ES a plum brandy

SLOB   *n* pl. -S a slovenly or boorish person

SLOBBER   *v* -ED, -ING, -S to drool

SLOBBERY   *adj* slobbering

SLOBBISH *adj* resembling a slob

SLOBBY *adj* SLOBBIER, SLOBBIEST characteristic of a slob

SLOE *n* pl. -S a plumlike fruit

SLOG *v* SLOGGED, SLOGGING, SLOGS to plod

SLOGAN *n* pl. -S a motto adopted by a group

SLOGGER *n* pl. -S one that slogs

SLOGGING present participle of slog

SLOID *n* pl. -S sloyd

SLOJD *n* pl. -S sloyd

SLOOP *n* pl. -S a type of sailing vessel

SLOP *v* SLOPPED, SLOPPING, SLOPS to spill or splash

SLOPE *v* SLOPED, SLOPING, SLOPES to slant

SLOPER *n* pl. -S one that slopes

SLOPPED past tense of slop

SLOPPING present participle of slop

SLOPPY *adj* -PIER, -PIEST messy **SLOPPILY** *adv*

SLOPWORK *n* pl. -S the manufacture of cheap clothing

SLOSH *v* -ED, -ING, -ES to move with a splashing motion

SLOSHY *adj* SLOSHIER, SLOSHIEST slushy

SLOT *v* SLOTTED, SLOTTING, SLOTS to cut a long, narrow opening in

SLOTBACK *n* pl. -S a type of football player

SLOTH *n* pl. -S a slow-moving arboreal mammal

SLOTHFUL *adj* sluggish

SLOTTED past tense of slot

SLOTTING present participle of slot

SLOUCH *v* -ED, -ING, -ES to sit, stand, or move with a drooping posture

SLOUCHER *n* pl. -S one that slouches

SLOUCHY *adj* SLOUCHIER, SLOUCHIEST slouching

SLOUGH *v* -ED, -ING, -S to cast off

SLOUGHY *adj* SLOUGHIER, SLOUGHIEST miry

SLOVEN *n* pl. -S a slovenly person

SLOVENLY *adj* -LIER, -LIEST habitually untidy or unclean

SLOW *adj* SLOWER, SLOWEST moving with little speed

SLOW *v* -ED, -ING, -S to lessen the speed of

SLOWDOWN *n* pl. -S a lessening of pace

SLOWISH *adj* somewhat slow

SLOWLY *adv* in a slow manner

SLOWNESS *n* pl. -ES the state of being slow

SLOWPOKE *n* pl. -S a slow individual

SLOWWORM *n* pl. -S a European lizard having no legs

SLOYD *n* pl. -S a Swedish system of manual training

SLUB *v* SLUBBED, SLUBBING, SLUBS to draw out and twist slightly

SLUBBER *v* -ED, -ING, -S to stain or dirty

SLUBBING *n* pl. -S a slightly twisted roll of textile fibers

SLUDGE *n* pl. -S a muddy deposit

SLUDGY *adj* SLUDGIER, SLUDGIEST covered with sludge

SLUE *v* SLUED, SLUING, SLUES to cause to move sideways

SLUFF *v* -ED, -ING, -S to discard a card or cards

SLUG *v* SLUGGED, SLUGGING, SLUGS to strike heavily

SLUGABED *n* pl. -S one inclined to stay in bed out of laziness

SLUGFEST *n* pl. -S a vigorous fight

SLUGGARD *n* pl. -S an habitually lazy person

SLUGGED past tense of slug

SLUGGER *n* pl. -S one that slugs

SLUGGING present participle of slug

SLUGGISH *adj* displaying little movement or activity

SLUICE *v* SLUICED, SLUICING, SLUICES to wash with a sudden flow of water

SLUICY *adj* falling in streams

SLUING present participle of slue

SLUM *v* SLUMMED, SLUMMING, SLUMS to visit slums (squalid urban areas)

SLUMBER *v* -ED, -ING, -S to sleep

SLUMBERY *adj* sleepy

SLUMGUM *n* pl. -S the residue remaining after honey is extracted from a honeycomb

SLUMISM *n* pl. -S the prevalence of slums

SLUMLORD *n* pl. -S a landlord of slum property

SLUMMED	past tense of slum
SLUMMER	*n* pl. -S one that slums
SLUMMING	present participle of slum
SLUMMY	*adj* -MIER, -MIEST resembling a slum
SLUMP	*v* -ED, -ING, -S to fall or sink suddenly
SLUNG	past tense of sling
SLUNK	a past tense of slink
SLUR	*v* SLURRED, SLURRING, SLURS to pass over lightly or carelessly
SLURB	*n* pl. -S a poorly planned suburban area **SLURBAN** *adj*
SLURP	*v* -ED, -ING, -S to eat or drink noisily
SLURRED	past tense of slur
SLURRING	present participle of slur
SLURRY	*v* -RIED, -RYING, -RIES to convert into a type of watery mixture
SLUSH	*v* -ED, -ING, -ES to splash with slush (partly melted snow)
SLUSHY	*adj* SLUSHIER, SLUSHIEST resembling slush **SLUSHILY** *adv*
SLUT	*n* pl. -S a slovenly woman **SLUTTISH** *adj*
SLUTTY	*adj* SLUTTIER, SLUTTIEST characteristic of a slut
SLY	*adj* SLIER, SLIEST or SLYER, SLYEST crafty **SLYLY** *adv*
SLYBOOTS	*n* pl. SLYBOOTS a sly person
SLYNESS	*n* pl. -ES the quality or state of being sly
SLYPE	*n* pl. -S a narrow passage in an English cathedral
SMACK	*v* -ED, -ING, -S to strike sharply
SMACKER	*n* pl. -S one that smacks
SMALL	*adj* SMALLER, SMALLEST of limited size or quantity
SMALL	*n* pl. -S a small part
SMALLAGE	*n* pl. -S a wild celery
SMALLISH	*adj* somewhat small
SMALLPOX	*n* pl. -ES a virus disease
SMALT	*n* pl. -S a blue pigment
SMALTI	a pl. of smalto
SMALTINE	*n* pl. -S smaltite
SMALTITE	*n* pl. -S a mineral
SMALTO	*n* pl. -TOS or -TI colored glass used in mosaics

SMARAGD	*n* pl. -S an emerald
SMARAGDE	*n* pl. -S smaragd
SMARM	*n* pl. -S trite sentimentality
SMARMY	*adj* SMARMIER, SMARMIEST marked by excessive flattery **SMARMILY** *adv*
SMART	*v* -ED, -ING, -S to cause a sharp, stinging pain
SMART	*adj* SMARTER, SMARTEST characterized by mental acuity
SMARTASS	*n* pl. -ES a smarty
SMARTEN	*v* -ED, -ING, -S to improve in appearance
SMARTIE	*n* pl. -S smarty
SMARTLY	*adv* in a smart manner
SMARTY	*n* pl. SMARTIES an obnoxiously conceited person
SMASH	*v* -ED, -ING, -ES to shatter violently
SMASHER	*n* pl. -S one that smashes
SMASHUP	*n* pl. -S a collision of motor vehicles
SMATTER	*v* -ED, -ING, -S to speak with little knowledge
SMAZE	*n* pl. -S an atmospheric mixture of smoke and haze
SMEAR	*v* -ED, -ING, -S to spread with a sticky, greasy, or dirty substance
SMEARER	*n* pl. -S one that smears
SMEARY	*adj* SMEARIER, SMEARIEST smeared
SMECTIC	*adj* pertaining to a phase of a liquid crystal
SMECTITE	*n* pl. -S a clayey mineral
SMEDDUM	*n* pl. -S ground malt powder
SMEEK	*v* -ED, -ING, -S to smoke
SMEGMA	*n* pl. -S sebum
SMELL	*v* SMELLED or SMELT, SMELLING, SMELLS to perceive by means of the olfactory nerves
SMELLER	*n* pl. -S one that smells
SMELLY	*adj* SMELLIER, SMELLIEST having an unpleasant odor
SMELT	*v* -ED, -ING, -S to melt or fuse, as ores
SMELTER	*n* pl. -S one that smelts
SMELTERY	*n* pl. -ERIES a place for smelting
SMERK	*v* -ED, -ING, -S to smirk
SMEW	*n* pl. -S a Eurasian duck
SMIDGE	*n* pl. -S a smidgen

SMIDGEN	*n* pl. -S a very small amount
SMIDGEON	*n* pl. -S smidgen
SMIDGIN	*n* pl. -S smidgen
SMILAX	*n* pl. -ES a twining plant
SMILE	*v* SMILED, SMILING, SMILES to upturn the corners of the mouth in pleasure
SMILER	*n* pl. -S one that smiles
SMILEY	*adj* exhibiting a smile (a facial expression)
SMIRCH	*v* -ED, -ING, -ES to soil
SMIRK	*v* -ED, -ING, -S to smile in an affected or smug manner
SMIRKER	*n* pl. -S one that smirks
SMIRKY	*adj* SMIRKIER, SMIRKIEST smirking
SMITE	*v* SMOTE, SMIT or SMITTEN, SMITING, SMITES to strike heavily
SMITER	*n* pl. -S one that smites
SMITH	*n* pl. -S a worker in metals
SMITHERS	*n/pl* small fragments
SMITHERY	*n* pl. -ERIES the trade of a smith
SMITHY	*n* pl. SMITHIES the workshop of a smith
SMITING	present participle of smite
SMITTEN	a past participle of smite
SMOCK	*v* -ED, -ING, -S to furnish with a smock (a loose outer garment)
SMOCKING	*n* pl. -S a type of embroidery
SMOG	*n* pl. -S an atmospheric mixture of smoke and fog **SMOGLESS** *adj*
SMOGGY	*adj* -GIER, -GIEST filled with smog
SMOKE	*v* SMOKED, SMOKING, SMOKES to emit smoke (the gaseous product of burning materials) **SMOKABLE** *adj*
SMOKEPOT	*n* pl. -S a container for giving off smoke
SMOKER	*n* pl. -S one that smokes
SMOKEY	*adj* SMOKIER, SMOKIEST smoky
SMOKING	present participle of smoke
SMOKY	*adj* SMOKIER, SMOKIEST filled with smoke **SMOKILY** *adv*
SMOLDER	*v* -ED, -ING, -S to burn with no flame
SMOLT	*n* pl. -S a young salmon
SMOOCH	*v* -ED, -ING, -ES to kiss
SMOOCHY	*adj* smudgy
SMOOTH	*adj* SMOOTHER, SMOOTHEST having a surface that is free from irregularities
SMOOTH	*v* -ED, -ING, -S or -ES to make smooth
SMOOTHEN	*v* -ED, -ING, -S to smooth
SMOOTHER	*n* pl. -S one that smooths
SMOOTHIE	*n* pl. -S a person with polished manners
SMOOTHLY	*adv* in a smooth manner
SMOOTHY	*n* pl. SMOOTHIES smoothie
SMOTE	past tense of smite
SMOTHER	*v* -ED, -ING, -S to prevent from breathing
SMOTHERY	*adj* tending to smother
SMOULDER	*v* -ED, -ING, -S to smolder
SMUDGE	*v* SMUDGED, SMUDGING, SMUDGES to smear or dirty
SMUDGY	*adj* SMUDGIER, SMUDGIEST smudged **SMUDGILY** *adv*
SMUG	*adj* SMUGGER, SMUGGEST highly self-satisfied
SMUGGLE	*v* -GLED, -GLING, -GLES to import or export illicitly
SMUGGLER	*n* pl. -S one that smuggles
SMUGLY	*adv* in a smug manner
SMUGNESS	*n* pl. -ES the quality or state of being smug
SMUT	*v* SMUTTED, SMUTTING, SMUTS to soil
SMUTCH	*v* -ED, -ING, -ES to smudge
SMUTCHY	*adj* SMUTCHIER, SMUTCHIEST smudgy
SMUTTED	past tense of smut
SMUTTING	present participle of smut
SMUTTY	*adj* -TIER, -TIEST obscene **SMUTTILY** *adv*
SNACK	*v* -ED, -ING, -S to eat a light meal
SNAFFLE	*v* -FLED, -FLING, -FLES to obtain by devious means
SNAFU	*v* -ED, -ING, -S to bring into a state of confusion
SNAG	*v* SNAGGED, SNAGGING, SNAGS to catch on a snag (a jagged protuberance)
SNAGGY	*adj* -GIER, -GIEST full of snags
SNAGLIKE	*adj* resembling a snag

SNAIL	*v* -ED, -ING, -S to move slowly
SNAKE	*v* SNAKED, SNAKING, SNAKES to move like a snake (a limbless reptile)
SNAKEBIT	*adj* unlucky
SNAKEY	*adj* SNAKIER, SNAKIEST snaky
SNAKY	*adj* SNAKIER, SNAKIEST resembling a snake **SNAKILY** *adv*
SNAP	*v* SNAPPED, SNAPPING, SNAPS to make a sharp cracking sound
SNAPBACK	*n* pl. -S a sudden rebound or recovery
SNAPLESS	*adj* lacking a snap (a type of fastening device)
SNAPPED	past tense of snap
SNAPPER	*n* pl. -S one that snaps
SNAPPIER	comparative of snappy
SNAPPIEST	superlative of snappy
SNAPPILY	*adv* in a snappy manner
SNAPPING	present participle of snap
SNAPPISH	*adj* tending to speak in an impatient or irritable manner
SNAPPY	*adj* -PIER, -PIEST snappish
SNAPSHOT	*v* -SHOTTED, -SHOTTING, -SHOTS to photograph informally and quickly
SNAPWEED	*n* pl. -S a flowering plant
SNARE	*v* SNARED, SNARING, SNARES to trap
SNARER	*n* pl. -S one that snares
SNARK	*n* pl. -S an imaginary animal
SNARKY	*adj* SNARKIER, SNARKIEST snappish
SNARL	*v* -ED, -ING, -S to growl viciously
SNARLER	*n* pl. -S one that snarls
SNARLY	*adj* SNARLIER, SNARLIEST tangled
SNASH	*n* pl. -ES abusive language
SNATCH	*v* -ED, -ING, -ES to seize suddenly
SNATCHER	*n* pl. -S one that snatches
SNATCHY	*adj* SNATCHIER, SNATCHIEST occurring irregularly
SNATH	*n* pl. -S the handle of a scythe
SNATHE	*n* pl. -S snath
SNAW	*v* -ED, -ING, -S to snow
SNAZZY	*adj* -ZIER, -ZIEST very stylish

SNEAK	*v* SNEAKED or SNUCK, SNEAKING, SNEAKS to move stealthily
SNEAKER	*n* pl. -S one that sneaks
SNEAKY	*adj* SNEAKIER, SNEAKIEST deceitful **SNEAKILY** *adv*
SNEAP	*v* -ED, -ING, -S to chide
SNECK	*n* pl. -S a latch
SNED	*v* SNEDDED, SNEDDING, SNEDS to prune
SNEER	*v* -ED, -ING, -S to curl the lip in contempt
SNEERER	*n* pl. -S one that sneers
SNEERFUL	*adj* given to sneering
SNEESH	*n* pl. -ES snuff
SNEEZE	*v* SNEEZED, SNEEZING, SNEEZES to make a sudden, involuntary expiration of breath
SNEEZER	*n* pl. -S one that sneezes
SNEEZY	*adj* SNEEZIER, SNEEZIEST tending to sneeze
SNELL	*v* -ED, -ING, -S to attach a short line to a fishhook
SNELL	*adj* SNELLER, SNELLEST keen
SNIB	*v* SNIBBED, SNIBBING, SNIBS to latch
SNICK	*v* -ED, -ING, -S to nick
SNICKER	*v* -ED, -ING, -S to utter a partly stifled laugh
SNICKERY	*adj* tending to snicker
SNIDE	*adj* SNIDER, SNIDEST maliciously derogatory **SNIDELY** *adv*
SNIFF	*v* -ED, -ING, -S to inhale audibly through the nose
SNIFFER	*n* pl. -S one that sniffs
SNIFFIER	comparative of sniffy
SNIFFIEST	superlative of sniffy
SNIFFILY	*adv* in a sniffy manner
SNIFFISH	*adj* haughty
SNIFFLE	*v* -FLED, -FLING, -FLES to sniff repeatedly
SNIFFLER	*n* pl. -S one that sniffles
SNIFFY	*adj* -FIER, -FIEST sniffish
SNIFTER	*n* pl. -S a pear-shaped liquor glass
SNIGGER	*v* -ED, -ING, -S to snicker
SNIGGLE	*v* -GLED, -GLING, -GLES to fish for eels
SNIGGLER	*n* pl. -S one that sniggles

SNIP	*v* SNIPPED, SNIPPING, SNIPS to cut with a short, quick stroke
SNIPE	*v* SNIPED, SNIPING, SNIPES to shoot at individuals from a concealed place
SNIPER	*n* pl. -S one that snipes
SNIPPED	past tense of snip
SNIPPER	*n* pl. -S one that snips
SNIPPET	*n* pl. -S a small piece snipped off
SNIPPETY	*adj* -PETIER, -PETIEST snippy
SNIPPING	present participle of snip
SNIPPY	*adj* -PIER, -PIEST snappish **SNIPPILY** *adv*
SNIT	*n* pl. -S a state of agitation
SNITCH	*v* -ED, -ING, -ES to tattle
SNITCHER	*n* pl. -S one that snitches
SNIVEL	*v* -ELED, -ELING, -ELS or -ELLED, -ELLING, -ELS to cry or whine with sniffling
SNIVELER	*n* pl. -S one that snivels
SNOB	*n* pl. -S one who tends to avoid or rebuff those regarded as inferior
SNOBBERY	*n* pl. -BERIES snobbish behavior
SNOBBIER	comparative of snobby
SNOBBIEST	superlative of snobby
SNOBBILY	*adv* in a snobby manner
SNOBBISH	*adj* characteristic of a snob
SNOBBISM	*n* pl. -S snobbery
SNOBBY	*adj* -BIER, -BIEST snobbish
SNOG	*v* SNOGGED, SNOGGING, SNOGS to kiss
SNOOD	*v* -ED, -ING, -S to secure with a snood (a net or fabric cap for the hair)
SNOOK	*v* -ED, -ING, -S to sniff
SNOOKER	*v* -ED, -ING, -S to trick
SNOOL	*v* -ED, -ING, -S to yield meekly
SNOOP	*v* -ED, -ING, -S to pry about
SNOOPER	*n* pl. -S one that snoops
SNOOPY	*adj* SNOOPIER, SNOOPIEST given to snooping **SNOOPILY** *adv*
SNOOT	*v* -ED, -ING, -S to treat with disdain
SNOOTY	*adj* SNOOTIER, SNOOTIEST snobbish **SNOOTILY** *adv*
SNOOZE	*v* SNOOZED, SNOOZING, SNOOZES to sleep lightly
SNOOZER	*n* pl. -S one that snoozes
SNOOZLE	*v* -ZLED, -ZLING, -ZLES to nuzzle
SNOOZY	*adj* SNOOZIER, SNOOZIEST drowsy
SNORE	*v* SNORED, SNORING, SNORES to breathe loudly while sleeping
SNORER	*n* pl. -S one that snores
SNORKEL	*v* -ED, -ING, -S to swim underwater with a type of breathing device
SNORT	*v* -ED, -ING, -S to exhale noisily through the nostrils
SNORTER	*n* pl. -S one that snorts
SNOT	*n* pl. -S nasal mucus
SNOTTY	*adj* -TIER, -TIEST arrogant **SNOTTILY** *adv*
SNOUT	*v* -ED, -ING, -S to provide with a nozzle
SNOUTISH	*adj* snouty
SNOUTY	*adj* SNOUTIER, SNOUTIEST resembling a long, projecting nose
SNOW	*v* -ED, -ING, -S to fall as snow (precipitation in the form of ice crystals)
SNOWBALL	*v* -ED, -ING, -S to increase at a rapidly accelerating rate
SNOWBANK	*n* pl. -S a mound of snow
SNOWBELL	*n* pl. -S a flowering shrub
SNOWBELT	*n* pl. -S a region that receives an appreciable amount of snow each year
SNOWBIRD	*n* pl. -S a small bird
SNOWBUSH	*n* pl. -ES a flowering shrub
SNOWCAP	*n* pl. -S a covering of snow
SNOWDROP	*n* pl. -S a European herb
SNOWFALL	*n* pl. -S a fall of snow
SNOWIER	comparative of snowy
SNOWIEST	superlative of snowy
SNOWILY	*adv* in a snowy manner
SNOWLAND	*n* pl. -S an area marked by a great amount of snow
SNOWLESS	*adj* having no snow
SNOWLIKE	*adj* resembling snow
SNOWMAN	*n* pl. -MEN a figure of a person that is made of snow
SNOWMELT	*n* pl. -S water produced by the melting of snow

SNOWMOLD *n* pl. -S a fungus disease of grasses near the edge of melting snow

SNOWPACK *n* pl. -S an accumulation of packed snow

SNOWPLOW *v* -ED, -ING, -S to execute a type of skiing maneuver

SNOWSHED *n* pl. -S a structure built to provide protection against snow

SNOWSHOE *v* -SHOED, -SHOEING, -SHOES to walk on snowshoes (oval frames that allow a person to walk on deep snow)

SNOWSUIT *n* pl. -S a child's garment for winter wear

SNOWY *adj* SNOWIER, SNOWIEST abounding in snow

SNUB *v* SNUBBED, SNUBBING, SNUBS to treat with contempt or neglect

SNUBBER *n* pl. -S one that snubs

SNUBBY *adj* -BIER, -BIEST blunt

SNUBNESS *n* pl. -ES bluntness

SNUCK a past tense of sneak

SNUFF *v* -ED, -ING, -S to use or inhale snuff (powdered tobacco)

SNUFFBOX *n* pl. -ES a box for holding snuff

SNUFFER *n* pl. -S one that snuffs

SNUFFIER comparative of snuffy

SNUFFIEST superlative of snuffy

SNUFFILY *adv* in a snuffy manner

SNUFFLE *v* -FLED, -FLING, -FLES to sniffle

SNUFFLER *n* pl. -S one that snuffles

SNUFFLY *adj* -FLIER, -FLIEST tending to snuffle

SNUFFY *adj* SNUFFIER, SNUFFIEST dingy

SNUG *adj* SNUGGER, SNUGGEST warmly comfortable

SNUG *v* SNUGGED, SNUGGING, SNUGS to make snug

SNUGGERY *n* pl. -GERIES a snug place

SNUGGEST superlative of snug

SNUGGIES *n/pl* women's long underwear

SNUGGING present participle of snug

SNUGGLE *v* -GLED, -GLING, -GLES to lie or press closely

SNUGLY *adv* in a snug manner

SNUGNESS *n* pl. -ES the quality or state of being snug

SNYE *n* pl. -S a side channel in a river or creek

SO *n* pl. SOS sol

SOAK *v* -ED, -ING, -S to saturate thoroughly in liquid

SOAKAGE *n* pl. -S the act of soaking

SOAKER *n* pl. -S one that soaks

SOAP *v* -ED, -ING, -S to treat with soap (a cleansing agent)

SOAPBARK *n* pl. -S a tropical tree

SOAPBOX *n* pl. -ES a box for soap

SOAPER *n* pl. -S a serial melodrama on radio or television

SOAPIER comparative of soapy

SOAPIEST superlative of soapy

SOAPILY *adv* in a soapy manner

SOAPLESS *adj* having no soap

SOAPLIKE *adj* resembling soap

SOAPSUDS *n/pl* suds (soapy water)

SOAPWORT *n* pl. -S a perennial herb

SOAPY *adj* SOAPIER, SOAPIEST containing or resembling soap

SOAR *v* -ED, -ING, -S to fly at a great height

SOARER *n* pl. -S one that soars

SOARING *n* pl. -S the sport of flying in a heavier-than-air craft without power

SOAVE *n* pl. -S an Italian wine

SOB *v* SOBBED, SOBBING, SOBS to cry with a convulsive catching of the breath

SOBBER *n* pl. -S one that sobs

SOBEIT *conj* provided that

SOBER *adj* SOBERER, SOBEREST having control of one's faculties

SOBER *v* -ED, -ING, -S to make sober

SOBERIZE *v* -IZED, -IZING, -IZES to sober

SOBERLY *adv* in a sober manner

SOBFUL *adj* given to sobbing

SOBRIETY *n* pl. -ETIES the quality or state of being sober

SOCAGE *n* pl. -S a form of feudal land tenure

SOCAGER *n* pl. -S a tenant by socage

SOCCAGE *n* pl. -S socage

SOCCER *n* pl. -S a type of ball game

SOCIABLE *n* pl. -S a social

SOCIABLY	*adv* in a friendly manner
SOCIAL	*n* pl. -S a friendly gathering
SOCIALLY	*adv* with respect to society
SOCIETY	*n* pl. -ETIES an organized group of persons **SOCIETAL** *adj*
SOCK	*n* pl. SOCKS or SOX a knitted or woven covering for the foot
SOCK	*v* -ED, -ING, -S to strike forcefully
SOCKET	*v* -ED, -ING, -S to furnish with a socket (an opening for receiving something)
SOCKEYE	*n* pl. -S a food fish
SOCKLESS	*adj* having no socks
SOCKMAN	*n* pl. -MEN socman
SOCKO	*adj* strikingly impressive
SOCLE	*n* pl. -S a block used as a base for a column or pedestal
SOCMAN	*n* pl. -MEN a socager
SOD	*v* SODDED, SODDING, SODS to cover with sod (turf)
SODA	*n* pl. -S a type of chemical compound **SODALESS** *adj*
SODALIST	*n* pl. -S a member of a sodality
SODALITE	*n* pl. -S a mineral
SODALITY	*n* pl. -TIES a society
SODAMIDE	*n* pl. -S a chemical compound
SODDED	past tense of sod
SODDEN	*v* -ED, -ING, -S to make soggy
SODDENLY	*adv* in a soggy manner
SODDING	present participle of sod
SODDY	*n* pl. -DIES a house built of sod
SODIUM	*n* pl. -S a metallic element **SODIC** *adj*
SODOM	*n* pl. -S a place notorious for vice and corruption
SODOMIST	*n* pl. -S a sodomite
SODOMITE	*n* pl. -S one who practices sodomy
SODOMIZE	*v* -IZED, -IZING, -IZES to engage in sodomy with
SODOMY	*n* pl. -OMIES unnatural copulation
SOEVER	*adv* at all
SOFA	*n* pl. -S a long, upholstered seat
SOFAR	*n* pl. -S a system for locating underwater explosions
SOFFIT	*n* pl. -S the underside of an architectural structure
SOFT	*adj* SOFTER, SOFTEST yielding readily to pressure
SOFT	*n* pl. -S a soft object or part
SOFTA	*n* pl. -S a Muslim theological student
SOFTBACK	*n* pl. -S a book bound in a flexible paper cover
SOFTBALL	*n* pl. -S a type of ball
SOFTEN	*v* -ED, -ING, -S to make soft
SOFTENER	*n* pl. -S one that softens
SOFTHEAD	*n* pl. -S a foolish person
SOFTIE	*n* pl. -S softy
SOFTIES	pl. of softy
SOFTISH	*adj* somewhat soft
SOFTLY	*adv* in a soft manner
SOFTNESS	*n* pl. -ES the quality or state of being soft
SOFTWARE	*n* pl. -S written or printed data used in computer operations
SOFTWOOD	*n* pl. -S the soft wood of various trees
SOFTY	*n* pl. SOFTIES a sentimental person
SOGGED	*adj* soggy
SOGGY	*adj* -GIER, -GIEST heavy with moisture **SOGGILY** *adv*
SOIGNE	*adj* carefully done
SOIGNEE	*adj* soigne
SOIL	*v* -ED, -ING, -S to make dirty
SOILAGE	*n* pl. -S green crops for feeding animals
SOILLESS	*adj* carried on without soil (finely divided rock mixed with organic matter)
SOILURE	*n* pl. -S a stain or smudge
SOIREE	*n* pl. -S an evening party
SOJA	*n* pl. -S the soybean
SOJOURN	*v* -ED, -ING, -S to stay temporarily
SOKE	*n* pl. -S a feudal right to administer justice within a certain territory
SOKEMAN	*n* pl. -MEN socman
SOKOL	*n* pl. -S an international group promoting physical fitness
SOL	*n* pl. -S the fifth tone of the diatonic musical scale
SOLA	a pl. of solum
SOLACE	*v* -LACED, -LACING, -LACES to console

SOLACER n pl. -S one that solaces

SOLAN n pl. -S a gannet

SOLAND n pl. -S solan

SOLANDER n pl. -S a protective box for library materials

SOLANIN n pl. -S solanine

SOLANINE n pl. -S a poisonous alkaloid

SOLANO n pl. -NOS a strong, hot wind

SOLANUM n pl. -S any of a genus of herbs and shrubs

SOLAR adj pertaining to the sun

SOLARIA a pl. of solarium

SOLARISE v -ISED, -ISING, -ISES to solarize

SOLARISM n pl. -S an interpretation of folk tales as concepts of the nature of the sun

SOLARIUM n pl. -IA or -IUMS a room exposed to the sun

SOLARIZE v -IZED, -IZING, -IZES to expose to sunlight

SOLATE v -ATED, -ATING, -ATES to change to a fluid colloidal system

SOLATION n pl. -S the act of solating

SOLATIUM n pl. -TIA a compensation given for damage to the feelings

SOLD past tense of sell

SOLDAN n pl. -S a Muslim ruler

SOLDER v -ED, -ING, -S to join closely together

SOLDERER n pl. -S one that solders

SOLDI pl. of soldo

SOLDIER v -ED, -ING, -S to perform military service

SOLDIERY n pl. -DIERIES the military profession

SOLDO n pl. -DI a former coin of Italy

SOLE v SOLED, SOLING, SOLES to furnish with a sole (the bottom surface of a shoe or boot)

SOLECISE v -CISED, -CISING, -CISES to solecize

SOLECISM n pl. -S an ungrammatical combination of words in a sentence

SOLECIST n pl. -S one who solecizes

SOLECIZE v -CIZED, -CIZING, -CIZES to use solecisms

SOLED past tense of sole

SOLEI pl. of soleus

SOLELESS adj having no sole

SOLELY adv singly

SOLEMN adj -EMNER, -EMNEST serious **SOLEMNLY** adv

SOLENESS n pl. -ES the state of being the only one

SOLENOID n pl. -S a type of electric coil

SOLERET n pl. -S solleret

SOLEUS n pl. -LEI a leg muscle

SOLFEGE n pl. -S a type of singing exercise

SOLFEGGI n/pl solfeges

SOLGEL adj involving some changes in the state of a colloidal system

SOLI a pl. of solo

SOLICIT v -ED, -ING, -S to ask for earnestly

SOLID adj -IDER, -IDEST having definite shape and volume

SOLID n pl. -S a solid substance

SOLIDAGO n pl. -GOS a flowering plant

SOLIDARY adj united

SOLIDI pl. of solidus

SOLIDIFY v -FIED, -FYING, -FIES to make solid

SOLIDITY n pl. -TIES the quality or state of being solid

SOLIDLY adv in a solid manner

SOLIDUS n pl. -DI a coin of ancient Rome

SOLING present participle of sole

SOLION n pl. -S an electronic detecting and amplifying device

SOLIQUID n pl. -S a fluid colloidal system

SOLITARY n pl. -TARIES one who lives alone

SOLITON n pl. -S a solitary wave in physics

SOLITUDE n pl. -S the state of being alone

SOLLERET n pl. -S a sabaton

SOLO n pl. -LOS or -LI a musical composition for a single voice or instrument

SOLO v -ED, -ING, -S to perform alone

SOLOIST n pl. -S one that performs a solo

SOLON n pl. -S a wise lawgiver

SOLONETS n pl. -ES solonetz

SOLONETZ n pl. -ES a type of soil

SOLSTICE n pl. -S the time of the year when the sun is at its greatest distance from the celestial equator

SOLUBLE	*n* pl. -S something that is soluble (capable of being dissolved)
SOLUBLY	*adv* in a soluble manner
SOLUM	*n* pl. -LA or -LUMS a soil layer
SOLUS	*adj* alone
SOLUTE	*n* pl. -S a dissolved substance
SOLUTION	*n* pl. -S a homogeneous liquid mixture
SOLVABLE	*adj* capable of being solved
SOLVATE	*v* -VATED, -VATING, -VATES to convert into a type of ion
SOLVE	*v* SOLVED, SOLVING, SOLVES to find the answer or explanation for
SOLVENCY	*n* pl. -CIES the ability to pay all debts
SOLVENT	*n* pl. -S a substance capable of dissolving others
SOLVER	*n* pl. -S one that solves
SOLVING	present participle of solve
SOMA	*n* pl. -MATA or -MAS the body of an organism **SOMATIC** *adj*
SOMBER	*adj* gloomy **SOMBERLY** *adv*
SOMBRE	*adj* somber **SOMBRELY** *adv*
SOMBRERO	*n* pl. -ROS a broad-brimmed hat
SOMBROUS	*adj* somber
SOME	*adj* being an unspecified number or part
SOMEBODY	*n* pl. -BODIES an important person
SOMEDAY	*adv* at some future time
SOMEDEAL	*adv* to some degree
SOMEHOW	*adv* by some means
SOMEONE	*n* pl. -S a somebody
SOMERSET	*v* -SETED, -SETING, -SETS or -SETTED, -SETTING, -SETS to roll the body in a complete circle, head over heels
SOMETIME	*adv* at some future time
SOMEWAY	*adv* somehow
SOMEWAYS	*adv* someway
SOMEWHAT	*n* pl. -S an unspecified number or part
SOMEWHEN	*adv* sometime
SOMEWISE	*adv* somehow
SOMITE	*n* pl. -S a longitudinal segment of the body of some animals **SOMITAL, SOMITIC** *adj*
SON	*n* pl. -S a male child

SONANCE	*n* pl. -S sound
SONANT	*n* pl. -S a sound uttered with vibration of the vocal cords **SONANTAL, SONANTIC** *adj*
SONAR	*n* pl. -S an underwater locating device
SONARMAN	*n* pl. -MEN a person who operates sonar equipment
SONATA	*n* pl. -S a type of musical composition
SONATINA	*n* pl. -TINAS or -TINE a short sonata
SONDE	*n* pl. -S a device for observing atmospheric phenomena
SONDER	*n* pl. -S a class of small yachts
SONE	*n* pl. -S a unit of loudness
SONG	*n* pl. -S a musical composition written or adapted for singing
SONGBIRD	*n* pl. -S a bird that utters a musical call
SONGBOOK	*n* pl. -S a book of songs
SONGFEST	*n* pl. -S an informal gathering for group singing
SONGFUL	*adj* melodious
SONGLESS	*adj* incapable of singing
SONGLIKE	*adj* resembling a song
SONGSTER	*n* pl. -S a singer
SONHOOD	*n* pl. -S the state of being a son
SONIC	*adj* pertaining to sound
SONICATE	*v* -CATED, -CATING, -CATES to disrupt with sound waves
SONICS	*n/pl* the science dealing with the practical applications of sound
SONLESS	*adj* having no son
SONLIKE	*adj* resembling a son
SONLY	*adj* pertaining to a son
SONNET	*v* -NETED, -NETING, -NETS or -NETTED, -NETTING, -NETS to compose a sonnet (a type of poem)
SONNY	*n* pl. -NIES a small boy
SONOBUOY	*n* pl. -BUOYS a buoy that detects and transmits underwater sounds
SONOGRAM	*n* pl. -S an image produced by ultrasound
SONORANT	*n* pl. -S a type of voiced sound
SONORITY	*n* pl. -TIES the quality or state of being sonorous
SONOROUS	*adj* characterized by a full and loud sound

SONOVOX *n* pl. -ES a sound effects device

SONSHIP *n* pl. -S the state of being a son

SONSIE *adj* -SIER, -SIEST sonsy

SONSY *adj* -SIER, -SIEST comely

SOOCHONG *n* pl. -S souchong

SOOEY *interj* — used in calling pigs

SOOK *n* pl. -S souk

SOON *adv* SOONER, SOONEST in the near future

SOONER *n* pl. -S one who settles on government land before it is officially opened for settlement

SOOT *v* -ED, -ING, -S to cover with soot (a black substance produced by combustion)

SOOTH *adj* SOOTHER, SOOTHEST true

SOOTH *n* pl. -S truth

SOOTHE *v* SOOTHED, SOOTHING, SOOTHES to restore to a quiet or normal state

SOOTHER *n* pl. -S one that soothes

SOOTHLY *adv* in truth

SOOTHSAY *v* -SAID, -SAYING, -SAYS to predict

SOOTY *adj* SOOTIER, SOOTIEST covered with soot **SOOTILY** *adv*

SOP *v* SOPPED, SOPPING, SOPS to dip or soak in a liquid

SOPH *n* pl. -S a sophomore

SOPHIES pl. of sophy

SOPHISM *n* pl. -S a plausible but fallacious argument

SOPHIST *n* pl. -S one that uses sophisms

SOPHY *n* pl. -PHIES a ruler of Persia

SOPITE *v* -PITED, -PITING, -PITES to put to sleep

SOPOR *n* pl. -S an abnormally deep sleep

SOPPED past tense of sop

SOPPING *adj* very wet

SOPPY *adj* -PIER, -PIEST very wet

SOPRANO *n* pl. -NOS or -NI the highest singing voice

SORA *n* pl. -S a marsh bird

SORB *v* -ED, -ING, -S to take up and hold by absorption or adsorption **SORBABLE** *adj*

SORBATE *n* pl. -S a sorbed substance

SORBENT *n* pl. -S a substance that sorbs

SORBET *n* pl. -S sherbet

SORBIC *adj* pertaining to a type of fruit

SORBITOL *n* pl. -S a chemical compound

SORBOSE *n* pl. -S a type of sugar

SORCERER *n* pl. -S one who practices sorcery

SORCERY *n* pl. -CERIES alleged use of supernatural powers

SORD *n* pl. -S a flight of mallards

SORDID *adj* filthy **SORDIDLY** *adv*

SORDINE *n* pl. -S a device used to muffle the tone of a musical instrument

SORDINO *n* pl. -NI sordine

SORDOR *n* pl. -S a sordid state

SORE *adj* SORER, SOREST painfully sensitive to the touch

SORE *n* pl. -S a sore area on the body

SOREHEAD *n* pl. -S a person who is easily angered or offended

SOREL *n* pl. -S sorrel

SORELY *adv* in a sore manner

SORENESS *n* pl. -ES the quality or state of being sore

SORER comparative of sore

SOREST superlative of sore

SORGHO *n* pl. -GHOS sorgo

SORGHUM *n* pl. -S a cereal grass

SORGO *n* pl. -GOS a variety of sorghum

SORI pl. of sorus

SORICINE *adj* belonging to the shrew family of mammals

SORING *n* pl. -S the practice of making a horse's front feet sore to force high stepping

SORITES *n* pl. SORITES a type of argument used in logic **SORITIC** *adj*

SORN *v* -ED, -ING, -S to force oneself on others for food and lodging

SORNER *n* pl. -S one that sorns

SOROCHE *n* pl. -S mountain sickness

SORORAL *adj* sisterly

SORORATE *n* pl. -S the marriage of a man usually with his deceased wife's sister

SORORITY *n* pl. -TIES a social club for women

SOROSIS *n* pl. -ROSES or -ROSISES a women's club or society

SORPTION	*n* pl. -S the act or process of sorbing **SORPTIVE** *adj*
SORREL	*n* pl. -S a reddish brown color
SORRIER	comparative of sorry
SORRIEST	superlative of sorry
SORRILY	*adv* in a sorry manner
SORROW	*v* -ED, -ING, -S to grieve
SORROWER	*n* pl. -S one that sorrows
SORRY	*adj* -RIER, -RIEST feeling grief or penitence
SORT	*v* -ED, -ING, -S to arrange according to kind, class, or size **SORTABLE** *adj* **SORTABLY** *adv*
SORTER	*n* pl. -S one that sorts
SORTIE	*v* -TIED, -TIEING, -TIES to attack suddenly from a defensive position
SORUS	*n* pl. -RI a cluster of plant reproductive bodies
SOT	*n* pl. -S an habitual drunkard
SOTH	*n* pl. -S sooth
SOTOL	*n* pl. -S a flowering plant
SOTTED	*adj* besotted
SOTTISH	*adj* resembling a sot
SOU	*n* pl. -S a former French coin
SOUARI	*n* pl. -S a tropical tree
SOUBISE	*n* pl. -S a sauce of onions and butter
SOUCAR	*n* pl. -S a Hindu banker
SOUCHONG	*n* pl. -S a Chinese tea
SOUDAN	*n* pl. -S soldan
SOUFFLE	*n* pl. -S a light, baked dish
SOUFFLED	*adj* made puffy by beating and baking
SOUGH	*v* -ED, -ING, -S to make a moaning or sighing sound
SOUGHT	past tense of seek
SOUK	*n* pl. -S a marketplace in northern Africa and the Middle East
SOUL	*n* pl. -S the spiritual aspect of human beings **SOULED, SOULLESS, SOULLIKE** *adj*
SOULFUL	*adj* full of emotion
SOUND	*adj* SOUNDER, SOUNDEST being in good health or condition
SOUND	*v* -ED, -ING, -S to make a sound (something that stimulates the auditory receptors)
SOUNDBOX	*n* pl. -ES a resonant cavity in a musical instrument
SOUNDER	*n* pl. -S one that sounds
SOUNDING	*n* pl. -S a sampling of opinions
SOUNDLY	*adv* in a sound manner
SOUNDMAN	*n* pl. -MEN a person who controls the quality of sound being recorded
SOUP	*v* -ED, -ING, -S to increase the power or efficiency of
SOUPCON	*n* pl. -S a minute amount
SOUPY	*adj* SOUPIER, SOUPIEST foggy
SOUR	*adj* SOURER, SOUREST sharp or biting to the taste
SOUR	*v* -ED, -ING, -S to make or become sour
SOURBALL	*n* pl. -S a sour candy
SOURCE	*v* SOURCED, SOURCING, SOURCES to obtain from a point of origin
SOURDINE	*n* pl. -S sordine
SOURISH	*adj* somewhat sour
SOURLY	*adv* in a sour manner
SOURNESS	*n* pl. -ES the quality or state of being sour
SOURPUSS	*n* pl. -ES a grouchy person
SOURSOP	*n* pl. -S a tropical tree
SOURWOOD	*n* pl. -S a flowering tree
SOUSE	*v* SOUSED, SOUSING, SOUSES to immerse
SOUTACHE	*n* pl. -S a flat, narrow braid
SOUTANE	*n* pl. -S a cassock
SOUTER	*n* pl. -S a shoemaker
SOUTH	*v* -ED, -ING, -S to move toward the south (a cardinal point of the compass)
SOUTHER	*n* pl. -S a wind or storm from the south
SOUTHERN	*n* pl. -S a person living in the south
SOUTHING	*n* pl. -S movement toward the south
SOUTHPAW	*n* pl. -S a left-handed person
SOUTHRON	*n* pl. -S a southern
SOUVENIR	*n* pl. -S a memento
SOUVLAKI	*n* pl. -S a Greek shish kebab
SOVIET	*n* pl. -S a legislative body in a Communist country
SOVKHOZ	*n* pl. -KHOZES or -KHOZY a state-owned farm in the Soviet Union

SOVRAN	*n* pl. -S a monarch
SOVRANLY	*adv* supremely
SOVRANTY	*n* pl. -TIES a monarchy
SOW	*v* SOWED, SOWN, SOWING, SOWS to scatter over land for growth, as seed **SOWABLE** *adj*
SOWANS	*n* pl. SOWANS sowens
SOWAR	*n* pl. -S a mounted native soldier in India
SOWBELLY	*n* pl. -LIES pork cured in salt
SOWBREAD	*n* pl. -S a flowering plant
SOWCAR	*n* pl. -S soucar
SOWENS	*n* pl. SOWENS porridge made from oat husks
SOWER	*n* pl. -S one that sows
SOWN	past participle of sow
SOX	a pl. of sock
SOY	*n* pl. SOYS the soybean
SOYA	*n* pl. -S soy
SOYBEAN	*n* pl. -S the seed of a cultivated Asian herb
SOYMILK	*n* pl. -S a milk substitute made from soybeans
SOYUZ	*n* pl. -ES a Soviet manned spacecraft
SOZIN	*n* pl. -S a type of protein
SOZINE	*n* pl. -S sozin
SOZZLED	*adj* drunk
SPA	*n* pl. -S a mineral spring
SPACE	*v* SPACED, SPACING, SPACES to set some distance apart
SPACEMAN	*n* pl. -MEN an astronaut
SPACER	*n* pl. -S one that spaces
SPACEY	*adj* SPACIER, SPACIEST weird in behavior
SPACIAL	*adj* spatial
SPACING	*n* pl. -S the distance between any two objects
SPACIOUS	*adj* vast or ample in extent
SPACKLE	*v* -LED, -LING, -LES to fill cracks or holes in a surface with paste
SPACY	*adj* SPACIER, SPACIEST spacey
SPADE	*v* SPADED, SPADING, SPADES to take up with a spade (a digging implement)
SPADEFUL	*n* pl. -S as much as a spade can hold
SPADER	*n* pl. -S one that spades
SPADICES	pl. of spadix
SPADILLE	*n* pl. -S the highest trump in certain card games
SPADING	present participle of spade
SPADIX	*n* pl. -DICES or -DIXES a flower cluster
SPADO	*n* pl. -DONES a castrated man or animal
SPAE	*v* SPAED, SPAEING, SPAES to foretell
SPAEING	*n* pl. -S the act of foretelling
SPAETZLE	*n* pl. -S a tiny dumpling
SPAGYRIC	*n* pl. -S a person skilled in alchemy
SPAHEE	*n* pl. -S spahi
SPAHI	*n* pl. -S a Turkish cavalryman
SPAIL	*n* pl. -S spale
SPAIT	*n* pl. -S spate
SPAKE	a past tense of speak
SPALE	*n* pl. -S a splinter or chip
SPALL	*v* -ED, -ING, -S to break up into fragments
SPALLER	*n* pl. -S one that spalls
SPALPEEN	*n* pl. -S a rascal
SPAN	*v* SPANNED, SPANNING, SPANS to extend over or across
SPANCEL	*v* -CELED, -CELING, -CELS or -CELLED, -CELLING, -CELS to bind or fetter with a rope
SPANDEX	*n* pl. -ES a synthetic elastic fiber
SPANDREL	*n* pl. -S a space between two adjoining arches
SPANDRIL	*n* pl. -S spandrel
SPANG	*adv* directly
SPANGLE	*v* -GLED, -GLING, -GLES to adorn with spangles (bits of sparkling metal)
SPANGLY	*adj* -GLIER, -GLIEST covered with spangles
SPANIEL	*n* pl. -S a dog with silky hair
SPANK	*v* -ED, -ING, -S to slap on the buttocks
SPANKER	*n* pl. -S one that spanks
SPANKING	*n* pl. -S the act of one that spanks
SPANLESS	*adj* having no extent
SPANNED	past tense of span
SPANNER	*n* pl. -S one that spans
SPANNING	present participle of span

SPANWORM	*n* pl. -S an inchworm
SPAR	*v* SPARRED, SPARRING, SPARS to provide with spars (stout poles used to support rigging)
SPARABLE	*n* pl. -S a type of nail
SPARE	*v* SPARED, SPARING, SPARES to refrain from punishing, harming, or destroying
SPARE	*adj* SPARER, SPAREST meager **SPARELY** *adv*
SPARER	*n* pl. -S one that spares
SPARERIB	*n* pl. -S a cut of pork
SPAREST	*adj* superlative of spare
SPARGE	*v* SPARGED, SPARGING, SPARGES to sprinkle
SPARGER	*n* pl. -S one that sparges
SPARID	*n* pl. -S any of a family of marine fishes
SPARING	present participle of spare
SPARK	*v* -ED, -ING, -S to give off sparks (small fiery particles)
SPARKER	*n* pl. -S something that sparks
SPARKIER	comparative of sparky
SPARKIEST	superlative of sparky
SPARKILY	*adv* in a lively manner
SPARKISH	*adj* jaunty
SPARKLE	*v* -KLED, -KLING, -KLES to give off or reflect flashes of light
SPARKLER	*n* pl. -S something that sparkles
SPARKLY	*adj* -KLIER, -KLIEST tending to sparkle
SPARKY	*adj* SPARKIER, SPARKIEST lively
SPARLIKE	*adj* resembling a spar
SPARLING	*n* pl. -S a young herring
SPAROID	*n* pl. -S a sparid
SPARRED	past tense of spar
SPARRIER	comparative of sparry
SPARRIEST	superlative of sparry
SPARRING	present participle of spar
SPARROW	*n* pl. -S a small bird
SPARRY	*adj* -RIER, -RIEST resembling spar (a lustrous mineral)
SPARSE	*adj* SPARSER, SPARSEST thinly distributed **SPARSELY** *adv*
SPARSITY	*n* pl. -TIES the quality or state of being sparse
SPARTAN	*adj* avoiding luxury and comfort
SPASM	*n* pl. -S an abnormal, involuntary muscular contraction
SPASTIC	*n* pl. -S one suffering from a paralysis with muscle spasms
SPAT	*v* SPATTED, SPATTING, SPATS to strike lightly
SPATE	*n* pl. -S a freshet
SPATHE	*n* pl. -S a leaflike organ of certain plants **SPATHAL, SPATHED, SPATHOSE** *adj*
SPATHIC	*adj* sparry
SPATIAL	*adj* of or pertaining to space
SPATTED	past tense of spat
SPATTER	*v* -ED, -ING, -S to scatter in drops
SPATTING	present participle of spat
SPATULA	*n* pl. -S a mixing implement **SPATULAR** *adj*
SPATZLE	*n/pl* spaetzle
SPAVIE	*n* pl. -S spavin **SPAVIET** *adj*
SPAVIN	*n* pl. -S a disease of horses **SPAVINED** *adj*
SPAWN	*v* -ED, -ING, -S to deposit eggs
SPAWNER	*n* pl. -S one that spawns
SPAY	*v* -ED, -ING, -S to remove the ovaries of
SPAZ	*n* pl. SPAZZES a clumsy, foolish, or incompetent person
SPEAK	*v* SPOKE or SPAKE, SPOKEN, SPEAKING, SPEAKS to utter words
SPEAKER	*n* pl. -S one that speaks
SPEAKING	*n* pl. -S a speech or discourse
SPEAN	*v* -ED, -ING, -S to wean
SPEAR	*v* -ED, -ING, -S to pierce with a spear (a long, pointed weapon)
SPEARER	*n* pl. -S one that spears
SPEARGUN	*n* pl. -S a gun that shoots a spear
SPEARMAN	*n* pl. -MEN a person armed with a spear
SPEC	*v* SPECCED, SPECCING, SPECS to write specifications for
SPECIAL	*adj* -CIALER, -CIALEST of a distinct kind or character
SPECIAL	*n* pl. -S a special person or thing
SPECIATE	*v* -ATED, -ATING, -ATES to undergo a type of evolutionary process
SPECIE	*n* pl. -S coined money

SPECIFIC   *n* pl. -S a remedy intended for a particular disease

SPECIFY   *v* -FIED, -FYING, -FIES to state in detail

SPECIMEN   *n* pl. -S a part or individual representative of a group or whole

SPECIOUS   *adj* having a false look of truth or authenticity

SPECK   *v* -ED, -ING, -S to mark with small spots

SPECKLE   *v* -LED, -LING, -LES to speck

SPECS   *n/pl* eyeglasses

SPECTATE   *v* -TATED, -TATING, -TATES to attend and view

SPECTER   *n* pl. -S a visible disembodied spirit

SPECTRA   a pl. of spectrum

SPECTRAL   *adj* resembling a specter

SPECTRE   *n* pl. -S specter

SPECTRUM   *n* pl. -TRA or -TRUMS an array of the components of a light wave

SPECULUM   *n* pl. -LA or -LUMS a medical instrument **SPECULAR** *adj*

SPEECH   *n* pl. -ES the faculty or act of speaking

SPEED   *v* SPED or SPEEDED, SPEEDING, SPEEDS to move swiftly

SPEEDER   *n* pl. -S one that speeds

SPEEDIER   comparative of speedy

SPEEDIEST   superlative of speedy

SPEEDILY   *adv* in a speedy manner

SPEEDING   *n* pl. -S the act of driving faster than the law allows

SPEEDO   *n* pl. SPEEDOS a speedometer

SPEEDUP   *n* pl. -S an acceleration of production without an increase in pay

SPEEDWAY   *n* pl. -WAYS a road designed for rapid travel

SPEEDY   *adj* SPEEDIER, SPEEDIEST swift

SPEEL   *v* -ED, -ING, -S to climb

SPEER   *v* -ED, -ING, -S to inquire

SPEERING   *n* pl. -S inquiry

SPEIL   *v* -ED, -ING, -S to speel

SPEIR   *v* -ED, -ING, -S to speer

SPEISE   *n* pl. -S speiss

SPEISS   *n* pl. -ES a metallic mixture obtained in smelting certain ores

SPELAEAN   *adj* spelean

SPELEAN   *adj* living in caves

SPELL   *v* SPELLED or SPELT, SPELLING, SPELLS to name or write the letters of in order

SPELLER   *n* pl. -S one that spells words

SPELLING   *n* pl. -S a sequence of letters composing a word

SPELT   *n* pl. -S a variety of wheat

SPELTER   *n* pl. -S zinc in the form of ingots

SPELTZ   *n* pl. -ES spelt

SPELUNK   *v* -ED, -ING, -S to explore caves

SPENCE   *n* pl. -S a pantry

SPENCER   *n* pl. -S a trysail

SPEND   *v* SPENT, SPENDING, SPENDS to pay out

SPENDER   *n* pl. -S one that spends

SPENSE   *n* pl. -S spence

SPENT   past tense of spend

SPERM   *n* pl. -S a male gamete **SPERMIC** *adj*

SPERMARY   *n* pl. -RIES an organ in which sperms are formed

SPERMINE   *n* pl. -S a chemical compound

SPERMOUS   *adj* resembling or made up of sperms

SPEW   *v* -ED, -ING, -S to vomit

SPEWER   *n* pl. -S one that spews

SPHAGNUM   *n* pl. -S a grayish moss

SPHENE   *n* pl. -S a mineral

SPHENIC   *adj* shaped like a wedge

SPHENOID   *n* pl. -S a bone of the skull

SPHERAL   *adj* of, pertaining to, or having the form of a sphere

SPHERE   *v* SPHERED, SPHERING, SPHERES to form into a sphere (a type of geometric solid)

SPHERIC   *adj* spheral

SPHERICS   *n/pl* the geometry of figures on the surface of a sphere

SPHERIER   comparative of sphery

SPHERIEST   superlative of sphery

SPHERING   present participle of sphere

SPHEROID   *n* pl. -S a type of geometric solid

SPHERULE   *n* pl. -S a small sphere

SPHERY	adj SPHERIER, SPHERIEST resembling a sphere	**SPIKY**	adj SPIKIER, SPIKIEST resembling a spike **SPIKILY** adv
SPHINGES	a pl. of sphinx	**SPILE**	v SPILED, SPILING, SPILES to stop up with a wooden plug
SPHINGID	n pl. -S the hawkmoth		
SPHINX	n pl. SPHINXES or SPHINGES a monster in Egyptian mythology	**SPILIKIN**	n pl. -S a strip of wood used in a game
SPHYGMUS	n pl. -ES the pulse **SPHYGMIC** adj	**SPILING**	n pl. -S a piling
		SPILL	v SPILLED or SPILT, SPILLING, SPILLS to cause to run out of a container
SPICA	n pl. -CAE or -CAS an ear of grain **SPICATE, SPICATED** adj		
SPICCATO	n pl. -TOS a method of playing a stringed instrument	**SPILLAGE**	n pl. -S something that is spilled
		SPILLER	n pl. -S one that spills
SPICE	v SPICED, SPICING, SPICES to season with a spice (an aromatic vegetable substance)	**SPILLWAY**	n pl. -WAYS a channel for surplus water in a reservoir
		SPILT	a past tense of spill
SPICER	n pl. -S one that spices	**SPILTH**	n pl. -S spillage
SPICERY	n pl. -ERIES a spicy quality	**SPIN**	v SPUN, SPINNING, SPINS to draw out and twist into threads
SPICEY	adj SPICIER, SPICIEST spicy		
SPICIER	comparative of spicy	**SPINACH**	n pl. -ES a cultivated herb **SPINACHY** adj
SPICIEST	superlative of spicy		
SPICILY	adv in a spicy manner	**SPINAGE**	n pl. -S spinach
SPICING	present participle of spice	**SPINAL**	n pl. -S an injection of an anesthetic into the spinal cord
SPICULA	n pl. -LAE spicule **SPICULAR** adj		
SPICULE	n pl. -S a needlelike structure	**SPINALLY**	adv with respect to the spine
SPICULUM	n pl. -LA spicule	**SPINATE**	adj bearing thorns
SPICY	adj SPICIER, SPICIEST containing spices	**SPINDLE**	v -DLED, -DLING, -DLES to impale on a slender rod
SPIDER	n pl. -S a type of arachnid	**SPINDLER**	n pl. -S one that spindles
SPIDERY	adj -DERIER, -DERIEST resembling a spider	**SPINDLY**	adj -DLIER, -DLIEST long and slender
SPIED	past tense of spy	**SPINE**	n pl. -S the vertebral column **SPINED** adj
SPIEGEL	n pl. -S a type of cast iron		
SPIEL	v -ED, -ING, -S to talk at length	**SPINEL**	n pl. -S a mineral
SPIELER	n pl. -S one that spiels	**SPINELLE**	n pl. -S spinel
SPIER	v -ED, -ING, -S to speer	**SPINET**	n pl. -S a small piano
SPIES	present 3d person sing. of spy	**SPINIER**	comparative of spiny
SPIFF	v -ED, -ING, -S to make spiffy	**SPINIEST**	superlative of spiny
SPIFFING	adj spiffy	**SPINIFEX**	n pl. -ES an Australian grass
SPIFFY	adj -FIER, -FIEST stylish **SPIFFILY** adv	**SPINLESS**	adj having no rotation
		SPINNER	n pl. -S one that spins
		SPINNERY	n pl. -NERIES a spinning mill
SPIGOT	n pl. -S a faucet	**SPINNEY**	n pl. -NEYS a thicket
SPIKE	v SPIKED, SPIKING, SPIKES to fasten with a spike (a long, thick nail)	**SPINNING**	n pl. -S the act of one that spins
		SPINNY	n pl. -NIES spinney
SPIKELET	n pl. -S a type of flower cluster	**SPINOFF**	n pl. -S a new application or incidental result
SPIKER	n pl. -S one that spikes		
SPIKEY	adj SPIKIER, SPIKIEST spiky	**SPINOR**	n pl. -S a type of mathematical vector
SPIKING	present participle of spike	**SPINOSE**	adj spiny

SPINOUS	*adj* spiny	**SPITFIRE**	*n* pl. -S a quick-tempered person
SPINOUT	*n* pl. -S a rotational skid by an automobile	**SPITING**	present participle of spite
		SPITTED	past tense of spit
SPINSTER	*n* pl. -S an unmarried woman who is past the usual age for marrying	**SPITTER**	*n* pl. -S a spitball
		SPITTING	present participle of spit
SPINTO	*n* pl. -TOS a singing voice that is lyric and dramatic	**SPITTLE**	*n* pl. -S saliva
		SPITTOON	*n* pl. -S a receptacle for saliva
SPINULA	*n* pl. -LAE spinule	**SPITZ**	*n* pl. -ES a dog having a heavy coat
SPINULE	*n* pl. -S a small thorn		
SPINY	*adj* SPINIER, SPINIEST bearing or covered with thorns	**SPIV**	*n* pl. -S a petty criminal
		SPLAKE	*n* pl. -S a freshwater fish
SPIRACLE	*n* pl. -S an orifice through which breathing occurs	**SPLASH**	*v* -ED, -ING, -ES to scatter a liquid about
SPIRAEA	*n* pl. -S spirea	**SPLASHER**	*n* pl. -S one that splashes
SPIRAL	*v* -RALED, -RALING, -RALS or -RALLED, -RALLING, -RALS to move like a spiral (a type of plane curve)	**SPLASHY**	*adj* SPLASHIER, SPLASHIEST showy
		SPLAT	*v* SPLATTED, SPLATTING, SPLATS to flatten on impact
SPIRALLY	*adv* in a spiral manner	**SPLATTER**	*v* -ED, -ING, -S to spatter
SPIRANT	*n* pl. -S a speech sound produced by the forcing of breath through a narrow passage	**SPLAY**	*v* -ED, -ING, -S to spread out
		SPLEEN	*n* pl. -S a ductless organ of the body
SPIRE	*v* SPIRED, SPIRING, SPIRES to rise in a tapering manner	**SPLEENY**	*adj* SPLEENIER, SPLEENIEST peevish
SPIREA	*n* pl. -S a flowering shrub	**SPLENDID**	*adj* -DIDER, -DIDEST magnificent
SPIREM	*n* pl. -S spireme	
SPIREME	*n* pl. -S a filament forming part of a cell nucleus during mitosis	**SPLENDOR**	*n* pl. -S magnificence
		SPLENIA	pl. of splenium
SPIRIER	comparative of spiry	**SPLENIAL**	*adj* pertaining to the splenius
SPIRIEST	superlative of spiry	**SPLENIC**	*adj* pertaining to the spleen
SPIRILLA	*n/pl* spirally twisted, aerobic bacteria	**SPLENIUM**	*n* pl. -NIA a surgical bandage
		SPLENIUS	*n* pl. -NII a muscle of the neck
SPIRING	present participle of spire	**SPLENT**	*n* pl. -S a splint
SPIRIT	*v* -ED, -ING, -S to carry off secretly	**SPLICE**	*v* SPLICED, SPLICING, SPLICES to join at the ends
SPIROID	*adj* resembling a spiral	**SPLICER**	*n* pl. -S one that splices
SPIRT	*v* -ED, -ING, -S to spurt	**SPLIFF**	*n* pl. -S a marijuana cigarette
SPIRULA	*n* pl. -LAE or -LAS a spiral-shelled mollusk	**SPLINE**	*v* SPLINED, SPLINING, SPLINES to provide with a spline (a key that connects two rotating mechanical parts)
SPIRY	*adj* SPIRIER, SPIRIEST tall, slender, and tapering	
SPIT	*v* SPITTED, SPITTING, SPITS to impale on a spit (a pointed rod on which meat is turned)	**SPLINT**	*v* -ED, -ING, -S to brace with a splint (a thin piece of wood)
SPITAL	*n* pl. -S a hospital	**SPLINTER**	*v* -ED, -ING, -S to split into sharp, slender pieces
SPITBALL	*n* pl. -S a type of pitch in baseball	**SPLIT**	*v* SPLIT, SPLITTING, SPLITS to separate lengthwise
SPITE	*v* SPITED, SPITING, SPITES to treat with malice	
SPITEFUL	*adj* -FULLER, -FULLEST malicious	**SPLITTER**	*n* pl. -S one that splits

SPLODGE	v SPLODGED, SPLODGING, SPLODGES to splotch	**SPOOF**	v -ED, -ING, -S to ridicule in fun
SPLORE	n pl. -S a carousal	**SPOOFER**	n pl. -S one that spoofs
SPLOSH	v -ED, -ING, -ES to splash	**SPOOFERY**	n pl. -ERIES good-natured ridicule
SPLOTCH	v -ED, -ING, -ES to mark with large, irregular spots	**SPOOFY**	adj humorously satiric
SPLOTCHY	adj SPLOTCHIER, SPLOTCHIEST splotched	**SPOOK**	v -ED, -ING, -S to scare
SPLURGE	v SPLURGED, SPLURGING, SPLURGES to spend money lavishly	**SPOOKERY**	n pl. -ERIES something spooky
		SPOOKISH	adj spooky
		SPOOKY	adj SPOOKIER, SPOOKIEST scary **SPOOKILY** adv
SPLURGER	n pl. -S one that splurges	**SPOOL**	v -ED, -ING, -S to wind on a small cylinder
SPLURGY	adj SPLURGIER, SPLURGIEST tending to splurge		
SPLUTTER	v -ED, -ING, -S to speak rapidly and confusedly	**SPOOLING**	n pl. -S the temporary storage of data for later output
SPODE	n pl. -S a fine china	**SPOON**	v -ED, -ING, -S to take up with a spoon (a type of eating utensil)
SPOIL	v SPOILED or SPOILT, SPOILING, SPOILS to impair the value or quality of	**SPOONEY**	adj SPOONIER, SPOONIEST spoony
SPOILAGE	n pl. -S something that is spoiled or wasted	**SPOONEY**	n pl. -EYS a spoony
		SPOONFUL	n pl. SPOONFULS or SPOONSFUL as much as a spoon can hold
SPOILER	n pl. -S one that spoils		
SPOILT	a past tense of spoil	**SPOONIER**	comparative of spooney
SPOKE	v SPOKED, SPOKING, SPOKES to provide with spokes (rods that support the rim of a wheel)	**SPOONIES**	pl. of spoony
		SPOONIEST	superlative of spooney
		SPOONSFUL	a pl. of spoonful
SPOKEN	past participle of speak	**SPOONY**	adj SPOONIER, SPOONIEST overly sentimental **SPOONILY** adv
SPOLIATE	v -ATED, -ATING, -ATES to plunder		
SPONDAIC	n pl. -S a spondee	**SPOONY**	n pl. SPOONIES a spoony person
SPONDEE	n pl. -S a type of metrical foot	**SPOOR**	v -ED, -ING, -S to track
SPONGE	v SPONGED, SPONGING, SPONGES to wipe with a sponge (a mass of absorbent material)	**SPORADIC**	adj occurring at irregular intervals
		SPORAL	adj of, pertaining to, or resembling a spore
SPONGER	n pl. -S one that sponges	**SPORE**	v SPORED, SPORING, SPORES to produce spores (asexual, usually single-celled reproductive bodies)
SPONGIER	comparative of spongy		
SPONGIEST	superlative of spongy		
SPONGILY	adv in a spongy manner		
SPONGIN	n pl. -S a fibrous material		
SPONGING	present participle of sponge	**SPOROID**	adj resembling a spore
SPONGY	adj SPONGIER, SPONGIEST resembling a sponge	**SPOROZOA**	n/pl parasitic one-celled animals
		SPORRAN	n pl. -S a large purse worn by Scottish Highlanders
SPONSAL	adj pertaining to marriage		
SPONSION	n pl. -S the act of sponsoring	**SPORT**	v -ED, -ING, -S to frolic
SPONSON	n pl. -S a projection from the side of a ship	**SPORTER**	n pl. -S one that sports
		SPORTFUL	adj sportive
SPONSOR	v -ED, -ING, -S to make oneself responsible for	**SPORTIF**	adj sporty
SPONTOON	n pl. -S a spear-like weapon	**SPORTIVE**	adj playful

SPORTY   *adj* SPORTIER, SPORTIEST showy **SPORTILY** *adv*

SPORULE   *n* pl. -S a small spore **SPORULAR** *adj*

SPOT   *v* SPOTTED, SPOTTING, SPOTS to mark with spots (small, roundish discolorations)

SPOTLESS   *adj* perfectly clean

SPOTLIT   a past tense of spotlight

SPOTTER   *n* pl. -S one that spots

SPOTTING   present participle of spot

SPOTTY   *adj* -TIER, -TIEST marked with spots **SPOTTILY** *adv*

SPOUSAL   *n* pl. -S marriage

SPOUSE   *v* SPOUSED, SPOUSING, SPOUSES to marry

SPOUT   *v* -ED, -ING, -S to eject in a rapid stream

SPOUTER   *n* pl. -S one that spouts

SPRADDLE   *v* -DLED, -DLING, -DLES to straddle

SPRAG   *n* pl. -S a device used to prevent a vehicle from rolling backward

SPRAIN   *v* -ED, -ING, -S to weaken by a sudden and violent twisting or wrenching

SPRANG   *n* pl. -S a weaving technique to form an openwork mesh

SPRAT   *n* pl. -S a small herring

SPRATTLE   *v* -TLED, -TLING, -TLES to struggle

SPRAWL   *v* -ED, -ING, -S to stretch out ungracefully

SPRAWLER   *n* pl. -S one that sprawls

SPRAWLY   *adj* SPRAWLIER, SPRAWLIEST tending to sprawl

SPRAY   *v* -ED, -ING, -S to disperse in fine particles

SPRAYER   *n* pl. -S one that sprays

SPREAD   *v* SPREAD, SPREADING, SPREADS to open or expand over a larger area

SPREADER   *n* pl. -S one that spreads

SPREE   *n* pl. -S an unrestrained indulgence in an activity

SPRENT   *adj* sprinkled over

SPRIER   a comparative of spry

SPRIEST   a superlative of spry

SPRIG   *v* SPRIGGED, SPRIGGING, SPRIGS to fasten with small, thin nails

SPRIGGER   *n* pl. -S one that sprigs

SPRIGGY   *adj* -GIER, -GIEST having small branches

SPRIGHT   *n* pl. -S sprite

SPRING   *v* SPRANG or SPRUNG, SPRINGING, SPRINGS to move upward suddenly and swiftly

SPRINGAL   *n* pl. -S a young man

SPRINGE   *v* SPRINGED, SPRINGEING, SPRINGES to catch with a type of snare

SPRINGER   *n* pl. -S one that springs

SPRINGY   *adj* SPRINGIER, SPRINGIEST resilient

SPRINKLE   *v* -KLED, -KLING, -KLES to scatter drops or particles on

SPRINT   *v* -ED, -ING, -S to run at top speed

SPRINTER   *n* pl. -S one that sprints

SPRIT   *n* pl. -S a ship's spar

SPRITE   *n* pl. -S an elf or fairy

SPRITZ   *v* -ED, -ING, -ES to spray

SPRITZER   *n* pl. -S a beverage of white wine and soda water

SPROCKET   *n* pl. -S a toothlike projection that engages with the links of a chain

SPROUT   *v* -ED, -ING, -S to begin to grow

SPRUCE   *adj* SPRUCER, SPRUCEST neat and trim in appearance **SPRUCELY** *adv*

SPRUCE   *v* SPRUCED, SPRUCING, SPRUCES to make spruce

SPRUCY   *adj* SPRUCIER, SPRUCIEST spruce

SPRUE   *n* pl. -S a tropical disease

SPRUG   *n* pl. -S a sparrow

SPRUNG   a past tense of spring

SPRY   *adj* SPRYER, SPRYEST or SPRIER, SPRIEST nimble **SPRYLY** *adv*

SPRYNESS   *n* pl. -ES the quality or state of being spry

SPUD   *v* SPUDDED, SPUDDING, SPUDS to remove with a spade-like tool

SPUDDER   *n* pl. -S a tool for removing bark from trees

SPUE   *v* SPUED, SPUING, SPUES to spew

SPUME   *v* SPUMED, SPUMING, SPUMES to foam

SPUMIER	comparative of spumy
SPUMIEST	superlative of spumy
SPUMING	present participle of spume
SPUMONE	n pl. -S an Italian ice cream
SPUMONI	n pl. -S spumone
SPUMOUS	adj spumy
SPUMY	adj SPUMIER, SPUMIEST foamy
SPUN	past tense of spin
SPUNK	v -ED, -ING, -S to begin to burn
SPUNKIE	n pl. -S a light caused by the combustion of marsh gas
SPUNKY	adj SPUNKIER, SPUNKIEST plucky **SPUNKILY** adv
SPUR	v SPURRED, SPURRING, SPURS to urge on with a spur (a horseman's goad)
SPURGALL	v -ED, -ING, -S to injure with a spur
SPURGE	n pl. -S a tropical plant
SPURIOUS	adj not genuine
SPURN	v -ED, -ING, -S to reject with contempt
SPURNER	n pl. -S one that spurns
SPURRED	past tense of spur
SPURRER	n pl. -S one that spurs
SPURREY	n pl. -REYS spurry
SPURRIER	n pl. -S one that makes spurs
SPURRING	present participle of spur
SPURRY	n pl. -RIES a European weed
SPURT	v -ED, -ING, -S to gush forth
SPURTLE	n pl. -S a stick for stirring porridge
SPUTA	pl. of sputum
SPUTNIK	n pl. -S a Soviet artificial earth satellite
SPUTTER	v -ED, -ING, -S to eject particles in short bursts
SPUTUM	n pl. -TA saliva
SPY	v SPIED, SPYING, SPIES to watch secretly
SPYGLASS	n pl. -ES a small telescope
SQUAB	n pl. -S a young pigeon
SQUABBLE	v -BLED, -BLING, -BLES to quarrel
SQUABBY	adj -BIER, -BIEST short and fat
SQUAD	v SQUADDED, SQUADDING, SQUADS to form into squads (small organized groups)
SQUADRON	v -ED, -ING, -S to arrange in squadrons (units of military organization)
SQUALENE	n pl. -S a chemical compound
SQUALID	adj -IDER, -IDEST marked by filthiness caused by neglect or poverty
SQUALL	v -ED, -ING, -S to cry or scream loudly
SQUALLER	n pl. -S one that squalls
SQUALLY	adj SQUALLIER, SQUALLIEST gusty
SQUALOR	n pl. -S the quality or state of being squalid
SQUAMA	n pl. -MAE a scale **SQUAMATE, SQUAMOSE, SQUAMOUS** adj
SQUANDER	v -ED, -ING, -S to spend wastefully
SQUARE	adj SQUARER, SQUAREST having four equal sides and four right angles; rigidly conventional
SQUARE	v SQUARED, SQUARING, SQUARES to make square
SQUARELY	adv in a straightforward or honest manner
SQUARER	n pl. -S one that squares
SQUAREST	superlative of square
SQUARING	present participle of square
SQUARISH	adj somewhat square
SQUASH	v -ED, -ING, -ES to press into a pulp or flat mass
SQUASHER	n pl. -S one that squashes
SQUASHY	adj SQUASHIER, SQUASHIEST soft and moist
SQUAT	v SQUATTED, SQUATTING, SQUATS to bend one's knees and sit on one's heels
SQUAT	adj SQUATTER, SQUATTEST short and thick **SQUATLY** adv
SQUATTER	v -ED, -ING, -S to move through water
SQUATTING	present participle of squat
SQUATTY	adj -TIER, -TIEST squat
SQUAWK	v -ED, -ING, -S to utter a loud, harsh cry
SQUAWKER	n pl. -S one that squawks
SQUEAK	v -ED, -ING, -S to make a sharp, high-pitched sound
SQUEAKER	n pl. -S one that squeaks
SQUEAKY	adj SQUEAKIER, SQUEAKIEST tending to squeak

SQUEAL   *v* -ED, -ING, -S to utter a sharp, shrill cry

SQUEALER   *n* pl. -S one that squeals

SQUEEGEE   *v* -GEED, -GEEING, -GEES to wipe with a squeegee (an implement for removing water from a surface)

SQUEEZE   *v* SQUEEZED, SQUEEZING, SQUEEZES to press hard upon

SQUEEZER   *n* pl. -S one that squeezes

SQUEG   *v* SQUEGGED, SQUEGGING, SQUEGS to oscillate in an irregular manner

SQUELCH   *v* -ED, -ING, -ES to squash

SQUELCHY   *adj* SQUELCHIER, SQUELCHIEST squashy

SQUIB   *v* SQUIBBED, SQUIBBING, SQUIBS to lampoon

SQUID   *v* SQUIDDED, SQUIDDING, SQUIDS to fish for squid (ten-armed marine mollusks)

SQUIFFED   *adj* drunk

SQUIFFY   *adj* -FIER, -FIEST squiffed

SQUIGGLE   *v* -GLED, -GLING, -GLES to wriggle

SQUIGGLY   *adj* -GLIER, -GLIEST wriggly

SQUILGEE   *v* -GEED, -GEEING, -GEES to squeegee

SQUILL   *n* pl. -S a Eurasian herb

SQUILLA   *n* pl. -LAS or -LAE a burrowing crustacean

SQUINCH   *v* -ED, -ING, -ES to squint

SQUINNY   *v* -NIED, -NYING, -NIES to squint

SQUINNY   *adj* -NIER, -NIEST squinty

SQUINT   *adj* SQUINTER, SQUINTEST cross-eyed

SQUINT   *v* -ED, -ING, -S to look with the eyes partly closed

SQUINTER   *n* pl. -S one that squints

SQUINTY   *adj* SQUINTIER, SQUINTIEST marked by squinting

SQUIRE   *v* SQUIRED, SQUIRING, SQUIRES to serve as a squire (an escort)

SQUIREEN   *n* pl. -S an owner of a small estate

SQUIRISH   *adj* of, resembling, or befitting a squire

SQUIRM   *v* -ED, -ING, -S to wriggle

SQUIRMER   *n* pl. -S one that squirms

SQUIRMY   *adj* SQUIRMIER, SQUIRMIEST wriggly

SQUIRREL   *v* -RELED, -RELING, -RELS or -RELLED, -RELLING, -RELS to store up for future use

SQUIRT   *v* -ED, -ING, -S to eject in a thin, swift stream

SQUIRTER   *n* pl. -S one that squirts

SQUISH   *v* -ED, -ING, -ES to squash

SQUISHY   *adj* SQUISHIER, SQUISHIEST squashy

SQUOOSH   *v* -ED, -ING, -ES to squash

SQUOOSHY   *adj* SQUOOSHIER, SQUOOSHIEST squashy

SQUUSH   *v* -ED, -ING, -ES to squash

SRADDHA   *n* pl. -S sradha

SRADHA   *n* pl. -S a Hindu ceremonial offering

SRI   *n* pl. -S mister; sir — used as a Hindu title of respect

STAB   *v* STABBED, STABBING, STABS to pierce with a pointed weapon

STABBER   *n* pl. -S one that stabs

STABILE   *n* pl. -S a stationary abstract sculpture

STABLE   *adj* -BLER, -BLEST resistant to sudden change or position or condition

STABLE   *v* -BLED, -BLING, -BLES to put in a stable (a shelter for domestic animals)

STABLER   *n* pl. -S one that keeps a stable

STABLEST   superlative of stable

STABLING   *n* pl. -S accommodation for animals in a stable

STABLISH   *v* -ED, -ING, -ES to establish

STABLY   *adv* in a stable manner

STACCATO   *n* pl. -TOS or -TI a musical passage marked by the short, clear-cut playing of tones

STACK   *v* -ED, -ING, -S to pile

STACKER   *n* pl. -S one that stacks

STACKUP   *n* pl. -S an arrangement of circling airplanes over an airport waiting to land

STACTE   *n* pl. -S a spice used by the ancient Jews in making incense

STADDLE   *n* pl. -S a platform on which hay is stacked

STADE   *n* pl. -S an ancient Greek unit of length

STADIA *n* pl. -S a method of surveying distances

STADIUM *n* pl. -S a structure in which athletic events are held

STAFF *v* -ED, -ING, -S to provide with a staff (a body of assistants)

STAFFER *n* pl. -S a member of a staff

STAG *v* STAGGED, STAGGING, STAGS to attend a social function without a female companion

STAGE *v* STAGED, STAGING, STAGES to produce for public view

STAGEFUL *n* pl. -S as much or as many as a stage can hold

STAGER *n* pl. -S an experienced person

STAGEY *adj* STAGIER, STAGIEST stagy

STAGGARD *n* pl. -S a full-grown male red deer

STAGGART *n* pl. -S staggard

STAGGED past tense of stag

STAGGER *v* -ED, -ING, -S to walk or stand unsteadily

STAGGERY *adj* unsteady

STAGGIE *n* pl. -S a colt

STAGGING present participle of stag

STAGGY *adj* -GIER, -GIEST having the appearance of a mature male

STAGIER comparative of stagey and stagy

STAGIEST superlative of stagey and stagy

STAGILY *adv* in a stagy manner

STAGING *n* pl. -S a temporary platform

STAGNANT *adj* not moving or flowing

STAGNATE *v* -NATED, -NATING, -NATES to become stagnant

STAGY *adj* STAGIER, STAGIEST having a theatrical quality

STAID *adj* STAIDER, STAIDEST sober and sedate **STAIDLY** *adv*

STAIG *n* pl. -S a colt

STAIN *v* -ED, -ING, -S to discolor or dirty

STAINER *n* pl. -S one that stains

STAIR *n* pl. -S a rest for the foot used in going from one level to another

STAIRWAY *n* pl. -WAYS a flight of stairs

STAITHE *n* pl. -S a wharf equipped for transferring coal from railroad cars into ships

STAKE *v* STAKED, STAKING, STAKES to fasten with a stake (a pointed piece of wood or metal)

STAKEOUT *n* pl. -S a surveillance of an area especially by the police

STALAG *n* pl. -S a German prisoner-of-war camp

STALE *adj* STALER, STALEST not fresh **STALELY** *adv*

STALE *v* STALED, STALING, STALES to become stale

STALK *v* -ED, -ING, -S to pursue stealthily

STALKER *n* pl. -S one that stalks

STALKY *adj* STALKIER, STALKIEST long and slender **STALKILY** *adv*

STALL *v* -ED, -ING, -S to stop the progress of

STALLION *n* pl. -S an uncastrated male horse

STALWART *n* pl. -S an unwavering partisan

STAMEN *n* pl. -S the pollen-bearing organ of flowering plants

STAMINA *n* pl. -S endurance **STAMINAL** *adj*

STAMMEL *n* pl. -S a red color

STAMMER *v* -ED, -ING, -S to speak with involuntary breaks and pauses

STAMP *v* -ED, -ING, -S to bring the foot down heavily

STAMPEDE *v* -PEDED, -PEDING, -PEDES to cause to run away in headlong panic

STAMPER *n* pl. -S one that stamps

STANCE *n* pl. -S a manner of standing

STANCH *adj* STANCHER, STANCHEST staunch

STANCH *v* -ED, -ING, -ES to stop the flow of blood from

STANCHER *n* pl. -S one that stanches

STANCHLY *adv* in a stanch manner

STAND *v* STOOD, STANDING, STANDS to assume or maintain an upright position

STANDARD *n* pl. -S an established measure of comparison

STANDBY *n* pl. -BYS one that can be relied on

STANDEE *n* pl. -S one who stands because of the lack of seats

STANDER *n* pl. -S one that stands

STANDING   *n* pl. -S a position or condition in society

STANDISH   *n* pl. -ES a receptacle for pens and ink

STANDOFF   *n* pl. -S a tie or draw, as in a game

STANDOUT   *n* pl. -S one that shows marked superiority

STANDPAT   *adj* resisting or opposing change

STANDUP   *adj* having an upright position

STANE   *v* STANED, STANING, STANES to stone

STANG   *v* -ED, -ING, -S to sting

STANHOPE   *n* pl. -S a light, open carriage

STANINE   *n* pl. -S one of the nine classes into which a set of scores are divided

STANING   present participle of stane

STANK   *n* pl. -S a pond

STANNARY   *n* pl. -RIES a tin-mining region

STANNIC   *adj* pertaining to tin

STANNITE   *n* pl. -S an ore of tin

STANNOUS   *adj* pertaining to tin

STANNUM   *n* pl. -S tin

STANZA   *n* pl. -S a division of a poem **STANZAED, STANZAIC** *adj*

STAPEDES   pl. of stapes

STAPELIA   *n* pl. -S an African plant

STAPES   *n* pl. -PEDES a bone of the middle ear

STAPH   *n* pl. -S any of various spherical bacteria

STAPLE   *v* -PLED, -PLING, -PLES to fasten by means of a U-shaped metal loop

STAPLER   *n* pl. -S a stapling device

STAR   *v* STARRED, STARRING, STARS to shine as a star (a natural luminous body visible in the sky)

STARCH   *v* -ED, -ING, -ES to treat with starch (a solid carbohydrate)

STARCHY   *adj* STARCHIER, STARCHIEST containing starch

STARDOM   *n* pl. -S the status of a preeminent performer

STARDUST   *n* pl. -S a romantic quality

STARE   *v* STARED, STARING, STARES to gaze fixedly

STARER   *n* pl. -S one that stares

STARETS   *n* pl. STARTSY a spiritual adviser in the Eastern Orthodox Church

STARFISH   *n* pl. -ES a star-shaped marine animal

STARGAZE   *v* -GAZED, -GAZING, -GAZES to gaze at the stars

STARING   present participle of stare

STARK   *adj* STARKER, STARKEST harsh in appearance **STARKLY** *adv*

STARKERS   *adj* naked

STARLESS   *adj* having no stars

STARLET   *n* pl. -S a small star

STARLIKE   *adj* resembling a star

STARLING   *n* pl. -S a European bird

STARLIT   *adj* lighted by the stars

STARNOSE   *n* pl. -S a burrowing mammal

STARRED   past tense of star

STARRING   present participle of star

STARRY   *adj* -RIER, -RIEST abounding with stars

STARSHIP   *n* pl. -S a spaceship for interstellar travel

START   *v* -ED, -ING, -S to set out

STARTER   *n* pl. -S one that starts

STARTLE   *v* -TLED, -TLING, -TLES to frighten or surprise suddenly

STARTLER   *n* pl. -S one that startles

STARTSY   pl. of starets

STARTUP   *n* pl. -S the act of starting something

STARVE   *v* STARVED, STARVING, STARVES to die from lack of food

STARVER   *n* pl. -S one that starves

STARWORT   *n* pl. -S a flowering plant

STASES   pl. of stasis

STASH   *v* -ED, -ING, -ES to store in a secret place

STASIMON   *n* pl. -MA a choral ode in ancient Greek drama

STASIS   *n* pl. STASES a stoppage of the normal flow of bodily fluids

STAT   *n* pl. -S a statistic

STATABLE   *adj* capable of being stated

STATAL   *adj* pertaining to a national government

STATANT   *adj* standing with all feet on the ground — used of a heraldic animal

STATE	v STATED, STATING, STATES to set forth in words	**STEADY**	v STEADIED, STEADYING, STEADIES to make steady
STATEDLY	adv regularly	**STEAK**	n pl. -S a slice of meat
STATELY	adj -LIER, -LIEST dignified	**STEAL**	v STOLE or STAW, STOLEN, STEALING, STEALS to take without right or permission
STATER	n pl. -S one that states		
STATIC	n pl. -S random noise produced in a radio or television receiver **STATICAL** adj	**STEALAGE**	n pl. -S theft
		STEALER	n pl. -S one that steals
STATICE	n pl. -S a flowering plant	**STEALING**	n pl. -S the act of one that steals
STATICKY	adj marked by static	**STEALTH**	n pl. -S stealthy procedure
STATING	present participle of state	**STEALTHY**	adj STEALTHIER, STEALTHIEST intended to escape observation
STATION	v -ED, -ING, -S to assign to a position		
STATISM	n pl. -S a theory of government	**STEAM**	v -ED, -ING, -S to expose to steam (water in the form of vapor)
STATIST	n pl. -S an adherent of statism		
STATIVE	n pl. -S a verb that expresses a condition	**STEAMER**	v -ED, -ING, -S to travel by steamship
STATOR	n pl. -S the part of a machine about which the rotor revolves	**STEAMY**	adj STEAMIER, STEAMIEST marked by steam **STEAMILY** adv
STATUARY	n pl. -ARIES a group of statues	**STEAPSIN**	n pl. -S an enzyme
STATUE	n pl. -S a three-dimensional work of art **STATUED** adj	**STEARATE**	n pl. -S a chemical salt
		STEARIN	n pl. -S the solid portion of a fat **STEARIC** adj
STATURE	n pl. -S the natural height of a human or animal body		
		STEARINE	n pl. -S stearin
STATUS	n pl. -ES relative position	**STEATITE**	n pl. -S a variety of talc
STATUSY	adj conferring prestige	**STEDFAST**	adj staunch
STATUTE	n pl. -S a law enacted by the legislative branch of a government	**STEED**	n pl. -S a horse
		STEEK	v -ED, -ING, -S to shut
STAUMREL	n pl. -S a dolt	**STEEL**	v -ED, -ING, -S to cover with steel (a tough iron alloy)
STAUNCH	adj STAUNCHER, STAUNCHEST firm and dependable		
		STEELIE	n pl. -S a steel playing marble
STAUNCH	v -ED, -ING, -ES to stanch	**STEELY**	adj STEELIER, STEELIEST resembling steel
STAVE	v STAVED or STOVE, STAVING, STAVES to drive or thrust away		
		STEENBOK	n pl. -S an African antelope
STAW	a past tense of steal	**STEEP**	adj STEEPER, STEEPEST inclined sharply
STAY	v STAYED or STAID, STAYING, STAYS to continue in a place or condition		
		STEEP	v -ED, -ING, -S to soak in a liquid
		STEEPEN	v -ED, -ING, -S to make steep
STAYER	n pl. -S one that stays	**STEEPER**	n pl. -S one that steeps
STAYSAIL	n pl. -S a type of sail	**STEEPISH**	adj somewhat steep
STEAD	v -ED, -ING, -S to be of advantage to	**STEEPLE**	n pl. -S a tapering structure on a church tower **STEEPLED** adj
STEADIED	past tense of steady		
STEADIER	n pl. -S one that steadies	**STEEPLY**	adv in a steep manner
STEADIES	present 3d person sing. of steady	**STEER**	v -ED, -ING, -S to direct the course of
STEADING	n pl. -S a small farm		
STEADY	adj STEADIER, STEADIEST firm in position **STEADILY** adv	**STEERAGE**	n pl. -S the act of steering
		STEERER	n pl. -S one that steers

STEEVE	*v* STEEVED, STEEVING, STEEVES to stow in the hold of a ship
STEEVING	*n* pl. -S the angular elevation of a bowsprit from a ship's keel
STEGODON	*n* pl. -S an extinct elephant-like mammal
STEIN	*n* pl. -S a beer mug
STEINBOK	*n* pl. -S steenbok
STELA	*n* pl. -LAE or -LAI an inscribed slab used as a monument **STELAR, STELENE** *adj*
STELE	*n* pl. -S the central portion of vascular tissue in a plant stem **STELIC** *adj*
STELLA	*n* pl. -S a former coin of the United States
STELLAR	*adj* pertaining to the stars
STELLATE	*adj* shaped like a star
STELLIFY	*v* -FIED, -FYING, -FIES to convert into a star
STEM	*v* STEMMED, STEMMING, STEMS to remove stems (ascending axes of a plant) from
STEMLESS	*adj* having no stem
STEMLIKE	*adj* resembling a stem
STEMMA	*n* pl. -MAS or -MATA a scroll recording the genealogy of a family in ancient Rome
STEMMED	past tense of stem
STEMMER	*n* pl. -S one that removes stems
STEMMERY	*n* pl. -MERIES a place where tobacco leaves are stripped
STEMMING	present participle of stem
STEMMY	*adj* -MIER, -MIEST abounding in stems
STEMSON	*n* pl. -S a supporting timber of a ship
STEMWARE	*n* pl. -S a type of glassware
STENCH	*n* pl. -ES a foul odor
STENCHY	*adj* STENCHIER, STENCHIEST having a stench
STENCIL	*v* -CILED, -CILING, -CILS or -CILLED, -CILLING, -CILS to mark by means of a perforated sheet of material
STENGAH	*n* pl. -S a mixed drink
STENO	*n* pl. STENOS a stenographer
STENOKY	*n* pl. -KIES the ability of an organism to live only under a narrow range of conditions
STENOSED	*adj* affected with stenosis
STENOSIS	*n* pl. -NOSES a narrowing of a bodily passage **STENOTIC** *adj*
STENTOR	*n* pl. -S a person having a very loud voice
STEP	*v* STEPPED, STEPPING, STEPS to move by lifting the foot and setting it down in another place
STEPDAME	*n* pl. -S a stepmother
STEPLIKE	*adj* resembling a stair
STEPPE	*n* pl. -S a vast treeless plain
STEPPED	past tense of step
STEPPER	*n* pl. -S one that steps
STEPPING	present participle of step
STEPSON	*n* pl. -S a son of one's spouse by a former marriage
STEPWISE	*adj* marked by a gradual progression
STERE	*n* pl. -S a unit of volume
STEREO	*v* -ED, -ING, -S to make a type of printing plate
STERIC	*adj* pertaining to the spatial relationships of atoms in a molecule
STERICAL	*adj* steric
STERIGMA	*n* pl. -MAS or -MATA a spore-bearing stalk of certain fungi
STERILE	*adj* incapable of producing offspring
STERLET	*n* pl. -S a small sturgeon
STERLING	*n* pl. -S British money
STERN	*adj* STERNER, STERNEST unyielding
STERN	*n* pl. -S the rear part of a ship
STERNA	a pl. of sternum
STERNAL	*adj* pertaining to the sternum
STERNITE	*n* pl. -S a somitic sclerite
STERNLY	*adv* in a stern manner
STERNSON	*n* pl. -S a reinforcing post of a ship
STERNUM	*n* pl. -NA or -NUMS a long, flat supporting bone of most vertebrates
STERNWAY	*n* pl. -WAYS the backward movement of a vessel
STEROID	*n* pl. -S a type of chemical compound
STEROL	*n* pl. -S a type of solid alcohol
STERTOR	*n* pl. -S a deep snoring sound

STET	v STETTED, STETTING, STETS to cancel a previously made printing correction	**STIFFISH**	adj somewhat stiff
STEW	v -ED, -ING, -S to cook by boiling slowly	**STIFFLY**	adv in a stiff manner
STEWARD	v -ED, -ING, -S to manage	**STIFLE**	v -FLED, -FLING, -FLES to smother
STEWBUM	n pl. -S a drunken bum	**STIFLER**	n pl. -S one that stifles
STEWPAN	n pl. -S a pan used for stewing	**STIGMA**	n pl. -MAS or -MATA a mark of disgrace **STIGMAL** adj
STEY	adj steep	**STILBENE**	n pl. -S a chemical compound
STHENIA	n pl. -S excessive energy **STHENIC** adj	**STILBITE**	n pl. -S a mineral
STIBIAL	adj pertaining to stibium	**STILE**	n pl. -S a series of steps for passing over a fence or wall
STIBINE	n pl. -S a poisonous gas	**STILETTO**	v -ED, -ING, -S or -ES to stab with a stiletto (a short dagger)
STIBIUM	n pl. -S antimony	**STILL**	adj STILLER, STILLEST free from sound or motion
STIBNITE	n pl. -S an ore of antimony		
STICH	n pl. -S a line of poetry **STICHIC** adj	**STILL**	v -ED, -ING, -S to make still
		STILLMAN	n pl. -MEN one who operates a distillery
STICK	v -ED, -ING, -S to support with slender pieces of wood	**STILLY**	adj STILLIER, STILLIEST still
STICK	v STUCK, STICKING, STICKS to pierce with a pointed object	**STILT**	v -ED, -ING, -S to raise on stilts (long, slender poles)
STICKER	n pl. -S an adhesive label	**STIME**	n pl. -S a glimpse
STICKFUL	n pl. -S an amount of set type	**STIMULUS**	n pl. -LI something that causes a response
STICKIER	comparative of sticky		
STICKIEST	superlative of sticky	**STIMY**	v -MIED, -MYING, -MIES to stymie
STICKILY	adv in a sticky manner	**STING**	v STUNG, STINGING, STINGS to prick painfully
STICKIT	adj unsuccessful		
STICKLE	v -LED, -LING, -LES to argue stubbornly	**STINGER**	n pl. -S one that stings
STICKLER	n pl. -S one that stickles	**STINGIER**	comparative of stingy
STICKMAN	n pl. -MEN one who supervises the play at a dice table	**STINGIEST**	superlative of stingy
		STINGILY	adv in a stingy manner
STICKOUT	n pl. -S one that is conspicuous	**STINGO**	n pl. -GOS a strong ale or beer
STICKPIN	n pl. -S a decorative tiepin	**STINGRAY**	n pl. -RAYS a flat-bodied marine fish
STICKUM	n pl. -S a substance that causes adhesion	**STINGY**	adj -GIER, -GIEST unwilling to spend or give
STICKUP	n pl. -S a robbery at gunpoint		
STICKY	adj STICKIER, STICKIEST tending to adhere	**STINK**	v STANK or STUNK, STINKING, STINKS to emit a foul odor
STICTION	n pl. -S the force required to begin to move a body that is in contact with another body	**STINKARD**	n pl. -S a despicable person
		STINKBUG	n pl. -S an insect that emits a foul odor
STIED	a past tense of sty	**STINKER**	n pl. -S one that stinks
STIES	present 3d person sing. of sty	**STINKIER**	comparative of stinky
STIFF	adj STIFFER, STIFFEST difficult to bend or stretch	**STINKIEST**	superlative of stinky
		STINKO	adj drunk
STIFF	v -ED, -ING, -S to cheat someone by not paying	**STINKPOT**	n pl. -S a jar containing foul-smelling combustibles formerly used in warfare
STIFFEN	v -ED, -ING, -S to make stiff		

STINKY   *adj* STINKIER, STINKIEST emitting a foul odor

STINT   *v* -ED, -ING, -S to limit

STINTER   *n* pl. -S one that stints

STIPE   *n* pl. -S a slender supporting part of a plant **STIPED** *adj*

STIPEL   *n* pl. -S a small stipule

STIPEND   *n* pl. -S a fixed sum of money paid periodically

STIPES   *n* pl. STIPITES a stipe

STIPPLE   *v* -PLED, -PLING, -PLES to draw, paint, or engrave by means of dots or short touches

STIPPLER   *n* pl. -S one that stipples

STIPULE   *n* pl. -S an appendage at the base of a leaf in certain plants **STIPULAR, STIPULED** *adj*

STIR   *v* STIRRED, STIRRING, STIRS to pass an implement through in circular motions

STIRK   *n* pl. -S a young cow

STIRP   *n* pl. -S lineage

STIRPS   *n* pl. STIRPES a family or branch of a family

STIRRED   past tense of stir

STIRRER   *n* pl. -S one that stirs

STIRRING   present participle of stir

STIRRUP   *n* pl. -S a support for the foot of a horseman

STITCH   *v* -ED, -ING, -ES to join by making in-and-out movements with a threaded needle

STITCHER   *n* pl. -S one that stitches

STITHY   *v* STITHIED, STITHYING, STITHIES to forge on an anvil

STIVER   *n* pl. -S a former Dutch coin

STOA   *n* pl. STOAE, STOAI, or STOAS an ancient Greek covered walkway

STOAT   *n* pl. -S a weasel with a black-tipped tail

STOB   *v* STOBBED, STOBBING, STOBS to stab

STOCCADO   *n* pl. -DOS a thrust with a rapier

STOCCATA   *n* pl. -S stoccado

STOCK   *v* -ED, -ING, -S to keep for future sale or use

STOCKADE   *v* -ADED, -ADING, -ADES to build a type of protective fence around

STOCKCAR   *n* pl. -S a boxcar for carrying livestock

STOCKER   *n* pl. -S a young animal suitable for being fattened for market

STOCKIER   comparative of stocky

STOCKIEST   superlative of stocky

STOCKILY   *adv* in a stocky manner

STOCKING   *n* pl. -S a knitted or woven covering for the foot and leg

STOCKISH   *adj* stupid

STOCKIST   *n* pl. -S one who stocks goods

STOCKMAN   *n* pl. -MEN one who owns or raises livestock

STOCKPOT   *n* pl. -S a pot in which broth is prepared

STOCKY   *adj* STOCKIER, STOCKIEST having a short, thick body

STODGE   *v* STODGED, STODGING, STODGES to stuff full with food

STODGY   *adj* STODGIER, STODGIEST boring **STODGILY** *adv*

STOGEY   *n* pl. -GEYS stogy

STOGIE   *n* pl. -S stogy

STOGY   *n* pl. -GIES a long, slender cigar

STOIC   *n* pl. -S one who is indifferent to pleasure or pain **STOICAL** *adj*

STOICISM   *n* pl. -S indifference to pleasure or pain

STOKE   *v* STOKED, STOKING, STOKES to supply a furnace with fuel

STOKER   *n* pl. -S one that stokes

STOKESIA   *n* pl. -S a perennial herb

STOKING   present participle of stoke

STOLE   *n* pl. -S a long-wide scarf **STOLED** *adj*

STOLEN   past participle of steal

STOLID   *adj* -IDER, -IDEST showing little or no emotion **STOLIDLY** *adv*

STOLLEN   *n* pl. -S a sweet bread

STOLON   *n* pl. -S a type of plant stem **STOLONIC** *adj*

STOLPORT   *n* pl. -S an airport for aircraft needing comparatively short runways

STOMA   *n* pl. -MAS or -MATA a minute opening in the epidermis of a plant organ

STOMACH   *v* -ED, -ING, -S to tolerate

STOMACHY   *adj* paunchy

STOMAL   *adj* stomatal

STOMATA	a pl. of stoma	**STOPPED**	a past tense of stop
STOMATAL	*adj* pertaining to a stoma	**STOPPER**	*v* -ED, -ING, -S to plug
STOMATE	*n* pl. -S a stoma	**STOPPING**	present participle of stop
STOMATIC	*adj* pertaining to the mouth	**STOPPLE**	*v* -PLED, -PLING, -PLES to stopper
STOMODEA	*n/pl* embryonic oral cavities	**STOPT**	a past tense of stop
STOMP	*v* -ED, -ING, -S to tread heavily	**STORABLE**	*n* pl. -S something that can be stored
STOMPER	*n* pl. -S one that stomps	**STORAGE**	*n* pl. -S a place for storing
STONE	*v* STONED, STONING, STONES to pelt with stones (pieces of concreted earthy or mineral matter) **STONABLE** *adj*	**STORAX**	*n* pl. -ES a fragrant resin
		STORE	*v* STORED, STORING, STORES to put away for future use
STONEFLY	*n* pl. -FLIES a winged insect	**STOREY**	*n* pl. -REYS a horizontal division of a building **STOREYED** *adj*
STONER	*n* pl. -S one that stones		
STONEY	*adj* STONIER, STONIEST stony	**STORIED**	past tense of story
STONIER	comparative of stony	**STORIES**	present 3d person sing. of story
STONIEST	superlative of stony	**STORING**	present participle of store
STONILY	*adv* in a stony manner	**STORK**	*n* pl. -S a wading bird
STONING	present participle of stone	**STORM**	*v* -ED, -ING, -S to blow violently
STONISH	*v* -ED, -ING, -ES to astonish	**STORMY**	*adj* STORMIER, STORMIEST storming **STORMILY** *adv*
STONY	*adj* STONIER, STONIEST abounding in stones		
STOOD	past tense of stand	**STORY**	*v* -RIED, -RYING, -RIES to relate as a story (an account of an event or series of events)
STOOGE	*v* STOOGED, STOOGING, STOOGES to act as a comedian's straight man		
		STOSS	*adj* facing the direction from which a glacier moves
STOOK	*v* -ED, -ING, -S to stack upright in a field for drying, as bundles of grain	**STOTINKA**	*n* pl. -KI a monetary unit of Bulgaria
		STOUND	*v* -ED, -ING, -S to ache
STOOKER	*n* pl. -S one that stooks	**STOUP**	*n* pl. -S a basin for holy water
STOOL	*v* -ED, -ING, -S to defecate	**STOUR**	*n* pl. -S dust
STOOLIE	*n* pl. -S an informer	**STOURE**	*n* pl. -S stour
STOOP	*v* -ED, -ING, -S to bend the body forward and down	**STOURIE**	*adj* stoury
		STOURY	*adj* dusty
STOOPER	*n* pl. -S one that stoops	**STOUT**	*adj* STOUTER, STOUTEST fat
STOP	*v* STOPPED or STOPT, STOPPING, STOPS to discontinue the progress or motion of	**STOUT**	*n* pl. -S a strong, dark ale
		STOUTEN	*v* -ED, -ING, -S to make stout
		STOUTISH	*adj* somewhat stout
STOPBANK	*n* pl. -S an embankment along a river	**STOUTLY**	*adv* in a stout manner
		STOVE	*n* pl. -S a heating apparatus
STOPCOCK	*n* pl. -S a type of faucet	**STOVER**	*n* pl. -S coarse food for cattle
STOPE	*v* STOPED, STOPING, STOPES to excavate in layers, as ore	**STOW**	*v* -ED, -ING, -S to pack **STOWABLE** *adj*
STOPER	*n* pl. -S one that stopes		
STOPGAP	*n* pl. -S a temporary substitute	**STOWAGE**	*n* pl. -S goods in storage
STOPING	present participle of stope	**STOWAWAY**	*n* pl. -AWAYS one who hides aboard a conveyance to obtain free passage
STOPOVER	*n* pl. -S a brief stop in the course of a journey		
		STOWP	*n* pl. -S stoup
STOPPAGE	*n* pl. -S the act of stopping		

STRADDLE	*v* -DLED, -DLING, -DLES to sit, stand, or walk with the legs wide apart	**STRATI**	pl. of stratus
STRAFE	*v* STRAFED, STRAFING, STRAFES to attack with machine-gun fire from an airplane	**STRATIFY**	*v* -FIED, -FYING, -FIES to form or arrange in layers
		STRATOUS	*adj* stratal
STRAFER	*n* pl. -S one that strafes	**STRATUM**	*n* pl. -TA or -TUMS a layer of material
STRAGGLE	*v* -GLED, -GLING, -GLES to stray	**STRATUS**	*n* pl. -TI a type of cloud
STRAGGLY	*adj* -GLIER, -GLIEST irregularly spread out	**STRAVAGE**	*v* -VAGED, -VAGING, -VAGES to stroll
STRAIGHT	*adj* STRAIGHTER, STRAIGHTEST extending uniformly in one direction without bends or irregularities	**STRAVAIG**	*v* -ED, -ING, -S to stravage
		STRAW	*v* -ED, -ING, -S to cover with straw (stalks of threshed grain)
STRAIGHT	*v* -ED, -ING, -S to make straight	**STRAWHAT**	*adj* pertaining to a summer theater situated in a resort area
STRAIN	*v* -ED, -ING, -S to exert to the utmost	**STRAWY**	*adj* STRAWIER, STRAWIEST resembling straw
STRAINER	*n* pl. -S a utensil used to separate liquids from solids	**STRAY**	*v* -ED, -ING, -S to wander from the proper area or course
STRAIT	*n* pl. -S a narrow waterway connecting two larger bodies of water	**STRAYER**	*n* pl. -S one that strays
		STREAK	*v* -ED, -ING, -S to cover with streaks (long, narrow marks)
STRAIT	*adj* STRAITER, STRAITEST narrow **STRAITLY** *adv*	**STREAKER**	*n* pl. -S one that streaks
STRAITEN	*v* -ED, -ING, -S to make strait	**STREAKY**	*adj* STREAKIER, STREAKIEST covered with streaks
STRAKE	*n* pl. -S a line of planking extending along a ship's hull **STRAKED** *adj*	**STREAM**	*v* -ED, -ING, -S to flow in a steady current
STRAMASH	*n* pl. -ES an uproar	**STREAMER**	*n* pl. -S a long, narrow flag
STRAMONY	*n* pl. -NIES a poisonous weed	**STREAMY**	*adj* STREAMIER, STREAMIEST streaming
STRAND	*v* -ED, -ING, -S to leave in an unfavorable situation	**STREEK**	*v* -ED, -ING, -S to stretch
		STREEKER	*n* pl. -S one that streeks
STRANDER	*n* pl. -S a machine that twists fibers into rope	**STREEL**	*v* -ED, -ING, -S to saunter
STRANG	*adj* strong	**STREET**	*n* pl. -S a public thoroughfare
STRANGE	*adj* STRANGER, STRANGEST unusual or unfamiliar	**STRENGTH**	*n* pl. -S capacity for exertion or endurance
STRANGER	*v* -ED, -ING, -S to estrange	**STREP**	*n* pl. -S any of various spherical or oval bacteria
STRANGLE	*v* -GLED, -GLING, -GLES to choke to death	**STRESS**	*v* -ED, -ING, -ES to place emphasis on
STRAP	*v* STRAPPED, STRAPPING, STRAPS to fasten with a strap (a narrow strip of flexible material)	**STRESSOR**	*n* pl. -S a type of stimulus
		STRETCH	*v* -ED, -ING, -ES to draw out or open to full length
STRAPPER	*n* pl. -S one that straps	**STRETCHY**	*adj* STRETCHIER, STRETCHIEST having a tendency to stretch
STRASS	*n* pl. -ES a brilliant glass used in making imitation gems	
STRATA	*n* pl. -S a stratum	**STRETTA**	*n* pl. -TE or -TAS stretto
STRATAL	*adj* pertaining to a stratum	**STRETTO**	*n* pl. -TI or -TOS a concluding musical passage played at a faster tempo
STRATEGY	*n* pl. -GIES a plan for obtaining a specific goal	
STRATH	*n* pl. -S a wide river valley	**STREUSEL**	*n* pl. -S a topping for coffee cakes

STREW	*v* STREWED, STREWN, STREWING, STREWS to scatter about
STREWER	*n* pl. -S one that strews
STRIA	*n* pl. STRIAE a thin groove, stripe, or streak
STRIATE	*v* -ATED, -ATING, -ATES to mark with striae
STRICK	*n* pl. -S a bunch of flax fibers
STRICKEN	*adj* strongly affected or afflicted
STRICKLE	*v* -LED, -LING, -LES to shape or smooth with a strickle (an instrument for leveling off grain)
STRICT	*adj* STRICTER, STRICTEST kept within narrow and specific limits **STRICTLY** *adv*
STRIDE	*v* STRODE, STRIDDEN, STRIDING, STRIDES to walk with long steps
STRIDENT	*adj* shrill
STRIDER	*n* pl. -S one that strides
STRIDING	present participle of stride
STRIDOR	*n* pl. -S a strident sound
STRIFE	*n* pl. -S bitter conflict or dissension
STRIGIL	*n* pl. -S a scraping instrument
STRIGOSE	*adj* covered with short, stiff hairs
STRIKE	*v* STRUCK or STROOK, STRICKEN or STRUCKEN, STRIKING, STRIKES to come or cause to come into contact with
STRIKER	*n* pl. -S one that strikes
STRING	*v* STRUNG or STRINGED, STRINGING, STRINGS to provide with strings (slender cords)
STRINGER	*n* pl. -S one that strings
STRINGY	*adj* STRINGIER, STRINGIEST resembling a string or strings
STRIP	*v* STRIPPED or STRIPT, STRIPPING, STRIPS to remove the outer covering from
STRIPE	*v* STRIPED, STRIPING, STRIPES to mark with stripes (long, distinct bands)
STRIPER	*n* pl. -S a food and game fish
STRIPIER	comparative of stripy
STRIPIEST	superlative of stripy
STRIPING	*n* pl. -S the stripes marked or painted on something
STRIPPED	a past tense of strip
STRIPPER	*n* pl. -S one that strips
STRIPPING	present participle of strip
STRIPT	a past tense of strip
STRIPY	*adj* STRIPIER, STRIPIEST marked with stripes
STRIVE	*v* STROVE or STRIVED, STRIVEN, STRIVING, STRIVES to exert much effort or energy
STRIVER	*n* pl. -S one that strives
STROBE	*n* pl. -S a device that produces brief, high-intensity flashes of light
STROBIC	*adj* spinning
STROBIL	*n* pl. -S strobile
STROBILA	*n* pl. -LAE the entire body of a tapeworm
STROBILE	*n* pl. -S the conical, multiple fruit of certain trees
STROBILI	*n/pl* strobiles
STRODE	a past tense of stride
STROKE	*v* STROKED, STROKING, STROKES to rub gently
STROKER	*n* pl. -S one that strokes
STROLL	*v* -ED, -ING, -S to walk in a leisurely manner
STROLLER	*n* pl. -S one that strolls
STROMA	*n* pl. -MATA the substance that forms the framework of an organ or cell **STROMAL** *adj*
STRONG	*adj* STRONGER, STRONGEST having great strength **STRONGLY** *adv*
STRONGYL	*n* pl. -S a parasitic worm
STRONTIA	*n* pl. -S a chemical compound **STRONTIC** *adj*
STROOK	a past tense of strike
STROP	*v* STROPPED, STROPPING, STROPS to sharpen on a strip of leather
STROPHE	*n* pl. -S a part of an ancient Greek choral ode **STROPHIC** *adj*
STROPPER	*n* pl. -S one that strops
STROPPY	*adj* -PIER, -PIEST unruly
STROUD	*n* pl. -S a coarse woolen blanket
STROVE	a past tense of strive
STROW	*v* STROWED, STROWN, STROWING, STROWS to strew
STROY	*v* -ED, -ING, -S to destroy
STROYER	*n* pl. -S one that stroys
STRUCK	a past tense of strike
STRUCKEN	a past participle of strike

STRUDEL   *n* pl. -S a type of pastry

STRUGGLE   *v* -GLED, -GLING, -GLES to make strenuous efforts against opposition

STRUM   *v* STRUMMED, STRUMMING, STRUMS to play a stringed instrument by running the fingers lightly across the strings

STRUMA   *n* pl. -MAE or -MAS scrofula

STRUMMER   *n* pl. -S one that strums

STRUMMING present participle of strum

STRUMOSE   *adj* having a struma

STRUMOUS   *adj* having or pertaining to a struma

STRUMPET   *n* pl. -S a prostitute

STRUNG   a past tense of string

STRUNT   *v* -ED, -ING, -S to strut

STRUT   *v* STRUTTED, STRUTTING, STRUTS to walk with a pompous air

STRUTTER   *n* pl. -S one that struts

STUB   *v* STUBBED, STUBBING, STUBS to strike accidentally against a projecting object

STUBBIER   comparative of stubby

STUBBIEST   superlative of stubby

STUBBILY   *adv* in a stubby manner

STUBBING   present participle of stub

STUBBLE   *n* pl. -S a short, rough growth of beard **STUBBLED** *adj*

STUBBLY   *adj* -BLIER, -BLIEST covered with stubble

STUBBORN   *adj* unyielding

STUBBY   *adj* -BIER, -BIEST short and thick

STUCCO   *v* -ED, -ING, -ES or -S to coat with a type of plaster

STUCCOER   *n* pl. -S one that stuccoes

STUCK   past tense of stick

STUD   *v* STUDDED, STUDDING, STUDS to set thickly with small projections

STUDBOOK   *n* pl. -S a record of the pedigree of purebred animals

STUDDIE   *n* pl. -S an anvil

STUDDING   *n* pl. -S the framework of a wall

STUDENT   *n* pl. -S a person formally engaged in learning

STUDFISH   *n* pl. -ES a freshwater fish

STUDIED   past tense of study

STUDIER   *n* pl. -S one that studies

STUDIES   present 3d person sing. of study

STUDIO   *n* pl. -DIOS an artist's workroom

STUDIOUS   *adj* given to study

STUDLY   *adj* -LIER, -LIEST muscular and attractive

STUDWORK   *n* pl. -S studding

STUDY   *v* STUDIED, STUDYING, STUDIES to apply the mind to the acquisition of knowledge

STUFF   *v* -ED, -ING, -S to fill or pack tightly

STUFFER   *n* pl. -S one that stuffs

STUFFING   *n* pl. -S material with which something is stuffed

STUFFY   *adj* STUFFIER, STUFFIEST poorly ventilated **STUFFILY** *adv*

STUIVER   *n* pl. -S stiver

STULL   *n* pl. -S a supporting timber in a mine

STULTIFY   *v* -FIED, -FYING, -FIES to cause to appear absurd

STUM   *v* STUMMED, STUMMING, STUMS to increase the fermentation of by adding grape juice

STUMBLE   *v* -BLED, -BLING, -BLES to miss one's step in walking or running

STUMBLER   *n* pl. -S one that stumbles

STUMMED   past tense of stum

STUMMING   present participle of stum

STUMP   *v* -ED, -ING, -S to baffle

STUMPAGE   *n* pl. -S uncut marketable timber

STUMPER   *n* pl. -S a baffling question

STUMPY   *adj* STUMPIER, STUMPIEST short and thick

STUN   *v* STUNNED, STUNNING, STUNS to render senseless or incapable of action

STUNG   past tense of sting

STUNK   a past tense of stink

STUNNED   past tense of stun

STUNNER   *n* pl. -S one that stuns

STUNNING   *adj* strikingly beautiful or attractive

STUNSAIL   *n* pl. -S a type of sail

STUNT   *v* -ED, -ING, -S to hinder the normal growth of

STUNTMAN	*n* pl. -MEN a person who substitutes for an actor in scenes involving dangerous activities	**STYLUS**	*n* pl. -LI or -LUSES a pointed instrument for writing, marking, or engraving
STUPA	*n* pl. -S a Buddhist shrine	**STYMIE**	*v* -MIED, -MIEING, -MIES to thwart
STUPE	*n* pl. -S a medicated cloth to be applied to a wound	**STYMY**	*v* -MIED, -MYING, -MIES to stymie
STUPEFY	*v* -FIED, -FYING, -FIES to dull the senses of	**STYPSIS**	*n* pl. -SISES the use of a styptic
STUPID	*adj* -PIDER, -PIDEST mentally slow **STUPIDLY** *adv*	**STYPTIC**	*n* pl. -S a substance used to check bleeding
STUPID	*n* pl. -S a stupid person	**STYRAX**	*n* pl. -ES storax
STUPOR	*n* pl. -S a state of reduced sensibility	**STYRENE**	*n* pl. -S a liquid hydrocarbon
STURDY	*adj* -DIER, -DIEST strong and durable **STURDILY** *adv*	**SUABLE**	*adj* capable of being sued **SUABLY** *adv*
STURDY	*n* pl. -DIES a disease of sheep **STURDIED** *adj*	**SUASION**	*n* pl. -S persuasion **SUASIVE, SUASORY** *adj*
STURGEON	*n* pl. -S an edible fish	**SUAVE**	*adj* SUAVER, SUAVEST smoothly affable and polite **SUAVELY** *adv*
STURT	*n* pl. -S contention		
STUTTER	*v* -ED, -ING, -S to speak with spasmodic repetition	**SUAVITY**	*n* pl. -TIES the state of being suave
STY	*v* STIED or STYED, STYING, STIES to keep in a pigpen	**SUB**	*v* SUBBED, SUBBING, SUBS to act as a substitute
STYE	*n* pl. -S an inflamed swelling of the eyelid	**SUBA**	*n* pl. -S subah
STYGIAN	*adj* gloomy	**SUBABBOT**	*n* pl. -S a subordinate abbot
STYLAR	*adj* pertaining to a stylus	**SUBACID**	*adj* slightly sour
STYLATE	*adj* bearing a stylet	**SUBACRID**	*adj* somewhat acrid
STYLE	*v* STYLED, STYLING, STYLES to name	**SUBACUTE**	*adj* somewhat acute
		SUBADAR	*n* pl. -S subahdar
STYLER	*n* pl. -S one that styles	**SUBADULT**	*n* pl. -S an individual approaching adulthood
STYLET	*n* pl. -S a small, stiff organ or appendage of certain animals	**SUBAGENT**	*n* pl. -S a subordinate agent
STYLI	a pl. of stylus	**SUBAH**	*n* pl. -S a province of India
STYLING	*n* pl. -S the way in which something is styled	**SUBAHDAR**	*n* pl. -S a governor of a subah
		SUBALAR	*adj* somewhat alar
STYLISE	*v* -ISED, -ISING, -ISES to stylize	**SUBAREA**	*n* pl. -S a subdivision of an area
STYLISER	*n* pl. -S one that stylises	**SUBARID**	*adj* somewhat arid
STYLISH	*adj* fashionable	**SUBATOM**	*n* pl. -S a component of an atom
STYLISING	present participle of stylise	**SUBAXIAL**	*adj* somewhat axial
STYLIST	*n* pl. -S one who is a master of a literary or rhetorical style	**SUBBASE**	*n* pl. -S the lowest part of a base
STYLITE	*n* pl. -S an early Christian ascetic **STYLITIC** *adj*	**SUBBASIN**	*n* pl. -S a section of an area drained by a river
		SUBBASS	*n* pl. -ES a pedal stop producing the lowest tones of an organ
STYLIZE	*v* -IZED, -IZING, -IZES to make conventional	**SUBBED**	past tense of sub
STYLIZER	*n* pl. -S one that stylizes	**SUBBING**	*n* pl. -S a thin coating on the support of a photographic film
STYLOID	*adj* slender and pointed	**SUBBLOCK**	*n* pl. -S a subdivision of a block

SUBBREED *n* pl. -S a distinguishable strain within a breed

SUBCASTE *n* pl. -S a subdivision of a caste

SUBCAUSE *n* pl. -S a subordinate cause

SUBCELL *n* pl. -S a subdivision of a cell

SUBCHIEF *n* pl. -S a subordinate chief

SUBCLAN *n* pl. -S a subdivision of a clan

SUBCLASS *v* -ED, -ING, -ES to place in a subdivision of a class

SUBCLERK *n* pl. -S a subordinate clerk

SUBCODE *n* pl. -S a subdivision of a code

SUBCOOL *v* -ED, -ING, -S to cool below the freezing point without solidification

SUBCULT *n* pl. -S a subdivision of a cult

SUBCUTIS *n* pl. -CUTES or -CUTISES the deeper part of the dermis

SUBDEAN *n* pl. -S a subordinate dean

SUBDEB *n* pl. -S a girl the year before she becomes a debutante

SUBDEPOT *n* pl. -S a military depot that operates under the jurisdiction of another depot

SUBDUAL *n* pl. -S the act of subduing

SUBDUCE *v* -DUCED, -DUCING, -DUCES to take away

SUBDUCT *v* -ED, -ING, -S to subduce

SUBDUE *v* -DUED, -DUING, -DUES to bring under control

SUBDUER *n* pl. -S one that subdues

SUBDURAL *adj* situated under the dura mater

SUBECHO *n* pl. -ECHOES an inferior echo

SUBEDIT *v* -ED, -ING, -S to act as the assistant editor of

SUBENTRY *n* pl. -TRIES an entry made under a more general entry

SUBEPOCH *n* pl. -S a subdivision of an epoch

SUBER *n* pl. -S phellem

SUBERECT *adj* nearly erect

SUBERIC *adj* pertaining to cork

SUBERIN *n* pl. -S a substance found in cork cells

SUBERISE *v* -ISED, -ISING, -ISES to suberize

SUBERIZE *v* -IZED, -IZING, -IZES to convert into cork tissue

SUBEROSE *adj* corky

SUBEROUS *adj* suberose

SUBFIELD *n* pl. -S a subset of a mathematical field that is itself a field

SUBFILE *n* pl. -S a subdivision of a file

SUBFIX *n* pl. -ES a distinguishing symbol or letter written below another character

SUBFLOOR *n* pl. -S a rough floor laid as a base for a finished floor

SUBFLUID *adj* somewhat fluid

SUBFRAME *n* pl. -S a frame for the attachment of a finish frame

SUBFUSC *adj* dark in color

SUBGENRE *n* pl. -S a subdivision of a genre

SUBGENUS *n* pl. -GENERA or -GENUSES a subdivision of a genus

SUBGOAL *n* pl. -S a subordinate goal

SUBGRADE *n* pl. -S a surface on which a pavement is placed

SUBGRAPH *n* pl. -S a graph contained within a larger graph

SUBGROUP *n* pl. -S a distinct group within a group

SUBGUM *n* pl. -S a Chinese dish of mixed vegetables

SUBHEAD *n* pl. -S the heading of a subdivision

SUBHUMAN *n* pl. -S one that is less than human

SUBHUMID *adj* somewhat humid

SUBIDEA *n* pl. -S an inferior idea

SUBINDEX *n* pl. -DEXES or -DICES a subfix

SUBITEM *n* pl. -S an item that forms a subdivision of a larger topic

SUBITO *adv* quickly — used as a musical direction

SUBJECT *v* -ED, -ING, -S to cause to experience

SUBJOIN *v* -ED, -ING, -S to add at the end

SUBLATE *v* -LATED, -LATING, -LATES to cancel

SUBLEASE *v* -LEASED, -LEASING, -LEASES to sublet

SUBLET *v* -LET, -LETTING, -LETS to rent leased property to another

SUBLEVEL *n* pl. -S a lower level

SUBLIME *adj* -LIMER, -LIMEST of elevated or noble quality

SUBLIME *v* -LIMED, -LIMING, -LIMES to make sublime

SUBLIMER *n* pl. -S one that sublimes

SUBLIMEST	superlative of sublime
SUBLIMING	present participle of sublime
SUBLINE	*n* pl. -S an inbred line within a strain
SUBLOT	*n* pl. -S a subdivision of a lot
SUBLUNAR	*adj* pertaining to the earth
SUBMENU	*n* pl. -S a secondary list of options for a computer
SUBMERGE	*v* -MERGED, -MERGING, -MERGES to place below the surface of a liquid
SUBMERSE	*v* -MERSED, -MERSING, -MERSES to submerge
SUBMISS	*adj* inclined to submit
SUBMIT	*v* -MITTED, -MITTING, -MITS to yield to the power of another
SUBNASAL	*adj* situated under the nose
SUBNET	*n* pl. -S a system of interconnections within a communications system
SUBNICHE	*n* pl. -S a subdivision of a habitat
SUBNODAL	*adj* situated under a node
SUBOPTIC	*adj* situated under the eyes
SUBORAL	*adj* situated under the mouth
SUBORDER	*n* pl. -S a category of related families within an order
SUBORN	*v* -ED, -ING, -S to induce to commit perjury
SUBORNER	*n* pl. -S one that suborns
SUBOVAL	*adj* nearly oval
SUBOVATE	*adj* nearly ovate
SUBOXIDE	*n* pl. -S an oxide containing relatively little oxygen
SUBPANEL	*n* pl. -S a subdivision of a panel
SUBPAR	*adj* below par
SUBPART	*n* pl. -S a subdivision of a part
SUBPENA	*v* -ED, -ING, -S to subpoena
SUBPHASE	*n* pl. -S a subdivision of a phase
SUBPHYLA	*n/pl* divisions within a phylum
SUBPLOT	*n* pl. -S a secondary literary plot
SUBPOENA	*v* -ED, -ING, -S to summon with a type of judicial writ
SUBPOLAR	*adj* situated just outside the polar circles
SUBPUBIC	*adj* situated under the pubis
SUBRACE	*n* pl. -S a subdivision of a race
SUBRENT	*n* pl. -S rent from a subtenant
SUBRING	*n* pl. -S a subset of a mathematical ring that is itself a ring
SUBRULE	*n* pl. -S a subordinate rule
SUBSALE	*n* pl. -S a resale of purchased goods
SUBSCALE	*n* pl. -S a subdivision of a scale
SUBSEA	*adj* situated below the surface of the sea
SUBSECT	*n* pl. -S a sect directly derived from another
SUBSENSE	*n* pl. -S a subdivision of a sense
SUBSERE	*n* pl. -S a type of ecological succession
SUBSERVE	*v* -SERVED, -SERVING, -SERVES to serve to promote
SUBSET	*n* pl. -S a mathematical set contained within a larger set
SUBSHAFT	*n* pl. -S a shaft that is beneath another shaft
SUBSHELL	*n* pl. -S one of the orbitals making up an electron shell of an atom
SUBSHRUB	*n* pl. -S a low shrub
SUBSIDE	*v* -SIDED, -SIDING, -SIDES to sink to a lower or normal level
SUBSIDER	*n* pl. -S one that subsides
SUBSIDY	*n* pl. -DIES a grant or contribution of money
SUBSIST	*v* -ED, -ING, -S to continue to exist
SUBSITE	*n* pl. -S a subdivision of a site
SUBSKILL	*n* pl. -S a subordinate skill
SUBSOIL	*v* -ED, -ING, -S to plow so as to turn up the subsoil (the layer of earth beneath the surface soil)
SUBSOLAR	*adj* situated directly beneath the sun
SUBSONIC	*adj* moving at a speed less than that of sound
SUBSPACE	*n* pl. -S a subset of a mathematical space
SUBSTAGE	*n* pl. -S a part of a microscope for supporting accessories
SUBSTATE	*n* pl. -S a subdivision of a state
SUBSUME	*v* -SUMED, -SUMING, -SUMES to include within a larger group
SUBTASK	*n* pl. -S a subordinate task
SUBTAXON	*n* pl. -TAXA or -TAXONS a subdivision of a taxon
SUBTEEN	*n* pl. -S a person approaching the teenage years

SUBTEND	v -ED, -ING, -S to extend under or opposite to
SUBTEST	n pl. -S a subdivision of a test
SUBTEXT	n pl. -S written or printed matter under a more general text
SUBTHEME	n pl. -S a subordinate theme
SUBTILE	adj -TILER, -TILEST subtle
SUBTILIN	n pl. -S an antibiotic
SUBTILTY	n pl. -TIES subtlety
SUBTITLE	v -TLED, -TLING, -TLES to give a secondary title to
SUBTLE	adj -TLER, -TLEST so slight as to be difficult to detect **SUBTLY** adv
SUBTLETY	n pl. -TIES the state of being subtle
SUBTONE	n pl. -S a low or subdued tone
SUBTONIC	n pl. -S a type of musical tone
SUBTOPIA	n pl. -S the suburbs of a city
SUBTOPIC	n pl. -S a secondary topic
SUBTOTAL	v -TALED, -TALING, -TALS or -TALLED, -TALLING, -TALS to total a portion of
SUBTRACT	v -ED, -ING, -S to take away
SUBTREND	n pl. -S a subordinate trend
SUBTRIBE	n pl. -S a subdivision of a tribe
SUBTUNIC	n pl. -S a tunic worn under another tunic
SUBTYPE	n pl. -S a type that is subordinate to or included in another type
SUBULATE	adj slender and tapering to a point
SUBUNIT	n pl. -S a unit that is a part of a larger unit
SUBURB	n pl. -S a residential area adjacent to a city **SUBURBED** adj
SUBURBAN	n pl. -S one who lives in a suburb
SUBURBIA	n pl. -S the suburbs of a city
SUBVENE	v -VENED, -VENING, -VENES to arrive or occur as a support or relief
SUBVERT	v -ED, -ING, -S to destroy completely
SUBVICAR	n pl. -S a subordinate vicar
SUBVIRAL	adj pertaining to a part of a virus
SUBVOCAL	adj mentally formulated as words
SUBWAY	v -ED, -ING, -S to travel by an underground railroad
SUBWORLD	n pl. -S a subdivision of a sphere of interest or activity
SUBZERO	adj registering less than zero
SUBZONE	n pl. -S a subdivision of a zone
SUCCAH	n pl. -CAHS or -COTH sukkah
SUCCEED	v -ED, -ING, -S to accomplish something desired or intended
SUCCESS	n pl. -ES the attainment of something desired or intended
SUCCINCT	adj -CINCTER, -CINCTEST clearly expressed in few words
SUCCINIC	adj pertaining to amber
SUCCINYL	n pl. -S a univalent radical
SUCCOR	v -ED, -ING, -S to go to the aid of
SUCCORER	n pl. -S one that succors
SUCCORY	n pl. -RIES chicory
SUCCOTH	a pl. of succah
SUCCOUR	v -ED, -ING, -S to succor
SUCCUBA	n pl. -BAE a succubus
SUCCUBUS	n pl. -BI or -BUSES a female demon
SUCCUMB	v -ED, -ING, -S to yield to superior force
SUCCUSS	v -ED, -ING, -ES to shake violently
SUCH	adj of that kind
SUCHLIKE	adj of a similar kind
SUCHNESS	n pl. -ES essential or characteristic quality
SUCK	v -ED, -ING, -S to draw in by establishing a partial vacuum
SUCKER	v -ED, -ING, -S to strip of lower shoots or branches
SUCKFISH	n pl. -ES a remora
SUCKLE	v -LED, -LING, -LES to give milk to from the breast
SUCKLER	n pl. -S one that suckles
SUCKLESS	adj having no juice
SUCKLING	n pl. -S an unweaned mammal
SUCRASE	n pl. -S an enzyme
SUCRE	n pl. -S a monetary unit of Ecuador
SUCROSE	n pl. -S a type of sugar
SUCTION	v -ED, -ING, -S to remove by the process of sucking
SUDARIUM	n pl. -IA a cloth for wiping the face
SUDARY	n pl. -RIES sudarium
SUDATION	n pl. -S excessive sweating
SUDATORY	n pl. -RIES a hot-air bath for inducing sweating

SUDD	*n* pl. -S a floating mass of vegetation
SUDDEN	*adj* happening quickly and without warning **SUDDENLY** *adv*
SUDDEN	*n* pl. -S a sudden occurrence
SUDOR	*n* pl. -S sweat **SUDORAL** *adj*
SUDS	*v* -ED, -ING, -ES to wash in soapy water
SUDSER	*n* pl. -S one that sudses
SUDSLESS	*adj* having no suds
SUDSY	*adj* SUDSIER, SUDSIEST foamy
SUE	*v* SUED, SUING, SUES to institute legal proceedings against
SUEDE	*v* SUEDED, SUEDING, SUEDES to finish leather with a soft, napped surface
SUER	*n* pl. -S one that sues
SUET	*n* pl. -S the hard, fatty tissue around the kidneys of cattle and sheep **SUETY** *adj*
SUFFARI	*n* pl. -S a safari
SUFFER	*v* -ED, -ING, -S to feel pain or distress
SUFFERER	*n* pl. -S one that suffers
SUFFICE	*v* -FICED, -FICING, -FICES to be adequate
SUFFICER	*n* pl. -S one that suffices
SUFFIX	*v* -ED, -ING, -ES to add as a suffix (a form affixed to the end of a root word)
SUFFIXAL	*adj* pertaining to or being a suffix
SUFFLATE	*v* -FLATED, -FLATING, -FLATES to inflate
SUFFRAGE	*n* pl. -S the right to vote
SUFFUSE	*v* -FUSED, -FUSING, -FUSES to spread through or over
SUGAR	*v* -ED, -ING, -S to cover with sugar (a sweet carbohydrate)
SUGARY	*adj* -ARIER, -ARIEST containing or resembling sugar
SUGGEST	*v* -ED, -ING, -S to bring or put forward for consideration
SUGH	*v* -ED, -ING, -S to sough
SUICIDAL	*adj* self-destructive
SUICIDE	*v* -CIDED, -CIDING, -CIDES to kill oneself intentionally
SUING	present participle of sue
SUINT	*n* pl. -S a natural grease found in the wool of sheep
SUIT	*v* -ED, -ING, -S to be appropriate to
SUITABLE	*adj* appropriate **SUITABLY** *adv*
SUITCASE	*n* pl. -S a flat, rectangular piece of luggage
SUITE	*n* pl. -S a series of things forming a unit
SUITER	*n* pl. -S a suitcase holding a specified number of suits (sets of garments)
SUITING	*n* pl. -S fabric for making suits
SUITLIKE	*adj* resembling a suit (a set of garments)
SUITOR	*n* pl. -S one that is courting a woman
SUKIYAKI	*n* pl. -S a Japanese dish
SUKKAH	*n* pl. -KAHS or -KOTH or -KOT a temporary shelter in which meals are eaten during a Jewish festival
SULCATE	*adj* having long, narrow furrows
SULCATED	*adj* sulcate
SULCUS	*n* pl. -CI a narrow furrow **SULCAL** *adj*
SULDAN	*n* pl. -S soldan
SULFA	*n* pl. -S a bacteria-inhibiting drug
SULFATE	*v* -FATED, -FATING, -FATES to treat with sulfuric acid
SULFID	*n* pl. -S sulfide
SULFIDE	*n* pl. -S a sulfur compound
SULFINYL	*n* pl. -S a bivalent radical
SULFITE	*n* pl. -S a chemical salt **SULFITIC** *adj*
SULFO	*adj* sulfonic
SULFONE	*n* pl. -S a sulfur compound
SULFONIC	*adj* containing a certain univalent radical
SULFONYL	*n* pl. -S a bivalent radical
SULFUR	*v* -ED, -ING, -S to treat with sulfur (a nonmetallic element)
SULFURET	*v* -RETED, -RETING, -RETS or -RETTED, -RETTING, -RETS to treat with sulfur
SULFURIC	*adj* pertaining to sulfur
SULFURY	*adj* resembling sulfur
SULFURYL	*n* pl. -S sulfonyl
SULK	*v* -ED, -ING, -S to be sulky
SULKER	*n* pl. -S one that sulks
SULKY	*adj* SULKIER, SULKIEST sullenly aloof or withdrawn **SULKILY** *adv*

SULKY   *n* pl. SULKIES a light horse-drawn vehicle

SULLAGE   *n* pl. -S sewage

SULLEN   *adj* -LENER, -LENEST showing a brooding ill humor or resentment **SULLENLY** *adv*

SULLY   *v* -LIED, -LYING, -LIES to soil

SULPHA   *n* pl. -S sulfa

SULPHATE   *v* -PHATED, -PHATING, -PHATES to sulfate

SULPHID   *n* pl. -S sulfide

SULPHIDE   *n* pl. -S sulfide

SULPHITE   *n* pl. -S sulfite

SULPHONE   *n* pl. -S sulfone

SULPHUR   *v* -ED, -ING, -S to sulfur

SULPHURY   *adj* sulfury

SULTAN   *n* pl. -S the ruler of a Muslim country **SULTANIC** *adj*

SULTANA   *n* pl. -S a sultan's wife

SULTRY   *adj* -TRIER, -TRIEST very hot and humid **SULTRILY** *adv*

SULU   *n* pl. -S a Melanesian skirt

SUM   *v* SUMMED, SUMMING, SUMS to add into one total

SUMAC   *n* pl. -S a flowering tree or shrub

SUMACH   *n* pl. -S sumac

SUMLESS   *adj* too large for calculation

SUMMA   *n* pl. -MAE or -MAS a comprehensive work on a topic

SUMMABLE   *adj* capable of being summed

SUMMAND   *n* pl. -S an addend

SUMMARY   *n* pl. -RIES a short restatement

SUMMATE   *v* -MATED, -MATING, -MATES to sum

SUMMED   past tense of sum

SUMMER   *v* -ED, -ING, -S to pass the summer (the warmest season of the year)

SUMMERLY   *adj* summery

SUMMERY   *adj* -MERIER, -MERIEST characteristic of summer

SUMMING   present participle of sum

SUMMIT   *v* -ED, -ING, -S to participate in a highest-level conference

SUMMITAL   *adj* pertaining to the highest point

SUMMITRY   *n* pl. -RIES the use of conferences between chiefs of state for international negotiation

SUMMON   *v* -ED, -ING, -S to order to appear

SUMMONER   *n* pl. -S one that summons

SUMMONS   *v* -ED, -ING, -ES to summon with a court order

SUMO   *n* pl. -MOS a Japanese form of wrestling

SUMP   *n* pl. -S a low area serving as a drain or receptacle for liquids

SUMPTER   *n* pl. -S a pack animal

SUMPWEED   *n* pl. -S a marsh plant

SUN   *v* SUNNED, SUNNING, SUNS to expose to the sun (the star around which the earth revolves)

SUNBACK   *adj* cut low to expose the back to sunlight

SUNBAKED   *adj* baked by the sun

SUNBATH   *n* pl. -S an exposure to sunlight

SUNBATHE   *v* -BATHED, -BATHING, -BATHES to take a sunbath

SUNBEAM   *n* pl. -S a beam of sunlight **SUNBEAMY** *adj*

SUNBELT   *n* pl. -S the southern and southwestern states of the U.S.

SUNBIRD   *n* pl. -S a tropical bird

SUNBLOCK   *n* pl. -S a preparation to protect the skin from the sun's rays

SUNBOW   *n* pl. -S an arc of spectral colors formed by the sun shining through a mist

SUNBURN   *v* -BURNED or -BURNT, -BURNING, -BURNS to burn or discolor from exposure to the sun

SUNBURST   *n* pl. -S a burst of sunlight

SUNCHOKE   *n* pl. -S a type of sunflower

SUNDAE   *n* pl. -S a dish of ice cream served with a topping

SUNDECK   *n* pl. -S a deck that is exposed to the sun

SUNDER   *v* -ED, -ING, -S to break apart

SUNDERER   *n* pl. -S one that sunders

SUNDEW   *n* pl. -S a marsh plant

SUNDIAL   *n* pl. -S a type of time-telling device

SUNDOG   *n* pl. -S a small rainbow

SUNDOWN   *n* pl. -S sunset

SUNDRESS   *n* pl. -ES a dress with an abbreviated bodice

SUNDRIES   *n/pl* miscellaneous items

SUNDROPS   *n* pl. SUNDROPS a flowering plant

SUNDRY	adj miscellaneous
SUNFAST	adj resistant to fading by the sun
SUNFISH	n pl. -ES a marine fish
SUNG	past participle of sing
SUNGLASS	n pl. -ES a lens for concentrating the sun's rays in order to produce heat
SUNGLOW	n pl. -S a glow in the sky caused by the sun
SUNK	a past participle of sink
SUNKEN	a past participle of sink
SUNKET	n pl. -S a tidbit
SUNLAMP	n pl. -S a lamp that radiates ultraviolet rays
SUNLAND	n pl. -S an area marked by a great amount of sunshine
SUNLESS	adj having no sunlight
SUNLIGHT	n pl. -S the light of the sun
SUNLIKE	adj resembling the sun
SUNLIT	adj lighted by the sun
SUNN	n pl. -S an East Indian shrub
SUNNA	n pl. -S the body of traditional Muslim law
SUNNAH	n pl. -S sunna
SUNNED	past tense of sun
SUNNING	present participle of sun
SUNNY	adj -NIER, -NIEST filled with sunlight **SUNNILY** adv
SUNPORCH	n pl. -ES a porch that admits much sunlight
SUNPROOF	adj resistant to damage by sunlight
SUNRISE	n pl. -S the ascent of the sun above the horizon in the morning
SUNROOF	n pl. -S an automobile roof having an openable panel
SUNROOM	n pl. -S a room built to admit a great amount of sunlight
SUNSCALD	n pl. -S an injury of woody plants caused by the sun
SUNSET	n pl. -S the descent of the sun below the horizon in the evening
SUNSHADE	n pl. -S something used as a protection from the sun
SUNSHINE	n pl. -S the light of the sun **SUNSHINY** adj
SUNSPOT	n pl. -S a dark spot on the surface of the sun
SUNSTONE	n pl. -S a variety of quartz
SUNSUIT	n pl. -S a type of playsuit
SUNTAN	n pl. -S a brown color on the skin produced by exposure to the sun
SUNUP	n pl. -S sunrise
SUNWARD	adv toward the sun
SUNWARDS	adv sunward
SUNWISE	adv from left to right
SUP	v SUPPED, SUPPING, SUPS to eat supper
SUPE	n pl. -S an actor without a speaking part
SUPER	v -ED, -ING, -S to reinforce with a thin cotton mesh, as a book
SUPERADD	v -ED, -ING, -S to add further
SUPERB	adj -PERBER, -PERBEST of excellent quality **SUPERBLY** adv
SUPERBAD	adj exceedingly bad
SUPERCAR	n pl. -S a superior car
SUPERCOP	n pl. -S a superior police officer
SUPEREGO	n pl. -EGOS a part of the psyche
SUPERFAN	n pl. -S an exceedingly devoted enthusiast
SUPERFIX	n pl. -ES a recurrent pattern of stress in speech
SUPERHIT	n pl. -S something exceedingly successful
SUPERHOT	adj exceedingly hot
SUPERIOR	n pl. -S one of higher rank, quality, or authority than another
SUPERJET	n pl. -S a type of jet airplane
SUPERLIE	v -LAY, -LAIN, -LYING, -LIES to lie above
SUPERMAN	n pl. -MEN a hypothetical superior man
SUPERMOM	n pl. -S a superior mom
SUPERNAL	adj pertaining to the sky
SUPERPRO	n pl. -PROS a superior professional
SUPERSEX	n pl. -ES a type of sterile organism
SUPERSPY	n pl. -SPIES a superior spy
SUPERTAX	n pl. -ES an additional tax
SUPINATE	v -NATED, -NATING, -NATES to turn so that the palm is facing upward
SUPINE	n pl. -S a Latin verbal noun
SUPINELY	adv in an inactive manner
SUPPED	past tense of sup
SUPPER	n pl. -S an evening meal

SUPPING	present participle of sup	**SURFBIRD**	*n* pl. -S a shore bird
SUPPLANT	*v* -ED, -ING, -S to take the place of	**SURFBOAT**	*n* pl. -S a strong rowboat
SUPPLE	*adj* -PLER, -PLEST pliant **SUPPLELY** *adv*	**SURFEIT**	*v* -ED, -ING, -S to supply to excess
SUPPLE	*v* -PLED, -PLING, -PLES to make supple	**SURFER**	*n* pl. -S one that surfs
SUPPLIER	*n* pl. -S one that supplies	**SURFFISH**	*n* pl. -ES a marine fish
SUPPLY	*v* -PLIED, -PLYING, -PLIES to furnish with what is needed	**SURFIER**	comparative of surfy
		SURFIEST	superlative of surfy
SUPPORT	*v* -ED, -ING, -S to hold up or add strength to	**SURFING**	*n* pl. -S the act or sport of riding the surf (breaking waves)
SUPPOSAL	*n* pl. -S something supposed	**SURFLIKE**	*adj* resembling breaking waves
SUPPOSE	*v* -POSED, -POSING, -POSES to assume to be true	**SURFY**	*adj* SURFIER, SURFIEST abounding in breaking waves
SUPPOSER	*n* pl. -S one that supposes	**SURGE**	*v* SURGED, SURGING, SURGES to move in a swelling manner
SUPPRESS	*v* -ED, -ING, -ES to put an end to forcibly		
SUPRA	*adv* above	**SURGEON**	*n* pl. -S one who practices surgery
SUPREME	*adj* -PREMER, -PREMEST highest in power or authority	**SURGER**	*n* pl. -S one that surges
SUPREMO	*n* pl. -MOS one who is highest in authority	**SURGERY**	*n* pl. -GERIES the treatment of medical problems by operation
SUQ	*n* pl. -S souk	**SURGICAL**	*adj* pertaining to surgery
SURA	*n* pl. -S a chapter of the Koran	**SURGING**	present participle of surge
SURAH	*n* pl. -S a silk fabric	**SURGY**	*adj* surging
SURAL	*adj* pertaining to the calf of the leg	**SURICATE**	*n* pl. -S a burrowing mammal
SURBASE	*n* pl. -S a molding or border above the base of a structure **SURBASED** *adj*	**SURIMI**	*n* pl. SURIMI an inexpensive fish product
		SURLY	*adj* -LIER, -LIEST sullenly rude **SURLILY** *adv*
SURCEASE	*v* -CEASED, -CEASING, -CEASES to cease	**SURMISE**	*v* -MISED, -MISING, -MISES to infer with little evidence
SURCOAT	*n* pl. -S an outer coat or cloak	**SURMISER**	*n* pl. -S one that surmises
SURD	*n* pl. -S a voiceless speech sound	**SURMOUNT**	*v* -ED, -ING, -S to get over or across
SURE	*adj* SURER, SUREST free from doubt	**SURNAME**	*v* -NAMED, -NAMING, -NAMES to give a family name to
SUREFIRE	*adj* sure to meet expectations	**SURNAMER**	*n* pl. -S one that surnames
SURELY	*adv* certainly	**SURPASS**	*v* -ED, -ING, -ES to go beyond
SURENESS	*n* pl. -ES the state of being sure	**SURPLICE**	*n* pl. -S a loose-fitting vestment
SURER	comparative of sure	**SURPLUS**	*n* pl. -ES an excess
SUREST	superlative of sure	**SURPRINT**	*v* -ED, -ING, -S to print over something already printed
SURETY	*n* pl. -TIES sureness		
SURF	*v* -ED, -ING, -S to ride breaking waves on a long, narrow board **SURFABLE** *adj*	**SURPRISE**	*v* -PRISED, -PRISING, -PRISES to come upon unexpectedly
		SURPRIZE	*v* -PRIZED, -PRIZING, -PRIZES to surprise
SURFACE	*v* -FACED, -FACING, -FACES to apply an outer layer to	**SURRA**	*n* pl. -S a disease of domestic animals
SURFACER	*n* pl. -S one that surfaces	**SURREAL**	*adj* having dreamlike qualities

SURREY	*n* pl. -REYS a light carriage
SURROUND	*v* -ED, -ING, -S to extend completely around
SURROYAL	*n* pl. -S the topmost prong of a stag's antler
SURTAX	*v* -ED, -ING, -ES to assess with an extra tax
SURTOUT	*n* pl. -S a close-fitting overcoat
SURVEIL	*v* -VEILLED, -VEILLING, -VEILS to watch closely
SURVEY	*v* -ED, -ING, -S to determine the boundaries, area, or elevations of by measuring angles and distances
SURVEYOR	*n* pl. -S one that surveys land
SURVIVAL	*n* pl. -S a living or continuing longer than another person or thing
SURVIVE	*v* -VIVED, -VIVING, -VIVES to remain in existence
SURVIVER	*n* pl. -S survivor
SURVIVOR	*n* pl. -S one that survives
SUSHI	*n* pl. -S a dish of cold rice cakes topped with strips of raw fish
SUSLIK	*n* pl. -S a Eurasian rodent
SUSPECT	*v* -ED, -ING, -S to think guilty on slight evidence
SUSPEND	*v* -ED, -ING, -S to cause to stop for a period
SUSPENSE	*n* pl. -S a state of mental uncertainty or excitement
SUSPIRE	*v* -PIRED, -PIRING, -PIRES to sigh
SUSS	*v* -ED, -ING, -ES to figure out
SUSTAIN	*v* -ED, -ING, -S to maintain by providing with food and drink
SUSURRUS	*n* pl. -ES a soft rustling sound
SUTLER	*n* pl. -S one that peddles goods to soldiers
SUTRA	*n* pl. -S a Hindu aphorism
SUTTA	*n* pl. -S sutra
SUTTEE	*n* pl. -S a Hindu widow cremated on her husband's funeral pile to show her devotion to him
SUTURAL	*adj* pertaining to the line of junction between two bones
SUTURE	*v* -TURED, -TURING, -TURES to unite by sewing
SUZERAIN	*n* pl. -S a feudal lord
SVARAJ	*n* pl. -ES swaraj
SVEDBERG	*n* pl. -S a unit of time
SVELTE	*adj* SVELTER, SVELTEST gracefully slender **SVELTELY** *adv*
SWAB	*v* SWABBED, SWABBING, SWABS to clean with a large mop
SWABBER	*n* pl. -S one that swabs
SWABBIE	*n* pl. -S a sailor
SWABBING	present participle of swab
SWABBY	*n* pl. -BIES swabbie
SWACKED	*adj* drunk
SWADDLE	*v* -DLED, -DLING, -DLES to wrap in bandages
SWAG	*v* SWAGGED, SWAGGING, SWAGS to sway
SWAGE	*v* SWAGED, SWAGING, SWAGES to shape with a hammering tool
SWAGER	*n* pl. -S one that swages
SWAGGED	past tense of swag
SWAGGER	*v* -ED, -ING, -S to walk with a pompous air
SWAGGIE	*n* pl. -S a swagman
SWAGGING	present participle of swag
SWAGING	present participle of swage
SWAGMAN	*n* pl. -MEN a hobo
SWAIL	*n* pl. -S swale
SWAIN	*n* pl. -S a country boy **SWAINISH** *adj*
SWALE	*n* pl. -S a tract of low, marshy ground
SWALLOW	*v* -ED, -ING, -S to take through the mouth and esophagus into the stomach
SWAM	past tense of swim
SWAMI	*n* pl. -S a Hindu religious teacher
SWAMIES	pl. of swamy
SWAMP	*v* -ED, -ING, -S to inundate
SWAMPER	*n* pl. -S one that lives in a swampy area
SWAMPISH	*adj* swampy
SWAMPY	*adj* SWAMPIER, SWAMPIEST marshy
SWAMY	*n* pl. -MIES swami
SWAN	*v* SWANNED, SWANNING, SWANS to swear
SWANG	a past tense of swing
SWANHERD	*n* pl. -S one who tends swans (large aquatic birds)
SWANK	*adj* SWANKER, SWANKEST imposingly elegant

SWANK	*v* -ED, -ING, -S to swagger
SWANKY	*adj* SWANKIER, SWANKIEST swank **SWANKILY** *adv*
SWANLIKE	*adj* resembling a swan
SWANNED	past tense of swan
SWANNERY	*n* pl. -NERIES a place where swans are raised
SWANNING	present participle of swan
SWANPAN	*n* pl. -S a Chinese abacus
SWANSKIN	*n* pl. -S the skin of a swan
SWAP	*v* SWAPPED, SWAPPING, SWAPS to trade
SWAPPER	*n* pl. -S one that swaps
SWARAJ	*n* pl. -ES self-government in British India
SWARD	*v* -ED, -ING, -S to cover with turf
SWARE	a past tense of swear
SWARF	*n* pl. -S material removed by a cutting tool
SWARM	*v* -ED, -ING, -S to move in a large group
SWARMER	*n* pl. -S one that swarms
SWART	*adj* swarthy
SWARTH	*n* pl. -S turf
SWARTHY	*adj* -THIER, -THIEST having a dark complexion
SWARTY	*adj* swarthy
SWASH	*v* -ED, -ING, -ES to swagger
SWASHER	*n* pl. -S one that swashes
SWASTICA	*n* pl. -S swastika
SWASTIKA	*n* pl. -S a geometrical figure used as a symbol or ornament
SWAT	*v* SWATTED, SWATTING, SWATS to hit sharply
SWATCH	*n* pl. -ES a sample piece of cloth
SWATH	*n* pl. -S a row of cut grass or grain
SWATHE	*v* SWATHED, SWATHING, SWATHES to wrap in bandages
SWATHER	*n* pl. -S one that swathes
SWATTED	past tense of swat
SWATTER	*n* pl. -S one that swats
SWATTING	present participle of swat
SWAY	*v* -ED, -ING, -S to move slowly back and forth **SWAYABLE** *adj*
SWAYBACK	*n* pl. -S an abnormal sagging of the back
SWAYER	*n* pl. -S one that sways
SWAYFUL	*adj* capable of influencing
SWEAR	*v* SWORE or SWARE, SWORN, SWEARING, SWEARS to utter a solemn oath
SWEARER	*n* pl. -S one that swears
SWEAT	*v* -ED, -ING, -S to perspire
SWEATBOX	*n* pl. -ES a small enclosure in which one is made to sweat
SWEATER	*n* pl. -S a knitted outer garment
SWEATY	*adj* SWEATIER, SWEATIEST covered with perspiration **SWEATILY** *adv*
SWEDE	*n* pl. -S a rutabaga
SWEENY	*n* pl. -NIES atrophy of the shoulder muscles in horses
SWEEP	*v* SWEPT, SWEEPING, SWEEPS to clear or clean with a brush or broom
SWEEPER	*n* pl. -S one that sweeps
SWEEPING	*n* pl. -S the act of one that sweeps
SWEEPY	*adj* SWEEPIER, SWEEPIEST of wide range or scope
SWEER	*adj* lazy
SWEET	*adj* SWEETER, SWEETEST pleasing to the taste
SWEET	*n* pl. -S something that is sweet
SWEETEN	*v* -ED, -ING, -S to make sweet
SWEETIE	*n* pl. -S darling
SWEETING	*n* pl. -S a sweet apple
SWEETISH	*adj* somewhat sweet
SWEETLY	*adv* in a sweet manner
SWEETSOP	*n* pl. -S a tropical tree
SWELL	*v* SWELLED, SWOLLEN, SWELLING, SWELLS to increase in size or volume
SWELL	*adj* SWELLER, SWELLEST stylish
SWELLING	*n* pl. -S something that is swollen
SWELTER	*v* -ED, -ING, -S to suffer from oppressive heat
SWELTRY	*adj* -TRIER, -TRIEST oppressively hot
SWEPT	past tense of sweep
SWERVE	*v* SWERVED, SWERVING, SWERVES to turn aside suddenly from a straight course
SWERVER	*n* pl. -S one that swerves
SWEVEN	*n* pl. -S a dream or vision

SWIDDEN	*n* pl. -S an agricultural plot produced by burning off the vegetative cover
SWIFT	*adj* SWIFTER, SWIFTEST moving with a great rate of motion
SWIFT	*n* pl. -S a fast-flying bird
SWIFTER	*n* pl. -S a rope on a ship
SWIFTLET	*n* pl. -S a cave-dwelling swift
SWIFTLY	*adv* in a swift manner
SWIG	*v* SWIGGED, SWIGGING, SWIGS to drink deeply or rapidly
SWIGGER	*n* pl. -S one that swigs
SWILL	*v* -ED, -ING, -S to swig
SWILLER	*n* pl. -S one that swills
SWIM	*v* SWAM, SWUM, SWIMMING, SWIMS to propel oneself in water by natural means
SWIMMER	*n* pl. -S one that swims
SWIMMING	*n* pl. -S the act of one that swims
SWIMMY	*adj* -MIER, -MIEST dizzy **SWIMMILY** *adv*
SWIMSUIT	*n* pl. -S a bathing suit
SWIMWEAR	*n* pl. SWIMWEAR clothing suitable for swimming
SWINDLE	*v* -DLED, -DLING, -DLES to take money or property from by fraudulent means
SWINDLER	*n* pl. -S one that swindles
SWINE	*n* pl. SWINE a domestic pig
SWINEPOX	*n* pl. -ES a disease of swine
SWING	*v* SWUNG or SWANG, SWINGING, SWINGS to move freely back and forth
SWINGBY	*n* pl. -BYS a mission in which a spacecraft uses a planet's gravitational pull for making course changes
SWINGE	*v* SWINGED, SWINGEING, SWINGES to flog
SWINGER	*n* pl. -S one that swings
SWINGIER	comparative of swingy
SWINGIEST	superlative of swingy
SWINGING	*adj* -INGEST lively and hip
SWINGING	*n* pl. -S the practice of swapping sex partners
SWINGLE	*v* -GLED, -GLING, -GLES to scutch
SWINGMAN	*n* pl. -MEN a basketball player who can play guard or forward
SWINGY	*adj* SWINGIER, SWINGIEST marked by swinging
SWINISH	*adj* resembling or befitting swine
SWINK	*v* -ED, -ING, -S to toil
SWINNEY	*n* pl. -NEYS sweeny
SWIPE	*v* SWIPED, SWIPING, SWIPES to strike with a sweeping blow
SWIPLE	*n* pl. -S a part of a threshing device
SWIPPLE	*n* pl. -S swiple
SWIRL	*v* -ED, -ING, -S to move with a whirling motion
SWIRLY	*adj* SWIRLIER, SWIRLIEST swirling
SWISH	*v* -ED, -ING, -ES to move with a prolonged hissing sound
SWISHER	*n* pl. -S one that swishes
SWISHY	*adj* SWISHIER, SWISHIEST swishing
SWISS	*n* pl. -ES a cotton fabric
SWITCH	*v* -ED, -ING, -ES to beat with a flexible rod
SWITCHER	*n* pl. -S one that switches
SWITH	*adv* quickly
SWITHE	*adv* swith
SWITHER	*v* -ED, -ING, -S to doubt
SWITHLY	*adv* swith
SWIVE	*v* SWIVED, SWIVING, SWIVES to copulate with
SWIVEL	*v* -ELED, -ELING, -ELS or -ELLED, -ELLING, -ELS to turn on a pivoted support
SWIVET	*n* pl. -S a state of nervous excitement
SWIVING	present participle of swive
SWIZZLE	*v* -ZLED, -ZLING, -ZLES to drink excessively
SWIZZLER	*n* pl. -S one that swizzles
SWOB	*v* SWOBBED, SWOBBING, SWOBS to swab
SWOBBER	*n* pl. -S swabber
SWOLLEN	past participle of swell
SWOON	*v* -ED, -ING, -S to faint
SWOONER	*n* pl. -S one that swoons
SWOOP	*v* -ED, -ING, -S to make a sudden descent
SWOOPER	*n* pl. -S one that swoops
SWOOSH	*v* -ED, -ING, -ES to move with a rustling sound

SWOP	*v* SWOPPED, SWOPPING, SWOPS to swap
SWORD	*n* pl. -S a weapon having a long blade for cutting or thrusting
SWORDMAN	*n* pl. -MEN one skilled in the use of a sword
SWORE	a past tense of swear
SWORN	past participle of swear
SWOT	*v* SWOTTED, SWOTTING, SWOTS to swat
SWOTTER	*n* pl. -S one that swots
SWOUN	*v* -ED, -ING, -S to swoon
SWOUND	*v* -ED, -ING, -S to swoon
SWUM	past participle of swim
SWUNG	a past tense of swing
SYBARITE	*n* pl. -S a person devoted to pleasure and luxury
SYBO	*n* pl. -BOES the cibol
SYCAMINE	*n* pl. -S the mulberry tree
SYCAMORE	*n* pl. -S a North American tree
SYCE	*n* pl. -S a male servant in India
SYCEE	*n* pl. -S fine uncoined silver formerly used in China as money
SYCOMORE	*n* pl. -S sycamore
SYCONIUM	*n* pl. -NIA a fleshy multiple fruit
SYCOSIS	*n* pl. -COSES an inflammatory disease of the hair follicles
SYENITE	*n* pl. -S an igneous rock **SYENITIC** *adj*
SYKE	*n* pl. -S a small stream
SYLI	*n* pl. -S a former monetary unit of Guinea
SYLLABI	a pl. of syllabus
SYLLABIC	*n* pl. -S a speech sound of high sonority
SYLLABLE	*v* -BLED, -BLING, -BLES to pronounce syllables (units of spoken language)
SYLLABUB	*n* pl. -S sillabub
SYLLABUS	*n* pl. -BI or -BUSES an outline of a course of study
SYLPH	*n* pl. -S a slender, graceful girl or woman **SYLPHIC, SYLPHISH, SYLPHY** *adj*
SYLPHID	*n* pl. -S a young sylph
SYLVA	*n* pl. -VAS or -VAE the forest trees of an area
SYLVAN	*n* pl. -S one that lives in a forest
SYLVATIC	*adj* pertaining to a forest
SYLVIN	*n* pl. -S sylvite
SYLVINE	*n* pl. -S sylvite
SYLVITE	*n* pl. -S an ore of potassium
SYMBION	*n* pl. -S symbiont
SYMBIONT	*n* pl. -S an organism living in close association with another
SYMBIOT	*n* pl. -S symbiont
SYMBIOTE	*n* pl. -S symbiont
SYMBOL	*v* -BOLED, -BOLING, -BOLS or -BOLLED, -BOLLING, -BOLS to serve as a symbol (a representation) of
SYMBOLIC	*adj* pertaining to a symbol
SYMMETRY	*n* pl. -TRIES an exact correspondence between the opposite halves of a figure
SYMPATHY	*n* pl. -THIES a feeling of compassion for another's suffering
SYMPATRY	*n* pl. -RIES the state of occupying the same area without loss of identity from interbreeding
SYMPHONY	*n* pl. -NIES an orchestral composition
SYMPODIA	*n/pl* plant stems made up of a series of superposed branches
SYMPOSIA	*n/pl* conferences for the purpose of discussion
SYMPTOM	*n* pl. -S an indication of something
SYN	*adv* syne
SYNAGOG	*n* pl. -S a building for Jewish worship
SYNANON	*n* pl. -S a method of group therapy for drug addicts
SYNAPSE	*v* -APSED, -APSING, -APSES to come together in synapsis
SYNAPSID	*n* pl. -S one of a group of extinct reptiles
SYNAPSIS	*n* pl. -APSES the point at which a nervous impulse passes from one neuron to another **SYNAPTIC** *adj*
SYNC	*v* -ED, -ING, -S to cause to operate in unison
SYNCARP	*n* pl. -S a fleshy multiple fruit
SYNCARPY	*n* pl. -PIES the state of being a syncarp
SYNCH	*v* -ED, -ING, -S to sync
SYNCHRO	*n* pl. -CHROS a selsyn
SYNCLINE	*n* pl. -S a type of rock formation
SYNCOM	*n* pl. -S a type of communications satellite

SYNCOPE   *n* pl. -S the contraction of a word by omitting one or more sounds from the middle **SYNCOPAL, SYNCOPIC** *adj*

SYNCYTIA   *n/pl* masses of protoplasm resulting from cell fusion

SYNDESIS   *n* pl. -DESES or -DESISES synapsis

SYNDET   *n* pl. -S a synthetic detergent

SYNDETIC   *adj* serving to connect

SYNDIC   *n* pl. -S a business agent **SYNDICAL** *adj*

SYNDROME   *n* pl. -S a group of symptoms that characterize a particular disorder

SYNE   *adv* since

SYNECTIC   *adj* pertaining to a system of problem solving

SYNERGIA   *n* pl. -S synergy

SYNERGID   *n* pl. -S a cell found in the embryo sac of a seed plant

SYNERGY   *n* pl. -GIES combined action **SYNERGIC** *adj*

SYNESIS   *n* pl. -SISES a type of grammatical construction

SYNFUEL   *n* pl. -S a fuel derived from fossil fuels

SYNGAMY   *n* pl. -MIES the union of two gametes **SYNGAMIC** *adj*

SYNGAS   *n* pl. -GASES or -GASSES a mixture of carbon monoxide and hydrogen used in chemical synthesis

SYNOD   *n* pl. -S a church council **SYNODAL, SYNODIC** *adj*

SYNONYM   *n* pl. -S a word having the same meaning as another

SYNONYME   *n* pl. -S synonym

SYNONYMY   *n* pl. -MIES equivalence of meaning

SYNOPSIS   *n* pl. -OPSES a summary **SYNOPTIC** *adj*

SYNOVIA   *n* pl. -S a lubricating fluid secreted by certain membranes **SYNOVIAL** *adj*

SYNTAGMA   *n* pl. -MAS or -MATA a syntactic element

SYNTAX   *n* pl. -ES the way in which words are put together to form phrases and sentences

SYNTH   *n* pl. -S a synthesizer

SYNTONY   *n* pl. -NIES the tuning of transmitters and receivers with each other **SYNTONIC** *adj*

SYNURA   *n* pl. -RAE any of a genus of protozoa

SYPH   *n* pl. -S syphilis

SYPHER   *v* -ED, -ING, -S to overlap so as to make an even surface, as beveled plank edges

SYPHILIS   *n* pl. -LISES a venereal disease

SYPHON   *v* -ED, -ING, -S to siphon

SYREN   *n* pl. -S siren

SYRINGA   *n* pl. -S an ornamental shrub

SYRINGE   *v* -RINGED, -RINGING, -RINGES to cleanse or treat with injected fluid

SYRINX   *n* pl. -INGES or -INXES the vocal organ of a bird

SYRPHIAN   *n* pl. -S syrphid

SYRPHID   *n* pl. -S a winged insect

SYRUP   *n* pl. -S a thick, sweet liquid **SYRUPY** *adj*

SYSOP   *n* pl. -S the administrator of a computer bulletin board

SYSTEM   *n* pl. -S a group of interacting elements forming a unified whole

SYSTEMIC   *n* pl. -S a type of pesticide

SYSTOLE   *n* pl. -S the normal rhythmic contraction of the heart **SYSTOLIC** *adj*

SYZYGY   *n* pl. -GIES the configuration of the earth, moon, and sun lying in a straight line **SYZYGAL, SYZYGIAL** *adj*

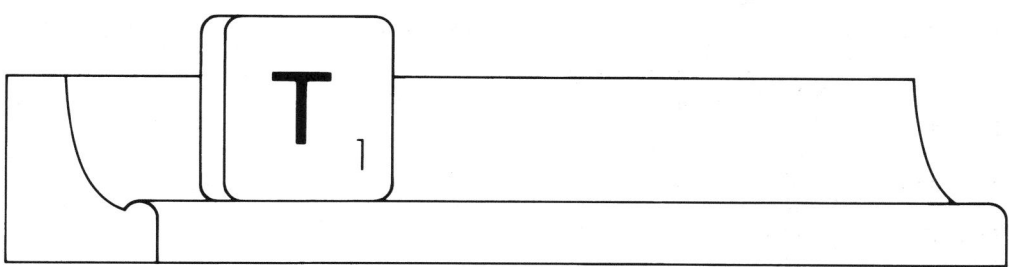

TA — *n* pl. -S an expression of gratitude

TAB — *v* TABBED, TABBING, TABS to name or designate

TABANID — *n* pl. -S a bloodsucking insect

TABARD — *n* pl. -S a sleeveless outer garment **TABARDED** *adj*

TABARET — *n* pl. -S a silk fabric

TABBED — past tense of tab

TABBIED — past tense of tabby

TABBIES — present 3d person sing. of tabby

TABBING — present participle of tab

TABBIS — *n* pl. -BISES a silk fabric

TABBY — *v* -BIED, -BYING, -BIES to give a wavy appearance to

TABER — *v* -ED, -ING, -S to tabor

TABES — *n* pl. TABES a syphilitic disease

TABETIC — *n* pl. -S one affected with tabes

TABID — *adj* affected with tabes

TABLA — *n* pl. -S a small drum

TABLE — *v* -BLED, -BLING, -BLES to place on a table (a piece of furniture having a flat upper surface)

TABLEAU — *n* pl. -LEAUX or -LEAUS a picture

TABLEFUL — *n* pl. TABLEFULS or TABLESFUL as much as a table can hold

TABLET — *v* -LETED, -LETING, -LETS or -LETTED, -LETTING, -LETS to inscribe on a small, flat surface

TABLETOP — *n* pl. -S the top of a table

TABLING — present participle of table

TABLOID — *n* pl. -S a small newspaper

TABOO — *v* -ED, -ING, -S to exclude from use, approach, or mention

TABOOLEY — *n* pl. -LEYS tabouli

TABOR — *v* -ED, -ING, -S to beat on a small drum

TABORER — *n* pl. -S one that tabors

TABORET — *n* pl. -S a small drum

TABORIN — *n* pl. -S taborine

TABORINE — *n* pl. -S a taboret

TABOULI — *n* pl. -S a Lebanese salad containing bulgur wheat, tomatoes, parsley, onions, and mint

TABOUR — *v* -ED, -ING, -S to tabor

TABOURER — *n* pl. -S taborer

TABOURET — *n* pl. -S taboret

TABU — *v* -ED, -ING, -S to taboo

TABULAR — *adj* of or pertaining to a list

TABULATE — *v* -LATED, -LATING, -LATES to arrange in a list

TABULI — *n* pl. -S tabouli

TABUN — *n* pl. -S a chemical compound

TACE — *n* pl. -S tasse

TACET — *interj* be silent — used as a musical direction

TACH — *n* pl. -S a device for indicating speed of rotation

TACHE — *n* pl. -S a clasp or buckle

TACHINID — *n* pl. -S a grayish fly

TACHISM — *n* pl. -S action painting

TACHISME — *n* pl. -S tachism

TACHIST — *n* pl. -S an action painter

TACHISTE — *n* pl. -S tachist

TACHYON — *n* pl. -S a theoretical subatomic particle

TACIT — *adj* unspoken **TACITLY** *adv*

TACITURN — *adj* habitually silent

TACK — *v* -ED, -ING, -S to fasten with tacks (short, sharp-pointed nails)

TACKER — *n* pl. -S one that tacks

TACKET	*n* pl. -S a hobnail
TACKEY	*adj* TACKIER, TACKIEST tacky
TACKIER	comparative of tacky
TACKIEST	superlative of tacky
TACKIFY	*v* -FIED, -FYING, -FIES to make tacky
TACKILY	*adv* in a tacky manner
TACKLE	*v* -LED, -LING, -LES to seize and throw to the ground
TACKLER	*n* pl. -S one that tackles
TACKLESS	*adj* having no tacks
TACKLING	*n* pl. -S equipment
TACKY	*adj* TACKIER, TACKIEST adhesive
TACNODE	*n* pl. -S a point of contact between two curves
TACO	*n* pl. -COS a tortilla folded around a filling
TACONITE	*n* pl. -S a low-grade iron ore
TACT	*n* pl. -S skill in dealing with delicate situations
TACTFUL	*adj* having tact
TACTIC	*n* pl. -S a maneuver for gaining an objective **TACTICAL** *adj*
TACTILE	*adj* pertaining to the sense of touch
TACTION	*n* pl. -S the act of touching
TACTLESS	*adj* lacking tact
TACTUAL	*adj* tactile
TAD	*n* pl. -S a small boy
TADPOLE	*n* pl. -S the aquatic larva of an amphibian
TAE	*prep* to
TAEL	*n* pl. -S a Chinese unit of weight
TAENIA	*n* pl. -NIAE or -NIAS a headband worn in ancient Greece
TAFFAREL	*n* pl. -S taffrail
TAFFEREL	*n* pl. -S taffrail
TAFFETA	*n* pl. -S a lustrous fabric
TAFFIA	*n* pl. -S tafia
TAFFRAIL	*n* pl. -S a rail around the stern of a ship
TAFFY	*n* pl. -FIES a chewy candy
TAFIA	*n* pl. -S an inferior rum
TAG	*v* TAGGED, TAGGING, TAGS to provide with a tag (an identifying marker)
TAGALONG	*n* pl. -S one that follows another
TAGBOARD	*n* pl. -S a material for making shipping tags
TAGGED	past tense of tag
TAGGER	*n* pl. -S one that tags
TAGGING	present participle of tag
TAGLIKE	*adj* resembling a tag
TAGMEME	*n* pl. -S the smallest unit of meaningful grammatical relation
TAGMEMIC	*adj* pertaining to a grammar in which a tagmeme is the basic unit
TAGRAG	*n* pl. -S riffraff
TAHINI	*n* pl. -S a paste of sesame seeds
TAHR	*n* pl. -S a goatlike mammal
TAHSIL	*n* pl. -S a district in India
TAIGA	*n* pl. -S a subarctic evergreen forest
TAIGLACH	*n* pl. TAIGLACH teiglach
TAIL	*v* -ED, -ING, -S to provide with a tail (a hindmost part)
TAILBACK	*n* pl. -S a member of the backfield in some football formations
TAILBONE	*n* pl. -S the coccyx
TAILCOAT	*n* pl. -S a man's coat
TAILER	*n* pl. -S one that secretly follows another
TAILFAN	*n* pl. -S a fanlike swimming organ at the rear of some crustaceans
TAILGATE	*v* -GATED, -GATING, -GATES to drive dangerously close behind another vehicle
TAILING	*n* pl. -S the part of a projecting stone or brick that is inserted into a wall
TAILLAMP	*n* pl. -S a light at the rear of a vehicle
TAILLE	*n* pl. -S a former French tax
TAILLESS	*adj* having no tail
TAILLEUR	*n* pl. -S a woman's tailored suit
TAILLIKE	*adj* resembling a tail
TAILOR	*v* -ED, -ING, -S to fit with clothes
TAILPIPE	*n* pl. -S an exhaust pipe
TAILRACE	*n* pl. -S a part of a millrace
TAILSKID	*n* pl. -S a support on which the tail of an airplane rests
TAILSPIN	*n* pl. -S the spiral descent of a stalled airplane
TAILWIND	*n* pl. -S a wind coming from behind a moving vehicle
TAIN	*n* pl. -S a thin plate

TAINT	*v* -ED, -ING, -S to touch or affect slightly with something bad	**TALIPOT**	*n* pl. -S a tall palm tree
TAIPAN	*n* pl. -S a venomous snake	**TALISMAN**	*n* pl. -S an object believed to possess magical powers
TAJ	*n* pl. -ES a tall, conical cap worn in Muslim countries	**TALK**	*v* -ED, -ING, -S to communicate by speaking
TAKA	*n* pl. TAKA a monetary unit of Bangladesh	**TALKABLE**	*adj* able to be talked about
TAKAHE	*n* pl. -S a flightless bird	**TALKER**	*n* pl. -S one that talks
TAKE	*v* TOOK, TAKEN, TAKING, TAKES to get possession of **TAKABLE, TAKEABLE** *adj*	**TALKIE**	*n* pl. -S a moving picture with synchronized sound
		TALKING	*n* pl. -S conversation
TAKEAWAY	*adj* designating prepared food that is sold for consumption elsewhere	**TALKY**	*adj* TALKIER, TALKIEST tending to talk a great deal
TAKEDOWN	*n* pl. -S an article that can be taken apart easily	**TALL**	*adj* TALLER, TALLEST having great height
TAKEOFF	*n* pl. -S the act of rising in flight	**TALLAGE**	*v* -LAGED, -LAGING, -LAGES to tax
TAKEOUT	*n* pl. -S the act of removing	**TALLAISIM**	a pl. of tallith
TAKEOVER	*n* pl. -S the act of assuming control	**TALLBOY**	*n* pl. -BOYS a highboy
TAKER	*n* pl. -S one that takes	**TALLIED**	past tense of tally
TAKEUP	*n* pl. -S the act of taking something up	**TALLIER**	*n* pl. -S one that tallies
TAKIN	*n* pl. -S a goatlike mammal	**TALLIES**	present 3d person sing. of tally
TAKING	*n* pl. -S a seizure	**TALLIS**	*n* pl. -LISIM tallith
TAKINGLY	*adv* in an attractive manner	**TALLISH**	*adj* somewhat tall
TALA	*n* pl. -S a traditional rhythmic pattern of music in India	**TALLIT**	*n* pl. -LITIM tallith
TALAPOIN	*n* pl. -S a small African monkey	**TALLITH**	*n* pl. TALLITHES, TALLITHIM, TALLITOTH, TALEYSIM, or TALLAISIM a Jewish prayer shawl
TALAR	*n* pl. -S a long cloak	**TALLNESS**	*n* pl. -ES the state of being tall
TALARIA	*n/pl* winged sandals worn by various figures of classical mythology	**TALLOL**	*n* pl. -S a resinous liquid
		TALLOW	*v* -ED, -ING, -S to smear with tallow (a mixture of animal fats)
TALC	*v* TALCKED, TALCKING, TALCS or TALCED, TALCING, TALCS to treat with talc (a soft mineral with a soapy texture) **TALCKY, TALCOSE, TALCOUS** *adj*	**TALLOWY**	*adj* resembling tallow
		TALLY	*v* -LIED, -LYING, -LIES to count
		TALLYHO	*v* -ED, -ING, -S to make an encouraging shout to hunting hounds
TALCUM	*n* pl. -S a powder made from talc		
TALE	*n* pl. -S a story	**TALLYMAN**	*n* pl. -MEN a person who tallies
TALENT	*n* pl. -S a special natural ability **TALENTED** *adj*	**TALMUDIC**	*adj* pertaining to the body of Jewish civil and religious law
TALER	*n* pl. -S a former German coin	**TALON**	*n* pl. -S a claw of a bird of prey **TALONED** *adj*
TALESMAN	*n* pl. -MEN a person summoned to fill a vacancy on a jury	**TALOOKA**	*n* pl. -S taluk
TALEYSIM	a pl. of tallith	**TALUK**	*n* pl. -S an estate in India
TALI	pl. of talus	**TALUKA**	*n* pl. -S taluk
TALION	*n* pl. -S a retaliation for a crime	**TALUS**	*n* pl. -LI a bone of the foot
TALIPED	*n* pl. -S a person afflicted with clubfoot	**TALUS**	*n* pl. -ES a slope formed by an accumulation of rock debris
TALIPES	*n* pl. TALIPES clubfoot	**TAM**	*n* pl. -S a tight-fitting Scottish cap

TAMABLE	*adj* capable of being tamed
TAMAL	*n* pl. -S tamale
TAMALE	*n* pl. -S a Mexican dish
TAMANDU	*n* pl. -S tamandua
TAMANDUA	*n* pl. -S an arboreal anteater
TAMARACK	*n* pl. -S a timber tree
TAMARAO	*n* pl. -RAOS tamarau
TAMARAU	*n* pl. -S a small buffalo of the Philippines
TAMARI	*n* pl. -S a Japanese soy sauce
TAMARIN	*n* pl. -S a South American monkey
TAMARIND	*n* pl. -S a tropical tree
TAMARISK	*n* pl. -S an evergreen shrub
TAMASHA	*n* pl. -S a public entertainment in India
TAMBAC	*n* pl. -S tombac
TAMBAK	*n* pl. -S tombac
TAMBALA	*n* pl. -S or MATAMBALA a monetary unit of Malawi
TAMBOUR	*v* -ED, -ING, -S to embroider on a round wooden frame
TAMBOURA	*n* pl. -S tambura
TAMBUR	*n* pl. -S tambura
TAMBURA	*n* pl. -S a stringed instrument
TAME	*adj* TAMER, TAMEST gentle or docile
TAME	*v* TAMED, TAMING, TAMES to make tame
TAMEABLE	*adj* tamable
TAMEIN	*n* pl. -S a garment worn by Burmese women
TAMELESS	*adj* not capable of being tamed
TAMELY	*adv* in a tame manner
TAMENESS	*n* pl. -ES the state of being tame
TAMER	*n* pl. -S one that tames
TAMEST	superlative of tame
TAMING	present participle of tame
TAMIS	*n* pl. -ISES a strainer made of cloth mesh
TAMMIE	*n* pl. -S tammy
TAMMY	*n* pl. -MIES a fabric of mixed fibers
TAMP	*v* -ED, -ING, -S to pack down by tapping
TAMPALA	*n* pl. -S an annual herb
TAMPAN	*n* pl. -S a biting insect
TAMPER	*v* -ED, -ING, -S to interfere in a harmful manner
TAMPERER	*n* pl. -S one that tampers
TAMPION	*n* pl. -S a plug for the muzzle of a cannon
TAMPON	*v* -ED, -ING, -S to plug with a cotton pad
TAN	*v* TANNED, TANNING, TANS to convert hide into leather by soaking in chemicals
TAN	*adj* TANNER, TANNEST brown from the sun's rays
TANAGER	*n* pl. -S a brightly colored bird
TANBARK	*n* pl. -S a tree bark used as a source of tannin
TANDEM	*n* pl. -S a bicycle built for two
TANDOOR	*n* pl. -DOORI a clay oven
TANG	*v* -ED, -ING, -S to provide with a pungent flavor
TANGELO	*n* pl. -LOS a citrus fruit
TANGENCE	*n* pl. -S tangency
TANGENCY	*n* pl. -CIES the state of being in immediate physical contact
TANGENT	*n* pl. -S a straight line in contact with a curve at one point
TANGIBLE	*n* pl. -S something palpable
TANGIBLY	*adv* palpably
TANGIER	comparative of tangy
TANGIEST	superlative of tangy
TANGLE	*v* -GLED, -GLING, -GLES to bring together in intricate confusion
TANGLER	*n* pl. -S one that tangles
TANGLY	*adj* -GLIER, -GLIEST tangled
TANGO	*v* -ED, -ING, -S to perform a Latin-American dance
TANGRAM	*n* pl. -S a Chinese puzzle
TANGY	*adj* TANGIER, TANGIEST pungent
TANIST	*n* pl. -S the heir apparent to a Celtic chief
TANISTRY	*n* pl. -RIES the system of electing a tanist
TANK	*v* -ED, -ING, -S to store in a tank (a container usually for liquids)
TANKA	*n* pl. -S a Japanese verse form
TANKAGE	*n* pl. -S the capacity of a tank
TANKARD	*n* pl. -S a tall drinking vessel
TANKER	*n* pl. -S a ship designed to transport liquids

TANKFUL	*n* pl. -S the amount a tank can hold
TANKLIKE	*adj* resembling a tank
TANKSHIP	*n* pl. -S a tanker
TANNABLE	*adj* capable of being tanned
TANNAGE	*n* pl. -S the process of tanning
TANNATE	*n* pl. -S a chemical salt
TANNED	past tense of tan
TANNER	*n* pl. -S one that tans
TANNERY	*n* pl. -NERIES a place where hides are tanned
TANNEST	superlative of tan
TANNIC	*adj* pertaining to tannin
TANNIN	*n* pl. -S a chemical compound used in tanning
TANNING	*n* pl. -S the process of converting hides into leather
TANNISH	*adj* somewhat tan
TANREC	*n* pl. -S tenrec
TANSY	*n* pl. -SIES a perennial herb
TANTALUM	*n* pl. -S a metallic element **TANTALIC** *adj*
TANTALUS	*n* pl. -ES a case for wine bottles
TANTARA	*n* pl. -S the sound of a trumpet or horn
TANTIVY	*n* pl. -TIVIES a hunting cry
TANTO	*adv* so much — used as a musical direction
TANTRA	*n* pl. -S one of a class of Hindu religious writings **TANTRIC** *adj*
TANTRUM	*n* pl. -S a fit of rage
TANUKI	*n* pl. -S a raccoon dog
TANYARD	*n* pl. -S the section of a tannery containing the vats
TAO	*n* pl. -S the path of virtuous conduct according to a Chinese philosophy
TAP	*v* TAPPED, TAPPING, TAPS to strike gently
TAPA	*n* pl. -S a cloth made from tree bark
TAPADERA	*n* pl. -S a part of a saddle
TAPADERO	*n* pl. -ROS tapadera
TAPALO	*n* pl. -LOS a scarf worn in Latin-American countries
TAPE	*v* TAPED, TAPING, TAPES to fasten with tape (a long, narrow strip or band)
TAPELESS	*adj* being without tape
TAPELIKE	*adj* resembling tape
TAPELINE	*n* pl. -S a tape for measuring distances
TAPER	*v* -ED, -ING, -S to become gradually narrower toward one end
TAPERER	*n* pl. -S one that carries a candle in a religious procession
TAPESTRY	*v* -TRIED, -TRYING, -TRIES to decorate with woven wall hangings
TAPETUM	*n* pl. -TA a layer of cells in some plants **TAPETAL** *adj*
TAPEWORM	*n* pl. -S a parasitic worm
TAPHOLE	*n* pl. -S a hole in a blast furnace
TAPHOUSE	*n* pl. -S a tavern
TAPING	present participle of tape
TAPIOCA	*n* pl. -S a starchy food
TAPIR	*n* pl. -S a hoofed mammal
TAPIS	*n* pl. -PISES material used for wall hangings and floor coverings
TAPPED	past tense of tap
TAPPER	*n* pl. -S one that taps
TAPPET	*n* pl. -S a sliding rod that causes another part of a mechanism to move
TAPPING	*n* pl. -S the process or means by which something is tapped
TAPROOM	*n* pl. -S a barroom
TAPROOT	*n* pl. -S the main root of a plant
TAPSTER	*n* pl. -S one that dispenses liquor in a barroom
TAR	*v* TARRED, TARRING, TARS to cover with tar (a black viscous liquid)
TARAMA	*n* pl. -S a Greek paste of fish roe, garlic, lemon juice, and olive oil
TARANTAS	*n* pl. -ES a Russian carriage
TARBOOSH	*n* pl. -ES a cap worn by Muslim men
TARBUSH	*n* pl. -ES tarboosh
TARDIER	comparative of tardy
TARDIES	pl. of tardy
TARDO	*adj* slow — used as a musical direction
TARDY	*adj* TARDIER, TARDIEST late **TARDILY** *adv*
TARDY	*n* pl. -DIES an instance of being late

TARDYON	*n* pl. -S a subatomic particle that travels slower than the speed of light
TARE	*v* TARED, TARING, TARES to determine the weight of a container holding goods
TARGE	*n* pl. -S a small, round shield
TARGET	*v* -ED, -ING, -S to make a goal of
TARIFF	*v* -ED, -ING, -S to tax imported or exported goods
TARING	present participle of tare
TARLATAN	*n* pl. -S a cotton fabric
TARLETAN	*n* pl. -S tarlatan
TARMAC	*n* pl. -S an asphalt road
TARN	*n* pl. -S a small mountain lake
TARNAL	*adj* damned **TARNALLY** *adv*
TARNISH	*v* -ED, -ING, -ES to dull the luster of
TARO	*n* pl. -ROS a tropical plant
TAROC	*n* pl. -S tarok
TAROK	*n* pl. -S a card game
TAROT	*n* pl. -S any of a set of playing cards used for fortune-telling
TARP	*n* pl. -S a protective canvas covering
TARPAN	*n* pl. -S an Asian wild horse
TARPAPER	*n* pl. -S a heavy paper coated with tar
TARPON	*n* pl. -S a marine game fish
TARRAGON	*n* pl. -S a perennial herb
TARRE	*v* TARRED, TARRING, TARRES to urge to action
TARRED	past tense of tar
TARRIED	past tense of tarry
TARRIER	*n* pl. -S one that tarries
TARRIES	present 3d person sing. of tarry
TARRIEST	superlative of tarry
TARRING	present participle of tar and tarre
TARRY	*v* -RIED, -RYING, -RIES to delay or be slow in acting or doing
TARRY	*adj* -RIER, -RIEST resembling tar
TARSAL	*n* pl. -S a bone of the foot
TARSI	pl. of tarsus
TARSIA	*n* pl. -S intarsia
TARSIER	*n* pl. -S a nocturnal primate
TARSUS	*n* pl. TARSI a part of the foot
TART	*adj* TARTER, TARTEST having a sharp, sour taste
TART	*v* -ED, -ING, -S to dress up
TARTAN	*n* pl. -S a patterned woolen fabric
TARTANA	*n* pl. -S a Mediterranean sailing vessel
TARTAR	*n* pl. -S a crust on the teeth **TARTARIC** *adj*
TARTISH	*adj* somewhat tart
TARTLET	*n* pl. -S a small pie
TARTLY	*adv* in a tart manner
TARTNESS	*n* pl. -ES the state of being tart
TARTRATE	*n* pl. -S a chemical salt
TARTUFE	*n* pl. -S tartuffe
TARTUFFE	*n* pl. -S a hypocrite
TARTY	*adj* resembling a prostitute
TARWEED	*n* pl. -S a flowering plant
TARZAN	*n* pl. -S a person of superior strength and agility
TASK	*v* -ED, -ING, -S to assign a job to
TASKWORK	*n* pl. -S hard work
TASS	*n* pl. -ES a drinking cup
TASSE	*n* pl. -S tasset
TASSEL	*v* -SELED, -SELING, -SELS or -SELLED, -SELLING, -SELS to adorn with dangling ornaments
TASSET	*n* pl. -S a piece of plate armor for the upper thigh
TASSIE	*n* pl. -S tass
TASTE	*v* TASTED, TASTING, TASTES to perceive the flavor of by taking into the mouth **TASTABLE** *adj*
TASTEFUL	*adj* tasty
TASTER	*n* pl. -S one that tastes
TASTING	present participle of taste
TASTY	*adj* TASTIER, TASTIEST pleasant to the taste **TASTILY** *adv*
TAT	*v* TATTED, TATTING, TATS to make tatting
TATAMI	*n* pl. -S straw matting used as a floor covering
TATAR	*n* pl. -S a ferocious person
TATE	*n* pl. -S a tuft of hair
TATER	*n* pl. -S a potato
TATOUAY	*n* pl. -AYS a South American armadillo
TATTED	past tense of tat
TATTER	*v* -ED, -ING, -S to become torn and worn
TATTIE	*n* pl. -S a potato

TATTIER comparative of tatty

TATTIEST superlative of tatty

TATTILY *adv* in a tatty manner

TATTING *n* pl. -S delicate handmade lace

TATTLE *v* -TLED, -TLING, -TLES to reveal the activities of another

TATTLER *n* pl. -S one that tattles

TATTOO *v* -ED, -ING, -S to mark the skin with indelible pigments

TATTOOER *n* pl. -S one that tattoos

TATTY *adj* -TIER, -TIEST shabby

TAU *n* pl. -S a Greek letter

TAUGHT past tense of teach

TAUNT *v* -ED, -ING, -S to challenge or reproach sarcastically

TAUNTER *n* pl. -S one that taunts

TAUPE *n* pl. -S a dark gray color

TAURINE *n* pl. -S a chemical compound

TAUT *adj* TAUTER, TAUTEST fully stretched, so as not to be slack

TAUT *v* -ED, -ING, -S to tangle

TAUTAUG *n* pl. -S tautog

TAUTEN *v* -ED, -ING, -S to make taut

TAUTLY *adv* in a taut manner

TAUTNESS *n* pl. -ES the state of being taut

TAUTOG *n* pl. -S a marine fish

TAUTOMER *n* pl. -S a type of chemical compound

TAUTONYM *n* pl. -S a type of taxonomic designation

TAV *n* pl. -S a Hebrew letter

TAVERN *n* pl. -S a place where liquor is sold to be drunk on the premises

TAVERNA *n* pl. -S a cafe in Greece

TAVERNER *n* pl. -S one that runs a tavern

TAW *v* -ED, -ING, -S to convert into white leather by the application of minerals

TAWDRY *adj* -DRIER, -DRIEST gaudy **TAWDRILY** *adv*

TAWDRY *n* pl. -DRIES gaudy finery

TAWER *n* pl. -S one that taws

TAWIE *adj* docile

TAWNEY *n* pl. -NEYS tawny

TAWNY *adj* -NIER, -NIEST light brown **TAWNILY** *adv*

TAWNY *n* pl. -NIES a light brown color

TAWPIE *n* pl. -S a foolish young person

TAWSE *v* TAWSED, TAWSING, TAWSES to flog

TAX *v* -ED, -ING, -ES to place a tax (a charge imposed by authority for public purposes) on

TAXA a pl. of taxon

TAXABLE *adj* subject to tax **TAXABLY** *adv*

TAXABLE *n* pl. -S a taxable item

TAXATION *n* pl. -S the process of taxing

TAXEME *n* pl. -S a minimum grammatical feature of selection **TAXEMIC** *adj*

TAXER *n* pl. -S one that taxes

TAXI *v* TAXIED, TAXIING or TAXYING, TAXIS or TAXIES to travel in a taxicab

TAXICAB *n* pl. -S an automobile for hire

TAXIMAN *n* pl. -MEN the operator of a taxicab

TAXINGLY *adv* in an onerous manner

TAXITE *n* pl. -S a volcanic rock **TAXITIC** *adj*

TAXIWAY *n* pl. -WAYS a paved strip at an airport

TAXLESS *adj* free from taxation

TAXMAN *n* pl. -MEN one who collects taxes

TAXON *n* pl. TAXA or TAXONS a unit of scientific classification

TAXONOMY *n* pl. -MIES the study of scientific classification

TAXPAID *adj* paid for by taxes

TAXPAYER *n* pl. -S one that pays taxes

TAXUS *n* pl. TAXUS an evergreen tree or shrub

TAXWISE *adj* pertaining to taxes

TAXYING a present participle of taxi

TAZZA *n* pl. -ZAS or -ZE an ornamental bowl

TEA *n* pl. -S a beverage made by infusing dried leaves in boiling water

TEABERRY *n* pl. -RIES a North American shrub

TEABOARD *n* pl. -S a tray for serving tea

TEABOWL *n* pl. -S a teacup having no handle

TEABOX *n* pl. -ES a box for tea leaves

TEACAKE *n* pl. -S a small cake served with tea

TEACART	n pl. -S a wheeled table used in serving tea	**TEASE**	v TEASED, TEASING, TEASES to make fun of
TEACH	v TAUGHT, TEACHING, TEACHES to impart knowledge or skill to	**TEASEL**	v -SELED, -SELING, -SELS or -SELLED, -SELLING, -SELS to raise a soft surface on fabric with a bristly flower head
TEACHER	n pl. -S one that teaches	**TEASELER**	n pl. -S one that teasels
TEACHING	n pl. -S a doctrine	**TEASER**	n pl. -S one that teases
TEACUP	n pl. -S a cup in which tea is served	**TEASHOP**	n pl. -S a tearoom
TEAHOUSE	n pl. -S a public establishment serving tea	**TEASING**	present participle of tease
		TEASPOON	n pl. -S a small spoon
TEAK	n pl. -S an East Indian tree	**TEAT**	n pl. -S a mammary gland **TEATED** adj
TEAKWOOD	n pl. -S the wood of the teak		
TEAL	n pl. -S a river duck	**TEATIME**	n pl. -S the customary time for tea
TEALIKE	adj resembling tea		
TEAM	v -ED, -ING, -S to form a team (a group of persons associated in a joint action)	**TEAWARE**	n pl. -S a tea service
		TEAZEL	v -ZELED, -ZELING, -ZELS or -ZELLED, -ZELLING, -ZELS to teasel
TEAMAKER	n pl. -S one that makes tea		
TEAMMATE	n pl. -S a member of the same team	**TEAZLE**	v -ZLED, -ZLING, -ZLES to teasel
TEAMSTER	n pl. -S a truck driver	**TECHED**	adj crazy
TEAMWORK	n pl. -S cooperative effort to achieve a common goal	**TECHIE**	n pl. -S a technician
		TECHNIC	n pl. -S technique
TEAPOT	n pl. -S a vessel used in making and serving tea	**TECHY**	adj TECHIER, TECHIEST tetchy **TECHILY** adv
TEAPOY	n pl. -POYS a small table used in serving tea	**TECTA**	pl. of tectum
		TECTAL	adj pertaining to a tectum
TEAR	v -ED, -ING, -S to emit tears (drops of saline liquid secreted by a gland of the eye)	**TECTITE**	n pl. -S tektite
		TECTONIC	adj pertaining to construction
TEAR	v TORE, TORN, TEARING, TEARS to pull apart or into pieces **TEARABLE** adj	**TECTRIX**	n pl. -TRICES a small feather of a bird's wing
		TECTUM	n pl. -TA a bodily structure resembling or serving as a roof
TEARAWAY	n pl. -AWAYS a rebellious person	**TED**	v TEDDED, TEDDING, TEDS to spread for drying
TEARDOWN	n pl. -S the process of disassembling		
TEARDROP	n pl. -S a tear	**TEDDER**	n pl. -S one that teds
TEARER	n pl. -S one that tears or rips	**TEDDY**	n pl. -DIES a woman's undergarment
TEARFUL	adj full of tears	**TEDIOUS**	adj causing weariness
TEARGAS	v -GASSED, -GASSING, -GASES or -GASSES to subject to a gas that irritates the eyes	**TEDIUM**	n pl. -S the state of being tedious
		TEE	v TEED, TEEING, TEES to place a golf ball on a small peg
TEARIER	comparative of teary		
TEARIEST	superlative of teary	**TEEL**	n pl. -S sesame
TEARILY	adv in a teary manner	**TEEM**	v -ED, -ING, -S to be full to overflowing
TEARLESS	adj being without tears		
TEAROOM	n pl. -S a restaurant serving tea	**TEEMER**	n pl. -S one that teems
TEARY	adj TEARIER, TEARIEST tearful	**TEEN**	n pl. -S a teenager
		TEENAGE	adj pertaining to teenagers

TEENAGED	*adj* teenage
TEENAGER	*n* pl. -S a person between the ages of thirteen and nineteen
TEENER	*n* pl. -S a teenager
TEENFUL	*adj* filled with grief
TEENIER	comparative of teeny
TEENIEST	superlative of teeny
TEENSY	*adj* -SIER, -SIEST tiny
TEENTSY	*adj* -SIER, -SIEST tiny
TEENY	*adj* -NIER, -NIEST tiny
TEENYBOP	*adj* pertaining to a young teenager
TEEPEE	*n* pl. -S tepee
TEETER	*v* -ED, -ING, -S to move unsteadily
TEETH	pl. of tooth
TEETHE	*v* TEETHED, TEETHING, TEETHES to cut teeth
TEETHER	*n* pl. -S an object for a baby to bite on during teething
TEETHING	*n* pl. -S the first growth of teeth
TEETOTAL	*v* -TALED, -TALING, -TALS or -TALLED, -TALLING, -TALS to abstain completely from alcoholic beverages
TEETOTUM	*n* pl. -S a spinning toy
TEFF	*n* pl. -S a cereal grass
TEFILLIN	*n/pl* the phylacteries worn by Jews
TEG	*n* pl. -S a yearling sheep
TEGMEN	*n* pl. -MINA a covering
TEGMENTA	*n/pl* anatomical coverings
TEGMINAL	*adj* pertaining to a tegmen
TEGUA	*n* pl. -S a type of moccasin
TEGULAR	*adj* resembling a tile
TEGUMEN	*n* pl. -MINA tegmen
TEGUMENT	*n* pl. -S a covering
TEIGLACH	*n* pl. TEIGLACH a confection consisting of balls of dough boiled in honey
TEIID	*n* pl. -S a tropical American lizard
TEIND	*n* pl. -S a tithe
TEKTITE	*n* pl. -S a glassy body believed to be of meteoritic origin **TEKTITIC** *adj*
TEL	*n* pl. -S an ancient mound in the Middle East
TELA	*n* pl. -LAE an anatomical tissue
TELAMON	*n* pl. -ES a male figure used as a supporting column
TELE	*n* pl. -S a television set
TELECAST	*v* -ED, -ING, -S to broadcast by television
TELEDU	*n* pl. -S a carnivorous mammal
TELEFILM	*n* pl. -S a motion picture made for television
TELEGA	*n* pl. -S a Russian wagon
TELEGONY	*n* pl. -NIES the supposed influence of a previous sire on the offspring of later matings of the mother with other males
TELEGRAM	*v* -GRAMMED, -GRAMMING, -GRAMS to send a message by telegraph
TELEMAN	*n* pl. -MEN a naval officer
TELEMARK	*n* pl. -S a type of turn in skiing
TELEOST	*n* pl. -S a bony fish
TELEPATH	*n* pl. -S one who can communicate with another by some means other than the senses
TELEPLAY	*n* pl. -PLAYS a play written for television
TELEPORT	*v* -ED, -ING, -S to transport by a process that involves no physical means
TELERAN	*n* pl. -S a system of air navigation
TELESIS	*n* pl. TELESES planned progress
TELESTIC	*n* pl. -S a type of acrostic
TELETEXT	*n* pl. -S a communications system in which printed matter is telecast to subscribers
TELETHON	*n* pl. -S a fund-raising television program
TELEVIEW	*v* -ED, -ING, -S to observe by means of television
TELEVISE	*v* -VISED, -VISING, -VISES to broadcast by television (an electronic system of transmitting images and sound)
TELEX	*v* -ED, -ING, -ES to send a message by a type of telegraphic system
TELFER	*v* -ED, -ING, -S to telpher
TELFORD	*n* pl. -S a road made of stones
TELIA	pl. of telium
TELIAL	*adj* pertaining to a telium
TELIC	*adj* directed toward a goal

TELIUM	*n* pl. -LIA a sorus on the host plant of a rust fungus
TELL	*v* TOLD, TELLING, TELLS to give a detailed account of **TELLABLE** *adj*
TELLER	*n* pl. -S one that tells
TELLIES	a pl. of telly
TELLTALE	*n* pl. -S a tattler
TELLURIC	*adj* pertaining to the earth
TELLY	*n* pl. -LIES or -LYS a television set
TELOME	*n* pl. -S a structural unit of a vascular plant **TELOMIC** *adj*
TELOMERE	*n* pl. -S the natural end of a chromosome
TELOS	*n* pl. TELOI an ultimate end
TELPHER	*v* -ED, -ING, -S to transport by a system of aerial cable cars
TELSON	*n* pl. -S the terminal segment of an arthropod **TELSONIC** *adj*
TEMBLOR	*n* pl. -S or -ES an earthquake
TEMERITY	*n* pl. -TIES foolish boldness
TEMP	*v* -ED, -ING, -S to work as a temporary employee
TEMPEH	*n* pl. -S an Asian food
TEMPER	*v* -ED, -ING, -S to moderate by adding a counterbalancing agent
TEMPERA	*n* pl. -S a technique of painting
TEMPERER	*n* pl. -S one that tempers
TEMPEST	*v* -ED, -ING, -S to agitate violently
TEMPI	a pl. of tempo
TEMPLAR	*n* pl. -S a lawyer or student of law in London
TEMPLATE	*n* pl. -S a pattern used as a guide in making something
TEMPLE	*n* pl. -S a house of worship **TEMPLED** *adj*
TEMPLET	*n* pl. -S template
TEMPO	*n* pl. -PI or -POS the rate of speed of a musical piece
TEMPORAL	*n* pl. -S a bone of the skull
TEMPT	*v* -ED, -ING, -S to entice to commit an unwise or immoral act
TEMPTER	*n* pl. -S one that tempts
TEMPURA	*n* pl. -S a Japanese dish
TEN	*n* pl. -S a number
TENABLE	*adj* capable of being held **TENABLY** *adv*
TENACE	*n* pl. -S a combination of two high cards in some card games
TENACITY	*n* pl. -TIES perseverance or persistence
TENACULA	*n/pl* hooked surgical instruments
TENAIL	*n* pl. -S tenaille
TENAILLE	*n* pl. -S an outer defense
TENANCY	*n* pl. -CIES the temporary occupancy of something that belongs to another
TENANT	*v* -ED, -ING, -S to inhabit
TENANTRY	*n* pl. -RIES tenancy
TENCH	*n* pl. -ES a freshwater fish
TEND	*v* -ED, -ING, -S to be disposed or inclined
TENDANCE	*n* pl. -S watchful care
TENDENCE	*n* pl. -S tendance
TENDENCY	*n* pl. -CIES an inclination to act or think in a particular way
TENDER	*adj* -DERER, -DEREST soft or delicate
TENDER	*v* -ED, -ING, -S to present for acceptance
TENDERER	*n* pl. -S one that tenders
TENDERLY	*adv* in a tender manner
TENDON	*n* pl. -S a band of tough, fibrous tissue
TENDRIL	*n* pl. -S a leafless organ of climbing plants
TENEBRAE	*n/pl* a religious service
TENEMENT	*n* pl. -S an apartment house
TENESMUS	*n* pl. -ES an urgent but ineffectual effort to defecate or urinate **TENESMIC** *adj*
TENET	*n* pl. -S a principle, belief, or doctrine held to be true
TENFOLD	*n* pl. -S an amount ten times as great as a given unit
TENIA	*n* pl. -NIAE or -NIAS a tapeworm
TENIASIS	*n* pl. -SISES infestation with tapeworms
TENNER	*n* pl. -S a ten-dollar bill
TENNIES	*n/pl* low-cut sneakers
TENNIS	*n* pl. -NISES an outdoor ball game
TENNIST	*n* pl. -S a tennis player
TENON	*v* -ED, -ING, -S to unite by means of a tenon (a projection on the end of a piece of wood)
TENONER	*n* pl. -S one that tenons

TENOR *n* pl. -S a high male singing voice

TENORIST *n* pl. -S one who sings tenor or plays a tenor instrument

TENORITE *n* pl. -S a mineral

TENOTOMY *n* pl. -MIES the surgical division of a tendon

TENOUR *n* pl. -S tenor

TENPENCE *n* pl. -S the sum of ten pennies

TENPENNY *adj* worth tenpence

TENPIN *n* pl. -S a bowling pin

TENREC *n* pl. -S a mammal that feeds on insects

TENSE *adj* TENSER, TENSEST taut **TENSELY** *adv*

TENSE *v* TENSED, TENSING, TENSES to make tense

TENSIBLE *adj* capable of being stretched **TENSIBLY** *adv*

TENSILE *adj* tensible

TENSING present participle of tense

TENSION *v* -ED, -ING, -S to make tense

TENSITY *n* pl. -TIES the state of being tense

TENSIVE *adj* causing tensity

TENSOR *n* pl. -S a muscle that stretches a body part

TENT *v* -ED, -ING, -S to live in a tent (a type of portable shelter)

TENTACLE *n* pl. -S an elongated, flexible appendage of some animals

TENTAGE *n* pl. -S a supply of tents

TENTER *v* -ED, -ING, -S to stretch on a type of frame

TENTH *n* pl. -S one of ten equal parts

TENTHLY *adv* in the tenth place

TENTIE *adj* TENTIER, TENTIEST tenty

TENTIER comparative of tenty

TENTIEST superlative of tenty

TENTLESS *adj* having no tent

TENTLIKE *adj* resembling a tent

TENTY *adj* TENTIER, TENTIEST watchful

TENUIS *n* pl. -UES a voiceless phonetic stop

TENUITY *n* pl. -ITIES lack of substance or strength

TENUOUS *adj* having little substance or strength

TENURE *n* pl. -S the holding of something **TENURED, TENURIAL** *adj*

TENUTO *n* pl. -TI or -TOS a musical note or chord held longer than its normal duration

TEOCALLI *n* pl. -S an Aztec temple

TEOPAN *n* pl. -S a teocalli

TEOSINTE *n* pl. -S an annual grass

TEPA *n* pl. -S a chemical compound

TEPAL *n* pl. -S a division of a perianth

TEPEE *n* pl. -S a conical tent of some North American Indians

TEPEFY *v* -FIED, -FYING, -FIES to make tepid

TEPHRA *n* pl. -S solid material ejected from a volcano

TEPHRITE *n* pl. -S a volcanic rock

TEPID *adj* moderately warm **TEPIDLY** *adv*

TEPIDITY *n* pl. -TIES the state of being tepid

TEPOY *n* pl. -POYS teapoy

TEQUILA *n* pl. -S a Mexican liquor

TERAI *n* pl. -S a sun hat with a wide brim

TERAOHM *n* pl. -S one trillion ohms

TERAPH *n* pl. -APHIM an image of a Semitic household god

TERATISM *n* pl. -S a malformed fetus **TERATOID** *adj*

TERATOMA *n* pl. -MAS or -MATA a type of tumor

TERAWATT *n* pl. -S one trillion watts

TERBIA *n* pl. -S an oxide of terbium

TERBIUM *n* pl. -S a metallic element **TERBIC** *adj*

TERCE *n* pl. -S tierce

TERCEL *n* pl. -S a male falcon

TERCELET *n* pl. -S tercel

TERCET *n* pl. -S a group of three lines of verse

TEREBENE *n* pl. -S a mixture of terpenes

TEREBIC *adj* pertaining to an acid derived from oil of turpentine

TEREDO *n* pl. -DOS or -DINES a bivalve mollusk

TEREFAH *adj* tref

TERETE *adj* cylindrical and slightly tapering

TERGA pl. of tergum

TERGAL	*adj* pertaining to a tergum
TERGITE	*n* pl. -S a tergum
TERGUM	*n* pl. -GA a back part of a segment of an arthropod
TERIYAKI	*n* pl. -S a Japanese food
TERM	*v* -ED, -ING, -S to give a name to
TERMER	*n* pl. -S a prisoner serving a specified sentence
TERMINAL	*n* pl. -S an end or extremity
TERMINUS	*n* pl. -NI or -NUSES a terminal
TERMITE	*n* pl. -S an insect resembling an ant **TERMITIC** *adj*
TERMLESS	*adj* having no limits
TERMLY	*adv* periodically
TERMOR	*n* pl. -S one that holds land for a certain number of years
TERMTIME	*n* pl. -S the time when a school or court is in session
TERN	*n* pl. -S a seabird
TERNARY	*n* pl. -RIES a group of three
TERNATE	*adj* arranged in groups of three
TERNE	*n* pl. -S an alloy of lead and tin
TERNION	*n* pl. -S a group of three
TERPENE	*n* pl. -S a chemical compound **TERPENIC** *adj*
TERPINOL	*n* pl. -S a fragrant liquid
TERRA	*n* pl. -RAE earth; land
TERRACE	*v* -RACED, -RACING, -RACES to provide with a terrace (a raised embankment)
TERRAIN	*n* pl. -S a tract of land
TERRANE	*n* pl. -S a rock formation
TERRAPIN	*n* pl. -S a North American tortoise
TERRARIA	*n/pl* glass enclosures for plants or small animals
TERRAS	*n* pl. -ES trass
TERRAZZO	*n* pl. -ZOS a mosaic flooring
TERREEN	*n* pl. -S terrine
TERRELLA	*n* pl. -S a spherical magnet
TERRENE	*n* pl. -S a land area
TERRET	*n* pl. -S a metal ring on a harness
TERRIBLE	*adj* very bad **TERRIBLY** *adv*
TERRIER	*n* pl. -S a small, active dog
TERRIES	pl. of terry
TERRIFIC	*adj* very good; fine
TERRIFY	*v* -FIED, -FYING, -FIES to fill with terror

TERRINE	*n* pl. -S an earthenware jar
TERRIT	*n* pl. -S terret
TERROR	*n* pl. -S intense fear
TERRY	*n* pl. -RIES an absorbent fabric
TERSE	*adj* TERSER, TERSEST succinct **TERSELY** *adv*
TERTIAL	*n* pl. -S a flight feather of a bird's wing
TERTIAN	*n* pl. -S a recurrent fever
TERTIARY	*n* pl. -ARIES a tertial
TESLA	*n* pl. -S a unit of magnetic induction
TESSERA	*n* pl. -SERAE a small square used in mosaic work
TEST	*v* -ED, -ING, -S to subject to an examination **TESTABLE** *adj*
TESTA	*n* pl. -TAE the hard outer coating of a seed
TESTACY	*n* pl. -CIES the state of being testate
TESTATE	*n* pl. -S a testator
TESTATOR	*n* pl. -S one that makes a will
TESTEE	*n* pl. -S one that is tested
TESTER	*n* pl. -S one that tests
TESTES	pl. of testis
TESTICLE	*n* pl. -S a testis
TESTIER	comparative of testy
TESTIEST	superlative of testy
TESTIFY	*v* -FIED, -FYING, -FIES to make a declaration of truth under oath
TESTILY	*adv* in a testy manner
TESTIS	*n* pl. TESTES a male reproductive gland
TESTON	*n* pl. -S a former French coin
TESTOON	*n* pl. -S teston
TESTUDO	*n* pl. -DINES or -DOS a portable screen used as a shield by the ancient Romans
TESTY	*adj* TESTIER, TESTIEST irritable
TET	*n* pl. -S teth
TETANAL	*adj* pertaining to tetanus
TETANIC	*n* pl. -S a drug capable of causing convulsions
TETANIES	pl. of tetany
TETANISE	*v* -NISED, -NISING, -NISES to tetanize
TETANIZE	*v* -NIZED, -NIZING, -NIZES to affect with convulsions

TETANUS   *n* pl. -ES an infectious disease **TETANOID** *adj*

TETANY   *n* pl. -NIES a condition marked by painful muscular spasms

TETCHED   *adj* crazy

TETCHY   *adj* TETCHIER, TETCHIEST irritable **TETCHILY** *adv*

TETH   *n* pl. -S a Hebrew letter

TETHER   *v* -ED, -ING, -S to fasten to a fixed object with a rope

TETOTUM   *n* pl. -S teetotum

TETRA   *n* pl. -S a tropical fish

TETRACID   *n* pl. -S a type of acid

TETRAD   *n* pl. -S a group of four **TETRADIC** *adj*

TETRAGON   *n* pl. -S a four-sided polygon

TETRAMER   *n* pl. -S a type of polymer

TETRAPOD   *n* pl. -S a four-footed animal

TETRARCH   *n* pl. -S one of four joint rulers

TETRODE   *n* pl. -S a type of electron tube

TETROXID   *n* pl. -S a type of oxide

TETRYL   *n* pl. -S a chemical compound

TETTER   *n* pl. -S a skin disease

TEUCH   *adj* teugh

TEUGH   *adj* tough **TEUGHLY** *adv*

TEW   *v* -ED, -ING, -S to work hard

TEXAS   *n* pl. -ES the uppermost structure on a steamboat

TEXT   *n* pl. -S the main body of a written or printed work

TEXTBOOK   *n* pl. -S a book used in the study of a subject

TEXTILE   *n* pl. -S a woven fabric

TEXTLESS   *adj* having no text

TEXTUAL   *adj* pertaining to a text

TEXTUARY   *n* pl. -ARIES a specialist in the study of the Scriptures

TEXTURAL   *adj* pertaining to the surface characteristics of something

TEXTURE   *v* -TURED, -TURING, -TURES to make by weaving

THACK   *v* -ED, -ING, -S to thatch

THAE   *adj* these; those

THAIRM   *n* pl. -S tharm

THALAMUS   *n* pl. -MI a part of the brain **THALAMIC** *adj*

THALER   *n* pl. -S taler

THALLIUM   *n* pl. -S a metallic element **THALLIC, THALLOUS** *adj*

THALLUS   *n* pl. -LI or -LUSES a plant body without true root, stem, or leaf **THALLOID** *adj*

THAN   *conj* — used to introduce the second element of a comparison

THANAGE   *n* pl. -S the land held by a thane

THANATOS   *n* pl. -ES an instinctual desire for death

THANE   *n* pl. -S a man holding land by military service in Anglo-Saxon England

THANK   *v* -ED, -ING, -S to express gratitude to

THANKER   *n* pl. -S one that thanks

THANKFUL   *adj* -FULLER, -FULLEST feeling gratitude

THARM   *n* pl. -S the belly

THAT   *pron* pl. THOSE the one indicated

THATAWAY   *adv* in that direction

THATCH   *v* -ED, -ING, -ES to cover with thatch (plant stalks or foliage)

THATCHER   *n* pl. -S one that thatches

THATCHY   *adj* THATCHIER, THATCHIEST resembling thatch

THAW   *v* -ED, -ING, -S to melt

THAWER   *n* pl. -S one that thaws

THAWLESS   *adj* never thawing

THE   *definite article* — used to specify or make particular

THEARCHY   *n* pl. -CHIES rule by a god

THEATER   *n* pl. -S a building for dramatic presentations **THEATRIC** *adj*

THEATRE   *n* pl. -S theater

THEBAINE   *n* pl. -S a poisonous alkaloid

THEBE   *n* pl. THEBE a monetary unit of Botswana

THECA   *n* pl. -CAE a protective anatomical covering **THECAL, THECATE** *adj*

THEE   *pron* the objective case of the pronoun thou

THEELIN   *n* pl. -S estrone

THEELOL   *n* pl. -S estriol

THEFT   *n* pl. -S the act of stealing

THEGN   *n* pl. -S thane **THEGNLY** *adj*

THEIN   *n* pl. -S theine

THEINE   *n* pl. -S caffeine

THEIR	*pron* a possessive form of the pronoun they
THEIRS	*pron* a possessive form of the pronoun they
THEISM	*n* pl. -S belief in the existence of a god
THEIST	*n* pl. -S one who believes in the existence of a god **THEISTIC** *adj*
THELITIS	*n* pl. -TISES inflammation of the nipple
THEM	*pron* the objective case of the pronoun they
THEMATIC	*n* pl. -S a stamp collected according to its subject
THEME	*v* THEMED, THEMING, THEMES to plan something according to a central subject
THEN	*n* pl. -S that time
THENAGE	*n* pl. -S thanage
THENAL	*adj* pertaining to the palm of the hand
THENAR	*n* pl. -S the palm of the hand
THENCE	*adv* from that place
THEOCRAT	*n* pl. -S a person who rules as a representative of a god
THEODICY	*n* pl. -CIES a defense of God's goodness in respect to the existence of evil
THEOGONY	*n* pl. -NIES an account of the origin of the gods
THEOLOG	*n* pl. -S a student of theology
THEOLOGY	*n* pl. -GIES the study of religion
THEONOMY	*n* pl. -MIES rule by a god
THEORBO	*n* pl. -BOS a stringed musical instrument
THEOREM	*n* pl. -S a proposition that is demonstrably true or is assumed to be so
THEORIES	pl. of theory
THEORISE	*v* -RISED, -RISING, -RISES to theorize
THEORIST	*n* pl. -S one that theorizes
THEORIZE	*v* -RIZED, -RIZING, -RIZES to form theories
THEORY	*n* pl. -RIES a group of propositions used to explain a class of phenomena
THERAPY	*n* pl. -PIES the treatment of illness or disability
THERE	*n* pl. -S that place
THEREAT	*adv* at that place or time
THEREBY	*adv* by that means
THEREFOR	*adv* for that
THEREIN	*adv* in that place
THEREMIN	*n* pl. -S a musical instrument
THEREOF	*adv* of that
THEREON	*adv* on that
THERETO	*adv* to that
THERIAC	*n* pl. -S molasses
THERIACA	*n* pl. -S theriac
THERM	*n* pl. -S a unit of quantity of heat
THERMAE	*n/pl* hot springs
THERMAL	*n* pl. -S a rising mass of warm air
THERME	*n* pl. -S therm
THERMEL	*n* pl. -S a device for temperature measurement
THERMIC	*adj* pertaining to heat
THERMION	*n* pl. -S an ion emitted by a heated body
THERMITE	*n* pl. -S a metallic mixture that produces intense heat when ignited
THERMOS	*n* pl. -ES a container used to keep liquids either hot or cold
THEROID	*adj* resembling a beast
THEROPOD	*n* pl. -S a carnivorous dinosaur
THESAURI	*n/pl* dictionaries of synonyms and antonyms
THESE	pl. of this
THESIS	*n* pl. THESES a proposition put forward for discussion
THESPIAN	*n* pl. -S an actor or actress
THETA	*n* pl. -S a Greek letter
THETIC	*adj* arbitrary
THETICAL	*adj* thetic
THEURGY	*n* pl. -GIES divine intervention in human affairs **THEURGIC** *adj*
THEW	*n* pl. -S a well-developed muscle
THEWLESS	*adj* weak
THEWY	*adj* THEWIER, THEWIEST brawny
THEY	*pron* the 3d person pl. pronoun in the nominative case
THIAMIN	*n* pl. -S thiamine
THIAMINE	*n* pl. -S a B vitamin
THIAZIDE	*n* pl. -S a drug used to treat high blood pressure
THIAZIN	*n* pl. -S thiazine
THIAZINE	*n* pl. -S a chemical compound

THIAZOL	*n* pl. -S thiazole
THIAZOLE	*n* pl. -S a chemical compound
THICK	*adj* THICKER, THICKEST having relatively great extent from one surface to its opposite
THICK	*n* pl. -S the thickest part
THICKEN	*v* -ED, -ING, -S to make thick
THICKET	*n* pl. -S a dense growth of shrubs or small trees **THICKETY** *adj*
THICKISH	*adj* somewhat thick
THICKLY	*adv* in a thick manner
THICKSET	*n* pl. -S a thicket
THIEF	*n* pl. THIEVES one that steals
THIEVE	*v* THIEVED, THIEVING, THIEVES to steal
THIEVERY	*n* pl. -ERIES the act or practice of stealing
THIEVES	pl. of thief
THIEVING	present participle of thieve
THIEVISH	*adj* given to stealing
THIGH	*n* pl. -S a part of the leg **THIGHED** *adj*
THILL	*n* pl. -S a shaft of a vehicle
THIMBLE	*n* pl. -S a cap used to protect the fingertip during sewing
THIN	*adj* THINNER, THINNEST having relatively little density or thickness
THIN	*v* THINNED, THINNING, THINS to make thin
THINCLAD	*n* pl. -S a runner on a track team
THINDOWN	*n* pl. -S a lessening in the number of atomic particles and cosmic rays passing through the earth's atmosphere
THINE	*pron* a possessive form of the pronoun thou
THING	*n* pl. -S an inanimate object
THINK	*v* THOUGHT, THINKING, THINKS to formulate in the mind
THINKER	*n* pl. -S one that thinks
THINKING	*n* pl. -S an opinion or judgment
THINLY	*adv* in a thin manner
THINNED	past tense of thin
THINNER	*n* pl. -S one that thins
THINNESS	*n* pl. -ES the quality or state of being thin
THINNEST	superlative of thin
THINNING	present participle of thin
THINNISH	*adj* somewhat thin
THIO	*adj* containing sulfur
THIOL	*n* pl. -S a sulfur compound **THIOLIC** *adj*
THIONATE	*n* pl. -S a chemical salt
THIONIC	*adj* pertaining to sulfur
THIONIN	*n* pl. -S a violet dye
THIONINE	*n* pl. -S thionin
THIONYL	*n* pl. -S sulfinyl
THIOPHEN	*n* pl. -S a chemical compound
THIOTEPA	*n* pl. -S a chemical compound
THIOUREA	*n* pl. -S a chemical compound
THIR	*pron* these
THIRAM	*n* pl. -S a chemical compound
THIRD	*n* pl. -S one of three equal parts
THIRDLY	*adv* in the third place
THIRL	*v* -ED, -ING, -S to thrill
THIRLAGE	*n* pl. -S an obligation requiring feudal tenants to grind grain at a certain mill
THIRST	*v* -ED, -ING, -S to feel a desire or need to drink
THIRSTER	*n* pl. -S one that thirsts
THIRSTY	*adj* THIRSTIER, THIRSTIEST feeling a desire or need to drink
THIRTEEN	*n* pl. -S a number
THIRTY	*n* pl. -TIES a number
THIS	*pron* pl. THESE the person or thing just mentioned
THISTLE	*n* pl. -S a prickly plant
THISTLY	*adj* -TLIER, -TLIEST prickly
THITHER	*adv* in that direction
THO	*conj* though
THOLE	*v* THOLED, THOLING, THOLES to endure
THOLEPIN	*n* pl. -S a pin that serves as an oarlock
THOLOS	*n* pl. -LOI a circular, underground tomb
THONG	*n* pl. -S a narrow strip of leather used for binding **THONGED** *adj*
THORAX	*n* pl. -RACES or -RAXES the part of the body between the neck and the abdomen **THORACAL, THORACIC** *adj*
THORIA	*n* pl. -S an oxide of thorium
THORIC	*adj* pertaining to thorium
THORITE	*n* pl. -S a thorium ore

THORIUM   *n* pl. -S a metallic element

THORN   *v* -ED, -ING, -S to prick with a thorn (a sharp, rigid projection on a plant)

THORNY   *adj* THORNIER, THORNIEST full of thorns **THORNILY** *adv*

THORO   *adj* thorough

THORON   *n* pl. -S a radioactive isotope of radon

THOROUGH   *adj* THOROUGHER, THOROUGHEST complete in all respects

THORP   *n* pl. -S a small village

THORPE   *n* pl. -S thorp

THOSE   pl. of that

THOU   *v* -ED, -ING, -S to address as "thou" (the 2d person sing. pronoun in the nominative case)

THOUGH   *conj* despite the fact that

THOUGHT   *n* pl. -S a product of thinking

THOUSAND   *n* pl. -S a number

THOWLESS   *adj* listless

THRALDOM   *n* pl. -S servitude

THRALL   *v* -ED, -ING, -S to enslave

THRASH   *v* -ED, -ING, -ES to beat

THRASHER   *n* pl. -S one that thrashes

THRAVE   *n* pl. -S a unit of measure for grain

THRAW   *v* -ED, -ING, -S to twist

THRAWART   *adj* stubborn

THRAWN   *adj* twisted **THRAWNLY** *adv*

THREAD   *v* -ED, -ING, -S to pass a thread (a very slender cord) through

THREADER   *n* pl. -S one that threads

THREADY   *adj* THREADIER, THREADIEST resembling a thread

THREAP   *v* -ED, -ING, -S to dispute

THREAPER   *n* pl. -S one that threaps

THREAT   *v* -ED, -ING, -S to threaten

THREATEN   *v* -ED, -ING, -S to be a source of danger to

THREE   *n* pl. -S a number

THREEP   *v* -ED, -ING, -S to threap

THRENODE   *n* pl. -S a threnody

THRENODY   *n* pl. -DIES a song of lamentation

THRESH   *v* -ED, -ING, -ES to separate the grain or seeds from a plant mechanically

THRESHER   *n* pl. -S one that threshes

THREW   past tense of throw

THRICE   *adv* three times

THRIFT   *n* pl. -S care and wisdom in the management of one's resources

THRIFTY   *adj* THRIFTIER, THRIFTIEST displaying thrift

THRILL   *v* -ED, -ING, -S to excite greatly

THRILLER   *n* pl. -S one that thrills

THRIP   *n* pl. -S a British coin

THRIVE   *v* THROVE or THRIVED, THRIVEN, THRIVING, THRIVES to grow vigorously

THRIVER   *n* pl. -S one that thrives

THRO   *prep* through

THROAT   *v* -ED, -ING, -S to utter in a hoarse voice

THROATY   *adj* THROATIER, THROATIEST hoarse

THROB   *v* THROBBED, THROBBING, THROBS to pulsate

THROBBER   *n* pl. -S one that throbs

THROE   *n* pl. -S a violent spasm of pain

THROMBIN   *n* pl. -S an enzyme

THROMBUS   *n* pl. -BI a clot occluding a blood vessel

THRONE   *v* THRONED, THRONING, THRONES to place on a throne (a royal chair)

THRONG   *v* -ED, -ING, -S to crowd into

THROSTLE   *n* pl. -S a songbird

THROTTLE   *v* -TLED, -TLING, -TLES to strangle

THROUGH   *prep* by way of

THROVE   a past tense of thrive

THROW   *v* THREW, THROWN, THROWING, THROWS to propel through the air with a movement of the arm

THROWER   *n* pl. -S one that throws

THRU   *prep* through

THRUM   *v* THRUMMED, THRUMMING, THRUMS to play a stringed instrument idly or monotonously

THRUMMER   *n* pl. -S one that thrums

THRUMMY   *adj* -MIER, -MIEST shaggy

THRUPUT   *n* pl. -S the amount of raw material processed within a given time

THRUSH   *n* pl. -ES a songbird

THRUST   *v* -ED, -ING, -S to push forcibly

THRUSTER	*n* pl. -S one that thrusts
THRUSTOR	*n* pl. -S thruster
THRUWAY	*n* pl. -WAYS an express highway
THUD	*v* THUDDED, THUDDING, THUDS to make a dull, heavy sound
THUG	*n* pl. -S a brutal ruffian or assassin
THUGGEE	*n* pl. -S thuggery in India
THUGGERY	*n* pl. -GERIES thuggish behavior
THUGGISH	*adj* characteristic of a thug
THUJA	*n* pl. -S an evergreen tree or shrub
THULIA	*n* pl. -S an oxide of thulium
THULIUM	*n* pl. -S a metallic element
THUMB	*v* -ED, -ING, -S to leaf through with the thumb (the short, thick digit of the human hand)
THUMBKIN	*n* pl. -S a screw that is turned by the thumb and fingers
THUMBNUT	*n* pl. -S a nut that is turned by the thumb and fingers
THUMP	*v* -ED, -ING, -S to strike so as to make a dull, heavy sound
THUMPER	*n* pl. -S one that thumps
THUNDER	*v* -ED, -ING, -S to produce a loud, resounding sound
THUNDERY	*adj* accompanied with thunder
THUNK	*v* -ED, -ING, -S to make a sudden, muffled sound
THURIBLE	*n* pl. -S a censer
THURIFER	*n* pl. -S one who carries a thurible in a religious ceremony
THURL	*n* pl. -S the hip joint in cattle
THUS	*adv* in this manner
THUSLY	*adv* thus
THUYA	*n* pl. -S thuja
THWACK	*v* -ED, -ING, -S to strike with something flat
THWACKER	*n* pl. -S one that thwacks
THWART	*v* -ED, -ING, -S to prevent the accomplishment of
THWARTER	*n* pl. -S one that thwarts
THWARTLY	*adv* athwart
THY	*pron* a possessive form of the pronoun thou
THYME	*n* pl. -S an aromatic herb
THYMEY	*adj* THYMIER, THYMIEST thymy
THYMI	a pl. of thymus
THYMIC	*adj* pertaining to thyme
THYMIER	comparative of thymey and thymy
THYMIEST	superlative of thymey and thymy
THYMINE	*n* pl. -S a chemical compound
THYMOL	*n* pl. -S a chemical compound
THYMOSIN	*n* pl. -S a hormone secreted by the thymus
THYMUS	*n* pl. -MI or -MUSES a glandular structure in the body
THYMY	*adj* THYMIER, THYMIEST abounding in thyme
THYREOID	*adj* pertaining to the thyroid
THYROID	*n* pl. -S an endocrine gland
THYROXIN	*n* pl. -S an amino acid
THYRSE	*n* pl. -S thyrsus
THYRSUS	*n* pl. -SI a type of flower cluster **THYRSOID** *adj*
THYSELF	*pron* yourself
TI	*n* pl. -S the seventh tone of the diatonic musical scale
TIARA	*n* pl. -S a jeweled headpiece worn by women **TIARAED** *adj*
TIBIA	*n* pl. -IAE or -IAS a bone of the leg **TIBIAL** *adj*
TIC	*n* pl. -S an involuntary muscular contraction
TICAL	*n* pl. -S a former Thai unit of weight
TICK	*v* -ED, -ING, -S to make a recurrent clicking sound
TICKER	*n* pl. -S one that ticks
TICKET	*v* -ED, -ING, -S to attach a tag to
TICKING	*n* pl. -S a strong cotton fabric
TICKLE	*v* -LED, -LING, -LES to touch lightly so as to produce a tingling sensation
TICKLER	*n* pl. -S one that tickles
TICKLISH	*adj* sensitive to tickling
TICKSEED	*n* pl. -S a flowering plant
TICKTACK	*v* -ED, -ING, -S to ticktock
TICKTOCK	*v* -ED, -ING, -S to make the ticking sound of a clock
TICTAC	*v* -TACKED, -TACKING, -TACS to ticktack
TICTOC	*v* -TOCKED, -TOCKING, -TOCS to ticktock
TIDAL	*adj* pertaining to the tides **TIDALLY** *adv*
TIDBIT	*n* pl. -S a choice bit of food

TIDDLER	*n* pl. -S a small fish
TIDDLY	*adj* slightly drunk
TIDE	*v* TIDED, TIDING, TIDES to flow like the tide (the rise and fall of the ocean's waters)
TIDELAND	*n* pl. -S land alternately covered and uncovered by the tide
TIDELESS	*adj* lacking a tide
TIDELIKE	*adj* resembling a tide
TIDEMARK	*n* pl. -S a mark showing the highest or lowest point of a tide
TIDERIP	*n* pl. -S a riptide
TIDEWAY	*n* pl. -WAYS a tidal channel
TIDIED	past tense of tidy
TIDIER	*n* pl. -S one that tidies
TIDIES	present 3d person sing. of tidy
TIDIEST	superlative of tidy
TIDILY	*adv* in a tidy manner
TIDINESS	*n* pl. -ES the state of being tidy
TIDING	*n* pl. -S a piece of news
TIDY	*adj* -DIER, -DIEST neat and orderly
TIDY	*v* -DIED, -DYING, -DIES to make tidy
TIDYTIPS	*n* pl. TIDYTIPS an annual herb
TIE	*v* TIED, TYING or TIEING, TIES to fasten with a cord or rope
TIEBACK	*n* pl. -S a loop for holding a curtain back to one side
TIECLASP	*n* pl. -S a clasp for securing a necktie
TIED	past tense of tie
TIELESS	*adj* having no necktie
TIEPIN	*n* pl. -S a pin for securing a necktie
TIER	*v* -ED, -ING, -S to arrange in tiers (rows placed one above another)
TIERCE	*n* pl. -S one of seven canonical daily periods for prayer and devotion
TIERCED	*adj* divided into three equal parts
TIERCEL	*n* pl. -S tercel
TIFF	*v* -ED, -ING, -S to have a petty quarrel
TIFFANY	*n* pl. -NIES a thin, mesh fabric
TIFFIN	*v* -ED, -ING, -S to lunch
TIGER	*n* pl. -S a large feline mammal
TIGEREYE	*n* pl. -S a gemstone
TIGERISH	*adj* resembling a tiger
TIGHT	*adj* TIGHTER, TIGHTEST firmly or closely fixed in place **TIGHTLY** *adv*
TIGHTEN	*v* -ED, -ING, -S to make tight
TIGHTS	*n/pl* a close-fitting garment
TIGHTWAD	*n* pl. -S a miser
TIGLON	*n* pl. -S the offspring of a male tiger and a female lion
TIGON	*n* pl. -S tiglon
TIGRESS	*n* pl. -ES a female tiger
TIGRISH	*adj* tigerish
TIKE	*n* pl. -S tyke
TIKI	*n* pl. -S a wood or stone image of a Polynesian god
TIL	*n* pl. -S the sesame plant
TILAK	*n* pl. -S a mark worn on the forehead by Hindus
TILAPIA	*n* pl. -S an African fish
TILBURY	*n* pl. -BURIES a carriage having two wheels
TILDE	*n* pl. -S a mark placed over a letter to indicate its sound
TILE	*v* TILED, TILING, TILES to cover with tiles (thin slabs of baked clay)
TILEFISH	*n* pl. -ES a marine food fish
TILELIKE	*adj* resembling a tile
TILER	*n* pl. -S one that tiles
TILING	*n* pl. -S a surface of tiles
TILL	*v* -ED, -ING, -S to prepare land for crops by plowing **TILLABLE** *adj*
TILLAGE	*n* pl. -S cultivated land
TILLER	*v* -ED, -ING, -S to put forth stems from a root
TILLITE	*n* pl. -S rock made up of consolidated clay, sand, gravel, and boulders
TILT	*v* -ED, -ING, -S to cause to slant **TILTABLE** *adj*
TILTER	*n* pl. -S one that tilts
TILTH	*n* pl. -S tillage
TILTYARD	*n* pl. -S an area for jousting contests
TIMARAU	*n* pl. -S tamarau
TIMBAL	*n* pl. -S a large drum
TIMBALE	*n* pl. -S a pastry shell shaped like a drum

TIMBER *v* -ED, -ING, -S to furnish with timber (wood used as a building material)

TIMBRE *n* pl. -S the quality given to a sound by its overtones **TIMBRAL** *adj*

TIMBREL *n* pl. -S a percussion instrument

TIME *v* TIMED, TIMING, TIMES to determine the speed or duration of

TIMECARD *n* pl. -S a card for recording an employee's times of arrival and departure

TIMELESS *adj* having no beginning or end

TIMELINE *n* pl. -S a schedule of events

TIMELY *adj* -LIER, -LIEST occurring at the right moment

TIMEOUS *adj* timely

TIMEOUT *n* pl. -S a brief suspension of activity

TIMER *n* pl. -S one that times

TIMEWORK *n* pl. -S work paid for by the hour or by the day

TIMEWORN *adj* showing the effects of long use or wear

TIMID *adj* -IDER, -IDEST lacking courage or self-confidence **TIMIDLY** *adv*

TIMIDITY *n* pl. -TIES the quality of being timid

TIMING *n* pl. -S the selection of the proper moment for doing something

TIMOLOL *n* pl. -S a drug used to treat glaucoma

TIMOROUS *adj* fearful

TIMOTHY *n* pl. -THIES a European grass

TIMPANO *n* pl. -NI a kettledrum

TIMPANUM *n* pl. -NA or -NUMS tympanum

TIN *v* TINNED, TINNING, TINS to coat with tin (a metallic element)

TINAMOU *n* pl. -S a South American game bird

TINCAL *n* pl. -S crude borax

TINCT *v* -ED, -ING, -S to tinge

TINCTURE *v* -TURED, -TURING, -TURES to tinge

TINDER *n* pl. -S readily combustible material **TINDERY** *adj*

TINE *v* TINED, TINING, TINES to lose

TINEA *n* pl. -S a fungous skin disease **TINEAL** *adj*

TINEID *n* pl. -S one of a family of moths

TINFOIL *n* pl. -S a thin metal sheeting

TINFUL *n* pl. -S as much as a tin container can hold

TING *v* -ED, -ING, -S to emit a high-pitched metallic sound

TINGE *v* TINGED, TINGEING or TINGING, TINGES to apply a trace of color to

TINGLE *v* -GLED, -GLING, -GLES to cause a prickly, stinging sensation

TINGLER *n* pl. -S one that tingles

TINGLY *adj* -GLIER, -GLIEST tingling

TINHORN *n* pl. -S a showily pretentious person

TINIER comparative of tiny

TINIEST superlative of tiny

TINILY *adv* in a tiny manner

TININESS *n* pl. -ES the quality of being tiny

TINING present participle of tine

TINKER *v* -ED, -ING, -S to repair in an unskilled or experimental manner

TINKERER *n* pl. -S one that tinkers

TINKLE *v* -KLED, -KLING, -KLES to make slight, sharp, metallic sounds

TINKLER *n* pl. -S one that tinkles

TINKLING *n* pl. -S the sound made by something that tinkles

TINKLY *adj* -KLIER, -KLIEST producing a tinkling sound

TINLIKE *adj* resembling tin

TINMAN *n* pl. -MEN a tinsmith

TINNED past tense of tin

TINNER *n* pl. -S a tin miner

TINNIER comparative of tinny

TINNIEST superlative of tinny

TINNILY *adv* in a tinny manner

TINNING present participle of tin

TINNITUS *n* pl. -ES a ringing sound in the ears

TINNY *adj* -NIER, -NIEST of or resembling tin

TINPLATE *n* pl. -S thin sheet iron coated with tin

TINSEL *v* -SELED, -SELING, -SELS or -SELLED, -SELLING, -SELS to give a showy or gaudy appearance to

TINSELLY	*adj* cheaply gaudy
TINSMITH	*n* pl. -S one who works with tin
TINSTONE	*n* pl. -S a tin ore
TINT	*v* -ED, -ING, -S to color slightly or delicately
TINTER	*n* pl. -S one that tints
TINTING	*n* pl. -S the process of one that tints
TINTLESS	*adj* lacking color
TINTYPE	*n* pl. -S a kind of photograph
TINWARE	*n* pl. -S articles made of tinplate
TINWORK	*n* pl. -S something made of tin
TINY	*adj* TINIER, TINIEST very small
TIP	*v* TIPPED, TIPPING, TIPS to tilt
TIPCART	*n* pl. -S a type of cart
TIPCAT	*n* pl. -S a game resembling baseball
TIPI	*n* pl. -S tepee
TIPLESS	*adj* having no point or extremity
TIPOFF	*n* pl. -S a hint or warning
TIPPABLE	*adj* capable of being tipped
TIPPED	past tense of tip
TIPPER	*n* pl. -S one that tips
TIPPET	*n* pl. -S a covering for the shoulders
TIPPIER	comparative of tippy
TIPPIEST	superlative of tippy
TIPPING	present participle of tip
TIPPLE	*v* -PLED, -PLING, -PLES to drink alcoholic beverages
TIPPLER	*n* pl. -S one that tipples
TIPPY	*adj* -PIER, -PIEST unsteady
TIPPYTOE	*v* -TOED, -TOEING, -TOES to tiptoe
TIPSIER	comparative of tipsy
TIPSIEST	superlative of tipsy
TIPSILY	*adv* in a tipsy manner
TIPSTAFF	*n* pl. -STAFFS or -STAVES an attendant in a court of law
TIPSTER	*n* pl. -S one that sells information to gamblers
TIPSTOCK	*n* pl. -S a part of a gun
TIPSY	*adj* -SIER, -SIEST slightly drunk
TIPTOE	*v* -TOED, -TOEING, -TOES to walk on the tips of one's toes
TIPTOP	*n* pl. -S the highest point
TIRADE	*n* pl. -S a long, vehement speech
TIRAMISU	*n* pl. -S a dessert made with ladyfingers, mascarpone, chocolate, and espresso
TIRE	*v* TIRED, TIRING, TIRES to grow tired
TIRED	*adj* TIREDER, TIREDEST sapped of strength **TIREDLY** *adv*
TIRELESS	*adj* seemingly incapable of tiring
TIRESOME	*adj* tedious
TIRING	present participle of tire
TIRL	*v* -ED, -ING, -S to make a vibrating sound
TIRO	*n* pl. -ROS tyro
TIRRIVEE	*n* pl. -S a tantrum
TISANE	*n* pl. -S a ptisan
TISSUAL	*adj* pertaining to tissue
TISSUE	*v* -SUED, -SUING, -SUES to weave into tissue (a fine sheer fabric)
TISSUEY	*adj* resembling tissue
TISSULAR	*adj* affecting an organism's tissue (structural material)
TIT	*n* pl. -S a small bird
TITAN	*n* pl. -S a person of great size
TITANATE	*n* pl. -S a chemical salt
TITANESS	*n* pl. -ES a female titan
TITANIA	*n* pl. -S a mineral
TITANIC	*adj* of great size
TITANISM	*n* pl. -S revolt against social conventions
TITANITE	*n* pl. -S a mineral
TITANIUM	*n* pl. -S a metallic element
TITANOUS	*adj* pertaining to titanium
TITBIT	*n* pl. -S tidbit
TITER	*n* pl. -S the strength of a chemical solution
TITFER	*n* pl. -S a hat
TITHABLE	*adj* subject to the payment of tithes
TITHE	*v* TITHED, TITHING, TITHES to pay a tithe (a small tax)
TITHER	*n* pl. -S one that tithes
TITHING	*n* pl. -S the act of levying tithes
TITHONIA	*n* pl. -S a tall herb
TITI	*n* pl. -S an evergreen shrub or tree
TITIAN	*n* pl. -S a reddish brown color
TITIVATE	*v* -VATED, -VATING, -VATES to dress smartly

TITLARK	*n* pl. -S a songbird
TITLE	*v* -TLED, -TLING, -TLES to furnish with a title (a distinctive appellation)
TITLIST	*n* pl. -S a sports champion
TITMAN	*n* pl. -MEN the smallest of a litter of pigs
TITMOUSE	*n* pl. -MICE a small bird
TITRABLE	*adj* capable of being titrated
TITRANT	*n* pl. -S the reagent used in titration
TITRATE	*v* -TRATED, -TRATING, -TRATES to determine the strength of a solution by adding a reagent until a desired reaction occurs
TITRATOR	*n* pl. -S one that titrates
TITRE	*n* pl. -S titer
TITTER	*v* -ED, -ING, -S to utter a restrained, nervous laugh
TITTERER	*n* pl. -S one that titters
TITTIE	*n* pl. -S a sister
TITTIES	pl. of titty
TITTLE	*n* pl. -S a very small mark in writing or printing
TITTUP	*v* -TUPED, -TUPING, -TUPS or -TUPPED, -TUPPING, -TUPS to move in a lively manner
TITTUPPY	*adj* shaky; unsteady
TITTY	*n* pl. -TIES a teat
TITULAR	*n* pl. -S one who holds a title
TITULARY	*n* pl. -LARIES a titular
TIVY	*adv* with great speed
TIZZY	*n* pl. -ZIES a state of nervous confusion
TMESIS	*n* pl. TMESES the separation of the parts of a compound word by an intervening word or words
TO	*prep* in the direction of
TOAD	*n* pl. -S a tailless, jumping amphibian
TOADFISH	*n* pl. -ES a marine fish
TOADFLAX	*n* pl. -ES a perennial herb
TOADIED	past tense of toady
TOADIES	present 3d person sing. of toady
TOADISH	*adj* resembling a toad
TOADLESS	*adj* having no toads
TOADLIKE	*adj* resembling a toad
TOADY	*v* TOADIED, TOADYING, TOADIES to engage in servile flattering
TOADYISH	*adj* characteristic of one that toadies
TOADYISM	*n* pl. -S toadyish behavior
TOAST	*v* -ED, -ING, -S to brown by exposure to heat
TOASTER	*n* pl. -S a device for toasting
TOASTY	*adj* TOASTIER, TOASTIEST comfortably warm
TOBACCO	*n* pl. -COS or -COES an annual herb cultivated for its leaves
TOBOGGAN	*v* -ED, -ING, -S to ride on a long, narrow sled
TOBY	*n* pl. -BIES a type of drinking mug
TOCCATA	*n* pl. -TAS or -TE a musical composition usually for an organ
TOCHER	*v* -ED, -ING, -S to give a dowry to
TOCOLOGY	*n* pl. -GIES the branch of medicine dealing with childbirth
TOCSIN	*n* pl. -S an alarm sounded on a bell
TOD	*n* pl. -S a British unit of weight
TODAY	*n* pl. -DAYS the present day
TODDIES	pl. of toddy
TODDLE	*v* -DLED, -DLING, -DLES to walk unsteadily
TODDLER	*n* pl. -S one that toddles
TODDY	*n* pl. -DIES an alcoholic beverage
TODY	*n* pl. -DIES a West Indian bird
TOE	*v* TOED, TOEING, TOES to touch with the toe (one of the terminal members of the foot)
TOEA	*n* pl. TOEA a monetary unit of Papua New Guinea
TOECAP	*n* pl. -S a covering for the tip of a shoe or boot
TOEHOLD	*n* pl. -S a space that supports the toes in climbing
TOELESS	*adj* having no toes
TOELIKE	*adj* resembling a toe
TOENAIL	*v* -ED, -ING, -S to fasten with obliquely driven nails
TOEPIECE	*n* pl. -S a piece of a shoe designed to cover the toes
TOEPLATE	*n* pl. -S a metal tab attached to the tip of a shoe

TOESHOE *n* pl. -S a dance slipper without a heel

TOFF *n* pl. -S a dandy

TOFFEE *n* pl. -S a chewy candy

TOFFY *n* pl. -FIES toffee

TOFT *n* pl. -S a hillock

TOFU *n* pl. -S a soft Oriental cheese made from soybean milk

TOG *v* TOGGED, TOGGING, TOGS to clothe

TOGA *n* pl. -GAS or -GAE an outer garment worn in ancient Rome **TOGAED** *adj*

TOGATE *adj* pertaining to ancient Rome

TOGATED *adj* wearing a toga

TOGETHER *adv* into a union or relationship

TOGGED past tense of tog

TOGGERY *n* pl. -GERIES clothing

TOGGING present participle of tog

TOGGLE *v* -GLED, -GLING, -GLES to fasten with a type of pin or short rod

TOGGLER *n* pl. -S one that toggles

TOGUE *n* pl. -S a freshwater fish

TOIL *v* -ED, -ING, -S to work strenuously

TOILE *n* pl. -S a sheer linen fabric

TOILER *n* pl. -S one that toils

TOILET *v* -ED, -ING, -S to dress and groom oneself

TOILETRY *n* pl. -TRIES an article used in dressing and grooming oneself

TOILETTE *n* pl. -S the act of dressing and grooming oneself

TOILFUL *adj* toilsome

TOILSOME *adj* demanding much exertion

TOILWORN *adj* worn by toil

TOIT *v* -ED, -ING, -S to saunter

TOKAMAK *n* pl. -S a doughnut-shaped nuclear reactor

TOKAY *n* pl. -KAYS a Malaysian gecko

TOKE *v* TOKED, TOKING, TOKES to take a puff on a marijuana cigarette

TOKEN *v* -ED, -ING, -S to serve as a sign of

TOKENISM *n* pl. -S the policy of making only a superficial effort

TOKER *n* pl. -S one that tokes

TOKING present participle of toke

TOKOLOGY *n* pl. -GIES tocology

TOKOMAK *n* pl. -S tokamak

TOKONOMA *n* pl. -S a small alcove in a Japanese house

TOLA *n* pl. -S a unit of weight used in India

TOLAN *n* pl. -S a chemical compound

TOLANE *n* pl. -S tolan

TOLBOOTH *n* pl. -S a prison

TOLD past tense of tell

TOLE *v* TOLED, TOLING, TOLES to allure

TOLEDO *n* pl. -DOS a finely tempered sword

TOLERANT *adj* inclined to tolerate

TOLERATE *v* -ATED, -ATING, -ATES to allow without active opposition

TOLIDIN *n* pl. -S tolidine

TOLIDINE *n* pl. -S a chemical compound

TOLING present participle of tole

TOLL *v* -ED, -ING, -S to collect or impose a toll (a fixed charge for a service or privilege)

TOLLAGE *n* pl. -S a toll

TOLLBAR *n* pl. -S a tollgate

TOLLER *n* pl. -S a collector of tolls

TOLLGATE *n* pl. -S a gate where a toll is collected

TOLLMAN *n* pl. -MEN a toller

TOLLWAY *n* pl. -WAYS a road on which tolls are collected

TOLU *n* pl. -S a fragrant resin

TOLUATE *n* pl. -S a chemical salt

TOLUENE *n* pl. -S a flammable liquid

TOLUIC *adj* pertaining to any of four isomeric acids derived from toluene

TOLUID *n* pl. -S toluide

TOLUIDE *n* pl. -S an amide

TOLUIDIN *n* pl. -S an amine

TOLUOL *n* pl. -S toluene

TOLUOLE *n* pl. -S toluol

TOLUYL *n* pl. -S a univalent chemical radical

TOLYL *n* pl. -S a univalent chemical radical

TOM *n* pl. -S the male of various animals

TOMAHAWK *v* -ED, -ING, -S to strike with a light ax

TOMALLEY *n* pl. -LEYS the liver of a lobster

TOMAN *n* pl. -S a coin of Iran

TOMATO *n* pl. -TOES the fleshy, edible fruit of a perennial plant **TOMATOEY** *adj*

TOMB *v* -ED, -ING, -S to place in a tomb (a burial vault or chamber)

TOMBAC *n* pl. -S an alloy of copper and zinc

TOMBACK *n* pl. -S tombac

TOMBAK *n* pl. -S tombac

TOMBAL *adj* pertaining to a tomb

TOMBLESS *adj* having no tomb

TOMBLIKE *adj* resembling a tomb

TOMBOLA *n* pl. -S a gambling game that is a type of lottery

TOMBOLO *n* pl. -LOS a sandbar connecting an island to the mainland

TOMBOY *n* pl. -BOYS a girl who prefers boyish activities

TOMCAT *v* -CATTED, -CATTING, -CATS to engage in sexually promiscuous behavior — used of a male

TOMCOD *n* pl. -S a marine fish

TOME *n* pl. -S a large book

TOMENTUM *n* pl. -TA a network of small blood vessels

TOMFOOL *n* pl. -S a foolish person

TOMMY *n* pl. -MIES a loaf of bread

TOMMYROT *n* pl. -S nonsense

TOMOGRAM *n* pl. -S a photograph made with X rays

TOMORROW *n* pl. -S the day following today

TOMPION *n* pl. -S tampion

TOMTIT *n* pl. -S any of various small active birds

TON *n* pl. -S a unit of weight

TONAL *adj* pertaining to tone **TONALLY** *adv*

TONALITY *n* pl. -TIES a system of tones

TONDO *n* pl. -DI or -DOS a circular painting

TONE *v* TONED, TONING, TONES to give a particular tone (a sound of definite pitch and vibration) to

TONEARM *n* pl. -S the pivoted part of a record player that holds the needle

TONELESS *adj* lacking in tone

TONEME *n* pl. -S a tonal unit of speech **TONEMIC** *adj*

TONER *n* pl. -S one that tones

TONETICS *n/pl* the phonetic study of tone in language **TONETIC** *adj*

TONETTE *n* pl. -S a simple flute

TONEY *adj* TONIER, TONIEST tony

TONG *v* -ED, -ING, -S to lift with a type of grasping device

TONGA *n* pl. -S a light cart used in India

TONGER *n* pl. -S one that tongs

TONGMAN *n* pl. -MEN a member of a Chinese secret society

TONGUE *v* TONGUED, TONGUING, TONGUES to touch with the tongue (an organ of the mouth)

TONGUING *n* pl. -S the use of the tongue in articulating notes on a wind instrument

TONIC *n* pl. -S something that invigorates or refreshes

TONICITY *n* pl. -TIES normal, healthy bodily condition

TONIER comparative of tony

TONIEST superlative of tony

TONIGHT *n* pl. -S the present night

TONING present participle of tone

TONISH *adj* stylish **TONISHLY** *adv*

TONLET *n* pl. -S a skirt of plate armor

TONNAGE *n* pl. -S total weight in tons

TONNE *n* pl. -S a unit of weight

TONNEAU *n* pl. -NEAUS or -NEAUX the rear seating compartment of an automobile

TONNER *n* pl. -S an object having a specified tonnage

TONNISH *adj* tonish

TONSIL *n* pl. -S a lymphoid organ **TONSILAR** *adj*

TONSURE *v* -SURED, -SURING, -SURES to shave the head of

TONTINE *n* pl. -S a form of collective life insurance

TONUS *n* pl. -ES a normal state of tension in muscle tissue

TONY *adj* TONIER, TONIEST stylish

TOO	*adv* in addition
TOOK	past tense of take
TOOL	*v* -ED, -ING, -S to form or finish with a tool (an implement used in manual work)
TOOLBOX	*n* pl. -ES a box for tools
TOOLER	*n* pl. -S one that tools
TOOLHEAD	*n* pl. -S a part of a machine
TOOLING	*n* pl. -S ornamentation done with tools
TOOLLESS	*adj* having no tools
TOOLROOM	*n* pl. -S a room where tools are stored
TOOLSHED	*n* pl. -S a building where tools are stored
TOOM	*adj* empty
TOON	*n* pl. -S an East Indian tree
TOOT	*v* -ED, -ING, -S to sound a horn or whistle in short blasts
TOOTER	*n* pl. -S one that toots
TOOTH	*n* pl. TEETH one of the hard structures attached in a row to each jaw
TOOTH	*v* -ED, -ING, -S to furnish with toothlike projections
TOOTHY	*adj* TOOTHIER, TOOTHIEST having or showing prominent teeth **TOOTHILY** *adv*
TOOTLE	*v* -TLED, -TLING, -TLES to toot softly or repeatedly
TOOTLER	*n* pl. -S one that tootles
TOOTS	*n* pl. -ES a woman or girl — usually used as a form of address
TOOTSIE	*n* pl. -S tootsy
TOOTSY	*n* pl. -SIES a foot
TOP	*v* TOPPED, TOPPING, TOPS to cut off the top (the highest part, point, or surface) of
TOPAZ	*n* pl. -ES a mineral **TOPAZINE** *adj*
TOPCOAT	*n* pl. -S a lightweight overcoat
TOPCROSS	*n* pl. -ES a cross between a purebred male and inferior female stock
TOPE	*v* TOPED, TOPING, TOPES to drink liquor to excess
TOPEE	*n* pl. -S topi
TOPER	*n* pl. -S one that topes
TOPFUL	*adj* topfull
TOPFULL	*adj* full to the top
TOPH	*n* pl. -S tufa
TOPHE	*n* pl. -S tufa
TOPHUS	*n* pl. -PHI a deposit of urates in the tissue around a joint
TOPI	*n* pl. -S a sun helmet
TOPIARY	*n* pl. -ARIES the art of trimming shrubs into shapes
TOPIC	*n* pl. -S a subject of discourse **TOPICAL** *adj*
TOPING	present participle of tope
TOPKICK	*n* pl. -S a first sergeant
TOPKNOT	*n* pl. -S an ornament for the hair
TOPLESS	*adj* having no top
TOPLINE	*n* pl. -S the outline of the top of an animal's body
TOPLOFTY	*adj* -LOFTIER, -LOFTIEST haughty
TOPMAST	*n* pl. -S a mast of a ship
TOPMOST	*adj* highest
TOPNOTCH	*adj* excellent
TOPOI	pl. of topos
TOPOLOGY	*n* pl. -GIES a branch of mathematics
TOPONYM	*n* pl. -S the name of a place
TOPONYMY	*n* pl. -MIES the study of toponyms
TOPOS	*n* pl. -POI a stock rhetorical theme
TOPOTYPE	*n* pl. -S a specimen selected from a locality typical of a species
TOPPED	past tense of top
TOPPER	*n* pl. -S one that tops
TOPPING	*n* pl. -S something that forms a top
TOPPLE	*v* -PLED, -PLING, -PLES to fall forward
TOPSAIL	*n* pl. -S a sail of a ship
TOPSIDE	*n* pl. -S the upper portion of a ship
TOPSIDER	*n* pl. -S one who is at the highest level of authority
TOPSOIL	*v* -ED, -ING, -S to remove the surface layer of soil from
TOPSPIN	*n* pl. -S a forward spin imparted to a ball
TOPSTONE	*n* pl. -S the stone at the top of a structure
TOPWORK	*v* -ED, -ING, -S to graft scions of another variety of plant on the main branches of

TOQUE   *n* pl. -S a close-fitting woman's hat

TOQUET   *n* pl. -S toque

TOR   *n* pl. -S a high, craggy hill

TORA   *n* pl. -S torah

TORAH   *n* pl. -RAHS, -ROTH, or -ROT a law or precept

TORC   *n* pl. -S a metal collar or necklace

TORCH   *v* -ED, -ING, -ES to set on fire

TORCHERE   *n* pl. -S a type of electric lamp

TORCHIER   *n* pl. -S torchere

TORCHON   *n* pl. -S a coarse lace

TORCHY   *adj* TORCHIER, TORCHIEST characteristic of a torch song

TORE   *n* pl. -S a torus

TOREADOR   *n* pl. -S a bullfighter

TORERO   *n* pl. -ROS a bullfighter

TOREUTIC   *adj* pertaining to a type of metalwork

TORI   pl. of torus

TORIC   *adj* pertaining to a torus

TORIES   pl. of tory

TORII   *n* pl. TORII the gateway of a Japanese temple

TORMENT   *v* -ED, -ING, -S to inflict with great bodily or mental suffering

TORN   past participle of tear

TORNADO   *n* pl. -DOES or -DOS a violent windstorm **TORNADIC** *adj*

TORNILLO   *n* pl. -LOS a flowering shrub

TORO   *n* pl. -ROS a bull

TOROID   *n* pl. -S a type of geometric surface **TOROIDAL** *adj*

TOROSE   *adj* cylindrical and swollen at intervals

TOROSITY   *n* pl. -TIES the quality or state of being torose

TOROT   a pl. of torah

TOROTH   a pl. of torah

TOROUS   *adj* torose

TORPEDO   *v* -ED, -ING, -ES or -S to damage or sink with an underwater missile

TORPID   *n* pl. -S a racing boat

TORPIDLY   *adv* in a sluggish manner

TORPOR   *n* pl. -S mental or physical inactivity

TORQUATE   *adj* having a torques

TORQUE   *v* TORQUED, TORQUING, TORQUES to cause to twist

TORQUER   *n* pl. -S one that torques

TORQUES   *n* pl. -QUESES a band of feathers, hair, or coloration around the neck

TORQUING   present participle of torque

TORR   *n* pl. TORR a unit of pressure

TORREFY   *v* -FIED, -FYING, -FIES to subject to intense heat

TORRENT   *n* pl. -S a rapid stream of water

TORRID   *adj* -RIDER, -RIDEST extremely hot **TORRIDLY** *adv*

TORRIFY   *v* -FIED, -FYING, -FIES to torrefy

TORSADE   *n* pl. -S a twisted cord

TORSE   *n* pl. -S a wreath of twisted silks

TORSI   a pl. of torso

TORSION   *n* pl. -S the act of twisting

TORSK   *n* pl. -S a marine food fish

TORSO   *n* pl. -SI or -SOS the trunk of the human body

TORT   *n* pl. -S a civil wrong

TORTE   *n* pl. TORTEN or TORTES a rich cake

TORTILE   *adj* twisted; coiled

TORTILLA   *n* pl. -S a round, flat cake of unleavened cornmeal

TORTIOUS   *adj* of the nature of a tort

TORTOISE   *n* pl. -S any of an order of reptiles having the body enclosed in a bony shell

TORTONI   *n* pl. -S a type of ice cream

TORTRIX   *n* pl. -ES a small moth

TORTUOUS   *adj* marked by repeated turns or bends

TORTURE   *v* -TURED, -TURING, -TURES to subject to severe physical pain

TORTURER   *n* pl. -S one that tortures

TORULA   *n* pl. -LAE or -LAS a type of fungus

TORUS   *n* pl. -RI a large convex molding

TORY   *n* pl. -RIES a political conservative

TOSH   *n* pl. -ES nonsense

TOSS   *v* TOSSED or TOST, TOSSING, TOSSES to throw lightly

TOSSER   *n* pl. -S one that tosses

TOSSPOT   *n* pl. -S a drunkard

TOSSUP   *n* pl. -S an even choice or chance

TOST   a past tense of toss

TOSTADA   *n* pl. -S a tortilla fried in deep fat

TOSTADO   *n* pl. -DOS tostada

TOT   *v* TOTTED, TOTTING, TOTS to total

TOTABLE   *adj* capable of being toted

TOTAL   *v* -TALED, -TALING, -TALS or -TALLED, -TALLING, -TALS to ascertain the entire amount of

TOTALISE   *v* -ISED, -ISING, -ISES to totalize

TOTALISM   *n* pl. -S centralized control by an autocratic authority

TOTALIST   *n* pl. -S one who tends to regard things as a unified whole

TOTALITY   *n* pl. -TIES the quality or state of being complete

TOTALIZE   *v* -IZED, -IZING, -IZES to make complete

TOTALLED   a past tense of total

TOTALLING   a present participle of total

TOTALLY   *adv* completely

TOTE   *v* TOTED, TOTING, TOTES to carry by hand

TOTEM   *n* pl. -S a natural object serving as the emblem of a family or clan **TOTEMIC** *adj*

TOTEMISM   *n* pl. -S a system of tribal division according to totems

TOTEMIST   *n* pl. -S a specialist in totemism

TOTEMITE   *n* pl. -S a totemist

TOTER   *n* pl. -S one that totes

TOTHER   *pron* the other

TOTING   present participle of tote

TOTTED   past tense of tot

TOTTER   *v* -ED, -ING, -S to walk unsteadily

TOTTERER   *n* pl. -S one that totters

TOTTERY   *adj* shaky

TOTTING   present participle of tot

TOUCAN   *n* pl. -S a tropical bird

TOUCH   *v* -ED, -ING, -ES to be in or come into contact with

TOUCHE   *interj* — used to acknowledge a hit in fencing

TOUCHER   *n* pl. -S one that touches

TOUCHUP   *n* pl. -S an act of finishing by adding minor improvements

TOUCHY   *adj* TOUCHIER, TOUCHIEST overly sensitive **TOUCHILY** *adv*

TOUGH   *adj* TOUGHER, TOUGHEST strong and resilient

TOUGH   *v* -ED, -ING, -S to endure hardship

TOUGHEN   *v* -ED, -ING, -S to make tough

TOUGHIE   *n* pl. -S a tough

TOUGHIES   pl. of toughy

TOUGHISH   *adj* somewhat tough

TOUGHLY   *adv* in a tough manner

TOUGHY   *n* pl. TOUGHIES toughie

TOUPEE   *n* pl. -S a wig worn to cover a bald spot

TOUR   *v* -ED, -ING, -S to travel from place to place

TOURACO   *n* pl. -COS an African bird

TOURER   *n* pl. -S a large, open automobile

TOURING   *n* pl. -S cross-country skiing for pleasure

TOURISM   *n* pl. -S the practice of touring for pleasure

TOURIST   *n* pl. -S one who tours for pleasure **TOURISTY** *adj*

TOURNEY   *v* -ED, -ING, -S to compete in a tournament

TOUSE   *v* TOUSED, TOUSING, TOUSES to tousle

TOUSLE   *v* -SLED, -SLING, -SLES to dishevel

TOUT   *v* -ED, -ING, -S to solicit brazenly

TOUTER   *n* pl. -S one that touts

TOUZLE   *v* -ZLED, -ZLING, -ZLES to tousle

TOVARICH   *n* pl. -ES comrade

TOVARISH   *n* pl. -ES tovarich

TOW   *v* -ED, -ING, -S to pull by means of a rope or chain

TOWAGE   *n* pl. -S the price paid for towing

TOWARD   *prep* in the direction of

TOWARDLY   *adj* favorable

TOWARDS   *prep* toward

TOWAWAY   *n* pl. -AWAYS the act of towing away a vehicle

TOWBOAT   *n* pl. -S a tugboat

TOWEL   *v* -ELED, -ELING, -ELS or -ELLED, -ELLING, -ELS to wipe with a towel (an absorbent cloth)

TOWELING   *n* pl. -S material used for towels

TOWER	*v* -ED, -ING, -S to rise to a great height
TOWERY	*adj* -ERIER, -ERIEST very tall
TOWHEAD	*n* pl. -S a head of light blond hair
TOWHEE	*n* pl. -S a common finch
TOWIE	*n* pl. -S a form of contract bridge for three players
TOWLINE	*n* pl. -S a line used in towing
TOWMOND	*n* pl. -S a year
TOWMONT	*n* pl. -S towmond
TOWN	*n* pl. -S a center of population smaller than a city
TOWNEE	*n* pl. -S a townsman
TOWNFOLK	*n/pl* the inhabitants of a town
TOWNHOME	*n* pl. -S one of a series of contiguous houses of two or three stories
TOWNIE	*n* pl. -S a nonstudent who lives in a college town
TOWNIES	pl. of towny
TOWNISH	*adj* characteristic of a town
TOWNLESS	*adj* having no towns
TOWNLET	*n* pl. -S a small town
TOWNSHIP	*n* pl. -S an administrative division of a county
TOWNSMAN	*n* pl. -MEN a resident of a town
TOWNWEAR	*n* pl. -S apparel that is suitable for wear in the city
TOWNY	*n* pl. TOWNIES townie
TOWPATH	*n* pl. -S a path along a river that is used by animals towing boats
TOWROPE	*n* pl. -S a rope used in towing
TOWY	*adj* resembling coarse hemp or flax fiber
TOXAEMIA	*n* pl. -S toxemia **TOXAEMIC** *adj*
TOXEMIA	*n* pl. -S the condition of having toxins in the blood **TOXEMIC** *adj*
TOXIC	*n* pl. -S a poisonous substance
TOXICAL	*adj* toxic
TOXICANT	*n* pl. -S a poisonous substance
TOXICITY	*n* pl. -TIES the quality of being poisonous
TOXIN	*n* pl. -S a poisonous substance
TOXINE	*n* pl. -S toxin
TOXOID	*n* pl. -S a type of toxin
TOY	*v* -ED, -ING, -S to amuse oneself as if with a toy (a child's plaything)
TOYER	*n* pl. -S one that toys
TOYISH	*adj* frivolous
TOYLESS	*adj* having no toy
TOYLIKE	*adj* resembling a toy
TOYO	*n* pl. -YOS a smooth straw used in making hats
TOYON	*n* pl. -S an ornamental evergreen shrub
TOYSHOP	*n* pl. -S a shop where toys are sold
TRABEATE	*adj* constructed with horizontal beams
TRACE	*v* TRACED, TRACING, TRACES to follow the course of
TRACER	*n* pl. -S one that traces
TRACERY	*n* pl. -ERIES ornamental work of interlaced lines
TRACHEA	*n* pl. -CHEAE or -CHEAS the passage for conveying air to the lungs **TRACHEAL** *adj*
TRACHEID	*n* pl. -S a long, tubular plant cell
TRACHLE	*v* -LED, -LING, -LES to draggle
TRACHOMA	*n* pl. -S a disease of the eye
TRACHYTE	*n* pl. -S a light-colored igneous rock
TRACING	*n* pl. -S something that is traced
TRACK	*v* -ED, -ING, -S to follow the marks left by an animal, a person, or a vehicle
TRACKAGE	*n* pl. -S the track system of a railroad
TRACKER	*n* pl. -S one that tracks
TRACKING	*n* pl. -S the placement of students within a curriculum
TRACKMAN	*n* pl. -MEN a railroad worker
TRACKWAY	*n* pl. -WAYS a trodden path
TRACT	*n* pl. -S an expanse of land
TRACTATE	*n* pl. -S a treatise
TRACTILE	*adj* capable of being drawn out in length
TRACTION	*n* pl. -S the act of pulling or drawing over a surface **TRACTIVE** *adj*
TRACTOR	*n* pl. -S a motor vehicle used in farming
TRAD	*adj* traditional
TRADE	*v* TRADED, TRADING, TRADES to give in exchange for another commodity **TRADABLE** *adj*
TRADEOFF	*n* pl. -S a giving up of one thing in return for another
TRADER	*n* pl. -S one that trades

TRADITOR   *n* pl. -ES a traitor among the early Christians

TRADUCE   *v* -DUCED, -DUCING, -DUCES to defame

TRADUCER   *n* pl. -S one that traduces

TRAFFIC   *v* -FICKED, -FICKING, -FICS to engage in buying and selling

TRAGEDY   *n* pl. -DIES a disastrous event

TRAGI   pl. of tragus

TRAGIC   *n* pl. -S the element of a drama that produces tragedy

TRAGICAL   *adj* of the nature of a tragedy

TRAGOPAN   *n* pl. -S an Asian pheasant

TRAGUS   *n* pl. -GI a part of the external opening of the ear

TRAIK   *v* -ED, -ING, -S to trudge

TRAIL   *v* -ED, -ING, -S to drag along a surface

TRAILER   *v* -ED, -ING, -S to transport by means of a trailer (a vehicle drawn by another)

TRAIN   *v* -ED, -ING, -S to instruct systematically

TRAINEE   *n* pl. -S a person receiving training

TRAINER   *n* pl. -S one that trains

TRAINFUL   *n* pl. -S as much as a railroad train can hold

TRAINING   *n* pl. -S systematic instruction

TRAINMAN   *n* pl. -MEN a railroad employee

TRAINWAY   *n* pl. -WAYS a railway

TRAIPSE   *v* TRAIPSED, TRAIPSING, TRAIPSES to walk about in an idle or aimless manner

TRAIT   *n* pl. -S a distinguishing characteristic

TRAITOR   *n* pl. -S one who betrays another

TRAJECT   *v* -ED, -ING, -S to transmit

TRAM   *v* TRAMMED, TRAMMING, TRAMS to convey in a tramcar

TRAMCAR   *n* pl. -S a streetcar

TRAMEL   *v* -ELED, -ELING, -ELS or -ELLED, -ELLING, -ELS to trammel

TRAMELL   *v* -ED, -ING, -S to trammel

TRAMLESS   *adj* having no tramcar

TRAMLINE   *n* pl. -S a streetcar line

TRAMMED   past tense of tram

TRAMMEL   *v* -MELED, -MELING, -MELS or -MELLED, -MELLING, -MELS to hinder

TRAMMING   present participle of tram

TRAMP   *v* -ED, -ING, -S to walk with a firm, heavy step

TRAMPER   *n* pl. -S one that tramps

TRAMPISH   *adj* resembling a vagabond

TRAMPLE   *v* -PLED, -PLING, -PLES to tread on heavily

TRAMPLER   *n* pl. -S one that tramples

TRAMROAD   *n* pl. -S a railway in a mine

TRAMWAY   *n* pl. -WAYS a tramline

TRANCE   *v* TRANCED, TRANCING, TRANCES to put into a trance (a semiconscious state)

TRANCHE   *n* pl. -S a portion

TRANGAM   *n* pl. -S a gewgaw

TRANK   *n* pl. -S a drug that tranquilizes

TRANQ   *n* pl. -S trank

TRANQUIL   *adj* -QUILER, -QUILEST or -QUILLER, -QUILLEST free from disturbance

TRANS   *adj* characterized by the arrangement of different atoms on opposite sides of the molecule

TRANSACT   *v* -ED, -ING, -S to carry out

TRANSECT   *v* -ED, -ING, -S to cut across

TRANSEPT   *n* pl. -S a major transverse part of the body of a church

TRANSFER   *v* -FERRED, -FERRING, -FERS to convey from one source to another

TRANSFIX   *v* -FIXED or -FIXT, -FIXING, -FIXES to impale

TRANSHIP   *v* -SHIPPED, -SHIPPING, -SHIPS to transfer from one conveyance to another

TRANSIT   *v* -ED, -ING, -S to pass across or through

TRANSMIT   *v* -MITTED, -MITTING, -MITS to send from one place or person to another

TRANSOM   *n* pl. -S a small window above a door or another window

TRANSUDE   *v* -SUDED, -SUDING, -SUDES to pass through a membrane

TRAP   *v* TRAPPED or TRAPT, TRAPPING, TRAPS to catch in a trap (a device for capturing and holding animals)

TRAPAN   *v* -PANNED, -PANNING, -PANS to trepan

TRAPBALL *n* pl. -S a type of ball game

TRAPDOOR *n* pl. -S a lifting or sliding door covering an opening

TRAPES *v* -ED, -ING, -ES to traipse

TRAPEZE *n* pl. -S a gymnastic apparatus

TRAPEZIA *n/pl* four-sided polygons having no parallel sides

TRAPEZII *n/pl* triangular muscles on the back

TRAPLIKE *adj* resembling a trap

TRAPLINE *n* pl. -S a series of traps

TRAPNEST *v* -ED, -ING, -S to determine the productivity of hens with a type of nest

TRAPPEAN *adj* pertaining to traprock

TRAPPED a past tense of trap

TRAPPER *n* pl. -S one that traps

TRAPPING *n* pl. -S a covering for a horse

TRAPPOSE *adj* trappean

TRAPPOUS *adj* trappean

TRAPROCK *n* pl. -S an igneous rock

TRAPT a past tense of trap

TRAPUNTO *n* pl. -TOS a decorative quilted design

TRASH *v* -ED, -ING, -ES to free from trash (worthless or waste matter)

TRASHMAN *n* pl. -MEN a person who removes trash

TRASHY *adj* TRASHIER, TRASHIEST resembling trash **TRASHILY** *adv*

TRASS *n* pl. -ES a volcanic rock

TRAUCHLE *v* -LED, -LING, -LES to trachle

TRAUMA *n* pl. -MAS or -MATA a severe emotional shock

TRAVAIL *v* -ED, -ING, -S to toil

TRAVE *n* pl. -S a frame for confining a horse

TRAVEL *v* -ELED, -ELING, -ELS or -ELLED, -ELLING, -ELS to go from one place to another

TRAVELER *n* pl. -S one that travels

TRAVELOG *n* pl. -S a lecture or film on traveling

TRAVERSE *v* -VERSED, -VERSING, -VERSES to pass across or through

TRAVESTY *v* -TIED, -TYING, -TIES to parody

TRAVOIS *n* pl. -ES a type of sled

TRAVOISE *n* pl. -S travois

TRAWL *v* -ED, -ING, -S to fish by dragging a net along the sea bottom

TRAWLER *n* pl. -S a boat used for trawling

TRAWLEY *n* pl. -LEYS a small truck or car for conveying material

TRAWLNET *n* pl. -S the large net used in trawling

TRAY *n* pl. TRAYS a flat, shallow receptacle

TRAYFUL *n* pl. -S as much as a tray will hold

TREACLE *n* pl. -S molasses **TREACLY** *adj*

TREAD *v* TROD, TRODE, or TREADED, TRODDEN, TREADING, TREADS to walk on, over, or along

TREADER *n* pl. -S one that treads

TREADLE *v* -LED, -LING, -LES to work a foot lever

TREADLER *n* pl. -S one that treadles

TREASON *n* pl. -S violation of allegiance toward one's country

TREASURE *v* -URED, -URING, -URES to value highly

TREASURY *n* pl. -URIES a place where funds are received, kept, and disbursed

TREAT *v* -ED, -ING, -S to behave in a particular way toward

TREATER *n* pl. -S one that treats

TREATISE *n* pl. -S a formal and systematic written account of a subject

TREATY *n* pl. -TIES a formal agreement between two or more nations

TREBLE *v* -BLED, -BLING, -BLES to triple

TREBLY *adv* triply

TRECENTO *n* pl. -TOS the fourteenth century

TREDDLE *v* -DLED, -DLING, -DLES to treadle

TREE *v* TREED, TREEING, TREES to drive up a tree (a tall, woody plant)

TREELAWN *n* pl. -S the strip of lawn between the street and the sidewalk

TREELESS *adj* having no tree

TREELIKE *adj* resembling a tree

TREEN *n* pl. -S an article made from wood

TREENAIL *n* pl. -S a wooden peg used for fastening timbers

TREETOP *n* pl. -S the top of a tree

TREF   *adj* unfit for use according to Jewish law

TREFAH   *adj* tref

TREFOIL   *n* pl. -S a plant having ternate leaves

TREHALA   *n* pl. -S a sweet, edible substance forming the pupal case of certain weevils

TREK   *v* TREKKED, TREKKING, TREKS to make a slow or arduous journey

TREKKER   *n* pl. -S one that treks

TRELLIS   *v* -ED, -ING, -ES to provide with a trellis (a frame used as a support for climbing plants)

TREMBLE   *v* -BLED, -BLING, -BLES to shake involuntarily

TREMBLER   *n* pl. -S one that trembles

TREMBLY   *adj* -BLIER, -BLIEST marked by trembling

TREMOLO   *n* pl. -LOS a vibrating musical effect

TREMOR   *n* pl. -S a shaking movement

TRENAIL   *n* pl. -S a treenail

TRENCH   *v* -ED, -ING, -ES to dig a long, narrow excavation in the ground

TRENCHER   *n* pl. -S a wooden platter for serving food

TREND   *v* -ED, -ING, -S to take a particular course

TRENDY   *adj* TRENDIER, TRENDIEST very fashionable **TRENDILY** *adv*

TRENDY   *n* pl. TRENDIES a trendy person

TREPAN   *v* -PANNED, -PANNING, -PANS to trephine

TREPANG   *n* pl. -S a marine animal

TREPHINE   *v* -PHINED, -PHINING, -PHINES to operate on with a surgical saw

TREPID   *adj* timorous

TRESPASS   *v* -ED, -ING, -ES to enter upon the land of another unlawfully

TRESS   *n* pl. -ES a long lock of hair **TRESSED** *adj*

TRESSEL   *n* pl. -S trestle

TRESSIER   comparative of tressy

TRESSIEST   superlative of tressy

TRESSOUR   *n* pl. -S tressure

TRESSURE   *n* pl. -S a type of heraldic design

TRESSY   *adj* TRESSIER, TRESSIEST abounding in tresses

TRESTLE   *n* pl. -S a framework for supporting a bridge

TRET   *n* pl. -S an allowance formerly paid to purchasers for waste incurred in transit

TREVET   *n* pl. -S trivet

TREWS   *n/pl* close-fitting tartan trousers

TREY   *n* pl. TREYS a three in cards, dice, or dominoes

TRIABLE   *adj* subject to judicial examination

TRIAC   *n* pl. -S an electronic device used to control power

TRIACID   *n* pl. -S a type of acid

TRIAD   *n* pl. -S a group of three

TRIADIC   *n* pl. -S a member of a triad

TRIADISM   *n* pl. -S the quality or state of being a triad

TRIAGE   *v* -AGED, -AGING, -AGES to practice a system of treating disaster victims

TRIAL   *n* pl. -S a judicial examination

TRIANGLE   *n* pl. -S a polygon having three sides

TRIARCHY   *n* pl. -CHIES government by three persons

TRIAXIAL   *adj* having three axes

TRIAZIN   *n* pl. -S triazine

TRIAZINE   *n* pl. -S a chemical compound

TRIAZOLE   *n* pl. -S a chemical compound

TRIBADE   *n* pl. -S a lesbian **TRIBADIC** *adj*

TRIBAL   *adj* pertaining to a tribe **TRIBALLY** *adv*

TRIBASIC   *adj* having three replaceable hydrogen atoms

TRIBE   *n* pl. -S a group of people sharing a common ancestry and culture

TRIBRACH   *n* pl. -S a type of metrical foot

TRIBUNAL   *n* pl. -S a court of justice

TRIBUNE   *n* pl. -S a defender of the rights of the people

TRIBUTE   *n* pl. -S something given to show respect, gratitude, or admiration

TRICE   *v* TRICED, TRICING, TRICES to haul up with a rope

TRICEPS   *n* pl. -ES an arm muscle

TRICHINA   *n* pl. -NAE or -NAS a parasitic worm

TRICHITE   *n* pl. -S a minute mineral body found in volcanic rocks

TRICHOID	adj hairlike	**TRIFOLD**	adj having three parts
TRICHOME	n pl. -S a hairlike outgrowth	**TRIFORIA**	n/pl galleries in a church
TRICING	present participle of trice	**TRIFORM**	adj having three forms
TRICK	v -ED, -ING, -S to deceive	**TRIG**	adj TRIGGER, TRIGGEST neat
TRICKER	n pl. -S one that tricks	**TRIG**	v TRIGGED, TRIGGING, TRIGS to make trig
TRICKERY	n pl. -ERIES deception		
TRICKIE	adj TRICKIER, TRICKIEST tricky	**TRIGGER**	v -ED, -ING, -S to actuate
TRICKIER	comparative of tricky	**TRIGGEST**	superlative of trig
TRICKIEST	superlative of tricky	**TRIGGING**	present participle of trig
TRICKILY	adv in a tricky manner	**TRIGLY**	adv in a trig manner
TRICKISH	adj tricky	**TRIGLYPH**	n pl. -S an architectural ornament
TRICKLE	v -LED, -LING, -LES to flow or fall in drops	**TRIGNESS**	n pl. -ES the quality or state of being trig
TRICKLY	adj -LIER, -LIEST marked by trickling	**TRIGO**	n pl. -GOS wheat
TRICKSY	adj -SIER, -SIEST mischievous	**TRIGON**	n pl. -S an ancient stringed instrument
TRICKY	adj TRICKIER, TRICKIEST characterized by deception	**TRIGONAL**	adj shaped like a triangle
TRICLAD	n pl. -S an aquatic flatworm	**TRIGRAM**	n pl. -S a cluster of three successive letters
TRICOLOR	n pl. -S a flag having three colors	**TRIGRAPH**	n pl. -S a group of three letters representing one sound
TRICORN	n pl. -S a hat with the brim turned up on three sides	**TRIHEDRA**	n/pl figures having three plane surfaces meeting at a point
TRICORNE	n pl. -S tricorn	**TRIJET**	n pl. -S an airplane powered by three jet engines
TRICOT	n pl. -S a knitted fabric		
TRICTRAC	n pl. -S a form of backgammon	**TRIKE**	n pl. -S a tricycle
TRICYCLE	n pl. -S a vehicle having three wheels	**TRILBY**	n pl. -BIES a soft felt hat
TRIDENT	n pl. -S a spear having three prongs	**TRILL**	v -ED, -ING, -S to sing or play with a vibrating effect
TRIDUUM	n pl. -S a period of three days of prayer	**TRILLER**	n pl. -S one that trills
		TRILLION	n pl. -S a number
TRIED	past tense of try	**TRILLIUM**	n pl. -S a flowering plant
TRIENE	n pl. -S a type of chemical compound	**TRILOBAL**	adj trilobed
		TRILOBED	adj having three lobes
TRIENNIA	n/pl periods of three years	**TRILOGY**	n pl. -GIES a group of three related literary works
TRIENS	n pl. -ENTES a coin of ancient Rome		
TRIER	n pl. -S one that tries	**TRIM**	adj TRIMMER, TRIMMEST neat and orderly
TRIES	present 3d person sing. of try	**TRIM**	v TRIMMED, TRIMMING, TRIMS to make trim by cutting
TRIETHYL	adj containing three ethyl groups		
TRIFECTA	n pl. -S a system of betting	**TRIMARAN**	n pl. -S a sailing vessel
TRIFID	adj divided into three parts	**TRIMER**	n pl. -S a type of chemical compound **TRIMERIC** adj
TRIFLE	v -FLED, -FLING, -FLES to waste time	**TRIMETER**	n pl. -S a verse of three metrical feet
TRIFLER	n pl. -S one that trifles	**TRIMLY**	adv in a trim manner
TRIFLING	n pl. -S a waste of time	**TRIMMED**	past tense of trim
TRIFOCAL	n pl. -S a type of lens	**TRIMMER**	n pl. -S one that trims

TRIMMEST superlative of trim

TRIMMING *n* pl. -S something added as a decoration

TRIMNESS *n* pl. -ES the state of being trim

TRIMORPH *n* pl. -S a substance existing in three forms

TRIMOTOR *n* pl. -S an airplane powered by three engines

TRINAL *adj* having three parts

TRINARY *adj* consisting of three parts

TRINDLE *v* -DLED, -DLING, -DLES to trundle

TRINE *v* TRINED, TRINING, TRINES to place in a particular astrological position

TRINITY *n* pl. -TIES a group of three

TRINKET *v* -ED, -ING, -S to deal secretly

TRINKUMS *n/pl* small ornaments

TRINODAL *adj* having three nodes

TRIO *n* pl. TRIOS a group of three

TRIODE *n* pl. -S a type of electron tube

TRIOL *n* pl. -S a type of chemical compound

TRIOLET *n* pl. -S a short poem of fixed form

TRIOSE *n* pl. -S a simple sugar

TRIOXID *n* pl. -S trioxide

TRIOXIDE *n* pl. -S a type of oxide

TRIP *v* TRIPPED, TRIPPING, TRIPS to stumble

TRIPACK *n* pl. -S a type of film pack

TRIPART *adj* divided into three parts

TRIPE *n* pl. -S a part of the stomach of a ruminant that is used as food

TRIPEDAL *adj* having three feet

TRIPHASE *adj* having three phases

TRIPLANE *n* pl. -S a type of airplane

TRIPLE *v* -PLED, -PLING, -PLES to make three times as great

TRIPLET *n* pl. -S a group of three of one kind

TRIPLEX *n* pl. -ES an apartment having three floors

TRIPLING present participle of triple

TRIPLITE *n* pl. -S a mineral

TRIPLOID *n* pl. -S a cell having a chromosome number that is three times the basic number

TRIPLY *adv* in a triple degree, manner, or number

TRIPOD *n* pl. -S a stand having three legs **TRIPODAL, TRIPODIC** *adj*

TRIPODY *n* pl. -DIES a verse of three metrical feet

TRIPOLI *n* pl. -S a soft, friable rock

TRIPOS *n* pl. -ES a tripod

TRIPPED past tense of trip

TRIPPER *n* pl. -S one that trips

TRIPPET *n* pl. -S a part of a mechanism designed to strike another part

TRIPPING *n* pl. -S the act of one that trips

TRIPPY *adj* -PIER, -PIEST suggesting a trip on psychedelic drugs

TRIPTANE *n* pl. -S a chemical compound

TRIPTYCA *n* pl. -S a triptych

TRIPTYCH *n* pl. -S an ancient writing tablet

TRIPWIRE *n* pl. -S a low-placed hidden wire that sets off an alarm or a trap

TRIREME *n* pl. -S an ancient Greek or Roman warship

TRISCELE *n* pl. -S triskele

TRISECT *v* -ED, -ING, -S to divide into three equal parts

TRISEME *n* pl. -S a type of metrical foot **TRISEMIC** *adj*

TRISHAW *n* pl. -S a pedicab

TRISKELE *n* pl. -S a figure consisting of three branches radiating from a center

TRISMUS *n* pl. -ES lockjaw **TRISMIC** *adj*

TRISOME *n* pl. -S an organism having one chromosome in addition to the usual diploid number

TRISOMIC *n* pl. -S a trisome

TRISOMY *n* pl. -MIES the condition of being a trisome

TRISTATE *adj* pertaining to an area made up of three adjoining states

TRISTE *adj* sad

TRISTEZA *n* pl. -S a disease of citrus trees

TRISTFUL *adj* sad

TRISTICH *n* pl. -S a stanza of three lines

TRITE *adj* TRITER, TRITEST used so often as to be made commonplace **TRITELY** *adv*

TRITHING *n* pl. -S an administrative division in England

TRITICUM *n* pl. -S a cereal grass

TRITIUM	*n* pl. -S an isotope of hydrogen
TRITOMA	*n* pl. -S an African herb
TRITON	*n* pl. -S a marine mollusk
TRITONE	*n* pl. -S a musical interval of three whole tones
TRIUMPH	*v* -ED, -ING, -S to be victorious
TRIUMVIR	*n* pl. -VIRS or -VIRI one of a ruling body of three in ancient Rome
TRIUNE	*n* pl. -S a trinity
TRIUNITY	*n* pl. -TIES a trinity
TRIVALVE	*n* pl. -S a type of shell
TRIVET	*n* pl. -S a small stand having three legs
TRIVIA	*n/pl* insignificant matters
TRIVIAL	*adj* insignificant
TRIVIUM	*n* pl. -IA a group of studies in medieval schools
TROAK	*v* -ED, -ING, -S to troke
TROCAR	*n* pl. -S a surgical instrument
TROCHAIC	*n* pl. -S a trochee
TROCHAL	*adj* shaped like a wheel
TROCHAR	*n* pl. -S trocar
TROCHE	*n* pl. -S a medicated lozenge
TROCHEE	*n* pl. -S a type of metrical foot
TROCHIL	*n* pl. -S an African bird
TROCHILI	*n/pl* trochils
TROCHLEA	*n* pl. -LEAE or -LEAS an anatomical structure resembling a pulley
TROCHOID	*n* pl. -S a type of geometric curve
TROCK	*v* -ED, -ING, -S to troke
TROD	a past tense of tread
TRODDEN	past participle of tread
TRODE	a past tense of tread
TROFFER	*n* pl. -S a fixture for fluorescent lighting
TROGON	*n* pl. -S a tropical bird
TROIKA	*n* pl. -S a Russian carriage
TROILISM	*n* pl. -S sexual relations involving three persons
TROILITE	*n* pl. -S a mineral
TROILUS	*n* pl. -ES a large butterfly
TROIS	*n* pl. TROIS the number three
TROKE	*v* TROKED, TROKING, TROKES to exchange
TROLAND	*n* pl. -S a unit of measurement of retinal response to light

TROLL	*v* -ED, -ING, -S to fish with a slowly trailing line
TROLLER	*n* pl. -S one that trolls
TROLLEY	*v* -ED, -ING, -S to convey by streetcar
TROLLIED	past tense of trolly
TROLLIES	present 3d person sing. of trolly
TROLLING	*n* pl. -S the act of one that trolls
TROLLOP	*n* pl. -S a prostitute **TROLLOPY** *adj*
TROLLY	*v* -LIED, -LYING, -LIES to trolley
TROMBONE	*n* pl. -S a brass wind instrument
TROMMEL	*n* pl. -S a screen used for sifting rock, ore, or coal
TROMP	*v* -ED, -ING, -S to tramp
TROMPE	*n* pl. -S a device used for supplying air to a furnace
TRONA	*n* pl. -S a mineral
TRONE	*n* pl. -S a weighing device
TROOP	*v* -ED, -ING, -S to move or gather in crowds
TROOPER	*n* pl. -S a cavalryman
TROOPIAL	*n* pl. -S troupial
TROOZ	*n/pl* trews
TROP	*adv* too much
TROPE	*n* pl. -S the figurative use of a word
TROPHIC	*adj* pertaining to nutrition
TROPHY	*v* -PHIED, -PHYING, -PHIES to honor with a trophy (a symbol of victory)
TROPIC	*n* pl. -S either of two circles of the celestial sphere on each side of the equator **TROPICAL** *adj*
TROPIN	*n* pl. -S tropine
TROPINE	*n* pl. -S a poisonous alkaloid
TROPISM	*n* pl. -S the involuntary response of an organism to an external stimulus
TROPONIN	*n* pl. -S a protein of muscle
TROT	*v* TROTTED, TROTTING, TROTS to go at a gait between a walk and a run
TROTH	*v* -ED, -ING, -S to betroth
TROTLINE	*n* pl. -S a strong fishing line
TROTTED	past tense of trot
TROTTER	*n* pl. -S a horse that trots
TROTTING	present participle of trot
TROTYL	*n* pl. -S an explosive

TROUBLE	*v* -BLED, -BLING, -BLES to distress	**TRUCKLE**	*v* -LED, -LING, -LES to yield weakly
TROUBLER	*n* pl. -S one that troubles	**TRUCKLER**	*n* pl. -S one that truckles
TROUGH	*n* pl. -S a long, narrow receptacle	**TRUCKMAN**	*n* pl. -MEN a trucker
TROUNCE	*v* TROUNCED, TROUNCING, TROUNCES to beat severely	**TRUDGE**	*v* TRUDGED, TRUDGING, TRUDGES to walk tiredly
TROUNCER	*n* pl. -S one that trounces	**TRUDGEN**	*n* pl. -S a swimming stroke
TROUPE	*v* TROUPED, TROUPING, TROUPES to tour with a theatrical company	**TRUDGEON**	*n* pl. -S trudgen
		TRUDGER	*n* pl. -S one that trudges
		TRUDGING	present participle of trudge
TROUPER	*n* pl. -S a member of a theatrical company	**TRUE**	*adj* TRUER, TRUEST consistent with fact or reality
TROUPIAL	*n* pl. -S a tropical bird	**TRUE**	*v* TRUED, TRUING or TRUEING, TRUES to bring to conformity with a standard or requirement
TROUPING	present participle of troupe		
TROUSER	*adj* pertaining to trousers		
TROUSERS	*n/pl* a garment for the lower part of the body	**TRUEBLUE**	*n* pl. -S a person of unwavering loyalty
TROUT	*n* pl. -S a freshwater fish	**TRUEBORN**	*adj* genuinely such by birth
TROUTY	*adj* TROUTIER, TROUTIEST abounding in trout	**TRUEBRED**	*adj* designating an animal of unmixed stock
TROUVERE	*n* pl. -S a medieval poet	**TRUED**	past tense of true
TROUVEUR	*n* pl. -S trouvere	**TRUELOVE**	*n* pl. -S a sweetheart
TROVE	*n* pl. -S a valuable discovery	**TRUENESS**	*n* pl. -ES the quality or state of being true
TROVER	*n* pl. -S a type of legal action		
TROW	*v* -ED, -ING, -S to suppose	**TRUER**	comparative of true
TROWEL	*v* -ELED, -ELING, -ELS or -ELLED, -ELLING, -ELS to smooth with a trowel (a hand tool having a flat blade)	**TRUEST**	superlative of true
		TRUFFE	*n* pl. -S truffle
		TRUFFLE	*n* pl. -S an edible fungus **TRUFFLED** *adj*
TROWELER	*n* pl. -S one that trowels	**TRUG**	*n* pl. -S a gardener's basket
TROWSERS	*n/pl* trousers	**TRUING**	a present participle of true
TROWTH	*n* pl. -S truth	**TRUISM**	*n* pl. -S an obvious truth **TRUISTIC** *adj*
TROY	*n* pl. TROYS a system of weights		
TRUANCY	*n* pl. -CIES an act of truanting	**TRULL**	*n* pl. -S a prostitute
TRUANT	*v* -ED, -ING, -S to stay out of school without permission	**TRULY**	*adv* in conformity with fact or reality
TRUANTRY	*n* pl. -RIES truancy	**TRUMEAU**	*n* pl. -MEAUX a column supporting part of a doorway
TRUCE	*v* TRUCED, TRUCING, TRUCES to suspend hostilities by mutual agreement		
		TRUMP	*v* -ED, -ING, -S to outdo
		TRUMPERY	*n* pl. -ERIES worthless finery
TRUCK	*v* -ED, -ING, -S to transport by truck (an automotive vehicle designed to carry loads)	**TRUMPET**	*v* -ED, -ING, -S to sound on a trumpet (a brass wind instrument)
		TRUNCATE	*v* -CATED, -CATING, -CATES to shorten by cutting off a part
TRUCKAGE	*n* pl. -S transportation of goods by trucks	**TRUNDLE**	*v* -DLED, -DLING, -DLES to propel by causing to rotate
TRUCKER	*n* pl. -S a truck driver	**TRUNDLER**	*n* pl. -S one that trundles
TRUCKFUL	*n* pl. -S as much as a truck can hold	**TRUNK**	*n* pl. -S the main stem of a tree **TRUNKED** *adj*
TRUCKING	*n* pl. -S truckage		

TRUNKFUL	n pl. -S as much as a trunk (a storage box) can hold
TRUNNEL	n pl. -S treenail
TRUNNION	n pl. -S a pin or pivot on which something can be rotated
TRUSS	v -ED, -ING, -ES to secure tightly
TRUSSER	n pl. -S one that trusses
TRUSSING	n pl. -S the framework of a structure
TRUST	v -ED, -ING, -S to place confidence in
TRUSTEE	v -TEED, -TEEING, -TEES to commit to the care of an administrator
TRUSTER	n pl. -S one that trusts
TRUSTFUL	adj inclined to trust
TRUSTOR	n pl. -S one that trustees his property
TRUSTY	adj TRUSTIER, TRUSTIEST worthy of trust **TRUSTILY** adv
TRUSTY	n pl. TRUSTIES one worthy of trust
TRUTH	n pl. -S conformity to fact or reality
TRUTHFUL	adj telling the truth
TRY	v TRIED, TRYING, TRIES to attempt
TRYINGLY	adv in a distressing manner
TRYMA	n pl. -MATA a type of nut
TRYOUT	n pl. -S a test of ability
TRYPSIN	n pl. -S an enzyme **TRYPTIC** adj
TRYSAIL	n pl. -S a type of sail
TRYST	v -ED, -ING, -S to agree to meet
TRYSTE	n pl. -S a market
TRYSTER	n pl. -S one that trysts
TRYWORKS	n/pl a type of furnace
TSADE	n pl. -S sade
TSADI	n pl. -S sade
TSAR	n pl. -S czar
TSARDOM	n pl. -S czardom
TSAREVNA	n pl. -S czarevna
TSARINA	n pl. -S czarina
TSARISM	n pl. -S czarism
TSARIST	n pl. -S czarist
TSARITZA	n pl. -S czaritza
TSETSE	n pl. -S an African fly
TSIMMES	n pl. TSIMMES tzimmes
TSK	v -ED, -ING, -S to utter an exclamation of annoyance
TSKTSK	v -ED, -ING, -S to tsk
TSOORIS	n pl. TSOORIS tsuris
TSORES	n pl. TSORES tsuris
TSORIS	n pl. TSORIS tsuris
TSORRISS	n pl. TSORRISS tsuris
TSUBA	n pl. TSUBA a part of a Japanese sword
TSUNAMI	n pl. -S a very large ocean wave **TSUNAMIC** adj
TSURIS	n pl. TSURIS a series of misfortunes
TUATARA	n pl. -S a large reptile
TUATERA	n pl. -S tuatara
TUB	v TUBBED, TUBBING, TUBS to wash in a tub (a round, open vessel)
TUBA	n pl. -BAS or -BAE a brass wind instrument
TUBAIST	n pl. -S a tuba player
TUBAL	adj pertaining to a tube
TUBATE	adj tubular
TUBBABLE	adj suitable for washing in a tub
TUBBED	past tense of tub
TUBBER	n pl. -S one that tubs
TUBBING	present participle of tub
TUBBY	adj -BIER, -BIEST short and fat
TUBE	v TUBED, TUBING, TUBES to provide with a tube (a long, hollow cylinder)
TUBELESS	adj having no tube
TUBELIKE	adj resembling a tube
TUBENOSE	n pl. -S a bird having tubular nostrils
TUBER	n pl. -S a thick underground stem
TUBERCLE	n pl. -S a small, rounded swelling
TUBEROID	adj pertaining to a tuber
TUBEROSE	n pl. -S a Mexican herb
TUBEROUS	adj pertaining to a tuber
TUBEWORK	n pl. -S tubing
TUBFUL	n pl. -S as much as a tub will hold
TUBIFEX	n pl. -ES an aquatic worm
TUBIFORM	adj tubular
TUBING	n pl. -S material in the form of a tube
TUBIST	n pl. -S a tubaist

TUBLIKE	*adj* resembling a tub
TUBULAR	*adj* shaped like a tube
TUBULATE	*v* -LATED, -LATING, -LATES to form into a tube
TUBULE	*n* pl. -S a small tube
TUBULIN	*n* pl. -S a protein that polymerizes to form tiny tubules
TUBULOSE	*adj* tubular
TUBULOUS	*adj* tubular
TUBULURE	*n* pl. -S a short tubular opening
TUCHUN	*n* pl. -S a Chinese military governor
TUCK	*v* -ED, -ING, -S to fold under
TUCKAHOE	*n* pl. -S the edible root of certain arums
TUCKER	*v* -ED, -ING, -S to weary
TUCKET	*n* pl. -S a trumpet fanfare
TUCKSHOP	*n* pl. -S a confectioner's shop
TUFA	*n* pl. -S a porous limestone
TUFF	*n* pl. -S a volcanic rock
TUFFET	*n* pl. -S a clump of grass
TUFOLI	*n* pl. TUFOLI a large macaroni shell
TUFT	*v* -ED, -ING, -S to form into tufts (clusters of flexible outgrowths attached at the base)
TUFTER	*n* pl. -S one that tufts
TUFTY	*adj* TUFTIER, TUFTIEST abounding in tufts **TUFTILY** *adv*
TUG	*v* TUGGED, TUGGING, TUGS to pull with force
TUGBOAT	*n* pl. -S a boat built for towing
TUGGER	*n* pl. -S one that tugs
TUGGING	present participle of tug
TUGHRIK	*n* pl. -S tugrik
TUGLESS	*adj* being without a rope or chain with which to pull
TUGRIK	*n* pl. -S a monetary unit of Mongolia
TUI	*n* pl. -S a bird of New Zealand
TUILLE	*n* pl. -S a tasset
TUITION	*n* pl. -S a fee for instruction
TULADI	*n* pl. -S a freshwater fish
TULE	*n* pl. -S a tall marsh plant
TULIP	*n* pl. -S a flowering plant
TULLE	*n* pl. -S a silk material
TULLIBEE	*n* pl. -S a freshwater fish
TUMBLE	*v* -BLED, -BLING, -BLES to fall or roll end over end
TUMBLER	*n* pl. -S one that tumbles
TUMBLING	*n* pl. -S the sport of gymnastics
TUMBREL	*n* pl. -S a type of cart
TUMBRIL	*n* pl. -S tumbrel
TUMEFY	*v* -FIED, -FYING, -FIES to swell
TUMID	*adj* swollen **TUMIDLY** *adv*
TUMIDITY	*n* pl. -TIES the quality or state of being tumid
TUMMLER	*n* pl. -S an entertainer who encourages audience participation
TUMMY	*n* pl. -MIES the stomach
TUMOR	*n* pl. -S an abnormal swelling **TUMORAL, TUMOROUS** *adj*
TUMOUR	*n* pl. -S tumor
TUMP	*v* -ED, -ING, -S to tip over
TUMPLINE	*n* pl. -S a strap for supporting a load on the back
TUMULAR	*adj* having the form of a mound
TUMULI	a pl. of tumulus
TUMULOSE	*adj* full of mounds
TUMULOUS	*adj* tumulose
TUMULT	*n* pl. -S a great din and commotion
TUMULUS	*n* pl. -LI or -LUSES a mound over a grave
TUN	*v* TUNNED, TUNNING, TUNS to store in a large cask
TUNA	*n* pl. -S a marine food fish
TUNABLE	*adj* capable of being tuned **TUNABLY** *adv*
TUNDISH	*n* pl. -ES a receptacle for molten metal
TUNDRA	*n* pl. -S a level, treeless expanse of arctic land
TUNE	*v* TUNED, TUNING, TUNES to put into the proper pitch
TUNEABLE	*adj* tunable **TUNEABLY** *adv*
TUNEFUL	*adj* melodious
TUNELESS	*adj* not tuneful
TUNER	*n* pl. -S one that tunes
TUNEUP	*n* pl. -S an adjustment to insure efficient operation
TUNG	*n* pl. -S a Chinese tree
TUNGSTEN	*n* pl. -S a metallic element **TUNGSTIC** *adj*
TUNIC	*n* pl. -S a loose-fitting garment

TUNICA *n* pl. -CAE an enveloping membrane or layer of body tissue

TUNICATE *n* pl. -S a small marine animal

TUNICLE *n* pl. -S a type of vestment

TUNING present participle of tune

TUNNAGE *n* pl. -S tonnage

TUNNED past tense of tun

TUNNEL *v* -NELED, -NELING, -NELS or -NELLED, -NELLING, -NELS to dig a tunnel (an underground passageway)

TUNNELER *n* pl. -S one that tunnels

TUNNING present participle of tun

TUNNY *n* pl. -NIES a tuna

TUP *v* TUPPED, TUPPING, TUPS to copulate with a ewe

TUPELO *n* pl. -LOS a softwood tree

TUPIK *n* pl. -S an Eskimo tent

TUPPED past tense of tup

TUPPENCE *n* pl. -S twopence

TUPPENNY *adj* twopenny

TUPPING present participle of tup

TUQUE *n* pl. -S a knitted woolen cap

TURACO *n* pl. -COS touraco

TURACOU *n* pl. -S touraco

TURBAN *n* pl. -S a head covering worn by Muslims **TURBANED** *adj*

TURBARY *n* pl. -RIES a place where peat can be dug

TURBETH *n* pl. -S turpeth

TURBID *adj* thick or opaque with roiled sediment **TURBIDLY** *adv*

TURBINAL *n* pl. -S a bone of the nasal passage

TURBINE *n* pl. -S a type of engine

TURBIT *n* pl. -S a domestic pigeon

TURBITH *n* pl. -S turpeth

TURBO *n* pl. -BOS a turbine

TURBOCAR *n* pl. -S an auto powered by a gas turbine

TURBOFAN *n* pl. -S a type of jet engine

TURBOJET *n* pl. -S a type of jet engine

TURBOT *n* pl. -S a European flatfish

TURDINE *adj* belonging to a large family of singing birds

TUREEN *n* pl. -S a large, deep bowl

TURF *n* pl. TURFS or TURVES a surface layer of earth containing a dense growth of grass

TURF *v* -ED, -ING, -S to cover with turf

TURFIER comparative of turfy

TURFIEST superlative of turfy

TURFLESS *adj* having no turf

TURFLIKE *adj* resembling turf

TURFMAN *n* pl. -MEN a person who is devoted to horse racing

TURFSKI *n* pl. -S a type of ski

TURFY *adj* TURFIER, TURFIEST covered with turf

TURGENCY *n* pl. -CIES turgor

TURGENT *adj* turgid

TURGID *adj* swollen **TURGIDLY** *adv*

TURGITE *n* pl. -S an iron ore

TURGOR *n* pl. -S the quality or state of being turgid

TURISTA *n* pl. -S intestinal sickness affecting a tourist in a foreign country

TURK *n* pl. -S one who eagerly advocates change

TURKEY *n* pl. -KEYS a large American bird

TURKOIS *n* pl. -ES turquois

TURMERIC *n* pl. -S an East Indian herb

TURMOIL *v* -ED, -ING, -S to throw into an uproar

TURN *v* -ED, -ING, -S to move around a central point **TURNABLE** *adj*

TURNCOAT *n* pl. -S a traitor

TURNDOWN *n* pl. -S a rejection

TURNER *n* pl. -S one that turns

TURNERY *n* pl. -ERIES the process of shaping articles on a lathe

TURNHALL *n* pl. -S a building where gymnasts practice

TURNING *n* pl. -S a rotation about an axis

TURNIP *n* pl. -S an edible plant root

TURNKEY *n* pl. -KEYS a person who has charge of a prison's keys

TURNOFF *n* pl. -S a road that branches off from a larger one

TURNOUT *n* pl. -S an assemblage of people

TURNOVER *n* pl. -S an upset or overthrow

TURNPIKE *n* pl. -S a toll road

TURNSOLE *n* pl. -S a plant that turns with the sun

TURNSPIT	*n* pl. -S one that turns a roasting spit
TURNUP	*n* pl. -S a part of a garment that is turned up
TURPETH	*n* pl. -S a medicinal plant root
TURPS	*n* pl. TURPS turpentine
TURQUOIS	*n* pl. -ES a greenish blue gem
TURRET	*n* pl. -S a small tower **TURRETED** *adj*
TURRICAL	*adj* resembling a turret
TURTLE	*v* -TLED, -TLING, -TLES to catch turtles (tortoises)
TURTLER	*n* pl. -S one that turtles
TURTLING	*n* pl. -S the act of one that turtles
TURVES	a pl. of turf
TUSCHE	*n* pl. -S a liquid used in lithography
TUSH	*v* -ED, -ING, -ES to tusk
TUSHIE	*n* pl. -S the buttocks
TUSHY	*n* pl. TUSHIES tushie
TUSK	*v* -ED, -ING, -S to gore with a tusk (a long, pointed tooth extending outside of the mouth)
TUSKER	*n* pl. -S an animal with tusks
TUSKLESS	*adj* having no tusk
TUSKLIKE	*adj* resembling a tusk
TUSSAH	*n* pl. -S an Asian silkworm
TUSSAL	*adj* pertaining to a cough
TUSSAR	*n* pl. -S tussah
TUSSEH	*n* pl. -S tussah
TUSSER	*n* pl. -S tussah
TUSSIS	*n* pl. -SISES a cough **TUSSIVE** *adj*
TUSSLE	*v* -SLED, -SLING, -SLES to struggle
TUSSOCK	*n* pl. -S a clump of grass **TUSSOCKY** *adj*
TUSSOR	*n* pl. -S tussah
TUSSORE	*n* pl. -S tussah
TUSSUCK	*n* pl. -S tussock
TUSSUR	*n* pl. -S tussah
TUT	*v* TUTTED, TUTTING, TUTS to utter an exclamation of impatience
TUTEE	*n* pl. -S one who is being tutored
TUTELAGE	*n* pl. -S the act of tutoring
TUTELAR	*n* pl. -S a tutelary

TUTELARY	*n* pl. -LARIES one who has the power to protect
TUTOR	*v* -ED, -ING, -S to instruct privately
TUTORAGE	*n* pl. -S tutelage
TUTORESS	*n* pl. -ES a female who tutors
TUTORIAL	*n* pl. -S a session of tutoring
TUTOYER	*v* -TOYERED or -TOYED, -TOYERING, -TOYERS to address familiarly
TUTTED	past tense of tut
TUTTI	*n* pl. -S a musical passage performed by all the performers
TUTTING	present participle of tut
TUTTY	*n* pl. -TIES an impure zinc oxide
TUTU	*n* pl. -S a short ballet skirt
TUX	*n* pl. -ES a tuxedo
TUXEDO	*n* pl. -DOES or -DOS a man's semiformal dinner coat **TUXEDOED** *adj*
TUYER	*n* pl. -S tuyere
TUYERE	*n* pl. -S a pipe through which air is forced into a blast furnace
TWA	*n* pl. -S two
TWADDLE	*v* -DLED, -DLING, -DLES to talk foolishly
TWADDLER	*n* pl. -S one that twaddles
TWAE	*n* pl. -S two
TWAIN	*n* pl. -S a set of two
TWANG	*v* -ED, -ING, -S to make a sharp, vibrating sound
TWANGER	*n* pl. -S one that twangs
TWANGIER	comparative of twangy
TWANGIEST	superlative of twangy
TWANGLE	*v* -GLED, -GLING, -GLES to twang
TWANGLER	*n* pl. -S one that twangles
TWANGY	*adj* TWANGIER, TWANGIEST twanging
TWANKY	*n* pl. -KIES a variety of green tea
TWASOME	*n* pl. -S twosome
TWATTLE	*v* -TLED, -TLING, -TLES to twaddle
TWEAK	*v* -ED, -ING, -S to pinch and twist sharply
TWEAKY	*adj* TWEAKIER, TWEAKIEST twitchy
TWEE	*adj* affectedly cute or dainty
TWEED	*n* pl. -S a coarse woolen fabric

TWEEDLE	*v* -DLED, -DLING, -DLES to perform casually on a musical instrument	**TWINGE**	*v* TWINGED, TWINGING or TWINGEING, TWINGES to affect with a sharp pain
TWEEDY	*adj* TWEEDIER, TWEEDIEST resembling tweed	**TWINIER**	comparative of twiny
TWEEN	*prep* between	**TWINIEST**	superlative of twiny
TWEENY	*n* pl. TWEENIES a housemaid	**TWINIGHT**	*adj* pertaining to a baseball doubleheader that begins in the late afternoon
TWEET	*v* -ED, -ING, -S to chirp	**TWINING**	present participle of twine
TWEETER	*n* pl. -S a loudspeaker designed to reproduce high-pitched sounds	**TWINJET**	*n* pl. -S an aircraft with two jet engines
TWEEZE	*v* TWEEZED, TWEEZING, TWEEZES to pluck with a tweezer	**TWINKLE**	*v* -KLED, -KLING, -KLES to shine with a flickering or sparkling light
TWEEZER	*n* pl. -S a pincerlike tool	**TWINKLER**	*n* pl. -S one that twinkles
TWELFTH	*n* pl. -S the number twelve in a series	**TWINKLY**	*adj* twinkling
TWELVE	*n* pl. -S a number	**TWINNED**	past tense of twin
TWELVEMO	*n* pl. -MOS a page size	**TWINNING**	*n* pl. -S the bearing of two children at the same birth
TWENTY	*n* pl. -TIES a number	**TWINSET**	*n* pl. -S a matching pair of sweaters to be worn together
TWERP	*n* pl. -S a small, impudent person	**TWINSHIP**	*n* pl. -S close similarity or association
TWIBIL	*n* pl. -S a battle-ax with two cutting edges	**TWINY**	*adj* TWINIER, TWINIEST resembling twine (a strong string)
TWIBILL	*n* pl. -S twibil	**TWIRL**	*v* -ED, -ING, -S to rotate rapidly
TWICE	*adv* two times	**TWIRLER**	*n* pl. -S one that twirls
TWIDDLE	*v* -DLED, -DLING, -DLES to play idly with something	**TWIRLY**	*adj* TWIRLIER, TWIRLIEST curved
TWIDDLER	*n* pl. -S one that twiddles	**TWIRP**	*n* pl. -S twerp
TWIDDLY	*adj* -DLIER, -DLIEST having many turns	**TWIST**	*v* -ED, -ING, -S to combine by winding together
TWIER	*n* pl. -S tuyere	**TWISTER**	*n* pl. -S one that twists
TWIG	*v* TWIGGED, TWIGGING, TWIGS to observe	**TWISTING**	*n* pl. -S a form of trickery used in selling life insurance
TWIGGEN	*adj* made of twigs (small branches)	**TWISTY**	*adj* TWISTIER, TWISTIEST full of curves
TWIGGY	*adj* -GIER, -GIEST twiglike	**TWIT**	*v* TWITTED, TWITTING, TWITS to ridicule
TWIGLESS	*adj* having no twigs	**TWITCH**	*v* -ED, -ING, -ES to move or pull with a sudden motion
TWIGLIKE	*adj* resembling a twig	**TWITCHER**	*n* pl. -S one that twitches
TWILIGHT	*n* pl. -S the early evening light	**TWITCHY**	*adj* TWITCHIER, TWITCHIEST fidgety
TWILIT	*adj* lighted by twilight	**TWITTED**	past tense of twit
TWILL	*v* -ED, -ING, -S to weave so as to produce a diagonal pattern	**TWITTER**	*v* -ED, -ING, -S to utter a succession of chirping sounds
TWILLING	*n* pl. -S a twilled fabric	**TWITTERY**	*adj* nervously agitated
TWIN	*v* TWINNED, TWINNING, TWINS to bring together in close association	**TWITTING**	present participle of twit
TWINBORN	*adj* born at the same birth	**TWIXT**	*prep* between
TWINE	*v* TWINED, TWINING, TWINES to twist together		
TWINER	*n* pl. -S one that twines		

TWO	*n* pl. TWOS a number
TWOFER	*n* pl. -S something sold at the rate of two for the price of one
TWOFOLD	*n* pl. -S an amount twice as great as a given unit
TWOPENCE	*n* pl. -S a British coin worth two pennies
TWOPENNY	*adj* worth twopence
TWOSOME	*n* pl. -S a group of two
TWYER	*n* pl. -S tuyere
TYCOON	*n* pl. -S a wealthy and powerful business person
TYE	*n* pl. -S a chain on a ship
TYEE	*n* pl. -S a food fish
TYER	*n* pl. -S one that ties
TYING	a present participle of tie
TYKE	*n* pl. -S a small child
TYLOSIN	*n* pl. -S an antibiotic
TYMBAL	*n* pl. -S timbal
TYMPAN	*n* pl. -S a drum
TYMPANA	a pl. of tympanum
TYMPANAL	*adj* tympanic
TYMPANIC	*adj* pertaining to the tympanum
TYMPANO	*n* pl. -NI timpano
TYMPANUM	*n* pl. -NA or -NUMS the middle ear
TYMPANY	*n* pl. -NIES a swelling of the abdomen
TYNE	*v* TYNED, TYNING, TYNES to tine
TYPAL	*adj* typical
TYPE	*v* TYPED, TYPING, TYPES to write with a typewriter **TYPABLE, TYPEABLE** *adj*
TYPEBAR	*n* pl. -S a part of a typewriter
TYPECASE	*n* pl. -S a tray for holding printing type
TYPECAST	*v* -CAST, -CASTING, -CASTS to cast in an acting role befitting one's own nature
TYPED	past tense of type
TYPEFACE	*n* pl. -S the face of printing type
TYPESET	*v* -SET, -SETTING, -SETS to set in type
TYPEY	*adj* TYPIER, TYPIEST typy
TYPHOID	*n* pl. -S an infectious disease
TYPHON	*n* pl. -S a type of signal horn
TYPHOON	*n* pl. -S a tropical hurricane **TYPHONIC** *adj*
TYPHOSE	*adj* pertaining to typhoid
TYPHUS	*n* pl. -ES an infectious disease **TYPHOUS** *adj*
TYPIC	*adj* typical
TYPICAL	*adj* having the nature of a representative specimen
TYPIER	comparative of typey and typy
TYPIEST	superlative of typey and typy
TYPIFIER	*n* pl. -S one that typifies
TYPIFY	*v* -FIED, -FYING, -FIES to serve as a typical example of
TYPING	present participle of type
TYPIST	*n* pl. -S one who types
TYPO	*n* pl. -POS a typographical error
TYPOLOGY	*n* pl. -GIES the study of classification according to common characteristics
TYPP	*n* pl. -S a unit of yarn size
TYPY	*adj* TYPIER, TYPIEST characterized by strict conformance to the characteristics of a group
TYRAMINE	*n* pl. -S a chemical compound
TYRANNIC	*adj* characteristic of a tyrant
TYRANNY	*n* pl. -NIES the rule of a tyrant
TYRANT	*n* pl. -S an absolute ruler
TYRE	*v* TYRED, TYRING, TYRES to furnish with a covering for a wheel
TYRO	*n* pl. -ROS a beginner **TYRONIC** *adj*
TYROSINE	*n* pl. -S an amino acid
TYTHE	*v* TYTHED, TYTHING, TYTHES to tithe
TZADDIK	*n* pl. -DIKIM zaddik
TZAR	*n* pl. -S czar
TZARDOM	*n* pl. -S czardom
TZAREVNA	*n* pl. -S czarevna
TZARINA	*n* pl. -S czarina
TZARISM	*n* pl. -S czarism
TZARIST	*n* pl. -S czarist
TZARITZA	*n* pl. -S czaritza
TZETZE	*n* pl. -S tsetse
TZIGANE	*n* pl. -S a gypsy
TZIMMES	*n* pl. TZIMMES a vegetable stew
TZITZIS	*n/pl* zizith
TZITZIT	*n/pl* zizith
TZITZITH	*n/pl* zizith
TZURIS	*n* pl. TZURIS tsuris

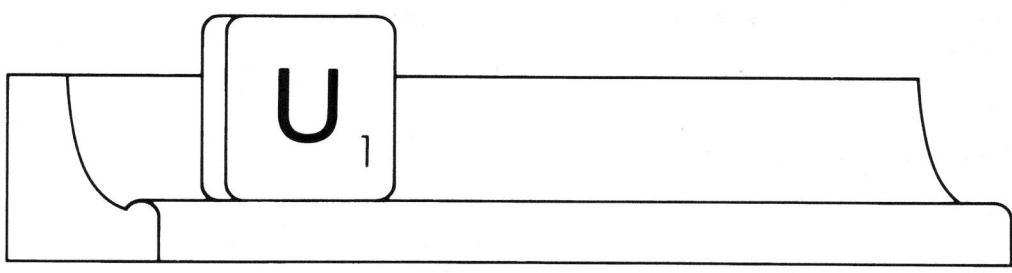

UBIETY	*n* pl. -ETIES the state of having a definite location
UBIQUE	*adv* everywhere
UBIQUITY	*n* pl. -TIES the state of being everywhere at the same time
UDDER	*n* pl. -S a mammary gland
UDO	*n* pl. UDOS a Japanese herb
UDOMETER	*n* pl. -S a rain gauge
UDOMETRY	*n* pl. -TRIES the measurement of rain
UFOLOGY	*n* pl. -GIES the study of unidentified flying objects
UGH	*n* pl. -S the sound of a cough or grunt
UGLIER	comparative of ugly
UGLIES	pl. of ugly
UGLIEST	superlative of ugly
UGLIFIER	*n* pl. -S one that uglifies
UGLIFY	*v* -FIED, -FYING, -FIES to make ugly
UGLINESS	*n* pl. -ES the state of being ugly
UGLY	*adj* -LIER, -LIEST displeasing to the sight **UGLILY** *adv*
UGLY	*n* pl. -LIES one that is ugly
UGSOME	*adj* disgusting
UH	*interj* — used to express hesitation
UHLAN	*n* pl. -S one of a body of Prussian cavalry
UINTAITE	*n* pl. -S a variety of asphalt
UKASE	*n* pl. -S an edict
UKE	*n* pl. -S ukelele
UKELELE	*n* pl. -S ukulele
UKULELE	*n* pl. -S a small guitar-like instrument
ULAMA	*n* pl. -S ulema
ULAN	*n* pl. -S uhlan
ULCER	*v* -ED, -ING, -S to affect with an ulcer (a type of lesion)
ULCERATE	*v* -ATED, -ATING, -ATES to ulcer
ULCEROUS	*adj* being or affected with an ulcer
ULEMA	*n* pl. -S a Muslim scholar
ULEXITE	*n* pl. -S a mineral
ULLAGE	*n* pl. -S the amount that a container lacks of being full **ULLAGED** *adj*
ULNA	*n* pl. -NAE or -NAS a bone of the forearm **ULNAR** *adj*
ULNAD	*adv* toward the ulna
ULPAN	*n* pl. -PANIM a school in Israel for teaching Hebrew
ULSTER	*n* pl. -S a long, loose overcoat
ULTERIOR	*adj* more remote
ULTIMA	*n* pl. -S the last syllable of a word
ULTIMACY	*n* pl. -CIES an ultimate
ULTIMATA	*n/pl* final proposals
ULTIMATE	*v* -MATED, -MATING, -MATES to come to an end
ULTIMO	*adj* of or occurring in the preceding month
ULTRA	*n* pl. -S an ultraist
ULTRADRY	*adj* extremely dry
ULTRAHIP	*adj* extremely hip
ULTRAHOT	*adj* extremely hot
ULTRAISM	*n* pl. -S advocacy of extreme measures
ULTRAIST	*n* pl. -S an advocate of extreme measures
ULTRALOW	*adj* extremely low
ULTRARED	*n* pl. -S infrared
ULU	*n* pl. -S an Eskimo knife
ULULANT	*adj* howling
ULULATE	*v* -LATED, -LATING, -LATES to howl
ULVA	*n* pl. -S an edible seaweed

UM	*interj* — used to indicate hesitation
UMANGITE	*n* pl. -S a mineral consisting of copper selenide
UMBEL	*n* pl. -S a type of flower cluster **UMBELED, UMBELLAR, UMBELLED** *adj*
UMBELLET	*n* pl. -S a small umbel
UMBER	*v* -ED, -ING, -S to color with a brown pigment
UMBILICI	*n/pl* navels
UMBLES	*n/pl* the entrails of a deer
UMBO	*n* pl. -BONES or -BOS the rounded elevation at the center of a shield **UMBONAL, UMBONATE, UMBONIC** *adj*
UMBRA	*n* pl. -BRAE or -BRAS a dark area **UMBRAL** *adj*
UMBRAGE	*n* pl. -S resentment
UMBRELLA	*v* -ED, -ING, -S to provide with an umbrella (a portable cover for protection from rain or sun)
UMBRETTE	*n* pl. -S a wading bird
UMIAC	*n* pl. -S umiak
UMIACK	*n* pl. -S umiak
UMIAK	*n* pl. -S an open Eskimo boat
UMIAQ	*n* pl. -S umiak
UMLAUT	*v* -ED, -ING, -S to modify a vowel sound by partial assimilation to a succeeding sound
UMM	*interj* um
UMP	*v* -ED, -ING, -S to umpire
UMPIRAGE	*n* pl. -S the function of an umpire
UMPIRE	*v* -PIRED, -PIRING, -PIRES to act as umpire (a person appointed to rule on the plays in a game)
UMPTEEN	*adj* indefinitely numerous
UMTEENTH	*adj* being the last in an indefinitely numerous series
UN	*pron* pl. -S one

U₁	N₁

Following is a list of self-explanatory adjectives and adverbs containing the prefix UN- (not):

UNABATED	*adj*
UNABLE	*adj*
UNABUSED	*adj*
UNACTED	*adj*
UNADULT	*adj*
UNAFRAID	*adj*
UNAGED	*adj*
UNAGEING	*adj*
UNAGILE	*adj*
UNAGING	*adj*
UNAIDED	*adj*
UNAIMED	*adj*
UNAIRED	*adj*
UNAKIN	*adj*
UNALIKE	*adj*
UNALLIED	*adj*
UNAMUSED	*adj*
UNANELED	*adj*
UNAPT	*adj*
UNAPTLY	*adv*
UNARGUED	*adj*
UNARTFUL	*adj*
UNASKED	*adj*
UNATONED	*adj*
UNAVOWED	*adj*
UNAWAKED	*adj*
UNAWARE	*adj*
UNAWED	*adj*
UNBACKED	*adj*
UNBAKED	*adj*
UNBANNED	*adj*
UNBARBED	*adj*
UNBASED	*adj*
UNBATHED	*adj*
UNBEATEN	*adj*
UNBENIGN	*adj*
UNBIASED	*adj*
UNBILLED	*adj*
UNBITTED	*adj*
UNBITTEN	*adj*
UNBITTER	*adj*
UNBLAMED	*adj*
UNBLEST	*adj*
UNBLOODY	*adj*
UNBONED	*adj*
UNBORN	*adj*
UNBOUGHT	*adj*
UNBOUNCY	*adj*
UNBOWED	*adj*
UNBRED	*adj*
UNBRIGHT	*adj*
UNBROKE	*adj*
UNBROKEN	*adj*
UNBULKY	*adj*

UNBURIED	adj	
UNBURNED	adj	
UNBURNT	adj	
UNBUSTED	adj	
UNBUSY	adj	
UNCALLED	adj	
UNCANDID	adj	
UNCARING	adj	
UNCASHED	adj	
UNCASKED	adj	
UNCATCHY	adj	
UNCAUGHT	adj	
UNCAUSED	adj	
UNCHARY	adj	
UNCHASTE	adj	
UNCHEWED	adj	
UNCHIC	adj	
UNCHICLY	adv	
UNCHOSEN	adj	
UNCIVIL	adj	
UNCLEAN	adj	-CLEANER, -CLEANEST
UNCLEAR	adj	-CLEARER, -CLEAREST
UNCLOYED	adj	
UNCOATED	adj	
UNCODED	adj	
UNCOINED	adj	
UNCOMBED	adj	
UNCOMELY	adj	
UNCOMIC	adj	
UNCOMMON	adj	-MONER, -MONEST
UNCOOKED	adj	
UNCOOL	adj	
UNCOOLED	adj	
UNCOUTH	adj	
UNCOY	adj	
UNCRAZY	adj	
UNCUFFED	adj	
UNCURED	adj	
UNCURSED	adj	
UNCUT	adj	
UNCUTE	adj	
UNDAMPED	adj	
UNDARING	adj	
UNDATED	adj	
UNDECKED	adj	
UNDENIED	adj	
UNDEVOUT	adj	
UNDIMMED	adj	
UNDOABLE	adj	
UNDOCILE	adj	
UNDOTTED	adj	
UNDREAMT	adj	
UNDRIED	adj	
UNDUBBED	adj	
UNDULLED	adj	
UNDYED	adj	
UNEAGER	adj	
UNEARNED	adj	
UNEATEN	adj	
UNEDIBLE	adj	
UNEDITED	adj	
UNENDED	adj	
UNENDING	adj	
UNENVIED	adj	
UNERASED	adj	
UNEROTIC	adj	
UNERRING	adj	
UNEVADED	adj	
UNEVEN	adj	-EVENER, -EVENEST
UNEVENLY	adv	
UNEXOTIC	adj	
UNEXPERT	adj	
UNFADED	adj	
UNFADING	adj	
UNFAIR	adj	-FAIRER, -FAIREST
UNFAIRLY	adv	
UNFAKED	adj	
UNFALLEN	adj	
UNFAMOUS	adj	
UNFANCY	adj	
UNFAZED	adj	
UNFEARED	adj	
UNFED	adj	
UNFELT	adj	
UNFILIAL	adj	
UNFILLED	adj	
UNFILMED	adj	
UNFIRED	adj	
UNFISHED	adj	
UNFLASHY	adj	
UNFLEXED	adj	
UNFOILED	adj	
UNFOND	adj	
UNFORCED	adj	
UNFORGED	adj	
UNFORKED	adj	
UNFORMED	adj	
UNFOUGHT	adj	
UNFOUND	adj	
UNFRAMED	adj	
UNFUNDED	adj	
UNFUNNY	adj	
UNFUSED	adj	
UNFUSSY	adj	
UNGALLED	adj	
UNGENIAL	adj	

UNGENTLE	adj		UNLIKE	adj
UNGENTLY	adv		UNLIKELY	adj -LIER, -LIEST
UNGIFTED	adj		UNLINED	adj
UNGLAZED	adj		UNLISTED	adj
UNGOWNED	adj		UNLIT	adj
UNGRACED	adj		UNLIVELY	adj
UNGRADED	adj		UNLOBED	adj
UNGREEDY	adj		UNLOVED	adj
UNGROUND	adj		UNLOVELY	adj -LIER, -LIEST
UNGUIDED	adj		UNLOVING	adj
UNHAILED	adj		UNLUCKY	adj -LUCKIER, -LUCKIEST
UNHALVED	adj		UNMACHO	adj
UNHAPPY	adj -PIER, -PIEST		UNMANFUL	adj
UNHARMED	adj		UNMANLY	adj
UNHASTY	adj		UNMAPPED	adj
UNHEALED	adj		UNMARKED	adj
UNHEARD	adj		UNMARRED	adj
UNHEATED	adj		UNMATED	adj
UNHEDGED	adj		UNMATTED	adj
UNHEEDED	adj		UNMEANT	adj
UNHELPED	adj		UNMELLOW	adj
UNHEROIC	adj		UNMELTED	adj
UNHEWN	adj		UNMENDED	adj
UNHIP	adj		UNMERRY	adj
UNHIRED	adj		UNMET	adj
UNHOLILY	adv		UNMILLED	adj
UNHOLY	adj -LIER, -LIEST		UNMINED	adj
UNHUMAN	adj		UNMIXED	adj
UNHUNG	adj		UNMIXT	adj
UNHURT	adj		UNMODISH	adj
UNIDEAL	adj		UNMOLTEN	adj
UNIMBUED	adj		UNMOVED	adj
UNIRONED	adj		UNMOVING	adj
UNISSUED	adj		UNMOWN	adj
UNJADED	adj		UNNAMED	adj
UNJOINED	adj		UNNEEDED	adj
UNJOYFUL	adj		UNNOISY	adj
UNJUDGED	adj		UNNOTED	adj
UNJUST	adj		UNOILED	adj
UNJUSTLY	adv		UNOPEN	adj
UNKEPT	adj		UNOPENED	adj
UNKIND	adj -KINDER, -KINDEST		UNORNATE	adj
UNKINDLY	adv -LIER, -LIEST		UNOWNED	adj
UNKINGLY	adj		UNPAID	adj
UNKISSED	adj		UNPAIRED	adj
UNKOSHER	adj		UNPARTED	adj
UNLAWFUL	adj		UNPAVED	adj
UNLEASED	adj		UNPAYING	adj
UNLED	adj		UNPEELED	adj
UNLETHAL	adj		UNPITIED	adj
UNLETTED	adj		UNPLACED	adj
UNLEVIED	adj		UNPLAYED	adj
UNLICKED	adj		UNPLIANT	adj

UNPLOWED	*adj*	UNSEEMLY	*adj* -LIER, -LIEST
UNPOETIC	*adj*	UNSEEN	*adj*
UNPOISED	*adj*	UNSEIZED	*adj*
UNPOLITE	*adj*	UNSENT	*adj*
UNPOLLED	*adj*	UNSERVED	*adj*
UNPOSED	*adj*	UNSEXUAL	*adj*
UNPOSTED	*adj*	UNSEXY	*adj*
UNPOTTED	*adj*	UNSHADED	*adj*
UNPRETTY	*adj*	UNSHAKEN	*adj*
UNPRICED	*adj*	UNSHAMED	*adj*
UNPRIMED	*adj*	UNSHAPED	*adj*
UNPRIZED	*adj*	UNSHAPEN	*adj*
UNPROBED	*adj*	UNSHARED	*adj*
UNPROVED	*adj*	UNSHARP	*adj*
UNPROVEN	*adj*	UNSHAVED	*adj*
UNPRUNED	*adj*	UNSHAVEN	*adj*
UNPURE	*adj*	UNSHED	*adj*
UNPURGED	*adj*	UNSHOD	*adj*
UNQUIET	*adj* -ETER, -ETEST	UNSHORN	*adj*
UNRAISED	*adj*	UNSHOWY	*adj*
UNRAKED	*adj*	UNSHRUNK	*adj*
UNRANKED	*adj*	UNSHUT	*adj*
UNRATED	*adj*	UNSIFTED	*adj*
UNRAZED	*adj*	UNSIGNED	*adj*
UNREAD	*adj*	UNSILENT	*adj*
UNREADY	*adj* -READIER, -READIEST	UNSINFUL	*adj*
UNREAL	*adj*	UNSIZED	*adj*
UNREALLY	*adv*	UNSLAKED	*adj*
UNRENTED	*adj*	UNSLICED	*adj*
UNREPAID	*adj*	UNSMART	*adj*
UNRESTED	*adj*	UNSMOKED	*adj*
UNRHYMED	*adj*	UNSOAKED	*adj*
UNRIFLED	*adj*	UNSOBER	*adj*
UNRIMED	*adj*	UNSOCIAL	*adj*
UNRINSED	*adj*	UNSOILED	*adj*
UNRISEN	*adj*	UNSOLD	*adj*
UNROPED	*adj*	UNSOLID	*adj*
UNROUGH	*adj*	UNSOLVED	*adj*
UNRULED	*adj*	UNSORTED	*adj*
UNRUSHED	*adj*	UNSOUGHT	*adj*
UNRUSTED	*adj*	UNSOUND	*adj* -SOUNDER, -SOUNDEST
UNSAFE	*adj*	UNSOURED	*adj*
UNSAFELY	*adv*	UNSOWED	*adj*
UNSALTED	*adj*	UNSOWN	*adj*
UNSATED	*adj*	UNSPENT	*adj*
UNSAVED	*adj*	UNSPILT	*adj*
UNSAVORY	*adj*	UNSPLIT	*adj*
UNSAWED	*adj*	UNSPOILT	*adj*
UNSAWN	*adj*	UNSPRUNG	*adj*
UNSCALED	*adj*	UNSPUN	*adj*
UNSEARED	*adj*	UNSTABLE	*adj* -BLER, -BLEST
UNSEEDED	*adj*	UNSTABLY	*adv*
UNSEEING	*adj*	UNSTEADY	*adj* -STEADIER, -STEADIEST

UNSTONED	adj	
UNSTUFFY	adj	
UNSTUNG	adj	
UNSUBTLE	adj	
UNSUBTLY	adv	
UNSUITED	adj	
UNSUNG	adj	
UNSUNK	adj	
UNSURE	adj	
UNSURELY	adv	
UNSWAYED	adj	
UNSWEPT	adj	
UNTAGGED	adj	
UNTAKEN	adj	
UNTAME	adj	
UNTAMED	adj	
UNTANNED	adj	
UNTAPPED	adj	
UNTASTED	adj	
UNTAXED	adj	
UNTENDED	adj	
UNTESTED	adj	
UNTHAWED	adj	
UNTIDILY	adv	
UNTIDY	adj	-DIER, -DIEST
UNTILLED	adj	
UNTILTED	adj	
UNTIMELY	adj	-LIER, -LIEST
UNTINGED	adj	
UNTIPPED	adj	
UNTIRED	adj	
UNTIRING	adj	
UNTITLED	adj	
UNTOLD	adj	
UNTORN	adj	
UNTRACED	adj	
UNTRENDY	adj	
UNTRIED	adj	
UNTRUE	adj	-TRUER, -TRUEST
UNTRULY	adv	
UNTRUSTY	adj	
UNTUFTED	adj	
UNTURNED	adj	
UNUNITED	adj	
UNURGED	adj	
UNUSABLE	adj	
UNUSED	adj	
UNUSUAL	adj	
UNVALUED	adj	
UNVARIED	adj	
UNVEINED	adj	
UNVERSED	adj	
UNVEXED	adj	

UNVEXT	adj	
UNVIABLE	adj	
UNVOCAL	adj	
UNWALLED	adj	
UNWANING	adj	
UNWANTED	adj	
UNWARIER	comparative of unwary	
UNWARIEST	superlative of unwary	
UNWARILY	adv	
UNWARMED	adj	
UNWARNED	adj	
UNWARPED	adj	
UNWARY	adj	-WARIER, -WARIEST
UNWASTED	adj	
UNWAXED	adj	
UNWEANED	adj	
UNWEARY	adj	
UNWED	adj	
UNWEDDED	adj	
UNWEEDED	adj	
UNWELDED	adj	
UNWELL	adj	
UNWEPT	adj	
UNWETTED	adj	
UNWHITE	adj	
UNWIELDY	adj	-WIELDIER, -WIELDIEST
UNWIFELY	adj	
UNWILLED	adj	
UNWISE	adj	-WISER, -WISEST
UNWISELY	adv	
UNWON	adj	
UNWOODED	adj	
UNWOOED	adj	
UNWORKED	adj	
UNWORN	adj	
UNWORTHY	adj	-THIER, -THIEST
UNWRUNG	adj	
UNYOUNG	adj	
UNZONED	adj	

UNAI	n	pl. -S unau
UNAKITE	n	pl. -S an igneous rock
UNANCHOR	v	-ED, -ING, -S to loosen from an anchor
UNARM	v	-ED, -ING, -S to disarm
UNARY	adj	consisting of a single element
UNAU	n	pl. -S a two-toed sloth
UNAWARES	adv	without warning

UNBAN   *v* -BANNED, -BANNING, -BANS to remove a prohibition against

UNBAR   *v* -BARRED, -BARRING, -BARS to remove a bar from

UNBATED   *adj* unabated

UNBE   *v* to cease to have being — UNBE is the only accepted form of this verb; it cannot be conjugated

UNBEAR   *v* -BEARED, -BEARING, -BEARS to free from the pressure of a rein

UNBELIEF   *n* pl. -S lack of belief

UNBELT   *v* -ED, -ING, -S to remove the belt of

UNBEND   *v* -BENT or -BENDED, -BENDING, -BENDS to make or allow to become straight

UNBID   *adj* unbidden

UNBIDDEN   *adj* not invited

UNBIND   *v* -BOUND, -BINDING, -BINDS to free from bindings

UNBLOCK   *v* -ED, -ING, -S to free from being blocked

UNBODIED   *adj* having no body

UNBOLT   *v* -ED, -ING, -S to open by withdrawing a bolt (a metal bar)

UNBONNET   *v* -ED, -ING, -S to uncover the head

UNBOSOM   *v* -ED, -ING, -S to reveal

UNBOUND   past tense of unbind

UNBOX   *v* -ED, -ING, -ES to remove from a box

UNBRACE   *v* -BRACED, -BRACING, -BRACES to free from braces

UNBRAID   *v* -ED, -ING, -S to separate the strands of

UNBRAKE   *v* -BRAKED, -BRAKING, -BRAKES to release a brake

UNBREECH   *v* -ED, -ING, -ES to remove the breeches of

UNBRIDLE   *v* -DLED, -DLING, -DLES to set loose

UNBUCKLE   *v* -LED, -LING, -LES to loosen a buckle

UNBUILD   *v* -BUILT, -BUILDING, -BUILDS to demolish

UNBUNDLE   *v* -DLED, -DLING, -DLES to price separately

UNBURDEN   *v* -ED, -ING, -S to free from a burden

UNBUTTON   *v* -ED, -ING, -S to unfasten the buttons of

UNCAGE   *v* -CAGED, -CAGING, -CAGES to release from a cage

UNCAKE   *v* -CAKED, -CAKING, -CAKES to break up a cake (a block of compacted matter)

UNCANNY   *adj* -NIER, -NIEST strange and inexplicable

UNCAP   *v* -CAPPED, -CAPPING, -CAPS to remove the cap from

UNCASE   *v* -CASED, -CASING, -CASES to remove from a case

UNCHAIN   *v* -ED, -ING, -S to free by removing a chain

UNCHANCY   *adj* unlucky

UNCHARGE   *v* -CHARGED, -CHARGING, -CHARGES to acquit

UNCHOKE   *v* -CHOKED, -CHOKING, -CHOKES to free from obstruction

UNCHURCH   *v* -ED, -ING, -ES to expel from a church

UNCI   pl. of uncus

UNCIA   *n* pl. -CIAE a coin of ancient Rome

UNCIAL   *n* pl. -S a style of writing

UNCIALLY   *adv* in the uncial style

UNCIFORM   *n* pl. -S a bone of the wrist

UNCINAL   *adj* uncinate

UNCINATE   *adj* bent at the end like a hook

UNCINUS   *n* pl. -NI an uncinate structure

UNCLAD   a past tense of unclothe

UNCLAMP   *v* -ED, -ING, -S to free from a clamp

UNCLASP   *v* -ED, -ING, -S to free from a clasp

UNCLE   *n* pl. -S the brother of one's father or mother

UNCLENCH   *v* -ED, -ING, -ES to open from a clenched position

UNCLINCH   *v* -ED, -ING, -ES to unclench

UNCLIP   *v* -CLIPPED, -CLIPPING, -CLIPS to remove a clip (a fastening device) from

UNCLOAK   *v* -ED, -ING, -S to remove a cloak from

UNCLOG   *v* -CLOGGED, -CLOGGING, -CLOGS to free from a difficulty or obstruction

UNCLOSE   *v* -CLOSED, -CLOSING, -CLOSES to open

UNCLOTHE	v -CLOTHED or -CLAD, -CLOTHING, -CLOTHES to divest of clothing	**UNDERCUT**	v -CUT, -CUTTING, -CUTS to cut under
UNCLOUD	v -ED, -ING, -S to free from clouds	**UNDERDO**	v -DID, -DONE, -DOING, -DOES to do insufficiently
UNCO	n pl. -COS a stranger	**UNDERDOG**	n pl. -S one who is expected to lose
UNCOCK	v -ED, -ING, -S to remove from a cocked position	**UNDEREAT**	v -ATE, -EATEN, -EATING, -EATS to eat an insufficient amount
UNCOFFIN	v -ED, -ING, -S to remove from a coffin	**UNDERFED**	adj fed an insufficient amount
UNCOIL	v -ED, -ING, -S to release from a coiled position	**UNDERFUR**	n pl. -S the thick, soft fur beneath the outer coat of certain mammals
UNCORK	v -ED, -ING, -S to draw the cork	**UNDERGO**	v -WENT, -GONE, -GOING, -GOES to be subjected to
UNCOUPLE	v -PLED, -PLING, -PLES to disconnect	**UNDERGOD**	n pl. -S a lesser god
UNCOVER	v -ED, -ING, -S to remove the covering from	**UNDERJAW**	n pl. -S the lower jaw
UNCRATE	v -CRATED, -CRATING, -CRATES to remove from a crate	**UNDERLAID**	past tense of underlay
		UNDERLAIN	past participle of underlie
UNCREATE	v -ATED, -ATING, -ATES to deprive of existence	**UNDERLAP**	v -LAPPED, -LAPPING, -LAPS to extend partly under
UNCROSS	v -ED, -ING, -ES to change from a crossed position	**UNDERLAY**	v -LAID, -LAYING, -LAYS to place under
UNCROWN	v -ED, -ING, -S to deprive of a crown	**UNDERLET**	v -LET, -LETTING, -LETS to lease at less than the usual value
UNCTION	n pl. -S the act of anointing	**UNDERLIE**	v -LAY, -LAIN, -LYING, -LIES to lie under
UNCTUOUS	adj greasy		
UNCUFF	v -ED, -ING, -S to remove handcuffs from	**UNDERLIP**	n pl. -S the lower lip
		UNDERLIT	adj lacking adequate light
UNCURB	v -ED, -ING, -S to remove restraints from	**UNDERLYING**	present participle of underlie
UNCURL	v -ED, -ING, -S to straighten the curls of	**UNDERPAY**	v -PAID, -PAYING, -PAYS to pay less than is deserved
UNCUS	n pl. -CI a hook-shaped anatomical part	**UNDERPIN**	v -PINNED, -PINNING, -PINS to support from below
UNDE	adj wavy	**UNDERRUN**	v -RAN, -RUNNING, -RUNS to pass or extend under
UNDEAD	n pl. UNDEAD a vampire		
UNDEE	adj unde	**UNDERSEA**	adv beneath the surface of the sea
UNDER	prep in a lower position than	**UNDERSET**	n pl. -S a current below the surface of the ocean
UNDERACT	v -ED, -ING, -S to act subtly and with restraint		
UNDERAGE	n pl. -S a shortage	**UNDERTAX**	v -ED, -ING, -ES to tax less than the usual amount
UNDERARM	n pl. -S the armpit	**UNDERTOW**	n pl. -S the seaward pull of receding waves breaking on a shore
UNDERATE	past tense of undereat		
UNDERBID	v -BID, -BIDDING, -BIDS to bid lower than	**UNDERWAY**	adv in progress
		UNDERWENT	past tense of undergo
UNDERBUD	v -BUDDED, -BUDDING, -BUDS to bud from beneath	**UNDID**	past tense of undo
		UNDIES	n/pl underwear
UNDERBUY	v -BOUGHT, -BUYING, -BUYS to buy at a lower price than	**UNDINE**	n pl. -S a female water spirit

UNDO   v -DID, -DONE, -DOING, -DOES to bring to ruin

UNDOCK   v -ED, -ING, -S to move away from a dock

UNDOER   n pl. -S one that undoes

UNDOING   n pl. -S a cause of ruin

UNDONE   past participle of undo

UNDOUBLE   v -BLED, -BLING, -BLES to unfold

UNDRAPE   v -DRAPED, -DRAPING, -DRAPES to strip of drapery

UNDRAW   v -DREW, -DRAWN, -DRAWING, -DRAWS to draw open

UNDRESS   v -DRESSED or -DREST, -DRESSING, -DRESSES to remove one's clothing

UNDRUNK   adj not swallowed

UNDUE   adj exceeding what is appropriate or normal

UNDULANT   adj undulating

UNDULAR   adj undulating

UNDULATE   v -LATED, -LATING, -LATES to move with a wavelike motion

UNDULY   adv in an undue manner

UNDY   adj unde

UNDYING   adj not subject to death

UNEARTH   v -ED, -ING, -S to dig up

UNEASE   n pl. -S mental or physical discomfort

UNEASY   adj -EASIER, -EASIEST marked by mental or physical discomfort **UNEASILY** adv

UNEQUAL   n pl. -S one that is not equal to another

UNFAITH   n pl. -S lack of faith

UNFASTEN   v -ED, -ING, -S to release from fastenings

UNFENCE   v -FENCED, -FENCING, -FENCES to remove a fence from

UNFETTER   v -ED, -ING, -S to free from fetters

UNFIT   v -FITTED, -FITTING, -FITS to make unsuitable

UNFITLY   adv in an unsuitable manner

UNFIX   v -FIXED or -FIXT, -FIXING, -FIXES to unfasten

UNFOLD   v -ED, -ING, -S to open something that is folded

UNFOLDER   n pl. -S one that unfolds

UNFORGOT   adj not forgotten

UNFREE   v -FREED, -FREEING, -FREES to deprive of freedom

UNFREEZE   v -FROZE, -FROZEN, -FREEZING, -FREEZES to cause to thaw

UNFROCK   v -ED, -ING, -S to divest of ecclesiastical authority

UNFURL   v -ED, -ING, -S to unroll

UNGAINLY   adj -LIER, -LIEST awkward

UNGIRD   v -GIRDED or -GIRT, -GIRDING, -GIRDS to remove a belt from

UNGLOVE   v -GLOVED, -GLOVING, -GLOVES to uncover by removing a glove

UNGLUE   v -GLUED, -GLUING, -GLUES to disjoin

UNGODLY   adj -LIER, -LIEST impious

UNGOT   adj ungotten

UNGOTTEN   adj not obtained

UNGUAL   adj pertaining to an unguis

UNGUARD   v -ED, -ING, -S to leave unprotected

UNGUENT   n pl. -S an ointment

UNGUENTA   n/pl ointments

UNGUIS   n pl. -GUES a nail, claw, or hoof

UNGULA   n pl. -LAE an unguis **UNGULAR** adj

UNGULATE   n pl. -S a hoofed mammal

UNHAIR   v -ED, -ING, -S to remove the hair from

UNHALLOW   v -ED, -ING, -S to profane

UNHAND   v -ED, -ING, -S to remove the hand from

UNHANDY   adj -HANDIER, -HANDIEST difficult to handle

UNHANG   v -HUNG or -HANGED, -HANGING, -HANGS to detach from a hanging support

UNHAT   v -HATTED, -HATTING, -HATS to remove one's hat

UNHELM   v -ED, -ING, -S to remove the helmet of

UNHINGE   v -HINGED, -HINGING, -HINGES to remove from hinges

UNHITCH   v -ED, -ING, -ES to free from being hitched

UNHOOD   v -ED, -ING, -S to remove a hood from

UNHOOK   v -ED, -ING, -S to remove from a hook

UNHOPED   adj not hoped for or expected

UNHORSE   *v* -HORSED, -HORSING, -HORSES to cause to fall from a horse

UNHOUSE   *v* -HOUSED, -HOUSING, -HOUSES to deprive of a protective shelter

UNHUSK   *v* -ED, -ING, -S to remove the husk from

UNIALGAL   *adj* pertaining to a single algal cell

UNIAXIAL   *adj* having one axis

UNICOLOR   *adj* of one color

UNICORN   *n* pl. -S a mythical horselike creature

UNICYCLE   *n* pl. -S a one-wheeled vehicle

UNIDEAED   *adj* lacking ideas

UNIFACE   *n* pl. -S a coin having a design on only one side

UNIFIC   *adj* unifying

UNIFIED   past tense of unify

UNIFIER   *n* pl. -S one that unifies

UNIFIES   present 3d person sing. of unify

UNIFILAR   *adj* having only one thread, wire, or fiber

UNIFORM   *adj* -FORMER, -FORMEST unchanging

UNIFORM   *v* -ED, -ING, -S to make uniform

UNIFY   *v* -FIED, -FYING, -FIES to make into a coherent whole

UNILOBED   *adj* having one lobe

UNION   *n* pl. -S a number of persons, parties, or political entities united for a common purpose

UNIONISE   *v* -ISED, -ISING, -ISES to unionize

UNIONISM   *n* pl. -S the principle of forming a union

UNIONIST   *n* pl. -S an advocate of unionism

UNIONIZE   *v* -IZED, -IZING, -IZES to form into a union

UNIPOD   *n* pl. -S a one-legged support

UNIPOLAR   *adj* showing only one kind of polarity

UNIQUE   *adj* UNIQUER, UNIQUEST existing as the only one of its kind; very unusual **UNIQUELY** *adv*

UNIQUE   *n* pl. -S something that is unique

UNISEX   *n* pl. -ES the condition of not being distinguishable as to sex

UNISON   *n* pl. -S complete agreement **UNISONAL** *adj*

UNIT   *n* pl. -S a specific quantity used as a standard of measurement

UNITAGE   *n* pl. -S amount in units

UNITARD   *n* pl. -S a leotard that also covers the legs

UNITARY   *adj* pertaining to a unit

UNITE   *v* UNITED, UNITING, UNITES to bring together so as to form a whole **UNITEDLY** *adv*

UNITER   *n* pl. -S one that unites

UNITIES   pl. of unity

UNITING   present participle of unite

UNITIVE   *adj* serving to unite

UNITIZE   *v* -IZED, -IZING, -IZES to divide into units

UNITIZER   *n* pl. -S one that unitizes

UNITRUST   *n* pl. -S a type of annuity trust

UNITY   *n* pl. -TIES the state of being one single entity

UNIVALVE   *n* pl. -S a mollusk having a single shell

UNIVERSE   *n* pl. -S the totality of all existing things

UNIVOCAL   *n* pl. -S a word having only one meaning

UNJOINT   *v* -ED, -ING, -S to separate at a juncture

UNKEMPT   *adj* untidy

UNKEND   *adj* unkenned

UNKENNED   *adj* not known or recognized

UNKENNEL   *v* -NELED, -NELING, -NELS or -NELLED, -NELLING, -NELS to release from a kennel

UNKENT   *adj* unkenned

UNKINK   *v* -ED, -ING, -S to remove curls from

UNKNIT   *v* -KNITTED, -KNITTING, -KNITS to unravel

UNKNOT   *v* -KNOTTED, -KNOTTING, -KNOTS to undo a knot in

UNKNOWN   *n* pl. -S one that is not known

UNLACE   *v* -LACED, -LACING, -LACES to unfasten the laces of

UNLADE   *v* -LADED, -LADEN, -LADING, -LADES to unload

UNLAID   past tense of unlay

UNLASH   *v* -ED, -ING, -ES to untie the lashing (a type of binding) of

UNLATCH   *v* -ED, -ING, -ES to open by lifting the latch (a fastening device)

UNLAY   *v* -LAID, -LAYING, -LAYS to untwist

UNLEAD   *v* -ED, -ING, -S to remove the lead from

UNLEARN   *v* -LEARNED or -LEARNT, -LEARNING, -LEARNS to put out of one's knowledge or memory

UNLEASH   *v* -ED, -ING, -ES to free from a leash

UNLESS   *conj* except on the condition that

UNLET   *adj* not rented

UNLEVEL   *v* -ELED, -ELING, -ELS or -ELLED, -ELLING, -ELS to make uneven

UNLIMBER   *v* -ED, -ING, -S to prepare for action

UNLINK   *v* -ED, -ING, -S to unfasten the links (connecting devices) of

UNLIVE   *v* -LIVED, -LIVING, -LIVES to live so as to make amends for

UNLOAD   *v* -ED, -ING, -S to remove the load or cargo from

UNLOADER   *n* pl. -S one that unloads

UNLOCK   *v* -ED, -ING, -S to unfasten the lock of

UNLOOSE   *v* -LOOSED, -LOOSING, -LOOSES to set free

UNLOOSEN   *v* -ED, -ING, -S to unloose

UNMAKE   *v* -MADE, -MAKING, -MAKES to destroy

UNMAKER   *n* pl. -S one that unmakes

UNMAN   *v* -MANNED, -MANNING, -MANS to deprive of courage

UNMASK   *v* -ED, -ING, -S to remove a mask from

UNMASKER   *n* pl. -S one that unmasks

UNMEET   *adj* improper **UNMEETLY** *adv*

UNMESH   *v* -ED, -ING, -ES to disentangle

UNMEW   *v* -ED, -ING, -S to set free

UNMINGLE   *v* -GLED, -GLING, -GLES to separate things that are mixed

UNMITER   *v* -ED, -ING, -S to depose from the rank of bishop

UNMITRE   *v* -TRED, -TRING, -TRES to unmiter

UNMIX   *v* -MIXED or -MIXT, -MIXING, -MIXES to separate from a mixture

UNMOLD   *v* -ED, -ING, -S to remove from a mold

UNMOOR   *v* -ED, -ING, -S to release from moorings

UNMORAL   *adj* amoral

UNMUFFLE   *v* -FLED, -FLING, -FLES to free from something that muffles

UNMUZZLE   *v* -ZLED, -ZLING, -ZLES to remove a muzzle from

UNNAIL   *v* -ED, -ING, -S to remove the nails from

UNNERVE   *v* -NERVED, -NERVING, -NERVES to deprive of courage

UNPACK   *v* -ED, -ING, -S to remove the contents of

UNPACKER   *n* pl. -S one that unpacks

UNPAGED   *adj* having no page numbers

UNPEG   *v* -PEGGED, -PEGGING, -PEGS to remove the pegs from

UNPEN   *v* -PENNED or -PENT, -PENNING, -PENS to release from confinement

UNPEOPLE   *v* -PLED, -PLING, -PLES to remove people from

UNPERSON   *n* pl. -S one who is removed completely from recognition

UNPICK   *v* -ED, -ING, -S to remove the stitches from

UNPILE   *v* -PILED, -PILING, -PILES to take or disentangle from a pile

UNPIN   *v* -PINNED, -PINNING, -PINS to remove the pins from

UNPLAIT   *v* -ED, -ING, -S to undo the plaits of

UNPLUG   *v* -PLUGGED, -PLUGGING, -PLUGS to take a plug out of

UNPUCKER   *v* -ED, -ING, -S to remove the wrinkles from

UNPUZZLE   *v* -ZLED, -ZLING, -ZLES to work out the obscured meaning of

UNQUIET   *n* pl. -S a state of unrest

UNQUOTE   *v* -QUOTED, -QUOTING, -QUOTES to close a quotation

UNRAVEL   *v* -ELED, -ELING, -ELS or -ELLED, -ELLING, -ELS to separate the threads of

UNREASON   *v* -ED, -ING, -S to disrupt the sanity of

UNREEL   *v* -ED, -ING, -S to unwind from a reel

UNREELER   *n* pl. -S one that unreels

UNREEVE   *v* -REEVED, -ROVE, -ROVEN, -REEVING, -REEVES to withdraw a rope from an opening

UNRENT   *adj* not torn

UNREPAIR   *n* pl. -S lack of repair

UNREST   *n* pl. -S a disturbed or uneasy state

UNRIDDLE   *v* -DLED, -DLING, -DLES to solve

UNRIG   *v* -RIGGED, -RIGGING, -RIGS to divest of rigging

UNRIP   *v* -RIPPED, -RIPPING, -RIPS to rip open

UNRIPE   *adj* -RIPER, -RIPEST not ripe
UNRIPELY *adv*

UNROBE   *v* -ROBED, -ROBING, -ROBES to undress

UNROLL   *v* -ED, -ING, -S to open something that is rolled up

UNROOF   *v* -ED, -ING, -S to strip off the roof of

UNROOT   *v* -ED, -ING, -S to uproot

UNROUND   *v* -ED, -ING, -S to articulate without rounding the lips

UNROVE   a past tense of unreeve

UNROVEN   a past participle of unreeve

UNRULY   *adj* -LIER, -LIEST difficult to control

UNSADDLE   *v* -DLED, -DLING, -DLES to remove the saddle from

UNSAFETY   *n* pl. -TIES lack of safety

UNSAY   *v* -SAID, -SAYING, -SAYS to retract something said

UNSCREW   *v* -ED, -ING, -S to remove the screws from

UNSEAL   *v* -ED, -ING, -S to remove the seal of

UNSEAM   *v* -ED, -ING, -S to open the seams of

UNSEAT   *v* -ED, -ING, -S to remove from a seat

UNSELL   *v* -SOLD, -SELLING, -SELLS to persuade to change an opinion or belief

UNSET   *v* -SET, -SETTING, -SETS to unsettle

UNSETTLE   *v* -TLED, -TLING, -TLES to make unstable

UNSEW   *v* -SEWED, -SEWN, -SEWING, -SEWS to undo the sewing of

UNSEX   *v* -ED, -ING, -ES to deprive of sexual power

UNSHELL   *v* -ED, -ING, -S to remove the shell from

UNSHIFT   *v* -ED, -ING, -S to release the shift key on a typewriter

UNSHIP   *v* -SHIPPED, -SHIPPING, -SHIPS to unload from a ship

UNSICKER   *adj* unreliable

UNSIGHT   *v* -ED, -ING, -S to prevent from seeing

UNSLING   *v* -SLUNG, -SLINGING, -SLINGS to remove from a slung position

UNSNAP   *v* -SNAPPED, -SNAPPING, -SNAPS to undo the snaps of

UNSNARL   *v* -ED, -ING, -S to untangle

UNSOLDER   *v* -ED, -ING, -S to separate

UNSONCY   *adj* unsonsie

UNSONSIE   *adj* unlucky

UNSONSY   *adj* unsonsie

UNSPEAK   *v* -SPOKE, -SPOKEN, -SPEAKING, -SPEAKS to unsay

UNSPHERE   *v* -SPHERED, -SPHERING, -SPHERES to remove from a sphere

UNSTACK   *v* -ED, -ING, -S to remove from a stack

UNSTATE   *v* -STATED, -STATING, -STATES to deprive of status

UNSTAYED   *adj* not secured with ropes or wires

UNSTEADY   *v* -STEADIED, -STEADYING, -STEADIES to make unsteady

UNSTEEL   *v* -ED, -ING, -S to make soft

UNSTEP   *v* -STEPPED, -STEPPING, -STEPS to remove from a socket

UNSTICK   *v* -STUCK, -STICKING, -STICKS to disjoin

UNSTITCH   *v* -ED, -ING, -ES to remove the stitches from

UNSTOP   *v* -STOPPED, -STOPPING, -STOPS to remove a stopper from

UNSTRAP   *v* -STRAPPED, -STRAPPING, -STRAPS to remove a strap from

UNSTRESS   *n* pl. -ES a syllable having relatively weak stress

UNSTRING   *v* -STRUNG, -STRINGING, -STRINGS to remove from a string

UNSTUCK   past tense of unstick

UNSWATHE   *v* -SWATHED, -SWATHING, -SWATHES to unbind

UNSWEAR   *v* -SWORE, -SWORN, -SWEARING, -SWEARS to retract something sworn

UNTACK	*v* -ED, -ING, -S to remove a tack from
UNTANGLE	*v* -GLED, -GLING, -GLES to free from tangles
UNTEACH	*v* -TAUGHT, -TEACHING, -TEACHES to cause to unlearn something
UNTENTED	*adj* not probed or attended to
UNTETHER	*v* -ED, -ING, -S to free from a tether
UNTHINK	*v* -THOUGHT, -THINKING, -THINKS to dismiss from the mind
UNTHREAD	*v* -ED, -ING, -S to remove the thread from
UNTHRONE	*v* -THRONED, -THRONING, -THRONES to remove from a throne
UNTIDY	*v* -DIED, -DYING, -DIES to make untidy
UNTIE	*v* -TIED, -TYING, -TIES to free from something that ties
UNTIL	*prep* up to the time of
UNTO	*prep* to
UNTOWARD	*adj* unruly
UNTREAD	*v* -TROD, -TRODDEN, -TREADING, -TREADS to retrace
UNTRIM	*v* -TRIMMED, -TRIMMING, -TRIMS to strip of trimming
UNTRUSS	*v* -ED, -ING, -ES to free from a truss
UNTRUTH	*n* pl. -S something that is untrue
UNTUCK	*v* -ED, -ING, -S to release from being tucked up
UNTUNE	*v* -TUNED, -TUNING, -TUNES to put out of tune
UNTWINE	*v* -TWINED, -TWINING, -TWINES to separate the twisted or tangled parts of
UNTWIST	*v* -ED, -ING, -S to untwine
UNTYING	present participle of untie
UNVEIL	*v* -ED, -ING, -S to remove a covering from
UNVOICE	*v* -VOICED, -VOICING, -VOICES to deprive of voice or vocal quality
UNWASHED	*n* pl. -S an ignorant or underprivileged group
UNWEAVE	*v* -WOVE, -WOVEN, -WEAVING, -WEAVES to undo something woven
UNWEIGHT	*v* -ED, -ING, -S to reduce the weight of

UNWIND	*v* -WOUND, -WINDING, -WINDS to reverse the winding of
UNWINDER	*n* pl. -S one that unwinds
UNWISDOM	*n* pl. -S lack of wisdom
UNWISH	*v* -ED, -ING, -ES to cease to wish for
UNWIT	*v* -WITTED, -WITTING, -WITS to make insane
UNWONTED	*adj* unusual
UNWORTHY	*n* pl. -THIES an unworthy person
UNWOUND	past tense of unwind
UNWOVE	past tense of unweave
UNWOVEN	past participle of unweave
UNWRAP	*v* -WRAPPED, -WRAPPING, -WRAPS to remove the wrapping from
UNYEANED	*adj* unborn
UNYOKE	*v* -YOKED, -YOKING, -YOKES to free from a yoke
UNZIP	*v* -ZIPPED, -ZIPPING, -ZIPS to open the zipper of
UP	*v* UPPED, UPPING, UPS to raise
UPAS	*n* pl. -ES an Asian tree
UPBEAR	*v* -BORE, -BORNE, -BEARING, -BEARS to raise aloft
UPBEARER	*n* pl. -S one that upbears
UPBEAT	*n* pl. -S an unaccented beat in a musical measure
UPBIND	*v* -BOUND, -BINDING, -BINDS to bind completely
UPBOIL	*v* -ED, -ING, -S to boil up
UPBORE	past tense of upbear
UPBORNE	past participle of upbear
UPBOUND	past tense of upbind
UPBOW	*n* pl. -S a type of stroke in playing a bowed instrument
UPBRAID	*v* -ED, -ING, -S to reproach severely
UPBUILD	*v* -BUILT, -BUILDING, -BUILDS to build up
UPBY	*adv* upbye
UPBYE	*adv* a little farther on
UPCAST	*v* -CAST, -CASTING, -CASTS to cast up
UPCHUCK	*v* -ED, -ING, -S to vomit
UPCLIMB	*v* -ED, -ING, -S to climb up
UPCOAST	*adv* up the coast
UPCOIL	*v* -ED, -ING, -S to coil up
UPCOMING	*adj* about to happen or appear

UPCURL	*v* -ED, -ING, -S to curl up
UPCURVE	*v* -CURVED, -CURVING, -CURVES to curve upward
UPDART	*v* -ED, -ING, -S to dart up
UPDATE	*v* -DATED, -DATING, -DATES to bring up to date
UPDATER	*n* pl. -S one that updates
UPDIVE	*v* -DIVED or -DOVE, -DIVING, -DIVES to spring upward
UPDO	*n* pl. -DOS an upswept hairdo
UPDRAFT	*n* pl. -S an upward movement of air
UPDRY	*v* -DRIED, -DRYING, -DRIES to dry completely
UPEND	*v* -ED, -ING, -S to set or stand on end
UPFIELD	*adv* into the part of the field toward which the offensive team is going
UPFLING	*v* -FLUNG, -FLINGING, -FLINGS to fling up
UPFLOW	*v* -ED, -ING, -S to flow up
UPFOLD	*v* -ED, -ING, -S to fold up
UPFRONT	*adj* honest; candid
UPGATHER	*v* -ED, -ING, -S to gather up
UPGAZE	*v* -GAZED, -GAZING, -GAZES to gaze up
UPGIRD	*v* -GIRDED or -GIRT, -GIRDING, -GIRDS to gird completely
UPGOING	*adj* going up
UPGRADE	*v* -GRADED, -GRADING, -GRADES to raise to a higher grade or standard
UPGROW	*v* -GREW, -GROWN, -GROWING, -GROWS to grow up
UPGROWTH	*n* pl. -S the process of growing up
UPHEAP	*v* -ED, -ING, -S to heap up
UPHEAVAL	*n* pl. -S the act of upheaving
UPHEAVE	*v* -HEAVED or -HOVE, -HEAVING, -HEAVES to heave up
UPHEAVER	*n* pl. -S one that upheaves
UPHELD	past tense of uphold
UPHILL	*n* pl. -S an upward slope
UPHOARD	*v* -ED, -ING, -S to hoard up
UPHOLD	*v* -HELD, -HOLDING, -HOLDS to hold aloft
UPHOLDER	*n* pl. -S one that upholds
UPHOVE	a past tense of upheave
UPHROE	*n* pl. -S euphroe
UPKEEP	*n* pl. -S the cost of maintaining something in good condition
UPLAND	*n* pl. -S the higher land of a region
UPLANDER	*n* pl. -S an inhabitant of an upland
UPLEAP	*v* -LEAPED or -LEAPT, -LEAPING, -LEAPS to leap up
UPLIFT	*v* -ED, -ING, -S to lift up
UPLIFTER	*n* pl. -S one that uplifts
UPLIGHT	*v* -LIGHTED or -LIT, -LIGHTING, -LIGHTS to light to a higher degree
UPLINK	*n* pl. -S a communications channel to a spacecraft
UPLOAD	*v* -ED, -ING, -S to transfer information from a small computer to a larger computer
UPMARKET	*adj* upscale
UPMOST	*adj* highest
UPO	*prep* upon
UPON	*prep* on
UPPED	past tense of up
UPPER	*n* pl. -S the part of a boot or shoe above the sole
UPPERCUT	*v* -CUT, -CUTTING, -CUTS to strike an upward blow
UPPILE	*v* -PILED, -PILING, -PILES to pile up
UPPING	*n* pl. -S the process of marking young swans for identification purposes
UPPISH	*adj* uppity **UPPISHLY** *adv*
UPPITY	*adj* tending to be snobbish and arrogant
UPPROP	*v* -PROPPED, -PROPPING, -PROPS to prop up
UPRAISE	*v* -RAISED, -RAISING, -RAISES to raise up
UPRAISER	*n* pl. -S one that upraises
UPRATE	*v* -RATED, -RATING, -RATES to improve the power output of an engine
UPREACH	*v* -ED, -ING, -ES to reach up
UPREAR	*v* -ED, -ING, -S to upraise
UPRIGHT	*v* -ED, -ING, -S to make vertical
UPRISE	*v* -ROSE, -RISEN, -RISING, -RISES to rise up
UPRISER	*n* pl. -S one that uprises
UPRISING	*n* pl. -S a revolt

UPRIVER *n* pl. -S an area lying toward the source of a river

UPROAR *n* pl. -S a state of noisy excitement and confusion

UPROOT *v* -ED, -ING, -S to pull up by the roots

UPROOTAL *n* pl. -S the act of uprooting

UPROOTER *n* pl. -S one that uproots

UPROSE past tense of uprise

UPROUSE *v* -ROUSED, -ROUSING, -ROUSES to rouse up

UPRUSH *v* -ED, -ING, -ES to rush up

UPSCALE *v* -SCALED, -SCALING, -SCALES to make appealing to affluent consumers

UPSEND *v* -SENT, -SENDING, -SENDS to send upward

UPSET *v* -SET, -SETTING, -SETS to overturn

UPSETTER *n* pl. -S one that upsets

UPSHIFT *v* -ED, -ING, -S to shift into a higher gear

UPSHOOT *v* -SHOT, -SHOOTING, -SHOOTS to shoot upward

UPSHOT *n* pl. -S the final result

UPSIDE *n* pl. -S a positive aspect

UPSILON *n* pl. -S a Greek letter

UPSOAR *v* -ED, -ING, -S to soar upward

UPSPRING *v* -SPRANG or -SPRUNG, -SPRINGING, -SPRINGS to spring up

UPSTAGE *v* -STAGED, -STAGING, -STAGES to outdo theatrically

UPSTAIR *adj* pertaining to an upper floor

UPSTAIRS *adv* up the stairs

UPSTAND *v* -STOOD, -STANDING, -STANDS to stand up on one's feet

UPSTARE *v* -STARED, -STARING, -STARES to stare upward

UPSTART *v* -ED, -ING, -S to spring up suddenly

UPSTATE *n* pl. -S the northern region of a state

UPSTATER *n* pl. -S an inhabitant of an upstate region

UPSTEP *v* -STEPPED, -STEPPING, -STEPS to step up

UPSTIR *v* -STIRRED, -STIRRING, -STIRS to stir up

UPSTOOD past tense of upstand

UPSTREAM *adv* toward the source of a stream

UPSTROKE *n* pl. -S an upward stroke

UPSURGE *v* -SURGED, -SURGING, -SURGES to surge up

UPSWEEP *v* -SWEPT, -SWEEPING, -SWEEPS to sweep upward

UPSWELL *v* -SWELLED, -SWOLLEN, -SWELLING, -SWELLS to swell up

UPSWING *v* -SWUNG, -SWINGING, -SWINGS to swing upward

UPTAKE *n* pl. -S an upward ventilating shaft

UPTEAR *v* -TORE, -TORN, -TEARING, -TEARS to tear out by the roots

UPTHROW *v* -THREW, -THROWN, -THROWING, -THROWS to throw upward

UPTHRUST *v* -THRUST, -THRUSTING, -THRUSTS to thrust up

UPTICK *n* pl. -S an increase or rise

UPTIGHT *adj* nervous

UPTILT *v* -ED, -ING, -S to tilt upward

UPTIME *n* pl. -S the time during which machinery is functioning

UPTORE past tense of uptear

UPTORN past participle of uptear

UPTOSS *v* -ED, -ING, -ES to toss upward

UPTOWN *n* pl. -S the upper part of a city

UPTOWNER *n* pl. -S one that lives uptown

UPTREND *n* pl. -S a tendency upward or toward growth

UPTURN *v* -ED, -ING, -S to turn up or over

UPWAFT *v* -ED, -ING, -S to waft upward

UPWARD *adv* toward a higher place or position **UPWARDLY** *adv*

UPWARDS *adv* upward

UPWELL *v* -ED, -ING, -S to well up

UPWIND *n* pl. -S a wind that blows against one's course

URACIL *n* pl. -S a chemical compound

URAEMIA *n* pl. -S uremia **URAEMIC** *adj*

URAEUS *n* pl. URAEI or URAEUSES the figure of the sacred serpent on the headdress of ancient Egyptian rulers

URALITE *n* pl. -S a mineral **URALITIC** *adj*

URANIA *n* pl. -S uranium dioxide

URANIC *adj* pertaining to uranium

URANIDE	*n* pl. -S uranium
URANISM	*n* pl. -S homosexuality
URANITE	*n* pl. -S a mineral **URANITIC** *adj*
URANIUM	*n* pl. -S a radioactive element
URANOUS	*adj* pertaining to uranium
URANYL	*n* pl. -S a bivalent radical **URANYLIC** *adj*
URARE	*n* pl. -S curare
URARI	*n* pl. -S curare
URASE	*n* pl. -S urease
URATE	*n* pl. -S a chemical salt **URATIC** *adj*
URB	*n* pl. -S an urban area
URBAN	*adj* pertaining to a city
URBANE	*adj* -BANER, -BANEST refined and elegant **URBANELY** *adv*
URBANISE	*v* -ISED, -ISING, -ISES to urbanize
URBANISM	*n* pl. -S the lifestyle of city dwellers
URBANIST	*n* pl. -S a specialist in city planning
URBANITE	*n* pl. -S one who lives in a city
URBANITY	*n* pl. -TIES the quality of being urbane
URBANIZE	*v* -IZED, -IZING, -IZES to cause to take on urban characteristics
URBIA	*n* pl. -S cities collectively
URCHIN	*n* pl. -S a mischievous boy
URD	*n* pl. -S an annual bean grown in India
UREA	*n* pl. -S a chemical compound **UREAL** *adj*
UREASE	*n* pl. -S an enzyme
UREDIA	pl. of uredium
UREDIAL	*adj* pertaining to a uredium
UREDINIA	*n/pl* uredia
UREDIUM	*n* pl. -DIA a spore-producing organ of certain fungi
UREDO	*n* pl. -DOS a skin irritation
UREIC	*adj* pertaining to urea
UREIDE	*n* pl. -S a chemical compound
UREMIA	*n* pl. -S an abnormal condition of the blood **UREMIC** *adj*
URETER	*n* pl. -S the duct that conveys urine from the kidney to the bladder **URETERAL, URETERIC** *adj*
URETHAN	*n* pl. -S urethane
URETHANE	*n* pl. -S a chemical compound
URETHRA	*n* pl. -THRAE or -THRAS the duct through which urine is discharged from the bladder **URETHRAL** *adj*
URETIC	*adj* pertaining to urine
URGE	*v* URGED, URGING, URGES to force forward
URGENCY	*n* pl. -CIES the quality of being urgent
URGENT	*adj* requiring immediate attention **URGENTLY** *adv*
URGER	*n* pl. -S one that urges
URGING	present participle of urge
URGINGLY	*adv* in an urging manner
URIAL	*n* pl. -S a wild Asian sheep
URIC	*adj* pertaining to urine
URIDINE	*n* pl. -S a chemical compound
URINAL	*n* pl. -S a fixture used for urinating
URINARY	*n* pl. -NARIES a urinal
URINATE	*v* -NATED, -NATING, -NATES to discharge urine
URINE	*n* pl. -S a liquid containing body wastes
URINEMIA	*n* pl. -S uremia **URINEMIC** *adj*
URINOSE	*adj* pertaining to urine
URINOUS	*adj* pertaining to urine
URN	*n* pl. -S a type of vase **URNLIKE** *adj*
UROCHORD	*n* pl. -S a rodlike structure in certain lower vertebrates
URODELE	*n* pl. -S a type of amphibian
UROLITH	*n* pl. -S a concretion in the urinary tract
UROLOGY	*n* pl. -GIES the branch of medicine dealing with the urinary tract **UROLOGIC** *adj*
UROPOD	*n* pl. -S an abdominal limb of an arthropod **UROPODAL** *adj*
UROPYGIA	*n/pl* the humps from which birds' tail feathers grow
UROSCOPY	*n* pl. -PIES analysis of the urine as a means of diagnosis
UROSTYLE	*n* pl. -S a part of the vertebral column of frogs and toads
URSA	*n* pl. -SAE a female bear
URSIFORM	*adj* having the form of a bear
URSINE	*adj* pertaining to a bear
URTEXT	*n* pl. -S the original text

URTICANT	*n* pl. -S an urticating substance
URTICATE	*v* -CATED, -CATING, -CATES to cause itching or stinging
URUS	*n* pl. -ES an extinct European ox
URUSHIOL	*n* pl. -S a toxic liquid
US	*pron* the objective case of the pronoun we
USABLE	*adj* capable of being used **USABLY** *adv*
USAGE	*n* pl. -S a firmly established and generally accepted practice or procedure
USANCE	*n* pl. -S usage
USAUNCE	*n* pl. -S usance
USE	*v* USED, USING, USES to put into service
USEABLE	*adj* usable **USEABLY** *adv*
USEFUL	*adj* serving a purpose **USEFULLY** *adv*
USELESS	*adj* serving no purpose
USER	*n* pl. -S one that uses
USHER	*v* -ED, -ING, -S to conduct to a place
USING	present participle of use
USNEA	*n* pl. -S any of a genus of lichens
USQUABAE	*n* pl. -S usquebae
USQUE	*n* pl. -S usquebae
USQUEBAE	*n* pl. -S whiskey
USTULATE	*adj* scorched
USUAL	*n* pl. -S something that is usual (ordinary)
USUALLY	*adv* ordinarily
USUFRUCT	*n* pl. -S the legal right to use another's property so long as it is not damaged or altered
USURER	*n* pl. -S one that practices usury
USURIES	pl. of usury
USURIOUS	*adj* practicing usury
USURP	*v* -ED, -ING, -S to seize and hold without legal authority
USURPER	*n* pl. -S one that usurps
USURY	*n* pl. -RIES the lending of money at an exorbitant interest rate
UT	*n* pl. -S the musical tone C in the French solmization system now replaced by do

UTA	*n* pl. -S any of a genus of large lizards
UTENSIL	*n* pl. -S a useful implement
UTERUS	*n* pl. UTERI or UTERUSES an organ of female mammals **UTERINE** *adj*
UTILE	*adj* useful
UTILIDOR	*n* pl. -S an insulated system of pipes for use in arctic regions
UTILISE	*v* -LISED, -LISING, -LISES to utilize
UTILISER	*n* pl. -S utilizer
UTILITY	*n* pl. -TIES the quality of being useful
UTILIZE	*v* -LIZED, -LIZING, -LIZES to make use of
UTILIZER	*n* pl. -S one that utilizes
UTMOST	*n* pl. -S the greatest degree or amount
UTOPIA	*n* pl. -S a place of ideal perfection
UTOPIAN	*n* pl. -S one who believes in the perfectibility of human society
UTOPISM	*n* pl. -S the body of ideals or principles of a utopian
UTOPIST	*n* pl. -S a utopian
UTRICLE	*n* pl. -S a saclike cavity in the inner ear
UTRICULI	*n/pl* utricles
UTTER	*v* -ED, -ING, -S to give audible expression to
UTTERER	*n* pl. -S one that utters
UTTERLY	*adv* totally
UVEA	*n* pl. -S a layer of the eye **UVEAL** *adj*
UVEITIS	*n* pl. -ITISES inflammation of the uvea **UVEITIC** *adj*
UVEOUS	*adj* pertaining to the uvea
UVULA	*n* pl. -LAE or -LAS the pendent, fleshy portion of the soft palate
UVULAR	*n* pl. -S a uvularly produced sound
UVULARLY	*adv* with the use of the uvula
UVULITIS	*n* pl. -TISES inflammation of the uvula
UXORIAL	*adj* pertaining to a wife
UXORIOUS	*adj* excessively submissive or devoted to one's wife

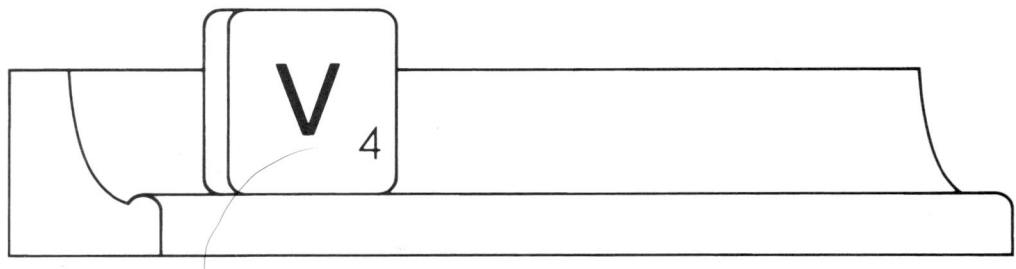

VAC	*n* pl. -S a vacuum cleaner
VACANCY	*n* pl. -CIES the quality or state of being vacant
VACANT	*adj* empty **VACANTLY** *adv*
VACATE	*v* -CATED, -CATING, -CATES to make vacant
VACATION	*v* -ED, -ING, -S to take a vacation (a period of time devoted to rest and relaxation)
VACCINA	*n* pl. -S vaccinia
VACCINE	*n* pl. -S a preparation given to produce immunity to a specific disease **VACCINAL** *adj*
VACCINEE	*n* pl. -S one that is vaccinated
VACCINIA	*n* pl. -S cowpox
VACUA	a pl. of vacuum
VACUITY	*n* pl. -ITIES an empty space
VACUOLE	*n* pl. -S a small cavity in organic tissue **VACUOLAR** *adj*
VACUOUS	*adj* empty
VACUUM	*n* pl. VACUUMS or VACUA a space entirely devoid of matter
VACUUM	*v* -ED, -ING, -S to use a device that cleans by suction
VADOSE	*adj* located above the permanent groundwater level
VAGABOND	*v* -ED, -ING, -S to live like a vagabond (a vagrant)
VAGAL	*adj* pertaining to the vagus nerve **VAGALLY** *adv*
VAGARY	*n* pl. -RIES a whim
VAGI	pl. of vagus
VAGILE	*adj* free to move about
VAGILITY	*n* pl. -TIES freedom of movement
VAGINA	*n* pl. -NAE or -NAS the passage leading from the uterus to the vulva **VAGINAL** *adj*
VAGINATE	*adj* enclosed in a sheath
VAGOTOMY	*n* pl. -MIES surgical division of the vagus nerve
VAGRANCY	*n* pl. -CIES the state of being a vagrant
VAGRANT	*n* pl. -S a wanderer with no apparent means of support
VAGROM	*adj* wandering
VAGUE	*adj* VAGUER, VAGUEST not clearly expressed or understood **VAGUELY** *adv*
VAGUS	*n* pl. -GI a cranial nerve
VAHINE	*n* pl. -S wahine
VAIL	*v* -ED, -ING, -S to lower
VAIN	*adj* VAINER, VAINEST filled with undue admiration for oneself **VAINLY** *adv*
VAINNESS	*n* pl. -ES the quality or state of being vain
VAIR	*n* pl. -S a fur used for lining and trimming medieval garments
VAKEEL	*n* pl. -S a native lawyer in India
VAKIL	*n* pl. -S vakeel
VALANCE	*v* -LANCED, -LANCING, -LANCES to furnish with a short drapery
VALE	*n* pl. -S a valley
VALENCE	*n* pl. -S the degree of combining power of an element or radical
VALENCIA	*n* pl. -S a woven fabric
VALENCY	*n* pl. -CIES valence
VALERATE	*n* pl. -S a chemical salt
VALERIAN	*n* pl. -S a perennial herb **VALERIC** *adj*
VALET	*v* -ED, -ING, -S to act as a personal servant to
VALGUS	*n* pl. -ES the position of a joint that is abnormally turned outward **VALGOID** *adj*
VALIANCE	*n* pl. -S valor
VALIANCY	*n* pl. -CIES valor

VALIANT   *n* pl. -S a courageous person

VALID   *adj* based on evidence that can be supported

VALIDATE   *v* -DATED, -DATING, -DATES to give legal force to

VALIDITY   *n* pl. -TIES the quality or state of being valid

VALIDLY   *adv* in a valid manner

VALINE   *n* pl. -S an amino acid

VALISE   *n* pl. -S a small piece of hand luggage

VALKYR   *n* pl. -S valkyrie

VALKYRIE   *n* pl. -S a maiden in Norse mythology

VALLATE   *adj* bordered by a raised edge

VALLEY   *n* pl. -LEYS a depression of the earth's surface

VALONIA   *n* pl. -S a substance obtained from dried acorn cups and used in tanning and dyeing

VALOR   *n* pl. -S courage

VALORISE   *v* -ISED, -ISING, -ISES to valorize

VALORIZE   *v* -IZED, -IZING, -IZES to establish and maintain the price of by governmental action

VALOROUS   *adj* courageous

VALOUR   *n* pl. -S valor

VALSE   *n* pl. -S a concert waltz

VALUABLE   *n* pl. -S a possession of value

VALUABLY   *adv* with value

VALUATE   *v* -ATED, -ATING, -ATES to appraise

VALUATOR   *n* pl. -S one that valuates

VALUE   *v* -UED, -UING, -UES to estimate the value (the quality that renders a thing useful or desirable) of

VALUER   *n* pl. -S one that values

VALUTA   *n* pl. -S the agreed or exchange value of a currency

VALVAL   *adj* resembling or pertaining to a valve

VALVAR   *adj* valval

VALVATE   *adj* having valves or parts resembling valves

VALVE   *v* VALVED, VALVING, VALVES to provide with a valve (a device for controlling the flow of a liquid or gas)

VALVELET   *n* pl. -S a small valve

VALVULA   *n* pl. -LAE valvule

VALVULAR   *adj* pertaining to a valve

VALVULE   *n* pl. -S a small valve

VAMBRACE   *n* pl. -S a piece of armor for the forearm

VAMOOSE   *v* -MOOSED, -MOOSING, -MOOSES to leave quickly

VAMOSE   *v* -MOSED, -MOSING, -MOSES to vamoose

VAMP   *v* -ED, -ING, -S to repair or patch

VAMPER   *n* pl. -S one that vamps

VAMPIRE   *n* pl. -S a reanimated corpse believed to feed on sleeping persons' blood **VAMPIRIC** *adj*

VAMPISH   *adj* seductive

VAN   *v* VANNED, VANNING, VANS to transport in a van (a type of motor vehicle)

VANADATE   *n* pl. -S a chemical salt

VANADIUM   *n* pl. -S a metallic element **VANADIC, VANADOUS** *adj*

VANDA   *n* pl. -S a tropical orchid

VANDAL   *n* pl. -S one who willfully destroys or defaces property **VANDALIC** *adj*

VANDYKE   *n* pl. -S a short, pointed beard **VANDYKED** *adj*

VANE   *n* pl. -S a device for showing the direction of the wind **VANED** *adj*

VANG   *n* pl. -S a rope on a ship

VANGUARD   *n* pl. -S the forefront of a movement

VANILLA   *n* pl. -S a flavoring extract **VANILLIC** *adj*

VANILLIN   *n* pl. -S a chemical compound used in flavoring

VANISH   *v* -ED, -ING, -ES to disappear

VANISHER   *n* pl. -S one that vanishes

VANITORY   *n* pl. -RIES a combined dressing table and basin

VANITY   *n* pl. -TIES inflated pride in oneself **VANITIED** *adj*

VANMAN   *n* pl. -MEN a person who drives a van

VANNED   past tense of van

VANNER   *n* pl. -S a person who owns a van

VANNING   present participle of van

VANPOOL   *n* pl. -S an arrangement whereby several commuters travel in one van

VANQUISH   v -ED, -ING, -ES to defeat in battle

VANTAGE   n pl. -S superiority over a competitor

VANWARD   adv toward the front

VAPID   adj insipid **VAPIDLY** adv

VAPIDITY   n pl. -TIES the quality or state of being vapid

VAPOR   v -ED, -ING, -S to emit vapor (visible floating moisture)

VAPORER   n pl. -S one that vapors

VAPORING   n pl. -S boastful talk

VAPORISE   v -ISED, -ISING, -ISES to vaporize

VAPORISH   adj resembling vapor

VAPORIZE   v -IZED, -IZING, -IZES to convert into vapor

VAPOROUS   adj vaporish

VAPORY   adj vaporish

VAPOUR   v -ED, -ING, -S to vapor

VAPOURER   n pl. -S vaporer

VAPOURY   adj vapory

VAQUERO   n pl. -ROS a cowboy

VAR   n pl. -S a unit of reactive power

VARA   n pl. -S a Spanish unit of length

VARACTOR   n pl. -S a capacitor with variable capacitance

VARIA   n/pl a collection of various literary works

VARIABLE   n pl. -S something that varies

VARIABLY   adv in a varying manner

VARIANCE   n pl. -S a license to perform an act contrary to the usual rule

VARIANT   n pl. -S a variable

VARIATE   v -ATED, -ATING, -ATES to vary

VARICES   pl. of varix

VARICOSE   adj abnormally swollen or dilated

VARIED   past tense of vary

VARIEDLY   adv in a varied manner

VARIER   n pl. -S one that varies

VARIES   present 3d person sing. of vary

VARIETAL   n pl. -S a wine designated by the variety of grape

VARIETY   n pl. -ETIES something differing from others of the same general kind

VARIFORM   adj having various forms

VARIOLA   n pl. -S smallpox **VARIOLAR** adj

VARIOLE   n pl. -S a foveola

VARIORUM   n pl. -S an edition containing various versions of a text

VARIOUS   adj of diverse kinds

VARISTOR   n pl. -S a type of electrical resistor

VARIX   n pl. VARICES a varicose vein

VARLET   n pl. -S a knave

VARLETRY   n pl. -RIES a group of common people

VARMENT   n pl. -S varmint

VARMINT   n pl. -S an animal considered to be a pest

VARNA   n pl. -S any of the four main Hindu social classes

VARNISH   v -ED, -ING, -ES to give a glossy appearance to

VARNISHY   adj glossy

VAROOM   v -ED, -ING, -S to vroom

VARSITY   n pl. -TIES the principal team representing a university, college, or school in any activity

VARUS   n pl. -ES a malformation of a bone or joint

VARVE   n pl. -S a deposit of sedimentary material **VARVED** adj

VARY   v VARIED, VARYING, VARIES to become or make different

VAS   n pl. VASA an anatomical duct **VASAL** adj

VASCULAR   adj pertaining to ducts that convey body fluids

VASCULUM   n pl. -LA or -LUMS a box used to hold plant specimens

VASE   n pl. -S a rounded, decorative container **VASELIKE** adj

VASIFORM   adj having the form of a vase

VASOTOMY   n pl. -MIES a surgical cutting of the vas deferens

VASSAL   n pl. -S a person granted the use of land by a feudal lord in return for homage and allegiance

VAST   adj VASTER, VASTEST of great extent or size

VAST   n pl. -S a vast space

VASTIER   comparative of vasty

VASTIEST   superlative of vasty

VASTITY   n pl. -TIES vastness

VASTLY   adv to a vast extent or degree

VASTNESS   n pl. -ES the quality or state of being vast

VASTY	*adj* VASTIER, VASTIEST vast
VAT	*v* VATTED, VATTING, VATS to put into a vat (a large container for holding liquids)
VATFUL	*n* pl. -S as much as a vat can hold
VATIC	*adj* pertaining to a prophet
VATICAL	*adj* vatic
VATICIDE	*n* pl. -S the killing of a prophet
VATTED	past tense of vat
VATTING	present participle of vat
VATU	*n* pl. -S a monetary unit of Vanuatu
VAU	*n* pl. -S vav
VAULT	*v* -ED, -ING, -S to provide with a vault (an arched ceiling)
VAULTER	*n* pl. -S one that leaps
VAULTING	*n* pl. -S the structure forming a vault
VAULTY	*adj* VAULTIER, VAULTIEST resembling a vault
VAUNT	*v* -ED, -ING, -S to brag
VAUNTER	*n* pl. -S one that vaunts
VAUNTFUL	*adj* boastful
VAUNTIE	*adj* boastful
VAUNTY	*adj* vauntie
VAV	*n* pl. -S a Hebrew letter
VAVASOR	*n* pl. -S a high-ranking vassal
VAVASOUR	*n* pl. -S vavasor
VAVASSOR	*n* pl. -S vavasor
VAW	*n* pl. -S vav
VAWARD	*n* pl. -S the foremost part
VAWNTIE	*adj* vaunty
VEAL	*v* -ED, -ING, -S to kill and prepare a calf for food
VEALER	*n* pl. -S a calf raised for food
VEALY	*adj* VEALIER, VEALIEST immature
VECTOR	*v* -ED, -ING, -S to guide in flight by means of radioed directions
VEDALIA	*n* pl. -S an Australian ladybug
VEDETTE	*n* pl. -S a small boat used for scouting
VEE	*n* pl. -S the letter V
VEEJAY	*n* pl. -JAYS an announcer on a program of music videos
VEENA	*n* pl. -S vina
VEEP	*n* pl. -S a vice president

VEEPEE	*n* pl. -S veep
VEER	*v* -ED, -ING, -S to change direction
VEERY	*n* pl. -RIES a songbird
VEG	*n* pl. VEG a vegetable
VEGAN	*n* pl. -S one that eats only plant products
VEGANISM	*n* pl. -S the practice of eating only plant products
VEGETAL	*adj* pertaining to plants
VEGETANT	*adj* characteristic of plant life
VEGETATE	*v* -TATED, -TATING, -TATES to grow in the manner of a plant
VEGETE	*adj* healthy
VEGETIST	*n* pl. -S one that eats only plant products
VEGETIVE	*adj* growing or capable of growing
VEGGIE	*n* pl. -S a vegetable
VEGIE	*n* pl. -S veggie
VEHEMENT	*adj* ardent
VEHICLE	*n* pl. -S a device used as a means of conveyance
VEIL	*v* -ED, -ING, -S to provide with a veil (a piece of sheer fabric worn over the face)
VEILEDLY	*adv* in a disguised manner
VEILER	*n* pl. -S one that veils
VEILING	*n* pl. -S a veil
VEILLIKE	*adj* resembling a veil
VEIN	*v* -ED, -ING, -S to fill with veins (tubular blood vessels)
VEINAL	*adj* of or pertaining to the veins
VEINER	*n* pl. -S a tool used in wood carving
VEINIER	comparative of veiny
VEINIEST	superlative of veiny
VEINING	*n* pl. -S a network of veins
VEINLESS	*adj* having no veins
VEINLET	*n* pl. -S a small vein
VEINLIKE	*adj* resembling a vein
VEINULE	*n* pl. -S venule
VEINULET	*n* pl. -S venule
VEINY	*adj* VEINIER, VEINIEST full of veins
VELA	pl. of velum
VELAMEN	*n* pl. -MINA a velum
VELAR	*n* pl. -S a kind of speech sound

VELARIUM   *n* pl. -IA an awning over an ancient Roman theater

VELARIZE   *v* -IZED, -IZING, -IZES to pronounce with the back of the tongue touching the soft palate

VELATE   *adj* having a velum

VELD   *n* pl. -S veldt

VELDT   *n* pl. -S a grassland of southern Africa

VELIGER   *n* pl. -S a larval stage of certain mollusks

VELITES   *n/pl* foot soldiers of ancient Rome

VELLEITY   *n* pl. -ITIES a very low degree of desire

VELLUM   *n* pl. -S a fine parchment

VELOCE   *adv* rapidly — used as a musical direction

VELOCITY   *n* pl. -TIES rapidity of motion

VELOUR   *n* pl. -S a fabric resembling velvet

VELOUTE   *n* pl. -S a type of sauce

VELUM   *n* pl. -LA a thin membranous covering or partition

VELURE   *v* -LURED, -LURING, -LURES to smooth with a velvet or silk pad, as a hat

VELVERET   *n* pl. -S a fabric resembling velvet

VELVET   *n* pl. -S a soft, smooth fabric **VELVETED, VELVETY** *adj*

VENA   *n* pl. -NAE a vein

VENAL   *adj* open to bribery **VENALLY** *adv*

VENALITY   *n* pl. -TIES the quality or state of being venal

VENATIC   *adj* pertaining to hunting

VENATION   *n* pl. -S an arrangement of veins

VEND   *v* -ED, -ING, -S to sell **VENDABLE** *adj*

VENDACE   *n* pl. -S a European fish

VENDEE   *n* pl. -S a buyer

VENDER   *n* pl. -S vendor

VENDETTA   *n* pl. -S a feud between two families

VENDEUSE   *n* pl. -S a saleswoman

VENDIBLE   *n* pl. -S a salable article

VENDIBLY   *adv* salably

VENDOR   *n* pl. -S a seller

VENDUE   *n* pl. -S a public sale

VENEER   *v* -ED, -ING, -S to overlay with thin layers of material

VENEERER   *n* pl. -S one that veneers

VENENATE   *v* -NATED, -NATING, -NATES to poison

VENENOSE   *adj* poisonous

VENERATE   *v* -ATED, -ATING, -ATES to revere

VENEREAL   *adj* involving the genital organs

VENERY   *n* pl. -ERIES sexual intercourse

VENETIAN   *n* pl. -S a flexible window screen

VENGE   *v* VENGED, VENGING, VENGES to avenge

VENGEFUL   *adj* seeking to avenge

VENIAL   *adj* easily excused or forgiven **VENIALLY** *adv*

VENIN   *n* pl. -S a toxin found in snake venom

VENINE   *n* pl. -S venin

VENIRE   *n* pl. -S a type of judicial writ

VENISON   *n* pl. -S the edible flesh of a deer

VENOGRAM   *n* pl. -S a roentgenogram of a vein

VENOM   *v* -ED, -ING, -S to inject with venom (a poisonous secretion of certain animals)

VENOMER   *n* pl. -S one that venoms

VENOMOUS   *adj* poisonous

VENOSE   *adj* venous

VENOSITY   *n* pl. -TIES the quality or state of being venous

VENOUS   *adj* full of veins **VENOUSLY** *adv*

VENT   *v* -ED, -ING, -S to provide with a vent (an opening for the escape of gas or liquid)

VENTAGE   *n* pl. -S a small opening

VENTAIL   *n* pl. -S the adjustable front of a medieval helmet

VENTER   *n* pl. -S the abdomen

VENTLESS   *adj* having no vent

VENTRAL   *n* pl. -S a fin located on the underside of a fish

VENTURE   *v* -TURED, -TURING, -TURES to risk

VENTURER   *n* pl. -S one that ventures

VENTURI   *n* pl. -S a device for measuring the flow of a fluid

VENTURING   present participle of venture

VENUE   *n* pl. -S the locale of an event

VENULE	*n* pl. -S a small vein **VENULAR, VENULOSE, VENULOUS** *adj*
VERA	*adj* very
VERACITY	*n* pl. -TIES conformity to truth
VERANDA	*n* pl. -S a type of porch
VERANDAH	*n* pl. -S veranda
VERATRIA	*n* pl. -S veratrin
VERATRIN	*n* pl. -S a poisonous mixture of alkaloids
VERATRUM	*n* pl. -S a poisonous herb
VERB	*n* pl. -S a word used to express an act, occurrence, or mode of being
VERBAL	*n* pl. -S a word derived from a verb
VERBALLY	*adv* in a spoken manner
VERBATIM	*adv* word for word
VERBENA	*n* pl. -S a flowering plant
VERBIAGE	*n* pl. -S an excess of words
VERBID	*n* pl. -S a verbal
VERBIFY	*v* -FIED, -FYING, -FIES to use as a verb
VERBILE	*n* pl. -S one whose mental imagery consists of words
VERBLESS	*adj* lacking a verb
VERBOSE	*adj* wordy
VERBOTEN	*adj* forbidden
VERDANCY	*n* pl. -CIES the quality or state of being verdant
VERDANT	*adj* green with vegetation
VERDERER	*n* pl. -S an officer in charge of the royal forests of England
VERDEROR	*n* pl. -S verderer
VERDICT	*n* pl. -S the decision of a jury at the end of a legal proceeding
VERDIN	*n* pl. -S a small bird
VERDITER	*n* pl. -S a blue or green pigment
VERDURE	*n* pl. -S green vegetation **VERDURED** *adj*
VERECUND	*adj* shy
VERGE	*v* VERGED, VERGING, VERGES to come near
VERGENCE	*n* pl. -S a movement of one eye in relation to the other
VERGER	*n* pl. -S a church official
VERGING	present participle of verge
VERGLAS	*n* pl. -ES a thin coating of ice on rock
VERIDIC	*adj* truthful
VERIER	comparative of very
VERIEST	superlative of very
VERIFIER	*n* pl. -S one that verifies
VERIFY	*v* -FIED, -FYING, -FIES to prove to be true
VERILY	*adv* in truth
VERISM	*n* pl. -S realism in art or literature
VERISMO	*n* pl. -MOS verism
VERIST	*n* pl. -S one who practices verism **VERISTIC** *adj*
VERITAS	*n* pl. -TATES truth
VERITE	*n* pl. -S the technique of filming so as to convey candid realism
VERITY	*n* pl. -TIES truth
VERJUICE	*n* pl. -S the juice of sour or unripe fruit
VERMEIL	*n* pl. -S a red color
VERMES	pl. of vermis
VERMIAN	*adj* pertaining to worms
VERMIN	*n* pl. VERMIN small, common, harmful, or objectionable animals
VERMIS	*n* pl. -MES a part of the brain
VERMOULU	*adj* eaten by worms
VERMOUTH	*n* pl. -S a liqueur
VERMUTH	*n* pl. -S vermouth
VERNACLE	*n* pl. -S vernicle
VERNAL	*adj* pertaining to spring **VERNALLY** *adv*
VERNICLE	*n* pl. -S veronica
VERNIER	*n* pl. -S an auxiliary scale used with a main scale to obtain fine measurements
VERNIX	*n* pl. -ES a fatty substance covering the skin of a fetus
VERONICA	*n* pl. -S a handkerchief bearing the image of Christ's face
VERRUCA	*n* pl. -CAE a wart
VERSAL	*adj* entire
VERSANT	*n* pl. -S the slope of a mountain or mountain chain
VERSE	*v* VERSED, VERSING, VERSES to versify
VERSEMAN	*n* pl. -MEN one who versifies
VERSER	*n* pl. -S a verseman
VERSET	*n* pl. -S a versicle
VERSICLE	*n* pl. -S a short line of metrical writing

VERSIFY	*v* -FIED, -FYING, -FIES to change from prose into metrical form
VERSINE	*n* pl. -S a trigonometric function of an angle
VERSING	present participle of verse
VERSION	*n* pl. -S an account or description from a particular point of view
VERSO	*n* pl. -SOS a left-hand page of a book
VERST	*n* pl. -S a Russian measure of distance
VERSTE	*n* pl. -S verst
VERSUS	*prep* against
VERT	*n* pl. -S the heraldic color green
VERTEBRA	*n* pl. -BRAE or -BRAS any of the bones or segments forming the spinal column
VERTEX	*n* pl. -TEXES or -TICES the highest point of something
VERTICAL	*n* pl. -S something that is vertical (extending up and down)
VERTICIL	*n* pl. -S a circular arrangement, as of flowers or leaves, about a point on an axis
VERTIGO	*n* pl. -GOES, -GOS, or -GINES a disordered state in which the individual or his surroundings seem to whirl dizzily
VERTU	*n* pl. -S virtu
VERVAIN	*n* pl. -S a flowering plant
VERVE	*n* pl. -S vivacity
VERVET	*n* pl. -S an African monkey
VERY	*adj* VERIER, VERIEST absolute
VESICA	*n* pl. -CAE a bladder **VESICAL** *adj*
VESICANT	*n* pl. -S a chemical warfare agent that induces blistering
VESICATE	*v* -CATED, -CATING, -CATES to blister
VESICLE	*n* pl. -S a small bladder
VESICULA	*n* pl. -LAE a vesicle
VESPER	*n* pl. -S an evening service, prayer, or song
VESPERAL	*n* pl. -S a covering for an altar cloth
VESPIARY	*n* pl. -ARIES a nest of wasps
VESPID	*n* pl. -S a wasp
VESPINE	*adj* pertaining to wasps
VESSEL	*n* pl. -S a craft for traveling on water **VESSELED** *adj*

VEST	*v* -ED, -ING, -S to place in the control of
VESTA	*n* pl. -S a short friction match
VESTAL	*n* pl. -S a chaste woman
VESTALLY	*adv* chastely
VESTEE	*n* pl. -S a garment worn under a woman's jacket or blouse
VESTIARY	*n* pl. -ARIES a dressing room
VESTIGE	*n* pl. -S a visible sign of something that is no longer in existence
VESTIGIA	*n/pl* vestiges
VESTING	*n* pl. -S the right of an employee to share in and withdraw from a pension fund without penalty
VESTLESS	*adj* being without a vest
VESTLIKE	*adj* resembling a vest (a short, sleeveless garment)
VESTMENT	*n* pl. -S one of the ceremonial garments of the clergy
VESTRY	*n* pl. -TRIES a room in which vestments are kept **VESTRAL** *adj*
VESTURAL	*adj* pertaining to clothing
VESTURE	*v* -TURED, -TURING, -TURES to clothe
VESUVIAN	*n* pl. -S a mineral
VET	*v* VETTED, VETTING, VETS to treat animals medically
VETCH	*n* pl. -ES a climbing plant
VETERAN	*n* pl. -S a former member of the armed forces
VETIVER	*n* pl. -S an Asian grass
VETIVERT	*n* pl. -S the essential oil of the vetiver
VETO	*v* -ED, -ING, -ES to forbid or prevent authoritatively
VETOER	*n* pl. -S one that vetoes
VETTED	past tense of vet
VETTING	present participle of vet
VEX	*v* VEXED or VEXT, VEXING, VEXES to annoy
VEXATION	*n* pl. -S a cause of trouble
VEXEDLY	*adv* in a vexed manner
VEXER	*n* pl. -S one that vexes
VEXIL	*n* pl. -S vexillum
VEXILLUM	*n* pl. -LA the web or vane of a feather **VEXILLAR** *adj*
VEXINGLY	*adv* in a vexing manner
VEXT	a past tense of vex

VIA	*prep* by way of
VIABLE	*adj* capable of living **VIABLY** *adv*
VIADUCT	*n* pl. -S a type of bridge
VIAL	*v* VIALED, VIALING, VIALS or VIALLED, VIALLING, VIALS to put in a vial (a small container for liquids)
VIAND	*n* pl. -S an article of food
VIATIC	*adj* pertaining to traveling
VIATICAL	*adj* viatic
VIATICUM	*n* pl. -CA or -CUMS an allowance for traveling expenses
VIATOR	*n* pl. -ES or -S a traveler
VIBE	*n* pl. -S a vibration
VIBIST	*n* pl. -S one who plays the vibraphone
VIBRANCE	*n* pl. -S vibrancy
VIBRANCY	*n* pl. -CIES the quality or state of being vibrant
VIBRANT	*n* pl. -S a sonant
VIBRATE	*v* -BRATED, -BRATING, -BRATES to move back and forth rapidly
VIBRATO	*n* pl. -TOS a tremulous or pulsating musical effect
VIBRATOR	*n* pl. -S something that vibrates
VIBRIO	*n* pl. -RIOS any of a genus of bacteria shaped like a comma **VIBRIOID** *adj*
VIBRION	*n* pl. -S vibrio
VIBRISSA	*n* pl. -SAE one of the stiff hairs growing about the mouth of certain mammals
VIBRONIC	*adj* pertaining to changes in molecular energy states resulting from vibrational energy
VIBURNUM	*n* pl. -S a flowering shrub
VICAR	*n* pl. -S a church official
VICARAGE	*n* pl. -S the office of a vicar
VICARATE	*n* pl. -S vicarage
VICARIAL	*adj* pertaining to a vicar
VICARLY	*adj* vicarial
VICE	*v* VICED, VICING, VICES to vise
VICELESS	*adj* having no immoral habits
VICENARY	*adj* pertaining to the number twenty
VICEROY	*n* pl. -ROYS one who rules as the representative of a sovereign
VICHY	*n* pl. -CHIES a type of mineral water

VICINAGE	*n* pl. -S vicinity
VICINAL	*adj* nearby
VICING	present participle of vice
VICINITY	*n* pl. -TIES the region near or about a place
VICIOUS	*adj* dangerously aggressive
VICOMTE	*n* pl. -S a French nobleman
VICTIM	*n* pl. -S one who suffers from a destructive or injurious action
VICTOR	*n* pl. -S one who defeats an adversary
VICTORIA	*n* pl. -S a light carriage
VICTORY	*n* pl. -RIES a successful outcome in a contest or struggle
VICTRESS	*n* pl. -ES a female victor
VICTUAL	*v* -UALED, -UALING, -UALS or -UALLED, -UALLING, -UALS to provide with food
VICUGNA	*n* pl. -S vicuna
VICUNA	*n* pl. -S a ruminant mammal
VIDE	*v* see — used to direct a reader to another item; VIDE is the only form of this verb; it cannot be conjugated
VIDEO	*n* pl. -EOS television
VIDEOTEX	*n* pl. -ES an electronic system for transmitting data to a subscriber's video screen
VIDETTE	*n* pl. -S vedette
VIDICON	*n* pl. -S a type of television camera tube
VIDUITY	*n* pl. -ITIES the quality or state of being a widow
VIE	*v* VIED, VYING, VIES to strive for superiority
VIER	*n* pl. -S one that vies
VIEW	*v* -ED, -ING, -S to look at **VIEWABLE** *adj*
VIEWDATA	*n* pl. VIEWDATA a videotex
VIEWER	*n* pl. -S one that views
VIEWIER	comparative of viewy
VIEWIEST	superlative of viewy
VIEWING	*n* pl. -S an act of seeing, watching, or looking
VIEWLESS	*adj* having no opinions
VIEWY	*adj* VIEWIER, VIEWIEST showy
VIG	*n* pl. -S a vigorish
VIGA	*n* pl. -S a ceiling beam in Spanish architecture

VIGIL   *n* pl. -S a period of watchfulness maintained during normal sleeping hours

VIGILANT   *adj* watchful

VIGNERON   *n* pl. -S a winegrower

VIGNETTE   *v* -GNETTED, -GNETTING, -GNETTES to describe briefly

VIGOR   *n* pl. -S active strength or force

VIGORISH   *n* pl. -ES a charge paid to a bookie on a bet

VIGOROSO   *adv* with emphasis and spirit — used as a musical direction

VIGOROUS   *adj* full of vigor

VIGOUR   *n* pl. -S vigor

VIKING   *n* pl. -S a Scandinavian pirate

VILAYET   *n* pl. -S an administrative division of Turkey

VILE   *adj* VILER, VILEST morally despicable or physically repulsive **VILELY** *adv*

VILENESS   *n* pl. -ES the state of being vile

VILIFIER   *n* pl. -S one that vilifies

VILIFY   *v* -FIED, -FYING, -FIES to defame

VILIPEND   *v* -ED, -ING, -S to vilify

VILL   *n* pl. -S a village

VILLA   *n* pl. -LAE or -LAS an agricultural estate of ancient Rome

VILLADOM   *n* pl. -S the world constituted by suburban residences and their occupants

VILLAGE   *n* pl. -S a small community in a rural area

VILLAGER   *n* pl. -S one who lives in a village

VILLAIN   *n* pl. -S a cruelly malicious person

VILLAINY   *n* pl. -LAINIES conduct characteristic of a villain

VILLATIC   *adj* rural

VILLEIN   *n* pl. -S a type of serf

VILLUS   *n* pl. -LI one of the hairlike projections found on certain membranes **VILLOSE, VILLOUS** *adj*

VIM   *n* pl. -S energy

VIMEN   *n* pl. -MINA a long, flexible branch of a plant **VIMINAL** *adj*

VINA   *n* pl. -S a stringed instrument of India

VINAL   *n* pl. -S a synthetic textile fiber

VINASSE   *n* pl. -S a residue left after the distillation of liquor

VINCA   *n* pl. -S a flowering plant

VINCIBLE   *adj* capable of being conquered **VINCIBLY** *adv*

VINCULUM   *n* pl. -LA or -LUMS a unifying bond

VINDALOO   *n* pl. -LOOS a curried dish made with meat, garlic, and wine

VINE   *v* VINED, VINING, VINES to grow like a vine (a climbing plant)

VINEAL   *adj* vinous

VINEGAR   *n* pl. -S a sour liquid used as a condiment or preservative **VINEGARY** *adj*

VINERY   *n* pl. -ERIES a place in which grapevines are grown

VINEYARD   *n* pl. -S an area planted with grapevines

VINIC   *adj* derived from wine

VINIER   comparative of viny

VINIEST   superlative of viny

VINIFERA   *n* pl. -S a European grape

VINIFY   *v* -FIED, -FYING, -FIES to convert into wine by fermentation

VINING   present participle of vine

VINO   *n* pl. -NOS wine

VINOSITY   *n* pl. -TIES the character of a wine

VINOUS   *adj* pertaining to wine **VINOUSLY** *adv*

VINTAGE   *n* pl. -S a season's yield of wine from a vineyard

VINTAGER   *n* pl. -S one that harvests wine grapes

VINTNER   *n* pl. -S a wine merchant

VINY   *adj* VINIER, VINIEST covered with vines

VINYL   *n* pl. -S a type of plastic **VINYLIC** *adj*

VIOL   *n* pl. -S a stringed instrument

VIOLA   *n* pl. -S a stringed instrument

VIOLABLE   *adj* capable of being violated **VIOLABLY** *adv*

VIOLATE   *v* -LATED, -LATING, -LATES to break or disregard the terms or requirements of

VIOLATER   *n* pl. -S violator

VIOLATOR   *n* pl. -S one that violates

VIOLENCE   *n* pl. -S violent action

VIOLENT	*adj* marked by intense physical force or roughness
VIOLET	*n* pl. -S a flowering plant
VIOLIN	*n* pl. -S a stringed instrument
VIOLIST	*n* pl. -S one who plays the viol or viola
VIOLONE	*n* pl. -S a stringed instrument
VIOMYCIN	*n* pl. -S an antibiotic
VIPER	*n* pl. -S a venomous snake **VIPERINE, VIPERISH, VIPEROUS** *adj*
VIRAGO	*n* pl. -GOES or -GOS a noisy, domineering woman
VIRAL	*adj* pertaining to or caused by a virus **VIRALLY** *adv*
VIRELAI	*n* pl. -S virelay
VIRELAY	*n* pl. -LAYS a medieval French verse form
VIREMIA	*n* pl. -S the presence of a virus in the blood **VIREMIC** *adj*
VIREO	*n* pl. -EOS a small bird
VIRES	pl. of vis
VIRGA	*n* pl. -S wisps of precipitation evaporating before reaching ground
VIRGATE	*n* pl. -S an early English measure of land area
VIRGIN	*n* pl. -S a person who has never had sexual intercourse
VIRGINAL	*n* pl. -S a musical instrument
VIRGULE	*n* pl. -S a diagonal printing mark used to separate alternatives
VIRICIDE	*n* pl. -S a substance that destroys viruses
VIRID	*adj* verdant
VIRIDIAN	*n* pl. -S a bluish-green pigment
VIRIDITY	*n* pl. -TIES verdancy
VIRILE	*adj* having masculine vigor **VIRILELY** *adv*
VIRILISM	*n* pl. -S the development of male secondary sex characteristics in a female
VIRILITY	*n* pl. -TIES the quality or state of being virile
VIRION	*n* pl. -S a virus particle
VIRL	*n* pl. -S a metal ring or cap put around a shaft to prevent splitting
VIROID	*n* pl. -S a viruslike plant pathogen
VIROLOGY	*n* pl. -GIES the study of viruses
VIROSIS	*n* pl. -ROSES infection with a virus
VIRTU	*n* pl. -S a love or taste for the fine arts
VIRTUAL	*adj* having the effect but not the actual form of what is specified
VIRTUE	*n* pl. -S moral excellence
VIRTUOSA	*n* pl. -SAS or -SE a female virtuoso
VIRTUOSO	*n* pl. -SOS or -SI a highly skilled artistic performer
VIRTUOUS	*adj* characterized by virtue
VIRUCIDE	*n* pl. -S viricide
VIRULENT	*adj* extremely poisonous
VIRUS	*n* pl. -ES any of a class of submicroscopic pathogens
VIS	*n* pl. VIRES force or power
VISA	*v* -ED, -ING, -S to put an official endorsement on, as a passport
VISAGE	*n* pl. -S the face or facial expression of a person **VISAGED** *adj*
VISARD	*n* pl. -S vizard
VISCACHA	*n* pl. -S a burrowing rodent
VISCERA	pl. of viscus
VISCERAL	*adj* pertaining to the internal organs
VISCID	*adj* thick and adhesive **VISCIDLY** *adv*
VISCOID	*adj* somewhat viscid
VISCOSE	*n* pl. -S a viscous solution
VISCOUNT	*n* pl. -S a British nobleman
VISCOUS	*adj* having relatively high resistance to flow
VISCUS	*n* pl. -CERA an internal organ
VISE	*v* VISED, VISING, VISES to hold in a vise (a clamping device)
VISE	*v* VISEED, VISEING, VISES to visa
VISELIKE	*adj* resembling a vise
VISIBLE	*adj* capable of being seen **VISIBLY** *adv*
VISING	present participle of vise
VISION	*v* -ED, -ING, -S to imagine
VISIONAL	*adj* imaginary
VISIT	*v* -ED, -ING, -S to go or come to see someone or something
VISITANT	*n* pl. -S a visitor
VISITER	*n* pl. -S visitor

VISITOR	*n* pl. -S one that visits
VISIVE	*adj* visible
VISOR	*v* -ED, -ING, -S to provide with a visor (a projecting brim)
VISTA	*n* pl. -S a distant view **VISTAED** *adj*
VISUAL	*n* pl. -S something that illustrates by pictures or diagrams
VISUALLY	*adv* with regard to sight
VITA	*n* pl. -TAE a brief, autobiographical sketch
VITAL	*adj* necessary to life
VITALISE	*v* -ISED, -ISING, -ISES to vitalize
VITALISM	*n* pl. -S a philosophical doctrine
VITALIST	*n* pl. -S an advocate of vitalism
VITALITY	*n* pl. -TIES exuberant physical strength or mental vigor
VITALIZE	*v* -IZED, -IZING, -IZES to give life to
VITALLY	*adv* in a vital manner
VITALS	*n/pl* vital organs
VITAMER	*n* pl. -S a type of chemical compound
VITAMIN	*n* pl. -S any of various organic substances essential to proper nutrition
VITAMINE	*n* pl. -S vitamin
VITELLIN	*n* pl. -S a protein found in egg yolk
VITELLUS	*n* pl. -ES the yolk of an egg
VITESSE	*n* pl. -S speed
VITIATE	*v* -ATED, -ATING, -ATES to impair the value or quality of **VITIABLE** *adj*
VITIATOR	*n* pl. -S one that vitiates
VITILIGO	*n* pl. -GOS a skin disease
VITRAIN	*n* pl. -S the material in the vitreous layers of banded bituminous coal
VITREOUS	*n* pl. -ES the jelly that fills the eyeball
VITRIC	*adj* pertaining to glass
VITRICS	*n/pl* the art of making or decorating glass articles
VITRIFY	*v* -FIED, -FYING, -FIES to convert into glass
VITRINE	*n* pl. -S a glass showcase for art objects
VITRIOL	*v* -OLED, -OLING, -OLS or -OLLED, -OLLING, -OLS to treat with sulfuric acid
VITTA	*n* pl. -TAE a streak or band of color **VITTATE** *adj*
VITTLE	*v* -TLED, -TLING, -TLES to victual
VITULINE	*adj* pertaining to a calf
VIVA	*n* pl. -S a shout or cry used to express approval
VIVACE	*n* pl. -S a musical passage played in a brisk spirited manner
VIVACITY	*n* pl. -TIES the quality or state of being lively
VIVARIUM	*n* pl. -IA or -IUMS a place for raising and keeping live animals
VIVARY	*n* pl. -RIES vivarium
VIVE	*interj* — used as an exclamation of approval
VIVERRID	*n* pl. -S any of a family of small carnivorous mammals
VIVERS	*n/pl* food
VIVID	*adj* -IDER, -IDEST strikingly bright or intense **VIVIDLY** *adv*
VIVIFIC	*adj* vivifying
VIVIFIER	*n* pl. -S one that vivifies
VIVIFY	*v* -FIED, -FYING, -FIES to give life to
VIVIPARA	*n/pl* animals that bring forth living young
VIVISECT	*v* -ED, -ING, -S to dissect the living body of
VIXEN	*n* pl. -S a shrewish woman **VIXENISH, VIXENLY** *adj*
VIZARD	*n* pl. -S a mask **VIZARDED** *adj*
VIZCACHA	*n* pl. -S viscacha
VIZIER	*n* pl. -S a high official in some Muslim countries
VIZIR	*n* pl. -S vizier **VIZIRIAL** *adj*
VIZIRATE	*n* pl. -S the office of a vizir
VIZOR	*v* -ED, -ING, -S to visor
VIZSLA	*n* pl. -S a Hungarian breed of dog
VOCABLE	*n* pl. -S a word
VOCABLY	*adv* in a manner that may be voiced aloud
VOCAL	*n* pl. -S a sound produced with the voice
VOCALIC	*n* pl. -S a vowel sound
VOCALISE	*v* -ISED, -ISING, -ISES to vocalize
VOCALISM	*n* pl. -S the act of vocalizing
VOCALIST	*n* pl. -S a singer

VOCALITY   *n* pl. -TIES possession or exercise of vocal powers

VOCALIZE   *v* -IZED, -IZING, -IZES to produce with the voice

VOCALLY   *adv* with the voice

VOCATION   *n* pl. -S the work in which a person is regularly employed

VOCATIVE   *n* pl. -S a grammatical case used in some languages

VOCES   pl. of vox

VOCODER   *n* pl. -S an electronic device used in transmitting speech signals

VODKA   *n* pl. -S a liquor

VODOUN   *n* pl. -S vodun

VODUN   *n* pl. -S a primitive religion of the West Indies

VOE   *n* pl. -S a small bay, creek, or inlet

VOGIE   *adj* vain

VOGUE   *v* VOGUED, VOGUING or VOGUEING, VOGUES to imitate poses of fashion models

VOGUER   *n* pl. -S one that vogues

VOGUISH   *adj* fashionable

VOICE   *v* VOICED, VOICING, VOICES to express or utter

VOICEFUL   *adj* sonorous

VOICER   *n* pl. -S one that voices

VOICING   present participle of voice

VOID   *v* -ED, -ING, -S to make void (of no legal force or effect) **VOIDABLE** *adj*

VOIDANCE   *n* pl. -S the act or process of voiding

VOIDER   *n* pl. -S one that voids

VOIDNESS   *n* pl. -ES the quality or state of being void

VOILA   *interj* — used to call attention to something

VOILE   *n* pl. -S a sheer fabric

VOLANT   *adj* flying or capable of flying

VOLANTE   *adj* moving with light rapidity — used as a musical direction

VOLAR   *adj* pertaining to flight

VOLATILE   *n* pl. -S a winged creature

VOLCANIC   *n* pl. -S a rock produced by a volcano

VOLCANO   *n* pl. -NOES or -NOS an opening in the earth's crust through which molten rock and gases are ejected

VOLE   *v* VOLED, VOLING, VOLES to win all the tricks in a card game

VOLERY   *n* pl. -ERIES a large birdcage

VOLITANT   *adj* volant

VOLITION   *n* pl. -S the power of choosing or determining

VOLITIVE   *adj* pertaining to volition

VOLLEY   *v* -ED, -ING, -S to return a tennis ball before it touches the ground

VOLLEYER   *n* pl. -S one that volleys

VOLOST   *n* pl. -S an administrative district in Russia

VOLPLANE   *v* -PLANED, -PLANING, -PLANES to glide in an airplane

VOLT   *n* pl. -S a unit of electromotive force

VOLTA   *n* pl. -TE a turning

VOLTAGE   *n* pl. -S electromotive force expressed in volts

VOLTAISM   *n* pl. -S electricity produced by chemical action **VOLTAIC** *adj*

VOLTE   *n* pl. -S a fencing movement

VOLTI   *interj* — used to direct musicians to turn the page

VOLUBLE   *adj* talkative **VOLUBLY** *adv*

VOLUME   *v* -UMED, -UMING, -UMES to send or give out in large quantities

VOLUTE   *n* pl. -S a spiral architectural ornament **VOLUTED** *adj*

VOLUTIN   *n* pl. -S a granular substance that is common in microorganisms

VOLUTION   *n* pl. -S a spiral

VOLVA   *n* pl. -S a membranous sac that encloses certain immature mushrooms **VOLVATE** *adj*

VOLVOX   *n* pl. -ES any of a genus of freshwater protozoa

VOLVULUS   *n* pl. -LI or -LUSES a twisting of the intestine that causes obstruction

VOMER   *n* pl. -S a bone of the skull **VOMERINE** *adj*

VOMICA   *n* pl. -CAE a cavity in the body containing pus

VOMIT   *v* -ED, -ING, -S to eject the contents of the stomach through the mouth

VOMITER   *n* pl. -S one that vomits

VOMITIVE   *n* pl. -S an emetic

VOMITO   *n* pl. -TOS the black vomit of yellow fever

VOMITORY	*n* pl. -RIES an emetic
VOMITOUS	*adj* pertaining to vomiting
VOMITUS	*n* pl. -ES vomited matter
VOODOO	*v* -ED, -ING, -S to hex
VORACITY	*n* pl. -TIES the quality or state of being ravenous
VORLAGE	*n* pl. -S a position in skiing
VORTEX	*n* pl. -TEXES or -TICES a whirling mass of fluid **VORTICAL** *adj*
VOTABLE	*adj* capable of being voted on
VOTARESS	*n* pl. -ES a female votary
VOTARIST	*n* pl. -S a votary
VOTARY	*n* pl. -RIES a person who is bound by religious vows
VOTE	*v* VOTED, VOTING, VOTES to cast a vote (a formal expression of will or opinion)
VOTEABLE	*adj* votable
VOTELESS	*adj* having no vote
VOTER	*n* pl. -S one that votes
VOTING	present participle of vote
VOTIVE	*adj* performed in fulfillment of a vow **VOTIVELY** *adv*
VOTRESS	*n* pl. -ES votaress
VOUCH	*v* -ED, -ING, -ES to give one's personal assurance or guarantee
VOUCHEE	*n* pl. -S one for whom another vouches
VOUCHER	*v* -ED, -ING, -S to establish the authenticity of
VOUSSOIR	*n* pl. -S a wedge-shaped building stone
VOUVRAY	*n* pl. -VRAYS a French white wine
VOW	*v* -ED, -ING, -S to make a vow (a solemn promise)
VOWEL	*n* pl. -S a type of speech sound
VOWELIZE	*v* -IZED, -IZING, -IZES to provide with symbols used to indicate vowels
VOWER	*n* pl. -S one that vows
VOWLESS	*adj* having made no vow
VOX	*n* pl. VOCES voice
VOYAGE	*v* -AGED, -AGING, -AGES to travel
VOYAGER	*n* pl. -S one that voyages
VOYAGEUR	*n* pl. -S a person employed by a fur company to transport goods between distant stations
VOYEUR	*n* pl. -S one who is sexually gratified by looking at sexual objects or acts
VROOM	*v* -ED, -ING, -S to run an engine at high speed
VROUW	*n* pl. -S a Dutch woman
VROW	*n* pl. -S vrouw
VUG	*n* pl. -S a small cavity in a rock or lode
VUGG	*n* pl. -S vug
VUGGY	*adj* -GIER, -GIEST abounding in vugs
VUGH	*n* pl. -S vug
VULCANIC	*adj* pertaining to a volcano
VULGAR	*adj* -GARER, -GAREST crude **VULGARLY** *adv*
VULGAR	*n* pl. -S a common person
VULGATE	*n* pl. -S the common speech of a people
VULGO	*adv* commonly
VULGUS	*n* pl. -ES an exercise in Latin formerly required of pupils in some English public schools
VULPINE	*adj* pertaining to a fox
VULTURE	*n* pl. -S a bird of prey
VULVA	*n* pl. -VAE or -VAS the external genital organs of a female **VULVAL, VULVAR, VULVATE** *adj*
VULVITIS	*n* pl. -TISES inflammation of the vulva
VYING	present participle of vie
VYINGLY	*adv* in a vying manner

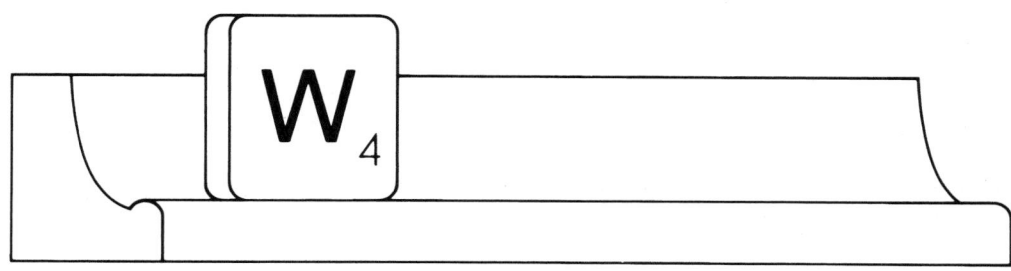

WAB	*n* pl. -S a web
WABBLE	*v* -BLED, -BLING, -BLES to wobble
WABBLER	*n* pl. -S one that wabbles
WABBLY	*adj* -BLIER, -BLIEST wobbly
WACK	*n* pl. -S a wacky person
WACKE	*n* pl. -S a type of basaltic rock
WACKO	*n* pl. WACKOS a person who is wacky
WACKY	*adj* WACKIER, WACKIEST very irrational **WACKILY** *adv*
WAD	*v* WADDED, WADDING, WADS to form into a wad (a small mass of soft material)
WADABLE	*adj* wadeable
WADDER	*n* pl. -S one that wads
WADDIE	*n* pl. -S a cowboy
WADDIED	past tense of waddy
WADDIES	present 3d person sing. of waddy
WADDING	*n* pl. -S a wad
WADDLE	*v* -DLED, -DLING, -DLES to walk with short, swaying steps
WADDLER	*n* pl. -S one that waddles
WADDLY	*adj* having or being a waddling gait
WADDY	*v* -DIED, -DYING, -DIES to strike with a thick club
WADE	*v* WADED, WADING, WADES to walk through water
WADEABLE	*adj* capable of being passed through by wading
WADER	*n* pl. -S one that wades
WADI	*n* pl. -S the bed of a usually dry watercourse
WADIES	pl. of wady
WADING	present participle of wade
WADMAAL	*n* pl. -S wadmal
WADMAL	*n* pl. -S a thick woolen fabric
WADMEL	*n* pl. -S wadmal
WADMOL	*n* pl. -S wadmal
WADMOLL	*n* pl. -S wadmal
WADSET	*v* -SETTED, -SETTING, -SETS to mortgage
WADY	*n* pl. -DIES wadi
WAE	*n* pl. -S woe
WAEFUL	*adj* woeful
WAENESS	*n* pl. -ES woeness
WAESUCK	*interj* waesucks
WAESUCKS	*interj* — used to express pity
WAFER	*v* -ED, -ING, -S to seal with an adhesive disk
WAFERY	*adj* resembling a wafer (a thin, crisp biscuit)
WAFF	*v* -ED, -ING, -S to wave
WAFFIE	*n* pl. -S a vagabond
WAFFLE	*v* -FLED, -FLING, -FLES to talk vaguely or indecisively
WAFFLER	*n* pl. -S one that waffles
WAFFLING	*n* pl. -S an indecisive statement or position
WAFT	*v* -ED, -ING, -S to carry lightly over air or water
WAFTAGE	*n* pl. -S the act of wafting
WAFTER	*n* pl. -S one that wafts
WAFTURE	*n* pl. -S waftage
WAG	*v* WAGGED, WAGGING, WAGS to move briskly up and down or to and fro
WAGE	*v* WAGED, WAGING, WAGES to engage in or carry on
WAGELESS	*adj* unpaid
WAGER	*v* -ED, -ING, -S to risk on an uncertain outcome
WAGERER	*n* pl. -S one that wagers
WAGGED	past tense of wag
WAGGER	*n* pl. -S one that wags

WAGGERY	*n* pl. -GERIES waggish behavior
WAGGING	present participle of wag
WAGGISH	*adj* playfully humorous
WAGGLE	*v* -GLED, -GLING, -GLES to wag
WAGGLY	*adj* waggling
WAGGON	*v* -ED, -ING, -S to wagon
WAGGONER	*n* pl. -S wagoner
WAGING	present participle of wage
WAGON	*v* -ED, -ING, -S to convey by wagon (a four-wheeled, horse-drawn vehicle)
WAGONAGE	*n* pl. -S conveyance by wagon
WAGONER	*n* pl. -S one who drives a wagon
WAGSOME	*adj* waggish
WAGTAIL	*n* pl. -S a songbird
WAHCONDA	*n* pl. -S wakanda
WAHINE	*n* pl. -S a Hawaiian woman
WAHOO	*n* pl. -HOOS a flowering shrub
WAIF	*v* -ED, -ING, -S to throw away
WAIFLIKE	*adj* resembling a waif (a homeless child)
WAIL	*v* -ED, -ING, -S to utter a long, mournful cry
WAILER	*n* pl. -S one that wails
WAILFUL	*adj* mournful
WAILSOME	*adj* wailful
WAIN	*n* pl. -S a large, open wagon
WAINSCOT	*v* -SCOTED, -SCOTING, -SCOTS or -SCOTTED, -SCOTTING, -SCOTS to line the walls of with wooden paneling
WAIR	*v* -ED, -ING, -S to spend
WAIST	*n* pl. -S the part of the body between the ribs and the hips **WAISTED** *adj*
WAISTER	*n* pl. -S a seaman stationed in the middle section of a ship
WAISTING	*n* pl. -S a type of dressmaking material
WAIT	*v* -ED, -ING, -S to stay in expectation of
WAITER	*n* pl. -S one who serves food in a restaurant
WAITING	*n* pl. -S the act of one who waits
WAITRESS	*v* -ED, -ING, -ES to work as a female server in a restaurant
WAIVE	*v* WAIVED, WAIVING, WAIVES to give up intentionally
WAIVER	*n* pl. -S the act of waiving something
WAKANDA	*n* pl. -S a supernatural force in Sioux beliefs
WAKE	*v* WAKED or WOKE, WOKEN, WAKING, WAKES to rouse from sleep
WAKEFUL	*adj* not sleeping or able to sleep
WAKELESS	*adj* unbroken — used of sleep
WAKEN	*v* -ED, -ING, -S to wake
WAKENER	*n* pl. -S one that wakens
WAKENING	*n* pl. -S the act of one that wakens
WAKER	*n* pl. -S one that wakes
WAKERIFE	*adj* wakeful
WAKIKI	*n* pl. -S shell money of the South Sea Islands
WAKING	present participle of wake
WALE	*v* WALED, WALING, WALES to mark with welts
WALER	*n* pl. -S an Australian-bred saddle horse
WALIES	pl. of waly
WALING	present participle of wale
WALK	*v* -ED, -ING, -S to advance on foot **WALKABLE** *adj*
WALKAWAY	*n* pl. -AWAYS an easy victory
WALKER	*n* pl. -S one that walks
WALKING	*n* pl. -S the act of one that walks
WALKOUT	*n* pl. -S a strike by workers
WALKOVER	*n* pl. -S a walkaway
WALKUP	*n* pl. -S an apartment house having no elevator
WALKWAY	*n* pl. -WAYS a passage for walking
WALKYRIE	*n* pl. -S valkyrie
WALL	*v* -ED, -ING, -S to provide with a wall (an upright structure built to enclose an area)
WALLA	*n* pl. -S wallah
WALLABY	*n* pl. -BIES a small kangaroo
WALLAH	*n* pl. -S a person engaged in a particular occupation or activity
WALLAROO	*n* pl. -ROOS a large kangaroo
WALLET	*n* pl. -S a flat folding case
WALLEYE	*n* pl. -S an eye having a white cornea **WALLEYED** *adj*
WALLIE	*n* pl. -S a valet
WALLIES	pl. of wally

WALLOP v -ED, -ING, -S to beat soundly

WALLOPER n pl. -S one that wallops

WALLOW v -ED, -ING, -S to roll about

WALLOWER n pl. -S one that wallows

WALLY n pl. -LIES waly

WALNUT n pl. -S an edible nut

WALRUS n pl. -ES a marine mammal

WALTZ v -ED, -ING, -ES to perform a ballroom dance

WALTZER n pl. -S one that waltzes

WALY n pl. WALIES something visually pleasing

WAMBLE v -BLED, -BLING, -BLES to move unsteadily

WAMBLY adj -BLIER, -BLIEST unsteady

WAME n pl. -S the belly

WAMEFOU n pl. -S a bellyful

WAMEFUL n pl. -S wamefou

WAMMUS n pl. -ES wamus

WAMPISH v -ED, -ING, -ES to throw about

WAMPUM n pl. -S a form of currency formerly used by North American Indians

WAMPUS n pl. -ES wamus

WAMUS n pl. -ES a heavy outer jacket

WAN adj WANNER, WANNEST unnaturally pale

WAN v WANNED, WANNING, WANS to become wan

WAND n pl. -S a slender rod

WANDER v -ED, -ING, -S to move about with no destination or purpose

WANDERER n pl. -S one that wanders

WANDEROO n pl. -ROOS an Asian monkey

WANDLE adj supple

WANE v WANED, WANING, WANES to decrease in size or extent

WANEY adj WANIER, WANIEST wany

WANGAN n pl. -S wanigan

WANGLE v -GLED, -GLING, -GLES to obtain or accomplish by contrivance

WANGLER n pl. -S one that wangles

WANGUN n pl. -S wanigan

WANIER comparative of waney and wany

WANIEST superlative of waney and wany

WANIGAN n pl. -S a supply chest used in a logging camp

WANING present participle of wane

WANION n pl. -S vengeance

WANLY adv in a wan manner

WANNED past tense of wan

WANNER comparative of wan

WANNESS n pl. -ES the quality of being wan

WANNEST superlative of wan

WANNIGAN n pl. -S wanigan

WANNING present participle of wan

WANT v -ED, -ING, -S to have a desire for

WANTAGE n pl. -S something that is lacking

WANTER n pl. -S one that wants

WANTON v -ED, -ING, -S to behave immorally

WANTONER n pl. -S one that wantons

WANTONLY adv immorally

WANY adj WANIER, WANIEST waning in some parts

WAP v WAPPED, WAPPING, WAPS to wrap

WAPITI n pl. -S a large deer

WAR v WARRED, WARRING, WARS to engage in war (a state of open, armed conflict)

WARBLE v -BLED, -BLING, -BLES to sing with melodic embellishments

WARBLER n pl. -S one that warbles

WARCRAFT n pl. -S the art of war

WARD v -ED, -ING, -S to turn aside

WARDEN n pl. -S the chief officer of a prison

WARDENRY n pl. -RIES the office of a warden

WARDER n pl. -S a person who guards something

WARDRESS n pl. -ES a female warden

WARDROBE n pl. -S a collection of garments

WARDROOM n pl. -S a dining area for officers on a warship

WARDSHIP n pl. -S the state of being under a guardian

WARE v WARED, WARING, WARES to beware of

WAREROOM n pl. -S a room in which goods are displayed for sale

WARFARE n pl. -S the act of engaging in war

WARFARIN n pl. -S a chemical compound

WARHEAD *n* pl. -S the front part of a missile containing the explosive

WARHORSE *n* pl. -S a musical or dramatic work that has been performed to excess

WARIER comparative of wary

WARIEST superlative of wary

WARILY *adv* in a wary manner

WARINESS *n* pl. -ES the state of being wary

WARING present participle of ware

WARISON *n* pl. -S a call to attack

WARK *v* -ED, -ING, -S to endure pain

WARLESS *adj* free from war

WARLIKE *adj* disposed to engage in war

WARLOCK *n* pl. -S a sorcerer

WARLORD *n* pl. -S a military leader of a warlike nation

WARM *adj* WARMER, WARMEST moderately hot

WARM *v* -ED, -ING, -S to make warm

WARMAKER *n* pl. -S one that wars

WARMER *n* pl. -S one that warms

WARMISH *adj* somewhat warm

WARMLY *adv* in a warm manner

WARMNESS *n* pl. -ES the state of being warm

WARMOUTH *n* pl. -S a freshwater fish

WARMTH *n* pl. -S warmness

WARMUP *n* pl. -S a preparatory exercise or procedure

WARN *v* -ED, -ING, -S to make aware of impending or possible danger

WARNER *n* pl. -S one that warns

WARNING *n* pl. -S something that warns

WARP *v* -ED, -ING, -S to turn or twist out of shape

WARPAGE *n* pl. -S the act of warping

WARPATH *n* pl. -S the route taken by attacking American Indians

WARPER *n* pl. -S one that warps

WARPLANE *n* pl. -S an airplane armed for combat

WARPOWER *n* pl. -S the power to make war

WARPWISE *adv* in a vertical direction

WARRAGAL *n* pl. -S warrigal

WARRANT *v* -ED, -ING, -S to give authority to

WARRANTY *n* pl. -TIES the act of warranting

WARRED past tense of war

WARREN *n* pl. -S a place where rabbits live and breed

WARRENER *n* pl. -S the keeper of a warren

WARRIGAL *n* pl. -S a dingo

WARRING present participle of war

WARRIOR *n* pl. -S one engaged or experienced in warfare

WARSAW *n* pl. -S a marine fish

WARSHIP *n* pl. -S a ship armed for combat

WARSLE *v* -SLED, -SLING, -SLES to wrestle

WARSLER *n* pl. -S a wrestler

WARSTLE *v* -TLED, -TLING, -TLES to wrestle

WARSTLER *n* pl. -S a wrestler

WART *n* pl. -S a protuberance on the skin **WARTED** *adj*

WARTHOG *n* pl. -S an African wild hog

WARTIER comparative of warty

WARTIEST superlative of warty

WARTIME *n* pl. -S a time of war

WARTLESS *adj* having no warts

WARTLIKE *adj* resembling a wart

WARTY *adj* WARTIER, WARTIEST covered with warts

WARWORK *n* pl. -S work done during a war

WARWORN *adj* showing the effects of war

WARY *adj* WARIER, WARIEST watchful

WAS 1st and 3d person sing. past indicative of be

WASABI *n* pl. -S a pungent herb

WASH *v* -ED, -ING, -ES to cleanse by immersing in or applying a liquid

WASHABLE *n* pl. -S something that can be washed without damage

WASHBOWL *n* pl. -S a bowl used for washing oneself

WASHDAY *n* pl. -DAYS a day set aside for washing clothes

WASHER *n* pl. -S one that washes

WASHIER comparative of washy

WASHIEST superlative of washy

WASHING *n* pl. -S articles washed or to be washed

WASHOUT *n* pl. -S an erosion of earth by the action of water

WASHRAG *n* pl. -S a small cloth used for washing oneself

WASHROOM *n* pl. -S a lavatory

WASHTUB   *n* pl. -S a tub used for washing clothes

WASHUP   *n* pl. -S the act of washing clean

WASHY   *adj* WASHIER, WASHIEST overly diluted

WASP   *n* pl. -S a stinging insect **WASPISH, WASPLIKE** *adj*

WASPY   *adj* WASPIER, WASPIEST resembling a wasp **WASPILY** *adv*

WASSAIL   *v* -ED, -ING, -S to drink to the health of

WAST   *n* pl. -S west

WASTABLE   *adj* capable of being wasted

WASTAGE   *n* pl. -S something that is wasted

WASTE   *v* WASTED, WASTING, WASTES to use thoughtlessly

WASTEFUL   *adj* tending to waste

WASTELOT   *n* pl. -S a vacant lot

WASTER   *n* pl. -S one that wastes

WASTERIE   *n* pl. -S wastry

WASTERY   *n* pl. -RIES wastry

WASTEWAY   *n* pl. -WAYS a channel for excess water

WASTING   present participle of waste

WASTREL   *n* pl. -S one that wastes

WASTRIE   *n* pl. -S wastry

WASTRY   *n* pl. -RIES reckless extravagance

WAT   *adj* WATTER, WATTEST wet

WAT   *n* pl. -S a hare

WATAP   *n* pl. -S a thread made from the roots of various trees

WATAPE   *n* pl. -S watap

WATCH   *v* -ED, -ING, -ES to observe carefully

WATCHCRY   *n* pl. -CRIES a password

WATCHDOG   *v* -DOGGED, -DOGGING, -DOGS to act as a guardian for

WATCHER   *n* pl. -S one that watches

WATCHEYE   *n* pl. -S a walleye

WATCHFUL   *adj* closely observant or alert

WATCHMAN   *n* pl. -MEN a man employed to stand guard

WATCHOUT   *n* pl. -S the act of looking out for something

WATER   *v* -ED, -ING, -S to sprinkle with water (a transparent, odorless, tasteless liquid)

WATERAGE   *n* pl. -S the conveyance of goods by water

WATERBED   *n* pl. -S a bed whose mattress is a plastic bag filled with water

WATERDOG   *n* pl. -S a large salamander

WATERER   *n* pl. -S one that waters

WATERIER   comparative of watery

WATERIEST   superlative of watery

WATERILY   *adv* in a watery manner

WATERING   *n* pl. -S the act of one that waters

WATERISH   *adj* watery

WATERLOG   *v* -LOGGED, -LOGGING, -LOGS to soak with water

WATERLOO   *n* pl. -LOOS a decisive defeat

WATERMAN   *n* pl. -MEN a boatman

WATERWAY   *n* pl. -WAYS a navigable body of water

WATERY   *adj* -TERIER, -TERIEST containing water

WATT   *n* pl. -S a unit of power

WATTAGE   *n* pl. -S an amount of power in terms of watts

WATTAPE   *n* pl. -S watap

WATTER   comparative of wat

WATTEST   superlative of wat

WATTHOUR   *n* pl. -S a unit of energy

WATTLE   *v* -TLED, -TLING, -TLES to weave into a network

WATTLESS   *adj* denoting a type of electric current

WAUCHT   *v* -ED, -ING, -S to waught

WAUGH   *adj* damp

WAUGHT   *v* -ED, -ING, -S to drink deeply

WAUK   *v* -ED, -ING, -S to wake

WAUL   *v* -ED, -ING, -S to cry like a cat

WAUR   *adj* worse

WAVE   *v* WAVED, WAVING, WAVES to move freely back and forth or up and down

WAVEBAND   *n* pl. -S a range of radio frequencies

WAVEFORM   *n* pl. -S a type of mathematical graph

WAVELESS   *adj* having no waves (moving ridges on the surface of a liquid)

WAVELET   *n* pl. -S a small wave

WAVELIKE   *adj* resembling a wave

WAVEOFF	*n* pl. -S the act of denying landing permission to an approaching aircraft
WAVER	*v* -ED, -ING, -S to move back and forth
WAVERER	*n* pl. -S one that wavers
WAVERY	*adj* wavering
WAVEY	*n* pl. -VEYS the snow goose
WAVIER	comparative of wavy
WAVIES	pl. of wavy
WAVIEST	superlative of wavy
WAVILY	*adv* in a wavy manner
WAVINESS	*n* pl. -ES the state of being wavy
WAVING	present participle of wave
WAVY	*adj* WAVIER, WAVIEST having waves
WAVY	*n* pl. -VIES wavey
WAW	*n* pl. -S vav
WAWL	*v* -ED, -ING, -S to waul
WAX	*v* -ED, -ING, -ES to coat with wax (a natural, heat-sensitive substance)
WAXBERRY	*n* pl. -RIES a berry with a waxy coating
WAXBILL	*n* pl. -S a tropical bird
WAXEN	*adj* covered with wax
WAXER	*n* pl. -S one that waxes
WAXIER	comparative of waxy
WAXIEST	superlative of waxy
WAXILY	*adv* in a waxy manner
WAXINESS	*n* pl. -ES the quality of being waxy
WAXING	*n* pl. -S the act of one that waxes
WAXLIKE	*adj* resembling wax
WAXPLANT	*n* pl. -S a tropical plant
WAXWEED	*n* pl. -S an annual herb
WAXWING	*n* pl. -S a type of passerine bird
WAXWORK	*n* pl. -S an effigy made of wax
WAXWORM	*n* pl. -S a moth that infests beehives
WAXY	*adj* WAXIER, WAXIEST resembling wax
WAY	*n* pl. WAYS a method of doing something
WAYBILL	*n* pl. -S a list of goods relative to a shipment
WAYFARER	*n* pl. -S a traveler
WAYGOING	*n* pl. -S the act of leaving
WAYLAY	*v* -LAID, -LAYING, -LAYS to ambush
WAYLAYER	*n* pl. -S one that waylays
WAYLESS	*adj* having no road or path
WAYSIDE	*n* pl. -S the side of a road
WAYWARD	*adj* willful
WAYWORN	*adj* fatigued by travel
WE	*pron* 1st person pl. pronoun in the nominative case
WEAK	*adj* WEAKER, WEAKEST lacking strength
WEAKEN	*v* -ED, -ING, -S to make weak
WEAKENER	*n* pl. -S one that weakens
WEAKFISH	*n* pl. -ES a marine fish
WEAKISH	*adj* somewhat weak
WEAKLING	*n* pl. -S a weak person
WEAKLY	*adj* -LIER, -LIEST weak and sickly
WEAKNESS	*n* pl. -ES the state of being weak
WEAKSIDE	*n* pl. -S the side of a basketball court with fewer players
WEAL	*n* pl. -S a welt
WEALD	*n* pl. -S a woodland
WEALTH	*n* pl. -S a great quantity of valuable material
WEALTHY	*adj* WEALTHIER, WEALTHIEST having wealth
WEAN	*v* -ED, -ING, -S to withhold mother's milk from and substitute other nourishment
WEANER	*n* pl. -S one that weans
WEANLING	*n* pl. -S a recently weaned child or animal
WEAPON	*v* -ED, -ING, -S to supply with a weapon (an instrument used in combat)
WEAPONRY	*n* pl. -RIES an aggregate of weapons
WEAR	*v* WORE, WORN, WEARING, WEARS to have on one's person
WEARABLE	*n* pl. -S a garment
WEARER	*n* pl. -S one that wears something
WEARIED	past tense of weary
WEARIER	comparative of weary
WEARIES	present 3d person sing. of weary
WEARIEST	superlative of weary
WEARIFUL	*adj* tiresome
WEARISH	*adj* tasteless

WEARY	*adj* -RIER, -RIEST tired **WEARILY** *adv*
WEARY	*v* -RIED, -RYING, -RIES to make or become weary
WEASAND	*n* pl. -S the throat
WEASEL	*v* -SELED, -SELING, -SELS or -SELLED, -SELLING, -SELS to act evasively
WEASELLY	*adj* resembling a weasel (a small carnivorous mammal)
WEASELY	*adj* weaselly
WEASON	*n* pl. -S weasand
WEATHER	*v* -ED, -ING, -S to expose to atmospheric conditions
WEAVE	*v* WOVE or WEAVED, WOVEN, WEAVING, WEAVES to form by interlacing threads
WEAVER	*n* pl. -S one that weaves
WEAZAND	*n* pl. -S weasand
WEB	*v* WEBBED, WEBBING, WEBS to provide with a web (an interlaced fabric or structure)
WEBBING	*n* pl. -S a woven strip of fiber
WEBBY	*adj* -BIER, -BIEST weblike
WEBER	*n* pl. -S a unit of magnetic flux
WEBFED	*adj* designed to print a continuous roll of paper
WEBFOOT	*n* pl. -FEET a foot having the toes joined by a membrane
WEBLESS	*adj* having no webs
WEBLIKE	*adj* resembling a web
WEBSTER	*n* pl. -S a weaver
WEBWORK	*n* pl. -S a weblike pattern or structure
WEBWORM	*n* pl. -S a web-spinning caterpillar
WECHT	*n* pl. -S weight
WED	*v* WEDDED, WEDDING, WEDS to marry
WEDDER	*n* pl. -S one that weds
WEDDING	*n* pl. -S a marriage ceremony
WEDEL	*v* -ED, -ING, -S to perform a wedeln
WEDELN	*n* pl. -S a skiing technique
WEDGE	*v* WEDGED, WEDGING, WEDGES to force apart with a wedge (a tapering piece of wood or metal)
WEDGIE	*n* pl. -S a type of woman's shoe
WEDGY	*adj* WEDGIER, WEDGIEST resembling a wedge

WEDLOCK	*n* pl. -S the state of being married
WEE	*adj* WEER, WEEST very small
WEE	*n* pl. -S a short time
WEED	*v* -ED, -ING, -S to remove weeds (undesirable plants)
WEEDER	*n* pl. -S one that weeds
WEEDIER	comparative of weedy
WEEDIEST	superlative of weedy
WEEDILY	*adv* in a weedy manner
WEEDLESS	*adj* having no weeds
WEEDLIKE	*adj* resembling a weed
WEEDY	*adj* WEEDIER, WEEDIEST resembling a weed
WEEK	*n* pl. -S a period of seven days
WEEKDAY	*n* pl. -DAYS any day of the week except Sunday
WEEKEND	*v* -ED, -ING, -S to spend the weekend (the end of the week)
WEEKLONG	*adj* continuing for a week
WEEKLY	*n* pl. -LIES a publication issued once a week
WEEL	*adj* well
WEEN	*v* -ED, -ING, -S to suppose
WEENIE	*n* pl. -S a wiener
WEENSY	*adj* -SIER, -SIEST tiny
WEENY	*adj* -NIER, -NIEST tiny
WEEP	*v* WEPT, WEEPING, WEEPS to express sorrow by shedding tears
WEEPER	*n* pl. -S one that weeps
WEEPIE	*n* pl. -S a very maudlin movie
WEEPING	*n* pl. -S the act of one that weeps
WEEPY	*adj* WEEPIER, WEEPIEST tending to weep
WEER	comparative of wee
WEEST	superlative of wee
WEET	*v* -ED, -ING, -S to know
WEEVER	*n* pl. -S a marine fish
WEEVIL	*n* pl. -S a small beetle **WEEVILED, WEEVILLY, WEEVILY** *adj*
WEEWEE	*v* -WEED, -WEEING, -WEES to urinate
WEFT	*n* pl. -S a woven fabric or garment
WEFTWISE	*adv* in a horizontal direction
WEIGELA	*n* pl. -S a flowering shrub
WEIGELIA	*n* pl. -S weigela

WEIGH v -ED, -ING, -S to determine the weight of

WEIGHER n pl. -S one that weighs

WEIGHMAN n pl. -MEN one whose occupation is weighing goods

WEIGHT v -ED, -ING, -S to add weight (heaviness) to

WEIGHTER n pl. -S one that weights

WEIGHTY adj WEIGHTIER, WEIGHTIEST having great weight

WEINER n pl. -S wiener

WEIR n pl. -S a fence placed in a stream to catch fish

WEIRD adj WEIRDER, WEIRDEST mysteriously strange

WEIRD n pl. -S destiny

WEIRDIE n pl. -S a very strange person

WEIRDIES pl. of weirdy

WEIRDLY adv in a weird manner

WEIRDO n pl. WEIRDOES or WEIRDOS a weirdie

WEIRDY n pl. WEIRDIES weirdie

WEKA n pl. -S a flightless bird

WELCH v -ED, -ING, -ES to welsh

WELCHER n pl. -S one that welshes

WELCOME v -COMED, -COMING, -COMES to greet cordially

WELCOMER n pl. -S one that welcomes

WELD v -ED, -ING, -S to join by applying heat **WELDABLE** adj

WELDER n pl. -S one that welds

WELDLESS adj having no welded joints

WELDMENT n pl. -S a unit composed of welded pieces

WELDOR n pl. -S welder

WELFARE n pl. -S general well-being

WELKIN n pl. -S the sky

WELL v -ED, -ING, -S to rise to the surface and flow forth

WELLADAY n pl. -DAYS wellaway

WELLAWAY n pl. -WAYS an expression of sorrow

WELLBORN adj of good birth or ancestry

WELLCURB n pl. -S the stone ring around a well (a hole dug in the ground to obtain water)

WELLDOER n pl. -S a doer of good deeds

WELLHEAD n pl. -S the source of a spring or stream

WELLHOLE n pl. -S the shaft of a well

WELLIE n pl. -S a Wellington boot

WELLIES pl. of welly

WELLNESS n pl. -ES the state of being healthy

WELLSITE n pl. -S a mineral

WELLY n pl. -LIES wellie

WELSH v -ED, -ING, -ES to fail to pay a debt

WELSHER n pl. -S one that welshes

WELT v -ED, -ING, -S to mark with welts (ridges or lumps raised on the skin)

WELTER v -ED, -ING, -S to roll about

WELTING n pl. -S a cord or strip used to reinforce a seam

WEN n pl. -S a benign tumor of the skin

WENCH v -ED, -ING, -ES to consort with prostitutes

WENCHER n pl. -S one that wenches

WEND v -ED, -ING, -S to proceed along

WENDIGO n pl. -GOS windigo

WENNISH adj wenny

WENNY adj -NIER, -NIEST resembling a wen

WENT past tense of go

WEPT past tense of weep

WERE a pl. and 2d person sing. past indicative, and past subjunctive of be

WEREGILD n pl. -S wergeld

WEREWOLF n pl. -WOLVES a person capable of assuming the form of a wolf

WERGELD n pl. -S a price paid for the taking of a man's life in Anglo-Saxon law

WERGELT n pl. -S wergeld

WERGILD n pl. -S wergeld

WERT a 2d person sing. past tense of be

WERWOLF n pl. -WOLVES werewolf

WESKIT n pl. -S a vest

WESSAND n pl. -S weasand

WEST n pl. -S a cardinal point of the compass

WESTER v -ED, -ING, -S to move toward the west

WESTERLY n pl. -LIES a wind from the west

WESTERN n pl. -S one who lives in the west

WESTING *n* pl. -S a shifting west

WESTMOST *adj* farthest west

WESTWARD *n* pl. -S a direction toward the west

WET *adj* WETTER, WETTEST covered or saturated with a liquid

WET *v* WETTED, WETTING, WETS to make wet

WETHER *n* pl. -S a gelded male sheep

WETLAND *n* pl. -S land containing much soil moisture

WETLY *adv* in a wet manner

WETNESS *n* pl. -ES the state of being wet

WETPROOF *adj* waterproof

WETTABLE *adj* capable of being wetted

WETTED past tense of wet

WETTER *n* pl. -S one that wets

WETTEST superlative of wet

WETTING *n* pl. -S a liquid used in moistening something

WETTISH *adj* somewhat wet

WHA *pron* who

WHACK *v* -ED, -ING, -S to strike sharply

WHACKER *n* pl. -S one that whacks

WHACKO *n* pl. WHACKOS wacko

WHACKY *adj* WHACKIER, WHACKIEST wacky

WHALE *v* WHALED, WHALING, WHALES to engage in the hunting of whales (large marine mammals)

WHALEMAN *n* pl. -MEN a whaler

WHALER *n* pl. -S a person engaged in whaling

WHALING *n* pl. -S the industry of hunting and processing whales

WHAM *v* WHAMMED, WHAMMING, WHAMS to hit with a loud impact

WHAMMO *interj* — used to indicate a startling event

WHAMMY *n* pl. -MIES a supernatural spell bringing bad luck

WHAMO *interj* whammo

WHANG *v* -ED, -ING, -S to beat with a whip

WHANGEE *n* pl. -S an Asian grass

WHAP *v* WHAPPED, WHAPPING, WHAPS to whop

WHAPPER *n* pl. -S whopper

WHARF *v* -ED, -ING, -S to moor to a wharf (a docking place for vessels)

WHARFAGE *n* pl. -S the use of a wharf

WHARVE *n* pl. -S a round piece of wood used in spinning thread

WHAT *n* pl. -S the true nature of something

WHATEVER *adj* being what or who it may be

WHATNESS *n* pl. -ES the true nature of something

WHATNOT *n* pl. -S an ornamental set of shelves

WHATSIS *n* pl. -SISES whatsit

WHATSIT *n* pl. -S something whose name is unknown or forgotten

WHAUP *n* pl. -S a European bird

WHEAL *n* pl. -S a welt

WHEAT *n* pl. -S a cereal grass

WHEATEAR *n* pl. -S a small bird of northern regions

WHEATEN *n* pl. -S a pale yellowish color

WHEE *interj* — used to express delight

WHEEDLE *v* -DLED, -DLING, -DLES to attempt to persuade by flattery

WHEEDLER *n* pl. -S one that wheedles

WHEEL *v* -ED, -ING, -S to convey on wheels (circular frames designed to turn on an axis)

WHEELER *n* pl. -S one that wheels

WHEELIE *n* pl. -S a maneuver made on a wheeled vehicle

WHEELING *n* pl. -S the condition of a road for vehicles

WHEELMAN *n* pl. -MEN a helmsman

WHEEN *n* pl. -S a fairly large amount

WHEEP *v* -ED, -ING, -S to wheeple

WHEEPLE *v* -PLED, -PLING, -PLES to give forth a prolonged whistle

WHEEZE *v* WHEEZED, WHEEZING, WHEEZES to breathe with a whistling sound

WHEEZER *n* pl. -S one that wheezes

WHEEZY *adj* WHEEZIER, WHEEZIEST characterized by wheezing **WHEEZILY** *adv*

WHELK *n* pl. -S a pustule

WHELKY *adj* WHELKIER, WHELKIEST marked with whelks

WHELM *v* -ED, -ING, -S to cover with water

WHELP	*v* -ED, -ING, -S to give birth to
WHEN	*n* pl. -S the time in which something is done or occurs
WHENAS	*conj* at which time
WHENCE	*adv* from what place
WHENEVER	*adv* at whatever time
WHERE	*n* pl. -S the place at or in which something is located or occurs
WHEREAS	*n* pl. -ES an introductory statement of a formal document
WHEREAT	*adv* at what
WHEREBY	*adv* by what
WHEREIN	*adv* in what
WHEREOF	*adv* of what
WHEREON	*adv* on what
WHERETO	*adv* to what
WHEREVER	*adv* in or to whatever place
WHERRY	*v* -RIED, -RYING, -RIES to transport in a light rowboat
WHERVE	*n* pl. -S wharve
WHET	*v* WHETTED, WHETTING, WHETS to sharpen by friction
WHETHER	*conj* if it be the case that
WHETTER	*n* pl. -S one that whets
WHETTING	present participle of whet
WHEW	*n* pl. -S a whistling sound
WHEY	*n* pl. WHEYS the watery part of milk **WHEYEY, WHEYISH** *adj*
WHEYFACE	*n* pl. -S a pale, sallow face
WHEYLIKE	*adj* resembling whey
WHICH	*pron* what particular one or ones
WHICKER	*v* -ED, -ING, -S to whinny
WHID	*v* WHIDDED, WHIDDING, WHIDS to move rapidly and quietly
WHIDAH	*n* pl. -S whydah
WHIFF	*v* -ED, -ING, -S to blow or convey with slight gusts of air
WHIFFER	*n* pl. -S one that whiffs
WHIFFET	*n* pl. -S an insignificant person
WHIFFLE	*v* -FLED, -FLING, -FLES to move or think erratically
WHIFFLER	*n* pl. -S one that whiffles
WHIG	*n* pl. -S one who interprets history as a continuing victory of progress over reactionary forces
WHILE	*v* WHILED, WHILING, WHILES to cause to pass pleasantly
WHILOM	*adv* formerly
WHILST	*conj* during the time that
WHIM	*n* pl. -S an impulsive idea
WHIMBREL	*n* pl. -S a shore bird
WHIMPER	*v* -ED, -ING, -S to cry with plaintive, broken sounds
WHIMSEY	*n* pl. -SEYS whimsy
WHIMSY	*n* pl. -SIES a whim **WHIMSIED** *adj*
WHIN	*n* pl. -S furze
WHINCHAT	*n* pl. -S a songbird
WHINE	*v* WHINED, WHINING, WHINES to utter a plaintive, high-pitched sound
WHINER	*n* pl. -S one that whines
WHINEY	*adj* WHINIER, WHINIEST whiny
WHINGE	*v* WHINGED, WHINGEING or WHINGING, WHINGES to whine
WHINIER	comparative of whiny
WHINIEST	superlative of whiny
WHINING	present participle of whine
WHINNY	*v* -NIED, -NYING, -NIES to neigh in a low or gentle manner
WHINNY	*adj* -NIER, -NIEST abounding in whin
WHINY	*adj* WHINIER, WHINIEST tending to whine
WHIP	*v* WHIPPED or WHIPT, WHIPPING, WHIPS to strike with a whip (an instrument for administering corporal punishment)
WHIPCORD	*n* pl. -S a strong, twisted cord
WHIPLASH	*n* pl. -ES the lash of a whip
WHIPLIKE	*adj* resembling a whip
WHIPPED	a past tense of whip
WHIPPER	*n* pl. -S one that whips
WHIPPET	*n* pl. -S a small, swift dog
WHIPPIER	comparative of whippy
WHIPPIEST	superlative of whippy
WHIPPING	*n* pl. -S material used to whip
WHIPPY	*adj* -PIER, -PIEST pertaining to or resembling a whip
WHIPRAY	*n* pl. -RAYS a stingray
WHIPSAW	*v* -SAWED, -SAWN, -SAWING, -SAWS to cut with a narrow, tapering saw
WHIPT	a past tense of whip

WHIPTAIL	*n* pl. -S a lizard having a long, slender tail
WHIPWORM	*n* pl. -S a parasitic worm
WHIR	*v* WHIRRED, WHIRRING, WHIRS to move with a buzzing sound
WHIRL	*v* -ED, -ING, -S to revolve rapidly
WHIRLER	*n* pl. -S one that whirls
WHIRLY	*adj* WHIRLIER, WHIRLIEST marked by a whirling motion
WHIRLY	*n* pl. WHIRLIES a small tornado
WHIRR	*v* -ED, -ING, -S to whir
WHIRRED	past tense of whir
WHIRRING	present participle of whir
WHIRRY	*v* -RIED, -RYING, -RIES to hurry
WHISH	*v* -ED, -ING, -ES to move with a hissing sound
WHISHT	*v* -ED, -ING, -S to hush
WHISK	*v* -ED, -ING, -S to move briskly
WHISKER	*n* pl. -S a hair on a man's face **WHISKERY** *adj*
WHISKEY	*n* pl. -KEYS a liquor
WHISKY	*n* pl. -KIES whiskey
WHISPER	*v* -ED, -ING, -S to speak softly
WHISPERY	*adj* resembling a whisper
WHIST	*v* -ED, -ING, -S to hush
WHISTLE	*v* -TLED, -TLING, -TLES to make a shrill, clear musical sound
WHISTLER	*n* pl. -S one that whistles
WHIT	*n* pl. -S a particle
WHITE	*adj* WHITER, WHITEST of the color of pure snow
WHITE	*v* WHITED, WHITING, WHITES to whiten
WHITECAP	*n* pl. -S a wave with a crest of foam
WHITEFLY	*n* pl. -FLIES a small whitish insect
WHITELY	*adv* in a white manner
WHITEN	*v* -ED, -ING, -S to make white
WHITENER	*n* pl. -S one that whitens
WHITEOUT	*n* pl. -S an arctic weather condition
WHITER	comparative of white
WHITEST	superlative of white
WHITEY	*adj* whity
WHITHER	*adv* to what place
WHITIER	comparative of whity

WHITIEST	superlative of whity
WHITING	*n* pl. -S a marine food fish
WHITISH	*adj* somewhat white
WHITLOW	*n* pl. -S an inflammation of the finger or toe
WHITRACK	*n* pl. -S a weasel
WHITTER	*n* pl. -S a large draft of liquor
WHITTLE	*v* -TLED, -TLING, -TLES to cut or shave bits from
WHITTLER	*n* pl. -S one that whittles
WHITTRET	*n* pl. -S a weasel
WHITY	*adj* WHITIER, WHITIEST whitish
WHIZ	*v* WHIZZED, WHIZZING, WHIZZES to move with a buzzing or hissing sound
WHIZBANG	*n* pl. -S a type of explosive shell
WHIZZ	*v* -ED, -ING, -ES to whiz
WHIZZED	past tense of whiz
WHIZZER	*n* pl. -S one that whizzes
WHIZZES	present 3d person sing. of whiz
WHIZZING	present participle of whiz
WHO	*pron* what or which person or persons
WHOA	*interj* — used to command an animal to stop
WHODUNIT	*n* pl. -S a mystery story
WHOEVER	*pron* whatever person
WHOLE	*n* pl. -S all the parts or elements entering into and making up a thing
WHOLISM	*n* pl. -S holism
WHOLLY	*adv* totally
WHOM	*pron* the objective case of who
WHOMEVER	*pron* the objective case of whoever
WHOMP	*v* -ED, -ING, -S to defeat decisively
WHOMSO	*pron* the objective case of whoso
WHOOF	*v* -ED, -ING, -S to make a deep snorting sound
WHOOP	*v* -ED, -ING, -S to utter loud cries
WHOOPEE	*n* pl. -S boisterous fun
WHOOPER	*n* pl. -S one that whoops
WHOOPLA	*n* pl. -S a noisy commotion
WHOOSH	*v* -ED, -ING, -ES to move with a hissing sound
WHOOSIS	*n* pl. -SISES an object or person whose name is not known

WHOP	*v* WHOPPED, WHOPPING, WHOPS to strike forcibly
WHOPPER	*n* pl. -S something unusually large
WHORE	*v* WHORED, WHORING, WHORES to consort with prostitutes
WHOREDOM	*n* pl. -S prostitution
WHORESON	*n* pl. -S a bastard
WHORING	present participle of whore
WHORISH	*adj* lewd
WHORL	*n* pl. -S a circular arrangement of similar parts **WHORLED** *adj*
WHORT	*n* pl. -S an edible berry
WHORTLE	*n* pl. -S whort
WHOSE	*pron* the possessive case of who
WHOSEVER	*pron* the possessive case of whoever
WHOSIS	*n* pl. -SISES whoosis
WHOSO	*pron* whoever
WHUMP	*v* -ED, -ING, -S to thump
WHY	*n* pl. WHYS the reason or cause of something
WHYDAH	*n* pl. -S an African bird
WICH	*n* pl. -ES wych
WICK	*n* pl. -S a bundle of loosely twisted fibers in a candle or oil lamp
WICKAPE	*n* pl. -S wicopy
WICKED	*adj* -EDER, -EDEST evil **WICKEDLY** *adv*
WICKER	*n* pl. -S a slender, pliant twig or branch
WICKET	*n* pl. -S a small door or gate
WICKING	*n* pl. -S material for wicks
WICKIUP	*n* pl. -S an American Indian hut
WICKYUP	*n* pl. -S wickiup
WICOPY	*n* pl. -PIES a flowering shrub
WIDDER	*n* pl. -S a widow
WIDDIE	*n* pl. -S widdy
WIDDLE	*v* -DLED, -DLING, -DLES to wriggle
WIDDY	*n* pl. -DIES a hangman's noose
WIDE	*adj* WIDER, WIDEST having great extent from side to side **WIDELY** *adv*
WIDE	*n* pl. -S a type of bowled ball in cricket
WIDEBAND	*adj* operating over a wide band of frequencies
WIDEN	*v* -ED, -ING, -S to make wide or wider
WIDENER	*n* pl. -S one that widens
WIDENESS	*n* pl. -ES the state of being wide
WIDEOUT	*n* pl. -S a receiver in football
WIDER	comparative of wide
WIDEST	superlative of wide
WIDGEON	*n* pl. -S a river duck
WIDGET	*n* pl. -S a gadget
WIDISH	*adj* somewhat wide
WIDOW	*v* -ED, -ING, -S to deprive of a husband
WIDOWER	*n* pl. -S a man whose wife has died and who has not remarried
WIDTH	*n* pl. -S extent from side to side
WIDTHWAY	*adv* from side to side
WIELD	*v* -ED, -ING, -S to handle or use effectively
WIELDER	*n* pl. -S one that wields
WIELDY	*adj* WIELDIER, WIELDIEST easily wielded
WIENER	*n* pl. -S a frankfurter
WIENIE	*n* pl. -S a wiener
WIFE	*n* pl. WIVES a woman married to a man
WIFE	*v* WIFED, WIFING, WIFES to wive
WIFEDOM	*n* pl. -S the status or function of a wife
WIFEHOOD	*n* pl. -S the state of being a wife
WIFELESS	*adj* having no wife
WIFELIKE	*adj* wifely
WIFELY	*adj* -LIER, -LIEST of or befitting a wife
WIFING	present participle of wife
WIFTY	*adj* -TIER, -TIEST ditsy
WIG	*v* WIGGED, WIGGING, WIGS to provide with a wig (an artificial covering of hair for the head)
WIGAN	*n* pl. -S a stiff fabric
WIGEON	*n* pl. -S widgeon
WIGGED	past tense of wig
WIGGERY	*n* pl. -GERIES a wig
WIGGIER	comparative of wiggy
WIGGIEST	superlative of wiggy
WIGGING	*n* pl. -S a scolding

WIGGLE   *v* -GLED, -GLING, -GLES to move with short, quick movements from side to side

WIGGLER   *n* pl. -S one that wiggles

WIGGLY   *adj* -GLIER, -GLIEST tending to wiggle

WIGGY   *adj* -GIER, -GIEST crazy

WIGHT   *n* pl. -S a living being

WIGLESS   *adj* having no wig

WIGLET   *n* pl. -S a small wig

WIGLIKE   *adj* resembling a wig

WIGMAKER   *n* pl. -S one that makes wigs

WIGWAG   *v* -WAGGED, -WAGGING, -WAGS to move back and forth

WIGWAM   *n* pl. -S an American Indian dwelling

WIKIUP   *n* pl. -S wickiup

WILCO   *interj* — used to indicate that a message received will be complied with

WILD   *adj* WILDER, WILDEST living in a natural state

WILD   *n* pl. -S an uninhabited or uncultivated area

WILDCAT   *v* -CATTED, -CATTING, -CATS to search for oil in an area of doubtful productivity

WILDER   *v* -ED, -ING, -S to bewilder

WILDFIRE   *n* pl. -S a raging, destructive fire

WILDFOWL   *n* pl. -S a wild game bird

WILDING   *n* pl. -S a wild plant or animal

WILDISH   *adj* somewhat wild

WILDLAND   *n* pl. -S uncultivated land

WILDLIFE   *n* pl. WILDLIFE wild animals and vegetation

WILDLING   *n* pl. -S a wilding

WILDLY   *adv* in a wild manner

WILDNESS   *n* pl. -ES the state of being wild

WILDWOOD   *n* pl. -S natural forest land

WILE   *v* WILED, WILING, WILES to entice

WILFUL   *adj* willful **WILFULLY** *adv*

WILIER   comparative of wily

WILIEST   superlative of wily

WILILY   *adv* in a wily manner

WILINESS   *n* pl. -ES the quality of being wily

WILING   present participle of wile

WILL   *v* -ED, -ING, -S to decide upon **WILLABLE** *adj*

WILL   *v* past sing. 2d person WOULD, WOULDEST, or WOULDST — used as an auxiliary followed by a simple infinitive to express futurity, inclination, likelihood, or requirement

WILLER   *n* pl. -S one that wills

WILLET   *n* pl. -S a shore bird

WILLFUL   *adj* bent on having one's own way

WILLIED   past tense of willy

WILLIES   present 3d person sing. of willy

WILLING   *adj* -INGER, -INGEST inclined or favorably disposed in mind

WILLIWAU   *n* pl. -S williwaw

WILLIWAW   *n* pl. -S a violent gust of cold wind

WILLOW   *v* -ED, -ING, -S to clean textile fibers with a certain machine

WILLOWER   *n* pl. -S one that willows

WILLOWY   *adj* -LOWIER, -LOWIEST pliant

WILLY   *v* -LIED, -LYING, -LIES to willow

WILLYARD   *adj* willful

WILLYART   *adj* willyard

WILLYWAW   *n* pl. -S williwaw

WILT   *v* -ED, -ING, -S to become limp

WILY   *adj* WILIER, WILIEST crafty

WIMBLE   *v* -BLED, -BLING, -BLES to bore with a hand tool

WIMP   *n* pl. -S a weak or ineffectual person

WIMPISH   *adj* wimpy

WIMPLE   *v* -PLED, -PLING, -PLES to pleat

WIMPY   *adj* WIMPIER, WIMPIEST weak, ineffectual

WIN   *v* WON or WAN, WINNING, WINS to be victorious

WIN   *v* WINNED, WINNING, WINS to winnow

WINCE   *v* WINCED, WINCING, WINCES to flinch

WINCER   *n* pl. -S one that winces

WINCEY   *n* pl. -CEYS a type of fabric

WINCH   *v* -ED, -ING, -ES to raise with a winch (a hoisting machine)

WINCHER   *n* pl. -S one that winches

WINCING   present participle of wince

WIND	*v* WOUND or WINDED, WINDING, WINDS to pass around an object or fixed center **WINDABLE** *adj*
WINDAGE	*n* pl. -S the effect of the wind (air in natural motion) on a projectile
WINDBAG	*n* pl. -S a talkative person
WINDBURN	*v* -BURNED or -BURNT, -BURNING, -BURNS to be affected with skin irritation caused by exposure to the wind
WINDER	*n* pl. -S one that winds
WINDFALL	*n* pl. -S a sudden and unexpected gain
WINDFLAW	*n* pl. -S a gust of wind
WINDGALL	*n* pl. -S a swelling on a horse's leg
WINDIER	comparative of windy
WINDIEST	superlative of windy
WINDIGO	*n* pl. -GOS an evil demon in Algonquian mythology
WINDILY	*adv* in a windy manner
WINDING	*n* pl. -S material wound about an object
WINDLASS	*v* -ED, -ING, -ES to raise with a windlass (a hoisting machine)
WINDLE	*v* -DLED, -DLING, -DLES to wind
WINDLESS	*adj* being without wind
WINDLING	*n* pl. -S a bundle of straw
WINDMILL	*v* -ED, -ING, -S to rotate solely under the force of a passing airstream
WINDOW	*v* -ED, -ING, -S to provide with a window (an opening in a wall to admit light and air)
WINDPIPE	*n* pl. -S the trachea
WINDROW	*v* -ED, -ING, -S to arrange in long rows, as hay or grain
WINDSOCK	*n* pl. -S a device used to indicate wind direction
WINDSURF	*v* -ED, -ING, -S to sail on a sailboard
WINDUP	*n* pl. -S a conclusion
WINDWARD	*n* pl. -S the direction from which the wind blows
WINDWAY	*n* pl. -WAYS a passage for air
WINDY	*adj* WINDIER, WINDIEST marked by strong wind
WINE	*v* WINED, WINING, WINES to provide with wine (the fermented juice of the grape)
WINELESS	*adj* having no wine
WINERY	*n* pl. -ERIES an establishment for making wine
WINESHOP	*n* pl. -S a shop where wine is sold
WINESKIN	*n* pl. -S a goatskin bag for holding wine
WINESOP	*n* pl. -S a food sopped in wine
WINEY	*adj* WINIER, WINIEST winy
WING	*v* -ED, -ING, -S to travel by means of wings (organs of flight)
WINGBACK	*n* pl. -S a certain player in football
WINGBOW	*n* pl. -S a mark on the wing of a domestic fowl
WINGDING	*n* pl. -S a lively party
WINGEDLY	*adv* swiftly
WINGER	*n* pl. -S a certain player in soccer
WINGIER	comparative of wingy
WINGIEST	superlative of wingy
WINGLESS	*adj* having no wings
WINGLET	*n* pl. -S a small wing
WINGLIKE	*adj* resembling a wing
WINGMAN	*n* pl. -MEN a pilot behind the leader of a flying formation
WINGOVER	*n* pl. -S a flight maneuver
WINGSPAN	*n* pl. -S the distance from the tip of one of a pair of wings to that of the other
WINGTIP	*n* pl. -S a type of man's shoe
WINGY	*adj* WINGIER, WINGIEST swift
WINIER	comparative of winey and winy
WINIEST	superlative of winey and winy
WINING	present participle of wine
WINISH	*adj* winy
WINK	*v* -ED, -ING, -S to close and open one eye quickly
WINKER	*n* pl. -S one that winks
WINKLE	*v* -KLED, -KLING, -KLES to displace, extract, or evict from a position
WINLESS	*adj* having no wins
WINNABLE	*adj* able to be won
WINNED	past tense of win (to winnow)
WINNER	*n* pl. -S one that wins
WINNING	*n* pl. -S money won in a game or competition
WINNOCK	*n* pl. -S a window
WINNOW	*v* -ED, -ING, -S to free grain from impurities

WINNOWER	*n* pl. -S one that winnows
WINO	*n* pl. WINOES or WINOS one who is habitually drunk on wine
WINSOME	*adj* -SOMER, -SOMEST charming
WINTER	*v* -ED, -ING, -S to pass the winter (the coldest season of the year)
WINTERER	*n* pl. -S one that winters
WINTERLY	*adj* wintry
WINTERY	*adj* -TERIER, -TERIEST wintry
WINTLE	*v* -TLED, -TLING, -TLES to stagger
WINTRY	*adj* -TRIER, -TRIEST characteristic of winter **WINTRILY** *adv*
WINY	*adj* WINIER, WINIEST having the taste or qualities of wine
WINZE	*n* pl. -S a steeply inclined mine shaft
WIPE	*v* WIPED, WIPING, WIPES to rub lightly in order to clean or dry
WIPEOUT	*n* pl. -S a fall from a surfboard
WIPER	*n* pl. -S one that wipes
WIPING	present participle of wipe
WIRE	*v* WIRED, WIRING, WIRES to fasten with wire (a slender rod, strand, or thread of ductile metal) **WIRABLE** *adj*
WIREDRAW	*v* -DREW, -DRAWN, -DRAWING, -DRAWS to draw into wire
WIREHAIR	*n* pl. -S a dog having a wiry coat
WIRELESS	*v* -ED, -ING, -ES to radio
WIRELIKE	*adj* resembling wire
WIREMAN	*n* pl. -MEN one who makes or works with wire
WIRER	*n* pl. -S one that wires
WIRETAP	*v* -TAPPED, -TAPPING, -TAPS to intercept messages by means of a concealed monitoring device
WIREWAY	*n* pl. -WAYS a tube for protecting electric wires
WIREWORK	*n* pl. -S an article made of wire
WIREWORM	*n* pl. -S a wirelike worm
WIRIER	comparative of wiry
WIRIEST	superlative of wiry
WIRILY	*adv* in a wiry manner
WIRINESS	*n* pl. -ES the quality of being wiry
WIRING	*n* pl. -S a system of electric wires
WIRRA	*interj* — used to express sorrow

WIRY	*adj* WIRIER, WIRIEST resembling wire
WIS	*v* past tense WIST to know — WIS and WIST are the only accepted forms of this verb; it cannot be conjugated further
WISDOM	*n* pl. -S the power of true and right discernment
WISE	*v* WISED, WISING, WISES to become aware or informed
WISE	*adj* WISER, WISEST having wisdom
WISEACRE	*n* pl. -S a pretentiously wise person
WISEASS	*n* pl. -ES a wiseacre
WISED	past tense of wise
WISELY	*adv* -LIER, -LIEST in a wise manner
WISENESS	*n* pl. -ES wisdom
WISENT	*n* pl. -S a European bison
WISER	comparative of wise
WISEST	superlative of wise
WISH	*v* -ED, -ING, -ES to feel an impulse toward attainment or possession of something
WISHA	*interj* — used to express surprise
WISHBONE	*n* pl. -S a forked bone in front of a bird's breastbone
WISHER	*n* pl. -S one that wishes
WISHFUL	*adj* desirous
WISHLESS	*adj* not wishful
WISING	present participle of wise
WISP	*v* -ED, -ING, -S to twist into a wisp (a small bunch or bundle)
WISPIER	comparative of wispy
WISPIEST	superlative of wispy
WISPILY	*adv* in a wispy manner
WISPISH	*adj* wispy
WISPLIKE	*adj* wispy
WISPY	*adj* WISPIER, WISPIEST resembling a wisp
WISS	*v* -ED, -ING, -ES to wish
WIST	*v* -ED, -ING, -S to know
WISTARIA	*n* pl. -S wisteria
WISTERIA	*n* pl. -S a flowering shrub
WISTFUL	*adj* yearning
WIT	*n* pl. -S intelligence

WIT	v WIST, WITING or WITTING, present sing. 1st person WOT, 2d WOST, 3d WOT, present pl. WITE to know	**WITTY**	adj -TIER, -TIEST humorously clever
WITAN	n/pl the members of a national council in Anglo-Saxon England	**WIVE**	v WIVED, WIVING, WIVES to marry a woman
WITCH	v -ED, -ING, -ES to bewitch	**WIVER**	n pl. -S wivern
WITCHERY	n pl. -ERIES sorcery	**WIVERN**	n pl. -S a two-legged dragon
WITCHING	n pl. -S sorcery	**WIVES**	pl. of wife
WITCHY	adj WITCHIER, WITCHIEST malicious	**WIVING**	present participle of wive
		WIZ	n pl. -ES a very clever or skillful person
WITE	v WITED, WITING, WITES to blame	**WIZARD**	n pl. -S a sorcerer **WIZARDLY** adj
WITH	prep in the company of	**WIZARDRY**	n pl. -RIES sorcery
WITHAL	adv in addition	**WIZEN**	v -ED, -ING, -S to shrivel
WITHDRAW	v -DREW, -DRAWN, -DRAWING, -DRAWS to move back or away	**WIZZEN**	n pl. -S weasand
		WO	n pl. WOS woe
WITHE	v WITHED, WITHING, WITHES to bind with flexible twigs	**WOAD**	n pl. -S a blue dye **WOADED** adj
WITHER	v -ED, -ING, -S to dry up and wilt	**WOADWAX**	n pl. -ES an ornamental shrub
WITHERER	n pl. -S one that withers	**WOALD**	n pl. -S a yellow pigment
WITHHOLD	v -HELD, -HOLDING, -HOLDS to hold back	**WOBBLE**	v -BLED, -BLING, -BLES to move unsteadily
WITHIER	comparative of withy	**WOBBLER**	n pl. -S one that wobbles
WITHIES	pl. of withy	**WOBBLY**	adj -BLIER, -BLIEST unsteady
WITHIEST	superlative of withy	**WOBBLY**	n pl. -BLIES a member of the Industrial Workers of the World
WITHIN	n pl. -S an interior place or area	**WOBEGONE**	adj affected with woe
WITHING	present participle of withe	**WODGE**	n pl. -S a chunk of something
WITHOUT	n pl. -S an exterior place or area	**WOE**	n pl. -S tremendous grief
WITHY	n pl. WITHIES a flexible twig	**WOEFUL**	adj -FULLER, -FULLEST full of woe **WOEFULLY** adv
WITHY	adj WITHIER, WITHIEST flexible and tough	**WOENESS**	n pl. -ES sadness
WITING	present participle of wit and wite	**WOESOME**	adj woeful
WITLESS	adj lacking intelligence	**WOFUL**	adj woeful **WOFULLY** adv
WITLING	n pl. -S one who considers himself witty	**WOK**	n pl. -S a cooking utensil
		WOKE	a past tense of wake
WITLOOF	n pl. -S chicory	**WOKEN**	a past participle of wake
WITNESS	v -ED, -ING, -ES to see or know by personal experience	**WOLD**	n pl. -S an elevated tract of open land
WITNEY	n pl. -NEYS a heavy woolen fabric	**WOLF**	n pl. WOLVES a carnivorous mammal
WITTED	adj having intelligence	**WOLF**	v -ED, -ING, -S to devour voraciously
WITTIER	comparative of witty		
WITTIEST	superlative of witty	**WOLFER**	n pl. -S one who hunts wolves
WITTILY	adv in a witty manner	**WOLFFISH**	n pl. -ES a marine fish
WITTING	n pl. -S knowledge	**WOLFISH**	adj wolflike
WITTOL	n pl. -S a man who tolerates his wife's infidelity	**WOLFLIKE**	adj resembling a wolf
		WOLFRAM	n pl. -S tungsten

WOLVER	*n* pl. -S wolfer
WOLVES	pl. of wolf
WOMAN	*n* pl. WOMEN an adult human female
WOMAN	*v* -ED, -ING, -S to play the part of a woman
WOMANISE	*v* -ISED, -ISING, -ISES to womanize
WOMANISH	*adj* characteristic of a woman
WOMANIZE	*v* -IZED, -IZING, -IZES to make effeminate
WOMANLY	*adj* -LIER, -LIEST having the qualities of a woman
WOMB	*n* pl. -S the uterus **WOMBED** *adj*
WOMBAT	*n* pl. -S a nocturnal mammal
WOMBY	*adj* WOMBIER, WOMBIEST hollow
WOMEN	pl. of woman
WOMERA	*n* pl. -S a device used to propel spears
WOMMERA	*n* pl. -S womera
WON	*v* WONNED, WONNING, WONS to dwell
WONDER	*v* -ED, -ING, -S to have a feeling of curiosity or doubt
WONDERER	*n* pl. -S one that wonders
WONDROUS	*adj* marvelous
WONK	*n* pl. -S an overly studious student
WONKY	*adj* -KIER, -KIEST unsteady
WONNED	past tense of won
WONNER	*n* pl. -S a prodigy
WONNING	present participle of won
WONT	*v* -ED, -ING, -S to make accustomed to
WONTEDLY	*adv* in a usual manner
WONTON	*n* pl. -S a pork-filled dumpling used in Chinese cooking
WOO	*v* -ED, -ING, -S to seek the affection of
WOOD	*v* -ED, -ING, -S to furnish with wood (the hard, fibrous substance beneath the bark of a tree or shrub)
WOODBIN	*n* pl. -S a bin for holding firewood
WOODBIND	*n* pl. -S woodbine
WOODBINE	*n* pl. -S a European shrub
WOODBOX	*n* pl. -ES a woodbin
WOODCHAT	*n* pl. -S a European shrike

WOODCOCK	*n* pl. -S a game bird
WOODCUT	*n* pl. -S an engraved block of wood
WOODEN	*adj* -ENER, -ENEST resembling wood in stiffness **WOODENLY** *adv*
WOODHEN	*n* pl. -S the weka
WOODIE	*n* pl. -S woody
WOODIER	comparative of woody
WOODIES	pl. of woody
WOODIEST	superlative of woody
WOODLAND	*n* pl. -S land covered with trees
WOODLARK	*n* pl. -S a songbird
WOODLESS	*adj* having no wood
WOODLORE	*n* pl. -S knowledge of the forest
WOODLOT	*n* pl. -S an area restricted to the growing of forest trees
WOODMAN	*n* pl. -MEN woodsman
WOODNOTE	*n* pl. -S a song or call of a forest bird
WOODPILE	*n* pl. -S a pile of wood
WOODRUFF	*n* pl. -S an aromatic herb
WOODSHED	*v* -SHEDDED, -SHEDDING, -SHEDS to practice on a musical instrument
WOODSIA	*n* pl. -S a small fern
WOODSMAN	*n* pl. -MEN one who works or lives in the forest
WOODSY	*adj* WOODSIER, WOODSIEST suggestive of a forest
WOODWAX	*n* pl. -ES woadwax
WOODWIND	*n* pl. -S a musical wind instrument
WOODWORK	*n* pl. -S work made of wood
WOODWORM	*n* pl. -S a wood-boring worm
WOODY	*adj* WOODIER, WOODIEST containing or resembling wood
WOODY	*n* pl. WOODIES a wood-paneled station wagon
WOOER	*n* pl. -S one that woos
WOOF	*v* -ED, -ING, -S to utter a gruff barking sound
WOOFER	*n* pl. -S a loudspeaker designed to reproduce low-pitched sounds
WOOINGLY	*adv* attractively
WOOL	*n* pl. -S the dense, soft hair forming the coat of certain mammals
WOOLED	*adj* having wool of a specified kind

WOOLEN *n* pl. -S a fabric made of wool

WOOLER *n* pl. -S a domestic animal raised for its wool

WOOLFELL *n* pl. -S woolskin

WOOLHAT *n* pl. -S one who works a small farm

WOOLIE *n* pl. -S a woolly

WOOLIER comparative of wooly

WOOLIES pl. of wooly

WOOLIEST superlative of wooly

WOOLLED *adj* wooled

WOOLLEN *n* pl. -S woolen

WOOLLIER comparative of woolly

WOOLLIES pl. of woolly

WOOLLIKE *adj* resembling wool

WOOLLY *adj* -LIER, -LIEST consisting of or resembling wool **WOOLLILY** *adv*

WOOLLY *n* pl. -LIES a garment made of wool

WOOLMAN *n* pl. -MEN a dealer in wool

WOOLPACK *n* pl. -S a bag for packing a bale of wool

WOOLSACK *n* pl. -S a sack of wool

WOOLSHED *n* pl. -S a building in which sheep are sheared

WOOLSKIN *n* pl. -S a sheepskin with the wool still on it

WOOLWORK *n* pl. -S needlework

WOOLY *adj* WOOLIER, WOOLIEST woolly

WOOLY *n* pl. WOOLIES a woolly

WOOMERA *n* pl. -S womera

WOOPS *v* -ED, -ING, -ES to vomit

WOORALI *n* pl. -S curare

WOORARI *n* pl. -S curare

WOOSH *v* -ED, -ING, -ES to whoosh

WOOZY *adj* -ZIER, -ZIEST dazed **WOOZILY** *adv*

WORD *v* -ED, -ING, -S to express in words (speech sounds that communicate meaning)

WORDAGE *n* pl. -S the number of words used

WORDBOOK *n* pl. -S a dictionary

WORDIER comparative of wordy

WORDIEST superlative of wordy

WORDILY *adv* in a wordy manner

WORDING *n* pl. -S the act or style of expressing in words

WORDLESS *adj* being without words

WORDPLAY *n* pl. -PLAYS a witty exchange of words

WORDY *adj* WORDIER, WORDIEST using many or too many words

WORE past tense of wear

WORK *v* WORKED or WROUGHT, WORKING, WORKS to exert one's powers of body or mind for some purpose

WORKABLE *adj* capable of being done

WORKADAY *adj* everyday

WORKBAG *n* pl. -S a bag for holding work instruments and materials

WORKBOAT *n* pl. -S a boat used for commercial purposes

WORKBOOK *n* pl. -S an exercise book for a student

WORKBOX *n* pl. -ES a box for holding work instruments and materials

WORKDAY *n* pl. -DAYS a day on which work is done

WORKER *n* pl. -S one that works

WORKFARE *n* pl. -S a welfare program that requires recipients to perform public-service work

WORKFOLK *n/pl* manual laborers

WORKING *n* pl. -S a mining excavation

WORKLESS *adj* unemployed

WORKLOAD *n* pl. -S the amount of work assigned to an employee

WORKMAN *n* pl. -MEN a male worker

WORKMATE *n* pl. -S a fellow worker

WORKOUT *n* pl. -S a period of physical exercise

WORKROOM *n* pl. -S a room in which work is done

WORKSHOP *n* pl. -S a workroom

WORKUP *n* pl. -S an intensive diagnostic study

WORKWEEK *n* pl. -S the number of hours worked in a week

WORLD *n* pl. -S the earth and all its inhabitants

WORLDLY *adj* -LIER, -LIEST pertaining to the world

WORM *v* -ED, -ING, -S to rid of worms (small, limbless invertebrates)

WORMER *n* pl. -S one that worms

WORMHOLE *n* pl. -S a hole made by a burrowing worm

WORMIER comparative of wormy

WORMIEST superlative of wormy

WORMIL *n* pl. -S a lump in the skin of an animal's back

WORMISH *adj* wormlike

WORMLIKE *adj* resembling a worm

WORMROOT *n* pl. -S pinkroot

WORMSEED *n* pl. -S a tropical plant

WORMWOOD *n* pl. -S a European herb

WORMY *adj* WORMIER, WORMIEST infested with worms

WORN *adj* affected by wear or use

WORNNESS *n* pl. -ES the state of being worn

WORRIED past tense of worry

WORRIER *n* pl. -S one that worries

WORRIT *v* -ED, -ING, -S to worry

WORRY *v* -RIED, -RYING, -RIES to feel anxious and uneasy about something

WORSE *n* pl. -S something that is worse (bad in a greater degree)

WORSEN *v* -ED, -ING, -S to make or become worse

WORSER *adj* worse

WORSET *n* pl. -S worsted

WORSHIP *v* -SHIPED, -SHIPING, -SHIPS or -SHIPPED, -SHIPPING, -SHIPS to honor and love as a divine being

WORST *v* -ED, -ING, -S to defeat

WORSTED *n* pl. -S a woolen yarn

WORT *n* pl. -S a plant, herb, or vegetable

WORTH *v* -ED, -ING, -S to befall

WORTHFUL *adj* worthy

WORTHY *adj* -THIER, -THIEST having value or merit **WORTHILY** *adv*

WORTHY *n* pl. -THIES a worthy person

WOST a present 2d person sing. of wit

WOT *v* WOTTED, WOTTING, WOTS to know

WOULD past tense of will

WOULDEST a 2d person sing. past tense of will

WOULDST a 2d person sing. past tense of will

WOUND *v* -ED, -ING, -S to inflict an injury upon

WOVE a past tense of weave

WOVEN *n* pl. -S a woven fabric

WOW *v* -ED, -ING, -S to excite to enthusiastic approval

WOWSER *n* pl. -S a puritanical person

WRACK *v* -ED, -ING, -S to wreck

WRACKFUL *adj* destructive

WRAITH *n* pl. -S a ghost

WRANG *n* pl. -S a wrong

WRANGLE *v* -GLED, -GLING, -GLES to argue noisily

WRANGLER *n* pl. -S one that wrangles

WRAP *v* WRAPPED or WRAPT, WRAPPING, WRAPS to enclose in something wound or folded about

WRAPPER *n* pl. -S one that wraps

WRAPPING *n* pl. -S the material in which something is wrapped

WRAPT a past tense of wrap

WRASSE *n* pl. -S a marine fish

WRASSLE *v* -SLED, -SLING, -SLES to wrastle

WRASTLE *v* -TLED, -TLING, -TLES to wrestle

WRATH *v* -ED, -ING, -S to make wrathful

WRATHFUL *adj* extremely angry

WRATHY *adj* WRATHIER, WRATHIEST wrathful **WRATHILY** *adv*

WREAK *v* -ED, -ING, -S to inflict

WREAKER *n* pl. -S one that wreaks

WREATH *n* pl. -S a band of flowers **WREATHY** *adj*

WREATHE *v* WREATHED, WREATHEN, WREATHING, WREATHES to shape into a wreath

WRECK *v* -ED, -ING, -S to cause the ruin of

WRECKAGE *n* pl. -S the act of wrecking

WRECKER *n* pl. -S one that wrecks

WRECKFUL *adj* destructive

WRECKING *n* pl. -S the occupation of salvaging wrecked objects

WREN *n* pl. -S a small songbird

WRENCH *v* -ED, -ING, -ES to twist suddenly and forcibly

WREST *v* -ED, -ING, -S to take away by force

WRESTER	*n* pl. -S one that wrests
WRESTLE	*v* -TLED, -TLING, -TLES to engage in a type of hand-to-hand contest
WRESTLER	*n* pl. -S one that wrestles
WRETCH	*n* pl. -ES a wretched person
WRETCHED	*adj* -EDER, -EDEST extremely unhappy
WRICK	*v* -ED, -ING, -S to wrench
WRIED	past tense of wry
WRIER	a comparative of wry
WRIES	present 3d person sing. of wry
WRIEST	a superlative of wry
WRIGGLE	*v* -GLED, -GLING, -GLES to turn or twist in a sinuous manner
WRIGGLER	*n* pl. -S one that wriggles
WRIGGLY	*adj* -GLIER, -GLIEST wriggling
WRIGHT	*n* pl. -S one who constructs or creates
WRING	*v* WRUNG or WRINGED, WRINGING, WRINGS to twist so as to compress
WRINGER	*n* pl. -S one that wrings
WRINKLE	*v* -KLED, -KLING, -KLES to make wrinkles (small ridges or furrows) in
WRINKLY	*adj* -KLIER, -KLIEST having wrinkles
WRIST	*n* pl. -S the junction between the hand and forearm
WRISTLET	*n* pl. -S a band worn around the wrist
WRISTY	*adj* WRISTIER, WRISTIEST using much wrist action
WRIT	*n* pl. -S a written legal order
WRITE	*v* WROTE, WRITTEN, WRITING, WRITES to form characters or symbols on a surface with an instrument **WRITABLE** *adj*
WRITER	*n* pl. -S one that writes
WRITERLY	*adj* characteristic of a writer
WRITHE	*v* WRITHED, WRITHING, WRITHES to squirm or twist in pain
WRITHEN	*adj* twisted
WRITHER	*n* pl. -S one that writhes
WRITHING	present participle of writhe
WRITING	*n* pl. -S a written composition
WRITTEN	past participle of write
WRONG	*adj* WRONGER, WRONGEST not according to what is right, proper, or correct
WRONG	*v* -ED, -ING, -S to treat injuriously or unjustly
WRONGER	*n* pl. -S one that wrongs
WRONGFUL	*adj* wrong
WRONGLY	*adv* in a wrong manner
WROTE	past tense of write
WROTH	*adj* very angry
WROTHFUL	*adj* wroth
WROUGHT	a past tense of work
WRUNG	a past tense of wring
WRY	*adj* WRIER, WRIEST or WRYER, WRYEST contorted **WRYLY** *adv*
WRY	*v* WRIED, WRYING, WRIES to contort
WRYNECK	*n* pl. -S a European bird
WRYNESS	*n* pl. -ES the state of being wry
WUD	*adj* insane
WURST	*n* pl. -S sausage
WURZEL	*n* pl. -S a variety of beet
WUSS	*n* pl. -ES a wimp
WUSSY	*n* pl. -SIES a wuss
WUSSY	*adj* WUSSIER, WUSSIEST wimpy
WUTHER	*v* -ED, -ING, -S to blow with a dull roaring sound
WYCH	*n* pl. -ES a European elm
WYE	*n* pl. -S the letter Y
WYLE	*v* WYLED, WYLING, WYLES to beguile
WYN	*n* pl. -S wynn
WYND	*n* pl. -S a narrow street
WYNN	*n* pl. -S the rune for W
WYTE	*v* WYTED, WYTING, WYTES to wite
WYVERN	*n* pl. -S wivern

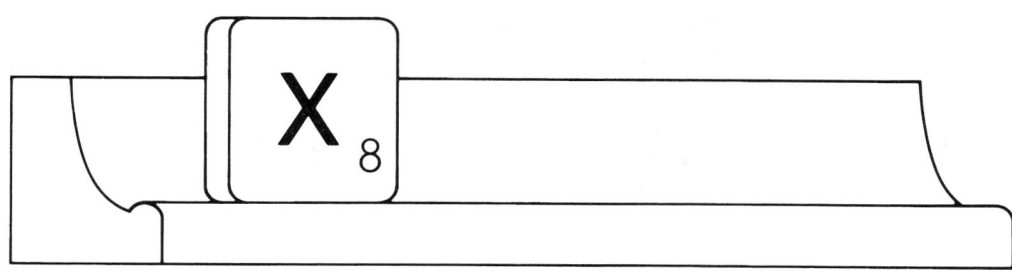

XANTHAN   *n* pl. -S a gum produced by bacterial fermentation

XANTHATE   *n* pl. -S a chemical salt

XANTHEIN   *n* pl. -S the water-soluble part of the coloring matter in yellow flowers

XANTHENE   *n* pl. -S a chemical compound

XANTHIC   *adj* tending to have a yellow color

XANTHIN   *n* pl. -S a yellow pigment

XANTHINE   *n* pl. -S a chemical compound

XANTHOMA   *n* pl. -MAS or -MATA a skin disease

XANTHONE   *n* pl. -S a chemical compound

XANTHOUS   *adj* yellow

XEBEC   *n* pl. -S a Mediterranean sailing vessel

XENIA   *n* pl. -S the effect of pollen on certain plant structures **XENIAL** *adj*

XENIC   *adj* pertaining to a type of culture medium

XENOGAMY   *n* pl. -MIES the transfer of pollen from one plant to another

XENOGENY   *n* pl. -NIES the supposed production of offspring totally different from the parent

XENOLITH   *n* pl. -S a rock fragment included in another rock

XENON   *n* pl. -S a gaseous element

XERARCH   *adj* developing in a dry area

XERIC   *adj* requiring only a small amount of moisture

XEROSERE   *n* pl. -S a dry-land sere

XEROSIS   *n* pl. -ROSES abnormal dryness of a body part or tissue **XEROTIC** *adj*

XEROX   *v* -ED, -ING, -ES to copy on a xerographic copier

XERUS   *n* pl. -ES an African ground squirrel

XI   *n* pl. -S a Greek letter

XIPHOID   *n* pl. -S a part of the sternum

XU   *n* pl. XU a monetary unit of Vietnam

XYLAN   *n* pl. -S a substance found in cell walls of plants

XYLEM   *n* pl. -S a complex plant tissue

XYLENE   *n* pl. -S a flammable hydrocarbon

XYLIDIN   *n* pl. -S xylidine

XYLIDINE   *n* pl. -S a chemical compound

XYLITOL   *n* pl. -S an alcohol

XYLOCARP   *n* pl. -S a hard, woody fruit

XYLOID   *adj* resembling wood

XYLOL   *n* pl. -S xylene

XYLOSE   *n* pl. -S a type of sugar

XYLOTOMY   *n* pl. -MIES the preparation of sections of wood for microscopic examination

XYLYL   *n* pl. -S a univalent radical

XYST   *n* pl. -S xystus

XYSTER   *n* pl. -S a surgical instrument for scraping bones

XYSTOS   *n* pl. -TOI xystus

XYSTUS   *n* pl. -TI a roofed area where athletes trained in ancient Greece

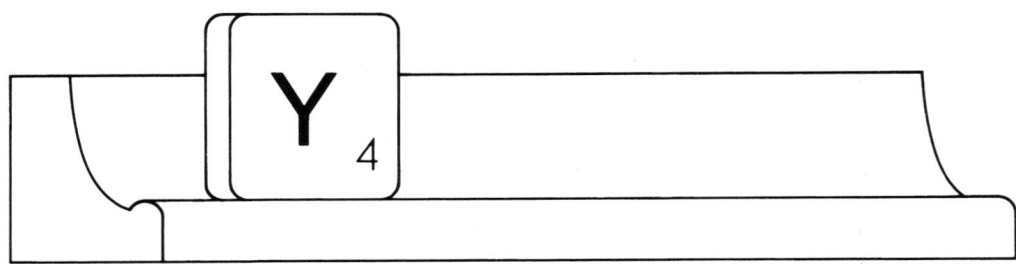

YA	*pron* you
YABBER	*v* -ED, -ING, -S to jabber
YACHT	*v* -ED, -ING, -S to sail in a yacht (a vessel used for pleasure cruising or racing)
YACHTER	*n* pl. -S one who sails a yacht
YACHTING	*n* pl. -S the sport of sailing in yachts
YACHTMAN	*n* pl. -MEN a yachter
YACK	*v* -ED, -ING, -S to yak
YAFF	*v* -ED, -ING, -S to bark
YAGER	*n* pl. -S jaeger
YAGI	*n* pl. -S a type of shortwave antenna
YAH	*interj* — used as an exclamation of disgust
YAHOO	*n* pl. -HOOS a coarse, uncouth person
YAHOOISM	*n* pl. -S coarse, uncouth behavior
YAHRZEIT	*n* pl. -S an anniversary of the death of a family member observed by Jews
YAIRD	*n* pl. -S a garden
YAK	*v* YAKKED, YAKKING, YAKS to chatter
YAKITORI	*n* pl. -S marinated chicken pieces on skewers
YAKKER	*n* pl. -S one that yaks
YALD	*adj* yauld
YAM	*n* pl. -S a plant having an edible root
YAMALKA	*n* pl. -S yarmulke
YAMEN	*n* pl. -S the residence of a Chinese public official
YAMMER	*v* -ED, -ING, -S to whine or complain peevishly
YAMMERER	*n* pl. -S one that yammers
YAMULKA	*n* pl. -S yarmulke
YAMUN	*n* pl. -S yamen
YANG	*n* pl. -S the masculine active principle in Chinese cosmology
YANK	*v* -ED, -ING, -S to pull suddenly
YANQUI	*n* pl. -S a United States citizen
YANTRA	*n* pl. -S a geometrical diagram used in meditation
YAP	*v* YAPPED, YAPPING, YAPS to bark shrilly
YAPOCK	*n* pl. -S an aquatic mammal
YAPOK	*n* pl. -S yapock
YAPON	*n* pl. -S yaupon
YAPPED	past tense of yap
YAPPER	*n* pl. -S one that yaps
YAPPING	present participle of yap
YAR	*adj* yare
YARD	*v* -ED, -ING, -S to put in a yard (a tract of ground adjacent to a building)
YARDAGE	*n* pl. -S the use of an enclosure for livestock at a railroad station
YARDARM	*n* pl. -S either end of a ship's spar
YARDBIRD	*n* pl. -S an army recruit
YARDLAND	*n* pl. -S an old English unit of land measure
YARDMAN	*n* pl. -MEN a man employed to do outdoor work
YARDWAND	*n* pl. -S a measuring stick
YARDWORK	*n* pl. -S the work of caring for a lawn
YARE	*adj* YARER, YAREST nimble **YARELY** *adv*
YARMELKE	*n* pl. -S yarmulke
YARMULKE	*n* pl. -S a skullcap worn by Jewish males
YARN	*v* -ED, -ING, -S to tell a long story
YARNER	*n* pl. -S one who yarns
YARROW	*n* pl. -S a perennial herb

YASHMAC	*n* pl. -S yashmak
YASHMAK	*n* pl. -S a veil worn by Muslim women
YASMAK	*n* pl. -S yashmak
YATAGAN	*n* pl. -S yataghan
YATAGHAN	*n* pl. -S a Turkish sword
YATTER	*v* -ED, -ING, -S to talk idly
YAUD	*n* pl. -S an old mare
YAULD	*adj* vigorous
YAUP	*v* -ED, -ING, -S to yawp
YAUPER	*n* pl. -S one that yaups
YAUPON	*n* pl. -S an evergreen shrub
YAUTIA	*n* pl. -S a tropical plant
YAW	*v* -ED, -ING, -S to deviate from an intended course
YAWL	*v* -ED, -ING, -S to yowl
YAWMETER	*n* pl. -S an instrument in an aircraft
YAWN	*v* -ED, -ING, -S to open the mouth wide with a deep inhalation of air
YAWNER	*n* pl. -S one that yawns
YAWP	*v* -ED, -ING, -S to utter a loud, harsh cry
YAWPER	*n* pl. -S one that yawps
YAWPING	*n* pl. -S a loud, harsh cry
YAY	*n* pl. YAYS yea
YCLEPED	*adj* yclept
YCLEPT	*adj* called; named
YE	*pron* you
YEA	*n* pl. -S an affirmative vote
YEAH	*adv* yes
YEALING	*n* pl. -S a person of the same age
YEAN	*v* -ED, -ING, -S to bear young
YEANLING	*n* pl. -S the young of a sheep or goat
YEAR	*n* pl. -S a period of time consisting of 365 or 366 days
YEARBOOK	*n* pl. -S a book published each year by a graduating class
YEAREND	*n* pl. -S the end of a year
YEARLIES	pl. of yearly
YEARLING	*n* pl. -S an animal past its first year and not yet two years old
YEARLONG	*adj* lasting through a year
YEARLY	*n* pl. -LIES a publication appearing once a year

YEARN	*v* -ED, -ING, -S to have a strong or deep desire
YEARNER	*n* pl. -S one that yearns
YEARNING	*n* pl. -S a strong or deep desire
YEASAYER	*n* pl. -S one that affirms something
YEAST	*v* -ED, -ING, -S to foam
YEASTY	*adj* YEASTIER, YEASTIEST foamy **YEASTILY** *adv*
YECCH	*n* pl. -S something disgusting
YECH	*n* pl. -S yecch
YECHY	*adj* disgusting
YEELIN	*n* pl. -S yealing
YEGG	*n* pl. -S a burglar
YEGGMAN	*n* pl. -MEN a yegg
YEH	*adv* yeah
YELD	*adj* not giving milk
YELK	*n* pl. -S yolk
YELL	*v* -ED, -ING, -S to cry out loudly
YELLER	*n* pl. -S one that yells
YELLOW	*adj* -LOWER, -LOWEST of a bright color like that of ripe lemons **YELLOWLY** *adv*
YELLOW	*v* -ED, -ING, -S to make or become yellow
YELLOWY	*adj* somewhat yellow
YELP	*v* -ED, -ING, -S to utter a sharp, shrill cry
YELPER	*n* pl. -S one that yelps
YEN	*v* YENNED, YENNING, YENS to yearn
YENTA	*n* pl. -S a gossipy woman
YENTE	*n* pl. -S yenta
YEOMAN	*n* pl. -MEN an independent farmer **YEOMANLY** *adj*
YEOMANRY	*n* pl. -RIES the collective body of yeomen
YEP	*adv* yes
YERBA	*n* pl. -S a South American beverage resembling tea
YERK	*v* -ED, -ING, -S to beat vigorously
YES	*v* YESSED, YESSING, YESSES or YESES to give an affirmative reply to
YESHIVA	*n* pl. -VAS, -VOT, or -VOTH an orthodox Jewish school
YESHIVAH	*n* pl. -S yeshiva
YESSED	past tense of yes

YESSES	a 3d person sing. of yes
YESSING	present participle of yes
YESTER	*adj* pertaining to yesterday
YESTERN	*adj* yester
YESTREEN	*n* pl. -S the previous evening
YET	*adv* up to now
YETI	*n* pl. -S the abominable snowman
YETT	*n* pl. -S a gate
YEUK	*v* -ED, -ING, -S to itch
YEUKY	*adj* itchy
YEW	*n* pl. -S an evergreen tree or shrub
YIELD	*v* -ED, -ING, -S to give up
YIELDER	*n* pl. -S one that yields
YIKES	*interj* — used to express fear or pain
YILL	*n* pl. -S ale
YIN	*n* pl. -S the feminine passive principle in Chinese cosmology
YINCE	*adv* once
YIP	*v* YIPPED, YIPPING, YIPS to yelp
YIPE	*interj* — used to express fear or surprise
YIPES	*interj* yipe
YIPPED	past tense of yip
YIPPEE	*interj* — used to express joy
YIPPIE	*n* pl. -S a politically radical hippie
YIPPING	present participle of yip
YIRD	*n* pl. -S earth
YIRR	*v* -ED, -ING, -S to snarl
YIRTH	*n* pl. -S yird
YLEM	*n* pl. -S hypothetical matter from which the elements are derived
YO	*interj* —used to call attention or to express affirmation
YOB	*n* pl. -S a hooligan
YOBBO	*n* pl. -BOS or -BOES a yob
YOCK	*v* -ED, -ING, -S to laugh boisterously
YOD	*n* pl. -S a Hebrew letter
YODEL	*v* -DELED, -DELING, -DELS or -DELLED, -DELLING, -DELS to sing with a fluctuating voice
YODELER	*n* pl. -S one that yodels
YODELLER	*n* pl. -S yodeler
YODELLING	a present participle of yodel
YODH	*n* pl. -S yod
YODLE	*v* -DLED, -DLING, -DLES to yodel
YODLER	*n* pl. -S yodeler
YOGA	*n* pl. -S a Hindu philosophy involving physical and mental disciplines
YOGEE	*n* pl. -S yogi
YOGH	*n* pl. -S a Middle English letter
YOGHOURT	*n* pl. -S yogurt
YOGHURT	*n* pl. -S yogurt
YOGI	*n* pl. -S a person who practices yoga
YOGIC	*adj* pertaining to yoga
YOGIN	*n* pl. -S yogi
YOGINI	*n* pl. -S a female yogi
YOGURT	*n* pl. -S a food made from milk
YOICKS	*interj* — used to encourage hunting hounds
YOK	*n* pl. -S a boisterous laugh
YOKE	*v* YOKED, YOKING, YOKES to fit with a yoke (a wooden frame for joining together draft animals)
YOKEL	*n* pl. -S a naive or gullible rustic
YOKELESS	*adj* having no yoke
YOKELISH	*adj* resembling a yokel
YOKEMATE	*n* pl. -S a companion in work
YOKING	present participle of yoke
YOKOZUNA	*n* pl. -S a champion sumo wrestler
YOLK	*n* pl. -S the yellow portion of an egg **YOLKED** *adj*
YOLKY	*adj* YOLKIER, YOLKIEST resembling a yolk
YOM	*n* pl. YOMIM day
YON	*adv* yonder
YOND	*adv* yonder
YONDER	*adv* over there
YONI	*n* pl. -S a symbol for the vulva in Hindu religion **YONIC** *adj*
YONKER	*n* pl. -S younker
YORE	*n* pl. -S time past
YOU	*pron* the 2d person sing. or pl. pronoun
YOUNG	*adj* YOUNGER, YOUNGEST being in the early period of life or growth
YOUNG	*n* pl. -S offspring
YOUNGER	*n* pl. -S an inferior in age

YOUNGISH	*adj* somewhat young
YOUNKER	*n* pl. -S a young gentleman
YOUPON	*n* pl. -S yaupon
YOUR	*adj* a possessive form of the pronoun you
YOURN	*pron* yours
YOURS	*pron* a possessive form of the pronoun you
YOURSELF	*pron* pl. -SELVES a form of the 2d person pronoun
YOUSE	*pron* you
YOUTH	*n* pl. -S a young person
YOUTHEN	*v* -ED, -ING, -S to make youthful
YOUTHFUL	*adj* young
YOW	*v* -ED, -ING, -S to yowl
YOWE	*n* pl. -S a ewe
YOWIE	*n* pl. -S a small ewe
YOWL	*v* -ED, -ING, -S to utter a loud, long, mournful cry
YOWLER	*n* pl. -S one that yowls
YPERITE	*n* pl. -S a poisonous gas
YTTERBIA	*n* pl. -S a chemical compound **YTTERBIC** *adj*
YTTRIA	*n* pl. -S a chemical compound

YTTRIUM	*n* pl. -S a metallic element **YTTRIC** *adj*
YUAN	*n* pl. -S a monetary unit of China
YUCA	*n* pl. -S yucca
YUCCA	*n* pl. -S a tropical plant
YUCCH	*interj* — used to express disgust
YUCH	*interj* yucch
YUCK	*v* -ED, -ING, -S to yuk
YUCKY	*adj* YUCKIER, YUCKIEST disgusting
YUGA	*n* pl. -S an age of time in Hinduism
YUK	*v* YUKKED, YUKKING, YUKS to laugh loudly
YULAN	*n* pl. -S a Chinese tree
YULE	*n* pl. -S Christmas time
YULETIDE	*n* pl. -S yule
YUM	*interj* — used to express pleasurable satisfaction
YUMMY	*adj* -MIER, -MIEST delicious
YUMMY	*n* pl. -MIES something delicious
YUP	*n* pl. -S a yuppie
YUPON	*n* pl. -S yaupon
YUPPIE	*n* pl. -S a young professional person working in a city
YURT	*n* pl. YURTA or YURTS a portable tent
YWIS	*adv* iwis

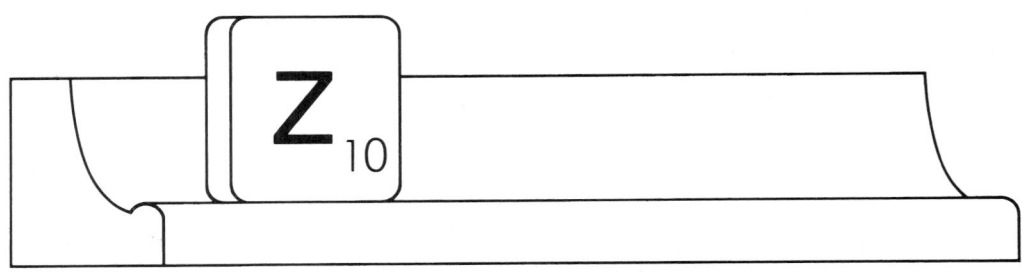

ZABAIONE   *n* pl. -S a dessert resembling custard

ZABAJONE   *n* pl. -S zabaione

ZACATON   *n* pl. -S a Mexican grass

ZADDICK   *n* pl. -DIKIM zaddik

ZADDIK   *n* pl. -DIKIM a virtuous person by Jewish religious standards

ZAFFAR   *n* pl. -S zaffer

ZAFFER   *n* pl. -S a blue ceramic coloring

ZAFFIR   *n* pl. -S zaffer

ZAFFRE   *n* pl. -S zaffer

ZAFTIG   *adj* full-bosomed

ZAG   *v* ZAGGED, ZAGGING, ZAGS to turn sharply

ZAIBATSU   *n* pl. ZAIBATSU a powerful family combine in Japan

ZAIKAI   *n* pl. -S the business community of Japan

ZAIRE   *n* pl. -S a monetary unit of Zaire

ZAMARRA   *n* pl. -S a sheepskin coat

ZAMARRO   *n* pl. -ROS zamarra

ZAMIA   *n* pl. -S a tropical plant

ZAMINDAR   *n* pl. -S a tax collector in precolonial India

ZANANA   *n* pl. -S zenana

ZANDER   *n* pl. -S a freshwater fish

ZANIER   comparative of zany

ZANIES   pl. of zany

ZANINESS   *n* pl. -ES the quality or state of being zany

ZANY   *adj* ZANIER, ZANIEST ludicrously comical **ZANILY** *adv*

ZANY   *n* pl. -NIES a zany person

ZANYISH   *adj* somewhat zany

ZANZA   *n* pl. -S an African musical instrument

ZAP   *v* ZAPPED, ZAPPING, ZAPS to kill or destroy instantaneously

ZAPATEO   *n* pl. -TEOS a Spanish dance

ZAPPER   *n* pl. -S a device that zaps

ZAPPY   *adj* -PIER, -PIEST zippy

ZAPTIAH   *n* pl. -S a Turkish policeman

ZAPTIEH   *n* pl. -S zaptiah

ZARATITE   *n* pl. -S a chemical compound

ZAREBA   *n* pl. -S an improvised stockade

ZAREEBA   *n* pl. -S zareba

ZARF   *n* pl. -S a metal holder for a coffee cup

ZARIBA   *n* pl. -S zareba

ZARZUELA   *n* pl. -S a Spanish operetta

ZASTRUGA   *n* pl. -GI sastruga

ZAX   *n* pl. -ES a tool for cutting roof slates

ZAYIN   *n* pl. -S a Hebrew letter

ZAZEN   *n* pl. -S meditation in Zen Buddhism

ZEAL   *n* pl. -S enthusiastic devotion

ZEALOT   *n* pl. -S one who is zealous

ZEALOTRY   *n* pl. -RIES excessive zeal

ZEALOUS   *adj* filled with zeal

ZEATIN   *n* pl. -S a chemical compound found in maize

ZEBEC   *n* pl. -S xebec

ZEBECK   *n* pl. -S xebec

ZEBRA   *n* pl. -S an African mammal that is related to the horse **ZEBRAIC** *adj*

ZEBRASS   *n* pl. -ES the offspring of a zebra and an ass

ZEBRINE   *adj* pertaining to a zebra

ZEBROID   *adj* zebrine

ZEBU   *n* pl. -S an Asian ox

ZECCHIN   *n* pl. -S zecchino

ZECCHINO   *n* pl. -NI or -NOS a former gold coin of Italy

ZECHIN	*n* pl. -S zecchino
ZED	*n* pl. -S the letter Z
ZEDOARY	*n* pl. -ARIES the medicinal root of a tropical plant
ZEE	*n* pl. -S the letter Z
ZEIN	*n* pl. -S a simple protein
ZEK	*n* pl. -S an inmate in a Soviet labor camp
ZELKOVA	*n* pl. -S a Japanese tree
ZEMINDAR	*n* pl. -S zamindar
ZEMSTVO	*n* pl. -VOS or -VA an elective council in czarist Russia
ZENAIDA	*n* pl. -S a wild dove
ZENANA	*n* pl. -S the section of a house in India reserved for women
ZENITH	*n* pl. -S the highest point **ZENITHAL** *adj*
ZEOLITE	*n* pl. -S a mineral **ZEOLITIC** *adj*
ZEPHYR	*n* pl. -S a gentle breeze
ZEPPELIN	*n* pl. -S a long, rigid airship
ZERK	*n* pl. -S a grease fitting
ZERO	*v* -ED, -ING, -ES or -S to aim at the exact center of a target
ZEROTH	*adj* being numbered zero in a series
ZEST	*v* -ED, -ING, -S to fill with zest (invigorating excitement)
ZESTER	*n* pl. -S a utensil for peeling citrus rind
ZESTFUL	*adj* full of zest
ZESTLESS	*adj* lacking zest
ZESTY	*adj* ZESTIER, ZESTIEST marked by zest
ZETA	*n* pl. -S a Greek letter
ZEUGMA	*n* pl. -S the use of a word to modify or govern two or more words, while applying to each in a different sense
ZIBELINE	*n* pl. -S a soft fabric
ZIBET	*n* pl. -S an Asian civet
ZIBETH	*n* pl. -S zibet
ZIG	*v* ZIGGED, ZIGGING, ZIGS to turn sharply
ZIGGURAT	*n* pl. -S an ancient Babylonian temple tower
ZIGZAG	*v* -ZAGGED, -ZAGGING, -ZAGS to proceed on a course marked by sharp turns
ZIKKURAT	*n* pl. -S ziggurat
ZIKURAT	*n* pl. -S ziggurat
ZILCH	*n* pl. -ES nothing
ZILL	*n* pl. -S one of a pair of finger cymbals
ZILLAH	*n* pl. -S an administrative district in India
ZILLION	*n* pl. -S an indeterminately large number
ZIN	*n* pl. -S a dry red wine
ZINC	*v* ZINCED, ZINCING, ZINCS or ZINCKED, ZINCKING, ZINCS to coat with zinc (a metallic element)
ZINCATE	*n* pl. -S a chemical salt
ZINCIC	*adj* pertaining to zinc
ZINCIFY	*v* -FIED, -FYING, -FIES to coat with zinc
ZINCITE	*n* pl. -S an ore of zinc
ZINCKED	a past tense of zinc
ZINCKING	a present participle of zinc
ZINCKY	*adj* resembling zinc
ZINCOID	*adj* zincic
ZINCOUS	*adj* zincic
ZINCY	*adj* zincky
ZINEB	*n* pl. -S an insecticide
ZING	*v* -ED, -ING, -S to move with a high-pitched humming sound
ZINGANO	*n* pl. -NI zingaro
ZINGARA	*n* pl. -RE a female gypsy
ZINGARO	*n* pl. -RI a gypsy
ZINGER	*n* pl. -S a pointed witty retort or remark
ZINGY	*adj* ZINGIER, ZINGIEST enjoyably exciting
ZINKIFY	*v* -FIED, -FYING, -FIES to zincify
ZINKY	*adj* zincky
ZINNIA	*n* pl. -S a tropical plant
ZIP	*v* ZIPPED, ZIPPING, ZIPS to move with speed and vigor
ZIPLESS	*adj* lacking vigor or energy
ZIPPER	*v* -ED, -ING, -S to fasten with a zipper (a fastener consisting of two rows of interlocking teeth)
ZIPPING	present participle of zip
ZIPPY	*adj* -PIER, -PIEST full of energy
ZIRAM	*n* pl. -S a chemical salt
ZIRCON	*n* pl. -S a mineral
ZIRCONIA	*n* pl. -S a chemical compound
ZIRCONIC	*adj* pertaining to a certain metallic element

ZIT	*n* pl. -S a pimple
ZITHER	*n* pl. -S a stringed instrument
ZITHERN	*n* pl. -S zither
ZITI	*n* pl. -S a tubular pasta
ZIZIT	*n/pl* zizith
ZIZITH	*n/pl* the tassels on the four corners of a Jewish prayer shawl
ZIZZLE	*v* -ZLED, -ZLING, -ZLES to sizzle
ZLOTY	*n* pl. ZLOTYS, ZLOTE, ZLOTIES, or ZLOTYCH a monetary unit of Poland
ZOA	a pl. of zoon
ZOARIUM	*n* pl. -IA a colony of bryozoans **ZOARIAL** *adj*
ZODIAC	*n* pl. -S an imaginary belt encircling the celestial sphere **ZODIACAL** *adj*
ZOEA	*n* pl. ZOEAE or ZOEAS a larval form of certain crustaceans **ZOEAL** *adj*
ZOECIUM	*n* pl. -CIA zooecium
ZOFTIG	*adj* zaftig
ZOIC	*adj* pertaining to animals or animal life
ZOISITE	*n* pl. -S a mineral
ZOMBI	*n* pl. -S zombie
ZOMBIE	*n* pl. -S a will-less human capable only of automatic movement
ZOMBIFY	*v* -FIED, -FYING, -FIES to turn into a zombie
ZOMBIISM	*n* pl. -S the system of beliefs connected with a West African snake god
ZONAL	*adj* pertaining to a zone **ZONALLY** *adv*
ZONARY	*adj* zonal
ZONATE	*adj* arranged in zones
ZONATED	*adj* zonate
ZONATION	*n* pl. -S arrangement in zones
ZONE	*v* ZONED, ZONING, ZONES to arrange in zones (areas distinguished from other adjacent areas)
ZONELESS	*adj* having no zone or belt
ZONER	*n* pl. -S one that zones
ZONETIME	*n* pl. -S standard time used at sea
ZONING	present participle of zone
ZONK	*v* -ED, -ING, -S to stupefy
ZONULA	*n* pl. -LAE or -LAS zonule
ZONULE	*n* pl. -S a small zone **ZONULAR** *adj*
ZOO	*n* pl. ZOOS a place where animals are kept for public exhibition
ZOOCHORE	*n* pl. -S a plant dispersed by animals
ZOOECIUM	*n* pl. -CIA a sac secreted and lived in by an aquatic organism
ZOOGENIC	*adj* caused by animals or their activities
ZOOGLEA	*n* pl. -GLEAE or -GLEAS a jellylike mass of bacteria **ZOOGLEAL** *adj*
ZOOGLOEA	*n* pl. -GLOEAE or -GLOEAS zooglea
ZOOID	*n* pl. -S an organic cell or body capable of independent movement **ZOOIDAL** *adj*
ZOOKS	*interj* — used as a mild oath
ZOOLATER	*n* pl. -S one that worships animals
ZOOLATRY	*n* pl. -TRIES the worship of animals
ZOOLOGY	*n* pl. -GIES the science that deals with animals **ZOOLOGIC** *adj*
ZOOM	*v* -ED, -ING, -S to move with a loud humming sound
ZOOMANIA	*n* pl. -S an excessive interest in animals
ZOOMETRY	*n* pl. -TRIES the measurement of animals or animal parts
ZOOMORPH	*n* pl. -S something in the form of an animal
ZOON	*n* pl. ZOA or ZOONS the whole product of one fertilized egg **ZOONAL** *adj*
ZOONOSIS	*n* pl. -NOSES a disease that can be transmitted from animals to man **ZOONOTIC** *adj*
ZOOPHILE	*n* pl. -S a lover of animals
ZOOPHILY	*n* pl. -LIES a love of animals
ZOOPHOBE	*n* pl. -S one who fears or hates animals
ZOOPHYTE	*n* pl. -S an invertebrate animal
ZOOSPERM	*n* pl. -S the male fertilizing element of an animal
ZOOSPORE	*n* pl. -S a type of spore
ZOOTOMY	*n* pl. -MIES the dissection of animals **ZOOTOMIC** *adj*

ZOOTY	*adj* ZOOTIER, ZOOTIEST flashy in manner or style
ZORI	*n* pl. ZORI or ZORIS a type of sandal
ZORIL	*n* pl. -S a small African mammal
ZORILLA	*n* pl. -S zoril
ZORILLE	*n* pl. -S zoril
ZORILLO	*n* pl. -LOS zoril
ZOSTER	*n* pl. -S a virus disease
ZOUAVE	*n* pl. -S a French infantryman
ZOUNDS	*interj* — used as a mild oath
ZOWIE	*interj* — used to express surprise or pleasure
ZOYSIA	*n* pl. -S a perennial grass
ZUCCHINI	*n* pl. -S a vegetable
ZWIEBACK	*n* pl. -S a sweetened bread
ZYDECO	*n* pl. -COS popular music of southern Louisiana
ZYGOID	*adj* pertaining to a zygote
ZYGOMA	*n* pl. -MAS or -MATA the cheekbone
ZYGOSIS	*n* pl. -GOSES the union of two gametes **ZYGOSE** *adj*
ZYGOSITY	*n* pl. -TIES the makeup of a particular zygote
ZYGOTE	*n* pl. -S a cell formed by the union of two gametes **ZYGOTIC** *adj*
ZYGOTENE	*n* pl. -S a stage in meiosis
ZYMASE	*n* pl. -S an enzyme
ZYME	*n* pl. -S an enzyme
ZYMOGEN	*n* pl. -S a substance that develops into an enzyme when suitably activated
ZYMOGENE	*n* pl. -S zymogen
ZYMOGRAM	*n* pl. -S a record of separated proteins after electrophoresis
ZYMOLOGY	*n* pl. -GIES the science of fermentation
ZYMOSAN	*n* pl. -S an insoluble fraction of yeast cell walls
ZYMOSIS	*n* pl. -MOSES fermentation **ZYMOTIC** *adj*
ZYMURGY	*n* pl. -GIES a branch of chemistry dealing with fermentation
ZYZZYVA	*n* pl. -S a tropical weevil